ENCYCLOPEDIA OF AMERICAN CULTURAL & INTELLECTUAL HISTORY

ADVISORY BOARD

ENCYCLOPEDIA OF
AMERICAN
CULTURAL &
INTELLECTUAL
HISTORY

VOLUME I

MARY KUPIEC CAYTON • PETER W. WILLIAMS
EDITORS

Charles Scribner's Sons
an imprint of the Gale Group
New York • Detroit • San Francisco • London • Boston • Woodbridge, CT

Charles Scribner's Sons
1633 Broadway
New York, New York 10019

3 5 7 9 11 13 15 17 19 20 18 16 14 12 10 8 6 4 2

Printed in the United States of America

The paper used in this publication meets the requirements of ANSI/NISO Z39.48–1992 (Permanence of Paper).

Library of Congress Cataloging-in-Publication Data

Encyclopedia of American cultural and intellectual history / Mary Kupiec Cayton, Peter W. Williams, editors.
    p. cm.
   Includes bibliographical references and index.
   ISBN 0-684-80561-8 (set : alk. paper) — ISBN 0-684-80558-8 (v. 1 : alk. paper) — ISBN 0-684-80559-6 (v. 2 : alk. paper) — ISBN 0-684-80560-X (v. 3 : alk. paper)
   1. United States—Civilization—Encyclopedias. 2. United States—Intellectual life—Encyclopedias. I. Cayton, Mary Kupiec. II. Williams, Peter W.

E169.1 .E624 2001
973′.03—dc21

2001020005

EDITORIAL STAFF

Managing Editor
JOHN FITZPATRICK

Project Editors
CHRISTA BRELIN
KATHERINE MOREAU
LAURA KATHLEEN SMID

Associate Editors
ALJA COLLAR   SARA FEEHAN
ANNA GROJEC   MARGARET KIM   KATE MILLSON

Manuscript Editors
GRETCHEN GORDON   ROBERT GRIFFIN   LOUISE B. KETZ
MICHAEL LEVINE   GINA MISIROGLU   LINDA SANDERS
DEBRA M. KIRBY   MICHAEL A. PARÉ

Proofreaders
JONATHAN G. ARETAKIS   TONY COULTER   MARY FLOWER   CAROL HOLMES
EVANGELINE LEGONES   ANDREW LIBBY   ALLISON MARION
LAURA SPECHT PATCHKOFSKY

Production Manager
EVI SEOUD

Designer
MICHELLE DIMERCURIO

Compositor
IMPRESSIONS BOOK AND JOURNAL SERVICES, INC., MADISON, WISC.

Picture Editor
DOUG PUCHOWSKI

Chronology
CHRISTOPHER WELLS

Indexer
KATHARYN DUNHAM, PARAGRAPHS

Publisher
KAREN DAY

TABLE OF CONTENTS

VOLUME 1

Part 1: EARLY AMERICA

Part 4: COMMERCIAL AND NATIONAL CONSOLIDATION: 1878–1912

VOLUME 2

VOLUME 3

Part 15: THE PURSUIT AND EXCHANGE OF KNOWLEDGE

Part 16: THE ARTS AND CULTURAL EXPRESSION

Part 17: METHODS AND CONCEPTS

ALPHABETICAL TABLE OF CONTENTS

Essay titles have been simplified to make a useful overview.
See index in volume 3 for a full analytical breakdown.

INTRODUCTION

Since the arrival of Europeans on New World soil over a half a millennium ago, "Americans" have been reflecting on human existence and expressing their thoughts and emotions in an extraordinary variety of ways. The encounter of native peoples with European newcomers initially led to mutual puzzlement and speculation on the nature of these reciprocal strangers. The importation of Africans as slaves generated further speculation on the part of Euro-Americans as to the essential character of humanity, its oneness or its manyness. Subsequent waves of voluntary immigrants, eventually from the entire world, further complicated and enriched the process, rendering the new republic both a microcosm of the planet as well as a unique society, continually shifting its physical, social, and cultural accommodation to the presence of novelty. For over five hundred years, the amalgam of peoples who have comprised the American experiment have made sense of their experience through the exchange of ideas and through artistic expression.

These three volumes are an attempt to comprehend the ever-changing character and rich variety of American thought and expression. Euro-Americans in particular have reflected the thought patterns of their transatlantic homelands, bending those patterns to fit New World realities. Britain contributed much of the initial framework for reflection on such matters as the nature of humanity, society, and divinity, as well as the primary language of discourse. Soon, however, competing paradigms emerged. In music and religion, for example, African elements rapidly complemented and rivaled the European in providing alternate patterns of expression. The coming together of Catholic and Jew, Saxon and Slav, black and white in the urban crucibles of the late nineteenth century set the groundwork for unparalleled cultural production. The image of "mongrel Manhattan" in the 1920s, might well be extended to describe an entire nation where periodic campaigns of cultural purification proved helpless against the ceaseless tides of adaptation, accommodation, and uninhibited invention.

With this *Encyclopedia of American Cultural and Intellectual History*, the editors are pleased to renew a collaboration begun with Scribners in the *Encyclopedia of American Social History* (1993). Like that set, the present work attempts to present systematically the most important scholarly insights and discussions in the field. In the manner of the earlier sets in the Scribner American Civilization series, these volumes are composed of entries in the systematic "reference essay" genre that Scribners is proud of having invented. More thoroughly than the usual encyclopedia entry and more accessibly than the typical academic journal article, each essay surveys a (limited) field of inquiry and provides an interpretation in the process.

As with the prior sets, we have decided to arrange the contents architectonically rather than alphabetically, so that the structure of the work itself provides an overview of the entire field. The first eight sections are chronological, surveying the major periods of American history from the arrival of Europeans to the beginning of the twenty-first century. Each section begins with an introductory overview essay that provides context for the more specialized topics which follow. We are well aware that many currents of thought cannot be neatly confined, say, to the Antebellum or Progressive eras, but we have tried to situate topical essays in the periods in which their subjects first attained major expression or influence.

Part 9 goes on to treat the thought and expression of several groups with distinctive identities derived from gender, race, religion, ethnicity, or sexual preference. In the interests of brevity, we were forced to make difficult decisions based on representativeness and distinctiveness. Similarly, in Part 10, we attempted to choose a variety of cities and regions with distinctive or influential cultural histories without attempting to include every possibility. Part 11 includes topics relating to the natural order, the divine, and the construction of the human personality in American thought. The next three sections address discourse about the political, economic, and social orders. Part 15 surveys the various ways in which knowledge of all sorts has been categorized, institutionalized, pursued, financed, and disseminated. The next section looks serially at the most important media and genres through which ideas and cultural products have been conveyed, addressing their distinctive characteristics and their unfolding in the American context. The final unit is theoretically oriented, and surveys a variety of major schools of thought in the interpretation of intellectual and cultural phenomena.

The 221 essays are supplemented by a variety of sidebars that excerpt original texts or provide other illustrative materials. In addition, many of the essays are accompanied by illustrations of works or figures dealt with in them. Each essay also includes a bibliography offering a selective guide to further reading.

Since the meanings of the terms "cultural" and "intellectual" are not self-evident, we submit the following as working definitions for our purposes. Within the realm of *intellectual history* we include the following:
· Institutions involved in the creation and dissemination of knowledge
· Public figures influential in the discourse of their times
· Concepts, ideas, and ideologies that have played significant roles in shaping public discourse
Within the realm of *cultural history,* we include these topics:
· Artifacts and modes of expression that serve as tangible evidence of the understandings and sensibilities of individuals and groups active in public discourse
· Institutions related to the creation and dissemination of these products
· Images or ideologies that transmit a vision of human behavior, human interaction, or human possibility
As a general rule, we have tried to include particular ideas or movements that had an impact on Americans in their own day; those that produced a continuing impact on American thought and expression; and those that have emerged as influential only in later times.

In 1993, our social history encyclopedia gained a certain coherence and by virtue of the pervasive Marxian or materialist strain and the determination to focus on groups of persons previously neglected historiographically. Race, class, and gender were—and to a very great extent still are—watchwords of the day. The field of social history, despite its new methodologies and subject matters, by and large maintained professional historians' faith in the existence of a recoverable past. Absent stories of various peoples and groups could be recovered and reconsidered in the light of new knowledge, making for a more accurate and just version of the past. It was not until the social history movement was well under way that questions about the objectivity of historical practice—first raised in a significant way in the 1930s—were revived in new guises. Contemporary cultural and intellectual historians of the last two decades have labored inescapably in their shadow.

The questions came from a variety of directions. Skepticism about authority and power, increasing in the United States from the 1960s through the scandals and disillusionments of subsequent decades, led to questioning of the motives and good faith of institutions and persons. Knowledge, no longer a neutral ideal discovered by credentialed experts, became a political commodity subject to popular debate. Within the academy, poststructuralist and postmodernist theory aimed to unsettle all forms of certainty, providing critiques of the taken-for-granted and the commonsensical. If, for much of the twentieth century, knowledge had been popularly seen pragmatically as a lever to move the world, by the end of the century, many feared that it was losing its fulcrum or grounding.

In the realm of theory, poststructuralism and postmodernism did not—or have not yet—altered in significant ways the basic practices of writing history. Most historians still see themselves reconstructing a past that really existed in some form, even if no historian will ever be able to recapture it in its entirety and without bias. At the same time, no historian has been immune to questions about the ways in which perspective colors our reconstructions of the past. Dealing with the issues raised by perspectivalism has been a particularly thought-provoking business for intellectual and cultural historians. Ideas and public artistic expression, the main subjects of these volumes, never operate at the level of raw experience; they are always at one remove. To articulate an idea or communicate through a work of art, we must always construct a way of experiencing the world: What things, drawn from the vast array of human utterance and expression, are worth examining, recording, and remembering? The choice, we have discovered, is always a political question, and always a question of values. What we say, or even think to say, depends on the experience and questions we bring to our investigation.

Readers will find that the essays in this encyclopedia reflect a number of issues and trends peculiar not only to cultural and intellectual history but to much contemporary historical practice. At the outset it was not our intent as editors to showcase these issues. But as essays were drafted on a wide variety of topics, it became clear that the field we examine here is in flux and full of creative challenge and tension.

First, readers will note little general agreement among authors on essential common denominators involved in the study of ideas, intellectuals, and public expression in the American past. Current scholarship is rich and diverse; and it sprawls without apology in many different directions. In contrast to our examination of social history scholarship, where themes converged and a few major paradigms ruled the day, we found few implicitly accepted assumptions about what should count as cultural or intellectual history today and what should not—and little debate about the question. As genres have expanded and their limits have blurred over the last generation, the boundaries defining these two categories of scholarship have become less than clear-cut, and perhaps less important as well.

Unable to deal with, or even to define, intellectual or cultural history in every possible sense, we (along with our board of editors) have made some fairly pragmatic and arbitrary decisions about the limits of the current project. For example, although many historians today might consider a variety of ethnographic histories and popular culture studies as falling under the rubric of either intellectual or cultural history, these are already well represented in the *Encyclopedia of American Social History* and we do not cover them here. We direct readers interested in such topics to the earlier set. For the sake of unity and clarity, we deal here with culture primarily as it manifests itself in concrete ways in the broader public sphere, most particularly as artifacts, institutions, and approaches identified with important public figures or groups.

Along with the blurring of lines among genres, readers may also note a certain division in these essays between attempts to *reconstruct* the past as it existed and those more nearly oriented to exploring the assumptions we use to *construct* the past. Contemporary intellectual and cultural history includes both kinds of scholarship. Authors have sometimes chosen to approach their topics by examining how we have come to think about a particular notion or topic in history rather than by looking directly at lived experience. In the essay on "Women," for example, Louise Stevenson might have chosen to narrate a story about particular contributions that particular women or groups of women have made to intellectual and cultural life in the United States. Instead, she chooses to tell a story about women's inclusion and exclusion in intellectual history over time, underlining the ways in which the categories and the definitions we use to produce knowledge may be as important as anything we may "discover" in the fabric of the past. Elsewhere in these volumes, readers will encounter other essays where the author looks more closely at change over time in the nature of knowledge than at concrete experience and accomplishment in the past.

As with the *Encyclopedia of American Social History*, readers will undoubtedly notice that the identity categories of race, gender, class, sexual preference, and ethnicity have made a difference in contemporary cultural and intellectual historical scholarship, although perhaps not nearly to as great an extent as in social history. When commissioning essays, we provided potential contributors with exactly the same guidelines with regard to inclusiveness as we did for *Social History*: wherever possible, consider the experiences and contributions of those with a variety of cultural affiliations and identities. The result this time has been different. Over time, we discovered some things that scholars working with the ideas and cultural expression of non-dominant groups have probably long known. First, the notion of a "general public sphere" of discourse with which we began is problematic. Because we focus here on public discourse and expression, the intellectual and cultural expression of persons and groups excluded from the public sphere at various times is less visible than any might wish. Second, because the general "public sphere" serves the needs of some groups better than others, many delimited spheres also exist. These reflect the experiences and ideas of particular groups defined along racial, ethnic, religious, gender, sexual, or regional lines. Aspects of African American public culture that become visible to nonblacks, for example, may represent only the tip of the iceberg, as topics or forms of expression mainly of interest to African Americans never make their way into the more general discourse. To deal thoroughly with cultural and intellectual expression among Americans, we need reconstructions on their own terms of the intellectual and cultural lives of peoples who have not dominated discussion and expression in the public sphere. Any future study of American cultural and intellectual history undoubtedly will look different as more scholarly studies of this sort become available. We hope such studies will benefit from our attempt to lay the groundwork.

Finally, readers will surely notice among the present essays an increased tendency among authors to take explicit or implicit political stands regarding their topics. Many scholars have questioned the ideal of objectivity in historical writing, particularly in disciplines where postmodern theory has exercised a strong influence. They believe that absolute neutrality in treating the past is neither possible nor desirable. The editors believe that a project such as this one should reflect the state of the art, and we have not insisted that authors attempt to conceal political biases. At the same time, we believe that in a comprehensive work, even essays with strong points of view need to present different sides of an issue fairly and accurately. Where an essay takes a perspective critical of existing institutions and practices, for example, we think that the author has an obligation to represent what may be at stake from a more conservative point of view as well. Conversely, an author who is critical of particular efforts to reform or change still has an obligation to represent them fairly. Our rule of thumb has been that even when all sides cannot be presented, the approach should be fair and complete enough so that a person holding an opposing point of view would acknowledge the representation to be accurate. Readers will note a fair number of essays in this set where the authors have not been shy about staking out positions on controversial topics.

As in any work such as this, the editors conclude their labor with mixed feelings. On the one hand, we are delighted with the collective contributions of some of the nation's finest established or newly minted scholars on a myriad of topics. Contributors have come from a wide variety of academic disciplines and methodological perspectives, ranging from history and American studies to religion and law. (A directory appears in volume 3.) Within broad limits we have tried to respect that variety of perspectives, insisting only on a broadly historical approach and accessibility to the informed general reader. We wish we could have covered even more topics. Difficult choices have been necessitated by spatial constraints or, occasionally, by our inability to find a qualified and available author.

In closing this introduction at the end of an editorial process of several years, we are pleased to acknowledge our indebtedness to a variety of individuals and institutions who have helped make this work possible. Karen Day, the publisher of Charles Scribner's Sons, has, as in past ventures, proven a stalwart believer in the enterprise, as has John Fitzpatrick, who has once again ably managed the editorial process. His assistants provided extraordinary help. It is our pleasure especially to acknowledge the aid of Andrew McCarthy, who helped to launch this project; Laura Smid, without whom it might have dragged on for far too long; and Christa Brelin and Margaret Kim, who saw it through to its conclusion. Our editorial advisory board has consisted of several outstanding scholars who have frequently provided assistance, especially in the area of suggesting potential contributors. They include Joyce Appleby, Casey Blake, Daniel Walker Howe, Eugene Leach, Angela Miller, Nell Irvin Painter, and Jon Roberts. We would also like to acknowledge the support of the Departments of Comparative Religion and History at our own institution, Miami University, for varieties of support and comfort.

Finally, we are delighted to acknowledge our most personal debts. Peter Williams has been sustained throughout this endeavor by Ruth Ann Alban Williams, to whom he dedicates these volumes with an abundance of affection, appreciation, and alliteration. Mary Cayton happily acknowledges her intellectual and emotional debt to Andrew Cayton, in this endeavor as in every other. Although he provided a number of helpful suggestions with regard to content and potential authors, they were not his principal contributions. Simply because he is who he is, these volumes are also dedicated to him.

Mary Kupiec Cayton
Peter W. Williams
Miami University
Oxford, Ohio
January 2001

CHRONOLOGY

YEAR	NATIONAL AND INTERNATIONAL EVENTS	CULTURAL AND INTELLECTUAL EVENTS
1600s	English settle Jamestown, Virginia (1607)	*Letters:* John Smith, *A True Relation of Occurrences in Virginia* (1608)
1610s	First Africans arrive in Virginia (1619)	*Letters:* John Smith, *A Description of New England* (1616)
1620s	Pilgrims settle at Plymouth (1620) Dutch settle New Netherland (1624) James I revokes Virginia Company's charter (1624)	*Art:* Anonymous, *Portrait of John Winthrop* (1629) *Letters:* Mayflower Compact signed (1620) John Smith, *New England's Trials* (1620) and *A Generall Historie of Virginia* (1624) Edward Winslow, *Good News from New England* (1624)
1630s	Puritans settle Massachusetts Bay colony (1630) "Great Migration" of English to American colonies (1630–1660) Lord Baltimore founds Maryland (1634) Pequot War in New England (1637) Anne Hutchinson banished to Rhode Island (1637)	*Institutions:* Harvard College founded (1636) *Letters:* John Winthrop, "A Modell of Christian Charity" (1630)

YEAR	NATIONAL AND INTERNATIONAL EVENTS	CULTURAL AND INTELLECTUAL EVENTS
1640s	English Civil War begins (1642) Roger Williams establishes legal government in Rhode Island (1644)	*The Bay Psalm Book* becomes first book printed in the colonies *Architecture:* Swedes introduce log cabins near the Delaware River Evolution of the "colonial style" (c. 1641–c. 1700) *Letters:* Roger Williams develops first dictionary of a Native American language (1643) Roger Williams, *The Bloudy Tenent of Persecution* (1644) John Winthrop, "Speech to the General Court" (1645)
1650s	First Navigation Act (1651)	*Letters:* William Bradford, *History of Plimmouth Plantation* (1650) Anne Bradstreet, *The Tenth Muse Lately Sprung up in America* (1650)
1660s	Charles II becomes king of England in restoration of Stuart dynasty (1660) Carolina becomes English colony (1663) English conquer New Netherland, which becomes New York (1664) New Jersey established (1664)	Half-Way Covenant in Massachusetts (1662) *Letters:* John Eliot, Algonquian translation of the Bible (1661) Michael Wigglesworth, *Day of Doom* (1662) *Theater: Ye Bare and Ye Cubb*, first known English play performed in colonies (1665)
1670s	King Philip's War in New England (1675–1676) Bacon's Rebellion in Virginia (1676) Quakers found West Jersey (1676)	*Art:* Anonymous, *Robert Gibbs* (1670) *Letters:* Increase Mather, *A Brief History of the Warr with the Indians* (1676)
1680s	William Penn founds Pennsylvania (1681) Dominion of New England (1686–1689) Insurrections in colonies following Glorious Revolution in England; James II deposed (1688–1691) William and Mary gain English throne (1689) King William's War (1689–1697)	*Architecture:* Parson Capen House, Topsfield, Massachusetts (1683) *Art:* Thomas Smith, *Self Portrait* *Letters:* Mary Rowlandson, *A Narrative of the Captivity and Restauration of Mrs. Mary Rowlandson* (1682, posthumous) Increase Mather, *An Essay for the Recording of Illustrious Providences* (1684)

YEAR	NATIONAL AND INTERNATIONAL EVENTS	CULTURAL AND INTELLECTUAL EVENTS
1690s	Salem witchcraft trials and executions (1692)	*Institutions:* William and Mary College founded (1693) *Letters:* First colonial newspaper founded (and suppressed) in Boston (1690) Cotton Mather, *The Wonders of the Invisible World* (1693)
1700s	Queen Anne's War (1702–1713)	*Architecture:* Evolution of English baroque style among the wealthy (c. 1700–c. 1750) *Institutions:* Yale College founded (1701) *Letters:* Robert Beverley, *The History and Present State of Virginia* (1705) John Williams, *The Redeemed Captive* (1707) Ebenezer Cook, *The Sot-Weed Factor* (1708)
1710s	New Orleans settled (1718) New York City slave revolt (1712)	*Letters:* Cotton Mather, *Bonifacius* (1710) John Wise, *A Vindication of the Government of the New England Churches* *Music: Mother Goose's Melodies for Children* (1719)
1730s	Georgia chartered as a colony (1732) Stono Slave Rebellion in South Carolina (1739)	Great Awakening sweeps over colonies (1734–1760) *Architecture:* Old Christ Church, Virginia (c. 1732) Drayton Hall, Charleston (1738) *Art:* Gustavus Hesselius, *Tishcohan* (1735) *Letters:* Benjamin Franklin, first issue of *Poor Richard's Almanac* (1732–1757)
1740s	King George's War (1744–1748) Franklin invents lightning rod (1749)	*Art:* Robert Feke, *Isaac Royall and Family* (1741) *Institutions:* College of New Jersey (later Princeton) founded (1746) *Letters:* Jonathan Edwards, "Sinners in the Hands of an Angry God" (1741) Jonathan Edwards, "Some Thoughts Concerning the Present Revival of Religion in New England" (1742) *Organizations:* American Philosophical Society founded (1743)

YEAR	NATIONAL AND INTERNATIONAL EVENTS	CULTURAL AND INTELLECTUAL EVENTS
1750s	Seven Years' War (1756–1763)	*Architecture:* Evolution of the Georgian style, the first truly American architectural style (c. 1751–c. 1789)
		Institutions: First American hospital established in Philadelphia (1752)
		Franklin's Academy (chartered 1754, reorganized as University of Pennsylvania 1779)
		Letters: Franklin, *Experiments and Observations in Electricity* (1752)
		Jonathan Edwards, *Freedom of the Will* (1754)
		Joseph Bellamy, *The Millennium* (1758)
		Benjamin Franklin, "The Way to Wealth" (1758)
		Music: Dr. Richard Schuckburg, "Yankee Doodle"
1760s	George III becomes king of Great Britain (1760)	*Art:* John Hesselius, *Charles Calvert and His Colored Slave* (1761)
	Proclamation of 1763 (1763)	Matthew Pratt, *The American School* (1765)
	Pontiac's Rebellion (1763–1764)	John Singleton Copley, *The Boy with the Squirrel* (1765) and *Paul Revere* (c. 1768–1770)
	Sugar, Stamp, and Currency Acts (1764–1765)	
	Sons of Liberty form in colonies (1765)	Benjamin West, *Agrippina Landing* (1768)
	Stamp Act Congress (1765)	*Institutions:* Rhode Island College (later Brown University) founded (1764)
	Colonists boycott British goods (1765)	
	Stamp Act repealed (1766)	Queen's College (later Rutgers) founded (1766)
	Declaratory Act (1766)	Dartmouth College founded (1769)
	Townshend duties (1767)	*Letters:* Jupiter Hammon, *Salvation by Christ with Penetential Cries* (1761)
		John Woolman, *A Plea for the Poor* (written 1763, published 1793)
		James Otis, *The Rights of the British Colonies Asserted* (1764)
		Jonathan Edwards, *The Nature of True Virtue* and *Concerning the End for Which God Created the World* (1765, posthumous)
		John Dickinson, *Letters from a Farmer in Pennsylvania* (1768)
		Theater: Southwark Theater in Philadelphia, first permanent colonial theater, opens

YEAR	NATIONAL AND INTERNATIONAL EVENTS	CULTURAL AND INTELLECTUAL EVENTS
1770	Townshend duties repealed (except on tea) Boston Massacre New England Quaker yearly meeting bans slaveholding	*Architecture:* Thomas Jefferson, Monticello (1770–1809), Charlottesville, Virginia *Art:* Benjamin West, *The Death of General Wolfe*
1771		*Art:* Benjamin West, *Penn's Treaty*
1772		*Art:* John Singleton Copley, *Samuel Adams* Benjamin West, *The Artist's Family*
1773	Tea Act and Boston Tea Party	*Art:* John Singleton Copley, *Mr. and Mrs. Thomas Mifflin* *Institutions:* First black Baptist church founded in Georgia *Letters:* Phillis Wheatley, *Poems on Various Subjects*
1774	Coercive Acts First Continental Congress meets	*Letters:* Thomas Jefferson, *A Summary View of the Rights of British America* John Woolman, *Journal* (posthumous)
1775	Battles of Lexington and Concord Second Continental Congress meets Olive Branch Petition Battles of Breed's Hill and Bunker Hill	*Organizations:* Pennsylvania Abolition Society, first antislavery organization, founded
1776	Battles of New York and Trenton Cherokee raids in North Carolina	*Letters:* Thomas Paine, *Common Sense* Thomas Jefferson, *Declaration of Independence* John Adams, *Thoughts on Government*
1777	Battles of Princeton, Saratoga, Brandywine Creek, Germantown Congress adopts Articles of Confederation	
1778	France recognizes United States and declares war on Great Britain British evacuate Philadelphia Battle of Monmouth Courthouse Iroquois attacks in Pennsylvania and New York	*Art:* John Singleton Copley, *Watson and the Shark* *Organizations:* New Jersey Society for Promoting Agriculture founded

YEAR	NATIONAL AND INTERNATIONAL EVENTS	CULTURAL AND INTELLECTUAL EVENTS
1780	British capture Charles Town	Pennsylvania begins gradual abolition of slavery *Organizations:* American Academy of Arts and Sciences founded
1781	Articles of Confederation become law Cornwallis surrenders at Yorktown	*Art:* Charles Willson Peale, *Washington and His Generals at Yorktown* *Organizations:* Massachusetts Medical Society founded
1782	British evacuate Savannah Peace negotiations begin in Paris	*Art:* Gilbert Stuart, *The Skater* *Institutions:* St. Mary's Church, Philadelphia, erects first parochial school *Letters:* Hector St. John de Crèvecouer, *Letters from an American Farmer*
1783	Treaty of Paris with Great Britain ends Revolutionary War Massachusetts Supreme Court declares slavery illegal	*Letters:* Noah Webster, *Spelling Book*
1784		*Art:* Charles Willson Peale, *Washington at the Battle of Princeton*
1785	Land Ordinance of 1785	*Architecture:* Thomas Jefferson, Virginia Capitol (1785–1791) *Letters:* Thomas Jefferson, *Notes on the State of Virginia*
1786	Virginia Statute for Religious Freedom Daniel Shays's Rebellion (1786–1787)	*Letters:* Philip Freneau, *Poems*
1787	Northwest Ordinance of 1787 Constitutional Convention meets in Philadelphia First American steamboat launched	*Art:* Charles Willson Peale, *Benjamin Franklin* John Trumbull, *The Declaration of Independence* (1787–1820) *Institutions:* Free African School established in New York City *Letters:* Alexander Hamilton, James Madison, and John Jay, *The Federalist* (1787–1788) Joel Barlow, *The Vision of Columbus* Benjamin Rush, "Thoughts upon Female Education"

YEAR	NATIONAL AND INTERNATIONAL EVENTS	CULTURAL AND INTELLECTUAL EVENTS
1788	U.S. Constitution ratified	*Letters:* Timothy Dwight, *Triumph of Infidelity*
1789	George Washington inaugurated French Revolution begins	Thanksgiving celebrated as national holiday *Architecture:* Roman revival (c. 1789–c. 1820) *Institutions:* State University of North Carolina opens *Letters:* Noah Webster, *Dissertations on the English Language* Olaudah Equiano, *Interesting Narrative*
1790	Samuel Slater's cotton mill opens First federal patent issued	Second Great Awakening begins *Letters:* Judith Sargent Murray, "On the Equality of the Sexes"
1791	Bank of the United States chartered Vermont statehood Bill of Rights adopted	*Letters:* Benjamin Franklin's *Autobiography* published (first American edition 1818) Alexander Hamilton, *Report on Manufactures* Thomas Paine, *The Rights of Man* (1791–1792) Susanna Rowson, *Charlotte Temple*
1792	Washington reelected Kentucky statehood	*Art:* Ralph Earl, *Chief Justice Oliver Ellsworth and His Wife* *Institutions:* New York Stock Exchange established *Letters:* Hugh Henry Brackenridge, *Modern Chivalry* (1792–1797)
1793	Fugitive Slave Law Washington's Neutrality Proclamation Eli Whitney invents cotton gin Citizen Genêt affair	*Architecture:* William Thornton, Stephen Hallet, Benjamin Henry Latrobe, and Charles Bulfinch, National Capitol, Washington D.C. *Letters:* Samuel Hopkins, *The System of Doctrines*

YEAR	NATIONAL AND INTERNATIONAL EVENTS	CULTURAL AND INTELLECTUAL EVENTS
1794	Whiskey Rebellion	**Institutions:** Bethel African Methodist Episcopal Church founded Philadelphia Museum established by Charles Willson Peale **Letters:** Thomas Paine, *The Age of Reason* (1794, 1796)
1795	Treaty of Greenville Jay Treaty with Great Britain	**Architecture:** Charles Bulfinch, Massachusetts State House, Boston (1795–1798) **Art:** Charles Willson Peale, *The Staircase Group* Rembrandt Peale, *George Washington* (1795–1823)
1796	John Adams elected president Tennessee statehood	**Art:** Benjamin West, *Death on the Pale Horse* Gilbert Stuart, *George Washington* and *Martha Washington* **Letters:** George Washington, "The Farewell Address"
1797	XYZ Affair	**Architecture:** Asher Benjamin, *The Country Builder's Assistant*
1798	Undeclared war with France Alien and Sedition Acts Naturalization Act Virginia and Kentucky Resolutions Eleventh Amendment	
1799		**Letters:** Nathaniel Bowditch, *Practical Navigator* Charles Brockden Brown, *Edgar Huntly* **Theater:** Gottlieb Graupner delivers first known minstrel performance
1800	Washington, D.C., becomes capital Gabriel Prosser's Rebellion Thomas Jefferson elected president	Great Kentucky Revival (1800–1801) **Institutions:** Library of Congress established **Letters:** Mason Weems, *Life of Washington*

YEAR	NATIONAL AND INTERNATIONAL EVENTS	CULTURAL AND INTELLECTUAL EVENTS
1801		**Art:** Rembrandt Peale, *Rubens Peale with a Geranium* **Print Media:** First issue *New York Evening Post* First issue *Port Folio* (1801–1827)
1803	*Marbury v. Madison* Louisiana Purchase Ohio statehood Lewis and Clark's expedition (1803–1806)	**Architecture:** Joseph F. Mangin and John McComb, New York City Hall (1803–1812)
1804	Twelfth Amendment Jefferson reelected Aaron Burr kills Alexander Hamilton in a duel	**Art:** John Vanderlyn, *Murder of Jane McCrea*
1805		**Letters:** Mercy Otis Warren, *History of the Rise, Progress, and Termination of the American Revolution*
1806		**Art:** Charles Willson Peale, *Exhumation of the Mastodon*
1807	Embargo Act *Chesapeake* affair Congress bans importation of slaves Robert Fulton's steamboat *Clermont* launched	**Letters:** Washington Irving, William Irving, and James Kirke Paulding, *Salmagundi* (1807–1808)
1808	James Madison elected president John Jacob Astor founds American Fur Company	
1809	Non-Intercourse Act of 1809 Tecumseh forms confederation	**Letters:** Washington Irving, *A History of New York* **Organizations:** Miami University (Ohio) founded
1810	Macon's Bill No. 2	**Art:** John Vanderlyn, *Ariadne Asleep*
1812	Western Florida annexed Madison reelected War declared against Great Britain Louisiana statehood	**Letters:** Benjamin Rush, *Medical Inquiries and Observations, upon the Diseases of the Mind* **Organizations:** American Antiquarian Society founded

YEAR	NATIONAL AND INTERNATIONAL EVENTS	CULTURAL AND INTELLECTUAL EVENTS
1813	Boston Manufacturing Company founded	
1814	Treaty of Ghent ends War of 1812 Andrew Jackson defeats Creeks at Horseshoe Bend Hartford Convention (1814–1815)	*Letters:* John Taylor, *An Inquiry into the Principles and Policy of the Government of the United States* *Music:* Francis Scott Key, "The Star Spangled Banner"
1815	Battle of New Orleans	*Music:* Handel and Haydn Society founded *Print Media:* First issue *North American Review* (1815–1939)
1816	Second Bank of the United States chartered First protective tariff passed James Monroe elected president Indiana statehood	
1817	American Colonization Society founded Mississippi statehood Erie Canal started	*Institutions:* University of Michigan founded *Letters:* William Cullen Bryant, "Thanatopsis" *Publishing:* J. & J. Harper established (later Harper and Bros.)
1818	Illinois statehood	*Print Media:* First issue *American Journal of Science and Arts*
1819	*Dartmouth College v. Woodward* *McCulloch v. Maryland* Panic of 1819 Spain cedes eastern Florida Alabama statehood Economic depression (1819–1821)	*Letters:* William Ellery Channing, "Unitarian Christianity" Washington Irving, *The Sketch Book* (1819–1820)
1820	Missouri Compromise Maine statehood Monroe reelected	*Architecture:* Greek revival (c. 1820–c. 1860)

YEAR	NATIONAL AND INTERNATIONAL EVENTS	CULTURAL AND INTELLECTUAL EVENTS
1821	Missouri statehood	***Institutions:*** Troy Female Seminary established First American high school opens in Boston ***Letters:*** James Fenimore Cooper, *The Spy* William Cullen Bryant, *Poems* Timothy Dwight, *Travels in New England and New York* (1821–1822)
1822	Denmark Vesey conspiracy, Charleston, South Carolina	***Architecture:*** Thomas Jefferson, University of Virginia Rotunda and Pavilions (1822–1826), Charlottesville ***Art:*** Charles Willson Peale, *The Artist in His Museum*
1823	Monroe Doctrine	***Letters:*** James Fenimore Cooper, *The Pioneers*
1824	Henry Clay's "American System" John Quincy Adams elected president by House of Representatives *Gibbons v. Ogden* Bureau of Indian Affairs established	***Print Media:*** First issue *Christian Examiner* (1824–1869)
1825	Erie Canal opens	Robert Owen founds New Harmony community ***Publishing:*** D. Appleton and Co. established
1826	American Temperance Society founded	Sequoyah creates Cherokee alphabet ***Art:*** Thomas Cole, *Falls of Kaaterskill* ***Institutions:*** Josiah Holbrook proposes idea for lyceums ***Letters:*** Cooper, *The Last of the Mohicans*
1827		***Letters:*** Sarah Josepha Hale, *Northwood* ***Print Media:*** First black newspaper, *Freedom's Journal,* New York City First issue *Western Monthly Review* (1827–1830)

YEAR	NATIONAL AND INTERNATIONAL EVENTS	CULTURAL AND INTELLECTUAL EVENTS
1828	Baltimore & Ohio Railroad chartered Andrew Jackson elected president "Tariff of Abominations"	**Architecture:** Isaiah Rogers, Tremont House **Letters:** John Calhoun, *South Carolina Exposition and Protest* Noah Webster, *An American Dictionary of the English Language* **Print Media:** First issue *Southern Review* (1828–1832) **Theater:** Thomas Dartmouth "Daddy" Rice introduces the minstrel character and song "Jim Crow" in Louisville, Kentucky
1829		**Letters:** *David Walker's Appeal* Moses Horton, *The Hope of Liberty*
1830	First commercial steam locomotive Indian Removal Act	Charles Finney's Rochester revival (1830–1831) **Institutions:** Church of Jesus Christ of Latter-day Saints founded **Print Media:** First issue *Godey's Lady's Book* (1830–1898)
1831	Nat Turner's Rebellion Alexis de Tocqueville begins visit to the United States	**Art:** John James Audubon, *The Birds of America* (1831–1839) Samuel F. B. Morse, *Gallery of the Louvre* (1831–1833) **Letters:** Thomas Gray, *The Confessions of Nat Turner* **Print Media:** First issue of William Lloyd Garrison's *The Liberator* (1831–1865)
1832	Jackson reelected Jackson vetoes Second U.S. Bank charter, begins removing funds to state banks South Carolina nullification crisis Samuel F. B. Morse invents telegraph	**Letters:** Thomas R. Dew, *Review of the Debate in the Virginia Legislature of 1831 and 1832*

YEAR	NATIONAL AND INTERNATIONAL EVENTS	CULTURAL AND INTELLECTUAL EVENTS
1833	Force Bill	*Art:* Karl Bodmer, *Mato-Tope* and *Mahchsi-Karehde* (1833–1834) *Institutions:* Oberlin College becomes first coeducational college in U.S. *Organizations:* American Anti-Slavery Society founded *Print Media:* First issue *New York Sun*, first penny newspaper
1834	Whig Party established Seminole Wars Lowell mill strike National Trades Union founded Cyrus McCormick patents reaper	*Art:* Edward Hicks, *Peaceable Kingdom* (1834–1849) *Letters:* George Bancroft, *History of the United States* (1834–1876) *Music:* George P. Morriss and Henry Russell, "Zip Coon" (later "Turkey in the Straw")
1835		*Letters:* Maria W. Stewart, *Productions*
1836	"Gag rule" Texas declares independence Battles of the Alamo and San Jacinto Specie Circular Arkansas statehood Martin Van Buren elected president Cherokee Trail of Tears	*Architecture:* Robert Mills, Washington Monument *Art:* Thomas Cole, *View from Mount Holyoke—The Oxbow* and the *Course of Empire* series *Letters:* Ralph Waldo Emerson, *Nature* William Holmes McGuffey, *Eclectic Readers* (1836–1857) Bronson Alcott, *Conversations with Children on the Gospels* (1836–1837) *Publishing:* J. B. Lippincott & Co. established
1837	Panic of 1837 John Deere invents steel plow Michigan statehood	*Institutions:* Mount Holyoke Female Seminary founded *Letters:* Ralph Waldo Emerson, "The American Scholar" Victor Séjour, *The Mulatto* Nathaniel Hawthorne, *Twice-Told Tales* George Catlin, *Gallery of Indians* *Print Media:* First issue *New York Review* (1837–1842)

YEAR	NATIONAL AND INTERNATIONAL EVENTS	CULTURAL AND INTELLECTUAL EVENTS
1838	Cherokee removal Morse code created Depression (1838–1844)	*Letters:* Ralph Waldo Emerson, "The Divinity School Address" Sarah Grimké, *Letters on the Condition of Women and the Equality of the Sexes* Angelina Grimké, *Letters to Catharine E. Beecher* William Ellery Channing, *Self-Culture* *Print Media:* First issue *Boston Quarterly Review* (1838–1842)
1839	Charles Goodyear invents vulcanized rubber Second Bank of the United States fails Liberty Party formed *Amistad* mutiny	*Letters:* Henry Wadsworth Longfellow, *Voices of the Night* *Publishing:* Dodd, Mead & Co. established
1840	Great migration via Oregon Trail William Henry Harrison elected president Independent Treasury Act	*Architecture:* Gothic revival (c. 1840–c. 1860) *Letters:* Orestes Brownson, "The Laboring Classes" Edgar Allan Poe, *Tales of the Grotesque and Arabesque* *Print Media:* First issue *Dial* (1840–1844)
1841	Harrison dies, John Tyler becomes president *Creole* revolt	Brook Farm founded *Letters:* Catharine Beecher, *A Treatise on Domestic Economy* Ralph Waldo Emerson, *Essays* (first series) *Print Media:* First issue *New-York Tribune* (1841–1966)
1842	Webster-Ashburton Treaty	*Institutions:* P. T. Barnum opens the American Museum in New York City *Music:* New York Philharmonic founded *Print Media:* First issue *Southern Quarterly Review* (1842–1857)
1843	New York Association for Improving the Condition of the Poor founded	*Theater:* First public full-length minstrel show *Letters:* Henry Highland Garnet, "Address to the Slaves"

YEAR	NATIONAL AND INTERNATIONAL EVENTS	CULTURAL AND INTELLECTUAL EVENTS
1844	James K. Polk elected president Oregon boundary dispute Morse sends first message via telegraph Senate rejects treaty for Texas statehood	Philadelphia Bible riots *Letters:* Emerson, *Essays* (second series) William Lloyd Garrison, "Address to the Friends of Freedom and Emancipation in the United States" *Organizations:* American Art Union formed *Print Media:* First issue *Brownson's Quarterly Review* (1844–1875)
1845	Texas and Florida statehood	*Letters:* Frederick Douglass, *Narrative of Frederick Douglass* Margaret Fuller, *Woman in the Nineteenth Century* Edgar Allan Poe, *The Raven and Other Poems* *Music:* William H. Fry, *Leonora*, first grand opera by an American *Print Media:* First issue *American Whig Review* (1845–1852) *Sports:* Knickerbocker Baseball Club formed in New York City
1846	Mexican War begins Wilmot Proviso Oregon boundary resolved Elias Howe invents sewing machine Iowa statehood	*Letters:* Herman Melville, *Typee* Charles Grandison Finney, *Lectures on Systematic Theology* Nathaniel Hawthorne, *Mosses from an Old Manse* *Music:* Daniel D. Emmett, "The Blue Tail Fly" (also known as "Jim Crack Corn") *Print Media:* First issue *De Bow's Review* (1846–1880) *Publishing:* Baker & Scribner established (later Charles Scribner's Sons)

YEAR	NATIONAL AND INTERNATIONAL EVENTS	CULTURAL AND INTELLECTUAL EVENTS
1847	Irish potato famine and immigration	*Art:* Tompkins Harrison Matteson, *The Last of the Race*
		Letters: Horace Bushnell, *Views of Christian Nurture*
		William Wells Brown, *Narrative*
		Music: Astor Place Opera House opens in New York
		Print Media: Frederick Douglass founds *North Star*
		Publishing: Little, Brown established
1848	Zachary Taylor elected president	Oneida community founded
	Free-Soil Party founded	*Letters:* James Russell Lowell, *The Biglow Papers* (first series)
	Treaty of Guadalupe Hidalgo	Edgar Allan Poe, *Eureka*
	Seneca Falls women's rights convention	*Music:* Stephen C. Foster, "Oh! Susanna"
	Gold discovered in California	
	Wisconsin statehood	
	William and Ellen Craft escape slavery	
1849	California gold rush	Astor Place theater riot
	Harriet Tubman becomes "conductor" on Underground Railroad	*Art:* Asher Durand, *Kindred Spirits*
		Letters: Horace Bushnell, *God in Christ*
		Francis Parkman, *The Oregon Trail*
		Henry David Thoreau, "Resistance to Civil Government"
1850	Taylor dies, Millard Fillmore becomes president	*Letters:* Nathaniel Hawthorne, *The Scarlet Letter*
	Compromise of 1850	Olive Gilbert, *Narrative of Sojourner Truth*
	California statehood	*Music:* Stephen C. Foster, "Frankie and Johnny"
	Fugitive Slave Law	American debut of Jenny Lind in New York
		Print Media: First issue *Harper's Monthly Magazine*

YEAR	NATIONAL AND INTERNATIONAL EVENTS	CULTURAL AND INTELLECTUAL EVENTS
1851	Maine prohibition law Fort Laramie Treaty Isaac M. Singer perfects sewing machine Women's Rights Convention in Ohio First American branch of Young Men's Christian Association (YMCA) Martin Delany advocates emigration for blacks	*Art:* George Caleb Bingham, *Daniel Boone Escorting Settlers* (1851–1852) *Institutions:* Northwestern University founded *Letters:* Herman Melville, *Moby-Dick* Nathaniel Hawthorne, *The House of Seven Gables* John C. Calhoun, *A Disquisition on Government* (posthumous) *Music:* Stephen C. Foster, "Old Folks at Home" ("Swanee River")
1852	Franklin Pierce elected president First school attendance law passed in Massachusetts Elisha Otis invents elevator	*Letters:* Harriet Beecher Stowe, *Uncle Tom's Cabin* Frederick Douglass, "What to the Slave Is the Fourth of July?" Nathaniel Hawthorne, *The Blithedale Romance* *Publishing:* Houghton, Mifflin established E. P. Dutton established
1853	Gadsden Purchase New York Children's Aid Society	*Letters:* William Wells Brown, *Clotel* *Music:* Stephen C. Foster, "My Old Kentucky Home" Debut of Louis Moreau Gottschalk in New York
1854	Know-Nothing Party and Republican Party formed Ostend Manifesto Kansas-Nebraska Act	*Architecture:* James Bogardus, Harper and Brothers Building, New York *Letters:* Henry David Thoreau, *Walden* Frances E. W. Harper, *Poems on Miscellaneous Subjects* P. T. Barnum, *Struggles and Triumphs*
1855	Struggle in Kansas between proslavery and antislavery governments	*Art:* Fitz Hugh Lane, *Boston Harbor* (1855–1858) *Letters:* Walt Whitman, *Leaves of Grass* Henry Wadsworth Longfellow, *Song of Hiawatha*
1856	James Buchanan elected president	

YEAR	NATIONAL AND INTERNATIONAL EVENTS	CULTURAL AND INTELLECTUAL EVENTS
1857	*Dred Scott v. Sandford* Lecompton Constitution Panic of 1857	New York's Central Park designed by Frederick Law Olmsted and Calvert Vaux *Art:* Frederic E. Church, *Niagara* *Letters:* Hinton R. Helper, *The Impending Crisis of the South* Louis Agassiz, *Contributions to the Natural History of the United States* *Music:* J. Pierpont, "Jingle Bells" *Print Media:* First issue *Atlantic Monthly*
1858	Lincoln-Douglas debates in Illinois Minnesota statehood	*Letters:* Horace Bushnell, *Nature and the Supernatural* Henry Wadsworth Longfellow, *The Courtship of Miles Standish*
1859	John Brown's raid on Harpers Ferry, Virginia; Brown's trial and execution Oregon statehood	*Art:* Frederic E. Church, *Heart of the Andes* Martin Johnson Heade, *Approaching Thunder Storm* *Letters:* Harriet E. Wilson, *Our Nig* *Music:* Daniel D. Emmett, "Dixie's Land"
1860	Abraham Lincoln elected president South Carolina secedes Pony Express begins	*Art:* Frederic E. Church, *Twilight in the Wilderness* (1860s) *Music:* Stephen C. Foster, "Old Black Joe"
1861	Confederate States of America formed Civil War begins First Battle of Bull Run First federal income tax First Confiscation Act Kansas statehood Morrill tariff	*Art:* Emanuel Leutze, *Westward the Course of Empire Takes Its Way* *Letters:* Harriet Jacobs, *Incidents in the Life of a Slave Girl* Frederick Law Olmsted, *The Cotton Kingdom* *Photography:* Mathew Brady begins to photograph Civil War scenes
1862	Battles of Shiloh, New Orleans, Second Bull Run, Antietam, and Fredericksburg 1st South Carolina Regiment (Colored) Homestead Act Robert Smalls seizes *Planter*	Morrill Land-Grant College Act *Art:* James Whistler, *The White Girl* *Music:* Julia Ward Howe, "The Battle Hymn of the Republic"

YEAR	NATIONAL AND INTERNATIONAL EVENTS	CULTURAL AND INTELLECTUAL EVENTS
1863	Emancipation Proclamation Battles of Gettysburg and Vicksburg New York City draft riots West Virginia statehood Massachusetts 54th and 55th Regiments (Colored)	*Art:* Albert Bierstadt, *The Rocky Mountains* *Letters:* Catharine Beecher, "Words of Comfort for a Discouraged Housekeeper" Abraham Lincoln, "Address Delivered at the Dedication of the Cemetery at Gettysburg" *Music:* Patrick Sarsfield Gilmore, "When Johnny Comes Marching Home"
1864	Sherman's March to the Sea Lincoln reelected Nevada statehood	*Letters:* George Perkins Marsh, *Man and Nature* Lyman Beecher, *Principles* (posthumous)
1865	Sherman's Field Order Number 15 Lee surrenders Civil War ends Freedmen's Bureau created Lincoln assassinated, Andrew Johnson becomes president Thirteenth Amendment First black codes passed	*Art:* Winslow Homer, *The Veteran in a New Field* *Institutions:* Vassar College and Cornell University founded *Letters:* Abraham Lincoln, "Second Inaugural Address" Walt Whitman, *Drum Taps* *Print Media:* First issue *The Nation*
1866	Riot in Memphis, Tennessee Civil Rights Act Ku Klux Klan formed National Labor Union formed	*Architecture:* M.I.T. opens first school of architecture
1867	First elevated railroad in New York City National Grange (Patrons of Husbandry) formed Nebraska statehood	*Art:* Albert Bierstadt, *Emigrants Crossing the Plains* and *Donner Lake from the Summit* *Institutions:* Howard University founded *Letters:* Horatio Alger, *Ragged Dick* *Music:* New England Conservatory of Music founded
1868	Johnson impeached, then acquitted Ulysses S. Grant elected president Fourteenth Amendment	*Letters:* Louisa May Alcott, *Little Women* (1868–1869) *Institutions:* Hampton Institute founded

YEAR	NATIONAL AND INTERNATIONAL EVENTS	CULTURAL AND INTELLECTUAL EVENTS
1869	Transcontinental railroad completed Knights of Labor founded Wyoming Territory grants woman suffrage Colored National Labor Union formed	*Commerce:* The Great Atlantic & Pacific Tea Company (A&P) opens a chain of grocery stores *Sports:* First intercollegiate football game Cincinnati Red Stockings organized
1870	Fifteenth Amendment Standard Oil Company incorporated Hiram Revels enters U.S. Senate	
1871	Great Fire in Chicago Tweed Ring exposed Civil Service Commission created	*Art:* James Whistler, *Arrangement in Gray and Black, No. 1* Thomas Eakins, *The Champion Single Sculls* *Letters:* Charles Hodge, *Systematic Theology* (1871–1872) Walt Whitman, *Democratic Vistas*
1872	Grant reelected Colfax, Louisiana, massacre Anthony Comstock founds New York Society for the Suppression of Vice Yellowstone National Park created	*Art:* John Frederick Kensett, *Eaton's Neck* James Whistler, *Nocturne in Blue and Gold* *Letters:* Mark Twain, *Roughing It*
1873	Panic of 1873	*Letters:* Mark Twain and Charles Dudley Warner, *The Gilded Age*
1874	Woman's Christian Temperance Union formed Greenback Party formed Barbed wire patented First electric streetcars in New York City	*Commerce:* Wanamaker's department store opens in Philadelphia *Institutions:* First Chautauqua Assembly *Letters:* Charles Hodge, *What Is Darwinism?* John Fiske, *Outlines of Cosmic Philosophy*
1875	Civil Rights Act Specie Resumption Act U.S.-Hawaii commercial treaty	*Art:* Thomas Eakins, *The Gross Clinic* *Institutions:* Smith College and Wellesley College founded in Massachusetts *Letters:* John Wesley Powell, *The Exploration of the Colorado River* *Music:* Henry Clay Work, "My Grandfather's Clock" *Sports:* First Kentucky Derby in Louisville

YEAR	NATIONAL AND INTERNATIONAL EVENTS	CULTURAL AND INTELLECTUAL EVENTS
1876	Alexander Graham Bell invents telephone Colorado statehood Battle of Little Bighorn Hamburg massacre, South Carolina	**Architecture:** Philadelphia Centennial Exhibition Romanesque revival (c. 1876–c. 1894) **Letters:** Mark Twain, *Adventures of Tom Sawyer* Washington Gladden, *Working People and Their Employers* **Sports:** National League of baseball established
1877	Rutherford B. Hayes becomes president following Compromise of 1877 Great Railway Strike *Munn v. Illinois* Reconstruction ends Nez Percé Indian insurrections Thomas Edison invents phonograph	**Architecture:** Henry Hobson Richardson, Trinity Church, Boston **Art:** Winslow Homer, *The Carnival* **Letters:** Henry James, *The American* Charles S. Peirce, "Fixation of Belief"
1878	Bland-Allison Act	**Letters:** John Wesley Powell, *Report on the Lands of the Arid Regions of the United States* Charles S. Peirce, "How to Make Our Ideas Clear"
1879	Edison perfects electric lightbulb	F. W. Woolworth opens "Five and Ten Cent Store" in Utica, New York **Letters:** Henry George, *Progress and Poverty*
1880	James A. Garfield elected president	**Art:** John Singer Sargent, *El Jaleo* Mary Cassat, *Five O'Clock Tea* **Letters:** Lew Wallace, *Ben-Hur* Joel Chandler Harris, *Uncle Remus* **Organizations:** U.S. branch of Salvation Army organized

YEAR	NATIONAL AND INTERNATIONAL EVENTS	CULTURAL AND INTELLECTUAL EVENTS
1881	Garfield assassinated, Chester A. Arthur becomes president Standard Oil Trust formed	*Architecture:* George B. Post, New York Produce Exchange (1881–1885) *Institutions:* Tuskegee Institute founded *Letters:* Helen Hunt Jackson, *A Century of Dishonor* William Graham Sumner, "Sociology" Henry James, *Portrait of a Lady* *Music:* Boston Symphony founded
1882	Chinese Exclusion Act New York Charity Organization Society founded	
1883	Pendleton Civil Service Act	William "Buffalo Bill" Cody founds Wild West Show Railroads separate country into time zones *Architecture:* George B. Post, New York Cotton Exchange (1883–1886) *Letters:* William Graham Sumner, *What Social Classes Owe to Each Other* Lester Frank Ward, *Dynamic Sociology* *Music:* Metropolitan Opera founded *Print Media:* first issue *Christian Science Journal*
1884	Grover Cleveland elected president Southern Farmers' Alliance formed	*Architecture:* William LeBaron Jenney, Home Insurance Building, Chicago (1884–1885) *Art:* John Singer Sargent, *Madame X* *Institutions:* Bryn Mawr College founded *Letters:* William Dean Howells, *The Rise of Silas Lapham* Lester Frank Ward, "Mind as a Social Factor"
1885	"New Immigration" begins	*Architecture:* McKim, Mead, and White, Henry Villard House, New York *Art:* Thomas Eakins, *Swimming* *Letters:* Mark Twain, *Adventures of Huckleberry Finn* Josiah Royce, *Religious Aspect of Philosophy* Josiah Strong, *Our Country*

YEAR	NATIONAL AND INTERNATIONAL EVENTS	CULTURAL AND INTELLECTUAL EVENTS
1886	*Wabash v. Illinois* American Federation of Labor founded Haymarket Riot	Richard Warren Sears opens first Sears, Roebuck store *Letters:* Henry James, *The Bostonians*
1887	Dawes Severalty Act Interstate Commerce Act	*Architecture:* Holabird and Roche, Tacoma Building, Chicago (1887–1888) *Art:* Thomas Wilmer Dewing, *The Days* *Letters:* John Dewey, *Psychology* *Organizations:* College Settlement House Association founded
1888	Benjamin Harrison elected president Colored Farmers' Alliance formed George Eastman introduces "Kodak" camera	*Architecture:* McKim, Mead, and White, Boston Public Library (1888–1898) Richard Morris Hunt, Marble House, Newport, Rhode Island (1888–1892) *Art:* John Singer Sargent, *Isabella Stewart Gardner* *Letters:* Edward Bellamy, *Looking Backward* Russell Conwell, "Acres of Diamonds"
1889	North Dakota, South Dakota, Montana, and Washington statehood	Hull-House established *Architecture:* George B. Post, Pulitzer Building, New York (1889–1892) Louis Sullivan, Chicago Auditorium *Art:* Albert Bierstadt, *The Last of the Buffalo* *Letters:* Mark Twain, *Connecticut Yankee in King Arthur's Court* Andrew Carnegie, "The Gospel of Wealth" Theodore Roosevelt, *The Winning of the West* (1889–1896)
1890	Battle of Wounded Knee Sherman Anti-Trust Act McKinley Tariff Yosemite National Park National American Women Suffrage Association founded Idaho and Wyoming statehood	*Architecture:* Louis Sullivan, Wainwright Building, St. Louis McKim, Mead, and White, Century Club, New York *Letters:* William James, *Principles of Psychology* Alfred Thayer Mahan, *Influence of Sea Power upon History* Jacob Riis, *How the Other Half Lives* Emily Dickinson, *Poems* (posthumous)

YEAR	NATIONAL AND INTERNATIONAL EVENTS	CULTURAL AND INTELLECTUAL EVENTS
1891		*Architecture:* Henry J. Hardenbergh, Waldorf Astoria Hotel, New York (1891–1896)
		Art: Mary Cassat, *The Letter*
		Institutions: Stanford University and University of Chicago founded
		Columbia University establishes Barnard College for women
		Letters: Hamlin Garland, *Main-Travelled Roads*
		Music: Chicago Symphony founded
		Carnegie Hall opens
		Sports: Basketball invented
1892	Populist Party formed	*Art:* Alfred Stieglitz, *The Terminal*
	Cleveland elected to (nonconsecutive) second term	*Letters:* Joseph Mayer Rice exposé of public schools in *Forum* magazine
	Sierra Club founded	Anna Julia Cooper, *A Voice from the South*
	Homestead strike	Charlotte Perkins Gilman, "The Yellow Wallpaper"
	Ellis Island opens	Elizabeth Cady Stanton, "Solitude of Self"
1893	Panic of 1893	City Beautiful movement begins
	American sugar growers rebel in Hawaii	*Architecture:* McKim, Mead, and White, Low Memorial Library, Columbia University
	Anti-Saloon League formed	Chicago's World Columbian Exposition
		Art: Thomas Moran, *The Grand Canyon of the Yellowstone* (1893–1901)
		Letters: Stephen Crane, *Maggie: A Girl of the Streets*
		Frederick Jackson Turner, "The Significance of the Frontier in American History"
1894	Pullman strike	*Architecture:* Louis Sullivan, Chicago Stock Exchange Building and Buffalo Guaranty Building
	"Coxey's Army" marches on Washington, D.C.	*Letters:* Mark Twain, *Pudd'nhead Wilson*
		Oliver Wendell Holmes Jr., "Privilege, Malice, and Intent"

YEAR	NATIONAL AND INTERNATIONAL EVENTS	CULTURAL AND INTELLECTUAL EVENTS
1895		Coney Island amusement park in Brooklyn opens
		Art: William Merritt Chase, *Shinnecock Hills*
		Letters: Stephen Crane, *Red Badge of Courage*
		Ida B. Wells, *A Red Record*
		Oliver Wendell Holmes Jr., "The Soldier's Faith"
		Booker T. Washington, "Atlanta Address"
		Elizabeth Cady Stanton, *Woman's Bible* (1895–1898)
1896	William McKinley elected president *Plessy v. Ferguson* Utah statehood	*Film:* First commercial motion picture exhibition using Vitascope
		Letters: Charles Sheldon, *In His Steps*
		Paul Laurence Dunbar, *Lyrics of Lowly Life*
		Music: First phonograph records marketed
1897		*Letters:* William James, *The Will to Believe*
1898	Spanish-American War	*Architecture:* Louis Sullivan, Bayard Building, New York
		Letters: Charlotte Perkins Gilman, *Women and Economics*
1899	First Open Door notes Filipino-American War begins (1899–1902)	*Architecture:* Louis Sullivan, Carson-Pirie-Scott Building, Chicago
		Letters: John Dewey, *School and Society*
		Charles Chesnutt, *The Conjure Woman*
		Kate Chopin, *The Awakening*
		Thorstein Veblen, *The Theory of the Leisure Class*
		Sutton E. Griggs, *Imperium in Imperio*
		Music: Scott Joplin, "Maple Leaf Rag"
1900	McKinley reelected U.S. officially adopts gold standard	*Art:* Winslow Homer, *West Point, Prout's Neck*
		Letters: Theodore Dreiser, *Sister Carrie*
		Print Media: *Colored American Magazine*

YEAR	NATIONAL AND INTERNATIONAL EVENTS	CULTURAL AND INTELLECTUAL EVENTS
1901	McKinley assassinated, Theodore Roosevelt becomes president Socialist Party of America formed U.S. Steel Corporation founded	*Letters:* Frank Norris, *The Octopus* Booker T. Washington, *Up from Slavery*
1902		*Architecture:* Daniel H. Burnham, "Flatiron" Building, New York George B. Post, College of the City of New York (1902–1911) *Letters:* Owen Wister, *The Virginian* Jane Addams, *Democracy and Social Ethics* William James, *Varieties of Religious Experience*
1903	Wright brothers' flight at Kitty Hawk, North Carolina	*Film: The Great Train Robbery*, first narrative film *Letters:* W. E. B. Du Bois, *The Souls of Black Folk* Jack London, *The Call of the Wild* *Sports:* First baseball World Series
1904	Chinese Exclusion Act Roosevelt reelected	*Architecture:* George B. Post, New York Stock Exchange Frank Lloyd Wright, Larkin Administration Building, Buffalo *Letters:* Lincoln Steffens, *The Shame of the Cities* Ida Tarbell, *History of the Standard Oil Company* Henry Adams, *Mont-St.-Michel and Chartres* Henry James, *The Ambassadors*
1905	Industrial Workers of the World (IWW) founded Niagara Movement founded	*Art:* George Luks, *The Wrestlers* *Film:* Nickelodeon, a movie house, established in Pittsburgh; became model for an estimated 8,000 to 10,000 theaters by 1908 *Letters:* Thomas Dixon, *The Clansman* Mary Boykin Chesnut, *A Diary from Dixie*

YEAR	NATIONAL AND INTERNATIONAL EVENTS	CULTURAL AND INTELLECTUAL EVENTS
1906	Hepburn Act Meat Inspection Act Pure Food and Drug Act San Francisco earthquake	*Architecture:* N. LeBrun and Sons, Metropolitan Life Insurance Company Tower, New York McKim, Mead, and White, J. Pierpont Morgan Library, New York *Letters:* Upton Sinclair, *The Jungle* Irving Fisher, *The Nature of Capital and Income*
1907	General Motors founded "Gentlemen's agreement" ends Japanese immigration Oklahoma statehood	*Architecture:* Henry J. Hardenbergh, Plaza Hotel, New York Ralph Adams Cram, Calvary Church, Pittsburgh *Letters:* Walter Rauschenbusch, *Christianity and the Social Crisis* William James, *Pragmatism* Henry Adams, *The Education of Henry Adams*
1908	William Howard Taft elected president *Muller v. Oregon* Model T Ford introduced	*Architecture:* Frank Lloyd Wright, Robie House, Chicago Louis Sullivan, National Farmers Bank, Owatonna, Minnesota *Theater:* First *Ziegfeld Follies* revue
1909	National Association for the Advancement of Colored People (NAACP) formed	*Art:* George Bellows, *Stag at Sharkey's* and *Both Members of This Club* *Letters:* Herbert Croly, *The Promise of American Life*
1910	Mann Act	*Architecture:* Henry J. Hardenbergh, Copley Plaza, Boston *Art:* John Marin, *Brooklyn Bridge* *Letters:* Jane Addams, *Twenty Years at Hull-House* William James, "The Moral Equivalent of War" *Music:* Portions of *Cavalleria Rusticana* and *Pagliacci* broadcast by radio from the Metropolitan Opera

YEAR	NATIONAL AND INTERNATIONAL EVENTS	CULTURAL AND INTELLECTUAL EVENTS
1911	Triangle Shirtwaist Company fire National Urban League founded	*Architecture:* Cass Gilbert, Woolworth Building, New York (1911–1913) Ralph Adams Cram, St. Thomas's Church, New York (1911–1913) *Letters:* Frederick W. Taylor, *The Principles of Scientific Management* *Music:* Irving Berlin, "Alexander's Ragtime Band"
1912	Woodrow Wilson elected president Arizona statehood	*Architecture:* Ralph Adams Cram, Fourth Presbyterian Church, Chicago *Art:* Marcel Duchamp, *Nude Descending a Staircase, No. 2* *Letters:* James Harvey Robinson, *The New History* Ezra Pound, *Ripostes* James Weldon Johnson, *The Autobiography of an Ex-Colored Man* (anonymous)
1913	Sixteenth and Seventeenth Amendments Federal Reserve established Department of Labor separates from Department of Commerce First assembly line at Ford Motor Company	*Art:* Art exhibition at the Armory in New York City Morgan Russell, *Synchromy in Orange: To Form* *Letters:* Willa Cather, *O Pioneers!* Charles Beard, *An Economic Interpretation of the Constitution*
1914	World War I begins in Europe; Wilson declares U.S. neutrality Panama Canal completed First long-distance telephone connection Marcus Garvey founds Universal Negro Improvement Association (UNIA)	*Art:* Marsden Hartley, *Portrait of a German Officer* *Letters:* Walter Lippmann, *Drift and Mastery* Louis Brandeis, *Other People's Money* *Music:* W. C. Handy, "St. Louis Blues" *Print Media:* first issue *The New Republic*
1915	*Lusitania* sinks Modern Ku Klux Klan organized	*Film:* *The Birth of a Nation* *Letters:* Charlotte Perkins Gilman, *Herland* *Publishing:* Alfred A. Knopf established

YEAR	NATIONAL AND INTERNATIONAL EVENTS	CULTURAL AND INTELLECTUAL EVENTS
1916	Wilson reelected Margaret Sanger forms New York Birth Control League Marcus Garvey arrives in Harlem	*Art:* Kenyon Cox, *Tradition* *Saturday Evening Post* hires Norman Rockwell as an illustrator *Film: Intolerance* *Letters:* John Dewey, *Democracy and Education* Randolph Bourne, "Trans-National America"
1917	U.S. enters World War I Espionage Act East Saint Louis (Illinois) race riot	*Art:* Georgia O'Keeffe, *Light Coming on the Plains III* *Letters:* Walter Rauschenbusch, *A Theology for the Social Gospel* Randolph Bourne, "Twilight of Idols" T. S. Eliot, *Prufrock and Other Observations* *Music:* Dixie Jass Band of New Orleans opens at Reisenweber's Cabaret, Chicago *Variety* magazine reports a jazz band in New York
1918	Influenza epidemic begins (1918–1919) World War I ends Wilson proposes Fourteen Points for peace	*Art:* Childe Hassam, *Celebration Day* *Film: Shoulder Arms* *Letters:* Willa Cather, *My Ántonia* *Music:* Eastman School of Music founded
1919	Eighteenth Amendment launches Prohibition Senate defeats Treaty of Paris Pan African Congress, Paris Chicago race riot	Harlem Renaissance (1919–1930) *Letters:* Sherwood Anderson, *Winesburg, Ohio* Thorstein Veblen, *Engineers and the Price System* *Publishing:* Harcourt Brace established
1920	Nineteenth Amendment Warren G. Harding elected president	*Letters:* F. Scott Fitzgerald, *This Side of Paradise* Sinclair Lewis, *Main Street* Edith Wharton, *The Age of Innocence* Ezra Pound, "Hugh Selwyn Mauberley" *Radio:* WWJ makes first commercial radio broadcast in Detroit *Sports:* Negro National League (baseball) founded

YEAR	NATIONAL AND INTERNATIONAL EVENTS	CULTURAL AND INTELLECTUAL EVENTS
1921	Washington Naval Conference (1921–1922); immigration restricted to 3% of each nationality's total in 1910 Tulsa, Oklahoma, race riot	**Film:** *The Kid, The Three Musketeers* **Letters:** James Harvey Robinson, *Mind in the Making* **Theater:** *Shuffle Along*, an all-black musical review
1922		**Film:** Will H. Hays organizes the Motion Picture Producers and Distributors of America, the industry's first self-censoring body **Letters:** Sinclair Lewis, *Babbitt* Herbert Hoover, *American Individualism* Walter Lippmann, *Public Opinion* T. S. Eliot, *The Waste Land* Harold E. Stearns, *Civilization in the United States* E. E. Cummings, *The Enormous Room*
1923	Harding dies, Calvin Coolidge becomes president Teapot Dome scandal	**Letters:** Jean Toomer, *Cane* Robert Frost, *New Hampshire* Emily Post, *Etiquette* Emma Goldman, *My Disillusionment with Russia* **Publishing:** Henry Luce founds *Time*
1924	Coolidge elected president Immigration restricted to 2% of each nationality's total in 1890	**Letters:** Jesse Fauset, *There Is Confusion* **Music:** Paul Whiteman performs at Aeolian Hall, New York, introducing George Gershwin's *Rhapsody in Blue* Juilliard Graduate School founded Curtis Institute of Music founded **Publishing:** Simon & Schuster established

YEAR	NATIONAL AND INTERNATIONAL EVENTS	CULTURAL AND INTELLECTUAL EVENTS
1925	First national convention of the Ku Klux Klan Ossian Sweet case, Detroit A. Philip Randolph founds Brotherhood of Sleeping Car Porters	Scopes trial in Dayton, Tennessee *Film:* The Gold Rush *Commerce:* A & W Root Beer becomes first national fast-food franchise *Letters:* Alain Locke, *The New Negro* Dorothy and DuBose Heyward, *Porgy* F. Scott Fitzgerald, *The Great Gatsby* William Carlos Williams, *In the American Grain* Bruce Barton, *The Man Nobody Knows* *Music:* Aaron Copland, *Symphony no. 1*
1926	Coolidge-Mellon tax reductions Carter G. Woodson founds Negro History Week	*Dance:* Martha Graham presents her first independent dance recital *Film:* The General *Letters:* Langston Hughes, *The Weary Blues* Sinclair Lewis, *Elmer Gantry* Ernest Hemingway, *The Sun Also Rises* H. L. Mencken, *Notes on Democracy* Will Durant, *Story of Philosophy* *Music:* "The Grand Ole Opry" begins broadcasts from Nashville, Tennessee *Publishing:* Book-of-the-Month Club begins distribution *Radio:* National Broadcasting Company (NBC) established
1927	Sacco and Vanzetti executed Marcus Garvey deported	Charles Lindbergh solos to Paris *Film:* Sunrise; The Jazz Singer, first feature-length movie with synchronized sound *Letters:* Willa Cather, *Death Comes for the Archbishop* *Music:* Aaron Copland, *Concerto for Piano and Orchestra* *Publishing:* Random House established *Radio:* Columbia Broadcasting System (CBS) established First car radios produced by Philco

YEAR	NATIONAL AND INTERNATIONAL EVENTS	CULTURAL AND INTELLECTUAL EVENTS
1928	Herbert Hoover elected president	**Art:** Charles Demuth, *The Figure 5 in Gold*
		John Steuart Curry, *Baptism in Kansas*
		Architecture: William Van Alen, Chrysler Building, New York (1928–1930)
		Commerce: Ford introduces the Model A
		Film: *Steamboat Willie*, *The Crowd*
		Letters: Nella Larsen, *Quicksand*
		Margaret Mead, *Coming of Age in Samoa*
		Claude McKay, *Home to Harlem*
		Music: Duke Ellington cuts first of over 160 records in four-year period (1928–1931)
		George Gershwin, *An American in Paris*
		Theater: Jerome Kern, *Show Boat*
1929	Stock market crash and onset of Great Depression	**Architecture:** Shreve, Lamb & Harmon, Empire State Building, New York (1929–1931)
		Raymond Hood, Rockefeller Center, New York (1929–1939)
		Film: *Hallelujah*, first all-black movie
		Broadway Melody, first film musical
		The Virginian
		Letters: William Faulkner, *The Sound and the Fury*
		Ernest Hemingway, *A Farewell to Arms*
		Thomas Wolfe, *Look Homeward, Angel*
		Robert and Helen Lynd, *Middletown*
		Walter Lippmann, *Preface to Morals*
1930	Veterans Adminstration established	**Art:** Georgia O'Keeffe, *Ranchos Church*
		Charles Sheeler, *American Landscape*
		Edward Hopper, *Early Sunday Morning*
		Grant Wood, *American Gothic*
		Film: *Animal Crackers*, *Little Caesar*, *All Quiet on the Western Front*
		Letters: John Dos Passos, begins *U.S.A.* trilogy (1930–1936)
		Twelve Southerners, *I'll Take My Stand*

YEAR	NATIONAL AND INTERNATIONAL EVENTS	CULTURAL AND INTELLECTUAL EVENTS
1931	Wickersham Commission Report on enforcement of the Eighteenth Amendment Scottsboro Boys case begins, Alabama	*Film:* *Frankenstein; The Public Enemy* *Institutions:* Black Muslims founded by Elijah Muhammad *Letters:* Pearl S. Buck, *The Good Earth* George Schuyler, *Black No More* Constance Rourke, *American Humor* *Music:* *Hansel and Gretel* broadcast by radio from the Metropolitan Opera
1932	Bonus March Franklin D. Roosevelt elected president Beginning of Tuskegee syphilis study	*Film:* *Scarface, I Am a Fugitive from a Chain Gang, Trouble in Paradise* *Letters:* James T. Farrell begins *Studs Lonigan* trilogy (1932–1935) Wallace Thurman, *Infants of the Spring* Reinhold Niebuhr, *Moral Man and Immoral Society* Erskine Caldwell, *Tobacco Road*
1933	Twentieth Amendment Twenty-First Amendment ends Prohibition Roosevelt's "Hundred Days" produce TVA, CCC, NIRA, PWA, and AAA, among others.	*Architecture:* Chicago World's Fair *Film:* *She Done Him Wrong, I'm No Angel, 42nd Street, Flying Down to Rio, Duck Soup* *Letters:* Nathanael West, *Miss Lonelyhearts* Jack Conroy, *The Disinherited* Erskine Caldwell, *God's Little Acre* Gertrude Stein, *The Autobiography of Alice B. Toklas*
1934	Indian Reorganization Act Securities and Exchange Commission (SEC) created	*Film:* Hollywood adopts self-regulating Production Code *It Happened One Night* *Letters:* Nathanael West, *A Cool Million* Lewis Mumford, *Technics and Civilization* Henry Roth, *Call It Sleep*

YEAR	NATIONAL AND INTERNATIONAL EVENTS	CULTURAL AND INTELLECTUAL EVENTS
1935	Social Security and WPA established National Labor Relations (Wagner) Act Huey Long assassinated Harlem race riot Popular Front emerges (1935–1937) Committee for Industrial Organization (CIO) formed	*Architecture:* WPA Federal Art Project organized *Art:* Thomas Hart Benton, *Social History of Missouri* *Film: Top Hat, A Night at the Opera* *Letters:* Walter Millis, *The Road to War: America, 1914–1917* Arna Bontemps, *Black Thunder* Sinclair Lewis, *It Can't Happen Here* *Music:* Debut of Kirsten Flagstad George Gershwin, *Porgy and Bess* *Theater:* WPA Federal Theater Project begins (1935–1939) Clifford Odets, *Waiting for Lefty*
1936	Roosevelt reelected United Auto Workers begins strike against General Motors in Flint, Michigan	*Architecture:* Frank Lloyd Wright, Fallingwater, Pennsylvania (1936–1939) *Film: Mr. Deeds Goes to Town, Swing Time, Modern Times* *Letters:* Dale Carnegie, *How to Win Friends and Influence People* Margaret Mitchell, *Gone with the Wind* Nathanael West, *Day of the Locust* William Faulkner, *Absalom, Absalom!* *Sports:* Jesse Owens wins four Olympic gold medals, Germany
1937	Wagner-Steagall Act Roosevelt's "court-packing" plan defeated William Hastie becomes first black federal judge	*Film: Snow White and the Seven Dwarfs,* first full-length animated feature *Letters:* Zora Neale Hurston, *Their Eyes Were Watching God* *Sports:* Joe Louis becomes heavyweight boxing champion

YEAR	NATIONAL AND INTERNATIONAL EVENTS	CULTURAL AND INTELLECTUAL EVENTS
1938	Fair Labor Standards Act Congress of Industrial Organizations (CIO) formed *Kristallnacht* in Germany	*Art:* Stuart Davis, *Swing Landscape* *Letters:* Thornton Wilder, *Our Town* Lewis Mumford, *The Culture of Cities* *Music:* Benny Goodman swing band concert at Carnegie Hall Aaron Copland, *Billy the Kid* Samuel Barber, *Adagio for Strings* and *Essay for Orchestra* *Radio:* Orson Welles, "The War of the Worlds"
1939	World War II begins in Europe	New York World's Fair *Architecture:* New York and San Francisco World's Fairs *Film: Stagecoach, The Wizard of Oz, Gone with the Wind* *Letters:* John Steinbeck, *The Grapes of Wrath* *Music:* Marian Anderson sings at the Lincoln Memorial *Publishing:* Pocket Books established *Television:* First scheduled television broadcast
1940	Roosevelt reelected for unprecedented third term	*Dance:* American Ballet Theatre founded *Film: The Grapes of Wrath, The Great Dictator, Fantasia* Hattie McDaniel wins Oscar *Letters:* Eugene O'Neill wins Nobel Prize for Literature Richard Wright, *Native Son* Ernest Hemingway, *For Whom the Bell Tolls* *Music:* First regular Texaco-sponsored radio broadcast from the Metropolitan Opera (1940–present) Charles "Bird" Parker and "Dizzy" Gillespie popularize "bop" (1940s)

YEAR	NATIONAL AND INTERNATIONAL EVENTS	CULTURAL AND INTELLECTUAL EVENTS
1941	Roosevelt bans discrimination in war industries Japan attacks Pearl Harbor Japan and Germany declare war on the United States A. Philip Randolph establishes March on Washington movement	*Film:* *Citizen Kane, The Maltese Falcon* *Letters:* James Agee and Walker Evans, *Let Us Now Praise Famous Men* W. J. Cash, *The Mind of the South* Sterling Brown and Arthur P. Davis, *Negro Caravan*
1942	Japanese Americans interned Allies invade North Africa Congress of Racial Equality formed	*Art:* Edward Hopper, *Nighthawks* *Film:* *Casablanca* *Letters:* William Faulkner, *Go Down, Moses* Margaret Mead, *And Keep Your Powder Dry* Margaret Walker, *For My People*
1943	Italy surrenders Detroit, New York City, Mobile (Alabama) race riots	*Art:* Norman Rockwell, *Four Freedoms* series *Letters:* Wendell Willkie, *One World* Ayn Rand, *The Fountainhead* *Radio:* FCC orders NBC to sell its "Blue network," later the American Broadcasting System (ABC) *Theater:* *Oklahoma!*
1944	Invasion of Normandy Roosevelt reelected for fourth term Bretton Woods Conference GI Bill of Rights *Smith v. Allwright* strikes down white primaries	*Art:* Arshile Gorky, *The Liver Is the Cock's Comb* *Film:* *Double Indemnity* *Letters:* Gunnar Myrdal, *An American Dilemma* Reinhold Niebuhr, *The Children of Light and the Children of Darkness* *Music:* Leonard Bernstein, *Jeremiah Symphony* Aaron Copland, *Appalachian Spring* *Theater:* Tennessee Williams, *The Glass Menagerie*
1945	Roosevelt dies, Harry Truman becomes president First atomic bombs dropped on Hiroshima and Nagasaki, Japan World War II ends	*Film:* *Anchors Aweigh* *Letters:* Vannevar Bush, *Science—The Endless Frontier* *Theater:* *Carousel* *Print Media:* *Ebony* magazine launched

YEAR	NATIONAL AND INTERNATIONAL EVENTS	CULTURAL AND INTELLECTUAL EVENTS
1946	Employment Act Winston Churchill's "Iron Curtain" speech	Baby boom takes off with 3.4 million births, 20% more than in 1945 *Computers:* ENIAC, first electric computer *Film: Best Years of Our Lives* *Letters:* Benjamin Spock, *Common Sense Book of Baby and Child Care* Ann Petry, *The Street* Robert Penn Warren, *All the King's Men* *Music:* Marc Blitzstein, *Airborne Symphony* Aaron Copland, *Symphony no. 3* Charles Ives, *Symphony no. 3* *Publishing:* Bantam Books established *Theater:* Eugene O'Neill, *The Iceman Cometh*
1947	Truman Doctrine Taft-Hartley Act HUAC investigates Hollywood Construction of Levittown, New York, begins Journey of Reconciliation (early freedom rides)	Designer Christian Dior introduces the "new look" for women *Film: The Secret Life of Walter Mitty* *Sports:* Jackie Robinson becomes first African American in major-league baseball *Theater:* Tennessee Williams, *A Streetcar Named Desire*
1948	Marshall Plan Berlin airlift Truman elected president Truman orders desegregation of armed forces	*Dance:* New York City Ballet founded *Film: Treasure of the Sierra Madre* *Letters:* Alfred Kinsey, *Sexual Behavior in the Human Male* Dorothy West, *The Living Is Easy* Norman Mailer, *The Naked and the Dead*
1949	NATO established Truman's Fair Deal	*Music:* Leonard Bernstein, *The Age of Anxiety* *Theater: South Pacific* Arthur Miller, *Death of a Salesman*

YEAR	NATIONAL AND INTERNATIONAL EVENTS	CULTURAL AND INTELLECTUAL EVENTS
1950	Alger Hiss convicted of perjury Korean War begins Joseph McCarthy charges communist influence in State Department *Sweatt v. Painter* and *McLaurin v. Oklahoma* desegregate graduate education	**Art:** Willem de Kooning, *Excavation* Jackson Pollock, *Number 1, 1950* and *Autumn Rhythm* **Film:** *All About Eve; Sunset Boulevard* **Letters:** David Riesman, *The Lonely Crowd* **Music:** Television broadcast of *Amahl and the Night Visitors* (1950 and 1951)
1950s		**Television:** *Ed Sullivan Show, Cheyenne, Gunsmoke, Maverick, Have Gun—Will Travel, Dragnet, 77 Sunset Strip, Perry Mason, Hawaiian Eye, Father Knows Best, The Adventures of Ozzie and Harriet, Leave It to Beaver, The Honeymooners, Your Show of Shows* **Theater:** Rapid growth of Off-Broadway theater
1951	Twenty-Second Amendment General Douglas MacArthur dismissed	**Architecture:** Louis I. Kahn, Art Gallery, Yale University **Film:** *A Streetcar Named Desire, An American in Paris, The African Queen* **Letters:** J. D. Salinger, *The Catcher in the Rye* Hannah Arendt, *Origins of Totalitarianism* C. Wright Mills, *White Collar* **Theater:** *The King and I*
1952	Dwight D. Eisenhower elected president First hydrogen bomb test	**Architecture:** Skidmore, Owings, and Merrill, Lever House, New York **Film:** *High Noon; Singin' in the Rain* **Letters:** Ralph Ellison, *Invisible Man* Norman Vincent Peale, *The Power of Positive Thinking* Paul Tillich, *The Courage to Be* **Music:** John Cage, *Imaginary Landscape No. 5* **Television:** NBC airs the *Today Show*

YEAR	NATIONAL AND INTERNATIONAL EVENTS	CULTURAL AND INTELLECTUAL EVENTS
1953	Federal "termination" policy to eliminate Indian tribes Julius and Ethel Rosenberg executed as atomic spies Korean War armistice	*Art:* Larry Rivers, *Washington Crossing the Delaware* *Film: From Here to Eternity, Shane* *Letters:* Gwendolyn Brooks, *Maud Martha* *Music:* Aaron Copland, *Tender Land* Duke Ellington performs *Black, Brown, and Beige* at Carnegie Hall *Print Media:* First issue of *Playboy* *Television:* 44 million (68% rating) tune in to the delivery of Lucille Ball's child on *I Love Lucy*
1954	Army-McCarthy hearings *Brown v. Board of Education of Topeka*	*Art:* Mark Rothko, *Ochre and Red on Red* Jasper Johns, *Flag* *Film: On the Waterfront, Rear Window* *Letters:* Wallace Stevens, *Collected Poems* *Music:* "Sh-Boom" (black version by Chords, white version by Crew Cuts) becomes first rock-and-roll hit Bill Haley and the Comets, "Rock Around the Clock" sells 16 million recordings Elvis Presley records his first single, "That's All Right" *Print Media:* First issue of *Sports Illustrated*
1955	AFL and CIO merge Montgomery bus boycott begins First McDonald's opens Polio vaccine pronounced safe Emmett Till lynched, Mississippi	*Art:* Jasper Johns, *Target with Four Faces* *Film: Rebel Without a Cause, East of Eden, Blackboard Jungle, The Man with the Golden Arm* *Letters:* James Baldwin, *Notes of a Native Son* Vladimir Nabokov, *Lolita* *Music:* Marian Anderson becomes first black singer with the Metropolitan Opera *Television:* Walt Disney airs one-hour TV show on Davy Crockett, sells $300 million in dolls, toys, t-shirts, and coonskin caps

YEAR	NATIONAL AND INTERNATIONAL EVENTS	CULTURAL AND INTELLECTUAL EVENTS
1956	Eisenhower reelected Interstate Highway Act	**Architecture:** Frank Lloyd Wright, Solomon R. Guggenheim Museum, New York **Film:** *The Ten Commandments* **Letters:** Grace Metalious, *Peyton Place* Allen Ginsberg, "Howl" C. Wright Mills, *The Power Elite* William H. Whyte, *The Organization Man* **Music:** Elvis Presley, "Hound Dog," "Heartbreak Hotel," and *Ed Sullivan Show* appearance Debut of Maria Callas at the Metropolitan Opera Leonard Bernstein, *Candide* **Theater:** *My Fair Lady*
1957	Crisis over school desegregation in Little Rock, Arkansas Russians launch *Sputnik* First nuclear power plant begins operating Civil Rights Act Southern Christian Leadership Council formed	Baby boom peaks **Film:** *Paths of Glory* **Letters:** Jack Kerouac, *On the Road* Vance Packard, *The Hidden Persuaders* **Theater:** Leonard Bernstein, *West Side Story* Eugene O'Neill, *Long Day's Journey into Night* (posthumous)
1958	National Aeronautics and Space Administration (NASA) founded	**Letters:** Grove Press's unexpurgated edition of D. H. Lawrence, *Lady Chatterley's Lover* John Kenneth Galbraith, *The Affluent Society* **Music:** Chuck Berry, "Johnny B. Goode" Samuel Barber, *Vanessa*
1959	Alaska and Hawaii statehood	**Film:** *Ben-Hur; Some Like It Hot* **Letters:** William Appleman Williams, *The Tragedy of American Diplomacy* C. Wright Mills, *The Sociological Imagination* Paule Marshall, *Brown Girl, Brownstones* **Television:** Quiz show scandals begin **Theater:** Lorraine Hansberry, *A Raisin in the Sun*

YEAR	NATIONAL AND INTERNATIONAL EVENTS	CULTURAL AND INTELLECTUAL EVENTS
Late 1950s		*Music:* Debbie Reynolds, "Tammy"; Bobby Darin, "Mack the Knife"; recordings by Perry Como, Frank Sinatra, Nat "King" Cole, Lena Horne, Pat Boone
1960s		*Television: Twilight Zone, Star Trek, Batman, The Monkees*
1960	U-2 incident First sit-ins in Greensboro, North Carolina John F. Kennedy elected president Civil Rights Act Students for a Democratic Society founded Student Nonviolent Coordinating Committee formed	Food and Drug Administration approves sale of "The Pill," the prescription drug Enovid *Film: Psycho* *Letters:* Dwight Macdonald, "Masscult and Midcult" Paul Goodman, *Growing Up Absurd* Daniel Bell, *The End of Ideology* *Music:* Chubby Checker, "The Twist" *Television:* Presidential campaign debates between Nixon and Kennedy
1961	Bay of Pigs invasion in Cuba Freedom rides in the South Twenty-Third Amendment	*Architecture:* Louis I. Kahn, Richards Medical Research Laboratories, University of Pennsylvania *Art:* Roy Lichtenstein, *The Kiss* *Letters:* Joseph Heller, *Catch-22*
1962	Cuban missile crisis First American orbits the earth	*Art:* Andy Warhol, *Gold Marilyn Monroe* *Film: The Longest Day* *Letters:* Rachel Carson, *Silent Spring* Marshall McLuhan, *The Gutenberg Galaxy* Michael Harrington, *The Other America* Thomas S. Kuhn, *The Structure of Scientific Revolutions* Ken Kesey, *One Flew Over the Cuckoo's Nest* *Music:* Bob Dylan, "Blowin' in the Wind" Lincoln Center opens

YEAR	NATIONAL AND INTERNATIONAL EVENTS	CULTURAL AND INTELLECTUAL EVENTS
1963	Kennedy assassinated, Lyndon B. Johnson becomes president Civil rights demonstrations in Birmingham March on Washington for Jobs and Freedom Birmingham, Alabama, church bombed Medgar Evers assassinated	**Architecture:** Paul Rudolph, Art and Architecture Building, Yale University **Art:** Robert Rauschenberg, *Estate* **Film:** *The Birds* **Letters:** Betty Friedan, *The Feminine Mystique* Martin Marty, *Second Chance for American Protestantism* Martin Luther King Jr., "Letter from a Birmingham Jail" **Print Media:** first issue *New York Review of Books* **Television:** Networks lengthen evening news shows to 30 minutes **Theater:** Edward Albee, *Who's Afraid of Virginia Woolf?*
1964	Civil Rights Act Free Speech Movement at the University of California, Berkeley "Freedom Summer" in Mississippi, three killed Gulf of Tonkin incident and resolution War on Poverty begins Twenty-Fourth Amendment Mississippi Freedom Democratic Party at Democratic National Convention Malcolm X leaves Nation of Islam Martin Luther King Jr. wins Nobel Peace Prize	**Art:** Romare Bearden, *The Dove* **Film:** *Dr. Strangelove, My Fair Lady, Mary Poppins* **Letters:** Saul Bellow, *Herzog* Martin Luther King Jr., *Why We Can't Wait* **Music:** The Beatles appear on Ed Sullivan Show, drawing largest ever audience (67 million) to that point **Theater:** Amiri Baraka (Leroi Jones), *Dutchman*
1965	Selma to Montgomery march in Alabama Voting Rights Act Escalation of American involvement in Vietnam Teach-ins begin Malcolm X assassinated Pope Paul VI makes first papal visit to U.S. Watts riots, Los Angeles	First "acid test" by Ken Kesey and the Merry Pranksters **Film:** *The Sound of Music* **Letters:** Ralph Nader, *Unsafe at Any Speed* Malcolm X, *Autobiography*

YEAR	NATIONAL AND INTERNATIONAL EVENTS	CULTURAL AND INTELLECTUAL EVENTS
1966	Stokeley Carmichael calls for "black power" National Organization for Women (NOW) formed Black Panther Party formed *Miranda v. Arizona*	*Letters:* Masters and Johnson, *Human Sexual Response* Jacqueline Susann, *The Valley of the Dolls* Truman Capote, *In Cold Blood*
1967	Race riots in many major American cities Twenty-Fifth Amendment Thurgood Marshall becomes first black on U.S. Supreme Court	*Film: Bonnie and Clyde, The Graduate, Guess Who's Coming to Dinner?* *Letters:* Haki Madhubuti, *Think Black!* John A. Williams, *The Man Who Cried I Am*
1968	Robert F. Kennedy assassinated First black woman elected to Congress Martin Luther King Jr. assassinated Richard Nixon elected president Kerner Commission report Poor People's Campaign, Washington, D.C.	*Film: M*A*S*H, 2001* *Letters:* James D. Watson, *The Double Helix* Norman Mailer, *Armies of the Night* Eldridge Cleaver, *Soul on Ice* Hoyt Fuller, "Towards a Black Aesthetic" *Theater: Hair*
1969	Nixon Doctrine Apollo 11 lands on the moon Two Black Panther leaders killed in Chicago police raid	Patrons of Stonewall Inn, a Greenwich Village gay bar, resist police raid *Film: Easy Rider* *Letters:* Kurt Vonnegut, *Slaughterhouse Five* *Music:* Woodstock and Altamont music festivals *Radio:* National Public Radio incorporates *Television: Sesame Street* airs Live broadcast of Neil Armstrong's first steps and words from the moon
1970s		*Television: Mary Tyler Moore Show, Rhoda, All in the Family, M*A*S*H, Rockford Files, Charlie's Angels, Dallas, Mary Hartman, Masterpiece Theatre,* miniseries *Roots*

YEAR	NATIONAL AND INTERNATIONAL EVENTS	CULTURAL AND INTELLECTUAL EVENTS
1970	Environmental Protection Agency created Kent State and Jackson State shootings First Earth Day	*Film:* Patton *Letters:* Joe McGinniss, *The Selling of the President, 1968* Toni Morrison, *The Bluest Eye* Maya Angelou, *I Know Why the Caged Bird Sings* Mari Evans, *I Am a Black Woman* Michael S. Harper, *Dear John, Dear Coltrane* Philip Roth, *Portnoy's Complaint* Mario Puzo, *The Godfather*
1971	Twenty-Sixth Amendment U.S. Supreme Court calls for widespread busing to facilitate school desegregation Jesse Jackson founds PUSH	*Film:* Shaft, *The Last Picture Show* *Letters:* New York Times publishes Pentagon Papers John Rawls, *A Theory of Justice* Sylvia Plath, *The Bell Jar* Addison Gayle, *The Black Aesthetic* Ernest J. Gaines, *The Autobiography of Miss Jane Pittman* Dee Brown, *Bury My Heart at Wounded Knee*
1972	Nixon visits China SALT I Watergate break-in Nixon reelected First National Black Political Convention	*Computers:* First minicomputers developed *Film:* The Godfather *Letters:* Sydney E. Ahlstrom, *A Religious History of the American People* Ishmael Reed, *Mumbo Jumbo* *Print Media:* Ms. magazine founded *Television:* television ownership reaches 99.8% of American homes, cigarette ads banned
1973	U.S. pulls out of Vietnam Battle of Wounded Knee OPEC raises oil prices after Yom Kippur War *Roe v. Wade*	*Art:* Philip Guston, *Painting, Smoking, Eating* *Letters:* Thomas Pynchon, *Gravity's Rainbow*

YEAR	NATIONAL AND INTERNATIONAL EVENTS	CULTURAL AND INTELLECTUAL EVENTS
1974	Nixon resigns, Gerald Ford becomes president	*Film: The Godfather, Part II* *Letters:* Carl Bernstein and Robert Woodward, *All the President's Men* Albert Murray, *Train Whistle Guitar* *Television:* rapid expansion of cable television systems (1974–1981)
1975	U.S. withdraws from Vietnam	*Architecture:* Charles W. Moore, Piazza d'Italia, New Orleans *Film: Jaws* *Letters:* E. O. Wilson, *Sociobiology* Samuel R. Delany, *Dhalgren* *Theater:* Ntozake Shange, *For Colored Girls Who Have Considered Suicide*
1976	Jimmy Carter elected president U.S. Supreme Court upholds constitutionality of capital punishment	*Film: Taxi Driver* *Theater:* David Mamet, *American Buffalo*
1977	Panama Canal treaties Department of Energy formed In first execution in nearly ten years Gary Gilmore is executed by firing squad in Utah	*Computers:* Apple II personal computer introduced *Film: Star Wars, Annie Hall* *Letters:* Toni Morrison, *Song of Solomon* *Music:* Television broadcast of *La Bohème*
1978		*Letters:* Herman Wouk, *War and Remembrance* *Television: Roots* series
1979	Nuclear accident at Three Mile Island SALT II OPEC raises oil prices again Iranian hostage crisis (1979–1981)	*Letters:* William Styron, *Sophie's Choice* Kurt Vonnegut, *Jailbird* Octavia Butler, *Kindred* *Television:* CNN airs, C-SPAN begins gavel-to-gavel coverage of the U.S. House of Representatives *Theater: Evita*

YEAR	NATIONAL AND INTERNATIONAL EVENTS	CULTURAL AND INTELLECTUAL EVENTS
1980s	Increasing number of deaths from AIDS	*Computers:* rising sales of personal computers for use at home *Television:* increasing sales of video games, satellite dishes, and camcorders *Cosby Show, Cheers, Murphy Brown, Dallas, Dynasty, L.A. Law, Hill Street Blues, Current Affair, Hard Copy,* talk shows, game shows
1980	Ronald Reagan elected president	*Architecture:* Michael Graves, Portland Building *Film: Raging Bull* *Letters:* June Jordan, "Poem about My Rights" Erma Bombeck, *Aunt Erma's Cope Book* *Television:* CNN established
1981	Sandra Day O'Connor appointed the first woman on the Supreme Court	*Letters:* David Bradley, *Chaneysville Incident* *Music:* Steve Reich, *Tehillim* *Television:* live broadcast of attempted assassination of Ronald Reagan, MTV airs
1982	Equal Rights Amendment fails Stock market boom begins	*Architecture:* Maya Lin, Vietnam Memorial *Film: Blade Runner, E.T., Tootsie* *Journalism:* First issue of *USA Today* *Letters:* Alice Walker, *The Color Purple* Gloria Naylor, *The Women of Brewster Place* *Music:* Philip Glass, *Glassworks* *Theater: Cats*
1983	U.S. invades Grenada Reagan proposes "Star Wars" defense system HIV, agent responsible for AIDS, is found	*Letters:* John Edgar Williams, *Sent for You Yesterday* *Theater:* Neil Simon, *Brighton Beach Memoirs*

YEAR	NATIONAL AND INTERNATIONAL EVENTS	CULTURAL AND INTELLECTUAL EVENTS
1984	Reagan reelected	*Letters:* Audre Lorde, *Sister Outsider* *Music:* Compact Discs enter the mass market Steve Reich, *The Desert Music* *Theater:* David Mamet, *Glengarry Glenn Ross*
1985	United States deploys cruise missiles in Europe	*Film:* Number of VCRs in American homes surpasses 17 million *The Color Purple* *Letters:* Jamaica Kincaid, *Annie John* *Music:* John Adams, *Harmonielehre* *Television:* LIVE-AID concert
1986	Tax reform bill passes Federal budget deficit peaks at $221 billion *Challenger* space shuttle explodes Iran-Contra controversy	*Film: Platoon* *Letters:* Rita Dove, *Thomas and Beulah* *Music:* Philip Glass, *Songs from Liquid Days* John Adams, *Nixon in China* *Television:* live broadcast of the explosion of the U.S. space shuttle *Challenger*
1987	Stock market crash	*Art:* Andres Serrano, *Piss Christ* *Film: Full Metal Jacket, Moonstruck* *Letters:* Allan Bloom, *The Closing of the American Mind* Toni Morrison, *Beloved* *Theater:* August Wilson, *Fences*
1988	Intermediate Range Nuclear Forces Treaty Iran-Contra scandal indictments George Bush elected president	*Architecture:* Michael Graves, Napa Valley Winery *Film: Who Framed Roger Rabbit?* *Theater: Phantom of the Opera*
1989	Federal bailout of savings and loan industry begins U.S. invades Panama Communist regimes collapse in central and eastern Europe *Exxon Valdez* oil spill	*Film: Do the Right Thing, The Little Mermaid*

YEAR	NATIONAL AND INTERNATIONAL EVENTS	CULTURAL AND INTELLECTUAL EVENTS
1990	Immigration reform implemented National debt reaches $3.1 trillion	*Computers:* Computers in use pass 50 million *Film: Goodfellas* *Letters:* Charles Johnson, *Middle Passage* Walter Mosley, *Devil in a Blue Dress*
1991	Strategic Arms Reduction Treaty (START) Persian Gulf War Tailhook scandal; Pan American Airways goes out of business	*Film: The Silence of the Lambs, Beauty and the Beast* *Theater:* Neil Simon, *Lost in Yonkers*
1992	Bill Clinton elected president Los Angeles riots	*Film: My Cousin Vinny, Malcolm X, Aladdin* *Letters:* Terry McMillan, *Waiting to Exhale* *Television:* Johnny Carson retires from *The Tonight Show*, draws over 55 million viewers
1993	NAFTA treaty approved	*Film: Jurassic Park, Schindler's List* *Letters:* Yusef Komunyakaa, *Neon Vernacular*
1994		*Television:* live broadcast of O. J. Simpson's car chase with police in Los Angeles; *Seinfeld* a hit sitcom
1995	Oklahoma City bombing	
1996	Clinton reelected	

ENCYCLOPEDIA OF
AMERICAN
CULTURAL &
INTELLECTUAL
HISTORY

Part 1

∽o∾

EARLY AMERICA

Part 1, *continued*

OVERVIEW:
EARLY AMERICA

Ned C. Landsman

In the middle of the twentieth century, a historian discussing the cultural and intellectual history of the colonial era of American history would have had little difficulty in devising a theme. Few doubted that American culture had progressed during that period from the hierarchical and constricted European forms American settlers had brought with them to the more democratic and independent ways that characterized Americans on the eve of the Revolution. Such an evolution was apparent in the principal survey of the topic produced during those years, Max Savelle's *Seeds of Liberty* (1948), which offered commendably nuanced portraits of a remarkable variety of topics in early American cultural history, only to conclude every section with a discussion of how each of those represented an aspect of American freedom.

At the end of the century, historians no longer shared that rosy view. For one thing, the earlier assumption of a static European background no longer sufficed as a description of the diverse and rapidly changing societies from which the settlers derived. Certainly an England that could send three hundred thousand or more people to the New World over the course of the seventeenth century would hardly seem to fit the picture of a culture in stasis; other western European nations had even higher rates of out-migration. Nor was the evolution of their settlements toward liberty, democracy, and American distinctiveness quite so straightforward as Savelle assumed. Indeed, by century's end, many historians would argue that in important respects the progression was more nearly the opposite: the cultures of the British colonies in North America evolved from an early period characterized by an almost unprecedented degree of unsettlement toward conditions that, by the years just before the American Revolution, were more orderly and hierarchical, and decidedly more British, than they had been in their initial stages.

That change in perception is the product of several historiographical trends. One is the abandonment of the assumption of American exceptionalism and the advent of a serious interest in comparative history. American historians no longer blindly set off their findings against a frozen image of the societies the settlers left behind. They are far more cognizant than before that the backgrounds the settlers brought with them varied by place of origin and over time. They are more likely to compare the cultures of British America to those of the neighboring settlements in New Spain and New France. Moreover, historical accounts also routinely notice the presence and the contributions of those who previously were rarely considered part of the story. Those include the native inhabitants of the lands, the African slaves whom the settlers purchased to work for them, and many others within colonial society who lacked a loud public voice: non-English speakers, laborers, indentured servants, and women. Their inclusion makes the story of the colonial era more complex and more diverse than was previously understood.

REGIONAL CULTURES

One way to treat that diversity is to divide early American culture into regions, which can be based roughly upon zones of settlement. Those regions were not wholly uniform, of course, nor was any one fully distinctive from the others; what makes them useful for our purposes is that they grew out of fairly distinctive migrations. Moreover, many early Americans developed recognizable, though certainly not all-encompassing, regional identities.

The Chesapeake The first region of settlement was the Chesapeake, dating from the founding of Jamestown in 1607, comprising the provinces of Virginia and Maryland. For much of the seventeenth century, Chesapeake culture reflected a society in considerable disarray. That was largely the result of horrific mortality, which precluded stable family life for the vast majority. Most of those who came arrived under terms of indenture, requiring them to labor for their masters, often under brutal conditions, for periods of up to seven years. Thus while many continued to seek the community, family, and stability to which they were accustomed—in short, the basic measures of civility in the seventeenth century—families and communities remained rather stunted. The situation discouraged certain kinds of cultural productions, such as literary ruminations upon the society in which they found themselves. For those who took the time to ponder it, a major theme was their isolation and remoteness from their cultural anchors abroad. "Wee are here att the end of the World," wrote planter William Byrd in 1690, "and Europe may bee turned topsy turvy ere wee can hear a Word of itt."

Toward the end of the century, social conditions began to stabilize. The mortality rate declined, and the increasing proportion of women in the region led to much greater stability in families and communities. About that time Chesapeake planters began to devote some effort to locating themselves and their society within the larger British world. One manifestation was the first efforts by the inhabitants to write about their region and its history. Thus, in short succession Virginians wrote *The Present State of Virginia, and the College* (1697) and the *History and Present State of Virginia* (1705), both intended to describe the background and circumstances of that settlement to a metropolitan audience.

By the middle of the eighteenth century, Chesapeake culture had settled into a far more stable pattern. At the top sat an increasingly interconnected class of planters, many of whom began to devote themselves to lives of politics, sociability, and learning as they sought to establish themselves as refined, civic-minded gentlemen. They identified especially with Whig traditions in political thought, which assumed superior virtue on the part of independent landed gentlemen and legitimated patriarchal authority over wives, children, servants, and slaves. Below them was a society of smaller farmers tied to the planters by a web of economic dependency and by the boundaries of race. As the basic labor force on the plantations shifted from European servant to African slave, even poorer white farmers attained a level of status and independence to which the great majority of Africans and their descendants could never aspire.

New England If the culture of the Chesapeake evolved partly in reaction to early conditions of pro-

found unsettlement, those who migrated to New England aimed from the beginning to establish conditions of order and settlement as substantial as could be found anywhere in the English world. Where migration to the Chesapeake was dominated by young, single men on the make, New England received a large number of families, many of whom were Puritans—extreme Protestants of the English Reformation—whose avowed intention was to remove themselves from what they perceived as the corruptions of England and the English church. They established a new and distinctive religious order in much of New England, based upon village-centered Congregationalist churches, the strict enforcement of Puritan orthodoxy, and a rigid moral code. Massachusetts was created to be a Bible commonwealth, and whatever was not in accord with their understanding of Scripture—that is to say, "innovation" of any sort—was resisted, persecuted, or warned away.

At the heart of Puritanism was the belief in the sovereignty of God, who determined the fates of nations and individuals according to his will, subject only to the limitations granted by specific scriptural promises. In that conviction, the Puritans were Calvinists, adherents to the general religious teachings of the sixteenth-century Genevan reformer John Calvin. Other important features of a Calvinist theology were the belief in justification by faith in God rather than by the performance of good works, and predestination, which held that some were irrevocably elected for salvation, and others for damnation.

The emphasis upon God's power led to considerable introspection among Puritans about their own fates and those of their colony. Puritans searched their lives and their feelings for signs of grace, or the lack thereof. Their leaders scrutinized the course of events in their region, recording its history right from the beginning and using it to persuade themselves that divine favor had been bestowed upon their mission. They found the signs of that approbation chiefly in "remarkable providences": unusual happenings, strange coincidences, or wondrous events that suggested supernatural intervention in the ordinary course of affairs. Thus would the early settler Edward Johnson in 1654 recount *The Wonder-Working Providence of Sions Saviour in New England*, a theme many would repeat thereafter.

The principal innovation of the Puritans was their emphasis upon purity, reflected in their effort to establish a church of "visible saints." Where Protestant orthodoxy had long maintained that the creation of a church restricted purely to the godly was impossible in a world where sinners and saints were hopelessly intermixed, the Massachusetts Puritans set out to try. While everyone in Puritan townships was not only expected but required to attend divine worship, only those who could recount the workings of God upon their souls in satisfactory fashion were allowed into full membership. In practice there was considerable variety in what was considered acceptable testimony from one congregation to the next, but the effort to achieve orthodoxy and visible sainthood distinguished New England Puritans from the mainstream of English Protestantism and even from their Puritan counterparts overseas.

The attainment of orthodoxy required the stifling of dissent, not only among non-Puritans but among key figures within the movement as well. Among those driven away was Thomas Hooker, whose misgivings about the attempt at purity led him to move to Connecticut. Another was Roger Williams, whose separatist belief that the secular state should not be given power over the godly church members became even more problematic when he insisted that the colony's patent from the king was invalid and the land wrongly taken from its Indian inhabitants. Still another exile was Anne Hutchinson, whose seeming endorsement of the "antinomian" heresy—she claimed she could hear the voice of the Holy Spirit—was rendered doubly threatening by the fact that she was a woman claiming that her connection to the spirit gave her greater authority than that of the established male religious leaders.

If the majority of lay Puritans dutifully attended to the lengthy rounds of preaching to which their ministers subjected them, they were not simply passive receivers of the word. Late-twentieth-century historians have depicted a laity that manifested an active interest in their own religious concerns, sometimes in ways that varied from orthodox doctrine. Among their primary concerns were to secure the baptism of their children, fearing that they might die outside of the church, and an often scrupulous reluctance to take communion where they felt that their thoughts and deeds had been less than pure.

During the last quarter of the seventeenth century, Puritan New England suffered a series of setbacks to their culture and their sense of divine favor. Those included King Philip's War (1675–1676), which destroyed frontier towns all over New England and led to the emergence of the captivity narrative as a popular literary genre, as in a work by Mary Rowlandson entitled *Soveraignty & Goodness*

of God, together, with the Faithfulness of His Promises Desplayed; Being a Narrative of the Captivity and Restauration of Mrs. Mary Rowlandson (1682). That was followed by the loss in 1684 of the Massachusetts charter and with it the ability of the Bay Colony to rule itself without outside interference. Thenceforth, New Englanders would have to accept the subordination of Puritan government to royal authority.

Perhaps most troubling of all was the witchcraft hysteria in Salem village in 1692, in which nearly two hundred people were accused of being witches, followed by trials leading to the conviction of twenty-seven and the execution of twenty. Most of those in each category were mature women. Many issues were at stake in Salem; recent studies have pointed out a range of conflicts over commerce and the changing nature of the village, the appearance of religious dissent, and the role of women in the community. It is clear that Puritan culture was extremely suspicious of older, unattached, or deviant women, whose presence seemed to challenge the normal order of patriarchal authority.

In the eighteenth century, New England would remain the most orthodox and orderly sector of British America. To be sure, religious affiliation would diversify, with Anglicans, Quakers, and Baptists all setting up meetings alongside of what remained a privileged Congregationalist establishment. Massachusetts would lose much of its autonomy to royal government. Still, the level of religiosity remained high. If the cultural landscape came to look less distinctly Puritan and New English and more Protestant and British, it was a British culture heavily imbued with Protestant faith.

The Middle Colonies In the three-province region known as the middle colonies, orthodoxy was never so large a concern. Even before the English conquest of New Netherland in 1664 made England the dominant power in the region, the mid-Atlantic was a land of many peoples. New Netherland was a medley of many groups that arrived by way of the Netherlands, the principal refuge center of Protestant Europe. Dutch speakers, German speakers, French speakers, English, Scots, and others all sought opportunities in this minor outpost of the Dutch commercial empire, where they were joined by Africans and Jews. New Sweden housed a mixed population of Swedes and Finns. Even the native population was an extremely varied mixture of Algonkian and Iroquoian speakers, including Lenape, Susquehannocks, members of the Five Nations, and many others, divided into diverse villages and nations.

The framework for mid-Atlantic culture was laid by its two principal proprietors. The first was James Stuart, the duke of York, and later James II of England and VII of Scotland, who would be ousted from the throne in the "Glorious Revolution of 1688." James received an extensive charter encompassing what would become New York and New Jersey, and much more, making him the dominant power in the region. James, a Catholic, established a form of religious toleration in the region, just as he would later in England, albeit one that represented considerably less than a complete freedom of religion. James's toleration was based in part upon a desire to make Protestant polities safe for Catholic worshippers, and Protestants thought that his real plan was to bring in Catholic rule by stealth.

Whatever his motives, James combined toleration with zealous protection of his own prerogatives. He certainly curtailed the power of any Protestant group to establish a dominance that would threaten either Catholic consciences or proprietary prerogatives, although his government did promote strong local establishments that would help preserve order without challenging colonial authority. The duke aggressively opposed militant Protestants, such as the Puritans of New England, whose governments he worked to confine. He approved the granting of a charter in 1681 to William Penn; the Society of Friends, to which Penn belonged, had abandoned its earlier militancy in favor of a far less threatening appeal to conscience. The first principle of Pennsylvania was liberty of conscience.

Thus, while toleration and pluralism came to seem among the most prominent characteristics of mid-Atlantic society, the colonies within the region maintained varying degrees of toleration and differing styles of pluralism. In New York, James's vision continued to have influence long after the end of his proprietorship. New York remained a colony of distinct cultural groups that only rarely intermixed, with a Dutch zone of influence in much of the Hudson Valley, a New English culture on eastern Long Island, and pockets dominated by various British cultures elsewhere. Beyond them all, a powerful Iroquois Confederacy sharply limited the prospects for expansion. Only New York City and its environs approached a true pluralism. Within most regions there was a dominant local church: Dutch Reformed, Congregationalist, or Anglican. By the duke's instructions the majority in each town chose the religion, with the whole of the inhabitants

taxed for its support. After James's ouster, a series of Anglican governors worked aggressively to make the Church of England into the dominant religion throughout the lower counties in and around New York City.

The development of New Jersey was considerably more complex. James granted the colony to two of his cronies, John Lord Berkeley and Sir George Carteret. They in turn sold their interests to a Quaker group that settled West Jersey, while a group of largely Scots proprietors acquired the eastern division. Although the two sections reunited in 1702, significant divisions remained. With authority divided, the Anglican Church was unable to attain the dominance it achieved around New York. Instead, the Presbyterian Church was able to forge alliances among the dissenting churches. With the establishment of the Presbyterian College of New Jersey in 1746, that church obtained an institutional voice more prominent than any other in the colony.

In Pennsylvania, toleration came closer to complete religious liberty, at least for Protestants, albeit not without frequent conflicts among competing religious and ethnic groups. Those groups were more often intermixed within the countryside than in New York, and in many areas no one communion was dominant. The principal exception was the backcountry, where Scots-Irish Presbyterians dominated large areas. There they fell into frequent military conflict with their Indian neighbors, which resulted in political troubles with the more peaceable colonial authorities. The most striking instance was the Paxton uprising of 1763, in which a group of predominantly Presbyterian frontiersmen from the town of Paxton and its surroundings, convinced that colonial authorities were not protecting them against Indian enemies, massacred the Christian Indians living under the colony's protection at the local workhouse. That produced a voluminous pamphlet war between east and west, Quaker and Presbyterian, in which religious and ethnic name-calling figured prominently. Still, the overriding facts of life elsewhere in Pennsylvania remained toleration and pluralism, deriving from Penn's initial plan.

The Quaker legacy gave the Delaware Valley a distinct moral tone. At the heart of the Quaker faith was the belief in the inner light, the small, still voice of God in everyone. While this had led some of the earliest Friends to follow the spirit into aggressive protests against the trappings of worldliness and social rank, by the time of Penn's proprietary most had opted to channel the light into less disruptive endeavors. For some Quakers, this meant causes such as the testimony of peace, a prominent role for Quaker women's meetings, and for a small but growing group, opposition to slavery.

Part of the reason that Quakers were able to maintain their testimony of peace was that for much of the period, Pennsylvania was spared the border conflicts that affected New England and New York, both of which bordered on New France. The elaborate alliance of the Covenant Chain that New York long maintained with its Five Nation neighbors provided much of the space within which Pennsylvania could conduct its holy experiment. Toward the middle of the eighteenth century, the expansion of British and French colonies finally brought those rival powers face to face in western Pennsylvania, effectively ending the Quaker era of peace.

The doctrine of the inner light resulted also in the adoption of distinctly modern notions of the family. Because the voice of the spirit resided in everyone, the mission of Friends was to convince others to listen to it, which implied the use of persuasion rather than brute force. Thus Quaker families emphasized nurturing in child rearing, in contrast to the authoritarian styles dominant elsewhere; one historian has portrayed Quakers as having the first modern families, based upon affection as much as authority. That implied raising children at home rather than sending them out to work as servants in other households, which in turn required extensive and prosperous farms, contributing to the decidedly commercial ethic of the mid-Atlantic countryside.

The middle colonies housed two main groups of non-English-speakers: the Dutch of New York and northern New Jersey, and the German speakers of Pennsylvania and its backcountry. For much of the colonial period, many in those groups remained largely to themselves. Some of the leading Dutch families of Albany and New York City mixed among the English elite, intermarrying and sometimes joining Anglican churches. In the process they separated themselves from other Dutch inhabitants, especially in rural areas, who continued to speak Dutch and worship in Dutch Reformed churches in communities that often remained largely separate from the English-speaking majority. German speakers, by contrast, settled principally in Pennsylvania and the southern backcountry. Lacking the experience of conquest, Germans developed a more articulate public culture than did their Dutch counterparts, with German-language newspapers and German community leaders engaging in political activity and discussion.

The Lower South   The other principal region of early America was the Lower South, comprising the colonies of South Carolina, Georgia, and East Florida. Unlike North Carolina, whose often modest farms and cultural diversity in many respects resembled society in the middle colonies, South Carolina from its beginnings was tied to the planter culture of the Caribbean, from which its first settlers arrived in 1669. There, they built a planter society surpassing any other on the North American mainland for wealth and grandeur; South Carolina became the only mainland colony with an African majority.

In the rest of mainland North America Africans were interspersed among predominantly European populations and often had only limited communication with other Africans, but the low country had a larger proportion of African-born slaves, who were sufficiently concentrated on large plantations to maintain distinct African elements within their cultures. Moreover, the fact that, before the middle of the eighteenth century, the low country received a high proportion of its slaves from Angola, meant the slaves had greater opportunity to maintain common African elements.

In the nineteenth century, northern observers would come to portray the plantation South as perpetually backwards, beholden to an ancient system of slave labor that undermined attempts to modernize. Such a view would hardly have been expressed the century before. Then, plantation society prospered and progressed so rapidly that planters there saw no contradiction between slavery and economic advance.

During the eighteenth century, planters of the Lower South devoted themselves to improving agriculture and the economies of their plantations, paying especially close attention to theories of economic development articulated by philosophers of the Scottish Enlightenment. Charleston was a cosmopolitan city with many clubs and institutions dedicated to intellectual improvement. Farther south, Georgia planters would come to argue that their colony, originally planned as a place for debtors to improve themselves through hard work, should end the prohibition on slavery so they could attain the same economic liberties as their slaveholding neighbors in other plantation colonies, a position they soon achieved.

Similar complaints at times emerged from the backcountry of the region, whose planters often thought that colonial authorities neglected their needs. Much of the backcountry was populated by a strand of settlement different from those who settled the low country, namely Scots-Irish and German farmers who migrated southward from Pennsylvania with their own distinct traditions. Many easterners looked with disdain upon those settlers. The younger William Byrd offered a witty depiction of his encounter with what he viewed as the barbarous inhabitants of "Lubberland" on the Carolina frontier in 1728, while the Anglican missionary Charles Woodmason castigated backcountry settlers as "Rude—Ignorant—Void of Manners, Education or Good Breeding—No Genteel or Polite Persons among them. . . . A mix'd Medley from all countries and the Off Scouring of America" (*The Carolina Backcountry*, pp. 6–7). In parts of the backcountry it seemed to colonial authorities as though the inhabitants had regressed from civility to savagery, a source of great concern to many.

In fact, many planters in the western lands were as desirous of civility and order as their coastal neighbors. The failure of authorities in the capital to provide basic institutions of order such as courts in some areas was a factor in the Regulator movements in the western territories of both Carolinas during the 1770s. With the growing prosperity of parts of the backcountry, and with the assistance of a growing network of churches, stores, and academies, some areas were transformed into full-fledged planter societies.

It had not always been that way. In their earliest stages, backcountry cultures displayed a unique character. In the "middle ground" between European and Indian, before any group had established full dominance, culture itself existed in a constant state of negotiation. People from various backgrounds engaged in a great variety of interactions with one another, from marriage to trade to diplomacy, each interpreting them in their own ways. In the Great Lakes region known to the French as the *pays d'en haut,* the constant influx of Indian refugees from the beaver wars and the delicate balance among British, French, and native power allowed the middle ground to endure for generations. Only after British authorities had attained sufficient power to impose their meanings upon the interactions of the peoples of that region did the backcountry begin to take on a British or European cultural style.

Much of the Lower South existed as a border culture, located between Spanish settlements to the south and the Creek and Cherokee nations to the west. An important reason for the founding of Georgia was to provide a buffer for South Carolina. There was an ongoing threat of Carolina slaves escaping to the south or west. Indians often returned the slaves; Spanish Florida did not. After the Seven Years' War (1756–1763), when British power became more secure in the region, British speculators began investing in exotic plantation regimes in the new colonies of East and West Florida, using African slaves or Europeans in slave-like conditions in an effort to create vast manors generating profitable goods and lordly lifestyles for planter-investors.

None had greater adjustments to make than the native inhabitants of the region, who constantly had to readjust their lifestyles to the movements of the various peoples around them. That resulted in the creation of new Indian nations from the remains of ones that had been diminished by warfare and disease; the Catawba, for example, were constituted out of a variety of smaller Indian nations in the southern borderlands in the eighteenth century. After failing in their efforts to resist Carolinian expansion by military force, the Catawba nation instead opted to develop friendship and trade relations with Europeans that let them survive on a portion of their homelands, albeit in a tenuous and dependent state.

EIGHTEENTH-CENTURY TRENDS

For all of the regional diversity, some general trends can be identified. One was a common tendency toward increased stability, order, and refinement. An important manifestation of this tendency was the growing participation of provincial Americans in the movement for a new, progressive model of learning called the Enlightenment. Beginning in the last decades of the seventeenth century, small groups of Americans from New England through the plantation colonies began immersing themselves in the new learning that was coming out of Europe. In New England, and later in the Chesapeake, students at Harvard College and at William and Mary were introduced to new writings in moral philosophy. These were generated especially by English and Scottish clergymen known as Latitudinarians, who deemphasized the particulars of denominational conformity, which had played so important a role in early New England, in favor of a common Protestant piety. Enlightened gentlemen also avidly followed other types of works from abroad, such as Joseph Addison and Richard Steele's witty *Tatler* (1709–1711) and *Spectator* (1711–1714) and other "polite" writings aimed at advancing civility and refinement.

The American Enlightenment took varied forms. It was evident in the many clubs and taverns where gentlemen and merchants congregated for purposes of commerce, conversation, and conviviality. It could also be discerned among urban tradesmen, such as the young Benjamin Franklin, who with a number of counterparts devoted much of his spare time to reading and discussing the latest theories in politics, science, philosophy, and religion. Even some women participated, such as Sarah Prince and Esther Edwards Burr, ministers' daughters who corresponded with one another in a series of journal-like letters modeled on those found in Samuel Richardson's moral novel *Clarissa* (1747–1748), which the women had read and discussed. They used these journals to converse about contemporary literature and the state of their souls, using reading and writing to spur one another to moral and intellectual improvement.

Burr and Prince were exemplars not only of the wide-ranging influence of the Enlightenment but of another, sometimes contrary trend in eighteenth-century cultural life: evangelical Protestantism, associated most dramatically with the religious revival known as the Great Awakening. That movement reached its apex during the American tours of the English evangelist George Whitefield between 1739 and 1741 and continued to influence religious life for decades thereafter. Whitefield and those who followed induced dramatic, emotional conversions among a broad populace in most of the Reformed denominations. Their tactics, including that of intruding themselves uninvited into the parishes of their fellow ministers, created lasting divides in several denominations and in American Protestantism generally.

The Enlightenment and the Awakening were long deemed opposing movements, the one representing the forces of modernity and reason, the other of traditionalism and emotion. Yet more than a few individuals, including Sarah Prince and Esther Burr, managed to straddle the divide. Nowhere was this more pronounced than at the College of New Jersey (later Princeton), where Burr's husband and father both presided. There, a succession of leaders managed to fuse much of the new learning in science and moral philosophy, along with the progressive intellectual framework of the Enlightenment, with a continuing commitment to evangelical piety. The greatest representative of that synthesis was John Witherspoon, who left Scotland in 1768 to lead the college and whose influence was felt in everything from religion and education to revolutionary politics and public morals and literary taste.

Witherspoon's influence helped cement an affinity on the part of Americans for intellectual trends emanating from Scotland in the eighteenth century, in areas from science and political economy to religion and moral philosophy. That was partly the result of their shared situation as expansive provincial cultures still removed from the center of imperial power. A common thread of those aspects of the Scottish Enlightenment assimilated by Americans was an emphasis on the demographic, economic, and even moral roots of prosperity and progress over those of traditional authority.

One thing that the evangelical movement shared with the Enlightenment was a marked reliance upon the expanding world of print. Americans were able to participate in the Enlightenment as much as they did largely because leading works were either imported into the colonies or, occasionally, printed there. The ability to read these works, and occasionally to write for enlightened audiences in such fields as natural philosophy and natural history, made educated Americans very much a part of the international movement that came to be called the republic of letters.

Americans also created an array of new cultural institutions. Prominent among them were colleges. For almost the entire seventeenth century, the English colonies housed only one college, Harvard, founded in 1636 for the purpose of training an orthodox Puritan clergy for New Englanders. To that was added William and Mary in Virginia in 1693 and Yale in Connecticut in 1701, the latter designed to combat emerging liberal tendencies at Harvard. Otherwise, until the mid-nineteenth century colonists looked across the Atlantic for higher education if they intended to pursue it at all.

The religious competition spurred by the Awakening and the impetus of the Enlightenment combined to produce an array of new institutions around the middle of the eighteenth century. Presbyterians created the College of New Jersey in 1746, along with an extensive network of academies that would extend to western Pennsylvania and southward into Virginia and the Carolinas. Presbyterians also shared the governance of the Benjamin Franklin's College of Philadelphia (later the University of Pennsylvania) with Anglicans, who controlled Kings College (later Columbia) in New York City. Baptists established Rhode Island College (later Brown), the Dutch Reformed Church founded Queens College (later Rutgers) in New Jersey, and the New Light Congregrationalist Eleazar Wheelock instituted an academy in Connecticut (later Dartmouth), ostensibly as an Indian school, which was subsequently transferred to New Hampshire. From the last of those came Samson Occum, the first Indian to be ordained as a missionary in New England.

Americans also created a variety of learned societies. Some were devoted to the advancement of science and useful knowledge, the principal concerns of the American Philosophical Society (1743, reorganized in 1769) and its rival, the American Society Held at Philadelphia for Promoting and Propagating Useful Knowledge (1768), which joined together in 1769. Others were designed to promote commerce or manufactures. A number were purely for entertainment, such as the Ancient and Honorable Tuesday Club, which met in an Annapolis tavern. Still others were devoted to the general Enlightenment goal of acquiring knowledge of any sort, such as the Masonic Lodges that sprung up among the most respectable gentlemen in most of the colonial cities, and some of Franklin's earliest associations for reading and discussion, which served to promote knowledge and self-improvement among city tradesmen.

All of these endeavors enhanced the relationship between the colonies and the cultural world of Britain, which American culture came more and more to resemble in important respects. The colonists were increasingly attracted to British goods, and provincial elites attempted to emulate the style and power of Britain's upper classes by controlling local politics and the colonial assemblies, a sign of growing colonial maturity and autonomy. The largest differences were the increasing rhetoric of social equality that emerged in the colonies, as well as a level of racial heterogeneity and hierarchy without precedent in Britain.

The cultural lives of slaves, and of African Americans generally, were also affected by increasing transatlantic connections, as Africans perhaps more than any other group inhabited nearly every port of call in the Atlantic trading world, from Africa to the West Indies to the New World. The life of the freed African mariner Olaudah Equiano, who traveled in Africa, the Caribbean, the mainland colonies, Central America, and Britain is immortalized in the *Interesting Narrative* of his life, first published in 1791. The connections these Africans wove among the many societies they inhabited, and the prominent influence they exerted in many places, helped to create the dimension of Atlantic culture that Paul Gilroy provocatively labeled the Black Atlantic.

One of the paradoxes of the Enlightenment in the Atlantic world was the extent to which it promoted the seemingly contradictory notions of antislavery and racism. For the first several centuries of American settlement, plantation slavery developed through what Winthrop Jordan referred to as an "unthinking decision." Slavery was an institution with a long and unquestioned place in many cultures, and not until the eighteenth century did one encounter the first significant declarations against slavery in the Western world. Quaker objections, by and large, came first, followed by protests from other groups influenced by the Atlantic culture of the Enlightenment. At almost the same time, Enlightenment inquiries into human nature were, for the first time, beginning to suggest the idea that human capabilities might vary by race, which was becoming a much clearer idea to Americans of European origin. Thomas Jefferson's famous aspersions on the intellectual capacity of Africans in his *Notes on the State of Virginia* (first English ed., 1787) was an early but important example.

If eighteenth-century trends were drawing the colonies culturally closer to Britain, the kind of relationship Americans desired with Britain is less clear. In many respects, metropolitan Britain constituted the height of fashion for provincial Americans, as it had been for colonials the century before. It ranked as the seat of knowledge and refinement. Moreover, in a world where Britons and Protestants felt themselves constantly under threat from the power of Catholic France, and British Americans felt imperiled by New France and its Indian allies, Britain and British power represented for Americans the source of their religion and security, their liberties, and their prosperity.

Alongside of those positive images of the metropolis grew others, deriving less from feelings of jealousy or inferiority and more from optimism and confidence. In the aftermath of the Seven Years' War, which removed the French threat from the colonies, some provincials began to view the metropolis as the source not only of power but of corruption and decay. Deriving their view both from Protestant dissent and Whiggish political traditions that emphasized the virtue of the independent citizen, those provincials increasingly came to view the provinces as the centers of liberty, prosperity, and true religion. Drawing in particular upon the new science of political economy and upon a new ethic of mobility well represented by Benjamin Franklin's *Poor Richard,* those Americans came to equate the relative liberty to be found in provincial life with the evident prosperity also found there. At their most optimistic, such provincials would portray the provinces as both the moral center and the most dynamic sector of the British Empire.

Even as Americans optimistically proclaimed the great and general benefit of provincial liberties, the prosperity of which they boasted for the whole of the colonies was built upon the labor of slaves to a far greater extent than many realized. Colonials thrived upon lands, moreover, that had been appropriated from their native inhabitants. Few saw any contradiction in the fact that those liberties extended only to Europeans. Thus in one of the earliest celebrations of the American character, the American Farmer, J. Hector St. John de Crèvecoeur, asked the famous question, "What, then, is the American, this new man?" (*Letters from an American Farmer*, p. 69). He answered, "He is either an European, or the descendant of an European.... Here individuals of all nations are melted into a new race of men" (pp. 69–70). The Farmer hardly felt compelled to notice that the unprecedented opportunities the descendants of Europeans of all nations enjoyed were leaving little room for the incorporation of non-Europeans, whether native peoples or slaves.

BIBLIOGRAPHY

Bonomi, Patricia U. *Under the Cope of Heaven: Religion, Society, and Politics in Colonial America.* New York, 1986.

Brown, Kathleen M. *Good Wives, Nasty Wenches, and Anxious Patriarchs: Gender, Race, and Power in Colonial Virginia.* Chapel Hill, N.C., 1996.

Burr, Esther Edwards. *The Journal of Esther Edwards Burr, 1754–1757.* Edited by Carol F. Karlsen and Laurie Crumpacker. New Haven, Conn., 1984.

Bushman, Richard L. *The Refinement of America: Persons, Houses, Cities.* New York, 1993.

Butler, Jon. *Awash in a Sea of Faith: Christianizing the American People.* Cambridge, Mass., 1990.

Chaplin, Joyce. *An Anxious Pursuit: Agricultural Innovation and Modernity in the Lower South, 1730–1815.* Chapel Hill, N.C., 1993.

Crèvecoeur, J. Hector St. John de. *Letters from an American Farmer and Sketches of Eighteenth-Century America.* Edited by Albert E. Stone. New York, 1981.

Davis, David Brion. *The Problem of Slavery in Western Culture.* Ithaca, N.Y., 1966.

Davis, Richard Beale. *Intellectual Life in the Colonial South, 1585–1763.* 3 vols. Knoxville, Tenn., 1978.

Equiano, Olaudah. *Interesting Narrative of the Life of Olaudah Equiano.* Edited by Vincent Carretta. New York, 1995.

Fischer, David Hackett. *Albion's Seed: Four British Folkways in America.* New York, 1989.

Franklin, Benjamin. *The Autobiography of Benjamin Franklin.* Edited by Leonard W. Labaree. New Haven, Conn., 1964.

Greene, Jack P. *The Intellectual Construction of America: Exceptionalism and Identity from 1492 to 1800.* Chapel Hill, N.C., 1993.

Hall, David D. *World of Wonder, Days of Judgment: Popular Religious Belief in Early New England.* New York, 1989.

Jefferson, Thomas. *Notes on the State of Virginia.* Edited by William Peden. Chapel Hill, N.C., 1954.

Jordan, Winthrop D. *White over Black: American Attitudes toward the Negro, 1550–1812.* Chapel Hill, N.C., 1968.

Karlsen, Carol F. *The Devil in the Shape of a Woman: Witchcraft in Colonial New England.* New York, 1987.

Landsman, Ned C. *From Colonials to Provincials: American Thought and Culture, 1689–1760.* New York, 1997.

Lepore, Jill. *The Name of War: King Philip's War and the Origins of American Identity.* New York, 1998.

May, Henry F. *The Enlightenment in America.* New York, 1976.

Merrell, James H. *The Indians' New World: Catawbas and their Neighbors from European Contact through the Era of Renewal.* Chapel Hill, N.C., 1989.

Miller, Perry. *The New England Mind: From Colony to Province.* Cambridge, Mass., 1953.

Morgan, Philip D. *Slave Counterpoint: Black Culture in the Eighteenth-Century Chesapeake and Lowcountry.* Chapel Hill, N.C., 1998.

Rowlandson, Mary. *The Soveraignty & Goodness of God, together, with the Faithfulness of His Promises Desplayed; Being a Narrative of the Captivity and Restauration of Mrs. Mary Rowlandson.* Cambridge, Mass., 1682.

Savelle, Max. *Seeds of Liberty: The Genesis of the American Mind.* New York, 1948.

Shields, David S. *Civil Tongues and Polite Letters in British America.* Chapel Hill, N.C., 1997.

Warner, Michael. *The Letters of the Republic: Publication and the Public Sphere in Eighteenth-Century America.* Cambridge, Mass., 1990.

White, Richard. *The Middle Ground: Indians, Empires, and Republics in the Great Lakes Region, 1650–1815.* New York, 1991.

Woodmason, Charles. *The Carolina Backcountry on the Eve of the Revolution: The Journal and Other Writings of Charles Woodmason, Anglican Itinerant.* Edited by Richard J. Hooker. Chapel Hill, N.C., 1953.

EUROPEAN AND INDIGENOUS ENCOUNTERS

Colin Calloway

The vast colonial encounter of early American history brought native men, women, and children from different nations, regions, and language groups into contact with European colonists from different countries and religious persuasions, as well as with other Indian peoples, in a world of shifting, porous, and contested cultural borderlands. In the sixteenth century, Spanish conquistadors invaded Indian America via Florida and New Mexico. By the seventeenth century, French, Dutch, Swedish, and English colonizers were contending for a foothold on the east coast. In the eighteenth century, Finns, Germans, Scots, Irish, and many other immigrants pushed west into Indian country; Spanish priests reached California and Russians began trading on the northwest coast. Throughout most of North America, Indian peoples interacted with other Indians, not with Europeans. But European people, animals, plants, plagues, products, and print all infiltrated Indian country while, conversely, contact with Indians influenced Europeans as well. Encounters were often marked with bloodshed, but many Indians and Europeans tried to understand each other, and in the process they sometimes gained new understanding of themselves. Various groups of people came to identify themselves as either "European" or "Indian" in opposition to the other, but even as they did so they were becoming more alike as a result of their encounters.

THE INVASION CONTEXT

Some Indians traveled to Europe as kidnap victims, slaves, or diplomats, but most Indian encounters with Europeans occurred on American soil. Armed with what they saw as a divine mandate to build their empire and extend Catholicism, Spanish soldiers and missionaries pushed north after their conquests in Mexico and Peru. Hernando de Soto's army blazed a trail of devastation from Florida to Texas between 1539 and 1542. Francisco de Coronado led an expedition of Spanish soldiers and Indian allies north into New Mexico from 1540 to 1542. They plundered food from the Pueblo Indians on the Rio Grande and wandered out on to the Great Plains looking for cities of gold but found only the farming villages of the Wichitas in Kansas. Juan de Oñate led a colonizing expedition into New Mexico in 1598 and, when Indians of Acoma Pueblo resisted his troops, he tried them, found them guilty of treason, and meted out mutilation and servitude as punishment. In 1680 the Pueblos synchronized a revolt that threw off Spanish economic and religious oppression and drove the Spaniards out of New Mexico for a dozen years. After Don Diego de Vargas reconquered New Mexico in 1692, most Pueblos resisted in more subtle ways, maintaining their culture and communities within a Spanish colony. Spaniards in turn reduced demands for labor and tribute and adopted more tolerance toward Pueblo religion.

Indians met, traded, and lived with French explorers, traders, and priests who paddled canoes to the Great Lakes and beyond, pushed south to the mouth of the Mississippi River, and, in the eighteenth century, ventured west onto the Great Plains from the Red River to Winnipeg. France built an empire on the fur trade, but Indians played crucial roles in its development. The French needed Indian allies to produce furs and provide assistance against rival English colonies. Indians saw the French as a source of merchandise and their best hope for assistance against English threats to their lands. But shared interests alone were not enough to maintain alliances. Constant mediation and compromise were required as each party adjusted to the cultural expectations of the other. Where French and Indian interests did not intersect bloody warfare sometimes occurred, as when the French tried to destroy the Fox, Natchez, and Chickasaw tribes early in the eighteenth century.

The English had extended dominion in the British Isles, but they were relative latecomers in the colonization of North America. The powerful Powhatan Indians of eastern Virginia did not see the English settlers at Jamestown as much of a threat: few in number and evidently inept in their new environment, half the settlers died in the first year. Indians supplied them with corn, and the paramount chief, Powhatan, seems to have tried to incorporate them into his chiefdom. But Englishmen began to seize corn and fighting broke out, culminating in bloody wars in 1622 and 1644. Elsewhere in the South, after the founding of Charles Town, South Carolina, in 1670, English traders pushed into the interior, and their demands for deerskin and Indian slaves reverberated as far as the Mississippi.

In New England, Pilgrims established Plymouth Colony on Cape Cod in 1620. They found the coast of Massachusetts depopulated by an earlier epidemic. The Pilgrims endured a harsh winter but benefited from the assistance of two Indians: an Abenaki Indian named Samoset, who had learned English from sailors on the coast of Maine, and Squanto, a Pawtuxet Indian, who had been kidnapped, taken to Spain and England, and made his way home only to find his village wiped out by disease. Squanto showed the Pilgrims how to plant corn and where to fish, and he acted as interpreter and intermediary for them in their dealings with local Indians. The English waged a brutal war against the Pequot Indians of Connecticut from 1636 to 1637, but elsewhere colonists and Indians remained economically interdependent despite escalating tensions. Metacom, a Wampanoag chief known to the English as King Philip, forged a multitribal coalition against English aggression and open war broke out in 1675. During what is known as King Philip's War, the Indians won early victories but fell victim to disease and Mohawk attacks while English captains like Benjamin Church learned to apply Indian guerrilla tactics. Some Indian people faced divided loyalties, and many Christian Indians supported the English. A Christian Indian killed Metacom, and the English stuck the Wampanoag leader's head on a post as the penalty for "treason."

By the end of the seventeenth century, Indian peoples in New England and New Mexico had fought and lost wars of independence against European invaders. In the eighteenth century, Indians participated in wars for empire between European powers, although for their own interests, not those of their European allies. When the contest for North American hegemony between Britain and France culminated in the Seven Years' War (1756–1763), the impacts of global conflict reverberated through Indian country. By the time the American colonies won their independence, Indians had fought for generations against and alongside European invaders and had endured almost one hundred years of recurrent warfare involving competing colonial powers. The experiences left indelible impressions on their communities and helped establish an enduring image of Indians as warriors.

As Europeans invaded America they brought with them new plants and crops, new grasses and weeds, and new fruits. Their domesticated animals trod down native grasses, trampled Indian cornfields, and drove away wild game. Colonists cut down forests, transformed wilderness into farmland, and introduced new ways of marking and managing land as property. Old world diseases, such as smallpox, measles, bubonic plague, and influenza, spread rapidly through Indian populations. Combined with increased warfare, famine, and other associated traumas of colonization, recurrent epidemics produced massive demographic decline.

The invaders brought new commodities that they exchanged for the resources of Native America. The Swedes, Dutch, French, British, Spaniards, and Russians all participated in the peltry trade. The search for new sources of fur and new customers fueled European penetration of Indian country, and cities like Springfield, Massachusetts; Albany, New York; Montreal; St. Louis; and Detroit originated as trading posts that were foci of cultural as well as economic interaction. Europeans provided capital, organization, manufactured goods, and equipment, but Indian men and women provided much of the labor force, as hunters, guides, packers, and paddlers; prepared skins and provided food; and operated as middlemen shuttling pelts and goods between Europeans and more distant tribes. In return for their pelts and services, Indians obtained goods that were cheaply produced in European factories but valuable in Indian country, where those goods sometimes replaced and supplemented existing items, were refashioned in traditional ways, or acquired new, Indian, meanings.

But the costs of exchange were high. Diseases spread along trade routes. Fur-bearing animals were hunted to the brink of extinction in some regions, and traditional rituals and relationships with animals broke down under the demands of European fur markets. New tools made life easier, but craft skills sometimes declined. Guns made warfare more lethal, and economic competition made it more frequent. People grew dependent on European goods and became tied to European markets as producers and consumers. They fell into debt to European traders who offered credit and alcohol, and sometimes they settled debts by selling land.

ATTITUDES AND UNDERSTANDINGS

From first contacts, Europeans and Indians were curious about the new peoples they encountered. Making sense of new people required explaining them within existing systems, and Indians and Europeans alike attempted to draw on ancient knowledge to understand new situations. Sometimes Europeans resorted to preconceived notions about "savages" and "heathens," but such preconceptions were inadequate in a world in which Indians were many and knew the land, whereas Europeans, as yet, were few and did not. Instead, making sense of new people often required rethinking assumptions about human nature and the world. Europeans were unprepared for the size, diversity, richness, and challenges of the American environment, and Indians thought them hopelessly ill equipped to deal with it. For their part, Indians were not prepared for European political, evangelical, commercial, and military motivations, which had few parallels in Native America.

Indians on the north Atlantic coast probably made contact with French fishermen in the fifteenth century. Native traditions from Algonquian peoples on the northeast coast tell how the first ships Indians saw appeared to them as floating islands. Other traditions recount that the Europeans first appeared to certain Indians in dreams, and that prophecies of their coming were marked by foreboding omens. Nevertheless, for the most part, Indian people greeted the newcomers with hospitality and goodwill, and Indian speakers in subsequent generations frequently reminded Europeans that Indian forefathers had assisted and befriended European forefathers when they were weak.

Indians and Europeans each had their own rituals of encounter that meant little to the people they encountered. Indians looked on while Europeans acted out ceremonies of conquest that, in their eyes, gave their king formal possession of the Indians' lands. Indians performed rituals of greeting that Europeans often misinterpreted as acts of submission. Indians often met invading Spaniards with offers of gifts and guides—assurances of great wealth in distant lands often proved the surest means to get them out of town. In the Midwest and Great Lakes, Indians danced the calumet ceremony and incorpo-

rated Frenchmen into their societies as symbolic kinsmen and real people. But hospitality often turned to hostility when people failed to understand each other and when pressures on land intensified.

When Indians and Europeans met in council to buy and sell land, they came with different expectations and understandings. Indians, living in an oral culture, attached most importance to the meeting, the spoken words, and the accompanying rituals; Europeans wanted a written document that recorded agreement to the terms of the transaction. Englishmen regarded treaties and deeds as a legitimate way to acquire Indian lands, even though they sometimes practiced fraud and deception in securing those treaties and deeds. Errors in translation created additional misunderstandings. Indians had good reason to voice their suspicion of the "pen and ink work" that went on during treaties. The written documents became the instruments by which much of America passed from Indian to non-Indian hands.

The Indians seem to have been impressed by the Europeans' technology, particularly their ships, guns, and metal tools, but shocked by their appearance, language, and behavior. Spanish conquistadors presented themselves to Indians as "children of the sun," and Europeans frequently claimed that Indians regarded them with awe, as godlike creatures. But Indians saw few godlike qualities in the invaders and regularly dismissed European pretensions to superiority. As early as 1524 the Florentine explorer Giovanni da Verrazzano found that Indians on the coast of Maine would not allow his crew ashore to trade; they had already had bad experiences with European sailors. The survivors of one disastrous Spanish expedition—Alvar Nuñez Cabeza de Vaca and three companions—lived and traveled for years among Indian peoples in the southern Plains and desert Southwest. They made their way as healers, and when they were reunited with Christians, a Spanish slave-raiding expedition, their Indian companions could not believe they were the same people: "We had come from the sunrise, they from the sunset; we came naked and barefoot, they clothed, horsed, and lanced; we coveted nothing but gave whatever we were given, while they robbed whomever they found and bestowed nothing on anyone." "You are always fighting and quarreling among yourselves," Micmac Indians in Nova Scotia told Frenchmen in the early seventeenth century. "You are envious and are all the time slandering each other; you are thieves and deceivers; you are covetous, and are neither generous nor kind; as for us, if we have a morsel of bread we share it with our neighbor" (Thwaites, ed., *Jesuit Relations*, vol. 1, p. 175).

Europeans had to describe and account for the presence of people who were not mentioned in the Bible, in ancient texts, or previous travel accounts. Some writers argued that "Indians" were proof of a second, separate creation. Other writers thought they were descendants of the Lost Tribes of Israel, an idea that sparked a pamphlet debate in seventeenth-century England and took up half of James Adair's *History of the American Indians* (1775). The concept of Asiatic origins gained credence in the eighteenth century, although some held that Indians were the descendants of a legendary twelfth-century Welsh prince named Madoc.

European explorers, missionaries, and colonists provided lengthy descriptions of the Indian people they met. Christopher Columbus called them *los Indios* and characterized the first natives he saw as gentle, generous, and innocent people who would make good servants and good Christians. But subsequent Spanish expeditions left more varied portrayals of Indian peoples in what is now the southeastern and southwestern United States. French explorers like Samuel de Champlain, travelers like Pierre de Charlevoix, and Jesuit missionaries in their massive body of *Relations*, annual reports sent to their superiors, provided detailed descriptions of native peoples in Canada and the Midwest. The works of John Smith in Virginia and William Wood, Roger Williams, and other New England colonists, together with well-read captivity narratives like that of Mary Rowlandson, contained information and commentary on English contacts with Indian people. Such written accounts, with their biases and limitations, provided the bases for subsequent Euro-American understandings of American encounters, whereas native understandings rested on tribal memories and oral accounts passed down through the generations.

Europeans measured Indians against European markers of "civilization": How did they dress? How did their languages sound to European ears? Did they live in settled and "orderly" societies? Did they live in patriarchal, nuclear families, and did their marriage customs and sexual practices conform to European notions of morality? Did their religion resemble Christianity? Did the men farm? They noted what Indians lacked—writing, wheeled vehicles, metal, guns, European codes of conduct—and frequently misunderstood their political systems, gender relations, religious ceremonies, and rituals of meeting. At a time when the development of the printing press greatly increased the circulation of

news and literature, Europeans soon had access to a variety of descriptions of the New World and its inhabitants. Those descriptions furnished evidence to support images of Indians as "savages" and as "noble savages."

European writers and thinkers debated what should be their proper relationship to and treatment of Indians. Some wondered whether Indians were human. Most recognized common human traits but saw Indians as occupying a lower stage of development. Some questioned whether the Indians' so-called state of nature was not, in many ways, superior to European society.

Spanish law required conquistadors to read to the Indians they encountered the *Requerimiento* (1513), a document, worked out by theologians at the request of the King of Spain, which called on Indians to acknowledge "the Church as the Ruler and Superior of the whole world," the Pope as high priest, and the king and queen of Spain as lords of their lands. If they refused or delayed, the Spaniards told the Indians that they would "forcibly enter into your country . . . make war against you in all ways and manners that we can," and "subject you to the yoke and obedience of the Church and of their Highnesses"; and the deaths that ensued would be "your fault, and not that of their Highnesses, or ours, nor of these gentlemen who come with us" (Hurtado and Iverson, pp. 58–59). Read in Spanish to Indian people who understood neither its language nor its concepts, the *Requerimiento* became little more than a formality allowing the Spaniards to justify conquest—and any accompanying atrocities.

But some protested the atrocities. Bartolomé de Las Casas, a Dominican priest who had worked as a missionary in the Caribbean, denounced the treatment of Native peoples in New Spain. *The Devastation of the Indies: A Brief Account* (originally published in Spanish in 1552), exposed a record of Spanish atrocity that caused public outrage and prompted royal reforms. It was quickly translated into other languages, cited by English, French, and Dutch colonial rivals as justification for breaking the Spanish hold on the Americas, and fueled long-standing "Black Legend" stereotypes (of the innocent Indian and the cruel Spaniard) by which Anglo-American historians characterized Spanish colonialism in the Americas. Arguing that the Indians' sophisticated cultures entitled them to the same political civil rights as those who conquered them, Las Casas participated in a series of formal debates in 1550 to 1551 with Juan Ginés de Sepúlveda before the Spanish court at Vallodolid. Sepúl-

CHRESTIEN LECLERQ'S "A MICMAC RESPONDS TO THE FRENCH"

Thou sayest of us that we are the most miserable and most unhappy of all men, living without religion, without manners, without honour, without social order, and, in a word, without any rules, like the beasts in our woods and our forests, lacking bread, wine, and a thousand other comforts which thou hast in superfluity in Europe. Well, my brother, if thou dost not yet know the real feelings which our Indians have towards thy country and towards all thy nation, it is proper that I inform thee at once. I beg thee now to believe that, all miserable as we seem in thine eyes, we consider ourselves nevertheless much happier than thou in this, that we are very content with the little that we have; and believe also once for all, I pray, that thou deceivest thyself greatly if thou thinkest to persuade us that thy country is better than ours. For if France, as thou sayest, is a little terrestrial paradise, art thou sensible to leave it? And why abandon wives, children, relatives, and friends? Why risk thy life and thy property every year, and why venture thyself with such risk, in any season whatsoever, to the storms and tempests of the sea in order to come to a strange and barbarous country which thou considerest the poorest and least fortunate of the world? Besides, since we are wholly convinced of the contrary, we scarcely take the trouble to go to France, because of fear, with good reason, lest we find little satisfaction there, seeing, in our own experience, that those who are natives thereof leave it every year in order to enrich themselves on our shores. We believe, further, that you are also incomparably poorer than we, and that you are only simple journeymen, valets, servants, and slaves, all masters and grand captains though you may appear, seeing that you glory in our old rags and in our miserable suits of beaver which can no longer be of use to us, and that you find among us, in the fishery for cod which you make in these parts, the wherewithal to comfort your misery and the poverty which oppresses you. As to us, we find all our riches and all our conveniences among ourselves, without trouble and without exposing our lives to the dangers in which you find yourselves constantly through your long voyages. . . . Learn now, my brother, once for all, because I must open to thee my heart: there is no Indian who does not consider himself infinitely more happy and more powerful than the French.

Source: LeClerq, pp. 50–51, 52.

---

veda, a lawyer, argued that Spanish aggression against Indians was intellectually defensible as just war waged to punish sins and convert Indians to Christianity and on the Aristotelian doctrine that some men were fitted by nature to be slaves.

In New England, Puritans viewed Indians as inhabitants of the wilderness they were trying to subdue and feared them as a threat to their moral character and the "new England" they were trying to build. Puritan ministers interpreted Indian captivity and King Philip's War as God's punishment for his people's sins. Cotton Mather, minister of

Boston's Second Church and an influential figure in the government of the Massachusetts Bay Colony, regarded Indians as descendants of one of the Lost Tribes of Israel who had been decoyed to America by Satan. He and other Puritan leaders regularly invoked Biblical parallels and terminology to understand and justify their treatment of the "heathen" Indians, driving out Canaanites as they created a new Israel. Others displayed more empathy. Roger Williams, founder of Rhode Island, offered a dissenting voice and a call for fair dealing with Indian people. His *A Key into the Language of America*

(1643) provided a dictionary of Algonquian language and customs and a positive portrayal of Indian life. Thomas Morton flouted Puritan authority by living with the Indians and establishing an experimental Anglo-Indian community at Merry Mount, Massachusetts, and expressed admiration for Indian ways in *New English Canaan* (1637). But for many Puritans these dissenters only emphasized the dangers of the wilderness and its inhabitants.

Some Europeans, like Joseph-François Lafitau in *Customs of the Savage Americans Compared with the Customs of the Earliest Times* (originally published in French in 1724), drew parallels between Native Americans and ancient peoples of Europe. Others employed native ways of life as a mirror by which to judge contemporary European society and used native critiques as a vehicle for satire of European conventions and pretensions. In seventeenth-century England, Thomas Hobbes believed that people who lacked what he regarded as organized government and the refinements of civilization were condemned to "nasty, brutish, and short lives," punctuated by violence. But John Locke argued that people who lived in a state of nature could enjoy peace and reason, free from the dictates and power of European-style governments. The Baron Louis-Armand de Lom d'Arce de Lahontan based his *Nouveaux voyages* (1703; New voyages) on his experiences as a soldier and explorer who fought against the Iroquois, traveled west beyond the Great Lakes, and lived ten years in Canada. Lahontan recounted conversations with a fictional Huron Indian chief named Adario, whose searching questions about French society revealed its brutality, corruption, and hypocrisy, in stark contrast to the natural and communal life of the Indians. Echoing Lahontan, the Baron de Montesquieu, Michel de Montaigne, and Jean Jacques Rousseau portrayed "noble savages" possessing virtues lacking in French society and living in a morally superior and happier natural state without the chains and corruptions of civilization. Long after the colonial era, opinions expressed about Indians often revealed more about the writers' attitudes toward their own society than about Native America.

COMPETING AND CHANGING CULTURES

Encounters between Indians and Europeans generated conflict and competition between radically different views of the world. Colonial governments, teachers, and missionaries endeavored to eradicate Indian ways and transform Indians into "civilized Christians." But some Europeans lived with Indians, or found that imitating Indian ways offered the best course of survival in America. Indians also tried to convert European captives into Indian people.

Most Europeans did not think they were displacing existing civilizations when they came to America; generally, they regarded Indians and Indianness as a threat that had to be removed to make way for "civilization." America's rich lands had to be put to good use and turn a profit. Indian peoples farmed but the farming was done primarily by women while the men, in European eyes, were improvident hunters who made no good use of the land and should not therefore be allowed to keep it out of the hands of European settlers, who would cultivate it and build homes and towns. If Indians were to survive in the new society that was being constructed they needed to renounce their "savage" ways.

They were required also to renounce their "heathen ways" and become Christians. Convinced of the righteousness of their work, Bible-bearing missionaries launched a sustained assault on Indian cultures in order to change the Indians' lives in this world and save their souls in the next, and they preached new ideas about Original Sin and the place of human beings in the cosmos. Spanish priests invaded sacred spaces, confiscated religious objects, tried to stamp out ceremonies, attempted to change attitudes toward sex and gender relations, and tried to transform Indian societies into communities of Christian peasants. Franciscan oppression and disruption of traditional lifeways produced suffering, resentment, and resistance, but thousands of Indians made Catholicism part of their lives.

Indians in New France seem to have been similarly syncretic and pragmatic in their responses to Christian missionaries. Often, missionaries brought their message of salvation at a time when Indians saw their world falling apart under the impact of new diseases, and hundreds of Indian people accepted baptism from Jesuit missionaries. Whereas French Jesuits went into Indian country and Indian communities in search of converts, in Massachusetts the Puritan missionary John Eliot gathered Indian converts into "praying towns" where they were expected to give up their old ways and live like their Christian English neighbors. Eliot shared the view that Indians were lost Hebrews who had been led to America by Satan and that their only hope of salvation lay in embracing Christianity and Puritan values. With the help of two Indian schoolteachers, Job Nesutan and John Sassamon, and an apprentice Indian printer, James Printer, Eliot translated the

Bible into Algonquian by 1663—the first Bible printed in America. The Society for the Propagation of the Gospel in Foreign Parts, founded in 1701, followed Eliot's methods of attempting to save Indian people by separating them into praying communities where they could be taught the Gospel and undergo cultural transformation.

Some Indian people found solace in Christianity as their world seemed to be unraveling amid sickness, alcohol, and violence. On Martha's Vineyard the Mayhew family established Indian churches after epidemic diseases swept the island in 1643 and 1645. A Christian congregation and community could offer refuge. Christian services and prayers supplemented and sometimes replaced traditional rituals that could not fend off new diseases. Women sometimes found that Christianity honored their traditional roles and gave them an opportunity to learn to read, write, and hold church office. Some leaders used Christianity to boost their status against more traditional rivals. Some Indians accepted the tenets and symbols of Christianity without abandoning their traditional beliefs and rituals; they blended the two and made Christianity an Indian religion.

Colonial authorities who saw themselves building civilization in the wilderness worried about the influence of Indian ways of life and the implications of "going Indian." Some individuals who lived with Indians even fought alongside them against Europeans. Indians took hundreds of captives from European settlements during the colonial wars. Captives might be tortured, but they might instead be ritually adopted to fill voids in kin-based Indian communities. Some European captives became accustomed to life in Indian communities and refused opportunities to return home. European women who were abducted and adopted sometimes preferred their new life to the one they had known in patriarchal colonial society. Captives who returned home sometimes did so with reluctance and broken hearts.

Benjamin Franklin and J. Hector St. John de Crèvecoeur both recognized a huge imbalance in the relative magnetism of Indian and colonial society: hundreds of Europeans became Indians but few if any Indians became Europeans by choice. Crèvecoeur asked: "By what power does it come to pass, that children who have been adopted when young among these people, can never be prevailed on to readopt European manners?" He decided there was "in their social bond something singularly captivating, and far superior to anything to be boasted of among us" (*Letters from an American Farmer,* 1962, pp. 214–216, 221). Some colonial legislatures passed measures to prevent their citizens from Indian influence. Thirty years before the French Revolution, Louis-Antoine de Bougainville, aide-de-camp to General Montcalm and later world traveler, worried about the effect on French soldiers of breathing "an air of independence" when they served alongside Indians and Canadians.

As Indians and Europeans came into increasing and more extensive contact, individuals crossed and straddled cultures, and the cultures themselves underwent change. Indian peoples in various regions rode horses, tended sheep and goats, and carried crucifixes. They interacted and intermarried with European colonists and African slaves, borrowed each other's foods, clothing, technologies, and words, and produced "new" people. In some areas, like New Mexico, Indian and Hispanic cultures coexisted and blended. Indians were drafted to work in Spanish mines, plantations, and households, and built Spanish missions and towns. Indian "cowboys" herded Spanish cattle on Spanish ranches. As traditional subsistence patterns eroded, many Indians found new economic opportunities in colonial towns and villages, served on colonial ships, and enlisted in colonial armies. Indian women sold food, baskets, and pottery in town markets. Indian healers applied their knowledge of herbal medicines to cure European as well as Indian patients. Some Indians attended colonial schools and colleges like William and Mary and Dartmouth; others worshiped, married, and were buried in colonial churches. Sometimes, they established and maintained their own churches with their own deacons and ministers. Some, like the Mohegan Samson Occom, became missionaries.

Indians who frequented European society often adopted European clothing and accoutrements, although what one wore and how one wore it might convey different meanings: military coats and medals indicated one's importance as a chief courted by European allies; wearing a European shirt hanging loose or a hat turned sideways might proclaim a preference for doing things "Indian-style"; wearing a mixture of Indian and European clothing to a council helped one look the part of cultural mediator. Europeans who mingled with Indians also adopted Indian clothes and Indian ways: many dressed in Indian hunting shirts, leggings, and moccasins; some wore their hair Indian style and displayed face paint and tattoos. They learned Indian languages, smoked Indian pipes, and hunted using Indian techniques.

WILLIAM SMITH'S ACCOUNT OF THE RETURN OF CAPTIVES TO COLONEL HENRY BOUQUET IN 1764

The Indians too . . . delivered up their beloved captives with the utmost reluctance; shed torrents of tears over them, recommending them to the care and protection of the commanding officer. Their regard to them continued all the time they remained in camp. They visited them from day to day; and brought them what corn, skins, horses, and other matters, they had bestowed on them, while in their families; accompanied with other presents, and all the marks of the most sincere and tender affection. Nay, they did not stop here, but, when the army marched, some of the Indians solicited and obtained leave to accompany their former captives all the way to Fort-Pitt, and employed themselves in hunting and bringing provisions for them on the road. . .

Among the children who had been carried off young, and had long lived with the Indians, it is not to be expected that any marks of joy would appear on being restored to their parents or relatives. Having been accustomed to look upon the Indians as the only connexions they had, having been tenderly treated by them, and speaking their language, it is no wonder that they considered their new state in the light of a captivity, and parted from the savages with tears.

But it must not be denied that there were even some grown persons who shewed an unwillingnesss to return. The Shawanese were obliged to bind several of their prisoners and force them along to the camp; and some women, who had been delivered up, afterwards found means to escape and run back to the Indian towns. Some, who could not make their escape, clung to their savage acquaintance at parting, and continued many days in bitter lamentations, even refusing sustenance.

For the honour of humanity, we would suppose those persons to have been of the lowest rank, either bred up in ignorance and distressing penury, or who had lived so long with the Indians as to forget all their former connections. For, easy and unconstrained as the savage life is, certainly it could never be put in competition with the blessings of improved life and the light of religion, by any persons who have had the happiness of enjoying, and the capacity of discerning, them.

Source: Smith, pp. 34, 36–37.

Even missionaries who entered Indian communities intent on transforming them spent years of their lives sharing their lodgings, learning their languages, eating their food, traveling in their canoes, and participating to a degree in the daily life of the societies they sought to change. Fur traders also took up residence in Indian communities. Some, particularly French and Scots, married Indian women and attained a place in their kinship networks: Scottish surnames were common among southeastern Indians. Traders' children often grew up to become leaders in Indian communities and mediators with colonial society.

Indians and Europeans alike learned new ways of communicating and dealing with each other. European Indian agents learned to follow the protocols of Indian country, to speak Indian languages, to read wampum belts, and to fulfill obligations of generosity and protection that Indians expected from men who claimed to be their "fathers." Indian leaders had to adjust and hone their diplomatic skills, walking a fine line to preserve their people's independence in a world of increasing dependency, and trying to negotiate the treacherous waters of diplomacy by pen and paper. Some Indians learned to read and write; all recognized the power of print.

Some individuals functioned as interpreters and culture brokers in the complex process of intercultural negotiation. Europeans learned how to do business in Indian country. Sir William Johnson, superintendent of Indian affairs for the northern department for more than a generation, lived with a Mohawk woman, immersed himself in Mohawk culture, spoke Mohawk, cultivated relations with important chiefs, gave generous gifts, and became a master in the intricate world of Iroquois politics. His home, Johnson Hall, was a meeting place of British and Indian cultures.

In *A Key into the Language of America* Roger Williams wrote that before the arrival of English, Dutch, and French, native peoples in New England did not have "any Names to difference themselves from strangers" but that after contact they began to "call themselves Indians, in opposition to English, &c." Instances of such Indian identity increased in the eighteenth century as native peoples from different tribes embraced movements of independence and resistance to European threats. At the same time, colonists from Europe who came into contact with Indians often self-identified in opposition to Indians. But new peoples and new societies were emerging that were quite different from anything seen in Europe or America before, indicating the pervasiveness of change resulting from European and indigenous encounters.

See also **Native Americans; The Frontier and the West; Borderlands** (*volume 2*).

BIBLIOGRAPHY

Axtell, James. *The Invasion Within: The Contest of Cultures in Colonial North America.* New York, 1985.

Berkhofer, Robert F. *The White Man's Indian: The History of an Idea from Columbus to the Present.* New York, 1978.

Calloway, Colin G. *New Worlds for All: Indians, Europeans, and the Remaking of Early America.* Baltimore, 1997.

Calloway, Colin G., ed. *The World Turned upside Down: Indian Voices from Early America.* Boston, 1994.

Canup, John. *Out of the Wilderness: The Emergence of an American Identity in Colonial New England.* Middletown, Conn., 1990.

Cronon, William. *Changes in the Land: Indians, Colonists, and the Ecology of New England.* New York, 1983.

Crosby, Alfred. *The Columbian Exchange: Biological and Cultural Consequences of 1492.* Westport, Conn., 1972.

Hurtado, Albert L., and Peter Iverson, eds. *Major Problems in American Indian History.* 2d ed. Boston, 2000.

Jennings, Francis. *The Invasion of America: Indians, Colonialism, and the Cant of Conquest.* New York, 1976.

Kupperman, Karen Ordahl. *Indians and English: Facing off in Early America.* Ithaca, N.Y., 2000.

LeClerq, Chrestien. "A Micmac Responds to the French." In *The World Turned Upside Down: Indian Voices from Early America,* edited by Colin G. Calloway. Boston, 1994.

Lepore, Jill. *The Name of War: King Philip's War and the Origins of American Identity.* New York, 1998.

Mancall, Peter C., and James H. Merrell, eds. *American Encounters: Natives and Newcomers from European Contact to Indian Removal, 1500–1850.* New York, 2000.

Merrell, James H. *The Indians' New World: Catawbas and Their Neighbors from European Contact through the Era of Removal*. Chapel Hill, N.C., 1989.

Moffitt, John F., and Santiago Sebastián. *O Brave New People: The European Invention of the American Indian*. Albuquerque, N. Mex., 1996.

Pagden, Anthony. *European Encounters with the New World from Renaissance to Romanticism*. New Haven, Conn., 1993.

Sayre, Gordon M. *Les Sauvages Américains: Representations of Native Americans in French and English Colonial Literature*. Chapel Hill, N.C., 1997.

Smith, William. *An Historical Account of the Expedition against the Ohio Indians in the Year 1764 under the Command of Henry Bouquet*. In *Warfare on the Colonial American Frontier*. Bargersville, Ind., 1997.

Thwaites, Reuben G., ed. *The Jesuit Relations and Allied Documents*. 71 vols. Cleveland, Ohio, 1896–1901.

Usner, Daniel H., Jr. *Indians, Settlers, and Slaves in a Frontier Exchange Economy: The Lower Mississippi Valley before 1783*. Chapel Hill, N.C., 1992.

Weatherford, Jack. *Indian Givers: How the Indians of the Americas Transformed the World*. New York, 1988.

———. *Native Roots: How the Indians Enriched America*. New York, 1991.

Weber, David J. *The Spanish Frontier in North America*. New Haven, Conn., 1992.

White, Richard. *The Middle Ground: Indians, Empires, and Republics in the Great Lakes Region, 1650–1815*. New York, 1991.

AFRICA AND AMERICA

John K. Thornton

THE SLAVE TRADE AND CULTURAL ASSIMILATION

The transatlantic slave trade was the largest-scale movement of human beings from one part of the world to another by sea before the nineteenth century. Something on the order of between 12 and 15 million Africans arrived in America between 1500 and 1850 from the long stretch of the African coast. There is little doubt of the demographic impact of this forced migration, but its cultural impact is much debated. As slaves, African immigrants suffered severely in their transit and upon arrival in America, in ways that might have impinged upon their ability to transmit cultures from Africa or to develop much of a unique culture of their own. Yet there is sufficient evidence of African influence in many American cultures to insure that the Africans did not come as culturally naked as was once believed.

The cultural impact of this movement was twofold. On the African side of the Atlantic, Europeans and Africans interacted with each other from the very beginnings of their contact in the fifteenth century. In the process, African societies absorbed some element of European culture. A few societies, like the Kongo in modern Angola, some states of Sierra Leone, and the small kingdom of Warri in modern Nigeria, adopted Christianity as their official religion. Literacy in one or another European language developed in places where Europeans colonized, like Angola, or where there was a large Christian community like Kongo, or where intense interaction favored its development. Crops and products were introduced to African consumers from Europe and from other areas of the world, such as India. Over the course of the long interaction, Africa gradually changed culturally as a result of this contact.

As that change took place, it affected the culture of those other Africans who were transported from Africa by the slave trade to the opposite shore of the Atlantic. But with the exception of Angola, these changes did not take place through conquest, and were not instituted by force. Even in Angola, conquest did not result in the same level of cultural pressure on Africans that the conquest in the Americas did. While African societies sometimes went through wars and disruptions that stemmed from the commercial contact (and perhaps from the slave trade), they themselves were in charge of the process of cultural absorption. It was just the opposite for their counterparts in America, however, who were enslaved and had little control over any aspect of their lives.

The African-oriented culture of the Atlantic was not primarily what would be considered "high culture" on the American side. Most Africans who were enslaved and brought to the Americas during the period of the slave trade were of humble estate. Peasants, petty artisans, small-scale traders, and professional soldiers made up a vast bulk of these unwilling immigrants. The political and social elites of African societies were rarely enslaved, and many of those who were, were able to ransom themselves. The handful of religious leaders, political authorities, or military officers who did make the crossing certainly had their impact in America, but for the most part it was representatives of several dozen folk cultures that came across the Atlantic.

There was not a single African culture, of course, but rather many, depending on how one determines the boundaries of culture. Many scholars have focused on language differences as diagnostic of cultural difference. Because languages are arbitrary systems of meaning, and require knowledge of a complex grammatical and lexical code to be comprehensible, their boundaries are often clear-cut. If one person speaks to another and is not understood, then a linguistic boundary is established. Sometimes such boundaries can be sharp and distinct, and miscomprehension is complete. But in other cases, languages shade off into each other, where adjacent dialects are close enough to allow some communication, and a boundary drawn by a linguist may be less sharp in reality than in theory. Still, even if one allows a fairly liberal definition of language differences, Africans who came to the Americas in the seventeenth and eighteenth centuries came from an area where as many as forty distinct languages were spoken, at least according to linguistically sophisticated observers in the Americas. From this point of view, Africans came from a wide variety of diverse cultures.

There were factors that worked against this sort of maximal diversity. The first was the widespread use of multilingualism and lingua francas (agreed-upon second languages) in areas of great linguistic diversity. For example, the Upper Guinea coast, especially the area of modern Guinea-Bissau and the Republic of Guinea whose capital is at Conakry (hereafter referred to as Guinea-Conakry), had great linguistic diversity, but it was also an area in which the Mande language served as a lingua franca. In the central African region, where languages are closely related linguistically, multilingualism was widespread among people who traveled within the region. These features tended to keep diversity limited, especially among those people who traveled within the region.

While languages rarely share much more than an occasional lexical borrowing, certainly not grammar, other elements of culture might be widely borrowed. Music, for example, is not called "the universal language" for nothing. Appreciation and borrowing of musical forms across cultural boundaries is easy, and it is probably safe to say that most adjacent societies, even if they do not communicate linguistically, might share musical cultures.

The same observation can be made about other elements of aesthetics. Although Kikongo and Kimbundu are mutually unintelligible languages spoken in modern Angola, both groups share substantial aesthetic norms. In the seventeenth century both groups had a great fondness for patterns of lozenge-shaped decorations, and such decoration appeared on cloth, on pottery, and sometimes in body scarification. All over Africa, archaeologists have confirmed that often pottery made and appreciated in one area with a particular pattern of decoration might be traded and appreciated in other regions, where different patterns were employed on works of local production. In fact, trading of culturally distinct items may destroy one's ideas of cultural particularism, just as the eighteenth-century Akan-speaking inhabitants of Ghana's fascination with Dutch bottles and jugs confounded an attempt to define distinct cultures. Under these circumstances, the best boundaries for decorated items of material culture are those that divided regions that had little or no mutual interactions. Patterns of European shipping had sometimes modified these, for one must still consider a seventeenth-century cloth hoard from Loango, in central Africa, that contained thousands of yards of cloth produced in Ijebu and Benin, in West Africa. Then again, during the eighteenth century, Africans from all along the Atlantic seaboard imported millions of yards of Indian-colored textiles, where they were worn in a variety of clothing, creating a certain uniformity across a wide region.

Other elements of culture, such as religion and ideology, are even more difficult to pin down to distinct and well-bounded groups of people. How many different systems of philosophy or ideology were there in Africa, and how distinct were they? Some have seen a single African way of thought, others as many different ones as there are different languages. Many African philosophical systems were expressed through proverbs and aphorisms. "They are all metaphysicians," wrote a Jesuit visitor to Kongo in 1548, "all their talk is in proverbs" (Brásio, ed., letter of Christóvão Ribero, *Monumenta Missionaria Africana*, vol. 15, p. 160). Proverbs are very dependent on specific lexical features of language. Puns and rhymes, for example, which are a frequent hallmark of proverbial speech, are specific to the meanings and pronunciations of particular words, and are therefore restricted to individual languages. The ideas expressed in such linguistic tools, however, may not be as distinct as their modes of expression. As someone who has learned proverbs in one language learns another, he or she may quickly learn and apply the language's proverbs because the philosophical system of the two languages is similar. Under these circumstances, it is difficult to say whether any fundamental philosophical change has occurred, or whether there was any cultural difference beyond that of language in early African culture that affected cultural assimilation in the Americas.

African religions, likewise, possessed strikingly pronounced local differences, contrasting with broadly similar philosophical tenets. Most religious traditions accepted the idea that after death people continued a new life as ancestors. They possessed the capacity to intervene in the lives of their descendants, and the living were advised to discover their desires through various means of revelation as well as to satisfy them with rituals, sacrifices, and other offerings. Ancestors were necessarily connected to families, although royal families' ancestors might require subjects of the former ruler to make sacrifices as well as the family. Beyond ancestors, a common tenet was that another class of deities existed, whose domains were typically territorial. Frequently such beings manifested themselves in strikingly shaped or unusual natural formations, or in woods, bodies of water, or other wastelands. Finally, most African religions also accepted the existence of a powerful creator God, with no particular earthly cults or functions; a last resort of the desperate, for whom the lesser supernatural entities might be intercessors.

Religious traditions from outside Atlantic Africa had also taken root in that region, and had a history of interaction with and syncretism to these more local systems. Islam had been present in the northern parts of West Africa since the tenth century at least, and local *marabouts* preached the Islamic law, while sometimes tacitly recognizing the concept of ancestors and integrating the territorial deities into their system as *jinn*, the mysterious spirits of Islam. Similarly, European traders introduced Christianity all along the coast from the late fifteenth century. In most of West Africa it was the religious ideal of only small parcels of the coastal population who lived in close proximity to European settlements or were descended from European visitors. There were occasional exceptions, for example, the states of Sierra Leone in the seventeenth century, or in a more permanent sense, the kingdom of Warri (whose official religion was Christianity). In central Africa, Christianity was much more widespread and deeply rooted. The kingdom of Kongo was Christianity's greatest triumph in Africa, an independent state with a well-organized church and a deep commitment to the religion. The Portuguese colony of Angola included thousands of Christian Africans, while adherence in the smaller surrounding states was spotty and incomplete. In all these traditions, however, ample elements of the previous African tradition were integrated, in the acceptance of the role of ancestors, and in the merging of territorial deities with Christian saints.

Taking all these factors into consideration, it is possible to define African regions in which a great deal of interaction on many levels took place and set them against their interactions beyond the region. Using this definition allows scholars to define three very broad cultural regions, divided into seven less distinct subregions; areas in which considerable intercommunication through trade and political contact created zones of cultural interchange. These interchanges included the use of lingua francas in the region as well as multiple and frequent exchanges of items of material culture. The first re-

gion, which can be designated as Upper Guinea, following older usage by European sailors, is the area drained by the rivers, which rise in the Foura Djallon highlands of modern Guinea-Conakry. It includes the Senegal and Gambia, as well as the many coastal rivers that flow into the modern-day Guinea-Bissau, Guinea-Conakry, and the Sierra Leone. The various drainage basins of the Sénégal River, Gambia River, and other coastal rivers form subregions with distinctive cultural styles within the larger zone. The ancient empire of Mali once defined much of the region, and the Mande language was a lingua franca in most of it. The kingdom of Jolof of the fifteenth century also shaped the Sénégal Valley portions of the zone, and Wolof was a second important lingua franca. Islam played a religious role throughout and, not surprisingly, Arabic was the language of literacy and high culture.

The coast south and then east of this great zone did not participate much in the slave trade, although the region known as the "Kwa Kwa Coast" in traders' guides did participate in international trade, but in pepper, cloth, and ivory rather than in human beings. The next great region, Lower Guinea, commenced in the eastern parts of what is today the Côte d'Ivoire, and ran across to the western border of Cameroon. It included a number of languages and linguistic groups (of which the Akan group, the Yoruba-Aja, and the Igbo group were only the most numerous). One can recognize three subregions in this zone, one focused on the Akan and related languages on the Gold Coast that borders the swampy region around the mouth of the Volta River. There it divides from the Allada-Dahomey-Yoruba zone, which in turn is divided in the Niger River delta from the Igbo area. Coastwise navigation, which allowed cargoes to travel along the seaside by means of lagoons and creeks, tended to bring these subregions into greater contact. In addition, the Volta border zone was subject to large-scale physical migrations by refugees from both adjoining regions created by wars, especially in the late seventeenth and early eighteenth centuries.

The final region was the greater Angola region, which stretched from the kingdom of Loango in modern Congo-Brazzaville, down to the lands of the Benguela highlands in central Angola. The three most important languages, Kikongo, Kimbundu, and Umbundu, are all closely related linguistically and may be learned by native speakers of one relatively quickly. Christianity in Kongo and Angola created some common religious bonds, at least between those who accepted a Christian identity. People from the farther interior, beyond the Kwango

River, did not join the flood of exported people until the middle of the eighteenth century, but they too spoke reasonably closely related languages and followed broadly similar customs. For these reasons, the central African zone is not subdivided as the two West African zones are. These broad regions, then, defined the cultural diversity of Africans who began arriving in the Americas shortly after the Spanish explorer Christopher Columbus did.

Scholarly opinion has varied widely over the years concerning the cultural contribution of Africans who came as slaves to the civilization of the larger Atlantic world. Because of their low social standing, their capacity to make contributions of the most dramatic sort was lacking. On the other hand, the contribution of Africans in other elements of culture has gradually been recognized. At present, the tendency is as much to exaggerate their contribution as it is to downplay it. However, because of the nature of the slave trade, the ways in which culture was transmitted was fundamentally different from transmission of European culture to the Americas.

Clearly, the slave trade was not a willing immigration, and did not involve either families in the initial group, or a first pioneering group subsequently sending for families from the home territories. Similarly, the break from the older, home traditions was more radical; few Africans revisited their homelands or had any further contact with them. Only through the arrival of new people from the same region could Africans in America learn of events of their homelands, including new cultural trends. Yet the slave trade did provide a steady stream of such new arrivals, and the possibility of some sort of renewal of African culture was always present to some degree.

COLONIAL LIFE AND SLAVE CULTURE

In addition to the problems inherent in the slave trade, there was the problem of the attitude of masters. Owners of slaves had varying views about their slaves' cultural lives. Some may well have sought to deculturate the newly arrived, by demanding that they not speak their home language or by discouraging other cultural manifestations. Such policies were especially popular where evidence of social solidarity among slaves, no matter what its manifestation, could also be perceived as conspiracies to revolt. Other masters, however, were probably not much interested in forcing cultural change as long as the required labor was performed and their stan-

dards of discipline were met. Even where masters were anxious to change cultures, however, the project would require significant effort, as occasional nationalistic modern dictatorships have discovered. In most countries, deculturation of minority groups is linked to mass education, an expensive undertaking that was rarely attempted in the pre-modern American world, and then not on a large scale.

Finally, there is also the issue of the role of work routines and practices. Slaves were badly treated, deprived of free time, and forced to work such long hours that they had little or no energy for other activities. In the opinion of some writers, this led to deculturation in spite of the intentions or lack of intentions of masters. While this may have been true in some cases, even widely, the development of culture and its dissemination has never been dependent on full participation. As long as some number of the slaves possessed sufficient time and energy to perform cultural tasks and develop cultural ideas, they could do it for others. Moreover, the transmission of culture from one generation to the next was naturally dependent upon the successful rearing of children. In the harshest labor regimes, this did not occur, and although culture might have been lost, the people themselves were also lost. Since they were typically replaced with more Africans, the cycle of transmission would renew each generation.

The Africans who crossed the Atlantic on slave ships did not have any control over their destination, and moreover traveled as individuals rather than as social groups. In many respects, then, these unwilling immigrants had to start over in the Americas, possessing neither family, former governments, nor former neighbors and friends with whom to work. Building a society began during the so-called Middle Passage, the ocean voyage that carried them to the Americas. People who traveled on the same ship, *malungos* in Brazil, or "shipmates" in the English-speaking world, formed tight bonds, which in eighteenth-century Jamaica, at least, were regarded as a new form of kinship. These particular bonds, which might be strained considerably when cargoes of ships were sold to separate masters often residing miles apart, were joined by the more permanent bond of first-generation Africans: the "nation" or "country."

"Nations" or "countries" were concepts of unity formed in America that linked people who spoke the same language. In an environment where much was strange and new and communication was difficult, meeting others who spoke one's own language with native proficiency was a natural source

26

of friendship and association. National groupings typically reinforced the smaller, though tighter ship-mate bonds, since socialization on ships was only really possible between people who spoke the same language—and many if not most ships carried groups of people (sometimes the entire cargo) who spoke the same language. The nation provided a new unit of organization unique to America, since in Africa political boundaries were not linguistic ones, and social units of various sizes were not organized by linguistic criteria.

Because they were American creations, the African nations often bore names that did not reflect either modern or older African terms of identity. Thus people who called themselves "Akan" or "Twi" in Africa might be called "Coromantees" from the small English-controlled port from which they first departed for Anglo-America. They might also be called "Minas" in Portuguese, "Aminas" in Danish or Dutch, "Mines" in French, and so on. In Africa, their tongue was often simply called the "language of Fante" or "language of Mina," or "language of Akwamu" or other small state entities, even though its uniformity was recognized throughout the area where it was spoken. While "Congo" clearly referred to the kingdom of Kongo, an identity shared on both sides of the Atlantic, it also clearly referred to people who did not live in Kongo, but only spoke the Kikongo language. The designation "Ibo," already in use in Jamaica in the late seventeenth century, fixed a name on an ethnolinguistic group that had no common name in Africa, though ironically it would come to use this term for itself in the twentieth century.

The languages of American nations might not be exactly the same as in Africa. Some dialects might prevail over others, and people from groups that were not numerous in the American slave population might end up speaking a lingua franca rather than their native language. In general the tendency was toward simplification, and with a goal of creating the largest group of people sharing some element of language that allowed for maximum communication.

In America, where family and community had to be established anew from scratch, the first step in mutual communication was the location and bonding with people who spoke the same languages. With commonality in language often came commonality in other aspects of culture and an attempt to continue satisfying elements of the home culture wherever conditions of labor, supervision, and residence permitted it. This solidarity might not be manifested in a formal organization, but it was likely to form recognizable patterns of socialization.

Africans enslaved in America often sought out marriage partners from their own group when they could. Statistical information from Latin regions where ethnicity was regularly recorded show that as many as three-quarters of all marriages were between people from the same nation. It is quite likely that similar patterns were also displayed in areas where no such records were kept. Clearly the children of such unions might find their home lives included many elements of a particular African culture.

Transplanted Africans met socially by nations, and their activities included performance of music and dance, funerals, mutual aid and assistance, and religious observations. In addition, nations sometimes elected symbolic "kings" or "queens" in many parts of the Americas, to form a sort of shadow government over the people of a single nation resident in a district, a town, or even a whole colony. Because nations were also active in plots and revolts, the colonial authorities had varying degrees of toleration for such meetings, especially those that were held off estates, or by people who traveled from one estate to another to attend such a gathering. At times, these meetings were forbidden, but even then they were often held clandestinely. In other places and times, however, national meetings were tolerated. Documentation mentions them in South Carolina and in New York, and there are other hints that they were held in other parts of English North America. They were even more extensive in the Caribbean.

In Catholic areas, such as the French, Spanish, or Portuguese colonies, including Louisiana and Florida (when under Spanish or French rule), the church sometimes helped to organize lay congregations built around national identity. While these organizations rarely took in all the people from a language group in a district or colony, they did serve as a focal point for the elite of the group to enjoy social contact. The Protestant areas never had equivalent organizations and often frowned on national organizations, which were frequently accused of fomenting plots.

The fear of plots was a real one, though in some specific cases it was probably unjustified, for national meetings or even organizations were not necessarily any more threatening than social and mutual aid meetings. But they certainly could engage in plotting, and many of the most powerful revolts were organized on national lines. A revolt like the Jamaican revolt of 1760, called "Tacky's

War," derived from its leader's name, was organized simultaneously in five Jamaican parishes, but involved only members of one ethnic background, the Coromantees, or Akan, from modern Ghana. The fact that the patterns of shipment and purchase meant that co-nationals were widely dispersed also meant that they could form a network that might stretch over several plantations, or in this case, parishes. National feeling played a role in other big revolts, such as the revolt on St. Jan in 1733 and the Haitian revolution of 1791 to 1804. In North America, the Stono rebellion of South Carolina in 1739 was mostly composed of Angolans (or Kongolese), while the New York revolt of 1712 was organized by Coromantees. In the Denmark Vesey revolt in Charleston, South Carolina, in 1822, plotters hoped that national organizations would group large numbers of rebels to support them in the rural areas.

As important as social and cultural contact with fellow nationals was for providing comfort and memories of home, Africans were often forced to live in close proximity to people of other nations. Whether on a rural plantation or in a small town or city, slaves were not at liberty to live where they chose, and were typically required to live in special quarters or sections of houses where they were placed without much regard to their own national feelings. Such a unit of co-residence can be called an estate, whether it was urban or rural, large or small.

Thus Africans in America were simultaneously members of a wide ranging national group that might be dispersed widely in many different estates, and of a local community which was almost always multinational. Moreover, they were also subject to a broader community, which spoke a colonial language such as English, French, Spanish, Portuguese, or Dutch, which few of the Africans knew from their home environment. This multinational background could have important implications for the survival, continuation, and growth of an African American culture; on one hand condemning African languages to rapid extinction, while creating powerful musical forms that would come to define American music for people of all backgrounds.

The multilingual aspect of the estate meant that Africans would be forced to find common languages in which to communicate. There were several possibilities—they could become multilingual; they could all learn a common African lingua franca; or they could adopt the colonial language as a lingua franca. In the end, the colonial language won out as a lingua franca. This should not be surprising, considering that knowledge of the colonial language would be essential for communicating beyond the slave community, and that colonial masters surely favored it.

The colonial languages English, French, Dutch, Portuguese, Spanish, and Danish were sometimes also spoken as lingua francas in coastal parts of Africa. In the seventeenth century, Portuguese was a common lingua franca in much of West and Central Africa, at least along the coast, where it joined other African lingua francas. In the eighteenth century, it was joined by English, which gradually replaced the Portuguese-based language by mid-century in the Lower Guinea regions, and was joined by French in Senegambia as well. This situation meant that a good many Africans came to America with some knowledge of the colonial languages, at least if they came to colonies where the lingua franca was spoken. These bi- and multilingual Africans may have played a crucial role in establishing the colonial languages, as in teaching others to speak them.

Africans, in both Africa and the Americas, spoke a creole dialect of the colonial languages. That is, they spoke a dialect that differed quite sharply from the metropolitan form of the language in grammar and phonology, though usually containing much of the same vocabulary. There has been considerable debate among linguists about the origins and nature of these creole languages. Some have argued that they arose first in Africa and then spread with bilingual slaves to the Americas; others maintain that they originated primarily in the Americas. Even within the Americas, there are competing theories that place their ultimate origins in some places, and has them spread to others. For example, the English language creoles of the West Indies show variants from island to island that suggest to some linguists that they originated in St. Christopher (St. Kitts) and spread from this early English colony to other Caribbean colonies. But the theory is contested, on the one hand by those who see the ultimate origin of the West Indies Creoles in the creole English lingua franca of West Africa, and on the other by those who argue for separate developments on the various islands.

There has been equally sharp debate about the nature of the creole languages, especially their grammar. Some linguists maintain that they represent simplified forms of grammar of African languages, so that language learning might be simplified by attaching new vocabulary to a familiar grammar. Others maintain that they are not originally from any specific language, but rather represent a sot of pan-human minimum grammar, and indeed might even provide insight into the nature of language itself. The resolution of these conflicting theories may never come about, though certainly there is a great deal to be said for the idea that the forms of grammar would be relatively easy for any learner to acquire, and the problem of language learning reduced to memorization of new vocabulary.

In North America, even early variants of the English of Africans were much closer to metropolitan languages or even the regional dialects of English that developed in America from English roots than they were to the creoles of the Caribbean. This has created its own explanatory problems, but one common suggestion is that in the earliest North American colonies (Virginia, Maryland, New York, New Jersey) there was a long period (roughly from about 1620 to 1670), attested in archaeology among other things, in which slaves did not live separately from their masters. During this time their cultural norms may have been shaped to a large degree by the dialects of the colonial language spoken by European native speakers. They would then have provided speech models for later, more numerous Africans that had arrived in the eighteenth century. The one exception, the coastal regions of South Carolina and Georgia, seems to have been a place in which Caribbean-style settlements were the norm from very early in the colonial period.

In any case, the colonial language, in either its metropolitan form or a creole form, became a second language for newly arrived Africans, who continued speaking their native language with their co-nationals and often with their spouses and children when they married within their nation. Runaway advertisements and other forms of evidence suggest that very few failed to learn a working proficiency of the colonial language within a few years. Those who were forced to work with non-nationals in intimate settings, like marriages, were thus likely to communicate in the colonial languages, whatever their level of proficiency.

For children born in America or in Africa, however, the colonial language also became a native language. Since they learned the language as children, they could and did acquire native proficiency in the language. While they might continue to speak their parents' African language (if that was regularly used in the home) as a second language, and they might also participate in affairs of their parents' co-nationals, where the African language would also be used, they might not do so. In common with many second generation immigrants, they may have failed to learn the African language, learned it imperfectly, or focused more attention on the colonial language. Their children would have been even less inclined to learn the African language, assuming that second

generation Africans continued to choose marriage partners from their nation and to speak the national language at home. In time the result of these factors would make African languages disappear, even as the stream of new immigrants constantly brought new native speakers of them into the Americas.

Masters' policies and attitudes probably helped to influence the direction of language change as well. Many masters were indifferent to the issue of languages spoken among their slaves, but they were anxious to be able to communicate with them in a minimal sense, and thus surely favored them acquiring some proficiency in the colonial language. Others, anxious about revolt for the same reasons that they also feared national gatherings and social events, took active steps to discourage the use of African languages, prohibiting slaves from speaking it except on intimate occasions. But either way, the language change toward exclusive use of the colonial language was driven by processes internal to the slave community much more strongly than by the policies of masters. No masters showed any inclination to allow time and opportunity for study of any language—a necessary component of forced language change.

The role of the slave community in developing a colonial language is well revealed in the case of communities of runaways. Many slaves ran away to concealed hideouts in areas that were difficult to access all over the Americas. Often these runaways formed communities along ethnolinguistic lines, with separate settlements for people from one or another African group, even if they worked in tandem for their defense. Yet, in these settlements colonial languages eventually took over. Thus, runaway communities that won official recognition and became formally independent soon spoke colonial languages even when they continued to identify themselves as coming from one African nation. Sometimes these creole languages that have survived until today have high rates of lexical borrowing from African languages, such as the borrowings from Akan in Suriname, or Kimbundu in Brazil and Columbia; however, the basic form of the language is that of the colonial language.

The case is best proved by the linguistic development of Haiti. At the time of its independence in 1804, a slim majority of the inhabitants of the island were African born and thus native speakers of African languages. The politics and tactics of revolution had caused many to resettle in single-nation communities, just as they often fought in single-nation military units. The slave condition and community were fundamentally altered and the master class eliminated. Thus, the conditions for the survival of African languages might seem assured, especially since many were ideologically hostile to Europeans and all their culture. Yet, within a generation, African languages were virtually unspoken in Haiti, and by the end of the nineteenth century one could not find anyone speaking an African language, though of course, as in runaway communities, there were ample lexical borrowings from a variety of African languages.

BLENDING AFRICAN CULTURAL NORMS INTO COLONIAL POPULAR CULTURE

The transmission of religions and religious norms from Africa to America provides a different model from that of the loss of languages. Like African languages, African religions were quite regionally specific, but unlike them were not dependent upon the kind of specific code that holds languages together. Ancestors were the forebears of particular people, and their propitiation took place in specific locations, often around their tombs. Similarly the deities of Africa were, with the exception of the creator God, generally localized around their shrines and territories. Clearly these specific places and the supernatural beings that served them were incapable of being transported to America, but this did not mean that the underlying theology of the religion that supported the tombs and shrines would be lost.

African theologies, unlike Christianity and Islam, were based on continuous revelation. That is, instead of having a sacred text whose interpretation might vary over time, Africans received a stream of new revelations from the "other world," which defined, and potentially could change, the religious system at any time. These revelations were received by a variety of people in a variety of ways, ranging from divination—determining messages from the other world by creating random acts that spiritual powers would shape—to being possessed by those beings themselves. The priests who received these revelations had to demonstrate through miracles that they were continuously in contact with the other world; if they failed to do so, they were no longer recognized. This was also true of holy places, rituals, shrines, and the other paraphernalia of religion. While the potential for change was certainly not realized, documented early forms of African religions were not much different from their modern forms, at least in basic cosmology. The idea of continuous revelation made Africans potentially willing to accept revelations from many different sources.

This led to the absence of orthodoxy and specifically religious conflict.

But this would not mean that the general African cosmology would not cross the Atlantic. In any new location, Africans could reason, there would be some deity responsible for its security. Locating and offering sacrifices to this deity would be an important first step in gaining insight into their new homes. This was something that could be done by continuous revelation, and anyone able to perform the requisite miracles could be considered an authority on it. It might be a Native American spirit that would fulfill the task, or perhaps a church or other holy place of the European colonists. Ancestors would also be lost in the crossing, only to be replaced as people died and left descendants who would sacrifice to them.

Historians know from colonial records that both processes did take place. Many Africans came to offer sacrifices at tombs, for example, even for several generations. The acceptance of holy places accompanied, and in some places preceded, conversion to Christianity. The syncretic models of Christianity often offered models for Africans even from non-Christian parts of Africa, as to how to come to grips with the second type of holy places.

In this context it is important to consider that African religions were not orthodoxies. That is, they did not attempt to convert others, nor was there a particular religious interpretation. The African priesthood was "precarious"; that is, Africans' own acceptance as leaders was dependent upon demonstrable performance of miracles and successful predictions about the other world. Likewise, in a cosmology where many different types of revelations were accepted as valid, there were few barriers to the acceptance of religious ideas and the practices of others. Thus, African identities were not bound up in a particular interpretation of the cosmic order, and they were unlike the Christian and Muslims who impinged upon them with evangelism and concepts of heresy. Thus, Africans were quite open to religious change.

In Catholic areas, they undoubtedly became convinced that patron saints of towns, plantations, ships, or other places had them under their protection. Certainly witnesses describe the fondness with which Africans fell in with the cult of the saints. They were, not surprisingly, fond of saints with African characteristics, such as St. Benedict, who was often represented as being black-skinned. Africans were also drawn to Baltazar, the black figure in the traditional European depiction of the Magi kings, and so were fond of Epiphany as a holiday. In addition, they were drawn to lay brotherhoods that traditionally served African people, such as the brotherhood of Our Lady of the Rosary. Founded in Portugal, the brotherhood spread in the sixteenth century to São Tomé, and Angola, as well as to Brazil. Chapters were also found in Spanish-speaking areas, and in all these regions probably represented either a syncretism of local deities (as in Kongo) or a recognizably local deity of the land where slaves were brought.

There is less certainty about what happened in Protestant areas, since Protestants made few efforts to convert Africans and believed firmly that conversion as opposed to acceptance was necessary. In most areas it would take the sort of direct revelation that accompanied the Great Awakening to bring Africans and their descendants to Christianity. Between their arrival and that of the Baptist and Methodist ministers, there were years of time when their folk religion was barely described. Presumably, however, they located sources of divine spirits, and approached them in acceptable ways.

Beyond religion as a formal system, Africans also brought philosophies and folk wisdom with them. The failure of African languages to survive in the situation of slavery meant that the exact forms of folktales and proverbs, which might be described as philosophies, were lost with the language. But this need not be particularly significant, for equivalent forms of wisdom soon replaced them. Even in creole languages a new stock of proverbs grew up. In some cases, one can argue that the new proverbs were simply translations of African language proverbs into a new language. There are some striking similarities between the general tenor of these new proverbs and those of Africa. But proving that these proverbs are simply translations is difficult, just as it is difficult to prove that they were simply borrowed from colonial languages.

The case for folktales, however, is clearer. While language change affected the details of these too, their general plot and characters clearly were translated. A striking case is the Anancy stories of the Akan region of modern Ghana. Anancy is the name of a clever spider who manages to extricate himself from difficult situations through his wits and good (though sometimes less than kind) humor. Mid-eighteenth-century accounts noted that these stories were being told in Jamaica, though without revealing much of their plots. However, the Anancy stories of today's Caribbean and South Carolina are strikingly similar to those of West Africa in both plot and characters. There are divergences today in both traditions, and the lack of historical records

does not allow historians to see how these changes developed, but the transmission of wisdom and moral values that these stories convey suggests a strong transmission of African culture.

In North America tales of the trickster rabbit, best known as Brer Rabbit, have a similar African analog in the rabbit tales of central Africa, where "Kalulu" performs the same functions as Anancy does in Ghana and the Caribbean. In the North American case and in the Caribbean, however, explaining variants in two traditions and possibly the borrowing of European tales, stories of Native American origin, and those of other African traditions into the Anancy or Brer Rabbit corpus have not yet been examined systematically. Again, as in the case of the development of each tradition, the lack of systematic historical records hampers research. The earliest collections of the tales come from the late nineteenth century, where there were already several hundred years separating the first Africans from their descendants.

The transmission of folk wisdom from one continent to another may not also take into consideration that the situation the wisdom addresses changes. Presumably any system of moral economy alters as the circumstances of the bearers change. Thus, the wisdom of free people in Africa may have differed from that of slaves in America. The slaves' vision as reflected in their selections of favorite tales from a particular corpus might have differed markedly from that of free people in Africa. In general, people who are discontented are likely to find some stories less satisfactory than others, which might be favored by people in better circumstances. Thus variants in the corpus of stories between the continents might not simply reflect transmission of an African culture to another location, but an evolution within that culture as it addresses new problems. While the idiom might be the same, the content is different, and over time this might lead to new patterns of creating stories of borrowing from traditions outside of the African one. This would certainly have been the case, for example, with the borrowing of North American slaves from the biblical tradition.

Even in African areas where Christianity had taken root, such as Kongo, and even in American areas where Christians might have been a significant number of African arrivals, as in South Carolina, the Kongolese form of Christianity was not Bible based. Like other Catholic forms, it was catechism based, and the wisdom of proverbs and folktales was supplied by the non-Christian culture. But when biblical tradition and biblical literacy was introduced into African-descended populations by Baptist and Methodist preachers in the late eighteenth century, in South Carolina as elsewhere, the tradition was appropriated and turned to new uses. There is little question that African slaves borrowed folktales and proverbial wisdom from the Bible, but their choices of these sources varied according to their conditions. They often diverged quite sharply from the choices and interpretations of the European or Euro-American ministers who introduced Bible-based wisdom, as one might expect, given their situation. This model might also help historians speculate about how African Americans decided to retain folk wisdom from African cultures, or which elements of which African culture would be borrowed.

The problem of the transmission of ethical ideas might be elaborated by considering the way in which Africans seeking a new American politics expressed themselves. For Coromantee (Akan) slaves in the Caribbean, for example, independent political choices might have been borrowed from a corpus of ideas elaborated in the Gold Coast. When Court, an African from the Akan region and enslaved in Antigua, was to be crowned "king" of the Coromantees, he took some pains to model his coronation on one from Africa. He chose a form called *ikyem*, or shield, from the tradition. In the Gold Coast, the title obtained through this ceremony was accorded by state authorities on a person who had achieved a great deal of wealth and was prepared to spend some of it in an elaborate entertainment. But Court was not chosen or accepted by the political authorities of Antigua for his coronation in 1736; rather it was from the nation of Coromantees and in part through his own lavish entertainment of them in the year or two before the event. In fact, the colonial authorities saw his coronation as part of a plot and eventually had him killed. Thus, in America the content of a political celebration was altered by new circumstances. Court was chosen by his nation, from below, rather than being recognized from above, as would have taken place in Africa.

Similarly, just two years later, Jamaican Maroons of the same origin as Court, having fought the colonial authorities for their freedom, accepted the new condition by performing a horn celebration, also borrowed from the Gold Coast political tradition. While the authorities recognized the Maroons and made significant grants to them, the celebration did not quite represent the same sort of recognition as in Africa, though it was closer in the Jamaican case than that of Court. Clearly the situation in America had changed some elements of the political ideology, even as it borrowed the idiom from Africa.

How other coronation ceremonies borrowed or changed African coronations has not yet been fully investigated. The idea that slaves might be crowned as kings is itself something which few African rulers would have countenanced, though ennobling ceremonies such as those of the Akan operated upon by Court and the Jamaica Maroons might provide models that would preserve the monarchical model while giving it a new substance. Certainly the power and authority of an African American king would reflect a different set of political ideals than those of the African rulers of their home countries.

Such a set of political modifications must have also underlay the African-based elements of the Haitian revolution of 1791. Leaders of the Kongo nation, like Macaya, who declared himself to be a subject of the "King of Congo, lord of all the blacks," were not thinking of simply reestablishing the kingdom of Kongo in Haiti. Rather, they and their followers were carving out new ideologies from old political idioms. This is not to say that African radicals and revolutionaries could not and did not do this—D. Beatriz Kimpa Vita had done the same nearly a century earlier in Kongo, when, as a woman possessed by St. Anthony, she had led a movement to reestablish the kingdom and end wars—rather, only that the transmission of wisdom concerning the right ordering of society and its government would not be the same on both sides of the Atlantic. Political traditions, like all forms of wisdom, are not necessarily static nor do they always reinforce the status quo.

The situation is quite different with aesthetic norms than it is with intellectual and philosophical traditions. In music and art the specifically African component is not dependent upon language and can travel and change freely. As already stated, decorative arts, and probably music, were readily exchangeable in Africa and hardly restricted to a single culture as defined by language. There was not likely to be a one-to-one transmission of African arts to the Americas, but rather a fantastic mixture of African, European, and Native American traditions.

To understand how art forms might cross the Atlantic and be transformed, it is worthwhile to start with music, probably the most immediately recognizable element of African culture to influence the general culture of the New World. In order to understand the way in which music would be transformed, one must consider how music is created and performed in general.

Although almost everyone can sing and keep simple rhythm, the advent of musical instruments, an innovation at least eight thousand years old in Africa, placed some emphasis on individual virtuosity. Not everyone played an instrument and those who either possessed the talent or acquired the skill necessarily produced it for others. Such a person would receive some sort of material gratification for his or her efforts, as well as a certain amount of prestige. As a result, there developed a fairly early relationship of reciprocity between a musician, most clearly defined by using instruments (though possibly also by virtuosity of singing), and an audience composed of nonmusicians. This relationship may well have extended to the creation of music as well as the performance of time-honored, traditional music.

The professionalization of music is exemplified in seventeenth- and eighteenth-century Atlantic Africa by the presence of patronage. Rulers had their own bands, sometimes with many members, who played on state occasions and for the pleasure of their patrons. At times their patronage even extended to Europeans who possessed either musical talent or training and found themselves in Africa, such as the German horn player who, in the early seventeenth century, found himself playing at the court of a Sierra Leone ruler and giving lessons to aspiring local musicians. When offered a chance to return to Europe, he refused, no doubt having found suitable patronage in Africa. While European influence on African music may have been small in most areas, it was likely to have been greater in central Africa, where Portuguese settlement and Christian conversion surely resulted in new musical forms developing among the musicians of the region. In addition to rulers, it is possible that the system of traveling musicians evidenced in later times was also prevalent in the earlier period, in which case musicians might have also been supported by ordinary people as well.

The patronage relationship, whether it is between rulers and their bands or common people and a semiprofessional musician, put pressures on musicians to be creative, and one way was by crossing cultural lines, while carefully fudging the sensibilities of the audience. What started in Africa surely also developed in the Americas.

Africans with musical abilities found employment in the Americas, for historians know that musicians playing instruments were present at the various national gatherings mentioned in travelers' and colonists' accounts. But while the national system surely allowed musicians from particular parts of

Africa to continue to enjoy the limited patronage available from their enslaved countrymen, the estate organization also insured that musicians would be exposed to and anxious to gain patronage from people of other nations. Thus, the tendency to cross musical traditions was particularly strong.

Such music was recorded in Jamaica in 1688 in one of the few cases where a sophisticated observer used modified western musical notation to record the music of slaves. Sir Hans Sloane, to whom history owes these observations, carefully noted the music that each nation played at a gathering he attended. The music that Sloane collected matches, in a general way, the modern music of the same African regions, confirming that African music had made the passage across the Atlantic. But there was another interesting aspect of the music: one piece had two parts, one of which was derived from an Akan tradition (modern Gold Coast) and the other from an Angolan one. Already musicians were crossing African traditions to produce a new music, one that would be distinctively African American.

Even as these developments were taking place, African musicians were also anxious to be patronized by their masters. Europeans in America often had disparaging comments to make about African music, but some also found it interesting. At some point, African musicians or their American descendants managed to create musical forms that crossed their still-blending African American music with that of Europe, including the adding of new instruments of European origin. At the end of the process they had created a special new music, one that appealed widely to the sensibilities of Africans from many different regions as well as to people of European origin. Another early traveler to Barbados spoke with an African musician who both entertained the slaves of his estate and also learned to play European instruments. Africans' central position in the creation of the new music, the result of their being forced to live in and please multicultural audiences, guaranteed that they personally, as well as their music, would come to define American music.

Scholars cannot determine more about music's relative, dance. Certainly there were named African dances, and these probably went with a limited number of musical forms. But there is a lack of choreographic information that allows scholars to match these matters up. American observers wrote that Africans performed dances of their nations, but it is quite likely that they learned dances of other nations as well. At least one Jamaican witness observed that a woman of the Coromantee (Akan) nation was good at performing dances of the Kongo nation, so historians have to assume that the sort of crossing that took place in music did so in dance as well. That masters may have watched and even imitated slave dances is possible, as is the converse, for witnesses do attest to African Americans performing their own version of colonial dances, no doubt with an additional mixture of their own multicultural dancing thrown in.

The fate of African music reveals what must have happened, in many different ways, in other aesthetic forms. Here, too, one must understand patterns of virtuosity in the production of art and the role of cultural mixing. The production of art, like that of music, depends upon the transportation of artists, and perhaps also upon a patronage network which allows them to work and develop. If the American labor regimes and low status of slaves in general prohibited the development of such a patronage pattern, then perhaps the result would be relatively low and uniform quality.

Such an interpretation might easily be made of early African American decorative arts as manifested in pottery decoration. Careful excavation of early colonial sites in the United States and some Caribbean areas reveals the presence of what archaeologists often call "Colono ware" on sites associated with occupation by people of African descent. The decorative motifs of this strong, utilitarian pottery is remarkably uniform from Virginia to South Carolina, and from there to the West Indies. Furthermore, it is no more than suggestive of any specific African motifs, even though it imitates no other European, Euro-American, or Native American style. Some archaeologists have suggested that perhaps the patterns of enslavement did not bring the best potters, who tended to be older women not favored by slave traders, to the Americas. But one must not confuse a statistical generality with the transmission of arts, for there need not be many skilled potters to create or retain a tradition. Colono ware suggests that while Africans might have grouped themselves socially into nations by their languages, they did not necessarily do so in other aspects of culture. Apparently in this small manifestation of culture, Colono ware represents a mixed tradition that emerged almost as soon as the Africans arrived. Perhaps the production of finer pottery was wholly at the masters' bidding and following their aesthetic norms entirely.

This is not to say that some culturally specific artistic decorations did not arrive in the Americas in other uses. Pipestems found in excavations in Virginia seem to be derived from models from a region around the southeastern part of modern Nigeria and the western parts of modern Cameroon. The timing of the appearance of these pipes in Virginia and the importation of people from this part of Africa suggests that the makers might have come from that area. The wide variety of patterns and high quality of some of the workmanship suggest that more than ordinary skill was required to make them. Similarly, excavators of the African Burial Ground in New York City found a decoration in the form of an Akan *sankofa* on the lid of one of the coffins, suggesting a connection between the African region's decorations and those of descendent populations. Other excavators have found other types of artifacts whose decorations suggest one or another African tradition; for example, the patterns associated with cosmograms from Kongo have also turned up in archaeological excavations. Clearly decoration outside of pottery was personal and, of course, reflected African regional backgrounds.

The problems of determining African origins or survivals in other matters or aesthetics are equally complex. In the issue of fashion, for example, historians know that Africans exported considerable amounts of cloth to the Americas, though research has yet to establish how much and to where in any systematic way. Certainly, Mexican documentation, for example, mentions "Congo mantles" as an item of daily wear, but without specifying whether these were of central African manufacture, or simply in some style that the African Americans identified as a Congo style or that others might have designated so. Any and all interpretations are possible, considering that people in Kongo wore European clothing on occasion, and that the designation of "Congo mantle" might refer to the fabric, style, coloring, or even just manner of wearing.

African Americans did make textiles, but not apparently just for their own consumption, nor did they make any input other than labor directed by others. Many were also clothed by their masters, as many supply lists and inventories reveal. Yet there seems to have developed a style of clothing that distinguished the African American population. In many respects, too, it resembled the clothing of Africans in Africa who wore European-style clothing, especially those who lived around European forts or in Angola. Was this style an imposition of Europeans? In Africa, probably not, but in America, the question is clearly more clouded. As a small example, it appears African women had begun covering their heads with cloth in the European-influenced parts of Africa in the late sixteenth century. Elsewhere fashion in hair treatment focused on braiding styles. Yet the idea of covering heads was rapidly adopted throughout the Americas, even though it never completely supplanted braiding—indeed, ultimately braiding and cutting are both essential to hair care.

Finally, in matters of cuisine, African food was certainly consumed in America. A few important food items of African origin (okra being one of the best known) crossed the Atlantic, and the method of preparation frequently approached that of Africa, particularly in those items that involved the concept of placing a gravy over a starchy foundation dish. Though such a style of preparation might not be unique to Africa and indeed was probably also shared with some parts of Europe, an African component is likely when it is African Americans engaged in it. But in cuisine as elsewhere, the possibility of cultural crossing was strong. When members of the Coromantee nation in Antigua gathered for an elaborate feast hosted by the prominent member Court in 1736, they feasted on a diet that would have made an Englishman proud—with roast leg of pork, tarts, and cider—with scarcely an item of African origin in it. Yet, somehow, modern Antiguans, like other Caribbean islands, have managed to produce a regional cuisine that is neither African nor European.

In conclusion, one of the remarkable features of the forced migration of Africans to the Americas, and the unique situation that slavery produced, especially the forced mixing of people of different areas, was the production of a new culture. This new culture possessed a dynamism that made it attractive and comfortable not only to the Africans who built it, but to later arrivals as well, and also to Europeans who imitated or incorporated much of it into their own culture. The dynamism was not the product of some unique African characteristic, but of the fact that its makers were forced from very early on to please a wide variety of cultural expectations and so created cultural expressions that were widely accepted. While patterns of segregation, social scorn, and later racism tended to marginalize the new culture, it was remarkably successful even in areas where Africans were only a small component of the population.

See also **Slavery and Race; Slave Culture and Consciousness; Thought and Culture in the Free Black Community; Antislavery** *(in this volume);* **African Americans** *(volume 2); and other articles in this section.*

BIBLIOGRAPHY

Alleyne, Mervyn. *Roots of Jamaican Culture.* London, 1988.

Berlin, Ira. *Many Thousands Gone: The First Two Centuries of Slavery in North America.* Cambridge, Mass., 1998.

Brásio, António, ed. *Monumenta Missionaria Africana.* 15 vols. Lisbon, 1952–1988.

Frey, Sylvia, and Betty Wood. *Come Shouting to Zion: African American Protestantism in the American South and British Caribbean to 1830.* Chapel Hill, N.C., 1998.

Gomez, Michael A. *Exchanging Our Country Marks: The Transformation of African Identities in the Colonial and Antebellum South.* Chapel Hill, N.C., 1998.

Hancock, Ian. "A Provisional Comparison of the English-Based Atlantic Creoles." *African Language Review* 8 (1969): 7–72.

Haviser, Jay B. *African Sites: Archaeology in the Caribbean.* Princeton, N.J., 1999.

Hall, Gwendolyn Midlo. *Africans in Colonial Louisiana: The Development of Afro-Creole Culture in the Eighteenth Century.* Baton Rouge, La., 1992.

Mullin, Michael. *Africa in America: Slave Acculturation and Resistance in the American South and the British Caribbean, 1736–1831.* Champaign-Urbana, Ill., 1992.

Palmié, Stephan, ed. *Slave Cultures and the Cultures of Slavery.* Knoxville, Tenn., 1995.

Rath, Richard. "African Music in Seventeenth-Century Jamaica: Cultural Transit and Transmission." *William and Mary Quarterly,* 3d ser., 50, no. 4 (1993): 700–726.

Schwegler, Armin. *"Chi ma nkongo": Lengua y rito ancestrales en El Palenque de San Basilio (Colombia).* 2 vols., Frankfurt and Madrid, 1996.

Slenes, Robert. "'Malungu, Ngoma vem!' África encoberta e descoberta no Brasil." *Revista da Universidade de São Paulo* 12 (1991–1992): 48–67.

Sobel, Mechal. *Trabelin' On: The Slave Journey to an Afro-Baptist Faith.* 1979. Reprint, Princeton, N.J., 1988.

———. *The World They Made Together: Black and White Values in Eighteenth-Century Virginia.* Princeton, N.J., 1987.

Stuckey, Sterling. *Slave Culture: Nationalist Theory and the Foundations of Black America.* New York and Oxford, 1987.

Thornton, John K. *Africa and Africans in the Making of the Atlantic World, 1400–1800.* 2d ed. London and New York, 1988.

———. "Central African Names and African-American Naming Patterns." *William and Mary Quarterly,* 3d ser. 50, no. 4 (1993): 727–742.

———. "Les raciness du vaudou: Religion africaine et société haïtienne dans la Saint-Domingue prérévolutionnaire." *Anthropologie et Sociétés* 22, no. 1 (1998): 85–104.

Vogt, Carlos, and Peter Fry. *Cafundó: A África no Brasil.* São Paulo, 1996.

Warner-Lewis, Maureen. *Trinidad Yoruba: From Mother Tongue to Memory.* Mona, Jamaica, 1997.

COLONIAL IMAGES OF EUROPE AND AMERICA

David S. Shields

The intellectual history of the discovery and settlement of America by the various European powers characteristically explores the Christian pretexts of imperial ventures, the commercial imperatives during the transatlantic enterprise, and the fantasy of the revival of ancient imperial glory entertained by early modern monarchs and their agents. It also attempts to capture colonists' sense of how their activities participated in an international project to extend western culture—European "civility"—into the western hemisphere. This essay will survey the images of Europe that occupied the imaginations of literate Euro-Americans until the American Revolution and evaluate their role in articulating a sense of American civil society.

While the imperial powers of Europe sponsored the colonization and occupation of North America, the settlers tended not to envision Europe as an integral cultural or political entity until the eighteenth century. This is not to say that writers and thinkers in America did not detect in the pattern of imperial rivalry common models and purposes directing territorial expansion and commercial dominion. In nearly every exposition of English, French, Spanish, or Dutch colonial enterprise lurked recollections of ancient Rome or Alexander's empire. These memories of classical empire supplied a symbolism of national enterprise that would warrant, in time, the naming of a "Western tradition" and a "European civilization" extending from ancient Greece to the modern era. Furthermore, the memory of Christendom, that international panoply of Western Christian states mobilized in the crusades against Islam, remained alive in the minds of early modern evangelists and imperial enterprisers. For instance, Captain John Smith (1580–1631), the most assiduous of Anglo-America's early seventeenth-century imperial publicists, won his martial reputation fighting the Ottoman Turks at Alba Regis as a mercenary for the German princes. Some historians also claim that a martial cant descended from the rhetoric of the Crusades incited the "invasion of America" and the English attack on native cultures. Yet for all the resonance of these images of transnational cultural and political community, few Americans formed these impressions into a focused vision of Europe until taught to do so by literary speculators concerned about America's place in world history.

The discovery of America was one of several "crises" that contributed to the eclipse of the vision of a Holy Roman Empire of Europe in the sixteenth century (the Reformation and the collapse of Charles V's imperial scheme were others). Colonial enterprise became an expression of competing imperial ambitions by nation states asserting individual and absolute sovereignty. Yet the discovery also stimulated a new conceptualization of the communal interests of nations, expressed in the formulation of international law—Hugo Grotius's *jus gentium* (the law of the people) and Francisco de Vitoria Suaréz's legal vision of the international Christian commonwealth, whose preservation was the imperative that constrained the ambition of nation states. The incursions of the Ottoman Turks into Hungary and Austria, culminating in the siege of Vienna in 1552, gave point to the idea of a common Christian political interest. Yet competition and war among the Western nations and divisions in theology and religious polity between Rome and Protestant states made many aware of how the notion of a commonwealth was phantasmal.

One who resented war's disruption of the old vision of an integral Christian community was Captain John Smith. In his memoir, *The True Travels, Adventures, and Observations of Captaine John Smith, in Europe, Asia, Africke, and America* (1630), Smith says he was "desirous to see more of the world, and trie his fortunate against the Turkes, both lamenting and repenting to have seene so many Christians slaughter one another" (*The Complete Works of Captain John Smith*, 1986, vol. 3, pp. 156–157). Smith was one of the few men of his era to develop an exquisite sense of Europe. He cites

THE
TRUE TRAVELS,
ADVENTVRES,
AND
OBSERVATIONS
OF
Captaine IOHN SMITH,

In *Europe*, *Asia*, *Affrica*, and *America*, from *Anno*
Domini 1593. to 1629.

His Accidents and Sea-fights in the Straights; his Service
and Stratagems of warre in *Hungaria*, *Transilvania*, *Wallachia*, and
Moldavia, against the *Turks*, and *Tartars*; his three single combats
betwixt the *Christian* Armie and the *Turkes*.

After how he was taken prisoner by the *Turks*, sold for a Slave, sent into
Tartaria; his description of the *Tartars*, their strange manners and customes of
Religions, Diets, Buildings, Warres, Feasts, Ceremonies, and
Living; how hee slew the Bashaw of *Nalbritz* in *Cambia*,
and escaped from the *Turkes* and *Tartars*.

Together with a continuation of his generall History of *Virginia*,
Summer-Iles, *New England*, and their proceedings, since 1624. to this
present 1629; as also of the new Plantations of the great
River of the *Amazons*, the Iles of St. *Christopher*, *Mevis*,
and *Barbados* in the *West Indies*.

All written by actuall Authours, whose names
you shall finde along the History.

LONDON,
Printed by *J. H.* for *Thomas Slater*, and are to bee
sold at the Blew Bible in *Greene Arbour*. 1630.

The True Travels, Adventures, and Observations of Captain John Smith, London 1630, printed by J. H. for Thomas Slater. Many of Smith's books were written to encourage immigration to the colonies and frequently contained maps detailing the coastline. © BETTMANN/CORBIS

two books as being central to his intellectual formation: "His studie was Machiavills Art of warre, and Marcus Aurelius" (p. 2). No doubt Smith pondered that portion of Book 2 of *L'arte della guerra* (1560) in which Machiavelli argued that the profusion of states in Europe occasioned conflicts that favored the emergence of military talent. Neither Asia nor Africa, according to Machiavelli, had a political organization that necessitated the honoring or encouraging of military merit, so had failed to produce as many significant men of arms. Smith personally benefited from Europe's theater of arms, building a reputation for valor that permitted him to pass from army to army eastward to the Turkish frontier. Yet he was clearly moved by a vision of a Christian commonwealth that made warring on behalf of one European state against another distasteful. Indeed, upon his return to England after his adventures in the East, his reluctance to reenter the service of any European power and his decision to

affiliate with the Virginia Company, the chartered corporation empowered by the English throne to colonize North America, may be attributable to his scruples concerning violence against Christian powers.

One wonders whether Smith's account of his motives was constructed retrospectively. His writings after his return from Virginia display a growing political radicalism. Criticisms of the organization of the government of Virginia, the Virginia Company, and the importation of aristocracy increase with each imprint. His vision of a New World meritocracy with property made available to the commonality becomes more pronounced. This growing radicalism reveals Smith's engagement with the contemporary recovery of republicanism. His political mentor was Sir Robert Bruce Cotton (1571–1631), the famous antiquarian and collector of the foremost library of Anglo-Saxon manuscripts. Cotton through his collecting pursued an atavistic vision of a primal Germanic culture, one that was republican, heroic, and free of the privilege of blood. For his imaginings he was executed as an enemy of the Crown. If we are to credit the first paragraph of Smith's *True Travels*, Cotton asked Smith to write his memoir. Cotton's image of an ancient Germano-European commonwealth is transferred into the New World in Smith's hopes for a reformed Virginia, and, later, New England.

Smith saw America's possibility in the light of an antiquarian fantasy of ancient European commonwealth. William Penn was moved by a more traditionally Christian ideal of the peaceable kingdom when founding his colony in America. The enterprise of making peace practicable in America prompted the Quaker proprietor to turn his thought to the problem of instituting a lasting political order in Europe. From 1692 to 1694, Penn drafted a plan whereby Europe might be drawn into a federal commonwealth that would ensure civil tranquility. *Essay Towards the Present and Future Peace of Europe* (1693) spoke to an international scene ravaged by the 1689–1714 war between Louis XIV and the Grand Alliance. The desirability of peace was being widely recognized, and to this desire Penn spoke his political postulates: "Peace is maintained by Justice, which is a Fruit from Society, and Society from Consent." An instrument was needed through which to work consent and to enact justice, so Penn proposed the "Soveraign or Imperial Dyet, Parliament or State of Europe."

Penn's scheme showed a familiarity with two prominent utopian schemes for European order composed during the seventeenth century: the Duc de Sully's Grand Design, published in 1662, which proposed a General Council of Europe overseeing regional councils to which all elective and hereditary monarchies and sovereign republics belonged; and Émeric Crucé's *Le nouveau Cynée* (1623) with its scheme of a permanent Assembly designed to maintain peace. Yet Penn's plan supplied a more elaborate rationale for a federated Europe than those of his predecessors. The "real benefits" that flowed from an institutionally enforced "Peace of Europe" were the following:

1. It would prevent the loss of lives and the depopulation of the nations.
2. It would recoup the reputation of Christianity in the "sight of infidels."
3. It would save money by forestalling the expenses of war.
4. It would prevent the destruction of towns, city, and countryside and all its attendant costs.
5. It would secure the highways and borders, enabling travel and encouraging trade.

The list of benefits mixes financial incentives for peace with wishes for Christian solidarity. Yet this admixture of worldly policy and utopian speculation made it no more enticing to the executives of Western nations than any of the other seventeenth-century "grand schemes." Penn would content himself with making peace practicable in his American enclave.

Chiliastic Christians, believers in the Christian millennium of Revelation 20, believed that neither kings nor parliaments in the end would bring peace and justice to the world. Only the Prince of Peace in his Second Coming as the Son of Man would put an end to the jealousies of the nations. The reign of God would be instituted despite the political machinations of men. American oracles of apocalypse, of which there were many, had a particular concern with the place of America in the drama of global judgment. The American role was often conceived as being in tension with the fate of Europe. In particular, the legend of the westward transit of religion popularized in early modern works such as George Herbert's "The Church Militant" imagined that the final things would not take place until sanctity had found refuge in America from the degeneracies of Rome, France, and England, and then passed westward to return to the Holy Lands again. To the New England Puritans the evacuation of religion to America was a congenial concept that explained their own history. England under the Stuart Kings seemed as Babylonian in Puritan eyes as Rome or

the court of the Sun King. In their thralldom to sin, the nations of the West formed a community of sin that made Europe a byword for degeneracy. Cotton Mather, introducing his magisterial history of American religion, *Magnalia Christi Americana* (1702), framed his story in terms of the contrast: "I write the Wonder of the Christian Religion flying from the Depravations of Europe to the American Strand."

The myths of the *translatio studii* and the *translatio imperii*—the westward course of learning and empire—derive from and often appeared in conjunction with the legend of Christianity's circumnavigation of the globe. Henricus Selijns, a Dutch Reformed minister in New York, noted in his prefatory poem to Mather's *Magnalia*:

Thou Science older climes befits
And Europe swarms with academic wits.
Yet see scholastic shades these wilds adorn.
Such as the Old World may not wisely scorn.
That world we left; But Science has made known,
Out of the world, a new world of our own:
A hemisphere, imperial let to rise—
In arts proficient, and in Learning wise.

In his prophecy of the rise of arts and learning Selijns regarded the movement of academic enterprise into the New World as beneficial. This benignant view was not shared by everyone moved by the vision of the *translatio studii*.

One question that troubled the prospect of learning's transit was that of scholastic degeneracy. Had the schools and schoolmen of the Old World codified superstitions, ancient suppositions, and "human inventions" into dogma? The question whether learning paralleled religion in depravation in Europe was complicated by the quarrel between the moderns and ancients in London and Paris during the 1690s. The insistence on the part of the partisans of the modern wisdom that the ancient wisdom failed to understanding nature as well as the science of modern analysts became attached to an image of America as the place where nature asserted her truth most clearly. Some British American writers suggested that in America an access to the truths of nature might be had free of the mediation of ancient, scholastic inventions. An intellectual genealogy for Emerson's "The American Scholar" (1837) can be traced back through dozens of minor New England and Pennsylvanian poets to the pages of Mather's *Magnalia*, where Selijns observed, "Philosophy and Science here / Will find new secrets and a broader sphere" (p. 87).

Ideas that patterns of virtue were inscribed in nature, and that the state of nature coincided with the state of liberty, had the effect of imbuing with moral and political meaning the science of American nature. Throughout the eighteenth century British American poets elaborated a myth about the New World as a place where the renovation of learning would take place coincidentally with the accomplishment of political liberty. In Pennsylvania, Benjamin Franklin's sometime friend George Webb supplied a neoclassical gloss to Penn's Quaker utopia of peace (*Leeds American Almanack for 1730*):

> E'er Time has Measured out a hundred Years
> Westward from Britain, shall an Athens rise.
> Which soon shall bear away the learned Prize;
> Hence Europe's Sons assistance shall implore,
> And learn from her, as she from them before.

The precondition for the transfer of learning to Philadelphia was the liberty instituted in the colony by Penn's charter:

> No Unjust Sentence we have cause to fear,
> No Arbitrary Monarch rules us here;
> Our Lives, our Properties, and all that's Ours,
> Our happy Constitution here secures.

A generation later, the early graduates of Philadelphia's academy would elaborate these themes repeatedly, in Francis Hopkinson's *Science: A Poem* (1756), Thomas Godfrey Jr.'s "A Cantata on Peace 1763," Nathaniel Evans's "Verses Addressed to the the Trustees of the College of Philadelphia" (1765), and Jacob Duche's "Seventh Letter" in *Tamoc Caspipina's Observations on a Variety of Subjects, Literary, Moral and Religious* (1774). But the great expositor of *translatio studii* was their teacher, Rev. William Smith, provost of the College of Philadelphia.

William Smith, trained at the University of Aberdeen when the Scottish Enlightenment had attained full luminosity, came to the New World fired with pedagogic ambitions. To the New York legislature (*Some Thoughts on Education*, p. 19) in 1752 he proposed to educate native youths in Western arts and sciences, warning:

> On this long-neglected Work depends
> No less, perhaps, then whether our New-World
> (When by the sad Vicissitude of Things
> The Old has sunk back to its pristin Sloth
> And Barbarism) shall be the last Retreat
> Of Arts, imperial Liberty and Truth.

Later in Smith's poem we see, literally, the enlightenment of America as the sun fires "her sluggish and unthinking Sons." Once aroused, they boldly "assert their native Rights as Men / Enjoy by turns, their Day of polish'd Bliss." Smith then offers the first of a long tradition of visions revealing "California" as the place where America's destiny has its culmination. Once learning rises and falls there, God will stretch forth his "strong right Arm, and Renovation give / To Nature."

There are a number of things to note about Smith's renovations to the myths of the *translatio studii* and *translatio imperii*. Earlier Christian writers envisioned the circuit of illumination proceeding from Jerusalem and circumnavigating the world westward, returning to Jerusalem. America's time of eminence was the penultimate stage in the transit. Asia would follow, and with its illumination then the heavenly Jerusalem would appear above the earthly Jerusalem. Smith made California the terminus of the transit because he envisioned learning and the arts as having emanated from China. Then, too, America would follow the pattern of empire, rising and falling. When California in future times became degenerate, then the precondition for the renovation of nature would have been met. Smith, too, popularized the idea that America's emergence onto the world stage was occurring before his generation's eyes, occasioned by the flight of virtue from Europe. When the "old World / Spuurning all Cure, in broad Corruption lies" (ibid., p. 24), then America would be exalted. Smith and his lineage of cultural prophets set Americans looking for signs of Europe's exhaustion, for such portents betokened America's coming into fullness.

The depravities of Europe were registered as featured matter in colonial newspapers. The *Boston News-Letter,* the first regularly published gazette in British America, set the pattern for the arrangement of contents in public papers in 1704. On the front page appeared notices of European and English affairs, digested from foreign journals or extracted from merchants' letters. Local notices were confined to a brief column in the body of the paper. Advertisements took up the rear. The criteria governing the selections of news was much the same as that devised by Grub Street, the untrammeled free market for print that came to be in London after the lapse of press censorship in the 1690s: wars, court intrigues, religious contentions, discoveries, adventures, prodigies, crimes, and inventions. In 1719 John Campbell, the editor of the *Boston News-Letter,* expanded the size of his paper to accommodate the wealth of news from abroad: "It's Impossible with half a Sheet in the Week to carry on all the Publick of Europe."

If Europe was the theater of political sensation in the minds of American colonials, it was also the model of civility and propriety. Nature did not eradicate the culture that settlers brought with them, nor immediately suggest to them alternatives to the patterns of civil order, sociability, commerce, consumption, and family they learned before immigrating to America. Indeed, contact with the variety of native nations confronted colonists with a sense of cultural difference that made them conscious of the character of Old World civility. The cultural mythology that bolstered English, later British, commercial imperialism celebrated the spread of the "arts of peace" with the spread of settlement.

Theoretically, these arts would flourish and in time ripen into luxurious degeneracy, as aesthetic indulgence besotted virtue. But luxury remained something of a phantom in countrysides and cityscapes as unformed and rude as prevailed in North America. In disheveled landscapes dotted with provisional buildings and fields still scarred by the effort of extirpating wild vegetation, tokens of finish, polish, gentility were sufficiently rare to be matters of comment, if not celebration, by travelers. The process of improvement that preoccupied the ambitious meant adjustment to a European model of estate and life. William Byrd, that Virginian champion of agricultural improvement and civility, had no anxiety about the dangers of luxury. What he feared was a collapse into a North Carolinian lubberland—a state of incivility, as farmers despairing at the labors entailed in betterment gave up the effort, fled into the frontiers of North Carolina, and went native. In such a state European civility was abandoned completely. Gazing at the ramshackle huts and free-range hogs of white men in rags made William Byrd and others of his kind understand the extent to which their images of life, estate, society, and culture reflected a European vision of genteel existence.

The avidity with which the most ambitious and well connected planters and merchants embraced a vision of the good life of the metropolis is baldly registered in the furnishings of the plantations and great town houses that have survived. London and Parisian goods became markers of social potency in provincial settings. The aping of metropolitan fashion became so ostentatious by the time of the American Revolution that English and Parisian satirists made the à la mode West Indian the butt of the Old World's laughter. Richard Cumberland's *The West Indian* (1771) was the most popular work on the London stage in the 1770s. The arriviste exuberance with which the sugar nabobs plunged into luxurious consumption stood hilariously at odds with the rhetoric of republican sumptuary morality that poured out of British America in the wake of the Stamp Act (1765) troubles, giving the satire much of its pungency. Franklin's masquerade through the European capitals as a simple Quaker, or Benjamin West's shirtless "natural man" reception of visitors to his Italian and London studios, must be understood as stratagems of publicity counterposed to the extravagance of planter travesty.

Of all the ironies implicit in the spectacle of modish planters, none was more pointed than the feudal grandeur of their way of talking. The plantation was the last great expression of the hierarchical vision of social order that had characterized the ancient and medieval worlds in the West. In political theory, feudalism had become synonymous with the politics of Europe. John Adams's *Dissertation on the Canon and Feudal Law* (1765) argued that the greatest enemy to the free inquiry into truth was a European conspiracy between clergy and feudal princes to introduce canon and feudal law into America. If one wished to forestall the transit of learning, liberty, and power to the New World, the quickest way would be to institute the legal and political arrangements characteristic of feudalism. To the extent that this was already accomplished in the staple colonies supported by African slavery, America already had the tincture of European feudal corruption within it.

The American Revolution was a political contention with Great Britain, not a contest with European culture. Yet the success of the Revolution and the reformist impulse it liberated among a range of political actors in the United States brought the question of American cultural dependency to the fore in the 1780s. Had a new order been instituted with the new nation, or was the United States an extension of European civilization, sharing language, arts, and manners? No intellectual troubled over this question more than Noah Webster. For Webster the work of revolution was not done. Until independence from European manners had been won, there would be no American independence: "This country is independent in government; but totally dependent in manners, which are the basis of government. Men seem not to attend to the difference between Europe and America, in point of age and improvement; and are disposed to rush, with heedless emulation, into an imitation of manners, for which we are not prepared" (Webster, "Remarks on Manners," pp. 83–85). The focus of Webster's critique was the American hunger for Europe's "fashionable amusements." Fashion was appropriate only for European countries where there was a disproportion in the arrangement of property. The eighty artisans needed to keep a gentleman or lady well coifed, stylishly dressed, and modishly powdered required whimsical changes in fashion in order to have regular work necessary for subsistence. In a republic where property was more equally dispersed among the population, fashion was not needed to support a population, and could only lead to the depravations of pleasure for its own sake.

Webster's subordination of aesthetics to a moralized political economy was characteristic of republican thought of his generation. Yet it was the great weakness of republicanism. What is liberty if it is not freedom to enjoy whatever one wishes to enjoy? Happiness may entail the pleasures of arbitrary consumption—even the class-ridden, genteel artifacts of Old World court cultures. If one wishes to understand the impetus behind the rise of liberalism and market individualism, one need look no further than this issue. In the contest between moral idealism and pleasure, the immediacy of pleasure triumphs over the abstraction of moral principle.

After the collapse of the French Revolution into Napoleonic imperialism, Europe lost its significance as a model in American political discourse, a loss that not even nineteenth-century scientific socialism would ever wholly redeem. Yet Europe never lost its aesthetic significance; it remained *the* culture of artistic potency. When the political segment of America's genteel propertied classes was finally excluded from the halls of government with the Jacksonian ascendancy, they created high culture—the world of museums, orchestras, opera houses, associations—in which to exercise their sway. The values of high culture were insistently European—German in instrumental music, Italian in opera, French in fine arts, English in literature. Europe's preeminence in the aesthetic realm of high culture would not be seriously challenged until the twentieth century, when American vernacular forms gave rise to the American pop culture that now dominates Western media.

See also **The Classical Vision** *(in this volume);* **Weberian Approaches** *(volume 3).*

BIBLIOGRAPHY

Ferguson, Robert A. *American Enlightenment, 1750–1820.* Cambridge, Mass., 1997.

Lemay, J. A. Leo. *The American Dream of Captain John Smith.* Charlottesville, Va., 1991.

Mikkeli, Heikki. *Europe as an Idea and an Identity.* New York, 1998.

Rougemont, Denis de. *The Idea of Europe.* New York, 1966.

Shields, David S. *Oracles of Empire.* Chicago, 1990.

PURITANISM AS A CULTURAL AND INTELLECTUAL FORCE

Rachelle E. Friedman

In coming to New England, the Puritans had the opportunity to do what few other people have: to construct a new society and to imprint it with their values and beliefs. Unlike the colonists who settled Virginia, the Puritans were concerned, perhaps even obsessed, with establishing a system wherein religion would flourish and their values and beliefs would penetrate every aspect of life, both sacred and secular. Despite the fact that the Puritans brought with them more than vestiges of their Englishness and that the roughness of the wilderness and the Native Americans would shape Puritan attitudes, the Puritans defined the intellectual and cultural life of colonial New England. So, too, Puritanism dictated social organization, the structure and philosophy of government, and religious life. In fact, it is impossible to regard any aspect of life in seventeenth-century New England as separate from Puritanism. This influence did not disappear along with the Puritans; rather, Puritanism continues to be a cultural and intellectual force in American life. As such, it has been one of the most dominant forces to occur over the course of American history.

Even before 1630, when the Puritans began to arrive in Massachusetts, they had a sense of the gravity of their endeavor and that they would leave a significant, permanent imprint on New England. Theirs was to be an "Errand into the Wilderness," one with a "positive sense of mission," as Perry Miller, the foremost scholar of American Puritanism, termed it. John Winthrop, the first governor of the Massachusetts Bay Colony, was cognizant of this when he listed the reasons for traveling to New England. He noted, "It will be a service to the church of great consequence to carry the gospel ... into those parts of the world." Writing in the winter of 1628–1629 in England, Winthrop already knew that Puritanism would effect New England. In reality, it gained momentum much beyond spreading the gospel, and went in directions he and the other settlers could not anticipate.

From the beginning, the Puritans tried to create a milieu in which the life of the mind as well as the spirit could flourish. They embraced evidence of intellectual activity, and thus their written expressions survive today. As a result of New England's "first flowering," the region continued to foster intellectualism and put forth most of the nation's literature, at least until the mid-nineteenth century. In contrast, other regions of the country did not have literary and intellectual traditions as highly esteemed. When authors such as Washington Irving began to tell the stories of their own regions, they did not have the same local, intellectual past on which to draw. They felt compelled to create a past that did not really exist in order to give their work the legitimacy and tradition that the intellectual heirs of the Puritans already had.

PURITANISM IN ENGLAND

The New England Puritans had, of course, come from England, with a theology created both in Britain and on the Continent. Their identity had been shaped as a persecuted opposition group. Though puritan, reformist strands had been present in England for more than a century before the Great Migration, what historians recognize as the direct intellectual heirs of the New England Puritans had formed in response to the church of Queen Elizabeth's design. The Puritans saw severe ills at work; the Anglican Church still bore too much resemblance to Rome and had not been purified enough. Infused by the ideas of the Protestant theologian John Calvin, the Puritans believed that their faith would transform them and give them a new way of life.

At the heart of English Puritan belief was the idea that humans in nature were sinful, but that they could grow in grace. Of course knowledge of genuine grace was impossible, as the Puritans believed in the doctrine of predestination. However, living a life of grace and belief offered evidence that God had predestined one's soul for election to heaven. Puritanism tried to be more than a religious system in England. As Calvin had taught, moral conduct and social organization were integral aspects of a godly community. The Puritans thus offered a sociocultural critique of English life. As part of their reforming efforts, they sought to eradicate the festivals, recreation, and sports which were consuming the English.

Neither the English government nor the Anglican Church looked upon the Puritans too favorably, and this status shaped both their belief system and their decision to leave England for America. Under Queen Mary, they had suffered the most; many had been exiled to Geneva. In Geneva, which had come under the influence of and indeed embraced Calvinism, the Marian exiles studied and further developed their religious ideas freely. In Switzerland, they publicized the persecution to their supporters in England; this "martyrdom" dramatized their plight and gave the movement a radical flavor. After Queen Mary's death, many Protestants returned to England, where some took posts at Cambridge University. There, armed with a sense of power and with cutting-edge knowledge of theology, they educated many of the ministers who later became the spiritual leaders of New England. When they realized that their ultimate goal, reorganizing the Church of England and recreating England's ecclesiastical system, was impossible, many Puritans decided to go to America. There, starting anew, they could create a covenanted community.

PURITANISM IN NEW ENGLAND: THEOLOGY

At the heart of New England Puritanism was covenant theology. A covenant spelled out both civil and spiritual relationships (the former undergirded by and subservient to the latter) and relationships between individuals and between individuals and God. Joining into a "federal covenant" with God, a community declared publicly that theirs was to be one based on social order as well as faith. Members of the federal covenant promised external obedience; in return, God promised outward prosperity. Individuals also entered into their own covenants with God, "covenants of grace." Those who had entered into a covenant of grace were known as "visible saints" and would, it was believed, receive eternal salvation. In the meetinghouse before church leaders, they gave a profession of faith or conversion narrative, which was a testimony of their religious experience. Although true sainthood was known only by God, a person who had given a profession of faith acceptable to the ministers was thought to be justified or possessing an understanding that he or she had been redeemed by God's grace. This person then became a church member. Visible sainthood had its privileges: these church members not only were entitled to partake in the Lord's Supper, but males had the right to vote in civil elections.

Puritan churches were congregational. In contrast to England, where a single system was controlled by a central governing body, the New England churches were independent entities. The faithful covenanted with one another to form their own community of faith, and were free to call their own ministers. This is not to say that ministers or congregations had the freedom to stray from orthodoxy. Ministers were often trained in the same schools, first in England and later at Harvard College. They formed ministerial associations and participated in communal religious life. However, they were not bound by one authoritative body as they were in England.

As such, differences in theological opinion arose and have had a long-term influence on American religious belief and thought. Some ministers, most notably the colonial clergymen Thomas Shepard and Thomas Hooker, believed that a Christian had some power in the spiritual journey. Through good works and a particular effort to seek conversion—a process called preparation—one might effect the desired outcome. In contrast, John Cotton, the acclaimed minister of Boston, was less certain that an individual could hasten justification; grace could only come as a gift from God. Though the ministers co-existed, their differences were apparent. To avoid the appearance of disagreement, Hooker ultimately left with his flock and founded the Connecticut colony. These two strands of thought did not end with the ministers who proffered them. Their congregants imbibed their respective theological systems week after week: Puritans attended church several times a week for several hours at a stretch. Hearing their ministers' ideas about the "morphology of conversion" in turn influenced the conversion narratives they gave to gain church membership. (No one "correct" form of narrative existed; the person seeking membership needed to sound honest, aware of the sight of his or her own sin, and sufficiently contrite.) After Puritanism had ceased to be the defining system of New England religious belief, American Christianity continued to be defined by both strands: one preparationist, rational strand, characterized best by the Unitarians; and the other strand emphasizing grace and pure faith, signified best by evangelical Christians such as Baptists.

CHALLENGES TO THE PURITAN ORTHODOXY

Puritanism was, in the cases of two of the most feared religious leaders, Roger Williams and Anne Hutchinson, an inflexible force. In his search for spiritual purity, Williams, as early as 1631, offered several opinions that resulted in his banishment from Massachusetts. His beliefs constituted a challenge to the social and political order of the Bay Colony. Williams argued for the separation of church and state, and thus, for liberty of conscience. He advocated a separation from the world and its evils. He also challenged the idea that anyone besides God might know if an individual had been justified. He favored limiting church membership, fearing that too many wicked people would be allowed to join in holy communion. With all sorts of sectaries coming to Massachusetts and tempting Puritans with their false beliefs (at least the orthodoxy perceived them as such), John Winthrop and the other officials knew that, in spreading his ideas, Williams was opening up the colony to failure. While Williams had been a respected minister and Winthrop gave him several opportunities to recant his errors, the governor knew that the young settlement was fragile. Disturbing as well to colonial officials was Williams's taking the Puritans to task for refusing to separate from the Church of England. The Anglican Church was filled with heresies, Williams argued, and the Puritans' continuing association meant that New England could never be the "New Israel." To keep him from spreading his false beliefs and to preserve the structure of the colony, Williams was banished to Rhode Island, where as one of the colony's founders he helped to institute freedom of religion.

Like Williams, Anne Hutchinson's fate was banishment from the Bay Colony, also for encouraging dangerous beliefs. She had followed her minister, John Cotton, from England to America in 1634. Her meetings to discuss Cotton's weekly sermons, at first only for women, soon began to include male participants and discussions of other ministers' sermons. She soon began spreading her belief, known as Antinomianism, that other ministers were under "covenants of works," that is, they told their parishioners that outward behavior might indicate justification. The faithful could not work toward or ef-

Governor John Winthrop, 1588–1649. The challenges Winthrop and the Massachusetts Bay Colony faced, among them the relationship between freedom and authority, would continue to shape America's history. © BETTMANN/ CORBIS

fect their salvation; only God could give it to them, as a gift. Cotton was questioned by other ministers, and in Winthrop's words, "gave satisfaction to them." Hutchinson, however, continued to argue that most Massachusetts clergymen preached works and not grace. The colony became divided, with Winthrop leading the side against Hutchinson and one of Winthrop's political opponents, Henry Vane, a leader of the Hutchinsonians. Winthrop even lost brief reelection because religious differences had turned political. Once Winthrop regained authority, measures against the Antinomians continued. These culminated in Hutchinson's being brought to trial in 1637. She demonstrated that her intelligence and knowledge of the Bible was as good as, if not better than, her opponents'. However, her admittance of receiving revelations from God gave the Puritan orthodoxy evidence that she was a heretic and should be banished from the colony. Historians continue to debate whether the Antinomian controversy was

Anne Hutchinson Preaching (**detail**). Hutchinson's exile from the Massachusetts Bay Colony has drawn numerous interpretations of varying viewpoints. This view is a painting by Howard Pyle (1853–1911). © BETTMANN/ CORBIS

church membership. With the Cambridge Platform of 1648, the Puritan orthodoxy demonstrated that they recognized the growing gap between members (who had come forth with conversion stories) and the population at large. At the same time, the Cambridge Platform was hardly a radical statement, rather one that reaffirmed that the godly were to join in a covenant and that a congregation had the right to elect its own minister.

A more extreme way of attracting church members, or at least keeping Puritans within the orthodox purview, was the Half-Way Covenant of 1662. As they reached adulthood, the baptized children of members were failing to apply for their own membership. They were not approaching the ministers to give their conversion narratives. However, as these unregenerate individuals were having children of their own, they did want to present their offspring for baptism. This created a quandary in Massachusetts: Were the grandchildren of church members eligible for baptism? Baptism, the Puritans believed, was a first step in the road to conversion. Some Puritans argued that in order to maintain a pure church, the children of nonmembers were *not* entitled to baptism. Others, however, recognized that closing the churches would encourage neither parents nor eventually their children to join the church. And, full membership in the church was necessary for male participation in political life. The compromise known as the Half-Way Covenant allowed the grandchildren of full members to be baptized. Remaining faithful to the ideal of congregationalism, many churches did not put the measure into practice. Opposition to the Half-Way Covenant indicated that many in New England remained committed to a pure church.

Scholars argue that Puritanism as the dominant religious system in New England ended with the evangelical revivals known as the Great Awakening of the 1730s and 1740s. Congregationalism had been losing its hold intellectually, socially, and politically by the end of the seventeenth century. Church membership continued to fall, accompanied by a general lack of interest. New churches, which did not adhere to orthodox ideas—such as Brattle Street Church and the Anglican King's Chapel—had appeared in Boston at the end of the seventeenth century. While they were, in the words of the Puritan Minister Cotton Mather, "full of Malignity to the Holy Wayes of our Churches," they nonetheless did not devour Puritanism. By the 1730s ministers were calling for more than reformation and recommitment (as they had earlier). They recognized the need for an outright revival.

so threatening to the Puritans because Antinomian religious beliefs were genuinely dangerous, or because the instigator was a popular woman who not only overstepped her gender role but also succeeded in turning her supporters against the government.

If religious mavericks such as Roger Williams and Anne Hutchinson did not bring down Puritanism, the Puritans might have argued that they themselves challenged its primacy. Everywhere they looked, the Puritans found signs of "declension," or a decline in piety and the willingness to sacrifice to make America the New Israel. Although no other system was successful in challenging Puritanism as a cultural or intellectual force for several decades to come, its authority was being eroded. Wishing to maintain their hold over New England, the Puritans sought innovative ways to renew religiosity and especially to preserve the goal of achieving the pure church ideal by the end of the seventeenth century. The clearest sign of declension was the falling off of

The revivals began in New England in western Massachusetts, where ministers like Jonathan Edwards began to inspire young people "to be full of the presence of God." News of the revival spread from Northampton to other towns, and those who had been, in Edwards's estimation, "very insensible of the things of religion," soon were experiencing religious transformations.

Awakening preachers in New England and throughout America began exhorting their listeners to feel God within themselves. No longer were prospective converts to follow the steps recommended by their ministers—this was too formulaic and too much of an intellectual process. Shunning "preparation," ministers instead urged the faithful to allow their hearts to be swayed. The "New Birth" came about instantaneously. Preachers, most of whom had not been trained at either Harvard or Yale, evangelized in passionate, emotional speeches meant to influence the affections.

Not everyone embraced the Great Awakening. The minister Charles Chauncy decried it in his sermon, "Seasonable Thoughts on the State of Religion" (1743). He argued that the revivals were "things of a bad and dangerous tendency." The resulting conversions were "precarious" at best, as they arose from the "passions" rather than "any thorow Change in the understanding and Will." The hysteria, "shriekings and screamings" were especially dangerous. The "Old Lights," or those who remained faithful to the traditional Calvinist system, were particularly disturbed by charges that their clergy belonged to an "unconverted ministry." Chauncy and other like-minded ministers charged that the Awakening was not an act of God.

The divisions and effects of the revivals exceeded the life of the Great Awakening. Puritan New England was now sundered between the revivalists and anti-revivalists. Although Congregationalism continued to be the official church of both Massachusetts and Connecticut, its system no longer dictated religious belief nor did it have the same impact on political and social institutions. Though Puritanism as a formal system was dead, elements of it continued to be an intellectual and cultural force.

AMERICAN RELIGIOUS CULTURE

Puritanism created the tradition of religious innovation in America that persists today. Not only did the Puritans create the dichotomy that continues today between the evangelical and rational strands of Christianity, through their vision of a New Israel they planted the idea that a perfect society or utopia might be realized in America. Today, religious groups ranging from the Shakers to the Church of Jesus Christ of Latter-day Saints (the Mormons) believe that creating the New Israel in America is possible. In the nineteenth century, more secular groups such as the communal living experiments Brook Farm and the Oneida Community strove for perfection. Like the Puritans, all of these groups have tried to create closed covenanted communities such as the founders had. Religious culture, not only that connected to any particular denomination, still thrives in America. While the Puritan ideal that the Sabbath was a day for going to the meetinghouse and for abstaining from all forms of work, school, and play is no longer pervasive, vestiges of their beliefs remain. In many parts of the United States, blue laws are still in force. For instance, in Massachusetts, it is illegal to purchase liquor on Sundays, and throughout the country many stores do not open until noon on Sundays. America remains an overwhelmingly religious country, with high percentages of people professing belief in God and attending services on a regular basis.

THE PURITAN INFLUENCE ON LITERATURE

The Puritan desire to understand God translated into a literary ethos. Sermons, along with poetry and history, were the most popular forms of literature in New England. The same was not true for drama, which the Puritans found to be immoral. Sermons were the most important literary genre: hearing or reading ministers' words would bring listeners closer to the divine. After a day in the meetinghouse, a church member might go home and record the sermon based on notes he or she had taken. Sermon series were often published in New England so that Puritans might consult them and edify themselves. The "jeremiad," or political sermon, was a literary genre native to Puritan New England. A fear of declension beginning in the 1650s and 1660s led ministers to preach jeremiads, which employed what would soon become formulaic rhetoric. First, the jeremiad listed the calamities—"savage raids" or crop failure, for instance—and reminded Puritans that God had sent these ills to indicate his displeasure. The sermons went on to remind listeners that God might show mercy if they repented. Jeremiads were, thus, at once both lamentations and celebrations. As they lamented their failings, the Puritans also recognized that they could reform themselves, that God still cared, and that New England could still be the New Israel. Thus, in jeremiads, the Puritans mythicized themselves and their mission. The jeremiad continued to be an appealing rhetorical strategy to politicians to stir listeners. President Abraham Lincoln employed it in the Cooper Institute Address of 1860, and, over one hundred years later, the presidential candidate George McGovern used it in his "Come Home America" speech (1972).

Poems were another means by which the Puritans expressed their faith and their sense of life in the New World. Anne Bradstreet, a woman living in Boston, is one of Puritan New England's best-known poets. Beginning in the 1630s, she wrote on topics ranging from those proper to her "sphere," such as household responsibilities and her affection for family members, to more spiritual concerns. Her work is not didactic, yet, for the most part, her writing adheres to Puritan and feminine sensibilities. Bradstreet ventured to offer her own veiled criticism of the "New England Way," though in a manner subtle enough to avoid notice. She wrote her poetry not for publication; indeed, her brother-in-law took her manuscripts to London, possibly without her knowledge, for it was improper for women to write and publish. Her work received critical acclaim: Cotton Mather praised her poems in his *Magnalia Christi Americana* (1702). The other most prominent Puritan poet was Edward Taylor. A Harvard-educated minister in the frontier town of Westfield, Massachusetts, Taylor wrote poetry in part to help the Christian pilgrim on the journey toward sanctification and justification. His preparatory "Meditations" as well as the long "God's Determinations" (c. 1680) are expressions of the Calvinist quest for faith. In these lines of "God's Determinations," the soul sees that it must separate from the world:

> Wherefore thy heart doth ake
> That it such Amorous Objects must forsake.
> The Love whereto so stuffs thy heart; no place
> Is left therein for any Saving Grace.
>
> (Stanford, p. 423)

The religio-poetic tradition continued in New England after the Puritan era. In the nineteenth century Emily Dickinson took up biblical themes and the search for spirituality. So, too, in the twentieth century did Robert Frost, whose poetry, though lacking Calvinist ideas, nonetheless takes up themes of morality and the individual's journey through life.

The Puritan habit of self-consciousness was evident in other literary forms, even those which did not exist in seventeenth-century New England or in those which the Puritans might have thought inappropriate. Several New England authors, prominent in the mid-nineteenth-century movement known as the American Renaissance, expressed and reflected Puritan ideas. To these authors, New England was a moral haven, and they shared the view that the Puritans were an ideal type whose faith and sacrifice should be celebrated. Ralph Waldo Emerson emphasized this view of the Puritans: "What is to replace for us the piety of that race?" Most famously, Nathaniel Hawthorne took up the problem of the Puritans in his work. His novels and stories, many of which are situated in Puritan New England, convey his attempt to understand the beliefs and actions of his ancestors and to reflect on their influence on his own times, while not necessarily embracing their culture. Henry David Thoreau, in retreating to Walden Pond, sought to find and deepen the relationship between himself—the soul—and God, if in terms devoid of a Calvinist vocabulary. One of the most prominent Unitarians, Ralph Waldo Emerson, participated in the continuity of ideas that had begun with Jonathan Edwards. Man was unfallen, Emerson argued, in contrast to Edwards. Having derived their ideas from covenant theology, both Edwards and Emerson made the "effort to confront, face to face, the image of a blinding divinity in the physical universe" (Miller, *Errand into the Wilderness,* p. 185). Emerson and his Unitarian and Transcendentalist colleagues shared a belief in pietism and right action with their Puritan forebearers, even as he wrote of being "happily rid" of "being tormented with the fear of sin" (vol. 8, p. 36).

PURITAN HISTORICAL WRITING

More than by any other genre, the Puritans expressed how they defined themselves and their experiment and how they wished to be remembered in their histories. From their beginnings in New England, they began the process of mythicizing their own past and wrote histories. There was nothing new about pilgrims chronicling their experiences: history writing was an appropriate means by which to celebrate saints, memorialize martyrs, and locate themselves in holy history. Several Christian histories served as models to the Puritans, including the work of Eusebius, the fourth-century bishop of Caesarea, and John Foxe's *Actes and Monuments of these Latter and Perillous Dayes.* History writing soon became more than a way to see themselves as a part of a Christian continuum. The Puritans wrote histories to remind others of their accomplishments, to set the terms in which those accomplishments would be remembered, and, above all, to ensure that they and their names would not be forgotten. Their goals were met: American historical writing since the seventeenth century has often reflected the Puritans' sense of history, often using the terms they used to define themselves.

At the same time as they were engaged in colony building, several first-generation Puritans also wrote histories. William Bradford, the first governor of Plymouth, emphasized in his history of Plymouth Plantation that future generations should remember their parents' sacrifices and struggles and how God had favored the Pilgrims by coming to their rescue. John Winthrop, in his *Journal,* told his readers that despite enduring various trials and being challenged by various enemies, the Puritans always remained virtuous. Indeed, he believed that their presence hallowed the Massachusetts ground. The greatest champion of New England history was Cotton Mather. His *Magnalia Christi Americana* is, on the one hand, a defense of his and his prominent family's often unpopular stance over a number of controversial political, social, and religious issues in Puritan New England. On the other hand, it is a mythicization of the first seventy years of New England's history. "I write the wonders," Mather began, and for over a thousand pages he channeled into his history abundant evidence, saintly lives, and godly institutions, supported by God's numerous providences, to prove the Puritans' success in creating a New Israel. Bolstered by his vivid language and unparalleled belief in America's potential, his vision of New England exceeded that of other historians in scope. Mather marshaled decades' worth of experience and evidence unavailable to Puritan historians who preceded him, and thus his work is filled with a certain confidence that New England would continue to succeed.

The myths of New England proffered in the works of Bradford, Winthrop, and Mather, and other Puritan historians have continued to fashion a strand in American historical writing. Following the American Revolution, as histories were used to help create a national identity, writers looked to Puritan works for early examples of American virtue and democracy in action. Mercy Otis Warren, in her 1805 history, praised the Puritans for their "persevering and self-denying virtues." Like her predecessors, she recognized the central role of Providence in both New England and America. Two prominent nineteenth-century historians, George Bancroft and John Gorham Palfrey, were not uncritical of the Puritans. However, both men recognized their contributions and, like their predecessors, wrote of New England's elect status. Bancroft believed that America was favored by Providence and that the Puritans had brought democracy (a virtue Bancroft tremendously valued) to New England. Palfrey exalted the Puritans as paragons of religiosity and virtue, and complained that some of his contemporaries were forgetting the founders' sacrifices. During the Progressive Era of the early twentieth century, the Puritans and their conception of New England fell into disfavor with historians. However, their reputation was soon repaired. The American historian Samuel Eliot Morison, himself an heir of Puritan families, wrote about the founders of New England in ways they would have recognized and applauded: "They appear . . . a courageous, humane, brave, and significant people." Though more recent histories have not been as laudatory of the Puritans, early New England has received more scholarly attention than most other subjects in American history.

PURITANS AND EDUCATION

The value that the Puritans placed on education has continued to be an important American tenet. Both at the primary and college levels, the Puritans supported and fostered education. Literacy rates for both New England men and women were higher than in other regions of colonial America. In a 1679 sermon, Puritan minister Increase Mather wrote that "If ignorance overspread the land apostasy will do so too." Most young children were at least taught reading and the catechism at home by their mothers or in "dame schools" run by neighborhood women. Many towns soon began to realize the value of Latin grammar schools, where boys from the age of seven to seventeen would study Latin, Greek, and Hebrew and perhaps prepare for further education at Harvard College. Boston Latin School, the first public school in North America, was founded in 1635, followed by Roxbury Latin School in 1645 and the Hopkins Grammar School in New Haven in 1660. Indeed, several Latin schools founded in the colonial era continue to flourish today.

Although many towns funded schools or teachers voluntarily, a 1647 law made it mandatory. The Old Deluder Act was the first provision for free public education, acting upon the theory that the Old Deluder (Satan) would have less influence if Puritan youth were taught to read and interpret the Bible for themselves. Towns of more than one hundred families were required to maintain a grammar school, and those towns with fifty of fewer families had to support a teacher.

The first American college, Harvard, was founded in 1636, largely as a training ground for future generations of ministers. Named for the Puritan minister John Harvard of Cambridge, England, who donated £770 and a library of 260 volumes, the college also received an initial £400 from the Massachusetts General Court. Harvard was the pride of Massachusetts, as the first commencement program stated:

> After God had carried us safe to *New England*, and wee had builded our houses, provided necessaries for our livli-hood, rear'd convenient places for God's worship, and setled the Civill Government: One of the next things we longed for, and looked after was to advance *Learning* and perpetuate it to Posterity; dreading to leave an illiterate Ministery to the Churches, when our present Ministers shall lie in the Dust.

Harvard was more than a divinity school; while its founders had always emphasized arts and sciences as well as theology, it soon became a college for boys who wanted an education beyond grammar school. Harvard College trained many of the colony's doctors and lawyers as well as ministers. Other colleges in New England followed, including Yale in 1701 and Dartmouth in 1769. Indeed, New England is still highly regarded for its concentration of colleges and universities, a fact which remains a point of pride for the region.

THE PURITAN LEGACY

The Puritans' imprint on American ideology and culture is inestimable. Their belief system has influenced the way Americans think and act, not only in the United States, but how Americans regard the rest of the world and how the rest of the world regards the United States. America is a special place, the Puritans believed, and later generations have taken the founders' self-mythicization to heart. Though the journalist H. L. Mencken claimed the founders of New England were a dour people—a belief that has penetrated popular thought—the myths of the Puritans (and their heirs) as superior and America as a "City on a Hill" remain. Though the more Calvinist aspects of Puritanism have disappeared, other vestiges remain. The Puritans' influence on America's intellectual life cannot be doubted—in religious culture, literature, education, and other areas, the founders' ideas are resoundingly at work. Governor Bradford need not have feared that the Puritans and their name would be forgotten.

See also **The New England Theology from Edwards to Bushnell; The Tranformation of American Religion: 1776–1838** *(in this volume);* **Hermeneutics and American Historiography** *(volume 3); and other articles in this section.*

BIBLIOGRAPHY

Bercovitch, Sacvan. *The American Jeremiad.* Madison, Wisc., 1978.

Bradford, William. *Of Plymouth Plantation 1620–1647.* Edited by Samuel Eliot Morison. New York, 1952.

Buell, Lawrence. *New England Literary Culture: From Revolution to Renaissance.* New York, 1986.

Colacurcio, Michael. "Puritans in Spite." In *Religion and Literature* 26 (1994): 27–54.

Cremin, Lawrence A. *American Education: The Colonial Experience, 1607–1783.* New York, 1970.

Delbanco, Andrew. *The Puritan Ordeal.* Cambridge, Mass., 1989.

Dunn, Richard S., James Savage, and Laetitia Yeandle, eds. *The Journal of John Winthrop, 1630–1649.* Cambridge, Mass., 1996.

Emerson, Ralph Waldo. *Journals and Miscellaneous Notebooks.* 16 vols. Edited by William H. Gilman et al. Cambridge, Mass., 1960–1982.

Friedman, Rachelle E. "Writing the Wonders: Puritan Historians in Colonial New England." Unpublished dissertation, University of California, Los Angeles, 1991.

Gura, Philip F. *A Glimpse of Sion's Glory: Puritan Radicalism in New England, 1620–1660.* Middletown, Conn., 1984.

Hall, David, ed. *The Antinomian Controversy, 1636–1638, A Documentary History.* Durham, N.C., 1990.

Hall, David D. *Worlds of Wonder, Days of Judgment: Religious Belief in Early New England.* New York, 1989.

Heimert, Alan, and Andrew Delbanco, eds. *The Puritans in America: A Narrative Anthology.* Cambridge, Mass., 1985.

Hensley, Jeannine. *The Works of Anne Bradstreet.* Cambridge, Mass., 1967.

Kamensky, Jane. *Governing the Tongue: The Politics of Speech in Early New England.* New York, 1997.

Knight, Janice. *Orthodoxies in Massachusetts: Rereading American Puritanism.* Cambridge, Mass. 1994.

Mather, Cotton. *Magnalia Christi Americana.* London, 1702.

Miller, Perry. *Errand into the Wilderness.* Cambridge, Mass., 1956.

——. *The New England Mind: From Colony to Province.* Cambridge, Mass., 1953.

Morgan, Edmund. *Visible Saints: The History of a Puritan Idea.* Ithaca, N.Y., 1963.

Morison, Samuel Eliot. *The Founding of Harvard College.* Cambridge, Mass., 1935.

Stanford, Donald, ed. *The Poems of Edward Taylor.* New Haven, Conn., 1960.

EDUCATION IN EARLY AMERICA

Siobhan Moroney

English settlers in America cobbled together a hybrid of ideas and institutions carried over from British practices, adapting them as needed by religious devotees in a new and often hostile land. Education—both in theory and in practice—focused on the depravity of human beings and therefore the need for salvation as reconciliation with God. The religious nature of education put it under the control of the clergy. By the revolutionary era, though, the United States had begun to develop what would become a unique, republican philosophy of education and mass schooling. Religion, although still present, eventually gave way as the civic aspects of the training of youth and citizen education became more established. A new, secular education required not church control but civil authority, in the form of state or municipal schools.

Early-twentieth-century historians of education viewed the American public school system created in the late nineteenth and early twentieth centuries, with its mandatory attendance policies and tax support, as the inevitable culmination of Puritan practices. In the second half of the twentieth century, a revision, led by the Harvard professor and historian Bernard Bailyn, occurred: public schools were not the inevitable outcome of colonial educational policies but required a transformation in thinking about schools and the purposes of schooling. This view has dominated the discipline of the history of American education until the twenty-first century. The Puritans laid certain foundations of education that ultimately served postcolonial needs, but there is no doubt that early American educational thinking differed significantly from the republican, civic enterprise that led to the creation of America's modern public school system.

THE SEVENTEENTH CENTURY

Education among New World natives was a tribal, not familial, affair; small communities easily transmitted knowledge through an oral tradition. Without advanced mechanical arts and no strict division of labor, apprenticeships were informal; children learned by watching and participating with adults in everyday life. The most formal method of education, storytelling, fell to the leaders and elders of the tribe. English settlers to the New World, especially those in Puritan colonies, never looked at native traditions, however, when addressing their own colonial educational problems.

While the early settlers left behind very little formal philosophy of education, they nonetheless devoted a great deal of attention and thought to how best to educate their community. Protestant theology insisted that each soul find salvation through reading the Scriptures; thus both religion and technological changes that increased the availability of printed matter drove the demand for literacy. While the Puritans were not wealthy or aristocratic, many had received fine educations, even attending Oxford or Cambridge Universities. Immigrants to America enjoyed higher than average literacy when compared to other English. Their religious culture married to an educational tradition, they sought to continue that tradition in the New World.

Certainly one distinctive marker of the Puritan settlements was their assertion that education concerned everyone, not just a select few. Although salvation remained an individual affair, John Winthrop, one of the Puritan founders of New England, reminded listeners to his 1630 sermon, "A Model of Christian Charity," that in this new City on a Hill "we must be knit together in this work as one man." Seeking religious community, early settlements viewed education as a means to that end, for shared faith and scriptural knowledge would bind them together. A strong patriarchal system gave family the primary responsibility for educating the young, but early laws confirmed the settlers' interest in insuring families, especially fathers, discharged their duties. Massachusetts Bay Colony's law of 1642 decried parental neglect, and demanded parents and masters fulfill both their religious and political responsibility by ensuring that children "read and understand the principles of religion and the capitall lawes of this country"; the law imposed both inspectors and fines. Five years later, the colony, worried about Satan keeping "men from the knowledge of the Scriptures," and also concerned that "learning . . . not be buried in the grave of our fathers in the church and commonwealth," again acted, requiring towns of fifty or more households to appoint one within the town to teach, his wages paid either by parents and apprentice's masters or the town's inhabitants in general. Although poorly enforced, probably due to the scattered population, these laws nonetheless indicate the seriousness with which the Puritans approached educational matters.

Churches held the place as the central educational institutions, with the sermon serving as the primary method of transmitting religious knowledge to all members of the community. The minister of a community served as its moral, and sometimes political, head, with authority to teach and rebuke any member of that community. Sabbath days were reserved solely for prayer and contemplation, churchgoing was an all-day affair, and sermons continued on for many hours. Both children and adults, equally susceptible to sin, benefited from the sermons' lessons; Sunday schools, separating children from adults, would not arrive for another two centuries. The content of these teachings varied little: humankind's wickedness and depravity jeopardized a place in heaven, and in order to escape hell the wicked must repent and resolve to sin no more.

But some aspects of learning could not take place within the church walls. The unstable and harsh New World economy permitted little leisure time, as each adult member of the community had to work constantly just to provide the material needs of basic subsistence. Advancing literacy, then, meant establishing formal educational institutions: schools. In the 1640s, soon after their arrival, Puritans fell back on the familiar, adapting institutions they already knew. Dame schools, often little more than neighborhood child care centers run by virtuous townswomen, would at least teach the alphabet and some early reading in English. Most children, especially girls, began and completed their formal educations this way. At around the age of seven or eight, children, usually boys, enrolled in grammar schools, encountering for the first time the Latin curriculum that would prepare them for membership in the adult community. Classical languages and texts formed the cornerstone of all learning;

without them, no person could be viewed as learned. Languages were also entrance requirements to the colleges that quickly sprang up to ensure a steady supply of ministers. Colonists eventually divided over the value of a classical curriculum, but initially they attempted to duplicate their own experiences in English schools, relying on similar pedagogical methods and even the same schoolbooks.

One practice, however, could not be imported: private tutors for children educated at home. The New World did not produce the kind of wealth that could afford private, one-on-one education and, as a consequence, parents relied on public schools: communal schooling of many students rather than teaching members of one family within a home. (Thus, "public" education meant education in a school, with other pupils, not a publicly financed school.) The South served as an exception to this practice. Virginia settlers were more likely to be single men looking for a quick fortune to take back to England, in contrast to northern colonists who set up permanent communities. When Southern communities were more firmly established, greater wealth, greater interest in imitating the English nobility, and geographical dispersal of large plantations meant schools did not foster there. Parents either sent their sons back to England or imported English tutors. The College of William and Mary excepted, the few formal institutions of education imitated what the northern colonies did more excellently. In New England and even the mid-Atlantic region, however, philanthropists began endowing academies as early as the 1650s, while municipalities and sometimes colonial governments contributed tax monies to keep them going.

Although Latin and Greek eventually exposed children to the humanistic classical tradition, English education invariably emphasized religion. Colonists associated ignorance with evil, knowledge with salvation. Seventeenth- and early-eighteenth-century schoolbooks served all parts of the curriculum. Given the expensiveness of books, many children had no more than an English Bible, from which they learned literacy, spelling, and even history. A catechism or primer might be available, but Puritans viewed secular books with some skepticism. All sermons, and nearly all literature in English, reminded children of their original sin, their susceptibility to evil influences, and the awaiting punishments for those unprepared and unworthy for the next world. High mortality in the colonies meant children could enjoy no season of innocence; from their earliest ages they readied themselves for God's mighty judgment. Even Dr. Isaac Watts's *The*

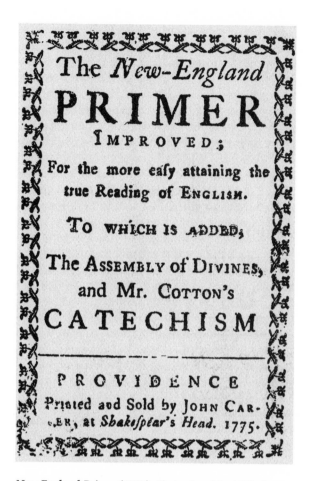

New England Primer (1775). First printed in 1690, the *New England Primer* was the most widely used textbook in eighteenth-century America. © BETTMANN/CORBIS

the establishment of the Massachusetts Bay Colony, in 1636. Modeled on Cambridge University, Harvard itself became a model for William and Mary (1693), Yale (1701), the College of New Jersey (1746, later Princeton), and other colonial colleges that continued the classical tradition dominant in England. Like other educational institutions, the colleges' first mission was religious: to instill piety, to create men of God who would minister to communities and lead churches, and to train upright schoolmasters who would scatter throughout the region, spreading learning and religious virtue. Since Puritans eschewed religious tolerance, most of the early conflicts within and between colleges involved religious factionalism, with periodic purges of students and faculty considered heretical by the administration.

Puritans never interpreted their religious commitment as devotion only to the Scriptures, at least in higher education. The college curriculum revolved around another, less religious purpose: to bring civilization to the barbarous New World. Colonists did not want to live in a world without culture and learning; they wanted the classical tradition preserved not only because of its service to religion but because the classics provided enlightenment. To that end, entrance requirements emphasized classical languages, and the unvaried reading lists for students (there were no electives) celebrated the great literary tradition college administrators and professors had learned in their English schools and colleges, even to the inclusion of the pagan Greeks and Romans. The City on a Hill's example lay in both its piety and its learning.

Where were the regular folk in all this? Unlike the Europeans, the settlers drew no formal class distinctions, recognized no lords or ladies; their theology meant even servants had to be taught to read. But the colonists accepted without question a class system in which the English curriculum would serve the poor and the working people, with the classical tradition accessible only to those who could afford it. Philanthropic and civic support of schools and schoolmasters rarely supplied a free education. While in some places—most notably Massachusetts and Connecticut—the underwriting of schools made tuition affordable to all but the destitute, in other places schooling required parental payment. Thus parents contributed, economically, to their own children's schooling, whether in the form of coin, lodging, or firewood. Attendance at a Latin grammar school, with a real schoolmaster, or enrollment at a boarding school was available to a minority; although college tuition remained inex-

Young Child's Catechism, considered a model of restraint and beneficence in the 1730s, reminded three- and four-year-old children of God's wrath, and concluded, "If I am wicked, I shall be sent down to everlasting Fire in Hell among wicked and miserable creatures." In the service of saving these young souls, teachers did not spare the rod; corporal punishment not only enforced good learning but beat out laziness, impiety, and all manner of evils.

Early on, higher education received a great deal of attention, for if elementary education saved souls, higher education saved communities. Again, high mortality contributed to the sense of urgency in getting educational institutions underway; the loss of a minister would leave a village bereft of religious and sometimes secular leadership, and often robbed it of its schoolmaster as well. Cost and perhaps risk prohibited most parents from sending their sons back to England for study. Thus colonists founded Harvard College less than ten years after

pensive, it was still prohibitive for most. Religious commitments led many with wealth to establish charity schools, but attending such a school marked a child and his family as poor, and parents often refused to burden their children with such a stigma. What resulted was a two-tiered educational system: English education for most, Latin education for an elite. It would only be in the late eighteenth century, after the Revolutionary War, that Americans would turn their attention to the problems created by class differences in educational opportunity.

European settlers viewed the indigenous peoples as threatening barbarians or potential converts to Christianity or, in the case of the Spanish, potential slaves. A hierarchical Catholic Church and the strength of the Spanish military made missions easy to establish in Spanish-held territory, and the dominance of Catholicism in South America through Mexico is the lingering result. A similar pattern occurred in French-influenced Canada. Protestant denominations, however, enjoyed neither wealth nor organization, and missionary work was more piecemeal in New England and the mid-Atlantic region. Although creating docile slaves was not part of the Puritan agenda, creating Christians was. Education of the natives meant "civilizing" them (teaching them European ways) and Christianizing them. Mission efforts drew European interest and money, too, from the first English settlements up through the nineteenth century.

For both Catholics and Protestants, education of the natives meant native assimilation, and of course it did not hurt that forming alliances with tribes and regional tribal confederations created political and military benefits, advantages especially important to the Spanish and French. Assimilation meant American-style clothes, speaking European languages, and conversion to Christianity. Protestant missionary efforts further demanded mastering a literary tradition, one with the Bible at the center. New England academies and colleges viewed native education as central to stemming the barbarity of the New World. Harvard College initiated an Indian college as early as the 1650s, with a plan to recruit and educate talented native youth so that they might return as Christian missionaries to their own tribes. The college drew few students, however, and graduated fewer still.

Efforts to assimilate the natives, however, never succeeded as well as the colonists hoped. Eventually, missionaries realized that older pupils were too entrenched in native ways, and that continued exposure to tribal culture compromised efforts at eliminating all traces of tribal speech and custom. They thus shifted tactics; beginning about the time of the revolutionary era, and continuing throughout the nineteenth century, boarding schools became the institution of choice for native children. Within the confines of a school, with children separated from parents for months or years at a time and forbidden to speak the native language, native assimilation, in the eyes of Christians, stood a real chance of succeeding. Without question, the spread of Christianity would not have reached as far without the aid of boarding schools. But the assimilationist education also contributed to the destruction of tribal societies; young adults, westernized and Christianized, had no alternative but to return to their tribes upon completion of their formal schooling. As whites found even westernized and Christianized natives difficult to embrace, so too did tribes uneasily welcome those who now spoke only English and knew absolutely nothing of tribal custom. Along with colonial and then national policies robbing natives of their land and resources, generations of boarding school natives weakened tribes at their cores by eliminating their languages, religions, and customs.

THE EIGHTEENTH CENTURY

An increasing population, new settlements, and a greater concentration of population in cities created, at the end of the seventeenth century, a new diversity in the colonies. Catholics settled in Maryland, while the Germans and Quakers went to Pennsylvania; southern colonies and their promise of riches attracted speculators from all parts of Europe. Educational systems diversified, settlers borrowing not just from England but from France or Scotland. This heterogeneity invited fear; Pennsylvanians worried that the English would become Germanized rather than the other way around.

New England communities had always opposed religious dissent of any kind, but along with diversity grew ideas of political and even religious tolerance. The British philosopher John Locke's *The Reasonableness of Christianity*, published in 1695, made its way to the colonies; for those without access, Locke's many populizers readily sufficed. The English Enlightenment, stressing as it did reason and the inalienable rights of man, suggested free inquiry might not hasten the end of civilization. Ideas about tolerance influenced theologians and ministers, who eventually admitted some religious dissent. A new openness blew through the colonies, transforming their strict, Puritan culture. Rather than fearing a wrathful God angered by human-kind's sinful nature, colonists learned to view God as a more benevolent presence. An emphasis on human reasonableness meant people could be taught to curb their sinful nature in order that they might live a life of virtue. These changes obviously affected schools and curriculum, and education transformed from a system by which evil children must be whipped into obedience to a guidance of the children's reason so that they might live an enlightened and thus virtuous life. In fact, neither the rod nor harsh religious precepts disappeared from schooling, but colonists discussed and were sometimes open to other educational methods.

The Great Awakening, the religious movement among the colonies in the 1730s and 1740s, emphasized not doctrine nor obedience to law but spiritual conversion, in the process turning colonists' attention away from the structure of the church and the minister. Religious conflicts in New England seemed to cause an overall religious weakening, and as diversity opened colonial thinking to new ideas, Puritanism waned. Remaining, however, was a well-established tradition of education, uneven and limited as it was, for all members of society. New England's eventual turn to republicanism occurred in part because of the foundations set by Puritan theories and sometimes the practice of widespread schooling.

In the South, a different story unfolded. Southern settlers were much more likely to come from, or aspire to, the aristocracy, more likely than their northern counterparts to amass wealth. If the Puritans educated for salvation, southerners educated to gentrify their sons. Latin and Greek were necessary for that, but so were riding, dancing, music, and courtly manners, subjects the Puritans rejected as worldly and frivolous. The "ornamental" education of Europe took hold in the South, for women as well as for men. It was cosmopolitan, it was social, and it was designed to create ladies and gentlemen. Without the religious impetus behind universal literacy, the poorer classes received no attention; the wealthy supported education for their own children but not for others. The southerner's educational practices changed little from the colonial era through the antebellum era; only after the Civil War did the South even attempt to imitate New England in matters of schooling.

Along with the acceptance of aristocracy, southern culture also accepted another class differential, as slavery created an entire class based solely on race and labor. To the extent that the South educated the Africans at all, it was strictly for creating obedience,

even docility; in whites' eyes, enslavement itself taught the Africans what they needed to know. Missionaries from Europe and New England attempted to Christianize slaves, but without much support from the white southerners, at least some of whom realized Christianity's subversive power. Slave owners most often permitted education in the form of preaching, usually by white clergy, but occasionally by trusted and well-supervised slave preachers. Although other "free" states prided themselves on their repudiation of slavery, educational opportunities were not much greater in the North for free boys and girls of color. A few schools were established in New England and especially Pennsylvania, but only a tiny minority attended them.

Africans, as best they could, took matters into their own hands. Slaves created a shadow of a traditional, extended family, which often held on to family lore and transmitted to children or newly arrived slaves a Christianity infused with African culture. They adopted and reworked sermons and spirituals to create an oral tradition documenting both their past and their future. Some slaves, through white or black patronage, learned to read, especially before the nineteenth-century abolitionist movement spurred white southerners to enact laws forbidding teaching slaves to read and write. In the North, although opportunities were limited, free blacks, too, were often able to master basic literacy, which they could then pass on to their families.

Besides the religious changes in New England, the other major cultural shift in the eighteenth-century colonies was a political one. Especially in the former Puritan colonies, now several generations removed from England, people began to consider themselves less Englishmen than residents of Massachusetts or Connecticut. This divide would sharpen considerably after 1776, the onset of the American Revolution, but its roots stem from the mid-eighteenth century. England, indeed Europe, increasingly came to be seen as old and decaying, its monarchies corrupt, while the New World, with its freshness and vigor, represented the best of the human spirit. Conflicts over curricula reflected this political change; most essentially, people began to question whether the classical tradition, inherited from England, deserved its prominence. Why did colonists, who spoke English, need to spend ten years learning Latin? Why should people who mostly worked in farming or manual trades try to read Ovid when they really needed agricultural and mechanical knowledge?

Local responses to these questions pushed a practical curriculum. While the classical tradition

Benjamin Franklin. Franklin listed Cotton Mather's *Bonifacius: Essays to Do Good* (1710) among his early influences. LIBRARY OF CONGRESS

continued for the upper classes, middle-class educators and parents began to look for a tangible payoff in education. Since American boys did not become English gentlemen, a gentlemanly course of study hardly suited them. Reformists found their model in the works and person of the scientist-statesman Benjamin Franklin. In *Proposals Relating to the Education of Youth in Pennsylvania* (1749), Franklin noted the very limited time and money colonists had to spend on education. It would be good for children to learn everything, he wrote, "but art is long and their time is short. It is therefore proposed that they learn those things that are likely to be most useful and most ornamental, regard being had to the several professions for which they are intended." So he proposed a course of study rich in sciences (natural history, gardening, astronomy, mechanics), business (accounting, penmanship, history, and principles of commerce), and those humanities contributing to a well-rounded man (history, biography, ethics, and English). Such a curriculum would not be merely vocational, it would form a man of character, hardy enough to take advantage of the bountiful natural resources of the

New World, self-reliant enough to be trusted with new rights and responsibilities.

Growing republicanism was taking hold. Colonists, especially in New England and the mid-Atlantic region, chafed at the restrictions of the English monarchy and Parliament. They pursued a course of self-determination, and looked to the social contractarian John Locke and the ancient Romans for guidance. Colonial governments, the press, and even some of the pulpits became politicized over self-determination. By 1776, when the colonies both united and formally broke with England, a new "Americanism" reached school and curricula, and by the end of the Revolutionary War, a nativist tradition arose. Foreign schoolmasters were immediately regarded with suspicion; what could they teach American children? Likewise, the practice of sending children back to England for a course of study met with disapproval. As Americans sought to create their own political and social culture, eschewing English fashions and preferring coffee to tea, they also sought their own textbooks, which would teach children the correct version of history.

Into this fray stepped Noah Webster, the schoolmaster, revolutionary patriot, and without a doubt the most influential schoolbook author in American history. Webster, through his dictionary, sought to Americanize the language, changing "musick" to "music" and "favour" to "favor," but his contribution to American education permeated even further. His crusade for native authors helped create a New World textbook industry, and children's literature was Americanized. Geographies described North America, and histories praised not ancient kings but Revolutionary War heroes like George Washington. Anthologies of great speeches and essays included Washington's inaugural address or Patrick Henry's revolutionary "Give Me Liberty or Give Me Death" speech.

Now education had a purpose beyond the need to save souls, spread civilization, and prepare children for future occupations. No longer subjects of the king but free citizens, Americans needed instruction in being members of a republic. The New England tradition of free or subsidized local schools served as the ideal institution to satisfy this new need. In Virginia, the statesman Thomas Jefferson proposed dividing the state into districts, establishing schools within the districts, and providing a free education for all white boys and girls for a minimum of three years, with paying students continuing thereafter and scholarships available from the fourth year through college for the most talented

BENJAMIN FRANKLIN

Born in Boston, Franklin spent only one year in grammar school and another under a private teacher before being apprenticed at the age of ten, first as a candle and soap maker and then as a printer. Printing brought Franklin in contact with books and newspapers, and he learned a great deal by reading on the job, even picking up some foreign languages, although not enough to become fluent. As printing, editing, and contributing to publications were not at that time separate jobs for different people, Franklin did all of them, writing pieces for publication even as he typeset them.

Leaving Boston for Philadelphia, Franklin put himself in the economic and political center of the colonies. Philadelphia was arguably the most prominent colonial city, one of the most diverse and cosmopolitan, and here Franklin's talents were recognized. He made his mark on the city with *Poor Richard's Almanack* (1732), a compendium of useful advice on moderate living published under a pseudonym, which sold well. Franklin's political and scientific achievements, inventing the Franklin stove and the lightning rod, serving as a representative in the Pennsylvania Assembly, a delegate to the Second Continental Congress, and a member of the Constitutional Convention, dovetailed with his educational efforts: he founded the first public circulating library, helped establish the first museum of natural history, was a founder of the discussion club "Junto," which developed into the American Philosophical Society (devoted to sharing scientific knowledge), and founded the Academy of Pennsylvania (which later became the University of Pennsylvania).

That he did all of this with only two years of formal education made him the model of a new kind of educated man, one dedicated to self-improvement and self-education of the most practical kind. Much of his educational work was designed for the working man with neither time nor money to devote to fine schools or colleges. A man with ambition but no means improved himself through libraries, museums, newspapers, and learned societies, raising both his economic and social status. Franklin preached—and he himself represented—the first distinctly American educational philosophy: practical and self-educative, emphasizing a curriculum directly related to one's vocation. Such a curriculum, he argued, does more for the individual and the community than the classical one. With Franklin's example, and the changing nature of American society, the classical tradition began its decline, a relic of an old and increasingly disreputable European practice inapplicable to the New World.

boys. Thus drawing on a radical egalitarian idea of a "natural" aristocracy, Jefferson argued, no one's talents would be wasted because of circumstances of birth. Although few endorsed Jefferson's idea, the philosophy behind it was widely shared: education mattered to the state, for America could neither prosper nor achieve political stability without an educated citizenry.

Attitudes toward the education of women accompanied the political changes of the eighteenth century. Early colonial New England did not consider women appropriate beneficiaries of advanced education. Latin or Greek, consuming so much precious time, served them ill; basic literacy, to read the Scriptures, was all that was required. Wealthy southerners wanted their daughters to be refined and genteel, so they sent them to Europe for convent education or local boarding schools, which might teach them a little French, drawing, dancing, or whatever a lady of good birth needed to get a husband. But with the rise of republicanism and a new emphasis on American citizenship, the woman's role as wife and mother gained new power and prestige. As her children's first teacher, a woman's educative role meant she herself needed education. The concept, then, of "republican motherhood," coupled with the rise in practical education generally, created conditions under which a woman might pursue formal schooling without undermining her femininity or her traditional role as wife and mother. While in practice few families insisted their daughters receive the same educations as their sons, and most academies and colleges closed their doors to female pupils, the ideology of the period introduced the philosophy, later acted upon, that women were equally deserving of educational opportunities, in the name of service to the republic.

By the time of the American founding, Americans had a new way of thinking about education. As all white men were citizens, or at least potential citizens, with rights of political participation and suffrage, all men needed an education that would prepare them to exercise their political judgment, to safeguard their rights, and to ensure thoughtful—and thus moderate—voting. Mass schooling, even for the poor, could be the antidote to anarchy. As the Puritans wanted universal education for the salvation of souls, the founding generation sought universal education, often styled as the "dissemination of knowledge," to save the newly born and still fragile republic. How this would happen would still be debated, and not until the 1830s would most states institute a system of schools. But the principle of universal schooling was widely shared even if the methods of implementing it were not.

See also **Education; The Role of the Intellectual; The American University; Learned Societies and Professional Associations; Textbooks; Lyceums, Chautauquas, and Institutes for Useful Knowledge; Libraries; Books** *(volume 3).*

BIBLIOGRAPHY

Bailyn, Bernard. *Education in the Forming of American Society: Needs and Opportunities for Study.* New York, 1972.

Cremin, Lawrence A. *American Education: The Colonial Experience, 1607–1783.* New York, 1970. Cremin's three-volume history of American education, of which this is the first volume, is considered definitive.

——. *American Education: The National Experience, 1783–1876.* New York, 1980. Volume 2 of Cremin's three volumes.

Curti, Merle Eugene. *The Social Ideas of American Educators, with New Chapter on the Last Twenty-Five Years.* Totowa, N.J., 1959.

Johnson, Clifton. *Old-Time Schools and School-books.* New York, 1963.

Lockridge, Kenneth A. *Literacy in Colonial New England: An Enquiry into the Social Context of Literacy in the Early Modern West.* New York, 1974.

May, Henry F. *The Enlightenment in America.* New York, 1976.

Miller, Perry. *The New England Mind: The Seventeenth Century.* Cambridge, Mass., 1983.

——. *The New England Mind: From Colony to Province.* Cambridge, Mass., 1983.

Morgan, Edmund S. *The Puritan Family: Religion and Domestic Relations in Seventeenth-Century New England.* New York, 1985.

Morison, Samuel Eliot. *The Intellectual Life of Colonial New England.* New York, 1953.

——. *The Founding of Harvard College.* Cambridge, Mass., 1935.

Rudolph, Frederick. *Essays on Education in the Early Republic; Benjamin Rush, Noah Webster, Robert Coram, Simeon Dogget, Samuel Harrison Smith,*

Amable-Louis-Rose de Lafitte du Courteil, Samuel Knox. Cambridge, Mass., 1965.

Tyack, David B., ed. *Turning Points in American Educational History.* Waltham, Mass., 1967. An anthology of primary documents.

Wright, Louis B. *The Cultural Life of the American Colonies, 1607–1763.* New York, 1957.

THE MATERIAL SHAPE OF EARLY AMERICAN LIFE

Barbara G. Carson

In seventeenth- and eighteenth-century colonial America, colonists' material lives can be understood as two distinct phases: the earlier years, when most people lived very meagerly, and the later decades, when widespread improvements emerged in the patterns of everyday life. Once the uncertain economic conditions of the earliest decades of settlement had been overcome, economic development allowed colonists to invest in more substantial and larger dwellings that were better furnished. Their descendants, along with much of the population of western Europe, experienced a general rise in the standard of living. This picture of change created by late-twentieth-century scholars has transformed the older history of antique objects and technologic artifacts into a more historically and theoretically grounded investigation into the roles these objects played in people's lives, in creating and communicating individual and group identities. We tend to look for improvement, to envision progress, and to romanticize life in the past. In some ways conditions did become better, but we always need to ask, in what ways and for whom?

The material aspects of life represent more than a simple correlation of social and economic status. Arrangements of the landscape, the ways structures are designed and built, and the availability, affordability, and desirability of their furnishings affect the lives of their owners and users. People differ in their ability to use, and their familiarity with, the equipment of daily or special experience. If one is comfortable or awkward drinking tea, people in one's company will make judgments accordingly. The material world, then, is not passive; it plays an active role. Objects should not be thought of as isolated entities. To write a letter, a colonial correspondent needed a quill pen, paper, containers of ink and pounce, a desk or table, and a chair. People who could express themselves on paper differed in their orientation to others and to the world around them from those who could not write. Thus, the material objects required for correspondence influenced their owners' relation to the world.

GENERAL POINTS ABOUT MATERIAL CULTURE

The notion that the colonists were self-sufficient is a myth. White colonial families relied upon local, skilled artisans to build their houses and outbuildings and to make their better furniture. They did not spin and weave all the cloth for their clothing and bedding, or cast their own cooking pots. These and many other commercial products came from England. Although the production of goods for local consumption was not prohibited, as a practical matter, the colonial population that could afford higher quality consumer items was not large enough to justify an artisan's investment in the equipment required to make certain categories of goods. A potter might produce enough redware to earn a living or at least supplement an income from farming, but the better tablewares of ceramic and glass came from abroad. The textile story is more complex. Great quantities of cloth from coarse oznaburgs to elaborate silks and velvets were imported, but domestic production was extensive and tended to soar when income from the international agricultural markets dropped. Many women spun thread for extra income. Some were weavers, but in the colonial era this skill was still largely practiced by men.

The early American material world that survives in collections today represents a very small percentage of what once existed. It tells largely about the visually richer and more expensive side of production. Most objects are not documented, and we will never know precisely who made or used them, nor when or where they were manufactured. Cultural contexts have been lost. Many more objects are buried in the ground—mainly durable pieces of ceramics and glass, deteriorating metalwares, and occasionally under the right conditions, animal and vegetable products. Rarely do these deposits move before they are excavated, so they can often be identified with a specific time, place, and persons. Buildings and gravestones are other categories of more readily documented material culture.

Many once common objects are virtually unknown today. Bedding, bedsteads, everyday clothing, baskets, benches, and so forth, wore out or were not sufficiently valuable or visually interesting to compel later generations to preserve them. Archaeological excavations and written evidence—mainly descriptions and lists of probate inventories, created for the judicial recognition of a person's will—to some extent compensate for this loss. Combining all sources of information often produces the most complete picture. A look at the archaeological record would suggest that eighteenth-century families set their tables only with ceramics. Probate inventories tell us that the use of pewter plates was widespread. Collections of both categories of tablewares offer the best evidence for their appearance.

A WORLD OF MANY CULTURES

Many culturally diverse groups—Native Americans, European immigrants, and African Americans, mostly transported as slaves—occupied North America during the several centuries of colonization. They adjusted to each other, especially under pressure for economic survival, but neither Indians nor African Americans completely converted to the ways of whites. However, the material cultures of each group were influenced and altered by the interaction with the other groups.

Native Americans and Spaniards in the Southwest and Florida

In the Spanish Southwest and along the Atlantic coast of Florida, the native and European cultures intermingled for the first time in North America. Native Americans in the Southwest were a diverse people who lived in permanent, tight pueblo communities or spread out in hogans in the dry, desert country, while others were seminomadic pastoralists. They were in many ways unaltered from the stone age people to whom, in the sixteenth century, the Spanish introduced the horse, wheel, and European trade goods. The Spaniards engaged in brutal treatment of the native population while they also tried to convert them to Christianity. As part of their missionary efforts, the Spaniards also introduced their architecture to the Native Americans. Franciscan missionaries and Indian laborers built elaborate baroque churches. The earliest ex-

WHAT IS AN INVENTORY?

Probate inventories in all colonies listed the personal property of many people who died without wills. They were not a basis for taxation, but rather, they secured assets for the benefit of heirs or creditors. Although any single inventory may omit items given away before death or taken away before the appraisers did their work, the itemization of old furniture, broken ceramic vessels, and unfixed guns and the low value of many of the items catalogued suggests their relative completeness. When arranged chronologically and by ascending value, they show change over time and possessions particular to different socio-economic groups. It is important to note that slaves and indentured servants were not legal property holders, so they are not represented by probate inventories. Likewise, women and children, who were subsumed in the patriarch's legal identity, and the very poor appear rarely in these records. And finally, because these largely white, male property holders were dead and likely to have been older than the majority of the population, one must be cautious when generalizing about conditions among the living. But even with their biases and problems, these documents are among the best sources historians have to examine the material world of a broad range of the colonial population.

amples date from the 1620s and the last was established in California in 1832. Spanish landowners also built haciendas, large estates that consisted of a main house, small dwellings for laborers and cowboys, various outbuildings or rooms, and often a school and church. For security, living and service areas were organized around one or more courtyards with controlled access through a sturdy gate. Furnishings tended to be sparse, and their basically sixteenth-century design tradition continued into the nineteenth century. The Spaniards also built small fortified settlements and formally organized towns laid out in grids.

Both California and Florida boasted impressive forts. The Castillo de San Marcos, built in St. Augustine, Florida, from 1672 to 1756, whose open courtyard is surrounded by rectangular rooms and four star-shaped bastions, is the best surviving ex-

Main Portal San José y San Miguel de Aguay, San Antonio. This prosperous mission was dominated by its large church with a massive belfry and a sixty-foot hemispherical dome. It boasted the finest Spanish colonial facade north of Mexico. Two classical entablatures surmounted the arched entry on the lower level and a circular window above. Additional ornamentation, the work of the Mexican sculptor Pedro Huizan, takes the form of scrolls, niches, sculptural saints, shells, and foliage. The original eight-acre complex was surrounded by a high stone wall with fortified towers containing barracks for soldier, offices, storerooms, shops, a gristmill, an outdoor oven, a water supply, and an Indian pueblo of eighty-four compartments. © RICHARD CUMMINS/CORBIS

ample in the United States of the European type of fortress that was developed after the introduction of gunpowder in the late Middle Ages. Florida's climate allowed modest houses to be built and encouraged use of braziers rather than fireplaces for heating. Walls were whitewashed and the furnishings were meager.

Native Americans of the East Coast Farther north in the coastal and piedmont regions east of the Appalachian Mountains, Native Americans lived in tribal villages that were sometimes organized into

layers of communities for defensive and diplomatic purposes. These tribes were mostly seminomadic, and lived inside wooden palisades in wigwams, wood-framed structures that supported plant or animal coverings. Central hearths provided fires for warmth and cooking, and the smoke that floated through holes in the roofs helped keep insects at bay. Platform beds, animal skins, baskets, earthenware vessels, and mats and other textiles made of vegetable fibers furnished these wigwams. Some goods were utilitarian, while others were decorative. These Indians ornamented their bodies with colorful paint and cowrie shells and some special clothing. Most of the evidence about these tribes is archaeological or written, but a few rare objects survive in museum collections. For example, a large cape of deerskin with a pattern of deer and dots worked in shells has been in Oxford University's Ashmolean Museum since the mid-seventeenth century.

After the arrival of Europeans, these practices continued but were augmented by the acquisition of European goods. The Indians came to value iron tools and cooking utensils; textiles, especially blankets; firearms; and glass beads, mainly made in Venice or Amsterdam. For these items, they traded beaver pelts that were sent to Europe and made into hats. During treaty negotiations, colonial and Native American representatives exchanged gifts, with tribal members favoring armbands or neck ornaments of engraved silver. Despite these changes to their material culture, Indians for the most part adhered to their traditional patterns of living. In 1761, Ezra Stiles, who later became president of Yale University, while traveling around New England as a minister in the 1760s, drew a fascinating plan of the Connecticut house of two Native American women, Phoebe and Elizabeth Moheegan; it had platform beds around the perimeter of the walls and a tea table standing at one end.

Even in the later eighteenth century, Indians were a familiar presence in colonial communities; for example, they would show up to trade baskets and pottery. After the initial years of white immigration and the subsequent displacement of natives from tribal lands, Native Americans constituted a very small percentage of the population and had very little, if any, cultural influence on most whites. However, they were still important for land negotiations and military alliances. Their presence, too, reinforced ideological notions of the importance of Anglo conquest and religious conversion. Although the colonists' culture was largely unaltered by their interaction with the Native Americans, Native

65

American culture was transformed during the colonial period.

African Americans In the seventeenth century, few slaves from Africa reached the North American colonies, but as the supply of indentured servants declined, more slaves were purchased, some directly from Africa but most from the West Indies. Slavery was legal in all the colonies, but eighty percent of the slave population was found in the South. Slaves were property, economic assets to be bought, sold, rented, or inherited, and as such their ability to maintain their material culture was seriously diminished. Conditions on slave ships were dreadful and did not allow space for personal possessions, although some Africans did manage to transport small ornaments. As moveable or chattel property, slaves soon became familiar with the equipment of coercion—whips and chains.

Most masters provided housing; others left slaves to construct their own shelters. Conditions varied regionally—from the dormitory accommodations for six slaves and an overseer, a "miserable shell" that contained "no conveniences, no furniture, no comfort," to "little huts [which] are comfortably furnished." Conditions also varied according to a slave's status within the community. For example, house slaves lived in better conditions than field hands. John Custis, who lived on the eastern shore of Maryland, wrote his will in 1743 and specified that a good house and furnishings be provided for his slave Jack. "When the house is completely finished it is my will that the same be furnished with One Dozen high Russia Leather Chairs One dozen Low Russia Chairs a Russia Leather Couch good and Strong three Good Feather Beds and Bedsteads and furniture [the bedding] and two good Black Walnut Tables." Such luxury was very exceptional.

Theoretically, all property, including slaves' personal possessions, belonged to the master; the reality was more complex. Padlocks on cabin doors strongly suggest that slaves secured their personal items. Slaves had opportunities to earn money, and as artisans, they sold their wares. One example of such wares might be the baskets made by African Americans of the Sea Island, off the coast of Georgia. The materials, technology, and patterns of these baskets are similar to those made in Africa. While some scholars have questioned whether the baskets that are still sold today descend in a direct line from slave times or were reintroduced in the late nineteenth century, these baskets may be one of the types of wares that slaves sold to colonists. Although Native Americans may have made some of the low-temperature fired ceramics known as colonoware, much of it was probably the work of African Americans.

To what extent did masters prohibit slaves from reproducing the material world they had known in Africa? The answer varies regionally and locally. Huts with circular walls and conical roofs like those in West Africa were built on the Barrier Islands off the North Carolina coast. A rectangular house in the tradition of the Kongo in central Africa was constructed in Edenton, South Carolina. Other African traditions were less welcome; because drums could be instruments of communication, whites were suspicious of native drumming. After a slave rebellion they were banned in South Carolina in 1740; but they were allowed in the Chesapeake. When drums were banned, slaves found various substitutes—from baskets to bodies—to provide percussive rhythms. Skilled African American musicians had banjos and other stringed instruments, like the one-stringed guitar, that were of African origin. Fiddles of European origin were also adapted to African American music. While indigenous African traditions were often quelched by the constraints of slavery, some of these traditions did survive in the colonies and helped to create a unique African American material culture.

Divergent European Cultures in the Colonies
Those who emigrated from Europe were geographically, socially, and economically diverse, and each group brought their unique material culture to the colonies. In the early seventeenth century, Dutch culture dominated what became New York State. The distinctive appearance of their buildings included stepped gables and an H-shaped framing system that emphasized the horizontality of the buildings' proportions. French Catholics, who occupied the Mississippi Valley, built large, raised plantation houses with colonnaded galleries and sweeping hipped roofs. In the middle Atlantic colonies the architecture of French Protestants, or Huguenots, blended with that of the larger Anglo population, but they preserved their heritage in techniques of furniture construction and the design of baroque silver.

The largest group of non-Anglo immigrants came from the German Rhineland. With the founding of Pennsylvania in 1682, William Penn actively promoted their settlement in his colony. Although most farmed the rich valley lands, many settled in Philadelphia. The most curious of their communities was the austere communal cloister at Ephrata, settled from 1728 to 1733. The Germans were especially known for producing quality clocks and rifles. A relatively rare example of manufacturing in early America, the ironworks and glassworks—operational from 1753 to 1774 and 1769 to 1774, respectively—of Henry William Stiegel were briefly successful.

In 1753, a group of Moravians from Pennsylvania established a community at Bethabara, North Carolina. It thrived, and in 1766 a larger town, Salem, was founded. Although pietistic, the Moravians did not mortify the flesh and saw nothing contradictory in turning a commercial profit. The efficiency of their communal organization created surplus profits that tended to be invested in various enterprises that in turn led to a shared prosperity. Well-organized kitchens with running water and stoves fed those who lived in the large houses for single brothers and sisters. These dormitories and the houses for families were comfortably but not elaborately furnished. With the exception of some creamware made briefly in the 1770s, the Moravians' artisanal products were similar to those produced in Pennsylvania as a whole.

Indeed, the colonies were a world of many cultures. The population of early America was comprised of diverse groups that influenced and were influenced by the dominant Anglo culture. While the Native Americans in the early American period retained much of their native culture, the Africans who came to the colonies as slaves were not as free to nurture their African heritage. However, the traces of their African roots that they retained added a unique thread to the emerging American society. Likewise, the various non-Anglo European settlers brought the indigenous traditions of their homelands to the colonies, thus contributing yet another layer to the complex material culture that existed in early America. Of course, the predominant culture derived much of its traditions from the British Isles, and this culture materially influenced the Native Americans, African Americans, and non-Anglo immigrant groups.

AMERICAN PRODUCTION AND FOREIGN IMPORTATION

Most studies of early American products concentrate on the furniture and silver made in the colonies. Although large quantities of both were imported by Europeans, this early history has been lost and will never be recovered. Other categories of imported objects have had a different reception in

THE UNIQUENESS OF AMERICAN OBJECTS

The appearance of most American-made objects derives from European precedents, although exact duplication seems not to have been the goal. Modern collectors and curators who emphasize the aesthetic rather than the functional merits of design judge objects according to their approximation of European, especially English, models. In the 1920s, there was a significant effort to identity American art forms. Jazz with its African American origins was, of course, the principal achievement. But what about originality in the material world? Interest in folk art grew. The special vision of the Shakers was widely celebrated. Their unornamented furniture derived from more general vernacular models, such as ladder-back chairs, and they even patented a device for tilting chairs, a seating posture Europeans criticized as uncivilized. There were also the individual expressions of painters like Edward Hicks, with his vision of the Peaceable Kingdom, and sculptors like Wilhelm Schimmel, who carved eagles with a characteristic hatching for the feathers. American technology, especially of clocks, guns, farm machinery, and sewing machines, was generally acknowledged as innovative. Like the folk art, these were nineteenth-century developments. A somewhat earlier change in the design of American axes raises the question of the relationship between tools and their environment. The traditional European axe had a long handle and a long blade without a poll, or back end, that could be used as a sledge. The American axe, which appears at the end of the eighteenth century, when land clearing was more intensive than ever, had a shorter curvilinear handle that increased the user's accuracy. The blade was shorter and heavier, with V-and U-shaped lugs where head and handle met and a poll opposite the blade. In controlled tests it is more efficient but requires more human energy.

modern times. Because Britain discouraged manufacturing for all but local sales and because no locality in America could support a volume of sales in the better sort of glass and ceramic tablewares, architectural and furniture hardware, cooking utensils, and quality textiles, these British-made goods are granted a kind of courtesy status in American decorative arts scholarship.

In colonial times, transatlantic exchange of goods was not always mutually satisfying. In 1757, George Washington expressed his opinion of English goods:

> It is needless for me to particularise the sorts, quality, or taste I would choose to have them in Unless it is in their several kinds we often have Articles sent us that could only have been Used by our Forefathers in the days of yor—'Tis a custom, I have some Reason to believe, with Many shop keepers, and Tradesmen in London when they know Goods are bespoke for Exportation to palm sometimes, old, and sometimes very slight and Indifferent Goods upon Us taking care at the same time to advance 10, 15 or perhaps 20 pe Ct. upon them.

A few years later, in 1767, Josiah Wedgwood sarcastically told his partner what he thought of the American market:

> I am rejoyced to know you have ship'd off the Green & Gold — May the winds & seas be propitious, & the invaluable Cargo be wafted in safety to their destin'd Market, for the emolument of our American Bretheren & friends, & as this treasure will now no longer be locked up, or lost to the rest of the world, I shall be perfectly easy about the returns, be they much, little, or nothing at all.

One important distinction between the British and American markets was the effective apprenticeship system that prevailed in London and a few major centers in Great Britain. These organizations trained a limited number of workmen, kept prices high, controlled quality, and occasionally provided guild members with financial relief. In America the apprenticeship system was much less developed, but it did manage to transfer craft techniques from one generation to the next and provided for orphans and destitute children by allowing them to learn a trade.

Americans used a rough formula for calculating the components that contributed to the cost of a product: one third each for materials, labor, and profit. Masters, of course, made the profit, and many did well, but more money was to be made in mercantile activity. Journeymen and unskilled laborers struggled. There was no social security system to provide income during sickness or recovery from injury. Even bad weather affected one's ability to earn. Many could not feed and house their families, much less buy consumer goods. As a result, the incentives to manufacture commercial goods in the colonies were diminished, and the colonies relied heavily on importing goods from abroad.

A PRECONSUMER WORLD

The rudimentary quality of seventeenth-century life can first be glimpsed through several advertisements telling planters what they should provide for their servants. One list from 1630 New England includes clothing, "One Sea Cape or Gowne, of coarse cloth. Other apparel, as their purse will afford." Six shirts, twelve blue calico handkerchiefs used for headbands in summer, four pairs of Irish stockings, shoes, boots, and leather to mend them were also on the list, as were tools and firearms for a family of four or five, thus indicating the need for protection and to earn a living. Suggested building supplies included nails and locks for doors and other hardware for chests. For bedding and household implements, a list from 1635 Maryland is more informative. At sea, servants required straw-filled beds (mattresses) to sleep on and a coarse rug made of heavy pile for a cover. Once on land, each person needed canvas yardage for a mattress, a bolster, and a pair of canvas sheets. Six persons were to share an iron spit, kettle, frying pan, gridiron, and two iron skillets, and wood platters, dishes, and spoons. There is no mention of furniture or forks.

Let us look in on a poor planter's family, a composite, fictional portrait drawn from the poorest of the late-seventeenth-century colonists. A wife, husband, two children, and perhaps a servant are gathered together in the perpetual dusk of their shuttered cottage. This evening, like most evenings, their dinner is cornmeal mush boiled in an iron pot and ladled into five low, metal bowls, or porringers. The father straddles a large storage trunk, and his daughter is perched on the edge of a small chest, the only other furniture in the room. The rest either stand or squat along the walls. They spoon up the food from the bowls that they must hold in their hands or place on the floor. They drink milk or water from a common cup, tankard, or bowl. No candle or lamp is lighted now or later when the room goes completely dark except for the glow of embers on the hearth. Nightfall puts an effective end to all the day's activities. While someone rinses bowls in a bucket of cold water (there being only one pot), someone else drags out a cattail mattress and arranges it in front of the fire. The husband, wife, and daughter lie down there, covering themselves with a single canvas sheet and a worn-out bedrug. The son and servant roll up in blankets on the floor. For warmth, all sleep in their clothes.

While probate inventories are rare before mid-century, as their frequency grows, they confirm this picture of material deprivation among the majority of the colonial population. In a single all-purpose room, a bedstead, if there was one, commanded space permanently, though mattresses could be rolled up during the day. Cooking was simple, mainly food was boiled in a single pot. At least half the inventoried population did not own the combination of table, chairs, and required linen for formal dining, but boxes and chests were numerous. They were used for storage, work surfaces, beds, or even biers. Generally, there were no chamber pots, and lighting devices were very rare. A good working rifle was a prized possession. Living was not comfortable, but for the most part food was plentiful. The lack of furnishings persisted well into the middle of the eighteenth century and beyond. Travelers' descriptions confirm this picture.

Alexander Hamilton, an Annapolis physician traveling for his health in 1744, crossed the Susquehanna on a ferry. He noted that the ferry was

> kept by a little old man whom I found att vittles with his wife and family upon a homely dish of fish without any kind of sauce.... They had no cloth upon the table, and their mess was in a dirty, deep, wooden dish which they evacuated with their hands, cramming down skins, scales, and all. They used neither knife, fork, spoon, plate, or napkin because, I suppose, they had none to use. I looked upon this picture of that primitive simplicity practiced by our forefathers long before the mechanic arts had supplied them with instruments for the luxury and elegance of life.

A small percentage of the wealthiest at the top of the scale lived better furnished lives. Their beds, raised on bedsteads, were enclosed with curtains for warmth and some privacy. They cooked their food in a variety of iron utensils and used coarse earthenware in their dairies. They sat on chairs drawn up to tables covered with white linen cloths and wiped their hands and faces on napkins. Depending upon their resources, their tablewares were made of silver, pewter, Chinese export porcelain, tin-glazed earthenware or delft, and glass. They stored their personal possessions—books, clothing, and so forth—in numerous boxes or chests. The doors of rooms could often be locked, but many pieces of storage furniture were also made with locks, indicating both a need to secure goods and to provide access to spaces where servants needed to work. These chests and some other forms of furniture were occasionally marked with dates and the owner's initials or occasionally a complete name.

Rooms in the seventeenth century were not so functionally specialized as they later became. Food preparation generally was separated from other ac-

Court Cupboard (1660–1680). Oak, pine, and walnut, 47⅞ x 50 x 18⅞ in. Only two southern court cupboards are known. This atypical example has an open storage shelf at the top. More customary was a shallow shelf with cut-back sides before a trapezoidal storage area. The tops of these pieces of elegant furniture were likely to be covered with turkey carpets and silver. The black point imitated ebony and contrasted with the oak, which was nearly white until well-oxidized in later years. COLLECTION OF MUSEUM OF EARLY SOUTHERN DECORATIVE ARTS

tivities: in the North in lean-to sheds and in the South in detached kitchens, which reduced heat in the summer and distanced slaves from the family throughout the year. Sleeping, business activities, leisure, and entertaining all took place in a single space. Colors were vivid and visually important. Whitewashed walls that were framed with oak timbering provided a background for portraits, engravings, and maps. The blond color of the unseasoned oak panels of case pieces presented a strong contrast with black painted molding strips, split spindles, and circular applied bosses. Status was attached to valuable items such as silver; textiles, which represented the ability to buy others' labor; and especially fancy, prepared food. Although tea was introduced to Europe in the seventeenth century, it did not appear in American life until the eighteenth century.

Personal and community preferences in material goods varied from region to region. Rich planters in the South tended to be showier than those in the North. Urban living seems to have stimulated more competitive spending than rural life. Quakers

Dram Cup (c. 1650–1660). Silver, 1½ x 4⁹⁄₁₆ in. John Hull and Robert Sanderson of Boston made this dram cup, the earliest known piece of American-made silver, in the mid-seventeenth century. Along the coast, wealthy colonists invested in silver made domestically or imported. In 1688, when William Fitzhugh, a Virginia planter, sent a very large order for silver to London, he explained, "I esteem it as well politic and reputable, to furnish myself with an handsom Cupboard of plate which gives my self the present use and Credit, [and] is a sure friend at t? deadlift without much loss, or is a certain portion for a Child after my decease." YALE UNIVERSITY ART GALLERY/MABEL BRADY GARVAN COLLECTION

did not spare expense but they preferred to invest in quality materials and relatively undecorated surfaces rather than in ostentatious displays. On the other hand, despite popular conception, Pilgrims and Puritans of high status did not hesitate to set themselves apart with all manner of finery. Of course, not every rich man expressed a preference for a well-furnished life. A traveler to Virginia in 1715 noted that one of the colony's most prominent gentlemen, "though rich . . . has nothing in or about his house but what is necessary." There were "good beds," but no bed curtains, and instead of chairs with cane seats and backs, the traveler noted, "he hath stools made of wood."

LATER REFINEMENTS, 1750

General improvements in the colonists' material circumstances were evident at all economic levels beginning in the second quarter of the eighteenth century. Some of the motivation for these improvements was a desire for basic creature comforts. The poorest first opted for better bedding and more

cooking utensils. Then they purchased tables, chairs, linens, and even the newly introduced knives and forks. Tablewares seem not to have been matched, but generally, each member of the family had a set of basic equipment. Even at this level, competition with one's social set probably was another important motivation for spending.

Toward the top of the economic scale, living might be fashionable and occasionally rather grand. In 1774, one commentator observed that "A Gentleman from London would almost think of himself at home at Boston when he observes the Numbers of People, their Houses, their Furniture, their Tables, their Dress and Conversation, which perhaps is as splendid and showy as that of the most considerable Tradesman in London." Matched sets of chairs and tablewares, and more color in wallpaper and carpets, which were now on the floor, affected the overall appearance of rooms. Beds were moved into private spaces. Generally, people were made more comfortable by the increase in upholstered chairs and sofas. Clocks and lighting devices were prevalent. The cabinetmaker's more delicate work, supplemented by that of the carver, gilder, uphol-

Sugar Box (1702). Silver. Engraved on base: "O DE donum W. P. 1702," 5½ x 7½ in. Edward Winslow made four of the six known American examples of this sugar box. Used to serve sweetmeats, stick candy, or sugar, this repoussé box is one of the finest and most elaborate forms of American silver. The lobes and leaves that set up a rhythmic pattern on the base are interrupted by a hasp and three other panels decorated with the figure of a knight on horseback. The oval form may represent female attractions, while the symbols of virtuous love that decorate the body and cover may have warned against indulgence in its sweet contents. COURTESY, WINTERTHUR MUSEUM

sterer, and inlay maker, superceded that of the joiner. With these refinements, the cost of much of the furniture increased, while the cost of many other consumer goods declined. Diversity of price and varied appearances helped expand this new consumer world, which offered something for everyone. The consumption of tea increased dramatically and required a whole range of paraphernalia. The pursuit of gentility motivated much of this eighteenth-century spending spree. Unlike ownership of land, inherited titles, or even local reputation, which were the traditional European symbols of status, genteel behavior could be learned, theoretically, by everyone.

Take the example of Benjamin Franklin, who began writing his *Autobiography* in 1771 but here comments on a change in his life in the 1740s.

My Breakfast was a long time Bread and Milk, (no Tea) and I ate it out of a two-penny earthen Porringer with a Pewter Spoon. But mark how Luxury will enter Families, and make a Progress, in Spite of Principle, Being call'ed one Morning to Breakfast, I found it in a China Bowl with a Spoon of Silver. They had been bought for me without my Knowledge by my Wife, and had cost her the enormous Sum of Three and Twenty Shillings for which she had no other Excuse or Apology to make, but that she thought her husband deserv'd a Silver Spoon and China Bowl as well as any of his Neighbours.

George Washington and Thomas Jefferson stand at opposite ends of the spectrum of the ways in which wealthy consumers thought about and purchased furnishings. Although Washington intuitively knew how best to represent himself as a planter, militia officer, commander in chief, or president, when it came to furniture, he was essentially

71

Side Chair (1770). Mahogany, 37 x 23.5 in. When he built his elaborate house, John Cadwalader commissioned a portrait of himself, his wife, and his child. He also bought very fine furnishings, including a large group of mahogany chairs, looking glasses, tables, and fire screens, from Thomas Affleck. This legendary chair, with its heavy paw feet, saddle seat, and very-well-executed carving over all, is considered the most elaborate of American-made rococo chairs. COURTESY, WINTERTHUR MUSEUM

a customer interested in the best value for the least money. Before his marriage to Martha Custis, a wealthy widow, he bought fashionable secondhand furniture through his London broker. In later years, he ordered newly manufactured items. Among them were terrestrial and celestial globes and a harpsichord for his stepdaughter Martha Parke (Nelly) Custis. Sometimes he willingly deferred to the taste of others; on other occasions he was specific about his preferences. During the Revolution he entertained his officers with silver cups bearing his crest made by Richard Humphries in Philadelphia. At the time he expressed his desire to avoid buying British goods. As president he spent more than 665 pounds on fancy French furnishings belonging to a retiring French minister, among them two gilt armchairs, a sofa, six small chairs, and two large looking glasses. Somewhat later he ordered a gilt *plateau*, a mirrored table ornament, noting that he wished to make a good show for little expense.

When he returned to Mount Vernon, he sold many of the more elegant pieces of furniture from his presidential quarters. Windsor chairs lined the portico overlooking the Potomac, relatively simple sideboards, chairs, and a makeshift table that could accommodate an ever-varied number of diners filled the new reception room. These relatively simple furnishings were augmented with some luxurious gifts, among them a marble mantel and Worcester garniture for the new dining room and a tea set of Chinese export porcelain for Martha. He also owned an unusual "fan chair," which was described as "a great armed chair, with rockers, and a large fan placed over it, with which he fans himself, keeps off flies, etc. while he sits reading, with only a small motion of his foot."

Jefferson, who was younger, had a more complex relationship with his furnishings than Washington. Although his careful patronage and attention to production at his cabinet shop on the Monticello mountaintop came after the Revolution, Jefferson's interest in design, fine furniture, and interesting artifacts was well-established much earlier. In France, Jefferson designed and commissioned clocks and silver items that conformed to his personal preferences. He sent back to Monticello eighty-six crates of goods recorded in a sixteen-page invoice, including chairs, tables, looking glasses, a second-rate but representative collection of oil paintings, books, and ornamental knickknacks. At Monticello, his entrance hall was filled with archaeological finds, natural specimens, and Native American artifacts from the Lewis and Clark expedition. John Hemings, his principal slave cabinetmaker, turned out case pieces and chairs of simple design and sturdy workmanship. He also made an elaborate writing desk as a wedding present for Jefferson's granddaughter, Ellen Randolph. Jefferson himself is thought to have made a tall narrow bookcase that held his garden notebooks.

Although Jefferson and Washington exhibited different degrees of interest in their material possessions, both men, and even the reluctant Benjamin Franklin, represented the growing comfort and sometimes refinement that characterized colonial life in the late eighteenth century. This increased prosperity was not limited to the elite of colonial society but was manifest in the lives of even the poorest colonists. Another area that reflected the improving circumstances in the colonies was the public buildings of early America.

PUBLIC BUILDINGS
AND THEIR FURNISHINGS

Public buildings, notable for their materials, size, and design, stood prominently on the landscape of early America. The winding streets of Boston and early New York did not offer open vistas, but the early-eighteenth-century baroque arrangements of Williamsburg and Annapolis and the rectangular grids of Philadelphia and Savannah emphasized these cities' public buildings. Red bricks with white painted woodwork distinguished public structures from all but the most expensive private residences. Although only well-educated colonists could have identified their classical design features, the symmetry, columns, pediments, cupolas, clocks, and bell towers intuitively signaled their importance.

At the time of the Revolution, royal governors appointed by the British Crown occupied "palaces," official buildings that served both as administrative offices and residences. The governor's residence in Williamsburg, Virginia, is one of the best documented and most thoroughly studied. A sixteen-thousand-item inventory for Lord Botetourt dated 1770, numerous account books, a plan of the residence drawn by Thomas Jefferson, and several excellent descriptions illuminate the details of the "standing furniture" supplied by the colony and the far more numerous personal possessions belonging to the governor. The authority and power of the Crown were evident in the entrance hall, where visitors saw an elaborate display of brightly colored flags and an assortment of arms. In 1750, the tally of displayed armaments was 276 muskets, 100 carbines, 193 pistols, and 264 swords. They were arranged ornamentally in crisscrossed rows and circular patterns similar to displays in the Tower of London. The shelves of the butler's pantry were filled with enough luxury glass goblets and silver plates to set tables for more than forty diners invited to special dinners. A two-tiered iron stove with a combination of rococo and neoclassical ornamentation provided warmth in winter. Copperplate printed fabrics hung around the beds, woven English carpets in bright colors covered the floors, window curtains and Venetian blinds covered the windows, and portraits of the monarchs reminded those who entered the ballroom of their allegiance to the Crown.

The institutions of colonial government displayed a wide range of material culture marked by varied degrees of status. County and colonial governments needed places where their legislatures could meet and their courts could convene. The dif-ference in status between the upper house, which was appointed, and the lower house, which was elected, was apparent in their interior appointments and furnishings. In the former a raised dais and a balustrade separated members from visitors. Canopies of estate (elaborate fabric constructions) or very-high-backed chairs, some with seats so far off the floor they required stools, might be provided for the speaker. Cushions softened seats through the session hours. In county court houses similar distinctions in status were evident. Judges were comfortably accommodated. Witnesses and the general public sat on plain benches, and defendants stood, often in chains. In jails, the indigent slept on straw and were given minimal food in bowls, while wealthier lawbreakers could buy better accommodations and services. The jailer and his family bought their furnishings for their government-supplied quarters as their income allowed. In contrast to the prevalence of jails, only two public hospitals or accommodation for the insane were built in colonial America.

Status also marked the plan and furnishings of church interiors. Higher-ranking worshippers sat in enclosed pews; others perched on benches in the back or in balconies. The chancel with its altar; tablets with the Lord's Prayer, Ten Commandments, Beatitudes, or Apostles' Creed; pulpit; and low screen were frontal visual attractions. Many colonial churches were furnished with fine organs, chandeliers and other lighting devices, carved baptismal fonts, Bibles, and carved tombs set into the walls or floors. Major gifts from members of the congregation paid for communion services. Generally, Dissenters paid less attention than Anglicans to ecclesiastical forms and the terms for them, such as chalice, paten, and flagon, but both groups accepted the host from vessels either made especially for the Eucharist or originally intended for domestic use.

Churchyards were often fenced and surrounded by graves. Gravestones are among the best-documented examples of material culture because they stay put and, through their inscriptions, can be dated and associated with a specific person. Gravestone designs show change over time. This change has been explained as a simple diffusion pattern, in which new ideas travel so many miles per year, or as a more complex socio-economic pattern of interaction, in which a design could skip quickly over a wide geographic area if the person ordering the stone was communicating with other buyers or makers whose taste he or she shared.

Children lucky enough to learn to read and write did so either at home or in schools located in the schoolmaster's or mistress's house. Institutions of higher learning could be private or public. Their classically designed buildings met the demands for accommodations, teaching space, and library services. Harvard was fortunate to have an English donor for an impressive cabinet of scientific instruments that included an orrery (a model of the solar system), electrostatic machines, vacuum pumps, and models of mechanical principles.

The needs of commercial life were met in public market houses, which were usually open on the ground floor and may have housed various civic and private activities on the upper floors. Other commerce took place in the personal stores of small merchants and the shops of artisans. By the eighteenth century, large expanses of glazed windows displayed the shops' wares to entice city customers to buy all sorts of merchandise. Rural shopkeepers did not make the same level of investment in display; they stood behind sturdy counters and measured fabric by the yard; weighed coffee, tea, or spices; counted lemons and oranges; and sold household wares by the piece or set. They were probably a significant source of information for inexperienced customers aspiring to greater affluence.

Sarah Kemble Knight, traveling from Boston to New York in 1704, described country people who came to a general store in New Haven to buy silk fabric and ribbon for hatbands. "They generally stand after they come in a great while speechless, and don't say a word till they are asked what they want, which I impute to the awe they stand in of the merchants, who they are constantly almost indebted to, and must take what they bring without liberty to choose for themselves; but they serve themselves well, making the merchants stay long enough for their pay."

Orphanages, poor houses, hospitals, windmills, and theaters are among the vanished buildings of colonial America.

TRAVEL AND THE LANDSCAPE

Colonists were on the move more for business than pleasure. After the former Virginia tutor Philip Fithian washed in Augusta Warm Springs in the 1770s, he expressed the view that the road was too steep and stony and the attraction too distant from the nearest settlement, much less a major town or city to warrant the trip. He concluded, "the greatest Number of the Americans yet have . . . little leisure for travel." When they left home most people walked, whether to church or school, on business, or to visit friends. An adult could walk approximately ten miles a day, which gave people an effective neighborhood radius of roughly five miles. With a horse one could travel about six miles an hour during daylight. No wonder most people, especially women, stayed at home, reserving their time and energy to attend church and occasionally visit friends. Traveling could also be dangerous. Strangers had a hard time finding their destinations as there were no road maps or adequate signage to guide them. One early traveler complained, "We missed the road, although we were upon it, and could not find that or any other plantation, and meanwhile it became dark. . . . We followed the roads as we found them, now easterly and then westerly, now a little more on one side, and then a little more on the other until we were completely tired out."

Despite the difficulties associated with travel, economic, civic, military, and political activities put many men on the road. Carters loaded wagons and hauled farm produce over familiar roads and tracks to market. Most businessmen, court officials, members of militias, and government representatives saddled their horses and rode to meet their professional obligations. Two- and four-wheeled carriages were rare and mainly found in urban areas with adequate roads. These vehicles implied style, but not necessarily greater comfort. The leather straps that suspended the passenger compartment did not offer much protection from the bumpy road surfaces. Public transportation was virtually nonexistent except for carts or hacks in the larger cities. Very few bridges spanned the rivers, so travelers had to rely on irregular ferries. Some boats were so small that two trips were required to transport vehicles, horses, and riders.

En route or at their destinations, most travelers relied on taverns, licensed by local authorities to assure that basic services—food, drink, sleeping space, and accommodation for animals—would be provided at a fixed charge to all who applied. Travelers who wanted the luxury of a private room usually had to find a boarding house that rented entire rooms, not simply a portion of a bed or a corner of a room for sleeping. On the other hand, taverns offered their mostly male and local clientele many entertainments—drinking, conversation, gambling, billiards, and cockfights. Travel conditions did not change until the Revolution, when the postal service offered guaranteed contracts to owners of horses and coaches, which provided enough incentive for owners to press for improvements in roads and bridges, and commercialized leisure put many men and women on the road.

The changing picture of material life in colonial America shows that our ancestors valued their houses and possessions functionally, aesthetically, and symbolically. After the Revolution, artifacts of the early material culture were vested with another level of significance. They provided spiritual contact with the past and its people. When Thomas Jefferson's original wedding gift to his granddaughter Ellen Randolph was lost at sea, he replaced it with the simple traveling desk he had commissioned from the Philadelphia cabinetmaker Benjamin Randolph. He noted that it had "no merit of particular beauty" but that like a chair in which William Penn once sat, "Its imaginary value will increase with years" and "as the relics of the Saints are in those of the Church" it will be "carried in the procession of our nation's birthday."

See also **The City; Pastoralism and the Rural Ideal** *(volume 2).*

BIBLIOGRAPHY

Ames, Kenneth L., and Gerald W. R. Ward, eds. *Decorative Arts and Household Furnishings in America, 1650–1920: An Annotated Bibliography.* Winterthur, Del., 1989.

Blackburn, Roderic H., and Ruth Piwonka. *Remembrance of Patria: Dutch Arts and Culture in Colonial America, 1609–1776.* Albany, N.Y., 1988.

Bushman, Richard L. *The Refinement of America: Persons, Houses, Cities.* New York, 1992.

Carson, Cary, Ronald Hoffman, and Peter J. Albert, eds. *Of Consuming Interests: The Style of Life in the Eighteenth Century.* Charlottesville, Va., 1994.

Fairbanks, Jonathan L. *New England Begins: The Seventeenth Century.* Boston, 1982.

Fales, Martha Gandy. *Early American Silver.* New York, 1973.

Fleming, E. McClung. "Artiface Study: A Proposed Model." *Winterthur Portfolio* 9 (1974): 153–173.

Fleming, John, and Hugh Honour, *Dictionary of the Decorative Arts.* New York, 1977.

Forman, Benno M. *American Seating Furniture, 1630–1730: An Interpretive Catalogue.* New York, 1988.

Garrett, Elisabeth Donaghy. *At Home: The American Family, 1750–1870.* New York, 1990.

Gilliam, Jan Kirsten, and Betty Crowe Leviner. *Furnishing Williamsburg's Historic Buildings.* Williamsburg, Va., 1991.

Heckscher, Morrison H., and Leslie Greene Bowman. *American Rococo, 1750– 1775: Elegance in Ornament.* New York, 1992.

Hood, Graham. *American Silver: A History of Style, 1650–1900.* New York, 1971.

Hume, Ivor Noël. *A Guide to Artifacts of Colonial America,* 1st ed. New York, 1970.

Hurst, Ronald L., and Jonathan Prown. *Southern Furniture, 1680–1830: The Colonial Williamsburg Collection.* Williamsburg, Va., 1997.

Jobe, Brock, and Myrna Kaye, *New England Furniture: The Colonial Era: Selections from the Society for the Preservation of New England Antiques.* Boston, 1984.

Lynn, Catherine. *Wallpaper in America from the Seventeenth Century to World War I*. New York, 1980.

Montgomery, Charles F. *A History of American Pewter*. New York, 1973.

Montgomery, Florence M. *Printed Textiles: English and American Cottons and Linens, 1770–1850*. New York, 1970.

——. *Textiles in America, 1650–1870: A Dictionary Based on Original Documents, Prints and Paintings, Commercial Records, American Merchants' Papers, Shopkeepers' Advertisements, and Pattern Books with Original Swatches of Cloth*. New York, 1984.

Morgan, Philip D. *Black Culture in the Eighteenth-Century Chesapeake and Low-Country*. Chapel Hill, N.C., 1998.

Naeve, Milo M. *Identifying American Furniture: A Pictorial Guide to Styles and Terms, Colonial to Contemporary*. 2d ed. New York, 1989.

Nygren, Edward J. "Edward Winslow's Sugar Boxes: Colonial Echoes of Courtly Love." *Yale University Art Gallery Bulletin* 33, no. 2 (autumn 1971): 38–52.

Nylander, Jane C. *Our Own Snug Fireside: Images of the New England Home, 1760–1860*. New York, 1993.

Prown, Jules. "Mind in Matter: An Introduction to Material Culture Theory and Method." *Winterthur Portfolio* 17, no. 1 (spring 1982): 1–19.

Sack, Albert. *Fine Points of Furniture: Early American*. New York, 1950.

Sobel, Mechal. *The World They Made Together: Black and White Values in Eighteenth-Century Virginia*. Princeton, N.J., 1987.

Taylor, Lonn, and Dessa Bokides. *New Mexican Furniture, 1600–1940: The Origin, Survival, and Revival of Furniture Making in the Hispanic Southwest*. Santa Fe, N.M., 1987.

Ulrich, Laurel Thatcher, "Hannah Barnard's Cupboard: Female Property and Identity in Eighteenth-Century New England." In *Through a Glass Darkly: Reflections on Personal Identity in Early America*, edited by Ronald Hoffman, Mechal Sobel, and Fredrika J. Teute, pp. 238–273. Williamsburg, Va., 1997.

Ward, Barbara McLean, and Gerald W. R. Ward. *Silver in American Life*. New York, 1979.

Ward, Gerald W. R., and William N. Hosley Jr., eds. *The Great River: Art and Society of the Connecticut Valley, 1635–1820*. Hartford, Conn., 1985.

ANGLO-AMERICAN RELIGIOUS TRADITIONS

Charles H. Lippy

During the age of exploration and conquest, the distinctions between a sacred realm, where religion and faith hold sway, and a secular realm, where all things cultural and political flourish independently without holy nuance, were only beginning to take hold in Western societies. That division gained currency in the wake of the Enlightenment and the spate of democratic revolutions that accompanied it. The Native American tribal societies that European colonists encountered when settling in the Americas made no such sharp distinctions; for virtually all of them, although details differed, tribal life was an ideological whole. Indeed, it appears that no tribal community had a separate word for "religion" since, like much else, it was so intricately interwoven with the whole of culture that identifying it as something discrete was impossible. One result was the failure of European invaders to understand the dynamics of a tribal society; they tended to see all tribal peoples as polytheistic pagans who needed to be civilized as well as Christianized, though civilizing and Christianizing were two dimensions of one reality.

But Europeans who came to the New World also brought with them religious ideologies with significant implications for the shape of culture, the structures of society, and the institutions sustaining common life. The circumstances of building viable colonial settlements required adaptation; nevertheless, these ideologies buttressed very different visions of how life in the Western Hemisphere should be ordered. While not the first to arrive in the Americas, the Puritans who sought to build their holy commonwealth in New England had by far the most penetrating influence and most wide-reaching impact on developments in the United States. Rabidly Protestant, they fused constructs drawn from the Calvinist theological heritage and their affection for political developments in England to fashion a vision of a theocracy, a culture where religious ideals would dominate and determine the particulars of politics, economics, education, and all other dimen-

sions of both public and private life. In the area of North America that became the United States, the Puritan vision clashed not only with that of the indigenous tribal cultures but with that fostered in colonies where the Church of England was established. There, a different understanding of how faith and government—church and state in the parlance of a later age—formed the foundations of cultural and intellectual life. The Anglican vision revolved around the supremacy of monarch and government over things religious; after all, the king was declared to be the supreme governor of the church on earth and King Henry VIII, reigning while Spain was busily establishing its control over much of the Americas, held the title of Defender of the Faith. The definite article in that title was also important, for it presumed that there was a single religious approach that constituted "the" faith. The Puritan understanding emerged in part as a reaction to the Anglican viewpoint, as did that of another group, the Quakers, who gave voice to yet another religious ideology that would offer its own understanding of what should go into the making of a society and culture. Even though Quaker colonists in North America were relatively few, they in time exerted an enduring influence far in excess of their numbers.

Quakers, Anglicans, and Puritans were all Protestants. Yet when they sought to nurture a culture in colonial North America reflecting their individual perspectives, they not only encountered the alternatives represented by the many indigenous tribal societies, but they came into contact and often into conflict with Spanish and French Catholics. Following the Protestant Reformation of the sixteenth century, which erupted roughly twenty-five years after Christopher Columbus's initial voyage to the Americas, the Spanish monarchs had come to see themselves as the great protectors of religious truth that they thought Roman Catholicism alone encapsulated. In turn, that passion for Catholicism combined with a virulent nationalism to give Spanish colonialism a dynamism all its own. In France, where developing nationalism carried an undercurrent of anticlericalism, a suspicion of the intentions of the church as an institution was spurred in part by the close ties between Spain and the papacy. Nevertheless, in the age of colonialism, the French brought to their enterprise in the New World a complex religious-political ideology.

Although as vital to the North American colonial experience as were the French and Spanish styles and, in time, an African presence thwarted always by slavery, the focus here will fall on the ways English and then Anglo-American religious perspectives fashioned the culture that became the United States.

Understanding how these different religious ideologies gave shape to the culture that became the United States requires a closer look at the way each worked in those areas where they were dominant.

THE PURITAN CULTURAL VISION

At the center of the Puritan cultural vision lay the idea of covenant. With roots in John Calvin's doctrine of election (the idea that God before all time determined who would be chosen for salvation), covenant thinking owed much to the reshaping of Calvinist theology in the works of William Ames, William Perkins, Richard Sibbes, and other Puritan thinkers. Of signal import was the agreement between God and humanity at creation, the covenant of works. Abrogated in the fall of humanity, that covenant ceased to be operative. God chose to offer another covenant, the covenant of grace, first to Abraham but exemplified best in the work of Jesus Christ (which some also identified as the covenant of redemption). Covenants, transactions binding on both parties, were thus God's way of structuring relationships with humanity. By extension, covenant became humanity's way of structuring relationships with each other. More than their European ideological counterparts, the Puritans who peopled New England saw in covenant ideology a basis for organizing both religious life and common or public life.

In New England Puritanism, covenant thinking provided the basis for setting up churches. A local congregation came into being as those who could testify to their being elected to salvation through God's gracious decree and then covenanted with each other to follow the commandments of God found in Scripture. They thus became a godly people, visible saints devoted to worship of God and a holy life. The covenanted community of the faithful was the final authority in church matters; no bishops or external ecclesiastical authorities held power that superseded the simple church covenant and the responsibilities it gave to God's elect. Yet from the start Puritans recognized that God had not elected all persons to salvation. More vexing was the realization that not all the elect necessarily knew with certainty that they had been given the gift of salvation until there was a distinct work of grace that brought spiritual illumination. The elect, the uncertain, and all others had to live together in society, though those not elect were a perpetual spiritual threat to men and women committed to leading a pure life.

To keep the entire culture centered on God's way, the Puritans in Massachusetts Bay determined that only those men who had owned the church covenant, only those who could testify that they had experienced election to salvation and in turn submitted to the authority of the congregation, were given the vote. This practice assured that laws governing all residents would reflect the Puritan vision for a holy commonwealth. After all, even those who were not elect would receive some social benefit from following laws designed to support a godly life; some might even come to realize that they were indeed among the elect of God. Some commentators have labeled the Puritan approach a theocracy, literally the "rule of God." Others have suggested that it was more the "rule of the saints" or of those who were convinced they could discern the divine will. Regardless of the label, however, the Puritan thrust relied heavily on an understanding of Scripture and biblical warrant for civil law, although never was government thought to have coercive power over the churches. Hundreds of years later, those who claimed the United States is a nation founded on biblical principle would attempt to use the Puritans as evidence, usually in a more simplistic fashion than the historical record warrants.

There were other cultural and intellectual implications of the Puritan style. If biblical testimony undergirded both church and state, albeit in their distinct spheres, one had to be able to read the Bible in order to capture its meaning. Hence there was built into the Puritan enterprise an educational emphasis that received concrete manifestation in 1636, just six years after the settlement of Boston, in the founding of Harvard College. Harvard's initial mission was to train a learned clergy, but its early curriculum reflected a broader Puritan understanding. Their mindset reasoned that if all of creation is the handiwork of God, then nothing is excluded from scrutiny. Knowledge itself is a gift from God to be used to praise God even as it benefits humanity. Hence Puritanism gave a tremendous boost to scientific inquiry in the colonial period, albeit almost always placing higher priority on the application of scientific knowledge than on pure science and theory. John Winthrop Jr., whose father had been a leading figure in the settlement of Massachusetts Bay and longtime governor of the colony, amassed a significant scientific library and acquired considerable equipment for Harvard, especially in the area of astronomy. Cotton Mather, the prominent preacher, was also a leading advocate of scientific pursuits, lending his endorsement, for example, to such new endeavors as use of vaccines to prevent illness. In the eighteenth century, Jonathan Edwards, perhaps the greatest philosopher-theologian New England Puritanism produced, had a keen scientific mind as well; like Mather before him, he urged people to receive inoculation against smallpox. Edwards himself was inoculated, after assuming the presidency of the College of New Jersey (later Princeton University) in the midst of a smallpox epidemic that had taken the life of his son-in-law and predecessor as president. Unfortunately, Edwards contracted the disease from the vaccine and died. But the Puritan emphasis on education and on practical science left an enduring mark on American culture.

One other cultural implication of the Puritan style deserves mention, its esthetics. In part because of their Calvinist-based conviction that humanity's primary task in life is to worship God, they tended to dismiss anything that stood between themselves and the Almighty. Popular amusements were suspect because they distracted one from pursuing things holy. In England during the Puritan ascendancy, advocates of this plain style frequently demolished stone carvings and other forms of religious representation in churches and cathedrals lest the art itself become the focus of adoration rather than the God to whom the art pointed. In New England, this penchant for simplicity in style and avoidance of superfluous decoration manifested itself most obviously in the meetinghouses that were among the first structures erected in any Puritan settlement. Stripped of overt religious symbolism, the meetinghouse served not only as a place for Sunday worship, but as the location for town meetings and other public gatherings. In Puritan esthetics, the space reserved for worship was not in itself sacred or holy. Hence the community could appropriate it for other purposes. Even when the faithful gathered to hear the word of God proclaimed, they expected the divine presence to come more through spoken word than architectural style or setting. The Puritan meetinghouse became the prototype for one of the first distinctively American architectural expressions.

At the same time, however, the emphasis on the word of God—and thus on the spoken and written word—sustained another esthetic dimension with enormous cultural implications. Among the earliest commercial ventures was the development of a colonial printing industry, producing not just the text of Scripture, but other aids to worship, sermons preached by Puritan divines, and other literature that would spur the pursuit of holiness. The importance of communicating the word of God in sermons meant that preaching became central to public religious life, elevating the sermon to a place of prominence that it retains in much of twenty-first-century American Protestantism. In the eighteenth century, Jonathan Edwards drew from an understanding of language and the inherent power of words themselves in his preaching. Although Edwards spoke in a monotone without making eye contact with his hearers, his preaching frequently generated an extraordinarily potent emotional response. What later ages deemed secular literature also reflected this esthetic. The poetry of the seventeenth-century Puritan Anne Bradstreet, for example, burns with life and defies the popular perception of Puritans as stolid, passionless folk because of their devotion to holy simplicity.

By the middle of the eighteenth century, however, a dissenting presence challenged some of the Puritan cultural dominance. The revivals of the Great Awakening of the 1740s revealed an undercurrent of dissatisfaction especially with the arrangements between church and government and also with the practice of infant baptism. The most vocal of these coalesced into the Baptists, following the leadership of Isaac Backus (1724–1806), who became a popular champion of religious liberty in the later colonial period. With historic ties to one wing of English Puritanism, the Baptists came to look on Roger Williams, the seventeenth century religious seeker who left the Massachusetts Bay Colony to establish the settlement that became Providence, Rhode Island, as their ideological founder. Williams had insisted that the government had no power to intervene or control any religious community; its role was limited to maintaining common order and promoting the common welfare. Williams, like the later colonial Baptists, believed that true believers were few in number, but that their religious belief functioned separately from their civil responsibilities.

AN ANGLICAN ALTERNATIVE

Later generations of interpreters have often contrasted the Puritan way with the presumably rather different cultural and intellectual heritage promoted by Anglican settlers in other areas of English colonial America. If Puritans were wary of secular amusements, Anglicans relished them. If Puritans devoted their minds to theological inquiry, Anglicans developed a studied skepticism. If Puritans were zealous, Anglicans were genteel, particularly when it came to religious expression. Like many uncomplicated contrasts, these contain a measure of accuracy and distortion. Particularly in the later decades of the colonial period, when a variety of evangelical forms of Christianity were flourishing in colonies where the Church of England held favored status, the contrasts are facile, for not only did the evangelical presence undermine the Anglican dominance, evangelicals themselves sustained multiple approaches to what an ideal culture should be. Yet the Anglican approach was by no means identical to the Puritan way, and the differences demonstrate how competing ideologies left their mark as American culture developed.

From the time of the English Reformation in the sixteenth century, the Anglican perspective assumed a rather different relationship between church and state, sacred and secular, than did the Puritan understanding. Both the church and the Crown had intertwining concern for the commonweal. If Puritans separated the spheres of responsibility, since only the elect could be members of the church, Anglicans nearly collapsed the distinction. The Church of England, after all, was supported by the public treasury; bishops of the church, analogous in their role to the king and nobility in the political sector, held seats in the House of Lords. The Anglican arrangement recognized the social utility of religion in a way that the Puritan style could not. As early as the age of Elizabeth I, when Marian exiles of a Puritan persuasion began returning to England and fueling a religious underground movement at odds with the religious establishment, the Church of England called for a broad conformity to its liturgy and practice and, sometimes unwittingly, sanctioned considerable latitude in matters of personal belief. The idea was simple: If all in the realm engaged in common religious practice, they would ipso facto have bonds with one another and a loyalty to the nation whose monarch was both chief of state and supreme governor of the church. This functionalist appreciation of the social role of organized religion echoed the medieval conviction that religious uniformity is a necessary precondition for political stability, a conviction that had helped ignite an age of religious wars on the European continent in the wake of the Protestant Reformation.

In one sense the difference between Puritan ideology and Anglican ideology of how government should be related to the church was more a matter of degree than polar opposition. Both held it appropriate, for example, for tax monies to be used to support sanctioned religious institutions, and in the early decades of the federal republic, states where Puritan influence held sway, such as Connecticut and Massachusetts, were among the last to abandon such public support for religion. Both believed that church and state each had a critical role in supporting public order and morality. Puritans, however, objected to the civil authority exercised by the Church of England and its leaders, regarding it as unbiblical. Hence they shuddered at the political role of bishops in Parliament, at the influence (if not control) over church appointments exercised by government officials, and at the apparent regulation of the content of doctrine and practice evidenced in such actions as Parliamentary adoption of the Anglican *Book of Common Prayer* (first authorized for use in the Church of England in 1549) and articles of faith. Anglicans assumed that these were merely manifestations of how the state recognized the importance of true religion; Puritans regarded them as intrusions into a realm where Scripture alone was supreme.

Hence when the first permanent English settlement was formed in Jamestown, Virginia, in 1607, provisions for the support of the church figured prominently in the first colonial law codes. If many of those who guided the religious life of Virginia in its early decades were sympathetic to Puritan theological understanding, they supported the Anglican structure of the proper relationship between church and government. At the same time, church attendance—at least in the early years—was mandated by law, and statutes prohibited profanity, blasphemy, and other sacrilegious acts. But differences between the Anglican and Puritan visions come into focus in a profound way in the understanding of what it meant to be religious, to be a Christian. For the Puritan, the experience of election, God's covenant with humanity in Jesus Christ, was fundamental; all else followed on that. For the Anglican, the starting point of religious life tended to be more assent to the basics of Christian belief, an intellectual acceptance of the truth of Christian doctrine broadly construed. In time the Anglican style more clearly reflected the emerging Enlightenment currents that saw religion as a matter of private judgment, of assessing various truth claims and then affirming those that measured up to the canons of reason. For those operating within a Christian orbit, the assumption was that only the claims of Christianity would meet the tests of reason. How one elaborated on those beliefs was a matter of individual understanding. Hence for those imbued with the Anglican style, the Puritan emphasis on the experience of election sometimes seemed as if emotional abandon had displaced reasoned understanding. As well, by the end of the colonial era, the appreciation of reason associated with Anglicanism led many of the intellectually inclined to espouse forms of deism. Several of the nation's founding generation, such as Thomas Jefferson, were far more comfortable with a relatively mild expression of deism than any manner of orthodox Christianity.

Yet some consequences of both approaches were complementary rather than contradictory. For example, in differing ways, both finally placed great authority in the individual when it came to matters of religion. For Anglicans, use of reason in the intellectual assent to particular beliefs brought the individual to the fore. For Puritans, only the individual could realize the experience of election within. One may have been more rational and one more affective, but both highlighted the role of the individual. In the Anglican-dominated areas of the southern colonies, this individualism took other forms. The polity of the Church of England vested much ecclesiastical power in the office of the bishop. Throughout the colonial era, however, there were no Church of England bishops serving in the areas that became part of the United States. Theoretically, the ministrations of bishops were required for confirmation into the church and for ordination of priests. While the matter of confirmation was somewhat more fluid, colonists seeking holy orders did finally have to cross the Atlantic if they wished to receive ordination. On a practical level, the more ad hoc structures that supported colonial Anglicanism granted much de facto power to the lay vestries of individual parishes, which often encompassed such large geographic areas as to render real pastoral ministry ineffective. Hence the local vestry, in some ways the extension of the individual, exercised far more control over the parish and the priest, if there was one, than was the case in England. One result was that seeds of independence nourished within an Anglican orbit in the Age of Revolution brought a different style of support for political separation from the Crown than did the covenant theology of the Puritans.

The culture informed by Anglican sensibilities took a different direction than that shaped by Puritan impulses. Convinced that God intends creatures to enjoy the fruits of creation, Anglicans were more likely to see the arts as bringing a kind of wholeness to life, of stimulating the senses to appreciate the wonder and majesty of the world. They believed beauty itself is a gift from God, not something that interrupts the pursuit of holiness. The greatest challenges in this arena came more from the demographics in areas of Anglican concentration than from a lack of appreciation for such things as music and the theater. As a plantation economy sustained by a slave labor system took hold, there were few villages or cities, other than Charleston, South Carolina, and Savannah, Georgia, with sufficient population to support many artistic endeavors. The distribution of the population also posed challenges for formal education. Efforts to establish a college in Anglican Virginia, underway by the 1660s, did not come to fruition until the founding of the College of William and Mary in 1693. Although intended to offer a classical liberal arts education, similar to that at the Puritan-oriented Harvard, William and Mary lagged behind for its first few decades, perhaps in part because its vision was somewhat broader. A spirit of urgency propelled Harvard in the early years, for a literate and learned clergy was essential to the Puritan enterprise; William and Mary never had the training of clergy as its sole initial aim and experienced a somewhat slower development.

Its notion of a more intertwined relationship between church and state, its tendency to see faith more as intellectual assent to the truth of doctrine, its appreciation of a life shaped by more than a passion for purity and holiness—all made the Anglican approach and the ideology that sustained it an alternative to the Puritan perspective in colonial America. Both had a continuing influence long after the colonial epoch ended, although many would insist that the Puritan way was more deeply embedded in the character of American culture.

THE QUAKER ACCEPTANCE OF PLURALISM

Ironically perhaps, the religious ideology that reflected the shape of American cultural life by the dawn of the twenty-first century had roots not only in Puritan and Anglican viewpoints, but in one that both Puritans and Anglicans held suspect in the colonial period and one that had its greatest early

Edward Hicks, *Penn's Treaty with Indians.* Oil on canvas, c. 1840. This scene has been the subject of some debate, as no direct record of the actual treaty exists. The scene, recurrent in Hicks's work, originally was the subject of a famous Benjamin West painting of the same name. © FRANCIS G. MAYER/CORBIS

influence in Pennsylvania. In 1681, the Quaker William Penn received a grant of land from King Charles II; by the following year, the first colonists were en route and a frame of government was established for what Penn called his "holy experiment." Although earlier associated with Puritans in England, Penn had become a Quaker and had emerged as one of its major voices after the death of the Society of Friends (Quakers) founder George Fox. Quakers shared the Puritan distrust of the easy collaboration between the Church of England and the British government; indeed, they wanted even greater distinction between the realm of civil authority and the realm of religion.

At the heart of the Quaker approach that informed Penn's colonial venture lay a more radical individualism than that nurtured by the Puritan understanding of election. Convinced that the Holy Spirit communicated directly with individuals, bringing spiritual illumination or an inner light,

Quakers understood that the truth could come differently to each person. There was no formula set in creed or doctrine, no one mode of worship, not even an absolute reliance on Scripture that could bring genuine spiritual awakening to all. The truth came in its own way, arousing a spiritual presence filled with power and peace deep within the individual. By Penn's day, Quakers had shed much of the rabid enthusiasm that had led earlier generations to disrupt Church of England worship with their shouting and quaking. They attributed such demonstrations to the power of the Holy Spirit, but onlookers and civil authorities regarded such as evidence of dangerous disorder. Penn and his coreligionists were already moving toward the quietism that later generations have associated with the Quaker style.

This understanding of how authentic religion stirred within had numerous vital consequences for public life. Most obvious was the incompatibility of giving legal sanction or governmental support to any single organized religion. Tolerance, not even always a Quaker virtue in the seventeenth century, became the byword. Hence Penn demonstrated a far greater appreciation of the integrity of the Native American tribal cultures in the area than did English colonists elsewhere; they, too, could be bearers of spiritual truth. Even if one were convinced that another were in error, persecution or other efforts to eliminate alternative viewpoints by force were incompatible with the Quaker way. A strict pacifism followed. Abhorrence of persecution led Penn to welcome to his colony those who were victims of religious oppression in England and on the European continent. Numerous German sectarian groups, for example, found in Pennsylvania both religious and geographic space to cultivate their own understanding of faith and culture. There was also a practical dimension to Penn's recruiting of the persecuted; he needed to find persons willing to move to the New World if his enterprise were to succeed. In time, Pennsylvania became the haven for many. Even though popular lore identifies neighboring Maryland as an early haven for Roman Catholics, who were suspect in England, by the time of American independence Philadelphia boasted one of the most flourishing Catholic communities in the nation. Catholics had become a minority in Maryland within a decade of the colony's founding. The need to attract enough settlers to make the colony viable meant opening the doors to others. An Act of Toleration promulgated in 1649 provided a modicum of religious liberty. Protestants of a Puritan persuasion soon outnumbered Catholics. The Quaker experiment provided a more fertile environment to nurture Catholic sensibilities.

In the eighteenth century, when denominations assumed embryonic structures, Pennsylvania played a key role. The nation's first presbytery formed in Philadelphia in 1706; significant Scotch-Irish immigration in the eighteenth century assured that Pennsylvania would remain central to American Presbyterianism. The following year the Philadelphia Baptist Association, the first formal network of Baptists, was established in the city. As well, after the American Revolution, the Protestant Episcopal Church, the American successor to the Church of England, organized in Philadelphia.

Penn did assume, mistakenly as developments later revealed, that Quaker influence would dominate even if all were welcome. The pacifism that flowed from the Quaker approach created difficulties in providing a military defense for the various Pennsylvania settlements. Gradually the leading Quakers retreated from political life although they long overshadowed others in the colony's economic life. Nonetheless, in nourishing a culture where persons of a variety of ethnic backgrounds and persons of diverse religious persuasions lived in relative harmony, the Quaker "holy experiment" in Pennsylvania undermined the old assumption about the necessity of religious uniformity to social and political order. It also foreshadowed what the American nation became, a culture of many religions, many ethnic styles, and many understandings of what makes an ideal society.

The Quaker cultural style as it developed revealed a dimension of irony. Committed to a simple life, with an aesthetic as stark as that of New England Puritans, Quakers were also committed to honest labor and hard work. One result was that some Quaker merchants soon amassed considerable wealth, although riches were never consciously sought given the penchant for simplicity. Another touch of irony stemmed from the Quaker insistence on pacifism. Could a government controlled by Quakers who refused to bear arms provide an adequate defense? As Pennsylvania welcomed colonists of many religious persuasions, providing such defense became a critical issue. Many Quakers gradually withdrew from positions of leadership in government in order to remain faithful to pacifist principles, but in turn they had more time and energy to devote to business and achieved even greater economic success.

OTHER IDEOLOGICAL ALTERNATIVES

Numerous other religious ideologies were also part of the colonial cultural and intellectual landscape. In several areas that later became part of the United States, Roman Catholicism provided the basic religious understanding. Both Spanish and French styles of Catholicism left a significant imprint on American life in regions first conquered by persons of those backgrounds. The Spanish especially saw themselves as the defenders of Catholic truth in the wake of the Reformation, and their colonial ventures brought a mixture of military and religious endeavors to plant a culture that was both Spanish and Catholic in the New World. The harsh treatment of indigenous peoples central to military conquest often provoked anxiety among missionary priests, who sought to mitigate the brutality of conquest while at the same time converting native peoples. Yet Spanish Catholic leaders were generally as unsympathetic to religious alternatives as Spanish conquistadors were to the integrity of the native cultures they destroyed. Ironically, however, the mix of peoples and cultures gave the Catholicism that prevailed a unique ethos. The natives who converted or who married their conquerors fused elements of their pre-Christian religiosity with Catholicism to create a distinctive mode of Catholic expression that endures into the twenty-first century.

The very presence of tribal peoples provided another undercurrent to the competing religious ideologies of the colonial period. The Spanish approach was the most severe in attempting to eradicate existing native cultures. In areas where the English were the first Europeans to establish colonial control, a greater ambivalence prevailed. Puritans and Anglicans alike faltered when it came to proselytizing among the natives, for every effort to promote conversion also required acceptance, albeit a reluctant one, of the integrity of the cultures and peoples being converted. That acceptance rendered conquest and control problematic on a theoretical level. The tribal style, where notions of private property and of the kind of individualism more characteristic of the colonists were unknown, remained a consistent challenge to the hegemony of European-based styles.

Perhaps the most significant challenge, however, came from Africans after the introduction of slavery in the English colonies in 1619. Despite efforts of slave traders and owners to destroy all obvious traces of African tribal life in order to render slaves more malleable, Africans retained many dimensions of their cultural and religious heritage. Throughout the colonial period, slavery itself provided a consistent challenge to the developing ideology of individualism and liberty fostered in different ways by Puritan, Anglican, and Quaker approaches. After all, slavery was by definition incompatible with freedom, whether it be the freedom to use reason to assent to belief, the freedom to seek signs of election, or the freedom to live according to the dictates of conscience. Sustained efforts to Christianize African Americans did not materialize until the eighteenth century, though there were a handful of persons earlier who took the Christian message to slaves. The work of the Anglican Society for the Propagation of the Gospel (SPG) after 1701 was in theory oriented toward the conversion of slaves and other non-Christian peoples, although the challenges posed by the nature of colonial culture meant that those efforts were always a minor part of the overall SPG endeavor. The evangelical revivals that spread through the English colonies in the 1740s spurred greater interest in converting slaves. Yet as was the case with the fusion of Spanish Catholicism and native tribal religiosity, when Christianity took root among African Americans, its expression reflected a syncretism of Christian belief and practice with tribal ways and often also with elements picked up in the Caribbean that gave African American Christianity a style of its own.

Europeans who colonized in America brought a variety of religious ideologies with them. As well, they confronted different approaches to cultural life among the peoples already living in the Americas and among those they forced into slavery. All of those ideologies had implications for the cultural and intellectual life that flourished during the colonial era. The Puritan presence may have left the most abiding influence on American culture, yet the Quaker enterprise in Pennsylvania more clearly cradled the mode of religious and cultural interaction that became characteristic of American life. Somewhere in between was the Anglican approach, always a middle way since the emergence of Anglicanism in sixteenth-century England. Yet from these competing ideologies and the challenges to them emerged an American culture.

See also **The Transformation of American Religion: 1776–1838** (*in this volume*) *and other articles in this section.*

BIBLIOGRAPHY

Baltzell, E. Digby. *Puritan Boston and Quaker Philadelphia.* New York, 1979.

Bercovitch, Sacvan. *The Puritan Origins of the American Self.* New Haven, Conn., 1975.

Bonvillain, Nancy. *Native American Religion.* New York, 1995.

Butler, Jon. *Awash in a Sea of Faith: Christianizing the American People.* Cambridge, Mass., 1990.

Commager, Henry Steele. *The Empire of Reason.* New York, 1982.

Dillenberger, John. *The Visual Arts and Christianity in America: From the Colonial Period to the Present.* New York, 1984.

Ellis, John Tracy. *Catholics in Colonial America.* Baltimore, 1965.

Frey, Sylvia R., and Betty Wood. *Come Shouting to Zion: African American Protestantism in the American South and British Caribbean to 1830.* Chapel Hill, N.C., 1998.

Gaustad, Edwin S. *Revival, Revolution, and Religion in Early Virginia.* Williamsburg, Va., 1994.

Heimert, Alan. *Religion and the American Mind: From the Great Awakening to the Revolution.* Cambridge, Mass., 1966.

Holmes, David L. "The Anglican Tradition and the Episcopal Church." In *Encyclopedia of the American Religious Experience,* edited by Charles H. Lippy and Peter W. Williams. Vol. 1. New York, 1988.

Howe, Daniel Walker. "The Impact of Puritanism on American Culture." In *Encyclopedia of the American Religious Experience,* edited by Charles H. Lippy and Peter W. Williams. Vol. 2. New York, 1988.

Isaac, Rhys. *The Transformation of Virginia, 1740–1790.* Chapel Hill, N.C., 1982.

Jones, Rufus M., et al. *The Quakers in the American Colonies.* New York, 1962.

Lippy, Charles H., Robert Choquette, and Stafford Poole. *Christianity Comes to the Americas, 1492–1776.* New York, 1992.

Marietta, Jack D. *The Reformation of American Quakerism, 1748–1783.* Philadelphia, 1984.

May, Henry F. *Religion and the Enlightenment in America.* New York, 1991.

Raboteau, Albert J. *Slave Religion: The "Invisible Institution" in the Antebellum South.* New York, 1978.

Rivera, Luis N. *A Violent Evangelism: The Political and Religious Conquest of the Americas.* Louisville, Ky., 1992.

Todorov, Tzvetan. *The Conquest of America: The Question of the Other.* Translated by Richard Howard. New York, 1992.

Tolles, Frederick B. *Meeting House and Counting House: The Quaker Merchants of Colonial Pennsylvania.* Chapel Hill, N.C., 1948.

Williams, Peter W. *Houses of God: Region, Religion, and Architecture in the United States.* Urbana and Chicago, 1997.

Williams, Peter W., ed. Pt. 2 of *Perspectives on American Religion and Culture.* Oxford, 1999.

Woolverton, John. *Colonial Anglicanism in North America, 1607–1776.* Detroit, Mich., 1984.

Ziff, Larzer. *Puritanism in America: New Culture in a New World.* New York, 1973.

PHILOSOPHY FROM PURITANISM TO THE ENLIGHTENMENT

Rick Kennedy

If philosophy is defined as the love of wisdom, the desire to understand one's place in the symphony of the cosmos, then colonial America probably had more than its share of philosophers and creative philosophies. The colonial period of United States history is defined by multiple contests of politics, religions, cultures, and ideas. Hopes were often artificially raised and the rate of failure was high. In such an unsettled situation, many people were encouraged to think deeply and pursue wisdom.

Using this definition, possibly the most creative and widespread philosophical movement in colonial America had nothing to do with either Puritanism or the Enlightenment. Beginning probably in the 1730s and spreading south, north, and east from the Ohio Valley was an intertribal discussion on what encroachment by Europeans meant for Indians. The most influential philosophers of this movement were prophets of a New World order. The most famous of these was Neolin, the Delaware Prophet, who preached that the Indians had collectively sinned by adopting "white people's ways and nature." He told a Descartes-style story of sitting alone by the fire, "musing and greatly concerned about the evil ways he saw prevailing among the Indians," when a man appeared who taught him a pure religion that would restore all Indians to a right relationship with the cosmos. Thousands of Indians, seeking wisdom and ready to act, followed Neolin and other prophets in ritual vomiting, witch-hunts, and rejection of European tools and alcohol. Some followers, such as the Ottawa warrior Pontiac, resorted to war in order to jump-start the new Indian renewal.

Lovers of wisdom like Neolin and his fellow prophets abound in stories of colonial America. So do Jesuits, Franciscans, Puritans, Quakers, German pietists, humanitarians, and political reformers. No doubt every colonial minister, like Neolin, mused by the fire about the sin of humanity and relied on the divine revelation of the Scriptures for a pro-gram of renewal. There were a number of highly educated missionaries, such as Jean de Brébeuf in New France, who developed ways to communicate Christianity to the Huron and the Iroquois. History reports many personal crises that led to deep introspection, for example when William Byrd II in Virginia disinterred and opened the coffin of his father in an attempt to understand his own place in the world. The love of wisdom was often made manifest in ephemeral ways, as when Judge Samuel Sewall and the Puritan clergyman Cotton Mather discussed the nature of humanity when they happened to meet in a Boston alley with the same purpose of relieving their bladders. Since the love of wisdom was not tied to formal education, women could participate fully, as when the poet Anne Bradstreet wrote a poem "upon the burning of our house":

> I, started up, the light did spye,
> And to my God my heart did cry
> To strengthen me in my Distresse
> And not to leave me succourlesse.
> Then coming out beheld a space
> The flame consume my dwelling place.
>
> And, when I could no longer look,
> I blest his Name that gave and took,
> That layd my goods now in the dust:
> Yea so it was, and so 'twas just.
> It was his own: it was not mine;
> Far be it that I should repine.
> (*The Works of Anne Bradstreet*, p. 40)

If philosophy is the love of wisdom, the desire to find one's place in the symphony of the cosmos, then colonial America had more than its share of philosophers and a multitude of creative philosophies. If philosophy, however, is defined as a focused project to understand a specific problem of reality using the tools of systematic reasoning, then only a small number of people in colonial America can be defined as philosophers and there was a limited amount of philosophical activity—all of it derived from European precedents. Defined this way, philosophy is a technical field within the tradition of

Western education, distinct from but overlapping theology and natural science. This latter definition is the traditional definition of philosophy and the definition used in this article. The goal is not to be exclusive; rather, using this limited definition helps clarify the intellectual relationship of British colonials to their European intellectual tradition.

Significant participation in technical philosophy usually requires a particular environment. There needs to be access to great books and ideas. There need to be means of communication—regular meetings, institutions, and probably a printing press. There also needs to be a community of people who share an educational heritage where they learned the same vocabulary and techniques of inquiry. In the seventeenth century north of Mexico, only the Puritans of the Boston area offered such a situation. The Puritans' most intellectually technical debates were in theology and their most influential practical thinking was political; however, they were also much interested in logic and moral philosophy. In 1636 they founded Harvard College and nurtured it for the next hundred years by imitating the highest standards of English and Dutch universities along with the innovative dissenting academies of England. Printing presses were available in the Boston area throughout the century along with booksellers, private libraries, and a community of philosophically minded men and women.

PHILOSOPHY PRACTICED BY
THE PURITANS

Puritanism is not a philosophy. The term was created to describe the extremist tendencies of people who thought the Elizabethan Settlement, as an attempt to establish a middle course between Roman Catholicism and the ideas of Protestant reformers, fostered an impure, compromised Protestantism. Puritan leaders were often highly educated and believed strongly in rational religion. Puritanism was initially nurtured in the 1560s and 1570s at several colleges at Cambridge University in England. The founders of Harvard College were by and large Cambridge graduates who desired to re-create their alma mater in America—hence renaming the college town Cambridge. The curriculum included first one year, then two years of logic, much math and natural philosophy, metaphysics, and divinity. Master of arts degree requirements included the option of writing a synopsis of a logic system. Yearly commencements were also well-attended intellec-

tual fiestas where Latin speeches attempted to answer knotty philosophical questions such as:

- Is form derived from the power of matter?
- Does the will always follow the last dictate of the intellect?
- Is the spirit of man distinct from his soul?
- Is metaphysical infinity to be distinguished from mathematical infinity?

As much as Cambridge in America fostered a lively intellectual atmosphere, the Puritans tended to encourage students to follow the lead of accepted authors, usually fellow Puritans who manifested a dynamic mix of piety and intellect. The two most influential of these accepted authors were Alexander Richardson and William Ames. The philosophic influence of Richardson and Ames on Harvard's first fifty years would be hard to overestimate, especially their support for the logic system of the French philosopher Petrus Ramus. The Boston minister and Harvard president Increase Mather described "the profoundly learned and godly" Richardson as an intellectual Gideon with Ames as a later champion who "hath improved Richardson's method and Principles to great advantage" (in Fitch, p. 5).

The role of Richardson and Ames as model textbook authors was what made each so influential in America. Colonial American philosophy thrived because of textbooks. The problem, of course, with philosophy practiced upon a foundation of textbooks is that teachers and students rarely read the actual works of the people the books talked about. The names of Plato, Aristotle, and Descartes, and even Ramus, were tossed about by people who had only read textbook authors discussing these thinkers. Also, because textbooks (as a genre) are almost always simplifications rather than amplifications, complexities and intricate technical matters were often lost in the transition into textbook form.

Aside from mere student synopses, the first philosophy books written in America were John Eliot's *The Logick Primer* (1672) and Increase Mather's *Catechismus Logicus ex Petri Rami, Alexandri Richardsoni, et Guilielmi Amesii* (1675). Eliot's *The Logick Primer* was a highly reductionist missionary venture, written in English and Natick, to teach logic to local Indians. Mather's *Catechismus Logicus* reduced Ramist logic to a short catechism. The most influential textbooks written at Harvard were by William Brattle, who, after being hired as a tutor by Increase Mather in 1685, wrote two Cartesian logic textbooks that were long used at Harvard. Charles Morton's *A Logick System* embodied Renaissance Aristotelianism and was the most pedagogically creative of all the logic textbooks used at Harvard, but it was probably written in England before he came to America in 1686. All of these logic textbooks, except Eliot's, appeared only in student notebooks as manuscript transcriptions. Harvard's first formally published logic textbook was *Compendium Logicae* in 1735, a work misattributed to William Brattle.

The various types of logic taught by Puritans at Harvard followed Renaissance patterns of emphasis first on analysis of knowledge itself, then synthesizing axioms and demonstrations. Logic was not narrowly abstract, but rather was at the core of a well-lived Puritan life. In the Ramist system the student dug deep to discover the fundamental bits of what is known. These bits were called *arguments*. *Arguments* must then be assembled together into *axioms*, then into *syllogisms* and geometry-style *demonstrations*. Alexander Richardson's *The Logicians School-Master* proclaimed that

> to see a thing in the cause, that is, the argument . . . that is our *intelligentia*, to make axioms is our *scientia*, to discourse is our *sapientia* [wisdom], to apply everything in time and place is our *prudentia*, to work the like our Art [of logic], these are the things that make a man a scholler, a wise man, *ergo* a man that shall take this course in his studies shall be an exquisite man in every way. (p. 252)

Puritans were optimistic. They believed that the pursuer of truth would find it. Entwined with this, they believed that the pursuer of the good would be set on the right path. William Brattle wrote in 1686:

> Man's mind being obnoxious to much error both in its searches for truth, and pursuits after that which is good, two arts have been sought out; the one to aid the understanding, the other to direct the will; this being called Ethics; that Logick. ("The Prolegomenon," in Kennedy, p. 257)

Logic and ethics were the two great concerns of Puritan philosophy. Even though the tutor Brattle might have categorized them separately, they overlapped extensively. Ethics, or moral philosophy, encompassed the study of the soul and its faculties, especially the intellect and the will. Right reasoning and right living were rooted in a well-functioning soul. Charles Morton was Puritan New England's most systematic student of moral philosophy. The historian Norman Fiering calls him "America's first professional philosopher." Morton was born in Cornwall, England, educated at Cambridge and Oxford, and for many years operated a private academy out of his house on the south edge of London. During this time he wrote thoughtful and intertwined textbooks on logic, physics, ethics, and

CHARLES MORTON

This Dividing asunder of *Soul* and *Spirit;* Is it a Philosophical Distinction, of the Powers and Faculties, into *Superior* and *Inferiour* (as some would have it)? I pray to what purpose? Is it to shew the *Superior,* as clear, and untainted by the Fall; but that the *Inferiour* and Bruital, or sensual part is violated and corrupt, as some of the Heathen Philosophers have confusedly suggested? They say indeed that NOUS (the mind) is . . . a Sacred, and Divine Thing not inclined to any thing Disallowed by Right Reason; till it come to be Incarcerated in the Body; and then clog'd by a Dull Material Flesh, and yoked with a couple of other silly Souls (the *Sensitive* of Brutes, and the *Vegetative* of Plants). It became obstructed in all vertuous aspiring; and born down to Sensual and Inferiour *Acts* and *Objects.* Thus they Dreamt; and does the Scripture give any Countenance to such Fancies? I think not.

Source: *The Spirit of Man,* p. 16–17.

pneumatology. Writing multiple textbooks was normal for a dynamic educator in the seventeenth century; however, Morton, after immigrating in 1686, went further by publishing in Boston America's first purely philosophical work not designed as a textbook: *The Spirit of Man* (1692).

Before the great theologian Jonathan Edwards, Morton was America's best student of souls—the souls of animals, humans, and angels. Morton's *Pneumaticks* was written as a textbook-style overview of souls in general while *The Spirit of Man* was a monograph on various characteristics and temperaments (spirits) within the human soul. Although Morton offered much descriptive psychology, the goal of the book was to help readers "know thyself" and pursue habits and temperaments consistent with divine grace.

The existence of Harvard College, multiple locally written manuscript textbooks in logic, and the formal publication of Eliot's *The Logick Primer* and Morton's *The Spirit of Man* in seventeenth-century Massachusetts is extraordinary in the context of what can be expected from a provincial colony in its first century. New England's dominant claim on the intellectual history of the United States was staked early on by an amazingly vigorous people who honored rationality and the Western tradition of liberal arts education far beyond any other American colony.

Philosophy was always the handmaid of theology for the Puritans, but logic was to be applied in theology. This dynamic relationship kept Puritans from complacent dogmatism. Their emphasis on rational religion also encouraged the study of natural philosophy.

The most significant work in natural philosophy done by the Puritans was in alchemy and astronomy. George Starkey graduated from Harvard in 1646 and was part of an alchemical circle in New England. After immigrating to England in his twenties, he took the pen name Eireneaus Philalethes and became one of England's most influential alchemists. John Foster and Thomas Brattle were the most influential students of astronomy when their measurements of the Comet of 1680 were used by the English physicist and mathematician Sir Isaac Newton to support his work on universal gravitation.

In natural philosophy, as in logic, the Puritans of New England were very provincial, depending much on whatever books or ideas might accidentally come their way in a bookseller's box or might appear in one of the intellectual periodicals that made it to America. Although quoted in Newton's *Philosophiae Naturalis Principia Mathematica* of 1687, Thomas Brattle wrote in 1705 that he had still never seen a copy. In 1723 the Harvard library still did not own copy of the English philosopher John Locke's *Essay concerning Human Understanding* (1690). The library owned only the short, preview form contained within *The Young Students Library* (1692), a book that probably did not reach the colonies until the turn of the century. Cotton Mather's *The Christian Philosopher* (1721), mostly a collection of English descriptions of "the best discoveries in Nature," was written a quarter to a half century earlier.

Possibly the most innovative area of moral philosophy practiced by the Puritans was political. The creation of a republican system mixing church membership and voting, the many sermons and published treatises on civil polity, and the body of judicial arguments and decisions constituted a large mass of practical philosophy. Civil polity for the Puritans, however, was rarely discussed in terms of technical philosophy: one exception being the clergyman John Wise's *Vindication of Government of New England Churches* (1717) that argued from the foundation of the "natural" and "civil being of

man." Wise argued the cause of democracy and for the state's responsibility to protect each citizen's rights and happiness. In having risen above practical Puritan politics into political philosophy, however, Wise left behind what was most creative in Puritan politics and fell into simply importing British political philosophy to the colony.

Maybe Wise's tract should not be considered Puritan at all since it was published in New York at one of the new presses in America outside Puritan control and its publication date crosses over into the period of the American Enlightenment.

PHILOSOPHY PRACTICED IN THE ENLIGHTENMENT

The American Enlightenment began in the 1690s and was fully alive by the 1730s when philosophy began to be practiced outside of the bounds of Puritan New England, and when Philadelphia, Williamsburg, and New York established communities of imported books, indigenous printing, and philosophical training. Like the term "Puritanism," the term "Enlightenment" does not signify a school of philosophy. For the study of technical philosophy in colonial America the phrase "from Puritanism to the Enlightenment" must be understood as the cultural context that expanded from the Boston-area and Puritan-supported works of the seventeenth century to more economically and religiously diverse urban-oriented pockets throughout the colonies in the eighteenth century. This transition is best seen in the wild expansion of small religious colleges in the eighteenth century. Harvard was founded in 1636, but at the turn of the century two new colleges in Connecticut and Williamsburg, Virginia, were founded. By the American Revolution there were nine colonial colleges, one in the South, four in the middle colonies, and four in New England. Philosophy, no longer practiced only by the Puritans, was being practiced widely in the colonies by diverse communities.

In general "the Enlightenment" is a dangerous term. So many definitions and characteristics have been attached to the term that it has almost become meaningless. Careful scholars usually speak of types and regions of enlightenments rather than "the Enlightenment." In American history, the term is useful as an umbrella over the general intellectual culture of British America from the 1690s through the Age of Adams, Jefferson, and Madison. Optimism was a key feature of this enlightenment—optimism about the powers of the human mind and the place of modern thought in relation to that which had come before it. "In the beginning," John Locke wrote, "all the world was America." Colonial Americans during the Enlightenment seemed to have taken for granted the English philosopher Francis Bacon's argument that ancient thinkers were the young while modern thinkers were the mature.

Americans in every colony and eventually in the Revolution embraced the chance of creating innovative governments. Long before the political philosopher Thomas Paine declared that Americans have it in their power to create the world anew, cities on a hill were being created throughout America. John Locke, himself, apparently played a major role in writing the Fundamental Constitutions of Carolina, and Anglican clergy such as Thomas Bray joined with soldier-politicians such as Francis Nicholson and James Oglethorpe to transform Virginia, Maryland, and Georgia into innovative, rationally constructed, colonies.

Granting the increasing ethnic and social diversity of eighteenth-century America, it is remarkable to find that the college curricula, philosophical activity, and general intellectual life of those interested in an intellectual life in the northern, southern, and middle colonies were amazingly unified. The books read, the ideas most popular, and even terms and phrases used appear to have been standardized throughout the colonies. When the Second Continental Congress gathered to edit Thomas Jefferson's draft of the Declaration of Independence there was no discussion of the preamble's assumptions and language about natural law, nature's God, and the unalienable rights of man. Upon later reflection, John Adams noted that Thomas Jefferson was simply saying what everyone in the room already believed. Such unanimity of thought was the result of an American Enlightenment. The fact that the Second Continental Congress cited no biblical authorities in support of its action is also a measure of the difference between seventeenth-century Puritanism and the eighteenth-century colonial Enlightenment.

The American Enlightenment expanded beyond seventeenth-century Puritanism the range of accepted authorities and the allowable boundaries of philosophical discussion. The culture remained generally Christian, but Christianity no longer dominated the intellectual culture in the way it had for Puritans. Divine revelation came to be treated in widely diverse ways and sometimes even denied. The laws of Carolina made merely the cursory demand that every property owner must "acknowledge a God." The American Philosophical Society,

following the lead of the Royal Society of London, had a rule disallowing religion as a topic of discussion. Jonathan Edwards and America's most famous thinker, Benjamin Franklin, could both believe deeply in the sovereignty and goodness of God, one working within the constraints of orthodox Christianity and the other freely unconcerned with orthodoxy.

Logic, moral philosophy, and divinity remained at the core of every college curriculum, but it is characteristic of the American Enlightenment that there was an increasing emphasis on natural philosophy. John Locke and Sir Isaac Newton were the names every student had to be able to discuss, but textbook reductions of major European systems of thought were still the dominant means of spreading the new learning.

The most popular logic textbook of the age was the hymn writer Isaac Watts's *Logic; or, The Right Use of Reason* (1724) which praised and simplified Locke's *Essay concerning Human Understanding* (1690). Watts's textbook emphasized the orthodox Christian aspects of Locke: it assumed the existence of God, clarified the highest certainty of divine revelation in Holy Scripture, and advocated procedures of analysis and synthesis not much different from Brattle's *Compendium of Logick*. It is hard to judge, but the logic and other philosophical works of Isaac Watts may have been the most widely read philosophy books of the century. A popular story of the American Revolution said that when the British were attacking Princeton, an American commander declared that if the ammunition ran out, soldiers would stuff the cannons with Watts's books and continue firing.

Another source for much of the American philosophy taught in colonial colleges was the Scottish universities that were in the midst of a golden age that produced the philosophers Francis Hutcheson, Thomas Reid, David Hume, and Adam Smith. The term "common sense" that Thomas Paine used to spur the American Revolution was the theme of the Scottish philosophers. Scottish common sense philosophy decreed the ability of all people to immediately grasp important aspects of reality. Politically, the philosophy tended to support democratic individualism. Religiously, it focused on individual experience and intuition. In logic and ethics it supported the ability of people to reason and live rightly if they followed their *common sense*. Thomas Jefferson was greatly influenced philosophically at the College of William and Mary by the Scottish professor William Small, and the Scot John Witherspoon, who, as the president of the College of New

BENJAMIN FRANKLIN

I had form'd most of my ingenious Acquaintances into a Club, for mutual Improvement, which we call'd the Junto. We met on Friday Evenings. The Rules I drew up, requir'd that every Member in his Turn should produce one or more Queries on any Point of Morals, Politics, or Natural Philosophy, to be discuss'd by the Company, and once in three Months produce and read an Essay of his own Writing on any Subject he pleased. Our Debates were to be under the Direction of a President, and to be conducted in the sincere Spirit of Enquiry after Truth, without fondness for Dispute, or Desire of Victory; and to prevent Warmth, all Expressions of Positiveness in Opinion, and of direct Contradiction, were after some time made contraband & prohibited under small pecuniary Penalties.

Source: *Writings*, p. 1361.

Jersey (now Princeton University), was a powerful philosophical influence in the middle colonies.

Witherspoon came to America in 1768, and his posthumously published *Lectures on Moral Philosophy and Eloquence* (1800) were gathered from the course on moral philosophy he taught every year to the seniors. For Witherspoon, ethics did not need to be derived from divine revelation but could instead be constructed out of simple observation with a bit of common sense. In his classes sat many of the leaders of the American Revolution, especially James Madison, and his greatest influence may have been to shield his students from the deeply abstract and religious influence of his predecessor Jonathan Edwards, encouraging instead a simpler, more straightforward pursuit of virtue.

In general, the American Enlightenment was led by conscientious teachers such as Witherspoon. Teaching duties encouraged people to think systematically, integrating epistemology, logic, natural philosophy, mathematics, metaphysics, divinity, and ethics. Genteel dilettantes might spend short spurts of time on particular topics, especially observational natural science, but systematic philosophic inquiry and publication were largely in the hands of teachers.

Samuel Johnson, a Puritan convert to Anglicanism, a tutor at Yale, a minister, and the eventual president of King's College in New York (now Columbia University), exemplified the connection between America's most systematic philosophical work and its educational institutions. As an eighteen-year-old grammar school tutor in Connecticut, he compiled a Ramist logic. Diligent study out of a box of books that had been sent over for what would eventually become Yale College caused the young tutor to repudiate Ramus for Locke and the "New Learning." In 1729 he was drawn to the immaterialism of the Irish philosopher George Berkeley who happened to settle in Rhode Island for two years. Berkeley argued that, since the primary distinction of the cosmos was between the perceived and the perceiver, humankind should think of reality as mental rather than physical. For Berkeley, this recognition allowed him to merge the essentials of Christianity, Locke, and Newton into a rational synthesis.

Johnson appreciated this synthesis and was in close contact with Berkeley for two years. When Berkeley returned to Britain in 1731 he left a legacy of nearly 900 books to the Yale library and a deep impression on Johnson. In 1746 Johnson published an elementary textbook on ethics, then in 1752 his *Elementa Philosophica,* which included systematic discussions of epistemology, logic, and ethics. The *Elementa Philosophica* was dedicated to Berkeley and designed to serve young students in colonial colleges. Like the work of Charles Morton, Johnson's *Elementa Philosophica* exemplified the creative efforts of a diligent and open-minded provincial teacher. As with Morton, and again with Edwards, the reward for a life of diligent philosophy was the offer of a college presidency.

Although America's colonial colleges were the focal points for integrated and serious thinking about philosophy during the American Enlightenment, colonial America's two most significant philosophers, the only two to have transatlantic influence, were not teachers and would not call themselves philosophers. Benjamin Franklin always referred to himself as a printer, and Jonathan Edwards was a minister.

Benjamin Franklin, like most colonial Americans, was highly interested in natural philosophy and ethics—and the role of a sovereign God in each. Not formally educated, Franklin liked to participate in self-help philosophic groups such as the Junto and the American Philosophical Society. His brilliance on the subject of electricity and light-hearted writing often clouds recognition of his years of disciplined study and intimate correspondence and conversation with men more recognized for deeper thinking.

Born among the Puritans of Boston, at age sixteen Franklin's first published writings spoofed Cotton Mather's *Essays to Do Good*. At nineteen, a runaway in London, he published *A Dissertation on Liberty and Necessity, Pleasure and Pain* (1725), which exposed his high philosophical aspirations. But Franklin realized he could never play the role of gentleman-philosopher. He would always be socially constricted by his tradesman status. For the rest of his life, even after attaining wealth and fame, Franklin brilliantly lived a role as a homespun, American philosopher. His best work was in grasping the mathematical principles of what would become social science and supplying a foundation for personal and social ethics based on usefulness. Never again attempting anything close to a systematic or serious book on ethics, he encouraged an image of himself as embodying a particular American and enlightened ethic. In popular literature—often bawdy or humorous—he presented his moral philosophy in a way more influential than most of his contemporaries.

Jonathan Edwards was a Puritan minister who responded to the practical religious matters of his day with books so deep, disciplined, and richly integrated that they gained a transatlantic following and continue to be studied for more than mere historical interest. The existence of Edwards in colonial America should not be used as evidence that colonial America was maturing intellectually. Edwards was an anomaly. He was a provincial thinker reliant on whatever books made their way to the colonies, while at the same time he so far outdid every other colonial philosopher in his work that he cannot be considered representative.

Edwards's most significant philosophical interest was in moral philosophy, especially psychology. His books *A Treatise concerning Religious Affections* and *Freedom of the Will*, essay "The Nature of True Virtue," and the unfinished collection "Notes on the Mind" stand as major creative works rooted in an Augustinian-Calvinistic tradition yet fully engaged in the dynamic philosophical dialogue of the early British and French enlightenments.

Fundamental to Edwards's philosophy was a radical view of God's transcendence and sovereignty. Similar to Berkeley, Edwards believed that the existence of the world was in the mind of God, that all that was perceived—matter, gravity, friction, etc.—was nothing but God's activity. According to Edwards, the ideas of God so constituted reality that the Trinity had to exist: the Son is the

JONATHAN EDWARDS

When we spake of Excellence in Bodies, we were obliged to borrow the word, *Consent,* from Spiritual things; but Excellence in and among Spirits is in its prime and proper sense, Being's consent to Being. There is no other proper consent by that of *Minds,* even of the Will; which, when it is of Minds toward Minds, it is *Love,* and when of Minds towards things, it is Choice. Wherefore all the Primary and Original beauty or excellence, that is among Minds, is Love; and into this may all be resolved that is found among them.

Source: *Notes on the Mind,* quoted in Faust and Johnson, eds., *Selections from Jonathan Edwards,* p. 35.

perfect idea God has of himself, and the love of God for the image he has begotten is so real that it is the Holy Spirit. Excellency, along with the highest beauty and virtue, could only occur in concert with God. People were morally free in that they could follow their wills, but deep within the soul God's grace had predisposed the will to choose at is did.

The works of Franklin and Edwards show the highest possibilities for philosophy on the intellectual frontier of the British Empire. The teachers, students, and textbooks of the colleges, first in Massachusetts then throughout the colonies, were the lifeblood of philosophy in the colonies. Logic and moral philosophy were the principal focus of pure philosophical inquiry with theology and natural philosophy usually intricately entwined.

Colonial political philosophy was of increasing importance; however, it was curiously unphilosophical. Colonial politicians, especially those who would support the American Revolution, seemed to have unreflectively adopted a jumble of assumptions about God, natural rights, personal autonomy, political corruption, and civic virtue developed by opposition politicians in England over the course of the seventeenth and eighteenth centuries. This jumble of assumptions has been called by scholars "republicanism," "radical Whig ideology," and other names; however, such names should not be taken to imply a philosophical consistency or systematic organization. The delegates who signed the Declaration of Independence shared vague terms and assumptions, but their work was not the result of intentional inquiry into political philosophy. The aftermath of the Revolution itself would encourage creative and systematic political philosophy; however, colonial American political philosophy never got beyond the relatively superficial way John Wise imported English ideas.

To define philosophy in the way this article does should not diminish the thousands of deeply thoughtful people in colonial America; however, with this definition students of the era grasp better the meaning of *colonial* America: a place to which the Course of Empire was making its way westward in the seventeenth and eighteenth centuries.

See also **Constitutional Thought** *(volume 2);* **The Humanities; The Role of the Intellectual** *(volume 3).*

BIBLIOGRAPHY

Primary Sources

Bradstreet, Anne. *The Works of Anne Bradstreet.* Edited by John Harvard Ellis. Gloucester, Mass., 1962.

Edwards, Jonathan. *The Works of Jonathan Edwards.* 13 vols. New Haven, Conn., 1957–1994.

Faust, Clarence H., and Thomas H. Johnson, eds. *Selections from Jonathan Edwards.* New York, 1935.

Fitch, James. *The First Principles of the Doctrine of Christ.* Boston, 1679.

Franklin, Benjamin. *Writings.* New York, 1987.

Johnson, Samuel. *The Philosopher,* vol. 2. *Samuel Johnson: His Career and Writings.* Edited by Herbert and Carl Scheider. New York, 1929.

Kennedy, Rick, ed. *Aristotelian and Cartesian Logic at Harvard: Charles Morton's "A Logick System" and William Brattle's "Compendium of Logick." Publications of the Colonial Society of Massachusetts* 67 (1995).

Kennedy, Rick, and Thomas Knowles. "Increase Mather's 'Catechismus Logicus': A Translation and Analysis of the Role of a Late Ramist Catechism in Harvard's Curriculum." *Proceedings of the American Antiquarian Society* 109 (1999).

Mather, Cotton. *The Christian Philosopher.* Edited by Winton U. Solberg. Urbana, Ill., 1994.

Morton, Charles. *The Spirit of Man.* Boston, 1692.

Richardson, Alexander. *The Logicians School-Master.* London, 1657.

Secondary Sources

Anderson, Douglas. *The Radical Enlightenments of Benjamin Franklin.* Baltimore, 1997.

Bridenbaugh, Carl, and Jessica Bridenbaugh. *Rebels and Gentlemen: Philadelphia in the Age of Franklin.* New York, 1965.

Butterfield, L. H. *John Witherspoon Comes to America.* Princeton, N.J., 1953.

Daniel, Stephen H. *The Philosophy of Jonathan Edwards: A Study in Divine Semiotics.* Bloomington, Ind., 1994.

Ellis, Joseph J. *The New England Mind in Transition: Samuel Johnson of Connecticut, 1696–1772.* New Haven, Conn., 1973.

Fiering, Norman. *Jonathan Edwards' Moral Thought in Its British Context.* Chapel Hill, N.C, 1981.

————. *Moral Philosophy at Seventeenth-Century Harvard.* Chapel Hill, N.C., 1981.

————. "The Transatlantic Republic of Letters: A Note on the Circulation of Learned Periodicals to Early Eighteenth-Century America." *William and Mary Quarterly* 33, no. 4 (1976): 642–660.

Flower, Elizabeth, and Murray G. Murphey. *A History of Philosophy in America.* 2 vols. New York, 1977.

Gaustad, Edwin S. *George Berkeley in America.* New Haven, Conn., 1979.

Howell, Wilbur S. *Eighteenth-Century British Logic and Rhetoric.* Princeton, N.J., 1971.

————. *Logic and Rhetoric in England, 1500–1700.* Princeton, N. J., 1956.

May, Henry. *The Enlightenment in America.* New York, 1976.

Miller, Perry. *The New England Mind: The Seventeenth Century.* Cambridge, Mass., 1939.

Morison, Samuel Eliot. *Harvard in the Seventeenth Century.* 2 vols. Cambridge, Mass., 1936.

Morris, William Sparkes. *The Young Jonathan Edwards: A Reconstruction.* Brooklyn, N.Y., 1991.

Sher, Richard, and Jeffrey R. Smitten, eds. *Scotland and America in the Age of Enlightenment.* Edinburgh, 1990.

Shuffelton, Frank, ed. *The American Enlightenment.* Rochester, N.Y., 1993.

POPULAR BELIEF AND EXPRESSION

Douglas L. Winiarski

D r. Alexander Hamilton loathed the company of men like Dutch colonist Marcus Van Bummill. Unschooled in the refined art of genteel conversation, such vulgar people made bad traveling companions, as the Annapolis, Maryland, doctor quickly learned during a brief voyage up the Hudson River in 1744. The Dutchman was a contradiction in terms. Van Bummill lectured both passengers and crew on the finer points of the Tower of Babel and other biblical tales, though he was prone to swearing and often drunk; he arrogantly dismissed Hamilton's medical practice as fraudulent, yet naively inquired after the meaning of the English word superstition.

Unfortunately for Hamilton, people like Marcus Van Bummill were legion in colonial North America. During his summer tour through the northern colonies, the doctor was beset by village pundits who reveled in the opportunity to share their local knowledge with an illustrious southern gentleman. From Maryland to Maine, Hamilton recorded conversations with a staggering number of men and women of varying races, ethnicities, social classes, religious persuasions, and educational backgrounds. Along with the bombastic Van Bummill, Hamilton encountered a drunken taverner with "bubbies like a woman," a humpbacked barber, a group of singing Quakers, foul-smelling Mohawks, the humorously named "Captain Scrotum," an effeminate falsetto singer, promenading buxom belles, a gentleman addicted to swearing by the devil's name, and a frightened woman who had recently dreamed of her own death. He dined with an impoverished family who hungrily consumed their plain fare without knives, forks, spoons, plates, or napkins, listened to lewd tales of sexual conquest narrated by a ferry operator, and witnessed the "antick tricks" of an elderly Long Island man who vaulted his body six inches off the ground using only the muscles in his buttocks. And everywhere Hamilton traveled, people were conversing about matters of the spirit: from the intricacies of Calvinist theology to the vi-

sions of New Light itinerants, from ethics and metaphysics to judicial astrology, haunted houses, and the devil.

Hamilton was ill at ease in the strange world he discovered beyond the polite society of his native Annapolis. Religion, supernatural wonders and the occult, medicine and healing, dreams and visions— these were the issues that dominated colonial popular culture. Indeed, by 1800, few Americans had embarked down the enlightened road to modernity. After all, anything was possible in a land where ordinary people like Marcus Van Bummill literally did not understand the meaning of the word superstition.

WONDERS

North America was often a dangerous and fearful place for migrating Europeans, though, in many ways, it was quite similar to the world they had left behind. Disease menaced the health of families; pestilence and drought plagued agricultural production; warfare with Indian and imperial adversaries disrupted commerce and destabilized village life. For most settlers, life was a cycle of unremitting toil, as families struggled to wrest their subsistence needs from an unfamiliar and often hostile environment.

Immigrants attempting to rationalize their New World experiences relied upon the "lore of wonders": an ancient stock of folk wisdom that explained how the world worked and how to survive in it. North American colonials, like their European counterparts, ascribed supernatural agency to comets and earthquakes, ghosts and witches, God and Satan. These invisible powers governed events in the visible world. The lore of wonders thus provided psychic consolation for Europeans living in a strange new land. Tales of the supernatural rendered seemingly random events comprehensible and familiar.

New England Puritans, in particular, chronicled countless wonders in their diaries and journals.

◦◦◦

THE PHANTOM SHIP OF LYNN, MASSACHUSETTS, 1682

Harvard tutor Noahdiah Russell's journal is typical of Puritan religious diaries. Murders, accidents, suicides, and sudden deaths; storms and astronomical anomalies; visions and diabolic possessions all find a place in the diary, as Russell attempted to gauge the providential meaning of the portentous events occurring in late-seventeenth-century New England. Perhaps the most intriguing wonder described in the diary is the appearance of a phantom ship in the skies over the town of Lynn, Massachusetts, in 1682.

It being Sabbath day [1 March, 1682], the morning very cold. At noon very warm. At night between 4 & 5 of the clock there was a thunder shower which came from the south West wherein was a great Storm of hail. The hail stones were nearly the bigness of a bullet; they broke several squares of glass at College, for they came with a strong wind. They broke glass at Roxbury and at Lyn it shattered many windows; moreover at Lyn after sun down as it began to be darkish an honest old man Mr. Handford went out to look for a new moon thinking the moon had changed when in the west he espied a strange black cloud in which after some space he saw a man in arms complete standing with his legs straddling and having a pike in his hands which he held across his breast, which sight the man with his wife saw and many others; after a while the man vanished in whose room appeared a spacious ship seeming under sail though she kept the same station. They saw it they said as apparently as ever they saw a ship in the Harbor which was to their imagination the handsomest of every they saw, with a lofty stem, the head to the south, the hull black the sails bright; a long and resplendent streamer came from the top of the mast. This was seen for a great space both by these and other of the same town. After this they went in where tarrying but a while and looking out again all was gone and the sky as clear as ever.

This news was sent in a letter to Mrs. Margaret Mitchell of Cambridge dated 3d 2d 1682 [3 April, 1682] from Mr. Jeremiah Shephard Minister at Lynn.

Source: S. V. Talcott, ed. "Copy of the Diary of Noahdiah Russell, Tutor at Harvard College, Beginning Anno Dom. 1682." *New England Historical Genealogical Register* 7 (1853), pp. 53–54; spelling and punctuation have been modernized.

Massachusetts residents claimed to have spied a spacious ship appearing in the heavens; a Connecticut man received credible intelligence that blood rained from the sky; and a Boston mason noted with curiosity the slaying of a two-headed snake. Others described acts of witchcraft, demonic possession, and monstrous births. Godly Puritans typically interpreted these unnatural events as tokens of divine displeasure signaling impending doom for the unregenerate. Seizing upon the providential significance of wars, epidemics, storms, and earthquakes, clergymen demanded corporate repentance for the collective sins of their congregations; numerous religious revivals followed the frowns of providence,

attesting to the pervasive influence of wonders in Puritan popular culture.

But New Englanders were not unique in their preoccupation with omens and prodigies. Credulous New Jersey magistrates believed that the guilt of a murderer could be adduced by forcing the accused to touch the victim's corpse; two decades later, in 1717, residents in a neighboring county claimed to have witnessed rain falling beneath two magical white oak trees on a cloudless day. Merchant seamen working in port towns throughout the colonies were attuned to omens of all kinds. The appearance of certain sea creatures signaled changes in the weather, while comets, shooting stars, and the haunting lights of St. Elmo's Fire carried warnings of impending misfortune.

The European lore of wonders, in turn, squared with the supernatural wisdom of Native Americans and African slaves. The Algonquian-speaking peoples of the eastern woodlands, for example, spoke of giants that roamed the earth, great serpents that lived beneath rivers, and mythic ancestors who taught villagers how to grow corn. Slaves believed that the specters of the dead haunted villages and they often ascribed personal misfortune to the actions of neighborhood conjurors and witches. In such an enchanted universe, pleasing the spirits was the key to prosperity. Indians offered frequent tobacco sacrifices to the *manitou* spirits that animated natural landforms; Africans constructed their dwellings in alignment with the powers of the four cardinal directions; and both groups buried their dead with utilitarian objects in order to ensure safe passage to the spirit realm of the ancestors.

POPULAR RELIGION

Along with their livestock, plows, weeds, diseases, and stock of wonder tales, European settlers arrived at their colonial outposts equipped with religious institutions which they quickly transplanted to their fledgling villages. They attempted to carve meaning out of the chaos of their new environment by sacralizing both time and space. Churches of various denominations proliferated, dotting the landscape with steeples and spires; pious settlers attempted to "redeem the time" by participating in various religious rituals both in churches and in their homes.

From baptism to extreme unction, the seven Roman Catholic sacraments marked major transitional periods in the lives of the faithful living near French and Spanish papal strongholds. In addition to these rites of passage, weekly masses, saints' day feasts, and processions structured the year, providing opportunities for celebration, mourning, and pious reflection on the blessings and afflictions of everyday life. In the widely dispersed settlements of the southern colonies, moreover, Anglican worship services, court days, and militia musters brought together all ranks of society. The civil and religious rituals enacted during these gatherings reinforced values of social order and deference to gentry elites. Scottish communion rituals and Methodist "love feasts," by contrast, tended to dissolve social distinctions between rich and poor, master and slave, as hearts "melted" together in communal worship.

In New England, similar devotional ordinances shaped popular consciousness, despite the reformers' zealous attempts to purge their Bible commonwealth of Catholic and Anglican ceremonialism. Families attended "meeting" twice each Sabbath; over the course of an average lifetime, Puritan churchgoers listened to an average of seven thousand sermons. Stimulated by wondrous events such as wars, epidemics, and natural disasters, periodic days of public fasting and thanksgiving provided opportunities for congregations to renew their covenanted obligations to God. Between meetings, pious New Englanders engaged in a variety of private devotional disciplines, including secret prayer, meditation, and spiritual journal writing. Together, these rituals helped the godly chart the course of their spiritual pilgrimage toward salvation.

Families unable to attend church frequently conducted religious exercises in their own homes by reading godly literature. One New Hampshire man read his Bible from Genesis to Revelation twelve times between 1677 and 1715. Others owned popular devotional tracts such as John Bunyan's *Pilgrim's Progress* or Lewis Bayly's *The Practice of Piety,* purchased cheaply printed English chapbooks and broadsides that contained scores of wonder tales, or studied the works of natural philosophers. Meanings gleaned from private reading, in turn, effected patterns of thought and speech. People learned to express themselves through the language of religion in their diaries, court testimonies, and public relations of faith; biblical passages darted into the minds of laymen and women as they worked on their farms or socialized together in homes and taverns, shaping their understanding of themselves, their society, and their world.

WITCHCRAFT, CUNNING FOLK, AND THE DEVIL

Few wonders stimulated as much controversy as witchcraft. Fueled by personal misfortune, gender ideologies, and neighborhood feuds, witch-hunting campaigns flared in villages from New France to the Spanish borderlands throughout the seventeenth and early eighteenth centuries. Allegations typically involved *maleficium,* or occult harm. Disgruntled settlers blamed local witches for the illnesses of their livestock, for the deaths of their children, or for common household misfortunes such as soured milk. Witchcraft was also a gendered crime. Barren wives, postmenopausal mothers, independent single women, midwives, and young girls suspected of

99

sexual deviance were particularly susceptible to accusation. Suspected witches, in turn, were subjected to a host of humiliating examinations including river duckings and bodily inspections for the witches' teat.

Scattered evidence suggests that a few colonials actually practiced the black arts on their unwitting neighbors. Gaelic-speaking Goodwife Glover confessed that she ensorcelled the children of Boston resident John Goodwin by stroking rag dolls—poppets—with her spittle-moistened fingers. Similar figurines were discovered in a Long Island, New York, dwelling and in the house of executed Salem, Massachusetts, witch Bridget Bishop. Appearing before the Holy Office of the Inquisition in Mexico City, numerous Spanish women claimed to have laced their cooking with bits of pubic hair, blood, and drams of bathwater in order to restrain their abusive and philandering husbands. Indians and African slaves, too, frequently attempted to dispatch their masters and enemies with spells and potions.

To protect themselves from occult assault, many people engaged in countermagic. Cakes baked from flour and urine unmasked the identity of afflicting witches; horseshoes hung over the door, pins driven into the floor, and witch bottles buried beneath the hearth protected houses from the intrusion of supernatural agents. In the Carolina backcountry, moreover, spiritual vigilantes known as witchmasters peddled their countermagical services to families afflicted by neighborhood sorcerers. One such adept, a Revolutionary War veteran named Joshua Gordon, composed a book of spells designed to undo the damage caused by attack magic such as the "evil eye."

The majority of magic practitioners in the colonial New World were cunning folk who plied traditional European occult trades: fortune-telling, palmistry, divination, sleight-of-hand, and astrology. Although wise people were often subjected to witchcraft investigations, men and women from all ranks of society eagerly solicited their unique talents. Tidewater planter William Byrd II, for example, consulted a Williamsburg witch before embarking on a sea voyage; a Massachusetts cunning woman fashioned protective charms for several soldiers preparing to invade the French fortress at Louisbourg; still others turned sieves and gazed into egg yolks hoping to catch a glimpse of future events. Astrology, in particular, drew considerable attention from both leading intellectuals, who packed the shelves of their libraries with arcane alchemical and astrological tracts, and middling families, who carefully recorded the planetary sign under which each child was born. In addition, many pious Christians practiced bibliomancy, a divination technique in which one's future was predicted by opening the Bible randomly. Still others consulted with Native and African American conjurers in order to locate lost or stolen possessions.

Satan maintained a physical presence in the New World throughout the colonial era. Ministers and lay people believed that he could possess the bodies of discontented servants or godly enthusiasts. Typically, Satan appeared reeking of brimstone and gnashing his teeth; in some cases, he assumed the form of social outsiders—Africans and Indians. Puritan goodwives described fantasies in which the devil offered to alleviate their endless toil, provide them with sumptuous clothing, or restore their dead children to life. He urged the dying to forsake God and tempted the melancholy to take their own lives. In the Spanish borderlands, moreover, women removed their rosaries and prayed to Satan for power over their sexual rivals, while male laborers believed that tattoos bearing the devil's image enhanced physical strength and sexual virility.

HEALING

By European standards, the New World was a relatively healthy place. North American settlers nonetheless faced a continuous barrage of health-related misfortunes ranging from broken bones, hernias, and toothaches to malaria, tuberculosis, and dysentery. The mere rumor of a smallpox outbreak sent urbanites fleeing into the countryside; childhood diseases such as diphtheria claimed countless young lives each year. Newspapers and broadsides throughout the colonies reported remarkable sudden deaths—women carried away in childbirth, healthy men struck down in their prime by an apoplectic fit—while diarists filled their journals with daily accounts of bodily pain and reports of sick neighbors or family members.

Responding to the endless round of agues, fevers, and fluxes, wealthy families typically consulted male doctors, who proscribed a battery of gruesome remedies designed to restore balance to the body's four humors. Others relied upon home remedies drawn from the accumulated herbal lore of female healers. Numerous men and women kept journals filled with medicinal recipes passed down through the generations; or they consulted published pharmacological handbooks, often marking successful cures in the margins.

THE DEVIL IN PHILADELPHIA, PENNSYLVANIA: 1716

The devil's name was not to be invoked casually in early modern Europe or North America, as a Philadelphia housewife learned following a heated exchange with her husband in 1716. Her unique story, recounted in the diary of Lutheran pastor Andreas Sandel, attests to the corporeal presence of Satan in the everyday lives of ordinary men and women.

1716, January 12—A dreadful thing happened in Philadelphia to the wife of a butcher, who had quarreled with her husband. He asked her to make their bed, but she refused. Continuing to refuse, he told her he would turn her out of the house, but she told him if he did so, she would break every window pane, and invoked the devil to come for her if she did not do it. The husband led her out of the house, she became highly excited, broke some of the panes, and through the kitchen made her way up to the attic, with a candle, and laid down on the bed greatly disturbed on account of her promise. Then she heard somebody coming up the stairs, but saw no one—this was repeated for half an hour. Becoming more and more agitated, fearing her awful invocation was about to be realized, she went down to her husband, telling him of her anguish and asking him to aid her. Laying down on a bench near the hearth, she perceived a dark human face, making horrid grimaces with mouth wide open and the teeth gnashing. Then she became thoroughly terrified, and asked her husband to read to her Psalms XXI, which he did, and the face disappeared. Soon afterwards she perceived at the window, one of which she had broken panes, that someone was standing there with both arms extended through the window, by which her fright was made greater. Then the figure approached and passed her, but she could not see where it disappeared. Her husband then clasped his arms around her, when the fumes of brimstone became so strong they could not remain in doors, and these fumes were apparent to all who came in later. At one o'clock she sent for the minister, who also came and prayed with her the next day. Many persons visited her, but she had to fold her hands over her knees to keep from trembling. A few days later the same woman related the story to me and two other clergymen, Mr. Ross and Smith, this story.

Source: "Extracts from the Journal of the Rev. Andreas Sandel, Pastor of 'Gloria Dei' Swedish Lutheran Church, Philadelphia, 1702–1719." *Pennsylvania Magazine of History and Biography* 30 (1906), p. 450.

Pious families turned to prayer and devotional routines for relief. For the godly, disease and misfortune constituted afflictions, signs of providential displeasure requiring personal or collective repentance. German pastors laboring among exiled Salzburgers in Georgia, for example, recorded hundreds of encounters with parishioners who ascribed their illnesses to human sin and pleaded for spiritual intervention. The weekly prayer bids submitted to Connecticut clergyman Jonathan Edwards by the members of his congregation, moreover, frequently included prayers for afflicted family members. Parents sought access to the ordinance of baptism in the hope of safeguarding both the temporal and eternal welfare of their children; women heightened their devotional routines in the weeks surrounding dangerous periods of childbirth travail; and individuals recovering from grave illness or injury fulfilled their duty to God by joining churches as full members. Protestant devotional behavior, in turn, paralleled Roman Catholic practices in which laymen and women sponsored feasts and masses to

LIFE AND DEATH IN CHARLESTON, SOUTH CAROLINA, 1769–1770

The terse, line-a-day diary of Charleston, South Carolina, gentlewoman Ann Ashby Manigault reveals the centrality of health concerns in the lives of colonial women. In Manigault's diary, family illnesses, neighborhood mortalities, doctor's housecalls, and childbirth reports overshadow prominent community events, such as a visit from the famous itinerant preacher George Whitefield.

Oct. 5 [1769]. My Grandson G. [Gabriel] not well. Took Hippo [ipecac, a purgative]. 6. He continues not well. Took Rhubarb. 7. Better. 8. Not so well. 9. Took physick again. 11. Still not well. 8. Mrs. Burn l[ay in]. 9. Mrs. Gordon l[ay in]. 23. Mrs. Colcock l[ay in]. 24. Mrs. T. L. Smith l[ay in]. 26. Went to Dr. Milligans's who had been very sick.

Nov. 4. Mr. Nightingale died. 6. Mrs. Wragg very ill. 18. Charlotte l. 26. Mrs. William Drayton l. 27. Went to see Mrs. Wragg. 28. Lady Mary, Mrs. Brewton, and Mr. Beresford's family came in. 29. Miss Moncriefe married. 30. Mr. [George] Whitefield came in.

Dec. 4. I went to hear him preach. 12. Went to my sons to enquire about Mrs. Wragg. Mrs. William Wragg had a son. 16. Mrs. Wragg died. Buried the 20th. 19. My Grandson G. has had a Flux for a week past. 21. My daughter came to see him. 22. He is a little better. 26. Took a purge of roses. 27. A little better. 28th. I rode out with him and carried him to see his mother. Jan. 1. Very much indisposed. 5th. Worse 7th. Better. 9th. Rode out with him. Dec. 24. I had a little Gout. 29. Parson Smith and his wife arrived.

1770. Jan. 5. Old Mrs. Austen died. 10. I was taken with the Gout at night. 11. No better. 11. M. T. Gadsen came in. 16. Mrs. Downes l. 18. Waldron's boat lost and 2 men drowned. 22. Mrs. Nowell l. 30. My grandson G. not well. 31. My leg broke out. Feb. 14. Not better. 18. No better. 20. A little better. 28. Sent for Dr. Moultrie. Mar. 9. Still the same.

Feb. 4. Mrs. John Harleston l. 8. Mrs. Roger Pinckney l.

Mar. 24. My son broke his Thumb. 25. Doctors, Mr. Eusebuis and Mrs. Gervais at dinner. 30. To Mr. Pike's Ball. 31. Mary lay in.

April 9. To Mrs. Arthur Middleton's. 20. Mrs. Bacot l. 26. Miss Nancy Sinclair married. 30. My Son and Daughter went to Goose-creek. I brought my Grandson J. home sick. He was better the 2d. May.

May 5. Mrs. Ben: Huger l. Mr. M[anigault]. was taken very ill with his old disorder, and was obliged to have Dr. Moultrie. 6th. A little better. 7th. Better but not well. 13. Better. 12th May. My Sons house was raised. 16. Heard of Mr. Doyley's death. 17. My Son and Daughter and Betsey H. came down. 18. Betsy H. not well. 23. Mrs. Laurens died. 29. Dillon's House on fire. My Grandson had a fever. Mr. M. to Silkhope by water. Returned 1st. June. 31. Mrs. Harleston went off.

June 2. My son took my two Grandsons to Goose creek. Mrs. Ben. Smith went off. 6. Peter Timothy died. 7. A great Storm at night. 8. Mrs. Branford's son died. 16. Very hot weather. 18. Mrs. Motte died. 19. A good many children die of the Hooping-cough. 23. Very hot weather. 24. Betsy H. not well. 27. Went to James Isld. Returned 16th. July not much better. 28. Mrs. A. Wright l. 30. I went to Goosecreek. Came down 3d. July very hot weather.

Source: Mabel L. Webber, "Extracts from the Journal of Mrs. Ann Manigault, 1754–1781." *South Carolina Historical Genealogical Magazine* 21 (1920), pp. 16–19.

celebrate the healing intercession of patron saints. Occasionally, gifted individuals claimed to possess miraculous curing powers, as was the case with Baptist faith healer John Blunt and immortalist Sarah Prentice, who maintained that her spiritually perfected body would never decay.

Other colonials coping with pain and illness turned to occult cures and cunning folk. Attempting to tap the unseen powers of nature, one Virginia woman applied a cobweb to an aching tooth in 1760. A generation later, backcountry witchmaster Joshua Gordon performed curing rituals on everything from bewitched muskets to young children, using arcane ingredients such as human urine and a deer phallus. Many of Gordon's spells required the invocation of the divine name, as did the magical talismans criticized by Boston clergyman Cotton Mather and a paper charm against malaria worn by a young Virginian boy. Some occult healing techniques, moreover, were borrowed from African and Indian specialists, whose services were in constant demand.

DREAMS, VISIONS, AND SPIRITUAL SEEKERS

In a fluid mental universe that blurred the boundaries of nature and the supernatural, revelations from the invisible world were common. Europeans, Indians, and Africans alike, for example, paid close attention to dreams, generally treating such nocturnal phenomena as omens portending future events. Many dreams, of course, reflected mundane concerns and anxieties—future travels, impending business transactions, or family matters—and they were treated as such. Others were more unsettling. Death dreams, for example, plagued the slumbers of prominent colonists Samuel Sewall and William Byrd II. Some dreamers confronted the devil, were transported to heavenly mansions on angelic wings, or encountered apocalyptic messengers. For the Iroquoian-speaking peoples of the northeast, moreover, dreams revealed repressed desires or communications from the spirit world; villagers sought to fulfill them through elaborate rituals.

During the religious revivals of the 1740s, visions and trances proliferated in the organized churches of New England, despite the best efforts of ordained clergymen to restrain the enthusiasm of their congregations. An unlettered Connecticut man received complete assurance of his eternal salvation following an extraordinary vision in which he was transported to heaven by a talking dove and

shown his name written in blood in the Book of Life by Jesus Christ himself. In a similar vision, converted Narraganset Indian Toby Coyhes proudly told missionary Joseph Fish of a revelation in which he was approached by Christ—who appeared in the form of a wealthy gentleman—and numerous heavenly beings resembling butterflies of various colors. Across the colony, minister Jacob Eliot was appalled to hear the news of a Connecticut man who interpreted a strange light in the night sky as a divine imperative to murder his own wife; his attempt failed and the unnamed man ran away distracted. Other New Light converts were moved by the Holy Spirit to sing and dance, exorcise demons, convulse on the floor, or exchange their spouses for spiritual soulmates.

Throughout the colonial period, religious seekers gathered small groups of devoted followers; many of these adepts firmly believed in the direct inspiration of the Holy Spirit. Antinomian Anne Hutchinson was banished to Rhode Island after teaching scripture to mixed audiences of men and women based on what she called the immediate voice of God. Sixty years later, Johannes Kelpius relied upon the leadings of the spirit to bring his small band of German followers to Wissahickon Creek on the outskirts of Philadelphia. There, for over a decade, Kelpius's group lived as hermits, practicing a perfectionist spirituality that blended elements of Lutheran pietism with Renaissance hermetic magic and Jewish mysticism. Apparently, Kelpius was not the only hermit to reside in the region. During the eighteenth century, travelers recorded visits with a man named Francis the Hermit, a sojourner from the western frontier who spoke no English and died in 1778 after living for a quarter of a century in a cave near Mount Holly, New Jersey.

DEBATE AND REFORMATION

Few people, of course, embraced the entire lore of wonders without hesitation; instead, incessant and often rancorous debates over the sources and meanings of wondrous events fragmented popular culture in colonial North America into a kaleidoscopic diversity of configurations. During the late seventeenth century, educated laymen and ministers consciously attempted to reform popular culture by labeling certain beliefs superstitious and by branding ordinary men and women vulgar. Recoiling against the radicalism of the English Civil War, they embraced the new literary standards of polite society and eagerly studied the new scientific thought of natural philosophers. Consequently, learned elites revised their understanding of comets and earthquakes, railed against the fraudulent practices of cunning folk, questioned the sanity of religious seekers, and exposed bogus witchcraft impostures.

Some laymen and women, on the other hand, seemed uninterested in supernatural forces of causation. During the two years in which the young Delaware planter Caesar Rodeney maintained his daily diary, for example, he described his wife's difficult childbirth, a solar eclipse, and a protracted drought—all without godly improvement. Instead, the future signer of the Declaration of Independence focused on genteel pursuits such as pipe smoking, card games, hunting and fishing, shooting competitions, elegant dining, weddings, and social visits (typically involving fiddling, dancing, and drinking). "Fare weather and Good Health" was the recurring refrain of his diary; no doubt numerous colonials lived their lives with similar disregard for either the dangers of hell or the glories of heaven.

In other cases, conflict over the veracity of wonders stemmed from social isolation. In the dark corners of the land—such as the New Jersey Pine Barrens, the northern New England hill country, or the Carolina frontier—families lived for decades without organized churches or regular preaching. During infrequent forays into these sparsely inhabited regions, educated clergymen such as Charles Woodmason lamented the fragility of religious and social institutions and vehemently criticized the theological ignorance and retrograde superstition of their backcountry audiences. In fact, what Woodmason had discovered was a creolized supernatural economy in which individuals cobbled together an eclectic worldview from a surprising variety of sources, including the Bible, European hermetic magic, Native American healing practices, and African spirit possession.

The vast majority of people in the New World, however, inhabited the untidy space between extremes of belief and skepticism; most remained judicious and pragmatic in what they chose to believe about the invisible world. When the tenants of a Plymouth, Massachusetts, mansion complained in 1733 that their house was bewitched by evil spirits, for example, neighborhood residents initiated a rigorous debate concerning the existence of witches, spirits, and ghostly apparitions. The Harvard-educated landlord maintained that believing in haunted houses was patently absurd and irrational; he eventually filed a slander suit against his vulgar tenants. But the majority of Plymouth townspeople were less certain. Most carefully weighed the evidence; some lampooned their more credulous neighbors, while others tacked back and forth between poles of outright belief and exclusive skepticism as personal experiences conspired to modify their opinions.

SURVIVALS

Despite the cessation of witchcraft trials and the self-congratulatory pronouncements of enlightened elites, popular traditions involving the lore of wonders survived the colonial period intact. Fears of neighborhood *maleficium,* for example, persisted well into the nineteenth century. Backcountry witch-masters prosecuted an impromptu trial against a neighborhood hag at the home of a prominent Carolina citizen in the 1790s, while a Philadelphia mob murdered a suspected female sorcerer during the Constitutional Convention in 1787. Cunning folk, too, profited from the decline in official witchcraft proceedings. Eighteenth-century herbalists, fortune-tellers, dream interpreters, and necromancers congregated in occult enclaves like Dogtown, a squalid, multiracial settlement hewn into the rocky recesses of Gloucester, Massachusetts. Confidence men such as Continental Army deserter Henry Tufts capitalized on the widespread popularity of cunning magic. Itinerating across northern New England, he peddled fraudulent occult services under the guise of an Indian doctor and a "Salem Wizard." In fact, the skills of these wise men and women expanded during the eighteenth century, as a spiritual treasure-seeking craze engulfed the burgeoning mercantile world of the northeast.

Godly Christians and religious visionaries perpetuated earlier supernatural beliefs as well. Stimulated by the hellfire preaching of Great Awakening itinerants and frontier evangelicals, accounts of satanic temptation and demonic possession actually increased in the eighteenth century, as tormented souls grappled with issues of sin and salvation. In the decades following independence, a host of religious seekers—including notable sectarian leaders Joseph Smith, Jemima Wilkinson, Ellen G. White, and Robert Matthews—surfaced, claiming to possess the power to heal, raise the dead, and commune with the divine through dreams, visions, and trances. Native American revitalization movements and slave revolts, too, incorporated popular Christian notions regarding apocalypticism, prophecies, and cunning magic.

Taken together, popular wonder traditions form a direct line pointing toward the beliefs and expressions of what one scholar has called the antebellum "spiritual hothouse." Evangelicals and spiritualists, communitarians and medical sectarians, Indian doctors and slave conjurors all inherited a vibrant tradition of supernatural beliefs from the colonial period.

See also **Rhetoric and Belles Lettres** *(in this volume);* **Elite vs. Popular Cultures; Culture for Mass Audiences; Journalism; Periodicals; Rhetoric; Fashion** *(volume 3).*

BIBLIOGRAPHY

Anecdotal evidence employed in this essay was drawn primarily from the published diaries cited in Laura Arksey, Nancy Pries, and Marcia Reed, comp., *American Diaries: An Annotated Bibliography of Published American Diaries and Journals,* vol. 1 (Detroit, 1983), and Carl Bridenbaugh, ed., *Gentleman's Progress: The Itinerarium of Dr. Alexander Hamilton, 1744* (Chapel Hill, N.C., 1948).

Popular Culture in Early Modern Europe

Burke, Peter. *Popular Culture in Early Modern Europe.* New York, 1978.

Christian, William. *Local Religion in Sixteenth-Century Spain.* Princeton, N.J., 1981.

Cressy, David. *Birth, Marriage & Death: Ritual, Religion, and the Life-Cycle in Tudor and Stuart England.* New York, 1997.

Duffy, Eamon. *The Stripping of the Altars: Traditional Religion in England, c. 1400–c. 1580.* New Haven, Conn., 1992.

Ginzburg, Carlo. *The Cheese and the Worms: The Cosmos of a Sixteenth-Century Miller.* Translated by John and Anne Tedeschi. Baltimore, 1980.

Thomas, Keith V. *Religion and the Decline of Magic.* New York, 1971.

Popular Religion and the Occult in Early Modern North America

Benes, Peter, ed. *Wonders of the Invisible World: 1600–1900.* Dublin Seminar for New England Folklife, *Annual Proceedings 1992.* Boston: Boston University, 1995.

Brooke, John. *The Refiner's Fire: The Making of a Mormon Cosmology, 1644–1844.* New York, 1994.

Butler, Jon. *Awash in a Sea of Faith: Christianizing the American People.* Cambridge, Mass., 1990.

Cervantes, Fernando. *The Devil in the New World: The Impact of Diabolism in New Spain.* New Haven, Conn., 1994.

Garrett, Clarke. *Origins of the Shakers: From the Old World to the New World.* Baltimore, 1998.

Godbeer, Richard. *The Devil's Dominion: Magic and Religion in Early New England.* New York, 1992.

Hall, David D. *Worlds of Wonder, Days of Judgment: Popular Religious Belief in Early New England.* New York, 1989.

Hambrick-Stowe, Charles E. *The Practice of Piety: Puritan Devotional Disciplines in Seventeenth-Century New England.* Chapel Hill, N.C., 1982.

Heyrman, Christine. *Southern Cross: The Beginnings of the Bible Belt.* New York, 1997.

Isaac, Rhys. *The Transformation of Virginia, 1740–1790.* Chapel Hill, N.C., 1982.

Johnson, A. J. B. *Religion in Life at Louisbourg, 1713–1758*. Kingston, Quebec, 1984.

Leventhal, Herbert. *In the Shadow of the Enlightenment: Occultism and Renaissance Science in Eighteenth-Century America*. New York, 1976.

Schmidt, Leigh Eric. *Holy Fairs: Scottish Communions and American Revivals in the Early Modern Period*. Princeton, N.J., 1989.

Seeman, Erik R. *Pious Persuasions: Laity and Clergy in Eighteenth-Century New England*. Baltimore, 1999.

Stout, Harry S. *The New England Soul: Preaching and Religious Culture in Colonial New England*. New York, 1986.

Taylor, William B. *Magistrates of the Sacred: Priests and Parishioners in Eighteenth-Century Mexico*. Stanford, Calif., 1996.

The Cultural World of Women, Slaves, and Indians

Brown, Kathleen. *Good Wives, Nasty Wenches, and Anxious Patriarchs: Gender, Race, and Power in Colonial Virginia*. Chapel Hill, N.C., 1996.

Calloway, Colin G. *New Worlds for All: Indians, Europeans, and the Remaking of Early America*. Baltimore, 1997.

Morgan, Philip D. *Slave Counterpoint: Black Culture in the Eighteenth-Century Chesapeake and Lowcountry*. Chapel Hill, N.C., 1998.

Piersen, William D. *Black Yankees: The Development of an Afro-American Subculture in Eighteenth-Century New England*. Amherst, Mass., 1988.

Rediker, Marcus. *Between the Devil and the Deep Blue Sea: Merchant Seamen, Pirates, and the Anglo-American Maritime World, 1700–1750*. New York, 1987.

Sobel, Mechal. *The World They Made Together: Black and White Values in Eighteenth-Century Virginia*. Princeton, N.J., 1987.

Trigger, Bruce. *Natives and Newcomers: Canada's "Heroic Age" Reconsidered*. Kingston, Quebec, 1985.

Ulrich, Laurel T. *Good Wives: Image and Reality in the Lives of Women in Northern New England, 1650–1750*. New York, 1982.

———. *A Midwife's Tale: The Life of Martha Ballard, Based on Her Diary, 1785–1812*. New York, 1990.

Wallace, Anthony F. C. *The Death and Rebirth of the Seneca*. New York, 1969.

THE FINE ARTS IN COLONIAL AMERICA

Barbara G. Carson

The traditional understanding of the fine arts in colonial America focuses on artists and their paintings and graphic works and gentlemen builders and architects and their private and public designs. The more contemporary scholarly position holds that economic conditions and cultural predispositions did not encourage artistic expression or expenditure, but that as general prosperity increased and the consumer revolution changed people's ideas about spending, the colonists' taste for amenities and luxuries—some of which might be considered art—grew. However, if one takes a broad view of people's interest in the visual enhancement of their world, the early colonists did not ignore the visual arts. This essay includes maps, samplers, needlework pictures, scenic wallpapers, and even ornamental arrangements of military arms as art; garden plans and ornaments as architecture; and weathervanes, shop signs, ceramic figurines, and portrait busts incorporated into furniture as sculpture—all evidence of the early colonists' interest in the visual arts. It could be argued that collectively these possessions and achievements were the foundation of America's creative, artistic future.

The early colonists themselves had differing perspectives on the place of fine art in colonial society. As early as 1743, in *A Proposal for Promoting Useful Knowledge among the British Plantations in America*, Benjamin Franklin wrote, "The first drudgery of settling new colonies, which confines the attention of people to mere necessaries, is now pretty well over; and there are many in every province in circumstances, that set them at ease, and afford leisure to cultivate the finer arts, and improve the common stock of knowledge." On the other hand, John Adams, who walked in various Parisian gardens and admired their statues in 1780, did not think Americans so advanced. He wrote to his wife, Abigail, that although he wished, "to observe these objects with taste, and describe them so as to be understood," his duty called him to more pragmatic endeavors.

> It is not indeed the fine arts which our country requires; the useful, the mechanic arts are those which we have occasion for in a young country as yet simple and not far advanced in luxury, although perhaps much too far for her age and character. I could fill volumes with descriptions of temples and palaces, paintings, sculptures, tapestry, porcelain, etc., etc., etc., if I could have time; but I could not do this without neglecting my duty. The science of government is my duty to study, more than all other sciences; the arts of legislation and administration and negotiation ought to take place of, indeed to exclude, in a manner, all other arts. I must study politics and war, that my sons may have liberty to study mathematics and philosophy. My sons ought to study mathematics and philosophy, geography, natural history and naval architecture, navigation, commerce, and agriculture, in order to give their children a right to study painting, poetry, music, architecture, statuary, tapestry, and porcelain.

Much of the early artistic work that was created in the colonies was intended for practical purposes such as decoration and illustration. The first European artists on American shores ornamented Catholic churches in French and Spanish colonies. The earliest views of the American landscape were not intended as art for the early settlers, but as information for those back home. Executed before the development of Enlightenment standards for accurate recording of the natural world, the handful of surviving works displayed the wonders of newly discovered land handsomely, but imaginatively. These early fantasies contrasted with more precise efforts to depict the world with greater objectivity. Jacques Le Moyne de Morgues (d. 1588), a Huguenot settler in an early French colony in Florida that the Spanish destroyed, and John White (active 1584–1593), who traveled to Roanoke, North Carolina, and to Virginia, were the first two naturalist artists to portray a more realistic view of the Americas. Of the former's works, only one original watercolor survives, but his published narrative was illustrated with engravings based on lost drawings, and these images were used for the next two centuries to illustrate books on America. White's surviving sixty-five watercolor drawings in the British Museum provide vivid details about indigenous plants and native people.

PAINTINGS AND GRAPHIC ARTS, 1650–1750

In the early colonial period, fine art traveled westward from the old to the new world. For example, large oil portraits of Governors John Winthrop and Edward Winslow were probably painted in London before their subjects emigrated. Wealthy colonists also imported less accomplished sets of family likenesses. In addition to reinforcing the social positions of their owners, the portraits probably served as reminders of loved ones across the seas and offered continuity and comfort in people's lives. Governor Peter Stuyvesant also brought family portraits to New Amsterdam in 1647. In the 1670s, Nicholas Roberts of London sent three works to his daughter Elizabeth, who had married a Boston merchant. Another group of five portraits from the Whettenhall family of Kent, England, reached Maryland around 1700. Neither the flow of images nor their emotional impact diminished in the eighteenth century. A member of the Lee family visited Stratford, his ancestral home, in 1783 and recorded his response.

> What a delightful occupation did it afford me sitting on one of the sophas of the great Hall, to have the family resemblance in the portraits of all my dear mother's fore-fathers—her father & mother grandfather & grandmother and so upwards for four generation! Their pictures have been drawn by the most eminent English artists and in large gilt frames adorn one of the most spacious & beautiful Halls I have seen.

Although landscapes are mentioned in seventeenth-century documents, works honoring individuals were more important. A handful of seventeenth-century paintings and a few more examples from the early eighteenth century survive from the collections of Dutch families in New York. Stuyvesant was painted around 1663, and Gansevoort Limner produced several charming and colorful full-length portraits of young colonists. Among the most vivid achievements of visual artists in New England were the objects created for funerary processions honoring prominent persons. Mourners carried hatchments or escutcheons, lozenge-shaped panels painted with the armorial bearings of the deceased. Although after the ceremonies the panels were hung on the front doors and later inside the homes of the deceased's families, no seventeenth-century examples have survived.

On the other hand, the tally for paintings identified as seventeenth-century New England portraits stands at approximately forty. This relatively low figure contrasts with the later eighteenth century, when John Singleton Copley alone is known to have painted 350 portraits before leaving for England in 1774. Clearly, the market for art had expanded significantly. One group of artists who benefitted from this expanding market were the limners. The early limners were miniaturists, hired to "limn" or to depict a likeness, although in the seventeenth century the term may have been used more widely to include other subjects.

At this time painting was considered a "useful" profession and was not classed as "polite" or one of the "liberal" arts. Only gradually did the elevation of painting to a higher status come to affect American artists' sensibilities. Limners were trained and accomplished in a fashionable, naturalistic style and they rendered their subjects rather flatly with a downward perspective. The main objectives of this portraiture were to highlight an individual's place in society, honor his memory upon or after death, and serve as a reminder of the transience of earthly life. Subjects were elegantly dressed and shown with appropriate attributes of their status, gender, and age, such as gloves, canes, books, flowers, fans, and toys. Arriving later in the century, but overlapping with the earlier tradition, was a provincial version of the baroque in the manner of Sir Godfrey Kneller, the fashionable English portrait painter. This style emphasized linear perspective and three-dimensional forms in space. It was rich in its depiction of light, shade, and texture, and allowed more candid observation of personality, sometimes showing its subjects as more than a little pompous.

Artists working in colonial America are identified in three ways. Most are known only by name, not by signed or attributed works. Then there are paintings, either single examples or groups of works, that cannot be assigned to known individuals. For example, in the South, one of these unknown artists left twelve portraits from Jamestown dated around 1723. Of course, at any time evidence could emerge to connect a name to an unattributed work. There are also limited cases that pair names with works. Henrietta Dearing Johnson, one of the rare women who earned their living through art, painted portraits in pastels in Charleston in the first quarter of the eighteenth century. In Annapolis for the decade from roughly 1708 to 1719, Justis Englehardt Kuhn died in debt, and his creditor noted that he had augmented his income by painting coats of arms. His portrait legacy is about a dozen, most showing their subjects in elaborate scenic backgrounds of columns, balustrades, and formal gardens that are unlikely to have been part of the real plantation landscape. Kuhn's portrait of Henry Darnall III, of Prince George's County, Maryland, painted around 1710, is the best known of his works. Deep in the background are a formal garden and a large country house. The elegantly dressed young Darnall holds a bow and arrow, and to his left stands a black servant, perhaps in a red livery jacket lined with blue and wearing a silver neck collar, holding a dead bobwhite.

A few other colonial works depict African Americans, mainly with their owners. The well-known scene of eleven musicians, dancers, and onlookers in front of several outbuildings dates to the end of the eighteenth century. As subject matter for art, Native Americans did not hold much interest for colonists, beyond documenting them for natural history. For the family of William Penn, in 1735, John Hesselius portrayed Tishcohan and Lapwinsa, two Delaware Indians who had taken part in the infamous "walking purchase," which secured extra acreage for Pennsylvania by anticipating the route of the transaction.

PAINTINGS AND ENGRAVINGS, 1750 TO THE REVOLUTION

Because the colonies were governed by the British crown, royal portraits were often hung in public buildings. In 1730, Boston's Council Chamber boasted "Pictures of their Majesties King George II, and Queen Caroline, beautifully drawn at length . . . the gift of His Majesty, to this His Province of the *Massachusetts Bay.*" Ten years later, in a retroactive move, portraits of King William and Queen Mary of "Blessed memory" were hung in the same room. More evidence of royal portraits is found in the 1770s. Governor Botetourt's inventory taken in Williamsburg, Virginia, in 1770, records "2 large paintings of the King & Queen gauze covers." Governor Robert Eden, who abandoned his post at Annapolis in 1776, left behind "1 Elligant portrait of Charles 1st by Vandike" and "1 . . . do of his Excellency by Peale." Eden also had paintings of landscapes, ruins, the Death of Woolf, and "The Marquis of Granby distributing Charity to the Soldier." Governor William Tryon's collection of royal portraits was extensive. In his Fort George, New York, residence he displayed "King William and Queen Ann," "King George the first," "King George the second and Queen," and "King George the third and Queen Charlotte." Visitors to Tryon's home could also see Mary Queen of Scots, the Marquis of Granby, and an individual identified simply as Mr. Reid. Although no royal portraits are listed among the personal possessions of Lord William Campbell who fled from Charleston, South Carolina, several that hung in the State House Council Chamber were surrounded by drapery.

Probably ordinary people would not have seen these portraits, but in 1740 Bostonians could pay a shilling and sixpence to view a series of "Landscapes, beautiful Seats, Water Works, Alcoves, Groves, and Sea Pieces" through a "certain Machine . . . lately arrived from Holland." In the same decade for two shillings New Yorkers could see "nine French Prospects," including the canal at Fontainebleau and the chestnut groves at Versailles through a "philosophical optical machine."

The range of subject matter in paintings and engravings offered to private customers was surprisingly varied. In May 1735 in Boston, John Smibert offered "A Collection of valuable PRINTS, engrav'd by the best Hands, after the finest Pictures in Italy, France, Holland, and England, done by Raphael, Michael Angelo, Poussin, Rubens, and other of the greatest Masters, containing a great Variety of Subjects, as History, etc." Nearly half a century later another seller advertised a "Variety of Metzitento Pictures, painted on Glass, double Frames, neatly carved and gilt, viz. The Royal Family, the Judges of England, the months, seasons, the four Parts of the Day, the senses, the Elements: very handsome Views of Sea Pieces; the Rakes and Harlots Progress, Maps, Gold Leaf, &c." A competitor offered, "Statesmen, Generals, and Admirals, that have distinguished themselves this War[French and Indian War]" along with "all the celebrated and reigning Beauties in *Britain.*" Less edifying were "Two small Pictures of dead Game in their proper Colours, the one representing a Hare hanging by the hind Feet emboweled; the other a Lark falling." Somewhat later a Philadelphia artist was selling "One landscape of cattle going out in the morning, being four feet six inches by three feet six inches in the straining frame, . . . one other landscape, representing the evening, painted after the manner of Pusine; also, a fire piece, representing a large pile of buildings on fire."

Approximately twenty-five artists of the mid-eighteenth century are associated with documented works, mainly portraits. But other subjects—such

Charles Willson Peale, *William Paca* **(c. 1772)** Oil on mattress ticking, 224.4 x 147.9 cm. William Paca (1740–1799), governor of Maryland, began building his house and garden in 1765. His pose, standard for an eighteenth-century gentleman, shows off his elegant legs in silk stockings and his sloping shoulders in a tightly fitted coat. One hand rests on his hip; the other is splayed out on the midsection of a plinth topped by an unidentifiable portrait bust, clearly an ornamental feature of his garden. In the rear left, other landscape features, confirmed by archaeology, are visible. A bridge of Chinese design crosses a canal in front of a two-story domed octagonal pavilion with a classical doorway. If Paca faced the opposite direction, he would view a series of three steps and broad terraces leading up to his two-story brick house. THE MARYLAND HISTORICAL SOCIETY, BALTIMORE, MARYLAND

as religious, mythological, historical, and genre—are known. John Hesselius (1728–1778) painted Bacchus and Ariadne and a lost version of the Last Supper. Along with his powerful portrait of Jersey Nanny, from 1748, John Greenwood (1728–1792) depicted a tavern scene in his painting from 1757–1758, *American Sea Captains Carousing in Surinam.* During his two years of study in London with Benjamin West, Matthew Pratt (1734–1805) painted *The American Academy,* a study of a group of Amer-

ican artists, one at an easel and another whose work is being criticized by West. Pratt also copied Correggio's *Madonna of St. Jerome and a Holy Family* after Raphael. The diverse subject matter captured by Charles Willson Peale (1741–1827) does not appear until after the Revolution.

American artists struggled with the limitation imposed on them by their talents, education, time, and situation. First Benjamin West (1738–1820) and then John Singleton Copley (1738–1815) fled the confines of America for London where both remained for the rest of their lives. Before leaving, Copley wrote to West:

> The taste of painting is too much wanting in Boston to afford any kind of help; and was it not for preserving the resemblance of particular persons, painting would not be known in the place. The people generally regard it as no more than any other useful trade, as they sometimes term it, like that of carpenter, tailor, or shoemaker, not as one of the most noble arts in the world.

About the same time Peale wrote to his friend John Beale Bordley in Philadelphia:

> What little I do is by mere imitation of what is before me ... A good painter of either portrait or history must be well acquainted with the Greesian [sic] and Roman statues, to be able to draw them at pleasure by memory, and account for every beauty.... These are some of the requisites of a good painter.... These are more than I shall ever have time or opportunity to know, but as I have a variety of characters to paint, I must, as Rembrandt did, make these my antiques and improve myself as well as I can while I am providing for my support.

With his artistic activities, intellectual curiosity, practical outlook, and promotional schemes, Peale suited the needs of his times and those of his Baltimore public.

Like Pratt, Ralph Earl (1751–1801) returned to America. His career is instructive because it contradicts the tendency of scholars to see paintings and artisanal products as becoming ever more sophisticated and skillful. Before leaving for London in 1777, Earl painted the American statesman, Roger Sherman, seated in a green and red Windsor chair in the corner of a room simply indicated by an angle on the floor and some looped drapery. Sherman wears a three-piece suit—coat, vest, and breeches of the same garnet-colored wool. In an egalitarian gesture, he does not cover his head with a wig. Earl, in spite of his loyalist sympathies, painted the (now lost) four views of the Battles of Lexington and Concord on which Amos Doolittle based his engravings. In London, Earl quickly developed a completely acceptable court style. However, when he returned to the United States in 1785, he did not always paint in that manner. Surviving portraits show considerable variety in sophistication with no particular correspondence to the years executed. They range from the large elegant renderings of the Boardman family in New Milford, Connecticut, painted from 1789 to 1793, to the conservative portrait of the Reverend Nathaniel Taylor also of New Milford, from around 1790. Many of Earl's subjects are shown in pastoral outdoor settings or seated next to windows through which, with artistic economy, Earl shows the house and landscape in which they live. Although these differences may have resulted from Earl's bouts with alcoholism, it is more likely that he adapted his renderings of clients according to their local tastes and pocketbooks.

For financial solvency, artists turned to a wide range of expression. Warwell, a "PAINTER from London," placed an elaborate advertisement in the *South Carolina Gazette and Country Journal* in 1766. He said he could paint history-pieces, heraldry, altarpieces, coaches, landscapes, window blinds, sea-pieces, chimney blinds, flowers, screens, and fruit. He offered to paint rooms in oil or water in "a new taste." He could also do "Deceptive Temples, Triumphal Arches, Obelisks, Statues, etc. for Groves and Gardens." Pierre Du Smitiers, who was active between 1769 and 1772, compiled careful lists of Philadelphians, New Yorkers, and Bostonians who owned coaches, coachwagons, and chariots or post chaises, an imaginative approach to obtaining portrait commissions among the carriage trade. Others taught drawing, and at least one hopeful instructor claimed that it was:

> a most ingenious, interesting and elegant art, and the study of it ought to be encouraged in every youth, . . . its utility being so extensive, that there are few arts or professions in which it is not serviceable.
>
> All designs and models are executed by it—Engineers, architects, and a multitude of professions, have frequent occasion to practice it, from the general who commands an army, to the mechanic who supports himself by handicraft. A young gentleman possessed of an accomplishment so exceedingly desireable, both for amusement and use, is qualified to take the sketch of a fine building—a beautiful prospect of any curious production of art, or of any uncommon and striking appearance in nature, expecially to persons of leisure and fortune, it affords a most pleasing entertainment, and enables them to construct and improve plans to their own taste and judge of designs, &c. with propriety.

Two skillful artist-explorers or artist-naturalists were also working in America in the eighteenth century. Mark Catesby (1679?–1749) made two trips to the South. On the first (1722–1726), he painted a large number of American birds, adding examples of plants associated with them. Because he found working with a Dutch engraver too expensive, he prepared himself the 220 plates for his *The Natural History of Carolina, Florida, and the Bahama Islands* published in London in 1731. Another series, undoubtedly prepared by Catesby but never published, survives as copper plates intended to illustrate William Byrd II's *A History of the Dividing Line between Virginia and North Carolina.* Byrd probably wrote the text between 1739 and 1741, more than ten years after Catesby would have completed the so-called Bodlein engravings. William Bartram (1739–1823) was the son of John Bartram, the famous Philadelphia botanist. His paintings of nature are exact and graceful. *Travels through North and South Carolina, Georgia, East and West Florida, etc. . . .* was published in 1791 and within ten years had gone through seven European editions.

Another mode of visual expression prevalent in eighteenth-century America was the engravings used by several colonial cities and institutions to promote themselves. The earliest engraving is that of New York City drawn around 1716 by William Burgess and engraved two years later in London. His view of Boston was offered to the public in the early 1720s. Harbors full of commercial ships, wharves lining the shore, and sturdy buildings crowding the streets indicate development and prosperity, attractive enticements to future investors and immigrants. Farther south, Bishop Rogers depicted Charleston in the 1730s. Paul Revere occasionally turned his hand from cartouches and coats of arms on silver to pictorial subjects. He executed two views of Boston in 1768 and 1774, one of Harvard College in 1767, and the famous *Bloody Massacre before the Boston State House* in 1770.

Large or small, most artworks were framed. Sets were closely grouped in available wall space, often in surprisingly large numbers—twelve, eighteen, or twenty-four. Engravings were usually under glass, and, in the case of the royal oil portraits in Williamsburg, kept free of fly spots with gauze covers. Prints were often advertised as framed and under glass, but a cheaper way to display them was simply to nail or paste them to the wall. In 1726, one Boston shopkeeper advertised "Picture Varnishes, which preserves them from the Smoak & Flies, &c."

GRAPHIC AND DOMESTIC ARTS

Maps covering areas varying from a small locality to all of North America were vital to colonial de-

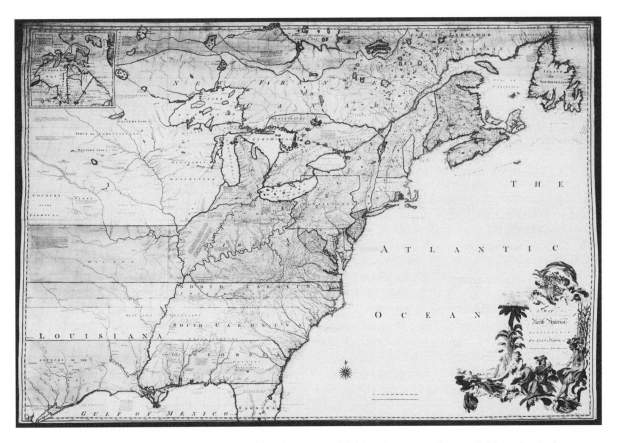

A Map of the British Colonies in North America (1755). Cartographic historians generally regard this as the single most important map in colonial history. It was drawn by John Mitchell, a doctor and botanist who practiced in Urbanna, Virginia, from about 1732 to 1746, when poor health forced his return to England. Growing concern over the expansion of French occupation in northwestern North America probably prompted him to begin work on the map in 1750. An inscription indicates he undertook the project with official approbation and undoubtedly had access to maps and reports of the British Board of Trade and the Admiralty. Engraved by Thomas Kitchen, the first edition was issued in 1755 and the second and third revised editions in 1757. The map was used in negotiating the Treaty of Paris. COURTESY OF THE COLONIAL WILLIAMSBURG FOUNDATION

velopment. They confirmed the boundaries of governmental authority and identified personal ownership of real estate. They had to be accurate. No wonder that surveying and mapmaking provided solid employment for many Americans. Maps were widely distributed and many were prominently displayed. Large maps were folded, and some were in slipcases. As small wall ornaments, they might be framed under glass. Larger examples were secured to rollers and could be taken from the walls for use in serious discussions about travel routes and jurisdictions.

In his letter to Abigail, John Adams mentions tapestries as art. In 1682, William Fitzhugh of Stafford County, Virginia, asked his agent, "Please to procure me a Suit of Tapestry hangings for a Room twenty foot long, sixteen foot wide, and nine foot high and half a dozen chairs suitable." Offered at a public sale in Boston in 1745 were "Beautiful Arras-

Hangings for a Room," and eight years later someone else wanted to dispose of "A Compleate sett of Tapestry Hangings." Beds were an elaborate feature of rooms used for entertainment throughout much of the colonial era, and, although functional, the quality of their artistic expression and the quality of the work should put them in the category of art. In 1687, Samuel Sewall of Boston ordered needlework supplies from London for his daughters, "white Fustian drawn, enough for Curitins, wallens [valances], counterpaine for a bed, and half a duz. chairs, with four threeded green worsted to work it." In the same city in 1736, Mrs. Susanna Condy offered for sale "a fine Fustian Suit of Curtains, with a Cornish and Base Mouldings of a beautiful Figure, drawn in London, on Frame full already worked; as also enough of the same for half a dozen Chairs." Tightly rolled colored paper formed into flowers, arranged in vases, and sprinkled with sparkling

112

mica kept elite women busy. These achievements were carefully preserved in glass boxes, sometimes with sconces, and hung on parlor walls. Needlework pictures, probably drawn by professionals but worked by women and girls, also were framed and hung. Eighteenth-century ladies enjoyed fishing, and needlework pictures of their sporting activities were a popular subject in mid-century Boston. Samplers were more likely to have been both drawn and wrought at home.

Wall painting and scenic papers surely qualify as art. The hallway of the McPhaedris-Warner House, Portsmouth, New Hampshire, from around 1710, was decorated with full-length portraits of two of the five Mohawk chieftains who were taken to England by Colonel Peter Schuyler in 1710. Among the assortment of other subjects, was Abraham about to sacrifice Isaac, a figure on a prancing steed, and a curious scene of a lady spinning while a dog protects her from an attacking eagle grasping a chicken in its talons. Four of eleven wall panels of landscapes, some with lively cartouches in the sky, survive from the William Clark House of Boston, built early in the eighteenth century. They were painted sometime before Clark's death in 1742. Plans for hand-painted papers were sent from London to the Van Rensselaer Manor House in Albany, New York, where the completed versions were installed in 1768. Roman ruins after paintings by Giovanni Paolo Pannini alternate with smaller panels showing views of fall and winter. Both types are executed in grisaille, a technique used to produce a three-dimensional effect, on a mustard-yellow ground. Similar treatment was used in Jeremiah Lee's house in Marblehead, Massachusetts, also in the mid-1760s. Chinese scenic wallpaper was purchased but not hung in a New England parlor in the late eighteenth century. It is now in the Winterthur Museum.

Fireplaces were the focal points of colonial rooms. They were embellished with elaborate, classical architectural details and surprisingly often with over-mantel paintings, usually a building set in a landscape. Bishop Roberts in Charleston advertised in 1735 that "Gentlemen may be supplied with Landscapes for Chimney Pieses of all Sizes." In 1757, George Washington sent an order to London that specified his desire for "A Neat Landscape after Claude Lorrain." Other advertisements placed by artists can be found in newspapers from Annapolis, Philadelphia, and Boston, including one that made it clear that the work was done by a "Genuine Painter." Surprisingly, considering the pride Americans seem to have taken in their grand houses, most of these mantelpiece paintings do not show their owners' residences, but are completely fanciful.

Undoubtedly the most surprising colonial artistic expressions were the ornamental arrangements of arms or the circular compositions of muskets and pistols with crisscrossed columns of swords as found in the Tower of London. The governor of New York, Benjamin Fletcher, installed one as early as 1697 in Fort St. George. A few years later Governor Spotswood revealed his version in Williamsburg, Virginia. By mid century that display numbered 276 muskets, 100 carbines, 193 pistols, and 264 swords. Spotswood planned a similar treatment for his residence in Annapolis. These military weapons remained functional, and their display expressed official authority, power, and artistic awareness.

ARCHITECTURE

The buildings of colonial America, whether rural or urban, public or private, are usually thought of as either polite or vernacular, that is refined or common. The essay on material life elsewhere in this collection touched on the latter. Here the emphasis falls on the classical tradition. Although earlier scholars have identified the principle works and detailed most of their important features, several important scholarly developments need to be raised. Dendrochronology, or the scientific use of tree-ring dating, and the precise observation and sequencing of ornamental details have confirmed or revised the dates of a number of well-known structures. For instance, Bacon's Castle, traditionally dated to about 1655, is now known to have been built from trees cut in 1665. Westover, once credited to the taste of the scholarly William Byrd II, is most likely the result of the extravagance of his son, the gambler, who built it in 1748–1749. Unfortunately, little of this information has been published. Second, paint analysis has significantly altered our view of interior and exterior color schemes. The colonial revival vision of pastel hues had been replaced by new information that reveals the use of vibrant color schemes. Third, the term "medieval" has largely been abandoned in favor of "early modern" because at the time of settlement features characteristic of the early modern period—such as chimneys, glazed windows, and full second stories—were commonplace. Fourth, although log structures were known, most buildings, even small, inexpensive ones along the coast, were timber-framed. However, log building did become increasingly common in the eighteenth century, especially in the southern backcountry. And finally, while a good part of the study of architecture focuses on design and building practices, its interpretive thrust has moved on to discuss patterns of room use and issues of social hierarchies.

The architecture of colonial America principally used its most plentiful material—wood. Brick or stone public buildings and a small number of brick residences of prominent colonists stood out on the landscape. Official or elite status was further stressed by size and by placement within a well-thought-out composition of urban streets and greens or an arrangement of roads, outbuildings, and gardens in which the country seat was usually high and central in its landscape.

By the end of the seventeenth century, classical design was beginning to emerge as the standard for better buildings. Little specific evidence survives about the interaction between those who did the work and their clients; more is known about printed sources for design. Titles of at least 106 architectural books offering suggestions for plans, elevations, and details have been identified in colonial libraries or booksellers lists. All but eight were British, and of these four were in the library at Harvard.

The architectural profession was in its infancy in the mid-eighteenth century. Three individuals, all immigrants, represent the range of activities of the best colonial practitioners. Peter Harrison (1716–1775) worked in Rhode Island and Massachusetts. He was an amateur and a gentleman who never earned a penny for his considerable skill. His diversity of achievements—navigation, woodcarving, military engineering, commerce, and agriculture—were widely recognized. As a ship owner and merchant he amassed considerable wealth, which he augmented by marrying a heiress. He could well afford his twenty-seven architectural design books which he used in responding to the call of public service. He designed the Redwood Library, Newport, Rhode Island, 1748–50; Kings Chapel, Boston, 1749–54; Christ Church, Cambridge, 1760; and the Tourc Synagogue, Newport, 1759–63. In 1766 he left Newport to take on the post of Collector of customs in New Haven where he died shortly before a revolutionary mob destroyed his extensive library and records.

William Buckland (1734–1774), born in Oxford, England, was apprenticed to an uncle in London who was a master builder and proprietor of a bookstore specializing in architectural books. That exposure influenced his interests, and at his death he owned sixteen books on architecture. In 1755,

CLASSICAL DESIGN

The ancient worlds of Greece and Rome profoundly influenced the design of western art. Classical public architecture, which endured throughout the centuries, affected not only the buildings of later millennia, but also the forms, proportions, and selection of motifs across all categories of furnishings. Inspiration and creative adaptation were more significant than any direct copying. Design information in colonial America was communicated mainly by seeing exhibited examples and by studying architectural books. The best-known author was the north Italian architect and writer Andrea Palladio (1508–1580) whose influence persisted in the English world through the eighteenth century.

In the classical tradition, five formally accepted orders of columns—Tuscan, Doric, Ionic, Corinthian, and composite—control the familiar proportions on temple facades. Pediments and balustrades emphasize the skyward profile, and the geometric, floral, and faunal details found on capitals and friezes provide an ornamental vocabulary. Classicism, which was reintroduced during the Renaissance, stretched forward to the American Revolution in four phases across two centuries. Dominating the seventeenth century, mannerism, a sophisticated distortion of high Renaissance stability, featured forms that were heavier on top than on bottom, keystones and other elements that dropped out of their accustomed places, and a visual device called strapwork that tied motifs together. The baroque, a style noted for its extravagant forms and sometimes grotesque ornamentation, was a response to the Reformation. The Roman Catholic Church used dramatic effects of light and space and the emotional power of paintings and sculpture to hold the attention of worshipers. Its imagery also reinforced the divine right of kings that was so effectively expressed by Louis XIV. The offshoot of Roman Catholic imagery—the rococo with its French C and S curves, Chinese asymmetry, and gothic pointed arches—relaxed the pomp of church and court. Finally, a new interest in history, wider travel around the Mediterranean, and archaeological discoveries introduced the neoclassical style. Only a handful of examples of it are known in America before the Revolution.

he emigrated from England under indenture to George Mason who built Gunston Hall in Westmoreland County, Virginia. Its rich interiors are of Buckland's design and execution. After working for Colonel John Tayloe at Mount Airy, Buckland turned north to Annapolis, where he found wealthy merchants willing to spend lavishly to live classically. The Hammond-Harwood House of 1774 stands as his best-known work.

These elegant and carefully planned structures contrast with the general run of colonial buildings. A generation of archaeologists, digging mainly in the Chesapeake Bay area, have discovered that well into the nineteenth century most dwellings and outbuildings were "impermanent" or built without brick or stone foundations. They were earth-fast, that is constructed on posts set directly into holes dug in the ground and therefore unprotected from rotting. The great rebuilding of America occurred only in the second quarter of the nineteenth century. A federal tax document from 1798, which survives for Maryland, Pennsylvania, Massachusetts, and a few other isolated locations, lists residential structures by materials and size. The vast majority were built of wood and had only one room, $12' \times 12'$, $12' \times 16'$, or $12' \times 20'$. Outbuildings provided more space for certain activities—cooking, smoking meat, dairying, or even accommodating servants—but for most families most of their lives were spent in one dimly-lit room, probably with a loft or out-of-doors. Except for the details of their molding profiles, classicism did not influence the design of any of these buildings.

SCULPTURE

Sculpture in the early colonial period encompassed monumental works, as well as works intended for private consumption such as funerary monuments, garden sculpture, and sculpture placed in elite homes. There was also sculpture intended for public entertainment in the form of waxwork figures and scenes, created for public occasions or to document prominent or interesting people. Finally, ornamental works were also sculptured for the decoration of colonial buildings and homes. This range of sculptural works is evidence of the colonists' interest in the visual enhancement of their lives and the importance of fine arts in the emerging colonial culture.

Monumental Sculpture Four monumental sculptural works were erected in colonies. A much-damaged marble statue of William Pitt, first Earl of Chatham, whose stand against the Stamp Act of 1765 won him the affection of colonists, still stands in Charleston. It is one of three by Joseph Wilton of London. His second of Pitt, in New York, was destroyed during the Revolution, as was his lead equestrian statue of King George II. Richard Hayward's statue of Norborne Berkeley, Baron de Botetourt and governor of Virginia from 1768 to 1770, was originally positioned before the capitol in Williamsburg. The marble figure temporarily lost its head during the French Revolution, but the restored Botetourt still stands proudly in the library of the College of William and Mary. It is one of the earliest examples of neoclassical design identified in the colonies. The first known portrait bust made in the colonies is again of the popular Pitt, placed on "a piller of Liberty" in Dedham, Massachusetts, in 1767 and destroyed by the British two years later. Although no works have been definitely attributed to Simeon Skillen Sr. (1716–1778), he may have executed the wooden "Little Admiral" who wears a uniform of the 1740s. The date 1770 is probably a later edition.

Garden Sculpture There is more evidence of sculpture in private gardens up and down the coast. Judge Samuel Sewall in Boston noted in 1718 that a strong wind "blew down the southernmost of my cherubim's heads at the Street Gates . . . they have stood there near thirty years." Several references cite statues of Italian marble; a few specify the subjects as Roman gods. The best surviving examples of such statues are at Cliveden in Germantown, Pennsylvania, traditionally said to have been mid-century wedding presents. Other noteworthy garden sculptures are the lead eagles and the pairs of stone finials at Westover, Virginia. The former are a play on the Byrd family name. The latter are symbolic of eighteenth-century values—acorns for perseverance, pineapples for hospitality, Greek keys for the world of knowledge, beehives and cornucopia for industry and plenty, and urns of flowers for beauty.

There is also evidence that sculptures may have adorned some colonial homes. Inside elite houses, mantel shelves, a few wall niches, and pedestals in the architectural compositions over doors indicate places where sculptures may have been placed. The entry hall at Tryon's Palace in North Carolina had four of these niches, but they may have been empty because no statuary is mentioned in the estate sale. The Chase-Lloyd House, built in Annapolis between 1769 and 1774, has two niches on the upstairs landing. The pedestals over the doors at Gunston Hall, Virginia, may have supported sculpture.

Funerary Monuments Funerary monuments are an ancient tradition. In parts of colonial America, they took the form of upright slate slabs carved with a death's-heads, winged skulls, hourglasses, and crossbones. As early as the mid-1670s, a stonecutter in Charleston, Massachusetts, used forms and iconography borrowed from print sources and English precedents. In his compositions, the winged skull fills the pediment. The cranium is enlarged, thin eyebrows terminate in little hooks, the nose is triangular, and the wings are carved with tiers of feathers. In the eighteenth-century cherubs' heads with wings, which represent the flight of the soul heavenward, appeared on gravestones. Wealthy southerners sent to England or to New England for carvers for their gravestones. Since slate is not conducive to any carving other than flat surface imagery, table tombs throughout the colonial era and effigy portraits introduced in the 1740s were made of stone or marble. Sir William Pepperrell ordered "a handsome marble tombstone with proper marble pillars or supporters to set it on" and an engraving of the three pineapples of the family coat of arms.

Waxworks Waxworks were another medium of artistic expression for private and public consumption. Governor Botetourt displayed thirteen wax portraits at the Governor's Palace in Williamsburg. Samuel Fraunces, proprietor of the famous Fraunces Tavern in New York, was a wax modeler. To commemorate Washington's farewell to his troops, he fashioned in wax a scene of Hector and his wife, Andromache, with a mother holding a baby. The figures are in modified Turkish or exotic dress from about 1780 with much use of metallic threads. Fraunces probably purchased the heads and little animals that are included in the scene. A small looking glass in the temple grotto suggests that a candle, creating a theatrical effect, may have been nearby. The mythological story connects the devotion of Hector and Andromache to that of George and Martha Washington.

Waxworks seem to have been a popular form of public entertainment in Boston throughout most of the eighteenth century. In 1733, for example, one could see a "very curious set . . . being a lively Representation of Margaret, Countess of Heininburg, who have 365 Children at one Birth, occasioned by the rash Wish of a poor Beggar Woman, who is represented asking her charity. Price 6 pence." A

Armchair for Masonic Master. Possibly the most unusual chair made in colonial America, this mahogany masonic seat incorporates features such as dolphins and lion's paw terminals from Thomas Chippendale's design book of 1754, many tools and symbols of Freemasonry and a portrait bust of the famed English poet, philosopher, and diplomat Matthew Prior (1664–1721). The choice of Prior is curious since he died shortly after the creation of the Grand Lodge in England and had little to say about Freemasonry. The bust derives from a mid-eighteenth-century ceramic image showing Prior in an artist's smock and turban. The chair, stamped with the name Benjamin Buckout, is the only known documented piece of Williamsburg furniture. COLONIAL WILLIAMSBURG FOUNDATION

royal waxworks was advertised in 1739, and nearly twenty years later "a fine Sett of Wax-work, consisting of Kings, Queens, &c. at full-Length" could be seen for six pence. In New York in 1771, a fire destroyed the waxwork of Mrs. Wright with its "Figures so nearly resembling the life, which have for some time past been exhibited in the City to general satisfaction." Nearly all Mrs. Wright's figures were "destroyed, amounting to several hundred pounds, yet she was so fortunate as to save the curious Piece of the Rev. Mr. Whitefield, the Pennsylvania Farmer, and some others."

Ornamental Works Early weather vanes were not sophisticated, but they were a form of public art. The earliest known, made for the second meetinghouse in Lynn, Massachusetts, is an iron banner that bears the cutout date, 1682. A rooster in copper from 1715 still has traces of paint and gold leaf. And a banner from 1699 decorated a Pennsylvania mill operated by William Penn, Samuel Carpenter, and Caleb Pusey. By 1742, Shem Drowne's grasshopper flew above the directional letters on Faneuil Hall in Boston. Throughout America, numerous shop signs carefully communicated goods an services in cities, villages, and along roadways.

Ceramic figurines adorned colonial houses. The Van Cortlandt family of New York had a pair of Chinese *blanc de Chine,* or white-on-white porcelain, compositions of three figures with a large lion and three cubs, each 11½″ high. One survives. The pair was recorded as "2 china Lion Images" in a 1774 inventory. In 1760, George Washington spent over twelve pounds on a number of sculptural ornaments "in copper, enamel or glazed." His supplier instructed him in "the manner of placing them on ye Chimney piece." There were five: "A group of Flora - Vase - Aeneas - Vase - Group of Bacchus." The vases were ornamented with "Faces & Festoons of Grapes & Vine Leaves &c finished Neat & bronzed w' Copp." The central group comprised "Aeneas carrying his Father out of Troy with 4 statues viz - his father Anchises, his wife Creusa, himself and his sone Ascanius." Washington also ordered and obtained "2 Furious Wild Beasts of any kind," which, of course, proved to be lions. Unfortunately, the great military leaders—Alexander the Great, Julius Caesar, Charles XII of Sweden, and Frederick the Great, King of Prussia—were not available. Neither were two other requests for Prince Eugene of Saxony and the Duke of Marlborough. In 1774, at the Belvoir sale, Washington was able to buy "a bust of the Imortal Shakespere." In Williamsburg in 1770, Governor Botetourt's inventory lists two separate sets of "11 Chelsea China figures." Governor Robert Eden left behind "2 China India figures" when he fled from Annapolis in 1776. "A Variety of curious fine China in Statuary," was offered at public auction in Boston in 1762, Closely related to these were "three Plaister Figures of Shakespear, Milton and Poppe" and "all sorts of Images, Birds, Cats, Dogs, & all other sorts of curious Animals, all of Plaster of Paris" offered in the 1760s by two Boston sellers.

Occasionally sculpture found its place on furniture. A portrait bust of the English philosopher John Locke (1632–1704) caps the pediment of a desk and bookcase, from around 1770–1780 in the Diplomatic Reception Rooms in Washington, D.C. A female bust affectionately named "Madame Pompadour" adorns a casepiece now housed in the Metropolitan Museum of Art. Most outlandish is the treatment of the back of a chair for a Masonic lodge that includes a bust of Matthew Prior.

As these examples of colonial fine art demonstrate, Americans took to prevalent classical expressions in the large efforts of public and private architecture. In painting, they chose portraits, landscapes, and a few religious and classical subjects. They bought engravings ranging from Hogarths's series, cityscapes, and maps. Neither American artists nor architects exerted any influence on European taste in these centuries, but they were generally aware of current European trends which they executed according to the tastes and pocketbooks of their clients. Their visual horizons were expanding.

See also **The Visual Arts; Architecture; Painting, Sculpture; Music** *(volume 3).*

BIBLIOGRAPHY

Colonial Society of Massachusetts, *Boston Prints and Printmakers, 1670–1775.* Boston, 1973.

Craven, Wayne. *American Art: History and Culture.* Madison, Wis., 1994.

Craven, Wayne. *Sculpture in America,* rev. ed. Newark, Del., 1984.

Cummings, Abbott Lowell. *The Framed Houses of Massachusetts Bay, 1625–1725.* Cambridge, Mass., 1979.

Little, Nina Fletcher. *American Decorative Wall Painting, 1700–1850,* enl. ed. New York, 1972.

Lounsbury, Carl R. *An Illustrated Glossary of Early Southern Architecture and Landscape.* New York, 1994.

Morrison, Hugh. *Early American Architecture from the First Colonial Settlements to the National Period.* New York, 1952.

Park, Helen. *A List of Architectural Books Available in America before the Revolution,* rev. ed. Los Angeles, 1973. Partly superceded by Janice Schimmelman, "Architectural Treatises and Handbooks Available in American Libraries and Bookstores through 1800," *Proceedings of the American Antiquarian Society* 95 (1985): 317–500.

Poesch, Jessie J. *The Art of the Old South: Painting, Sculpture, Architecture, and the Products of Craftsmen, 1560–1860.* New York, 1983.

Richardson, Edgar Preston. *Painting in America: The Story of 450 Years.* New York, 1963.

Sarudy, Barbara. *Gardens and Gardening in the Chesapeake, 1700–1805.* Baltimore, 1998.

Schwartz, Seymour I., and Ralph E. Ehrenberg. *The Mapping of America.* New York, 1980.

MERCANTILISM

Cathy Matson

Although it was never a complete system of laws and ideas, mercantilism guided the economic policy making of states throughout the Atlantic world during the early modern era. As the handmaiden of political nationalism and the consolidation of nation states following a long era of instability and war, mercantilism was a powerful rubric for understanding rapid changes and for giving coherence to particular new interests in Europe and England. Commerce was displacing landed interests in importance, and new ideas and policies began to privilege the people and goods related not to an organic, fixed economic order, but to an expansive commercial enterprise. Whereas in the past rents and direct land taxes provided the Crown with much of its operating revenue, by the early 1600s landed interests resisted higher taxes and so officials turned to merchants and taxes on their international trade as a source of support for the Crown.

By the early 1600s many writers began to reason that commerce was of vital importance to rising nation states because of its central role in overcoming scarcities, poverty, and the unemployment of European societies before then. In 1691 the English economist Sir Dudley North set forth one of the central tenets of mercantilism: "The whole World as to Trade, is but one Nation or People, and therein Nations are as Persons." Commerce united peoples across the globe in the satisfaction of their mutual wants and needs. As other writers insisted, commerce brought conveniences and pleasures to persons, strength and glory to the nation state.

The risks that merchants took to export and import goods produced beneficial results for the entire national community. Merchants offered the prospect of returning more gold and silver to crown coffers, and also demanded more special legislation to protect their interests against foreign competitors. Despite lingering suspicions about the nature of merchants' activities, many writers argued that merchants were also the ones who would organize international exchange, and return their ships laden with goods to satisfy consumer appetites. In an important reversal of traditional scorn for merchants, mercantilists argued that merchants served the nation by venturing into a world that was hostile, often at war, infested by pirates, plagued by deceitful debtors, and alarming in its degree of private competition. Merchants could navigate this world of risk and, in the process, exchange national surpluses for the "necessaries" and "superfluities" that citizens came to demand.

Although mercantile tenets were only loosely construed, politicians and ideological advocates shared a few notions that gave rough shape to the collective body of policies. One of the core concepts of mercantilism was "a balance of trade," by which it was argued that the best way to ensure that one nation's treasures was greater than all others was for its merchants to send out goods of greater value overall than they brought in. Such thinking did not imply mutuality or equality in exchange, any more than a balance of power implied political equality in the unwritten English constitution. The "overplus" of profits returned to England from foreign exchange would be in the form of specie (coins) and bills of exchange, assets that represented not only private gain but also enrichment of the nation's "stock" of money and goods. Mercantilists further emphasized the constancy of the world's wealth and a domestic economy operating on the basis of simple exchanges that satisfied individual needs. In this thinking, what one nation gained, another had to lose; for, as the English philosopher and writer Sir Francis Bacon observed, "whatsoever is somewhere gotten is somewhere lost."

But keeping a balance of trade in a country's favor was difficult to sustain over time, so that at the center of mercantile thinking was the assumption that government had a right and responsibility to shape the economic exchanges of citizens. By regulating producers, consumers, and merchants alike, the government would create a national interest and channel economic activities toward greater stability and prosperity than any particular interest could hope to achieve on its own. Policies were designed, for example, to exploit the consuming appetites of foreigners by sending commodities to them of greater value than what the home country imported. If one nation exported more than it imported, foreign nations would pay the balance of trade to the most active nation. A host of import restrictions, export incentives, revenue schedules, and collection officials, as well as drawbacks on reexports, rebates on raw materials used in manufactures, bounties to encourage new enterprise, inducements to import specie and keep it in the home country, and temporary embargoes or monopolies to spur commercial risk taking were all devised to enhance England's favorable balance of trade. Laws to encourage production of exportable commodities, to ease international trade on the high seas, and to restrain importation of competing goods proliferated over the early modern period. Private interests and government together, argued mercantilists, would secure a union of ambition, risk taking, and protection that would in turn benefit people nationwide and compete effectively against hostile external governments.

Since mercantilists shaped the commercial greatness of nations in the shadow of the diminishing stature of competing nations, warfare was a logical consequence. In the case of England, Queen Elizabeth I, who reigned from 1558 to 1603, understood the rising importance of commerce to England when she determined to defeat the Spanish Armada and clear the high seas of foreign pirates; subsequent efforts to create joint stock companies for foreign trade in different parts of the world expanded England's foreign dominion, too. By the early 1600s, Queen Elizabeth's nascent mercantile policies led to the creation of colonies such as Barbados and Virginia, and by then a host of English leaders anticipated war with the Dutch, who were England's most formidable commercial competitor.

With the Restoration in 1660, and the reign of King Charles II put in place, England's mercantile policy making began in earnest. Statute after statute stipulated that commercial regulations would contribute to the mutual rise of the imperial nation and its satellite colonies. Collectively called the Acts of Trade and Navigation (or the Navigation Acts), these laws set the requirements that imperial trade be channeled through England; they set the limits of colonial production within the empire and exchange outside of it; and, above all, they raised revenue from the colonies for the Crown.

The Navigation Act of 1651, which privileged English carriers of goods to the English colonies and limited the role of Dutch carriers, was the first of a long line of statutes that refined mercantile policies ever more clearly. Acts of 1660 and 1663 brought even more of the young empire's commerce under the aegis of English merchants and English ports. The 1660 Act ensured that no trade into or out of any English colony could take place in anything but an English ship built and registered in England, sailed by an English captain and a crew that was at least three-quarters English. The act further "enumerated" particular goods that were to bear import duties at any British ports—and thereby be the basis for revenue carried into the mother country from imperial trade. Early enumerated goods included a category of "European goods" that encompassed grain, wine, salt, Turkish commodities, and timber originating in non-English ports; and "colonial goods" such as tobacco, sugar, ginger, cotton wool, and dyes. Later acts would supplement the enumerated goods with rice, naval stores, copper, furs, finished iron goods, and other colonial exports. The 1663 Act further stipulated that all goods imported from European ports had to travel first through English ports to pay English customs duties. In order to enter the colonies, many items would have to be transferred from foreign vessels onto English or colonial ones, thereby guaranteeing English wholesalers more of the carrying trade and ensuring the English government more revenues. By then, belligerence turned into warfare against the Dutch, and mercantile goals of profit and power were inextricably tied together. Shortly thereafter, mercantilists reinforced commercial legislation with a host of bureaucratic appointments providing for the collection of duties and inspection of vessels; an Act of 1696 clarified admiralty court procedures for the prosecution of violators.

Mercantilists helped liberate commercial competition from traditional fears about merchants, luxury, foreigners, and extended credit and debt. The array of goods becoming available to consumers showed that commerce could give shape and purpose to private ambitions. If, in the process of acquiring necessary goods, consumers were exposed to fashion, arts, and even luxury, the laws of the state would curb excesses. Consumers would be able to enjoy refinement, become more civilized, and not bend to their base passions, thanks to the watchful guidance of the state. Laws that facilitated the exportation of goods to customers abroad were balanced by those that regulated the flow of imports and thus checked the deleterious consequences of luxury consumption on private character. Within a nation, and among nations, trade linked people in a Chain of Dependence on each other. Indeed, after 1720 many mercantilists differentiated between the evils of stockjobbing or usury, and the civilized virtues of a cultured society that a nation's material rise enhanced.

After 1720 certain mercantile thinking and policies began to change focus. Manufacturers in England were becoming an important presence in the domestic economy, and they had gained a voice in circles close to the Crown and Parliament. Their interests centered less on revenue making and more on obtaining lower duties on imported raw materials and exported English finished goods, as well as lower interest rates, lower exchange rates for currency, easier credit for private interests, incentives to settle and develop new lands, and deterrents to piracy and the flight of specie.

During the 1730s lobbyists representing the "West Indies interest" and manufacturers in England argued that shifting commercial and producing interests required a new view of the colonies as well. For example, while the Caribbean's plantation economy had continued to occupy the most important place in transatlantic imperial exchanges, argued lobbyists, the North American colonists had systematically violated Acts of Trade that prohibited their trade at foreign islands. Colonists also frequently rejected legitimate trade with fellow colonists at British islands. In ensuing debates over policy, colonists were increasingly reminded that they were subordinate, dependent satellites of the mother country. There would be no even "balance of power" between the English state and the colonies. Rather, mercantilists reinforced mercantile laws governing West Indies and other trade relations. Colonies, they insisted, should never buy goods directly from foreign nations if they could purchase the equivalent from the mother country; nor should colonists send their ships and goods to peoples outside the empire unless they had it cleared through imperial customs officers and paid the requisite duties and fees. In all, imperial leaders were entitled to enjoy a "monopoly" of commercial rights over colonists.

By the Seven Years' War, a substantially altered view of the North American colonists was emerging overseas. As the Iron Act of 1750 underscored, colonial production was to be controlled and restricted, so as to complement but never compete with English manufacturing. Colonists were to provide important markets for the purchase of English finished commodities, and thereby subsidize the ris-

ing productivity of the mother country. Although international commerce remained the chief conceptual realm for most imperial writers throughout the 1700s, a decided shift toward privileging the special interests of English manufacturing was beginning to occur just as the Imperial Crisis set in.

How did North Americans respond to this re-conceptualization of their place in the empire? Most scholars would agree that there was no immediate outcry. The Molasses Act of 1733, intended to levy a tax on sugar, molasses, and rum, and to enforce the collection of duties and channeling of English ships into legal West Indies voyages, was in fact systematically sidestepped over the following three decades. Colonists were legally permitted a wide latitude of trade with some foreign ports during times of peace. And although some important items of colonial transport were taxed—including peltry, dyewoods, sugar, and naval stores—many goods that were shipped in very large quantities were never enumerated at all, including the wheat and flour exported from the middle Atlantic colonies, livestock, processed meats, staves and boards, and salt. Wine, an increasingly important import, was taxed only after 1705, and the enumerated commodities potash, pearl ash, whale oil, iron, indigo, ginger, and cotton wool were exported in large quantities only after the opening of the eighteenth century. A few colonial merchants made fortunes privateering and trading within the mercantile system; many more did not grow rich, but readily agreed that they benefited from the privileged commercial status all English colonists were granted within the empire.

Then, too, although mercantilism was not solely responsible for the rising standards of living throughout the empire, contemporaries associated state protection with the unparalleled opportunities of that era. In the North American colonies, which reached over one-third of the British empire's population by the mid-1700s, colonists boasted the highest standard of living anywhere in the known world. Whether by slave or servant labor, hardscrabble family farming, rich soil and good waterways, or sheer luck, colonists were aided in their endeavors to prosper by the many ways that mercantilism protected their commerce and defended their polities. Furthermore, mercantile writers issued a series of promotional tracts that gave optimism to colonists contemplating the compelling prospects for economic success as members of the English empire, and replaced many long-standing ethical injunctions against expansive private material wealth with praise for expansive appetites. Such optimism paralleled the opportunities of protected markets, channeling of foreign competition, deterrents to the flight of valuable currencies, and arguments for the suppression of piracy against the empire's ships. For these reasons, most colonial merchants continued to adhere, ideologically, to mercantile tenets.

However, some of the most influential writers on economic policies began to chip away at portions of the mercantile edifice. Their concerns often began with attempts to reconcile the individual's quest for continual improvement with the restraining hand of the state. How, some writers asked, can policy makers simultaneously celebrate the private search for greater wealth, and restrain waste of one's property, encroachments on others' property, or greed and passion to acquire without limit? How, they also asked, can the state free ambitious interests to seek markets and at the same time define and limit commercial choices?

In England, this tension between the acquisitive individual and the restraining state was addressed more fully than in continental Europe. The second of John Locke's second treatise *Two Treatises of Government,* which was highly influential at the time of the Glorious Revolution, warned of the dangers that followed from "ceaseless ambitions," but also exuded confidence in the ability of individuals to control and coordinate their appetites. By invoking the hypothetical vision that when "all the world was America," there had been no need for government, Locke opened the door to considerations about reducing the influence of government in contemporary England.

Some voices spoke out more emphatically than Locke against mercantile policies. Traditionalists of many kinds raised doubts very early in the 1600s about whether Britons should eschew customary wisdoms about specie, prices, and economic exchanges in order to prop up the "mushroom" merchants rising from below in the new commercial order. Some critics worried about legislation being passed for factional reasons, on behalf of shifting interests that did not hold a stake in the social order of the nation. Still others objected to the great national debt associated with mercantile objectives, especially the establishment of the Bank of England at the end of the seventeenth century, through which the government became the nation's largest debtor, borrowing systematically from individuals and monopolied companies to fuel competition and wars abroad. The specter of "mere paper credits" arose by the early 1700s, when speculation in government securities rose to alarming heights.

Alongside Locke and traditionalists, another strain of criticism of mercantilism arose. Appeals for "economic freedom," or "free trade," appeared frequently during seventeenth-century discussions about how empires grew, acquired dominion abroad, and sustained far-flung peoples in their orbits. Some English observers disagreed that Dutch commercial supremacy should be merely squashed; instead, perhaps, the "natural liberty" of Dutch trade, including open ports through the Dutch empire and the absence of restrictions at markets, ought to be emulated. Governors and merchants of West Indies islands in the early seventeenth century demanded more freedom for merchants visiting their ports, and numerous rising interests clamored for an end to great trading monopolies.

By the late 1600s, economic freedom was pitted against mercantilism more subtly. Holland, it turned out, was never so "perfectly free" as some English writers imagined, and almost all writers advocated particular kinds of regulations for particular economic interests from time to time. Merchants who were most vulnerable in trade and least empowered in politics often argued the loudest for eliminating commercial restraints; but these comparatively weaker economic groups were also unable to sustain such efforts. Nevertheless, the appeal of arguments for economic freedom—as distinguished from mercantilism—remained alive in work that extolled the natural competition of buyers and sellers in personally responsive exchanges. Coastal and West Indian traders in eighteenth-century North America used arguments about economic freedom to justify their growing illegal trade. Retailers and reflective consumers began to turn away from older notions of political and moral obligation to society, and from prescriptive rights of landownership, toward the "sweet" effects of self-interested commerce. As a consequence, it became more and more difficult for provincial governments in the empire to create monopolies, declare embargoes, or discriminate against neighboring ports because there was widespread public sentiment for simply ignoring such mercantile efforts.

By the mid-1700s writers in the Scottish Enlightenment tradition added their voices to those who would soften the influence of mercantilism, especially as they distanced themselves from the problems of political corruption and addressed more directly the economic goals of mercantilism. The Scottish philosopher and historian David Hume, who published influential tracts in the 1740s and 1750s, deemphasized the necessity of a strong state in creating economic success and downplayed the dangers of merchant greed. He recognized a universal love of gain in human beings, as well as the increasing bounty available for consumption. Although mild mercantile regulations might be necessary to protect and encourage "infant interests" Hume maintained, an elaborate edifice of legislation over extensive periods of time would probably interfere with individual economic initiatives. Moreover, Hume came close to recognizing a self-correcting mechanism in economies that were relatively unfettered by mercantile legislation: over the long term, he believed, setbacks, scarcities, and gluts would come and go; if regulations were held to a minimum and people were free to create markets as collectives of individuals, then there was no reason to fear temporary disturbances in the overall rising prosperity of a nation. The Scottish economist Adam Smith would challenge mercantilism even more forcefully along these lines in his famous Book 4 of *The Wealth of Nations,* which was published in 1776.

Concepts of regulation and freedom functioned as poles of a single powerful discourse which might be labeled economic liberalism. Although advocates of mercantilism thought of free trade arguments as absolutely antithetical to their goals, and thus not an equal possibility to be chosen or modified, both sets of economic ideas were in fact nurtured together in public debates about the delicate equipoise between such other concepts as authority and liberty, scarcity and plenty, and war and peace. Both poles of thought validated the commercial claims of merchants in the Western world against the countervailing interests of the landed aristocracy and customary traditions, promoting a radical shift in thinking about trade, commodities, and international exchange. Mercantilists and free traders alike subscribed to the notion of human perfectibility over time and believed in the universal human desire for refinement. The connections they made between self-interest, property, and national wealth overturned ancient and scholastic conceptions of the common interest by proposing that the promise of material reward lay at the heart of individual inducements to labor and that profits were a justified gain from commercial risk taking. Seeking to avoid the scarcities, insecurities, and widespread unemployment of previous eras, both mercantilists and the advocates of free trade extolled brisk circulation of, and more demand for, all kinds of goods. The resultant wealth, they believed, was the stuff that would make nations and satellite colonies great.

As noted, until the Imperial Crisis of 1763–1776, little organized resistance to mercantile restrictions occurred in the mainland colonies. Mercantilism had protected and nurtured colonial trade for many years with convoys, bounties, military defense, and a wide latitude of unenumerated trade—all of which counterbalanced the long list of commodities that bore duties, and the restrictions made on who carried goods, how they were carried, and where they were permitted to go.

However, as colonists perceived that the laws were tightening, they began to petition more vigorously and to publicly discuss the more widespread ramifications of changes in commercial laws that emanated from England after the Seven Years' War. In this dissent, colonists referred to their long-standing habits of ignoring imperial laws or smuggling, which had been endured relatively quietly on all sides of the empire for decades, but took on more poignant meanings in the context of heightened colonial unhappiness with the legal and constitutional contours of empire after 1763. Larger numbers of merchants were willing to flaunt their smuggling, and great numbers of colonists were willing to tolerate and even promote it. Illegal trade not only became a widely sanctioned form of informal protest against mercantilism, it also became a popular conduit of expansive consumer desires for new commodities.

Colonists also were inspired by the countervailing ideas of economic freedom, which had never been a successful antidote to the unequal balance of power between parts of the empire, but endured as a vision of human potential. Indeed, although revolutionary Americans had no clear conception about the role government should play in their future economy, tenets of economic freedom pointed toward dismantling the regulatory apparatus of British mercantilism and releasing individual energies into marketplaces. In the process of achieving independence, the vision of a collective of unfettered individuals interacting in benign market relations remained alive. During the nonimportation movements of 1765, 1768, and 1770 rhetoric about the potential for colonial self-sufficiency in future years ran high.

However, in the exigencies of the Revolutionary War, Americans were forced to use their new state governments to create policies that interfered more extensively in the economy than the hated British mercantilism itself. The Continental Association of 1774 enjoined Americans to cease importing, exporting, and consuming goods of English "taint." Price controls and local enforcement committees were part of the new machinery of public virtue, and often the trade to the foreign West Indies was curtailed. Whatever latitude they gave individual economic freedom, the exigencies of war led to dramatic expansion of public authority over the lives of private citizens and their markets.

Moreover, despite the rhetoric of economic freedom during the American Revolution, most citizens were wary of fulfilling such a promise after the war. The new nation's experiments with unregulated foreign and domestic exchange raised troubling questions about whether Americans had virtue enough to sustain independence; foreign powers constantly warned that the "thirteen disunited states" were falling into political anarchy and commercial luxury. Free trade, just like unfettered individual self-interest, could never hold a people together, according to eighteenth-century wisdom. And even the groups of southern planters and northern merchants who wished to increase their sphere of economic freedom called often on Congress to negotiate favorable trade agreements. Land speculators, commercial farmers, and urban artisans all sought state legislation to further their ambitions.

Nationalists during the 1780s felt certain that some degree of neo-mercantilism would shape America's economy in the future. The problem was, however, that state legislatures had steadily gained popular support for regulations of conflicting and discriminatory sorts. Such differentiation among the states was not conducive to holding the federal republic together; in fact, it raised the specter of selfish state interests vying with each other and annihilating the joint interests of all states. Without adequate regulation at the national level, a uniform commercial policy transcending state particularisms, and the creation of a viable national domain in the West, the states would destroy Americans' best hopes for stability and expansion.

The pessimism of the 1780s that surrounded commentaries about America's economic future were set aside by reconceptualizing the value of their mercantilist past. Instead of individual state regimes of regulation, and instead of one continental consolidated union that regulated from afar, the framers at the Philadelphia Constitutional Convention began to see the virtues of mixing regulatory powers at both the state and national levels. The federal system they proposed in 1787, while typically addressed by scholars as a series of interlocking political measures, was undergirded by the realization that America comprised many distinctive economic interests at local and regional levels. Economic interests, according to the Federalist solution, need not be fractured and mutually contradictory; economic regulations, properly understood and expediently shaped, could preserve and strengthen the Union. It was a winning formula—for the time being—and even Anti-Federalists had to agree about the value of government's protective hand in the economy; for Federalists and their detractors alike, the issue was not whether government regulation was necessary, but rather the extent and nature of that regulation. Into the 1790s mercantilism continued to shed much of its association with special interest legislation and restraint on commercial opportunities. It became one of the cornerstones of the Federalist promises to create a natural union of economic interests in America, and new political configurations after Federalists also continued to insist that far from stifling individual citizens' entrepreneurial ambitions, government regulations would protect and serve them.

See also **Political Economy; Consumerism; Technological Enclaves** *(volume 3).*

BIBLIOGRAPHY

Classic Sources

Goldsmiths'-Kress Library of Economic Literature: Resources in the Economic, Social, Business and Political History of Modern Industrial Society, pre-1800–1850. Woodbridge, Conn., 1975– .

Hume, David. *Writings on Economics.* Edited by Eugene Rotwein. Madison, Wisc., 1955.

Jensen, Merrill, et al. *The Documentary History of the Ratification of the Constitution.* 10 vols. to date. Madison, Wisc., 1976– .

Locke, John. *Two Treatises of Government.* Edited by Peter Laslett. New York, 1965.

Petty, William. "Political Arithmetick." In *The Economic Writings of Sir William Petty,* edited by Charles Henry Hull. Cambridge, Mass., 1899.

Smith, Adam. *An Inquiry into the Nature and Causes of the Wealth of Nations.* Book 4. 1776. Edited by Edwin Cannan, 1904. Reprint, Chicago, 1976.

Yaranton, Andrew. *England's Improvement by Sea and Land.* London, 1677.

Secondary Sources

Andrews, Charles M. *The Colonial Period of American History.* 4 vols. New Haven, Conn., 1934–1938. Volume 4 is especially relevant.

Appleby, Joyce Oldham. *Economic Thought and Ideology in Seventeenth-Century England.* Princeton, N.J., 1979.

Harper, Lawrence. *The English Navigation Laws: A Seventeenth-Century Experiment in Social Engineering.* New York, 1939.

Hirschman, Albert O. *The Passions and the Interests: Political Arguments for Capitalism before its Triumph.* Princeton, N.J., 1977.

Letwin, William O. *The Origins of Scientific Economics: English Economic Thought, 1660–1776.* London, 1963.

Macpherson, C. B. *The Political Theory of Possessive Individualism: Hobbes to Locke.* Oxford, 1962.

Wilson, Charles. *England's Apprenticeship, 1603–1763.* London, 1965.

LAW (COLONIAL)

Sally E. Hadden

American law did not develop from purely American experiences but evolved from European legal ideas and experiences, which migrated to the New World in the minds of settlers and in the books they brought with them. The most significant source of America's legal tradition was England's common and constitutional law. In addition, the civil law of France and Spain also influenced American legal thought, as did the ad hoc system of slave law created by European slave owners in the course of supervising their plantations in the Caribbean. The transmission of European legal ideas, combined with ideas forged in a New World crucible, created a colonial legal culture that continues to have a lasting effect upon American society.

ENGLISH BACKGROUND

Residents of early modern England were familiar with law as it operated in their society, even if they never saw the interior of London's exalted Westminster law courts. In their daily lives, legal norms, procedures, and penalties surrounded and regulated everyday experiences. The lord's manorial court, the local borough court, or the traveling assizes that brought justices from London to towns across England ensured that most English men and women had seen a judge or trial—perhaps the arrival of justices to open the local assize, or the hanging of a thief at the trial's conclusion—at some point during their lifetimes. These courts were surrounded by enough ritual pomp and ceremony to convey the seriousness of legal events to even the illiterate of English society, in much the same way that stained glass windows transmitted visual knowledge of the Bible to the illiterate faithful who gathered in English cathedrals.

Aside from dispensing justice, judges were primarily responsible for keeping the populace in check at a time when England had no police force

or effective penitentiaries to monitor or discipline public behavior when it went wrong. For English criminals who transgressed the law in the sixteenth, seventeenth, or eighteenth centuries, the options for punishment were limited. Fines, public shaming mechanisms like the stocks, mutilation (through branding, ear cropping, and whipping), or execution remained the judges' only options, until transportation to a New World colony became a viable possibility. The threat of execution became particularly severe in the seventeenth and eighteenth centuries, as the list of capital crimes grew lengthy, but scholars believe that in actual practice criminal execution was used relatively sparingly. Marxist historians, foremost among them E. P. Thompson and scholars trained by him, have explored this phenomena as an exercise of class-based domination. Why would a society create laws so severe that hanging should have been an almost daily event, but was not? The process of inspiring terror in the general population seemed necessary to ruling elites who enacted laws and passed sentence from the bench, but terror could be tempered with mercy; for example, clemency was ritually extended to the convicted on a routine basis through "benefit of clergy" (a one-time exemption allowing the offender to read a Bible verse and receive a lighter sentence). By granting mercy to the convict, judges subtly convinced the masses that law was dispensed fairly to everyone, thus inspiring support for law and lawgivers from all ranks of English society, not just the elites who wrote laws and then enforced them from the bench. The convicted man was expected to pronounce a judge honest and the law fair, even when sent to the gallows for his crimes; printers in early modern England published pamphlets containing the final contrite musings of many a condemned man, in which he would usually fault himself (or law or society) for his failings. This method of doing justice to criminals would find imitators in the colonies, where police and penitentiaries were also unknown; as a result, the "terror-mercy" spectacle of many criminal trials passed from England to America.

Yet the ordinary Englishman need not have watched a criminal hang or a judge process into his courtroom with majestic robes and a white wig to know about law. Daily life brought law into many English households. The transmission of property (through sales, mortgage, or lease) and the making of contracts (for labor or goods) meant that most families entered into legal relations with others as a part of everyday living. Goods sold had to be warranted for soundness; property mortgaged had to have proper documentation. As a result, lawyers became more common in early modern England, for they handled the daily transaction of business, land, and goods that passed from hand to hand in a market economy, although not everyone could participate. English law disabled women; while it enabled men to conduct business, the common law technically restricted women to legally subordinate positions. Women who married passed from legal subservience under their fathers to legal invisibility under their husbands (a status known as *feme covert*). Only widows escaped the supervision of an adult male for their legal dealings. In theory, married women could not contract debts or run businesses; whatever property they brought with them in marriage became their husbands', and wealthy families took extreme measures to control property given to daughters, so that husbands could not exploit or waste their lands. In reality, some boroughs passed laws permitting married women to trade and own property, effectively admitting that a few women operated outside their sex's legal norms. One feature of modern life would have been completely unknown to the common inhabitant of early modern England: divorce was virtually unheard of. Only the wealthy could afford to petition for divorce through the ecclesiastic courts of England (another realm of legal contests) and even then divorce was only granted for limited reasons, such as impotence. Beginning in 1670, legislative divorces became possible, effected by private bill through Parliament, but they too remained outside the reach of average English citizens.

Law regulated relationships between man and wife, seller and purchaser, and even community member and outsider. The Elizabethan poor law mandated that indigent persons be returned to the parish of their birth; regardless of personal choice, a woman with no means of support could be legally evicted from village after village ("warned out") until she was forced back to her birthplace. This process was adopted in English colonies, particularly in the mid-eighteenth century when poverty rates rose following a series of wars between England and France. But even residents who never left home for an entire lifetime lived in a world ringed with laws. Incorporated (chartered by the Crown) towns like London created their own laws about roads, fires, markets, and worship, to name only a few areas regulated by civic authority.

CONQUEST AND SETTLEMENT

Following the discovery of land in the New World, Spaniards, Frenchmen, Dutchmen, and Englishmen alike made their way westward, hoping to find wealth. According to European law, claims made by explorers such as Christopher Columbus, John Cabot, Jacques Cartier, and Hernán Cortés transferred (through the antiquated means of feudal vassalage) land in the New World to their monarchs. Despite the fact that the monarchs never saw the new lands or that Native Americans had lived on them for generations—explorers claimed the Americas for king and country. The Spanish sent administrators and soldiers to exploit what wealth they could from Central and South America; Spanish monarchs became the envy of other European rulers as they profited from the gold and silver that flowed back across the ocean to them. Many Spanish soldiers went to the New World because Spanish law typically favored the transfer of land from father to eldest son, limiting the inheritance of real property by younger sons (a legal rule known as primogeniture, common in England as well). Spanish administrators set up governments-in-miniature in each New World colony, establishing *audencias,* which served as both local councils to territorial viceroys and as courts of law in each region. True political authority remained in Spain, but local customs or viceregal decisions achieved the status of law to such a widespread extent that Spanish New World ordinances and bylaws were compiled and published as the *Recopilación de leyes de los reinos de las Indias* in 1681.

Initially, England's monarchs sent no administrators to America in the way the Spanish did. Although the charters they granted required that English law be observed in the new colonies, colonists would have the chance to develop local laws suited to their own principles. English kings used the new American lands as royal favors (given in return for promises of future economic royalties or used as payoffs for services rendered to the Crown) whether the charter went to a merchant company (as in the case of Virginia) or a group of noble proprietors (as with Maryland and the Carolinas). The charters provided the legal foundation for local colonial authority, and any disputes about governance would ultimately be judged by whether a law, a governor's action, or a court decision exceeded the original mandate given by the Crown to settlers. By the eighteenth century, the majority of charters establishing English colonies in America had been revoked and replaced, dispossessing companies and proprietors in favor of the Crown, so that the king could select royal governors and council members for the colonies. What the Crown gave, the Crown could take back—medieval feudal relations and royal prerogative dictated that the English king was the ultimate legal owner of all his country's lands, even those in America.

LEGALLY DISENFRANCHISED: NATIVE AMERICANS AND SLAVES

The native peoples who had resided throughout North America for ages were reluctant to lose their best hunting, fishing, and planting grounds to European settlers who flocked to the continent, relying upon charters to stake their land claims. Both the Spaniards and English tried to reduce indigenous peoples to slavery, but the Spanish had greater success. To work their mines and plantations, the Spanish imported Africans to the New World to labor beside the native peoples as slaves. The Catholicism that dominated Spanish settlements, in addition to the civil law tradition that the Spaniards brought with them, dictated that slaves should be treated with dignity and that their personhood should be recognized: for example, Spanish law mandated that slaves who married should not be separated, slaves should be allowed to rest and attend worship services on Sunday, and slaves should be able to keep and own property. This last legal consideration, a remnant of Roman law that had survived within Spain's civil law, permitted slaves to amass money so that they could purchase their own freedom, a process known as *coartación.* Similar protections appeared in French New World colonies and were codified in the *Code noir,* a compilation of French slave-related laws published in 1685. Legally, the lot of slaves under French and Spanish regimes appeared milder than the form of slavery that evolved under English control; slaves working on English plantations had no such safeguards under law. However, scholars have disputed whether Spanish and French laws were actually enforced and gave

protection to the (legally speaking) weakest of all residents in the New World.

In English Caribbean settlements, slavery forced some of the first legal innovations that became part of America's laws. Unlike the Spanish and French, who derived many of their slave laws from Roman legal sources, the English had no common-law tradition regarding slaves. Serfdom and villenage—forms of legal unfreedom in the Middle Ages—had disappeared from early modern England, so the English borrowed many laws and practices for controlling slaves from their colonial Spanish and French Caribbean counterparts. Crudely constructing slave laws using the forms of English common law (for example, confusing whether slaves could have legal volition or were to be treated as mere pieces of property), seventeenth-century Englishmen crafted slave codes in the Caribbean that were copied—in whole or in part—by English settlers who moved to continental North America later in the century. Although American slave law appeared orderly and precise by the nineteenth century, it remained chaotic and unsystematic in the colonial period. Slaves had no direct impact upon the shaping of American law as lawmakers or legal interpreters, but their actions of resistance (such as running away, vagrancy, and shirking) inspired the creation of American laws to curb their perceived misbehavior. Slaves on New World plantations may have used African legal procedures during the first few generations, but their European masters either did not know or care about such traditions; Spanish, French, or English laws and procedures prevailed whenever slaves were brought to court, usually for capital crimes (like arson, rape, or murder) committed against whites. Simpler, less violent crimes—and punishments—were handled by the individual master, and most slaves never encountered any transplanted, formal European legal procedures during their lifetimes. For many slaves, the master *was* the law.

Like the Africans, Native Americans found themselves disempowered through legal procedures utilized by Europeans who tried to dominate them. Whether reduced to slavery or not, Native Americans discovered that their legal practices and tribal laws were routinely ignored by Europeans, who dismissed them as barbaric or quaint customs. Few legal concepts derived from Native Americans became part of mainstream American legal thought, in part because Europeans could not accommodate the cultural implications that would follow such acceptance. For example, native couples could readily divorce, but this was unthinkable in both Catholic and Protestant settlements, where law and religion combined to prevent such family divisions. A clear example of the dissonance between native and European legal traditions can be seen in attitudes toward real property. Native tribes tended to treat land as a spiritual commodity that was shared communally by all living things, and the land itself might be endowed with mystical qualities as the home of higher entities. Tribes recognized that some lands "belonged" to rival groups or that a specific planting ground "belonged" to a particular family group, but in general, native peoples considered land a community asset filled with spiritual meaning that should not be desecrated by excessive fishing or hunting. The European practice of treating land as an individually held piece of property, with which the owner could do anything, was alien to Native American legal conceptions. Sometimes Europeans "purchased" lands from Native Americans for settlement via treaties, but whether Indians understood European ideas about exclusive property rights remains unclear. More often than not, however, European-born settlers simply considered the land to be theirs, and they relied upon royal charters to justify selling and leasing that property to others. When indigenous peoples returned to traditional hunting grounds and found permanent settlers there who claimed exclusive use of a specific piece of land, the stage was set for conflict between the groups. Such legal-cultural misunderstandings were common throughout the New World and persisted until the twentieth century, when the treaties became the legal basis for reclaiming territory by modern tribal entities.

DISPUTES IN CHURCH AND COURT

Within English colonial settlements, a complex legal regime developed to resolve disputes among settlers. Justices of the peace decided minor problems with low financial costs. Justices of the peace came from the ranks of colonial gentry, and their social status helped enforce decisions that they made individually. Collectively, justices of the peace rendered judgment in county courts, where more costly issues came before them four times a year. Gentlemen frequently held multiple positions of authority, and it was not uncommon in the seventeenth and eighteenth century for justices of the peace to serve as members of their colonial assembly, muster the local militia as officers, and rule on cases from the county court bench. In their individual capacity, justices of the peace were the most

familiar face of colonial legal authority in each community. Armed with Michael Dalton's *The Countrey Justice* (1618), an English-printed manual to cover all legal occasions and the first book most Americans imported for legal guidance, justices of the peace resolved a variety of legal disagreements.

Above the justices of the peace and the county courts on which they sat were courts of appeal, including colonial supreme courts. Unlike modern America's courts, in which virtually all appeals are based upon an error in arrest or at trial (and where the appellate trial is about the technical error), colonial appeals frequently required a completely new trial of facts before new judges. Ultimately, a decision rendered by the highest colonial court might be appealed back to England and the Board of Trade and Plantations (a royal advisory group), in a process that the historian Joseph Smith has described as one that foreshadowed judicial review. Likewise, colonial laws were reviewed for their conformity to English law and were voided if they violated English law. No laws or legal decisions could ever be considered final in the colonies, so long as they could be appealed to England. Nonetheless, through locally created colonial assemblies and court systems, American colonists in the eighteenth century grew accustomed to managing their own legal affairs without interference from imperial authorities in London.

Other groups also resolved legal disputes within the colonial world. In the seventeenth century, especially in New England, churches frequently intervened between feuding members to settle both spiritual and secular arguments. As the historians David Konig and William Nelson have described, church-based dispute resolution kept many causes from actually reaching the courthouse. The methods varied by congregation, but it was common to appoint a group of arbitrators who met with each of the aggrieved parties; the arbitrators would attempt to conciliate the combatants so that Puritan community harmony could be restored. Dispute resolution worked best in homogenous communities where all residents belonged to the same church. Church-based solutions declined in popularity and efficacy in the eighteenth century when New World community populations diversified and dispersed, churches multiplied in number and denominational variety, and economic competition increased. As financial contacts expanded across the Atlantic and down the seaboard in the eighteenth century, traders and merchants in coastal towns conducted business with far-flung inland proprietors who might not be known to them through face-to-face dealings. Women routinely appeared in court to sue and be sued. Not surprisingly, the number of lawsuits rose almost exponentially in the eighteenth century due to the booming colonial population, decline of church-based dispute resolution, and tremendous economic growth.

LAWYERS AND THEIR TRAINING: THE EXPERIENCE OF JOHN ADAMS

In the seventeenth century, few lawyers migrated to American colonial settlements. A very few settlers in these early groups may have had two or three years' training at the Inns of Court (the method of legal apprenticeship in London) but from the beginning, lawyers were disdained in the new communities or lacked sufficient work to be employed full-time. In New England, the religious covenant that bound together individuals with God and each other in loving relations discouraged those same individuals from prosecuting cases through court. In the South, some high-born settlers preferred resolving their disputes without courtrooms, for conceptions of honor or deference gave face-to-face solutions greater moral weight than allowing judges to decide problems impersonally. In addition to societal opprobrium, some legislatures prevented lawyers from plying their trade; the Massachusetts General Court originally barred advocates from pleading in court in return for client fees. In such a hostile climate, few lawyers willingly journeyed to America where judges and court clerks in every colony knew virtually nothing about formal adjudication. This may have made for rough, intuitive justice in the seventeenth century (in which judges sometimes resorted to biblical solutions, as New England justices occasionally did), but professional lawyers disdained such proceedings as anything but law. Despite the absence of trained attorneys, many individuals—including a few women—carried on thriving legal practices, using their memory of English legal procedures and rough knowledge of the law to plead cases in colonial courts. These individuals almost always worked as attorneys on strictly a part-time basis, in addition to their regular vocations as farmers or merchants.

Only in the eighteenth century were educated, full-time lawyers present in the colonies—some trained at the Inns of Court, while others sought legal education through apprenticeship to established American attorneys. Learning from a working attorney provided access to a lawyer's library and provided examples of how to handle clients and

John Adams (c. 1766). Benjamin Blyth, pastel on paper. This portrait was done shortly after Adams began his legal career. COURTESY OF THE MASSACHUSETTS HISTORICAL SOCIETY

win cases. Having completed his bachelor's degree at Harvard the future president John Adams apprenticed himself in 1756 to the attorney James Putnam. Adams studied Roman civil law texts like Justinian's *Institutes* during his apprenticeship in addition to the English common law, and he probably helped Putnam draft simple bills and letters for delivery to court and clients. For a lawyer, the most important books were written in Latin; Adams's college education guaranteed that he was comfortable reading and writing that language. After two years of study, Adams returned home to Braintree, Massachusetts, and continued his studies; later he applied for admission to the local bar association (Boston was one of the rare colonial cities that had a bar association, limiting who practiced law in the courts). The best lawyers in Boston questioned him on legal matters before signing his certificate and allowing him to be sworn in as a bona fide attorney. Even after admission to the bar, Adams recognized how poorly he had been trained during his apprenticeship. He applied to Jeremy Gridley, the leading lawyer in Boston, to guide him to clients and further learning. Gridley did both, and Adams's practice flourished during the next fifteen years. Even into the nineteenth century, many American lawyers relied upon patronage to improve their skills and word of mouth to bring them business. For the next hundred years, young struggling attorneys could secure access to better libraries and more clients by marrying the daughters of leading lawyers, or at the very least marrying the daughters of well-situated families that could ensure a steady stream of business. Adams attained the latter through his marriage to Abigail Smith, who was related to the respected, powerful Quincy, Shepard, and Smith clans of Boston.

Adams collected his own library of legal literature, much the same way that Thomas Jefferson of Virginia did. Adams owned books on common law, civil law, court opinions from England (nearly twenty volumes), and abridgments that summarized important opinions under topical headings. To stay up-to-date on legal developments, Adams made arrangements with English booksellers to send him new law books as they were published (as did many well-read colonial gentlemen, whether they practiced law or not); almost no books about the law were published in America during the colonial period. Until the end of the eighteenth century, opinions rendered in American courtrooms were usually recorded only by lawyers who were present to hear them. Adams, like other practicing attorneys, took copious notes about judgments he heard delivered in court. Adams and other colonial lawyers would also have read Sir Edward Coke's *Institutes of the Laws of England* (a four-volume, seventeenth-century guide to English law and process) and William Blackstone's *Commentaries* on English law (published in the 1760s). Much of Adams's studies were given over to understanding actions about contract and property, with some time devoted to admiralty law and commercial matters like bailment. Like most eighteenth-century lawyers, his legal practice gave him little reason to study, or to use, material about criminal law or torts. The orderly presentation of law in Coke and Blackstone—which organized English legal opinions by topic, subtopic, and sub-subtopic—gave a formal structure and systematic feel to the otherwise chaotic legal decisions rendered in English courts. Coke and Blackstone's carefully arranged series of legal authorities reinforced the sense colonial lawyers had that their field of study was growing clearer and more mathematically precise with each opinion. The scientific precision (verging on biological taxonomy in its orderliness) of English legal opinions presented in digests like these connected colonial readers with the Enlightenment spirit that pervaded European legal writing through the eighteenth century.

While authorities like Coke or Blackstone could show Adams much about the correct form for pleading a case, and give numerous examples of cases won in support of a specific legal principle, they did not always carry the day in American courtrooms. Colonial judges, even in the eighteenth century, frequently were not well read in technical legal matters as lawyers like Adams or Jefferson were. Moreover, individuals who had no legal training continued to appear before eighteenth-century courts to plead their own causes and those of their neighbors. Adams's worst nightmare became real during the first case he pleaded—and lost—to an untrained man who knew much less law than Adams did, but who knew how to persuade a judge and jury with commonsense arguments. The decisions made by judges, learned or not, remained so crucial to a budding legal career that Adams attended court sessions incessantly to watch and learn all that he could not understand from books alone.

The great mass of legal cases handled by Adams and other colonial attorneys concerned contracts and property. The getting and selling of services or goods in the New World was important, since labor was scarce and many finished goods had to be imported from abroad. Property, on the other hand, was readily available, for land in America seemed endless to European settlers. If land was plentiful, disputes about it also arose with profusion: routine quarrels involving botched surveyors' maps, faulty deeds, or squatters versus owners provided a steady stream of business for colonial courts. The abundance of real property prompted some important changes in legal doctrine that would have seemed unusual back in the Old World, where land was relatively scarce. For example, instead of providing land for only the eldest son (primogeniture), at the time of inheritance many colonial families subdivided their property and gave land to each of their children, or gave land to each son and moveable goods (like household furnishings) to each daughter. Outside of Kent, an English county where such equitable divisions were common (a practice known as gavelkind), equal or near-equal division of lands among a family's children was uncommon in England.

LEGISLATURES, LOCAL COURTS, AND THE AMERICAN REVOLUTION

Although modern readers are accustomed to a strong distinction between legislative enactments (laws affecting groups) and judicial opinions (cases usually affecting individuals), in the colonial period there seems to have been little difference between work done by legislatures and courts. Multiple officeholding—the same men serving as both representatives and judges—was common to the period, and may have contributed to this blurring effect. In the seventeenth century, particularly, colonial assemblies engaged in actions that we would normally associate with the judiciary. "Private" legislation could be passed by an assembly to resolve an individual's problems; for example, to arbitrate a land dispute or divorce a married couple. Except in South Carolina, colonial assemblies began granting divorces, a comparative innovation. These so-called private laws remained common through the colonial period, and only in the early national period would some of these actions become the exclusive jurisdiction of courts. In addition to private laws, legislatures of the seventeenth and eighteenth centuries passed laws affecting a wide range of activities in everyday life. Contrary to what one might suspect about colonial lawmakers, legislators passed laws touching upon many aspects of daily life: establishing ports, towns, roads, markets, price structures for commodities, fences and ferries, legal procedures, religious observances, schools, health ordinances, trade with Native Americans, and much more. Lawmaking was not "laissez-faire" in colonial America.

Lacking direction on many of these matters from the English government (under a policy called "salutary neglect"), colonists resorted to making their own laws to regulate and improve conditions. Colonists could hardly do otherwise: if London refused to act, the legal void demanded that colonists themselves take steps to remedy local problems. Without close supervision from the English government in most matters, American colonists became accustomed to crafting their own laws and running their own courtrooms or legislatures in the seventeenth and most of the eighteenth century. In the 1760s, when "salutary neglect" ended and England began to intervene more directly in colonial affairs, Americans perceived the shift in supervision as an attempt to deprive them of their legal liberties and rights as Englishmen. England's efforts to raise revenues through numerous taxes and rigorous enforcement of the Navigation Acts in the 1760s and 1770s, coupled with the presence of English military troops stationed in American port towns, created an explosive situation that culminated in the American Revolution.

Historians have long considered the American Revolution an unusual type of rebellion. When contrasted with other uprisings, like the French or Russian Revolutions, America's attempt to break with its mother country looks remarkably civilized. Although poverty and indebtedness had been on the rise during the mid-eighteenth century, few would argue that Americans rebelled solely because of financial distress; the taxes proposed by the English government in the 1760s or 1770s were not protested primarily because of the financial havoc that they caused. Indeed, Americans in the 1760s were taxed at roughly one-twentieth the rate of Englishmen in the same period. Nor was the Revolution in America accompanied by violent upheavals and ritual slaughtering of the aristocracy or landed nobility. Outraged colonists spoke against the Parliament's taxes or the blindness of King George III in squandering his colonists' goodwill, but they did not talk of guillotining the king or killing off the English landed gentry. In part, this was due to the physical distance separating the colonies from England, but it was also a reflection of widespread dissatisfaction at all levels of American society with English rule. In America, landed gentry—men like Thomas Jefferson and George Washington—helped lead the rebellion; colonists did not slaughter representatives of the colonial aristocracy, but venerated them for their guidance during the Revolution.

Although money and tyranny were elements of the Revolutionary story, the leading cause of revolution was the shared sense among Americans that their rights were being trampled upon. The language of rights and legal liberties had been current among the English Radical Whigs (men like John Wilkes) for decades, as they complained of the political corruption that they viewed running rampant in the English government. As Bernard Bailyn has described, the Revolution was grounded in the force of ideas about the proper role of government and the basic rights of Englishmen. Colonial Americans appropriated these ideas, transformed them in the New World context, and reached the conclusion suggested by Jefferson's Declaration of Independence: when government ceases to be just toward the governed, revolution is a necessary remedy. The Declaration itself had a legal formula embedded within it; Jefferson accused the king of immoral or illegal behavior in what amounted to a royal bill of indictment. At the time of the Revolution, Americans still admired English law and the unwritten English Constitution, which they believed was the best in all the world; they merely wanted to continue enjoying their rights without interference from English politicians. The American Revolution (though fought in battles and debated by diplomats) was at bottom about the legal position and legal rights that Americans wanted for themselves. If England would not accord them the degree of lawmaking and tax-making responsibilities that colonists had grown accustomed to, then Americans would revolt and form a new government based upon laws of their own creation. The colonists' first actions would be to create new governments built upon state constitutions in the 1770s, a repudiation of Old World beliefs that government flowed downward from kingly prerogative and divine right, and an affirmation of law's central importance in the new nation. While changing the basis for government power, Americans would cling to the English common law in the courtroom; for decades to come, American lawyers and judges would continue to look to English legal opinions for guidance.

LAW AS A CULTURAL ICON

Americans take for granted that the founding of their country was based upon a series of legal grievances about taxes and inadequate representation. The cohesive force of this nation-founding story is so strong that it remains among the most powerful cultural myths in America even in the twenty-first century—every schoolchild knows the claim "no taxation without representation." The notions that legal rights are of paramount concern and that American citizens should have some form of legal representation in their governments form core elements of American cultural identity. Indeed, some scholars have argued that, lacking a shared religion, a shared ancient heritage, and (even today) a shared national language, the formation of the United States during the Revolution and the primary role of law and Constitution-making during the 1770s and 1780s are the principal ties that bind American society together. In measuring the impact of law upon American cultural and intellectual life, the cohesive force of law in the country's creation is outmatched only by the omnipresence of law in every facet of American daily life. Englishmen of the early modern world considered law to be a ubiquitous part of their lives, as did Americans—rich, poor, and middling—at the end of the eighteenth century. Although modern-day Americans may take for granted their legal rights or responsibilities, they would readily admit law continues to dominate the landscape of American society.

See also **Constitutional Thought** (volume 2); **Government** (volume 3).

BIBLIOGRAPHY

Allen, David G. *In English Ways: The Movement of Societies and the Transferal of English Local Law and Custom to Massachusetts Bay in the Seventeenth Century.* Chapel Hill, N.C., 1981.

Bailyn, Bernard. *The Ideological Origins of the American Revolution.* Rev. and enlarged ed. Cambridge, Mass., 1992.

Baker, John Hamilton. *An Introduction to English Legal History.* 3d ed. London, 1990.

Cohen, Morris, ed. *Bibliography of Early American Law.* 6 vols. Buffalo, N.Y., 1998.

Coquillette, Daniel, ed. *Law in Colonial Massachusetts, 1630–1800.* Publications of the Colonial Society of Massachusetts, vol. 62. Boston, 1984.

Dayton, Cornelia. *Women before the Bar: Gender, Law, and Society in Connecticut, 1639–1789.* Chapel Hill, N.C., 1995.

Hoffer, Peter. "Honor and the Roots of American Litigiousness." *American Journal of Legal History* 33, no. 4 (1989): 295–319.

———. *Law and People in Colonial America.* Rev. ed. Baltimore, 1998.

Hull, N. E. H. *Female Felons: Women and Serious Crime in Colonial Massachusetts.* Urbana, Ill., 1987.

Katz, Stanley. "The Problem of a Colonial Legal History." In *Colonial British America: Essays in the New History of the Early Modern Era,* edited by Jack Greene and J. R. Pole. Baltimore, 1984.

Konig, David. *Law and Society in Puritan Massachusetts: Essex County, 1629–1692.* Chapel Hill, N.C., 1979.

Mann, Bruce. *Neighbors and Strangers: Law and Community in Early Connecticut.* Chapel Hill, N.C., 1987.

Nelson, William E. *Americanization of the Common Law: The Impact of Legal Change on Massachusetts Society, 1760–1830.* Cambridge, Mass., 1975.

——. *Dispute and Conflict Resolution in Plymouth Colony, Massachusetts, 1725–1825.* Chapel Hill, N.C. 1981.

Offutt, William. *Of "Good Laws" and "Good Men": Law and Society in the Delaware Valley, 1680–1710.* Urbana, Ill., 1995.

Prest, Wilfrid, ed. *Lawyers in Early Modern Europe and America.* New York, 1981.

Roeber, A. G. *Faithful Magistrates and Republican Lawyers: Creators of Virginia Legal Culture, 1680–1810.* Chapel Hill, N.C., 1981.

——. "'He Read It to Me from a Book of English Law': Germans, Bench, and Bar in the Colonial South, 1715–1770." In *Ambivalent Legacy: A Legal History of the South,* edited by David Bodenhamer and James Ely. Jackson, Miss., 1984.

Salmon, Marylynn. *Women and the Law of Property in Early America.* Chapel Hill, N.C., 1986.

Sharpe, J. A. *Crime in Early Modern England, 1550–1750.* London, 1984.

Smith, Joseph Henry. *Appeals to the Privy Council from the American Plantations.* New York, 1950.

Sosin, Jack M. *The Aristocracy of the Long Robe: The Origin of Judicial Review in America.* New York, 1989.

Watson, Alan. *Slave Law in the Americas.* Athens, Ga., 1989.

William and Mary Quarterly 3d ser., 50 (January 1993) special issue on "Law and Society in Early America," which includes articles by Cornelia Dayton, James Henretta and James Rice, Peter Hoffer, David Konig, Bruce Mann, J. R. Pole, Richard Ross, and Terri Snyder.

Wood, Gordon. *The Creation of the American Republic, 1776–1787.* Chapel Hill, N.C., 1969.

CONFLICTING IDEALS OF COLONIAL WOMANHOOD

Ann M. Little

Women in colonial British America were called to live up to conflicting and contradictory cultural ideals: all women were to be submissive to patriarchal authority, and yet many were also expected to exercise their authority as competent household managers. They were required to defer to male-run institutions like the church and the state, but of course many European women came to America as members of dissident congregations. Indian and African women were considered inferior by European settlers because they labored in the fields, and yet African American women were kept at agricultural labor by the coercion of their Euro-American masters. Enslaved African American and Indian women, even if they were Christianized, were almost never granted the privileges of Euro-American women, and yet were expected to adopt their manners and perform their duties. Married women had few economic privileges and no sure claim to the fruits of their labor or their wombs, despite their lifetime of vital contributions to household wealth in labor and capital. All women were considered intellectually inferior, yet it was the custom of limiting girls' education and not an innate dullness that was responsible for crediting colonial men with far greater intellectual achievements. Women were also believed to be more prone to sin than men and in need of men's spiritual leadership, yet over the colonial period women were increasingly held accountable for men's transgressions of the civil and religious order.

"God Almighty in His most holy and wise providence hath so disposed of the condition of mankind, as in all times some must be rich, some poor, some high and eminent in power and dignity, others mean and in subjection." These words, written by the first governor of Massachusetts John Winthrop on his journey to America in 1630, demonstrate the kind of hierarchical social order most English founders of American colonies desired to recreate. In colonial America as in Renaissance and Reformation Europe, all women were in theory subordinate

to men in the "great chain of being" that ordered all of humanity. As Winthrop's words illustrate, men and women of his era believed that all just authority on earth emanated from God, who reigned supreme. Since God had delegated his authority on earth to Adam, men were to rule over women, children, servants, and slaves. Of course, real life for women in colonial America was much messier and more complicated than any neat hierarchy could hope to organize, largely because many different kinds of women led very different lives. For a long time the term "colonial women" was a theoretically inclusive concept, but in fact most historians wrote only about free Anglo-American women, and focused almost exclusively on their lives as married women and mothers of children. Since the mid-1980s, historians have laid the foundations for a more complicated understanding of women's history that includes enslaved African and African American women, European servants, Native American women, and widows and single women. These women occupied very different positions in colonial society and accordingly led very different lives. The historiography on colonial women is beginning to explore this diversity of experience.

THE LEGAL, ECONOMIC, AND CULTURAL LIMITS

Whichever colonial women are under consideration, the ideals of colonial womanhood were not simply matters of culture or custom: in colonies under English colonial rule, they were grounded in a large number of enforceable laws inherited from the common law tradition. The most important of these were the laws of coveture, which operated on the fiction that a married couple was, for the purposes of political representation and economic rights, united into a single being represented by the husband. Therefore, married women as *femes covertes* (literally "covered women") could not own property or conduct business in their own names, and were similarly invisible in the civil sphere as household dependents who could neither vote nor represent themselves in courts of law. Children, servants, and slaves were also theoretically represented in the person of the household patriarch as well, but male children and servants usually outgrew their dependent status and upon marriage became heads of households themselves. Daughters and female servants would also move up the hierarchy, although ideally they would pass from coveture under a father or a master to that of a husband. Enslaved men as well as women, however, were destined to live under household government for the rest of their lives. Free women without husbands, either widows or never-married women, were permitted to exercise economic rights as *femes soles,* but they were only very rarely granted the political rights shared broadly by male heads of households. While many women spent significant portions of their lives as *femes soles,* most women in colonial America, bound or free, spent most of their lives as *femes covertes.*

Given the supposedly divine origins of women's subordination and the powerfully coercive political and economic system, it is no wonder that women in colonial America were instructed to display behavior and virtues that demonstrated their cheerful deference to patriarchal authority. Seventeenth- and eighteenth-century sermons and courtesy literature emphasized the importance of submissiveness to the feminine ideal. But religion played a complex role in the lives of colonial women, as it both demanded that they defer to earthly patriarchal authority, and at the same time resist unjust and ungodly authority. English puritans, members of the Society of Friends (the Quakers), and Catholics in the seventeenth century, as well as German pietists and Moravians in the eighteenth century, came to America as members of dissenting communities who were well practiced in the art of resisting unjust authority in European churches and states. Yet in America, women in even these communities were expected to defer to established authority. According to ministers of all denominations, piety in women should be expressed first and foremost by a quiet acceptance of the authority and righteousness of God. But this put godly women in a difficult position if they believed themselves subject to unjust political, ministerial, or household authority. What was a woman's duty if she were kept from religious observance by a husband who scorned the church? What if the town minister preached incorrect doc-

trine, according to the judgment of others in the community? Many women decided that their duty to follow God's way necessarily superseded their earthly obligations to obey husbands, ministers, and magistrates. But flouting earthly hierarchies was difficult and dangerous, and frequently earned women the rage of civil and religious authorities who had recourse to a number of punishments: they might fine the woman; whip, brand, or confine her (among other corporal punishments); excommunicate her from the church; expel her from the colony; or even put her to death, a fate met by Quaker women and convicted witches in the New England colonies.

While religion may have played an equivocal role in women's submission to patriarchal authority, education was a less ambiguous means by which this gendered hierarchy was enforced: both girls and boys were taught to read, but in the seventeenth century only boys were regularly taught to write. Furthermore, through the colonial period only young men had the opportunity to pursue a college or seminary education. This division of literacy skills and educational attainment reflect quite starkly the gendered divisions of colonial society, where men were designated as the producers of both religious and secular knowledge, and women only as consumers. Even the Puritan poet Anne Bradstreet, whose verse celebrates the virtues of dutiful, loving wife- and motherhood, and efficient and clever huswifery, acknowledged the hostility her work might meet in the prologue to her first book:

> I am obnoxious to each carping tongue
> who says my hand a needle better fits
> a poet's pen all scorn I should thus wrong
> for such despite they cast on female wits
> if what I do prove well it won't advance
> they'll say it's stol'n, or else it was by chance.
> (*The Tenth Muse, Lately Sprung up in America,*
>   1650, p. 4)

Moreover, written language was not the only means by which men and women were divided; there were very different rules governing men's and women's speech in colonial America, and women's rebellious words—even if they remained only threats or jokes—were treated in courtrooms as very real threats to the social order.

Submission to male authority was not the only necessary quality in women who inhabited a frontier frequently visited by war and privation. There was a lot of work to be done in colonial America, and women were responsible for at least half of it. The "virtuous woman" praised in Proverbs 31:10–31 provided a worthy model for colonial women to emulate, as the verses detail the hard work, frugality, fortitude, and foresight she demonstrates in caring for her husband and family. The colonial sense of "virtue" was not so closely tied to sexual morality as the Victorian understanding of the word. Female virtue in daughters, wives, and servants had more to do with their productive labor than with their abstinence outside of marriage, or their sexual fidelity within. Just as men and women were assigned different rights and privileges within the political and economic spheres of colonial America, so too the world of work was divided along the lines of gender.

In the agricultural communities that shaped the experiences of most early Americans, girls and women were responsible for the care and maintenance of the household and kitchen garden, whereas men worked primarily in the barn, livestock pens, and fields. Women's labors included the tedium of thrice daily meal preparation and cleanup, the daily chores of child care, looking after smaller domesticated animals (such as chickens, pigs, or goats), and perhaps spinning, weaving, knitting, and making new linens or clothing for the family and the seasonal challenge of laundry and cleaning. Women also were chiefly responsible for key nutrition and variety in the family's diets, as they brewed beer, made cheese, churned butter, and baked bread. (These items had good market value, and some women supplemented their families' incomes by selling beer, cheese, or butter.) They also planted and tended kitchen gardens not only for the nutritional value of the vegetables, but for the medicinal qualities of the herbs they grew there. Besides the various demands of "women's work," many women were called to the field seasonally, to help out with such labor-intensive tasks as planting or harvesting. Women in the urban seaport cities were responsible for all labor inside the household and for maintaining their family's (or their master's and mistress' family's) well-being. In addition to this, some worked in the family shop or market stall, and some even worked in skilled trades like dressmaking. Many others worked at low-skill jobs for wages or hawked their wares, but even these women were selling female labor and goods that reflected their household responsibilities. For example, poor women sold shellfish or prepared foods, and took in laundry.

INDIAN AND AFRICAN WOMEN

While Euro-American women struggled with their duties to defer to male authority and to work for the benefit of their families, they were negotiating the contradictions within their own culture. In contrast, Indian and African American women who lived in or near Euro-American colonies were judged by European ideals of womanhood, and if they served or were enslaved in Euro-American households or plantations were often forced to conform to these foreign standards of female behavior. Indian women were represented and described by Europeans in contradictory ways, alternately objects of desire and contempt: on the one hand, Europeans saw Indian women as ill-kempt drudges, because they performed almost all of the agricultural labor for their communities and because their body adornments of tattoos and animal fats were unattractive to Europeans; on the other hand, they were described as enticing and sexually promiscuous because their manner of dress was immodest according to European standards, and some Indian women engaged in casual-seeming sexual relations with Europeans. Additionally, some Native cultures allowed for fairly easy divorce and remarriage. Indian women had a much greater measure of economic and political power in their communities than Euro-American women, as they retained ownership of the fruits of their labor, and they sometimes even held the position of tribal leader, or sachem. In the eyes of Europeans, the kind of power and autonomy exercised by Indian women made them seem inappropriately strong and Indian men alarmingly weak. This served to reinforce European suspicions that Indian cultures were inherently unstable and ungodly.

Because most African and African American women in colonial America were enslaved, the contradictions that shaped their lives were even more difficult to endure. On the one hand, Europeans disdained Africans as they did Indians because women were the farmers in their respective societies. But slavery in the Americas meant that the vast majority of African and African American women were forced into arduous field work on a daily basis. In *Good Wives, Nasty Wenches, and Anxious Patriarchs* (1995), Kathleen Brown argues that this contradiction was not accidental, but instrumental to the construction and elaboration of racial hierarchies in colonial America. Through her painstaking analysis of the evolution of slavery in the law, she examines how the shifting terrain of gender ideology became the means by which racial hierarchies were first imagined and then implemented. Hierarchies of gender and class in the seventeenth century changed to incorporate race as Virginia's labor force changed from being composed mostly of indentured servants to the use of enslaved Africans. Where once only class distinctions among women were necessary to tell the "good wives" from the "nasty wenches," the use of African labor created "a racial opposition in which women of English descent embodied the privileges and virtues of womanhood while women of African descent shouldered the burner of its inherently evil, sexual lust" (p. 2). Thus, the labor of one class of women purchased the leisure and social prestige of the other. "By the mid-eighteenth century, the social categories of gender and race had become mutually implicated in supporting the claims of a wealthy slaveholding planter class to social and political authority" (p. 1).

Another burden enslaved women bore was the exploitation of their sexuality and their maternity. Like Indian women, African American women were alternately portrayed as unattractive or even monstrous on the one hand, and as enticing and always eager for sex on the other. Their masters or other white men assumed sexual access to enslaved women, who had absolutely no rights to either their labor or bodily self-determination. While it's impossible to discover how frequently sex (either coercive or consensual) across the color line happened, the large numbers of children described as "mulatto" indicate that it was a common occurrence in most communities, North and South. Even if an enslaved woman was not lured or forced into sexual liaisons with white men and was permitted to marry within the slave community, she was not entitled to the rights of free wives. Slave marriages were commonly broken by a master's desire to sell one or the other spouse; even more frequently, the children of enslaved parents were sold away from them, as masters were entitled not only to their productive but their reproductive labors.

IDEALS AND COLONIAL REALITIES

Thus, women were abjured to be submissive, while simultaneously called to develop their skills and work hard for the benefit of their households and masters. The fruits of their labor were crucial to the survival of colonial families, yet as household dependents most of them were denied the right to legal ownership of their labor or wages. Widows were entitled only to one-third of a deceased husband's estate, and of that portion they might only be granted a "lifetime share," which meant that it was theirs to use only while they lived, and the remainder was already entailed to another (usually male) beneficiary. Daughters who labored faithfully

in their fathers' households might expect to get a measure of their labor back in the form of their "marriage portion," granted to them by most parents when they left the paternal home to begin a new household with a husband. But, because of the law of coveture, the daughter's labors legally enriched only her husband, as the moment she married she transferred her coveture from her father to her husband. Notions of ideal conduct for colonial women get even more complicated when historians consider that some women, as mothers and mistresses of servants or slaves, were in positions of authority over several members of their household, including other women. Even single or widowed *femes soles* were caught in these contradictions, for while they might not have a patriarch in their household to answer to, men and women in their communities could and did hold them to the same standards of ideal female conduct.

Historians have described and attempted to explain these contradictions from a variety of different perspectives. While no serious scholars foster the myth that the colonial period was a "golden age" for American women, there are great differences in the ways in which historians describe and interpret women's lives. Some historians believe that although women were denied real political and economic power, their productive labor and skills earned them considerable (if informal) influence in their communities. In both of her major works, Laurel Thatcher Ulrich paints portraits of heroic colonial womanhood, focusing on the creative ways in which Anglo-American women supported their families and earned influence in fledgling frontier settlements. Ulrich's women are not heroes in the sense of being exceptional, but in their ordinary hard work and dutifulness to husbands, families, and communities. As she states in her preface to *Good Wives* (1982), Ulrich intentionally emphasizes "*good* wives" in her effort to highlight the "normative elements in a history which from the time of Hawthorne has been dominated by outcasts and witches" (p. xiii). She uses typological models from the Old Testament to outline the range of appropriate and inappropriate roles for puritan women: Bathsheba, the dutiful wife engaged in energetic huswifery; Eve, the sin-prone female and mother of humanity; and Jael, heroic defender of her family and faith. Despite these divergent identities, Ulrich's "good wives" successfully negotiate the complex and contradictory demands their culture placed on them.

In *A Midwife's Tale* (1991), Ulrich puts the life of midwife Martha Ballard at the center of the life of Hallowell, Maine, and uses both the life and the history of the community to illuminate each other. Although her story takes place after the American Revolution, Ulrich insists that Ballard is "more a colonial goodwife than a Republican Mother" (p. 32). Indeed, she is a typical Ulrich heroine, a woman who embodies the contradictory virtues required of colonial women and who is thus rewarded with some measure of social prestige and local influence. Ballard is devoted to her work as a midwife, responding to calls of women in labor no matter the hour or the weather, and achieving an impressive record of safe births for both mothers and babies. Because of Ballard's position as the midwife, when called upon she cooperates with local officials in investigating crimes. She is a churchgoing woman, a meet help for her husband, a loving mother, and a considerate mistress to the young women who work in her household. Despite Ballard's knowledge of intimate and public affairs, Ulrich's portrayal of Ballard remains focused on her work as a midwife and on her womanly duties at home, sealed off from political controversies or family troubles. For example, when the wife of a controversial minister confides in Ballard that she was assaulted by a wealthy and influential man, she counsels the woman to keep the allegations to herself, and Ulrich dismisses the case as an "ugly tear in local history, an unexplained rent in the social web" (p. 105).

Ulrich seems reluctant to address the conflicts that inevitably arose among Ballard's many loyalties to her family and community. When Ballard was in her seventies, her husband Ephraim was imprisoned for debt at age seventy-nine because of his failures as a tax collector; their impulsive, troublesome son Jonathan exploited his mother's vulnerability and moved his family into her house, relegating her to a single room which she was sometimes forced to heat with wood she gathered and chopped herself. Despite her years of service, she received little assistance from either family or community in the seventeen months of Ephraim's imprisonment. Yet Ulrich describes her in the last years of her life as finding "an eye of peace in a heroic commitment to her neighbors and in a passionate, almost lyrical devotion to the small patch of earth for which she was responsible" (p. 308).

Other historians have been more sanguine when evaluating the effects of political and economic disenfranchisement on women. Indeed, they argue that women not only didn't make any gains over the course of the colonial period, they probably lost ground over the 150 years before the American Rev-

olution. Elaine Forman Crane demonstrates that even female-majority communities couldn't outrun patriarchal control in *Ebb Tide in New England* (1998). While Ulrich portrays Martha Ballard, whose life spanned the Revolution and stretched into the nineteenth century, as essentially the same as her seventeenth-century "goodwives," Crane sees dramatic changes over the colonial period that created a "growing dependence of women on men and the increasingly regulated nature of their lives" (p. 3). Focusing on women who lived in female-majority towns and who, because of their husbands' seafaring occupations, were left to run their own households for several months or even years at a time, Crane first thought that the story she would tell would be one of "empowerment . . . with a more positive, or at least egalitarian, ending" (p. 5). Despite women's importance to the building of the New England towns of Boston, Salem, Newport, and Portsmouth and the "wide variety of mercantile pursuits" (p. 6) that were the basis of their economies, women's importance and influence declined because of the increasing importance of long-distance trade and the replacement of the barter economy by cash. Both of these developments privileged men's activities over women's work and, combined with reforms in the civil law, served to increase women's dependence on men.

Similarly, Cornelia Hughes Dayton's *Women before the Bar* uses the civil and criminal court records of early Connecticut to argue that women were increasingly marginalized through the colonial period. She argues that the gradual "Anglicization" of the law in early Connecticut increased the expense and formal requirements of filing or answering to civil and criminal charges. This decreased women's access to and influence in courts of law, and thus had the effect of elevating men's rights and privileges. An excellent example of this is the ways in which fornication prosecutions changed over time, from the seventeenth century's concern for an equal-opportunity rooting out of sin among the sinners, to the eighteenth century's increasing concern with protecting men's liberties at women's expense. Because any kind of sex outside of marriage was considered not just immoral but illegal in colonial America, fornication was a very popular crime prosecuted when evidence in the form of an untoward pregnancy came to light. Seventeenth-century courts prosecuted not just the women, who bore the evidence of their sin on their bodies, but their male partners whom they made great efforts to discover and punish. Although most couples resolved their problem with a speedy marriage, even these

WARS OF WORDS

While the ideal woman was quiet and submissive, few women in colonial America of any age, status, or ethnicity could have lived up to such a strict standard. Mistresses Brewster, Moore, and Leach were three elite women whose outspoken views on religion earned them a lengthy examination in a New Haven courtroom in the late spring of 1646. Their complaints about the town's minister, rejection of infant baptism, and threats to run off to Rhode Island and join other dissidents fleeing Puritan orthodoxy had become public knowledge, and their position as elite women meant that they might have the social prestige to attract converts. This was not an unfounded fear, as Anne Hutchinson had rent Massachusetts a decade earlier with her popular teachings in the Antinomian controversy, and Anne Eaton had threatened a similar uprising in New Haven, leading to her excommunication in 1645.

In this excerpt from her court examination, Mrs. Leach's servants Elizabeth Smith and Job Hall testify about Lucy Brewster's unorthodox religious ideas and resentment of local authorities, as well as about how she turned her anger at them when she learned they were cooperating with the officials investigating her. The conflict between the women is especially interesting, as it reveals how women used ideals of womanhood against one another: Smith accuses Brewster of threatening both church and political authority, while Brewster accuses Smith of promiscuity. Smith might have testified because she feared Brewster's religious unorthodoxy, or the consequences of not cooperating with court officials, or simply because she resented the elite woman's prestige in the community. In her responses to the charges below, Brewster clearly resents what she sees as Smith's efforts to curry favor with a magistracy that would otherwise punish her for her pregnancy out of wedlock. The following excerpt illustrates several themes in colonial history: an intolerance of outspoken women and the state's readiness to enforce womanly ideals; anxiety about women living outside of the laws of coverture; conflict between masters and servants; and the ways in which women as well as men evoked womanly ideals of sexual purity or submission to authority to malign their antagonists.

> Elizabeth Smith saith, that haveing bin forth & comming in to her Mrs. howse she heard Mrs. Brewster, speaking lowd to Mrs. Eaton concerninge banishment, say, they could not banish her but by a Gennerall Court, & if it came to that shee wished Mrs. Eaton to come to her & acquaynt her wth her judgment & grownds about baptizing, & she would by them seduce some other weomen, & then she, the said Mrs. Brewster, would complayne to the court of Mrs. Eaton & the other weoman should complayne of her as being thus seduced, and soe they would be banished together & she spake of going to Road Island.

> Mrs. Brewster confesseth the chardge, but saith she spake it in jest & laughing, she was told, foolish & uncomely jesting are sinfull, but to harden one agaynst the truth who already lyeth under guilt, may not passe under a prtence of jesting.

> Job saith, that the last day of the weeke, being May the 9th, he was called upp before Mrs. Brewster, Mrs. Moore, & Mrs. Leach, at Mr. Leaches howse. Mrs. Brewster told him shee had bin where she had justified herselfe agaynst a great manny of his lyes & added, she would have him & his slutt, you & yor harlott, to the whipping post. Elizabeth saith that she being below the howse at this time, heard the former words. Mrs. Brewster spake them soe lowd that, (as she conceiveth) they might be heard into the midst of the streate.

CONTINUED NEXT PAGE

Mrs. Brewster denied those words, you & yor slutt, you & yor harlott, to the whipping post. . . .

Elizabeth said that onn the same day, May the ninth, Mrs. Brewster told her that she went about carrying lyes, to currey favor to keep her whores back from whipping, adding, she would call her nothing but whore and harlott till she had bin whipped and was marryed, then she must call her so noe more. . . . Mrs. Brewster further said Elizabeth told halfe truthes & halfe lyes. Eliza answered, her halfe truthes will prove whole truthes. Mrs. Brewster replyed, will they so, you brasen facd whore. . . .

Mrs. Brewster denied the word whore, she said she called her only harlott, she was told such rayling landguadge was uncomely & sinfull, Micaell the Archangell durst not carry it soe wth the Divell, though he had matter enough against him . . .

Source: Hoadly, *Records of the Colony and Plantation of New Haven, 1638–1649,* pp. 246–247.

instances of "bridal pregnancy" were brought before the courts. After 1690 Dayton shows that men were increasingly inclined to deny responsibility for women's pregnancies, and that Connecticut courts, now held to stricter standards for evaluating evidence, ended up prosecuting women alone because their pregnancies meant they couldn't deny their guilt. Fornication prosecutions are only one example of the transformation of the courtroom from "an inclusive forum representative of community to a rationalized institution serving the interests of commercially active men" (p. 3).

Other scholars have embraced exceptional women and the controversies they created as an important means by which to understand the limitations on women in early America. Carol Karlsen's work demonstrates that seventeenth-century accusations of witchcraft reveal assumptions about normative behavior as well as fascinating insight into Puritan fantasies about terrifyingly powerful women. In *The Devil in the Shape of a Woman* (1989), Karlsen argues that women who seemed to overstep their accepted roles were much more vulnerable to witchcraft accusations than women who appeared to fulfill womanly ideals: whatever their marital status, women over forty were more vulnerable than women of childbearing age; unmarried women were more vulnerable than their married sisters safely enclosed by the laws of coveture; and women who challenged God's supremacy or violated the prescribed norms of female conduct were much more likely to be accused than women who did not appear to present challenges to the patriarchal power in their homes and communities. Perhaps most importantly, Karlsen's research demonstrates that the variable that made women most

vulnerable to witchcraft accusations had nothing whatsoever to do with their own behavior or position within their communities, but with inheritance laws. Women without brothers or sons who inherited their families' estates or stood to inherit them blocked the "orderly transmission of property from one generation of males to another" that coveture was designed to protect (p. 116). Thus, even the most dutiful good wives of colonial New England might have fallen prey to deadly community fears of their self-sufficiency and influence if they had the misfortune not to have brothers or sons.

Like accused witches, female religious radicals can also teach us something about the standards to which colonial women were held, because they frequently were prosecuted by local authorities for their flouting of the accepted standard for women's behavior as well as for their theological unorthodoxies. Susan Juster's *Disorderly Women* (1994) documents the transformation of New England's Baptists from a religious community committed to sexual egalitarianism that permitted women leadership roles in the church in the mid-eighteenth century, to a denomination that by the end of the century marginalized women. She links this to the rhetoric and effects of the American Revolution, which left in its wake a "republican America" whose new, secular language and ideas were "quintessentially masculine" (p. 10). Because of their religion's leveling tendencies, New England Baptists were drawn to the Revolution and worked on behalf of the political movement whose goal was secular equality. The success of the Revolution meant that Baptists moved from the periphery of New England's religious life and closer to its center, and in so doing returned to the patriarchal values that had characterized New England's leadership from the start. Male Baptist leaders ensured their denomination's survival in the new nation by aligning themselves against "disorderliness" in family and society, a disorderliness that was closely associated with women because of old ideas about women's spiritual weakness and inherent sinfulness. This narrative arc concerning women and religion in colonial America is useful for understanding the histories of women in other reformed Protestant traditions. In *Women and Religion in Early America, 1600–1850* (1999), Marilyn Westerkamp examines the radical implications and conservative transformations of various sects and denominations, and documents the tensions inherent in being a submissive Puritan or evangelical woman as well as an instrument for the Lord's work.

REVOLUTION AND THE RIGHTS OF WOMEN

For Anglo-American men the American Revolution represented a rejection of the patriarchal authority of a king; however, the Revolution did little to change the legal, economic, or political status of American women. Slavery ended gradually in the North and divorces became somewhat easier to obtain, but Euro-American and African American women led lives very similar to those of their colonial mothers and grandmothers as slavery and coveture continued uninterrupted by the laws of the new republic. Furthermore, the aggressive continental expansionism of the United States served to disrupt the lives of increasing numbers of Native American women, either by "removing" them into exile, or by subjecting them to the gendered expectations of Anglo-American culture. After the Revolution, Euro-American women made some educational gains and took charge of the religious education and spiritual life of their households. Through these means, they determinedly carved out a role for themselves as citizens of the nation. However, their new identity as "republican mothers," charged with the intellectual, moral, and spiritual education of their children as future American citizens, was one that still relied on their enclosure in coveture and submission to male political authority. Furthermore, it relied on the continued submission of Indian, African American, and newly arrived immigrant women, who continued to be perceived and portrayed by Euro-Americans as slovenly, amoral, and neglectful of their children. These working women served not only in the households and plantations of Euro-American women, but also as foils for their patriotic and virtuous brand of womanhood.

See also **Women** *(volume 2);* **Family; Gentility and Manners; Gender** *(volume 3).*

BIBLIOGRAPHY

Brown, Kathleen. *Good Wives, Nasty Wenches, and Anxious Patriarchs: Gender, Race, and Power in Colonial Virginia.* Chapel Hill, N.C., 1995.

Crane, Elaine Forman. *Ebb Tide in New England: Women, Seaports, and Social Change, 1630–1800.* Boston, 1998.

Dayton, Cornelia Hughes. *Women before the Bar: Gender, Law and Society in Connecticut, 1639–1789.* Chapel Hill, N.C., 1995.

Hoadly, Charles J., ed. *Records of the Colony and Plantation of New Haven.* Hartford, Conn., 1857.

Juster, Susan. *Disorderly Women: Sexual Politics and Evangelicalism in Revolutionary New England.* Ithaca, N.Y., 1994.

Karlsen, Carol F. *The Devil in the Shape of a Woman: Witchcraft in Colonial New England.* New York, 1989.

Kerber, Linda K. *Women of the Republic: Intellect and Ideology in Revolutionary America.* New York, 1986.

Norton, Mary Beth. *Founding Mothers and Fathers: Gendered Power and the Forming of American Society.* New York, 1996.

Salmon, Marylynn. *Women and the Law of Property in Early America.* Chapel Hill, N.C., 1986.

Ulrich, Laurel Thatcher. *Good Wives: Image and Reality in the Lives of Women in Northern New England, 1650–1750.* New York, 1982.

——. *A Midwife's Tale: The Life of Martha Ballard, Based on Her Diary, 1785–1812.* New York, 1991.

Westerkamp, Marilyn J. *Women and Religion in Early America, 1600–1850: The Puritan and Evangelical Traditions.* London and New York, 1999.

Wilson, Lisa. *Life after Death: Widows in Pennsylvania, 1750–1850.* Philadelphia, 1992.

Wulf, Karin A. *Not All Wives: Women of Colonial Philadelphia.* Ithaca, N.Y., 2000.

RACE AS A CULTURAL CATEGORY

Joshua Lane

"RACE MATTERS"

At the dawn of the twenty-first century, scientists, historians, and humanists have arrived at a common conclusion about "race": race reflects arbitrary ideas about perceived—not genetic—differences among human populations. Race categories are grounded in culture rather than nature. In the words of the historian Barbara Fields, "Race is a purely ideological and therefore, historical, notion." Dictionary editors confirm: the once-assumed genetic basis of race is no longer acceptable. Compilers of the *Random House Webster's Unabridged Dictionary* (second edition, revised), for example, had by 1987 defined race as "persons related by common descent or heredity . . . any of the traditional divisions of humankind, the commonest being Caucasian, mongoloid, and Negro, characterized by supposedly distinctive and universal characteristics. No longer in technical use."

While no longer in technical use, biologically based definitions of "race" nonetheless continue their grip on American culture and transcend dictionary definitions and time. The United States census, for example, still categorizes inhabitants as Caucasian, Asian, African American, and Native American. The hues of white, yellow, black, and red with which these racial categories have often been associated are so deeply woven into the fabric of American culture that most Americans take them for granted. Although the 2000 census clarifies that "race" or "racial group" is a "classification indicating general racial or ethnic heritage based on self-identification," the racial labels commonplace in the census, employment forms, and elsewhere, are often still linked in the popular imagination to a baseless but entrenched belief system rooted in nineteenth-century biology that posits that human identities are genetically fixed in racial groupings that exist outside of history and that these groupings somehow predetermine human character. Race in this sense is ubiquitous not simply in its application but

in its profound and often deleterious consequences for American culture. The crux of the matter, the historian David Brion Davis observed, is that despite the fact that "responsible scientists . . . have long discredited any biological or genetic definition of racial groups," racial distinctions remain at the core of American history and experience. Racial profiling and racial discrimination continue to the present; though historians have come to understand race as a cultural invention, it nonetheless has exerted, and continues to exert, real power over Americans' lives. The historian and contemporary commentator Cornel West put it most simply: "Race matters."

Why race matters and *how* race has mattered historically are the central concerns of this essay. How did America develop from linguistically, culturally, and ethnically diverse local communities at the time of European settlement into a nation starkly divided by the chromatic categories red, white, and black by the turn of the nineteenth century? How did a polyglot America become a nation perceived to be composed of "three naturally distinct, one might almost say hostile, races" in the eyes of the French observer Alexis de Tocqueville, describing his impressions of the country's inhabitants in his *Democracy in America* (1835)? Most mainstream historians have avoided race in their historical accounts of colonial America until the late twentieth century. This essay is based on the premise that the questions how and why race came to matter to past Americans are central to the study of American culture from the time of European settlement onward. Race matters because identity politics have always mattered to Americans.

EUROPEANS CONSTRUCT A DISCOURSE OF RACE

Modern race ideology differs markedly from colonial Americans' ideas about race and identity. A historic review of changing notions of race reveals that the definition of race did not acquire a genetic underpinning until the mid-nineteenth century. Compilers of the *Oxford English Dictionary* point out that race did not acquire the meaning "a group of several tribes or peoples, regarded as forming a distinct ethnical stock" until the mid-nineteenth century and that it was not paired with other words to mean "caused by, based on, or pertaining to race," such as with the phrases "race war," "race consciousness," and "race gap," until the end of the nineteenth century.

What was the meaning of race before the nineteenth century? The very concept of race emerged only gradually and race categories were created out of differing local contexts of contact between various indigenous and immigrant groups—Indians, Africans, individuals of mixed ethnic parentage, poor Europeans and wealthy Europeans, the non-religious, and religious groups of Jews, Catholics, and Protestants. Jointly, America's varied inhabitants shaped ideas about race. According to the historian Robert Berkhofer, categories of national and cultural identity were becoming increasingly important to literate and ambitious Europeans, who, beginning in the early 1500s, underwrote and engaged in the charting of new oceanic trade routes, the colonization of new lands, and the escalation of religious wars against one another's countries. Beginning in the 1400s, Europeans referred to themselves not only as "Christians" but also as "Europeans," "English," "French," and "Spanish." They strengthened their senses of national allegiance with newly defined or reinforced religious convictions, which were part of a general tightening of relations between church and state. Inhabitants throughout England, for example, began to see themselves as both English and Anglican, and inhabitants across Spain began to identify themselves as both Spanish and Catholic.

The etymology of race reveals that Europeans framed an imprecise discourse of race about the same time that they were beginning to expand their geographical horizons. English-speaking peoples first used the word race at the end of the fifteenth century to identify categories of humans. Akin to the French *race,* Italian *razza,* Spanish *raza,* and Portuguese *raca,* the English word "race" ultimately derived from the Latin root *ratio* meaning a sort, kind. Sometime around the 1500s, the English adopted the term race to differentiate between sorts, or kinds, of people. Editors of the *Oxford English Dictionary* have documented some early sixteenth-century writers' use of race to describe "a limited number of persons," "a tribe, nation, or people" regarded as of common class, family, or stock, "a set or class of persons" (e.g. "race of beggars" c. 1500), "one of the sexes" (e.g. "race of womankind," c. 1590), even a "line or succession of persons holding office" (e.g. "race of bishops" c. 1570).

The introduction of the movable-type printing press in 1455 provided the means to disseminate the new vocabulary of race, in all its varied meanings, quickly. News of European adventurers' travels in Africa and the Americas, and stories about their initial encounters with the peoples of newly colonized lands quickened Europeans' interest in new ways of seeing, naming, and understanding the visible world and categorizing its various inhabitants. With the advent of the printing press, European audiences could satisfy their hunger for news of the latest discoveries abroad, by devouring published accounts about foreign places and peoples. Into the accounts seeped ideas that added new meaning to the term race—ideas that were informed as much by traditions that Europeans brought to the New World as by any actual colonial inhabitants' immediate encounter with New World inhabitants.

One printed text in particular, Sir John Mandeville's *Travels* (c. 1356), encouraged readers to generalize their perceptions of human differences in terms of race—loosely understood sense of groups of similar humans—and newly, in terms of color. Europeans knew a variety of Africans, all with variously different complexions and physical attributes—moors, Christian blacks, Africans from northern Africa. Further, European observers characterized native West Africans (whom the Portuguese and Spanish began to enslave before 1550) as utterly different from the other Africans they had known for centuries. Despite this knowledge, Mandeville assigned the simplistic chromatic label of "right blacke," and "black of colour" to all Africans whom he identified as "Thiops" and "Numidians." Eventually the reading public followed suit and generically applied labels of "Thiops" and "Numidians," "black," and "negro" (following the Spanish use of the term *negre*) to frame all Africans in the same color-coded terms.

Not only did Mandeville reinforce Europeans' perceptions of Africans' generic blackness, but he underscored a widely sustained interpretation of black as the color of brutishness. In his *Travels* he encouraged readers to view all Africans as black and as uncivil. Assigning negative connotations to "blackness," Mandeville both constructed and problematized blackness as a category of human identity. According to the historian Winthrop Jordan, Mandeville's *Travels* established a "popular baseline of spatial and human geography until the late sixteenth century," and contributed to Europeans' sharpening perception of all Africans' identity as black.

The strength of Mandeville's text to establish black as a category of human identity ultimately cannot be understood separately from European attempts to create a self-identity in terms of whiteness, based on positive associations with that color. Elizabethan Anglos linked white with benevolence, cleanliness, purity, and Christianity. As Anglos, they associated white with cleanliness, goodness, and godliness; so they associated black with its opposite: malevolence, filth, corruption, and paganism. This ranking of color among humans harmonized with a concept received from medieval Christianity known as the Great Chain of Being. According to this idea, all living things were organized into a vertically aligned continuum with God positioned as the highest, whitest entity and the devil as the lowest, blackest being. By the time of the American Revolution, European settlers had established a hierarchy of color that affirmed Europeans' identity as white, and therefore as closer to God. By association, "black" humans were viewed as closer to the devil than to God.

However, for some Christian thinkers trying to make sense of a growing flood of reports about newly encountered peoples throughout the world, the idea of hierarchically ranked humans by chromatic grouping (specifically black and white) raised a serious question. If God brought man and woman forth from one source, how had the world's peoples come to differ so much, from one group to another and from one place to another? The cultural authorities of the fifteenth century, biblical scholars, turned to the Bible to search for answers. Whether deliberate or not, some scholars' interpretations of the biblical story of Noah's son, Ham, stigmatized Africans as "black" and "slavish." By the 1610 publication of the King James Bible, most English theologians argued that the accursed Ham had been banished to Africa, where he and his descendants for all time had assumed the color black and lived in bondage to Ham's brothers, Japeth and Shem, and their descendants. Some Anglo commentators, such as the British naval surgeon John Atkin, simply skipped over biblical teachings altogether in explaining Africans' differences from Europeans and formed theories of their own about the origin of Africans. In 1735 Atkin advocated the radical idea of Africans' and Europeans' separate genesis. Wary about challenging the interpretations of biblical

scholars, other scientifically inclined commentators developed alternative theories about human genesis that were compatible with biblical teachings. Sir Thomas Browne, for one, drew on environmental and medical beliefs to explain perceived human differences. In his 1646 essay "Of the Blackness of Negroes" he asserted that the sun pigmented Africans' skins, producing a trait that African men passed on to their children, but that was reversible in subsequent generations.

Still other seventeenth-century theorists harmonized their environmental explanations of racial differences with contemporaneous theories about the role that bodily "humors" (fluids such as blood, urine, sweat, and bile) played in determining such attributes as skin pigmentation, hair color and texture, the shapes of facial features, character, and capacity for thought. Humoral theory gained additional credence as an explanation of human difference in the eighteenth century when the Swedish scientist Linnaeus [Karl von Linne] incorporated it in his chromatic classification of humans. In the 1740 expanded second edition of his comprehensive taxonomy, *General System of Nature,* he grouped humankind into four hierarchically ranked chromatic categories starting with the highest group, white Europeans, followed by red Americans (Indians) and yellow Asians, and ending with black Africans. With its air of scientific authority, Linnaeus's biological ranking of human beings gave new credence to chromatic notions about race that had already taken hold in the public imagination.

IMPLICATIONS OF RACE IN THE ADVENT OF CHATTEL SLAVERY

Whatever its theoretical basis, a hierarchy of color being established in the European mind loosely conformed to a social hierarchy being set in place in North America at the time. How, why, and by what processes did whites in Virginia and elsewhere throughout the colonies codify the race-based slavery of Africans? And how did slavery solidify racial identity? Thomas Jefferson relied on Linnaeus's seemingly scientific ideas about the humoral differences between peoples to provide some answers to these questions in his 1785 *Notes on the State of Virginia.* In Jefferson's view, Africans' physiology not only differed from that of whites, but also predisposed them to lives as slaves. "Whether the black of the negro resides in the reticular membrane between the skin and scarf-skin, or in the scarf-skin itself; whether it proceeds from the colour of the blood, the colour of the bile, or from that of some other secretion, the difference is fixed in nature, and is as real as if its seat and cause were better known to us" (p. 133). Jefferson further observed that members of the "African race" required less sleep than whites, which suited them to long hours of labor. Concerning their cognitive abilities, he asserted that although "in memory they are equal to whites . . . in reason [they are] much inferior." In other words, Jefferson implied, they were mentally unsuited for any but the most menial labor; biologically, they were destined to perform the work of slaves.

But Europeans' attitudes about blackness by themselves do not explain the development of American-style race categories or the advent of race-based slavery on North American soil. The historian Edmund Morgan's class-based analysis of southern race-based slavery provides a compelling theory that links Europeans' anxieties about non-property-holding whites to the institution of African slavery. Morgan focused his examination on larger plantation owners and their fears of anarchy at the hands of their poor white neighbors who vastly outnumbered them in the New World. These planters' concerns about the poor whites of the colonial South grew out of their English forefathers' experience attempting to control the antisocial behavior of the landless poor. At the start of Anglo colonization in North America, "Tudor England was undergoing social ferment, generated by an increasingly commercialized economy," Winthrop Jordan observed, as well as by Parliament's passage of the Enclosure Acts—legislation that dissolved landowners' traditional obligations toward their tenant laborers and allowed for tenant eviction and demolition of homes in order to make room for livestock. The resulting dislocations added to the ranks of London's homeless population and to a rising number of vagrants in the countryside, angry at the landed aristocracy. Members of England's middle and upper classes worried about these "masterless men" wandering around in their midsts, capable of begging, stealing, or worse, in their minds. Wealthy colonists in Virginia and elsewhere in the South saw the propertyless free whites, white servants, Africans, and Indians who had participated in the peasant rebellions of the late 1600s, notably Bacon's rebellion in 1676, in much the same light: as "ranging" and "roaming" vagrants prone to rebel, kill, and plunder, unable to control their sexual impulses and violent appetites, unmindful of personal property. At this point, at least for the property-holding plantation owners in the southern colonies, poor Europans, Africans, and Indians *together* posed a problem.

Plantation owners seized upon the institution of race-based slavery to address their fear of anarchy at the hands of what seemed to be a growing population of unrestrained and racially undifferentiated poor. Understanding that the expansion of slavery would curtail indentured servitude, and thus potentially limit the number of poor whites arriving in the colony, Virginia planters completed the switch from white servitude to African slavery by 1708, according to the planter Edmund Jennings. In 1708 Jennings wrote that no white servants had arrived in the colony in the previous six years. By contrast, between 1708 and 1750, nearly 40,000 African slaves were brought into the colony.

Morgan argued that emerging race-based slavery offered a way to brand Africans—and later Indians—as inherently different from poor whites and to co-opt poor whites such as those who had once threatened their property interests during Bacon's rebellion. Once Africans and Indians were enslaved on a racial premise the wealthy owners could separate freed poor whites from poor Africans and from the stigma of poverty, signaling the idea that poor whites were fit for freedom, property ownership, and the responsibility of self-government. The enactment of slave laws between 1650 and 1700 brought racial conceptions of whiteness into focus for those who sought to benefit from slavery. The gradual enactment of racially coded slave laws restricted the rights and behaviors of poor African slaves rather than poor free whites. It freed—and encouraged—poor free whites to participate in the emerging slave system as overseers, patrols, and supporters. Even though most poor whites would never own slaves of their own, their freedom allowed them to dream of upward mobility, dreams that the institution of slavery denied to Africans and Indians.

The institution of slavery encouraged whites to fuse their fears about the poor with their chromatically coded perceptions of "black" Africans and Indians (whom some commentators also labeled "black"). The logic of these slave codes circled around. Virginia's colonial leaders framed slave laws that not only defined the institution of slavery, but defined blackness—that is, crystallized ideas about Africans' separate racial identity as supposedly violent, sexually aggressive, venal, and idle—seeming in turn to obviate the need for their legal restraint and coercion.

AFRICANS, INDIANS, AND SLAVERY

Morgan's work asserts the negative implications of the color labels of black and white not simply for Africans in southeastern colonies but for Native Americans as well. From the moment of contact some Europeans lumped Indians and Africans together as "heathens" fit only for slavery. At the behest of colonial officials and promoters, some settlers subjected Indians to the same treatment that they reserved for Africans: they kidnapped them or rounded them up as war captives and sold them into slavery at home and abroad. Instances of European colonists' enslavement of Indians are legion. The followers of the Virginia planter-rebellion leader Nathaniel Bacon accepted the Virginia Assembly's offer of land and as many Indian slaves as they could capture on Virginia's frontier in return for their promise of peace. Whites in Virginia's hinterlands were not alone in their desire to enrich themselves off of Indian slave labor. Working for English sugar planters on the West Indies island of Barbados, the explorer William Hilton returned from a reconnaissance mission along the Carolina coast in the 1660s with several southeastern Indians on board his vessel whom he immediately sold as slaves to Barbadian planters upon reaching port. Even if they were not directly involved in the enslavement of Indians and Africans, some Europeans such as the Anglican missionary Morgan Godwyn, author of the 1680 missionary tract *The Negro's and Indians' Advocate,* treated both groups conceptually as one and the same. Godwyn regarded Indians and Africans in the New World as debased and heathen populations equally in need of the same Christian education.

Indians and Africans, however, were not interchangeable. White slave owners placed a lower monetary value on Indian slaves than on African slaves, suggesting a perception of difference in their productive worth. Unlike their African counterparts who had no place of escape, Indian slaves held within the mainland colonies often found refuge in nearby communities of free Indians when they absconded from their masters. As Native Americans escaped from slavery into what was, for them, familiar countryside, or refused to the death to labor as slaves, European colonists recognized the inadvisability of attempting systematically to subdue and enslave them. They were left with the central question: who were the Indians and how should they be treated?

IMPLICATING RACE IN NATIVE AMERICAN GENOCIDE

Native Americans and Europeans regarded each other with deep ambivalence: some initially greeted one another with curiosity and interest, others with hostility and distrust. Some Native Americans embraced Europeans as potential allies against their tribal enemies, other Native Americans feared Europeans as powerful antagonists in their own right. During the first 150 years of colonization, Europeans pursued a myriad of contradictory policies toward Indians. They negotiated land deals, formed political alliances, signed peace treaties with them, traded with them, hired them as translators and day laborers, attempted to Christianize them, married them, and occasionally adopted native culture and lived with them in their villages. In Pennsylvania, the Quaker leader William Penn actively pursued a policy of peaceful Indian-white co-existence. In the Carolinas, officials supplied arms both to European settlers and to a constantly shifting constellation of Indian allies in the hopes that they would engage in wars of attrition against Indian enemies newly armed by the French and Spanish. In all the colonies, however, most colonists simply wanted title to native lands. Indians protested whites' expansion into their territories with raids on whites' newly surveyed farms. Everywhere Europeans settled, it seemed, Indian war soon followed. Early on, even Pennsylvania's policy of peace had failed.

Soon after the English settlement of New England in the early 1620s, Indians and colonists clashed. In 1637, Captain John Mason attacked the Pequot's main settlement in coastal southeastern Connecticut, with more on his mind than the idea of subduing the Indians: he aimed for Indian genocide. Sporadically throughout the seventeenth and eighteenth centuries similar attacks followed in nearly every other colony. Settlers in the Carolinas pursued the same goal in their efforts to eliminate the Yamasee and then the Tuscarora in the early eighteenth century. In the 1760s, a vigilante group on Pennsylvania's frontier who called themselves the Paxton Boys attempted to decimate the Conestoga. A few eighteenth-century commentators such as the North Carolina naturalist, landowner, and surveyor-general John Lawson, the Virginia naturalist and planter Robert Beverley, and Thomas Jefferson continued to call for Indian assimilation, but by the mid-eighteenth century, most colonists uniformly supported the idea of native extirpation.

From the 1790s to the 1820s the federal government adopted an Indian policy that treated Indians as members of foreign nations with sovereign, communal rights over their recognized lands. The federal government exercised sole authority to ratify treaties negotiated with individual tribes and it devoted funds to support Indian assimilation. When Andrew Jackson became president in 1829, however, he reversed this policy to reflect overwhelming popular support for solving the "Indian problem" once and for all by removing Indians from their homelands within the states. With the full support of Congress, he passed the Indian Removal Act in 1830.

What allowed white Americans so aggressively to pursue the extirpation and removal of Native Americans? There are no simple answers. However, what is clear upon examining divergent sources is how profoundly race mattered in the formulation of public perceptions of, and policies about, the Indians. Divergent sources together begin to tell a larger story of how white Americans came to label diverse nations of Native Americans generically as Indians, to chromatically code this label as red, and then to forge this label (and their prejudice about its meaning and biological basis) into anti-Indian racism.

NEW WORLD COLONISTS RAISE THE "PROBLEM OF THE INDIAN"

When the paltry number of European settlers of the early 1600s (less than 100,000 in 1650) first encountered the 5.5 million Native Americans (by conservative estimates) representing at least 500 diverse nations on North American soil, the Native Americans struck Europeans as different from anyone else they had ever encountered in their explorations of the fifteenth century. Further, according to the historian James Merrell, the Europeans in fact knew their myriad native neighbors to be as distinct from each other as they were from whites and blacks. Just as the wealthy southern planters spoke of the various tribes of Africa, they understood as well about the differences between "northern Indians" of the Iroquois League, the Tuscarora, the Yuchi, the Savannah, the Cherokee, and members of various Muskogean (Creek) communities of the Southeast. Despite their knowledge of this diversity of inhabitants, commentators quickly adopted and universally applied to all native peoples, the Genoese explorer Christopher Columbus's precedent-setting term "Indians" (*indios* in Spanish)—a name

documenting his mistaken understanding that he had found a trade route to India when he first landed on the small Caribbean island he named San Salvador and encountered its inhabitants, the Tainos. Other explorers added another label to describe New World peoples: "savages," the anglicized version of the French *sauvage,* a term that ultimately derived from the Latin *silvaticus* meaning "of the wood, wild," (*silva* referring to "woods" or "forest"). Whereas Europeans quickly adopted these two labels (often using them together), many Europeans weren't entirely certain of the meaning of the terms for, nor the true identity of, diverse natives. Thus emerged simultaneously both the term "Indian" in European glossaries, and what Europeans referred to as "the problem of the Indian" in the European popular imagination. The problem raised was one of identity. Who were the Indians?

If unsure of native identity, many observers agreed upon the Indians' seeming docility and physical attractiveness. Early commentators such as Thomas Hariot, an observer who accompanied the English adventurer Sir Walter Raleigh in his exploration of the Carolina coastline in the 1580s, described the local inhabitants as childlike innocents. More than one hundred years later, in his 1709 travelogue *A New Voyage to Carolina,* John Lawson observed that the "Indians of North Carolina are well-shap'd clean-made People . . . they are a very streight People."

Wherever positive opinion of Indian body and character traits existed, explorers such as Sir Martin Frobisher could be found who cast Indians in less than favorable terms: he labeled northern Indians in the mid-sixteenth century as cannibalistic half-humans. The word "cannibal" entered the English language via Columbus's mischaracterization of the "Canuba" Indians in his diary as human flesh-eating "Cannibals" with an "addiction to war." The sobriquet stuck as observers such as Frobisher quickly applied it to communities of native inhabitants not openly friendly toward the English. Such criticism obscured Europeans' historical role in the escalation of Indian violence by implying that the Indians' "addiction to war" was a function of their character. In reality, from the start of colonization, European traders had supplied Indians with firearms, fueling their feuds and making their wars more deadly.

The very ambiguity and contradictions of observers' commentary on the Indians ended up creating more negative stereotypes in the European mind. Some observers used their own failure to "read" Indian identity, as evidence that the Indians were mentally incompetent. So frustrated was John Lawson at his failure to understand the Tuscarora Indians' behaviors, customs, and languages that he labeled them "Bedlamites," comparing them to the inmates of Bedlam, London's notorious insane asylum.

NATIVE AMERICANS EN ROUTE TO "REDSKINS"

New World commentators began to speak about Indian identity in color-coded terms although they could not agree on Indians' skin color. They described native peoples variously as tawny, yellow, olive, the color "of a sad French green," drab, brown, red-brown, russet, "the colour of the juyce of mulberries," and even black. Some argued that Indians were born with dark-hued skin. Other commentators asserted that Indians were born with the same skin pigmentation as whites but that they acquired darker complexions through early exposure to the sun and repeated applications of bear's grease. Europeans' preoccupation with Indian skin color signaled their larger questions about Indian identity. Whereas they came to perceive Indians as distinct from Africans, many wondered, How close were they to Europeans? Were Indians, after all, like themselves? Were they whites whose physical and cultural differences could be explained by environmental factors and geographic isolation?

Writers such as the Presbyterian minister Thomas Thorowgood, attempting to resolve these questions about Indians' identity, argued that the Indians were of the same ancient stock as Jews from which the English Protestants traced their lineage. In his 1650 book *Jewes in America, or Probabilities That the Americans Are of That Race,* he identified Native Americans as descendants of the lost tribes of Israel. Nonconformist divines such as the Reverend John Eliot, a Puritan missionary to Massachusetts' "praying Indians" at Natick, eagerly subscribed to this theory because it allowed them to pursue the larger Puritan aim of identifying and converting Indians, supposed latter-day Jews, to Christianity and to white Anglo culture.

Although Eliot gathered apparent evidence of a Jewish connection from his own Indian contacts early in his career, he later withdrew his support for this hypothesis. As his knowledge of Natick Indian culture deepened, he realized that the linguistic and cultural differences between the Natick and Puritans were far greater than any affinities upon which Thorowgood had based his book. For Eliot and other commentators it became clear the Indians' origins were not linked to either black or white cultural origins. Indian identity would remain to them a mystery.

THE PROBLEM OF THE INDIAN RAISES THE PROBLEM OF WHITE IDENTITY

Questions about the Indians' cultural and physical similarities to whites spurred commentators to refocus their attention on whites. Perhaps the most pressing aspect of the "problem of the Indians" in the European mind was the problem of whites; that is, Who were whites becoming as they interacted with Indians? Some wondered, Did Indians represent the future of white frontierspeople? Would the whites living on the margins of European colonial settlements regress to the putatively savage state of Indians? Commentators' ambiguous and contradictory statements about the Indians are revealing in the level of anxiety they reflect about European settlers' identity. Commentators found their uncertainty over Indians' identity advantageous for commenting on white settlers. Their ambiguity left them room to identify Indian attributes that they sought both to encourage and suppress in whites. Writers praised only those aspects of Indian character and culture that conformed to their own ideal values. For example, John Lawson instructed readers in his vision of a perfected Anglo colonial culture through his commentary about members of various local Indian communities, including the Tuscarora, whom he visited during an extended tour of Carolina's Indian country in 1701. He praised the Tuscarora for their generosity, their deference toward their elders, their patience and persistence—qualities he urged readers to emulate in their own fledgling settlements.

Likewise, many observers used their commentaries on the Indians indirectly to address what they viewed as white colonists' social and cultural problems. Typically for natural history writers of the early eighteenth century, Lawson condemned the Indians' supposed predisposition to steal, their apparent inability to plan for the future, and their seeming addiction to retaliatory wars as behaviors inimical to the patriarchal values that his propertied, profit-oriented, slave-owning contemporaries were attempting to normalize. Whereas European commentators like Lawson associated Africans with the ideas of absolute poverty and dependence, they linked Indians with the opposite notion of absolute freedom. Either condition, if left unchecked, ultimately would destroy colonial society, Lawson argued. One particular lesson that he inscribed in his observations about Indians was the idea that whites who criticized or ignored planter-class interests—lawless "white Indians" who "ranged" the land as woodsmen, traders, cattle-rustlers, hunters, poachers, trespassers, and squatters—had no place in colonial society.

DEFINING "REDSKINS"

When and why did the Indians become "redskins" with the connotation of a status inferior to "whites" that went along with it? No clear evidence emerges from the documentary record to provide an easy answer. Two influential sources, however, one from European scientific circles, the other from southeastern Indians themselves, emerged in the eighteenth century to inform popular perceptions of the Indians as red.

The epithet "redskin" did not come into popular usage until after the American Revolution even though scientists began systematically to categorize different human communities by color in the 1730s. In his correspondence with Linnaeus, the French naturalist Georges Louis Leclerc de Buffon, took exception to Linnaeus's view that the Indians were uniformly "red." He argued in his influential, multivolume *Natural History* (begun in 1749) that their complexions varied considerably. Nonetheless, Buffon concluded his commentary on Native Americans with the remark that "the whole continent of America contains but one race of men, who are all more or less tawny." From these two internationally known scientists, mid-eighteenth-century audiences learned that America's Indians comprised a distinct race, possibly red, certainly darker than, and inferior to, themselves.

At the same time that Americans were finding support for their color-coded notions of racial identity in European scientific writings, they were also discovering parallels in race labels that their southeastern Indian cohorts were devising to create their own categories of difference in the context of their widening contacts with Europeans and Africans. According to the historian Nancy Shoemaker, the color-coded race labels that Cherokees and others repeated in their creation stories, diplomatic speeches, and answers to missionaries' and natural historians' seemingly interminable questions reinforced Europeans' own emerging notions of race. In their interactions with whites, Shoemaker has found that many southeastern Indians identified

themselves as red, accentuating the link between their traditional names for themselves, their words for the color red, and their understandings of their divine origin in the red clay earth of their homelands. Others additionally embraced the label red as an expression of their attachment to war moieties—communities politically dominated by younger male warriors who distinguished themselves by the color red. Even though these war moieties were balanced by peace moieties largely composed of male and female elders and their clans who identified themselves by the color white, most Indians, whether from "white" or "red" communities, nonetheless represented themselves as "red Indians" to their "white European" counterparts.

Southeastern Indians developed color categories in tandem with their non-native neighbors to define the characteristics and obligations of the many "others" moving among them: various white Europeans and African slaves. In this mutual enterprise of creating race labels based on generalizations about skin color, then, they shared the same goals. Yet, even though southeast Indians seemed to echo and confirm whites' color categories, they did not share whites' moral associations with these labels. They resisted the pejorative connotations that whites were attaching to the label red.

For their part, whites not only tightened their perception of the link between the labels "Indian" and "red" and "European" and "white," but also found ways to further separate Indians from whites and stigmatize them as an inferior people. John Lawson, for one, asserted that the very diversity and apparent unintelligibility of southeastern Indians' languages evidenced the Indians' inferiority. Their different tongues, he asserted, functioned to divide and isolate their communities, thereby weakening them as a people. He argued that the Indians' mutual misunderstandings of one another's languages was at the root of "the continual Wars these Savages maintain." Their many languages, he believed, indicated their collective incapacity to reason and to act responsibly. Their extreme cultural localism and attachment to various languages and dialects only provided further evidence, in his mind, that they were "Bedlamites" unable to develop a pan-Indian culture devoted to peace rather than war. In his criticism of their putative linguistic deficiency, he strengthened the foundations for a biologically rooted conception of an inferior Indian race: the Indians lacked the mental capacity to develop a single, unifying language upon which to secure their survival. In his view, their habit of speaking in tongues rendered them a savage people whom whites were justified in subduing.

Europeans further layered their race category of "red Indian" with negative meaning in their commentary about the Indians susceptibility to European diseases. With no immunological defenses against such European scourges as smallpox, historians estimate population losses of up to 80 percent wherever Europeans settled along the coast. Some Europeans such as John Winthrop, the first governor of the Massachusetts Bay Colony, were quick to interpret the spread of disease among the Indians as the work of divine providence. Lawson argued that Europeans' ability to withstand the diseases that were ravaging Southeast coastal Indians proved Europeans better adapted than the Indians to a radically changing New World environment. In his view, Europeans' drive to survive upon, "improve," and profit from the land positioned whites as the natural and rightful successors to the countryside that the weakened Indians once dominated. Writing after the American Revolution during a time when white Americans were building consensus over the Indians' "redness," Thomas Jefferson interpreted the Indians' high death rate due to disease as a sign of their permanent alienation from the land and justification for their elimination.

Before the American Revolution, Anglo colonial officials attempted to secure Native American groups as military allies against the French and Spanish, rival European powers who were competing to enlist Indians in their efforts to advance their own imperial ambitions in North America. After the Revolution, the French and the Spanish stopped supplying arms to the Indians and the Indians found that they commanded less respect from white Americans than ever. White Americans' perception of the Indians shifted in the era of the new republic. Because Indians had sided with the British during the war, white Americans regarded them as enemies in their own land. Many saw the Indians as powerless and vulnerable—shunned from the white world, sinking deeper into poverty and succumbing to disease. As Indians on the frontier began to coalesce a pan-Indian resistance to the frontierspeople flooding onto their lands, whites fought back with words as well as weapons: they solidified their label of "redskin" into an epithet that at once derided Indians and justified their own calls to isolate, contain, and, ultimately, remove them from their midsts.

This essay is suggestive of how European settlers constructed race as an expedient category to make sense of their world, and how they devised a racial ideology to divide and oppress large segments of a diverse and growing New World population. The hold of race categories on Anglo colonists' imaginations grew stronger as North American society gained in complexity. After the Revolution, citizens of the new nation divided fellow inhabitants into the stark categories red, white, and black, defying the intermixed reality of the expanding population. As race became embedded as an unquestioned cultural premise, Americans found it ever more difficult to recognize the intermingling of inhabitants in every region of the country. To the present day, race as a cultural category has exerted the power to limit America's choices of identity and to mask the demographic reality of the nation's complex and diverse society.

See also **Whites and the Construction of Whiteness** *(volume 2);* **Race** *(volume 3).*

BIBLIOGRAPHY

Bartels, Emily C. "Othello and Africa: Postcolonialism Reconsidered." *William and Mary Quarterly* 54, no. 1 (January 1997): 45–64.

Berkeley, Edmund, and Dorothy Smith Berkeley. *The Reverend John Clayton: A Parson with a Scientific Mind—His Scientific Writings and Other Related Papers.* Charlottesville, Va., 1965.

Berkhofer, Robert F. *The White Man's Indian: Images of the American Indian from Columbus to the Present.* New York, 1979.

Bragdon, Kathleen J. *Native People of Southern New England, 1500–1650.* Norman, Okla., 1996.

Braude, Benjamin. "The Sons of Noah and the Construction of Ethnic and Geographical Identities in the Medieval and Early Modern Periods." *William and Mary Quarterly* 54, no. 1 (January 1997): 103–142.

Browne, Thomas. "Of the Blackness of Negroes." 1646. In *The Works of Sir Thomas Browne,* 3 vols., edited by Charles Sayle. London, 1904–1907.

Davis, David Brion. "Constructing Race." *William and Mary Quarterly* 54, no. 1 (January 1997): 7–18.

Fields, Barbara. "Ideology and Race in American History." In *Region, Race, and Reconstruction,* edited by James M. McPherson, pp. 143–177. New York, 1982.

Godwyn, Morgan. *The Negro's and Indians' Advocate.* 1680.

Hudson, Charles M., ed. *Red, White and Black: Symposium on Indians in the Old South.* Athens, Ga., 1971.

Jefferson, Thomas. *Notes on the State of Virginia.* 1785. Reprint, New York, 1964.

Jordan, Winthrop D. *White over Black: American Attitudes toward the Negro, 1550–1812.* Chapel Hill, N.C., 1968.

Kupperman, Karen Ordahl. "Presentment of Civility: English Reading of American Self-Presentation in the Early Years of Colonization." *William and Mary Quarterly,* 3d ser., vol. 54, no. 1 (January 1997): 193–229.

Lawson, John. *A New Voyage to Carolina.* 1709. Reprint, edited by Hugh Talmage Lefler. Chapel Hill, N.C., 1968.

Merrell, James H. *The Indians' New World: Catawbas and their Neighbors from European Contact through the Era of Removal.* New York, 1998.

Montagu, Ashley. "Race: The History of an Idea." In *Race Awareness,* edited by Ruth Miller and Paul J. Dolan. New York, 1971.

Morgan, Edmund S. *American Slavery American Freedom: The Ordeal of Colonial Virginia.* New York, 1975.

Morgan, Jennifer L. "'Some Could Suckle Over Their Shoulders: Male Travelers, Female Bodies, and the Gendering of Racial Ideology, 1500–1770." *William and Mary Quarterly* 54, no. 1 (January 1997): 167–192.

Nash, Gary B. "The Image of the Indian in the Southern Colonial Mind." In *Shaping Southern Society: The Colonial Experience,* edited by T. H. Breen, pp. 75–99. New York, 1976.

Shoemaker, Nancy. "How Indians Got to Be Red." *American Historical Review* (June 1997): 625–644.

Vaughan, Alden T. *Roots of American Racism: Essays on the Colonial Experience.* New York, 1995.

Vaughan, Alden T., and Virginia Mason Vaughan. "Before *Othello*: Elizabethan Representations of Sub-Saharan Africans." *William and Mary Quarterly* 54, no. 1 (January 1997): 19–44.

Wood, Peter H. *Black Majority; Negroes in Colonial South Carolina from 1670 through the Stono Rebellion.* New York, 1974.

Part 2

REVOLUTION, CONSTITUTION, AND THE EARLY REPUBLIC TO 1838

OVERVIEW:
THE REVOLUTIONARY ERA
AND THE EARLY REPUBLIC

Andrew R. L. Cayton

In the late eighteenth and early nineteenth centuries, the population of the United States doubled roughly every twenty years. Just over 2 million people in 1776 had become slightly more than 17 million by 1840. They were a remarkably diverse group. In 1800, approximately 20 percent were Africans; another 10 percent were Germans; over half were female; and around two-thirds were under the age of twenty-one. In fact, it would be perfectly reasonable to construct an overview of American intellectual and cultural life in this period as a collection of relatively discrete ways of considering and organizing the world.

Still, there were great similarities in the patterns of people's lives. Most Americans devoted themselves to ensuring the survival of their households through the production of food and goods and the reproduction of children. They entertained themselves in time-honored fashion and they conceived of the world much as their ancestors had. Large numbers of people believed strongly in supernatural occurrences and saw themselves as parts of a larger drama over which they and other human beings had little control. Virtually all thought in terms of families, local communities, or religions; only a few, disproportionately known to historians, spoke of an American identity.

Historians do not know as much about popular or vernacular cultures as they would like. But they do know that, despite the multiplicity of cultures in eastern North America, a hegemonic culture had emerged by the middle of the eighteenth century. Variations on one kind of discourse predominated—and that was British, male, Protestant, and Enlightened.

Within this Anglo-American community, there was a growing tendency to think in universal terms. Full of prejudices (most especially against Catholics), they nonetheless longed to create a common world, as long as it was dominated by the British and full of people who thought and acted as they did. In a larger sense, the Age of Revolution was an era of generalizations about human beings. People everywhere talked about universal notions of liberty, equality, and fraternity. As the political philosopher Thomas Paine, an Englishman who witnessed both the American and French Revolutions, wrote in his pamphlet *Common Sense,* "The cause of America is in a great measure the cause of all mankind" (*Thomas Paine Reader,* p. 65). The key document of the French Revolution spoke not of the rights of Frenchmen but of the rights of man and citizen.

Class, race, and gender inequalities in British North America were as obvious to enslaved African Americans, women, American Indians, and ordinary laborers as they have been to recent historians. But when the Methodist preacher Richard Allen and the scientist Benjamin Banneker advocated the rights of Africans, or the young African Phillis Wheatley composed poetry, they did so within the language of Protentantism and the Enlightenment. The writers Mercy Otis Warren and Judith Sargent Murray expressed themselves in a gender-neutral rhetoric that gave few clues that women were in any way different from men. Many people hoped that the upheavals of the late eighteenth century would inaugurate a new age in which men (and some women) would come together and, transcending religious and local peculiarities, create through commercial and intellectual exchanges a better world.

Nothing was more central to this enterprise than the word "citizen." Not only did the word connote political participation, it suggested a status that cut across all borders. But what did it mean? No notion was more contested in the Early American Republic than that of citizenship. Was it a matter of birth, residence, property ownership, race, gender? These questions were not idle ones. The major thing Americans did in this period, after all, was to create a nation. The republican empire they fashioned was a revolutionary concept. The whole idea of a nation was still very fluid. The belief that it could operate democratically (however much that term was compromised by the racial, class, and gender exclusiveness of democracy) was radical. There was, in short, much to consider.

PROTESTANTISM AND ENLIGHTENMENT

Of all the intellectual traditions in eighteenth-century North America the most important by far was religion. Protestantism created the most common framework for understanding the world and human beings. No book was more widely read than the Bible. No figures were more important in conveying information to large groups of people (at least until the early nineteenth century) than ministers. No images or metaphors had wider acceptance than those of Christianity. To the extent that there was a pervasive culture in British North America it was Protestant. Even as secular a document as *Common Sense* was replete with biblical allusions.

The only truly continental figure in the colonies—and the most well-known celebrity of his day—was the Anglican minister George Whitefield. His extensive speaking tours, which took him from Georgia to New England in the 1740s, were models of charismatic communication. All kinds of Americans turned out to hear Whitefield and to listen to his message of hope. Democratic in style, Whitefield and other evangelicals assured Americans of the possibility of salvation achieved through utter devotion to God and his benevolent works. They also reinforced traditional beliefs in the Calvinist God's transcendent presence in their world and in the role of the North American colonies as a New Israel—a "City on a Hill" to the rest of the world—whose success or failure rested on the behavior of individuals. Salvation, in short, depended on the ways in which human beings conducted themselves. In a paradoxical combination of predestinarian theology and an Arminian sense of freedom of choice, they believed that while human beings could not control their destinies, they did have the power to shape their contours.

At the same time, a scientific rationalism associated with European intellectual developments lumped together under the label of the Enlightenment was gaining ground. The most famous American exemplar of the inclination to exalt human reason about superstitious faith was Benjamin Franklin, the Boston-born printer who became one of the leading figures of the eighteenth-century Anglo-American world. Franklin's efforts to understand and master nature (as in his experiments with lightning, which led to his invention of the lightning rod—a practical solution to an age-old problem) and his struggle to reduce his life to a science have made him an icon of American rationality.

Protestantism and the Enlightenment were not incompatible, however. The Calvinist minister Jonathan Edwards, surely the most brilliant writer in eighteenth-century North America, wrestled all of his life with efforts to reconcile science and revelation, to mix reason and faith. No one was more deeply versed in the world of the Enlightenment than Edwards. Indeed, it was the tension between science and religion that fueled most of his most powerful prose. To understand the predictable workings of this world (including those of the human brain) as testaments to the power of God was sublime.

Edwards was neither popular nor influential in his lifetime. Much more important in transmitting a mixture of religion and reason to prominent Americans was the clergyman John Witherspoon, the president of the College of New Jersey (now Princeton University) from 1768 to 1794. Witherspoon was a native Scot and a devotee of that country's particular take on the Enlightenment. At Princeton, the statesman James Madison and dozens of other white men became familiar with the works of the philosophers Francis Hutcheson, David Hume, and Adam Smith. They were introduced to fundamental questions about the nature of human beings, about the possibility of self-improvement and social reform, about the ways in which human beings' very flaws—their passions, impulses, and needs—can be turned to social advantage. The Scottish Enlightenment emphasized the need for orderly economic development and polite manners and propounded the idea of common sense—a pragmatic, enlightened approach to human society which drew on humans' instinctive moral sense.

American Protestantism and the Scottish Enlightenment shared much in common. Both emphasized the essential degradation of humankind and they struggled with trying to fathom the ways, if any, to attain grace in this world and the next. And both focused on the strengthening of individual character as the foundation of all human achievement.

Indeed, human nature obsessed thoughtful British Americans in the eighteenth and early nineteenth centuries. The eighteenth-century Anglo-American world was alive with rumors of conspiracies and betrayals, stories of the rise and fall of empires and individuals, and investigations of the reliability and durability of human relationships. Many people were profoundly distrustful of human nature. Weaned in a Protestant culture of sin and divine intervention but exposed to an enlightened mentality in which there was supposedly a direct cause for every effect, they saw uncivilized human beings as cauldrons of seething passions, besotted with greed, lust, and ambition.

The peculiarity of British North Americans was not their belief in the imperfections of human beings, however. Rather, their distinctiveness lay in the nature of their reflections on the possibilities of controlling human failings, or at least channeling them into socially beneficial directions. At the heart of this enterprise was a tension (a creative one, more often than not) between the universal tendencies of an enlightened interest in general laws of human conduct and the particular experiences of the American environment. The latter involved confronting not just the natural or constructed landscape of North America but the development of a largely British and increasingly bourgeois sense of civilization as a triumph of manners over impulses.

PATRICIANS AND PLEBEIANS

Although far more Americans were influenced by religion than by the Enlightenment, the latter was especially important to members of the gentry, or patricians, who valued their connections with Great Britain. There was, it is important to emphasize, no such thing as an eighteenth-century intellectual. All European Americans wealthy enough to live an independent existence assumed that reading and writing were quintessential marks of their status as refined persons. To reflect on the state of the world was to be civilized; it was to differentiate oneself from plebeians, the "meaner sort" of human beings who made up the mass of humankind.

Patricians, whether they were planter families in Virginia or mercantile households in Boston, lived off of the labor of their dependents; they did not work themselves. Instead, they devoted—or made a great show out of devoting—much of their time to acquiring the accoutrements of gentility. Wealthy Americans literally rebuilt their worlds in the eighteenth century. They constructed the brick homes with glass windows, elegant entrance halls, and separate dining rooms, stuffed with all kinds of utensils, tables, chairs, paintings, draperies that most Americans associate with the colonial era. Patricians were fascinated with detail. A young John Adams, raised in a family of middling means, was alternately awestruck and appalled on his visit to the

mansion of the wealthy Boston merchant Nicholas Boylston in January 1766:

> Went over [to] the House to view the Furniture, which alone cost a thousand Pounds sterling. A seat it is for a noble Man, a Prince. The Turkey Carpets, the painted Hangings, the Marble Table, the rich Beds with crimson Damask Curtains and Counterpins, the beautiful Chimny Clock, the Spacious Garden, are the most magnificent of any Thing I have ever seen. (*Diary and Autobiography of John Adams*, vol. 1, p. 294)

Patricians believed that such displays separated them from the plebeian cultures of their inferiors. Ordinary people could not afford the plates and tea services of a gentry household. More important, they did not know how to use them properly. They were unrefined, lacking the taste that denoted gentility even more than wealth. So critical was the mastery of social performance to patricians that fashions in clothing and wigs became subtler over the course of the eighteenth century in order to make emulation more difficult. The true mark of gentle people was not the value of their clothes or trinkets, the amount of lace on their bodies or silver in their houses, but rather the way in which they wore and used them. All the money in the world could not teach someone how to dance with grace or appreciate a fine meal. Social climbers and parvenus beware: a rise in status depended on style as well as cash.

THE PERFORMANCE OF CIVILITY

The most admired American of the late eighteenth century was the statesman George Washington, a man who appeared publicly to be so restrained as to be without any distinctive personality at all. Washington was an exemplary human being not because he was a wealthy landowner or a powerful leader but because of extraordinary personal mastery. He commanded others by virtue of his command of himself. Washington lived his life as if he were always on stage, performing for the approbation and improvement of other human beings.

Critical to the culture of genteel politeness was the cultivation of the mind. Men and women of patrician status necessarily exposed themselves to the finest in art, literature, music, and drama. The idea was that reading and seeing and hearing the right things elevated one's taste and one's sense of the possibilities of human achievement. Here was the sensationalist theory of the seventeenth-century English philosopher John Locke in his *Essay concerning Human Understanding*, the notion that human beings are to a great extent the product of the sensations they receive from the environment in which they exist, in action. A walk in a well-ordered garden or a graceful dance helped human beings subdue their baser instincts as much as it exercised them physically. Viewing paintings of famous people by artists such as John Singleton Copley or, even more important, decisive events in human history, encouraged the observer to try harder at living a life of elegance or doing some transcendent. Thus Benjamin West's huge canvas detailing the death of General James Wolfe during the Battle of Quebec in 1759 became all the rage in London, while John Trumbull's massive paintings of the major events of the American Revolution were eventually placed in the great halls of American public buildings.

Architecturally, this didactic trend reached its peak in the neoclassical federal style that dominates Washington, D.C., a city constructed with an eye to affecting visitors. The balanced proportions of public and private buildings from the 1780s to the 1820s reflected a widespread interest in instilling order and harmony into the artificial as well as the natural environment. New England towns were rebuilt in the decades after the American Revolution; cities such as New York adopted rectangular, block designs. Federal architecture and urban planning emphasized symmetry, subtlety, and sophistication.

Drama's role in creating an uplifting environment was more ambiguous. Theaters in eighteenth-century Anglo-America were never models of decorum. Patrons were generally unruly and disheveled; they thought nothing of talking during a performance or commenting loudly on what they were seeing (much as Americans behave now when they watch television in their own homes). Most entertainments were frankly popular in nature, their goal to make money more than educate. There were exceptions, of course. The English playwright William Shakespeare was very popular. Some Americans, most notably the playwright Royall Tyler in his comedy *The Contrast,* tried to bring the culture of politeness to the stage. The difficulty was that Tyler's comic relief character, a servant named Jonathan, proved far more popular than his wooden hero, Colonel Manly. The fact that there were permanent theaters and professional acting troupes in Philadelphia and New York by the early 1800s reflected the popularity rather than the morality of drama.

None of this immersion in the world of the arts could have taken place without the emergence of institutions and an infrastructure which made its flourishing possible. Following the lead of the British, Americans in the late 1700s and early 1800s constructed public parks and public spaces. Entrepreneurs and organizations opened rudimentary art galleries and developed musical concerts in and out of private homes. Perhaps the most ambitious of these concerns was the Peale Museum in Philadelphia. Mixing a collection of bones and other natural artifacts with paintings by himself and his talented children, topped off by a moving picture show, the artist Charles Willson Peale attracted thousands of paying customers to his entertaining and enlightening exhibition.

No effort to structure an environment that would elevate the behavior of human beings and bring order to the world by confronting their inevitable passions was more far-ranging than the Constitution of the United States. Written in Philadelphia in the summer of 1787 and ratified over the course of the next two years, the Constitution created a government dedicated to the proposition that human beings were essentially self-interested and passionate creatures. The scheme of a federal republic sought, in the tradition of the Scottish Enlightenment, to put human failings to use in the greater cause of humankind. James Madison and others envisioned their political structure as a system of counterbalancing passions, seeking harmony not in repression but in a symmetrical juxtaposition of human impulses, represented by Congress, the president, and the judiciary. Madison, Alexander Hamilton, and John Jay explained this vision in detail in newspaper essays collected in *The Federalist Papers.*

More than an intellectual experiment, the Constitution was an arrangement of power in the new republic. One of the most important things it did in this regard was to create a national political community and encourage a national political discourse. The Federalists who dominated the national government in the 1790s went to great lengths to develop an infrastructure that would facilitate maximum exchange within the republic and inculcate self-discipline in the vulgar masses. These political efforts paralleled and promoted other institutional developments that would make possible the realization of a truly national framework in the United States by the 1830s.

THE REVOLUTION IN PRINT

By far the most important development was in the world of print. In North America as elsewhere, the major technological development was the revolution in communication, particularly the expansion of print culture to greater numbers of people. While most people probably still functioned in a primarily oral culture, there was a dramatic increase, particularly after the American Revolution, in the number of people who read newspapers or mailed letters. Technological improvements made possible the publication of inexpensive books and periodicals that circulated widely among ordinary people.

At least through the end of the eighteenth century, Americans were as likely to communicate with people in western Europe as they were with people in other regions of North America. In the small French town of Vincennes on the Wabash River in the 1770s, people read books printed in Paris. English newspapers made their way into the coffeehouses and drawing rooms of seaboard cities from Boston, Massachusetts, to Charleston, South Carolina. Educated Americans followed events in Europe with the kind of intensity only someone who feels themselves provincial can muster.

No wonder that the ambitious Maryland cleric Mason Weems—a man in search of a fortune by whatever means possible—saw possibilities in a biography of the recently deceased George Washington. "I've got something to whisper in your lug," he wrote to the Philadelphia printer Mathew Carey in January 1800. "Washington, you know is gone! Millions are gaping to read something about him. I am very nearly primd and cockd for 'em." Weems confided that he had "enlivend" the hero's life "with *Anecdotes apropos interesting* and *Entertaining*" (Cunliffe, p. xv). Sold for twenty-five or thirty-seven cents, the book would cost only ten cents to produce. Carey never replied and Weems had to find another publisher. His strategy, however, was an excellent one; his biography ultimately went through several editions in his lifetime. There was indeed a large audience in North America for entertaining books and periodicals.

By the 1830s, inexpensive newspapers abounded in American cities. A cornucopia of books and pamphlets existed to satisfy the desires of a multitude of eager readers. Religious tracts, novels, etiquette books—whatever was requested was available. Voluntary organizations, most notably the American Tract Society and others that made up the informal "Benevolent Empire," dispersed vast quantities of didactic printed material.

Eighteenth-century English novels such as *Tristram Shandy* and *Clarissa* were widely read in North America and eventually produced imitations. Intended to sell, these fictional works were full of melodrama, coincidences, and contrived plots. But

they also had an educational purpose. In *Modern Chivalry,* Hugh Henry Brackenridge composed an eighteenth-century variation on *Don Quixote* in which he gleefully lampooned the democratic excesses and pretensions of the "meaner sort" in the aftermath of the American Revolution. Susanna Haswell Rowson's *Charlotte Temple* was a warning to young women to mind the advice of parents and resist the temptations of attractive men in colorful uniforms who would inevitably seduce them into a life of disgrace, penury, and humiliation. Charles Brockden Brown, a young Federalist lawyer, used Gothic conventions to reflect on the dark side of human nature. His *Wieland,* an account of an educated young man who falls victim to the games of a ventriloquist and kills his wife and children, suggested that in a struggle between reason and emotion, science and superstition, the latter would normally prevail.

Not all published work was religious or fictional. Historians such as David Ramsay, Mercy Otis Warren, and John Marshall retraced the American Revolution in an effort to draw lessons from the experience. Essayists such as Judith Sargent Murray reflected on the status of women and argued for a greater political role for women of education and taste. Most of their works were published in periodicals, which became leading advocates of didactic roles for women as "republican" wives and mothers.

This expansion of a reading public fostered at least two major developments in American society. The first was the growth of an incipient consumer mentality. Readers become more discriminating, driving the market with demand, and writers and publishers became more adept at advertising their wares and manipulating their customers. Books were well on their way to becoming a commodity, something to be bought and sold like a piece of cloth or an enslaved African in any American market.

The second development was a democratization of knowledge. All kinds of people all over the United States in the Early Republic had access to data that had simply been unavailable to their grandparents. Reading was no longer an activity limited to the leisured or the pious. The loosening of control over information meant that more and more people could acquire the illusion of power over themselves and their worlds. The vulgar mob now had the means, literally, to think and reason. So what if few people could match the beau ideal of the Salem, Massachusetts, clergyman William Bentley, who devoted his entire life to the acquisition of knowledge apparently for no other purpose than to collect it?

No other American home had Bentley's massive library or the breadth of his intellectual interests, but many of them had a small shelf of books that went well beyond the proverbial Bible and almanacs of the eighteenth century.

THE RISE OF ROMANTICISM

The fascination with the universal faded in the Early Republic. Disillusionment with the outcomes of revolutions had a lot to do with that shift in thinking, a disillusionment nurtured by the availability of newspaper reports of events in faraway places. The French Revolution, which had commenced in grand discussion of liberty, equality, and fraternity, produced a volatile 1790s, full of terror, executions, a succession of governments, and continental war, and ended with a self-crowned emperor. The French emperor Napoleon Bonaparte's conquests exported the ideas of the revolution; they also encouraged the growth of nationalist feelings among conquered peoples in Germany, Spain, Italy, and the Austrian Empire. The Haitian Revolution of the 1790s frightened European Americans throughout the Western Hemisphere; white southerners, in particular, came to associate revolutionary ardor with race-based massacre. In Mexico, most patricians abetted in the ruthless suppression of revolutionary movements until they decided in 1821 that a liberal Spain was a more dangerous threat to their positions and created a new nation; elsewhere in Spanish America calls for reform seemed to produce either anarchy or reaction. No wonder the South American revolutionary leader Simon Bolívar likened efforts to reform Spanish America to plowing the seas.

Disillusionment in the United States was less pronounced but present nonetheless. Few of the so-called founding fathers died pleased with the outcome of the American Revolution. Even the most sanguine of them, Thomas Jefferson, retired from the presidency in 1809 disgusted with the American people's failure to support his national experiment in commercial coercion as an alternative to war, the Embargo Act of 1807. Concerned about the divisive issue of slavery and worried about the rise of uneducated, passionate leaders such as Andrew Jackson, Jefferson moaned in 1820 "that the useless sacrifice of themselves by the generation of 1776, to acquire self-government and happiness to their country, is to be thrown away by the unwise and unworthy passions of their sons, and my only consolation is to be, that I live not to weep over it" (*Jefferson: Writings,* p. 1434).

Of all the Founding Fathers, Jefferson had the least reason to express such misgivings. He had triumphed over the Federalists in 1801 and downsized the American government they had established in the 1790s. Jefferson took office under the assumption that society could regulate itself better than the institutions of state power. He well knew that men were not angels but he hoped that affection or friendship would prove stronger bonds among people than attachments based on force.

Or rather, Jefferson hoped that affection among white males would suffice. Whereas the Federalists had maintained a modified patriarchal model of human society, the Jeffersonians claimed to be a band of brothers or friends. Fraternity was a key term in their lexicon. They were creating a democracy of civilized white males. Other peoples (Indians, for example) might join this fraternity but only if they became like Jefferson and his friends. Blacks, however, were not invited; the enslaved blacksmith Gabriel Prosser and a couple dozen other enslaved men paid with their lives when they made the mistake of thinking otherwise and planned an aborted rebellion in Richmond, Virginia, in 1800. Nor were women invited to the Jeffersonian party. The Jeffersonians' substitution of fraternity for patriarchy meant that there was no clear place for dependents in their world. They, therefore, had to come up with reasons why some people could not belong, which led them to focus on the differences among human beings, to become more articulate in expressions of scientific racism and sexism.

Disillusionment and the politics of exclusion were only parts of the reasons for the demise of enlightened universalism, however. As important was the growing assertiveness of ordinary people. Romanticism—the celebration of vernacular, popular cultures, the elevation of the particular, the association of place with behavior—was never as fully developed in the United States as it was in Europe. Still, decades of revolution had persuaded many people that they were better off asserting their personal interests rather than those of humankind. Americans, in general, became more nationalistic in the Early Republic. As important, they became more self-conscious about regional, racial, gender, and class divisions. The kind of universal discourse that had dominated the late eighteenth century gave way to a vocabulary of the peculiar and the specific.

In part, the actions of disillusioned, frightened white males in excluding people from their fraternity on the basis of race or gender forced people to develop their own consciousness; the process, however, also involved the transformation of the hegemonic rhetoric of independence and equality into a vocabulary of liberation. Working people celebrated the dignity of work. African Americans formed their own churches and began to find a public voice that would reach expression in the writings of the abolitionists David Walker, Frederick Douglass, and Sojourner Truth. Women in private correspondence and public periodicals began to consider womanhood as something distinct from the rights of man and citizen. If women never inhabited a separate sphere, they no longer used the universal language of enlightenment as had Judith Sargent Murray and Mercy Otis Warren. The Seneca leader Handsome Lake, the Shawnee Indian chief Tecumseh and his brother Tenskwatawa, and, to a lesser extent, the Cherokee leader Sequoyah, rejected calls for assimilation into the Jeffersonian paradise of farmers and families and enjoined others to preserve, protect, and defend their traditions.

European American literature became more concerned with national and regional themes. Southerners and westerners began to think and speak more often of being southern or western, accentuating differences rooted in particular kinds of places. By the 1840s, the former were discussing the existence of a Southern nation different in style and purpose from that in the North. To be sure, men of letters such as the American essayist Ralph Waldo Emerson prided themselves on maintaining connections with prominent Europeans. But there was now a merging of universal and national themes in American literature. Historians such as Francis Parkman, William Hickling Prescott, and George Bancroft had associated the great themes of the eighteenth century (liberty, equality, fraternity) with certain kinds of people, specifically, with Protestant, Caucasian, English-speaking Americans. James Fenimore Cooper and other novelists, along with artists, celebrated the indigenous American environment, the great expanse of land, the imposing skies and natural formations. Somehow the experience of living in North America had transformed Europeans into something new, something unlike anybody else in the world.

In all of these emerging communities, emotion was a key factor. The very kind of passion that enlightened Christians had tried to control became a source of pride in the nineteenth century. Unitari-anism, which espoused as enlightened and reasonable an approach to matters of faith as was imaginable to contemporaries, failed to win many converts beyond the patrician families of Boston. In the denominational diversity of the Second Great Awakening (c. 1795–1825), religion became more emotional, more evangelical, more dependent on personal experiences for the achievement of salvation.

Writing in general became more sentimental, more popular; drama, poetry, and novels appealed far more to emotion than reason for their persuasive power. Public orations now matched the popular style associated with Patrick Henry and George Whitefield in the 1700s; speakers depended on personal charisma to make their points. They intended to have a dramatic impact on their listeners. They were less concerned with reasoning with audiences than with overpowering them. These changes are most evident in contrasting the most important mobilizing document in the American Revolution, Paine's *Common Sense,* with that of the Civil War, Harriet Beecher Stowe's *Uncle Tom's Cabin.*

Symbolic of all these changes was the construction of the American Napoleon, the president of the United States in the 1830s, Andrew Jackson. A man of temper and impulse, uneducated and only moderately refined, Jackson was a hero to many Americans and the Antichrist to others precisely because they imagined him as the antithesis of the enlightened Christian vision of the late eighteenth century. Americans admired Jackson for his (apparent) simplicity and sincerity and his (apparent) honesty and hubris, not for his universal qualities but for his embodiment of American qualities. "Born a simple citizen," Andrew Stevenson of Richmond, Virginia, informed his audience on the news of Jackson's death in 1845, "he became great by no other means than the energy of his own character, and being, as he seems to have been, the favourite of nature and Heaven! Had he been born to wealth and influence, he might probably have lived and died, an obscure and ordinary man." Instead, he became "the architect of his own fortunes!" (Ward, p. 166). From Washington to Jackson, the eighteenth century's suspicion of the universal tendencies of human nature had given way to a celebration of the peculiar natures of Americans.

BIBLIOGRAPHY

Adams, John. *Diary and Autobiography of John Adams.* 4 vols. Edited by Lyman H. Butterfield. Cambridge, Mass., 1961.

Appleby, Joyce. *Liberalism and Republicanism in the Historical Imagination.* Cambridge, Mass., 1992.

Banning, Lance. *The Sacred Fire of Liberty: James Madison and the Founding of the Federal Republic.* Ithaca, N.Y., 1995.

Brewer, John. *The Pleasures of the Imagination: English Culture in the Eighteenth Century.* New York, 1997.

Brown, Richard D. *Knowledge is Power: The Diffusion of Information in Early America, 1700–1865.* New York, 1989.

Bushman, Richard. *The Refinement of America: Persons, Houses, Cities.* New York, 1992.

Butler, Jon. *Awash in a Sea of Faith: Christianizing the American People.* Cambridge, Mass., 1990.

Conforti, Joseph A. *Jonathan Edwards, Religious Tradition, and American Culture.* Chapel Hill, N.C., 1995.

Cunliffe, Marcus, ed. *The Life of Washington.* Cambridge, Mass., 1962.

Davidson, Cathy N. *Revolution and the Word: The Rise of the Novel in America.* New York, 1986.

Davis, David Brion. *The Problem of Slavery in the Age of Revolution, 1770–1823.* Ithaca, N.Y., 1975.

Dowd, Gregory Evans. *A Spirited Resistance: The North American Indian Stuggle for Unity, 1745–1818.* Baltimore, 1992.

Ellis, Joseph J. *After the Revolution: Profiles of Early American Culture.* New York, 1979.

Fliegelman, Jay. *Declaring Independence: Jefferson, Natural Language, and the Culture of Performance.* Stanford, Calif., 1993.

Grimsted, David. "Anglo-American Racism and Phillis Wheatley's 'Sable Veil,' 'Length'ned Chain,' and 'Knitted Heart.'" In *Women in the Age of the American Revolution,* edited by Ronald Hoffman and Peter J. Albert. Charlottesville, Va., 1989.

Hatch, Nathan O. *The Democratization of American Christianity.* New Haven, Conn., 1989.

Howe, Daniel Walker. *Making the American Self: Jonathan Edwards to Abraham Lincoln.* Cambridge, Mass., 1997.

Jefferson, Thomas. *Writings.* New York, 1984.

John, Richard R. *Spreading the News: The American Postal System from Franklin to Morse.* Cambridge, Mass., 1995.

Kerber, Linda K. *Women of the Republic: Intellect and Ideology in Revolutionary America.* Chapel Hill, N.C., 1980.

May, Henry F. *The Enlightenment in America.* New York, 1976.

McLoughlin, William G. *Cherokee Renascence in the New Republic.* Princeton, N.J., 1986.

Paine, Thomas. *Thomas Paine Reader.* Edited by Michael Foot and Isaac Kramnick. New York, 1987.

Sher, Richard B., and Jeffrey R. Smitten, eds. *Scotland and America in the Age of the Enlightenment.* Princeton, N.J., 1990.

Taylor, Alan. *William Cooper's Town: Power and Persuasion on the Frontier of the Early American Republic.* New York, 1995.

Waldstreicher, David. *In the Midst of Perpetual Fetes: The Making of American Nationalism, 1776–1820.* Chapel Hill, N.C., 1997.

Ward, John William. *Andrew Jackson: Symbol for an Age.* New York, 1955.

Watts, Steven. *The Republic Reborn: War and the Making of Liberal America, 1790–1820.* Baltimore, 1987.

Wood, Gordon S. *The Radicalism of the American Revolution.* New York, 1992.

Young, Alfred F., and Terry J. Fife, with Mary E. Janzen. *We the People: Voices and Images of the New Nation.* Philadelphia, 1993.

LIBERALISM AND REPUBLICANISM

Cathy Matson

The strains of thought known as liberalism and republicanism profoundly influenced colonial and revolutionary Americans. Both bodies of ideas took shape over a long period of time, and then gave inspiration and voice to political developments that frequently set North American colonists on a dissenting course within the empire, especially after 1760. Through the revolutionary years and into the Early Republic, Americans regularly turned to some mixture of liberal and republican reasoning to justify actions that they claimed were not innovative, but instead were within tested political and social parameters. Ironically, liberal and republican reasoning actually propelled early Americans toward thoroughly making over their polity and society during those heady times.

REPUBLICANISM

The oldest forms of republicanism took root deep in the past. "Classical republicanism," or the civic-humanist tradition, emerged from the writings of Aristotle, Cicero, Tacitus, Plutarch, and others at the opening of the first millennium. These men extolled an earlier time before great imperial wars and large city-states, when Roman farmers lived in agricultural simplicity and exercised a civic virtue dedicated to love of country and fellow citizens. The price of advancing civilization, they said, was greater than its benefits; following the era of rustic virtue was one of greed and luxury that came out of rising commerce, and political corruption that came out of contentions among rich and poor, or families vying for power. Citizens no longer served a public welfare, but instead served their own self-interests. The Roman republic had declined due to the internal decline of collective virtue.

Renaissance writers revived classical republicanism and meshed its teachings with political and philosophical wisdom prevalent in southern Europe, especially the writings of the Italian Niccolò Machiavelli. His work posited that human beings gained meaning and accomplishment through participation in public life. That public life, "civic humanists" insisted, had to be channeled through the rights and responsibilities of citizenship in a *res publica,* or republic. Good government was made of virtuous, good men, all of whom wished to zealously guard the commonweal, not as interested individuals, but as members of a community or polity.

By the 1600s, these ideas gained a wide acceptance in northern Europe, especially among the "commonwealth" writers of England such as John Milton, Algernon Sidney, and James Harrington. Republicans in England appeared as an opposition against the rapid social and economic changes that followed the Glorious Revolution of 1688. By definition, they feared the emergent commercial spirit of the early modern period, as well as the new kinds of wealth it engendered. They set the terms for a critique of the financial and administrative changes in the English Empire following the Glorious Revolution. Traditional, static agricultural relations, in which freeholders did not depend on credit at interest or risk their property in speculative enterprises, was extolled above the modernizing tendencies in England. During the seventeenth century, republicans held merchants and manufacturers in suspicious regard. The great international traders borrowed, loaned, and set up international networks of credit, and profited from small producers at home and needy people abroad.

Republicanism informed people that political rights and personal virtue flowed from the ownership of hereditary and transmissible land, often in modest freeholds. Such holdings would, argued republicans, give individuals a "stake in society" that provided personal independence from the whims of others, as well as from overwhelming political authority. Land, a possession of relatively stable value over time, also provided safeguards against self-interest and excessive debt. Title to an unencumbered freehold guaranteed one's personal identity and political liberty itself.

In addition, the main purpose of republican government was to further not ambitious private or group interests, but the public good. This required the constant sacrifice of individual interests to the greater needs of the people. The latter were typically conceived of as a relatively homogeneous mass, whose interests and accomplishments were held together by social harmony and a relatively static conceptualization of satisfying economic needs.

By the early 1700s, and especially in the wake of Queen Anne's War, the new order of commercial and financial relations had clearly established itself, and the republican critique of these changes grew correspondingly shrill. Republicans redoubled their criticism as the new order became increasingly associated with not only commerce but political patronage and government debt, especially during the 1720s and 1730s when the first lord of treasury, Sir Robert Walpole, set new parameters for Crown Finance. The republican opposition melded scorn for Walpolean patronage and political corruption in government with warnings against the dangers of large personal debt, stock speculation, and luxury consumption. Republican writers, including John Trenchard, Thomas Gordon, Henry St. John, and Viscount Bolingbroke, formulated a commonwealth or "country" ideology that confronted the policies of Walpole and his "court party" and saw corruption on all sides—in the failing virtue of the general citizenry as well as in the venal policies of self-interested politicians. At stake, they insisted, was nothing less than the public virtue of the nation. Irrational and unpredictable relations based upon credit, fluctuating prices, and the pursuit of exotic goods in foreign markets drew citizens' attention away from the general welfare of the nation. In time, said republicans, the welfare of the nation could break apart into nothing more than myriad splintered pieces of selfish private interests or special interest groups.

The remedy for such corruption was wholesale reform of personal life, including the elimination of luxury spending and careful attention to the proper economic direction for sustaining the morality of a people. Furthermore, republican people would reject overreliance on government banks and public credit, reject building a public debt, eliminate political patronage, and abolish standing armies. Their means to do this lay with the widespread distribution of modest independent landholdings. In practice, however, republicans did not usually support an equal share of political authority for small land-holders and the elite. Rather, republicanism was quite tradition-bound: only men with more land than most, with a great deal of personal virtue, and with the habits of ruling others in the social hierarchy should be entrusted to hold political offices. High birth, refinement, and good fortune were not requisites of office holding, but they enhanced the dignity of politics.

Many historians have proposed that although republicanism did not bring about deep and enduring change in England, where the commonwealth tradition first took shape, it was the intellectual strand with the greatest amount of influence on Revolutionary Americans. In this view, republicanism gave voice to opponents of unconstitutional taxation, plural office holding, the threat of bishops, the weakening of the colonial judiciary, and attacks against the long-held privileges of colonial assemblies. Moreover, republicanism gave colonists the language to see this corruption not as accumulated slippage away from responsible rule, but as a conspiracy against their liberty. Americans feared the corruption of English government and the modernizing tendencies of the English people. Americans, republicans argued during the 1760s and 1770s, had been subjected to the degeneracy of England, its corruption and scheming attempts to oppress colonists—American liberty was itself under attack. In order to surmount the dangers of such English corruption, Revolutionary Americans would have to display a far higher level of virtue and a commitment to roughly equal opportunity for all of its citizens, based upon their attachment to independent landholdings.

The republican viewpoint gave Americans a way to understand the bewildering array of changes imposed upon them during the 1760s and 1770s. It informed them that men in power would seek to extend their domination over others. Indeed, it was the nature of power to expand beyond the limits of equity, liberty, and justice; power was relentless and aggressive, while liberty was meek and passive. Liberty could be preserved only if a people was vigilant and consistently virtuous. Such virtue, argued Americans, was in fact present among them and could regenerate the body politic into the great moral force that was necessary for preserving and expanding the new "American republic." American virtue was also supposedly embodied in their frugality, temperance, industry, simplicity, and self-restraint. Republics, if they were to survive, needed a preponderance of egalitarian, independent, small-landed citizens whose differences were based not on heredity and patronage, but on merit.

During the revolutionary years and into the 1780s, Americans widely agreed upon rejecting aristocracy and monarchy; they eliminated many forms of inherited authority and built safeguards to protect merit and talent. But how could republicans describe the society they intended to make? And what were the structures of their government going to be? For many years, they could not say. Most republicans wished to keep elements of a corporate, traditional society; they often wished to fend off the competitive, materialistic values that were slowly evolving before their eyes. Indeed, republicanism had won over so many Americans because it offered a critique of spreading market conditions, financial and commercial transformations, and myriad proof of the potential for widespread accumulation of new wealth. Tensions between old values and new behaviors persisted after the American Revolution and endured well into the Republic's formative years. Yet even though Americans thought they encountered greedy farmers and rapacious contractors during the war, merchants who wantonly imported luxuries, absconding militiamen, deceitful privateers, and new layers of corrupt politicians in their own midst, they continued to believe that their revolution was republican in character.

Traditionally, said Revolutionary leaders, republics were fragile and short-lived; only small and relatively homogeneous countries could sustain republican forms of governance over an extended period of time. But clearly America was an extensive domain of many new states, and the revolutionary victory added the potential for great territorial expansion in the future. In order to sustain the civic virtue of this vast and diverse place, and to prevent the decay that Rome or Civil War England had endured, founders proposed a new philosophy and a new structure for the American republic.

America's new extended republic, embodied in public arguments during the 1780s, the Constitution of 1787, and the writings of Federalists, boldly departed from traditional republican wisdom and yet also retained many elements of republicanism. The gigantic territory that American republican government encompassed mortified hesitant observers. The realignment of political powers that emerged from the experiments in state government–making and the Constitutional Convention also represented major steps away from existing beliefs. The acceptance of diverse, often conflicting, interests that cut across class, occupation, talent, region, and family lines, and their incorporation in the very design of government, also created a stir in every corner of America. But republican character would save these new forms of government from corruption: national leaders promised that their experiments in government could be accomplished by experienced leaders who remained free of partisanship and separated private gain from office holding.

Commitment to republicanism seemed to grow, not shrink, during the 1780s and into the early 1800s, most likely because it shed some direct social and political meanings and took on more attenuated cultural meanings. Immigration, migration, territorial expansion, and market relationships all stretched original meanings of republicanism. Americans overall became less committed to the sacrifice of personal self-interest for the common good, even as they continued to insist on their virtuous republican characters. The success of their own revolution, which had legitimated an expansive economy and prompted thinking about social equality, had broken down the deference upon which republicanism leaned. Distinction slowly gave way to merit. Restoration of traditional harmony gave way to a brave new world of goods and new men of wealth. Even the pace of change defied republican attachments to stasis.

In time, republicanism was disembodied from the nature and extent of social and economic change across the country. Even as citizens continued to invoke the older images of republicanism, they were rapidly becoming a people that republicans would not recognize. But republicanism also allowed Americans to soften the impact of rapid, deep-going change during the early national years; republicanism continued to present the picture of order, community, harmony, and civic responsibility that made changes *away from* those ideals possible.

LIBERALISM

The few general tenets that have come to be associated with liberalism took shape later than republicanism, primarily during Europe's early modern era. By then, leading participants in the Renaissance and Protestant Reformation had already deeply altered notions about the role of individuals in many cultural and religious contexts. By the late 1500s these issues began to appear in more sustained, widespread discussions, and to be more and more closely linked to merchant and entrepreneurial interests brimming with enthusiasm about future commercial and productive opportunities.

By the early 1600s unprecedented rivalries arose among imperial states in Europe for dominion over lands, resources, and native peoples of distant places. Internal transformations also marked the era, including the consolidation of more centralized governments, powerful military establishments, and national financial institutions. Stabilizing populations in Europe and England made it possible for producers to grow and make more goods for rising merchants and manufacturers to accumulate significant amounts of capital, and for policymakers to recognize the needs and demands of the great mass of consumers. The pace and extent of this change called forth intense reexamination of notions about the relationship of rulers and commoners, the rights and obligations of individuals in society, and the antimonarchical forms a government might take. Writers began to celebrate the ability of individuals to know their own best interests. Separated from considerations about the church and the state, individuals were free to contemplate their positions vis-à-vis material accumulation. Moreover, individual striving and achievement were made conceptually distinct from traditional moral and legal restraints, so that entering a competitive marketplace and becoming the desirous consumer of shifting fashion and taste were no longer subjects of scorn to liberal thinkers. It also seemed clear to liberals that human reason and talents outweighed both God's interventions and nature's dictates over human well-being. All of these ideas had been circulating for some time already, but they became more useful during the moments of economic scarcity, profound commercial and employment crises, and political turmoil that often marked the 1500s and 1600s.

Beyond these basic characteristics of the liberal individual, however, writers during the 1600s and 1700s proposed various understandings about individuals in relationship to society and government. The English philosopher John Locke, who wrote the influential second treatise of *Two Treatises of Government* after the mid-1600s, systematically examined the natural rights, reasoning faculties, potential to prosper, and other qualities of individuals and linked them to a social compact that extolled the virtues of representative government. Individuals, the new wisdom also held, would form collectives of consenting citizens to protect their private rights and property and to form legitimate governments in a chain of mutual benefits and obligations. One of the first significant moments in which emerging liberalism affected political change occurred in the formulation of the creed that gave coherence to ascendant Whig dissenters in England during and after the Glorious Revolution of 1688. Departing from an older view that insisted on static social ranks premised on the privileges of inheritance, family name, and custom, liberal Whigs advocated support for new social groups that demanded to be recognized, protected, and elevated to favorable political and economic stature.

Like many others of his time, Locke proposed that at one time all humans were born equal in nature and possessed equal natural rights to enjoy the fruits of their labor, or property. In the process of protecting their individual private rights from encroachments by others, argued Locke, the collective of individuals in society agreed to come together to protect their many interests by creating a representative government, founded by their mutual consent. One of the most significant arguments Locke presented was the denial of a place for God, inheritance, divine right, or conquest as the basis for political rulership. There was no room in Locke's arguments for monarchs and nobles. Government was to be representative of consenting citizens, increasingly associated with an emergent bourgeois order, but also made up of myriad aspiring middling producers and consumers. Liberal government, based upon the consent of the governed, would be responsible directly to its citizenry. Any government that either failed in its mission or invaded the lives and property of individuals—as tyrants or corrupted ministries might do—stood to be dismantled and replaced with a representative one. Furthermore, it was Locke who gave later publicists the formula that government was merely the servant of the collective of individual wills, and its powers were strictly limited by the laws made by the people. Taxes, they further insisted, were "gifts of the people" to their representatives for the efficient running of their governments.

Out of the Lockean tradition there also emerged a celebration of citizens in marketplaces seeking unlimited personal gain. Those who worked hard and had good luck in their efforts deserved to enjoy the fruits of their labor. Lockean liberal notions about labor were not, in fact, very far removed from Protestant thinking about "industry" and the "calling." Such thinking helped justify the rising prosperity of many middling people in the Atlantic world and spurred the ambitions of many others regarding international commerce and agricultural exporting. Locke held that there was no natural limitation on the acquisition of wealth, including land, goods, or money; all restraints, regulations, fixed limits, and even taxation did not emanate naturally from society, but were rather the acts of governments. There was, wrote Locke, no inherently immoral or unjust quality to unlimited acquisition, as long as an individual did not impinge on the wealth of another person in unfair actions such as physical force against a competitor, as long as individuals avoided wanton and wasteful use of nature, and as long as individuals obeyed the justified laws of their government.

Lockean liberals did not propose that such tenets would lead to equality of results socially, for some people would work harder than others, and some would have greater natural or acquired talents than others. But free competition for the fruits of one's labor was the best guarantee of the political freedom of a people in society. Liberal arguments privileged personal achievement over ordained place of birth and rank. Individuals and social groups were decreasingly viewed as being a part of a preordained, unchanging order; energy, enterprise, "improvement," and commerce—in their personal and larger social meanings—were early modern liberal terms that reflected the newfound enthusiasm for growth and change.

By the 1700s, liberalism was related to dissenting Protestant and Enlightenment influences, too. The latter, an intellectual movement unfolding in England and all of western Europe during the eighteenth century, extolled secular reason, education, legal reform, scientific inquiry, freedom in the marketplace, and the unleashing of human potential in general. In the American colonies, the clergyman-writer Joseph Priestley, the philosopher Richard Price, and, by the 1770s, the political philosopher Thomas Paine were among the many publicists who were influenced by the blending of these trends and who in turn helped motivate colonists to create a resistance movement during the 1760s and 1770s. It is not an exaggeration to say that the mixture of dissenting, Lockean, and Enlightenment ideas was a powerful aid to American colonists to understand their right to resist tyranny and eventually to break from the English Empire.

In addition to Lockean liberalism's contributions to understanding the individual in society and politics, another liberal tradition tended to emphasize the role of the individual more directly in the economy. Emergent ideas that were often identified as "free trade" or "economic freedom" helped people set aside the lingering appeal of customary notions about production and exchange in the hinterlands and international trade. Liberal economic ideas challenged the value of moral and ethical restrictions placed on individuals pursuing economic opportunities; rising traders and merchants applauded material plenty, fuller employment, swifter and more secure trade, and the greater material comforts that many people enjoyed in Western empires.

A small but significant number of early modern traders employed economic liberalism to defeat or circumvent mercantilism, the body of increasingly stringent regulations that purported to channel and promote productive and commercial activities for the benefit of rising imperial interests. In contrast to the principle of regulation, some economic liberals offered the allure of unfettered commerce. The Dutch example of commercial freedoms proved especially appealing to many merchants and consumers in Western empires. Mercantilists, they argued, had unnecessarily constrained their traffic by imposing excessive amounts of regulation, including fixing the prices and quality of exports, prohibiting commerce with foreign ports on occasion, limiting the quantities or types of commodities that could be transported between imperial locations, and constraining new kinds of manufacturing in colonial satellite regions. Ambitious rising traders throughout the Western Hemisphere supported opening up the commercial boundaries between colonies and their imperial centers, and between foreigners and themselves. They actively sought elimination of embargoes and reduction of trade duties, and they were among myriad traders who felt fully justified by liberal notions to pursue trade in illicit channels. Economic liberalism, like its Lockean cousin, proved especially helpful to North American colonists for many decades of commercial and intercolonial economic activities. By the time of the Imperial Crisis, arguments for economic freedom influenced the ambitions of small producers, millers, and commercial farmers throughout the North American countryside. Although alliances of economic interests were still too ephemeral to affect long-ranging policies in the revolutionary and postrevolutionary years, ideas about, and opportunities for, economic freedom were together powerful enough to dash lingering attachments to customary forms of exchange.

Still, Americans were not ready for bold references to self-interest or universal individual rights to enter competitive marketplaces without government restraint; indeed, they never would be. For one thing, liberalism never purported to be a coherent body of policies and many aspects of liberal thought were still inchoate during the late colonial years. And even though ever more individuals began to extol the virtues of the marketplace and to accept elaborate credit and debt linkages, few of them argued that Americans should rid themselves of watchful local and regional political regimes during the revolutionary years. As a consequence, along with economic liberalism's great promise of opportunity and material rise, persistent voices continued to direct attention to a "common interest" or a "will of the people." Into the heady 1780s, few Americans argued for far-reaching individual freedoms associated with an unbridled economy. And even the Scottish economist Adam Smith, who is associated with a strident critique of government regulations and promotion of self-interested economic exchanges, knew that completely unharnessed free-market capitalism was impossible.

LIBERALISM AND REPUBLICANISM

For decades, scholars have presented liberalism and republicanism as distinct, often incompatible strains of thought that represented the extreme ends of early modern intellectual and political life. But such antitheses reflect more the way scholars work than contemporary transatlantic thinking and behavior. Late-twentieth-century investigations of liberalism and republicanism tended to see where the two bodies of thought overlap and incorporate other intellectual traditions that date from various eras, some in the distant past. Equally important, scholars have tempered their appreciation of liberalism and republicanism by admitting that each set of ideas was less pervasive *on its own* than they might have supposed, although together, and in combination with other traditions, they endured long into the nineteenth century.

In the case of liberalism, writers have retained an emphasis on the rise of individual accountability, rights consciousness, and personal opportunity, though most of them reject the argument that liberalism accounted for a full-blown capitalism in the Early American Republic. In the case of republicanism, writers continue to insist that it contributed to

awareness about the definitions and roles of citizenship during the late eighteenth century, and inspired the realignment of political forces often associated with a republican government. In distinction to liberalism, republicanism did not focus as much on the individual as on public relationships, especially institutional ones.

Today most writers do not find a direct correspondence between classical republicanism and the way Americans sustained their American Revolutionary War, or the way they recovered in the 1780s. Scholars tend to agree that during the Revolution, Americans believed unbridled self-interest would subvert military mobilization and civilian morale; but it was also true that Americans combined the dream of creating a virtuous republic with their hopes of accomplishing self-interested prosperity. The economic imperatives of the war saved Americans from an excess of virtuous self-denial, for myriad farmers and urban producers sought unfettered enterprise. More often than not, work at the end of the twentieth century insisted on a multilingual intellectual tradition and the uneven emergence of a liberal economy within enduring elements of a republican political structure.

As it happened, the founding generation of Americans created a federal union based upon republican principles that would promote and protect the liberal interests of individuals. The new states formed during the Revolution began the dialogue among agricultural, commercial, and manufacturing interests, and aligned new interests with some old ones so that they reinforced one another. A new political economic order was beginning to emerge in these state-level efforts. Notwithstanding the inspiration of liberals, however, state governments subjected the economy to myriad neomercantile restraints. In fact, far into the subsequent years of the Early Republic, liberalism and republicanism both lent a hand in the shaping of new productive efforts, westward settlement, and sectional distinctions.

See also **Nationalism; Liberalism; Constitutional Thought; Anti-Statism** *(volume 2);* **Individualism and the Self** *(volume 3); and other articles in this section.*

BIBLIOGRAPHY

Appleby, Joyce. *Capitalism and a New Social Order: The Republican Vision of the 1790s.* New York, 1984.

Bailyn, Bernard. *The Ideological Origins of the American Revolution.* Cambridge, Mass., 1967.

LIBERALISM AND REPUBLICANISM

Kloppenberg, James T. "The Virtues of Liberalism: Christianity, Republicanism, and Ethics in Early American Political Discourse." *Journal of American History* 74 (1987): 9–33.

Matson, Cathy, and Peter Onuf. *A Union of Interests: Political and Economic Thought in Revolutionary America.* Lawrence, Kans., 1990.

Pocock, J. G. A. *The Machiavellian Moment: Florentine Political Thought and the Atlantic Republican Tradition.* Princeton, N.J., 1975.

Shalhope, Robert E. "Toward a Republican Synthesis: The Emergence of an Understanding of Republicanism in American Historiography." *William and Mary Quarterly* 29 (1972): 49–80.

———. "Republicanism and Early American Historiography." *William and Mary Quarterly* 39 (1982): 334–356.

Wood, Gordon. *The Creation of the American Republic.* Chapel Hill, N.C., 1969.

FEDERALISTS AND ANTIFEDERALISTS

Peter S. Onuf

Federalist proponents of the new federal Constitution, drafted in Philadelphia in May through September 1787, battled their Antifederalist opponents in state ratifying conventions and in the First Congress convened under the Constitution's aegis in New York City in March 1789. Seeking to assuage Antifederalist concerns about the concentration or "consolidation" of power in the new central government, James Madison of Virginia spearheaded congressional passage of twelve amendments to the Constitution in September 1789; ten of these amendments, subsequently known as the Bill of Rights, became effective on 15 December 1791 with their ratification by ten states. The triumphant Federalists dominated the new government under President George Washington (1789–1797), while Antifederalism disappeared as a coherent opposition movement.

With the Constitution and the Bill of Rights in place, Antifederalist concerns continued in the republican opposition—led by Madison and Thomas Jefferson (Washington's first Secretary of State, 1789–1793)—to the executive administration. Republicans professed loyalty to the new Constitution but were fiercely critical of Treasury Secretary Alexander Hamilton and his Federalist allies, charging that Federalists were acting on dangerously broad interpretations of constitutional provisions in a way that jeopardized the ratifiers' original understanding. With oppositionists representing themselves not as critics of the Constitution, but as its true friends, the legitimacy of the new regime was at least temporarily secured. By focusing on questions of constitutional interpretation, however, Republicans guaranteed that the concerns articulated by Antifederalists during the ratification debate would remain compelling through the partisan controversies of the 1790s. The Antifederalist legacy was most conspicuous in the strict-constructionist "Principles of 1798" set forth in the Virginia and Kentucky Resolutions (penned by Madison and Jefferson respectively), the ideological lodestone of the Republicans who subsequently dominated national politics. The Resolutions interpreted the Constitution as the guarantor of states' rights, insisting that the sovereign people, convened in state ratifying conventions, had delegated limited powers to the federal government. Federalists may have won the struggle for constitutional reform, but their short-term success gave new life to the spirit of provincial, libertarian opposition that had animated patriot revolutionaries in 1776 and critics of the Constitution a decade later.

Though the loosely organized, ad hoc coalitions of the ratification controversy quickly gave way to new partisan alignments, the great debate between Federalists and Antifederalists had an enduring impact on American political discourse. The specific political and economic interests that shaped positions in the debate are easily discernible in the various compromises—on representation, the regulation of commerce, and slavery—woven through the Constitution. Polemicists did not hesitate to underscore suspect motives. Federalists depicted Antifederalists as advocates of parochial interests: according to James Wilson of Pennsylvania, "every person . . . who either enjoys or hopes to enjoy a place of profit under the present establishment" opposed the Constitution (Kaminski et al., *Documentary History*, vol. 2, pp. 171–172). Antifederalists responded in kind, accusing the reformers of being "aristocrats" and crypto-monarchists who intended to reverse the outcome of the American Revolution. Writing as "Centinel," Samuel Bryan, former clerk of the Pennsylvania General Assembly and "Constitutionalist" defender of his state's radical 1776 Constitution, asserted that the new system was "far from being a regular balanced government," but "would be in practice a *permanent* Aristocracy" (ibid., pp. 165–166).

The logic of constitution-writing made the Philadelphia framers into political mechanics, intensely conscious of the need to accommodate powerful interests through compromise and concession;

ALLIES AND OPPONENTS: MADISON AND HAMILTON

James Madison of Virginia and Alexander Hamilton of New York were unlikely allies in the Constitutional reform movement. After studying at the College of New Jersey (now Princeton University), the studious Madison (1751–1836) returned to Virginia where he was soon swept up in the Revolutionary movement. As a member of the state legislature and of Virginia's congressional delegation, Madison struggled to balance the conflicting claims of his beloved commonwealth and the American union. Finding himself on the defensive in Virginia, where the popular Patrick Henry appealed to local prejudices, Madison sought to curb state particularism by strengthening the central government. Born and raised in the West Indies and educated at King's College (Columbia University), Hamilton (1755–1804) had a much weaker attachment to his state, establishing his brilliant reputation in the Continental army and as a member of congress. As a long-committed "nationalist," Hamilton feared that the Constitution drafted at the Philadelphia Convention had not gone nearly far enough in energizing the central government and subordinating the states. Madison, whose original design for the Constitution had been significantly compromised, also had serious misgivings about the proposed system. But both men saw ratification as the only hope for a union in desperate straits.

The success of Madison and Hamilton's great collaboration in the *Federalist,* a series of eighty-five essays (including five by New Yorker John Jay [1745–1829]) published in various New York papers between November 1787 and August 1788 and in two volumes (March and May 1788), depended on "Publius's" ability to overcome these misgivings, merge the authors' distinctive perspectives and agendas, and reassure skeptical Antifederalists who dominated the state ratifying convention. Though the *Federalist* probably had little impact on the vote in New York or other states, it was soon widely accepted as the most authoritative exposition of the Constitution.

When the new federal government was inaugurated in April 1789 Treasury Secretary Hamilton expected that Congressman Madison would be a staunch supporter of the Washington administration. But Madison was instead increasingly drawn into the ranks of the Republican opposition that coalesced around Hamilton's fellow cabinet member and political enemy, Secretary of State Thomas Jefferson (1743–1826). Virginians Madison and Jefferson, lifetime friends and allies, became convinced that Hamilton's bold initiatives, particularly in the realm of fiscal policy, would lead to a dangerous concentration of power in the central government, thus destroying their cherished federal balance. Hamilton never took Jefferson seriously and had no regrets about their growing alienation; by contrast, Madison's defection to the opposition party struck him as a personal betrayal. Madison insisted that he remained a true friend to the Constitution that he and his erstwhile ally had so eloquently and persuasively defended.

by contrast, ratifiers in the states, facing a stark choice with momentous implications for the future of republican government, necessarily operated on a loftier, more theoretical plane. As they mobilized to persuade skeptical voters and delegates, Federalists and Antifederalists argued about the meaning of the American Revolution for the future of republicanism in America and in the world.

CRISIS OF UNION

Exploiting a broad consensus among politically active Americans that the existing scheme of continental government under the Articles of Confederation (ratified in 1781) was woefully inadequate, Federalists seemed to hold all the cards in the ratification debate. Lacking the power to raise revenue, the Confederation Congress depended on requisitions from the states to survive; by 1787, few states were willing or able to comply with these assessments. Meanwhile, Congress was powerless to enforce its will against recalcitrant states, most conspicuously in fulfilling the terms of the treaty of 1783 with Britain ending the Revolution. The choice, Federalists insisted, was between union and disunion, between preserving the republican legacy of the Revolution and reverting to the condition of independent, sovereign states (or regional unions) with conflicting, potentially hostile interests and ambitions. Without an effective, energetic union, the disunited states would become the image of Europe, constantly at war, or preparing for war, with one another. Antifederalists questioned this horrible outcome: when a real crisis came, Americans surely would rally against internal as well as external threat, as they had in the Revolution. But they could hardly deny that an "imbecilic" Congress was incapable of negotiating and enforcing engagements with foreign powers crucially necessary to securing the new nation's territorial claims—most notably in the Mississippi Valley and the Old Northwest—as well as favorable terms of trade for American staple producers.

Thoughtful Antifederalists recognized that the tendency of American politics in the mid-1780s was centrifugal, with state governments taking on more responsibilities (for instance, in servicing Revolutionary War debts) as the Confederation Congress found it increasingly difficult even to muster a quorum. Thus, when Federalists likened the drafting of the Constitution to a "miracle," they were not proclaiming its perfection, for all of the framers had had to accept unpalatable provisions. What was miraculous was the very existence of any document at all. Federalists could insist that this was the last real chance at national constitutional reform because the framers, despite their recognition that something had to be done, had been so hard-pressed to come to terms with one another. It would never again be possible to assemble delegates from so many states (only Rhode Island was not represented at Philadelphia) who were prepared to undertake such a comprehensive negotiation in such a concessive spirit.

The Federalists accurately defined the problem of American politics, signaling in their crisis rhetoric their determination to secure and promote their interests, either within or beyond the existing structure of the union. Federalists predicted the emergence of separate regional unions (most famously in the early numbers of the *Federalist*) because many of them were prepared to support such unions if the existing Confederation failed. Antifederalists worried about the potential abuses of consolidated power if the new regime were established. But they also had very good reason to be concerned about what might happen if the reform project collapsed altogether. For years, "nationalists" had been floating trial balloons about alternative strategies, including the consolidation of authority at the regional level and even, for bolder spirits, the reestablishment of monarchical rule. While Federalists promised that the proposed government would be thoroughly republican, thus preempting the political and social aspirations of would-be "aristocrats," they threatened that rejection of the Constitution would unleash the very forces that Antifederalists professed to fear the most.

As they emphasized the dangers of disunion, Federalists insisted on their own fealty to fundamental American Revolutionary principles. Scholars see the reformers' appropriation of the name "Federalist" as a clever ruse to disguise their nationalist ambitions and disarm opponents who had a better claim to the name. But the delegates at Philadelphia, whatever their original predilections, recognized that Americans would never consent to the destruction of the states; furthermore, the distribution of authority between central and state governments promised to safeguard local and regional interests that the consolidation of power (in the wrong hands) could jeopardize. Madison thus came into the Philadelphia Convention as a "nationalist," determined to reduce the states to a clearly subordinate position by giving Congress a veto over state legislation, but he emerged as a genuine federalist who would assure fellow delegates at

179

the state ratifying convention that Virginia's vital corporate interests would be most secure under the new regime. Negotiating the great compromises at Philadelphia made nationalists into federalists; as they promoted ratification in the states, Federalists could plausibly argue that the whole point of strengthening the union was to preserve the states, not to destroy them.

Federalists were slower off the mark in responding to broad popular sentiment for protection of individual liberties in a bill of rights. The framers failed to anticipate this sentiment because they understood the new government to be one of limited, delegated powers. "The people surrender nothing," Hamilton insisted in *Federalist* 84, "and as they retain every thing, they have no need of particular reservations" (Cooke, *The Federalist,* p. 578). But it was also true that the new central government would have direct authority over individuals, thus imperiling rights defined and secured in the state constitutions. If "supreme power . . . remains and flourishes with the people," as James Wilson claimed in the Pennsylvania debates, then why shouldn't their rights be as fully protected as those of the "peoples" of the respective states? (Kaminski et al., *Documentary History,* vol. 2, p. 348). Wilson's argument for (national) popular sovereignty may have been a brilliant rhetorical move to short-circuit state sovereignty, but it also exposed defects in the Constitution that the framers—focused on the distribution of powers within and among governments—had overlooked. Proponents of ratification sought to allay fears about the concentration of power and threats to liberty by underscoring the similarity of the new federal Constitution to the state constitutions that preceded it. By this standard, the absence of a bill of rights was increasingly conspicuous and indefensible; not surprisingly, critics of the Constitution seized their opportunity, demanding amendments that would secure popular rights against the federal Leviathan.

CONVERGENCE AND CONSENSUS

The ratification debate led Federalists to emphasize ways in which their system would secure states' rights and interests and Antifederalists to acknowledge the need for a much more energetic national government—provided their liberties were adequately protected. As a result of these exchanges, and of the momentum of successive state ratifications, Federalist and Antifederalist positions moved toward convergence, with the most heated debate focused on questions of procedure and timing. Should states that had not yet acted withhold ratification until a second convention had a chance to act on proposed amendments? Or should ratification be unconditional, thus enabling the new regime to begin functioning, with a good faith pledge to consider recommended amendments in a timely fashion? By the time Massachusetts delegates convened in January 1788, five states had ratified (Delaware, New Jersey, and Pennsylvania in December; Georgia and Connecticut in January), all by decisive votes. But the haste with which these states (particularly Pennsylvania) had acted stoked Antifederalist suspicions in Massachusetts and the remaining states. Massachusetts Federalists, recognizing that they would lose a straight up or down vote, hit on the formula of unconditional ratification and recommendatory amendments. They urged convention delegates to vote for the Constitution in its present, unamended form, promising that the new federal Congress would seriously consider amendments recommended by the convention that would better define the powers of state governments and secure individual civil liberties. Prominent Antifederalists Samuel Adams and John Hancock found these terms attractive enough to justify throwing their support behind ratification, and the Federalists were able to eke out a narrow 187 to 168 victory. Antifederalist delegates in the Pennsylvania Convention who sought to block ratification by staying away from the proceedings and thereby preventing a quorum were thwarted when two dissenters were forcibly brought to the convention hall. The rush to ratify elsewhere reflected the obvious benefits of a stronger central government for smaller, economically dependent, and strategically vulnerable states. But Antifederalist opposition in the remaining states was much more formidable, gaining in strength even while proponents of the new system enjoyed early successes.

The Massachusetts pattern was replicated in subsequent ratifications, most crucially in the key states of Virginia (in June, by a vote of 89 to 79) and New York (in July, by 30 to 27). Delegates in all these states understood that their votes would determine the future of the union. But they also recognized that the two sides differed little on substantive issues. Antifederalists conceded the key point, that a more energetic central government was necessary to secure the union and its vital interests abroad; for their part, Federalists disclaimed any intention of subverting the states or jeopardizing individual liberties. The issue came down to one of trust: would Antifederalists follow through on their promise of a second convention if they succeeded in aborting the current campaign? Could the Federalists guarantee that the new federal government would enact a bill of rights? Antifederalists might well question Federalist campaign promises. Yet if the Federalists failed to keep their promises, they could be turned out of office, according to the provisions of their own Constitution. It was far less likely that Antifederalists would be able to mobilize another, more effective national constitutional reform movement. Even if they could, the resulting document probably would differ little from the one they were now rejecting.

The closeness of the ratification votes is deceptive. Recognizing that they could offer no viable alternative to ratification, sufficient numbers of Antifederalists were willing to switch sides in each of the key states in order to permit a positive vote while their dissenting colleagues acquiesced in the outcome. At the same time, however, the close votes sent a powerful message that a vigilant electorate would be on the lookout for abuses of power according to standards elaborated by Federalists themselves as they sought to allay Antifederalist anxieties. By pledging to work for subsequent amendments, Federalists took a further, crucial step, publicly embracing their opponents' account of the Constitution's shortcomings—even if they continued to privately discount the efficacy of what Madison called "parchment barriers" (in a letter to Jefferson, 17 October 1788, in Stagg et al., *Papers of James Madison* vol. 11, p. 297). What in fact constituted an abuse of power or threat to liberty was subject to interpretation, but the new administration's failure to act on the recommended amendments would be unmistakable. In the first federal Congress, Madison thus became the champion of the Bill of Rights (carefully selecting amendments that would not jeopardize the effectiveness of the new government) because he understood the need to placate his own constituents and to win the support of moderate Antifederalists everywhere. Ratification may have been technically unconditional, but a large body of dissenters had clearly expressed serious misgivings about the responsiveness of the new regime to its concerns. Madison recognized that the legitimacy of any government rested on public opinion: action on the amendments would be a crucial test of the government's good faith.

Antifederalists and their Republican successors were strict constructionist, textual literalists. But it was the Constitution as interpreted by Federalists in the ratification debates that authorized their textual fetishism. The culmination of these debates in

votes for ratification by the state conventions gave life and legitimacy to the new federal Constitution. When, during the party battles of the 1790s, Federalists sought to expand the central government's powers by expansive constructions of the Constitution, Republican oppositionists emphasized the state conventions' pivotal role in establishing the new regime: Madison's compact theory, the notion that the Constitution was the act of the sovereign people as assembled in their respective state conventions, authorized a strict construction of the document that relied heavily on the representations its advocates had made during the state debates. The *Federalist* thus remained a key source for Republican constitutionalists, notwithstanding the justifications for a broader construction of federal powers offered in some of its numbers, particularly those by Hamilton.

In the ratification debates, politically active Americans articulated a broad ideological consensus on key issues. Federalists and Antifederalists were all "republicans" of a recognizably modern sort: no one advocated a return to monarchy or the establishment of a legally privileged, aristocratic ruling class; nor did anyone promote the cause of a socially homogenous, "classical" republic in which virtuous citizens sacrificed private interest for the public good. All associated liberty with property rights, agreeing on the centrality of market relations in the American political economy: though most were "mercantilists" who continued to see a constructive regulatory role for governments, the strong tendency of their thought and practice was "liberal," toward free trade and private enterprise. Federalists and Antifederalists also drew on a common stock of influences and experience in their thinking about questions of constitutional design. Devotees of liberty in the Anglo-American common-law tradition, they believed in the efficacy of the separation and balance of governmental powers for preserving rights. Friends and foes of the proposed federal Constitution looked to experience in the states both for examples and inspiration. They all accepted the premise of state constitution-writing, that the sovereign people were the source of all legitimate authority. The ratification debate itself represented the logical extension of this premise to the constitution of government on a continent-wide scale. If the federal Constitution were finally ratified, advocates and critics agreed, its authority would derive directly from the sovereignty of the people.

Yet fundamental agreement on so many issues did not preempt bitter controversy in the ratification debates. To the contrary, the degree of apparent agreement only served to exaggerate mutual suspicions about underlying intentions. Combatants on both sides made major concessions in order to command broad public support: Federalists had to represent themselves as genuine federalists, solicitous of states' rights and civil liberties; Antifederalists had to grant the possibility of a continental republic in order to justify their campaign for a federal bill of rights. Though these converging positions made sense politically, they easily could be portrayed as opportunistic and internally incoherent. What did it mean to say, as Federalists did, that the new regime was both national and federal, that for some purposes the central government would be supreme, but that the states would retain their sovereignty for others? Antifederalists were no better off in proclaiming their support for the federal union, without ever defining what sort of powers its government should properly exercise. Both sides insisted, against the conventional wisdom, that it was possible to split the difference between "a perfect consolidation and a mere confederacy of States" (Gunning Bedford of Delaware at the Philadelphia Convention, in Farrand, ed., *Records,* vol. 1, p. 490). But neither could invoke traditional language or experience to explain how this might be done. Federalism, the Americans' great contribution to modern political science, thus was the product of exchanges between mutually suspicious Federalists and Antifederalists, seeking to define and capture this ambiguous middle ground. Its viability depended on transcending (or ignoring) the conventional wisdom: that, for instance, "imperium in imperio" (a sovereignty within a sovereignty) was a contradiction in terms. Beyond the conceptual problem was an even more compelling concern: Would it be possible to reconcile the divergent geopolitical perspectives and agendas that distinguished national constitutional reformers from Antifederalist defenders of local rights and interests?

CONFLICTING PERSPECTIVES

Federalists were primarily concerned about the new nation's standing in the family of nations, focusing on the central government's credit with European bankers (and hence with its ability to raise tax revenues), its capacity to negotiate favorable commercial treaties, and its capacity to mobilize resources effectively in the event of future wars. From this diplomatic perspective, the devolution of power to the state governments was as ominous as the "im-

becility" of the Confederation Congress. For, as Edmund Randolph warned at the Virginia Convention, disunion would unleash "the dogs of war," as sovereign states sought to gain advantage over each other in conflicts for territory or trade (Kaminski et al., *Documentary History,* vol. 9, p. 1020). Federalists hammered home the dangers of disunion in countless depictions of incipient anarchy: American politics would increasingly come to resemble the European antitype, with a never-ending cycle of wars subverting republican governments and destroying liberty. Oliver Ellsworth predicted that in the event of disunion "European powers will form alliances, some with one state and some with another, and play the states off one against another, and that we shall be involved in all the labyrinths of European politics" (Kaminski et al., *Documentary History,* vol. 3, p. 545). The Europeanization model linked external threats with the collapse of the union and the outbreak of internal conflict. Counterrevolutionary imperial powers would forge alliances with individual states, or regional unions of states, thus drawing Americans into the conflicts of the European system and exacerbating their conflicts with each other. Disunion would lead to Europeanization; anarchy would give rise to despotism.

The challenge for Federalists in the ratification debates was to reconcile the need for an energetic, unitary national government that could secure America's independence and vital interests with a regime that would sustain liberty and republican government. Antifederalists, positioning themselves as tribunes of the "people" and defenders of the American Revolutionary legacy, warned that the concentration of power advocated by nationalist reformers jeopardized liberty. In contrast to Federalists who conceptualized the crisis of the union within the framework of European statecraft, Antifederalists continued to see their world within the imperial framework of the Revolutionary generation. Provincial patriots struggled to secure their rights against the specter of metropolitan domination: if they submitted to parliamentary sovereignty, Americans would be reduced to the condition of slaves, with no will of their own. Before independence, imperial authorities sought to establish direct rule over subject provinces; to secure the legacy of the Revolution, vigilant Americans must preempt the possibility of a new metropolis emerging in their midst, capable of wielding despotic power at the expense of their liberties. As they warily encountered the framers' handiwork, skeptical Antifederalists asked if the proffered solution was perhaps more dangerous for the future of American republicanism than the problem it was supposed to solve. Instead of defending the Revolution from external and internal threats, would a more energetic central government destroy liberty and therefore reverse the Revolution's outcome?

Federalists insisted that their proposed system would avoid either extreme and that the anarchy that must follow its rejection inevitably would lead to despotism. (They depicted Daniel Shays, the putative leader of agrarian disturbances in western Massachusetts, as a prototype despot.) Insisting that union would not survive without a new Constitution, Hamilton in *Federalist* 6 contemptuously dismissed any hope that "peace and cordiality" would reign among the disunited states as "the deceitful dream of a golden age" (in Cooke, ed., *The Federalist*, p. 35). Antifederalists could not imagine that conflicts among the state-republics would ever lead to war. This "deceitful dream" flowed from their understanding of American experience: for Revolutionary patriots, the unity of the British empire in America was a given; metropolitan efforts to enslave the colonists made them conscious of their common cause and the successful war effort sealed their union. It was the assumption of these bonds that made civil war seem like a moral impossibility to critics of the Constitution such as Virginia's Patrick Henry: "there were no tyrants in America, as there are in Europe"; "instead of being dangerous to one another," citizens of the American republics "mutually support one another's liberties" (Kaminski et al., *Documentary History*, vol. 9, pp. 1042–1043).

Yet, as Hamilton outlined in *Federalist* 7 and 8, there was ample scope for "hostile pretensions" among the states in conflicts over western land, commercial regulation, and the distribution of the national debt: "we should be in a short course of time, in the predicament of the continental powers of Europe—our liberties would be prey to the means of defending ourselves against the ambition and jealousy of each other" (Cooke, ed., *The Federalist*, pp. 38, 49). The Antifederalists' mistake was to continue to think in imperial terms, to take the union of the former colonies for granted even after the old metropolitan authority was vanquished. But it was an illusion to think that the American empire could survive without a central government. The challenge was to make sure that the powers of this government remained strictly limited, to find a genuinely republican alternative to monarchical authority. Here was the key issue in the ratification debates. For if few Antifederalists really believed that union would survive without some sort of government, they were all genuinely skeptical about the

possibility of reconstructing metropolitan authority along republican lines.

Antifederalists may have been on tenuous ground when arguing that republics were naturally peaceful and union among them was spontaneous, but they could invoke the best authorities of contemporary political science against the Federalists' continental republic. Republics, the esteemed French political theorist Baron de Montesquieu had written persuasively, could only survive in small territories where a virtuous citizenry would zealously guard their own and their country's liberties. The American experience in the British Empire offered powerful confirmation of the corollary proposition, that a government would have to be despotic to sustain effective rule over an extensive domain. Massachusetts' royal governor Thomas Hutchinson famously affirmed this conventional wisdom when he wrote that British liberties necessarily diminished at the peripheries of the empire: the need for centrally directed, energetic government increased proportionally with distance from the metropolis. Arguing from these premises, Antifederalists could offer no viable alternative to the Federalists' plan: if a stronger central government did prove necessary, the best they could hope for would be something akin to the old empire, benignly neglectful of Americans' internal affairs while effectively protecting them from foreign threats and promoting their commercial interests abroad. But Antifederalists could invoke Monstequieuan principles and American experience to much better effect in criticizing the proposed federal Constitution. Antifederalist skepticism about the possibility of establishing a republican government for the entire continent was as well grounded as Hamilton's prediction that republicanism in the states would not long survive under the anarchic conditions of disunion.

The Federalists' success in countering Antifederalist criticism depended not simply on exposing the limitations of their opponents' logic, for this was a game both sides could play. Advocates of constitutional reform needed to take a more constructive tack, acknowledging the legitimacy of their opponents' concerns and reconciling the Antifederalists' understanding of the Revolution and its legacy with their own. To avoid the imputation of being counter-revolutionaries, Federalists had to reconcile the Revolutionary framework of 1776, when provincial patriots mobilized against metropolitan despotism, with their understanding of the new nation's increasingly vulnerable diplomatic situation in 1787.

TOWARD FEDERALISM

Federalists met the Antifederalist challenge with two complementary lines of argument. First, they argued that the new federal government would be one of delegated powers, so constrained by constitutional limitations that it could never jeopardize the liberties secured by the Revolution. They thus posed the simple, but crucial question: Was it possible for the government of the union to have a republican constitution or not? Answering this question in the affirmative did not mean that Americans would have to jettison their state governments and submit to an all-powerful, if nominally "republican" central government. To the contrary, as Federalists insisted in their second line of argument, a more energetic and effective federal government would best secure the rights and interests of the states as republics. Federalists created a framework for consensus by deploying republicanism as both means and end: the elaborate machinery of republican constitutionalism would curb the despotic tendencies of the new central government even while securing the peace and stability that would enable republican governments to flourish in the states. By professing equal solicitude for the future of republicanism at different levels of governance, Federalists presented themselves as genuine "federalists." If they could be taken at their word, the new regime would be true to the legacy of the Revolution as both Antifederalists and Federalists understood it. The American states would not be subjected to the despotic rule of a distant metropolis, nor would they claim the illusory freedom and equality of fully sovereign states, always poised to make war on one another and so to sacrifice the lives and liberties of their citizens.

Madison made the most famous argument for the "extended republic" in *Federalist* 10. Following Montesquieu, Antifederalists argued that republicanism could only survive in compact territories where a homogenous citizenry was virtuous and vigilant. Madison turned this argument on its head, suggesting that there was no check to majority tyranny in a small republic. But where the sphere of republican government was extended, "you take in a greater variety of parties and interests; you make it less possible that a majority of the whole will have a common motive to invade the rights of other citizens." Yet if Madison's "Republican remedy for the diseases most incident to Republican government" has enthralled subsequent generations of theorists, his evident hostility to the states, where "factious leaders" were all too prone to "kindle [the] flame" of popular politics, limited the effectiveness of his argument in the context of the ratification debates (Cooke, ed., *The Federalist*, pp. 64–65). As long as Madison and his fellow Federalists assumed an adversarial relation between federal and state governments, they would only reinforce their opponents' misgivings, for few voters wanted to replace their state republics with a national republic.

Ironically, it was Hamilton, the future High Federalist, who offered a more effective response to Antifederalist anxieties. In the *Federalist* 9, Hamilton invoked the authority of the Antifederalists' favorite philosopher Montesquieu on behalf of the "CONFEDERATE REPUBLIC as the expedient for extending the sphere of popular government and reconciling the advantages of monarchy with those of republicanism." Where Madison conceived of the states and the union on the same level, as republics small or large, and therefore implicitly in conflict with one another, Hamilton and Montesquieu distinguished governments according to level or sphere. The "Confederate Republic" was an "assemblage of societies," an association of states designed to preserve their integrity and independence, not to dissolve them in a larger whole (Cooke, ed., *The Federalist*, pp. 53, 55). As they acknowledged the states as crucial components in the new system, Federalists pushed themselves further toward a genuinely federal understanding of their own handiwork. Madison himself moved in this direction in the next few months. In the *Federalist* 51 (published in February 1788), he argued that "in the compound republic of America, the power surrendered by the people, is first divided between two distinct governments, and then the portion allotted to each, subdivided among distinct and separate departments" (Cooke, ed., *The Federalist*, p. 351). Rather than deny that the large size of the union was a problem, Madison could now suggest that the American people, in their sovereign wisdom, could have it both ways by delegating different powers to distinct levels of government. Once those levels were distinguished, it became logically possible to argue that the enhancement of federal authority in its own sphere of operations—conducting foreign policy, managing interstate relations—would enhance, not diminish, the effective authority of the states.

LEGACIES

Over the course of the ratification debates, Federalists made significant concessions to their opponents. If the original point of the reform movement had been to create an energetic central government that could deal more effectively with foreign powers, advocates increasingly portrayed the Constitution as the best possible guarantee of states' rights and individual liberties. Recognizing the need to accommodate their opponents' antimetropolitan perspective, Federalists moved progressively toward genuine federalism. This conceptual realignment began with efforts to rationalize the complex of compromises negotiated at the Philadelphia Convention. As they resisted the Antifederalist campaign for conditional ratification and a second constitutional convention, Federalists insisted that a properly strict interpretation of the new government's delegated powers would secure the federal balance. Federalists assured skeptics that the new Congress, acting according to this understanding of its powers, would proceed to adopt appropriate amendments. The Bill of Rights did not alter the structure of the new government, but by securing civil liberties against encroachments by the federal government (and not the states), it harked back to the American Revolutionaries' resistance to metropolitan tyranny.

For many Federalists, the balance had shifted too far. Eager to get on with the business of establishing an effective central government, Federalists in the First Congress were reluctant to waste time on amendments most considered meaningless. As Treasury Secretary Alexander Hamilton's bold financial plan soon showed, the administration had little interest in binding itself by narrow interpretations of its own powers. But for Madison and the emergent opposition, loyalty to the Constitution did not require submission to an administration that claimed the seemingly limitless powers authorized by loose construction of the constitutional text. The reconciliation of perspectives that made ratification possible thus proved ephemeral. In the resulting party divisions of the 1790s, Republicans recurred to the Revolutionary principles of 1776, elaborating on Antifederalist anxieties about the abuses of metropolitan authority at the expense of provincial liberties. Turning away from federalism, Federalists sought to buttress central government authority against domestic as well as foreign threats. Where advocates of ratification had once seen distinct and complementary spheres of authority in a "composite" or federal republic, Federalists in power saw state governments as strictly subordinate jurisdictions—or as dangerous competitors. The conflicting perspectives that Federalists and Antifederalists had brought to the ratification debates and that had apparently been reconciled with the establishment of the new regime would thus prove compelling for partisans in the 1790s and throughout the antebellum era, until the union itself finally collapsed during the Civil War.

See also **Nationalism; Constitutional Thought; Anti-Statism** *(volume 2); and other articles in this section.*

BIBLIOGRAPHY

For a comprehensive and definitive collection of sources on the ratification debates, see John P. Kaminski et al., eds., *The Documentary History of the Ratification of the Constitution,* 18 vols. to date (Madison, Wisc., 1976–). The Kaminski edition will supersede Jonathan Elliot, ed., *The Debates in the Several State Conventions on the Adoption of the Federal Constitution,* 5 vols. (Philadelphia, 1876). James Madison's career as a constitutional reformer can be followed through J. C. A. Stagg et al., eds., *The Papers of James Madison: Congressional Series,* 17 vols. (Chicago and Charlottesville, Va., 1959–1991). Madison's notes on debates at the Constitutional Convention may be found in Max Farrand, ed., *The Records of the Federal Convention of 1787,* 4 vols. (New Haven, Conn., 1911–1937). The best edition of the most notable contribution to the ratification debates is Jacob E. Cooke, ed., *The Federalist* (Middletown, Conn., 1961), including essays by James Madison, Alexander Hamilton, and John Jay. For a generous sampling of Antifederalist writings, see Herbert J. Storing, ed., *The Complete AntiFederalist,* 7 vols., (Chicago, 1981).

The scholarly literature on the ratification debates is enormous. The best place to start is with Jack N. Rakove, *Original Meanings: Politics and Ideas in the Making of the Constitution* (New York, 1996). For a collection of essays discussing the debates in each state see Michael Gillespie and Michael Lienesch, eds., *Ratifying the Constitution* (Lawrence, Kans., 1989). The most important and influential study of the development of constitutional thought in the period is Gordon S. Wood, *The Creation of the American Republic, 1776–1787* (Chapel Hill, N.C., 1969). Lance Banning's *The Sacred Fire of Liberty: James Madison and the Founding of the Federal Republic* (Ithaca, N.Y., 1995) is the best study of Madison in this period; it is particularly notable for emphasizing the importance of federalism, a theme slighted in much of the literature. The varieties of Antifederalist thought are ably surveyed in Saul Cornell, *The Other Founders: Anti-Federalism and the Dissenting Tradition in America, 1788–1828* (Chapel Hill, N.C., 1999). The debate over the Bill of Rights is fully discussed in an excellent collection, Ronald Hoffman and Peter J. Albert, eds., *The Bill of Rights: Government Proscribed* (Charlottesville, Va., 1997).

On federalism see Peter S. Onuf, *The Origins of the Federal Republic: Jurisdictional Controversies in the United States, 1775–1787* (Philadelphia, 1983) and Cathy D. Matson and Peter S. Onuf, *A Union of Interests: Political and Economic Thought in Revolutionary America* (Lawrence, Kans., 1990), where the Europeanization theme is elaborated. Antifederalist anxieties about metropolitan power are further discussed in Peter S. Onuf, "Federalism, Republicanism, and the Origins of American Sectionalism," in Edward L. Ayers et al., *All Over the Map: Rethinking American Regions* (Baltimore, 1996), pp. 11–37. For the history of conflicting geopolitical perspectives in Anglo-American constitutionalism, see Jack P. Greene, *Peripheries and Center: Constitutional Development in the Extended Polities of the British Empire and the United States, 1607–1788* (Athens, Ga., 1986).

For further reading see the citations in Peter S. Onuf, "Reflections on the Founding: Constitutional Historiography in Bicentennial Perspective," *William and Mary Quarterly*, 3d ser., 46 (1989): 341–375.

JACKSONIAN IDEOLOGY

William E. Gienapp

At the beginning of March 1829 Washington, D.C., was overrun with strangers. The hotels were full and boarding houses were overflowing; hardly a room could be found anywhere in the city. Experienced political observers were simply astonished at the number of ordinary citizens who descended on the capital from every "point on the compass" to witness Andrew Jackson's inauguration as president.

On 4 March an immense crowd gathered in front of the capital to witness the inauguration of the new president. When Jackson walked out to take the oath of office, a deafening cheer rent the air. "Never can I forget . . . the electrifying moment," commented one eyewitness, "when the eager, expectant eyes of that vast and motley multitude caught sight . . . of their adored leader."

When the mass of humanity flocked to the reception at the White House after the ceremony, pandemonium ensued. Jackson had to flee to avoid being crushed by well-wishers, and the crowd smashed the china and nearly destroyed the furnishings before servants finally carried the refreshments out onto the lawn to reduce the press of people inside. To one dismayed observer, "the reign of KING MOB seemed triumphant," but a Jacksonian editor insisted: "It was a proud day for the people. General Jackson is *their own* President."

The response to Jackson's inauguration was striking evidence of the powerful emotions he generated among the populace. Observers sensed a vague, half-articulated feeling among his supporters that something was seriously wrong in the Republic. "People have come five hundred miles to see General Jackson," Massachusetts senator Daniel Webster commented with a mixture of amazement and condescension, "*and they really seem to think that the country is rescued from some dreadful danger!*" Without realizing it, Webster had distilled the real significance of the occasion.

ORIGINS

Jacksonian ideology drew on a variety of political and intellectual antecedents, but its roots were located in two major events of the early 1820s.

The first was the Panic of 1819 and the popular response to it. In the years after 1815, the country entered a long period of accelerating economic growth. The creation of a domestic market was the key to this change. Improved inland transportation and a growing urban population created a ready market for farmers' crops, and many began to abandon semisubsistence agriculture. With commodity prices, led by cotton, at record heights, Americans poured westward across the Appalachian Mountains and land sales, largely on credit, soared. A new commercial orientation took hold of many Americans who had access to market, and a heady euphoria, fueled by good times, seized the country.

Economic growth was further stimulated by the new policies of the federal government. Following the War of 1812, Congress established a protective tariff to stimulate manufacturing, chartered a new national bank to expand credit, and promoted a series of internal improvements projects to improve transportation. Caught up in the era's economic exuberance, the directors of the Second Bank of the United States, which had been chartered in 1816, recklessly promoted the prevailing speculative mania.

Then suddenly, in 1819, the bubble burst and the United States entered the first national depression in its history. The price of cotton on the world market collapsed, and almost overnight land values plummeted 50 to 75 percent. Not until 1823 would the economy finally pull out of the depression.

The severity of the 1819 depression, and the fact that many more Americans were affected than in earlier downturns, made the decade of the 1820s a time of national soul-searching. Enmeshed in a bewildering new economic system, overcome with a

Andrew Jackson's Inaugural Reception. Despite the disruptive White House revels for Jackson's inaugural reception, public parties continued throughout the administration. © CORBIS

sense of powerlessness in the face of vast economic forces, and beholden to impersonal economic institutions often located hundreds of miles distant, countless ordinary citizens concluded that something was seriously wrong in the Republic.

Groups that would come together in the Jacksonian movement focused in particular on the national bank and its role in the depression. Shortly before the Panic began, a new set of directors took charge of the Bank and began to rigorously reduce credit by calling its loans. This ruthless policy of contraction ruined many farmers and businessmen who had borrowed from the bank. As William Gouge, a leading Jacksonian monetary theorist, noted, "The Bank was saved and the people were ruined." Critics charged that through foreclosure proceedings the Bank owned entire western towns. "All the flourishing cities of the West are mortgaged to this money power," stormed Missouri senator Thomas Hart Benton, who would become a major Jacksonian leader. "They are in the jaws of the monster! A lump of butter in the mouth of a dog! One gulp, one swallow, and all is gone!" Long before

Andrew Jackson became president, the Bank already was a monster in the eyes of many Americans.

The other important influence on Jacksonian ideology was the 1824 presidential election. In that contest, Andrew Jackson demonstrated unexpected popularity and surprised observers by finishing first in both the popular and the electoral vote. Since he lacked an electoral majority, however, the election went into the House of Representatives, which ignored the popular will and selected Secretary of State John Quincy Adams.

Adams's victory stemmed from the support he received from Jackson's western rival, Henry Clay of Kentucky. When Adams subsequently appointed Clay as secretary of state, Jackson was convinced he—and the people—had been cheated by a corrupt bargain. Raising the cry "Jackson and reform," the general's supporters called for the restoration of the sovereign power of the people.

Popular anger over Adams's election drew sustenance from the democratic impulse of the era. The Panic of 1819 heightened mass interest in politics, precipitated a demand for new leaders responsive to the popular will, transformed elections into referenda on policy, and stimulated the effort to bring all government institutions under popular control. This new democratic tone first appeared in state and local politics, but it was Andrew Jackson who came to symbolize these changes nationally.

In 1828 Jackson capitalized on the electorate's discontent and became the first political outsider in American history to win the presidency. During his presidency (1829–1837), Jackson and his advisers, together with party editors, Democratic officeholders, and a group of intellectuals and reformers, formulated a powerful political ideology that fused popular anxiety over the market revolution with an unrestrained faith in democracy. By giving a sharp focus to the popular malaise, this ideology mobilized an unprecedented number of voters and established the Democrats as the country's dominant party in the years before the Civil War.

THE RULE OF THE PEOPLE

Jacksonians constantly trumpeted their belief in democracy, which they considered the foundation of the country's political system. In his first message to Congress, delivered 8 December 1829, Andrew Jackson affirmed that "the first principle of our system" was that *the majority is to govern.* Indeed, in what proved to be a tactically brilliant move, Jackson's supporters took the name Democrats to emphasize their faith in the masses. The "imperishable basis of Democratic faith," the *Washington Globe,* the party's national organ, proclaimed, was "that the mass of the people are honest and capable of self-government." Democrats extolled the wisdom of the people, favored white manhood suffrage, endorsed removing property requirements for officeholding, and advocated making most appointed offices elective instead.

Following the 1840 election, in which the triumphant Whigs aped Democratic campaign techniques, a few party reformers, such as the clergyman Orestes Brownson, lost faith in democracy. Jackson, however, never wavered in this belief. He declared in 1841, "A long and intimate acquaintance with the character of the American people inspired me with the most implicit faith in their disposition to pursue and maintain truth, virtue, patriotism and independence with a single purpose." Like Jackson, the large majority of Democrats looked to the "sober second thoughts" of the people to restore the party to power.

The Jacksonians' democratic creed included a deep suspicion of elitism. Consequently, Democrats sought to break down the traditional barrier separating officeholders from the people. Jackson was convinced that too many federal officeholders believed that they held their office as a matter of right and considered it "a species of property." When Jackson removed a number of federal officeholders and appointed his supporters in their place, a New York Democrat defended this policy on the grounds that "to the victor belong the spoils." Because of the vigor with which Jackson defended these removals, he became widely identified with the spoils system. Periodically requiring public servants to resort to "the same means of obtaining a living" as "the millions who never hold office" would make government more responsive and officeholders less aloof.

In celebrating the wisdom of the common people, Jacksonian ideology nurtured a pronounced anti-intellectualism, which was manifested in Jackson's insistence that special training was not necessary to hold most government offices. In Jackson's view, ordinary citizens were quite capable of staffing the government bureaucracy. "The duties of all public officers are, or at least admit of being made, so plain and simple that men of intelligence may readily qualify themselves for their performance," he affirmed in his first annual message, "and I cannot but believe that more is lost by the long continuance of men in office than is generally to be gained by their experience." Indefinite tenure made government "an engine for the support of the few at the expense of the many"; hence rotation in office was "a leading principle in the republican system."

Following Jackson's lead, the Democratic Party shrewdly portrayed itself as the champion of the people battling the forces of aristocracy in the country. This image was self-serving, since like all parties the Democrats were led by social and economic elites. Yet it was also politically effective, for it perfectly mirrored the prevailing popular mood. So strong was the democratic faith of the age that the opposition had no choice but to follow suit. Stimulated by the Democratic Party's effective techniques, elections regularly featured activities and symbols designed to link the parties with the masses. Political speeches routinely celebrated the virtues of the people and, tarring the opposition with aristocratic pretensions, became a campaign staple.

More controversial was Democrats' conception of presidential power. Influenced by Jackson's style of leadership and his numerous battles with Congress, the Supreme Court, and even his cabinet, the party favored a strong executive. Jackson made the veto a substantial presidential power by using it far more frequently than had his predecessors. (During his two terms in office Jackson vetoed twelve pieces of legislation compared to only nine for all previous presidents combined.) Moreover, Jackson had no compunction about vetoing bills simply because he disliked them. Opponents cried that "King Andrew I" was concentrating all power in the hands of one man, but Jackson shrewdly invoked democratic principles to defend the role of a strong executive. Noting that the president was the only federal official elected by a national electorate, Jackson lectured the Senate, "The President is the direct representative of the American people. He was elected by the people, and is responsible to them."

THE BANK WAR

The defining event of Jackson's presidency—and the issue that defined the core of Jacksonian ideology—was the destruction of the Second Bank of the United States. Jackson's hostility to banks and paper money was rooted in bitter personal experience. As a young man eager to rise in Tennessee society, Jackson had engaged in various speculative activities that eventually brought him to the brink of financial ruin. It had taken Jackson years of painful struggle to pay his debts and restore his wealth.

As he pondered his personal situation, he increasingly came to the conclusion that banks threatened the Republic and that the only constitutional currency was specie (gold and silver), or hard money. The Panic of 1819 intensified these feelings, and Jackson entered the presidency determined to reform the national banking system. While Jackson had little understanding of the nature of banking, of the currency, or of the role the national bank played in the economy, he intuitively comprehended the fears of a large segment of the population, particularly those who clung to the old semisubsistence way of life and those who felt victimized by the new commercial institutions of the market.

When Congress approved a bill in 1832 rechartering the national bank, Jackson promptly vetoed it. His veto message invoked a number of arguments, but the most important was the claim that the bank was an aristocratic institution of special privilege. Jackson charged that the bank's unique position as the depository of federal funds served to enrich the bank's stockholders by making government subject to "the rich and the powerful," and he pledged, as president, to protect the people against

"the advancement of the few at the expense of the many." Congress failed to override the veto, and Jackson's reelection in 1832 sealed the doom of the Bank.

More than any other event, the "Bank War" defined the economic outlook of the Jacksonian movement. Jackson considered his veto as the first step to restoring a hard money currency in the country. Because paper money fluctuated widely in value and could be manipulated by insiders, he viewed it as a fraud designed to cheat honest workers and farmers out of fair payment for their labor. "We have been providing facilities for those engaged in extensive commerce and have left the mechanic and the laborer to all the hazards of an insecure and unstable circulating medium," charged Roger Taney, who served in 1833–1834 as Jackson's secretary of the Treasury. Jackson agreed: it was "the duty of every government, so to regulate its currency as to protect this numerous class, as far as practicable, from the impositions of avarice and fraud."

From the perspective of Jacksonians, banks had become a great power in the land that threatened the government itself. Arrogant and bloated, the money power was "ready to thwart" the government's "purposes and defy its power" if it dared oppose its wishes. To Democratic senator Robert Walker of Mississippi (1836–1845) the question was "whether this shall be a Government of the Banks or of the people." Thus the banking system had to be curtailed, even abolished, if democracy was to survive, and in the aftermath of the bank war hardmoney Democrats in various states attempted to restrict or eliminate state banks, which issued the bulk of the notes that circulated in the economy. Banks, a Pennsylvania paper warned, were always ready to "overpower, and bind the liberties of any people."

THE SPECTER OF ARISTOCRACY

The Jacksonians' antibank crusade raised the specter of aristocracy, since banks, under their legislative charters, enjoyed unique privileges. "A national bank is the bulwark of the aristocracy; its outpost, its rallying point," Massachusetts Democrats resolved in 1837. "It is the bond of union for those who hold that Government should rest on property." The *Washington Globe* succinctly remarked: "The Jackson cause is the cause of democracy and the people, against a corrupt and abandoned aristocracy."

This aristocracy included not just bankers, but also those who served the interests of and benefited from the activities of banks. Unrepublican in their attitudes, members of this homegrown aristocracy displayed a sense of superiority toward Americans in more humble walks of life. Class resentment suffused Jacksonian rhetoric. Banks "have attempted to seize upon the government of the Union and of the States, and make use of the revenues and loans upon the people's credit to uphold their villainy and grind the people to earth with oppression," the *Ohio Statesman* alleged in 1839. "In these attempts these corporations have been supported by the powerful array of mercantile wealth—by city and county court lawyers largely in their pay—by the benighted and mercenary portion of the priesthood—by village doctors who love the shade of an awning better than the golden fields of husbandman or the workshop of the mechanic."

In attacking the Bank as an aristocratic institution, Jacksonians portrayed the bank war as part of a larger struggle to preserve equality, "the grand fundamental principle" that lay "at the heart" of democracy. Jacksonians warned that under the onslaught of the money power the principle of equality was rapidly being lost sight of in the United States. The "natural tendency" of banks, Democrats charged, was "to make the rich richer and the poor poorer—to create a broad distance between the conditions of the few—very rich, and the many—very poor."

Democrats traced this alarming development primarily to the action of government. Bank charters and government-created monopolies interfered with the natural working of society by favoring one group at the expense of others. Any act that "tends in the smallest degree, to give *legal* advantages to *capital* over *labor* . . . must necessarily increase the natural inequality in society," the *Washington Globe* argued, "and finally, make two distinct classes: namely—masters and slaves." To counteract this trend, Jacksonians called for a limited government that would not intervene in the economy.

At the same time, Democrats firmly rejected the idea of equality of property. "Distinctions in society will always exist under every just government," Jackson acknowledged in his bank veto message of 10 July 1832. "Equality of talents, of education, or of wealth can not be produced by human institutions." Instead, Democrats condemned what they termed "artificial inequality," which they believed was created by government action. No government legislation produced greater inequality, according to Democrats, than did the banking system. "It is a system of credit whose very essence is inequality," contended the *Globe*; "not an inequality

TOO MUCH GOVERNMENT

Too much government has a direct tendency to aid one man or one set of men in . . . the "acquiring, possessing, and protecting [of] property," if not at the expense of the rest, at least without rendering them the like assistance . . . there is very little difference in the ability of all men to provide for themselves and families; and if all were left without any special aid from government, both land and the products of industry would be far more equally distributed than they are. . . . Four-fifths of the action of all legislation is, by law, to promote the accumulation of prosperity in a few hands.

Source: *Democratic Review* 20, March 1847, pp. 202–203.

founded on the external basis of a difference in personal vigor, personal activity, superior talent, prudence or enterprise, . . . but an inequality created by legislative enactments, and sustained by the partiality of the law." Government should be limited to its proper role of providing equal opportunity and equal protection of the law, not equal outcomes. Jacksonians confidently predicted if banks and paper money were abolished and government generally left people alone, "nature's own leveling process" would restore "that happy mediocrity of fortune which is so favorable to the practice of Christian and republican virtues."

For this reason, Democrats favored, as Jackson declared in his first message, "a government of limited and specific, and not general, powers." Summarizing the party's creed, the *Democratic Review* put on its masthead, "The best government is that which governs least." Thus Democrats opposed not only banks but also a protective tariff and aid to internal improvements, which they believed benefited one group in society at the expense of others.

THE RESTORATION OF THE OLD REPUBLIC

Democrats' defense of equality was closely tied to their acceptance of the labor theory of value, which held that labor produced all wealth in society. This perspective led party members to reject the idea of a fundamental harmony of interests and to think of society instead in terms of a basic conflict between capital and labor.

Jacksonians praised the contributions and virtue of farmers, mechanics, and laborers, "the bone and sinew of the country," who worked with their hands and knew that success was gradual and depends on industry and hard work. Opposed to these groups—the real people—was the financial aristocracy—the bankers, stockjobbers, lawyers, and financiers whose wealth came from manipulating paper and other commercial instruments rather than from performing any productive work. From the perspective of the Jacksonians, these individuals, who were identified with the developing market economy, were parasites who lived off other people's labor. "Bankers and capitalists enrich no part of our country, nor improve no part of its soil," contended one Democratic spokesman, "and many of them, as priests of old, . . . are mere drones in society, that live upon the labor of the more industrious of the hive."

Moreover, these members of the financial aristocracy were enemies of morality and the Republic because they fostered the antirepublican habits of idleness and extravagance by encouraging speculation and the desire for sudden, unearned wealth. Democrats recognized the temptations that speculation and the new market economy posed. Unless they were constantly vigilant, the people would lose their liberties, because banks used "every inducement to attract the confidence of the unwary and seduce into their grasp the most watchful and shrewd." Near the end of his presidency, Jackson emphasized that those he considered the real working classes were threatened by a "gradual consuming corruption, which is spreading and carrying stockjobbing, Land jobbing, and every species of speculation." By stimulating "idleness," "extravagance," and an "eager desire to amass wealth without labor," the credit system and the accompanying spirit of speculation threatened the morals and character of the American people.

Such rhetoric harkened back to the republicanism of the American Revolution. Like this earlier tradition, Jacksonians linked the moral character of the people to the survival of the Republic and celebrated the values of simplicity, frugality, and hard work. They were haunted by the fear of internal threats and conspiracies and believed, as Jackson declared in his Farewell Address (1837), that "eternal vigilance" was "the price of liberty." The main treat to the Republic, he continued, was not from a foreign power. Rather, he warned, "it is from

THE TRUE SOURCE OF WEALTH

The paper system . . . naturally engender[s] a spirit of speculation injurious to the habits and character of the people. . . . If your currency continues as exclusively paper as it now is, it will foster this eager desire to amass wealth without labor . . . and inevitably lead to corruption, which will . . . destroy at no distant day the purity of your Government. . . . The planter, the farmer, the mechanic, and the laborer all know that their success depends upon their own industry and economy, and that they must not expect to become suddenly rich by the fruits of their toil. Yet these classes of society form the great body of the people of the United States.

Source: Andrew Jackson, Farewell Address, 4 March 1837.

within, among yourselves—from cupidity, from corruption, from disappointed ambition and inordinate thirst for power—that factions will be formed and liberty endangered." Jacksonians saw agriculture as essential to the preservation of republican values. Echoing Thomas Jefferson, Jackson affirmed that "independent farmers are everywhere the basis of society and true friends of liberty."

Hostility to banks expressed a more basic suspicion of cities, the world of commerce, and the power of the market in people's lives. Jackson's antibank rhetoric appealed to Americans uncomfortable with, and sometimes outside of, the new market economy, with its impersonal long-distance dealings, dependence on credit, and inherent uncertainty and risk. Farmers and workers who clung to traditional ideas and attitudes rooted in the premodern world rallied to Jackson's standard and embraced this ideology, which gave expression to their own feelings. Banks, paper money, and commercial attitudes were, from this perspective, invisible forces inexorably drawing the virtuous into their web. Money exerted "a secret and invisible influence over the actions of man," a Mississippi Democrat observed, and thereby threatened to become "the ruler, the master, the disposer of his temporal destinies."

At the heart of Jacksonian ideology was a call to restore the old Jeffersonian Republic. Adherents of this ideology longed for a return to the simple agrarian republic of Jefferson's day when labor was honored, community ties were strong, and dealings were face-to-face. The summons to restore the old Republic reflected a desire to preserve the values of the past: simplicity, frugality, hard work, self-reliance, and independence. By destroying the corporate power that menaced the Republic, the bank war was the first step toward this goal. A hard money currency, Jackson confidently predicted, "will do more to revive and perpetuate those habits of economy and simplicity which are so congenial to the character of republicans than all the legislation which has yet been attempted."

The Jacksonians were agrarian-minded and clung to the Jeffersonian view that cities were evil and commercial society corrupt. Ill at ease with a competitive, changing society, Jacksonians sought to flee the psychological uncertainties of the market without sacrificing the economic rewards it offered to honest toil.

RACE, SLAVERY, AND EXPANSION

It was one of the era's seeming paradoxes that Jacksonian ideology united a vigorous defense of white equality with a virulent racism directed against blacks and Indians. The Democratic Party more consistently supported slavery, opposed black rights, and favored Indian removal than did the Whigs. A veteran Indian-fighter, Jackson strongly advocated removing the eastern tribes to the west of the Mississippi River, and indeed during his administration and the administration of Martin Van Buren (1837–1841), a total of approximately 100,000 Indians suffered the trauma of removal from their homelands.

In endorsing this policy, Jackson adopted a paternalistic attitude and insisted he was acting in the best interests of the tribes themselves. Unless they were isolated from contact with whites, he argued, they would certainly be exterminated, and thus it was in their interest to move west. Yet Jackson also knew at stake were some 100 million acres of land, and that land-hungry whites were determined to seize tribal lands. Furthermore, American attitudes on race were hardening in this period, as racial differences came to be seen as permanent and ineradicable rather than the product of culture and environment.

Jackson's defense of Indian removal reflected and appealed to these new racial attitudes. In his annual message in 1830, Jackson defended his policy of removal by observing:

> What good man would prefer a country covered with forests and ranged by a few thousand savages to our extensive Republic, studded with cities, towns, and prosperous farms, embellished with all the improvements which art can devise or industry execute, occupied by more than 12,000,000 happy people, and filled with all the blessings of liberty, civilization, and religion?

Antiblack sentiment was a key component of the ideology of the Jacksonian movement. Democrats strongly opposed black suffrage, favored black-exclusion laws, and resisted granting additional civil liberties to free blacks. Democratic speeches and newspapers often resorted to racist demagoguery. In 1845, for example, the *Ohio Statesman*, the party's state organ, reacted to a proposal to allow blacks to testify against whites by asking its readers: "Are you ready to [be] placed on a level with 'the niggers' in the political rights for which your fathers contended? Are you ready to share with them your hearths and homes?" Following the same script, Democrats bitterly denounced the abolitionist movement and argued that slavery was strictly a state and not a national concern. Even the free soil wing of the party, which in the 1840s opposed the expansion of slavery, rarely voiced any opposition to slavery where it existed or any concern for the welfare of African Americans, slave or free.

The New York writer and loyal Jacksonian James Kirke Paulding outlined the Democratic view of race in a defense of slavery published in 1836. He argued that racial distinctions in society were legitimate because unlike class divisions, which were artificial, they were based on natural inequality. The most outspoken champions of white equality were frequently at the forefront of the effort to exclude blacks from the promise of the Declaration of Independence. "The signers of the Declaration of Independence had no reference to negroes at all when they declared all men to be created equal," insisted Illinois senator Stephen A. Douglas on the campaign stump. "They did not mean [the] negro, nor the savage Indians, nor the Fejee Islanders, nor any other barbarous race. They were speaking of white men."

At the same time, Jacksonians were strong boosters of American expansionism. Indeed, it was a Jacksonian editor, John O'Sullivan, who coined the expression "Manifest Destiny" in the 1840s to describe American geographic expansion. Looking to the West as the means to reinvigorate American values and preserve the agrarian Republic, Democrats eagerly supported westward expansion. Jackson, who unsuccessfully tried to acquire Texas, spoke of "extending the area of freedom," while another Democrat assured Congress that acquiring new lands would induce "half-starved" workingmen in eastern cities to migrate to the West to obtain a "farm on which to subsist and . . . get rid of that feeling of dependence which made them slaves." In upholding this vision, Democratic president James K. Polk (1845–1849) pushed the nation's boundaries to the Pacific by acquiring the southern half of the Oregon country as well as the Mexican provinces of New Mexico and California.

In 1846 the *Democratic Review* succinctly summarized the Democratic creed:

> The general policy of the democracy is to favor the settlement of the land, spread the bounds of the future empire, and to favor, by freedom of intercourse and external commerce, the welfare of the settlers, . . . men of simple habits and strong hands, looking to mother-earth for their only capital, and to their own labor as the sole means of making it productive.

PUBLIC AND PRIVATE

In discussing the proper role of government in society, Jacksonians drew a sharp line between public and private matters. They did not believe that questions of personal morality and behavior were the proper concern of government, and they resisted efforts of religiously motivated reformers to blur the line between church and state in American society. This outlook was well expressed by Richard M. Johnson of Kentucky, who would be Martin Van Buren's vice president, in his 1830 congressional report defending Sunday mail service. Johnson scornfully rejected the demand of church members that the post office cease transporting mail on the Sabbath. "It is not the legitimate province of the Legislature to determine what religion is true, or what false," he lectured. "Our government is a civil, and not a religious institution."

Jacksonians believed that the public and private spheres were distinct and separate, but their object in both spheres was to free individuals from government power. Democrats applied their concept of limited government to private matters as well. "Law-made wealth and law-made religion are equally obnoxious," Massachusetts Democrats averred in 1841.

This outlook made Jacksonians less sympathetic to the humanitarian reform movements of the era,

particularly the efforts of various reformers to use the political system to achieve their goal of reform. Just as party members did not favor an activist, interventionist government in the economy, they likewise did not want the government to scrutinize and regular private behavior. To do so would be an infringement of personal liberty. In general, the *Democratic Review* maintained, government should just leave people alone and "have as little as possible to do" with their "general business and interests."

Votes in state legislatures on various reform issues in the 1830s and 1840s demonstrate there were distinct limits to the Democratic party's common man ideology. Democratic legislators were more likely to support bills to abolish imprisonment for debt and provide debtor relief. On the other hand, they opposed establishing tax-supported public schools, temperance laws, and prison and asylum reform. And they were far less sympathetic to antislavery measures and problack legislation.

The Democratic party's opposition to clerical meddlers, Sabbatarians, and middle-class reformers gave it a special appeal to groups that felt culturally marginalized. Cloaking themselves in the aura of social respectability, reformers condemned groups that resisted modernity, opposed middle-class ideals, and did not quickly and easily assimilate into American culture. These groups, including traditionalist workers and farmers, Catholics, non-British immigrants, and the nonchurched, found a natural home in the Democratic Party. Just as the struggle over banks pitted modernists against those who clung to the earlier agrarian ideal, the Democratic Party's suspicion of humanitarian reformers and its demand to keep religion out of politics pitted culturally dominant groups against those on the periphery.

HOPE AND MEMORY

Like many political ideologies, Jacksonianism was Janus-faced, looking forward and backward at the same time. Its belief in democracy and faith in the common people anticipated the country's future path of development, while its crusade against banks and paper money represented a vain effort to stem the forces of modernism and preserve a traditional way of life that was being rapidly swept away. In extolling the sovereignty of the people and celebrating the potential of a democratic society, the Jacksonians spoke to the hopes of the American people; in their opposition to banks and their negative view of government power, they spoke to their fears.

Jacksonian ideology gave voice to many Americans' anxiety over the country's emerging new economic order, but in the end the lure of the market was too powerful, and the Jacksonian program too limited, to seriously impede the forces of capitalism that were fundamentally transforming the republic.

See also **Nationalism; Democracy; Constitutional Thought** *(volume 2);* **Political Economy** *(volume 3); and other articles in this section.*

BIBLIOGRAPHY

Ashworth, John. *"Agrarians" and "Aristocrats": Party Political Ideology in the United States, 1837–1846.* New York, 1987.

Baker, Jean H. *Affairs of Party: The Political Culture of Northern Democrats in the Mid-Nineteenth Century.* Ithaca, N.Y. 1983.

Ellis, Richard E. *The Union at Risk: Jacksonian Democracy, States' Rights, and the Nullification Crisis.* New York, 1987.

Ershkowitz, Herbert, and William G. Shade. "Consensus or Conflict? Political Behavior in the State Legislatures during the Jacksonian Era." *Journal of American History* 58 (1971): 591–621.

Fredrickson, George M. *The Black Image in the White Mind.* New York, 1971.

Hietala, Thomas R. *Manifest Design: Anxious Aggrandizement in Late Jacksonian America.* Ithaca, N.Y., 1985.

Hofstadter, Richard. *The American Political Tradition and the Men Who Made It.* New York, 1948.

Holt, Michael F. "The Democratic Party, 1828–1860." In his *Political Parties and American Political Development: From the Age of Jackson to the Age of Lincoln.* Baton Rouge, La., 1992.

Horsman, Reginald. *Race and Manifest Destiny: The Origins of American Racial Anglo-Saxonism.* Cambridge, Mass., 1981.

Kohl, Lawrence Frederick. *The Politics of Individualism: Parties and the American Character in the Jacksonian Era.* New York, 1989.

McFaul, John M. *The Politics of Jacksonian Finance.* Ithaca, N.Y., 1972.

Meyers, Marvin. *The Jacksonian Persuasion: Politics and Belief.* Stanford, Calif., 1957.

Remini, Robert V. *The Legacy of Andrew Jackson.* Baton Rouge, La., 1988.

———. *The Life of Andrew Jackson.* New York, 1988.

Richards, Leonard L. "The Jacksonians and Slavery." In *Antislavery Reconsidered: New Perspectives on the Abolitionists,* edited by Lewis Perry and Michael Fellman. Baton Rouge, La., 1979.

Richardson, James D., ed. *A Compilation of the Message and Papers of the Presidents, 1789–1908.* Vols. 2 and 3. Washington, D.C., 1908.

Satz, Ronald N. *American Indian Policy in the Jacksonian Era.* Lincoln, Nebr., 1975.

Schlesinger, Arthur M., Jr. *The Age of Jackson.* Boston, 1945.

Sellers, Charles. *The Market Revolution: Jacksonian America, 1815–1846.* New York, 1991.

Sharp, James Roger. *The Jacksonians versus the Banks: Politics in the States after the Panic of 1837.* New York, 1970.

Watson, Harry L. *Liberty and Power: The Politics of Jacksonian America.* New York, 1990.

Welter, Rush. *The Mind of America, 1820–1860.* New York, 1975.

Wilson, Major L. *Space, Time, and Freedom: The Quest for Nationality and the Irrepressible Conflict, 1815–1861.* Westport, Conn., 1974.

WHIG IDEOLOGY

Allen C. Guelzo

The Whig ideology was a cluster of political ideas that had its long-term origins in the resistance of the English Parliament and the English Puritans to the Stuart monarchy of the 1600s. The American Whig ideology was derived from this English Whig or "Commonwealth" tradition, and actually had two lives: one in the eighteenth century, the other in the nineteenth. In the eighteenth century, it became one component in the larger ideology of colonial resistance to British overlordship in the 1760s and the American Revolution. In the nineteenth century, it referred to the emergence of a political party opposed to the policies and personality of the seventh United States president, Andrew Jackson. The American Whig Party, begun in 1834 with the Senator Henry Clay's application of the term to organized anti-Jacksonianism, developed a fresh recension of the Whig ideology, which combined political elements unique to the onset of the industrial revolution as well as elements harking back to the older forms of Whiggism. This second Whig ideology outlasted the practical dissolution of the Whig Party in 1856, and was absorbed into the new Republican Party, where it played a major role in the coming of the American Civil War and the establishment of a Republican political ascendancy in the six decades following the Civil War.

WHIG ORIGINS AND THE FIRST WHIG IDEOLOGY

The term "whig" came into use, probably as early as the 1670s, to describe the political faction in England with the greatest sense of continuity with the grievances of Parliament and the Puritans in the English Civil War (1642–1651) and with their determination to resist the repeated attempts of the Stuart monarchs, especially Charles I and James II, to impose forms of monarchial absolutism on English governance. The word itself seems to have been derived from "whiggamore," a term of abuse

suggesting a country yokel. And indeed the Whigs liked to think of themselves as the heirs of the "country" party of the 1630s and 1640s, characterized by a simple, strict Protestantism and concerned with the promotion of the good of their rural communities.

If Whiggery could be distilled to four propositions, they would be:

1. Liberty is natural, and cannot be a gift of a monarch.
2. Liberty, however, can be destroyed, normally by the corrupt elite who strive to concentrate power in themselves and corrupt others.
3. Liberty therefore requires an alliance with virtue for protection from corruption and power, whether in the form of the natural virtues (like modesty, productive work, or self-restraint), or religious ones (such as would be found in strict Protestant moralism).
4. Because Whigs prefer virtue to power, they are most often the "country" party, and are found outside the centers of power.

On these terms, Whiggism had tremendous appeal to the British colonists of North America. Like the English Whigs, Americans felt themselves marginalized from the centers of imperial decision-making, yet convinced that their lives in the "countryside" of the empire were better examples of virtue than the gin-crazed mobs they saw depicted in William Hogarth's paintings. They found first-hand confirmation of this, first, when the Seven Years' War (1756–1763) for the first time compelled the British government to garrison regular British infantry in the colonies, where they could then become enforcers of imperial policy; and, second, when the costs of that war finally impelled the imperial government in London to begin restraining the freewheeling activities of the colonial legislatures and colonial economy and harness them to the overall development of the English Empire. The Americans responded with a revolution that

197

severed their ties to England and left them free to erect a Whiggish republic, without any obligations to the English Crown.

But as experience had shown in England, the Whig ideology proved a far better weapon for criticizing the powerful than for prescribing actual techniques for governing. It was not virtue but self-interest that eventually governed the construction of a new American federal constitution in 1787. The Revolutionary War itself threw up new leaders who were more interested in equality than virtue, while the new governments in the American states frequently became pits of interest-group politics and competitive individualism.

THE RISE OF THE AMERICAN WHIG PARTY

English Whig thought was republican rather than democratic in nature. It was juxtaposed to corrupt monarchs, not a self-interested commons, but a virtuous, disinterested gentry who acted on the commons' behalf. The revolutionary leaders were sometimes drawn from the ranks of such gentry elites; but they were just as often not, and in the Early Republic, nearly the only place where a landed gentry retained anything close to political dominance was in the slaveholding plantation South.

This agrarian elite, as typified by Thomas Jefferson, John Randolph of Roanoke, and John Taylor of Carolina, still believed that the purpose of their revolution had been the establishment of virtue. But it was a virtue linked explicitly to a carefully recruited meritocracy and the pursuit of gentry agriculture. "Corruption of morals in the mass of cultivators," remarked Jefferson in his *Notes on the State of Virginia* (1782), "is a phenomenon which no age nor nation has furnished an example." Taylor impressed the Democratic leader Thomas Hart Benton as the embodiment of a republican squire, "plain and solid . . . innately republican—modest, courteous, benevolent, hospitable—a skillful, practical farmer, giving his time to his farm and his books, when not called by an emergency to the public service—and returning to his books and his farm when the emergency was over."

Confident of their virtue, and free at last of the manipulations of imperial planners in London, the fears of the republican gentry gravitated instead to the new class of upwardly mobile merchants and entrepreneurs whom the American Revolution had also released from imperial restraint, and who were now turning up new fortunes from commerce, investments, and banking. At first, this took the form of Jeffersonian Democratic Party opposition to Alexander Hamilton and Hamilton's Federalist plans for a federally sponsored Bank of the United States and federally backed investment in manufacturing. But the Federalists proved politically inept in challenging the southern squirearchs. Jefferson's election as president in 1800 seemed to symbolize the triumph of the agrarian elite as the new Republican order, and the charter of Hamilton's Bank of the United States ran out without renewal.

There was, of course, a twofold difficulty with this: the first was that an elite, even a gentry one, clashed strongly with the democratic energies let loose by the American Revolution, and lesser southern farmers questioned why they should tamely welcome the virtuous direction of Jeffersonian cotton planters. The answer to that was found in race. The work force of the Jeffersonian countryside was predominantly black and enslaved, and small white farmers who viewed the great planters with envy could always be placated by having their interests, not as small farmers but as white men, played off against the interests of black slaves. The instant that interest was pointed out, the small farmers could readily be predicted to take the Jeffersonian side and vote Democratic.

The second problem was that a nation of Cincinnatuses at the plow was ill fitted to compete in the new nineteenth-century world of transatlantic capitalism and diplomacy. This was dramatically demonstrated in 1808, when Jefferson attempted to punish both France and Britain for pillaging American ships on the high seas by imposing an embargo on all American exports to either country. Contrary to what one might have expected from a virtuous, self-sufficient agrarian republic, the bottom fell out of the American economy, which turned out to be far more dependent on commercial exchange than Jefferson imagined. Then, in 1812, Jefferson's successor, James Madison, allowed himself to be pushed by ardent Jeffersonians, who blamed all of their economic distress on British plots, into a war with Great Britain. The War of 1812 was an American disaster, as the agrarian republic proved unable to feed, clothe, and equip its ill-led armies.

In the wake of the War of 1812, members of Jefferson's Democratic Party began to count the costs of agrarianism. John Pendleton Kennedy recalled:

> Our commerce was put in fetters by non-importation acts and embargoes; and the crisis that succeeded found us without the most ordinary resources of an independent people. Our armies went

to the frontier clothed in the fabrics of the enemy; our munitions of war were gathered as chance supplied them from the four quarters of the earth; and the whole struggle was marked by the prodigality, waste and privation of a thriftless nation, taken at unawares and challenged to a contest without the necessary armor of a combatant. . . . These disasters opened our eyes to some important facts. They demonstrated to us the necessity of extending more efficient protection, at least, to those manufactures which were essential to the defence of the nation. They proved to us the value of a national currency, and the duty of protecting it from the influence of foreign disturbance; and among other things of equal moment, they made us acquainted with the fact that the British manufacturers could find a large and, if necessary, a complete supply of cotton from other soils than our own. (*Political and Official Papers*, pp. 119–120)

Foremost among these sadder but wiser Jeffersonians was Henry Clay, who in 1816 spearheaded a drive to establish a second Bank of the United States. Clay reasoned that America's defenselessness in the War of 1812 rose from its inability to compete with the European powers as a manufacturing and commercial power. In 1824, Clay laid out a series of economic policies that he named "the American System," involving a return to federal financing for manufacturing, a system of steep tariffs to protect infant American industries from cheap European imports, and a system of "internal improvements" (funded through the sales of public lands) in the form of canals, roadways, and, eventually, railroads to promote the opening of the agrarian hinterlands to European markets. The Jeffersonian Democrats vilified Clay's program as a threat to liberty (as well as a threat to slavery, since a federal government powerful enough to perform interventions of that nature in the economy might have the power to regulate, or even abolish, slavery). When they succeeded in electing the arch-Jeffersonian Andrew Jackson as president in 1828, Jackson dismantled by veto each element of Clay's "American System," including the withdrawal of all federal funds from the second Bank of the United States and a veto of the renewal of its congressional charter in 1834.

Clay had once considered himself as good a Jeffersonian as Jackson, but the bank veto destroyed all illusion that the party of Jefferson was still one party. In the run-up to the 1832 election, Clay's followers organized their own national nominating convention and ran Clay against Jackson (Clay lost). The final divorce came in April 1834, when Clay bestowed on his new party organization its own name: the Whigs. Some of this was simply a calculated rhetorical gesture, as Clay sought to wrench

the claim to genuine republicanism out of the hands of Jackson and the Democratic Party. But it also reflected Clay's belief that his followers were the real heirs of the old Whig tradition, struggling once again against the concentration of power at the center of government. Not only was Andrew Jackson a "military chieftain" and a "President General" with a long record of high-handedness and arbitrary punishments, but he had also overridden both Congress and the Constitution by hurling one executive veto after another at the bank and the "American System" legislation. "The Whigs of the present day are opposing executive encroachment," Clay claimed, "and a most alarming extension of executive power and prerogative. They are ferreting out the abuses and corruptions of an administration, under a chief magistrate who is endeavoring to concentrate in his own person the whole powers of the government."

This was an unusual claim for Clay to make, since Jackson, as a plantation owner and slaveholder, had far better title than Clay's followers in banking and commerce to the fundamental identity of all Whigs as the "country" party. But for the Whigs, the exact significance of the "country" had changed with the immense shifts in the world economy since the term "whig" had first been heard. The farmer, argued the journalist Horace Greeley, "is now too nearly an isolated being. . . . Of the refining, harmonizing, expanding influences of general society, he has little experience." If only Jacksonian farmers could be synonymous with the "country," then Whiggism would have to become synonymous with slavery rather than liberty. "Could those patriots of former days, who so zealously guarded the security of personal independence and the freedom of individual opinion against the arbitrary exercise of executive power" return and give their opinion? asked a New York Whig convention in 1836. Would it be likely that they would identify their aspirations with the likes of Andrew Jackson and his followers?

If, on the other hand, the original intent of the "country" had been to designate the industrious small producer, the energetic individualist with no inherited assets except talent and imagination, the entrepreneur eager to engage the new transatlantic capitalist markets, the self-disciplined Protestant moralist, then surely such people were the real "Whigs of the present day." As Francis Bacon put it in 1844, "Those who labor in poverty, with intelligence, honesty, virtue, and HOPE, are Whigs, ten to one; those who labor not, or labor in ignorance and vice, and in despair of improving their condition under any system of government are [Democrats]—a hundred to one."

THE SECOND WHIG IDEOLOGY

The second Whig ideology came to rest around three important amendments of the first Whig ideology:

(1) The substitution of economic mobility for physical location in the "country": In other words, the Whigs redefined their location outside the centers of power in conceptual rather than spatial terms, although this shift did not mean any real alteration in the American Whigs' conviction that this located them on the side of virtue. The Whigs became the party of small-scale urban business and finance, and usually urban businesses and financiers who were parts of transatlantic networks of investment and trade or of trade that crossed state and regional boundaries. "The spirit of improvement is abroad upon the earth," urged John Quincy Adams, and Americans, "while foreign nations less blessed with that freedom which is power than ourselves are advancing with gigantic strides in the career of public improvement," ought not "to cast away the bounties of Providence and doom ourselves to perpetual inferiority." Edward Everett, in his Fourth of July oration at Lowell, Massachusetts, extolled the Lowell factory system "as a specimen of other similar seats of American art and industry" which "may with propriety be considered as a peculiar triumph of our political independence." Manufacturing and commerce are, said Everett, "the complement of the revolution. They redress the peculiar hardships of the colonial system." This did not mean that the Whigs were entirely a city-oriented party: in fact, the Whigs drew a large measure of support from farmers, skilled artisans, and free blacks. But Whig farmers tended to be large-scale commercial farmers, who produced agricultural products for distant markets, and who were tied into networks of trade that benefited from the regulation of state or even national controls on trade.

Whigs were not, as such, a party whose members identified themselves strictly with their state or their locality, either economically or socially. Most often, the Whigs looked to escape the restraints of locality and community, seeking to refashion themselves on the basis of new economic identities in a larger world of trade, based on self-improvement and free wage-paid labor. They wanted, no less than Jacksonian farmers and laborers, to pursue equality; but for the Whigs, equality meant equality of economic opportunity. "It is through high wages that we make the laboring man a partner in the gains of the rich," argued John Pendleton Kennedy. Unlike the great Jacksonian planters, the New York Whigs believed that "it accords with the republican spirit of our institutions to give to all our citizens, as far as possible, equal means and opportunities of acquiring property," all of which required a national banking system, federal "internal improvements," and the other components of the "American System."

(2) The definition of virtue as self-improvement, whether through commerce, thrift, or religious transformation: The Whigs described themselves as the "sober, industrious, thrifty people," which is a statement, not only about economic behavior, but about moral behavior as well. The Jeffersonians believed that virtue originated in the private sphere, in the farm or at least away from the public forum of commercial transactions. The Whigs reversed this, and located the origins of virtue in the public sphere of commercial society. Instead of commerce being subordinate to refinement and culture, it became the very means of perfecting it.

Just as Whig economics depended upon regularizing the national economy, the Whigs also relied upon regularity of moral behavior, and this led the Whigs into a close alliance with another form of publicly located virtue, the ambitious and aggressive Protestant evangelicalism of the Second Great Awakening. "Out of all doubt, the moral training of mankind—since this cannot be separated from religion—is committed to the Church," wrote the Whig congressman Daniel Barnard. "Political leaders and social reformers, who never look to Christianity and the Church for the meaning of these terms and the doctrines properly involved in them, are only blind guides to lead the people to their destruction." (Democrats, according to the Presbyterian clergyman Lyman Beecher, were "Sabbathbreakers, rum-selling tippling folk, infidels, and ruff-scuff generally"; Democrats, according to the Massachusetts Whig Charles Sumner, "underbid the Whigs in *vulgarity*.")

Certainly not every Protestant evangelical was a Whig, nor were all Whigs evangelicals. (Clay was notorious for his personal womanizing and gambling; some of the most energetic evangelical revivalists, especially among the Baptists and Methodists, were ardent Democrats.) But there was a broad band of Protestant opinion—which the historian Charles C. Sellers called the "Moderate Light"—that saw as its principal task, not revivalism (which they regarded as too undependable and irregular) but the creation of a Christian consensus within society. This Moderate Light aimed to reestablish through "influence" the once-legal church establishments of the prerevolutionary period and leaven (rather than revive) society with Christian interest. The great theological minds of the Moderate Light were northerners—Nathaniel William Taylor of Yale University, and Taylor's pupil, Horace Bushnell, and Charles Hodge of Princeton University—but their great activist was Lyman Beecher, a New Englander who left New England for Cincinnati in 1832 to ensure that the American West would be made safe for Protestantism. In the ongoing Moderate Light quest for Christian influence over society, Beecher happily struck up a close alliance with the Whigs, and the Whigs found in Moderate Light influence the ideal rule for promoting the kind of national unity necessary for the smooth operation of an American System.

(3) The relocation of power and Whig nationalism: The first Whig ideology had been preoccupied with the toxicity of power, and the lethal results when it became concentrated at the center. The victories of the Jacksonians, however, convinced Clay and the second Whig ideology that power could be just as toxic when concentrated on the peripheries, like the American South, since then the power-holding could constantly threaten a political breakup of the Union as the cost of defying their will. The situation of Jacksonian America seemed to demonstrate the need to counterbalance the tyrannical Democratic power on the peripheries with some form of power near the center. Not only would that offset the jealousies of the agrarians, but it would assist in the establishment of a national economy and the spread of a uniform Protestant morality. The middle ground, then, for the Whigs would be in the legislatures, and especially in Congress, as opposed to the executive branch. As John Pendleton Kennedy wrote:

[The Whigs] fearing this administrative arm, and believing that the safety of free institutions is best secured by watching and restraining the Executive, disdain to seek its favor by any act of adulation or by any relaxation of their distrust. These naturally put great faith in the National Legislature. They see in the Executive the fountain of political honors, rank, emolument, consideration with the world: that it is prone to be selfish, ambitious, crafty: that it has a motive to reward subserviency; that it may so dispense them as to gratify those who defend and applaud it: that it may convert public servants into political minions; that it may work in secret and corrupt enterprises, and gloss them over with pretenses of public good. In all these attributes and propensities of Executive power they find strong

motive to regard it with jealousy. (*Political and Official Papers,* pp. 320–321)

In practical terms, this also meant that Whig legislators saw themselves as fighting two battles: against overweening executive aggrandizement and against a raging Democratic populism at the peripheries. Whigs like Maine's William Pitt Fessenden were no more confident of the virtue of the mob than they were of "King Andrew," and they saw their task as the use of a representative legislature to chart out a path of independent wisdom for the whole nation, even if it meant setting aside the demands of their local constituencies for favors. "On questions of local interest, connected with ourselves alone, my constituents have a right to instruct me," Fessenden wrote. He continued:

But sir, on questions of general interest, I have a higher obligation. I am bound to form my own opinions and to act upon them. . . . Sir, did I know that the opinions of every one of my constituents differed from my own, I would act according to my own conviction of right. I am willing to be the servant of the people, but I will never be their slave. (Fessenden, *Life and Public Services of William Pitt Fessenden,* vol. 1, p. 8)

The model of the Whig politician, therefore, was that of the "statesman," the farseeing, wise elder who rises above the clamor of partisan and sectional loyalties to forge nation-saving compromises. Indeed, the Whigs were reluctant to consider themselves *as* a mere party. "All legislation, all government, all society, is formed upon the principle of mutual concession, politeness, comity, courtesy," Clay remarked, and not on the passionate and divisive triumphalism of Democratic populism. "On the American statesman, then," declaimed the financier Nicholas Biddle, in his 1835 commencement address at Princeton, "devolves the solemn charge of sustaining its institutions against temporary excesses, either of the people or their rulers—and protecting them from their greatest foes—which will always lie in their own bosom" (in Howe, ed., *The American Whigs*).

This made Clay and the new Whigs into political nationalists; which is to say that it forced them to the Lockean end of the Whig spectrum, emphasizing common natural rights and a common national identity irrespective of ethnic or regional diversity. In the Whig mind, wrote the great Whig jurist and political theorist Rufus Choate:

The exclusiveness of state pride, the narrow selfishness of a mere local policy, and the small jealousies of vulgar minds, would be merged in an expanded, comprehensive, constitutional sentiment of old, family, fraternal regard. It would reassemble, as it were, the people of America in one vast congregation. It would rehearse in their hearing all things which God had done for them in the old time; it would proclaim the law once more; and then it would bid them join in the grandest and most affecting solemnity—a national anthem of thanksgiving for deliverance, of honor for the dead, of proud prediction for the future! (in Howe, ed., *The American Whigs*, p. 171)

Henry Clay, especially, appeared to embody this commitment to Whig nationalism. "Whatever he did, he did for the whole country," declared Abraham Lincoln (an early Whig who admired Clay as his "beau ideal of a statesman") after Clay's death in 1852:

Feeling, as he did, and as the truth surely is, that the world's best hope depended on the continued Union of these States, he was ever jealous of, and watchful for, whatever might have the slightest tendency to separate them. . . . He loved his country, partly because it was his own country, but mostly because it was a free country; and he burned with a zeal for its advancement, prosperity and glory, because he saw in such, the advancement . . . of human liberty, human right and human nature. He desired the prosperity of his countrymen partly because they were his countrymen, but chiefly to show to the world that freemen could be prosperous (*Collected Works*, vol. 3, p. 126)

This national prosperity not only embraced all sections, but all classes. The Whigs would appeal to a "harmony" of economic interests as well as national ones, claiming that manufacturers and workers, far from representing two antagonistic class loyalties, actually complemented each other. "The interests of the capitalist and the laborer," wrote the economist-sociologist Henry Carey, "are . . . in perfect harmony with each other, as each derives advantage from every measure that tends to facilitate the growth of capital." This allowed the Whigs to claim that the promotion of manufacturing and high tariffs actually benefitted the workingman fully as much as the capitalist. "Looking at the gigantic and horrible evils resulting from the competition among laborers for the same employment," wrote the *American Whig Review*, "every thoughtful statesman must be led to the conclusion, that here is discovered the pitfall of modern civilization." But protected industries meant protected jobs, and under the banner of protection, factory owner and factory worker could labor together in a great nation-building enterprise. "A freedom thus secured and thus protected appears to us to go beyond the mere political idea usually attached to the term," continued the *American Whig Review*, and, if thoroughly understood and carried out, to be the solution for

most of the social enigmas that perplex and distract the age."

Whig nationalism would also force Clay and the Whigs into deploring both slaveholding southern sectionalists and impatient northern abolitionists as equally destructive to the Union. Clay, for instance, was a Kentucky slaveholder, which aligned him with southern slaveholding interests; but he also publicly condemned the morality of slave ownership, actively sought to restrict the spread of slaveholding in the United States, promoted colonization schemes for freed slaves (not so much for the good of the slaves as to remove a potential irritant to national harmony), and was the architect of one compromise after another to hold the southern slave states in the Union. For the Whigs, the antidote for the risks of power at the center was the exercise of "statesmanship," of virtuous and disinterested compromise between competing national priorities.

The cumulative effect of these amendments in the second Whig ideology, together with its glorification of national union, small-business opportunism, and public morality, pushed Whiggism into a convergence with European liberalism in the 1840s. At the same time, however, this also meant that the Jacksonians found themselves speaking for slave-based agriculture and for industrial workers along the same lines that European socialism was already beginning to do in the German states and in England. As the historian Daniel Walker Howe put it, the Whigs promoted a society which would be economically diverse but culturally uniform; Democrats preferred economic uniformity and equality, but tolerated the spread of cultural, ethnic, and moral diversity.

THE FUTURE OF THE WHIG IDEOLOGY

The Whig Party of the 1830s has often been dismissed as a party of no ideas at all, rather than the party of a second Whig ideology. It has also been dismissed as the party of failure, or at least of bad electoral luck. Whig presidential candidates won only two national elections, in 1840 and in 1848, and both of those candidates (William Henry Harrison and Zachary Taylor) died without completing a full term in office. The unhappy Henry Clay ran three times for the presidency and lost on each occasion.

But these dismissals of the Whigs may be little more than a reflection of the sympathies of modern historians for Jeffersonianism, and a severe underestimation of the difficulties Clay and the Whigs faced as a minority party in winning elections. Far from a lack of ideas, the second Whig ideology was linked to the first, and to Whiggery's seventeenth-century origins, by its concern over the relationship of power and liberty. The Whigs feared Jackson, but even more they feared the strangling hand of an agrarian elite on the throat of middle-class economic mobility. They were also more successful politically than they have often been portrayed: they fought the Democratic Party on uneven terms from 1834 to 1848, but they managed to capture the White House twice, the House of Representatives from 1846 to 1848, and majorities in numerous important state legislatures, including New York, Pennsylvania, and Virginia, between 1838 and 1852.

But being a minority party meant that their successes rested very largely on their ability to distance themselves decisively from the Democrats, and to capitalize on the failures of Democratic promises, while their anxiety to be seen as high-minded nationalists undermined the low-minded necessity for party discipline and organization. The decision of the Whig Party leadership, led by Clay, to embrace a compromise settlement over slavery in the newly acquired western lands won from Mexico in the Mexican War wiped out the element of difference over the most critical emerging issue of the 1850s. Yet, the leadership lacked the strength to impose uniformity in rallying behind the compromise. "Our policy has been adherence to the Whig party, believing that through that organization we might accomplish the greatest good," wrote Charles Sumner in 1847, but if the party "under slaveholding influence, should decline to sanction what seem to us cardinal truths . . . can we sustain its course?" Northern Whigs who opposed the compromise, and southern Whigs who endorsed it, at once set

incompatible political courses that split the Whig Party along sectional lines. Within six years, the disruptive power of the slavery question, and the ease with which new parties based solely on the slavery issue could be formed, had permanently torn the Whig Party to pieces, and after one last fruitless effort in 1856, the Whig Party disintegrated.

Sumner and many northern Whigs would form the antislavery core of the new Republican Party in 1856. Southern Whigs, meanwhile, would either align with the Democrats or attempt to keep local southern Unionist movements afloat in southern state politics (many of these southern Whigs would form the center of Unionist resistance to secession in 1861, and become cooperating "scalawags" during Reconstruction). However, the nomination of Abraham Lincoln as the Republican presidential candidate in 1860 once more placed "an old Henry Clay Whig" at the top of a national ticket. And though Lincoln's election helped trigger the South's secession and then the Civil War, Lincoln's domestic agenda during the war was literally the revival of Clay's "American System"—a national banking system, direct aid for internal improvements, a new tariff system, and the definitive establishment of the Union as a single nation. Lincoln, the Whig-turned-Republican, set out a policy direction that governed Republican and national initiatives until 1932 and the advent of the New Deal, by which point American liberals had lost the old Whiggish confidence that commercial society could enrich and cultivate the personality. The Whig ideology, in its successive versions, played a significant (if frequently the minority) role in the history of Anglo-American political theory, and created an even more significant alternative in American affairs for the dominance of Jeffersonian and Jacksonian democracy.

See also **Nationalism** *(volume 2);* **Political Economy** *(volume 3); and other articles in this section.*

BIBLIOGRAPHY

Whig Origins

Appleby, Joyce. *Liberalism and Republicanism in the Historical Imagination.* Cambridge, Mass., 1992.

Bailyn, Bernard. *The Ideological Origins of the American Revolution.* Cambridge, Mass., 1967.

Colbourn, H. Trevor. *The Lamp of Experience: Whig History and the Intellectual Origins of the American Revolution.* Chapel Hill, N.C., 1965.

Pocock, J. G. A. *The Machiavellian Moment: Florentine Political Thought and the Atlantic Republican Tradition.* Princeton, N.J., 1975.

Wood, Gordon S. *The Radicalism of the American Revolution.* New York, 1992.

The American Whigs and the Second Whig Ideology

American Review (vols. 1–10) and *American Whig Review* (vols. 11–16). January 1845–December 1852.

Ashworth, John. *Slavery, Capitalism, and Politics in the Antebellum Republic.* Cambridge, Mass., 1995.

Beecher, Lyman. *Autobiography, Correspondence, etc., of Lyman Beecher.* Edited by Charles Beecher. 2 vols. New York, 1865.

Brown, Thomas. *Politics and Statesmanship: Essays on the American Whig Party.* New York, 1985.

Brownlow, William G. *Political Register, Setting Forth the Principles of the Whig and Locofoco Parties in the United States with the Life and Public Services of Henry Clay.* 1844.

Carwardine, Richard J. *Evangelicals and Politics in Antebellum America.* New Haven, Conn., 1993.

Choate, Rufus. *The Works of Rufus Choate, with a Memoir of His Life.* Edited by Samuel Gilman Brown. 2 vols. 1862.

Clay, Henry. *The Papers of Henry Clay.* Edited by J. F. Hopkins et al. 10 vols. Lexington, Ky., 1959– .

Fessenden, Francis. *Life and Public Services of William Pitt Fessenden.* 2 vols. Boston and New York, 1907.

Holt, Michael F. *Political Parties and American Political Development from the Age of Jackson to the Age of Lincoln.* Baton Rouge, La., 1992.

——. *The Rise and Fall of the American Whig Party: Jacksonian Politics and the Onset of the Civil War.* New York, 1999.

Howe, Daniel Walker. *Making the American Self: Jonathan Edwards to Abraham Lincoln.* Cambridge, Mass., 1997.

——. *The Political Culture of the American Whigs.* Chicago, 1979.

Howe, Daniel Walker, ed. *The American Whigs: An Anthology.* New York, 1973. An excellent anthology of Whig writings, including Clay, Everett, Webster, Biddle, Barnard, Beecher, Choate, Sumner, and Lincoln.

Kennedy, John Pendleton. *Political and Official Papers.* New York, 1872.

Lincoln, Abraham. *The Collected Works of Abraham Lincoln.* Edited by Roy P. Basler. 8 vols. New Brunswick, N.J., 1953.

Ormsby, Robert McKinley. *A History of the Whig Party.* Boston, 1860.

Poage, George Rawlings. *Henry Clay and the Whig Party.* Chapel Hill, N.C., 1936.

Remini, Robert V. *Henry Clay: Statesman for the Union.* New York, 1991.

Sumner, Charles. *The Selected Letters of Charles Sumner.* Edited by Beverly Wilson Palmer. 2 vols. Boston, 1990.

Thompson, Charles M. *The Illinois Whigs before 1846.* Urbana, Ill., 1915.

THE NEW ENGLAND THEOLOGY FROM EDWARDS TO BUSHNELL

Joseph A. Conforti

The decades that extend from Jonathan Edwards's ministry in the middle of the eighteenth century to Horace Bushnell's in the middle of the nineteenth constitute perhaps the most theologically creative period in American religious history. Edwards's voluminous writings gave birth to the New England Theology, the only distinctively American school of Calvinism. The New England Theology evolved in the aftermath of what has been called the Great Awakening, a series of religious revivals that swept through New England and other colonies in the early 1740s. Edwards devoted lengthy volumes to explaining and defending the theological implications of revival religion, which emphasized the need for spiritual rebirth. Edwards attracted clerical followers who extended his theological work in a movement that became known as the New Divinity. Responding to Enlightenment rationalism and Revolutionary republicanism, Edwards's disciples developed a Calvinist theology that emphasized moral accountability, promoted revivalistic religion, encouraged Christian activism, and remained vital well into the nineteenth century. Edwards and his New Divinity students made significant contributions to the theological development of evangelical Protestant America in the nineteenth century. Horace Bushnell's influential writings, however, signaled the demise of the New England Theology and its American Calvinist tradition.

EDWARDS AND THE GREAT AWAKENING

Edwards's revivalistic preaching and writings transformed the Northampton, Massachusetts, Congregational minister into an intellectual spokesman for evangelical Calvinism. In the mid-1730s, Edwards led revivals in Northampton and other Connecticut River Valley towns and described this religious stir in *A Faithful Narrative of the Surprising Work of God in the Conversion of Many Hundred Souls* (1737).

Edwards's account stands as the first American revival narrative—the first detailed report of a series of spiritual awakenings. Edwards's *Faithful Narrative* would be frequently reprinted, especially in the revivalistic era of the early nineteenth century. The volume became a model for subsequent revival narratives, an important form of religious writing that was used to publicize and encourage the spread of religious conversion.

The religious "harvests" of the mid-1730s were followed by more geographically extensive revivals in the early 1740s—a "Great Awakening"—in New England. The brilliant and prolific Edwards emerged as the leading interpreter of the Awakening's theological significance; he also defended revivalistic Calvinism against its critics. As a result, Edwards produced major theological works whose influence reverberated in American religious and intellectual life for a century.

In his *Treatise concerning Religious Affections* (1746), Edwards confronted the question of what constitutes authentic, divine-inspired piety, or, in other words, how does the believer gain some assurance that saving grace has been experienced? The question acquired a religious urgency in the 1740s. The revivals of the Great Awakening had provoked emotional outbursts, including shrieks and groans of spiritually aroused worshipers. Most disturbing, the Awakening had given birth to spiritually self-assured believers; these radicals often attacked ministers who did not enthusiastically support revivalism. Such excesses persuaded rationalist critics that the Awakening was not an outpouring of supernatural grace but an unleashing of natural emotions that threatened to subvert reason.

Edwards's challenge in *Religious Affections,* then, was to offer a balanced theological defense of the Awakening's evangelical religion and of true holiness. On the one hand, Edwards had to disarm rationalist critics of revivalistic religion; on the other, he had to admonish so-called antinomians, participants in the Awakening whose confidence in their

JONATHAN EDWARDS, 1703–1758

Jonathan Edwards is widely recognized as the most important religious thinker America has produced. But Edwards is also popularly perceived as a fire and brimstone preacher, the last powerful Puritan and a precursor of modern biblical Fundamentalists and perhaps even of television evangelists. Edwards's graphic revival sermon, "Sinners in the Hands of an Angry God," is widely used in high school and college texts as a prime example of his thought and writings. The sermon, with its famous comparison of the sinner's peril to that of a spider suspended by a thread over a blazing pit, enables modern readers, unfamiliar with the religious world from which Edwards emerged, to categorize him as a fiery, even fanatical Puritan. But Edwards was a complex man of daunting intellect and deep piety, characteristics that he displayed at an early age.

Born in East Windsor, Connecticut, in 1703, Edwards was the only son in a family of eleven children. His father, Timothy, was the Congregational minister in East Windsor, and his mother, Esther, was the daughter of Solomon Stoddard, a renowned pastor in Northampton, Massachusetts, who was sometimes called "the pope of the Connecticut River Valley." Edwards followed his father and grandfather into the Congregational ministry.

Edwards graduated from Yale in 1720 at the age of seventeen and remained at the college for two more years preparing for the ministry. During these years Edwards kept a diary that consisted of a series of "Resolutions" that documented his intense introspection. He sought the signs of true holiness in his religious experience and struggled to mold his behavior to a lofty standard of self-denying Christian virtue. In his "Personal Narrative," a lyrical account of his youthful conversion that was written years later (in 1739), Edwards recorded the doubt and hope that framed his religious life. In much of his theological writing Edwards would return to the issues raised by his early religious experience and his quest to distinguish authentic from false religion in his own heart and behavior.

In 1727 Edwards moved to Northampton to assist his grandfather as associate minister of the First Congregational Church. Two years later Solomon Stoddard died, and Edwards succeeded to the pastorate. His grandfather had been a successful revivalist. By the mid-1730s, Edwards led his own revivals in Northampton and in other towns in the Connecticut Valley; he was beginning to emerge from the long shadows cast by both his grandfather and his father.

When the Great Awakening erupted in New England in the early 1740s, Edwards was already acknowledged as an authority on evangelical Calvinism. The Awakening transformed Edwards into a national and international religious figure. Writings such as *Some Thoughts concerning the Present Revival of Religion* (1742) reached a broad audience. People flocked to Northampton seeking his spiritual counsel. Ministerial candidates sought out his theological guidance. Edwards had attained a reputation and level of influence that even his illustrious grandfather had not achieved. But Edwards's personal fortunes quickly spiraled downward.

In New England, the Great Awakening receded by 1744. Troubles in Edwards's own church, which he often did not handle like a skilled pastor, soon consumed the famous preacher. In particular, Edwards insisted that only spiritually converted members were eligible to receive communion, a position that overturned the

CONTINUED NEXT PAGE

practices of his grandfather. Strife accelerated in the church that had been in the vanguard of revivalism. In 1750 Edwards was dismissed by his congregation.

A year later he accepted a position as a missionary to the Indians in Stockbridge, Massachusetts. The distinguished divine labored in exile in what was then a frontier outpost. In addition to preaching to the Native American residents of Stockbridge and trying to defend them against land-hungry white settlers, Edwards continued his theological writing. Indeed, during the Stockbridge years Edwards produced some of his most important theological works, including *Freedom of the Will.*

Edwards's writings and the assistance of his clerical supporters helped win his release from exile in Stockbridge. Edwards was offered the presidency of the College of New Jersey (later renamed Princeton), and he assumed the position in early 1758. Within weeks, however, the renowned Calvinist theologian died from a smallpox inoculation. Edwards perished well short of his fifty-fifth birthday and while he appeared to be at the height of his intellectual power. But his writings and ideas would shape American theology and revivalism for decades.

personal piety seemed to place them above the human laws of this world. Edwards defined "affections" as inclinations or exercises of the heart or will (what we might call "motives"). Saving grace did not alter the understanding, that is, the individual's rational faculty; it reoriented the affections. Edwards rejected a rationalist theology of conversion prominent among critics of the Awakening. Conversion involved a shift from self-centered affections to a new spiritual sense of the excellency and sovereignty of God. Supernatural grace transformed selfish, sinful inclinations into self-denying, holy affections centered on a love of God.

Edwards defined conversion out from under the rationalist critics of the Awakening. But he also interpreted the "signs" of holy affections in ways that undermined the spiritual smugness and moral complacency of believers who saw their moment of conversion as the culmination of salvation. For Edwards conversion—the transformation of the affections—only marked the beginning of a life of Christian action. Holy affections manifested themselves in self-denial, charity, and meekness—what Edwards described as "evangelical humility"—not spiritual pride or self-indulgence. Edwards made Christian practice "the chief of all signs of grace, both as an evidence of the sincerity of professors unto others, and also to their own consciences" (*Works,* vol. 2, p. 406). In a rebuke to the spiritual antinomians of the Awakening, Edwards insisted that sanctified behavior as a sign of holy affections was "much to be preferred to the method of first convictions, enlightenings and comforts in conver-

sion, or any immanent discoveries of grace whatsoever, that begin and end in contemplation" (*Works,* vol. 2, p. 426).

Thus the Awakening compelled Edwards to develop a theology that located conversion in the heart or will, not the understanding, and that linked this internal change of affections to Christian practice. Edwards reiterated this theology in works such as *The Nature of True Virtue* (1765), in which he defined authentic holiness as affections and behavior rooted in disinterested benevolence "or selfless-love" toward God and his creation. Edwards bequeathed a major intellectual legacy to the architects of the New England Theology who succeeded him. He gave the evangelical Calvinist theologians, revivalists, and reformers who extended his ideas a powerful interpretation of the inner workings of saving grace on the affections and a summons to Christian practice in the world. Even more important, Edwards formulated an understanding of freedom of the will in ways that brilliantly developed the evangelical Calvinism of works like *Religious Affections.*

Where *Religious Affections* sought to balance personal piety and Christian practice, Edwards's greatest work, *A Careful and Strict Inquiry into the Modern Prevailing Notions of that Freedom of the Will* (1754), attempted to reconcile moral accountability and determinism. Enlightenment critics offered a rationalist critique of evangelical Calvinism focusing on its determinism. Traditional Calvinism held that humans were born with the moral corruption of Adam's original sin. The human race was naturally depraved and could only be redeemed by

Jonathan Edwards. Philosopher, theologian, and critic of religious awakenings. LIBRARY OF CONGRESS

supernatural grace. But Calvinism seemed to rob humans of their moral accountability; they were not free to choose right from wrong, to elect salvation over damnation. Edwards, for example, held that humans' natural affections or inclinations of the will were corrupted by selfishness, the moral legacy of Adam's fall. Only divine intervention could regenerate human affections. As a result, the will was not self-determining; its moral choices were shaped by the corrupt or holy inclinations (affections) that lay behind it. Such a view of the will suggested that individuals were not free to choose sin or salvation. To eighteenth-century rationalists, Calvinism seemed to be an absurd theological system because in depriving people of freedom of the will it made them morally unaccountable for their behavior.

In *Freedom of the Will*, Edwards ingeniously reconciled Calvinist views of divine sovereignty and determinism with free will and moral accountability. Edwards brought about this reconciliation, and extended the psychology of *Religious Affections*, by carefully distinguishing natural from moral necessity.

For Edwards, natural necessity referred to physical and intellectual capacities. Individuals suffered under a necessary natural inability if they faced a physical or intellectual obstacle external to their will. A person cannot lift a thousand-pound boulder; an infant cannot solve complex mathematical problems. Such "cannots" of the natural world differed, however, from the "will not" of the moral realm. Moral necessity referred to the certainty between the affections—the inclinations, dispositions, or motives—behind the will and volition and actions. Moral necessity meant that individuals acted voluntarily, according to the disposition (the affections) of their wills. Human beings were free as long as they could do as they willed, that is, as long as they could act according to the affections or the inclination of their wills. Sinners were *naturally* able to repent; their moral inability only amounted to the lack of holy affections and therefore of the inclination to choose salvation over sin; their *cannot* was merely a *will* not.

Edwards believed that he had defended evangelical Calvinism against Enlightenment charges that it deprived individuals of their free will and thus of their moral accountability. "Edwards on the Will," as his weighty defense of Calvinism came to be called, inspired theological debate for the next century. *Freedom of the Will* proved to be a seminal text in the development of the New England Theology. Edwards suggested to his followers a means of protecting traditional Calvinist notions of divine sovereignty over creation while at the same time emphasizing the voluntary character of sin and the sinner's natural ability to repent. *Freedom of the Will, Religious Affections, The Nature of True Virtue,* and other works stimulated one of the most theologically creative movements in American religious history.

THE NEW DIVINITY MOVEMENT

During the Great Awakening, Edwards's preaching and writing brought him notoriety. He began to attract candidates for the ministry to his Northampton parsonage. These students became ministers and theologians who then acquired their own disciples, fashioning through their writing and instruction an influential movement that came to be called the "New Divinity." Samuel Hopkins (1721–1803), Joseph Bellamy (1719–1790), Jonathan Edwards Jr. (1745–1801), and Nathanael Emmons (1745–1840) were the most important followers of Edwards. The name "New Divinity" was coined by opponents who accused them of advocating novel and dangerous theological ideas drawn from Edwards.

Edwards's clerical disciples were not just skilled Calvinist theologians. Their mentor's work also encouraged them to promote religious revivals and to engage in the practice of true virtue—to exercise holy affections—in the world. But the New Divinity men were nonetheless ridiculed by their theological opponents as arid scholastics who lacked both Edwards's acumen and his vital piety. More often than not, the theological history of America from the decades after the colonial Awakening to the middle of the nineteenth century has involved a narrative that acknowledges Edwards's brilliance but diminishes his historical importance and dismisses his New Divinity adherents. In this view, the rise of religious rationalism under the influence of the Enlightenment, the emergence of Unitarianism in the early nineteenth century, and the birth of Transcendentalism at midcentury form the main lines of New England, and American, intellectual development. From this perspective, Edwards squandered his brilliance defending an outmoded and doomed Calvinist theological system that his New Divinity followers hurried to the grave.

Only recently have we come to appreciate that Edwards's theology had a long life and that his New Divinity followers developed a powerful Edwardsian Calvinist tradition that endured into the nineteenth century. Edwards died unexpectedly in 1758. He left incomplete and unpublished writings. His New Divinity students worked to extend, systematize, and apply Edwards's thought in ways that continued to revitalize Calvinism, encourage revivalism, and provide a rationale for religious reform. Edwards and his New Divinity disciples, then, made major contributions to the emergence of nineteenth-century evangelical America—the broad Protestant investment in individual conversion, religious revivalism, and Christian reform.

The New Divinity's doctrine of immediate conversion looked back to Edwards and forward to the revivalistic culture of the Second Great Awakening in the nineteenth century. Edwards's students rejected an older, gradual approach to spiritual regeneration, which urged people to rely on the so-called means of grace—prayer, Bible reading, and church attendance. Such a gradualist approach obscured how conversion could be experienced immediately. New Divinity theologians stressed that individuals possessed the natural ability to embrace the gospel immediately, but they lacked the will; they continued *willfully*, as Edwards argued, to resist the promise of salvation offered in the gospel. The doctrine of immediate conversion reveals how *Freedom of the Will* gave the New Divinity both a Calvinist definition of liberty and an evocative vocabulary that supported the evangelical work of the pulpit. By preaching that sinners can do what they will not do, New Divinity ministers promoted conversions and revivalistic religion.

The New Divinity position on immediate conversion was a direct application of Edwards's *Freedom of the Will*. But other New Divinity doctrines required an "improvement" of Edwards. The New Divinity men preferred to call themselves "Consistent Calvinists." They worked to extend to all the major tenets of Calvinism the kind of theological balance between divine sovereignty and human moral accountability that Edwards had developed in *Freedom of the Will*. To achieve this doctrinal consistency and to refute Enlightenment critics of Calvinism, the New Divinity had to extend Edwards's ideas to doctrines that he had not reinterpreted.

For example, Edwards's theological followers revised the traditional Calvinist understanding of the atonement to make the doctrine more compatible with their mentor's ideas. In the process, they incorporated the republican political discourse of the Revolutionary era into New Divinity theology. The accepted doctrine of the atonement held that Christ substituted for sinners, paid the penalty of their guilt with his crucifixion, and thereby satisfied the moral debt that was owed to God. As a consequence, Christ's righteousness was "imputed" or transferred to a limited portion of humankind, the "elect," who would be saved. But *Freedom of the Will* encouraged New Divinity theologians to view sin and salvation as personal, voluntary choices; moral evil and good were not transferable. Furthermore, the limited consequences of the atonement seemed to undermine Edwards's argument that all sinners possessed the natural ability to be saved.

The governmental theory of the atonement resolved these inconsistencies. Sin was a transgression of the divine law; a punishment—Christ's death—had to be exacted to defend the sanctity of God's moral government of the world. Christ's sacrifice was necessary to uphold the divine law, not to pay the moral debt of sinners. Moral good or evil could not be transferred. Christ's righteousness was not imputed to the elect; rather, his death enabled God to offer salvation to *all* sinners in a manner that was consistent with the rule of divine law.

The governmental theory of the atonement reconciled God's sovereignty and humans' moral accountability, just as *Freedom of the Will* had. Equally

209

important, the new understanding of the doctrine reflected elements of Revolutionary republican discourse, which suggests that Edwards's disciples were not closeted intellectuals but ministers engaged in the world and trafficking in eighteenth-century ideas that they deployed to shore up and revitalize Calvinism. Their theory of the atonement described God as a sovereign but not an arbitrary ruler. He was a moral governor of the universe who ruled according to divine law. The universal laws that framed God's government of the world established a kind of divine constitution that regulated the moral and natural order of the universe.

Important aspects of their theology encouraged New Divinity men to support both the American Revolution and the antislavery campaign that it promoted. Samuel Hopkins and other New Divinity ministers emerged as leaders of the Revolutionary antislavery cause. Slavery came to be seen not only as a sign of selfish affections and therefore as a betrayal of true holiness; it was also a violation of universal divine law that invited God's punishment. America was threatened with "enslavement" at the hands of the British. But America had the ability and the duty to eradicate slavery immediately, satisfy the requirements of divine law, and assure Providential blessing of the Revolution.

New Divinity ministers became strong supporters of the Constitution and of the Federalist Party. Yet their Revolutionary patriotism did not culminate in a nationalism that held up America as a chosen nation. The universalism of their theology made Edwards's disciples uneasy with the earlier Puritan belief that America was a covenanted nation—a country bound in a special relationship with God. From Enlightenment thinkers New Divinity theologians had accepted the idea that the moral and natural order of the universe was governed by divinely established law. All nations were rewarded or punished based on whether they adhered to God's moral law. America would be blessed or afflicted not as a uniquely covenanted nation but because it, like all nations, was subject to divine law. Even though the Constitution incorporated compromise over slavery and the slave trade, New Divinity ministers supported ratification while expressing moral reservations. Their New Divinity theology restrained its advocates' Revolutionary nationalism.

In the decades after the Revolution, New Divinity theology helped propel Edwards's disciples to the forefront of other reform movements in addition to the campaign against slavery. They led the foreign missionary cause from its home base in New England, for example. Edwardsian missionaries drew inspiration from a stock of theological ideas: the definition of true holiness as consisting of self-denying, benevolent affections and practice; the universalism of the moral government theory of the atonement, which held that the offer of salvation was extended to all sinners; and the evangelical impulse derived from the belief that sinners possessed the natural ability to repent. Such Edwardsian doctrines, rooted in the evangelicalism of the colonial Awakening, also thrust the New Divinity men into the front ranks of the Second Great Awakening in New England, which began in the 1790s and continued through the first three decades of the nineteenth century. Thus the New Divinity men fashioned an evangelical Calvinist tradition whose vitality persisted long after Edwards's death.

SEMINARIES, NATHANIEL W. TAYLOR, AND THE NEW HAVEN THEOLOGY

Following Edwards's example and colonial practice, New Divinity ministers accepted clerical aspirants into their parsonages for theological study. Joseph Bellamy and Nathanael Emmons were particularly popular teachers, instructing nearly two hundred ministers between them. New Divinity theologians' commitment to clerical instruction helps explain how Edwards's ideas were extended across time. Ministers and their students coalesced into a New Divinity community of intellectuals who generated and circulated religious ideas and writings.

The rise of seminaries in the early nineteenth century transformed the study of theology, preparation for ministry, and communities of religious intellectuals. Theological instruction became more professional and academic. A new clerical figure—the seminary minister-professor—appeared and recast the old town parson–theologian's claim to intellectual leadership. Seminaries published their own journals, where religious discussion and debate took place. In nineteenth-century evangelical America, seminaries developed into the leading centers of intellectual life.

Andover Seminary in Massachusetts, America's first postgraduate theological school, opened in 1808. Between that date and 1836, thirteen more seminaries and divinity schools were founded, including Princeton (1812), Harvard (1816), and Yale (1822). Andover was cofounded by Edwards's New Divinity adherents, who came to dominate the seminary. Andover developed into antebellum America's largest seminary. It transmitted the New England Theology to hundreds of ministers, sent scores of graduates into nineteenth-century religious reform movements such as the Bible and Sunday School societies, and served as the center of the foreign missionary movement. Andover had been established in part as a reaction to the growing theological liberalism of Harvard College, which was the center of American Unitarianism. A rational, Enlightenment faith, Unitarianism rejected Calvinist dogma such as belief in the moral corruption of the human race. Unitarians, therefore, disdained revivalism, dismissed the need for a radical transformation of a believer's affections, and denied the divinity of Christ. As the leading evangelical Calvinist seminary in America, Andover led the intellectual defense of the New England Theology and of revivalistic religion against Unitarian onslaughts.

Other seminaries did as well. Edwards's writings continued to inspire these evangelical schools to defend Calvinism against nineteenth-century critics. Nathaniel W. Taylor, the leading proponent of the so-called New Haven Theology of the Yale Divinity School, stands out as one of the most important nineteenth-century "improvers" of the New England Theology.

The pastor of New Haven's First Congregational Church, Taylor joined the Yale Divinity School when it was formed in 1822. Committed to Calvinist tradition and the revivalism of the Second Great Awakening, Taylor, like Edwards's earliest New Divinity students, sought to extend the New England Theology's balance between divine sovereignty and human moral accountability in ways that would continue to promote conversions and revivals. The familiar Calvinist belief in the human race's natural depravity, which derived from Adam's original sin, struck Taylor as ill-suited to the "voluntaristic" republican religious and political culture of nineteenth-century America. Critics of Calvinism such as the Unitarians held up natural depravity as a moral grotesquerie. Even Edwards's *Freedom of the Will*, with its heralded analysis of natural and moral ability, had not fended off critics of natural depravity. While arguing for freedom of the will, Edwards clung to a heavily traditional Calvinist belief in depravity as an inborn corruption that people did not possess the natural ability to change. To Calvinism's nineteenth-century opponents, Edwards's view of the innate corruption of the human race suggested that his distinction between natural and moral ability was merely a semantic sleight of hand that did not establish human accountability.

Taylor's principal theological task, then, was to build on the work of earlier New Divinity "improvements" of Edwards and clearly reconcile the central arguments of *Freedom of the Will* with a new understanding of original sin. Taylor advanced a view of original sin that was consistent with the New England Theology's emphasis on the voluntary character of moral choices. With Taylor's revised, updated interpretation of "Consistent Calvinism," which he began systematically explaining in the 1820s, the New England Theology entered the final phase of its one-hundred-year history.

Taylor rejected the idea that the human race inherited a corrupt nature from Adam. Adam's sin merely provided God with the "occasion" for creating humans with selfish "affections," Taylor argued with Edwardsian terminology. The human race was not punished for Adam's sin; people were only responsible for their own sins. In fact, the selfish natural affections of human beings were not inherently sinful; they were simply the "occasion" of sin. That is, humans were not sinful by their nature but by their actions; before they "exercised" their selfish affections in moral agency, sinners were not guilty. For Taylor, sin consisted in sinning—in personal, voluntary choices of the will and not in some passive, corrupt human nature that existed prior to the exercise of the will.

Taylor extended the moral voluntarism of the New England Theology that was inspired by *Freedom of the Will*. He detached Edwards's notion of moral inability from its association with the old Calvinist idea of original sin. Human nature was morally neutral, comprising selfish affections that were not sinful in themselves. Through spiritual conversion these affections could be redirected toward love of God. But moral good, like sin, involved choice. The converted believer needed to exercise regenerated affections to become virtuous. Even as he significantly revised Edwards for a new revivalistic era, Taylor invoked language regarding the affections, moral voluntarism, and Christian practice that reflected his continuing attachment to Edwardsian theological tradition.

HORACE BUSHNELL AND THE DECLINE OF THE NEW ENGLAND THEOLOGY

By the middle of the nineteenth century, decades of theological debate had produced a richly textured Edwardsian Calvinist tradition. Moreover, far from smothering the fires of revivalism with a blanket of doctrinal abstractions, the New England Theology coexisted with and furnished Calvinist support for the Second Great Awakening. But the New England

THE TAYLOR-TYLER CONTROVERSY

Taylor's creative "improvements" to Edwardsian and Calvinist tradition won supporters and provoked critics. Lyman Beecher (1775–1863), one of Yale's most influential graduates and a leader of the Second Great Awakening, embraced the New Haven theology. Taylor, Beecher believed, offered an interpretation of Consistent Calvinism that neutralized Unitarian criticisms of the Edwardsians' doctrinal severity and that supported the evangelical work of the Second Great Awakening. Conservative Calvinists disagreed. Bennett Tyler emerged as Taylor's sharpest critic. He engaged Taylor in a "paper war" over the New Haven Theology, one of the most famous doctrinal disputes of the first half of the nineteenth century.

Tyler, a graduate of Yale, served as a Congregational minister in Connecticut and Maine and spent six years (1822–1828) as president of Dartmouth College. Tyler accused Taylor of abandoning traditional Calvinist interpretations of human depravity and original sin when the New Haven theologian argued that sin consisted in sinning rather than in a passive corrupt nature inherited from Adam. In 1833 Tyler and his conservative Calvinist supporters formed a new seminary, the Theological Institute of Connecticut (later renamed Hartford Theological Seminary), to counteract the influence of Taylor and Yale. From the presidency of the new seminary, Tyler defended Calvinist tradition and pursued his war of words with Taylor and advocates of the New Haven Theology.

A complex and prolonged doctrinal debate, the Taylor-Tyler controversy is sometimes viewed as evidence of a theological tradition that had run its course. Yet the dispute also suggests the importance of theology in nineteenth-century intellectual life and the way seminaries were institutions that generated new ideas and sparked controversy.

Theology and Calvinism in general were highly contested intellectual traditions in the nineteenth century. Seminaries waged an ongoing "paper war" over Calvinism, Edwards, the New Divinity, and the New Haven Theology. In addition, Unitarians kept up their rationalist critique of all Calvinist thought and of the revival system. While the Second Great Awakening receded after 1840, theological dispute intensified. In this context a new, powerful voice appeared in New England and offered a postrevival, post-Calvinist theology that signaled the end of the era inaugurated by the colonial Awakening one hundred years earlier.

Horace Bushnell was a native of Connecticut and a graduate of Yale Divinity School. He was ordained as the pastor of a Congregational church in Hartford, Connecticut, in 1833. But while he had studied under Nathaniel Taylor and had been converted in a revival in 1831, Bushnell rejected both the penetrating logical theological reasoning of New England tradition and the Edwardsian dependence on revivalism to advance religion. Bushnell developed important theological foundations for the liberal Protestantism that would emerge in the second half of the nineteenth century.

Bushnell was a church pastor, not a seminary professor. He was influenced by Romanticism and its emphasis on intuition and the inward-dwelling presence of God. Bushnell criticized the kind of religious investment in strict logical deduction and doctrinal systematizing that characterized the New England Theology. In major works such as *God in Christ* (1849) and *Christ in Theology* (1851), Bushnell challenged the dogmatic rationalism of both Calvinists and Unitarians whose goal was to produce logically consistent statements of religious belief. This scholastic impulse, a hallmark of the New England Theology and of seminaries, yielded creeds which led to divisive doctrinal disputes that undermined what Bushnell saw as the primary purpose of religion: the encouragement of a personal, spiritual relationship with God.

Bushnell was antidogmatic, not anti-intellectual. He emphasized the importance of an inwardly experienced God as the basis of Christian life. Therefore, he questioned the power of language, as in formal theological statements, to convey religious truths precisely and definitively. Even the language of the Bible was suggestive, metaphorical, poetic. Attempts to extract linguistic and doctrinal consistency from the Bible—to translate its often paradoxical truths into logical creedal statements—were ill-founded. Doctrinal creeds embodied partial religious truths that were amplified into dogmatic certainty, with resulting theological controversy. But neither authentic religious experience nor biblical language could be reduced to the kind of rational argumentation that characterized the New England Theology and seminary doctrinal polemics.

Bushnell also found fault with nineteenth-century revivalism, whose religious culture was so indebted to Edwards's writings. Revivals disrupted church life and made ministers who, like Bushnell, were not good preachers, appear to be deficient. Revivalism encouraged a boom-bust view of parish life. Revivals could not be sustained indefinitely; the inevitable retreat of revivalism was received as a discouraging sign of religious declension. Evangelical churches, Bushnell believed, had overinvested in revivalism and sudden conversion to sustain institutional growth.

In *Christian Nurture* (1847), his most famous book, Bushnell offered an antirevival alternative for churches. He advocated a return to a more gradual approach to conversion. From childhood to adulthood, the individual should be spiritually nurtured by a Christian community that extended from church to home. A child would "grow up as a Christian and never know himself as being otherwise" (Bushnell, p. 126). Conversion was redefined as spiritual growth over time, a faith sustained by communal institutions. The future of a church would not depend on revivalism nor require of believers a wrenching spiritual change. Even more than Taylor, his mentor, Bushnell's belief in Christian nurture relegated such Calvinist doctrines as natural depravity to a dogmatic past. Bushnell's controversial works announced a major intellectual departure from Edwards, the New England Theology, and Calvinism in general.

Bushnell's ideas pointed toward the liberal Protestantism that rapidly replaced evangelical Calvinism in the decades after the Civil War. In his rejection of biblical literalism, his belief that no denominational creed cornered the market on religious truth, and his emphasis on the social sources and practices of Christian faith, Bushnell left an important theological legacy for post–Civil War Protestantism. Bushnell helped silence the ghost of Jonathan Edwards and turn mainline Protestant denominations away from revivalism and toward a Social Gospel.

See also **Evangelical Thought** *(in this volume);* **Evangelical Protestants; New England; God, Nature, and Human Nature** *(volume 2);* **Organized Religion** *(volume 3); and other articles in this section.*

BIBLIOGRAPHY

Primary Sources

Bellamy, Joseph. *Works.* 3 vols. Edited by Tryon Edwards. Boston, 1850.

Bushnell, Horace. *Horace Bushnell* [Twelve Selections]. Edited by H. Shelton Smith. New York, 1965.

Edwards, Jonathan. *A Jonathan Edwards Reader.* Edited by John E. Smith, Harry S. Stout, and Kenneth Minkema. New Haven, Conn., 1995.

———. *Works.* 17 vols. Edited by Perry Miller. New Haven, Conn., 1957– .

Hopkins, Samuel. *The Works of Samuel Hopkins.* 3 vols. Edited by Edwards A. Park. Boston, 1852.

Taylor, Nathaniel W. *Lectures on the Moral Government of God.* 2 vols. New York, 1859.

Secondary Sources

Cherry, Conrad. *The Theology of Jonathan Edwards: A Reappraisal.* 1966. Reprint, Bloomington, Ind., 1990.

Conforti, Joseph A. *Jonathan Edwards, Religious Tradition, and American Culture.* Chapel Hill, N.C., 1995.

———. *Samuel Hopkins and the New Divinity Movement: Calvinism, the Congregational Ministry, and Reform in New England between the Great Awakenings.* Grand Rapids, Mich., 1981.

Guelzo, Allen C. *Edwards on the Will: A Century of American Theological Debate.* Middletown, Conn., 1989.

Haroutunian, Joseph. *Piety versus Moralism: The Passing of the New England Theology.* New York, 1932.

Hatch, Nathan O., and Harry S. Stout, eds. *Jonathan Edwards and the American Experience.* New York, 1988.

Jenson, Robert W. *America's Theologian: A Recommendation of Jonathan Edwards.* New York, 1988.

Kling, David W. *A Field of Divine Wonders: The New Divinity and Village Revivals in Northwestern Connecticut, 1792–1822.* University Park, Pa., 1993.

Kuklick, Bruce. *Churchmen and Philosophers: From Jonathan Edwards to John Dewey.* New Haven, Conn., 1985.

McDermott, Gerald R. *One Holy and Happy Society: The Public Theology of Jonathan Edwards.* University Park, Pa., 1992.

McLoughlin, William G. *Revivals, Awakenings, and Reform: An Essay on Religion and Social Change in America, 1607–1977.* Chicago, 1977.

Mead, Sidney Earl. *Nathaniel William Taylor, 1786–1888: A Connecticut Liberal.* Chicago, 1942.

Smith, David L. *Symbolism and Growth: The Religious Thought of Horace Bushnell.* Chico, Calif., 1981.

Stein, Stephen J., ed. *Jonathan Edwards's Writings: Text, Context, Interpretation.* Bloomington, Ind., University Press, 1996.

Tracy, Patricia J. *Jonathan Edwards, Pastor: Religion and Society in Eighteenth-Century Northampton.* New York, 1980.

Valeri, Mark. *Law and Providence in Joseph Bellamy's New England: The Origins of the New Divinity in Revolutionary America.* New York, 1994.

THE TRANSFORMATION OF AMERICAN RELIGION, 1776–1838

Mark Stoll

The American religious scene underwent a remarkable transformation between the Revolution and the era of Andrew Jackson. In 1776 the Congregationalist Church was dominant in New England, and the Church of England (or Anglican—then later Episcopal—Church) was the leading denomination elsewhere. These churches tended to be officially established: ministers were supported in all colonies by public taxes, and many, especially in New England, were educated and trained at public expense as well. The dominant theology was Calvinism. Other denominations and sects—Presbyterians, Quakers, Huguenots, Catholics, Dutch and German Reformed, and various German sects—like the leading churches, had their origins in Europe. One-fifth of the settled population, the African slaves, was largely non-Christian.

Sixty years later, the Methodist and the Baptist churches, which had been tiny before the Revolution, had become by far the two largest denominations. Moreover the Campbellites, or Disciples of Christ, who did not exist at all in 1776, had taken a place among the major denominations. From Campbellites to Mormons to Transcendentalists, new American-born denominations and religious movements proliferated. With establishment a thing of the past, churches competed freely for members in the religious "marketplace," in which the Episcopal, Congregational, and Presbyterian churches steadily lost "market share." Calvinism was in eclipse, and Arminianism was triumphant. The "up-start" churches often downplayed theological training, and many congregations selected ministers according to spiritual and oratorical gifts rather than formal education. Evangelization of African slaves proceeded rapidly. An intense religion-mindedness electrified the nation, with dramatic effects on politics, gender roles, and social movements, whose issues now often became moral issues. If a number of religious groups that would emerge as significant in the twentieth century—for instance, Pentecostals, Catholics, and Jews (only

15,000 in 1840)—had yet to become consequential, nevertheless during this period American religion took on a shape far more recognizable today than the religious world of the colonial era.

These religious changes paralleled the remarkable changes in American political and social life between the Revolution and the Age of Jackson. While the seeds of change had certainly been sown in the colonies, the American Revolution brought them into dramatic and rapid fruition. Change worked more rapidly in the South than in the North and in the West than in the East, but change came everywhere. The rhetoric of revolution and independence and the principles of republicanism undermined the legitimacy of established churches. Republican faith in the virtue of the yeoman farmer evolved into Jacksonian celebration of the common man, which undercut distinctions based on education and wealth. As the common white man participated more and more in politics, so did the common person press to participate in decisions relating not only to ecclesiology and theology but also and especially to his or her own salvation. The consequence was a religious scene fitted to a self-confident, aggressive democratic republic.

RELIGION AND REVOLUTION

The Revolution itself favored some denominations over others. Congregationalists, Presbyterians, Lutherans, and Catholics enthusiastically supported resistance to British tyranny. Congregationalists' Dissenter heritage, not to mention their Puritan ancestors' participation in two seventeenth-century revolutions, excited revolutionary ardor. Particularly in the early years of the conflict, many New Englanders also interpreted events to mean that the millennium was near, which redoubled their fervor. The war did, however, force New Englanders to consider new viewpoints: France's 1777 alliance with Americans against Britain induced them to

CALVINISM

Calvinism, named for the sixteenth-century French theologian John Calvin, was the dominant Protestant theology outside of Lutheran areas. In 1619 Protestant divines convened in the Dutch city of Dort to consider a challenge against Calvinism brought by Arminians, the advocates of the Dutch theologian Jacob Armin. The Synod of Dort condemned Arminianism as unscriptural and reaffirmed what became known as the "Five Points of Calvinism." These were:

1. *Total Depravity:* Due to Original Sin, humans cannot by themselves comprehend the Gospel.

2. *Unconditional Election:* God chooses certain individuals (the "elect") for salvation solely from his own sovereign will.

3. *Limited Atonement:* Christ's redeeming work and atoning death save the elect only.

4. *Irresistible Grace:* Individuals cannot reject God's saving grace.

5. *Perseverance of the Saints:* Those who receive God's grace will be saved.

During the reign of Elizabeth I, the Church of England tended toward Calvinism but stopped short of adopting it in its official statement of theological principle, the Thirty-Nine Articles. However, under James I and Charles I, the Church of England moved toward Arminianism. While some Puritans were Arminian, the majority fiercely defended Calvinism, which in turn became the orthodox theology of Puritan New England. Later Puritans, such as Cotton Mather and Jonathan Edwards, blended Calvinism with current European philosophical and scientific ideas. Edwards also adapted Calvinism for the revivals of the Great Awakening of the 1730s and 1740s.

By the early nineteenth century the Five Points were the subject of intense controversy. Arminians denied the first four points and believed that humans respond to God's initiative: God provides salvation for all, but only those who freely choose it will be saved. Methodists denied the fifth point and affirmed the possibility of a fall from grace.

bury their traditional virulent anti-Catholicism. (Later Protestant revivals brought the embers to life again: anti-Catholicism burst forth in 1834 riots and burning of the Ursuline Convent in Massachusetts.) Scots-Irish Presbyterians, German Lutherans, and Catholics had long had either little love for or loyalty to the English crown.

Tied to Tory mother churches, Anglicans and Methodists suffered divided loyalties during the Revolution that left them weakened at the war's end. In the years just preceding 1776, some Anglicans had pressed hard for an American bishop, who would eliminate certain difficulties such as having to send candidates for ordination to England and would strengthen ties to the English church. Yet as the colonies grew increasingly estranged from Brit-

ain, the bishop controversy engendered suspicion of motives. Its loyalty divided, the Anglican church lay vulnerable to the drive to disestablish religion, which culminated in 1786 when deistic elite including Thomas Jefferson and James Madison, in concert with Baptists (led by Isaac Backus) and Presbyterians, ended the long reign of Anglicanism as Virginia's established church. Methodism lost most of its prewar clergy, and some churches in the southern Piedmont seceded and reorganized without bishops as Republican Methodists.

The battle to disestablish the Anglican Church had sweeping implications. In the mood of the 1770s, when the states were eliminating vestiges of the old regime and experimenting with new forms of state and society, established churches every-

216

where found themselves on the defensive. Old and new arguments about freedom of conscience and the free competition of religious claims before the bar of public opinion persuaded the legislatures of one state after another to disestablish religion and influenced Madison's phrasing of the First Amendment to the Constitution after 1789. Patriotism, clerical influence, and public support of Congregationalism protected the established position of that church for a generation, but between 1817 (New Hampshire) and 1833 (Massachusetts) even the New England states ended tax support for churches.

Churches struggled to define themselves after independence. Devastated by the Revolution, the Anglican church ordained its first American bishop in 1784 and restructured itself as the Protestant Episcopal Church in 1793 with organizing principles that pointed toward significant democratization: lay representation, elected bishops, and strong local vestries. Methodists organized an independent American church in 1784. In 1788 Presbyterians adopted a new constitution with a new American structure of presbyteries, synods, and a general assembly. The Dutch Reformed Church formalized its existing independence in a reorganization of 1792–1794. The Vatican selected the Reverend John Carroll of Maryland to lead the American Catholic Church in 1784, authorized American priests to elect him bishop in 1789, and made him archbishop in 1808. Carroll pressed for the elevation of an American as the first American bishop because a foreign-born bishop was not as likely to be as sympathetic as he to republicanism and would not understand the unique situation of the American Catholic church in a heavily Protestant country. Due to a shortage of priests, Carroll initiated trusteeism, a kind of congregationalism that was unique to American Catholicism.

RATIONALISM ASCENDANT

Popular interest in revivals and theological issues appeared at low ebb in the generation after the Revolution, although there were some revival flurries around 1780 and 1790. Ministers across the nation bemoaned religious coldness and indifference. The vital political and military issues of the day distracted the people and attracted intellectual energy from religion. Also, as British power crumbled, obstacles to westward movement vanished and southerners left the poorer land of the Piedmont for rich lands in Kentucky and Tennessee. The depleted and

empty congregations left in their wake had difficulty sustaining the evangelism and revivals that had spread and strengthened Baptist and other churches in the region.

Enlightenment rationalism abetted religious liberalism and skepticism not only among the educated elite but among all classes. The Reverend Lyman Beecher later recalled that it seemed as if every farmboy was reading Thomas Paine's skeptical and deistic *Age of Reason* (1794). Many urban Congregational churches moved toward Unitarianism. In 1805 Unitarians took over Harvard University, founded in 1636 to train Puritan ministers, and in response, orthodox Calvinists led by Jedidiah Morse in 1808 founded Andover Theological Seminary, the first American graduate school for theology. After 1819, William Ellery Channing took the lead in proclaiming Unitarian principles. Unitarians believed that the American was a new Adam, humanity's great second chance, sinless and innocent, a free agent capable of working out his own salvation. They doubted the divinity of Jesus and tended toward belief in universal salvation. More strongly than revivalists, Unitarians emphasized philanthropy, humanitarianism, civic concern, and education. The "New England Renaissance" of the mid-nineteenth century, in which William Cullen Bryant, Henry Wadsworth Longfellow, James Russell Lowell, and Oliver Wendell Holmes were leading figures, was also a flowering of Unitarianism.

Unitarians were primarily located in urban Massachusetts, but rationalists like Jefferson hoped that Unitarianism would replace Anglicanism as the dominant southern church; ministers across the nation noted significant numbers of skeptics, deists, and rationalists. Many Revolution-era leaders, including Jefferson as well as Benjamin Franklin and John Adams, abandoned orthodox Christianity to become deists and Unitarians, if rarely atheists. Jefferson, for example, would later edit miracles and resurrection out of the Gospels, leaving the sermons and parables, to re-create what he thought was the truest version of Jesus' life, undistorted by later hands.

Although it is clear in retrospect that events were passing them by, the turn of the nineteenth century was the era of the last of the great theologians of the Puritan tradition. With Yale as their bastion, proponents of the New Divinity included Joseph Bellamy, Samuel Hopkins, Jonathan Edwards Jr., and Nathanael Emmons. They continued the task of the senior Jonathan Edwards: bringing the Enlightenment to Calvinist theology and keeping Ed-

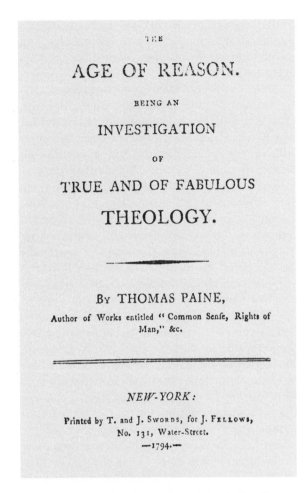

The Age of Reason **by Thomas Paine (1794).** "I believe in the equality of man; and I believe that religious duties consist in doing justice, loving mercy, and endeavoring to make our fellow creatures happy. . . . I do not believe in the creed professed by . . . any church that I know of. My own mind is my own church." LIBRARY OF CONGRESS

wardsian revival theology alive and available for the coming revivals.

THE SECOND GREAT AWAKENING BEGINS: THE SOUTH

In the 1790s, the anticlerical excesses of the French Revolution terrified and galvanized the New England clergy, who were certain that Jefferson and his party threatened the same purpose in the United States. Several clergymen led small, local revivals between 1797 to 1801, including some at Yale organized by its president, Timothy Dwight. These revivals were the first glimmerings of that religious explosion called the Second Great Awakening. Although its roots lay in the First Great Awakening that began in New England in the 1730s and 1740s,

the Second Great Awakening burst into life not in New England, but on the western frontier, a rough, profane region where easterners despaired that religion would ever prosper.

In the late 1790s, Presbyterian ministers invited Methodist preachers to join in traditional Scots-Irish extended communion celebrations at many small churches throughout central Kentucky. There, as previously along the Piedmont and in Scotland, these days-long affairs erupted into emotional revivals accompanied by fainting and fits of shaking. At an 1800 communion service organized by James McGready in Gasper Ridge, Kentucky, several wagonloads of people arrived prepared to camp for the duration of the services, and the "camp meeting" was born.

Camp meetings of all sizes appeared all over the region in 1801. The most famous (or notorious) was a weeklong revival organized by Barton W. Stone at Cane Ridge, Kentucky. Thousands showed up, perhaps ten thousand on Sunday, the largest day, and perhaps twenty thousand over the week, astonishing numbers for the scattered rural population of the time. People of all races and classes were caught up in the excitement, with Presbyterian and some Methodist ministers preaching sermons day and night, and "exhorters" and Baptist preachers preaching to crowds all over the grounds. (Exhorters were laymen who worked with ministers to encourage revival participants through the conversion experience.) Hundreds fainted, some spoke or laughed unintelligibly, and others shook, or "jerked," in religious excitement.

Organizers praised Cane Ridge as the "greatest outpouring of the spirit since Pentecost." While some East Coast commentators acclaimed this extraordinary event as the dramatic beginning of religion in a godless region, others condemned its emotional excesses or ascribed them to Satan. But Cane Ridge unleashed a new, aggressive evangelicalism in the South, marked by itinerant evangelists and use of the camp meeting. It also engendered controversy and schism. Prorevival Presbyterians under Stone joined some Republican Methodists to form the "Christian" or "Stonite" movement. Another Presbyterian schism produced the prorevival Cumberland Presbyterian denomination.

Methodists had no problem with the emotional outpourings and, indeed, tried to keep the revival spirit alive in their regular meetings. Led by the tireless Francis Asbury, they adopted the camp meeting with enthusiasm, which along with their circuit-rider system made them the nation's largest denomination by 1840. Baptists, too, profited by the reviv-

THE CAMP MEETING

Perfectly suited to the rural South, camp meetings took place in forest clearings. Organizers prepared the scene by constructing a raised platform before rows of benches. Revivalists would stay in tents or wagons around the perimeter. An aisle through the middle of the congregation divided the sexes, men on one side, women on the other. Daytime was taken up by hymn singing, prayers, testimony, and didactic preaching. The real work of conversion went on at night. Bonfires and candles lent an unearthly glow to the scene, especially for rural folk unused to staying up late. A few benches known as "mourners' benches" were reserved at the front. As the preacher's sermon rose in intensity, decrying the congregations' sins and urging change of heart before it was too late, he invited the moaning, weeping (and often fainting and shaking) sinners to come forward to the reserved benches. There he and other preachers and lay exhorters moved in to aid the "mourners" with prayer and encouragement through conversion to salvation.

Some elements, such as conversion and individual testimony, would have been familiar to the Puritans, while others, like exhorters, itinerant preachers, shortened stages of conversion, and the emphasis on religion of the heart rather than the head, were legacies of the First Great Awakening. The outdoor camp meeting (appropriate for rural areas with few, small churches) and mourners' benches were innovations. Decidedly un-Puritan was the self-consciously Arminian theology of many preachers. Democratic-republican America had no use for a theology that allowed no self-determination, particularly in an area as important as one's personal salvation, and predestination, particularly of infants, appeared cruel. A popular anti-Calvinist satire ran,

> You can and you can't,
> You will and you won't,
> You're damned if you do,
> And you're damned if you don't.

als, although they made less use of camp meetings. Their rejection of educated ministers in favor of farmer-preachers and their congregational polity was both practical and appealing to the scattered settlers of the frontier and the South. In 1801 Presbyterians worked out a Plan of Union with Congregationalists to deal with the problems of rapid frontier growth. Nevertheless, Presbyterians, who retained an educated ministry, examined converts for doctrinal correctness, and clung to their official Calvinism, grew but slowly and lost their initial numerical frontier advantage.

EVANGELICALS, SLAVERY, AND AFRICAN AMERICANS

At first southern evangelism tended toward a fervent opposition to the institution of slavery. Early Baptists, Methodists, and many prorevival Presbyterians regarded slave ownership as unchristian. This view raised so much hostility that over time evangelists accommodated their message to southern society, arriving at positions on slavery from silence to outright support. These young, upstart churches also faced considerable opposition in their desire to proselytize slaves. Slave owners had a variety of reasons to oppose Christianizing their slaves. Many feared that the implications of equality in the church might ultimately make their slaves intractable, a fear amplified by the prospect of slaves gaining literacy in order to read the Bible. The fact that several slave revolts, including the notorious 1831 rebellion of Nat Turner, were plotted at religious gatherings gave many southerners pause. To win over slave owners, by the 1830s evangelicals asserted that Christianity's black converts made better

Religious Camp Meeting. Watercolor by J. Maze Burbank (c. 1839). Place and date are unknown, but the artist worked "from a sketch taken on the spot." OLD DARTMOUTH HISTORICAL SOCIETY—NEW BEDFORD WHALING MUSEUM, NEW BEDFORD, MASS.

slaves because they had absorbed the proper message of Christian meekness and Pauline obedience to masters. The evangelical effort downplayed literacy altogether. Often converted themselves, slave owners increasingly relented. Nevertheless, black Christianity developed essentially in isolation from whites, to such a large degree that scholars sometimes call the black church an "invisible" institution.

It was during this period that the first independent black churches and black denominations began to form. The first black congregations were Baptist, formed in the middle eighteenth century. Unequal treatment by white Methodists in Philadelphia led dissatisfied blacks under Richard Allen to establish the African Methodist Episcopal Church by 1816, and in New York blacks organized the African Methodist Episcopal Zion Church in 1821. Not surprisingly, both denominations strongly emphasized abolitionism.

Many African Americans found the emotional tenor of the Second Great Awakening revivals quite congenial and similar to half-remembered African religious forms. They attended camp meetings and church, although they were restricted to the back benches and church galleries. In the Deep South blacks often outnumbered whites at religious gatherings. Slaves took Christianity, conformed it to the still active elements of African culture alive in the slave quarters, and created a syncretic Christianity unlike any church in white America. They identified with the unjust sufferings of Jesus, the slavery, trials, and liberation of Moses and Israel, and the message of salvation for the meek and powerless, and they made Christianity an element of racial unity. They added Africanisms like the ring shout and the call-and-response spiritual. Black congregations responded to preaching in vocal and musical ways that had no precedent in European-American religion. Many whites disapproved strongly of these "heathen" changes to their churches, but the presence of blacks at camp meetings and in churches had an inevitable and considerable influence. By the twentieth century, for example, white southern church hymnals were full of spirituals and call-and-response music. The Christianization of African Americans had its counterpart in the Africanization of American Christianity.

THE SECOND GREAT AWAKENING: THE NORTH

The political and military concerns of the War of 1812 quieted revivalism, but it also heightened awareness that Americans seemed to have fallen far from their view of themselves as a moral example to the nations. The war ended with much discussion about Americans' need for moral reform. The great popularity of Parson Mason Locke Weems's famous moral tales of George Washington—"I cannot tell a lie"—reflected widespread concern about the moral improvement of American youth. Magnified moral concern provided fertile ground for an explosive religious awakening.

The Second Great Awakening manifested itself in the North dramatically after 1814. The war ended British support for Indian resistance west of the Alleghenies, which, combined with the building of the Erie Canal and population pressures in New England, encouraged a huge movement out of New England, across upstate New York, and throughout the Great Lakes region. By the 1820s, as tumultuous frontier conditions (which inspired the name "burnt-over district" as an infertile place for religion) gave way to a more settled landscape, evangelists found the region ripe for revival. New York's leading revivalist, the Presbyterian minister Charles Grandison Finney, adapted camp-meeting tactics for an area with more towns and church buildings and publicized his formula as his "New Methods." At the invitation of local ministers, he would arrive in town to begin what he called the "protracted meeting," staying for several weeks. As he preached nightly at various churches around town, he would reserve the front pews as the "anxious bench" for the would-be Christians who were ready to receive the spirit. Women throughout the country were the foot soldiers of revival, bringing in doubtful or reluctant fathers, husbands, and sons to convert. Women in northern towns and cities, having the advantage of proximity, would visit door-to-door to bring in other women and organize prayer groups to plan the campaign. With their help, Finney and other revivalists enjoyed tremendous success in upstate New York cities, most spectacularly in Rochester in 1831.

Evangelists turned from their victories in small towns and farms to tackle the problem of the cities. The minister Lyman Beecher, one of Dwight's Yale converts, took a Boston congregation in 1826, but found that his revival message did not fall on fertile ground there. A wealthy merchant and abolitionist, Lewis Tappan, financed Finney's assault on New York in 1832, using a converted theater, Chatham Street Chapel. The architecture of a theater proved to be so practical and successful that in 1836 Finney had an amphitheater built, the Broadway Tabernacle. By the late 1830s, however, he realized that the revival was over, that he was not preaching to poor lost souls in need of salvation, but to the comfortable and converted. Nevertheless evangelicals, especially Methodists, did achieve success among urban working classes and artisans.

WOMEN AND RELIGION

Since the days of the Puritans, women underwent the majority of conversion experiences. As colonial church-attendance laws lapsed and establishment ended, ministers found themselves preaching to increasingly female congregations. Those in established churches found themselves no longer filling a state office but a profession funded by voluntary contributions. As most of the membership was female, ministers depended on women for much of the work of the church and for its financial support. Women's auxiliary groups became essential for the functioning of the church and later proved a training ground for women's participation in religious, benevolent, and reform societies, to which they similarly offered their numbers, energy, and skills. Still, few churches accepted women in leadership positions. An exception was domestic and foreign missionary work, in which women were often important figures.

Religion influenced changing concepts of women's social role, especially for middle-class women. As these women found themselves restricted to noneconomic activities such as child raising, housework, and church, the home became known as the women's "sphere." The men's sphere was outside the house, in active, less godly affairs like business and politics. Many saw women's separation from "amoral" economic activity and their greater involvement in churches as signs of spiritual superiority. "Angels of the home," women took responsibility for the moral uplift of their household, including husband and children. So significant to society were these roles that women for the first time regarded their activities and their sphere as equal to men's, a significant step toward modern equality of the sexes. Clergy and women themselves saw women's activity in the church and at home as essential to the evangelization of the nation. Indeed, Catharine Beecher, a popular women's author and the daughter of Lyman Beecher, reflected a widely held sentiment in describing women's contribution as crucial to preparation for the millennium itself.

NEW RELIGIOUS MOVEMENTS

The intense religious-mindedness of the age presented theological problems. Farmers had visions as they plowed or walked alone in the woods. While most were of a personal nature, what status ought churches grant such visions? Moreover, which church was a new Christian to join? Each denomination proclaimed itself to be the denomination truest to the Gospel and the Reformation, often to the exclusion of other churches. Denominations proliferated, creating confusion and anxiety among believers, who wanted the power of choice over their eternal destiny, but found themselves bewildered by the variety of choices.

Thomas Campbell and his son Alexander, immigrants from Scotland, offered a solution to this dilemma: a denomination that purported to be no denomination, calling itself simply "Christian." Rather than quibble over moot points of doctrine, Campbellites accepted all Christians who accepted just five basic points of Christian doctrine. This simple, commonsensical, broad-minded approach appealed to many, especially in the Ohio Valley, where the Campbellites won many converts and in 1832 were joined by Barton Stone's followers. However, the Campbells combined their broad theology with a strict restorationist ecclesiology designed to re-create exactly the early church as described in the New Testament. They went so far as to bar organs in their churches because Christ and the disciples sang hymns without them.

Joseph Smith proclaimed a different solution to the problem of denominational proliferation: a church (ostensibly a restoration of the true church) built upon a new revelation that answered the theological controversies of the day. A son of hardscrabble New England farmers, raised amid the pervasive revivalism of upstate New York, an erstwhile treasure hunter and religious seeker, the young Smith reported having visions in which the angel Moroni revealed to him the location of buried golden tablets. As Smith miraculously translated them, they revealed the story of the lost tribes of Israel in America, the Book of Mormon. He published it in 1830 and established the Church of Jesus Christ of Latter-day Saints, whose organization he based on biblical descriptions of the Jewish priesthood and temple. His church grew, drawing especially from the ranks of the unprosperous and from women, but his religious community had a knack for alienating its neighbors. Smith and his followers found themselves hounded out of successive locations in New York, Ohio, Missouri, and Illinois, where a mob killed Smith in 1844. His successor, Brigham Young, then led most Mormons in an exodus to the isolation of the Great Salt Lake, now in Utah, where they flourished.

The intense religious activity of the Second Great Awakening led many to believe that the Last Days were near. Revivalist success in 1835 led Finney to predict the evangelization of the world in three years, which surely would precede the millennium. Alexander Campbell's *Christian Baptist* magazine was renamed the *Millennial Harbinger* in 1830, reflecting denominational expectations of an imminent Second Coming. Mormons believed that they were preparing the earth for Christ's impending return. In New York in the 1830s, the Baptist preacher and farmer William Miller interpreted biblical prophecy to predict the millennium in 1843. Thousands prepared themselves for the prophesied ascent into heaven of the elect, but when the appointed day passed, the date was recalculated for 1844. After another disappointment, Miller retired into obscurity. One of Miller's followers then had a vision that the "cleansing of the temple" had indeed occurred on the expected date, but in heaven, not on earth, which inspired Millerites to organize the Adventist church. Under the leadership of the "Adventist Prophetess," Ellen Gould White, the Seventh-Day Adventists gradually took shape as a denomination.

Belief in the imminent Second Coming of Christ, or the desire as old as the Puritans to live apart from society in a godly community, led to the creation of utopian religious communities across the North and upper South. The best-known and longest-lived were Shaker communities, which reached their peak after 1830. Founded in America by the English immigrant Ann Lee Stanley in 1774, Shakers believed "Mother Ann" (d. 1784) to be the feminine manifestation of God, as Christ was the masculine. A ritual dance and shaking associated with inspiration from the Holy Ghost inspired the name "Shakers." Because in the incarnation of Mother Ann the Second Coming had already occurred, procreation was unnecessary and Shakers were to remain celibate. Their communities emphasized equality of labor and reward; members held property in common; and ultimately the Shakers became famous for their commitment to simplicity and hard work and for their beautifully designed and crafted furniture and household items. They picked up a number of converts in the wake of the Cane Ridge revival; six of their eventual nineteen communities were in the Ohio Valley. Shaking, direct inspiration of the Holy Spirit, and other characteristics linked Shakers with early camp meetings, the original Quakers, and modern Pentecostalism.

NATURE AND THE SPIRIT

The individual experience of visions, the abandonment of the old churches, and the rejection of over-intellectualized religion were phenomena that manifested not just among the uneducated, farmers, and westerners, but among the old New England elite as well. Rejecting "corpse-cold" Unitarianism, a rationalist Christianity that had removed all that was mysterious, miraculous, and "unreasonable" from religion, Ralph Waldo Emerson left his Unitarian congregation to proclaim the need for an "original relation" with nature and the Spirit. In his essay *Nature* (1836) and other writings, Emerson urged people to go into the wild, where, far from grasping, materialistic Jacksonian America, amid the beauty of the ongoing creation of God, one could experience the divine spirit directly, without the intermediaries of priest or church. Emerson's circle, the Transcendentalists, which included Henry David Thoreau, had great influence on Unitarians and, in later decades, upon the mind of the nation.

Themes of associating nature, spirit, and moral regeneration appeared also in the works of eminent nineteenth-century New England writers and poets such as William Cullen Bryant, John Greenleaf Whittier, and Henry Wadsworth Longfellow. Similar themes pervaded the paintings of the Hudson River school and its successor, a style of landscape painting that came to be known as Luminist. Born or brought up in New England, such artists as Thomas Cole, Frederic Church, and Albert Bierstadt depicted divine light streaming into scenes of natural beauty in paintings intended to morally uplift viewers.

THE REFORM MOVEMENTS

The Puritan ideal of constructing a godly society never died. In the early nineteenth century, the de-

scendants of Puritans transformed that ideal into a potent national political movement for reform. Religion-mindedness, intense revivalism, and hopeful millennialism revitalized the desire to perfect the nation. Drawing energy from the new voluntarism of postestablishment churches, reform societies combined the energies and resources of people of more than one denomination. The founders of the first societies desired only to further the work of evangelization by publishing and distributing religious tracts and literature in frontier and unchurched areas. Modeled on similar English societies, the American Bible Society, American Tract Society, American Education Society, and American Sunday School Union rapidly appeared after 1814. American home and foreign missionary societies began appearing in the years before the War of 1812 and grew rapidly after the war was over. Opponents of Sunday mail delivery and commercial activities founded Sabbatarian societies. Many gave a characteristically Protestant interpretation to the enormous national alcohol consumption of the early republic, viewing alcoholism as a moral failing. They established temperance societies that originally promoted temperate drinking but later demanded abstinence and total prohibition. Eventually both the Sabbatarians and temperance advocates for a time successfully won the adoption nationwide of "blue laws" (restricted Sunday business activity) and prohibition.

If America was to become a moral and Christian example to the nations, or even lead the world into the millennium, it must eliminate national sins as much as possible. To a growing number of northern revivalists, the biggest obstacle to national redemption was the glaring sin of slavery. Northern evangelical abolitionists such as Theodore Dwight Weld, a protégé of Finney's, believed that the institution of slavery by its nature promoted unchristian abuses: sexual exploitation of women, separation of women from their children, prohibition of slave marriage, consequent extramarital promiscuity, and "irresponsible power." By irresponsible power they meant that slave owners were responsible to no legal authority for their treatment of slaves, which exposed slaves to severe beatings, maiming, or death at the whim of masters. In his 1839 best-seller, *Slavery as It Is,* Weld documented these abuses. William Lloyd Garrison, the editor of the Boston-based *Liberator* and a former editor of a Baptist temperance journal, took evangelical antislavery arguments to their extreme, calling the Constitution an unholy document because it mentioned slavery and demanding that the free states secede from the

United States so that they would not be united with sinful slave states.

Evangelical antislavery and its contention that slavery was immoral and unchristian alienated southern revivalists and congregations, laying the basis for the later split in the Methodist, Baptist, and Presbyterian organizations into northern and southern churches. In the 1830s southerners defensively began to develop arguments that slavery was not an evil but in fact a positive good for slave and master alike. Much of the "positive good" argument was religious; slavery was defended as an agency of uplift that civilized and Christianized the slave, inculcating Christian values and habits. Southern churches also developed a biblical defense of slavery based on the so-called curse of Ham (interpreted as an ancestor to Africans) and on the many passages in both the Old and New Testaments accepting the institution.

By the late 1830s, religion was transformed. The denominations that once dominated the colonies, Congregationalism, Anglicanism, and Presbyterianism, had lost much of their influence. Most Americans attended newly formed or much enlarged churches: the Methodist, Baptist, and Campbellite. The Puritan theological tradition and Calvinism were in permanent decline. Rising numbers of Americans, including free and enslaved blacks, attended church. Whereas the ideas that shaped the country in the years after 1776 largely arose from secular ideas of republicanism, citizenship, and democracy, by the 1830s Protestant moralism increasingly intruded into public discussions of social and political issues. Nineteenth-century American Protestantism was forged in the fires of the camp meeting and revivalism, with cultural, social, and political consequences that still affect Americans at the turn of the twenty-first century.

See also **Evangelical Thought** *(in this volume);* **Evangelical Protestants; God, Nature, and Human Nature** *(volume 2);* **Organized Religion** *(volume 3); and other articles in this section.*

BIBLIOGRAPHY

Abzug, Robert H. *Cosmos Crumbling: American Reform and the Religious Imagination.* New York, 1994.

Ahlstrom, Sydney. *A Religious History of the American People.* New Haven, Conn., 1972.

Bloch, Ruth. *Visionary Republic: Millennial Themes in American Thought, 1756–1800.* Cambridge, U.K., 1985.

Boles, John B. *The Great Revival, 1787–1805: The Origins of the Southern Evangelical Mind.* Lexington, Ky., 1972.

Bruce, Dickson D. *And They All Sang Hallelujah: Plain-Folk Camp-Meeting Religion, 1800–1845.* Knoxville, Tenn., 1974.

Bushman, Richard L. *Joseph Smith and the Beginnings of Mormonism.* Urbana, Ill., 1984.

Butler, Jon. *Awash in a Sea of Faith: Christianizing the American People.* Cambridge, Mass., 1990.

Conkin, Paul Keith. *Cane Ridge, America's Pentecost.* Madison, Wisc., 1990.

Cott, Nancy F. *The Bonds of Womanhood: "Women's Sphere" in New England, 1780–1835.* 1977. 2d ed., New Haven, Conn., 1997.

Cross, Whitney R. *The Burned-Over District: The Social and Intellectual History of Enthusiastic Religion in Western New York, 1800–1850.* 1950. Reprint, New York, 1965.

Gaustad, Edwin S. *Neither King nor Prelate : Religion and the New Nation, 1776–1826.* Rev. ed., Grand Rapids, Mich., 1993.

Hatch, Nathan O. *The Democratization of American Christianity.* New Haven, Conn., 1989.

Heyrman, Christine Leigh. *Southern Cross: The Beginnings of the Bible Belt.* Chapel Hill, N.C., 1997.

Isaac, Rhys. *The Transformation of Virginia, 1740–1790.* 1982. Reprint, Chapel Hill, N.C., 1988.

Johnson, Paul E. *A Shopkeeper's Millennium: Society and Revivals in Rochester, New York, 1815–1837.* New York, 1978.

Mathews, Donald G. *Religion in the Old South.* Chicago, 1977.

——. "The Second Great Awakening as an Organizing Process, 1780–1830: An Hypothesis." *American Quarterly* 21, no. 1 (1969): 23–43.

Miller, Perry. *The Life of the Mind in America: From the Revolution to the Civil War.* New York, 1965.

Novak, Barbara. *Nature and Culture: American Landscape and Painting, 1825–1875.* 1980. Rev. ed., with a new preface, New York, 1995.

Raboteau, Albert J. *Slave Religion: The "Invisible Institution" in the Antebellum South.* New York, 1978.

Shipps, Jan. *Mormonism: The Story of a New Religious Tradition.* Urbana, Ill., 1985.

THE BLACK CHURCH: INVISIBLE AND VISIBLE

Tracey E. Hucks

BACKGROUND

The "invisible" and "visible" forms of the black church have been the central hosts for African American religious agency in North America for several centuries. As an institution, the black church has historically serviced not only the religious needs of African American communities but also their social, political, and educational needs in the United States. In both its "invisible" form during the enslavement of Africans and its "visible" form after Emancipation, the black church has functioned as a repository of African American social resistance, political critique, and religious innovation. Throughout the years, the black church has assumed religious postures ranging from radicalism and resistance to conservatism and accommodationism. However, despite its diverse responses, the black church remained one of the few institutions that attempted to exercise religious autonomy in early America. Overall, its identity during the colonial and post-Emancipation eras was shaped largely by the content of its theological message, its negotiation of the Christian tradition, its geographic diversity, and its fidelity to African orientations and styles.

The American black church emerged within the institution of slavery. In British North America, the enslavement of Africans began in the early seventeenth century with the first importation to Jamestown, Virginia, in August 1619. The establishment of Virginia under the royal charter of the Virginia Company of London twelve years previously marked the first settlement in the English South. Also present in the South were the Spanish, who had come much earlier to the New World and by that time had dominated European colonization for more than a century. The Spanish and the English who settled in the Americas and the Caribbean saw the New World in terms of its potential wealth. However, some scholars contend that, as representatives of the Catholic and Protestant faiths, the Spanish and the English launched their conquests of the New World, in part, as a possible stage for "religious crusade." The likely targets for this venture would have been the indigenous peoples of the Americas, and eventually those of Africa, both of whom would inevitably be designated as the New World's official labor force.

The population development of these two early labor forces inversely paralleled one another. The decline of the indigenous population directly corresponded to the rise of African populations throughout the Americas and the Caribbean. For example, the indigenous population in Virginia had declined from approximately twenty thousand in 1607 to two thousand in 1669, whereas the African population increased to fifteen thousand by 1700. Unlike their Spanish counterparts, who initially utilized their forced labor to mine gold, extract various natural resources, and eventually harvest cash crops, the British colonizers in North America used their enslaved African labor primarily for agricultural purposes in the South and for domestic purposes in the North.

THE INVISIBLE INSTITUTION IN COLONIAL NEW ENGLAND

Within colonial New England, an area largely unexplored with regard to the invisible institution, the religious life of enslaved Africans remained virtually neglected by early Puritans. Enslaved Africans were first transported to the colony of Massachusetts in 1638. According to John Winthrop's journal entry dated 10 December 1638, Captain W. Pierce returned to Salem on the ship *Desire* from the Tortugas, where he had exchanged a group of Pequod Indian warriors for "salt, cotton, tobacco, and Negroes" (A. L. Higginbotham, *In the Matter of Color*, p. 413, n. 1). In terms of geographic origins, the enslaved African community in New England was quite diverse. Although Africans were largely brought into the region from English Caribbean colonies, at least three-quarters of all Africans in New England were African born, originating from Senegal, Gambia, Sierra Leone, Guinea, and Angola.

A major impediment to the development of plantation slavery in colonial New England was that the total population of Africans never rose above 2 percent, and of this percentage the highest concentration of Africans resided in Massachusetts. On average, slaveholding New Englanders owned some two to five Africans per household; they were either hired out or assumed full domestic responsibilities for the master's family. Thus, a system of "family slavery" was established in which masters and slaves generally inhabited the same domestic sphere.

African religious life in New England remained largely uninformed by Christianity. In fact, it is argued that between 1619 and 1719, Christianity had very little influence upon the religious orientation of Africans within the British North American colonies.

In Puritan New England, several ideological and concrete barriers prevented the early proselytization of Africans. First, it was believed by many slaveholders that Christianity was incompatible with the enslaved status of Africans. It was feared that it would jeopardize the institution of slavery by elevating the status of Africans through baptism, and also that their new Christian status might warrant certain rights and privileges within English society. Second, it was suggested that Africans did not possess the innate intelligence to grasp Christianity; that conversion to Christianity would make them resist their condition; and that it was both time-consuming and costly to Christianize a population destined exclusively for labor. Although New England had its first black convert to Christianity in 1641, just three years after the initial arrival of Africans, the bulk of its African population remained outside the boundaries of the Christian faith well into the next century. Finally, the more obvious reasons that prevented widespread conversion of Africans included the exclusive nature of New England Puritanism, language barriers, literacy requirements, stylistic and worship differences, indifference to the new faith of Christianity, and the passive theological message of subservience and obedience taught by Puritan ministers. As the eighteenth century approached, concentrated missionary activity attempted to overcome these practical impediments.

In 1701 the Anglican Church formed the Society for the Propagation of the Gospel in Foreign Parts (SPG) as a missionary enterprise in North America.

Commissioning more than three hundred missionaries, the SPG dedicated its mission work to the Christianization of English colonists, of the indigenous population in the colonies, and of enslaved Africans. To the latter group, it emphasized obedience to their masters as well as submission to their lot as slaves. A major part of the Christian indoctrination process involved the catechism method, which entailed a lengthy process of memorization and an even slower process of developing literacy among Africans through written instruction and the creation of mission schools. As a result, the success rate remained relatively low, and ultimately the SPG had very little impact on the overall religious lives of Africans.

As a result, African religious practices and beliefs persisted throughout colonial New England. They were, however, most often understood by New Englanders within a pejorative framework of black magic, devil worship, and witchcraft. Traditions of witchcraft and magic existed within European societies, and many of the perceptions about these traditions were transplanted to the British colonies. Using them, white New Englanders began to formulate their own interpretations of African religious practices.

In recent studies on race and ethnicity in seventeenth-century New England, scholars have begun to explore the correlation between African-derived practices and the meaning of witchcraft and magic within the European imagination. During the late seventeenth century, several Africans in colonial New England were formally accused of engaging in witchcraft and satanic practices. More specifically, two African women and one African man were accused of practicing witchcraft during the witch trials of the early 1690s. Several primary sources that document the testimonies of accused witches indicate that the symbolic representations of the devil were closely connected to black Africans. Several court records indicate confessions that the appearance of the devil was likened to that of "a Black" or a "Black man." According to the Puritan minister Cotton Mather in his 1693 text, *The Wonders of the Invisible World: Being an Account of the Tryals of Several Witches Lately Executed in New England:*

> The Devil, exhibiting himself ordinarily as a small Black man has decoy'd a fearful knot of proud, froward, ignorant, envious and malicious creatures to lift themselves in his horrid service, by entering their Names in a Book by him tendred unto them.

Images of blacks and the connection of their religious rites and practices to evil and Satan were prevalent throughout colonial New England documents.

These documents show that New England colonists interpreted the practices of Africans through the lenses of magic and witchcraft shaped by their own religious orientations. For example, in his 1706 work *The Negro Christianized,* Cotton Mather attempted to explain the rites of New England's enslaved blacks.

> A roaring Lion who goes about seeking whom he may devour, hath made a seizure of them [enslaved Africans]. Very many of them to with Devillish Rites actually worship Devils, or maintain a magical conversation with Devils. And all of them are more slaves to Satan than they are to You, until a Faith in the Son of God has made them free indeed. Will you do nothing to pluck them out of the jaws of Satan the Devourer?

The "invisible institution" of slave religion in colonial New England can be found not so much within the created magical lore of Cotton Mather as within concrete African practices of conjuration, divination, herbalism, and funeral/burial rites. Within these practices, blacks in New England maintained the vestiges of a religious world rooted in Africa. At times, African folk practices paralleled those of European masters and were, on occasion, tolerated in New England. The historian William Piersen notes that divination practices were performed by respected black men and women within the slave community. Moreover, these diviners were readily consulted by white New Englanders. According to Piersen, one African woman, Silvia Tory, was known for her divination skills in Salem, Massachusetts. It was recorded by a white New Englander that "did a cow stray beyond boundaries, or was a horse stolen, the bereaved owner hastened to inquire to Silvia, who would obligingly furnish him with various occult directions, by a strict adherence to which, the lost might be found" (Piersen, *Black Yankees,* p. 85). Piersen concluded that the more closely the worlds of black and white folk beliefs converged, the more African practices were regarded as "harmless superstitions" and indulged.

The theology of enslaved Africans in colonial New England revealed myriad beliefs. Many of these beliefs centered on the notion of death resulting from physical and spiritual causes; the human soul returning to Africa after death; dreams as prophetic entities that provide an outlet into the spiritual world; the spirit world as accessible through multiple divination techniques; herbs as having both spiritual and medicinal powers; and the use of charms as an effective means of thwarting evil. Often the practices of charm making, herbalism, conjuration, and divination were interconnected,

blending a complex tradition of healing and protection. White New Englanders labeled the practitioners of these rites as "fetish" worshipers and "fortunetellers," and by the early eighteenth century the elaborate world of African religious lore came to be classified under the general category of "Negro-Mancy."

Although colonial New England can be viewed as a prism for examining the invisible world of African religious culture, it can equally be seen as the region that set the stage for the event that marked large-scale African conversions to Christianity in both the North and the South. The Great Awakening, out of which developed new styles of religious interaction and worship, was perhaps the most pivotal moment in American religious history regarding the intersection between Africans and Christianity. In the 1730s and 1740s, the Great Awakening launched new modes of religious engagement based on emotional preaching, the conversion experience, ecstatic behavior, and revivalism. The religious culture of evangelicalism throughout New England, and eventually the South, deemphasized the need for a collective convenant, a learned clergy, a solemn worship service, and a strict literacy requirement. Revival preachers such as Jonathan Edwards, George Whitefield, and Gilbert Tennent often noted the large participation of African Americans as converts and as lay preachers at revivals. What appealed most to Africans regarding this new form of Christianity was its emphasis on the conversion experience, the emotionalism of the revival meetings, the rhythmic and melodic style of hymn singing, the call-and-response of psalm reading, the accessibility of the evangelical priesthood, and the use of the human body as the medium for spirit possession. Many of these practices overlapped in style with those of African traditional religions, thus making the new evangelical tradition readily attractive.

Colonial New England's shift in religious climate from Puritanism to revivalism launched a transformation in the religious identity of enslaved Africans in the region. Evangelical Christianity made the Christian message more accessible to Africans and made it more possible to accommodate the retention of indigenous religious practices.

THE INVISIBLE INSTITUTION IN THE AMERICAN SOUTH

In contrast to colonial New England, the religious life of Africans in the South has been documented much more extensively, revealing a diversity of practices and interpretations.

The South contained 90 percent of North America's enslaved population. Of the estimated 596,000 Africans brought to North America before the close of the slave trade in 1808, the vast majority were transported and concentrated in the South. By 1860 this population had grown to 4.5 million. The invisible institution of religion formed by this enslaved population involved a delicate balance between their own African cultural styles and characteristics and the European religious heritage that they encountered. Therefore, according to black religionist Gayraud Wilmore, African American Christianity cannot be understood without "its rapidly disintegrating but persistent base" of an "African substratum."

The plantation system in the South fostered the invisible institution. Within this context, New World African systems of religious thought and practice, such as the ring shout, in which enslaved Africans danced in a circle, in a counterclockwise direction, in order to invoke divine presence and spirit possession; conjure; hoodoo; and voodoo were pervasive throughout the South. Often interpreted through a Christian prism, these practices nonetheless revealed the vestiges of an endangered African culture attempting to adjust to the demands of a New World context.

As in New England, the predominance of Baptist, Methodist, and Presbyterian revivalists in the South helped to facilitate numerous black conversions to Christianity. These denominations, however, would have to endure sectional divisions in the first half of the nineteenth century for their disputes on slavery.

By the 1740s and 1750s, evangelical Protestantism began to penetrate the religious lives of the South's enslaved communities. During the post-Revolutionary period, camp meetings of evangelical Christians became the central forum for the religious transformations that would occur in the lives of the South's enslaved communities. What appealed most to these enslaved communities was evangelical Protestantism's ability to privilege the spoken word over the written word in preaching; to incorporate hymn singing and ecstatic religious dance into revival services; to invoke religious conversion through appeals to emotionalism; to embody the Holy Spirit through possession; and, for some denominations, to purify the body and spirit through full-immersion baptismal rites.

Journals, diaries, and correspondence of church-appointed and itinerant ministers provide testimony for the widespread curiosity that enslaved Africans had for Christianity and their attraction to it. According to a Presbyterian minister, Samuel Davies, who labored among enslaved communities in the South, "Never have I been so struck with the appearance of an assembly, as when I have glanced my eyes to one part of the Meeting-house adorned (so it has appeared to me) with so many black countenances, especially attentive to every word they heard, and some of them washed with tears" (Freye and Wood, *Come Shouting to Zion,* p. 97). Moreover, Davies noted a distinct theological interpretation that enslaved Africans had concerning baptismal rites: "They have very high notions of the necessity and efficacy of Baptism. Indeed, it seems to be their common opinion, when they first become a little thoughtful, and uneasy in a state of Heathenism, that if they were but baptized, they should become Christians instantaneously; and it is hard to convince them of the necessity of proper preparatory qualifications for it" (*Come Shouting to Zion,* p. 99).

The continuity of black Christian conversions was ensured with the coming of black evangelical clergy. Many of the black evangelical preachers who emerged during this period became directly responsible not only for the spread of Christianity throughout enslaved communities in North America but also for its spread throughout the British Caribbean islands. In addition, black evangelical preachers on occasion were given the opportunity to preach to audiences consisting of both blacks and whites. Harry Hosier, one such individual, often accompanied the Methodist preacher Francis Asbury on his revival circuit.

Within the network of black Christianity, slave communities sought to maintain religious fellowship by means of the "hush harbors." These were densely forested areas, some distance away from plantations, that served to shield the secret religious meetings of enslaved Africans. Because of its physical isolation, the hush harbor preserved the invisible institution of slave communities. Moreover, this need for secrecy heightened after legal persecution intensified as a result of the slave plots and revolts of Gabriel Prosser (Virginia, 1800), Denmark Vesey (South Carolina, 1822), and Nat Turner (Virginia, 1831).

Subsequently, following widespread conversions, there emerged a complex theological tradition surrounding black Christianity. African Americans began to formulate their own intepretations of the Christian message that reflected their enslaved and oppressed condition. Traditional Christian theological doctrines of providential design, eschatology, the cross, and sin and humanity were challenged daily by enslaved African communities. They readily rejected the notion that the institution of slavery was preordained and that the Hamitic curse—claiming a mythic typology, that Africans were the cursed descendants of Noah's son Ham—divinely decreed Africans as slaves. They also rejected the "rule of gospel order," which stated that the salvation of the slave population was contingent upon their obedience to their earthly masters. Catechisms written by Christian missionaries in the South, such as the Presbyterian minister Charles Colcock Jones, reflected this rule of sacred obedience. Jones, who owned three rice plantations and 129 Africans, became the first appointed missionary of the Association for Religious Instruction of Negroes in December 1832. Established by the planter class in Liberty County, Georgia, the association echoed the sentiments Jones would eventually put forth in his *Catechism*:

> Q. What are the Servants to count their Masters worthy of?
> A. All honour.
> Q. How are they to try to please their Masters?
> A. Please them well in all things, not answering again.
> Q. Is it right for a Servant when commanded to do anything to be sullen and slow, and answering his master again?
> A. No.
> Q. But suppose the Master is hard to please, and threatens and punishes more than he ought, what is the Servant to do?
> A. Do his best to please him.
> Q. Are servants at liberty to tell lies and deceive their Masters?
> A. No.
> Q. If servants will faithfully do their duty and Serve God in their stations as Servants, will they be respected of men, and blessed and honoured of God, as well as others?
> A. Yes.
>
> (Johnson, *African-American Christianity*, p. 22)

Within this artificially constructed, divinely ordained social order, bondsmen and women sought to create a theological world of negotiation and agency. Interpretations of traditional Christian doctrines, especially the doctrine of sin, were overtly and subtly contested. African Americans developed their own criteria for moral conduct with an elasticity that expanded according to their needs as human chattel. In order to accommodate the moral contradictions of slavery, the boundaries of the slave moral order often stretched to include acts of resistance traditionally labeled as "sins"—such as deception, lying, and stealing—as well as extreme acts such as infanticide, escape, and rebellion.

As was the case with sin, eschatological issues were profoundly ambiguous within the slave context. Slave religion was highly critical of the otherworldly theology it encountered. Because liberation and freedom from captivity were foreseeable in the temporal world, enslaved blacks did not readily comply with the belief that rewards for their earthly service would be granted in the afterlife. Instead, slave communities questioned the theological contradictions under which their slaveholders lived, and many predicted that their masters and mistresses would spend eternity in hell rather than in heaven. John Anderson, who managed to escape captivity, stated that "some folks say slaveholders may be good Christians, but I can't and won't believe it, nor do I think that a slaveholder can get to heaven" (Raboteau, *Slave Religion,* pp. 291–292). Like Anderson, many who suffered under the harsh conditions of bondage condemned the proslavery theological tenets that provided justification for their suffering.

Permeability and fluidity were fundamental characteristics of slave religion. Throughout Southern slave plantations, Christianity and African-inspired practices such as conjure, hoodo, and voodoo existed within a complementary and dialogical relationship. In order to meet their spiritual needs, members of the enslaved population sought to access the powers that both Christianity and African-inspired traditions offered. According to the religious historian Albert Raboteau, "Conjure could, without contradiction, exist side by side with Christianity in the same individual and in the same community because, for the slaves, conjure answered purposes which Christianity did not and Christianity answered purposes which conjure did not" (*Slave Religion*, p. 288). Within slave communities, conjure encompassed a set of African-inspired beliefs and practices often having unspecified roots, origins, or systematic rituals. It relied heavily on divination, herbalism, and the creation of protective charms. Sources of power associated with these practices were commonly identified as God, the devil, unknown African powers and spirits, or natural intuitive abilities. Conjurers, root doctors, voodoo specialists, and seers became the surrogate priests and priestesses who maintained this African-influenced New World tradition in southern North America. According to Mechel Sobel, "The chief evidence that African world views came into America and that they coalesced into a more or less singular cosmos is the fact that Voodoo actively permeated all of slave life. . . . The world of spirits and the practices surrounding their supplication and control remained an overarching reality throughout the slave era. . . . No slave area was without spirit-workers, and virtually no slave was without contact with spirits" (*Trabelin' On,* p. 41).

In all, the invisible expressions of slave religion in America's northern and southern regions reflected the varied and diverse attempts of Africans to maintain a religious identity that resisted their economic and social status as chattel. Invisible to the larger world around them, these very real and innovative practices created an alternative religious reality that helped to sustain the inner world of American slave life.

THE VISIBLE CHURCH IN SLAVERY AND FREEDOM

The first known "visible" black Christian churches in the antebellum period emerged primarily from the Baptist and Methodist denominations. The historical connection between the Baptists and Methodists and the Great Awakenings, along with the primacy of local church governance, especially within the Baptist denomination, made them likely candidates for hosting black ecclesial autonomy. The first of these black church efforts developed in the South with the formation of the First African or Bluestone Baptist Church on the plantation of William Byrd III in Virginia in 1758. Less than two decades later, between 1773 and 1775, the Silver Bluff Baptist Church was formed in South Carolina under the leadership of David George and George Liele. Over the course of the next two centuries, black Baptist activity in the North and South would culminate in a separate black denomination in 1895, the National Baptist Convention.

The early movement of black church separation in the North was fueled largely by the efforts of black Methodists. Bethel Church, the first of these black independent churches, was established in Philadelphia by Richard Allen, a former slave, in 1794. The Union Church of Africans was formed in 1813 in Wilmington, Delaware, as a result of segregatory practices in the local white church. The spread of black Methodism came, however, with Allen's denominational formation of the African Methodist Episcopal (A.M.E.) Church in 1816. Shortly thereafter, the A.M.E. Church evolved into a national network of black Methodist churches that extended from the East to the Midwest: Maryland,

Richard Allen (1760–1831). Allen was founder and first bishop of the African Methodist Episcopal Church. © BETTMANN/CORBIS

Delaware, New York, New Jersey, Ohio, Indiana, and Missouri.

This newly formed denomination stressed a social platform of racial unity, mutual aid, education, and abolitionism. According to one A.M.E. minister speaking at the 1856 denominational General Convention, "Every colored man is an abolitionist, and slaveholders know it" (Wilmore, *Black Religion and Black Radicalism,* p. 85). In addition to its antislavery mission, many educational institutions and colleges, such as Wilberforce, Morris Brown, Allen, Paul Quinn, and Shorter Junior were founded under the auspices of the A.M.E. Church. Finally, as a direct result of its missionary endeavors in the South, the A.M.E. Church increased its pre–Civil War membership of twenty thousand persons to almost a half million in 1896.

The African Methodist Episcopal Zion Church ranked as the second largest black Methodist denomination following its official organization in New York in 1822. Like the A.M.E. Church, the A.M.E. Zion Church strongly opposed the institution of slavery, and its independent churches became important stops along the Underground Railroad. Third in black Methodist membership was the Colored (later Christian) Methodist Episcopal Church, founded in 1870 by former slaves in Jackson, Tennessee. Black Methodists were linked by their early commitment to antislavery and their later commitment to missions throughout the Caribbean and Africa. Their missionary activity spread as far as Haiti, Cuba, Jamaica, Antigua, the Virgin Islands, Trinidad, Tobago, Barbados, Bahamas, Bermuda, Dutch Guiana, British Guiana, South Africa, Sierre Leone, and Liberia. Through domestic and foreign missionary endeavors, black Methodists, as well as black Baptists, sought to cultivate racial uplift while ushering in a new era of black Christendom.

With the coming of Emancipation, the demands upon the black church intensified. Given the short-lived efforts of government agencies such as the Freedmen's Bureau, the burden of acclimating African Americans to freedom fell disproportionately upon independent black churches. Privately, these churches had to negotiate the challenges involved in absorbing the membership of the "invisible" institution while easing the new divisions caused by class, education, and worship styles. Publicly, the most immediate challenges facing black churches were how to acquire literacy and education, political enfranchisement and full citizenship, social integration and public respectability.

Despite the passage of the Fourteenth and Fifteenth Amendments and the Civil Rights Acts of 1866 and 1875, American society was still not prepared to embrace as equals its former enslaved population. Continued local and state tactics of disenfranchisement in the form of poll taxes, grandfather clauses, and literacy tests, plus increased violence and physical intimidation in the form of lynching, as well as rigid division and social segregation forced postbellum black churches to assume a social as well as a religious posture.

Throughout the nineteenth century, black churches responded in various ways to the numerous social and political impediments that thwarted black mobility. Thus, a crucial priority of black churches became institution-building. Important institutions that emerged out of black churches in the postslavery years were schools and colleges, in order to elevate the 5 to 10 percent literacy rate; newspapers and periodicals; women's societies and conventions; and self-help programs and companies. In addition to institution-building, many black churches invested their time and energy in fashioning respectable public images of African Americans. Strategically, this meant that many black churches embraced accommodationist stances in order to prove worthy of full and equal citizenship. According to the historian Evelyn Brooks Higgenbotham, black Christian churches embraced a "politics of respectability" aimed at assimilating black social behavior, conduct, and manners to the norms of Victorian America.

At times, this platform of respectability permeated larger national church debates. For example, the A.M.E. Church sustained much internal debate as to whether it should retain "African" in its nomenclature. Some church leaders and clergy saw its retention as antithetical to the Americanization process. Others, like A.M.E. minister George Rue in the 1860s, opposed the name change, asking, "What is there so detestable in that word?" He added that no other name "seems to be so frightful to our oppressors as the word African. It is a terror to evildoers, and is destined to loose the captive from his chain, through the power of God's great arm" (Montgomery, *Under Their Own Vine and Fig Tree*, p. 124). In agreement, J. T. Jenifer added some three decades later: "Why, then, should the Negro of this country, with African blood and African parentage, be ashamed of Africa? . . . To the proscribed and downtrodden colored people of this country this name was a symbol of hope; it was an *asylum and an inspiration*—a protest against religious oppression or proscription at the altar of God" (Montgomery, p. 225).

An active minority of black church leaders took their affinity for Africa one step further by advocating emigration as an alternative to remaining in America. Although many African emigration plans were short-lived, they reflected an effort on the part of black Christian churches to expand their vision of racial uplift to the African continent. Regardless of the various responses to racial and spiritual subjugation, the collective impulse of black churches in the post-Emancipation era was to provide religious guidance to their newly freed adherents, as well as social and political leadership to their black constituency.

CONCLUSION

The "invisible" and "visible" black churches of slavery and freedom have historically attempted to create safe havens for black Christians in North America. From these churches there emerged a religious tradition of freedom and liberation as well as a solid denominational structure that shaped black religious agency well into the twenty-first century. The

Franklin McMahon, *St. Paul's A.M.E. Church,* **1978.** Located on Chicago's South Side, St. Paul's African Methodist Episcopal Church was founded in 1919. © FRANKLIN MCMAHON/ CORBIS

invisible church of colonial New England and the plantation South, along with the independent black churches of postcolonial America, formed a distinct black Christian identity imbued with its own theology and African religious expression. Hans Baer and Merrill Singer label this unique black perspective a "reworked Christianity" with its "own character, style, and outlook, but one which incorporated elements of African religion." Ultimately, this reworked Christianity became a mechanism for sustaining black survival by structuring new meaning for black Christian identity and promoting an alternative religious reality that affirmed black humanity.

See also **Slave Culture and Consciousness; Thought and Culture in the Free Black Community** *(in this volume);* **African Americans; Evangelical Protestants** *(volume 2).*

BIBLIOGRAPHY

Ahlstrom, Sydney E. *A Religious History of the American People.* New Haven, Conn., 1972.

Albanese, Catherine L. *America: Religions and Religion.* Belmont, Calif., 1992.

Baer, Hans A., and Merrill Singer. *African American Religion in the Twentieth Century: Varieties of Protest and Accommodation.* Knoxville, Tenn., 1992.

Butler, Jon. *Awash in a Sea of Faith: Christianizing the American People.* Cambridge, Mass., 1990.

Cornelius, Janet Duitsman. *"When I Can Read My Title Clear": Literacy, Slavery, Religion in the Antebellum South.* Columbia, S.C., 1991.

Fitts, Leroy. *A History of Black Baptists,* Nashville, Tenn., 1985.

Freye, Sylvia, and Betty Wood. *Come Shouting to Zion: African American Protestantism in the American South and British Caribbean to 1830.* Chapel Hill, N.C., 1998.

Greene, Lorenzo Johnston. *The Negro in Colonial New England 1620–1776.* New York, 1942.

Higginbotham, A. Leon. *In the Matter of Color: Race and the American Legal Process, the Colonial Period.* New York, 1978.

Higginbotham, Evelyn. *Righteous Discontent: The Women's Movement in the Black Baptist Church 1880–1920.* Cambridge, Mass., 1993.

Holloway, Joseph, ed. *Africanisms in American Culture.* Bloomington, Ind., 1990.

Johnson, Paul E., ed. *African-American Christianity: Essays in History.* Berkeley, 1994.

Mather, Cotton. *The Negro Christianized: An Essay to Excite and Assist the Good Work, the Instruction of Negro-Servants in Christianity.* Boston, 1706.

——. *The Wonders of the Invisible World. Being an Account of the Tryals of Several Witches Lately Executed in New England.* Amherst, Mass., 1862.

McMillan, Timothy. "Black Magic: Witchcraft, Race, and Resistance in Colonial New England." *Journal of Black Studies* 25, no. 1 (1994).

Montgomery, William E. *Under Their Own Vine and Fig Tree: The African-American Church in the South 1865–1900.* Baton Rouge, La., 1993.

Murphy, Larry G., J. Gordon Metlon, and Gary L. Ward, eds. *Encyclopedia of African American Religions.* New York, 1993.

Nash, Gary. *Red, White and Black: The Peoples of Early America.* 2d ed. Englewood Cliffs, N.J., 1982.

Piersen, William D. *Black Yankees: The Development of an Afro-American Subculture in Eighteenth-Century New England.* Amherst, Mass., 1988.

Raboteau, Albert. *Slave Religion: The "Invisible Institution" in the Antebellum South.* New York, 1978.

Schomburg Center for Research in Black Culture. *African American Religion: Research Problems and Resources for the 1990s.* New York, 1992.

Sernett, Milton C. *Black Religion and American Evangelicalism: White Protestants, Plantation Missions, and the Flowering of Negro Christianity, 1787–1865.* Metuchen, N.J., 1975.

Sobel, Mechal. *Trabelin' On: The Slave Journey to an Afro-Baptist Faith.* Westport, Conn., 1979.

——. *The World They Made Together: Black and White Values in Eighteenth-Century Virginia.* Princeton, N.J., 1987.

Washington, James Melvin. *Frustrated Fellowship: The Black Baptist Quest for Social Power.* Macon, Ga., 1986.

Wilmore, Gayraud S. *Black Religion and Black Radicalism: An Interpretation of the Religious History of Afro-American People.* 2d ed., rev. and enl. Maryknoll, N.Y., 1983.

THE CLASSICAL VISION

Susan Ford Wiltshire

In 1663 a tract of land on the Maryland side of the Potomac River was given the name "Rome" by its new owners, perhaps because it adjoined a small creek named "Tiber" after the great river of ancient Rome. In time Washington, D.C., for many the "New Rome on the Potomac," was built around this site.

Adopting place names from Greek and Roman antiquity illustrates one compelling characteristic of the American imagination from colonial times through the nineteenth century: the eagerness to endow what was new with the dignity and stability of the old. In over twenty states one will find at least one city, town, or village named Rome, Athens, Sparta, or Troy, along with numerous others such as Corinth, Delphi, Ithaca, Marathon, or Syracuse. Other cities were named from Greek or Roman heroes, for example Cicero, Cato, or Cincinnatus.

In the national period, the dignifying use of classical themes pervaded national iconography from the outset. After declaring independence on 4 July 1776, the Continental Congress resolved later on the same day "that Dr. Franklin, Mr. J. Adams and Mr. Jefferson, be a committee, to bring in a device for a seal for the United States of America." Their design, assisted by others, was approved by the Continental Congress in 1782. The obverse of the Great Seal—with its shield of thirteen stripes, eagle with thirteen arrows in one talon and an olive branch with thirteen leaves in the other—is the more familiar side. The eagle, the symbolic bird of the Greek god Zeus or the Roman god Jupiter in the classical world, also adorned the standards of Roman legions. On the Great Seal the eagle carries a ribbon in its beak with the national motto, *e pluribus unum,* "out of many, one." On the reverse of the seal, which appears only on the back of a U.S. one dollar bill, is an unfinished pyramid with thirteen steps. Below the pyramid are the words *novus ordo seclorum,* "a new order of the ages," and above, *annuit coeptis,* "he has nodded approval on our be-

ginnings." All three Latin phrases are adapted from the Roman poet Vergil (70–19 B.C.).

The usefulness of classical antiquity, however, was not limited to the topographic, decorative, or symbolic. After winning the American Revolution, the first order of business for the founders was to create a form of governance reflecting their hopes, beliefs, and experience. Following hard on the adoption of the Constitution came the design of a new capital city for the nation. Throughout the early American period, to be educated meant to have studied the classical languages and literature, with an eye always on mining the Old World for edifying examples for the New. Out of this grew a literature grounded in classical themes, an influence that continued in some quarters into the twentieth century. And when the United States finally had to confront the evil of slavery, classical precedents provided arguments for both sides of the debate.

CREATING A NEW FORM OF GOVERNMENT

After saying farewell to his troops at Fraunces Tavern in New York City, the commander in chief of the Continental Army, George Washington, proceeded to Annapolis to meet with the Congress in session there. On this occasion he did something no victorious revolutionary general has done before or since: he voluntarily gave up his power. After returning the parchment commission granted him in Philadelphia eight and a half years earlier, Washington told the Congress with conviction that he was leaving behind "all employments of public life." The next day, 24 December 1783, he returned home to Mount Vernon at last.

Washington's voluntary resignation of command astonished everyone, but it did not happen in a vacuum. Firmly fixed in his mind, as the historian Garry Wills has amply demonstrated, was the example of the ancient Roman citizen-soldier Lucius Quinctius Cincinnatus, who likewise assumed military command at the request of the citizens to save the Roman state. Then, when his work was done, he happily returned to the work of his farm. Cincinnatus, selfless guardian of the Roman republic, was the explicit model for the precedent Washington thus established of the ideal public servant. Washington's veterans formed the Society of the Cincinnati, and a mural of the Roman citizen-soldier returning to his plow occupies a conspicuous place in the decoration of the United States Capitol.

The impact of Washington's decision to resign rather than exploit power reached far beyond American shores. In his efforts to unify Italy nearly a century later, the nationalist leader Giuseppe Garibaldi said that the examples of bad dictators should teach leaders "to seek more diligently for a Cincinnatus and a Washington." A lithograph of 1860, *The Most Worthy Triumvirate* by Giuseppe Fochetti and Pietro Sindico, depicts Cincinnatus handing Garibaldi a sword from one side and General Washington offering a rifle from the other.

As the weaknesses of America's first written constitution, the Articles of Confederation, became increasingly apparent, a convention of fifty-five delegates was called in Philadelphia during the summer of 1787 to amend them. Reluctantly, Washington agreed to serve as a delegate from Virginia. His steadying presence as president of the assembly provided the cover for his younger contemporaries to transgress the mandate of the convention, and propose a new constitution instead. Now delegates could bring to bear on the practical demands of contemporary governance their immense knowledge of history, especially of constitutional history, ancient and modern. Now their classical vision could provide examples not for war but for peace.

Scholars differ on the origins of the U.S. Constitution. J. G. A. Pocock, for example, argued that the founders derived their classical republican ideology from the British Whigs, who fashioned their beliefs from Florentine thinkers of the Renaissance. Bernard Bailyn considered any classical thought of the founders to be superficial or illustrative rather than substantive. Until the late twentieth century, however, few studies examined in detail the extent of the classicism of the founders in both their education and their habits of thought. This lack was due largely to traditional barriers among the academic disciplines: American historians tended to discount classical influences and the classics in general, while classicists knew little about American intellectual and political history. Beginning with the

pioneering work of Meyer Reinhold since 1968 and especially with the publication of his *Classica Americana* (1984), the academic study of the classical tradition in America has grown increasingly nuanced and elaborated. Carl J. Richard's *The Founders and the Classics: Greece, Rome, and the American Enlightenment* (1994) extends and in some ways corrects the earlier work of both Americanists and classicists. *The Founders* contends that the classics extended a formative influence on the founders, an influence that then was mediated through their knowledge of Whig and American intellectual history. Their educational and social conditioning tended to link the founders more directly back to the works of antiquity than often is thought.

No one questions the ancient origins of the most important of all principles sustained in the body of the Constitution, the separation of powers buttressed with compound checks and balances. By the time of the Constitution, the framers knew from the accumulated record of antiquity, as well as from their own recent experience, that limits on the exercise of power were crucial to the new institutions they were creating.

In tracing the ancient origins of the separation of powers, it is important to distinguish among three closely related theories: mixed government, the separation of powers, and checks and balances. A mixed government results from the understanding that elements of monarchy, aristocracy, and democracy are all required if a political order is to be stable and harmonious. The notion here is that opposing forces *should* coexist within the same government so as to prevent their clash outside it. The New York delegate Alexander Hamilton spoke to that issue at the Constitutional Convention of 18 June 1787, when he cited the Greek philosopher Aristotle together with the Roman orator Cicero and the French political philosopher Montesquieu as corroborating his views on the proper mixture of oligarchy and democracy.

Separation of powers has to do not with conflicting interests but with the separate *functions*, or powers, of government. Traditionally these are three in number: the legislative, the executive, and the judicial branches. The notion of checks and balances is closely connected with the first two and could not exist without the presence of a mixed government, the separation of powers, or both. Checks and balances serve as a "control mechanism" to prevent one interest group or one branch of government from increasing its power at the expense of the others. In the convention of 1787, the framers constructed a document that combined all three theories.

The earliest origins of these ideas may be traced back to the ancient Pythagoreans of the sixth century B.C. The Greek philosopher-mathematician Pythagoras and his followers believed that antithetical forces exist on a cosmic level, but that instead of pulling things apart, the tension between them keeps the universe in balance. One early Pythagorean distinguished three forms of government: democratic, oligarchic, and aristocratic—and worked out a mathematical relationship among the three that would create the most stable order.

This idea of mathematics and balance kindled the Greek philosopher Plato's imagination, and it may be in Plato's political writings that the theory of a mixed constitution first appeared. In *Laws*, Plato's longest and most practical work, written in 360 B.C., he maintained, "If we disregard due proportion by giving anything what is too much for it, too much canvas to a boat, too much nutriment to a body, too much authority to a soul, the consequence is always shipwreck." Although Aristotle disagreed with Plato's leanings toward oligarchy, he too sought a balanced constitution as the solution for the dangerous concentration of political power. Aristotle wrote in *Politics* (335–323 B.C.): "The better, and the more equitable, the mixture in a 'polity,' the more durable it will be." After Aristotle, the most extensive arguments concerning mixed government were tendered by Polybius, the Greek historian, in his *Histories,* a recounting of Rome from 220 to 146 B.C. Polybius attributed Rome's greatness to its mixed constitution. He saw the powers of the consuls, the senate, and the people as interdependent, with each providing checks on the powers of the other two. There could be no better political system than this, he concluded, because "every part remains in its established position, partly because it is checked by the others if it tries to increase its power, and partly because, from the beginning, it fears the reaction of the others."

Many of the Constitutional Convention delegates referred frequently to their colleague John Adams's 1778 study of the origins of constitutional government, *A Defense of the Constitutions of Government of the United States of America,* which consists largely of long discussions virtually copied from Greek and Roman authors. It was the Virginia delegate James Madison who constructed the more elaborate adaptation of the separation of powers to the American experience. In *Federalist* 47, Madison acknowledged that opponents of the Constitution objected to it partly out of fear that it violates the principles of separation.

A great problem remained, as the Virginia delegate George Mason noted on his working copy of the draft of the Constitution: "There is no Declaration of Rights." This omission, which one scholar called the "Achilles' heel" and "tactical error" of the convention, cost the support of Mason and may have jeopardized ratification altogether if Madison had not turned all his attention to the issue. Madison promised the state ratifying conventions that if the Constitution were ratified and he were elected to Congress, his first act would be to submit amendments for a Bill of Rights.

Ratification occurred, and Madison was elected. The House of Representatives approved seventeen of Madison's amendments, the Senate consolidated them to twelve, and on 25 September 1789, these were submitted to the states for ratification. The ten that were ratified in 1791 constitute the Bill of Rights.

As an instrument of governance, the Bill of Rights is an American invention. Only six of the provisions, or about 20 percent, were first stated in the Magna Carta of 1215. Of the twenty-seven provisions of the Bill of Rights, however, all but one—freedom of the press—have roots in classical antiquity.

The English mathematician Alfred North Whitehead intuitively recognized the debt of the framers to classical antiquity when he observed, "I know of only three times in the Western world when statesmen consciously took control of historic destinies: Periclean Athens, Rome under Augustus, and the founding of your American republic." The political scientist Hannah Arendt put the matter more directly: "Without the classical example . . . none of the men of the revolutions on either side of the Atlantic would have possessed the courage for what turned out to be unprecedented action."

ROME ON THE POTOMAC: A CLASSICAL CAPITOL IS BUILT

After the Revolution was won and the manner of governance determined, the United States was faced with creating a civic architecture that would reflect its new aspirations. During the colonial period, public buildings generally reflected those of the same period in Europe. The reconstructed buildings of colonial Williamsburg, Virginia, for example, follow the Georgian architecture of the era. Now Americans wanted to offer a new face to the world, one that would nevertheless symbolize stability and continuity.

In the matter of the new capital city, historians know exactly when, where, and to whom to look for the formative inspiration and ethos. In 1785, Thomas Jefferson paid a visit to the Maison-Carrée in Nîmes, France, a Roman temple built in 16 B.C. By his own account he sat there gazing at it for hours, "like a lover at his mistress." For Jefferson this one building represented an entire culture. "The city of Rome is actually existing in all the splendor of its empire," he wrote. Jefferson modeled his design for the state capitol of Virginia in Richmond (erected in 1788) on this temple. Later he chose classical models, especially the domed Roman Pantheon, for his home at Monticello, near Charlottesville, and for the central rotunda at the University of Virginia.

While in 1790 Washington chose the site for the new national capital at the head of the Potomac River, it was Jefferson who worked with the architect Pierre L'Enfant to envision the layout and aspect of the city. As Garry Wills put it, "Jefferson took the first steps that stamped America's federal city as a Roman town. . . . New ideas were more daring the older they could claim to be." Washington, D.C., was not going to be another London, but a new instantiation on American shores of a now truly democratized Roman republic. Thus Jefferson rebuked the architect Benjamin Latrobe for not offering a design for the Capitol along Roman lines, which Jefferson's own anonymous submission embraced. The most significant precedent of all was the soaring dome of the ancient Roman Pantheon, which still survives.

Besides their grandeur, the new public buildings were to represent purity of form, symmetry, and proportion. American tastes changed in about 1840, and no new public buildings were built in Washington in the neoclassical style until the twentieth century, when L'Enfant's plan was resurrected. The Lincoln Memorial, completed in 1922 and easily compared with the Athenian Parthenon, and the Jefferson Memorial, completed in 1943 and referring both to the Roman Pantheon and Jefferson's own Monticello, completed the grand plan.

Of a different exterior architectural style is the Library of Congress, built at the end of the nineteenth century. The presiding presence within, however, is the Greek goddess Athena. In the massive mosaic at the landing of the main staircase, Athena is represented as having laid aside her armor. Her shield and helmet lie on the ground. Instead she has assumed the sponsoring role for the liberal arts in a free society. The time for full expression in all the arts and practical sciences had come.

GREECE AND ROME IN AMERICAN LITERATURE

Classical education in the colonial and national period in some ways waned in the nineteenth century, when the emphasis on progress often eclipsed classical learning. Three factors helped stir an interest in Greek over Latin in the early nineteenth century: travel by Americans to Greece, starting with the financier Nicholas Biddle in 1806; study by Americans in the great German universities, especially Göttingen; and the War of Greek Independence from the Turks, from 1821 to 1832. Even as some of this intellectual Hellenism faded by the 1830s, it gained strong acceptance in another form, that of Greek Revival architecture.

In the field of literature, the influence of one classical author remained powerful from the outset. For explorers first and then settlers from Europe, Vergil's great Latin epic poem the *Aeneid*, started in circa 30 B.C. and unfinished at his death, provided an analogy for the American experiment almost from the beginning. The theme of heading into an unknown future had strong purchase on the American imagination because so much of the nation's still relatively brief history had been concerned with going west: first to the New World; then across the mountains to Ohio, Kentucky, and Tennessee; and finally on to Texas, California, and beyond.

When Vergil's hero Aeneas flees the burning city of Troy with his father on his shoulders and his son at his side, all he carries with him into an uncertain future is what he knows of the past. In time this proves sufficient. Through many wanderings and false starts toward the west, the young man eventually is able to combine his sense of history with his own practical experience in order to establish a new Troy on the Tiber—the powerful city of Rome.

Because Vergil located the destiny of Aeneas literally in the west, in Hesperia, it is no surprise that the figure of Aeneas as explorer and colonizer had become conspicuous to America's founders. Aeneas is a prominent analogue, for instance, in seventeenth-century English travelogues describing voyages to the New World and promoting colonial expansion. The explorer William Strachey's account of an expedition to Virginia in 1609 includes this description of Captain Newport's voyage up the James River in search of a safe landing:

Maison-Carrée, Nîmes, France, built 16 B.C. The ancient Roman temple inspired Thomas Jefferson's vision for American public architecture. © GIANNI DAGLI ORTI/CORBIS

At length, after much and weary search (with their barge coasting still before, as Vergil writeth Aeneas did, arriving in the region of Italy called Latium, upon the banks of the River Tiber) . . . they had sight of an extended plain . . . the trumpets sounding, the admiral struck said . . . and here . . . the colony disembarked. (Wright, pp. 78–79)

Strachey noted that part of the landfall was a low plain of about half an acre, adding in parentheses, "Or so much as Queen Dido might buy of King Iarbas, which she compassed about with the thongs cut out of one bull hide and there built her castle of Byrsa."

The historian Howard Mumford Jones has shown that the Aeneas image formed the organizing conception behind *The Proceedings of the English Colonie in Virginia,* published at Oxford in 1612. Composed in twelve books like the *Aeneid,* Captain John Smith is portrayed as an epic hero who also transplants his people to new shores and encounters a hero of equal stature, Powhatan, echoing Aeneas's encounter with Turnus. The parallels include also the appeals of each nation to its own deities, skill in

diplomacy, single combat, and even a mysterious wound in the hour of triumph.

In 1835 Francis Glass published a biography in Latin of George Washington, a subject, wrote his editor, "above all Greek; above all Roman fame." Praised by leading classics professors of the day for the Ciceronian purity of its Latin, it exhibited, according to one, "a narrative in Latinized English" but savoring throughout of "an original Roman idiom." The *New Yorker* in its pages urged that it become a school text: "It is well to place in the hands of our youth this record of the Father of his country, in the same language in which they read of the valour of Caesar, of the prudence of Fabius, and the virtues of Cincinnatus; for it will enable them, with a glow of honest pride, to feel that in Washington all these rare and exalted attributes were combined."

When George Washington finally was able to retire from military service to his beloved Mount Vernon, he placed an order for a bronze sculpture to decorate his mantlepiece. The subject of the sculpture was the Trojan hero Aeneas, father on his shoul-

241

Minerva mosaic by Elihu Vedder at the Library of Congress. The Roman divinity Minerva was the goddess of wisdom. LIBRARY OF CONGRESS

A EULOGY FOR JOHN ADAMS AND THOMAS JEFFERSON

The lawyer-statesman Daniel Webster presented this eulogy for two of America's Founding Fathers at Fanueil Hall in Boston on 2 August 1826.

Literature sometimes disgusts, and pretension to it much oftener disgusts, by appearing to hang loosely on the character, like something foreign or extraneous . . . this has exposed learning, and especially classical learning, to reproach. Men have seen that it might exist without mental superiority, without vigor, without good taste, and without utility. . . . The question after all, if it be a question, is, whether literature, ancient as well as modern, does not assist a good understanding, improve natural good taste, add polished armor to native strength, and render its possessor, not only more capable of deriving private happiness from contemplation and reflection, but more accomplished also for action in affairs of life, and especially for public action. Those whose memories we now honor were learned men; but their learning was kept in its proper place and made subservient to the uses and objects of life. They were scholars, not common nor superficial; but their scholarship was so in keeping with their character, so blended and inwrought, that careless observers or bad judges, not seeing an ostentatious display of it, might infer that it did not exist; forgetting, or not knowing, that classical learning in men who act in conspicuous public stations, perform duties which exercise the faculty of writing, or address popular, deliberative, or judicial bodies, is often felt where it is little seen, and sometimes felt more effectually because it is not seen at all.

Source: Wiltse, *The Papers of Daniel Webster: Speeches and Formal Writings,* vol. 1 (1800–1833), p. 266.

ways in which Vergilian metaphor lies behind the novel *The Great Meadow* (1930) by Elizabeth Madox Roberts. The novel recounts the migration by Diony Hall and her new husband from Albemarle County, Virginia, to a new home in Kentucky in the 1790s. The Vergilian connection is suggested at the outset, as Dione is the name of the mother of Venus, Aeneas's mother. Diony Hall's father Thomas, a great lover of books, brings the myth and the story together explicitly when he bids his daughter farewell with the words, in Latin, of the opening three and a half lines of the *Aeneid.* Other episodes in the novel are analogous to the gathering of the household Penates, the preparation for the journey, the stop at Buthrotum, the attention given to the burial of the dead, and even a symbolic journey to the underworld. The use of the past here is to make the new country seem like home.

Laura Krey's 1938 novel *And Tell of Time* spans the years 1775 to 1888 and several generations of the families of Lucina and Calvin Darcy, who migrate from Georgia to the Brazos River area of Texas in 1865. The quotation prefacing the final section of the novel is from the third book of the *Aeneid* and confirms the relocation of Troy on the banks of the Brazos. Lucina Darcy sees herself consciously as a mediator of a cultural tradition as she contemplates the importance of a sense of history as a means of establishing oneself and one's family in a new terrain. A small glass bottle, found in a field in England and handed down through her family in Virginia, carried then to Georgia and finally to Texas, serves as a material sign of continuity. "Some Roman may have dropped it," Lucina's father had told her, "unaware that his would be the last generation to refer thus easily, as if by right of kinship, to great Rome on the Tiber."

The Darcys migrated to Texas because the South, their Troy, had fallen. Southerners tended to identify closely their own lost cause with the fall of Troy, as appears in the stanzas of an untitled poem, sent by P. S. Worsley to General Robert E. Lee after Appomattox:

Thy Troy is fallen, thy dear land
Is marred beneath the spoiler's heel.
I cannot trust my trembling hand
To write the things I feel.

An angel's heart, an angel's mouth
Not Homer's, could alone for me
Hymn the great Confederate South,
Virginia first, and Lee.

(in Douglas Southall Freeman, *R. E. Lee: A Biography.* Vol. 4. New York, 1935, p. 236)

ders and son at his side, setting out resolutely to establish with his people a new civilization in the west.

In the westering tradition within the United States, settlers often took knowledge or symbols of the classical tradition with them as a kind of talisman, not unlike the Penates or household gods carried by Aeneas and his father as they set out from Troy. The explorer Joan Reinhard Smith showed the

The great classicist Basil Lanneau Gildersleeve, born in South Carolina and a professor first at the University of Virginia, then at the Johns Hopkins University, wrote a far more apt and compelling comparison of the Civil War with Greek antiquity in his essay "A Southerner in the Peloponnesian War," first published in the *Atlantic Monthly* in 1897. Drawing on his experiences as both a scholar and a soldier, Gildersleeve wrote: "I went from my books to the front, and went back from the front to my books, from the Confederate war to the Peloponnesian war, from Lee to Early to Thucydides and Aristophanes. I fancy I understood my Greek history and my Greek authors better for my experience in the field." That kind of learning, however, is not to be wished. Recalling the horror, Gildersleeve wistfully quoted the Greek poet Pindar: "A sweet thing is war to those who have not tried it." The essay concludes with: "No wonder that all these details of daily hardship come back even now to the old student when he reopens his Aristophanes. No wonder that the ever present Peloponnesian war will not suffer him to forget those four years in which the sea of trouble rose higher and higher."

In the twentieth century, classical analogies again became useful in understanding warfare. The psychiatrist Jonathan Shay wrote in his *Achilles in Vietnam* (1994) that he could not understand the dilemmas of Vietnam veterans until he made his own careful study of the Greek poet Homer's epic the *Iliad*. The classicist William H. Race, himself a Vietnam veteran, combined the experience of Gildersleeve with the acumen of Shay in his 1996 essay "A Classicist in the Vietnam War."

For the poets known as the Fugitives who first met at Vanderbilt University in the 1920s, the classics paradoxically provided a means of freeing southern literature from the thrall of the Civil War. Allen Tate especially, but also Robert Penn Warren and others, appropriated Vergil's *Aeneid* as a universalizing rather than parochializing text. Three of Tate's major poems, "The Mediterranean" (1932), "Aeneas at Washington" (1933), and "Aeneas at New York" (1932), employ Aeneas as narrator. His only novel, *The Fathers* (1938), likewise explores the conflict of tradition with modernity. The Aeneas image likewise informs one of Warren's final novels, *A Place to Come To* (1977). Part two compares Jed Tewksbury's arrival in Nashville with Aeneas's arrival in Carthage.

JEFFERSON, CALHOUN, AND THE SLAVERY DEBATE

In the American South, not one but two classical traditions evolved in the early period. One, represented best by Thomas Jefferson and informed by the American Enlightenment, looked to antiquity for models of free institutions, the inspiration of striking personalities, and lessons in moral virtue. The other was one of conservative reaction, seeking justification in the past for maintaining the status quo in the present. These divisions were to some extent geographical even within the South, one spreading out from Virginia into Kentucky and Tennessee, the other centered in South Carolina and greatly influencing the intellectual and social climate of the Deep South, especially Alabama and Mississippi. Charlottesville and Charleston were never mutually exclusive, of course, but the flashpoint between them came in the nineteenth century with the debates about slavery, the subject that had been acknowledged but muted—painfully by some and angrily by others—at the convention that produced the U.S. Constitution.

From the classical perspective, the ancient author most frequently adduced was Aristotle. Jefferson had little regard for Aristotle, advising a young acquaintance: "The full experiment of a government democratical, but representative, was and is still reserved for us. . . . The introduction of this new principle of representative democracy has rendered useless almost everything written before on the structure of government; and, in a great measure, relieves our regret, if the political writings of Aristotle, or of any other ancient have been lost, or are unfaithfully rendered or explained to us." On the other hand, the champion of slavery and the Southern cause, John C. Calhoun of South Carolina, counseled his young friend: "I would advise a young man with your views to . . . read the best elementary treatises on Government, including Aristotle's, which I regard as among the best."

The compelling difference in these assessments rests on Aristotle's formulation of the organic theory of society, which maintains that the needs of the polity supercede those of the individual, who is born into a certain place with the function of contributing to the welfare of the whole from that position. The organic theory contrasts radically with the ideals of the Enlightenment dear to Jefferson, in which the welfare of the individual supersedes that of society. Jefferson was instead committed to the idea of the social contract and to a "natural aristocracy" based on virtue and talent—fostered by education provided by the state—rather than on birth, position, or wealth.

Although Calhoun began his career as a Jeffersonian and a nationalist, he had become by the late 1820s an ardent defender of states' rights. By 1838 he could say of the institution of slavery: "Many in the South once believed that it was a moral and political evil. That folly and delusion are gone. We see it now in its true light, and regard it as the most safe and stable basis for free institutions in the world." Calhoun nourished with special zeal a contempt for the proposition that all men are created equal. "We now begin to experience," he said in his 1848 speech on the Oregon Territory Bill, which prohibited slavery in the area, "the danger of admitting so great an error to have a place in the Declaration of our Independence. It had strong hold on the mind of Mr. Jefferson, the author of that document, which caused him to take an utterly false view of the subordinate relation of the black to the white race in the South, and to hold, in consequence, that the latter, though utterly unqualified to possess liberty, were as fully entitled to both liberty and equality as the former."

Writing in *De Bows Review* in 1860, the slavery defender and staunch South Carolina antisecessionist William J. Grayson made explicit the genealogy of Calhoun's position: "The maxim of Mr. Calhoun is, that a democratic government cannot exist unless the laboring class be slaves. . . . It is not a new thing, but is two thousand years old. So far from being 'first enumerated' by Mr. Calhoun, it is as ancient as Aristotle. In his 'Politics'—which should be a textbook in all Southern colleges—in words as clear and emphatic as language can furnish, he lays down the maxim, that *a complete household or community is one composed of freemen and slaves* [emphasis in original]. . . . The whole proposition, both as to slavery and the race of the slave, is distinctly stated by the Greek philosopher" (pp. 59–60).

The more liberal classical tradition in the South did have successors. A Virginian named Jesse Burton Harrison, highly trained in the classics, wrote a refutation of the pro-slavery argument in 1833. He urged the young men of Virginia not to fear the unpopularity attendant on championing such a cause, invoking the name of Jefferson as the Great Democrat, and quoting Cicero, the last great defender of the Roman republic: "In great enterprises some are called to risk their lives, some their reputation, and some the good will of their fellow citizens" (pp. 398–399).

Another notable was Sam Houston, the self-educated classicist who claimed to have memorized all five hundred pages of Pope's English translation of the *Iliad* as a youth. As a member of Congress from Tennessee, Houston compared the politician Henry Clay with the Trojan War hero Ajax in the thick of battle. As president of the Republic of Texas, he likened the heroes of the Alamo to King Leonidas and the Spartans at Thermopylae. As a senator from Texas, it was Houston's support of the admission of Oregon as a free state, with slavery expressly prohibited, that identified him among southerners with the abolitionist cause. In the summer of 1848, Houston cast one of the two decisive votes for the bill to organize the Oregon Territory, for which he won the undying enmity of John C. Calhoun. He was by many a betrayer of his region: "With this single vote," one Charleston newspaper proclaimed, "the South has been beaten by the South." Houston's position, nevertheless, was consistent. As governor of Texas in 1859 he was bodily removed from the governor's office for his opposition to slavery and for his refusal to take the oath of allegiance to the Confederacy.

THE USES OF THE PAST

In the multitude of appropriations of the Greek and Roman past, there was never one classical vision but many, each embraced for different ends and purposes. Some encouraged adaptation and freedom of thought; others were erected as a bulwark against change. In the end, however, the founders were a practical people. Because of their extensive classical education, they had a very long sense of history. From this perspective they learned how to avoid mistakes of the past even as they were crafting a workable plan for the future.

In governance, civic architecture, literature, and politics, Americans, like the ancient Athenians, have never been afraid to innovate. Like the Romans of the republic, however, Americans also yearned to preserve what is good. This combination of innovation and preservation, encoded in the Constitution and implanted in habits of heart and mind, gives Americans the continuing capacity to adapt the guidance of the past to an uncharted future.

See also **Colonial Images of Europe and America; The Arts in the Republican Era; Slavery and Race; Antislavery; Southern Intellectual Life** *(in this volume);* **Constitutional Thought** *(volume 2);* **Education; The American University; Architecture; Monuments and Memorials; Fiction; Poetry; Myth and Symbol; History and the Study of the Past** *(volume 3).*

BIBLIOGRAPHY

Albu, Emily, and Michele Valerie Ronnick. *Teaching the Classical Tradition.* New York, 1999.

Bailyn, Bernard. *The Ideological Origins of the American Revolution.* Cambridge, Mass., 1967.

Bondanella, Peter. *The Eternal City: Roman Images in the Modern World.* Chapel Hill, N.C., 1987.

Boswell, Jeannetta. *Past Ruined Ilion: A Bibliography of English and American Literature Based on Greco-Roman Mythology.* Metuchen, N.J., 1982.

Gildersleeve, Basil Lanneau. "A Southerner in the Peloponnesian War." In *Soldier and Scholar: Basil Lanneau Gildersleeve and the Civil War,* edited by Ward W. Briggs Jr., pp. 389–413. Charlottesville, Va., 1998.

Glass, Francis. *A Life of George Washington in Latin Prose.* 1835. Reprint, edited by J. N. Reynolds, Washington, D.C., 1976. See also the translated edition: *A Composite Translation of A Life of George Washington in Latin Prose,* edited by John Francis Latimer. Washington, D.C., 1976.

Grayson, William J. "Mackay's Travels in America, The Dual Form of Labor." *De Bow's Review* 28 (1860): 59–60.

Harrison, Jesse Burton. "The Slavery Question in Virginia" (Richmond, 1832). In *Aris Sonis Facisque, The Harrisons of Skimono,* edited by Fairfax Harrison. New York, 1910.

Jones, Howard Mumford. *O Strange New World. American Culture: The Formative Years.* New York, 1964.

Kelsey, Francis W. *Latin and Greek in American Education.* New York, 1928.

Miles, Edwin A. "The Old South and the Classical World." *North Carolina Historical Review* 48 (1971): 258–275.

Mills, Lane. *Architecture of the Old South: Greek Revival and Romantic.* Savannah, Ga., 1996.

Parrington, Vernon Louis. *Main Currents in American Thought: An Interpretation of American Literature from the Beginnings to 1920.* New York, 1930.

Pocock, J. G. A. *The Machiavellian Moment: Florentine Political Thought and the Atlantic Republican Tradition.* Princeton, N.J., 1975.

——, ed. *Three British Revolutions, 1641, 1688, 1776.* Princeton, N.J., 1980.

——, ed. *The Varieties of British Political Thought 1500–1800.* Cambridge, England, 1993.

Race, William H. "A Classicist in the Viet Nam War." Nashville, Tenn., 1996. Unpublished presidential address at the meeting of the Classical Association of the Middle West and South.

Rahe, Paul A. *Republics Ancient and Modern: Classical Republicanism and the American Revolution.* Chapel Hill, N.C., 1992.

Reinhold, Meyer. *Classica Americana: The Greek and Roman Heritage in the United States.* Detroit, Mich., 1984.

——. *The Classick Pages: Classical Reading of Eighteenth-Century Americans.* University Park, Pa., 1975.

Richard, Carl J. *The Founders and the Classics: Greece, Rome, and the American Enlightenment.* Cambridge, Mass., 1994.

Sellers, M. N. S. *American Republicanism: Roman Ideology in the United States Constitution.* Basingstoke, England, 1994.

Smith, Jo Reinhard. "New Troy in the Bluegrass: Vergilian Metaphor and *The Great Meadow*." *Mississippi Quarterly* 22 (1968–1969): 39–46.

Stewart, George R. *Names on the Land: A Historical Account of Place-Naming in the United States*. Boston, Mass., 1958.

Vance, William. *America's Rome*. 2 vols. New Haven, Conn., 1989.

Whitehead, Alfred North. *Dialogues of Alfred North Whitehead, As Recorded by Lucien Price*. Boston, Mass., 1954.

Wills, Garry. *Cincinnatus: George Washington and the Enlightenment*. New York, 1984.

Wiltshire, Susan Ford. *Greece, Rome, and the Bill of Rights*. Norman, Minn., 1992.

——. "Jefferson, Calhoun, and the Slavery Debate: The Classics and the Two Minds of the South." *Southern Humanities Review* special issue (1977): 33–40.

——. "Rome on the Potomac: Virgil and Public Life in America." *Augustan Age* 6 (1987): 219–226.

——. "Thomas Jefferson and John Adams on the Classics." *Arion* 6, no. 1 (1967): 116–132.

——. "Vergil, Allen Tate, and the Analogy of Experience." *Classical and Modern Literature* 5, no. 2 (1985): 87–98.

Wiltshire, Susan Ford, ed. *The Classical Tradition in the South*. Special issue, *Southern Humanities Review*, 1977.

——. *The Usefulness of Classical Learning in the Eighteenth Century*. N.p., 1975.

Winkler, Martin M. *Classics and the Cinema*. Lewisburg, Pa., 1991.

Wolk, Allan. "Classical Names." Chap. 8 in *The Naming of America*. Nashville, Tenn., 1977.

Wood, Gordon S. *The Creation of the American Republic, 1776–1787*. Chapel Hill, N.C., 1969.

Wright, Louise B., ed. "True Reporting." In *A Voyage to Virginia in 1609*. Charlottesville, Va., 1964.

Wyke, Maria. *Projecting the Past: Ancient Rome, Cinema and History*. New York, 1997.

AGRARIANISM AND THE AGRARIAN IDEAL IN EARLY AMERICA

R. Douglas Hurt

Agrarianism is the imagined and sentimental idealization of rural life. It is the mental image of a gardenlike Eden where farm men and women live in idyllic and harmonious innocence with themselves and a benevolent nature. At the heart of this concept is the premise that rural life is superior to all other forms of occupation and living. As such, the agrarian ideal represents a middle ground between the cities and the wilderness, and it has been a symbol of American civilization since the colonial period. In the countryside, men and women could live independent, egalitarian, and democratic lives that provided the foundation for the republic. Although the most articulate expression of agrarianism came during the eighteenth century, it remained a viable interpretation through the twentieth century for those who chose to see the countryside as a place where small-scale, family farm men and women lived wholesome and self-sufficient lives far removed from the corruption, poverty, and savagery of the cities.

CRÈVECOEUR

Although the concept of American life based on the philosophy of agrarianism is usually traced to Thomas Jefferson, J. Hector St. John Crèvecoeur, a naturalized citizen and the author of *Letters from an American Farmer* (1782), provided an earlier explanation of the agrarian ideal in the development of America. Crèvecoeur made an impassioned and unqualified defense of an agrarian life in America. He believed that people are inherently benevolent and good and that the environment determines nearly everything. He wrote: "Men are like plants; the goodness and flavour of the fruit proceeds from the peculiar soil in which they grow" (p. 50). As a result, men and women were best able to achieve goodness when they remained close to the soil. They could do so by leaving corrupt Europe behind for America and earning a living as farmers in their new nation.

In America, he wrote, "Nature opens her broad lap to receive the perpetual accession of new-comers" (p. 17). There, they would prosper and flourish as farmers.

Crèvecoeur believed that the most distinctive aspect of America was its agrarian character. The abundance of land enabled all who so chose to become small-scale farmers, which ensured that Americans would lead self-sufficient, independent lives. Like Jefferson, Crèvecoeur based his agrarian ideal on the philosophy of John Locke, contending that the ownership of land ensured liberty and freedom. Still, the ownership of property in the form of a small farm meant more than material success and political liberty. It also imparted spiritual benefits. Crèvecoeur wrote: "it is as we silently till the ground and move along the odoriferous furrows of our low lands, uninterrupted either by stones or stumps; it is there that the salubrious effluvia of the earth animate our spirits and serve to inspire us" (p. 22). The uniquely benevolent effects of farming the native soil made it possible for Americans to remain close not only to nature but also to a higher spiritual force. Small-scale farmers, then, could confidently look forward to living happy, full, and independent lives far removed from the crowded cities where they would neither be close to nature nor free to lead ethical and moral lives based on farming.

For Crèvecoeur, American society was characterized by a special form of cultivation and farmer. His agrarian vision beheld a freeholder, that is, a landowning farmer or yeoman. These farmers were different from the peasants in feudal Europe and from the planters in the American South. Crèvecoeur believed that the small-scale American farmers were "a new race of men," a class of people unknown anywhere else in the world (p. 49). These farmers were unique because they were independent and self-sufficient. But Crèvecoeur believed that the achievement of material success and independence was based on a moral journey and personal transformation. In the American wilderness, immigrants shed their former dependency, subservience, and poverty. As the farmer worked his land, he mastered the virtues of sobriety, honesty, and industry, which Crèvecoeur believed were the principal requirements for success in America. In this sense, then, farming became a school in moral virtue and a training ground for the building of character.

Crèvecoeur's transformation of farmers from peasants to independent men was political as well as moral. He believed that the ownership of property in the form of a small farm developed men who were more jealous of their civil liberties and more resistant to despotism than any other people. He wrote: "Tyranny never can take a strong hold in this country, the land is too widely distributed; it is poverty in Europe that makes slaves" (p. 194). Crèvecoeur, then, linked a series of images and ideas in his writing: nature to property, property to independence, and independence to equality, virtue, and civil liberty. Jefferson would express these ideas with greater clarity a few years later, when he too located the physical setting of republican virtue in the countryside. There, honest and self-reliant farmers cultivated the soil and lived in harmony with nature and their fellow men and there they mastered the code of moral and political virtue. Crèvecoeur's writing, apart from Jefferson's, constitutes the most enthusiastic support of the agrarian idea in eighteenth-century America. For Crèvecoeur, America was an agrarian paradise where farmers could experience regeneration and renewal in a bucolic setting located midway between the cities and the frontier.

JEFFERSON

Despite Crèvecoeur's writing, the concept of agrarianism is most often traced to Thomas Jefferson, who believed in the moral superiority of farmers. In 1785, Jefferson wrote to John Jay: "Cultivators of the earth are the most valuable citizens. They are the most vigorous, the most independent, the most virtuous, and they are tied to their country, and wedded to its liberty and interests, by the most lasting bonds" (*The Life and Selected Writings of Thomas Jefferson*, p. 377). Two years later Jefferson affirmed his belief that farmers provided the moral strength of the nation when he wrote that:

> Those who labour in the earth are the chosen people of God, if ever he had a chosen people, whose breasts he has made his peculiar deposit for sub-

stantial and genuine virtue. . . . Corruption of morals in the mass of cultivators is a phaenomenon of which no age nor nation has furnished an example. (*Notes on the State of Virginia*, pp. 164–165)

Jefferson's thoughts on American farmers and rural life rank among the most frequently quoted political values in American history. It is from these writings that nineteenth-century Americans were taught that rural life, particularly farming, was, if not sacred, then at least the most desirable, ethical, moral, and free, that is, ideal, way of living.

Agrarianism and Government Although many political and social commentators and farmers have used Jefferson's words to justify assertions that the family farm is the foundation of the American economy, his thoughts more appropriately reconcile self-interest and the public good through landownership and an agricultural life. Jefferson committed his views to paper between the Declaration of Independence of 1776 and the U.S. Constitution of 1787. In the debate over ratification of the Constitution, Jefferson and the Federalists, particularly Alexander Hamilton, argued about the location of political power and public responsibility. The Federalists believed that some people were better prepared to recognize the public good than others and that political power should be concentrated in the hands of a few individuals, particularly merchants, professionals, and large-scale land or estate owners. Jefferson, a follower of John Locke's labor theory of property, which held that men established their right to property ownership through their own labor, contended that the state, that is, government, existed to protect property, which in the new nation consisted of many farms. Jefferson believed that farmers would be the most loyal supporters of the new government and that a nation of farmers would be easier to govern than a country composed of merchants, manufacturers, large landowners, and landless workers. The small-scale farmer, or yeoman, who owned his farm and worked the land with his family was, to Jefferson, the most honest and independent citizen. Because farmers lived close to a beneficent nature by necessity, he believed they adopted special values that enabled them to lead wholesome lives and exhibit a personal integrity that would serve the nation well in political forums.

By living close to a benevolent nature, farmers created an agrarian lifestyle based on moral principles and hard work for both the benefit of their fellow citizens and the glory of God. The agrarian ideal, then, for Jefferson, Crèvecoeur, and those who accepted their philosophy was based on the own-

THOMAS JEFFERSON

Although Thomas Jefferson was the principal exponent of the agrarian ideal, he did not write extensively on the subject. His most important thoughts on agrarianism are contained in his only published book, *Notes on the State of Virginia* (1787), which he wrote during the early 1780s. He argued that the new nation should not attempt to develop its own industry, but rather strive to preserve its agricultural and rural character. In America, Jefferson argued, a society or class of independent, small-scale landowning farmers gave economic, social, and moral strength to the new nation. Jefferson's praise for the agricultural life was unlimited:

Those who labour in the earth are the chosen people of God, if ever he had a chosen people, whose breasts he has made his peculiar deposit for substantial and genuine virtue. It is the focus in which he keeps alive that sacred fire, which otherwise might escape from the face of the earth. Corruption of morals in the mass of cultivators is a phaenomenon of which no age nor nation has furnished an example. It is the mark set on those, who not looking up to heaven, to their own soil and industry, as does the husbandman, for their subsistence, depend for it on the casualties and caprice of customers. Dependence begets subservience and venality, suffocates the germ of virtue, and prepares fit tools for the designs of ambition. . . . While we have land to labour then, let us never wish to see our citizens occupied at a work-bench, or twirling a distaff . . . for the general operations of manufacture, let our work-shops remain in Europe. It is better to carry provisions and materials to workmen there, than bring them to the provisions and materials, and with them their manners and principles. The loss by the transportation of commodities across the Atlantic will be made up in happiness and permanence of government. The mobs of great cities add just so much to the support of pure government, as sores do to the strength of the human body. It is the manners and spirit of a people which preserve a republic in vigour. A degeneracy in these is a canker which soon eats to the heart of its laws and constitution. (pp. 164–165)

ership of land, which gave people a stake in society and a desire to protect and preserve its government. Jefferson contended that freeholders, or property-owning farmers, as opposed to renters or tenants, had the character to carry out the responsibilities of a free citizenry, because property ownership in the form of small-scale farms made it necessary for them to participate in government to ensure the protection of their lands. Jefferson believed that because farmers were tied to their lands through ownership, they would necessarily resolve political differences in ways that would not endanger the stability of the government, that is, the nation-state. He contended that landowners in the form of small-scale farmers made the strongest identification between self-interest and the public good, and that consequently they were the most virtuous citizens. Moreover, agrarianism and democracy were inextricably linked. Since most men in the early republic were farmers and because landownership usually conveyed the right to vote, agriculture made an important contribution to democracy. Farmers by their numbers alone gave weight and significance to democratic government. Agrarianism also was a political ideology of the majority that supported limited government.

Agrarianism in this context, then, stressed the belief that a landed population, that is, a nation of small-scale, family farmers, would seek the common good through governmental actions. As a result, government would ensure a high quality of life for all citizens based on social justice, freedom, and economic prosperity. Jefferson's agrarian writings were intended to counter the Federalist desire to centralize government in the hands of the elite, and instead to place the ultimate responsibility for achieving the common good through government in the hands of farmers. In this context, Jeffersonian democracy meant that a society based on small-scale farmers would check both tyranny by the few and mob rule by the many. For Jefferson, farmers were the most important citizens because they could see, direct, and control the convergence of personal interest and the public good and provide stability and fiscal responsibility for society. The ability, then, to understand the relationship between public and private interests is the mark of citizenship, and for Jefferson, it was based on property ownership in the form of land and occupation in the form of farming—that is, on an agrarian life.

Jefferson, of course, understood that the structure of American society would change, but he hoped that if the government of the new nation could be based on small-scale farmers, changing conditions and circumstances could be managed for the public good. Indeed, Jefferson believed that an agrarian life would establish long-term patterns of conduct that would become broadly characteristic of American society, such as morality, independence, virtuosity, and democracy. Accordingly, Jefferson contended that a nation of property-owning farmers would never suffer poverty or second-class citizenship because they would not only take care of their families but also the nation by their energetic, independent thought and action, all of which would be public-spirited and directed to achieving the common good.

Certainly, Jefferson's writings embodied the essential concepts of agrarianism: belief in the independence and virtue of the small-scale, property-owning (yeoman) farmer; the idea that property ownership was a natural right; a preference for landownership without restrictions on use or disposition; the conviction that land provided a safety valve for overcrowded cities; the belief that anyone could gain a good life through hard work on their own farm; and the view that family farms provided the primary source of wealth for the nation. In this sense, farmers had the moral superiority and civic responsibility to guarantee freedom, liberty, and order.

At first, Jefferson's agrarian philosophy had nearly universal appeal among the well-educated, upper-class landowners of the late eighteenth century, who welcomed a philosophy of living that gave order to their political, social, and economic world. Many landowning Americans at that time linked the concepts of a simple agricultural life, in which people lived close to nature, with John Locke's formal philosophy of property rights. By so doing they created a natural rights philosophy based on landownership that became especially popular among mass society during the nineteenth century.

The Farm Wife

Agrarianism, with its emphasis on property and civil rights for men as owners of land in the form of small-scale farms, meant something else for rural women. Jefferson's image of an agrarian nation in which the republic was protected by a landowning, democratic citizenry of small-scale farmers did not include women as agrarian equals of men. Technically, women were not farmers, although they labored in the fields and barns, and few bought land as a result of their own labor. African American women worked land as agricultural laborers, but as slaves they did so without the rights of citizens.

For Jefferson, the house and the farm occupied different spheres, and the male head of the household controlled the farm. To the extent that the farm woman had a place in the agrarian image of American rural life it was in the context of a helpmate who churned butter, gathered eggs, or tended the garden, all in a peaceful, bucolic, and romantic setting. The farmer, not the farm wife, was the canonical citizen, and the farm family was his canonical family. The farmer's wife supported the citizen farmer while she worked in the home. Jefferson wrote: "The order and economy of a house are as honorable to the mistress as those of the farm to the master, and if either be neglected, ruin follows, and children destitute of the means of living" (*The Life and Selected Writings of Thomas Jefferson*, p. 689). The agrarian vision of America, then, placed women in a subordinate position. They were necessary to the success of the farm operation, but they were viewed as appendages to male farmers.

The Impact of Jeffersonian Ideology

Jefferson's belief that agriculture was a fundamental industry, that independent farmers benefited society, and that farming was a moral and virtuous occupation became an agrarian creed during the late eighteenth and early nineteenth centuries. The public readily accepted Jefferson's agrarian ideology because most Americans believed that independent farmers by necessity took care of their families in the best possible way and that they stood equal to any other men. In essence, farmers were superior because their occupation was the most essential and legitimate. Landownership created a self-sufficient, independent, conservative people to guard American liberties. These yeomen easily transferred their reverence for land and freedom to love of the nation in which they were the most patriotic citizens.

Farmers also believed that nonfarm people relied on farmers for their sustenance and prosperity. Farmers fed and clothed people through hard work.

AGRARIAN ART

The concept of agrarianism and the rural ideal can best be seen in the pictures of the artists collectively known as the Hudson River school, which dominated the American art scene from approximately 1825 to the 1880s. The landscape painters Thomas Cole, Asher B. Durand, Frederic Edwin Church, and George Inness, among others, painted rural scenes in which they portrayed nature in great detail, and also as a benevolent force that farm men and women altered for their own purposes. For these artists a tamed nature gave strength of character to those who worked the land and brought order to the countryside. The painters of the Hudson River school essentially believed that their pictures would have a moral effect, and they often painted nature as a garden in which small-scale farmers lived in harmony with the land and their neighbors.

During the 1930s, the agrarian ideal can best be seen in the paintings of Grant Wood, John Steuart Curry, and Thomas Hart Benton, the primary members of the Regionalist school in American art. Although their techniques differed from the artists of the Hudson River school a century earlier, the Regionalists concerned themselves particularly with the symbols of American rural life. The small-scale farms in the countryside enabled them to portray the public's continued belief that an agrarian life was not only the American ideal, but reality itself.

West Rock, New Haven (1849), by Frederic Edwin Church; *Delaware Water Gap* (1861), by George Inness; and *Stone City, Iowa* (1930), by Grant Wood, portray the agrarian ideal in rural life. In each picture the artist painted a benevolent nature in which farmers live a peaceful, secure, well-ordered life that is the foundation of a strong nation. An agrarian life ensured social stability far removed from the grim and crowded industrial cities. The painters of the Hudson River and Regionalist schools, then, provided visual images of the agrarian ideal or myth. Their paintings show idyllic landscapes where farmers have never known physical hardship, natural disaster, or economic troubles. Their pictures also show a bountiful and beneficent nature as well as the virtues of family, manual labor, and cooperative efforts among farmers. For these painters, the family farm is a cultivated state of nature, between the untamed wilderness and urban civilization. The result is the visualization of the concept of agrarianism in American life.

The artists of the Hudson River and Regionalist schools both painted pictures that reinforced America's image of itself, particularly its inherent dignity, basic goodness, and commitment to hard work and the right to enjoy the rewards that come from it. They portray farm life as harmonious with nature, even though farmers altered it for their own purposes. Through their pictures, generations of Americans came to better understand the written words of Crèvecoeur, Jefferson, Emerson, and Thoreau. As a result, the agrarian symbols of both political philosophers and artists merged to create a lasting image of America as an agrarian nation where rural life provided a strong economic, political, and social foundation in a gardenlike setting and made America exceptional among all nations.

Stone City, Iowa. Oil on wood panel by Grant Wood (1930). The artist's first major landscape. Estate of Grant Wood/ VAGA, New York, and Joslyn Art Museum, Omaha, Nebr. Gift of the Art Institute of Omaha

In contrast, nonfarmers such as lawyers, bankers, and merchants did not produce products that met basic human needs. Artisans met wants but seldom needs. Farmers rightly thought that they were the most important part of the economy. With approximately 80 percent of the population engaged in farming in 1800, farmers provided most exports, and merchants processed, handled, or sold agricultural products. Also, most investment capital was expended on land and slaves. Agriculture made the American economy function, and agrarianism provided the underlying philosophy that supported personal commitment to it as a way of life. In this sense farming, not manufacturing or trade, was the fundamental American industry that provided the wealth of the nation. Farmers also contended that the agricultural life was natural and good as well as the corollary that urban life was unnatural and not good. Accordingly, commercialism, excessive leisure and luxuries, and uncalloused hands corrupted individuals, drained their virtue, and ruined their mo-

rality. In contrast, farmers followed a sanctified calling.

Americans accepted the agrarian creed because it met most of the pressing needs of the early republic. Belief in the importance of independence, virtue, and patriotism enabled agrarians to assert cultural independence and democratic superiority and create a national identity in a world of monarchical nation-states. Agrarianism, then, provided the foundation for the creation of an American national consciousness. Agrarianism also influenced the cultural life of the Early Republic, particularly regarding the development of transcendentalism as reflected in the reverence for nature in the writings of Ralph Waldo Emerson and Henry David Thoreau and in the many rural communitarian experiments that became popular before the Civil War.

Jefferson's concept of agrarianism is, of course, a romantic view of the world, because it ignored urban citizens and others who did not make their living as small-scale farmers. Rapid growth of the republic significantly altered Jefferson's agrarian vision as cities expanded, and universal, white manhood suffrage allowed individuals other than landowning farmers to vote. In addition, the farm population began to decline during the late nineteenth century as industry expanded. Even so, Jefferson's vision of democracy based on ethical simplicity deriving from an agrarian life remained basic to American political ideology. During the nineteenth century, Jefferson's view of the role of the citizen-farmer in American society became even more romanticized, with two major themes predominating. The first held that nature played a formative role in the development of the American character. The second stressed that hard, physical labor, particularly farming, served as a prerequisite for achievement, success, and self-fulfillment.

The agrarian ideal that championed landownership as a natural right and small-scale farmers as the foundation of freedom, independence, and democracy, as well as the concept that wealth and virtue derived from the land and family, permeated American thought into the late nineteenth century. This agrarian creed also continued to hold that country people were morally virtuous and superior to those who lived in towns and cities. In 1896 Democratic presidential candidate William Jennings Bryan said: "Burn down your cities and leave our farms, and your cities will spring up again as if by magic; but destroy our farms and the grass will grow in the streets of every city in the country" (*Speeches of William Jennings Bryan*, p. 248).

By the twentieth century the concept of agrarianism reminded people of the virtues of independence, self-reliance, and the importance of community and common purpose. The agrarian ideal would continue to associate farming and agriculture with morality, politics, and the economy well into the twentieth century.

See also **Expansion and Empire** *(in this volume);* **Pastoralism and the Rural Ideal; The Natural World** *(volume 2);* **Individualism and the Self** *(volume 3).*

BIBLIOGRAPHY

Primary

Bryan, William Jennings. *Speeches of William Jennings Bryan.* Edited by William Jennings Bryan. Vol. 1. New York, 1913.

Crèvecoeur, J. Hector St. John. *Letters from an American Farmer.* 1782. Reprint, Gloucester, Mass., 1968.

Jefferson, Thomas. *Notes on the State of Virginia.* 1785. Reprint, edited by William Peden, New York, 1954.

Koch, Adrienne, and William Peden, eds. *The Life and Selected Writings of Thomas Jefferson.* New York, 1944.

Secondary

Adams, William. "Natural Virtue: Symbol and Imagination in the American Farm Crisis." *Georgia Review* 39, no. 4 (1985): 695–712.

Danbom, David B. *Born in the Country: A History of Rural America.* Baltimore, 1995.

Dennis, James M. *Renegade Regionalists: The Modern Independence of Grant Wood, Thomas Hart Benton, and John Steuart Curry.* Madison, Wisc., 1998.

Fink, Deborah. *Agrarian Women: Wives and Mothers in Rural Nebraska, 1880–1940.* Chapel Hill, N.C., 1992.

Hofstadter, Richard. "The Myth of the Happy Yeoman." *American Heritage* 7, no. 3 (1956), 42–53.

Howat, John K. *The Hudson River and Its Painters.* New York, 1972.

Machor, James I. "The Garden City in America: Crèvecoeur's Letters and the Urban-Pastoral Context." *American Studies* 23, no. 1 (1982): 69–83.

Montmarquet, James A. "Philosophical Foundations for Agrarianism." *Agriculture and Human Values* 2, no. 2 (1985): 5–14.

Peterson, Tarla Rai. "Jefferson's Yeoman Farmer as Frontier Hero: A Self-Defeating Mythic Structure." *Agriculture and Human Values* 7, no. 1 (1990): 9–19.

Rohrer, Wayne C., and Louis Douglas. *The Agrarian Transition in America: Dualism and Change.* Indianapolis, Ind., 1969.

Smith, Henry Nash. *Virgin Land: The American West as Symbol and Myth.* Cambridge, Mass., 1950.

Thompson, Paul B. "Agrarianism and the American Philosophical Tradition." *Agriculture and Human Values* 7, no. 1 (1990): 3–8.

Wilson, Douglas L. "The American *Agricola:* Jefferson's Agrarianism and the Classical Tradition." *South Atlantic Quarterly* 80, no. 3 (1981): 339–354.

THE ARTS IN THE REPUBLICAN ERA

David Jaffee

"A taste of painting is too much Wanting. . . . The people generally regard it no more than any other useful trade, as they sometimes term it, like that of a Carpenter tailor or shew maker, not as one of the most noble Arts in the World," the Boston-born portrait painter John Singleton Copley lamented in 1767. Yet Copley went on to claim an annual income of three hundred guineas that supported him "handsomely for a Couple of Years with a family." The plight of the arts in colonial British North America in the 1760s was a contradictory one, a situation that would continue in the post-revolutionary years. Without the ancient regime or a court style to sustain them, artists and their patrons still looked to European models in the late eighteenth and early nineteenth centuries, and they continued to lament the lack of European institutions and tastes. However, forces for innovation and support were appearing with the republican desires to escape the degeneration of the Old World and define new forms—in politics and in the arts. A new kind of society was emerging; one without an aristocracy, but with an elite of merchants and large landowners, still seeking recognition of their social status, who provided patronage for artists and artisans. Distinctions were fluid in American society, between the fine and useful arts, high and low, and art and artisanship.

COMMERCE AND CONSUMPTION IN THE COLONIAL WORLD

The bustling port cities of colonial British North America contained increasing numbers and varieties of craftsmen, communities of artisans who fashioned sophisticated objects. In portraiture for example, relatively stable clusters of artists and patrons gathered along with the growing availability of artists' supplies, books, and lessons in painting. When Charles Willson Peale left Annapolis, Maryland, on a visit to Philadelphia, Pennsylvania, in 1763, he was able to view the work of James Claypoole Jr., visit the painter Christopher Steele, and go to a bookstore and color shop: "at this store [Rivington] I bought the hand maid to the arts, it was the only Book he had on colours or painting, this I began to study art at my lodgings in order to enable me to form some judgment on what Colours I ought to purchase also the quantity [of]. Mr. Marshall in Chestnut Street, the only colour shop in the City, obligingly gave me a list of what colours he had and the prices annexed" (Miller, *Selected Papers* 3, p. 174). Port cities were centers of government as well as commercial entrepôts, with their merchants, magistrates, and other professionals; all these social groups offered potential sources of patrons. The presence of public buildings with their opportunities for display of the portraits of public figures and ornate decoration promoted the training of craftsmen and encouraged consumption on the part of the larger population.

Historians have hailed an eighteenth-century consumer revolution that spilled across the Atlantic from Great Britain to encompass the British North American colonies. In *The Refinement of America* (1992), Richard Bushman showed how the provincial gentry borrowed the genteel codes of Europe to offer visible evidence of their social status in the guise of stately homes, grander domestic furnishings, and more polite social conduct. From Virginia to Massachusetts aspiring gentry began to build mansion houses—imposing structures that materially set them apart from their merely middling neighbors. These structures, based on English Georgian forms, presented symmetrical facades to the viewer while a central hall provided a proper entry and parlor for formal entertainment; they stood out in the cultural landscape due to their size, elegance, and, often, their building materials and decorations. The few New World painters, often visitors or immigrants, filled the limited demand. However, newspaper advertisements and household inventories all indicate an increasing volume of furniture, textiles, ceramics, glassware, and utensils that were available to people at all social levels starting in the second quarter of the eighteenth century.

The midcentury colonial wars and flood of money in British North America only quickened the competition for display and decoration. In the colonies' few urban areas display reached new heights in the 1760s and 1770s—splendid carriages and sumptuous portraits made their appearance in the streets and houses of patrician Boston and New York. The statesman John Adams described in his diary his visit to a Boston merchant: "Went over [to] the House to view the Furniture, which alone cost a thousand Pounds sterling. A seat is for a noble Man, a Prince. The Turkey Carpets, the painted Hangings, the Marble Table, the rich Beds with crimson Damask Curtains and Counterpins, the beautiful Chimny Clock, the Spacious Garden, are the most magnificent of any Thing I have ever seen" (*Diary*, edited by L. H. Butterfield, 1:294). Even among the rural gentry the scale of country seats rose. Artisans continued their migration to the port cities of North America throughout the eighteenth century, looking for work and the opportunity to practice a trade. The European ornate rococo style, today called Chippendale, made its way across the Atlantic, brought by English craftsmen and objects, with its "gothick" and "Chinese" decorative motifs. Furniture and silver were festooned with rococo motifs such as shells and leaves and produced in the craft shops of colonial centers such as Williamsburg, Virginia, or Portsmouth, New Hampshire.

Other craftsmen sought the exposure and training only available in a cosmopolitan environment, yet they returned to the hinterlands where the rising consumer demand of the revolutionary era meant a demand for their services and products. Finally, the growing social distress and economic uncertainty of revolutionary hotbeds such as Boston caused recent arrivals such as Thomas Harland, the "watch and clockmaker from London," in 1773, to relocate almost immediately to Norwich, Connecticut, a town of about 7,500 inhabitants with a growing cluster of craftsmen. It was here he made the latest design of British clocks and trained a rising generation of Connecticut clockmakers. The direction of change, similar to the diffusion of mansion houses, or knives and forks for that matter, went from the urban towns to the elite of rural areas, those commercial and well-placed regions of the countryside, and continued down the social hierarchy to the aspiring rural genteel. However, rural people, or even the urban elite, did not simply copy the designs of British portraits or urban products.

When the furniture maker Eliphalet Chapin returned to his rural Connecticut home from a stint in Philadelphia, he offered the local notables rococo furniture, cosmopolitan in form but plainer and cheaper.

The growing sophistication of the arts in the colonies comes across in the life and career of the first great native-born painter, John Singleton Copley. Raised for a time by his stepfather, the engraver Peter Pelham, who died in Copley's youth, the young, largely self-taught Copley took advantage of the available resources: immigrant portraitists, mezzotints, and picture galleries. His rapid progress in graphic designs and rich color schemes made him the portraitist of the colonial merchant princes of Boston beginning in the 1760s; later he visited New York and Philadelphia. Not content with his mastery of the provincial scene, he sent his portrait of Henry Pelham (*Boy with a Squirrel*, 1765) for exhibition in London, where it met with a favorable reception. Copley considered the advice to pursue European training, but as his letter replying to that advice indicates (see sidebar), despite the provincial nature of the patronage that he enjoyed, he held a comfortable status as the leading painter in the colonies. Only the renewal of those European invitations a decade later, as the escalating political crisis

John Singleton Copley, *Boy with a Squirrel (Henry Pelham)*, 1765. Oil on canvas, Museum of Fine Arts, Boston. © BURSTEIN COLLECTION/CORBIS

JOHN SINGLETON COPLEY, 1767

The painter John Singleton Copley laments the state of the artist and the arts in the colonies; he debates leaving America for Europe:

I observe the Critisisms made on my last picture were not the same as those made on the first. I hope I have not in this as in the last by striving to avoid one error fallen into another. I shall be sorry if I have. However it must take its fate. Perhaps You may blame me for not taking anoth[e]r subject that would aforded me more time, but subjects are not so easily procured in this plac[e]. A taste of painting is too much Wanting to affoard me any kind of helps; and was it not for preserving the resembla[n]ce of perticular persons, painting would not be known in the plac[e]. The people generally regard it no more than any other usefull trade, as they somtimes term it, like that of a Carpenter tailor or shew maker, not as one of the most noble Arts in the World. Which is not a little Mortifiing to me. While the Arts are so disregarded I can hope for nothing, eith[e]r to incourage or assist me in my studies but what I receive from a thousand Leagues Distance, and be my improvements what they will, I shall not be benefited by them in this country, neighther in point of fortune or fame. This is what I at large in my last letter Datted [ ] as the only reason that discourages me from going to Europe, least after going I shall not find myself so good an artist, as to merit that incouragement that would make it worth my while. It would by no means be [ ] to go th[e]re to improve myself, and than return to America; but if I could make it worth my [while] to stay there, I would remove with Moth[e]r and Broth[e]r, who I am bound by all the ties of Duty and Effe[c]tion not to Desert as Long as I live. My income in this Country is about three hund'd Guineas a Year, out of which I have been able to Lay up as much as would carrie me thru and support me handsomly for a Couple of Years with a family.

Source: John Singleton Copley [to Benjamin West or Captain R. G. Bruce?], 1767. In Guernsey Jones, ed. *Letters and Papers of John Singleton Copley and Henry Pelham, 1739–1776.* Boston, 1914. Pp. 65–66.

divided families and communities, creating havoc among his artistic clientele as well as personal turmoil for Copley, led to his decision to leave America in 1774. Other portraitists continued to visit the middle and southern colonies.

Artisan-artists also made an appearance in the countryside. The services of a "limner," once reserved exclusively for residents of or visitors to Boston or New York or Charleston, South Carolina, could be had much closer to home if performed by a native artist such as Winthrop Chandler or Ralph Earl. When the Reverend Ebenezer Devotion wanted to celebrate his fifty-sixth birthday he turned to his artisan-artist neighbor Winthrop Chandler, who had just returned to northwestern Connecticut after serving an apprenticeship in Boston. Chandler would spend his career offering a variety of decorative services such as gilding or house painting to his neighbors with an occasional portrait or landscape. However, the most memorable images of events in these crisis years came from the

engraver's pen. The American patriot Paul Revere, the subject of a striking Copley portrait in which he is clad simply in a shirt, holding one of his rococo teapots, produced engravings of the Boston Massacre and the Boston Tea Party. Others issued scenes of critical battles or new heroes, bringing the pictorial arts to a broad popular audience and contributing to the politicization of the populace.

NEW STYLES FOR THE NEW NATION

The Peace of Paris of 1783 that severed the colonial ties of the North Americans from the British Empire and created the new American republic did not automatically secure the status of the arts in the new nation. Great purposes emerged—to celebrate the republic in a variety of decorative elements such as eagles or the figure of Liberty, as well as artistic forms such as grand history paintings, imposing public buildings, or even household furnishings in the new Federal style. European styles such as neo-

The Bloody Massacre, 1770. Hand-colored copperplate engraving by Paul Revere. The Boston silversmith, engraver, and entrepreneur rushed to advertise and print this version of the encounter between British troops and Boston residents, first designed and engraved by Henry Pelham (the half-brother of John Singleton Copley). Pelham entitled his version *The Fruits of Arbitration Power; or, The Bloody Massacre.* CLEMENTS LIBRARY, UNIVERSITY OF MICHIGAN. © BURSTEIN COLLECTION/CORBIS

classicism made their way across the Atlantic, often obtained through artists' and architects' experience in Europe. Some considered the fine arts to be a luxury for people busy with the work of building a nation. John Adams wrote, "It is not indeed the fine arts which our country requires: the useful, the mechanic arts are those we have occasion for in a young country." Others looked to continue the experimentation of the political process into the realm of the arts and obtain the support of the new republic's expanding citizenry.

The war years had sent many promising painters across the Atlantic to Benjamin West's studio, which would serve as a springboard for several generations of painters who had great expectations for the arts. John Trumbull came from a prominent Connecticut family, served as an officer in the Continental Army during the American Revolution, then went to London in 1784 to study with West and to pursue a career as an artist. Inspired by West's history paintings, Trumbull painted a series of canvases based upon the defining events of the new nation's birth. His bold command of color and strong compositions adopted West's techniques for the purpose of building national sentiment, as in *The Death of General Warren at the Battle of Bunker's Hill* (1786). However, his countrymen showed little interest in supporting Trumbull's work by joining lists of subscribers for engravings; Trumbull, like many of his generation, turned to portraiture for his sustenance.

Gilbert Stuart, who was born in Rhode Island and practiced as a provincial portraitist in the 1770s, also embarked for London, where he learned the current painterly styles. Stuart showed less resistance to a career as a face painter, and he relocated to America, moving from New York to Philadelphia to Boston, where he finally settled in 1805. His most famous work became his three portraits of George Washington, which produced defining national icons of the war hero and first president. In his *Athenaeum Portrait* (1796) he deftly offered a bust portrait that was both ideal and real, depicting a mythic figure as well as a burdened individual. Entrepreneurial engravers transformed that portrait into the iconic image of Washington, the national hero. Schoolchildren also learned to paint "mourning pictures" of Washington after his death in 1799, as drawing and other decorative arts became part of the curriculum in the new nation's female academies. Stuart remained in Boston until his death, becoming the leading portrait painter in America and transforming fashionable portraiture in the nation's urban centers. His cosmopolitan "painterly" style had rapid facile brushwork and the subtle blending of color to create an atmospheric effect.

Others found the hinterlands to be a growing market for their cultural wares. Another member of West's circle, Ralph Earl, was one of the first to resume his activity in New England; in the 1790s he traveled as an itinerant artist in rural areas of Connecticut, Massachusetts, and Vermont, where he transformed his British portrait style to suit the plainer tastes of his rural patrons, who desired appropriate images of themselves as citizens of the new republic. In the rural gentry Earl found a new clientele for portraiture: Oliver Ellsworth and Abigail Wolcott Ellsworth, painted in Windsor, Connecticut, in 1792, provoked a burst of artistic production in the region and inspired numerous imitators.

European ideas and craftsmen also contributed to the rise of the new Federal style. The style, which had gained popularity in England during the 1760s and 1770s as neoclassical, provided an obvious mode for those Americans who sought to communicate status and understated style. "Because of the emphasis on plain and planar surfaces, rectilinear forms, and restrained use of carving," the historian Kevin Sweeney wrote, "neoclassical interiors, furniture, and metalwares were invariably described as 'neat and plain.'" Cabinetmakers shifted direction, fashioning lighter and more rectilinear forms;

the furniture's plainer surfaces were decorated with veneers and inlays rather than heavy rococo carving. British craftsmen such as John and Thomas Seymour and Duncan Phyfe, and English pattern books by the cabinetmakers George Hepplewhite and Thomas Sheraton, contributed to the development of American neoclassical furniture. Neoclassicism with its reawakening of interest in antiquity appealed to republicans looking to establish associations with the great republics of classical Greece and Rome.

The Scottish-born Duncan Phyfe, the best known of the era's furniture makers, was more entrepreneur than craftsman. He operated a large manufactory where hundreds of elegant items were fashioned by a variety of specialists, complete with a wareroom where customers could purchase a variety of ready-made items, marking a new development in the movement away from the older traditions of bespoke craft production. By the 1820s Phyfe operated the largest shop in the United States and exported his furniture to the South and the West Indies. Phyfe was soon joined in New York City by the French cabinetmaker Charles Honoré Lannuier, bringing the new Empire style of Napoleon Bonaparte's Paris to America. Based on imperial Rome, the style was heavier in scale than the neoclassical, with bold sculptural carving and greater use of gilt and brass ornamentation. The door was open to a succession of revivals—Greek, Roman, Gothic, Egyptian, and Near Eastern—in the early nineteenth century. With the coming of the Greek War of Independence in the 1820s, there was a craze for things Greek: gilt cornucopia and imperial eagles graced tables or chairs as well as silver bowls and other household decorations.

In the buildings—public and private—of the new nation, neoclassical forms entered through the travels and advocacy of gentlemen-architects such as Charles Bulfinch and Thomas Jefferson. Thomas Jefferson, an architect as well as a scientist, statesman, and farmer, served as the principal author of the Declaration of Independence, the minister to France, and the president of the United States for two terms. While living in Paris Jefferson gazed at the proportion and beauty of the buildings around him and became friends with Charles-Louis Clérisseau, an archaeologist, an architect, and the author of *Antiquitiés de la France* (1778). When the Virginia legislature turned to Jefferson for a design for the new state capitol in Richmond, he consulted with Clérisseau to produce a building based on the Maison-Carrée, a first-century B.C. Roman building that had made a powerful impression upon him.

Regency-style Mahogany Couch (c. 1810–1820). Part of a large set of furniture attributed to Duncan Phyfe and owned by the wealthy New York City merchant Thomas Cornell Pearsall. The design derives from Greco-Roman forms illustrated in the 1808 edition of the London *Chairmakers' and Carvers' Book of Prices.* THE METROPOLITAN MUSEUM ART. GIFT OF C. RUXTON LOVE, 1960. ALL RIGHTS RESERVED, THE METROPOLITAN MUSEUM OF ART. (60.4.1)

With its classical portico, the new state capitol announced the arrival of a new style of architecture and the values of republicanism. Later, Jefferson would address the remodeling of his home at Monticello and the construction of an entire institution, the neoclassical University of Virginia. For the new capital city, the District of Columbia, the national leaders turned to the Frenchman Pierre-Charles L'Enfant. His plan gave the city a spacious atmosphere, its grand schemes and monumental boulevards symbolizing balance and rationality.

BUILDING AN "AMERICAN ATHENS"

While America was busy redecorating itself, a cadre of artists came back from Europe with English designs foremost in mind. Samuel McIntire and Charles Bulfinch built federal mansions for the merchant princes of New England, who had grown rich in the China trade and other commercial opportunities of the bustling economy. Bulfinch, the first native-born professional architect, was impressed with London town houses and modeled the Harrison Gray Otis house in Boston, with its flat roof and three-story brick structure, after London's Somerset House. He also created the Massachusetts State House, with its spacious interior chambers and great dome, after the Scottish designers Robert and James Adam, among the leading proponents of neoclassicism. These Adamesque designs moved to the southern and western United States as carpenters and builders adopted their form. The carpenter-turned-architect Asher Benjamin began his career building neoclassical structures in the Connecticut Valley, while his writings distributed those ideas throughout the new nation. *The Country Builder's Assistant* (1797), the first American architectural design book, contained plans for meetinghouses and homes; earlier American architectural imprints were compilations of English material or local editions of works by English authors. By 1803 Benjamin had moved to Boston and brought Bulfinch's innovations to a wider public in *The American Builder's Companion* (1806). South Carolina's Robert Mills moved from designing Charleston's County Records Building to working on the United States Treasury Building, with its monumental classicism and its maze of office spaces. Other architects began to promote Greek Revival styles with the first great architectural firm, Town and Davis (founded by Ithiel Town and Alexander Jackson Davis), designing numerous state capitols in the Greek mode, imitating the Parthenon. Southern antebellum mansions featured rows of two-story Doric columns. By the 1830s Asher Benjamin's writings had incorporated the new Greek Revival designs, thus constructing a republican culture extending to all the arts.

The promise of the American Revolution to build an "American Athens" in the westward-moving progress of the arts was part of the post-revolutionary optimism. For many Americans, including Charles Willson Peale, the Revolution meant the bursting of old categories. Peale, apprenticed as a saddler, had received some local instruction in painting and advertised as a sign painter; he left for London under the patronage of a local Maryland grandee—the traditional means of artistic support at the time. He took an active part in the Revolution while also producing a grand full-length portrait of General George Washington before the Battle of Princeton (1777). This son of the Enlightenment brought together art and science like the heroes of the day, Benjamin Franklin and Thomas Jefferson; he took seriously the joining of his life and art with the national mission, a mission that he saw as placing the arts on a broader base. As early as 1782 he began to envision a museum of natural history and fine arts, "a great school of nature . . . to bring into one view a world in miniature." He went about collecting portraits of distinguished Americans as well as specimens of American birds. He set about creating the first art academy, the Columbianum, which, although unsuccessful, paved the way for the founding of the Pennsylvania Academy of the Fine Arts in 1805. Peale exhibited his eclectic collection of paintings, gadgets, and stuffed animals initially in his own house, which he later moved to Independence Hall as the Peale Museum, while he tried to obtain governmental support. His broadside *To the Citizens of Philadelphia* (1790) solicited popular support for the venture, which he called a "Temple of Wisdom." As the artist discovered, the marketplace became the means of his survival; he staged shows in the museum along with his scientific displays. His self-portrait *The Artist in His Museum* (1822) brings up the curtain on his life's work: an American bird, a turkey, and a taxidermist's tools lie to the left, and the bones of the great mastodon that he had helped excavate are positioned to the right along with a painter's palette; in the background stretch several cases of specimens and rows of portraits while several visitors engage the exhibits. Peale's children, imaginatively named Raphaelle, Angelica Kauffmann, Rembrandt, Titian, Linnaeus, and Franklin, represented his hopes for the triumph of the arts and science in republican America; they continued many of his activities in art and science.

Others followed in the style of Peale or Earl while making available plain portraits to urban and rural families. The first professional African American artist, Joshua Johnston, was born in the West Indies and completed an apprenticeship as a blacksmith; he painted prominent families in Baltimore, Maryland, in the first two decades of the nineteenth century. He received his freedom in 1782 and advertised in local newspapers as "a self-Taught genius" who had "experienced many insuperable obstacles in the pursuit of his studies."

ARTIST AND ARTISAN IN THE COMMERCIAL REPUBLIC

For many of the artists and painters of the new generation, born during the American Revolution and anticipating a career in the fine arts, the so-called Grand Tour through Europe to view the monuments of the past became a necessary pilgrimage. Some came back seeking to extend European culture to the New World, to paint canvases in the grand manner, though ultimately that goal would be too difficult to sustain in the new bourgeois world of nineteenth-century America. John Vanderlyn put Paris on the artistic itinerary. He looked at the work of the old masters in the Louvre and the work of French contemporaries of the revolutionary era. His *Death of Jane McCrea* (1804) followed French models. It was painted as a model for the later engraving in Joel Barlow's epic poem *The Columbiad* (1807) to depict a Revolutionary incident, the murder of the heroine by two Mohawk Indians sympathetic to the British cause. By 1815 Vanderlyn, having hoped that an ambitious panorama of the *Palace and Gardens of Versailles,* his project of several years, could appeal to a popular audience, turned to the local scene as he became disillusioned with the taste of the masses. Samuel F. B. Morse likewise availed himself of a European tour and training, but found upon his return to America that he needed to travel in the hinterlands, painting portraits while he planned a major history painting. He emerged with *The Old House of Representatives* (1822), a dramatic interior view of the chamber, depicting the deliberations of a democratic institution. He went on tour with the painting

Erastus Salisbury Field, *Joseph Moore and His Family* **(1839).** Oil on canvas. Field, a rural painter who had trained in New York City with Samuel Morse, traveled throughout the countryside painting the emerging rural bourgeoisie. In this large and imposing portrait, he depicted the family of the itinerant hat maker, dentist, and professor of religion, surrounded by their stenciled furniture and other strikingly decorated household possessions. GIFT OF MAXIM KAROLIK FOR THE M. AND M. KAROLIK COLLECTION OF AMERICAN PAINTINGS, 1815–1865, 1958 (58.25). COURTESY OF MUSEUM OF FINE ARTS, BOSTON.
© 2000 MUSEUM OF FINE ARTS BOSTON, ALL RIGHTS RESERVED

hoping that admissions fees would finance another trip abroad. (Instead, he was forced to paint copies after the old masters to raise the funds.) Upon his return, he resumed portraiture and his energies went toward founding the National Academy of Design in 1826, which soon became a flourishing academy for New York's growing community of artists. As the borders between art and science remained flexible, Morse's interests turned to science and new inventions, including the telegraph and, in 1839, the daguerreotype, an inexpensive early photograph produced on a silver or silver-coated copper plate.

Another group of artists and patrons transformed the artisan-artist tradition. After the Revolutionary War the new middling market of rural consumers wanted affordable objects that signified cultural authority—the furniture, books, clocks, and portraits that had once been the province of the aristocratic few—to advance their social claims in the bustling mobile commercial society of early nineteenth-century America. The destruction of the aristocracy, "the real American Revolution," as the historian Gordon Wood wrote in *The Radicalism of the American Revolution* (1966), created in its wake a fluid middling society where everyone claimed to be a gentleman. "Under such circumstances gentlemanly distinctiveness was hard to sustain," Wood noted. Cultural commodities became key props in the universal drama of proving one's genteel status. Spurred on by these developments, rural artisans transformed limited quantity high-style objects into mass-marketed goods. The French historian and politician Alexis de Tocqueville saw how the destruction of the aristocratic and hierarchical colonial system created new opportunities for craftsmen:

> In an aristocracy he [the artisan] would seek to sell his workmanship at a high price to the few; he now conceives that the more expeditious way of getting rich is to sell them at a low price to all. But there are only two ways of lowering the price of commodities. The first is to discover some better, shorter, and more ingenious method of producing them; the second is to manufacture a larger quantity of goods, nearly similar, but of less value. (vol. 2, pp. 49–50)

Tocqueville went on to say how those who were rising as well as those who were falling in society would want goods, dramatically expanding the domestic market.

Windsor chairmakers specialized in making this originally English design with its sturdy construction and interchangeable parts. In the 1820s colorful Hitchcock chairs, mass-produced in Lambert Hitchcock's Connecticut factory, combined the European elegance of urban neoclassical chairs with the simplicity of Windsor chair production. As stenciled forms replaced freehand painted decoration, and painted striping replaced turned forms, this cheap yet elegant design (and its numerous imitations) became a part of every class of household. Connecticut clockmakers utilized wooden parts to replace the expensive metal ones in a Harland clock and embarked upon an era of faster and cheaper methods of clock manufacturing. The shelf clock, invented by Eli Terry in 1814, "*constituted a new form* of clock, *a new article,* and a *new manufacture*" (emphasis in original), claimed the inventor's son Henry Terry. The shelf clock sold for ten dollars with its wooden case grained to imitate more costly woods (case included)—a standardized and mass-marketed object which signified status to a vast market. Even in the far reaches of the frontier, one Arkansas traveler found "in every cabin where there was not a chair to sit on there was sure to be a Connecticut clock."

Portrait painters combed the countryside pioneering the rapid (and sometimes mechanically

Star of Bethlehem Quilt with Chintz Appliqués, c. 1835. Cotton, 122 x 122 in. Quilts provided utilitarian and decorative design for antebellum households. This large quilt was characteristic of the fine work done in Baltimore-style quiltmaking, a tradition that reached its zenith with the famous album quilts of the 1840s. THE METROPOLITAN MUSEUM OF ART, SANSBURY-MILLS FUND, 1973. ALL RIGHTS RESERVED, THE METROPOLITAN MUSEUM OF ART (1973.204)

aided) manufacture of likenesses using stylized two-dimensional templates, but with bold decorative designs. They increased their production and scaled their artistic efforts to suit their customers' pocketbooks. Some innovative artisans offered profiles (silhouettes), using a camera obscura (a dark box fitted with a lens and mirror to throw the sitter's image onto a piece of paper) that reduced their artistic labors; they could produce perhaps twenty in an evening's work in a local tavern. Other popular portraitists priced their offerings according to size, materials used, and time spent on execution. Their products were standardized by stock poses, but they distinguished among subjects through the inclusion of personal possessions. Academically trained artists recognized the opportunities of the emerging middle-class market. In the 1820s and 1830s Erastus Salisbury Field, a student of Samuel Morse in New York, found a means of portraying the rural bourgeoisie of central New England in grand poses and lavish surroundings while relying on stock poses to increase volume and satisfy sitters' expectations. By displaying their personal possessions, Field evolved a formula that simultaneously individualized his sitters and emphasized their status. (See *Joseph Moore*

CHESTER HARDING

About this time [1818] I fell in with a portrait painter by the name of Nelson, one of the primitive sort. He was a sign, ornamental, and portrait painter. He had for his sign a copy of the 'Infant Artists' of Sir Joshua Reynolds, with this inscription, 'Sign, Ornamental, and Portrait Painting executed on the shortest notice, with neatness and dispatch.' It was in his sanctum that I first conceived the idea of painting heads. I saw his portraits, and was enamored at once. I got him to paint me and my wife, and thought the pictures perfection. He would not let me see him paint, nor would he give me the least idea how the thing was done. I took the pictures home, and pondered on them, and wondered how it was possible for a man to produce such wonders of art. At length my admiration began to yield to an ambition to do the same thing. I thought of it by day, and dreamed of it by night, until I was stimulated to make an attempt at painting myself. I got a board; and, with such colors as I had for use in my trade, I began a portrait of my wife. I made a thing that looked like her. The moment I saw the likeness I became frantic with delight: it was like the discovery of a new sense; I could think of nothing else. From that time sign painting became odious, and was much neglected. (*A Sketch*, p. 18)

So Chester Harding began his career as an artist. Harding—farmhand, chairmaker, saloonkeeper, peddler, and sign painter—turned to painting "heads" after his encounter with Nelson. He traveled through new western regions of the United States seeking clients before a brief period of study in Philadelphia, where he discovered the limitations of his techniques. He returned to the West and paid a call to the aging frontiersman Daniel Boone in 1820. When he returned to St. Louis, he quickly produced and marketed an engraving of a full-length Boone holding a rifle. By 1821 he had paid a "pilgrimage" to Gilbert Stuart in Boston, opened a studio in western Massachusetts, and went abroad at age twenty-one; the chairmaker from Conway, Massachusetts, remained unimpressed by the European masters, however. Eventually, Harding, his reputation buoyed by his persona as the "backwoodsman, newly caught, " moved to Boston, from where he traveled to Washington and New Orleans, painting the wealthy and influential figures of his time.

and His Family, 1839.) Several women artists also utilized periods of itinerancy to reach the middle market of patrons; Ruth Henshaw Bascom, a minister's wife and portraitist, recorded over one thousand portraits painted in her journal.

An American-born generation of sculptors emerged from eighteenth-century wood-carvers and artisan-stonecutters. With the arrival of European influences, many worked on monumental public buildings or created sculpture like those from European studios. William Rush, who was trained by his father, a Philadelphia ship's carpenter, began as a vernacular and then later became a successful maker of ships' figureheads who incorporated new influences into his designs. He helped found the

Pennsylvania Academy of the Fine Arts with Peale, then began modeling in clay, producing public sculpture in Philadelphia. As with painting, the next generation of sculptors formed an American school. Many sculptors had spent long periods as expatriates, and they built upon the incorporation of neo-classical goals as well as American wood-carving traditions. Both Horatio Greenough and Hiram Powers, one a Boston Yankee and the other a rural artisan, were born in 1805 and spent their careers in Florence, Italy. In 1832 Greenough was given the important commission by Congress of creating "a full-length pedestrian statue of Washington," which followed his own fascination with things Greek and depicted Washington as a Greek God, nude to the waist. Few appreciated the neoclassical allusions, and scandalized Americans forced the statue's removal from the Capitol.

The expanding nation incorporated other regional traditions. German artisans in Pennsylvania and other areas brought with them German traditions in style and techniques of decoration, producing complex decorated pottery in quantity. They made rich red earthenware, the most prized known as graffito, in which their design was cut through the cream-colored slip or into the clay, so that the outer coating revealed the red body underneath. The pottery was known for its stylized compositions with flowers and birds, often embellished with humorous German inscriptions reflective of the potters' heritage. In Spanish New Mexico a small number of artists worked in wood or painted on hides, crafting religious images for use in village churches and homes, often modeled on imported Mexican religious prints but with their own bold and colorful style. Santa Fe's José Rafael Aragón created monumental altar screens as well as panel paintings and sculptures as he moved up and down northern New Mexico's valleys and communities. He signed the San Calletano panel with its striking details and balance. And throughout the United States women made quilts and other bed coverings, often with a high degree of artistry as traditions of needlework and design were passed down through the generations.

Increasingly, American artists and art patrons found a fascination with things American; engravings of Hudson River views or portraits of Indian leaders circulated in the early republic. Print shops opened in every city where one could buy scenes or urban views. The first lithograph, a new technique of producing images, celebrated the opening of the Erie Canal in 1825. The firm of Currier and Ives would bring colored lithographs or "chromos" to every home after midcentury. Scenes of the American land and the ordinary daily life of the common folk came from academic artists and anonymous vernacular painters. Led by English craftsmen and the tradition of eighteenth-century topographical views, Robert Salmon, Thomas Birch, and Francis Guy produced views of harbor scenes and street scenes that drew upon northern European art and displayed the bustling nature of American life. Others were drawn to local scenery; Joshua Shaw traveled from Massachusetts to Georgia making direct observations and romantic interpretations of nature. Assembled in a portfolio entitled *Picturesque Views of American Scenery*, the prints were pub-

lished from 1819 to 1821 in collaboration with the engraver John Hill. Hundreds bought the prints, and the portfolio became a milestone in American printmaking. John James Audubon spent two decades tracking and drawing his four-volume *Birds of America* (1827–1838). His life-size bird studies, like the Wild Turkey, probably painted in 1822 while he was in Louisiana, had natural backgrounds, and greatly expanded the range of American arts. Others stuck closer to home like the Long Islander William Sidney Mount, who painted genre scenes of farmers and villagers, just as a nostalgia grew for a rural life in the midst of a changing nation.

With the expansion of the American nation across the continent, the most striking development became the identification of the American landscape. Instead of the grand manner history paint-

James Otto Lewis, *Colonel Daniel Boon,* **n.d.** Stipple engraving after Chester Harding, St. Louis Museum, St. Louis, Missouri. In 1820 Chester Harding sought out America's best-known backwoodsman, Daniel Boone. He made two portraits, including this one of Boone leaning on a rifle with a dog at his feet. PURCHASE OF SAINT LOUIS ART MUSEUM

ings, artists and patrons looked to the landscape to celebrate the American republic, but also to indulge their longing for a wilderness that was being destroyed. Thomas Cole, the first painter of what became known as the Hudson River school, came from England and resided in New York City, which was rapidly becoming the cultural capital of the United States. There he found the patronage of the elite. His early work bore literary characteristics, based on the novelist James Fenimore Cooper's Leatherstocking tales. In his *Essay on American Scenery* (1836) Cole said, "The most distinctive, and perhaps the most impressive, characteristic of American scenery is its wildness. It is the most distinctive, because in civilized Europe, the primitive features of scenery have long since been destroyed or modified." After his encounter with the scenery from the Hudson River to the Catskill Mountains and a trip to Europe, he fashioned the series *The Course of Empire* (1836), portraying various scenes of American progress, from savagery through the creation and the destruction of the empire to the final desolation, as nature reclaims the scene. Depicting a real rather than an imaginary place, Cole painted *The Ox-Bow* (1846), portraying a dramatic vista, where the artist in the foreground sits before an "improved" landscape with its cultivated fields and foreboding storm. Other self-taught artists emerged out of the hinterlands to ascend to the highest ranks of academic art in the expanding republic.

Cole, rooted in the eighteenth-century republicanism and the patronage of his elite sponsors, grew disillusioned with the democratic drift of American society. In his later work his pessimism grew as he depicted the republic besieged, a stark contrast to his midcentury nationalist artistic colleagues who had a more self-confident response to the rise of the American empire. Cole saw foreboding storm clouds on the horizon, as did his fellow painter Gilbert Stuart. When an aging Stuart asked, "How goes the Harding fever?" he sarcastically acknowledged his successor Chester Harding in Boston and the distance traveled since his own eighteenth-century rise in the exciting but precarious revolutionary era. As represented in the rise of Chester Harding and his self-authored story, a new generation had come of age with their roots deep in the North American continent as well as in the new commercial republic.

See also **Artistic, Intellectual, and Political Refugees** *(volume 2);* **The Visual Arts; Elite vs. Popular Cultures; Museums; Architecture; Painting; Sculpture; Drama; Poetry; Music; Dance** *(volume 3); and other articles in this section.*

BIBLIOGRAPHY

Primary

Benjamin, Asher. *The American Builder's Companion.* 1806. Reprint, New York, 1965.

Dunlap, William. *History of the Rise and Progress of the Arts of Design in the United States.* 1834. Reprint, New York, 1965.

Harding, Chester. *A Sketch of Chester Harding, Artist, Drawn by His Own Hand.* Edited by his daughter, Margaret E. White, 1890. Reprint, New York, 1970.

Miller, Lillian, et al., eds., *The Selected Papers of Charles Willson Peale and His Family.* 4 vols. Sidney Hart, assistant editor. New Haven, Conn., 1983.

Secondary

Breen, T. H. " 'Baubles of Britain': The American and Consumer Revolutions of the Eighteenth Century." In *Of Consuming Interests: The Style of Life in the Eighteenth Century,* edited by Cary Carson et al., pp. 444–482. Charlottesville, Va., 1994.

Bushman, Richard L. *The Refinement of America: Persons, Houses, Cities.* New York, 1992.

Cooke, Edward. *Making Furniture in Preindustrial America: The Social Economy of Newtown and Woodbury, Connecticut*. Baltimore, 1996.

Craven, Wayne. *American Art: History and Culture*. New York, 1994.

Ellis, Joseph J. *After the Revolution: Profiles of Early American Culture*. New York, 1979.

Harris, Neil. *The Artist in American Society, The Formative Years, 1790–1860*. New York, 1966.

Heckscher, Morrison H. *American Rococo, 1750–1775: Elegance in Ornament*. New York, 1992.

Hurst, Ronald L., and Jonathan Prown. *Southern Furniture 1680–1830: The Colonial Williamsburg Collection*. Williamsburg, Va., 1997.

Kornhauser, Elizabeth Mankin. *Ralph Earl: The Face of the Young Republic*. New Haven, Conn., 1991.

Miller, Angela. *The Empire of the Eye: Landscape Representation and American Cultural Politics, 1825–1875*. Ithaca, N.Y., 1993.

Miller, Lillian B., ed. *The Peale Family: Creation of a Legacy 1770–1870*. New York, 1996.

Reaves, Wendy Wick. *George Washington, an American Icon: the Eighteenth-Century Graphic Portraits*. Washington, D.C., 1982.

Rebora, Carrie. *John Singleton Copley in America*. New York, 1995.

Silverman, Kenneth. *A Cultural History of the American Revolution: Painting, Music, Literature, and the Theatre in the Colonies and the United States from the Treaty of Paris to the Inauguration of George Washington, 1763–1789*. New York, 1976.

Sloat, Caroline, ed. *Meet Your Neighbors: New England Portraits, Painters, & Society, 1790–1850*. Sturbridge, Mass., 1992.

Staiti, Paul J. *Samuel F. B. Morse*. New York, 1989.

Sweeney, Kevin. "High Style Vernacular: Lifestyles of the Colonial Elite." In *Of Consuming Interests: The Style of Life in the Eighteenth Century*, edited by Cary Carson et al., 1–58. Charlottesville, Va., 1994.

Tocqueville, Alexis de. *Democracy in America*. Edited by Phillips Bradley. 2 vols. New York, 1945.

Vlach, John Michael. *The Afro-American Tradition in Decorative Arts*. Cleveland, Ohio, 1979.

Wallach, Alan. *Thomas Cole: Landscape into History*. New Haven, Conn., 1994.

Wood, Gordon S. *The Radicalism of the American Revolution*. New York, 1966.

Zea, Philip. *Clock Making in New England, 1725–1825: An Interpretation of the Old Sturbridge Village Collection*. Sturbridge, Mass., 1992.

THE PRINT REVOLUTION

Robert A. Gross

One generation's revolution is another's status quo. That rule seemingly characterizes Americans' experience of print in the passage from the small, colonial world of Benjamin Franklin to the expansive democracy of the newspaper editors James Gordon Bennett and Horace Greeley.

At the start of the conflict with Britain triggered by the Stamp Act in 1765, John Adams proclaimed the American colonists a liberty-loving people and attributed that remarkable devotion to widespread literacy and a free press. "A native of America who cannot read and write," he declared, "is as rare an appearance as a Jacobite or a Roman Catholic, that is, as rare as a comet or an earthquake." Among such people, "none of the means of information are more sacred, or have been cherished with more tenderness and care by the settlers of America, than the press." Yet, time and again, in the new nation founded by Adams and his generation, citizens found themselves living in an unprecedented era of popular knowledge and communication change. In 1801, as Adams was vacating the presidency for his rival Thomas Jefferson, the Federalist minister Samuel Miller was decrying the so-called progress of the times. The eighteenth century had been the "Age of Printing," when books and periodicals poured forth from the press, stirring a broad "taste for reading" and promising a general "diffusion of knowledge." Had enlightenment ensued? In Miller's severe judgment, a mass of "hasty, superficial works," gotten up for profit, was driving the best books from view, while in the partisan battles of the day, periodicals spread "erroneous opinions" and "coarse invective." Alas, America was no longer Adams's land of "rational liberty."

Within two decades, the republic recovered; in the 1820s, a new generation took stock of the publishing scene and rejoiced at the abundance of books and periodicals reaching the people. "This is emphatically the age of reading," decided the Supreme Court justice Joseph Story. "At other times this was the privilege of the few; in ours, it is the possession of the many." To other observers, the era was an Age of Print, stirred into life by the momentous events of the Napoleonic wars, when "Bullets and bulletins together sped/Joint couriers of the living and the dead," and sustained through the pursuits of peace, "Ours the campaigns and victories of mind." Those testimonials were premature, at least in the eyes of the New York publishers who gathered in 1855 to celebrate the astonishing growth of "the Printing Press in the Age of Steam and Electricity." Twenty years before, no bookseller had dreamed of "editions of 100,000 or 75,000, or 30,000, or even the now common number of 10,000." Thanks to new machinery, publishers could serve a mass audience across the nation. In its triumphant progress, the Reverend E. H. Chapin told his assembly, "the troublesome democrat" of the press was "stalking into the world among kings and priests," releasing truth from chains, and promoting liberty, peace, and divine truth. John Adams would have recognized that message.

Was there a "print revolution" every thirty years, from the 1760s to the Civil War? To judge from the testimony, the story is always the same: an explosion of publications; an expanding reading public; a democratization of politics, society, and culture. It suggests a single transformation from scarcity to abundance unfolding in successive waves of change and striking each generation, in its turn, as altogether new. It points as well to a common ideological lens, dating back to the invention of the printing press in the fifteenth century, through which white Protestants had come to interpret advances in communications as progressive steps in the fulfillment of God's plan for humankind. "Print revolution" thus designates a social process in the past and registers the cultural perceptions of those living through it. Not surprisingly, contemporary witnesses often seized on the new, whether in enthusiasm or disgust; the persistence of old ways went unnoticed or unremarked. In this perspective,

271

a more complex narrative emerges. Although print culture did become more abundant, diverse, and far-reaching in the first half century of the republic, it did so gradually through modest innovations in business, politics, and technology. For the most part, the rhetoric of revolution was overblown. Not until the mid-1830s did the pace and scale of change foretell the coming of a new age of mass communications through print.

THE AMERICAN REVOLUTION IN PRINT

When the thirty-year-old lawyer John Adams singled out the press as a safeguard of "public interest, liberty, and happiness," he was calling attention to a prominent development in his lifetime: the rise of the newspaper. Back in 1704, the royal postmaster of Massachusetts had launched America's first newspaper, the *Boston News-Letter,* as a quasi-official organ of government, "published by Authority." Issued weekly to 250 subscribers, the *News-Letter* filled its columns with public proclamations, shipping news, and extensive reprints from the London press. It had the market to itself for fifteen years, but from the 1720s on, newspapers spread to the principal ports of British North America. Typically, they served the interests of political and merchant elites and steered clear of faction; though free from prior censorship, the press could be prosecuted for seditious libel if it brought the government into disrepute. Printers, who ran twenty-one papers in ten towns by 1763, played it safe, opening their columns to all parties and affirming their attachment to none. Nonetheless, in towns with rival presses, newspapers were enlisted in the recurrent contests between royal governors and popular assemblies, in the course of which they disseminated an alternative view of the press as a champion of liberty and check on tyranny. The Stamp Act crisis obliged printers to choose between competing visions; most took a stand against British imperial policy and, to their surprise, found that partisanship paid. Enjoying expanding circulation in the intense climate leading up to independence—the *Massachusetts Spy* claimed 3,000 subscribers in 1775—the Patriot press propagated a republican ideal of print. In its pages, citizens were invited to discuss principles, not personalities, and to speak impersonally for the common good. From such rational discourse among anonymous individuals, it was expected, would emerge the true voice of the people. Speaking for everyone in general and nobody in particular, the newspaper claimed to rep-

resent a new force in politics—public opinion—that was constituted in its columns of type. It thereby played a crucial role in the creation of the "classic public sphere" of the eighteenth century, that complex of institutions and practices, including coffeehouses, clubs, and salons as well as the press, that fostered critical, independent debate about church and state throughout the Atlantic world.

Newspapers were not alone in promoting a vigorous print culture. On the eve of independence, America was the leading export market for London publishers, absorbing more English books than all of Europe. A growing corps of booksellers competed to bring the "latest print"—notably, novels and periodicals—from the mother country to colonial readers; in Boston, the Scottish-born John Mein boasted in 1765 "the most extensive trade of any person on the American Continent," with some ten thousand volumes in stock. These merchants supplied both individual patrons and the various voluntary associations of booklovers springing up in the land, such as Benjamin Franklin's Library Company of Philadelphia. They also rented out books through circulating libraries based in their shops. By these means, Anglo-Americans fashioned a provincial version of the sophisticated literary culture back "home."

Yet all of this activity, vital as it was for transmitting radical whig thought and Enlightenment ideals from the Old World to the New, rested atop what the historian David Hall called a "traditional world of literacy" extending over the countryside. For the vast majority of white colonists, books were scarce; few rural households ever possessed more than a Bible, an almanac, a hymnal, and a school primer. Such "devout and useful" books (apart from the Bible) were the common products of the colonial press, short, cheap imprints designed for local consumption. Whatever their origin or appearance, religious works held a special meaning. To the pious, the gospel was the living word of God; consequently, any spiritual text imparting its message—a sermon, devotional guide, or conversion narrative—could carry a sacred aura. The faithful were urged by ministers to approach these writings in a godly spirit, digesting the words slowly and carefully, literally chewing them over like a cow its cud. At any moment, the Holy Spirit could shine through the page and illuminate the soul with grace. This was the style that has come to be known as "intensive reading"—the reverent return to the same sacred texts day by day, year by year, during the course of one's life. Politically, the practice could be double-edged; it could prompt Puritan saints to uphold authority in Massachusetts Bay and inspire Quaker dissidents to defy it. Either way, it was culturally conservative. In a rural world where print was scarce, common folk turned to familiar sources for essential information. The mass medium was word of mouth. Through the filter of oral culture, ordinary people read the newspapers and other printed texts that with increasing frequency and urgency entered their lives in the second half of the eighteenth century.

The American Revolution secured the ascendancy of the newspaper in print culture. Jettisoning the notion of neutrality, two out of three printers enlisted their presses in the struggle for independence. Through their efforts, colonists gained immediate knowledge of the momentous events at Lexington and Concord and of the Declaration of Independence. A few suffered British retaliation; John Hunter Holt's Norfolk paper was seized by the Virginia governor the earl of Dunmore for "poisoning the minds of the people." Far more Loyalists lost their presses to Patriot mobs and vigilance committees. Even so, whig printers portrayed themselves, as did Benjamin Edes of the *Boston Gazette,* as "an underrated Centinel in those times that 'tried men's souls.'" It was of no matter that they violated the republican canon of impersonality with abandon, assailing neutrals, Loyalists, and war profiteers alike, by name, as enemies of the country. Even Thomas Paine, who published *Common Sense* anonymously on the grounds that "the Object for Attention is the *Doctrine Itself,* not the *Man,*" could not resist the temptation to brag publicly of his authorship. In the campaign for the Constitution, printers, overwhelmingly Federalist, played the politics of personality to the hilt. While they publicized the endorsement of the new frame of government by George Washington and Benjamin Franklin, they declined to publish anonymous objections to the plan. Anti-Federalists would have to reveal their names or stay silent. Once their identities as common farmers and mechanics were exposed, the critics would lose all credibility. Anti-Federalists were obliged to air their opinions anonymously in separate presses.

POLITICS AND THE PRESS

Printers were well rewarded for their services. Federalists valued the press as a conduit of "correct intelligence" from the government to the people; Anti-Federalists and later Republicans regarded it as a "watchman on the tower of liberty." All paid tribute to the ideal of an informed citizenry. Under the new nation, politicians joined together to promote the circulation of information. The First Amendment denied Congress the power to abridge "the freedom of speech, or of the press." The Copyright Act of 1790 enabled the free flow of publications from abroad. Congress subsidized the distribution of newspapers through the mails at low rates. Executive and legislative branches awarded printing contracts to supporters; state governments did the same. Even new communities on the frontier offered bounties to printers to settle in their midst. In 1790, there were 84 newspapers up and down the coast and as far west as Pittsburgh and Lexington, Kentucky. Ten years later, the ranks surged to 201. That spurt far outpaced the growth and dispersal of a burgeoning population, and it was fueled by more than public largesse. What galvanized the astonishing takeoff was, ironically, the Federalist campaign to rein in hostile critics. Empowered by the Sedition Act of 1798, the Adams administration set out to punish offending editors for libel—the "coarse invective" that so troubled Reverend Samuel Miller. To Federalists, the campaign was consistent with the traditional understanding of a free press; indeed, it marked an advance over English precedent in allowing truth as a defense. But the crusade only succeeded in galvanizing the opposition. A loose network of press critics was transformed into an electoral arm of the Republicans. Where prosecution failed, the Federalists tried patronage, greatly expanding the number of papers of record designated to print the laws. Thanks to the joint efforts of Federalists and Republicans, a party press took shape, one that came to employ informal, popular rhetoric to appeal to voters. The competition spurred the continuing growth of newspapers to 366 in 1810; that figure climbed to 861 by 1828, at the dawn of the Age of Jackson, and rose to some 1,400 by 1840, the year of the Log Cabin campaign. The press played a leading part in the democratization of American politics.

James Parker, a farmer in the central Massachusetts town of Shirley, enlisted early in the swelling ranks of newspaper readers. Thirty-one years old, with a wife and three children at the outbreak of the American Revolution, Parker was an industrious yeoman who minded his own business, leaving the burdens of government to others. After two months' service during the siege of Boston in the winter of 1776, he returned to his farm and concentrated on raising crops for the booming wartime market. His education had been limited to a few years in the district schools of rural Massachusetts;

he had little care for books. Nonetheless, one of the first items he got as his fortunes improved was a subscription to the *Massachusetts Spy*, which he ordered in 1778, not long after buying himself a watch. With "a great many flying stories consirning the Army" running through town, Parker was determined to keep up with the latest, most authoritative news. As his status rose, his horizons expanded. In the 1790s, by then an aspiring gentleman, Parker joined the Masons and became a founder of the Shirley library society. That experience was common. The Revolution drew men and women into public life, like it or not, and quickened desires for social mobility. The political strife of the Early Republic deepened those interests. Out of such experiences Americans became what the *Portfolio* dubbed in 1800 "a nation of newspaper readers."

The reach of the press and the enthusiasm for print can be exaggerated. Though newspapers appeared to be popping up everywhere in the Early Republic, they were, in fact, far less numerous in the South. As in the colonial era, the press in such states as Virginia and South Carolina stayed close to the coast and to the interests of the gentry. That was owing, in part, to the lower levels of literacy among whites below the Mason-Dixon line. Yet even in the Northeast, barriers of class and gender limited access to the press. A newspaper subscription was costly, equal to one or two days' wages for an ordinary laborer, and an entire year's run had to be paid for in advance. Current issues were not for sale; they could be readily found in coffeehouses and taverns. Linked to masculine spaces and concerns, notably politics and commerce, newspapers seem to have appealed chiefly to male readers, though that changed, especially in the 1820s, when contents broadened to include poetry, fiction, and moral essays, and editors aspired to reach the entire American family. Technology, in any case, set severe limits on the capacity of the press. Until the 1830s, printers still relied on the basic hand press invented by Johannes Gutenberg in the fifteenth century, albeit one with improved materials and design, to turn out a four-page weekly paper; under these constraints, the usual press run seldom exceeded one thousand. Many papers did not last for long. While printers scattered across the countryside after 1790, they were often just passing through; one out of two newspapers was destined to fail within three years of publication. No wonder, then, that political parties could not depend wholly on the press to mobilize voters. Particularly in rural areas, they relied on the familiar methods of a largely oral culture—

stump speeches at barbecues, court days, and rallies—to get out the vote, so successfully that the turnout in many parts of the South reached or exceeded that in the North. Valuable as the press was to facilitate partisan politics, it was not indispensable.

PUBLISHING IN AN EXTENSIVE REPUBLIC

Similar difficulties beset the first generation that set out to publish and distribute books to a diverse population rapidly expanding across an extensive, decentralized republic. In late colonial America, publishing hardly existed as a separate branch of business. The book trade was divided broadly between booksellers and printers. The former imported books from England and marketed them in their shops. The latter issued few titles at their own risk, apart from almanacs, schoolbooks, and newspapers; it was more profitable to do custom work, printing books to order, the way a cabinetmaker produced highboys, at the customer's expense. Only occasionally did even Benjamin Franklin venture into the modern world of publishing, that is, choosing a text, putting it in print, and managing its sale; and when he did so, he mainly opted to reprint English works that had already proven their popularity overseas. On the eve of the Revolution, there were harbingers of change. The bookseller Robert Bell, who arrived in Philadelphia in 1768, recreated the aggressive trade practices he had learned in Dublin. Exploiting a loophole in British copyright law—the lack of protection for English books in Ireland—Dublin publishers made a handsome specialty out of reprinting books popular in London and selling them cheaply wherever they pleased. Bell took the business of literary piracy to America and justified it on the grounds of free trade. Though neither Bell nor most of his compatriots in the book trade were around after the war, his example set the direction for American publishing.

The rising generation of booksellers faced a twofold challenge. On the one hand, they were eager to follow Bell's lead, cast off the role of importer, and seize the profits from the reprint trade; on the other, they needed a wide market to absorb their products. The key to success lay in cooperation. Instead of importing titles in small quantities to supply limited, local demand, publishers combined forces to create a national market. With nothing to stop them—United States copyright law afforded no protection to foreign works—entrepreneurs adopted a code of conduct, known as "courtesy of trade," to regulate the practice of piracy. The rule was simple: first come, first serve. Under that compact, a single reprint of an English title could circulate up and down the nation, free from competing editions. To disseminate such texts, booksellers tried a variety of expedients, including holding trade fairs, purveying one another's works on commission and exchange, and sending traveling salesmen throughout the countryside. By these means, the fledgling "men of capital," many of whom had started out in printing, turned themselves into general publishers cum retailers, with a diverse stock of books, their own and others' productions, from all over the land.

In practice, the development of publishing was never easy. Despite their best efforts to restrain competition, booksellers were plagued by recurrent overproduction, brought on by the need to have titles for exchange and by the readiness of local printers to issue publications as well. It was thus imperative to control costs. Happily, foreign authors were not entitled to payment, though publishers were willing to invest in American writers. Journeymen printers endured constant downward pressure on wages, owing to such bookseller tactics as resorting to the labor of semiskilled teenagers and women and putting out jobs to cheaper craftsmen in the countryside. Seeking to reduce competition among themselves while stirring it among others, publishers sought stable markets and steady prices for their wares—to no avail. The mortality rate for booksellers rivaled that of printers. Capital was scarce, supplies, such as paper, expensive, and the trade was hampered by continuing problems of distribution. Those who survived and even prospered managed to secure exclusive control over a title in steady demand. Philadelphia's Mathew Carey, an Irish Catholic émigré, built his house on the solid rock of the King James Bible, which he kept in standing type, issuing quarto and duodecimo editions as needed, without having to pay for new composition. To the same end, Carey and his colleagues welcomed the invention of stereotyping, a technique for preserving cast type on metal plates, from which reprints could be efficiently and repeatedly issued.

On the foundation of British reprints was built an independent American publishing industry, centered in Boston, New York, and Philadelphia. Older titles predominated. In the first flush of expansion, booksellers plundered the perennials of British and European print. Devotional works, such as the Puritan clergyman Richard Baxter's *Call to the Unconverted* (1657), constituted the bulk of these "steady sellers." They were joined by a host of traditional tales—*Little Red Riding Hood, Jack the Giant Killer, Guy of Warwick*—that had entertained nobles and peasants alike since the Middle Ages and that with their sex and gore were deemed anathema by Protestant moralists. The chapbook "godlies" and "romances" flowed from rural presses. The leading booksellers focused on more recent British and European titles in various fields—history, biography, science, poetry, fiction, belles lettres—from the eighteenth and early nineteenth centuries. In 1820, 70 percent of the books published in the United States were British originals. That suited the tastes of readers in a "postcolonial" nation, who were eager to keep up with the latest ideas and styles in the cultural capitals of the Old World. To be sure, for basic knowledge, the public was glad to consult original American texts, such as Noah Webster's speller and Jedidiah Morse's textbook on geography, and "Americanized" versions of British works, the content of which was adapted to native interests. Schoolbooks, like Bibles and dictionaries, generated the regular revenues that supported booksellers' riskier ventures. But serious and fashionable reading alike came from the other side of the Atlantic, pretested for popular appeal.

READING REVOLUTION

Did all this activity spark a "reading revolution," as some scholars have argued? It certainly bore fruit in a greater abundance of printed matter. As early as 1816, it was a "common objection," one writer noticed, that "there are already too many books in the world." Along the upper Connecticut River Valley of New Hampshire and Vermont in the Early Republic, the proof was found in ordinary homes. Roughly six out of ten households kept a family library. These holdings steadily increased in size, from an average of five books at the close of the eighteenth century to four times that number following the War of 1812. There were not only more books available, but a greater variety, issued by publishers far and wide. At the heart of the reading revolution was the invention and proliferation of new genres for a large, diverse public. The cultural fare became more secular and cosmopolitan. Not that "intensive reading" disappeared; religious publishing actually expanded, and people continued to cherish the Bible daily, in a practice that continues into the twenty-first century. But piety was sustained in a pluralistic milieu. Many cultivated "extensive" reading habits, in a spirit of openness to new ideas circulating in the wider world. It was the largely white, native-born inhabitants of the Northeast, especially New England, who led the way, though no region was without its participants in the cultural transformation. Justice Joseph Story was correct. By the 1820s, the middle and upper classes had entered "an age of reading."

Of special interest is the role of the sentimental novel in fostering a new sensibility. Born in the eighteenth century and popularized by such figures as Daniel Defoe and Samuel Richardson in England, Jean-Jacques Rousseau in France, and Johann Wolfgang von Goethe in Germany, the genre was, as the name indicates, a novel form of fiction. Myth, allegory, and folklore had long been the stuff of literature in the West. The novel offered a different scene for the imagination. In its pages unfolded narratives of concrete individuals, moving through recognizable social worlds. Readers could readily identify with the characters' trials and adventures, the sentiments they felt, the moral lessons they learned. They raged at the profligate arts of the licentious Lovelace and wept over the tragic seduction of the innocent Clarissa. They were lured by glittering images of high society and instructed in polite manners. They fantasized themselves in the story. That, to orthodox moralists, was the fatal flaw of the genre. Though such fiction claimed to be "founded on fact," it fostered, in the words of the Yale president Timothy Dwight, "false and exaggerated notions of life." Young people, especially women, were particularly vulnerable to such "corruption." Caught up in stirring scenes, they built "castles in the air" and neglected social duties; worse, they were tempted to turn art into life, seeking the pleasures and imitating the vices they tasted in print. Such condemnation, however exaggerated, captured an important truth. As feminist scholars have shown, sentimental fiction addressed the situation of the sexes in an emerging bourgeois age, with old-style patriarchy on the wane and young people claiming greater power to make their own lives. Would women enjoy greater autonomy in this new world? Could they marry freely for love? Or would they stumble like Charlotte Temple, the title character in the popular novel by Susanna Rowson, and die alone, seduced and abandoned, in urban squalor? In sentimental fiction, Cathy Davidson has argued, women gained a medium to explore these questions. The genre enacted a revolution in culture parallel to that in politics. It offered women representation in the realm of letters that was denied them in the sphere of the state.

There is much to credit in this interpretation. Women did identify powerfully with such characters as Charlotte Temple; they decorated copies of the text, inscribed their feelings in the margins— "My Treasure," wrote one—and even made pilgrimages to her supposed grave. But the argument goes too far. Booksellers did not rush to publish fiction. Between 1789 and 1820, a total of ninety American novels appeared in print, a mere three a year. Reprints of British fiction were far more numerous. Even so, the genre played only a minor role in American publishing before 1820. Rather than buy novels, readers preferred to rent them from the circulating libraries organized in major towns. That confined the fashion to urban centers; the countryside proved lukewarm, if not indifferent, as the Merriam printing firm of Brookfield, Massachusetts, discovered, to its cost, when it issued an edition of *Charlotte Temple* in 1819. Half the copies remained unsold on the shelves, read only by idle apprentices. Nor did young women limit their fare to fiction. Educated at the nearly four hundred female academies and seminaries founded between 1790 and 1830, they came to cultivate interests in geography, history, classics, and natural science. The most ambitious aspired to be "learned women." Gender did not dictate genre.

Actually, sentimental fiction did not act alone in assaulting the traditional order. The magazine of print was stockpiled with diverse weapons. Agricultural experts summoned the rising generation to abandon customary ways and start farming "by the book." *The Farmer's Almanac* advised it to shun the tavern and read by the fireside. Domestic manuals proclaimed authority on the proper way to raise a child. Abolitionist literature reached blacks in the South, where slave literacy was not uncommon and not always a crime, stirring dreams of freedom in a twelve-year-old boy named Frederick Bailey on the Baltimore docks, who found in a schoolbook called *The Columbia Orator* confirmation of his inner beliefs. Years later, having fled to freedom in the North and remade himself into the antislavery activist Frederick Douglass, he recalled vividly that moment of discovery. "The more I read, the more I was led to abhor and detest my enslavers."

No wonder, then, that Silas Felton, a farmboy in Marlborough, Massachusetts, could not keep his mind on his chores after the Revolution. Happier at school than in the field and "becoming more fond of books" than work, he "used at every convenient opportunity to take my book and step [out] of sight," for which he acquired a general reputation as lazy. Felton never tired of books. At the age of twenty-six, he compiled a record of his reading, 106 titles in all, classified into ten "Professions or Arts." "Religion or Morality" ranked first, followed closely by history and novels. He pondered both the "Christian Bible" and the "Mahometan Bible or Alcoran," determined, like his hero Benjamin Franklin, to rise above "prejudice of any kind whatever, always to practice reason and truth." "Nature," he concluded, "never formed me to follow an Agricultural Life." Deserting the farm, he taught school as a stopgap, then started a successful store in Marlborough village. Like many in the postrevolutionary generation, male and female alike, he was "ruined" by a book.

THE RISE OF MASS PUBLISHING

The pace of change in print culture accelerated after 1820, in tandem with the growth of an increasingly urban, industrial society. The Erie Canal, completed in 1825, opened up the great heartland from New York to the Old Northwest and linked it to markets on the coast; the first railroads began operating in the mid-1830s, with hubs in Boston, Baltimore, and Philadelphia. As old obstacles to transportation fell, the trend toward decentralization was reversed. From major urban centers, entrepreneurs manufactured and shipped goods directly to customers integrated into regional and national markets. In publishing, the lead was taken not by commercial booksellers but by benevolent societies, motivated by religion. From a base in New York City, the American Bible Society and the American Tract Society employed stereotype plates and steam-powered presses to turn out testaments and tracts by the millions, which they distributed through a chain of auxiliaries and paid agents. Disgusted by the "vicious literature" that unprincipled publishers produced for profit, the reformers provided not what the public wanted, but what it needed. That meant the Bible, of course, but also the same "steady sellers"—Richard Baxter, Philip Doddridge, and the like—that evangelical Protestants had been digesting since the Puritans. Advanced technology could serve traditional ends.

Not always. Prompted by the astonishing popularity of Sir Walter Scott's novels, booksellers forgot courtesy of trade. No longer did they wait to determine if a British title would sell enough to merit reprinting. They raced to get the latest works from London, paid for advance sheets, issued competing editions of the same texts, and aggressively invaded each other's territory. It was new books the public demanded, and the booksellers supplied them. In 1832, Henry C. Carey informed his aging father, Mathew, that the finances of the business no longer rested on the Bible. "Five-sixths of the whole sales are of books manufactured within the year." For the Carey firm, as for publishing generally, new books were, more and more, written as well as printed in the United States by such top-selling authors as Washington Irving, James Fenimore Cooper ("the American Scott"), Catharine Sedgwick, and others. Alert to current tastes, Carey and Lea in Philadelphia contended fiercely against Harper Brothers in New York. It was ultimately a losing cause; Manhattan was on the way to becoming the publishing capital of America.

As they fought for dominance, the booksellers were outflanked by a new rival around 1840, the upstart "story papers" like *Brother Jonathan*, which used steam-powered presses to turn out massive editions of novels in huge, newspaper format and shipped them cheaply to subscribers through the mail. Sold for twelve cents a copy, the story papers unleashed an era of ruinous competition in the book trade. In journalism, too, novelty, speed, and centralization were the driving themes. In the Age of Jackson, the party press, both Democrat and Whig, was integrated into rival national networks taking their cues from Washington, with editors drawn from the ranks of lawyers and politicians, not working printers, and hired and fired as the political winds shifted. The leading commercial papers in the major port cities stepped up the competition for news, with pony expresses running between New York and Philadelphia and fast boats racing to intercept ships arriving in harbor. In the mid-1830s, the New York *Courier and Enquirer* claimed the largest circulation in the nation—4,500 papers a day—but it was soon dwarfed by the penny press, which changed the rules of urban journalism. Instead of charging high rates for advance subscriptions (six cents an issue or sixteen dollars a year), the *Sun*, the *Transcript*, and the *Herald* in New York and their counterparts in Boston, Philadelphia, and Baltimore sold copies daily on the city streets for only one cent. The target audience for the newcomers was not the business and political elite but the expanding middle and working classes of the burgeoning cities. Boasting their independence from the political parties, the editors, most prominently, the Scottish-born James Gordon Bennett of the *Herald*, appealed to readers with entertaining stories of crime, sex, high society, and scandal and fought furiously to be the first with the news, even dispatching flocks of carrier pigeons to speed delivery.

With daily circulations of 15,000 to 20,000 by the early 1840s, the penny press was an advance agent of the new machine age of telegraph, railroad, and steam power.

Custodians of authority and radical reformers alike were appalled at the raucous popular culture in the new print media. Henry David Thoreau, the Concord Transcendentalist, derided the mania for fiction and the hunger for news. "Hardly a man takes a half hour's nap after dinner, but when he wakes he holds up his head and asks, 'What's the news?' as if the rest of mankind had stood his sentinels." Absorbed in the transient and the superficial, Americans were heedless of the classics, "the recorded wisdom of mankind," and blind to the divine potential within themselves. The age of reading was a sham. This critique was reminiscent of Reverend Samuel Miller, and for good reason. Despite the greater quantity, speed, and scale of the press, the issues at the heart of print culture—authority and liberty, knowledge and power—remained. Every advance of communication complicated the discussion but did not change the fundamental terms. Looking back at the "print revolution" in the first half century of the republic, Americans in the electronic age may understandably have a sense of déjà vu. One generation's revolution is another's status quo.

See also **Authorship, Intellectual Property, and Copyright; Culture for Mass Audiences; Literary Reviews and "Little Magazines"; Textbooks; Almanacs and Ephemeral Literature; Journals of Opinion; Books; Journalism; Periodicals;** *(volume 3); and other articles in this section.*

BIBLIOGRAPHY

Amory, Hugh, and David D. Hall, eds. *The Colonial Book in the Atlantic World.* Vol. 1 of *A History of the Book in America.* Cambridge, Mass., 2000.

Bailyn, Bernard, and John B. Hench, eds. *The Press and the American Revolution.* Worcester, Mass., 1980.

Blondheim, Menahem. *News over the Wires: The Telegraph and the Flow of Public Information in America, 1844–1897.* Cambridge, Mass., 1994.

Botein, Stephen. "'Meer Mechanics' and an Open Press: The Business and Political Strategies of Colonial American Printers." *Perspectives in American History* 9 (1975): 127–225.

Brooke, John L. "'To Be Read by the Whole People': Press, Party, and the Public Sphere in the United States, 1790–1840." *Proceedings of the American Antiquarian Society* 110 (2000).

Brown, Richard D. *Knowledge Is Power: The Diffusion of Information in Early America, 1700–1865.* New York, 1989.

———. *The Strength of a People: The Idea of an Informed Citizenry in America, 1650–1870.* Chapel Hill, N.C., 1996.

Charvat, William. *Literary Publishing in America, 1790–1850.* Amherst, Mass., 1993.

Clark, Charles E. *The Public Prints: The Newspaper in Anglo-American Culture, 1665–1740.* New York, 1994.

Cornelius, Janet Duitsman. *"When I Can Read My Title Clear": Literacy, Slavery, and Religion in the Antebellum South.* Columbia, S.C., 1991.

Davidson, Cathy N. *Revolution and the Word: The Rise of the Novel in America.* New York, 1986.

Gilmore, William J. *Reading Becomes a Necessity of Life: Material and Cultural Life in Rural New England, 1780–1835.* Knoxville, Tenn., 1989.

Green, James N. "Book Publishing in Early America." The A. S. W. Rosenbach Lectures for 1993.

Gross, Robert A. *Books and Libraries in Thoreau's Concord.* Worcester, Mass., 1988.

Hall, David D. *Cultures of Print: Essays in the History of the Book.* Amherst, Mass., 1996.

Hall, David D., and John B. Hench, eds. *Needs and Opportunities in the History of the Book: America, 1639–1876.* Worcester, Mass., 1987.

Jaffee, David. "The Village Enlightenment in New England, 1760–1820." *William and Mary Quarterly,* 3rd ser., 47 (July 1990): 327–346.

John, Richard R. *Spreading the News: The American Postal System from Franklin to Morse.* Cambridge, Mass., 1995.

Joyce, William L., David D. Hall, Richard D. Brown, and John B. Hench, eds. *Printing and Society in Early America.* Worcester, Mass., 1983.

Kelley, Mary. "Reading Women/Women Reading: The Making of Learned Women in Antebellum America." *Journal of American History* 83 (1996): 401–424.

Larkin, Jack. "The Merriams of Brookfield: Printing in the Economy and Culture of Rural Massachusetts in the Early Nineteenth Century." *Proceedings of the American Antiquarian Society* 96 (1986): 39–73.

Nerone, John. *Violence against the Press: Policing the Public Sphere in U.S. History.* New York, 1994.

Nord, David. "Systematic Benevolence: Religious Publishing and the Marketplace in Early Nineteenth-Century America." In *Communications and Change in American Religious History.* Edited by Leonard I. Sweet, pp. 239–269. Grand Rapids, Mich., 1993.

Remer, Rosalind. *Printers and Men of Capital: Philadelphia Book Publishers in the New Republic.* Philadelphia, 1996.

Schudson, Michael. *Discovering the News: A Social History of American Newspapers.* New York, 1981.

Silver, Rollo G. *The American Printer, 1787–1825.* Charlottesville, Va., 1967.

Smith, Jeffery. *Printers and Press Freedom: The Ideology of Early American Journalism.* New York, 1988.

Tebbel, John. *The Creation of an Industry, 1630–1865.* Vol. 1 of *A History of Book Publishing in the United States.* New York and London, 1972.

Tucher, Andie. *Froth and Scum: Truth, Beauty, Goodness, and the Ax Murder in America's First Mass Medium.* Chapel Hill, N.C., 1994.

Warner, Michael. *The Letters of the Republic: Publication and the Public Sphere in Eighteenth-Century America.* Cambridge, Mass., 1990.

Zboray, Ronald J. *A Fictive People: Antebellum Economic Development and the American Reading Public.* New York, 1993.

RHETORIC AND BELLES LETTRES

Jill Swiencicki

Rhetoric is both a practice and a philosophy: the practice of effective, persuasive speech, and the study of the strategies of effective language use and of the relationship between language and knowledge. In the West, since the birth of Athenian democracy in the fifth century B.C., rhetoric has flourished as the codes through which citizens speak to one another in legal, political, and ceremonial arenas. Philosophers such as the Sophists, Plato, and Aristotle theorized about what counts as persuasive speech and whether rhetoric is an adequate means of representing truth and reality. From classical times until the nineteenth century, rhetorical practice required privileged social status: those who were authorized to speak in varied public arenas were literate, propertied men with citizen status. The rhetorical tradition's purview in the West was challenged as social orders shifted, showing that, as a central aspect of creating community and expressing knowledge, rhetoric reflects the beliefs, values, and conflicts of the culture that produced it.

The story of rhetoric and belles lettres in the eighteenth and early nineteenth centuries in America reveals radical shifts in social, economic, and intellectual thought. Americans were no longer a group of colonized subjects who looked to a sovereign ruler for direction. Merchants and the emergent middle class stepped into the space where monarchy once prevailed, offering less formal styles of speech and less hierarchical ways of organizing society. Throughout the contest with Britain in the eighteenth century, a well-defined and independent public emerged in America—a space of opinion outside the state in which citizens could have rational discussions about matters of local, national, and international importance. This public sphere was fueled by increasing literacy rates, a dramatic increase in printed material, and the appearance of coffeehouses and meetinghouses in cities and towns that furnished spaces for debate. Intellectual ideas about rhetoric were shifting, as it moved from being an ornament of thought that threatened to obscure truth to the center of discussions of science, morals, philosophy, and letters. Finally, as society democratized further, a critique of rhetoric as a male, privileged, Euro-American domain was launched on several fronts, as women, the working classes, African Americans, and Native Americans used established rhetorical strategies—and created new rhetorical practices—to diversify cultural and intellectual landscapes.

THE AMERICAN CIVIC IDEAL

In mid-eighteenth-century America, discussions about rhetoric revealed a larger anxiety about the future of a nation without social hierarchies or courtly standards in place. Influential political and cultural figures such as John Quincy Adams and the lawyer-statesman Daniel Webster connected eloquence—moving, persuasive speech—to a specific kind of audience, self, and social order. Rhetoric focused on teaching the skills needed in a civilized society. A rhetorical ideal emerged in this period that was civic, educated, refined (but not highbrow), and moral, demanding that one demonstrate "virtue," which in this context implied a devotion to the public good that eschewed personal interests on behalf of social cohesion. Linking eloquent speech with civil society promoted a national identity as well as reinforced the interests, tastes, and language practices of enfranchised leaders of the period.

The Orator and Eloquence Like many in the young democracy, John Quincy Adams, first a Boylston Professor of rhetoric and oratory at Harvard and later the sixth president of the United States, believed that a gifted individual could drive a nation's history. Adams embodied this civic ideal and in his lectures he charged his students to do the same: "Let him catch the relics of ancient oratory those unresisted powers, which mould the mind of man to the will of the speaker, and yield the guidance of a nation to the dominion of the voice." In what was a developing oratorical culture (a political, scholarly, and public culture centered on the power of speech), the practice of persuasion was the ultimate democratic skill. The oratorical culture was neoclassical, focusing on classical rhetorical aims of debate and consensus on matters of civic and national interest. Oratory was valued as the main vehicle for shaping collective values, and orators who demonstrated eloquence were leaders who could unite disparate sets of beliefs and maintain cultural unity.

Eloquence and Social Difference   The oratorical culture's interest in a neoclassical, or hierarchical, unified civic body was in part a reaction against the increasingly diverse public cultures and communicative practices emerging in the late eighteenth and early nineteenth centuries. In the schools and courts Latin was replaced with the vernacular, and dialects as well as regional and class differences emerged in speech and affected the political, religious, and cultural arenas. Backwoods, unschooled speakers such as Patrick Henry were both admired for their ability to move audiences and feared for new linguistic practices, as seen in the statesman Thomas Jefferson's criticism of Henry as "a man who had read nothing and had no books," and a speaker whose "pronunciation was vulgar and vicious, but it was forgotten while he was speaking." Literacy rates were the highest they had ever been in this period, and a developing print culture created an informed public who vigorously shared speakers' views. The emergence of linguistic and social differences was met by the publishing of grammars from such figures as the lexicographer Noah Webster. These grammars attempted to expand knowledge, but they also codified the language and social interests of the enfranchised class.

If eloquence restricted linguistic difference, it also restricted racial difference. The influential rhetorical philosopher Hugh Blair asserted, "Never did a slave become an orator" because "liberty is the nurse of true genius." Such rhetorical polemics challenged African American orators such as Frederick Douglass, who in his first public address in 1841 made a disclaimer in which he vowed to refrain from using black vernacular. While acquiring rhetorical skill often meant cultural assimilation, figures such as Douglass used their knowledge of dominant rhetorical practices in political and pulpit oratory to critique the culture and become leading voices for the antislavery cause. For Douglass, as-

THE COLUMBIAN ORATOR

That gem of a book, *The Columbian Orator*, with its eloquent orations and spicy dialogues, denouncing oppression and slavery—telling of what had been dared, done and suffered by men, to obtain the inestimable boon of liberty—was still fresh in my memory, and whirled into the ranks of my speech with the aptitude of well trained soldiers, going through the drill. The fact is, I here began my public speaking.

Source: Frederick Douglass, *My Bondage and My Freedom*, pp. 305–306.

sociating himself with the white abolitionist lecture circuit and reading Caleb Bingham's *The Columbian Orator* (1797), a text that offered rhetorical education through speeches on republican values and political reformism, helped him to argue forcefully on behalf of an oppressed people. A successful abolitionist lecturer, he appealed to his mainly white audiences in a refined style, for which Sojourner Truth chastised him. Truth, an African American preacher turned suffragette and abolitionist, could not read, had rhetorical roots in evangelical Christianity, and always spoke in black dialect, turning the traditional notion of eloquence on its head.

RHETORIC AND BELLES LETTRES IN THE UNIVERSITY

The eighteenth century was the period when the human sciences were born: anthropology, psychology, sociology, economics, and rhetoric and belles lettres. It was a time when universities did not have strict divisions of knowledge into departments and programs; science and philosophy were considered compatible realms of inquiry, and poetry, drama, oratory, and history comprised a single body of knowledge. Extending the trivium of rhetoric, grammar, and logic, liberal education became a mixture of classics, history, literature, theology, mathematics, and the natural and moral sciences. The classics remained a core feature of rhetorical study, but rhetorical philosophy at this time was transatlantic in its nature, and American students, intellectuals, and scholars were heavily influenced by theories of rhetoric set forth from the British cultural provinces of Ireland and Scotland, as well as from the rest of Europe.

Classical Rhetoric   Even though the eighteenth century marked the period during which Latin was replaced with English in university instruction, legal proceedings, and intellectual circles, and even though classical studies were in decline, classics remained the basis of rhetorical education for the practical guides it offered students. The writings of Aristotle frame rhetoric in several useful ways: in judicial, deliberative, epideictic domains; in ethical, pathetic, and logical appeals; in canons of invention, arrangement, style, memory, and delivery; and in aims of information, persuasion, and pleasure for audiences. Curricula regularly included the Roman rhetorical writings of Cicero and Quintilian, which see rhetoric as an art that can be taught and offer rules for effective communication. The Boylston chair of rhetoric at Harvard was endowed by a wealthy merchant in 1771 and in 1806 John Quincy Adams filled the post, which was intended to foster classical pedagogies in rhetorical education such as readings in Cicero, and weekly declamations, where students composed and delivered speeches on a given topic for the university and city communities.

As commercial interest and influence grew in America, classical rhetoric was reoriented toward a combination of eighteenth-century British aesthetics, republican ideals, and print culture. By the early nineteenth century rhetoricians challenged the Aristotelean and Ciceronian assumptions that rhetoric related only to political, ceremonial, and forensic discourse. In the spirit of the English philosopher Francis Bacon's empiricism, the "new rhetoric" asserted that arguments should be made from the facts of the case under debate rather than drawn from set topics or commonplaces, and favored a rhetoric of persuasion broadly understood as the active art of moving and influencing the passions, extending rhetoric into new realms, such as literary criticism. Eighteenth-century precursors such as the English philosopher John Locke connected rhetoric with epistemology (how people know what they know) by identifying belief and knowledge not as abstract entities but as firmly entrenched within the act of persuasion.

The Scottish School   The "new rhetoric" was borne of a group of rhetorical philosophers from Ireland and Scotland known as the Scottish school. These intellectuals were members of a close intellectual community interested in the new aesthetics

and psychology. Adam Smith gave his *Lectures on Rhetoric and Belles Lettres* in 1748 at Edinburgh, and was succeeded as a lecturer by Hugh Blair in 1759, whose published lectures became the most frequently used text on rhetoric in American colleges and universities from the late eighteenth to the mid-nineteenth centuries. In 1757 George Campbell lectured on pulpit oratory at Aberdeen, later publishing his *Philosophy of Rhetoric* (1776). The Irishman Thomas Sheridan lectured all over Britain and Europe on his theories of delivery, or elocution. The Scottish school offered students of rhetoric fresh ideas in that it assimilated into rhetoric recent ideas on taste, beauty, sublimity, orality, and psychology. It is most frequently associated with a synthesis of belle lettres, faculty psychology, and elocutionary theories.

Belles Lettres   Belletrism loosely refers to practices of literary theory and criticism of the eighteenth century. If rhetoric refers to oratory and eloquence, belletrism sees its domain as the language arts, such as biography, drama, history writing, philology, poetry, and science. According to belletrism, scholars believed each of these genres shared essential features whose rules could be extrapolated and taught, and a discovery of these features would make one more acquainted with appropriate morals, "tastes," and "sympathies." In this way belletristic rhetoric appealed to the middle classes who longed for an education equal to their increasing economic power, and they believed that an education in belletristic rhetoric would prepare them to join the cultural elite. The Scottish philosopher David Hume saw them as "agents of improvement" devoted to drawing their country "from a state of rudeness to one of cosmopolitan refinement." If Cicero was interested in how to speak to the common people, Scottish belletrism taught readers how to speak to refined, enlightened people like themselves.

The main belletristic theorist of the period was Hugh Blair, whose two-volume *Lectures on Rhetoric and Belles Lettres* (1783) was delivered as a series of lectures at the University of Edinburgh. For Blair, the goal of rhetoric is to teach others to be effective critics of all of the arts of discourse as well as to be effective speakers. Blair's belletristic criticism hinges on two concepts: appreciating and cultivating taste and style. He described taste as "the power of receiving pleasure from the beauties of nature and art" and in his lectures he attempted to discover qualities in language that transcend time and place. Blair concluded that taste is neither wholly rational nor wholly a product of internal sensibility, and believed that standards of taste are negotiated publicly through discussion and debate: "While accidental causes may occasionally warp the proper operations of taste," ultimately corrupt tastes are overturned. Similar to the moral implications of his theories of taste, Blair believed that a writer's style reveals his character and the innate virtues of the text under consideration. He culled his examples of style largely from the vernacular, as he attended to such contemporary writers as Joseph Addison and Jonathan Swift in explanations of their vices and virtues. Blair approached style as the key to a text's meaning and a person's psychology. His form of textual analysis is easily corrupted into appreciative analysis of the surface features of language, and his attention to taste has persisted in contemporary arguments to remedy current university English curricula with texts that scholars maintain represent core cultural values.

Faculty Psychology   George Campbell's *Philosophy of Rhetoric* rivaled Blair's *Lectures* as most frequently taught in American colleges and universities. Inspired by the writings of Francis Bacon, Campbell came to believe that the mind is separated into faculties, or categories of understanding. These faculties comprise a hierarchy ranging from the elementary faculty of "understanding" to the more complex faculty of the "will." Persuasion therefore is a result of instruction in appealing to the imagination, passion, and will. As Campbell argued, "If the orator would prove successful, it is necessary that he engage in his service all these different powers of the mind, the imagination, the memory, and the passions. These are not the supplanters of reason, or even rivals in her sway; they are her handmaids, by whose ministry she is enabled to usher truth into the heart, and procure it there a favorable reception" (in Golden et al., p. 26). Richard Whately carried on the psychological-philosophical trend in rhetoric with his *Elements of Rhetoric* (1828). Popular in American colleges, and in the curricula of less traditional teachers, such as the social reformer Margaret Fuller, Whately's text emphasizes forms of reasoning in argument that are audience motivated.

Elocution   Elocution was a reaction to the new print culture and focused on orality in language. In his well-known *Lectures on Elocution* (1762), Thomas Sheridan wrote, "Our greatest men have been trying to do that with the pen, which can only be performed by the tongue; to produce effects by

the dead letter, which can never be produced by the living voice, with its accompaniments." Pronouncing dictionaries, rhetorical grammars, lectures, and books on elocution were in fashion in the late eighteenth and early nineteenth centuries, and ranked the powers of speech above writing. Study in delivery aimed to help speakers affect not just the literate gentry but a general public meant to create consensus. In this way, crucial to the new rhetoric of the Scottish philosophers was elevating the performative element of speech over the argumentative, and the study of tonal and gestural delivery took a central place in rhetorical philosophy. James Burgh's *The Art of Speaking* (1761) was the most influential American elocutionary manual of the late eighteenth century and addresses the revelation of internal moral dispositions and passions as registered by vocal tones, physical comportment, and facial expressions. Ironically, elocution, the study of the performance of rhetorical sincerity, was meant to promise real sincerity in a diverse new republic.

WOMEN, RHETORIC, AND THE PUBLIC SPHERE

Until the late nineteenth century, the phrase "public woman" generally referred to actresses and prostitutes. While women struggled to be heard in the church, courts, professions, and press, social factors constrained the study and practice of rhetoric for women. Rhetorical education was linked with universities, and women were almost completely excluded from university education until the end of the nineteenth century. University training aimed at preparing lawyers, clergymen, and business leaders, occupations closed to women until the end of the nineteenth century. Further, rhetorical philosophy largely excluded women from its purview for much of its history, as discourse on rhetoric and eloquence associated rhetoric with power and masculinity, and ornate, emotional, effusive speech was deemed by rhetoricians from Cicero to Blair as weak and feminine. But by the end of the seventeenth century women's access to literacy changed, and by the end of the eighteenth at least 50 percent of women in North America were literate, gaining their education at home or in village schools. They read the Bible, newspapers, and popular literature, wrote letters, practiced penmanship, and soon began making inroads into the public sphere and the rhetorical tradition, creating some of its most dramatic changes.

Religion and Women's Rhetoric In the Bible, St. Paul's letter to the Corinthians declares: "Let your women keep silence in the churches: for it is not permitted unto them to speak; but they are commanded to be under obedience, and also saith the law. And if they will learn any thing, let them ask their husbands at home" (1 Cor. 14:34). Known as the Pauline injunction against women's speech, it produced centuries-old justifications for denying a woman's right to speak publicly with authority. But just as religious doctrine prohibited women's speech, religious practice became a space for women to gain a meaningful voice in their communities, often presenting themselves rhetorically as prophetesses of divine truth, as feminine voices in dependent relation to a masculine deity.

One challenge to the Pauline injunction came from the African American abolitionist Maria Stewart early in the nineteenth century: "Did St. Paul but know of our wrongs and deprivations, I presume he would make no objection to our pleading in public for our rights." Living as a servant in a clergyman's family until her marriage, Stewart underwent a transformative religious experience that intensified her opposition to slavery and linked religious, female, and political rhetoric. At one of her speeches delivered in 1832 at Franklin Hall, she pleaded: "My beloved brethren, as Christ has died in vain for those who will not accept his offered mercy, so will it be vain for the advocates of freedom to spend their breath in our behalf, unless with united hearts should you make some mighty efforts to raise your sons and daughters from the horrible state of servitude and degradation in which they are placed. It is upon you that woman depends; she can do but little besides using her influence; and it is for her sake and yours that I have come forward and made myself a hissing and a reproach among the people." A vessel for the work of a male deity, Stewart made influential public, political arguments within religious discourse. She delivered three public addresses in 1832, after which public resistance made her cease.

The Quaker sisters Sarah and Angelina Grimké represented a new kind of rhetoric for religious women who wanted public influence, as seen in Sarah's lament: "I have blushed for my sex when I have heard of their entreating ministers to attend their associations, and open them with prayer. The idea is inconceivable to me, that Christian women can be engaged in doing God's work, and yet cannot ask his blessing on their efforts, except through the lips of a man." The Grimkés were southern women who renounced the slave system, became devout Quakers, and, with the benefit of a family inheritance, moved north to Philadelphia and worked on behalf of antislavery and women's rights. The Quakers were the first to recognize women's equal capacity to feel the propensity toward an "inward light" and express it. This focus gave women authority both in the family and the outside world. While still working within a strict patriarchal institution, Quaker women spoke freely at meetings, often held separate meetings, and traveled extensively as preachers. Like Maria Stewart, the Grimké sisters' faith led them into the political sphere. In *Letters on the Equality of the Sexes and the Condition of Women* (1838), Sarah argued—in biblical language and in images derived from Christian iconography—the first fully developed women's rights argument in America. In 1837 both sisters embarked on an antislavery lecture tour of New England, arguing at the podium and in print both against slavery and for a woman's right to speak out against it. This nettled proponents of female domesticity such as Catharine Beecher who, in a published letter exchange with Angelina Grimké, argued that women's moral influence is best kept within the bounds of the home.

"True Womanhood" The Grimké sisters responded to the gendered social norms of the period that prescribed appropriate roles for women based on sex. Sarah wrote: "Intellect is not sexed . . . strength of mind is not sexed, and . . . our views about the duties of men and the duties of women, the sphere of man and the sphere of woman, are mere arbitrary opinions, differing in different ages and countries, and depending solely on the will and judgement of erring mortals." Such beliefs were radically opposed to the ideology of true womanhood, in which women were attributed by "nature" to be pious, pure, and moral, and to be associated exclusively with the private sphere of home and family. Such beliefs also took shape in the notion of republican motherhood, the idea that it was women's highest calling to educate their children and thus morally strengthen the nation by nurturing its citizenry.

One of true womanhood's major proponents was Sarah Josepha Hale. Hale was the editor of *Godey's Lady's Book,* one of the largest circulating magazines in the nineteenth century, one that combined fiction, belletristic essays, book reviews, embroidery patterns, and fashion plates for its middle-class, white, female readers.

Hale never directly mentioned the rise of political, female orators in *Godey's,* but did write a

SARAH HALE ON WOMEN'S LETTER WRITING

Typical of the worldview of true womanhood, in a *Godey's* article on women and letter writing, the focus of the article lies not in the content of the composition but in the physical manner in which a woman composes. With tips from Mr. Shaw, a "writing-master," the article advises women on how to maintain proper posture while writing so as not to become "disfigured" and ungraceful. Writing is assumed to be an apolitical, unthoughtful, private activity which should not disturb the presumed ideal of the white, upper-middle-class woman's body as a graceful, delicate ornament.

Source: *Godey's Lady's Book* 12, p. 59.

novel, *The Lecturess, or Woman's Sphere* (1839), about the threat that one woman's desire for political, public lecturing poses for her family, her nation, and her "nature." Speaking through the ideology of true womanhood, the lecturess Marian's husband, William, argues that "woman's sphere is distinct from that of man. True, her natural rights are equal and the same. Her social and conventional rights, though equally honorable, are not the same." He then goes on to exult in the "high, glorious privileges" bestowed upon women, such as being a "beloved companion," "soother of sorrows," and a "mother of his children." Marian, echoing predecessors such as the English novelist Mary Wollstonecraft and contemporaries such as the Grimkés, boldly critiques this ideology: "The proper sphere of woman! Where is it? In the kitchen, or the laundry room? or, to rise one step in civilized life, to sit besides the cradle, and bow her head meekly in acquiescence to her husband's will, be it ever so arbitrary or unreasonable? or, still higher, is it woman's sphere to spend her days in listless inactivity, or in a giddy race after amusement? *I* do not believe that her creator ever intended her life to be spent in any of these ways."

Women and Reform Rhetoric
The nineteenth century saw women challenging the rhetoric of true womanhood by orating on behalf of political re-

forms. Scottish-born Frances Wright was the first woman in the United States to speak before mixed audiences that numbered in the thousands. Wright began her activism by arguing for alternate public roles for women from those related to popular religious revivalism, mandatory motherhood, and marriage. She advocated for women's education, antislavery, and even women's reproductive freedom. Wright created new public arenas around these issues through journalism, trade unionism, Quakerism, and most notoriously as the originator of the 1825 Nashoba, Tennessee, project for emancipating slaves through a communal work project. To ensure a space to speak in the face of increasing public hostility, Wright purchased a lecture hall. Still, her speeches were riddled with mob unrest and threats of bombfire and her short-lived speaking career, from 1828 to 1830, came to a close.

By the end of the 1830s solo women orators like Wright became a chorus of voices working together on social issues such as slavery, prostitution, temperance, and suffrage. Through moral and political reform societies, women participated in public dialogue on fundamental questions underlying the polity, such as, What constitutes a citizen? A human being? Who has the right to an education? These questions were pressed upon all-male societies and government officials in conventions and publications, sometimes stretching public toleration to the limit. For example, in 1838 an angry mob burned to the ground the newly erected Pennsylvania Hall, the site of the Second Antislavery Convention of American Women. The mob torched the hall upon hearing that the inaugural speeches of the antislavery meetinghouse would be given by white and African American women. With the steady emergence of female political speakers, the deluge of antislavery petitions to Congress bearing women's signatures, and women's organization into antislavery and suffrage societies, concerns were raised among the middle classes about women stepping out of their "proper" sphere of female activities, and about the rise in desegregated coalition activity within abolition and women's rights organizations as those oppressed by the dominant culture began to link race, class, and gender oppression in their activism. At the close of the decade, it appeared that the conservative factions of the argument were winning the public debate, as women's antislavery organizations whose publicity was based on true womanhood prevailed; as the congressional gag rules of 1836–1840 accepted antislavery petitions from women without reading them; as several female social activists withdrew from public lecturing; and as mob demonstrations at antislavery and suffrage meetings continued. But with feminist rhetorical milestones such as the Seneca Falls Convention of 1848 on the horizon, and with growing national and international women's movements for temperance, antislavery, labor reform, and suffrage, women's political rhetoric continued to agitate for meaningful reform throughout the nineteenth century.

THE IMPACT OF RELIGIOUS TRADITIONS ON RHETORIC

The republican period saw challenges to traditional Calvinism and Presbyterianism on a number of fronts, and these challenges produced radically new rhetorical practices and philosophies that influenced politics and reflected larger changes in diverse public cultures in the period. For its proponents, new religious rhetorics replaced elite traditions of Ciceronian and Scottish rhetorics, moving rhetoric away from textuality (an emphasis on learned, practiced speeches in a measured, plain style) and toward orality (an emphasis on unstudied, spontaneous speech). This shift popularized new modes of performance that would diversify ways of being in public. From the religious rhetorics of disenchanted Boston intellectuals to those of laborers suffering the dislocations of the market revolution, dissenting voices found expression in new religious sects, and their rhetorics became a way to challenge social as well as religious orders.

Religious Awakenings   The late eighteenth and early nineteenth centuries were the years of the great spiritual revivals that transformed the American culture. The revivals prompted a debate about the people's voice—its provenance and the scope and nature of its representativeness. The Great Awakening of the 1740s was a grassroots religious movement that democratized religion by shifting the balance of power between minister and congregation. It offered a direct challenge to clerical authority in stating that authority to preach depended not on having studied at Harvard or Yale but on experiential knowledge, and was not restricted to the four walls of a church. A new class of preachers emerged—women, people of color, and children—to preach the glories to the colonies of the promise of regeneration. Their evangelism was a fundamental challenge to the Puritan preaching system. Dramatic, emotionally disruptive, colloquial, extemporaneous speech offered a religious rhetoric whose transformation carried into the political and intellectual realms. Such an experience was offered by the English evangelist George Whitefield, who attracted more than twenty thousand to his 1740 Boston Common sermon. "The grand itinerant," Whitefield traveled through towns, rural outposts, and cities offering crowds a "new birth." This insistence that God was accessible to all intensified the revelatory aspects of religious experience, and privileged personal experience and emotion over formal knowledge. Whitefield's extempore preaching aroused audiences who responded to expressive vernacular over orthodox scholasticism, and his speech was marked by "roarings, agonies, screamings, tremblings, dropping down, ravings." This enthusiasm—eliciting response from worshipers rather than silence—is part of a revolutionary ideology of participation.

Unitarianism   Intellectuals and philosophers—specifically the northeastern elite—were offering their own challenge to traditions of pulpit oratory. One of the best received speakers of his day was the clergyman William Ellery Channing. His 1819 speech "Unitarian Christianity" is arguably the most important incident in American Unitarianism. Attacking Calvinism, Channing argued that "religion, in one or another form, has always been an engine for crushing the human soul. But such is not the religion of Christ. If it were, it would deserve no respect." His was a rhetoric of liberation, dwelling on traditional pastoral topics such as religion and philosophy but more so on pacifism, slavery, and social justice. Channing opposed the characteristics of Calvinist preaching, for which the most common appeal to emotion involved fear, and eschewed elitist theory and Latin phrases. Channing spoke in a plain style—simple, but not turgid—that was valued in the period, and offered rhetoric as a means to action. He deplored theatricality, arguing that plain truth reveals itself: "On no account, in your public services, try to exhibit by look or tone any emotion which you do not feel. If you feel coldly, appear so. The sermon may be lost, but your own truthfulness will be preserved."

Religious Rhetoric and Social Difference   These changes in the style and content of religious rhetoric were in part defined as a feminization of American religion, marking the shift from a Calvinist deity's inscrutability and omnipotent will to nurture, mercy, and love. Women's public conversion narratives became an important oral form available to women, whose association with piousness and morality allowed them public authority and eventually influenced belletristic forms like the novel and poetry.

Interesting class and racial alliances converged in evangelical religions to form new rhetorics. Those in the Second Great Awakening (1795–1835) often saw themselves as religions of outsiders battling against a reprobate elite. Worshipers joined in common experiences of economic dislocation, as swelling ranks of migrant labor faced social vulnerability, and the values of sobriety, piety, and honesty provided access routes to respectability. Some of these mostly Euro-American groups, such as Baptists and Methodists, disregarded hierarchies and created temporary, cross-racial alliances with African Americans, laboring whites, and Indians, and allowed marginalized people to maintain their racial communities through religion but also simultaneously forge bonds with oppressed whites. One such Methodist was the Pequot preacher William Apess, who drew on personal and religious experiences with cultural hybridization to defend native rights, offering a "new revelation" by holding up native values to Anglo ones through evangelism.

In the revolutionary period the rhetorical canon was expanded to include not just declamations from graduating students at Harvard and Yale, not just elocutionary textbooks, not just grammars and philosophies of rhetoric, but slave narratives, emotional speeches at religious camp meetings, and women orators who critiqued the rhetorical tradition, enriching it in the process. In the last half of the nineteenth century, while the practice of rhetoric waned in the expanding university systems and was replaced by composition, and while civic oratory was overtaken by commercial interests in the public sphere, the legacy of women and minority rhetors, and the intellectual and cultural developments they helped facilitate, invigorated and democratized the rhetorical tradition for years to come.

See also **Artistic, Intellectual, and Political Refugees** *(volume 2);* **The Role of the Intellectual; Learned Societies and Professional Associations; Literary Reviews and "Little Magazines"; Salons, Coffeehouses, Conventicles, and Taverns; Lyceums, Chautauquas, and Institutes for Useful Knowledge; Almanacs and Ephemeral Literature; Books; Periodicals; Rhetoric** *(volume 3).*

BIBLIOGRAPHY

Overviews

Aristotle. *On Rhetoric: A Theory of Civic Discourse.* Edited by George A. Kennedy. New York, 1991.

Bizzell, Patricia, and Bruce Herzberg, eds. *The Rhetorical Tradition: Readings from Classical Times to the Present.* Boston, 1990.

Cmiel, Kenneth. *Democratic Eloquence: The Fight for Popular Speech in Nineteenth-Century America.* Berkeley, Calif., 1990.

Isocrates. *Against the Sophists.* Translated by George Norlin. Vol. 2 of *Isocrates.* Cambridge, Mass., 1968.

The American Civic Ideal

Adams, John Quincy. *Lectures on Rhetoric and Oratory, Delivered to the Classes of Senior and Junior Sophisters in Harvard University.* Vol. 1. 1810. Reprint, Delmar, N.Y., 1997.

Bingham, Caleb. *The Columbian Orator: Containing a Variety of Original and Selected Pieces Together with Rules, Which are Calculated to Improve Youth and Others, in the Ornamental and Useful Art of Eloquence.* 1797. Reprint, edited by David W. Blight, New York, 1998.

Clark, Gregory, and S. Michael Halloran, eds. *Oratorical Culture in Nineteenth-Century America: Transformations in the Theory and Practice of Rhetoric.* Carbondale, Ill., 1993.

Douglass, Frederick. *Autobiographies: Narrative of the Life of Frederick Douglass, An American Slave; My Bondage and My Freedom; Life and Times of Frederick Douglass.* New York, 1994.

Fliegelman, Jay. *Declaring Independence: Jefferson, Natural Language, and the Culture of Performance.* Stanford, Calif., 1993.

Webster, Noah. *A Philosophical and Practical Grammar of the English Language.* 1807. Reprint, New Haven, Conn., 1822.

Rhetoric and Belles Lettres in the University

Berlin, James A. *Writing Instruction in Nineteenth-Century American Colleges.* Carbondale, Ill., 1984.

Blair, Hugh. *Lectures on Rhetoric and Belles Lettres.* 2 vols. 1783. Reprint, edited by Harold F. Harding, Carbondale, Ill., 1965.

Burgh, James. *The Art of Speaking.* 1761. Reprint, Delmar, N.Y., 1992.

Campbell, George. *The Philosophy of Rhetoric.* 1776. Reprint, Cambridge, Mass., 1969.

Cicero. *De Oratore, Books I-II.* Translated by E. W. Sutton and H. Rackham. Cambridge, Mass., 1942.

Ferreira-Buckley, Linda. "Hugh Blair." In *Eighteenth-Century British and American Rhetorics and Rhetoricians: Critical Studies and Sources,* edited by Michael G. Moran, pp. 21–35. Westport, Conn., 1994.

Golden, James L., Goodwin F. Berquist, and William E. Coleman. *Rhetoric of Western Thought.* Edited by James Golden et al. 4th ed. Dubuque, Iowa, 1989.

Howell, Wilbur Samuel. *Eighteenth-Century British Logic and Rhetoric.* Princeton, N.J., 1971.

Johnson, Nan. *Nineteenth-Century Rhetoric in North America.* Carbondale, Ill., 1991.

Locke, John. *An Essay concerning Human Understanding.* 1690. Reprint, edited by Peter Nidditch, Oxford, 1975.

McIntosh, Carey. *The Evolution of English Prose 1700–1800: Style, Politeness, and Print Culture.* New York, 1998.

Miller, Thomas P. *The Formation of College English: Rhetoric and Belles Lettres in the British Cultural Provinces.* Pittsburgh, Pa., 1997.

Quintilian. *Institutio Oratoria.* Translated by H. E. Butler. 4 vols. Cambridge, Mass., 1936.

Sheridan, Thomas. *A Course of Lectures on Elocution.* 1762. Reprint, North Stratford, N.H., 1968.

Smith, Adam. *Lectures on Rhetoric and Belles Lettres.* Edited by John Lothian. Carbondale, Ill., 1963.

Ulman, H. Lewis. *Things, Thoughts, Words, Actions: The Problem of Language in Late Eighteenth-Century British Rhetorical Theory.* Carbondale, Ill., 1994.

Whately, Richard. *Elements of Rhetoric . . . From the Third English Edition.* 1832. Reprint, Carbondale, Ill., 1969.

Witherspoon, John. *Selected Writings.* Edited by Thomas P. Miller. Carbondale, Ill., 1990.

Women, Rhetoric, and the Public Sphere

Brody, Miriam. *Manly Writing: Gender, Rhetoric, and the Rise of Composition.* Carbondale, Ill., 1993.

Campbell, Karlyn Kohrs, ed. *Women Public Speakers in the United States, 1800–1925: A Biocritical Sourcebook.* Westport, Conn., 1993.

Graff, Harvey J. *The Legacies of Literacy.* Bloomington, Ind., 1987.

Hale, Sarah Josepha. *The Lecturess, or Woman's Sphere.* Boston, 1838.

———. "On Letter Writing." *Godey's Lady's Book* 12 (February 1836): 57–59.

Lerner, Gerda, ed. *The Feminist Thought of Sarah Grimké.* New York, 1998.

Logan, Shirley Wilson. *"We Are Coming": The Persuasive Discourse of Nineteenth-Century Black Women.* Carbondale, Ill., 1999.

Lunsford, Andrea A., ed. *Reclaiming Rhetorica: Women in the Rhetorical Tradition.* Pittsburgh, Pa., 1995.

Matthews, Glenna. *The Rise of Public Woman: Women's Power and Women's Place in the United States, 1630–1970.* New York, 1992.

Peterson, Carla L. *"Doers of the Word": African-American Women Speakers and Writers in the North, 1830–1880.* New Brunswick, N.J., 1995.

Stewart, Maria W. "Lecture Delivered at the Franklin Hall." In *With Pen and Voice: A Critical Anthology of Nineteenth-Century African-American Women,* edited by Shirley Wilson Logan, pp. 6–10. Carbondale, Ill., 1995.

Welter, Barbara. *Dimity Convictions: The American Woman in the Nineteenth Century.* Athens, Ohio, 1976.

Rhetorics of Religious Traditions

Apess, William. *On Our Own Ground: The Complete Writings of William Apess, A Pequot.* Edited by Barry O'Connell. Amherst, Mass., 1992.

Channing, William Ellery. *The Works of William E. Channing.* 1845. Reprint, Temecula, Calif., 1990.

Haynes, Carolyn A. *Divine Destiny: Gender and Race in Nineteenth-Century Protestantism.* Jackson, Miss., 1998.

Ruttenberg, Nancy. "George Whitefield, Spectacular Conversion, and the Rise of Democratic Personality." In *The American Literary History Reader,* edited by Gordon Hunter, New York, 1995.

Tiro, Karim M. "Denominated 'Savage': Methodism, Writing, and Identity in the Works of William Apess, A Pequot." *American Quarterly* 48, no. 4 (December 1996): 653–679.

Whitefield, George. *The Works of the Reverend George Whitefield.* 6 vols. 1771.

PROPHETIC NATIVE AMERICAN MOVEMENTS

Michael D. McNally

Pontiac and Tecumseh, the warrior-diplomats who brought Native American peoples of eastern North America together across barriers of language, tribe, and culture in the late eighteenth and early nineteenth centuries, have so captured the American imagination that cities, summer camps, Civil War generals, cars, and chain saws all bear their respective names. To many Americans, they were legendary as statesmen who rose high above the supposed "tribalism" of their peoples to envision a united Native American stand against European encroachment.

Legend may have accorded each a sort of fame as an exemplary "noble savage," but it has also, among other interpretive violences, obscured the more significant and lasting cultural and religious transformations that their anticolonial revolts signaled and ushered in. First, the focus on Pontiac and Tecumseh as "idea men" has obscured the pivotal role played by spiritual leaders at their sides whose prophecies were arguably the real binding agent of the movements. Second and more important, the "great man" approach has eclipsed the broader religious dynamics that made intertribal resistance a surprisingly well-organized and urgent matter, for Pontiac's rebellion, Tecumseh's resistance, and other intertribal movements were rooted deeply, necessarily, in the sacred. Appreciating the extent to which they were thus rooted is crucial because it discloses how Native American religions have been at the heart of native struggles to negotiate the changes of history, and not simply the bulwarks of tradition that held their ground, unchanging and unchangeable, in the face of that history.

The native people who crossed boundaries of language and culture were not simply well marshaled by Pontiac and Tecumseh to defend a pre-Columbian status quo. They were engaged in a holy venture, called by the sacred to effect a viable future with integrity on native terms. The prophets called followers back to a life in balance with the land and the peoples of the land, but they did so by preaching a curious blend of old and new. Age-old ceremonies of purification and cyclical renewal that were associated with various tribal traditions merged with Christian-influenced millennial visions of heaven, hell, and the end of linear time. Out of intertribal resistance emerged a powerful new identity as "red people"—or perhaps it was the other way around: intertribal resistance emerged out of the ferment of the new identity. Though this new identity never completely displaced other ways of construing identity in terms of tribe, band, village, or clan, and though it invariably developed in outright tension with these other commitments, a "red" identity became an important part of the equation vesting intertribal alliances with a sacred necessity.

Coming to terms with these movements, then, requires taking religion seriously. As Joel Martin puts it in his study of the religious roots of the Red Stick Revolt, "prophetic talk about spiritual beings and ritual practices of shamans are treated as real and important historical forces, as real as the price of bullets in Pensacola in 1813" (*Sacred Revolt*, p. 4). Taking religion seriously, in turn, requires a recognition that the visions of prophets, outrageous as they could be, were potentially more than self-serving bids for personal influence. Historians who have paid the movements more sustained attention have noticed that they were much more than isolated flare-ups of frustration or the legerdemain of local charlatans. Gregory Evans Dowd argues that their "followers were . . . not the disciples of single charismatic leaders alone, but were the adherents of a broadly interconnected movement that produced many visionaries even as it divided communities" (p. xix). The many prophets who emerged from the mid-eighteenth to early nineteenth century were individual links in a chain of a larger pattern, an interdependent movement that sought to unite native peoples east of the Mississippi in a broad, spirited, anticolonial movement. Although it did not ultimately succeed in altering the basic contours of American expansion, this network of movements stands as strong evidence of the resourcefulness and resolve shown by native communities as they struggled to shape history.

DISPLACEMENTS

Crossing boundaries of tribe, language, and culture was part of native American experience well before 1492. Trade had long brought needed goods across such boundaries, alliances had long brought protection, and cultural exchanges had long made those alliances and that trade possible. What was new was the landscape in which native peoples undertook to negotiate a living amid peoples from across the Atlantic, the diseases that came with them, and the fur and deerskin trades.

By the end of the seventeenth century, smallpox and other diseases had taken a great toll on native populations and on the structures of clan, village, and community that gave their lives order and meaning. Such uprootings, combined with the new possibilities emerging with European goods and the trade that could secure them, led to a dramatic refashioning of Native American life in eastern North America. Trade brought some native peoples together in alliances with one or another European power; it also fanned the flames of small-scale ritualized intertribal conflicts into blazing arms races. A network of resettlement communities emerged that brought native peoples of different tribes and languages into close proximity to one another and to Europeans, with whom they created what Richard White has called "the middle ground," a cultural world mutually produced by Native Americans and Europeans to make trade possible. This was not a world in which European colonizers were able to wholly define native people; nor was it a world where powerless native people entered into cultural change only reluctantly.

The middle ground worked as such only when both sides could exercise power. It began to come apart first with the defeat of France and the consolidation of British control over eastern North America in the 1760s, and then more decidedly in the 1810s, with the consolidation of the United States' control. Between the 1760s and 1810s, declining demand for furs in Europe and overexploitation of furbearer and deer populations undercut the economic parity that had underwritten mutual authorship of the middle ground.

Encroaching settlers, less interested in trade than in controlling land, pushed westward a line of native refugee communities stretching up and down the East. Not surprisingly, displacement and migration increased competition for scarce resources and favor, exacerbating old tensions among different native peoples. This realignment also fueled new tensions within tribes, accentuating existing social differences into class distinctions. In most native communities, there emerged a fault line between those whose strategy for survival included broad accommodation of British and American interests, often traditional elder chiefs or people of mixed descent, and those who challenged such broad accommodations, often younger warriors.

SACRED VISIONS OF UNITY AND THE ANTICOLONIAL ACTION

With the collapse of the middle ground, new ways of imagining native identity began to emerge among the displaced who were living in those refugee villages not simply as Delawares, or Shawnees, or Odawas (Ottawas), but also as Native American "red people." It would be easy to overstate the novelty of intertribalism, were it not for the powerful economic, political, and military alliances with peoples of other tribes made on the middle ground and cemented with ceremonial exchanges that linked allies as relatives (fictive kin). But what emerged among some native people in these villages was an identification of their being fundamentally "red." In this, they asserted boundaries that stressed ontological difference between Indians and certain Europeans and, later, all whites, and that deemphasized distinctions of tribe or band. The significance of the prophetic resistance movements associated with Pontiac and Tecumseh was not their introduction of intertribalism, then, but rather their forging of powerful new identities from those intertribal alliances.

A pan-native identity was not an identity that was simply "out there" waiting to be discovered and embraced unequivocally by peoples previously stubborn in their tribalism. Any pan-native identity that emerged proved to be highly contested, because it forsook the political and spiritual authority of leaders and kin construed tribally for that of prophets and warriors and kin construed in other ways. What is more, the resulting tensions were aggressively exploited by European and American authorities seeking to extend influence and control. This made for no simple field of choices between being, say, Potawatomi or being simply "Indian," but an incredibly tenuous and complex layering of identities that shifted with circumstance. Following James

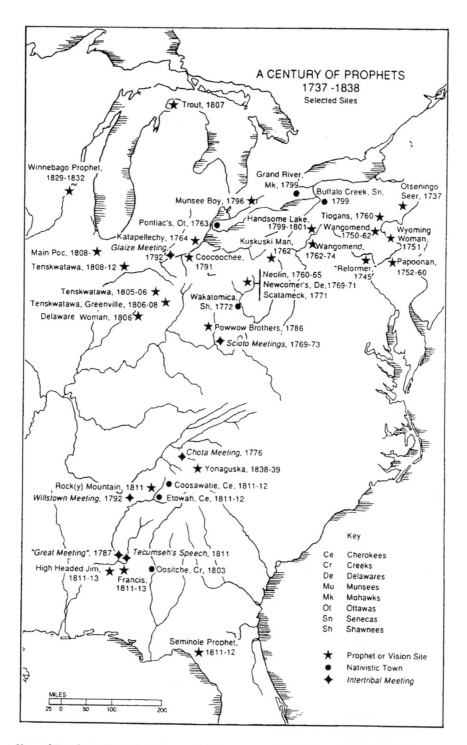

Sites of Prophecy. From the 1730s to the 1830s, Native American prophetic movements, noted here by geographical site, organized considerable anticolonial resistance along the shifting frontier of Euro-American settlement. FROM GREGORY EVANS DOWD, *A SPIRITED RESISTANCE: THE NORTH AMERICAN INDIAN STRUGGLE FOR UNITY, 1745–1815.* © JOHNS HOPKINS UNIVERSITY PRESS, 1991

Clifford, it is useful to think of identity not simply in terms of an either/or "boundary to be maintained but a fluid, shifting nexus of relations," a responsive resource for contending with changing circumstances of history (as cited in White, *Middle Ground,* p. ix).

But the identity of being "red" or "Indian," at least for those who staked their lives on that configuration of their identity, was no mere contingency of changing circumstance. It was experienced as rooted in the sacred, the really real. A consistent claim of the prophets in each of these movements was that resistance, renewal, and reconfiguration of identity were not simply the strategies of noble leaders, but commands of the sacred powers animating all life. Unlike seers of many native traditions whose visions were considered gifts of specific, local, or familiar spiritual sources, the men and women whose prophecy galvanized these movements often claimed they were receiving direct revelations from the high God, variously known as the Master of Life, the Breath-maker, the Great Spirit.

Although the details varied, each prophet told of a mythic polygenesis by which white and red peoples were created as intentionally different beings with separate destinies, and even representing distinct cosmic forces. Thus rooted in myth, the boundaries of identity separated not only "redness" from "Britishness," "Americanness," or "whiteness," but also purity from pollution and order from chaos. Consequently, maintaining the integrity of those boundaries took on a sense of sacred duty. Although the circumstances of lived experience would complicate how clearly such boundaries would, in fact, be maintained, prophets discouraged or prohibited intermarriage, but they also directed the maintenance of boundaries by means of ethics and ritual.

Ethically, the prophets called their followers back to a restoration of right relationships among people. They decried the violence that had broken out within and among native communities. They proclaimed that followers should shun the values of the market, and the wealth accumulation and class distinctions that came along with it, and return to economic ethics of subsistence and communalism. They called followers back to a lifeway free of the violence and disorientation associated with alcohol, wife beating, and child abuse. Prophets called for restored relations with plants and animals, especially those exploited in the fur trade, affirming their status as nonhuman beings and part of the moral community. Importantly, the prophets were not directing blame at Euro-Americans but a moral critique at their own people. By framing social and environmental ills in such moral terms, the prophets were empowering native people to take charge of their world through ethical action.

Moral criticism fused powerfully with visions of ritual renewal, for the restoration of relations was a matter of proper ceremonial behavior as well as one of restored ethical relations. In some cases, new songs, dances, and ceremonies were key parts of the prophets' visions, and performance of them was understood as generating new sources of power. In other cases, older seasonal ceremonies, like the annual Green Corn ceremonies of the Shawnee and Muskogee (Creek), took on a new cultural force as crisis rituals, ceremonies necessary not just for renewing the earth's cycles but also for reversing the tide of history. Common to such ceremonies of renewal were rites of purification in which emetics like "Black Tea" were consumed to cleanse body, mind, and spirit of pollutants. Ritual attention was directed especially to the purity of food and drink. Alcohol was uniformly forbidden. Foods associated with Europeans, like pork and beef and bread from imported grain, were denounced in favor of purer diets of foods indigenous to the land, like corn, beans, squash, maple syrup, and wild game.

Prophets called for the ritual reorganization of space. To dramatize their disassociation from polluted ways, the members of these movements removed themselves from the ordinary spaces of tribal or village life to create their own special "prophet towns." Like that of the Jerusalem Temple, the layouts of these villages were products of visions commanding a symbolic organization of space for the work of sacred restoration. The villages became important sites of pilgrimage for emissaries, warriors, desperadoes, and seekers from faraway native communities, and rose to the task of feeding and housing large groups for extended periods. One such town in Ohio became known commonly as Vomittown for the ceremonial purgations practiced regularly by its pilgrims and inhabitants.

The moral critique and ritual renewal of the prophets' visions served to forge a sense of shared identity that was remarkably powerful for those followers who embraced them. The moral critique was aimed most sharply at those native people, especially leaders, who tied their fortunes to treaty promises, Christian missions, and agrarian visions of a native future. Telling of their visionary journeys along the path of the dead, prophets warned of the ultimate demise awaiting those who set their courses by Anglo-American moral compasses. Such certainties fueled the conviction that it was necessary to rid the community of contaminating influences, sometimes leading to witch-hunts aimed at native people deemed impure for their Euro-American leanings. Here, ritual did not simply maintain a boundary against impurities without, but established and policed those boundaries within native communities.

Prophets called their followers back to identities, ceremonies, and ethics deemed purer, but that purity was based on a foundation of revelation, not nature, an assertion of structure like the seven-day week based on Genesis rather than a recognition of those structures in heredity or skin color. Seen in this light, it need not perplex us that boundaries which felt so powerful did not necessarily demarcate an all-out "race war" between red and white or a doctrinaire rejection of all things post-Columbian. The prophets' teachings may have had some nativistic elements, but they were emphatically forward-looking visions, hybrids that resonated with European notions of millennial time, heaven and hell, and a focus on the afterlife. The prophets themselves were typically well acquainted with missionary teachings and with lives of accommodation, and their teaching reflected that biculturalism.

It is beyond the scope of this essay to explore a number of important precedents of prophetic movements that linked spirited calls to intertribal unity with varying degrees of anticolonial resistance. Such might include the Pueblo revolts of the 1680s, in which a Tewa medicine man named Popé had a vision whose power brought the distinctive peoples of different Pueblos together in a remarkable, and initially successful, routing of the Spanish from the region. One might also include the renowned alliance that the five (later six) nations fashioned ceremonially as the Haudenosaunee, or Iroquois, Confederacy, or the renewal movement within that confederacy under the Seneca prophet Handsome Lake. For our purposes, a focus on the line of prophetic movements of eastern North America leading from Pontiac's rebellion in 1763–1764 to the Red Stick Rebellion in 1813–1814 will provide details enough to trace the contours of interpretive debate.

PONTIAC AND NEOLIN, THE DELAWARE PROPHET

The British defeat of the French in the Seven Years' War brought a dramatic shift in power relations. Unaccustomed to the dictates of the middle ground negotiated between French trader interests and na-

tive peoples of the western Great Lakes, the British assumed an imperious position over the native population as defeated and subject peoples. In the eighteenth century, such a program of rule proved unsustainable, for the native peoples of the region still maintained effective control over the trade and the land that supported it. British presumptions of power were tenuous in the face of the network of intertribal alliances forged on the old middle ground, an infrastructure ready at hand for an organized intertribal response. What catalyzed a response was the empowering teaching of Neolin, a Delaware prophet who envisioned intertribal peace, native self-sufficiency, and a return of sacred power; what organized it into an anti-British rebellion was the military leadership of Pontiac, an Odawa warrior leader and fervent believer in Neolin's message.

Neolin stood in a tradition of Delaware prophets that emerged in the 1740s and 1750s within scattered villages in central Pennsylvania. Papoonan, a Munsee Delaware, received visions from the Master of Life disclosing how that community's misfortunes were punishment for its departure from traditional ways. Wangomend, the Assinsink Prophet, was another Munsee Delaware who called people to abandon drinking alcohol and other ways deemed British. Both preached the need to assert boundaries against the colonizers, but their preaching also reflected familiarity with colonial ways, especially the ministrations of Quakers and Moravians—who, as it happens, preached a message in similar tension with much of their own settler culture.

With the erosion of French protection in North America during the last years of the Seven Years' War, the Delawares moved west of the Appalachians, and in one of the villages near the Ohio River, an even more far-reaching message came from the Delaware prophet Neolin. Neolin was gripped by his first vision in 1761, a vision that he depicted in terms of a path leading from earth to heaven that was blocked by white people. Though it is uncertain whether the distinction asserted here was a racial one between Indian and white as we might understand those terms, or a cultural one aimed at the British, Neolin preached the necessity of turning from rum, trade, and, ultimately, use of all European goods, and toward native self-sufficiency, peace among tribes, and a restoration of relations with the game animals. The message of peace and restored relations was also a message that criticized those native people who did not hearken to it. With time, that criticism developed into full-blown accusations of witchery, with Neolin calling for the elimination of any witches who worked against him, especially those who affiliated with Christian missions. Followers in a network of prophet villages in the upper Ohio Valley were to restore their purity and power by refusing foods not indigenous to the land and imbibing an emetic tea called "black drink."

Neolin's message made deep inroads in those villages and, through pilgrims and emissaries to the villages, extended far and wide to communities of Wendats (Wyandots), Shawnees, Odawas (Ottawas), Potawatomis, Ojibwes (Ojibwas), some Senecas, and peoples of the Illinois confederacy. In 1763, the movement, fueled by Neolin's visions, took up arms against the British, who had newly consolidated their power in an alliance with the Iroquois Confederacy. The rebellion took several British posts, but by 1765 the British had ground the rebellion down to a stalemate, and eventually made its leader Pontiac into the kind of go-between power broker scorned by the uprising in the first place. Although it failed to drive the British out, Pontiac's revolt nonetheless succeeded in forcing them to adopt a form of rule that recognized native peoples more as allies and less as imperial subjects.

The mixed outcome has led scholars to disagree about whether Pontiac—or Neolin, for that matter—sought a complete severance from whites (Dowd) or whether they sought its seeming opposite: a return to a mutually agreeable middle ground of continued interaction (White). The former option too quickly identifies the movement's cosmological and ritual boundaries as those between red and white. The latter option is too tidy to allow for the felt necessity of the cosmological and ritual distinctions of pure and impure, and their implications for an evolving identity as *native* American that would become more definitive as interactions with the nascent United States carried native experience farther and farther from the middle ground.

NATIVE-BRITISH ALLIANCES AND THE AMERICAN REVOLUTION

Developments related to the American Revolution infused prophetic pan-native movements with more vigor still. With the fracturing of a consolidated British North America, native peoples once again were able to exploit a division of "foreign" interests to their own ends, and came increasingly to see that the respective fortunes of all native communities rose and fell together. The intertribal networks developed in the western Great Lakes under prophets and warrior-diplomats of Neolin's and Pontiac's

generation were being augmented by emerging alliances with Shawnees and other peoples threatened by settler encroachments in southern Ohio and Kentucky, and with militant wings of the Cherokees and Muskogees in the south.

A resulting large-scale pan-Indian force that had been orchestrated and envisioned by councils of native peoples from north and south in 1779 never made it into the history books because it was thwarted by colonial forces at Vincennes, Indiana. Even after the British resolve and capacity to quash the American Revolution yielded ground in the Peace of Paris in 1783, the broad pan-Indian alliance intensified by that revolution remained poised for action.

Once independence was won, American settlement west of the Appalachians activated many native communities that had pledged neutrality during the Revolutionary War to join forces with the broad pan-Indian alliance. In 1792, thousands of native militants and former neutralists from the Great Lakes to the Gulf, including many who had been once again displaced from Ohio and Kentucky, formed an intertribal resistance village known as The Glaize in northwestern Ohio. In this village, ceremonial and diplomatic exchanges generated the spiritual support and resolve to stem westward encroachments of settlers. A series of linked raids in both north and south increased the alliance's confidence, but without more aggressive support of the British or Spanish, the alliance suffered a massive defeat by "Mad" Anthony Wayne at the Battle of Fallen Timbers. The Treaty of Greenville (1795) ceded most of what is today Ohio for American settlement. Recognizing the threat posed by concerted native action, the United States carried out aggressive policies of divide and conquer to eat away at the bonds of the alliance.

TECUMSEH AND TENSKWATAWA, THE SHAWNEE PROPHET

Fifty years after Pontiac and Neolin, a second major attempt to unite native peoples of the Old Northwest emerged around the vision of the Shawnee Prophet, Tenskwatawa, brother of Tecumseh. The alliance galvanized by the brothers formed a crucial part of the British force in the War of 1812. Tecumseh died in that war while fighting for the vision, and he thus received praise as the visionary leader who sought to unite native people against American encroachment. Less famous was his brother, who survived the War of 1812 and lived out his years less heroically on a reservation in what is now north-eastern Kansas. Conventional wisdom and some historians have roundly dismissed Tenskwatawa as something of a nuisance to Tecumseh's cause, an impetuous fanatic who sought the promotion of his personal influence at the expense of better judgment, who promoted witch-hunts instead of unity. A closer look, however, shows Tenskwatawa's charismatic authority at the foundations of the movement that has gone down in American history bearing the name of his brother. To get that closer look, the historian must move beyond the presumption that prophecy is false in order to appreciate the ways in which followers found meaning, orientation, and possibility in the words that prophets spoke. The charisma that Tenskwatawa possessed from his first vision in 1805 through the tumultuous decade that followed was an authority granted him by peoples of many different cultures, languages, and political dispositions by virtue of the attested power of his visions from the Master of Life.

Sons of a Shawnee father and a Muskogee mother, Tenskwatawa and Tecumseh entered a world that was tumultuous, uncertain, and painful for the native peoples of Ohio. Tenskwatawa became a drunk and the family ne'er-do-well, called The Noisemaker for his boastful manner. In the winter of 1804–1805, The Noisemaker collapsed and was taken for dead. To the amazement of those who had begun to prepare his body for burial, the young man awakened, and spoke of a journey he had taken at the behest of the Master of Life, to peer into paradise. This paradise would be "a rich, fertile country, abounding in game, fish, pleasant hunting grounds and fine corn fields," the prophet was told, off-limits to sinful Shawnees, who would be consigned to a large lodge with a torturous, never-quenching fire (Edmunds, *Shawnee Prophet,* p. 33).

The vision conferred upon him a new name, The Open Door, or Tenskwatawa, for the possibilities that his prophecy would present to restore prosperity in this world and to guide his followers to paradise in the next. His prediction of a solar eclipse in 1806 furthered his reputation as a seer. He admonished followers to pray regularly each day with symbolic prayer sticks, and to abandon many of the traditional dances and ceremonies and teachings of other medicine people. They were to extinguish old fires, and light new ones with brands from a ceremonial fire made without use of European steel. They were to renounce beef, pork, and bread, and to eat only foods of the land: wild game, fish, corn, squash, beans, and maple syrup. Subsequent visions taught the prophet that Americans were in

reality "children of the Evil Spirit," and that if native people would follow the directions of the vision, the Master of Life would send a great crab to "overturn the land, so that all the white people will be covered and you alone shall inhabit the land" (Edmunds, *Shawnee Prophet,* p. 38). Pilgrims and seekers arriving at his village could become initiates by confessing sins and performing gestures considered symbolically to be "shaking hands with the Prophet."

Tenskwatawa was spiritually directed to establish a village that became known as Prophet's Town, near the junction of the Tippecanoe and the Wabash Rivers in what is now Indiana. This was particularly significant because the vision directed Prophet's Town to be located in the land that accommodationist leaders had ceded in the Treaty of Greenville.

Tenskwatawa preached the spiritual urgency of political unity among native villages and peoples. "If, as the Shawnee Prophet said, Americans were unchangeably inimical to Indians, if 'the Great Spirit did not mean that the white and red people should live near each other' because whites 'poison'd the land,' and if all Indians came from a common creation different from that of others, then it only made sense that Indians should unite against the American threat" (Dowd, p. 142). At Prophet's Town, Tenskwatawa received, housed, and fed large numbers of pilgrims from the Delawares, Miamis, Shawnees, Wendats, Potawatomis, Odawas, and Ojibwes from areas that are now Michigan, Illinois, Wisconsin, Minnesota, Iowa, Ohio, and Kentucky. Other prophets whose visions emerged to minister to the times, like an Odawa named "The Trout," joined with Tenskwatawa and brought new recruits to the movement. As momentum grew at Prophet's Town, so did the significance of Tecumseh's strategic leadership in bringing that momentum to bear in tangible diplomatic and military ways. With Tecumseh's diplomacy, the following at Prophet's Town included delegations of potential allies and followers among Muskogees and militant Cherokees far to the south.

Prophet's Town and all it represented posed no small threat to the United States, but it also posed an increasing threat to the traditional Shawnee and Miami leaders who had signed the Treaty of Greenville. Even more boldly than Neolin, Tenskwatawa preached the urgency of identifying such accommodationist leaders not only as sellouts but also as wielders of witchery.

In 1809, the more accommodationist traditional chiefs ceded much of Indiana in the Treaty of Fort Wayne. This only served to fuel the resistance movement and galvanize alliances; prompt unified action would be required to stem the expansion of the United States and its settlers. Even after suffering a severe setback in 1811 at the battle of Tippecanoe, which might otherwise have preempted a future for the alliance, the movement rebounded under Tecumseh's leadership to join the British when the War of 1812 broke out. When adequately provisioned and armed by the British, this was perhaps the high point of the pan-native movement, a culmination of several generations of prophets and a vision shared by many native people: that an alliance rooted in sacred power could overcome American expansion and restore balance to peoples of the land. Ultimately, the Americans defeated the British-Indian alliance, but perhaps it was more the result of an erosion of Britain's interest and resources in defending North America, preoccupied as it was in Europe, than of the supposition that native peoples could never fully rise above their tribalism to stem the tide of colonialism.

THE RED STICK REVOLT

During the War of 1812, Tecumseh sought several times to tap into an organized resistance in the deep South among militant Cherokees and the Muskogees or Creeks, a people comprised of autonomous villages along rivers in what is now Georgia and Alabama. In a manner similar to those of the Ohio and Indiana region, some Muskogees protested the more accommodationist positions of traditional leadership by withdrawing from ordinary life in those villages to "the woods," where they lived according to the spiritual direction of prophets and mounted a sacred revolt. As more lands were ceded to the United States and its settlers, as fewer game animals were able to sustain the deerskin trade or even subsistence, and as traders continued to call in their debts, many Muskogees grew disenchanted with the accommodation. A series of earthquakes in 1811–1812 focused attention on a group of emerging prophets who related Muskogee struggles to deeper matters of cosmic imbalance.

Finding that the earthquake was the doing of Tie-Snake, a sacred being associated with wild stretches of rivers and chaos, a prophet named Sam Isaacs returned from a shamanic visionary journey to a river bottom where he had been entrusted by Tie-Snake with the power and knowledge to help usher in a new creation signaled by the quake. According to Joel Martin, this combined with apocalyptic imagery contributed to Muskogee thought by

the African Americans who had joined their ranks, and a version of the Busk, or Green Corn ceremony, a ritual that Muskogees observed annually as necessary to renew the cosmos. Their version of the Busk included a war dance of Shawnee origin, which had been shared with them during one of Tecumseh's missions.

Like that of the Shawnee prophet, the message of the Muskogee prophets called for purification, and those Muskogees who broke with the villages sought to cleanse their bodies and their community of any influences, and people, thought to defile them. The purgation included many of the practices commonly associated with the Busk: extinguishing old fires, fasting, drinking emetic teas, and singing and dancing in a renewed world. It also included the destruction of American food, clothing, weapons—and of those Muskogees accommodating the Americans.

Fighting against all odds in a manner that only confirms the felt necessity of their sacred purpose, in 1813, seven to nine thousand Muskogees took up red war clubs, by which the Red Stick Revolt would be known, against the United States. In March 1814, a thousand Red Stick warriors were defeated at Tohopeka (Horseshoe Bend) by the United States, whose forces included a young Andrew Jackson and Davy Crockett, some Cherokees, and other Muskogees. In the subsequent Treaty of Fort Jackson, the defeated Muskogees ceded fourteen million acres, much of what is considered the Deep South.

INTERPRETING THE SIGNIFICANCE OF THESE MOVEMENTS

A brief history of the interpretation of prophetic movements led by such figures offers an instructive introduction to the significance these movements hold for the broader concerns of American intellectual and cultural history. The first wave of historical writing about these movements consisted of biographies of their leaders, especially Pontiac and Tecumseh, identifying these figures as forward-thinking individuals rising above the tribalisms of their cultures to lead a noble resistance to the seemingly inevitable forces of Manifest Destiny (Parkman, Peckham, Gilbert). Later biographies of individual prophets drew detailed attention to the power of prophecy and its authority in the movements, but focused largely on the charisma of the figures rather than on the social and cultural context in which that charisma became a social fact (Edmunds, *Shawnee Prophet;* Herring).

From Biography to Ethnohistory Biographies of the charismatic leaders gave way to a renewed appreciation of the importance of such movements in the wake of Anthony F. C. Wallace's case study of a prophetic movement among the Seneca nation of the Iroquois alliance. *Death and Rebirth of the Seneca* (1969) offers a detailed consideration of the revitalization spurred by the visions and leadership of the prophet Handsome Lake at the turn of the nineteenth century.

Wallace initially challenged the unidirectional view of acculturation and assimilation implied in the *death* portion of his title, to appreciate the significant revitalization movements that also characterize Native American history. As a work of ethnohistory, *Death and Rebirth* focused on the cultural and social forces generating the Handsome Lake movement, and not simply on the ideas or charisma of Handsome Lake himself. Specifically, Wallace considered the demoralization of "cultural deprivation" stemming from contact with Euro-Americans and its attendant disease, dispossession, alcoholism, and social fracture. The details of this historical work complicate the earlier theory formulated in the wake of his studies of the Delaware, but the overall interpretation remains: prophetic movements of cultural revitalization are driven by the demoralizing experience of cultural deprivation. As such they are flashes in the pan, short-lived syncretic phenomena that not only are products of their circumstances but also, in most respects, derivatives from them.

From Cultural Deprivation to Sacred Renewal Since the early 1990s, a number of important reappraisals of pan-Indian prophetic movements have built on Wallace's work, but have roundly criticized the notion that these movements are derivatives of cultural deprivation. They suspend an objectivist bias that dismisses the messages of such prophets as irrational rant or blatant grabs for personal power, but they depart significantly from Wallace's framework in seeing the prophetic movements merely as nativist attempts to return to a golden age before Euro-Americans. As Joel Martin notes, the deprivation theory would not explain how the movements proceeded not simply with desperation, but also with a resolve born of hope, confidence in the power of the sacred. "Colonialism may have pushed," Martin concludes, "but even more important, the sacred pulled Native American peoples into a new religious world" (*Sacred Revolt,* p. 182). It is nonetheless crucial to remember that although these new religious worlds involved change for native people, they were hardly altogether new. The prophetic movements that helped reconfigure identity also reaffirmed long-standing indigenous ways of imagining the relationships among people, land, and the sacred.

Richard White, for example, overstates the novelty of the prophetic movement of Pontiac and Neolin with his argument that it marked a sea change from established traditions. "This was not the restoration of tradition," White concludes, "but rather its invention" (*Middle Ground,* p. 285).

Perhaps "tradition" and "invention" are both too blunt to appreciate the fluidity with which tradition and change intermingle in these prophetic movements and in native traditions generally. In each case, though in different ways, the new religious worlds of native peoples entertained an approach to change that itself was a continuity with what had gone before.

As the nineteenth century wore on, Native American prophetic movements continued, some breathing new life into a pan-native identity, others rekindling tribal-specific traditions and identities. Best known are the peyote-centered Native American Church, the Indian Shaker movement of the prophet Smohalla, and the Ghost Dance of the 1890s; but through many prophets in different contexts, the sacred called native people together in new ways to honor the past and greet the future.

See also **Native Americans; The Frontier and the West** *(volume 2).*

BIBLIOGRAPHY

Dowd, Gregory Evans. *A Spirited Resistance: The North American Indian Struggle for Unity, 1745–1815.* Baltimore, 1992.

Edmunds, R. David. *The Shawnee Prophet.* Lincoln, Neb., 1983.

———. *Tecumseh and the Quest for Indian Leadership.* Boston, 1984.

Gilbert, Bil. *God Gave Us This Country: Tekamthi and the First American Civil War.* New York, 1989.

Herring, Joseph B. *Kenekuk, the Kickapoo Prophet.* Lawrence, Kans., 1988.

Jacobs, Wilbur. *Dispossessing the American Indian: Indians and Whites on the Colonial Frontier.* Norman, Okla., 1985. First published 1972.

Martin, Joel. *Sacred Revolt: The Muskogees' Struggle for a New World.* Boston, 1991.

———. "From 'Middle Ground' to 'Underground.'" In *Religion and American Culture.* Edited by David Hackett. New York, 1995.

Merrell, James H. *The Indians' New World: Catawbas and Their Neighbors from European Contact Through the Era of Removal.* Chapel Hill, N.C., 1989.

Mooney, James. *The Ghost-Dance Religion and Wounded Knee.* New York, 1973. First published 1896.

Parkman, Francis. *The Conspiracy of Pontiac and the Indian War After the Conquest of Canada.* Boston, 1898.

Peckham, Howard. *Pontiac and the Indian Uprising of 1763.* Princeton, N.J., 1947.

Richter, Daniel K., and James H. Merrell, eds. *Beyond the Covenant Chain: The Iroquois and Their Neighbors in Indian North America, 1600–1800.* Syracuse, N.Y., 1987.

Wallace, Anthony F. C. *King of the Delawares: Teedyuscung 1700–1763.* Philadelphia, 1949.

———. "Revitalization Movements." In *American Anthropologist* 58 (May 1956): 264–281.

———. *Religion: An Anthropological View.* New York, 1966.

———. *The Death and Rebirth of the Seneca.* New York, 1972. First published 1969.

White, Richard. *The Middle Ground: Indians, Empires, and Republics in the Great Lakes Region 1650–1815.* Cambridge, U.K. 1991.

Part 3

ANTEBELLUM, CIVIL WAR, AND RECONSTRUCTION: 1838–1877

Part 3, continued

OVERVIEW:
THE ANTEBELLUM, CIVIL WAR,
AND RECONSTRUCTION ERAS

William E. Gienapp

The period 1840–1877 was a time of momentous change in American history. During these years the United States expanded to the Pacific, slavery became a major issue in American thought and politics, antagonism between the North and the South eventually led to civil war, and following its victory the North undertook to reconstruct southern institutions and society. These developments had long-lasting ramifications in American thought and culture.

ABOLITIONISM AND
PROSLAVERY THOUGHT

In the years before the Civil War, American society pulsated with the contagion of reform. "In the history of the world, the doctrine of reform never had such scope as at the present hour," the poet and essayist Ralph Waldo Emerson observed in his 1841 essay "Man the Reformer." This reform impulse was expressed in both utopian communities and humanitarian reform movements directed against specific social problems. Of the many antebellum reform movements, abolitionism ultimately had the most profound impact on the nation.

Abolitionism, which began in the 1830s, was increasingly confined to the North. Abolitionists condemned slavery as anti-Christian and contrary to the American ideals of liberty and equality and demanded its immediate end in the republic. The movement's radical program and harsh rhetoric generated intense opposition, and prior to 1861 it never attracted more than a small minority of northerners. But abolitionism's importance cannot be measured in numbers alone. Its supporters raised the moral issue of slavery in American life and kept it constantly before the public mind, thereby fostering the growing conflict between the North and the South. Equally important, their harsh rhetoric and uncompromising demands provoked southerners into adopting extreme positions that alarmed a growing number of northerners.

To meet the challenge of abolitionism, southern intellectual life during this period focused on the defense of slavery. Discarding the region's earlier condemnation of the institution, southern leaders fashioned a set of religious, historical, and social arguments upholding slavery as a positive good, but they were never able to escape the reality that slavery was based on race. Southern clergymen and churches were leading defenders of the institution, and the section's most important intellectuals contributed to the proslavery argument as well. Increasingly, southern public opinion tolerated no deviation on slavery, and an intellectual conformity descended over the region that rendered southern intellectual life increasingly sterile.

EXPANSIONISM AND THE
SLAVERY ISSUE

The nation's geographic expansion westward in the 1840s also stimulated sectional tensions. In the 27 December 1845 issue of the *New York Morning News,* the editor John L. O'Sullivan proclaimed that it was the nation's "manifest destiny to overspread and to possess the whole of the continent which providence has given us for the development of the great experiment of liberty and federated self-government entrusted to us." The term "manifest destiny," which brought together a number of ideas that had been percolating in American thought for some time, quickly caught on and became a popular slogan justifying American expansion. The concept of manifest destiny expressed the widespread belief that the United States was destined to expand to the Pacific and dominate the North American continent.

Political support for expansion was linked to the growing factionalism of the two major parties after 1840. Shortly after he took office in 1841, William Henry Harrison, the first Whig president, died. He was succeeded by John Tyler of Virginia, who soon broke with the Whigs in Congress over economic policies. Hoping to strengthen himself politically, Tyler promoted the annexation of Texas, which had revolted against Mexico in the 1830s and became an independent slaveholding republic in 1836. Tyler's activity made the annexation of Texas a major political issue and helped elect James K. Polk of Tennessee, the Democratic candidate, president in 1844 on an expansionist platform. In the last days of Tyler's term in 1845, Congress formally approved the annexation of Texas.

An ardent expansionist, Polk was determined to push the U.S. boundaries to the Pacific. He got the British to agree to divide the Oregon Country, but he could not induce Mexico to accept the annexation of Texas or sell any of its northern provinces. The United States finally went to war with Mexico in 1846 and won an easy victory by 1848. Under the terms of the peace treaty, Mexico ceded the provinces of New Mexico and Upper California, some 500,000 square miles, to the United States, in exchange for $15 million. Polk's continental vision had become a reality.

This acquisition of territory, however, came at enormous political cost to the nation. In August 1846 a group of northern Democrats, angered that Polk, a southern slaveholder, had surrendered half of Oregon and convinced that he had gone to war with Mexico in order to acquire territory suitable for slavery, introduced the Wilmot Proviso in Congress as an amendment to a war appropriations bill. The Proviso, which sought to prohibit slavery from any territory acquired from Mexico, split the two parties along sectional lines and marked the emergence of the issue of the expansion of slavery that would eventually lead to civil war. Emerson was prophetic when he wrote in his journals in 1846, "The United States will conquer Mexico, but it will be as the man who swallows the arsenic which brings him down in turn. Mexico will poison us" (*Journals of Ralph Waldo Emerson,* eds. Edward Waldo Emerson and Waldo Emerson Forbes, vol. 7, p. 206).

Congress wrangled for several years over the status of slavery in the Southwest until the Compromise of 1850 defused the sectional crisis. In organizing the Mexican cession, Congress rejected the Wilmot Proviso and adopted the principle of popular sovereignty, which authorized the residents of the newly created New Mexico and Utah territories to decide the status of slavery for themselves.

The passage of the Compromise of 1850 produced a national sigh of relief. The sectional storm seemed to have passed, and Americans eagerly turned their attention to developing the continent, for the economy was again roaring with speculative enthusiasm.

NATIONALISM AND SECTIONALISM

The expansion of the railroad network, the accelerating process of industrialization, the arrival of thousands of European immigrants, and the high price cotton commanded on the world market all promoted the rapid expansion of the economy in the 1850s. This growth produced dislocation in both the North and the South.

The exuberance of the decade was captured by the Young America movement, which celebrated the ascendancy of a new generation of political, cultural, and intellectual leaders in American life. An expression of American nationalism, Young America advocated an expansionist foreign policy and extolled the uniqueness and achievements of American culture. Above all, it captured the sense of excitement over the nation's boundless potential that prevailed as the decade opened.

This optimism, however, was soon challenged by growing anxiety over immigration. From 1845 to 1854 nearly three million immigrants, largely from Germany and Ireland and mostly Roman Catholic, came to the United States. Their arrival precipitated a powerful if short-lived nativist movement in American society that reflected both American nationalism and popular fears for the preservation of traditional American values and institutions.

The South was unusually prosperous throughout the 1850s, yet southern thought also reflected a growing sense of crisis. With prosperity came a sharp rise in the price of both land and slaves, which economically squeezed smaller farmers. Southern leaders worried that the South was running out of land suitable for agriculture, and that without new territory white opportunity would be closed off. These fears stimulated the growing confrontation with the North over the expansion of slavery.

The South's internal crisis also strengthened the idea of southern nationalism, which drew upon the romantic idea that nationalism was rooted in culture. Insisting that the South had developed a distinctive culture, southern nationalists argued that the South should also be a separate nation. In this decade, southern nationalists promoted a series of schemes to strengthen the South and enhance southern cultural distinctiveness, but none was very successful.

THE ROAD TO WAR

The passage in 1854 of the Kansas-Nebraska Act, which opened the remainder of the Louisiana Purchase to slavery, was the final blow that destroyed the already weakened Jacksonian party system. This law reinvigorated the slavery extension issue and led to the formation of the Republican Party. A northern, sectional organization, the Republican Party opposed the expansion of slavery and the admission of any more slave states. It upheld the ideal of free labor and lauded the superiority of northern society, with its emphasis on opportunity and social mobility.

Many northerners feared that the party threatened the Union, but, aided by the sectional violence in Kansas and elsewhere, the Republicans carried most of the free states in the 1856 election. It was further strengthened by the depression that began in 1857 and the disruption of the Democratic Party over the attempt to admit Kansas under the pro-slavery Lecompton Constitution in 1858.

In 1860 the Republican Party elected Abraham Lincoln president. His election stimulated southern fears for the security of slavery, and in response the seven states of the Lower South—the entire tier of cotton-growing states from South Carolina across to Texas—seceded from the Union. Representatives from these states quickly established the Confederate States of America and elected Jefferson Davis of Mississippi as president.

While Lincoln hoped to devise a peaceful solution, he was prepared to use force to preserve the Union. When he dispatched a relief expedition to Fort Sumter in Charleston harbor, Confederate batteries on 12 April 1861 opened fire on the fort, which surrendered the next day. When Lincoln called for volunteers to put down the rebellion in the South, the four states of the Upper South, led by Virginia, seceded and joined the Confederacy. The Civil War had begun.

Neither side foresaw the magnitude of the contest they now faced. And neither side comprehended the revolutionary forces that the war would release.

THE SECOND AMERICAN REVOLUTION

The Civil War was the first modern war in history. It involved the mobilization of some three million men in the two armies, unprecedented government expenditures, and the rapid expansion of industry. Furthermore, victory depended on civilian morale and the willingness of the home front to sustain the armies in the field. In short, the two sides had to bring all their resources—political, economic, social, and intellectual—to bear on the war effort.

In both societies, the war produced a dramatic expansion of government power. From the beginning of the conflict, Lincoln took the position that under the U.S. Constitution the government could exercise powers in war that would be unconstitutional in peacetime. He also believed that because the president was commander in chief, the bulk of these war powers belonged to the executive branch and not Congress. "I conceive that I may in an emergency do things on military grounds," he declared to Senator Zachariah Chandler in 1864, "which cannot be done constitutionally by Congress" ("Lincoln and the Civil War" in the *Diaries of John Hay*, p. 204). Lincoln consistently argued that it was his responsibility, and not that of Congress, to determine the policies on which the war was conducted, and he successfully turned back all congressional challenges to his authority. The powers Lincoln exercised during the war were breathtaking in their extent and revolutionary in their significance. He spent money without congressional authorization, suspended the writ of habeas corpus throughout the Union and authorized the arbitrary arrest of thousands of civilians, instituted a program of reconstruction in the South, and made emancipation a Union war aim.

In addition, Congress passed a series of laws that promoted the forces of centralization in American life by concentrating power in the hands of the federal government at the expense of the states. Prior to the war, Americans paid no taxes to the federal government, but from 1861 to 1865 Congress enacted a system of internal taxes, including the first national income tax in American history, that brought the tax collector into the home of virtually every northerner. It drastically increased the tariff duties to protect American industry, established a national banking system, and created a uniform national currency. It also enacted a federally controlled system of conscription, authorized the construction of a transcontinental railroad, approved a homestead law to provide free farms from the public domain, and helped fund higher education through the Land Grant College Act (Morrill Act) in 1862. The war marked a decisive turning point in the role of the federal government in promoting economic development.

The South was a more localistic society, but Jefferson Davis also centralized power in the national government at Richmond, Virginia, to a striking degree. Davis correctly understood that a Confederate victory depended on a centrally directed war effort. Because the ideology of states' rights was stronger in the Confederacy, Davis's policies precipitated very strong opposition. While Davis was more circumspect than Lincoln in suspending the writ of habeas corpus, the Confederate army arrested thousands of civilians for disloyalty. Moreover, the Confederacy adopted a much more sweeping conscription law than the Union, and the Confederate Congress authorized the army to impress private property, including slaves, for use in the war effort. In addition, the Confederate War Department seized southern mines and railroads and operated its own war factories.

Critics raised the cry that Davis was a dictator trampling on the rights of the states. They focused in particular on the issues of conscription and civil liberties, which directly impinged on individual liberty. Ordinary farmers also bitterly protested the policy of impressment, which inflicted economic hardship on rural families. These internal divisions hamstrung Davis's leadership and badly weakened the Confederate war effort.

EMANCIPATION

The most critical decision that Lincoln confronted was on emancipation. Unlike antislavery Radical Republicans, Lincoln put saving the Union ahead of emancipation. Moreover, as a conservative, he feared the social consequences of such a radical step as emancipation. "In considering the policy to be adopted for suppressing the insurrection," he commented in his Annual Message to Congress on 3 December 1861, "I have been anxious and careful that the inevitable conflict for this purpose shall not degenerate into a violent and remorseless revolutionary struggle."

At the beginning of the war Lincoln considered his greatest political problem to be retaining the loyalty of the border slave states, and he feared that any interference with slavery would drive those states into the Confederacy. Northern public opinion endorsed Lincoln's caution. In late July 1861, following the Union defeat at Bull Run in Virginia, Congress passed a resolution asserting "that this war is not waged for any purpose of overthrowing or interfering with the rights or established institutions of these States, but to defend and maintain the supremacy of the Constitution and to preserve the Union." Lincoln adhered to this policy throughout the first year of the conflict, and he revoked proclamations issued by two of his generals (John C.

Frémont in 1861 and David Hunter in 1862) abolishing slavery in their districts. Matters relating to emancipation, he explained, "are questions which, under my responsibility, I reserve to myself."

Lincoln hoped to end slavery by state action, but border state representatives twice rejected his proposal. In the wake of their refusal and the military setbacks the Union suffered in 1862, especially in Virginia, Lincoln concluded that a more vigorous war policy was needed. He was also increasingly convinced by the radicals' argument that emancipation would strike a military blow at the Confederacy. On 22 September 1862, following the Union victory at Antietam, Lincoln issued the preliminary emancipation proclamation, which he made final on 1 January 1863.

The Emancipation Proclamation only applied to areas designated to be in rebellion and thus did not free all the slaves in the United States. Nor was its legality beyond challenge, since the Constitution gave the federal government no power over slavery in a state. Indeed, Lincoln justified his action solely on military grounds. Despite its limitations, the Emancipation Proclamation was of immense symbolic significance, and African Americans were correct in hailing it as a liberating document. By making emancipation a war aim, the Proclamation redefined the nature of the war. The North was fighting to create a new Union and not restore the old one. The war had become a revolution.

UNION POLITICS

Emancipation marked the turning point in the Democratic Party's attitude toward the war as well. At the beginning of the conflict, northern Democrats had rallied behind the war to save the Union, but they condemned conscription and arbitrary arrests, and they vehemently opposed any interference with slavery. These policies increasingly estranged the majority of Democrats. A vocal peace faction of Democrats, dubbed Copperheads by the Republicans, advocated an armistice and negotiations with the Confederacy. In addition, Democrats exploited the race issue in northern politics by charging that emancipation would cause former slaves to come to the North and thus lead to race mixing. Adopting the slogan "the Union as it was, the Constitution as it is, and the negro where he is," Democrats made significant political gains in the 1862 fall elections.

With time, however, northern opinion began to shift in favor of emancipation. The performance of black troops in combat in 1863 helped change popular opinion, both in the army and on the home front. In addition, the political ascendancy of peace Democrats and the draft riot in New York City in July 1863, in which Irish Democrats played the major role, tainted the party with the image of disloyalty, and in key races that year notorious peace Democrats were defeated.

Nevertheless, Lincoln still faced an uphill battle in the upcoming presidential election. The mounting death toll and new draft calls had brought northern will to the breaking point by the summer of 1864. Yet Lincoln resisted the growing clamor for peace negotiations, knowing that the Confederacy would never agree to reunion, and he refused to retreat on the issue of emancipation in the face of Democratic charges that he was stubbornly prolonging the war solely to end slavery. Many observers expected Lincoln to be defeated, but the improvement in the military situation, particularly the Union's capture of Atlanta, secured his reelection. Lincoln's victory confirmed the decision for emancipation and ended any chance of a Confederate victory. In January 1865 Congress approved the Thirteenth Amendment, abolishing slavery throughout the United States, which was ratified in December.

THE HOME FRONT

The war directly involved the home front to a greater degree than in previous American wars. In both the North and the South, women actively supported the war effort and assumed new jobs and responsibilities. They ran farms and plantations, took up nursing in military hospitals, and entered factories in increased numbers. They also became much more outspoken concerning public affairs and circulated petitions, delivered speeches, wrote letters to public officials, and even participated in mob protests. This activity laid the basis for the women's rights movement in the postwar years.

The lives of slaves changed even more dramatically. In the Confederacy, the absence of so many men and the chaotic situation significantly loosened the bonds of slavery. On plantations slaves enjoyed much greater personal freedom and became much more rebellious and defiant. At the same time, the war opened a host of new employment opportunities for slaves. In addition, the Union began to accept black recruits in the South, and eventually 180,000 African Americans, most of whom were former slaves, served in the Union army. Nothing so strikingly illustrated the revolutionary potential

of the war as the sight of armed black men in uniform marching along the roads of the South.

The mounting casualty lists stimulated efforts to relieve the immense suffering produced by the war. The best-known example was the United States Sanitary Commission (USSC), which was the most important volunteer reform organization during the war. The USSC served as an umbrella organization to coordinate local efforts to collect money and supplies for Union military hospitals. It also recruited doctors and nurses and promoted greater efficiency and regulation in the army medical service. The Confederacy, in contrast, lacked any national relief organizations and volunteer work remained local and state-oriented.

Both northern and southern churches were important means to rally the populace behind the war effort. Northern and southern ministers alike assured volunteers that God was on their side, and countless sermons portrayed the war as a test of whether the people were worthy of God's favor. Both presidents proclaimed fast days to renew the population's commitment, and in the last two winters of the war extensive religious revivals occurred among Confederate soldiers.

In the North, a number of cultural leaders took up their pens to promote the war effort. In February 1863 a group of northern intellectuals organized the Loyal Publication Society in New York City to disseminate propaganda in favor of the Union cause. The society eventually published some ninety different pamphlets totaling over 900,000 copies.

As the contest became a war of attrition, Lincoln and Davis bore the main responsibility for sustaining popular morale in their respective societies. Lincoln was more adept at this task. Throughout the struggle, he repeatedly placed the war in its largest ideological context by portraying it as a struggle to preserve democracy, not just in the United States, but throughout the world. In his Gettysburg Address of 19 November 1863, Lincoln called for a new birth of freedom to redeem the unprecedented sacrifices of the war.

Davis also confronted the enormously difficult task of creating from scratch a sense of Confederate nationalism, although he was unable to match Lincoln's eloquence. In the end, Davis was unable to forge a viable nationalism capable of withstanding the growing hardship on the southern home front, and in the second half of the war he emphasized fear of the North rather than any positive ideals in a desperate effort to sustain popular morale. In the last months of the war southern civilians, feeling militarily overwhelmed and emotionally exhausted, simply abandoned the Confederate cause and gave up.

THE WAR'S LEGACY

The Civil War ended in April 1865 when the main Confederate armies surrendered. Its final toll was more than 620,000 dead and a cost of more than $20 billion. These figures, however, do not measure either the war's legacy or its true cost.

The war preserved the Union, destroyed slavery, and made the North politically and economically dominant. In burying forever the notion that the Union was a compact of sovereign states, the war greatly expanded the powers of the national government and made it supreme in the federal system. The war also significantly enlarged presidential powers, particularly in wartime.

Economically, the war accelerated the process of industrialization and promoted the organization of the economy on a truly national scale. It substantially increased northern wealth, especially in the industrial Northeast, while at the same time it transformed the South into the nation's poorest region.

The conflict also had a profound impact on American values and the American spirit. "The Civil War," Henry James observed in his life of Hawthorne in 1879, "marks an era in the history of the American mind." By changing the national consciousness, it "left a different tone from the tone it found." The war had increasingly been characterized by widespread fraud and corruption, immorality, selfishness, and extravagance, which left a pervasive sense of moral disillusionment after the war. At the same time, the war seriously weakened the humanitarian reform impulse that had been so powerful before 1861. Many Americans blamed reformers for the war, and in the face of the war's staggering loss of life, it was difficult to believe in the earlier ideals, such as millennialism or perfectionism. In their place the war enshrined the values of order and control, and gave impetus to the emerging idea that science could impartially adjudicate social and economic conflict. It also focused attention on mass society over the individual, accustomed Americans to ruthless behavior, and paved the way for the ascendancy of the ideology of social Darwinism in the postwar years.

George Ticknor, the Boston literary figure who was sensitive to intellectual and social currents, was amazed at the changes that had occurred in just a few years. The war, he declared in a letter in 1869, had left "a great gulf between what happened before it in our century and what has happened since. . . . It does not seem to me as if I were living in the country in which I was born."

PRESIDENTIAL AND CONGRESSIONAL RECONSTRUCTION

Abraham Lincoln inaugurated a program of reconstruction in several southern states during the war. His assassination in 1865, however, cut short his attempt to devise a workable program to restore loyal governments in the former states of the Confederacy. The problem of reconstruction fell into the hands of his successor, Andrew Johnson of Tennessee. Events would demonstrate that Johnson lacked the political skills necessary to make Reconstruction succeed.

A staunch Unionist, Johnson had worked with the Radical Republicans during the war, but their grounds of agreement were in reality quite narrow. Unlike the radicals, Johnson, who was an inveterate racist, had no interest in the welfare of African Americans and no desire to extend political rights to the former slaves, or freedpeople. Instead, he directed his animosity at the former slaveholding aristocrats, whom he blamed for the war. Nevertheless, Johnson shrank from the prospect of drastic social or economic upheaval, and in the end he failed to sustain his program's original goals, a failure that brought him into growing conflict with Republicans in Congress.

The challenges of Reconstruction were enormous. The South's economy had been wrecked, its society uprooted, and its traditional leaders repudiated. Slavery had been the South's most important social, racial, and economic institution, and its destruction rendered fundamental change inevitable. Southern agriculture had to be reorganized on a free labor basis, the political and legal privileges of the former slaves determined, and the nature of race relations in the postwar South fixed. In addition, new state governments had to be created, and the political rights of former supporters of the Confederacy decided.

Reconstruction also involved a struggle between the Republican and Democratic parties for national power. Republicans were determined to preserve the Union's fruits of victory, in which they included not just emancipation and the Union but also the economic system of banks, currency, and industry that the war had created. For Republicans, that meant they had to retain control of the federal government and Republican state governments had to be established in the South. "The whole fabric of Southern society *must* be change," radical Republican leader Thaddeus Stevens explained in a speech in Lancaster, Pennsylvania, in 1865, "or all our blood and treasure have been spent in vain" (*Selected Papers of Thaddeus Stevens,* ed. Beverly Wilson Palmer, vol. 2, pp. 16, 23). Believing that a quick restoration of the southern states would bring their party back to power in 1868, Democrats argued that no conditions could be imposed on the seceded states. Republicans rejected this view, but there was no agreement among party members over what those conditions should be.

Johnson put his program of Reconstruction into operation in the summer of 1865. His program varied in some ways from that of Lincoln, but more critical was his failure to respond firmly when southern whites flouted the requirements he set. In establishing new governments, southern whites denied African Americans any political rights, enacted a series of discriminatory laws (the black codes) that applied only to blacks, and elected ineligible former leaders of the Confederacy to state and federal offices. Refusing to confront the state of affairs in the South, Johnson announced that Reconstruction had been successfully completed.

Alarmed by these developments, northern public opinion considered the black codes a form of quasi-slavery and concluded that defiant southern whites had not accepted the lessons of defeat. When Congress assembled in December, the Republican majority refused to seat the representatives of Johnson's governments and appointed a joint committee to devise a new program of Reconstruction.

In the meantime, Congress passed laws over Johnson's vetoes to extend the life of the Freedmen's Bureau and to guarantee minimal civil rights for blacks in the South. Without such protection, the Republican Senator Lyman Trumbull contended in Congress in 1866, the freedpeople would "be tyrannized over, abused, and virtually reenslaved." The joint committee drafted a new constitutional amendment to protect black rights, make blacks citizens, and limit the president's pardoning power. By indirect means it also tried to impose black suffrage on the South while exempting the North from this requirement. After Congress passed the proposed Fourteenth Amendment, Tennessee was the only former Confederate state that ratified it. Congress responded in July 1866 by restoring Tennessee to its congressional representation. The other southern states remained under military control.

Following the 1866 congressional elections, which produced a resounding repudiation of Johnson, Congress enacted its own program of Reconstruction. In a series of laws, it specified the steps the remaining former Confederate states had to follow to create new state governments and regain their representation in Congress. This legislation mandated black suffrage and required the states to ratify the Fourteenth Amendment (those that failed to complete the process by 1868 also had to ratify the Fifteenth Amendment, which prohibited racial tests for voting). Johnson vetoed these laws and accused congressional Republicans of seeking "to Africanize the [southern] half of our country," but Congress promptly overrode his vetoes. After Johnson attempted to remove Secretary of War Edwin Stanton from office for a second time in 1868, which was a violation of the Tenure of Office Act, the House of Representatives impeached the president, but the Senate failed by one vote to convict him and remove him from office. In subsequent years Congress also passed laws to combat terrorist organizations like the Ku Klux Klan, safeguard the social rights of blacks, and grant amnesty to all but the highest leaders of the Confederacy.

RECONSTRUCTION IN THE SOUTH

Under the terms of congressional Reconstruction, new governments were established in the South that included significant black participation. Initially perhaps 20 percent of the southern white voters supported the Republican Party but most eventually abandoned the party, reducing it to a coalition of blacks and transplanted northern whites.

The new radical governments in the South were not without significant achievements. They expanded government services, established public school systems, and made government more democratic. While these regimes sought to protect black rights, they were conservative on the issues of social intermixing and land reform.

Southern Democrats bitterly assailed the new Republican state governments as illegitimate. They attacked the native southern whites who held office under the radical governments as traitors to their race and dismissed northern officeholders as foreign adventurers bent on plundering the South. They chafed at black voting and portrayed black voters and officeholders as ignorant dupes. Critics devoted particular attention to the issue of corruption. While corruption undeniably existed, the real source of southern whites' hostility to these governments was that they tried to protect black rights and gave some offices to blacks.

Reconstruction also involved social and economic developments. In freedom former slaves sought to remove all reminders of bondage and refused to work in gangs, be disciplined by the whip, or live in the old slave quarters. In response to black demands, sharecropping eventually became the means of organizing black agricultural labor in the South. Under this system, a black family farmed a plot of land and at the end of the season divided the crop with the white landowner. Sharecropping was a harshly exploitive system, but blacks preferred it because it gave them greater independence and freed them from constant supervision. But it also mired southern blacks in poverty and retarded southern development.

Blacks were "*crazy* to learn," one official reported, and families often sent their children to school rather than have them work in the fields. At the same time, most black members left white-controlled churches and established independent black Methodist and Baptist churches. Indeed, black churches became the most important institutions in the black community after the war.

THE END OF RECONSTRUCTION

Congressional Reconstruction began to wane almost as soon as it commenced. Republican governments in the South came under mounting pressure from Democrats on the race issue, violence drove thousands of blacks from the polls, and northern public opinion became increasingly tired of the disorder that regularly accompanied elections in the South. Voicing growing doubts about the capabilities of blacks, northerners more and more spoke of leaving the race question to southern whites.

Compounding growing northern disillusionment was the widespread corruption that saturated northern public life at all levels of government. A series of scandals wracked President Ulysses S. Grant's administration (1869–1877) and made "Grantism" a term for cronyism and venality. Although well intentioned, Grant lacked the political skill or moral will to make Reconstruction a success, and he displayed no zeal to eradicate wrongdoing in his administration.

The Panic of 1873 further undercut northern support for Reconstruction. The onset of hard times enabled the Democrats in 1874 to gain control of the House for the first time since the war began. Republican leaders increasingly spoke of cutting loose from the remaining radical regimes in the South, which they viewed as dead weights that hurt the party politically in the North. When Democrats resorted to widespread violence to carry the 1875 Mississippi election, Grant, fearing a northern backlash, refused to intervene.

After Grant's successor, Rutherford B. Hayes, withdrew military support in 1877 for the remaining Republican governments in the South, they promptly collapsed. With the fall of these governments, Democrats controlled every southern state, and Reconstruction came to an end.

Despite its failure, Reconstruction had written the goal of racial equality into the Constitution with the Fourteenth and Fifteenth Amendments. In the twentieth century, reformers would utilize these amendments to undermine segregation, disfranchisement, and second-class citizenship. The immediate consequence of the overthrow of Reconstruction, however, was intensifying racism, black poverty, and racial segregation. The country's initial effort to establish racial equality had floundered on the rock of antiblack racism.

BIBLIOGRAPHY

The Coming of the Civil War

Boritt, Gabor S., ed. *Why the Civil War Came*. New York, 1996.

Foner, Eric. *Free Soil, Free Labor, Free Men: The Ideology of the Republican Party before the Civil War*. New York, 1970.

Freehling, William W. *The Road to Disunion: The Secessionists at Bay, 1776–1854*. New York, 1990.

Gienapp, William E. *The Origins of the Republican Party, 1852–1856*. New York, 1987.

Hietala, Thomas R. *Manifest Design: Anxious Aggrandizement in Late Jacksonian America*. Ithaca, N.Y., 1985.

Holt, Michael F. *The Political Crisis of the 1850s*. New York, 1978.

Horsman, Reginald. *Race and Manifest Destiny: The Origins of American Racial Anglo-Saxonism.* Cambridge, Mass., 1981.

Jimerson, Randall C. *The Private Civil War: Popular Thought during the Sectional Conflict.* Baton Rouge, La., 1988.

McCardell, John. *The Idea of a Southern Nation: Southern Nationalists and Southern Nationalism, 1830–1860.* New York, 1979.

Morrison, Michael A. *Slavery and the American West: The Eclipse of Manifest Destiny and the Coming of the Civil War.* Chapel Hill, N.C., 1997.

Potter, David M. *The Impending Crisis, 1848–1861.* Edited and completed by Don E. Fehrenbacher. New York, 1976.

Stewart, James Brewer. *Holy Warriors: The Abolitionists and American Slavery.* New York, 1976.

Walters, Ronald G. *American Reformers, 1815–1860.* New York, 1978.

Widmer, Edward L. *Young America: The Flowering of Democracy in New York City.* New York, 1999.

The Civil War

Escott, Paul. *After Secession: Jefferson Davis and the Failure of Confederate Nationalism.* Baton Rouge, La., 1978.

Faust, Drew Gilpin. *Mothers of Invention: Women of the Slaveholding South in the American Civil War.* Chapel Hill, N.C., 1996.

Fredrickson, George M. *The Inner Civil War: Northern Intellectuals and the Crisis of the Union.* New York, 1965.

Gallagher, Gary W. *The Confederate War.* Cambridge, Mass., 1997.

Genovese, Eugene D. *A Consuming Fire: The Fall of the Confederacy and the Mind of the White Christian South.* Athens, Ga., 1998.

Litwack, Leon F. *Been in the Storm So Long: The Aftermath of Slavery.* New York, 1979.

McPherson, James M. *Battle Cry of Freedom: The Civil War Era.* New York, 1988.

Moorhead, James H. *American Apocalypse: Yankee Protestants and the Civil War, 1860–1869.* New Haven, Conn., 1978.

Paludan, Phillip S. *A People's Contest: The Union and Civil War, 1861–1865.* New York, 1988.

———. *The Presidency of Abraham Lincoln.* Lawrence, Kans., 1994.

Rable, George C. *The Confederate Republic: A Revolution against Politics.* Chapel Hill, N.C., 1994.

Rose, Anne C. *Victorian America and the Civil War.* New York, 1992.

Thomas, Emory. *The Confederate Nation, 1861–1865.* New York, 1979.

Reconstruction

Belz, Herman. *Emancipation and Equal Rights: Politics and Constitutionalism in the Civil War Era.* New York, 1978.

Benedict, Michael Les. *The Impeachment and Trial of Andrew Johnson.* New York, 1973.

Carter, Dan T. *When the War Was Over: The Failure of Self-Reconstruction in the South, 1865–1867.* Baton Rouge, La., 1985.

Edwards, Laura F. *Gendered Strife and Confusion: The Political Culture of Reconstruction.* Urbana, Ill., 1997.

Foner, Eric. *Reconstruction: America's Unfinished Revolution, 1863–1877.* New York, 1988.

Gillette, William. *Retreat from Reconstruction, 1869–1879.* Baton Rouge, La., 1980.

Harris, William C. *With Charity for All: Lincoln and the Restoration of the Union.* Lexington, Ky., 1997.

Holt, Thomas. *Black over White: Negro Political Leadership in South Carolina during Reconstruction.* Urbana, Ill., 1977.

McPherson, James M. *The Struggle for Equality: Abolitionists and the Negro in the Civil War and Reconstruction.* Princeton, N.J., 1964.

Nieman, Donald. *To Set the Law in Motion: The Freedmen's Bureau and the Legal Rights of Blacks, 1865–1868.* Millwood, N.Y., 1979.

Perman, Michael. *The Road to Redemption: Southern Politics, 1869–1879.* Chapel Hill, N.C., 1984.

Rable, George C. *But There Was No Peace: The Role of Violence in the Politics of Reconstruction.* Athens, Ga., 1984.

Ransom, Roger L., and Richard Sutch. *One Kind of Freedom: The Economic Consequences of Emancipation.* New York, 1977.

Roark, James L. *Masters without Slaves: Southern Planters in the Civil War and Reconstruction.* New York, 1977.

Saville, Julie. *The Work of Reconstruction: From Slave to Wage Laborer in South Carolina, 1860–1870.* New York, 1994.

Silber, Nina. *The Romance of Reunion: Northerners and the South, 1865–1900.* Chapel Hill, N.C., 1993.

SLAVERY AND RACE

Paul Finkelman

Slavery has been present in almost every age and in almost every human society. Until the settlement of the New World, however, slavery was rarely tied to race. By the Revolution race had become a cultural category, and color and race had become a proxy for social and legal status. Colonists viewed race as an ideological category for organizing their society between free people and slaves. The revolutionary ideology also undermined slavery, however. The Declaration of Independence asserted that all people were "created equal," and "endowed by their Creator" with the "unalienable Rights," of "Life, Liberty and the Pursuit of Happiness." If this was really true, some patriots asked, then how could Americans own slaves?

In the North, the Revolution stimulated what has been called "the first emancipation," as one state after another took steps to end slavery. In the South, the Revolution led a few masters to privately liberate their slaves, and to suggest and support moderations to slave codes. Twin threats to slavery—political ideology and religious fervor—forced southern leaders to develop defenses for their institution. Before the mid-eighteenth century there had been so few challenges to the legitimacy of slavery that there were also few reasons to defend the institution. The British empire was a hierarchical one in which equality was a relatively unimportant concept. With few challenges to slavery, or its racial basis, there were few needs to defend either the institution or its racial presumptions. But following the revolutionary period this scenario changed.

RACE AND THE DEFENSE OF SLAVERY

The first clearly racist defense of slavery emerged from the pen of Thomas Jefferson. In a sense, there is a certain logic to Jefferson's defending slavery on racial grounds. In the Declaration of Independence,

Jefferson, who owned about one hundred and fifty slaves at the time, articulated that "all men are created equal." If this were literally true, then slavery could not survive. Thus, in his *Notes on the State of Virginia* (1785), Jefferson turned to "natural science," or at least his assertions of what science might be, and offered one of the first "scientific" rationales for racially based slavery. Jefferson argued that blacks were fundamentally different from and inferior to whites. He noted that a harsh bondage did not prevent Roman slaves from achieving distinction in science, art, or literature because "they were of the race of whites." But, in his mind, American slaves could never achieve such distinction because they were black. Jefferson argued that American Indians had "a germ in their minds which only wants [lacks] cultivation"; they were capable of "the most sublime oratory." But, he asserted he had never found a black who "had uttered a thought above the level of plain narration; never seen an elementary trait of painting or sculpture." He found "no poetry" among blacks. Jefferson argued that blacks' ability to reason was "much inferior" to that of whites, while "in imagination they are dull, tasteless, and anomalous," and "inferior to the whites in the endowments of body and mind." Jefferson even speculated that blacks might have been "originally a distinct race, or made distinct by time and circumstances." He conceded blacks were brave, but this was due to "a want of fore-thought, which prevents their seeing a danger till it be present." If they had natural rights, and Jefferson seemed uncertain on this point, they could only exercise them outside the United States. A scientist and naturalist, he nevertheless accepted and repeated absurdly unscientific and illogical arguments about the racial characteristics of blacks, speculating that blackness might come "from the colour of the blood" or that blacks might breed with the "Oran-ootan."

This excursion into racist science allowed Jefferson, and many other Americans, to accept both the egalitarian ideas of the Declaration of Independence and racially based slavery. All men, it would seem, were "endowed by their Creator" with natural rights, but because blacks were physically and mentally unequal, they were legitimately enslaved by whites. In a sense, the American Revolution made the scientific and racist defense of slavery necessary. With the abolition of royalty and formal class lines, America needed a new rationale for the legal subordination of one group—and one group only—under everyone else in society. Racism provided the rationale.

ATTACKS ON SLAVERY

The first great political debate over slavery came in 1819–1820, when Missouri sought to enter the Union as a slave state. Northerners argued that under the Northwest Ordinance of 1787 all territory north and west of the southernmost point of the Ohio River was forever free. This included most of the future state of Missouri. Southerners claimed that the ordinance only applied to the territory owned by the United States in 1787, and that in any event since the Ohio River ended at the Mississippi the ordinance could not possibly apply to territory that was not directly north of the river. These technical points had little impact on the debate. Most northern congressmen did not want another slave state; most southerners did. In the House of Representatives the northern majority was strong enough to block Missouri statehood; in the evenly divided Senate a few northern defectors joined the solid southern opposition to place a ban on slavery in Missouri. Debates over two sessions of Congress led to the Missouri Compromise (1820). Missouri entered the Union as a slave state, while Maine split off from Massachusetts and entered as a free state. Slavery would be forever banned, however, in all territory west and north of Missouri.

In the decade following the Missouri crisis the South felt under pressure in other ways. In 1822 authorities in Charleston, South Carolina, discovered the Denmark Vesey conspiracy shortly before this former slave planned to launch a revolt that may have included as many as eight thousand slaves in the region. The sheer scope of Vesey's plans amazed and frightened southern whites. In 1828 David Walker, a free black living in Massachusetts, began publishing his *Appeal*, which urged slaves to revolt if they were not granted freedom. In 1831 William Lloyd Garrison launched the *Liberator*, the first national abolitionist newspaper, and in 1833 he helped organize the American Anti-Slavery Society, which was dedicated to total abolition of slavery. In August 1831 the Virginia slave Nat Turner led a brief but bloody revolt in Southampton County, Virginia. When it was over, some sixty whites and over one hundred blacks were dead. From 1831 to 1832 the Virginia legislature debated the future of bondage in the state, but in the end reaffirmed the state's commitment to slavery.

The events from 1819 to 1831 shook the South deeply, and southerners responded with the development of what historians have generally called the proslavery argument. In the decades that followed southerners offered a detailed and complex defense of slavery, based on politics, economics, history, religion, and science. Undergirding this defense were theories of race.

PROSLAVERY THEORY

Southerners insisted that slavery was vital to the nation's economy, and that without slavery cotton production would stop in the South and the vitally important textile industry in the North would quickly collapse. Southerners never tired of pointing out that commodities produced by slave labor were the nation's most important exports. Along similar lines, southerners argued that the Constitution specifically protected slavery, and thus attacks on slavery were in effect attacks on the nation's founders. These arguments were obvious and were doubtless persuasive to northern conservatives who believed maintaining the Union and the economy were the most important issues of national politics.

Such arguments could not adequately respond to the new abolitionist movement, which based its assault on slavery on moral and religious grounds. The abolitionist attack on slavery was part of a larger moral revival, known as the Second Great Awakening. In this atmosphere economic and political arguments were unimpressive, not only to northerners but even to some southern whites. The abolitionists had a powerful answer to the economic or constitutional argument for slavery: economic prosperity was hardly a reason to violate the law of God or the natural rights of God's creatures. Such an answer might well have resonated with southern whites, who were also products of an evangelical

Protestant culture and were also influenced by the Second Great Awakening.

Thus, southern defenders of slavery turned to religion, and ironically to science as well, to defend slavery. They also used history and sociology to support their goals. Ultimately, these defenses were rooted in race and theories of race.

BIBLICAL UNDERSTANDINGS OF SLAVERY AND RACE

The abolitionist attack on slavery was predicated on the assumption that slavery violated Christian morality. How, one might ask, could one "do unto others," by enslaving them? Southern clergymen turned to their Bibles for a response and discovered one that supported slavery as an abstract institution and the more immediate form of racially based slavery.

Careful reading of the Bible produced numerous examples of how slavery was not inconsistent with God's law. While Jesus admonished people to treat each other well, the New Testament never condemned slavery. On the contrary, in many places it gave positive support for slavery. In his letter to Philemon, the apostle Paul urged the slave master Philemon to treat kindly his slave Onesimus, but he did not urge him to emancipate Onesimus. Furthermore, although Onesimus had been baptized, Paul did not declare him free, but urged him to return to his master. This example dovetailed with the language in Colossians, urging slaves to obey their masters (3:22) and masters to "give unto your servants that which is just and equal" (4:1). In other words, a Christian master treated his slaves kindly, and baptized them, but did not free them.

The Old Testament provided an elaborate legal code for the treatment of slaves, and indicated how a servant for a term of years could be turned into a slave for life. The Israelite patriarchs—Abraham, Isaac, and Jacob—had "slaves." Southerners found the story of Abraham useful. In the book of Genesis, when Hagar ran away from Abraham, the Angel of God found her in the desert and demanded of her, "Hagar, Sarah's maid, . . . whither wilt thou go?" Hagar answered, "I flee from the face of my mistress." The Angel told her, "Return unto thy mistress, and submit thyself under her hands" (16:8–9). What better source could southerners ask for when defending their right to capture runaway slaves?

Mosaic law clearly supported the idea that slavery was a permissible, even normal, human institution. Significantly, the legal code set out in Leviticus provided for the enslavement of foreigners and aliens, but not normally for fellow Israelites, who usually were treated as debt slaves for a term of six years. The implication of this for the racial defense of slavery is clear: it was legitimate to enslave outsiders, foreigners, aliens—"the other," in modern sociological terms—and people of African ancestry were the most obvious outsiders in America.

The story of Noah in Genesis also provided, for antebellum southerners, "proof" that God intended blacks to be the slaves of whites. According to the story, after the ark came to rest Noah planted grapes. "And he drank of the wine, and became drunken; and he uncovered himself within his tent. And Ham, the father of Canaan, saw the nakedness of his father, and he told his brothers." For Ham's indiscretion, Noah cursed Ham's son, Canaan, declaring, "Cursed be Canaan, a servant of servants he shall be unto his brethren" (9:21–25). Southern ministers interpreted the "curse" of Canaan to mean that he became black, and thus they argued that the Bible justified not merely slavery, but the enslavement of Africans, the descendants of Canaan. The story of Ham became a mainstay of southern defenses of slavery, and bolstered southern evangelicals in their debates with northern clergymen.

PROSLAVERY SCIENCE

Scientists and physicians of the mid-nineteenth century also supported the racial nature of slavery. Scientists offered an explanation for racial difference that ran counter to the Bible, but nevertheless supported the enslavement of blacks. Many scientists argued that the races were separately created, and that blacks were a distinct, and inferior, race of people. This dovetailed with Jefferson's speculations in his *Notes on the State of Virginia*. Such arguments were a significant corollary to the natural rights arguments of the Declaration of Independence. As a separate species, blacks might not be entitled to the same rights of liberty and the pursuit of happiness as whites.

Southern physicians joined in this debate. Josiah Nott, who practiced medicine in Mobile, Alabama, published "scientific" research in which he claimed that mulattoes were a genuine hybrid of two separate races—weaker and less fertile than either. Nott argued Negroes had major anatomical differences from whites, including a larger head, smaller brain, defective mental powers, and larger nerves. He wrote that Negroes reached their highest attainable goals when "tamed," and "educated to capacity" as slaves. Dr. Samuel Cartwright, a New Orleans physician specializing in "Negro diseases," believed that the internal organs and flesh of blacks—even brains—were biologically darker than whites'. He wrote that Negroes "under the compulsive power of the white man . . . are made to labor or exercise, which makes the lungs perform the duty of vitalizing the blood more perfectly than is done when they are left free to indulge in idleness. It is the red, vital blood sent to the brain that liberates their mind when under the white man's control, and it is the want of a sufficiency of red, vital blood that chains their mind to ignorance and barbarism when in freedom." Cartwright identified a disease called "drapetomania," which caused slaves to run away. The cure for the "running away disease" was to whip slaves who showed symptoms, such as sullenness or discontent. Other scientists, such as Samuel G. Morton, collected skulls of various races, and measured the cranial capacities to "prove" that blacks were intellectually inferior to whites. The thrust of these arguments is obvious: if blacks were inferior, then their enslavement was justified.

The medical and scientific arguments about race affected cultural views of blacks and their inherent suitability to be kept as slaves. Slaves who frequently escaped were considered "addicted to running away," as though the desire for freedom was unnatural in blacks. On the other hand, the Louisiana legislature declared that some blacks were "addicted" to theft. Dr. Cartwright asserted that the nerve endings of blacks were less developed than those of whites, which led to the logical conclusion that they felt less pain when whipped. Others observed, echoing Jefferson's *Notes on the State of Virginia*, that they were more "disposed to sleep" than whites—in other words they were inherently lazy. Jefferson's views that blacks were sexually immoral also echoed throughout the century. In his treatise on the law of slavery, Thomas R. R. Cobb argued that the legislatures of the South ought to consider "whether the offense of rape, committed upon a female slave, should not be indictable." He even suggested that if a master rapes a slave the owner/rapist should be required to sell the slave to a new master. Such a law, he believed, should be passed for "the honor of the statute-book." He doubted, however, that the crime of raping a slave could ever actually take place, because rape required a lack of consent, and "the known lasciviousness of the negro, renders the possibility of its occurrence very remote."

HISTORY, RACE, AND THE PRACTICALITY OF SLAVERY

At the Constitutional Convention of 1787 Charles Pinckney of South Carolina argued that "if slavery be wrong, it is justified by the example of all the world." He offered the examples of "Greece, Rome & other ancient States; the sanction given by France, England, Holland & other modern States." Pinckney asserted that "in all ages one half of mankind have been slaves."

In the antebellum period numerous southerners took up this argument, but often with a racial twist. They easily cited Plato, Aristotle, and other classical writers to show that slavery was found in the ancient world and to equate the South with Rome and Greece. In 1831, Alexander Knox, a Virginia politician, argued there was not "one solitary instance of a Government, since the institution of civil society, in which the principle of slavery was not tolerated in some form or other. . . . In the republics of Greece and Rome, the cradles of liberty, slavery was tolerated in the severest form." In essence, this meant that American liberty was predicated on slavery. This was a far stronger argument than the notion that cotton was "King," or that slavery was economically valuable. By the 1820s America's institutions had become part of a civil religion of democratic voting, republican government, and national progress. Southerners argued that slavery was at the heart of this trinity.

John C. Calhoun, the most important southern nationalist voice in the Senate, made similar arguments. In an 1837 debate over the reception of abolitionist petitions, Calhoun "denied having pronounced slavery in the abstract a good." Rather, he asserted, "it was an inevitable law of society that one portion of the community depended upon the labor of another portion, over which it must unavoidably exercise control." Here Calhoun rejected the validity of the concept of free labor, which, from the 1830s to the Civil War would come to dominate northern thought on this subject, and be reflected in the ideology of the Republican Party in the 1850s and 1860s.

Calhoun went from repudiating free labor to embracing racially based slavery, asserting that slavery "was good where a civilized race and a race of different description were brought together." Noting the "different color, and striking dissimilarity in conformation, habits, and a thousand other particularities," between blacks and whites, Calhoun boldly asserted, "here the existence of slavery was good to both." He told his Senate colleagues that "the Central African race . . . had never existed in so comfortable, so respectable, or so civilized a condition, as that which it now enjoyed in the Southern states."

Calhoun's articulation of the positive good of slavery tied together three concepts: a rejection of the value of free labor; the understanding that all societies need a subordinate class; and the idea that Africans are so inferior to whites that they benefit from slavery. In the next two and half decades other southerners would repeat these arguments, with different nuances and different thrusts.

In *An Inquiry into the Law of Negro Slavery* (1858), Thomas R. R. Cobb, a cofounder of the first law school in Georgia, quoted Plato, Euripides, Juvenal, and other classical writers to teach his readers that slavery, especially Negro slavery, was accepted by the greatest minds of Western culture. Cobb explicitly tied this argument to race, insisting that in an "early day" the "negro was commonly used as a slave at Rome." Implicitly comparing the South to the Roman republic, he noted that "for her footmen and couriers" the Roman "wife preferred always the negroes" and that "Negroes, being generally slaves of luxury, commanded a very high price." Similarly, Cobb asserted that in ancient Israel "many" of the slaves "were Africans of negro extraction," that "among the Egyptians . . . there were numbers of negro slaves." Making similar claims for Assyria and Alexander the Great's empire, he concluded the Negro "was a favorite among slaves" in the ancient world. While there is no historical support for these ideas, Cobb's assertions went unchallenged by most readers, who had no access to any serious works of history.

In the same year that Cobb's book came out, Senator James Henry Hammond of South Carolina tied the economic argument to the politics of race. In his first speech in the Senate Hammond asserted, "No, you dare not make war on cotton. No power on earth dares to make war on it. Cotton is King." Having asserted this, he then went on to argue that the enslavement of blacks was fundamental to American democracy. He noted that every society needed a "class to do the menial duties, to perform the drudgery of life." Members of this class required a "low order of intellect and but little skill. Its requisites are vigor, docility, fidelity." He condemned the North for reducing white people to such servitude and noted that because the members of this class could vote, there would always be political turmoil in the free states. Happily, however, Hammond

crowed, "the South" had "found a race adopted to that purpose. . . . We use them for our purposes, and call them slaves."

Hammond, like Calhoun and Cobb, reflected the proslavery theory of a public man, a politician or lawyer, who in the end appealed to his southern, racist, proslavery constituents, clients, and students. George Fitzhugh, however, never ran for office, and sought the endorsement of no group. Indeed, although a powerful intellectual, most southerners viewed him as something of a crackpot. That is because he took the final step in the proslavery argument, asserting that even without race, slavery was a valuable institution. Rejecting Lockean and Jeffersonian concepts of the formation of society, Fitzhugh asserted "There is no such thing as *natural human* liberty, because it is unnatural for man to live alone and without the pale and government of society." He characterized a "Free Society" as one which "makes the weak, ignorant, and poor, free, by turning them loose in a world owned exclusively by the few (whom nature and education have made strong, and whom property has made stronger) to get a living." He argued that "self-interest is everywhere the strongest motive to human conduct" and thus "the law of self-interest secures kind and humane treatment to Southern slaves." The essence of Fitzhugh's argument is that slaves are treated better than free workers because they are property, and the logical conclusion is that free workers ought to be enslaved.

In his most important book, *Cannibals All! or, Slaves without Masters* (1857) he denounced capitalism, which makes "the White Slave Trade . . . more exacting and fraudulent (in fact, though not in intention) than Black Slavery." He argued that the free enterprise system "is more cruel" than slavery, "in leaving the laborer to take care of himself and family out of the pittance which skill or capital have allowed him to retain." His defense of slavery is complete: "The negro slaves of the South are the happiest, and, in some sense, the freest people in the world." The logical end point of Fitzhugh's work is that all workers should be owned by kind masters, and that capitalism should be rejected for a kind of socialism in which the paternalistic leaders of society own, not merely the means of production, but the producers themselves. Race precludes blacks from ever having a leadership role in Fitzhugh's world, but it does not preclude whites from being left in a subordinate, slavelike role, to be cared for by their masters.

317

THE NORTHERN RESPONSE TO SLAVERY AND RACE

During and immediately after the Revolution the northern states took steps to end slavery, and by 1830 only a few aging slaves could be found in a handful of northern states. The new abolitionist movement, which began in the 1830s, initially met with hostility in much of the North. But by the 1840s most northerners had accepted a good deal of the abolitionist argument. Northerners saw the South as aggressively trying to foist its labor system on the nation, by pushing slavery into the territories and through the gag rule, which prevented even a discussion of slavery in Congress. By the 1850s only a tiny minority of northerners supported slavery, although most northerners were not ready to attack slavery in the South. In 1856 and 1860 the Republicans would appeal to a majority of northerners because the party's position was both moderate and firm: the Republicans would not let any more slave states into the Union, and would prevent slavery from spreading to the western territories. This position appealed to staunch opponents of slavery—like Salmon Chase or Charles Sumner—because they saw it as a constitutionally permissible method of strangling slavery until it suffocated. Similarly, it appealed to more moderate northerners, who feared chaos and change, and saw stopping the spread of slavery inherently conservative. Finally, it appealed to racist northerners, who worried more about the spread of blacks than slaves.

Racial attitudes in the North were extraordinarily complex. In most of New England blacks had all or almost all of the same legal rights as whites, but social segregation was common. As late as 1849 the Massachusetts Supreme Judicial Court, in *Roberts v. City of Boston*, refused to order the integration of Boston's public schools. However, in 1855 the state legislature banned all segregation in the state. In the 1830s most of the Midwest denied blacks access to public schools, but Ohio repealed such restrictions in 1849 and the newer states of Michigan and Wisconsin never adopted them. In the 1830s mobs attacked blacks and white abolitionists in Cincinnati, Utica, and other northern cities. However, by 1860 a black held elective office in Ohio, even though blacks were not allowed to vote in that state, and the Syracuse and Utica (New York) public schools were integrated.

Most whites in the North did not accept the idea of black equality and avoided social interaction with them. But when fugitive slaves were seized, whole towns might pour into the streets to protest, and hundreds of otherwise law-abiding whites, many of whom were not abolitionists, risked incarceration or fines to help fugitive slaves. Harriet Beecher Stowe's remarkable book *Uncle Tom's Cabin* (1852) became the most popular novel of the era, in part because she humanized slavery in ways that whites could accept. The heroine, Eliza, is nearly white, and Stowe effectively used common color prejudice of the period to lead northern whites to the conclusion that someone who is virtually white should not be treated as a slave. The most noble character in the book, the Christ-like Uncle Tom, is coal black. Tom is ultimately murdered by his master, Simon Legree, a New Englander by birth, because Tom will not divulge the hiding place of two slave women whom Legree wants to sexually abuse. Thus, the very black slave is the true Christian martyr, while the New Englander, under the corrupting influence of slavery, is the sinner.

The northern response to John Brown's abolitionist raid on the federal arsenal at Harpers Ferry, Virginia, in 1859 also suggests the variety of northern attitudes on race. Democrats throughout the North condemned Brown, and many Republicans initially tried to distance themselves from him. But northern intellectuals, like Henry David Thoreau and Ralph Waldo Emerson, embraced him. Emerson concluded that Brown was "the new saint awaiting his martyrdom, and who, if he shall suffer, will make the gallows glorious like the cross." Reverend Henry Ward Beecher gloried in the prospect of Brown on the gallows. "Let Virginia make him a martyr! Now, he has only blundered. . . . But a cord and gibbet would redeem all that, and round up Brown's failure with a heroic success." John A. Andrew, a rising star in the Republican Party and the future governor of Massachusetts, refused to commit himself on the wisdom of Brown's raid, but declared that "John Brown himself is right." At the time of his hanging millions in the North mourned him, bought pictures and busts of him, and read his authorized biography, James Redpath's *The Public Life of Captain John Brown* (1860), which went through forty-one editions by 1872. Clearly, Brown's attack on slavery resonated with northerners, just as did Stowe's *Uncle Tom's Cabin*.

The complexity of northern attitudes toward race and slavery would continue into the Civil War and beyond. In 1861 President Abraham Lincoln called on the North to defend the Constitution and the Union. He would not lift a finger against slavery, understanding that he had neither the constitutional or legal power to do so, nor sufficient political support. Moreover, he needed the border South to

318

remain in the Union. When a clergyman told Lincoln if he freed the slaves he would "have God on his side," the president allegedly responded, "I would like to have God on my side, but I *need* Kentucky." Northern troops nevertheless soon found themselves in the role of emancipators, and they rarely denied sanctuary to slaves escaping their traitorous masters. General Benjamin F. Butler applied his legal mind to the problem and determined that slaves were in fact "contrabands of war," and could not be returned to their masters. Lincoln and the North could accept this legal fix until 1862, when the preliminary Emancipation Proclamation was issued, committing the North to ending slavery. Most northerners accepted this, and with it black troops, although some did not. Riots, especially in New York City, against blacks revealed the deep racism of some northerners. But, the willingness of thousands of whites to serve as noncommissioned officers and officers for black troops, and to fight side by side with them in the last two years of the war also reveals the complexity of northern culture. That martyred Lincoln would be remembered not as the man who held the Union together but as the "Great Emancipator" suggests that slavery and race did matter to most northerners.

SOUTHERN IDEOLOGY AND AMERICAN CULTURE

Uncle Tom's Cabin was banned throughout the South. By the 1850s the South had become a closed society, where intellectual interchange on slavery was impossible. Criticism of the institution, even by native white southerners, was not acceptable. Hinton Rowan Helper was chased from his native North Carolina for his book *The Impending Crisis of the South* (1857) because he argued that slavery was an impediment to the welfare of the non-slaveholding whites in the South. Similarly, Francis Leiber was fired from the University of South Carolina for expressing doubts about the justice and good policy of slavery.

Shielded from debate on the central social issue of their culture, southerners created a proslavery ideology predicated on race and racism. Indeed, by the eve of the Civil War the need to defend the racial status quo had become as important as the need to defend slavery. Thus, the South cheered when Chief Justice Roger B. Taney, in *Dred Scott v. Sandford* (1857), declared that no black, slave or free, could ever be a citizen of the United States or claim the same rights as whites.

On the heels of *Dred Scott* came John Brown's raid at Harpers Ferry, which left southerners fearful and angry. Their anger was not so much against Brown. He was, after all, a fanatic. Moreover, his brave comportment on the gallows made him a worthy adversary. Rather, the South was furious at the northerners who did not denounce Brown, but instead praised him. Brown's raid culminated a decade of northern opposition to the return of fugitive slaves. Every northern sermon on fugitive slaves, every riot (although in reality there were very few) that freed a slave, every speech against the law, convinced southern intellectuals and politicians of the dangers of maintaining a Union with free states. The outpouring of support from the North for John Brown, followed by Lincoln's victory at the polls eleven months later, convinced the leaders and voters of seven southern states that the time had come to create a true slaveholders' republic. Alexander Stephens, the Confederate vice president, clearly stated the reason for secession. Slavery, he declared, was "the cornerstone" of the Confederacy.

The Civil War of course destroyed slavery, but not the intellectual arguments that the South had developed to defend the institution. They survived. The strongest legacy of slavery may well have been the racist defense of the institution. During Reconstruction racist ideology motivated President Andrew Johnson's vetoes of civil rights legislation and led the South to impose black codes on former slaves. The Ku Klux Klan thrived on white fears of black rule and black sexuality. In the North such ideas remained alive as well, in part because of the great energy of Dr. John H. Van Evrie of New York, who published numerous antiabolition and racist tracts from the 1850s and 1860s, culminating with his massive *White Supremacy and Negro Subordination; or, Negroes a Subordinate Race* (1868). As Reconstruction waned, new studies of science and Scripture resurrected the proslavery argument on black inferiority. Illustrative of this was A. Hoyle Lester's *The Pre-Adamite; or, Who Tempted Eve?* (1875), which sought to use passages of Scripture to support the widely held scientific view that blacks were a separate species. The Civil War may have ended slavery, but it clearly did not end its defense. Indeed, the ideology of slavery finally reemerged full blown in the demand for total segregation of all social interaction at the end of the nineteenth century. Thus in *Williams v. State of Mississippi* (1898), the Supreme Court endorsed the notion that blacks were inherently ignorant, and thus their disfranchisement was permissible. So too was the denial of equal educational opportunities for blacks a legacy of the proslavery arguments, articulated so well by Jefferson, that blacks were incapable of learning. Why educate those who were so inferior? Indeed, throughout much of the twentieth century the proslavery arguments reemerged as a rationale for segregation, discrimination, and ghettoization. At the dawn of the twenty-first century African Americans complained about being stopped by police for no other reason than "driving while black." Such social problems can be viewed as a modern consequence of the proslavery view that blacks are inherently criminal, which justifies their enslavement in a system that can control them and make them work hard for the profit of the master class.

See also **The Classical Vision; Racialism and Racial Uplift** *(in this volume);* **African Americans** *(volume 2);* **Race** *(volume 3); and other articles in this section.*

BIBLIOGRAPHY

Ambrose, Douglas. *Henry Hughes and Proslavery Thought in the Old South.* Baton Rouge, La., 1996.

Cobb, Thomas R. R. *An Inquiry into the Law of Negro Slavery.* Edited by Paul Finkelman. Athens, Ga., 1999.

Davis, David Brion. *Slavery and Human Progress.* New York, 1984.

Faust, Drew Gilpin. *The Ideology of Slavery: Proslavery Thought in the Antebellum South, 1830–1860.* Baton Rouge, La., 1981.

Finkelman, Paul. *Slavery and the Founders: Race and Liberty in the Age of Jefferson.* Armonk, N.Y., 1996.

Finkelman, Paul, and Joseph C. Miller. *The Macmillan Encyclopedia of World Slavery.* New York, 1998.

Genovese, Eugene D. *The World the Slaveholders Made: Two Essays in Interpretation.* Rev. ed. Middletown, Conn., 1988.

Horsman, Reginald. *Josiah Nott of Mobile: Southerner, Physician, and Racial Theorist.* Baton Rouge, La., 1987.

Jenkins, William S. *Proslavery Thought in the Old South.* Chapel Hill, N.C., 1935.

Smith, John David, ed. *Anti-Black Thought, 1863–1925.* 11 vols. New York, 1993.

Snay, Mitchell. *Gospel of Disunion: Religion and Separatism in the Antebllum South.* New York, 1993.

Stanton, William. *The Leopard's Spots: Scientific Attitudes toward Race in America, 1815–1859.* Chicago, 1960.

Tise, Larry E. *Proslavery: A History of the Defense of Slavery in America, 1701–1840.* Athens, Ga., 1987.

SLAVE CULTURE AND CONSCIOUSNESS

Dickson D. Bruce Jr.

The development of a distinctive slave culture and consciousness was one of the major events in American cultural history from the colonial era to the end of the Civil War. This culture took its most visible form during the antebellum period, as the product of a maturing slave system and of demographic processes producing a distinctively African American slave community. Nevertheless, it was the culmination of a lengthy series of developments going back to the earliest arrival of people of African descent in what would ultimately become the United States.

ORIGINS

From the initial arrival of Africans as slaves in the Western Hemisphere in the sixteenth century, through their emancipation in the nineteenth, slave communities engaged in the creation of distinctive cultural forms that were marked by ideas, values, and beliefs shaped by the slaves themselves. The process involved a synthesis of African elements, American institutional forces, and European cultural influences.

African traditions were a major part of slave cultural creation, and would continue to be so through the antebellum era. Of the roughly 10 million to 12 million people taken out of Africa during the era of the slave trade (about 430,000 of those going to what would ultimately become the United States), the vast majority came from West Africa. Their cultural backgrounds were not destroyed during the passage from Africa to America, and therefore played a major role in language, religion, oral traditions, kinship patterns, plastic arts, and technical skills under slavery.

American influences grew mainly out of the experiences of slavery. The character of slavery varied significantly from colony to colony. In New England and, to a lesser degree, in Virginia and the middle colonies, cultural interchanges among whites and blacks were frequent, creating adoptions and adaptation of European traditions that tended to dominate, though not entirely supplant, African cultural influences. In their earliest years, both denominations had strong antislavery tendencies (even if, subsequently, they were to compromise those principles in the interest of gaining white, slave-owning members). As a result, they developed an appeal to slaves that matched their appeal among whites.

The Colonial Background to Antebellum Slave Culture Within this framework of origins and variation, the most important aspect of cultural creation with implications for later slave culture and consciousness lay in the process of "creolization," the merging of African and European elements into distinctive forms. The earliest creolized languages appeared during the period. Combining English with African-based grammatical structures and vocabularies, these languages continued to develop through the antebellum period and beyond. No less fundamental were naming practices, in many cases preserving African patterns, as well as styles of appearance, music, and movement that showed similar processes of creolization.

Religion. Such a process of creolization was particularly visible in religion. Diversity marked the religious pasts of American slaves. Different groups brought unique traditions to the American colonies; at least a few slaves had been exposed to Christianity and Islam prior to arriving in the New World. However, it is possible to identify West African traditions that were broadly distributed and remained significant in the American setting. Spirit possession and visionary experiences, both within and outside the context of religious ritual, characterized many West African religions, as did highly personal, and personalized, conceptions of deities. Most West African religions were polytheistic, although many shared a belief in a high god ruling subordinate deities. West African religions also tended to share a reverence for ancestral spirits, along with strong components of magic, recognizing possibilities for using supernatural manipulation to affect human affairs.

Such African traditions endured through the colonial era. Although it is almost certainly the case that no single tradition survived intact among the slaves, specific elements did, especially possession beliefs and reverence for ancestors, reinforced by being widely shared among diverse peoples. Some, notably magic beliefs, were also reinforced by similar beliefs among European settlers and Native Americans, and continued as practices often labeled "folk beliefs," providing supernatural solutions to social and physical problems.

But, above all, many traditions found renewed life in the emergence of a distinctive slave Christianity during the colonial period. Although Christian conversion took place only fitfully, and more commonly in New England than elsewhere, there is some evidence that slaves maintained important African practices, including funerary rites and visionary beliefs, as they adopted and adapted the Christianity to which they were exposed in British North America.

Folk traditions. In addition to religious traditions, slaves developed a variety of other cultural forms during the colonial period that were carried forward into the antebellum era. Along with musical forms and dance styles that combined European and African elements, slaves created a material culture that synthesized diverse American and European practices.

Distinctive oral traditions, with roots in Africa and Europe, also began to appear during the period. A few slave stories became fairly well known to whites and blacks alike. The experience of enslavement evolved into a traditional tale of white betrayal and African victimization, a tale widely diffused by the end of the colonial period and current among slaves through the nineteenth century. Also well known was the story of a slave who refused to be buried in his master's family tomb, next to his master, for fear that the devil would take him by mistake (Piersen, *Black Yankees*, p. 109). The story not only circulated orally but even appeared in turn-of-the-century joke books and periodicals. It, too, remained a part of slave oral traditions through the antebellum period.

Thus, the traditions shaped during the colonial period provided an important basis for continuing cultural creation among slaves through the era of American independence and beyond.

CULTURAL TRANSFORMATIONS IN THE REVOLUTIONARY ERA AND THE EARLY REPUBLIC

If the colonial period laid the foundations for a distinctive slave culture and consciousness, the era of the American Revolution and the early years of American independence were settings for major transformations that would further determine directions for slave cultural creation in the years leading up to the Civil War.

One such transformation involved the increasing significance of ideas of freedom among slaves, as among others in the United States. The Revolution itself, with its emphasis on freedom and equality, had significant impact. Slaves showed the influence of Revolutionary ideals during the period by petitioning colonial legislatures for emancipation, using Revolutionary rhetoric. Many joined the war effort, on both sides, in a quest for freedom.

This heightened concern for freedom was reinforced by changes taking place in American religion at about the same time. Most important was the rise of the great evangelical denominations—the Methodists and the Baptists—in America. These denominations were built around an emphasis on personal religious experience as the foundation for faith—an emphasis compatible with both African and European traditions of visionary and possession experiences—and a conception of the church as a community of believers, a conception that looked in significant ways toward egalitarianism. They had strong antislavery tendencies, and developed an appeal to slaves that matched their appeal among whites. The growth of Christianity among the slaves reached unprecedented levels during the closing years of the eighteenth century. This growth encouraged the development of distinctive black churches, "visible" and "invisible," that were to serve as the institutional bases for slave religion through the antebellum period. Reinvigorating that synthesis of Christian and African traditions which had already begun to characterize slave religion, it also helped suffuse slave religion, more than ever before, with democratic ideals and notions of freedom that would reverberate until Emancipation.

Major developments in slave culture and consciousness were encouraged, finally, by demographic transformations in the Early Republic. On the one hand, late-eighteenth-century programs of

322

emancipation north of Delaware, influenced in part by Revolutionary and religious ideals, confined slavery increasingly to the southern states, reducing—though not eliminating—geographic diversity. At the same time, the expansion of southern slavery to the west, beginning in earnest during the early nineteenth century, ensured a diffusion of slave culture that, to some extent, transcended geographic lines. Finally, the closing of the African slave trade in 1808, anticipated by a burst of importations directly from Africa in the closing years of the eighteenth century and the early years of the nineteenth, simultaneously reinforced African cultural influences while ensuring that those influences would operate mainly within the context of an American experience.

ANTEBELLUM THOUGHT AND CULTURE

Processes of slave cultural creation, within a distinctively African American cultural frame, were characterized, during the antebellum period, by the ongoing adaptation of processes inaugurated during earlier periods to the developing character of slavery itself. The African influences that remained an important part of processes of cultural creation were apparent in virtually every aspect of antebellum slave culture, including religion, oral traditions, and even some social institutions. Such cultural forms as dance and musical styles continued to show strong African influences, and many customs—turning a pot upside down to protect the secrecy of a gathering, for example—were direct carryovers of African practices. Language, too, continued to show African influence. This was especially true of the much-studied Gullah, spoken mainly on the South Carolina coast and on the nearby Sea Islands. A melding of English and several West African languages, including vocabulary and grammatical structures, Gullah has remained one of the more important evidences of processes of African cultural retention in the United States.

Still, most scholars agree that however significant such forms were, African impulses, as a result of demographic factors, were far more subtly expressed in the United States than elsewhere in the Western Hemisphere. Even as, by the antebellum period, slave culture in the United States was shaped within an essentially American frame, slave populations elsewhere in the hemisphere continued to rely heavily on importation from Africa, resulting in stronger, ongoing African influence. Specific ties of ethnicity were preserved. An array of cultural forms, including religion and music, oral traditions and even family and kinship patterns, bore a much closer resemblance to often highly specific, readily identifiable African counterparts.

Some places saw the fairly direct carryover of religious institutions with African origins to an American setting: *vaudou* in Haiti, for example, and *candomblé* in Brazil. This level of cultural continuity was not unknown in the United States. Some historians have found evidence of the continuing existence of identifiable African "secret societies" among American slaves; and voodoo practices in New Orleans, though strongly infused with Roman Catholic elements, showed a high level of African influence in practices and organizational patterns. Nevertheless, such high levels of cultural retention were far less common than elsewhere in the Americas, reflecting the distinctive demographic character of slavery in the United States.

The major geographic differences that continued to influence slave cultural creation involved, particularly, significant differences between urban and rural slave communities, and important regional variations. Many urban slaves, in such cities as Charleston, Baltimore, and Richmond, occupied a quasi-free status, with ties to the larger slave community, and to slave culture, that were tenuous at best. In the South Carolina coastal regions, and especially on the Sea Islands, the linguistic formation of Gullah was only one aspect of a larger complex of African traditions more visible there than elsewhere in the United States. These were also the products of a plantation system more characterized by absentee ownership—and a diminution of European-American influences—than elsewhere. The cotton South, largely rural, and characterized by large plantations, seems not only to have conformed most clearly to classic ideas of southern slavery as an institution but also to have been the setting for the most influential slave cultural formations.

Again, however, given processes of cultural diffusion, one of the most notable things about antebellum slave life is the extent to which major cultural forms transcended regional and other barriers. Despite the diversity in the institution and its practices, it remains possible to speak of a "slave culture and consciousness" unifying large numbers of people in antebellum America.

Cultural Institutions Fundamental to slave culture and consciousness were the institutions that evolved within the world of slavery, sometimes at the sufferance of slaveholders, sometimes despite their opposition. Ties of family and kinship, often crossing plantation lines, appear to have been the primary anchor for the slave community and a source of identity for slaves as individuals. Although such ties were always vulnerable to disruption due to sale and separation, family loyalty remained a strong value in slave culture, and lines of descent were significant—reflected in, among other things, naming patterns.

Slave religion, in both its visible and its invisible forms, was another important institutional foundation for slave culture. The visible church, a product of denominational ministries to the slaves, reached increasing numbers of people through the antebellum period, including those who joined their masters and other whites for services—though usually sitting in segregated galleries—and those who attended urban churches intended mainly for African American congregations.

On the other hand, the invisible church, hidden from the purview of whites, encouraged the development of a set of beliefs and practices, drawing on both African and European sources, unique to the slave community, whether this involved forms of expression, ritual practices, or basic articles of faith. In some parts of the South, especially in coastal South Carolina, where African influences were strongest, such distinctive ritual forms as the "ring shout," a circular dance with African roots involving rhythmic clapping and hymn singing, further helped to make the institution a source for a distinctive identity.

Other elements of community life served a similar purpose. At the simplest level, off-times in the quarters provided an opportunity for a slave-initiated cultural life and a sense of identity and community. The social life available to slaves, including weekend parties and Sunday celebration, as well as the festivities allowed for holidays—especially Christmas—appears to have done much to cement a sense of community ties. So did some group work activities, such as corn shuckings, in which slaves were able to combine work with play, singing as they shucked the corn—often songs satirizing white society—and concluding the day with music and dance.

Some community activities were fairly elaborate. The Sunday dances in New Orleans's "Congo Square," involving hundreds of people and dominated by African musical and dance forms, represented an important focus for community among the city's people of African descent. Elsewhere, many slaves took part in a festival variously known as John Koonering or John Canoe. Also having roots in African traditions, this festival, usually occurring around Christmas, involved parading, flamboyant costumes, music, even wearing masks. It often included a burlesquing of slaveholders' ways, and was a visible assertion of a distinctive identity for the slave communities in which it occurred.

The distinctive identity found in such festivals, and in other cultural institutions, underlay the major tenets of slave thought and culture in the antebellum South.

The Content of Antebellum Slave Culture

Much of what is known about slave culture in the antebellum period comes from the accounts of contemporary observers. Travelers to the South, and even some white southerners, provided valuable evidence of slave cultural life. No less important were autobiographies written in the North by slaves who had fled. Encouraged by abolitionist and other antislavery organizations, such notable fugitives as Frederick Douglass, William Wells Brown, and Harriet Jacobs produced widely read narratives. If they were intended to serve the antislavery cause, they nonetheless provided reliable firsthand evidence of how the institution worked as well as portrayals of significant cultural practices and institutions within the slave community.

Still more evidence comes from oral traditions collected during and after slavery. Slave culture was, preeminently, founded in oral tradition. Literacy was certainly not absent from slave communities; estimates suggest that from 5 percent to 10 percent of slaves were literate, despite laws in several southern states intended to prohibit slaves from learning to read and write. Many fugitives had learned to read and write prior to their escape, and their literacy helped them to elude capture. Many slave preachers achieved their places in both the visible and the invisible institutions of slave religion precisely because they could read and convey Scripture to their congregations. Some literate slaves learned their skills from whites, for religious and other reasons; others, from connections within the slave community. Nevertheless, although literate men and women played an important role in slave cultural life, much of the everyday diffusion of cultural knowledge and practices was through oral forms: tales, songs, and popular customs and beliefs.

Slave folktales began to appear in popular sources during the antebellum era; they remained popular through the nineteenth century. The same is true of slave songs, especially religious songs called spirituals. Known before the Civil War, spirituals attracted great attention during the war, es-

AN EARLY SLAVE FOLKTALE

An old gentleman at the point of death, called a faithful negro to him, telling him he would do him an honour before he died. The fellow thanked him, and hoped massa would live long. I intend Cato, said the master, to allow you to be buried in the family vault. Ah massa, returns Cato, me no like dat, ten pounds would be better to Cato, he no care where he be buried; besides, massa, suppose we be buried togeder, and *de devil come looking for massa in de dark, he might take away poor negar man in mistake.*

Source: *American Museum* 5 (1789), p. 432.

pecially as Union troops and Northern teachers and missionaries began to move into liberated areas of the South. The songs were widely published in the Northern press during the war and, further disseminated by the concert performances of such groups as the Fisk University Jubilee Singers, retained their popularity through the end of the century.

The closing years of the nineteenth century and early years of the twentieth saw a great increase in the collecting of traditions with antebellum roots. Fisk University sponsored extensive collecting among ex-slaves, documenting everything from tales and songs to folk beliefs and reminiscences of slavery. Hampton Institute did so as well, creating a Folk-Lore Society and publishing many items in its journal, *The Southern Workman*. Scholarly collectors including Newbell Niles Puckett, Zora Neale Hurston, and Arthur Huff Fauset produced important collections that, although not concentrating on ex-slaves, included a great deal of material with antebellum origins. The 1930s federal Works Progress Administration (WPA) interviews with ex-slaves gathered not only personal memoirs but also oral traditions. All of these collections, and others, have provided an extensive body of evidence on which to base a description of slave culture and consciousness during the antebellum period.

Folktales. The richest source for insight into slave culture and consciousness is the large body of tales collected from slaves and ex-slaves. Although folktales were told primarily for entertainment, they had an important educational function. Presenting types of characters, dramatizing the slaves' own understanding of the kinds of situations they were likely to confront, and offering strategies for dealing with those situations, the tales were a major way in which cultural ideals and conventions were passed from community to community, and from generation to generation.

Slave folktales were of many types. Jokes were common. So were ghost stories and other supernatural tales, which often overlapped into the worlds of religion and folk belief. Most common, however, were trickster tales, many with African origins and others with clearer links to slavery itself. These tales usually involved a battle of wits, often between a strong figure and a weak figure, in which victory was far from certain and the contest often brutal.

A substantial body of trickster tales consisted of animal stories looking back specifically to trickster animal traditions from West Africa. The best-known involved the trickster rabbit, usually in competition with some larger animal, attempting to use his cleverness to get the better of his foe. The famous story of Bre'r Rabbit's tricking an angry Bre'r Bear (or some other antagonist) into throwing him into a brier patch, his natural home, was typical. Exemplifying trickery, wit, and possibilities for triumph over an ostensibly stronger antagonist, such animal tales were popular throughout the South.

No less common were tales featuring a slave everyman, "John," in his confrontations with "Old Master." Set within slavery, these tales were told throughout the South. Like the protagonists of the animal tales, John was a trickster hero living by his wits, relying on his cleverness to get the better of his master. In these tales, John might gain release from punishment, riches, or even freedom by tricking Old Master into believing it was his due.

The role of such stories seems obvious. By showing how slaves could outwit Old Master, the stories indicated the possibility of survival—sometimes more than survival—in a system based on brutality and domination. The stories showed that slaves were not without resources, however oppressive the system appeared to be. Such an explanation is only partial, however, given the range of trickster stories—including both animal stories and "John" tales—slaves told among themselves. Although, for example, in many the trickster came out on top, this was not always the case. In some, the trickster got caught in his own trickery; in a few John tales, Old Master used trickery of his own to get the better of the slave. In the popular "Master's Gone to Philly-Me-York," for example, Master, supposedly on a

EXTRACTS OF TWO TALES FROM *SOUTHERN WORKMAN:*

[Bre'r Elephant] say to Bre'r Rabbit, "I dono wedder to trow you in de fire or in de brier patch."

Bre'r Rabbit say, "Bre'r elephant what ever you do don't trow me in de briar patch but trow me in de fire." He keep on beggin' so hard to be trowed in de fire dat Bre'r Elephant tink dat hit would hurt him most, so he up wid him and trow him in de brier patch.

Time Bre'r Rabbit light on de ground he kick up his heels at Bre'r Elephant and say to 'em, "You fool, Bre'r Elephant dis where I is bred and born at" and wid dat he run off in de bushes.

Source: *Southern Workman* 23 (1894), p. 150.

Once an old slave used to make it his practice to steal hogs. The way he would be sure of the animal he would tie one end of a rope around his prey and the other around himself. The old Negro had been successful for many years in his occupation, but one time when he caught one of his master's hogs he met his equal in strength. He was fixing to have a big time on the next day, which was Sunday. He was thinking about it and had the old hog going along nicely, but at last as he was coming up on the top of a very high hill the hog got unmanageable and broke loose from the old fellow's arms. Still the old man made sure it was all right because of the rope which tied them together, so he puffed and pulled and scuffed, till the hog got the best of him and started him to going down the steep hill. The hog carried him clear to his master's house, and the master and his family were sitting on the porch. All the Negro could say, as the hog carried him around and around the house by his master was, "Master, I come to bring your pig home!"

Source: *Southern Workman* 26 (1897), p. 79.

trip to the north, relies on his own cleverness to catch John throwing an unsanctioned party in the plantation house (Levine, *Black Culture and Black Consciousness*, p. 129). In "Hog Thief," a story in which a slave is caught trying to steal one of Master's hogs, the slave's effort to extricate himself by using his wits—claiming to be returning rather than taking the hog—appeared to be something less than a clever ruse.

Thus, to the extent that these tales had an educational function, they did more than recommend the utility of trickery in an oppressive world. Rather, they helped to define the nature of that world itself, showing it to be the site of ongoing conflict and competition, a place in which trust was difficult and outcomes were unpredictable. Here was a series of messages, a worldview, conveyed across a broad range of stories and widely distributed throughout the slaveholding states.

The pervasiveness of these tales is a measure of how widely shared the views they implied must have been. With their stress on antagonism, such tales did much to define the world of slavery, presenting it as a place of conflict and uncertainty. Slaveowners were viewed not as benevolent protectors, but as men and women capable of acting arbitrarily, with no other purpose than keeping their slaves under control. Encapsulating such a view, the tales dramatized the extent to which a sense of antagonism underlay those other elements of slave cultural creation in which slaves expressed their distinctiveness from the white society in which they lived. Opposition as well as difference was a fundamental feature of slave culture and consciousness, if these tales are to be believed.

Religious traditions. No less revealing were religious traditions. These traditions were complex, operated at several levels, and, like the tales, brought together a range of sources. By the antebellum period, Christianity dominated slave religious life. The slaves' religious vocabulary was thoroughly Christian. But, as was the case with the tales, this vocabulary showed considerable adaptation to the environment created by slavery.

At one level of religious tradition were folk beliefs, including supernatural beliefs and those associated with witchcraft and related phenomena. The origins of these beliefs were various. Some were clearly of African origin; in many places, for example, slaves continued African practices of grave adornment that were tied to traditional forms of reverence for ancestral spirits. Others owed much to the European traditions preserved by whites in the South. There were also important Native American influences on slave magic and folk beliefs. Slaves synthesized a major complex of beliefs related to supernatural healing, to signs and omens—the screech owl's cry or a lowing cow as a sign of death, for example.

Southern Scenes—Cooking Shrimps. This domestic scene, reproduced from *Frank Leslie's Popular Monthly,* illustrates the common family—an anchor for slave culture and identity. COURTESY THE HISTORIC NEW ORLEANS COLLECTION, 1974.25.23.39, MUSEUM/RESEARCH CENTER, NEW ORLEANS, LA.

At the center of popular beliefs was the conjurer or "conjure doctor," present on virtually all plantations. Conjurers, whose role owed much to African witchcraft beliefs, were thought to control magical powers that could be mobilized in a broad array of situations, from healing to problems with love to a desire for revenge against another slave. They were also called upon to help with problems posed by the institution of slavery itself. Conjurers were consulted by potential runaways who hoped for magical protection. They also were sought for protection from plantation brutality, particularly by those facing a whipping. Although there is evidence that at least a few whites sought the service of noted conjurers, "hoodoo," as it was sometimes called, was thought by many slaves to be the exclusive property of African Americans, something white people could neither appreciate nor understand. It was thus, again, tied specifically to African American community and identity situated in the experiences of slavery.

Connections between conjure and more formal, Christian ideas and institutions were complex.

Many Christian slaves claimed to oppose conjure on religious grounds. However, there is little evidence that conjurers and their clients saw themselves as being in opposition to Christianity; most saw themselves as fully within the Christian orbit. Some conjurers also were plantation preachers. Slave Christianity did, however, offer a set of beliefs that was far more inclusive, more overarching, than the magical beliefs encompassed by conjuration. Like all religious systems, that created by American slaves served to describe, order, and explain the larger world within which they lived.

The independence of the slave religion is important to emphasize. Although it grew out of the mission to the slaves and took its vocabulary, and some of its practices, from the denominational messages to which slaves were exposed, it went in directions very different from those proposed by the denominational missionaries, and from the messages encouraged by the slaveholders who sponsored the missionary efforts. The missionary message, and that which slaveholders found acceptable, tended to focus on duty and obedience, and on the rewards a tractable slave could expect in heaven. Within the "invisible institution" of the slave church, however, a very different message was current, one that focused on the power of a personal God and, looking back to the revolutionary era, on the ultimate hope of freedom. This difference was significant to many Christian slaves, who rejected more than an outward compliance with denominational religion while cultivating an independent religious life free of slaveholder constraints.

The message of slave religion was expressed in a variety of ways. The sermons of slave preachers often focused on the centrality of spiritual and human equality as a principle of Christian belief. Mosaic themes of deliverance, especially the Exodus story, were incorporated into slave preaching, and the preachers drew parallels between the experience of the Israelites in Egypt and those of Africans in American bondage. Millennial elements figured in such rhetoric, as did notions of a "chosen peoplehood" that saw African slaves as having a special, providential relationship with God. Underlying all was a belief that God would protect his children and make them free.

This message was also incorporated into the conversion experiences many slaves claimed to have undergone and viewed as the foundation for their faith. Melding European and African vision traditions, slave conversions could be quite vivid. Many converts reported having had visions in which their bodies were temporarily "struck dead," allowing the soul to travel freely, often to encounter Jesus and even the devil. Accounts of such visions were not entirely unlike the slave folktales, emphasizing conflict and even containing trickster elements as Jesus and the devil battled for a convert's soul. More important, many converts reported that, as a result of conversion, they no longer perceived their situation as they had before. "Master" had been replaced, they said, by God as their real source of authority; obedience to God replaced obedience to the master as the basis for a Christian life. Many even said they feared the slaveholder's violence less than before, being able to rely on God's protection in a brutal world.

The most noted expression of both providential and personalistic ideas was found in religious song, especially the spirituals indigenous to slave religion. Although slaves used many of the same hymns sung by mainstream denominations—the popular hymns of Isaac Watts and Charles and John Wesley—and though one can find some similarities between folk hymns sung both by white and African Americans, slave communities also created a dis-

"LET MY PEOPLE GO"

When Israel was in Egypt's land,
  O, let my people go!
Oppressed so hard they could not stand,
  O, let my people go!
CHORUS—O go down, Moses,
  Away down to Egypt's land,
And tell king Pharaoh
  To let my people go! . . .
We need not always weep and mourn
  O, let my people go!
And wear these Slavery chains forlorn—
  O, let my people go!

Source: New York *Weekly Anglo-African,* 18 January 1862.

tinctive body of spirituals exclusive to the slave church.

The spirituals encapsulated key themes in slave religion. Personalistic beliefs were clear in "The Heavenly Road" as singers recounted "the rocks" Satan rolled in the Christian's way, declaring, "But Jesus is my bosom friend, /And roll 'em out de way" (Raboteau, *Slave Religion,* p. 252). The orientation toward deliverance that was no less important to slave religion was no less apparent in the popular "Go Down, Moses," with its evocation of the Exodus story and its application of that story to the lives of American slaves. Here, the message was strong enough that slaves were known to sing the song at their peril, doing so only when assured that slaveholding whites were not likely to hear it.

For most slaves, the power of religion was mainly as a consolation. The hope of freedom expressed in slave religion still looked mainly toward the future. For a few, however, the tendencies went farther. This was the case for such a slave rebel as Nat Turner, whose revolt had a major impact on Virginia in 1831. Turner in many ways epitomized tendencies in slave religion, at least if surviving accounts of his life are to be believed. A visionary, Turner felt himself personally directed by God to lead an insurrection of millennial proportions, one in which he would be the instrument of God's plan to bring slavery to an end. Few took the visionary, millennial tendencies in slave religion as far as Turner did, but his interpretation of religion was compatible with the tradition that underlay much of slave religious belief.

Cultural Traditions and the Institution of Slavery Thus, slave culture and consciousness, as they emerged in antebellum America, formed a complex product. Taking shape beginning in the seventeenth century, this culture brought together African, European, and Native American traditions with American experiences, receiving its ultimate expression in the antebellum period. There can be little doubt that the institution of slavery did much to determine the main directions of slave cultural creation. Not only did the crucible of slavery serve to forge a synthesis of diverse traditions, but the power of slavery in virtually every slave's life served to frame the development of ideals, values, and strategies that seemed workable in a difficult world.

See also **The Black Church: Invisible and Visible** (in this volume); **African Americans** (volume 2); and other articles in this section.

BIBLIOGRAPHY

Abrahams, Roger D. *Singing the Master: The Emergence of African American Culture in the Plantation South.* New York, 1992.

Berlin, Ira. *Many Thousands Gone: The First Two Centuries of Slavery in North America.* Cambridge, Mass., 1998.

Blassingame, John. *The Slave Community: Plantation Life in the Antebellum South.* Rev. and enl. ed. New York, 1979.

Butler, Jon. *Awash in a Sea of Faith: Christianizing the American People.* Cambridge, Mass., 1990.

Cornelius, Janet Duitsman. *"When I Can Read My Title Clear": Literacy, Slavery, and Religion in the Antebellum South.* Columbia, S.C., 1991.

Creel, Margaret Washington. *"A Peculiar People": Slave Religion and Community-Culture among the Gullahs.* New York, 1988.

Egerton, Douglas R. *Gabriel's Rebellion: The Virginia Slave Conspiracies of 1800 and 1802.* Chapel Hill, N.C., 1993.

Franklin, John Hope, and Loren Schweninger. *Runaway Slaves: Rebels on the Plantation.* New York, 1999.

Frey, Sylvia R. *Water from the Rock: Black Resistance in a Revolutionary Age.* Princeton, N.J., 1991.

———, and Betty Wood. *Come Shouting to Zion: African American Protestantism in the American South and British Caribbean to 1830.* Chapel Hill, N.C., 1998.

Genovese, Eugene D. *Roll, Jordan, Roll: The World the Slaves Made.* New York, 1974.

Gomez, Michael A. *Exchanging Our Country Marks: The Transformation of African Identities in the Colonial and Antebellum South.* Chapel Hill, N.C., 1998.

Gutman, Herbert G. *The Black Family in Slavery and Freedom, 1750–1925.* New York, 1976.

Joyner, Charles. *Down by the Riverside: A South Carolina Slave Community.* Urbana, Ill., 1984.

Kay, Marvin L. Michael, and Lorin Lee Cary. *Slavery in North Carolina, 1748–1775.* Chapel Hill, N.C., 1995.

King, Wilma. *Stolen Childhood: Slave Youth in Nineteenth-Century America.* Bloomington, Ind., 1995.

Kolchin, Peter. *American Slavery, 1619–1877.* New York, 1993.

Levine, Lawrence W. *Black Culture and Black Consciousness: Afro-American Folk Thought from Slavery to Freedom.* New York, 1977.

Malone, Ann Patton. *Sweet Chariot: Slave Family and Household Structure in Nineteenth-Century Louisiana.* Chapel Hill, N.C., 1992.

Morgan, Philip D. *Slave Counterpoint: Black Culture in the Eighteenth-Century Chesapeake and Lowcountry.* Chapel Hill, N.C., 1998.

Piersen, William D. *Black Yankees: The Development of an Afro-American Sub-culture in Eighteenth-Century New England.* Amherst, Mass., 1988.

Raboteau, Albert J. *Slave Religion: The "Invisible Institution" in the Antebellum South.* New York, 1978.

Sidbury, James. *Ploughshares into Swords: Race, Rebellion, and Identity in Gabriel's Virginia, 1730–1810.* Cambridge, U.K., 1997.

Sobel, Mechal. *The World They Made Together: Black and White Values in Eighteenth-Century Virginia.* Princeton, N.J., 1987.

Stampp, Kenneth M. *The Peculiar Institution: Slavery in the Ante-Bellum South.* New York, 1956.

Stuckey, Sterling. *Slave Culture: Nationalist Theory and the Foundations of Black America.* New York, 1987.

Thomas, Hugh. *The Slave Trade: The Story of the Atlantic Slave Trade, 1440–1870.* New York, 1997.

Webber, Thomas L. *Deep like the Rivers: Education in the Slave Quarter Community, 1831–1865.* New York, 1978.

White, Shane, and Graham White. *Stylin': African American Expressive Culture from Its Beginnings to the Zoot Suit.* Ithaca, N.Y., 1998.

Wood, Betty. *Women's Work, Men's Work: The Informal Slave Economies of Lowcountry Georgia.* Athens, Ga., 1995.

Wood, Peter H. *Black Majority: Negroes in Colonial South Carolina from 1670 through the Stono Rebellion.* New York, 1975.

THOUGHT AND CULTURE IN THE
FREE BLACK COMMUNITY

Graham Russell Hodges

The cultural and intellectual history of free African Americans is complicated by a number of factors. Fundamentally, they were identified by what they were not: slaves. However, hampered by punitive laws during the colonial and national eras, free blacks often could not own property, marry legally, vote, or hold office. Personal mobility and access to many occupations were often restricted. Common early in the seventeenth century, their numbers dwindled through enslavement and then remained few through colonial times. Their numbers soared after the American Revolution, and soon thereafter the overwhelming majority of northern blacks were free. Meanwhile, southern free people of color increasingly found their liberty sharply curtailed. Degrees of freedom, effected by the politics of each state, affected the cultural and intellectual traditions of free blacks.

Until recently, scant attention was given to these traditions. The existence of a record of free black cultural and intellectual accomplishments is owed first to emancipated African Americans themselves, beginning with pamphleteers who commemorated black achievements in the early nineteenth century. Black abolitionists in the antebellum period based much of their comprehension of black history on these examples. After the Civil War, historians led by George Washington Williams and, later, by W. E. B. Du Bois, chronicled the overall history of free blacks. In the twentieth century, the Association for the Study of Negro Life and History, founded in 1915 by Carter G. Woodson, its *Journal of Negro History,* and Du Bois's unceasing efforts sustained memory of free black traditions in defiance of white academic indifference.

In the late twentieth century, the subject of African American historiography became politicized over issues of acculturation versus African retention or Africanity, with *Slave Culture* (1987), by Sterling Stuckey, being a key work in this debate. Through the use of biographies, studies of the abolitionist movement, literary criticism of black narratives,

and the growing integration of African American history into American historiography, the importance of free black thought has become critical to the comprehension of slavery and freedom in early America. While significant institutions such as churches, political lobbying groups, and educational societies are discussed, attention is also given to free black culture as expressed in noninstitutional ways and in brief, evanescent moments.

THE COLONIAL ERA AND REVOLUTIONARY WAR

In the sixteenth century, free Africans joined exploring parties along the coast or in the interior of North America. Oceangoing pilots such as Jan Rodrigues in New Amsterdam and Esteban, who traveled along the Atlantic Coast and into New Spain (later the U.S. Southwest and Mexico) were *bricoleurs* (cultural brokers) who melded together African, European, and Native American cultures. Isabel de Olvera, a free black woman who arrived in Santa Fe in 1600, expected her free status would protect her from slavery. Assertions of freedom in former countries were made by many of the sixteenth-century black arrivals in New England, New Amsterdam and New York, Virginia, and Maryland. Frequently, people of color passed briefly through the tiny fortifications and ports along the coast, leaving behind commodities such as the cowrie shell, from Africa, which became a key component of wampum. Those who stayed often farmed and joined the dominant European religions, hoping that conversion would ensure their freedom. Methods of religious observance included rituals such as Pinkster (Pentecost) in New York and New Jersey; Negro Election Day, a mock plebiscite held by enslaved blacks in New England to elect a governor or king; and Jonne Canoe (Jonkonnu), in which enslaved blacks wore fantastic clothing including ox horns attached to the skin of raccoons, drawn over the head and face, in southern colonies and the West Indies. These rituals were, from the late seventeenth century onward, replete with African music, dancing, and song. They were aspects of "slave culture" or secular activities by a combination of enslaved blacks and a small number of free blacks that appeared in the taverns, streets, and wharves of port cities, combining African retentions with hybrids of the music, dance, and language of European conquest nations. Free blacks and enslaved Africans regularly frolicked together to the consternation of white authorities. As Du Bois has noted, from these frolics emerged the first forms of African American music.

Acculturation began in earnest after 1700 via the missionary arm of the Church of England. Under Crown orders, the Society for the Propagation of the Gospel in Foreign Parts (SPG) catechized free blacks and slaves in New England, the Middle Colonies, and the Upper and Lower South. To appease worried slave owners anxious about the effects of education on enslaved Africans, the SPG sponsored successful legislation that separated conversion to Christianity from civil freedom. At the same time, the Atlantic colonies passed black codes that denied free blacks access to property ownership, politics, and many occupations, and that, overall, lowered their status perilously close to enslavement. Despite these controls, the SPG schools remained controversial and small, with only domestic slaves and free blacks permitted to attend lessons. Education remained an elusive talisman of freedom for the rest. Du Bois identified SPG schools as the original source of the Talented Tenth, even though most clerical instructors cowed before slave masters and taught only on the latter's terms. Near the end of the colonial period, Anglican clerics in New York City described educated blacks as being capable of performing religious services for their own kind. The historian Jon Butler subsequently revised Du Bois by insisting that the SPG schools created a holocaust of African culture and made free blacks mere emulators of European mores. Though not going as far as Butler, similar findings by William Pierson regarding black Yankees and Joyce Goodfriend regarding New York City blacks point to a small, strongly acculturated sector of the free black population. By contrast Stuckey, in his *Slave Culture,* and Margaret Washington Creel in her study *A Peculiar People: Slave Religion and Community-Culture among the Gullahs* (New York, 1988), point to the connections between African *poro* and *sande* secret cultures, which initiated young Africans into

W. E. B. Du Bois. A prolific journalist and author, Du Bois (1868–1963) also edited *The Crisis,* the journal of the NAACP, from 1910 to 1934. © CORBIS

adulthood and were the precursors of subsequent free black fraternal organizations in South Carolina.

The high barriers to emancipation in all colonies forced discontented blacks to liberate themselves through flight. Self-emancipated blacks found refuge in the cities, on the frontier, or on the ocean. Studies of runaways in New York, East Jersey, and South Carolina have found that fiddling was common among fugitives, marking a glimpse of a tradition of African American popular music. In the cities, free blacks sought confederacy in urban gangs, which occasionally turned revolutionary. For example, in New York City, free black "doctors," self-appointed medical practitioners skilled in the use of poisonous herbs and folk medicine who took leadership roles in black gangs through their positions as learned men, worked in tandem with slaves to spark revolts in 1712 and 1741. There were few free blacks in coastal colonies before the American Revolution.

Free blacks made notable contributions. The poet Phillis Wheatley and the enslaved poet Jupiter

Hammon secured praise from even the most critical whites late in the colonial period. Black autobiographical narratives represented an emerging black literary and intellectual tradition. The desire of paternalist Anglicans to produce perfect domestics brought education to favored servants. Influenced by their education, some of these blacks wrote narratives modeled upon *Pilgrim's Progress* (1678), by the Englishman John Bunyan. These black autobiographers described how they were enslaved, then educated and converted, and finally freed either by a kindly master or their own efforts. The narrators Venture Smith, James Albert Ukawsaw Gronniosaw, John Jea, and Britton Hammon depicted picaresque events that tossed them about the Atlantic, and went on to describe how, invariably, their faith and growing self-identification as free blacks eventually produced salvation.

In an important development that would inspire hopes for black freedom, the antislavery movement among whites arose in the Society of Friends (Quakers). In 1758 the Philadelphia Yearly Meeting of the Society of Friends concluded that enslavement was unchristian and called upon those within its jurisdiction to emancipate their bondspeople. This decision impacted powerfully upon slavery in Pennsylvania, Maryland, and, later, Delaware, New York, and New Jersey. By the Revolution about four hundred free blacks lived in Pennsylvania, by far the largest concentration in the colonies. Though Quakers rarely admitted blacks into their congregations, the society's message confirmed what blacks had always believed: that slavery was contrary to God's will. Free blacks flocked to churches, such as the nascent Methodist denomination, that supported this position and made it a central tenet of their culture.

The American Revolution produced a free black culture charged with revolutionary ideals and behavior. During the conflict, many blacks sided with the British. Though such practices were derided in patriot newspapers, descriptions of integrated balls indicate that British officers and soldiers mingled and danced with African Americans. In New York City and Charleston, which were occupied by the British for much of the war, free black musicians played openly at these racially integrated balls. Educated black leaders including ministers David George, John Marrant, Boston King, and George Liele went into exile in Nova Scotia, the Bahamas, and Jamaica after the close of the war. Though the British were as slippery in their promises as the patriots, most free blacks felt greater loyalty to Britain than to the American republic for decades after. For some free blacks the move to British-controlled areas of the Americas was not enough. In 1791 over one thousand black Loyalists made a hegira from Nova Scotia to Sierra Leone, popularizing a return to Africa among disaffected free blacks.

POSTREVOLUTIONARY FREE BLACKS

In the postrevolutionary era, the free blacks remaining in the United States sought greater liberty for themselves and for enslaved African Americans. Creation of an African American political identity involved building on the foundations of African beliefs and values mixed with the heady republicanism spawned by the Revolution.

Freedom became the dominant status for blacks in postrevolutionary New England and, after 1803, in New York, Pennsylvania, and New Jersey as well. Scarce before the Revolution, free blacks rose in number to almost 60,000 in 1790 and then trebled to 186,000 over the next twenty years. In 1810 there were as many free blacks in the Upper South as in the North, where slavery was in the process of gradual extinction by then. The Upper South (Maryland, Virginia, and North Carolina) was home to 75,000 free blacks, while 75,000 lived in the North. In the Lower South, only 6,000 blacks lived in freedom, though that was an increase of more than 200 percent over 1790 when there were only 2,200. In the newly acquired territories, variations of skin color complicated the makeup of black societies. The purchase of the Louisiana Territory in 1803 brought about 2,000 free blacks into the nation's population. These Creoles, as they were known, were largely the product of interracial relations between white men and black women. As in Charleston, South Carolina, light-skinned free blacks in New Orleans formed a conservative middle culture between whites and slaves and participated heavily in the territory's militia. In Charleston, light-skinned free blacks formed a Brown Fellowship Society in 1790 and opened a school three years later.

The drastic increase in the number of free blacks stemmed from postrevolutionary egalitarianism, the emergence of Methodism as an antislavery denomination, and rising disgust with the Atlantic slave trade. These factors induced all states in the North to abolish slavery, convinced many masters in all regions to bargain freedom with their slaves, and produced a vibrant free black community, particularly in the cities. Though Methodism's antislavery fervor soon cooled and white politics became more conservative, new factors came into play. Some blacks, taking advantage of liberal judicial attitudes after the Revolution, sued successfully for liberty. Freedom suits affected only a small number of African Americans. Flight remained the most common route to freedom as turbulent young blacks emancipated themselves by escaping from their masters. Finally, Toussaint Louverture's successful revolt against the French in Sainte Domingue (later Haiti) brought a number of newly freed blacks into New York City, Charleston, and New Orleans. Enlivening these cities with their Afrocentric culture, these migrants also brought heady news of the new black republic.

For two decades after the American Revolution, free blacks were a highly mobile group. Over eight thousand blacks left with the British in 1783. Their example spurred a strong current of thinking among postrevolutionary free blacks about migration to more hospitable climes. For example, Paul Cuffe, the noted black sea captain, visited black Loyalists in Africa and encouraged African Americans to repatriate. Though Cuffe was received very warmly in New York, Boston, Philadelphia, and Baltimore, few black Americans left for Africa. One reason was the American Colonization Society, founded a year before Cuffe's death in 1817. The society combined dubious racial attitudes with an intent of promoting black migration to Liberia, and soon free African Americans cooled on African return. Haiti became an alluring spot for resettlement, though few blacks actually moved there. The choice of exile or a quest for freedom and citizenship in the United States created what W. E. B. Du Bois called a double consciousness among free blacks; while Americans, they were also black people with a yearning for African culture, if not residence.

At first, free black life centered on the church. In the wake of the Revolution, a free black ministry sprang up in the cities. Emerging from African societies, which appeared first in Philadelphia, then in New York and Boston, clerics Richard Allen, Absalom Jones, Nathaniel Paul, Peter Williams Jr., and a host of others first aligned themselves with the Methodists, Baptists, and Episcopalians. Stymied by racial barriers to a black ministry and chafing under white controls, these clerics led their congregations out of the parent church into independence. Black churches, whether offspring of staid denominations such as the Episcopalians (former Anglicans) or more expressive creeds such as the Methodists and Baptists, soon produced their own protocols, hymnbooks and songs, and evocative styles of worship, which stressed the sacrifices and examples of Jesus and his disciples. Believing that the meek shall inherit the earth, African American Methodists perceived themselves as the true inheritors of those sacrifices. Overriding all these efforts was a fierce biblical independence and self-determination. The black church movement spread rapidly through the young nation. By the late 1820s, conferences of African Methodist Episcopal churches were held throughout the Mid-Atlantic states and Ohio. In the South such conferences became so controversial that they were banned after the Denmark Vesey conspiracy in 1822. Religious themes mixed with antislavery in the early poetry of Noah Calwell W. Cannon and John Jea, itinerant Methodist ministers. Cannon's poetry evokes the power of Jehovah to free blacks stolen from Africa in the slave trade, while Jea's poems reveal the sustaining strength of Christ's messages for a beleaguered free black sailor.

Free black churches shared membership with mutual aid societies, which began sprouting up in northern cities during the last two decades of the eighteenth century. Initially intended to help indigent free blacks and ensure proper burials, the black association movement quickly expanded into abolitionist activities. These organizations were often named in honor of white abolitionists, as with the Wilberforce Philanthropic Society (New York City, 1810), the Rush Benevolent Society (Philadelphia, 1805), the Female Benezet Society (Philadelphia, 1818), and the Humane and Friendly Society (Charleston, 1802). Such groups spread even more rapidly in the 1830s, when Philadelphia had as many as thirty of these organizations.

Free blacks created a historical narrative with political intentions. For example, clerical orations in New York, Boston, and Philadelphia in the first decade of the nineteenth century were intended to celebrate black achievements and were forwarded to Presidents Thomas Jefferson and James Monroe to convince them to end the foreign slave trade. The success of their endeavors brought a spate of pamphlets by black voices rejoicing in this abolitionist achievement. For example, each year in New York City, Peter Williams Jr. and others met to commemorate the end of the legal foreign trade in 1808 and then published an annual oration extolling black accomplishments. The translation and publication in 1810 of Henri Grégoire's *Enquiry concerning the Intellectual and Moral Faculties and Literature of Negroes* inspired free blacks to compose brief biographies of the accomplishments of historic men and women of color. Haiti remained an inspiration for free black artists. The poet Charles Boyer Fashon wrote odes to the heroism of Vincent Ogé, whose exploits are featured in Grégoire's narrative.

Key offshoots of the black church movement were schools for free blacks. Direct descendants of the SPG charity schools, free schools were sponsored by churches and were partially supported by city funds. Beginning in 1787, for example, the African Free School in New York educated over one hundred young blacks annually in the basics of literacy, classical literature, and mathematics and geared them for careers at sea with courses in navigation. By the early 1800s, graduates of the school formed a principal part of the free black middle class in the city. Among its most illustrious graduates were minister Peter Williams Jr., physician James McCune Smith, actor Ira Aldridge, and artist Patrick Reason. Other graduates included abolitionist leaders Henry Highland Garnet, Alexander Crummell, and Samuel Ringgold Ward. Charles Lewis Reason, another graduate, wrote poetry that reflected the melding of religious and antislavery themes. Although the school remained popular in the 1820s, free blacks tired of the paternalistic, veiled racism of its principal, Charles C. Andrews. When he announced his support for colonization of free blacks, parents quickly deserted the Free School for public schools and experimental, black-run institutions. As black identity swept the free black class in the North, adult students also left the church-supported Sunday schools, which provided literacy education to all ages.

Free blacks were frustrated in their desire for a college education. Talented young blacks such as James McCune Smith and Alexander Crummell had to travel to England to study because of discrimination at home. Oberlin College in north central Ohio, Bowdoin in Maine, and the Madison Institute (later Colgate) in upstate New York were among the few schools to admit blacks. In 1849, New York Central College in McGrawville, New York, near Cortland, opened as an explicitly antislavery, integrationist school. Funded by white philanthropists, its faculty included Charles Reason, professor of Greek, Latin, mathematics, and natural philosophy. The student body was, however, probably just 10 percent black. The school ran into financial difficulties and collapsed during the depression of 1857.

Outside of the churches and schools, the secular culture continued to flourish into the nineteenth century. Free blacks and enslaved African Americans frolicked together at festivals. Pinkster, a vulgarized religious holiday, became explicitly African after 1800. As with other black holidays such as General Training Day and Negro Election Day, Pinkster festivals sported processions of blacks in festive garb; much drinking, dancing, and music; and the crowning of a black king. In the 1990s, a debate between Sterling Stuckey and Shane White focused on Pinkster's basic message. Was it a fusion of African survivals in music and dance mixed with European culture, as Stuckey suggested, or an example of a momentary release of social pressures, as White maintained? Whatever the answer, the debate highlighted the continued significance of the origins of free black thought. White, in his book *Stylin'* (1998), took culture in new directions by pointing out the importance of black styles of dress, hair, dance, and drinking among urban blacks. For example, he described blacks wearing tea leads in hair braids, dancing at the Catherine Street market in New York City or at fancy-dress balls in Philadelphia. Poorer free blacks frequented taverns, much to the dismay of their middle-class brethren.

In the early 1840s, popular free black culture became fashionable among whites. Black entertainers had long been staples of public music and dance in the cities. Partly displaced in the late 1830s by Jim Crow artists (white singers performing Negro songs in blackface) free black musicians flourished in interracial neighborhoods like the Five Points in New York City. A trip to the Five Points was required for any international tourist. In his *American Notes* (1867), Charles Dickens recorded his observations of a free black band at Almack's Tavern where a black fiddler and tambourine player spurred on interracial dancers. Another writer chronicled how "negro melodies" were derived from Scottish or Irish tunes. As historians have pointed out, Jim Crow musicians reflected the nasty racial animosities of the period. While Jim Crow musicians were invariably white, they appropriated and ridiculed black artists. Genuine black artists, performing in basement dives around the Five Points, formed bands that created the first African American popular music. Almack's was a site where blacks advanced a performance style that still resonates. Similarly, in rural areas black taverns such as that of Sylvia Du Bois in Somerset County, New Jersey, were places where free blacks created a syncretic style of American popular music. Finally, free blacks using personal styles of dress, hair, and posture established in locales like these the prototypes for such legendary urban figures as Stagger Lee and Frankie and Johnny.

THE MILITANT 1830s

However expressed, free black culture was almost always political. James Forten, for example, a wealthy free sailmaker in Philadelphia, wrote an influential pamphlet entitled *A Series of Letters by a Man of Color* (1813), which protested discriminatory laws in Pennsylvania. Those who see revolutionary content in free black culture may point to contemporary studies of the freedmen Gabriel Prosser and Denmark Vesey. Enthused by revolutionary republicanism and Old Testament theology, and operating out of taverns, fields, and plantations, they planned massive revolts against slavery in Virginia in 1800 and South Carolina in 1822. Though defeated, their examples terrified southern whites and became inspirations to free blacks throughout the nation.

Walker's Appeal, published in 1829, announced the rise of militant free black abolitionist advocacy. David Walker, who lived in Boston and worked as a used clothing salesman and agent for black New York City newspapers, wrote his jeremiad as a dialogue between himself and President Thomas Jefferson, the author of the Declaration of Independence. Walker, in a series of pointed questions, asked how Jefferson could empower egalitarianism and yet describe blacks as intellectual inferiors in his *Notes on the State of Virginia* (1787). Walker concluded that because of Jefferson's contradictions, which had ramifications through American society, blacks had no choice but to follow the examples of Prosser and Vesey and revolt against slavery. Walker's work, which he smuggled hidden in secondhand clothing to southern slaves, became so controversial that ownership in some southern states was a capital offense, the only book in American letters to be so dangerous to its readers. Walker's book resonated through the free black middle class.

Black minister Samuel Cornish, aided by John Russwurm, the first black college graduate (Bowdoin, 1826), published the initial black newspaper, *Freedom's Journal*, from 1827 to 1829. Its weekly issues chronicled black history and current events and hosted lively debates over what constituted proper black culture. Cornish was intent, like many of his peers, on proving black equality with whites, and so promoted self-help, temperance, and manners along with staunch antislavery. The newspaper died after Cornish turned it over to Russwurm, who resigned suddenly to move to Liberia, a decision that scandalized the paper's readers. Free blacks anxious about proper manners, however, needed to look no further than *House Servant's Directory* (1827), by Robert Roberts, which described for servants the ways to perform their various tasks.

Historians have generally assumed that militant abolitionism stemmed from the demand by William Lloyd Garrison for the immediate abolition of slavery, made in Boston on 4 July 1829 and published in *The National Philanthropist*. Free blacks, however, had striven for an immediate end to slavery for over twenty years and had been opposed to the American Colonization Society (ACS) since its founding in 1816. After publication of *Walker's Appeal* in 1829, and in the same year of the firebrand pamphlet *The Ethiopian Manifesto*, by Robert Alexander Young, free blacks pursued a full antislavery agenda. Over the next two decades, free blacks built staunch resistance to slavery and northern racism through their literature and journalism. It is no exaggeration to state that their unceasing antislavery effort remains among the most politicized activities by intellectuals in American history.

Free black activists in northern cities were influenced by revolutionary republicanism, evangelical religion, and racial solidarity. They came from the ranks of ministers, artisans, and professionals; were educated at free African schools; and, in some cases, held advanced degrees. In time they were joined by self-emancipated slaves who came North. Frederick Douglass was but the most famous of these many former slaves.

There was much for them to do. Free blacks in all states and cities faced rising hostility in all sectors of society and politics. They experienced abuse when merely walking the streets, along with racial discrimination in housing, employment, and transport. Schools and colleges were generally segregated. White Americans from the president on down regarded colonization as the proper way to dispose of free blacks. Though free blacks rarely could vote or hold office, they responded in the 1830s by organizing annual national conventions, lobbying abolitionist groups and local and national politicians, creating a press, and working energetically on self-help projects. By 1840 they had established a shadow political order to oppose the worsening racial situation.

In 1833 white abolitionists formed the American Anti-Slavery Society (AASS), in which some blacks participated and a few held office. Meanwhile, the convention movement was the widest-ranging effort by free blacks. Initiated in 1830, the convention movement attacked slavery and racism and demanded civil rights for free blacks including the right to testify in court, the right to serve on juries, and unrestricted suffrage. Invariably, free blacks at conventions preached the value of temperance, morality, education, economy, and self-help. The conventions sought not special consideration, but equality or opportunity. The initial movement lapsed after a few years, then was revived once more in the 1840s. By the 1850s free blacks in California and other western states, many having moved to escape racism in the East, were holding their own conventions.

Free blacks published a wide variety of newspapers, pamphlets, books, poems, and magazines in the 1830s. They enthusiastically supported Benjamin Lundy's *Genius of Universal Emancipation,* William Lloyd Garrison's *Liberator,* and the *Emancipator,* published by the AASS; free blacks were regular correspondents for these newspapers. David Ruggles, an agent for the *Emancipator,* established his own imprint with the publication of his pamphlet, *Abrogation of the Seventh Commandment by the American Churches* (1835). He was also the author of several anti-ACS pamphlets and operated a bookstore on Lispenard Street that sold antislavery materials. In 1838 Ruggles, by then one of the most militant abolitionists, published the first black magazine, the *Mirror of Liberty,* of which five issues appeared over the next three years. Ruggles was a key writer for the *Colored American,* the second black newspaper, which Samuel Cornish and Philip Bell published from 1837 to 1841. The *Colored American* acted as a national paper for free blacks; although containing other news, the weekly concentrated on antislavery and anti-ACS articles. Other short-lived newspapers followed. In 1842 Henry Highland Garnet and William H. Allan published the *National Watchman Clarion* in Troy, New York. Stephen Myers edited and published the *Elevator* in Albany, New York. Martin R. Delaney issued the *Mystery* in Pittsburgh, Pennsylvania, in 1843. Among the most militant was the *Ram's Horn,* published by Willis Augustus Hodges in Brooklyn in 1847. After migrating to California, Philip Bell published the *Pacific Appeal* in 1862.

David Ruggles was noted for his activities as founder and secretary of the New York Vigilance Committee (1835), an organization of free blacks and whites intent on protecting northern blacks from kidnapping and sale in the South, and equally desirous of shielding self-emancipated slaves from recapture. Ruggles's name and his skills became widely known across the country. Angry whites attempted to smuggle him to the South. Ruggles fought against slave catchers in the streets, and to runaway bondspeople he was the most visible person in the Underground Railroad. Frederick Augustus Bailey came to Ruggles after slipping away from his home in Maryland in 1838. Ruggles transferred him to New Bedford, Massachusetts, where he became nationally famous as Frederick Douglass, the great orator, and in 1845 the author of the most famous slave narrative. Ruggles, however, was just one member of a network of free blacks and sympathetic whites. Along the northeastern coast, up the Appalachian Mountains through Pennsylvania and upstate New York, through Ohio and westward through Michigan, self-freed bondspeople found succor in a thousand homes. When southern politicians demanded that the free states and the federal government return the fugitives, free blacks banded together to "rescue" them.

During the 1830s free blacks sustained community through interconnected fraternal and educational societies. Black freemasonry, initiated in Boston in the 1780s, spread widely among urban free blacks. Black freemasons promoted education for blacks. The less elitist Order of Odd Fellows concentrated on mutual aid activities such as illness and burial insurance.

Scholars have criticized the black societies as exclusive and parochial. The Negro convention movement of the 1830s collapsed when it lost its focus on such issues as antislavery and the colonization movements in favor of general appeals for universal humanity and such specifically political protests as opposition to the annexation of Texas. Still, the presence of these societies helped buffer free blacks from the disappointments and disunion that plagued reform movements. For example, since black leadership and activities had an organizational base in the societies, they survived the 1840 split in the antislavery movement. Free blacks, therefore, continued to pursue their own goals. Among these was the quest for the vote. Blacks had voted in several northern states before their right to vote was burdened by oppressive property qualifications in the first decades of the nineteenth century. The creation of the Political Improvement Association of New York in 1838 and massive protests against disfranchisement by Philadelphia blacks the same year were signs that free blacks were unwilling to accept second-class citizenship. Protest continued through the Civil War period, paving the way for the Fifteenth Amendment to the Constitution. Historian Leonard Curry has highlighted five roles of black societies. First, they enabled individual blacks to act in concert with others to accomplish necessary tasks and protect themselves against personal disaster. Second, societies enhanced black knowledge of institutional management. Third, societies helped free blacks communicate with each other in a hostile world. Fourth, membership counteracted

337

anomie fostered by the fluidity, rootlessness, and apparent ephemerality of urban life. Fifth and last, they fostered a sense of community.

Black women joined males in self-help organizations. In Philadelphia they made up more than 60 percent of members in black beneficial societies. The African Dorcas Societies in Philadelphia and New York City dispensed clothing to indigent blacks and encouraged young people to attend schools. In New Orleans, the Colored Female Benevolent Society of Louisiana sought to suppress vice among poorer blacks. In New York City, the Female Literary Society promoted reading, as did the Philomathean Society and the Phoenix Society. Poets Francis Ellen Watkins Harper, Charlotte Forten Grimké, and Ann Plato produced verses extolling the courage of participants in the Underground Railroad. Hester Lane of New York City was a philanthropist who purchased whole families out of slavery and then freed them. Jarena Lee and Sojourner Truth were pentecostal preachers. Maria Stewart, who gave public lectures in Boston in the early 1830s, exhorted black males to learn trades and become businessmen to demonstrate their manliness. Perhaps the most famous black woman before the Civil War was Harriet Tubman, the "Moses of her people." After her escape from slavery in 1849, Tubman returned to the South again and again as a conductor on the Underground Railroad.

THE 1840s AND 1850s

Discouraged by the indifference of national politicians to their plight and angered by a worsening racial climate, free blacks began to rethink African migration in the late 1830s. Migration to Sierra Leone and Liberia, intellectually taboo for over twenty-five years, became newly attractive in the 1840s. This new trend was announced in Hosea Easton's *Treatise on the Intellectual Character and Civil and Political Condition of the Colored People of the United States* (1837). Easton raised strong doubts about the feasibility of African Americans' achieving equality in a racist United States. He argued that African Americans descended from peaceful civilizations in Egypt and Africa while white Americans came from naturally violent Europeans. Easton's positive accounts of Africa and its history resurrected black American interest in resettlement there. In 1841, James W. C. Pennington wrote *A Textbook of the Origin and History of Colored People,* which emphasized legacies of the African past. In 1836 Robert B. Lewis authored *Light*

and Truth, the first black-authored history of African Americans, constructed from the Bible and ancient and modern histories. Alexander Crummell in *The Duty of a Rising Christian State to Contribute to the World's Well-being and Civilization, and the Means by Which It May Perform the Same: The Annual Oration before the Common Council and the Citizens of Monrovia, Liberia—July 26, 1855* (1855), and Martin R. Delaney in *The Condition, Elevation, Emigration, and Destiny of the Colored People in the United States, Politically Considered* (1852), contended that African Americans could not only elevate Africa by bringing Christianity there, but also build societies on that continent which would bring relief from the racial hazards of life in the United States. Theirs were but the first of many articles and books by free blacks that sought to bring understanding and hope by examining the African past.

The 1840s were also notable for the rise of Frederick Douglass and the tradition of the slave narrative. After his successful flight from slavery in 1838, the abolitionist movement became aware of his oratorical skills and put him on tour in the early 1840s. The 1845 narrative by this handsome, charismatic, highly intelligent, and ambitious former slave was met with immediate acclaim and high sales. Other self-emancipated slaves had published their narratives before Douglass, but his was the first to achieve high literary status. It also attracted support for the antislavery cause. In 1847 Douglass started his own newspaper, *The North Star,* to the dismay of William Lloyd Garrison, and began canvassing the country as America's first major black leader. Soon, other black narrators took to the lecture circuit. Fugitives William and Ellen Craft told how she posed as a white male and he as a servant. Henry "Box" Brown delighted audiences on tour by describing how he mailed himself to the North in a large wooden box. In 1851 Sojourner Truth began entrancing audiences with her saga of enslavement in rural New York; after the talk, she sold the narrative of her life, her "book of life" along with *cartes de visite.* These itinerant narrators humanized the antislavery movement for Americans across the free states and led many to accept its views, once considered too radical. It has often been remarked that the novel *Uncle Tom's Cabin* (1852), by Harriet Beecher Stowe, transformed northern opinion toward slavery, but the way was unquestionably paved by the many free blacks who told their stories of bondage.

The decade before the Civil War began in a terrifying fashion for free blacks. The federal Fugitive Slave Act of 1850, designed to prevent disunion

Harriet Tubman with Former Slaves Whom She Rescued. Tubman (*at far left*) guided over three hundred slaves to freedom. © BETTMANN/CORBIS

among the states, powerfully suggested to black Americans that none among them was safe. Under the terms of the act, municipalities used militias to ensure the return of fugitive bondspeople to the slave states. Numerous black congregations in New York City lost half of their members as blacks fled to Canada, out of reach of slave catchers. No political party seemed interested in their plight. Slave traders moved easily in and out of the port of New York. The U.S. Supreme Court's Dred Scott decision of 1857 identified inferior legal status as the constitutionally ordained condition of blacks, slave or free.

Free blacks were determined to resist the Fugitive Slave Act. Boston's black community presents a good example. There, blacks organized to defend self-emancipated former slaves. Lewis Hayden, self-emancipated himself, turned his home into an armed fortress to defend Ellen and William Craft. The couple then left for England. In 1851 an armed black mob broke into a federal courthouse and spirited Fred "Shadrach" Wilkins off to Canada to save him from a return to southern enslavement. The

state and federal government had to bring in massive force to return to slavery Thomas Sims in 1851 and Anthony Burns in 1854. Free black members of the Twelfth Baptist Church then purchased Burns. These dramatic moments, in which thousands of white and black citizens tried to impede the enforcement of federal laws, demonstrated how the mainstream of northern society had moved closer to the perspectives of free black abolitionism.

To establish the principle that blacks were worthy of full equality, free black William Cooper Nell wrote *Colored Patriots of the American Revolution* in 1855 to describe African American support for the patriot cause in the American Revolution. Similarly, Boston blacks established Crispus Attucks Day to honor the hero of the Boston Massacre in 1770 and used the holiday to denounce the federal government and slavery. But with the government in Washington becoming ever more the handmaiden of the slave owners during the 1850s, many free blacks began giving up on protest; to them, migration to Africa seemed an increasingly appealing option.

THE CIVIL WAR

President Abraham Lincoln, who consulted regularly with Frederick Douglass and received Sojourner Truth in the White House, was far more open to black voices than any previous American president. Yet he was opposed to outright abolition, flirted with colonization schemes, and announced at the beginning of the Civil War that he was fighting only to preserve the Union. Free blacks, however, knew that the conflict was inseparably connected to slavery and that the war's outcome would determine the fate of that institution. "Our national sin has found us out," proclaimed *Douglass's Monthly* in 1861. They applauded Lincoln's careful steps toward the Emancipation Proclamation, issued finally on 1 January 1863. In San Francisco, blacks celebrated the proclamation with public speeches and festivals. Local black poet James Madison Bell honored the occasion with a poem entitled "A Fitting Time to Celebrate." In 1864, blacks in New York City hailed the formation of a black regiment when it paraded down Broadway. Across the free states, blacks swept into the Union army by the thousands. The frustration and anger of the preceding decades were cast aside as black soldiers played an instrumental role in defeating the Confederacy. In the North, free blacks welcomed people of color escaping from a crumbling Confederacy. Frederick Douglass, Henry Highland Garnet, and other black leaders planned for further postwar political efforts. Their lobbying helped to secure passage of the Thirteenth, Fourteenth, and Fifteenth Amendments to the Constitution, which respectively ended slavery, guaranteed black citizenship, and enfranchised black men. Every step occurred within the framework of a free black cultural and intellectual tradition that focused on collective needs and demanded reform of American society and politics.

See also **The Black Church: Invisible and Visible** *(in this volume);* **African Americans** *(volume 2);* **Race** *(volume 3).*

BIBLIOGRAPHY

Berlin, Ira. *Many Thousands Gone: The First Two Centuries of Slavery in North America.* Cambridge, Mass., 1998.

——. *Slaves without Masters: The Free Negro in the Antebellum South.* New York, 1974.

Blackett, R. J. M. *Beating against the Barriers: Biographical Essays in Afro-American History.* Baton Rouge, La., 1986.

Blight, David W. *Frederick Douglass' Civil War: Keeping Faith in Jubilee.* Baton Rouge, La., 1989.

Curry, Leonard P. *The Free Black in Urban America, 1800–1850: The Shadow of the Dream.* Chicago, 1981.

Gomez, Michael A. *Exchanging Our Country Marks: The Transformation of African Identities in the Colonial and Antebellum South.* Chapel Hill, N.C., 1998.

Hodges, Graham Russell. *Root and Branch: African Americans in New York and East Jersey, 1613–1863.* Chapel Hill, N.C., 1999.

Horton, James Oliver, and Lois E. Horton. *In Hope of Liberty: Culture, Community, and Protest among Northern Free Blacks, 1700–1860.* New York, 1997.

Nash, Gary B. *Forging Freedom: The Formation of Philadelphia's Black Community, 1720–1840.* Cambridge, Mass., 1988.

Nash, Gary B., and Jean R. Soderlund. *Freedom by Degrees: Emancipation in Pennsylvania and Its Aftermath.* New York, 1991.

Peterson, Carla L. *"Doers of the Word": African-American Women Speakers and Writers in the North (1830–1880).* New York, 1995.

Quarles, Benjamin. *Black Abolitionists.* New York, 1969.

———. *Black Mosaic: Essays in Afro-American History and Historiography.* Amherst, Mass., 1988.

Piersen, William D. *Black Yankees: The Development of an Afro-American Subculture in Eighteenth-Century New England.* Amherst, Mass., 1988.

Ripley, C. Peter, ed. *Witness for Freedom: African American Voices on Race, Slavery, and Emancipation.* Chapel Hill, N.C., 1993.

Sherman, Joan R. *Invisible Poets: Afro-Americans of the Nineteenth Century.* 2d ed. Urbana, Ill., 1989.

Stewart, James Brewer. *Holy Warriors: The Abolitionists and American Slavery.* Rev. ed. New York, 1996.

Stuckey, Sterling. *Slave Culture: Nationalist Theory and the Foundations of Black America.* New York, 1987.

Taylor, Quintard. *In Search of the Racial Frontier: African Americans in the American West, 1528–1990.* New York, 1998.

White, Shane. *Somewhat More Independent: The End of Slavery in New York City, 1770–1810.* Athens, Ga., 1991.

EXPANSION AND EMPIRE

Michael A. Morrison

Territorial expansion and the quest for an empire of liberty were coeval with the American nation itself. As part of the British Empire, most colonies held charters that granted them sovereignty all the way to the Pacific Ocean. British efforts to limit colonists' movements west helped to provoke a revolt in 1776 that had as its aim empire as much as independence. Once achieved, however, independence did not translate into empire. The Articles of Confederation provided that Congress should have authority over foreign affairs and, looking ahead, provided that Canada "shall be admitted into and entitled to all the advantages of this Union." Nonetheless, unable to control, much less expand, the boundaries and commerce of the new nation, the confederation government proved hopelessly inadequate to these ends.

James Madison, Alexander Hamilton, and others became convinced that only a powerful central authority could ensure union and, more important, promote the physical and economic growth necessary to an empire of liberty. In fact, in his defense of the Constitution, Madison declared in *Federalist* 10 that an empire of liberty was the function of territorial expansion. "Extend the sphere," Madison contended, "and . . . you make it less probable that a majority of the whole will have a common motive to invade the rights of other citizens." As Madison envisioned, the Constitution did much to empower the central government, enabling it to promote territorial aggrandizement and commercial expansion.

FOUNDING AN EMPIRE OF LIBERTY

Madison and Thomas Jefferson, among others, committed themselves to an unfolding empire of liberty premised on western expansion, commercial liberalism, and an open international commercial order. Although Madison's *Federalist* 10 stressed the advantages issuing from a widely dispersed population expanding over space, he and Jefferson also were convinced that commerce elevated the mind and promoted civilization and virtue. Without this bond to commerce, those agrarians who migrated west would lead a rudimentary, perhaps savage, existence. In that case, and based on that society, the republican experiment would fail.

Although Americans' access to foreign markets remained limited and problematic in the Early Republic, Jefferson's purchase of the Louisiana Territory in 1803 whetted the public's taste for more land. First the Adams-Onís Treaty (1819) secured East and West Florida and extended American interests to the Pacific Northwest. The Monroe Doctrine (1823) ensured hemispheric security and circumscribed Europe's ability to hedge about an expansive American republic. By the 1820s the idea of a national destiny—a Manifest Destiny—began to emerge. Speaking for millions of Americans, John Quincy Adams maintained that the United States was destined to be "coextensive with the North American Continent, destined by God and by nature to be the most populous and powerful people ever combined into one social contract" (Perkins, *Creation of a Republican Empire*, p. 4). The concepts it embraced—virtue, mission, geographic predestination, and national destiny—were melded into a powerful, if often disingenuous, argument for territorial expansion and commercial growth. By the 1840s, the term came to encompass a broad spectrum of expansionist rationalizations.

For all of that, territorial expansion stalled during the 1820s and 1830s. To be sure, tensions along the Canadian-American border erupted in the 1830s, eventually resulting in a formal settlement of the northeast boundary. In February 1839 American and Canadian lumberjacks brawled along a stretch of the Aroostook River in a region claimed by both New Brunswick and Maine. Each called out its militia. While singing "God Save the Queen," the Nova Scotia legislature appropriated war credits. Congressmen in Washington, lathering for a scrap, authorized President Martin Van Buren to raise

COASTING.
The old horse was too slow for Uncle Sam.

"Coasting. The Old Horse Was Too Slow for Uncle Sam."
Having abandoned his horse, on whose saddle appears
"Monroe Doctrine," Uncle Sam now rides a bicycle across
the globe. © BETTMANN/CORBIS

50,000 volunteers and appropriated $10 million in
the event of war. The "Aroostook War" remained
one of words, however. Nonetheless, the trial of a
Canadian citizen, Alexander McLeod, in a New
York state court in 1840 for the murder of an American citizen in a raid by pro-British Canadians
across the Niagara River in 1837 prompted more
talk of war. The Webster-Ashburton Treaty of 1842
relieved these strains in Anglo-American relations
and established a permanent boundary in the
northeast. By the terms of the pact, which slightly
favored Great Britain, the United States received a
little more than half of the disputed territory along
the Aroostook River. The treaty also firmly established a northern boundary from Lake Superior to
the Rocky Mountains.

To the south, Texas revolutionaries achieved a
semblance of independence when, under duress, the
Mexican president and general Antonio López de
Santa Anna signed the Treaty of Velasco, which
ended the fighting between the Texas rebels and the
Mexican army, which was to withdraw across the
Rio Grande. Once out of prison, Santa Anna, and
then the Mexican government, quickly repudiated
that agreement. Texas was an important element of
Jackson's vision of an American empire, yet his
unwillingness to risk either Martin Van Buren's

election or war with Mexico made the president
cautious. Following the lead of the Senate, however,
Jackson agreed to formal recognition of the Republic of Texas on 3 March 1837. Preoccupied with a
depression later that year, the newly elected Van Buren would go no further.

By the late 1830s, enthusiasm had taken wing in
the bombast of Manifest Destiny. Growing out of
fundamental principles of liberty, self-government,
and freedom broadly defined, the rhetoric of expansion proclaimed that "the far reaching, the
boundless future will be the era of American greatness." The principles of cohesion that bound Americans together and made possible the Union were
the love of "liberty itself for its own reward" and
the guarantee of personal autonomy by a limited
government. "We are the nation of human progress," John L. O'Sullivan boomed, "and who will,
what can, set limits to our onward march?" Ralph
Waldo Emerson, too, understood that national destiny, mixed motives, controversial means, and the
sheer force of expansionism gave meaning and force
to territorial expansion during the antebellum era.
"It is very certain," he observed, "that the strong
British race which have now overrun so much of
this continent, must also overrun [Texas], & Mexico
& Oregon also, and in the course of ages be of small
import by what particular occasions & methods it
was done. . . . It is a measure that goes not by right
nor by wisdom but by feeling."

A DESTINY MANIFEST: THE 1840s

Between 1845 and 1848 a surge of territorial expansion took the nation to the Pacific coast and made
it a true continental empire. With the annexation
of the Republic of Texas to the Union in 1845 and
the Mexican Cession of 1848, the United States acquired more than one million square miles of land.
The rhetoric of Manifest Destiny, which had begun
to take shape in the 1810s, became florid, exaggerated, and protean. National security, natural
boundaries, and Manifest Destiny were argued to
justify and explain expansion.

The context for this expansion was the steady
stream of immigrants who moved west from 1810
to 1860. The population of the Old Northwest and
the Southwest doubled every ten years, on average,
during this period. By 1860, the population of the
Midwest (Iowa, Minnesota, Nebraska, Kansas, and
the Dakota Territory) swelled to 988,000. From
1840 to 1860, the population of Iowa alone rose
from 43,000 to 675,000. Pushed to the frontier by

overcrowding and soil exhaustion in the East, settlers were also pulled westward by the prospects of personal independence and upward mobility. Wealth on the frontier, though somewhat lower than in the East, was more evenly distributed. Also, prospects for increased accumulation of wealth and self-sufficiency were considerable in the West.

Before the presidency of John Tyler, there were several concepts of republican freedom. Whigs wished to use government "to achieve through time the goods of increasing order and improvement" (Wilson, *Space, Time, and Freedom,* p. 4). Democrats looked to preserve personal liberty through expansion over space. These variant strains of republicanism—personal liberation and individual liberty—were merged in the issues of Texas, Oregon, and the Mexican Cession. Their fusion gave expansionism in the 1840s its particular force.

Thus, at a deeper level the desire to maintain and expand freedom, itself the essence of American nationalism, proved to be the catalytic element in expansion. Instructed by a political culture whose purpose was to realize and extend the basic republican tenets of equality and liberty, supporters of territorial aggrandizement understood its political power. It expanded freedom over space by extending American institutions to the Southwest and the Pacific coast. It also preserved personal liberty by meeting the territorial needs of a nation of autonomous agrarians. Finally, it enhanced freedom through time by providing the means of upward mobility through increased commercial opportunities and newly opened lands.

After years of ingenious and cautious maneuvering, the Tyler administration signed a treaty of annexation with the Texas Republic in early April 1844. The president sent it to the Senate later that month. In an atmosphere charged with political ambitions and ideological convictions, the Senate deliberated the merits of Tyler's treaty, and territorial expansion in general, in a series of high-voltage speeches. Fearing that premature and rapid expansion would preclude progress and promote social degeneration, Whigs stood solidly against Tyler's treaty of annexation. Joined by a handful of free-soil Democrats, they killed the treaty.

Despite the Whigs' best efforts, Texas annexation became an issue in the presidential campaign of 1844. Democrats ran James K. Polk on a platform that called for the "re-annexation" of Texas and the "re-occupation" of Oregon—and, for good measure, a tariff plank calculated to appeal to commercial-minded merchants and farmers. Although historians have made much of the connection between slavery

(or antislavery) and the Texas issue, the divisions between Democrats and Whigs and within the electorate over the measure were actually principled and structured and defined by the ideologies of both parties. Individual liberty, most Democrats believed, was incompatible with overcrowding, exhausted lands, and wage dependency. Believing that personal autonomy and true freedom depended on land ownership and economic independence, expansionists maintained that the addition of thousands of square miles of territory to the Union addressed the single most consequential prerequisite of republican freedom.

Texas also appealed to an emerging group within the Democratic Party that stressed territorial aggrandizement, commercial expansion, internal improvements, and free trade. Because expansion would enhance the liberation of Americans through the development of commercial opportunities, Oregon was easily and naturally woven into the Democratic campaign. Its importance to a future American empire on the Pacific neatly dovetailed with annexationists' market-expansion theme. Some believed that the Texas Republic would be the first essential link to the Pacific and, consequently, Asian trade. Sole occupation of Oregon and possession of the mouth of the Columbia River would open up a new commercial emporium there. Aggressive entrepreneurs would bring accessible markets in the Pacific and Far East within the scope of American commerce.

Whigs, to the contrary, feared that a Democratic empire based on unchecked territorial aggrandizement would subvert the evolution of American civilization. As the population grew increasingly nomadic, there would develop an aversion to peaceful, civilizing occupations. Individual capacities and that of the nation would remain undeveloped. The republic would then fragment and decline. Some in the party raised the specter of slavery extension. The party's opposition to annexation and rapid expansion to the Pacific, however, remained rooted in the fear that they would promote the enslavement of millions of whites to the degraded conditions of a primitive, colonial economy.

Polk, riding this new, powerful issue of expansion, defeated the Whig nominee, Henry Clay. Believing that the election was a referendum on Texas annexation, President Tyler urged Congress again to take up the measure. Bypassing the treaty ratification process (which requires a two-thirds majority in the Senate), Congress annexed Texas as a state by a joint resolution, with simple and fairly slim majorities in both houses. Tyler signed the bill on 1 March 1845.

Taking measure of Congress's action, on 21 April the London *Times* fretted that the recent annexation of Texas to the United States would lead assuredly to the eventual disruption of the Mexican confederacy. Once Texas was admitted to the Union, the *Times* predicted, "it would be found to embrace the distant objects of American ambition to the shores of the Pacific." Annexation, the *Times* claimed, "is only the prelude to [the United States's] ulterior designs. The claim to the exclusive possession of the Oregon territory is another indication of the *same* policy." This writer was right on both counts.

War between the United States and Mexico had been brewing since the annexation of Texas. Because it had never formally recognized Texas independence, the Mexican government broke off diplomatic relations in March 1845 in protest. Polk ordered troops to the Rio Grande. At the same time he pressured Mexico to cede Upper California and New Mexico to the United States in exchange for a settlement of the Texas boundary, surrender of American claims against Mexico, and an appropriately large remuneration. Negotiations proved fruitless. Following a border skirmish in late April 1846, Polk asked Congress to recognize that a state of war existed between the two countries.

Although the president had preferred to realize his grandiose scheme for empire (which by now included all of Oregon up to 54°40′, California, New Mexico, and perhaps some of the northern provinces of Mexico) by peaceful coercion or purchase, he did not shrink from the opportunity that war presented. He made clear, first to his cabinet and then to his supporters in Congress, that any settlement with Mexico would necessarily include territorial secession.

With Texas safely in the Union and the president on record as having his eye on an empire on the Pacific, Democrats, especially in the Old Northwest, expected Polk to make good on his—and the party's—claim, shadowy at best, to all of Oregon. To their minds, Oregon was at once an extension and a reflection of the appeal of annexation. Bringing Texas into the Union was not an end but part of an ongoing process of physical growth and commercial enhancement. Begging to disagree, the Whig editor of the New York *Courier* decried the "*mania* which is impelling so many of our better people to abandon the better climate, better soil, and altogether fairer regions of this better side of the Rocky Mountains, in order to seek a fortune in Oregon." To Democratic expansionists in Missouri this was so much twaddle; they were whooping "Woo ha! Go it boys! We're in a perfect *Oregon* fever!" (Independence *Expositor*, 3 May 1845).

Unwilling to risk war with England while waging one with Mexico, the president, however, coolly abandoned the Democratic platform on Oregon. Instead, after some saber rattling, a reiteration of Monroe's noncolonization principle, and a congressional resolution empowering him to terminate joint occupation with Britain, Polk and Secretary of State James Buchanan negotiated a compromise. The treaty divided the territory along the forty-ninth parallel to the Strait of Georgia, then along Puget Sound and the Strait of Juan de Fuca to the Pacific Ocean, leaving Vancouver Island to the British. The northwest boundary of the United States was now clearly defined—and complete.

Polk realized his empire on the Pacific and in the Southwest two years later. From the spring to the fall of 1847 American troops won a series of victories against an overmatched Mexican army. Democratic expansionists became increasingly convinced that the war must be the outcome of profound forces. "The principles of free government are destined to progress and extend and in due time they will be diffused all over Mexico," the *Nashville Union* proclaimed. Similarly a northern editor predicted that the army's success in the field "would seem to indicate, that the hand of Providence is directing our destiny, without regard to the policy of man." Expansion was the great movement of the age, the *Democratic Review* asserted, adding that until Americans occupied every acre of the North American empire, "the foundation of the future empire shall not have been laid" (quotations from Morrison, *Slavery and the American West*, p. 81).

Even Whigs who had been wary of unbridled territorial aggrandizement came close to adopting the expansionist designs of spread-eagle Democrats. Party members as diverse as William H. Seward and Alexander H. Stephens viewed territorial growth as a way to promote liberation and personal upward mobility through market expansion. The growth of commerce in the Pacific and the peaceful settlement of the Oregon dispute roused their enthusiasm for the addition to the Union of Upper California, with its fine bay of San Francisco. As a means to an enhanced American carrying trade in Asia, the acquisition of the Pacific port would strengthen the nation's maritime power and, by extension, promote the economic independence envisioned by the party's American System.

By the winter of 1848 the United States effectively controlled New Mexico and Upper California. Negotiations with the Mexican government, however, faltered. "Mexico is an ugly enemy," Daniel Webster observed in disgust. "She will not fight—& will not treat" (Van Alstyne, *Rising American Empire*, p. 145). Not until 2 February 1848 did Polk's peace emissary, Nicholas Trist, sign the Treaty of Guadalupe Hidalgo ending the Mexican-American War. By terms of the agreement, Mexico gave up all claims to Texas above the Rio Grande and ceded New Mexico and California. In return for the cession of 619,000 square miles of territory, the United States agreed to pay Mexico $15 million and assume the claims of American citizens against the government up to $3.25 million. The Senate ratified the treaty on 10 March 1848. Including Texas, the United States had acquired approximately half of Mexico. The ascendancy of republican freedom was, many believed, secure in a rising American empire.

A DESTINY DEBATED: THE 1850s

Growing out of the fundamental principles of individual liberty, self-government, and personal liberation, the rhetoric of expansion proclaimed that "the far reaching, the boundless future will be the era of American greatness." In some quarters, expansionist fervor even increased after the Mexican-American War. A navy lieutenant, for example, maintained that the war was "but the first step in that great movement southward, which will form part of our destiny," and compared Americans to the "northern hordes of the Alani" spreading their new energetic civilization over "an inferior people" (Pletcher, "Manifest Destiny," p. 526). *De Bow's Review* proclaimed—one would hardly say it proved—that the nation's destiny was not limited to the North American continent, but was to envelop the Hawaiian Islands, Central and South America, and parts of Asia and Europe.

Nevertheless, the sole expansionist achievement of the 1850s was modest. The Gadsden Purchase in 1853, which secured a small swath of Mexican territory (now comprising the southern portions of Arizona and New Mexico) was driven less by visions of empire than by a desire to acquire a good southern route for a railroad to the Pacific. The purchase completed the enormous territorial gains of the United States before the Civil War. Other expansionist initiatives—Cuba, Mexico, and parts of Central America—all failed.

The expansionist projects of the 1850s contained peoples that Americans refused to rule and to absorb. Americans had never viewed their ever-expanding frontier as a home for native peoples. To be sure, neither had they sought to enslave Native Americans or Mexicans, though their attempts to subordinate the former were particularly barbarous. They lusted after the land and its resources. It is suggestive that the enormous tract of land the United States wrested from Mexico contained only a few thousand inhabitants. Indeed, the Gadsden Purchase was so desolate that scout and Indian agent Kit Carson reported "a wolf could not make a living upon it."

The rhetoric of redemption and mission reached its apogee during the Mexican-American War. Opponents of the conflict—Whigs for the most part—declared that the United States could not extend its laws over the inhabitants of Mexican provinces without denigrating the principle of freedom and self-government. Furthermore, believing that governments embodied the moral sense of the race, dissidents declared in Congress that "representatives of ignorance & barbarism"—these "mongrel races"—would hold in their power the American birthright of republican government (Morrison, *Slavery and the American West*, p. 75).

Not surprisingly, as popular interest in the acquisition of Cuba grew, many in and out of government worried that expansion might endanger, not promote, their empire of liberty. William Brownlow, editor of the Knoxville *Whig*, doubted "whether the real people of Cuba have the spirit, intelligence and pluck ... not only to PROCLAIM themselves *free*, but to maintain their freedom." In like vein, the editor of the *Weekly Raleigh Register and North Carolina Gazette* charged that "the bigoted religious prejudice of the masses, (which are opposed to change,) are stronger than any sense of degradation arising from the arbitrary exactions of their masters."

A second obvious, but not always very enlightening, explanation for these failed expansionist projects is that the issue of slavery in newly acquired territory precluded further expansion. Once anxious to escape enslavement themselves and to unfetter individual potential, Americans felt their enthusiasm for further annexations cool after the Mexican Cession. Expansion became associated with either slavery or antislavery rather than freedom. Beginning with the Wilmot Proviso (1846), which would have banned slavery in any territory acquired from Mexico, the nation was forced to address the problem of slavery's relevance to its empire of republican liberty.

The standard and long-standing focus on slavery extension into the West and future acquisitions concentrates too narrowly on the institution itself. It underestimates the racism of nineteenth-century white Americans. Moreover, slavery had always been the central symbol of American political ideology. As an institution, and no less importantly as a trope, slavery negated liberty, contradicted equality, and precluded self-determination. Put in reductive terms, freedom as a symbol existed because the symbol of slavery existed.

As the issue was played out in the context of the expansionist designs of the 1840s and 1850s, it spoke to the present and the future. Were the institutions of the West and future acquisitions to resemble those of the North or the South? Slavery, Northerners believed, retarded the progress of the nation, degraded white workingmen, and contravened the fundamental republican principles of liberty and equality. To these free-soil Democrats and Republicans, the essence of the territorial issue was whether the national government would be administered in the spirit of the revolutionary heritage or handed over to an aristocratic power.

Southerners—slaveholders and nonslaveholders alike—replied that slavery promoted both equality, by ameliorating class conflict, and liberty, by making exploitation and manipulation of white workers unnecessary. They therefore linked slavery restriction to their constituents' future progress—or decline. Restricting slavery in recently acquired land and future additions of territory had the effect of vitiating true egalitarianism for settlers in territories and denying the equality of the South within the Union.

The origin and force of expansion had deep roots that stretched from Jefferson to the Jacksonian political system. The breakup of that political system explains the absence of widespread territorial growth in the 1850s. That is, the free-soil conflict pitting one section against the other for the right to expand and control the government disrupted Jacksonian party differences and then displaced them altogether. When expansion became identified with sectional, not national, objectives, it ceased.

The cases of Cuba and Central America are instructive. Narciso López, a Venezuelan by birth, resuscitated the issue of territorial expansion with two unsuccessful filibustering raids against Cuba in 1850 and 1851. The second raid cost him his life. Although López's supporters came from the free and slave states (he had a particularly strong follow-

ing in New York City), widespread objection in both sections to the raids reflected a diminished sense of national confidence and a sensitivity to residual sectional tensions. Even though Manifest Destiny was not yet in eclipse, to a growing number of Americans in 1851, expansion no longer appeared to promote automatically the ideals of liberty and expansion.

In 1854, at the urging of Secretary of State William Marcy, the United States ministers to Britain, France, and Spain met to exchange opinions and make recommendations for the acquisition of Cuba. Meeting in Ostend, Belgium, in October, James Buchanan, John Y. Mason, and Pierre Soulé drafted a remarkable document that recommended an immediate attempt to purchase Cuba for $120 million. If Spain would not sell, they declared that the United States would be justified by law—human and divine—in "wresting" the island away.

Even enthusiasts of territorial expansion found this hard to accept. They condemned the Ostend Manifesto as "a highwayman's plea." American diplomacy, they contended, was now given "to the habitual pursuit of dishonorable objects by clandestine means." The document, widely scorned, permanently discredited territorial aggrandizement, which had been considered respectable and necessary to the empire of liberty, by linking Manifest Destiny with naked aggression. Moreover, the annexation of Cuba—by any means fair or foul—meant expansion southward. Expansion southward seemed to imply the expansion of slavery.

When in 1859 the House Committee on Foreign Affairs proposed a $30 million appropriation to purchase Cuba, Republicans and Democrats alike reacted warily. Some Republicans, such as James Doolittle and Francis P. Blair Jr., suggested opening up Central America to free African Americans. Asserting that an "isothermal" line prevented whites from settling in the tropics, they argued that colonization had many advantages. It would rid the North of its race problem and keep Anglo-Saxon institutions—and blood—pure. Assuming that all African American colonists were incipient capitalists, they further maintained that colonization would produce the commercial advantages of annexation without the trouble and expense of acquisition. Finally and most important, colonization of free African Americans would produce something of a firewall that would prevent the spread of slavery.

Filibustering forays of William Walker, the "grey-eyed man of destiny," to Mexico and Central America engendered similar opposition to forcible territorial aggrandizement. Having abandoned medicine and failed as a lawyer, the diminutive Walker drifted into journalism, then filibustering. What Walker lacked in physical stature (he was 5′5″ tall and on the minus side of 120 pounds) he made up for in hubris and delusions of grandeur. Walker led a motley group of adventures ("the immortals") to Nicaragua in May 1855 to participate in a civil war. Approximately six months later he controlled the country; within a year he had made himself president. U.S. President Franklin Pierce recognized his government. Unfortunately for Walker, the American transportation magnate Cornelius Vanderbilt did not. When Walker revoked a franchise for a Vanderbilt-controlled steamship company, the Commodore withdrew his support for Walker. Walker's adversaries in Nicaragua then put down his regime, and he was forced to beat a hasty retreat on an American naval vessel in May 1857.

Walker invaded Nicaragua again in November to regain power. He did not even reach the coast. Commander Hiram Paulding arrested Walker for violation of American neutrality laws and returned him to the United States. Walker made a third attempt in 1860. A British officer arrested him off the coast of Honduras and turned the freebooter over to local authorities. Walker was tried and convicted on 11 September. And on 12 September, after receiving the last rites of the Catholic Church, Walker was executed. A firing squad fired two volleys into his body, and, for good measure, a soldier fired a single musket shot to his head.

The attacks on Walker in the press, though not so fatal, were telling. Separately and together they reflected a diminished sense of boundlessness that had characterized expansionism in the 1840s. Editors in both the North and South, while reiterating a belief in the nation's Manifest Destiny, also cautioned that territorial expansion, if it came at all, had to be by means honest and fair. Moreover, editors and congressmen alike insisted that new territory must be either unoccupied, or peopled by a race sympathetic to, and supportive of, the republican institutions of the United States. William Henry Seward, for example, envisioned territorial expansion as an extended process of peaceful emigration to, and Americanization of, Central America.

The failure to acquire Cuba and López's and Walker's successful filibustering expeditions also had coincided with the reemergence of sectional tensions in American politics, and each deepened a sense of declension and heightened concern over the future of free institutions in the United States.

The political vicissitudes and fragmentation that attended the sectional quarrels over territorial expansion and slavery extension were undercurrents that eroded the optimism of the 1840s.

This national self-doubt issued from a prevailing uneasiness of a nation increasingly at sea over the meaning of its own revolutionary past. The disorganization of political coherence in the years following the Mexican Cession reflected a diminished sense of national self-confidence and a widespread fear in the North and South that Americans were increasingly unable to recapture the spirit or, worse, agree on the essence of their Revolution. A strain of the American sense of self, which dated from John Winthrop's City on a Hill and was embodied in the Revolution, was a sense of national mission. By definition, for the American experiment to be a success, the eyes of the rest of the world had to be focused admiringly on her. The failures of López and Walker suggested that the people of Cuba and Nicaragua had chosen to ignore the American model. If so, Americans might be left with a polity that no one wanted and whose essence was very much in doubt and under debate.

James Madison had posited in *Federalist* 10 that expansive republics made it "more difficult for all who feel [a common interest] to discover their own strength, and to act in unison with each other." He miscalculated badly. The conflict over slavery in the newly acquired lands of the Southwest and potential acquisitions in Mexico, Central America, and the Caribbean engendered battle between the North and South for control of the government. Filibustering expeditions to Cuba, Mexico, and Central America exacerbated that struggle. By the end of the decade, opposition to territorial acquisitions reflected a growing conviction that the failure of American institutions to expand was due to moral retrogression. The destiny of slavery, so it seemed, had to be resolved before any further expansion of the empire of liberty.

AN EMPIRE TRANSFORMED: THE 1860s

Acquisition of an empire to the south never materialized. Still, the dwindling numbers of expansionists continued to advocate the acquisition of overseas colonies. They talked of seizing or acquiring by more traditional means Formosa, Hawaii, Okinawa, the Bonin Islands, and Santo Domingo. The more deluded called for the purchase of the island of Rhodes or the principality of Monaco. Understandably, public response was underwhelming.

Perhaps reflecting popular opinion, Secretary of State William Marcy maintained, "Remote colonies are not a source of strength to any Government, but of positive weakness, in the cost of their defense, and in the complications of policy which they impose to the prejudice of home-interests. Their supposed advantage to the mother-country, is the commercial monopoly, secured by such connection" (Brauer, "Economics and the Diplomacy of American Expansionism," p. 64). The U.S. government and members of both political parties, however, had opposed such monopolies, advocating at the very least commercial reciprocity. At the very most, they urged a liberal economic order based on free trade and open access to global markets.

Economic expansion, so critical to Jefferson's and Madison's idea of an empire of liberty, fared well in the three decades prior to the American Civil War. Throughout the 1830s, the U.S. Navy expanded the scope of its operations in the Caribbean, along the coast of South America, on the Pacific coast, and in the Far East to protect and encourage American trade in those areas. American diplomats, mindful of the importance of foreign markets, concluded commercial agreements at the rate of about one per year from 1815 to 1860.

Expansion of commercial ties to Latin America proved less successful. Although the government secured access to these economies, American merchants were unable to compete successfully or seriously challenge British hegemony in these markets. Though Americans were better able to gain a larger share of the carrying trade, Britain continued to command a disproportionate share of Latin American commerce. Although overseas commerce was becoming increasingly critical to the U.S. economy, trade with independent Latin American countries accounted for only about 5 percent of its exports. Less than 10 percent of U.S. imports came from Latin America.

Prospects in Asia proved somewhat brighter. After Britain forced China to open some of its ports to foreign trade in 1842 through the peace treaty ending the Opium Wars, the United States followed suit. Special envoy Caleb Cushing secured most-favored-nation privileges for the United States in the Treaty of Wanghia (1844). Over the next five years, American merchants sent more ships to Chinese ports than merchants of any other nation except Great Britain. By the mid-1850s, they controlled about one-third of the carrying trade between China and Europe. At Shanghai, which had replaced Canton as China's busiest seaport, they handled almost half of the trade.

President John Tyler later claimed that the treaty not only would expand American markets in China but also was the "nest egg" for opening up trade with Japan. So it was. In 1854, Commodore Matthew Perry combined suasion with threats to open the door, however slightly, to Japan with the Treaty of Kanagawa, which protected the lives of shipwrecked sailors and opened the ports of Shimoda and Hakodate, both relatively inaccessible. "The World has assigned this duty to us," Perry claimed; "we have assumed the responsibility and undertaken the task, and can not now hold back" (Van Alstyne, *Rising American Empire*, p. 173). In 1858 Townsend Harris negotiated a treaty of commerce and amity that provided for an exchange of diplomatic representatives, set tariff schedules, established the principle of extraterritoriality, and, most important, opened five Japanese ports for the purposes of trade.

On the eve of the Civil War, commercial expansion, which had been a function of, and a necessary adjunct to, an expansive agrarian empire of independent yeomen, eclipsed territorial aggrandizement. After the war, it transcended it altogether. Ironically and tragically, territorial expansion, which was to ensure Jefferson's empire of liberty, was nearly the occasion of its demise. Because it was such an intense force, the political source of the sectional conflict—and of the Civil War—came to be anchored in the meaning of national growth. In the postwar era and throughout Reconstruction, governmental and public interest in territorial acquisitions—Alaska, the Isthmus of Panama, the West Indies (particularly Santo Domingo), and in the Pacific—were means to an end. Global commercial supremacy, not territorial hegemony, defined and gave shape to an American empire if not an empire of the Americas.

The acquisition of Alaska in 1867 makes the case exactly. Secretary of State William Henry Seward, Gideon Welles once complained, was "almost crazy on the subject of territorial acquisition" (Paolino, *Foundations of the American Empire*, p. 14). The purchase of Alaska from Russia for $7.2 million would seem to prove Welles correct. Alaska totaled some 586,000 square miles. It was twice the size of Texas and nearly one-fifth the size of the continental United States. At two cents an acre, Alaska was indeed a bargain.

Yet the purchase represented no simple, indiscriminate land grab. Rather, Seward's interest in Alaska reflected his desire to secure an entrepôt in the Pacific Northwest for the trade of the Pacific and Asia. Seward's son Frederick later remembered that his father believed that the purchase would give Americans "a foothold for commercial and naval operations accessible from the Pacific states" (LaFeber, *American Search for Opportunity*, p. 14). On 31 March 1867, the *New York Times* discussed the treaty under the head "BRIGHT PROSPECTS FOR OUR JAPAN AND CHINA TRADE" while assuring its readers that the purchase of Alaska would "influence in our favor the vast trade of the Pacific." Writing in the Albany *Argus*, John Pruyn envisioned a very different destiny for the United States. "The day is coming," he predicted, "when the commerce of the Pacific will rival the Atlantic and be almost entirely under our control" (Paolino, p. 113).

CODA

In 1771 Timothy Dwight published the first of his many patriotic poems that both captured and inspired a national sense of destiny and empire:

> Hail land of light and glory! Thy power shall grow
> Far as the seas, which round thy regions flow;
> Through earth's wide realms thy glory shall
> extend, And savage nations at thy scepter bend.
> And the frozen shores thy sons shall sail, Or
> stretch their canvas to the ASIAN gale.

Dwight's paean (Perkins, *Creation of a Republican Empire*, p. 7) neatly summarizes the westward course of American expansion in the antebellum era. Jefferson's empire of liberty, which was premised on both expansion over space and enhanced commercial opportunities abroad, reached its apo-gee in the 1840s with the acquisition of Texas and the Mexican Cession, as well as increased commercial opportunities in the Pacific and Asia. The internal logic of this empire and the driving force of territorial and commercial aggrandizement were defined and informed by a political culture whose purpose was to reify and extend the basic republican tenets of political freedom and individual liberty. Expansion, as it took shape in the 1840s, had the effect of merging those republican desiderata into a single highly volatile issue, one that seemed to ensure both independence and personal liberation and growth.

Despite the ability of expansionists to quote chapter and verse from Madison's *Federalist* 10, they forgot or failed to comprehend that Madison premised his brief for a widespread republic on the recognition that liberty and equality—freedom and democracy—are fundamentally antagonistic. He said so explicitly. By the 1840s, however, expansionists insisted that they were mutually reinforcing and interchangeable. Therein lay the power of territorial growth. Yet by the 1850s, debate over the extension of slavery into the newly acquired lands of the West made salient the inherent tension between liberty and equality, freedom and democracy. The American Civil War, the tragic offspring of those assumptions and that debate, nearly destroyed Jefferson's empire of liberty. Sadly, it did nothing to make clear the muddled, contradictory, and at times arrogant constellation of beliefs that gave shape to that unhappy destiny.

See also **Agrarianism and the Agrarian Ideal in Early America; Nationalism and Imperialism** *(in this volume);* **The Frontier and the West; The Middle West; The Southwest; Borderlands** *(volume 2);* **Technological Enclaves** *(volume 3).*

BIBLIOGRAPHY

Historiography

Brauer, Kinley J. "The Great American Desert Revisited: Recent Literature and Prospects for the Study of American Foreign Relations, 1815–61." *Diplomatic History* 13 (summer 1989): 395–417.

Nelson, Anna Kasten. "Destiny and Diplomacy, 1840–1865." In *American Foreign Relations: A Historiographical Review*, edited by Gerald K. Haines and J. Samuel Walker. Westport, Conn., 1981.

Weeks, William Earl. "New Directions in the Study of Early American Foreign Relations." *Diplomatic History* 17 (winter 1993): 73–96.

Articles and Essays

Brauer, Kinley J. "Economics and the Diplomacy of American Expansionism." In *Economics and World Power: An Assessment of American Diplomacy since 1789,* edited by William H. Becker and Samuel F. Wells Jr. New York, 1984.

———. "The United States and British Imperial Expansion, 1815–60." *Diplomatic History* 12 (winter 1988): 19–37.

Crapol, Edward P. "John Tyler and the Pursuit of National Destiny." *Journal of the Early Republic* 17 (fall 1997): 467–491.

"Foreign Policy in the Early Republic Reconsidered: Essays from a SHEAR Symposium." *Journal of the Early Republic* 14 (winter 1994): 453–495.

Freehling, William W. "The Complex Career of Slaveholder Expansionism." In his *The Reintegration of American History: Slavery and the Civil War.* New York, 1994.

Pletcher, David M. "Manifest Destiny." In *Encyclopedia of American Foreign Policy: Studies of the Principal Movements and Ideas,* edited by Alexander DeConde. Vol. 2. New York, 1978.

Books

Belohlavek, John M. *"Let the Eagle Soar!" The Foreign Policy of Andrew Jackson.* Lincoln, Neb., 1985.

Brown, Charles H. *Agents of Manifest Destiny: The Lives and Times of the Filibusters.* Chapel Hill, N.C., 1980.

Graebner, Norman A. *Empire on the Pacific: A Study in American Continental Expansion.* New York, 1955.

Haynes, Sam W., and Christopher Morris, eds. *Manifest Destiny and Empire: American Antebellum Expansionism.* College Station, Tex., 1997.

Heald, Morrell, and Lawrence S. Kaplan. *Culture and Diplomacy: The American Experience.* Westport, Conn., 1977.

Hietala, Thomas R. *Manifest Design: Anxious Aggrandizement in Late Jacksonian America.* Ithaca, N.Y., 1985.

Holbo, Paul. *Tarnished Expansion: The Alaska Scandal, the Press, and Congress, 1867–1871.* Knoxville, Tenn., 1983.

Horsman, Reginald. *Race and Manifest Destiny: The Origins of American Racial Anglo-Saxonism.* Cambridge, Mass., 1981.

Jones, Howard. *To the Webster Ashburton Treaty: Anglo American Relations, 1783–1843.* Chapel Hill, N.C., 1977.

Jones, Howard, and Donald Rakestraw, eds. *Prologue to Manifest Destiny: Anglo-American Relations in the 1840s.* Wilmington, Del., 1997.

LaFeber, Walter. *The Cambridge History of American Foreign Relations,* vol. 2, *The American Search for Opportunity, 1865–1913.* Cambridge, U.K., 1993.

May, Robert E. *The Southern Dream of Caribbean Empire, 1854–1861.* Baton Rouge, La., 1973.

McCoy, Drew R. *The Elusive Republic: Political Economy in Jeffersonian America.* Chapel Hill, N.C., 1980.

Morrison, Michael A. *Slavery and the American West: The Eclipse of Manifest Destiny and the Coming of the Civil War.* Chapel Hill, N.C., 1997.

Paolino, Ernest N. *The Foundations of the American Empire: William Henry Seward and U.S. Foreign Policy.* Ithaca, N.Y., 1973.

Perkins, Bradford. *The Cambridge History of American Foreign Relations*, vol. 1, *The Creation of a Republican Empire*. Cambridge, U.K., 1993.

Pletcher, David M. *Diplomacy of Annexation: Texas, Oregon, and the Mexican War*. Columbia, Mo., 1973.

Potter, David M. *The Impending Crisis, 1848–1861*. New York, 1976.

Sellers, Charles. *The Market Revolution: Jacksonian America, 1815–1846*. New York, 1991.

Schroeder, John H. *Shaping a Maritime Empire : The Commercial and Diplomatic Role of the American Navy, 1829–1861*. Westport, Conn., 1985.

Stuart, Reginald C. *United States Expansionism and British North America, 1775–1871*. Chapel Hill, N.C., 1988.

Stephanson, Anders. *Manifest Destiny: American Expansion and the Empire of Right*. New York, 1995.

Van Alstyne, Richard W. *The Rising American Empire*. New York, 1960. Reprint, Chicago, 1965.

Weeks, William Earl. *Building the Continental Empire: American Expansion from the Revolution to the Civil War*. Chicago, 1996.

Weinberg, Albert K. *Manifest Destiny: A Study of Nationalist Expansionism in American History*. Baltimore, 1935.

Williams, William A. *Roots of the Modern American Empire: A Study of the Growth and Shaping of Social Consciousness in a Marketplace Society*. New York, 1969.

Wilson, Major L. *Space, Time, and Freedom: The Quest for Nationality and the Irrepressible Conflict, 1815–1861*. Westport, Conn., 1974.

ANTISLAVERY

Julie Roy Jeffrey

ORIGINS AND SIGNIFICANCE

In January 1831 the first issue of a new antislavery newspaper, the *Liberator,* appeared in Boston, Massachusetts. With his demand for the immediate emancipation of the slaves, the paper's editor, William Lloyd Garrison, announced a dramatic shift in the direction of American antislavery. In language foreshadowing the character of what would become the most important reform movement of the antebellum period, he insisted that he would be "harsh as truth, and as uncompromising as justice.... Urge me not to use moderation in a cause like the present. I am in earnest—I will not equivocate—I will not excuse—I will not retreat an inch and I WILL BE HEARD" (Stewart, *William Lloyd Garrison,* pp. 50, 51).

The uncompromising nature of Garrison's brand of antislavery quickly became apparent in his scathing attacks on the American Colonization Society (ACS), the major expression of organized antislavery in the 1820s. Founded in 1816, the society formulated a tepid program that hardly threatened prevailing social and economic arrangements. Advocating the gradual and voluntary emancipation of American slaves and the colonization of free blacks in Africa, the society proposed ending racism in the North by eliminating its free black population and encouraging emancipation by assuring slaveholders that freed slaves would be repatriated. The ACS attracted support from most major religious denominations, many northerners troubled by slavery but fearful of disruptions in national life, and southern slaveholders. Recognizing that the ACS's commitment to voluntary manumission actually offered little threat to their own slaves, slaveholders embraced the ACS's other goal of ridding their region of its free blacks.

Garrison recognized the irrelevance of the ACS's approach in a time when slavery was expanding rapidly. Furthermore, he had learned from free African Americans in Baltimore and elsewhere of their op-

position to colonization. Accusing the ACS of harboring a fundamental *"antipathy to blacks,"* Garrison rejected the society's professed concern for the slave and pointed out that it had never disavowed one of the main premises supporting slavery: the right to hold human beings as slaves (Stewart, *William Lloyd Garrison,* p. 57). Moreover, the ACS's emphasis on the degraded state of African Americans encouraged white racial prejudice. Garrison's *Thoughts on African Colonization* (1832) elaborated his views. In a technique that would become common in antislavery publications, he quoted from prominent colonizationists to reveal their racism and support for slavery. He also included statements made by African Americans in anticolonization meetings in 1831 and 1832 to undermine the validity of colonization as a solution for the race "problem" and to show that blacks, far from being degraded, were articulate and intelligent. The book won many over to immediatism and helped dislodge the ACS from its central position in antislavery.

For all its significance as a reform movement, however, abolitionism never gained support from a majority of northerners. While abolitionists drew upon political, social, religious, and economic ideas shared by many other Americans, the fundamental proposals to end slavery and to provide equal rights for African Americans threatened the status quo and, some early suggested, even the union. Particularly during the 1830s, abolitionism aroused furious reactions. In 1836 Congress, fearing the acriminious discussions of slavery that the presentation of abolitionist petitions prompted, passed the gag rule to curb debate. Northern mobs attacked abolitionist lecturers, broke up meetings, destroyed property, often owned by blacks, and in 1837 killed Elijah Lovejoy, the editor of an abolitionist newspaper in Alton, Illinois. Verbal attacks on women's involvement in abolitionism, while less threatening than physical violence, were harsh, suggesting that abo-

The Liberator, 23 April 1831. Although Garrison originally thought abolition would best be advanced by relocating free blacks to areas outside the United States, he reversed his position to one advocating anticolonization by the time the opening issue of the *Liberator* was published. © BETTMANN/CORBIS

litionism also threatened middle-class gender arrangements.

Scholars have debated the relationship between abolitionism, broad trends, like growing sectionalism or the growth of feminism, and specific events, like the division of Protestant denominations into northern and southern branches or the collapse of the second party system. While many historians recognize some relationship between abolitionism and the market economy, the nature of that relationship is unclear. One view links the rise of a humanitarianism to the market revolution, suggesting that economic change encouraged individuals to see themselves in control of their own lives and morally responsible for the less successful. Yet this interpretation does not account for the prominence in abolitionism of women, who, one scholar suggests, were less touched than men by the liberating tendency of capitalism that supposedly promoted humanitarianism. Less problematic is the argument that abolitionists shared the individualistic values that helped to fuel the market revolution. Their denunciation of slavery in part rested on the premise that each person had the right to make his way in the world—a right, of course, that slavery denied.

Because they do not believe that abolitionism transformed northern public opinion on the subject of slavery, few scholars at the end of the twentieth century see abolitionism as a cause of the Civil War. Yet many still perceive indirect connections between abolitionism and that conflict. The abolitionist campaign angered the South so profoundly, they suggest, that its spokesmen became increasingly aggressive in defending slavery. Such aggressiveness, in turn, prompted anti-southern feelings among northerners who had little sympathy for immediate emancipation. Others emphasize the ways in which extremist abolitionist rhetoric that depicted the South as a threatening and conspiratorial slave power and southern slaveholders as lustful, tyrannical masters shaped northern thinking, leaving little room for tolerance or negotiation of difference. Whatever part abolitionism may have played in setting the stage for war, abolitionists succeeded in keeping an unpopular topic alive as a subject for moral, political, and economic debate for three decades.

Abolitionism was a diffuse reform movement with diverse forms of expression between 1831 and 1865. During the 1830s, abolitionists tended to agree about how to carry on the campaign against slavery, both organizationally and tactically. The secular voluntary society, already familiar in evangelical and benevolent reform circles, was the site for antislavery activism. Moral suasion, based on the faith that an appeal to reason and moral sensibilities could transform public opinion, represented the means by which abolitionists expected to accomplish their goals.

At the end of the 1830s, the movement fragmented. The secular voluntary society became just one means of working for abolitionism. Political clubs and parties, antislavery fairs, religious voluntary societies, religious and political conventions, informal work groups like sewing societies, and the loosely coordinated Underground Railroad all provided different ways to be active in the antislavery cause. While many abolitionists continued to believe in the value of moral suasion, a host of other tactics, ranging from political action and lobbying to lawsuits, propaganda, and fund-raising, were used. While some scholars have stressed that division weakened abolitionism as a whole, others point out that all factions continued to work for the central goal of immediate emancipation. Indeed, they suggest that fragmentation may actually have helped the reform movement by offering individuals and groups alternative ways of pursuing immediate emancipation. Rather than dropping out of antislavery because of a disagreement over means, individuals could choose how to pursue their commitment. Moreover, at the grassroots level, particularly in the Middle West, arguments in New York and New England had little impact.

SHARED BELIEFS

Abolitionism did not represent a coherent system of thought, but most abolitionists agreed upon certain fundamental ideas. Even those who opposed slavery but rejected abolitionism subscribed to some of these ideas. The Democratic Cleveland newspaper, the *Plain Dealer,* denounced slavery in 1848 in terms most abolitionists would find acceptable as "an evil that stares you in the face from uncultivated fields, and howls in your ears with its horrid din of clanking chains and fetters, and the groans of wretched bondsmen" (Stokes and Conway, eds., *The Market Revolution,* p. 213).

Most obviously, abolitionists rejected gradualism as ineffective and old-fashioned in contrast to their own modern, progressive struggle of immediatism. Untroubled by the fact that the campaign

for immediate emancipation lacked a specific scheme to end slavery, abolitionists emphasized the importance of making the moral decision as a beginning. The disinterest in specificity may have led abolitionists to underestimate the social and economic difficulties and disruptions that emancipation involved. But they were not unrealistic about the time frame that might be necessary before their reform succeeded. While some, as Wendell Phillips pointed out, were "apt to be in a hurry and look for some immediate result," the task of re-educating "a whole people" might well take considerable time (Stewart, *Wendell Phillips,* p. 144).

The energies that abolitionists put into the campaign delayed careful consideration of what might happen when their cause prevailed and what sorts of accommodations, beyond legal freedom, might be necessary to make African Americans full participants in the country's life. Joshua Leavitt, an early convert to abolitionism, gave a rationale for putting off thinking about the post-emancipation world. "Whatever provisions of legislation, education, guardianship, etc. either prudence or humanity may decide to be necessary for such a multitude thus delivered from slavery, should all take effect subsequent to emancipation," he explained, "for they are all necessarily inconsistent with even the temporary existence of slavery (Davis, *Joshua Leavitt,* p. 102).

Because abolitionists thought about slavery within a national framework, they believed that all Americans, not just southerners, were implicated in its survival. As the antislavery newspaper the *Emancipator* emphasized in 1837, every northern "merchant or manufacturer . . . who has southern debts to collect, becomes more anxious than ever, to keep all quiet, and prevent any agitation, that will hazard the stability of commercial arrangements" (Davis, pp. 138, 139). Those who did business in the South, or who turned a blind eye to slavery because they had no obvious contact with it, or who supported the system by buying products of slave labor, all shared the guilt of slavery. This perspective suggested a northern focus for the reform effort, which became a practical necessity after the attempt to blanket the South with abolitionist literature failed in the mid-1830s.

Abolitionist language and thought suggests the profound influence of the evangelical revivals of the 1820s and 1830s. Abolitionists often described their "conversion" to abolitionist "doctrines," and spoke of abolitionism as a "moral" or "religious" duty. This terminology echoed that used by revivalists, who told sinners they must be converted to be saved, but that once saved, they must battle sin in the world. What distinguished abolitionists from other evangelicals was their refusal to view slavery as an economic, political, or social problem, an unfortunate fact, or a distinctly southern matter. Slavery was a sin, they insisted, that had to be stamped out; abolitionism was, in the words of one woman, "the *cause* of God" (Jeffrey, *The Great Silent Army of Abolitionism*, p. 37). Although nonevangelical Christians, especially Quakers and Unitarians, who embraced abolitionism did not share this evangelical perspective, they did agree that slavery was a sin and abolitionism a moral duty.

Like others in the antebellum period, abolitionists were affected by the economic, social, and political transformations that were altering American life. These changes made them fearful for political ideals and the appropriate balance between liberty and power, a concern of American political discourse since the eighteenth century. Slavery symbolized the threatening forces of their world. It encouraged license and tyranny by freeing slaveholders of all restraints. "The master-passion in the bosom of the slaveholder," Garrison warned, was not "the love of gain, but the possession of absolute power, unlimited sovereignty" (Walters, *The Antislavery Appeal*, p. 71).

The coupling of slavery with tyranny made the connection between slavery and the fate of the nation clear. It was impossible, Wendell Phillips argued in 1837, for the South to "be corrupt, and we sound." Slavery, he insisted, "sends out poisonous branches over the fair land, and corrupts the very air we breathe." Extending the meaning of the Revolution further than the founders had intended, he suggested that slavery conflicted with the basic ideals of the Revolution. Thus "the patriot as well as the abolitionist" should be "concerned in this struggle" to "finish what our fathers left unfinished when they declared all men free and equal" (Stewart, *Wendell Phillips*, pp. 69–70).

Fundamental to the abolitionist rejection of slavery was a view of human nature shared by other reformers and nineteenth-century moralists. Human beings enjoyed the capacity to make and act upon their moral decisions. While internal restraints were necessary for social order, external restraints on behavior and decision making robbed human beings of their essential freedom. Slavery was wrong because it violated slaves' basic right to make moral decisions and because it encouraged license on the part of slaveholders. Indeed, the

South presented a frightening example of what happened when a society abandoned moral restraint.

As an 1836 *Anti-Slavery Almanac* insisted, all blacks were "fellow immortals" (Jeffrey, p. 39). This belief that blacks and whites shared a common humanity highlighted the evil of racial prejudice that provided crucial support for the slave system and justified discriminatory treatment of free blacks in the North. Most antislavery society constitutions took a stand against northern practices by pledging members to strive to improve the situation of freed blacks, to "correct public opinion," and to "obtain for them equal civil and political rights and privileges with the whites" (Goodman, *Of One Blood*, p. 58). Although white abolitionists were not entirely free of prejudice themselves, many northerners saw their insistence on basic civil and political rights for blacks as being just as extreme as their call to eliminate slavery.

EARLY DEVELOPMENTS

Despite the radical implications of the idea of emancipation and enhanced rights for northern free blacks, the 1830s marked a period of rapid growth for organized antislavery in the North. In December 1831, Garrison and twelve other men formed the New England Anti-Slavery Society in Boston. By the next year the message of immediate emancipation had aroused enough interest to bring sixty-two men from eleven states together to establish a national antislavery organization, the American Anti-Slavery Society. The AAAS, based in New York City, was directed by a group of New York reformers, including Lewis Tappan. Its priority was, as one supporter noted, to "put on the muscle and transfuse the warm blood and breathe into . . . [the movement] the breath of life" (Davis, p. 104).

In their effort to bring the reform to life, abolitionists skillfully launched a far-ranging propaganda effort. Part of what has been called the information revolution, abolitionists successfully exploited changes in printing technology that made it possible to mass produce cheap printed materials. Antislavery tracts, books both factual and imaginative, almanacs, newspapers, broadsides, giftbooks, and slave narratives—often inexpensive, sometimes distributed free—poured forth to spread the antislavery message. Understanding that there were now several reading publics, abolitionist writers and printers skillfully targeted different groups of readers, ranging from those who preferred facts and figures about slavery, to those who wanted sentimental tales, to those who desired stories and alphabet books suitable for children. By 1838, some 750,000 publications had been dispersed in a massive attempt to transform public opinion.

In the 1830s the AAAS also initiated another grassroots recruiting effort that became a persistent feature of abolitionism. Building upon the system of itinerancy used by evangelical denominations and the general interest in public oratory and self-improvement, the AAAS established a national corps of antislavery speakers that included gifted orators like Theodore Weld. Partly for financial reasons, later in the decade the AAAS encouraged local lecturers to work as publicizers and organizers. These men (and later women) were invaluable in getting out the original message of abolitionism, renewing interest when adherents became discouraged, interpreting current events from an abolitionist perspective, and giving listeners a sense that they were part of a movement that stretched beyond their own communities. During the 1830s, lecturers played an important role not only in explaining what abolitionism was and why it was necessary but also in urging the formation of local and state antislavery societies. By 1838, the AAAS claimed thirteen hundred auxiliary societies, with more than 1.25 million members. Most were located in New England, western New York, along the Pennsylvania-Ohio border, and in those parts of the Midwest settled by Quakers and New Englanders. Evidence suggests that most abolitionists came from the middling ranks of rural and small-town society and from the fluid middle classes in urban areas.

Members of antislavery societies began their organizational lives by adopting constitutions, setting out goals and criteria for membership, soliciting signatures (and thus members) for the constitution, and electing officers. As they began to hold meetings, they shaped the character and specific purpose of their antislavery societies and created the procedures that were vital for successful associational life. In the annual meeting of the Lynn Female Anti-Slavery Society in 1837, for example, one member, realizing that "a free interchange of opinions and sentiments gives life and interest to our meetings," offered a resolution encouraging the women to overcome their "diffidence" (Jeffrey, p. 79). Making speeches, debating resolutions, delivering prayers, reading aloud from antislavery literature, the Bible, or letters from other antislavery societies, singing special antislavery songs, and discussing possible

projects all stimulated interest and contributed to the formation of a unique antislavery culture.

WOMEN IN ANTISLAVERY

Initially, as in Lynn, Massachusetts, women tended to form their own societies. Antislavery leaders originally sought women's involvement because given the association in nineteenth-century culture between women and morality, that involvement heightened the credentials of the reform. Another reason was that the role women played in the British emancipation movement suggested how valuable women could be. The constitutions adopted by many female societies show that women responded to the issue of slavery in gendered terms, perhaps partly because of the way antislavery lecturers shaped their appeals to women. The lecturer Amos Phelps, for example, waved an overseer's whip in front of his female audiences, driving home the point that it had lacerated the backs of slave women. In the preamble to their constitution, the women of Canton, Ohio, stated: "We consider that we are *not moving out of our proper sphere* as females when we assume a *public* stand in favor of our *oppressed sisters*" (Jeffrey, p. 57).

Although women responded to the abolitionist message because they felt it was their moral duty as women to do what they could for their slave sisters, the commitment unexpectedly encouraged many of them to engage in what conservatives labeled unwomanly activities. Societies provided not only an education about the evils of slavery, but also political and public experience. As was true in benevolence societies, adopting a constitution, electing officers, managing meetings, and debating resolutions all taught women democratic skills. More important, the work that many female societies adopted thrust them into the world of public controversy and debate. Circulating newspapers and other printed materials prompted women to learn how to explain why slavery was wrong, to defend immediate emancipation, and to persuade neighbors and acquaintances to accept or buy antislavery literature. Beginning in the mid-1830s and continuing into the Civil War period, petition drives relied upon women not only to sign but also to circulate antislavery petitions sent to Congress and anti-discrimination petitions sent to state legislatures. This effort to pressure political bodies on political questions, often carried out in public spaces or in the domestic spaces of strangers and involving women in discussion and even argumentation, drew much criticism from conservatives that women were out of their sphere. But as one circular reminded women, since petitoning was "the only means of direct political action . . . which we can exert upon our Legislatures," it must continue (Jeffrey, p. 92).

In 1834 the Boston Female Anti-Slavery Society initiated a project that also carried women beyond the domestic circle: the antislavery fair. Since abolitionism was poorly financed, antislavery fairs became an important means of fund-raising for many different groups of abolitionist women. Successful fairs relied upon women, working in groups or alone, to make attractive and useful items for sale. While this task could easily be accomplished at home, organizing and holding fairs involved women in the highly commercial world of buying and selling. Moreover, fairs were not just marketplaces but sites for publicizing the message of antislavery and influencing those who came to buy. In the decoration of fair halls, with their banners and visual depictions of slavery, and in the items sold, many with antislavery mottoes, women propagated the antislavery message while at the same time signifying their determination to participate in the political debate swirling around slavery.

AFRICAN AMERICANS

Although eventually most antislavery organizations in the 1830s admitted African Americans, it did not happen without some struggle. Usually, black members had to prove their respectability and adherence to middle-class norms before they could join white societies, and they were rarely considered for leadership roles. Although a few societies, like the Philadelphia Female Anti-Slavery Society, had a biracial membership for many years, blacks, particularly after the 1830s, often preferred their own societies. Uncomfortable with white prejudice, African Americans also were more concerned with improving the situation of free northern blacks than were white societies. Initially, they hoped that self-improvement efforts would weaken white hostility, but this faith was faltering by the end of the 1830s. At a time when over 90 percent of free blacks lacked the vote, men like William Whipper believed that "complexion [not culture] . . . deprived the man of color of equal treatment," and Charles Lenox Remond called for "more radicalism among us" (Ripley, ed., *The Black Abolitionist Papers*, vol. 3, p. 20). Many blacks embraced political abolitionism with

the franchise as their goal and participated in attempts to overturn northern discrimination.

In the 1840s, as Whipper's and Remond's comments suggest, many black abolitionists were dissatisfied not only with the lack of racial progress in the North but also with what they saw as their second-class status within the abolitionist movement as a whole. Seeking to assert their independence, many, like the former slave and abolitionist orator Frederick Douglass, abandoned Garrison and struck out in new directions. In the 1840s and 1850s many blacks embraced political abolitionism with the franchise as their goal. Others broadened the definition of abolitionism to include, as one leader explained, "the mere act of riding in public conveyances" as well as the "liberation of every slave" (Ripley, vol. 3, p. 24). The attack on northern discrimination accorded with the values and interests of a new generation of black leaders, many of whom were fugitives from slavery rather than mem-

Frederick Douglass (1817–1895). Drawing on his personal experience as a slave, Douglass formulated an insightful social commentary that he delivered with oratorical eloquence. He was arguably the most effective reformer of his day. © BETTMANN/CORBIS

bers of the free black elite who had been prominent in the 1830s.

The publication of black newspapers, among them Frederick Douglass's *North Star,* also helped to draw blacks into abolitionist activities. In the 1850s, vigilance work and assistance for fugitive slaves also widened the appeal of abolitionism in black communities.

DEVELOPMENTS AFTER 1840

In the late 1830s the movement began to fragment. The New England lecture tour in 1837 of the Grimké sisters, who broke with custom by speaking before mixed audiences, raised the question of the role and place of women in the movement. Garrisonians firmly supported an expanded role for women and mixed antislavery societies. But New York abolitionists were concerned that Garrison and his supporters were weakening and discrediting the cause by combining it with other reforms. Some abolitionists, including the New Yorkers Myron Holley and James Birney, concluded that moral suasion was a failure and favored pursuing antislavery through politics. Such differences boiled over during the yearly meeting of the AAAS in 1840. When Garrison and his supporters managed to place a woman, Abby Kelley, on the business committee, Arthur Tappan and almost three hundred other delegates walked out. They immediately established another organization, the American and Foreign Anti-Slavery Society (AFAS; often called the New Organization to distinguish it from the AAAS, the Old Organization).

During the 1840s and 1850s the AAAS, with Garrison as one of its guiding spirits, was nominally a national organization with a national newspaper, the *National Anti-Slavery Standard,* and a yearly meeting. In fact, however, it was largely a New England organization. The AFAS, based in New York, never had sufficient funding to play a vigorous national role. Although neither organization was capable of directing or controlling local and state antislavery efforts, neither was unimportant. The AAAS continued its efforts in moral suasion, and its views were well represented in abolitionist newspapers like Garrison's *Liberator* and Ohio's *Anti-Slavery Bugle.* The AFAS was active in encouraging church-based abolitionism that used moral suasion and later supported political action. Its monthly publication, the *American and Foreign Antislavery Reporter,* carried abolitionist news and, as a May 1846 issue made clear, promoted the abolitionist life as one of "unceasing activity, in some way for the slave."

Neither the division within the antislavery ranks nor the weakness of the two most prominent organizations emerging from it spelled the end of local or state antislavery activities. Some societies organized during the 1830s did divide or disband. But others continued their activities, relatively undisturbed by disagreements separating national antislavery leaders. Moreover, documentary evidence, though not abundant, suggests that a strong organizing impulse continued and that many antislavery activists retained their faith in working collectively toward their goals. They persisted in establishing new groups, some formal, like vigilante societies and political clubs, and others informal, like petition committees and sewing circles to do fair work or to aid black fugitives. These less formal groups were particularly important in keeping an antislavery commitment and culture alive. Fair work, for example, tied women in different communities into a network of like-minded people, all working to make items for a particular fair, often communicating with one another as sisters in the cause, sharing ideas for the fair and other abolitionist news. Making decisions for the profits earned—to support a state antislavery lecturer or an antislavery newspaper, for example—reinforced a feeling of achievement and connection with the larger cause. Some informal groups enjoyed continuity. The antislavery sewing society in Portland, Maine, for example, held regular meetings while the men's antislavery society lapsed. Other groups had an intermittent life that coincided with a particular task or purpose. During the 1850s outside events like the Fugitive Slave Act and the Kansas-Nebraska Act sparked another round in which secular antislavery societies were organized.

RITUAL EVENTS

The ritual events organized by abolitionists helped cement them to the cause and often brought together abolitionists with diverse agendas. Fairs were one such type of event. The annual anniversary gatherings held by the AAAS and AFAS, as well as by state antislavery societies, with their speeches, resolutions, and opportunities to see friends and meet leaders, were another. Religious and political conventions that encouraged the exchange of ideas provided excitement in what often seemed a never-ending struggle to change public opinion. Monthly prayer meetings for the slaves, which in Dover,

New Hampshire, lasted for over twenty years, drew members together in prayer and reinforced the sacred nature of the cause. Alternative celebrations of the Fourth of July and festivities to mark the anniversary of emancipation in the West Indies in 1833 provided a stirring mixture of pageantry, speeches, song, good food, and good cheer in attractive rural settings. All these events contributed to a distinctive antislavery culture that helped keep those supporting an unpopular reform committed and connected.

POLITICAL ABOLITIONISM

With the formation of the Liberty Party in 1840, political abolitionists signaled their rejection of the tacit bargain that had protected the second party system by keeping the issue of slavery out of politics. Insisting that political action represented the most effective way to work for emancipation and black rights, political abolitionists defined voting as a moral duty. The Liberty Party won some seven thousand votes (or 0.3 percent of the total) in the 1840 presidential election and never enjoyed great success at the polls. Although the party adopted much of the paraphernalia of popular politics, it did not try to broaden its appeal by compromising abolitionist principles. Even the majority of abolitionist voters, reluctant to vote for candidates with little chance of winning, did not vote for Liberty candidates.

Yet the Liberty Party was more important than the number of its votes suggested. Although technically abandoning moral suasion, the party actually played an important educational and moral role. In states ranging from Michigan to Wisconsin to Maine, the party's printed materials and political activities, which often included women, publicized antislavery views and exposed the failings of the existing political system. During a period when the rights of African Americans were being curtailed, the party supported black political and civil rights. In Ohio, the Liberty Party made the repeal of the state's black laws a major goal of its campaigns in the early 1840s while Wisconsin's Liberty Party's slogan proclaimed "no political distinction based on color." The party welcomed African Americans and also made special efforts to attract evangelical support, thus strengthening the moral and racial credentials of antislavery. In the long run, the Liberty Party contributed to the eventual collapse of the second party system by pressuring northern Whig politicians to become more forceful in opposition to slavery.

In 1848, Gerrit Smith drew a distinction between an abolitionist who "is one who is in favor of abolishing slavery, and who works for its abolition," and "an antislavery person . . . who may be but opposed to slavery" (Kraut, ed., *Crusaders and Compromisers*, p. 101). This distinction suggests that, at best, the Free-Soil Party that succeeded the Liberty Party in the late 1840s and the Republican Party that emerged out of the wreckage of the second party system in the 1850s were examples of moderate antislavery rather than abolitionism. Opposed to the slave power rather than slavery, neither party called for the abolition of slavery in states where it already existed. Also, their commitment to black rights was faltering. Yet the distinction should not be carried too far. Many Free Soilers were more enlightened on race issues than most northerners. Many felt that slavery was wrong. Republicans and Free Soilers alike believed that if the South was unable to expand into western territories, slavery would wither and die. Abolitionists like Frederick Douglass and the writer and newspaper editor Lydia Maria Child supported moderate antislavery politics as a way of undermining the slave system.

ABOLITIONISTS AND THE CHURCHES

The Massachusetts abolitionist Charles Whipple expressed a common view when in the late 1850s he stated that "the Anti-slavery movement . . . was at its commencement, and has ever since been, thoroughly and emphatically a religious enterprise" (McKivigan, p. 18). Because abolitionists were convinced that slavery was a sin, they initially expected that the evangelical churches would adopt the cause as their own. As the 1830s progressed, however, it became increasingly clear that the national bodies of the evangelical denominations wished to avoid taking a stand that would offend southern members, prevent denominational access to the slaves, and perhaps lead to formal division. On the local level, many ministers and congregations were not convinced that slavery was a sin. Some clergy feared that the contention over slavery would undermine the church's religious mission and possibly even threaten their own position. As a result, someone like Mrs. Cornelia Perry, a member of the Presbyterian Church in Seneca Falls, New York, knew nothing about the evils of slavery for "our ministers had never told us anything about it & I [had] sup-

Lydia Maria Child. An abolitionist, suffragist, and prolific writer, Child (1802–1880) undergirded her opposition to racism and sexism with a philosophy of individualism. © CORBIS

posed there was no very great sin in it" (Altschuler and Saltzgaber, p. 121).

The resistance at both national and local levels provoked abolitionists to keep up their pressure. Abolitionist clergy raised the question of slavery in national meetings and held their own conventions, highlighting the moral failure of their governing bodies. Individuals sent in petitions and forced discussions at the local level. In some congregations and places there was no disagreement about slavery, and the church became the site of antislavery activities. In Illinois, abolitionists who controlled the Congregational Association passed a ruling in 1845 that made the acknowledgment of slavery as a sin obligatory for those joining Congregational churches affiliated with the association. In other places committed abolitionists, although not in the majority, persisted in efforts to influence fellow church members. As they realized, the church provided access to a large group of people who might

avoid organized antislavery events but who would not stay away from Sabbath services.

In the 1840s, however, some church abolitionists became discouraged, denounced the moral laxity of their fellow Christians, and withdrew from their churches. Although some agonized over this decision, the democratizing trends that had affected Protestantism in the Early Republic reinforced their belief in the primacy of the individual conscience. As one woman declared, "with the Bible before me . . . I need not err" (Jeffrey, p. 146). In 1843 thousands of Methodists separated from their denomination to form the Wesleyan Methodist Church. The Indiana Yearly Meeeting of Orthodox Quakers split (along with meetings in Michigan, New York, Ohio, and Pennsylvania), while in New York State, "come-outers" from different denominations formed union churches. By the 1850s, there were six large "come-outer" sects. Separation weakened individual churches and denominations morally and financially.

Church and political abolitionism continued into the 1850s. The crises of that decade generated renewed interest in fugitive slaves, fugitive slave communities in Canada, and vigilance and underground railroad activities. They also reopened the question of colonization in African American abolitionist circles.

The crises that made many northern blacks despair of having a future in the United States ironically promoted more sympathy in the North for the abolitionists. Harriet Beecher Stowe's *Uncle Tom's Cabin,* published in 1852, reinforced changing feelings toward the abolitionist cause with its depiction of good-hearted slaves and the civil system under which they suffered. Many white abolitionists felt more a part of the mainstream than ever before. Carrying their ideals into wartime, they pressed the administration to make emancipation a war goal and promoted relief efforts among contraband slaves. With the end of the war, however, most societies considered their work finished. The slaves were free. In 1874 a group of abolitionists met in Chicago. They spent their time not contemplating what needed to be done among the newly freed people but reflecting upon "the success which we have been permitted to realize" (Jeffrey, p. 231).

See also **Africa and America; Race as a Cultural Category; The Black Church: Invisible and Visible; The Classical Vision; Secession, War, and Union** *(in this volume);* **African Americans** *(volume 2);* **Race** *(volume 3); and other articles in this section.*

BIBLIOGRAPHY

Biographies

Davis, Hugh. *Joshua Leavitt: Evangelical Abolitionist.* Baton Rouge, La., 1990.

Mayer, Henry. *All on Fire: William Lloyd Garrison and the Abolition of Slavery.* New York, 1998.

McFeely, William S. *Frederick Douglass.* New York, 1991.

Sterling, Dorothy. *Ahead of Her Time: Abby Kelley and the Politics of Antislavery.* New York, 1991.

Stewart, James Brewer. *Wendell Phillips: Liberty's Hero.* Baton Rouge, La., 1986.

———. *William Lloyd Garrison and the Challenge of Emancipation.* Arlington Heights, Ill., 1992.

Religious Abolitionism

Altschuler, Glenn C., and Jan M. Saltzgaber. *Revivalism, Social Conscience, and Community in the Burned-Over District: The Trial of Rhoda Bement.* Ithaca, N.Y., 1983.

Carwardine, Richard J. *Evangelicals and Politics in Antebellum America.* New Haven, Conn., 1993.

McKivigan, John R. *The War against Proslavery Religion: Abolitionism and the Northern Churches, 1830–1865.* Ithaca, N.Y., 1984.

Politics

Kraut, Alan M., ed. *Crusaders and Compromisers: Essays on the Relationship of the Antislavery Struggle to the Antebellum Party System.* Westport, Conn., 1983.

Race and Gender in Abolitionism

Finkelman, Paul, ed. *Fugitive Slaves: Articles on American Slavery,* vol. 6. New York, 1989.

Goodman, Paul. *Of One Blood: Abolitionism and the Origins of Racial Equality.* Berkeley, Calif., 1998.

Hewitt, Nancy A. *Women's Activism and Social Change: Rochester, New York 1822–1872.* Ithaca, N.Y., 1987.

Jacobs, Donald M., ed. *Courage and Conscience: Black and White Abolitionists in Boston.* Bloomington, Ind., 1993.

Jeffrey, Julie Roy. *The Great Silent Army of Abolitionism: Ordinary Women in the Antislavery Movement.* Chapel Hill, N.C., 1998.

Ripley, C. Peter, ed. *The Black Abolitionist Papers.* 5 vols. Chapel Hill, N.C., 1985–1992.

Yee, Shirley J. *Black Women Abolitionists: A Study in Activism, 1828–1860.* Knoxville, Tenn., 1992.

Yellin, Jean Fagan. *Women and Sisters: The Antislavery Feminists in American Culture.* New Haven, Conn., 1989.

Yellin, Jean Fagan, and John C. Van Horne, eds. *The Abolitionist Sisterhood: Women's Political Culture in Antebellum America.* Ithaca, N.Y., 1994.

Other

Friedman, Lawrence J. *Gregarious Saints: Self and Community in American Abolitionism, 1830–1870.* New York, 1982.

Magdol, Edward. *The Antislavery Rank and File: A Social Profile of the Abolitionists' Constituency.* Westport, Conn., 1986.

Stokes, Melvyn, and Stephen Conway, eds. *The Market Revolution in America: Social, Political, and Religious Expressions, 1800–1880.* Charlottesville, Va., 1996.

Walters, Ronald G. *The Antislavery Appeal: American Abolitionism after 1830.* Baltimore, 1976.

REFORM INSTITUTIONS

Ellen Dwyer

European visitors to the early-nineteenth-century United States were amazed at what they saw in the rapidly growing and changing new country. Twenty-three-year-old Isabella Bird was struck by the extraordinary number of political parties and religious groups. The census, she marveled, listed more than one hundred denominations among the American people. In addition to such standard religions as Methodism, Presbyterianism, Congregationalism, and Roman Catholicism, there were:

> Maronites, Antiburgers, Believers in God, Children of Peace, Disunionists; Danian, Democratic Gospel, and Ebenezer Socialists; Free Inquirers, Inspired Church, Millerites, Menonites, New Lights, Perfectionists, Pathonites, Pantheists, Tunkards, Restorationists, Superalists, Cosmopolites, and hosts of others. (p. 426)

Another Englishwoman, Harriet Martineau, more enthusiastically saluted the propensity of Americans to join organizations and work for change:

> I regard the American people as a great embryo poet: now moody, now wild, but bringing out results of absolute good sense; restless and wayward in action but with deep peace at his hearth; exulting that he has caught the true aspect of things past, and at the depth of futurity which lies before him, wherein to create something so magnificent as the world has scarcely begun to dream of. (p. 29)

Taken together (albeit with a grain of salt) these two commentaries capture an important aspect of antebellum America: the extraordinary perfectionist impulse, the energy for reform. Often reformers' rhetoric echoed Martineau's dream of creating "something so magnificent as the world has scarcely begun to dream of." Yet, the sheer number and range of reform organizations evoke Bird's bemusement when faced with what sometimes seemed like an absurdly large number of religious sects, political parties, and reform groups. The new country was growing rapidly, its industries expanding, its cities taking in large numbers of immigrants from Europe, its transportation network becoming ever larger and more sophisticated. Middle- and upper-class Americans viewed this situation with both excitement and alarm. Pleased by the increasing prosperity and power of the United States, they simultaneously worried that it might be changing so quickly that the social bonds that had once held the country together might weaken and even break. In response, they became involved in a wide range of reform movements, from abolition, temperance, and relief for the poor to free love, anti-masonry, and women's rights, some intended to reinvigorate traditional values and others to restructure more radically.

In addition to using persuasion and the law to change behavior and values, antebellum activists constructed a powerful pantheon of reform institutions, from prisons, houses of refuge, and county poorhouses to schools for the blind and orphanages. Probably the most important and long-lasting of these new arrangements were prisons, lunatic asylums, and common schools. Initially, antebellum reformers expressed enormous optimism about the potential of these institutions to meet not only specific goals—for example, the curing of madness—but to help reform the entire society. By inculcating disorderly lunatics, criminals, and schoolchildren with the values of hard work, self-discipline, and control, these institutions would demonstrate to the many restless, self-absorbed, and heedless Americans who lived outside their walls the order in a disorderly world. Antebellum reformers did not want to halt progress in America, but they wanted to slow down its pace and refine its rough edges. They also genuinely hoped that these new social institutions would help the poor and the weak.

Although interrupted by the Civil War, large-scale efforts to help and control poor and dependent Americans resumed as soon as the war ended. In many areas of the country, a new scientific charity emerged, tinged with the beginnings of the more pessimistic hereditarian ideology that ultimately saw certain individuals and groups as unimprovable

PRISON REFORM

This excerpt, written by Alexander H. Connor, the head of the educational division at the Indiana State Prison in Michigan City, suggests the ways in which the ideas of moral education, so powerful in the common school movement, influenced other reform institutions as well. To twentieth-century eyes, the rhetoric of salvation through learning appears somewhat incongruous, given the well-known harshness of prison life and the violent histories of many inmates.

The moral instructor's matter-of-fact description of his efforts to teach adult inmates to read reminds historians of the wide variations in basic literacy in the nineteenth-century United States, even in the industrializing Midwest. The intensity of his religious beliefs suggests the strong vein of evangelical Protestantism in much nineteenth-century reform work.

To the Board of Directors: Gentlemen—In this my Second Annual Report, I respectfully call your attention to the "Educational Department."

During the past year about fifty of the younger men of the convicts have been taken to the chapel one hour on each Sunday, and have so improved in reading that most of them are now placed in classes reading the Testament at a Sabbath-school, which is now held at 9 o'clock, A.M., every Sunday.

Those who cannot read are doing well in the primer, and may soon be advanced to reading classes. The Assistance of Messrs. Smith, Ford, and Miller, in the Sunday morning school, is proof of the magnetic power of personal contact for elevating human nature, not only teaching to read, but to sing and to pray and trust.

Many have, with their own funds, purchased copy books and slates and are practicing the art of writing in their cells.

Arithmetics and geographies have been furnished to all who would receive them, and public and private instruction given on all these subjects.

These are the "arts" required by law to be taught to all whom the Warden may send (by the Moral Instructor). . . .

As the rules contemplate a religious as well as educational work, I ask permission to report that all the convicts are taken to the chapel on every Sunday at 11½ o'clock, A.M., unless specially excused. One hour only is allowed for public service, consisting of singing, prayer, reading Scripture lessons, and lecture or sermon. . . .

While I speak as a man on the educational and financial part of my work, I must be permitted to speak as a minister of the Lord Jesus Christ, in the report on religion.

I have baptized three on profession of their faith, two more are catechumens for the same ordinance. Eight profess to be reclaimed from their backslidings, and four profess to have received the witness of pardon during the past six weeks.

What I have done for them I wait the judgment to decide, but what this work has done for me—I know now that its responsibilities have driven me to the Master. "All my springs are in Him," and His love has been greatly increased in my heart, as it has been enlarged by my "travail of soul" for the salvation of all who are in bondage to sin.

Source: *Annual Report of the Officers and Directors of the Indiana State Prison North. To the Governor, 1869.*

because of their "defective" genetic makeup. At the institutional level, states began to coordinate their multiple social welfare efforts under the umbrella Board of Charities. The first to act, in 1863, was Massachusetts, with its three state insane asylums, three almshouses, reform school for boys, industrial school for girls, hospital for sick and disabled aliens, and four other institutions that accepted state funds. By 1875, there was a Board of Charities in each of the northern and midwestern states. A bit later, at annual meetings of the National Conference of Charities and Corrections, reformers from an extraordinary range of public and private institutions came together to give papers, share fund-raising strategies, and discuss how to control and treat what seemed to be increasingly recalcitrant clients.

More than one hundred years later, as they look back with the advantage of hindsight, scholars argue bitterly over how best to understand the intentions and actions of nineteenth-century reformers, whether of the antebellum or postbellum variety, and of their institutions, many of which have proven surprisingly durable. Often the debate divides between those who emphasize the class-based social control motives of reformers and those who prefer to stress their idealism and benevolence. While the argument has yet to be settled, in the late twentieth century historians turned their attention to those who used and inhabited prisons, lunatic asylums, and common schools. Increasingly, they stressed the institutions' multiple roles (lunatic asylums, for example, functioned as hospitals, schools, old-age and rest homes, and prisonlike places of confinement) and the ways in which inmates and families, as well as elites and the state, shaped (albeit from a much weaker position) their internal environments and daily routines. Some scholars also noted the paradoxical impact of gender and race on institutional experiences. Kept out of southern schools for the feeble-minded by racist policies, for example, late-nineteenth-century African Americans also escaped the experiments in therapeutic sterilization carried on at some of these institutions. Gender as well as race shaped the experiences of reformers and their targets. For example, in the case of the prison movement, middle- and upper-class women led the campaign for the building of specialized reformatories where white female criminals would be protected from sexual exploitation and offered vocational training. They then filled those institutions with sexual delinquents, many with indefinite sentences for relatively minor offenses. Excluded from such institutions, African American women were crowded into custodial, sometimes mixed-sex prisons in the South. However, moral delinquencies alone seldom led to imprisonment for them. And regionalism shaped the timing of institutional innovation and change in ways historians have yet to fully capture.

While lunatic asylums, prisons, and common schools differed from one another in important ways, generally they were supported by many of the same people. For example, Horace Mann started out interested in prison reform and then got caught up in the common school movement. In 1832, Samuel Gridley Howe became the first director of the Perkins School for the Blind, the first such institution in the United States; he also helped the reformer Dorothea Dix lobby for funds for insane asylums in Massachusetts. Public schools, lunatic asylums, and prisons shared not only supporters but also similar organizational goals and reformative principles.

PRISON REFORM: ITS EMERGENCE IN THE EARLY-NINETEENTH-CENTURY UNITED STATES

Large, state-funded prisons, in the form of penitentiaries, were not unique to the antebellum United States. They first had been built in eighteenth-century England and France. Before the American Revolution, criminals had spent time in local jails or been punished with whippings, fines, and, in extreme cases, hangings. Afterward, as states drafted new constitutions, many attempted to revise criminal codes so as to make them more humane. In Pennsylvania, for example, Quaker legislators eliminated the death penalty for property offenses and sodomy, substituting ten years' imprisonment. The purpose of confinement, they argued, was not simply to punish but to "correct and reform" offenders. Because solitary confinement was considered more conducive to reflection than traditional public work projects, in 1790, Philadelphia's Walnut Street Jail was divided up into thirty-six cells, twenty-four for men and twelve for women. Thus, it became what many historians view as the first prison in the United States.

A number of other states quickly emulated Pennsylvania and, by the 1820s, imprisonment had become the preferred sanction for criminals in the Northeast and parts of the Midwest. Visitors came from all over western Europe to tour American prisons and report back to their home governments. At the heart of these new institutions was a set of daily routines, which, in combination with careful architectural arrangements, were expected to demonstrate the principles of sound social organization to those both within and without. Combining practicality with humanitarian ideals, penitentiaries became a source of much civic pride.

Despite their fervent embrace of prisons as rehabilitative institutions, reformers argued bitterly about which of two early-nineteenth-century systems worked best: the so-called separate system, developed in Pennsylvania, and New York's congregate system, initiated at Auburn Prison between 1819 and 1823 and then set up at Ossining (Sing Sing). Both arrangements kept convicts separate from one another but, at Auburn, they worked silently side by side during the day, while in Pennsylvania they were isolated for the term of their sentences, eating, working, sleeping, and reading the Bible alone in single-person cells. Given the intensity of the debate over their merits, it is surprising to see how much the two systems resembled one another. Both were based on the assumption that criminals are not innately evil but have been led astray by negligent families and corrupt communities. If removed from temptation and forced to follow a strict daily regimen of work and reflection, convicts learn the value of honesty, self-discipline, and hard work. In the end, the Auburn system won out, largely because congregate arrangements were cheaper than separate ones. By the 1850s, however, in many American prisons order was enforced through brutal discipline and the lockstep had replaced the Bible as a key symbol of American prison life.

THE POSTWAR EXPERIENCE: NEW ARRANGEMENTS FOR WOMEN, CHILDREN, AND AFRICAN AMERICANS

Even before the Civil War, reformers had begun to experiment with new penal institutions for women and children. For example, in the 1820s, private philanthropists worked together with state officials to build specialized institutions for white male juveniles in cities like New York, Philadelphia, and Boston. In 1849, Philadelphia's House of Refuge added a separate facility for African American delinquents. Seeing a close link between poverty and juvenile crime, legislatures made it legal to force children into these institutions not only when they broke criminal laws but when they committed status offenses (like school truancy) or were perceived to suffer from parental neglect.

The movement to reform delinquent girls took a slightly different shape. In 1854, Massachusetts created the first state training school for girls, the Lancaster Industrial School for Girls. It was structured so as to emulate the Victorian family, with a distant, paternal male superintendent overseeing the school and "mothers" put in charge of individual cottages. While reformers saw Lancaster as a refuge for girls whose families had failed to protect them, families too viewed the institution as useful and used it to control and educate adolescent daughters who had become difficult to control. The same, largely female, reformers who pushed for the establishment of Lancaster also called for separate prisons for adult (white) females in the years before the Civil War. These reformers felt themselves uniquely qualified because of their sex to help their weak and fallen sisters. The guiding principles of female prison reformers were threefold: women criminals should be kept in separate institutions from men; they needed special rehabilitation programs designed to teach domestic skills and sexual morality; and the prisons should be run exclusively by women. Beginning in the 1870s in Indiana, they succeeded in persuading a number of state legislatures to implement these ideas in the form of female reformatories.

For the most part, African American women were excluded from female reformation. In the North, they tended to be sent to male prisons. In the impoverished South, right after the Civil War, because plantation owners easily had managed to punish their slaves without recourse to prisons, states turned to convict leasing programs. These programs let private contractors use prisoners as laborers in return for providing minimal custodial care. Primarily used for African Americans who had broken the law, for a time they not only saved localities the cost of constructing prisons but made them money as well.

The other major institutional innovation of the 1870s was the reformatory, designed to offer young male first-time offenders an alternative to the increasingly harsh and violent state penitentiaries. The best known was the Elmira (New York) Reformatory, run from 1876 until 1900 by Zebulon R. Brockway. The first cycle of prison reform had ended ignominiously, its obituary written in a scathing 1867 *Report on the Prisons and Reformatories,* and a new era opened, at the National Congress of Penitentiary and Reformatory Discipline in October 1870. Here, what came to be known as "the new penology" was introduced by its most prominent spokesperson, Brockway. In most respects, Brockway and his peers continued to support the rehabilitative goals of earlier reformers but they had new ideas about how best to achieve them.

At Elmira, Brockway replaced repressive routines with educational programs and replaced set prison terms with indeterminate sentencing and parole. However, when faced with resistance, Brockway quickly reverted to harsh punishments to maintain discipline, at times whipping his young charges with rubber hoses and two-foot-long leather straps or confining them to isolated cells for months. The result was predictable: inmates rioted, injured themselves, and tried to escape. Eventually, Brockway was removed in disgrace. Thus this latest reform venture, heralded as part of the "March of Progress," instead once again revealed the rehabilitative limitations of institutions. Somewhat surprisingly, this failure, however, did not lead reformers to question seriously the prisons they had spent the century fighting for. The major problems lay not within but without: in legislatures that refused to fund prison programs adequately and in criminal codes.

THE ASYLUM MOVEMENT IN ANTEBELLUM AMERICA

Although they were not an invention of Jacksonian America, the number of state-funded lunatic asylums in the United States grew substantially during the years before the outbreak of the Civil War. Appearing first in the South, they then were constructed in industrializing states like New York and Massachusetts, from whence the movement spread to agricultural areas like Vermont, Ohio, Tennessee, and Georgia. By 1850, almost every northeastern and midwestern legislature had created an asylum; by 1860, twenty-eight of the thirty-three states had public asylums for the insane. Institutional solutions to madness were neither new nor uniquely American. However, they did assume a very different view of the agitated mentally ill than that of the eighteenth century, when lunatics had been treated more like raving animals than rational beings.

A particularly eloquent articulator of new views was the French doctor Philippe Pinel. Opposed to confining and secluding the insane, he developed a new psychologically oriented therapy, which he called "moral treatment." By "moral," Pinel meant oriented toward the mind, rather than the body. Far from being a hopeless disorder, Pinel argued, lunacy could be cured by confinement in quiet, well-ordered institutions. From the external order of their days, lunatics would learn internal order as well. Because rehabilitation demanded a special milieu, the asylum hospital became the center of Pinel's therapeutic system. Also influential in the development of institutional responses to insanity was the English Quaker William Tuke, who founded the York (England) Retreat in 1796. Unlike Pinel, however, the Quakers used lay managers to oversee patients and enforce treatment programs.

American doctors trained abroad, social reformers who visited English and French institutions, and publishers of the writings of doctors like Pinel and Tuke helped bring these European therapeutic innovations to the attention of middle- and upper-class Americans. Further contributing to the popularity of first private and then state-funded lunatic asylums was the need for new forms of social control. Traditional ways of coping with the insane, especially the violent, were increasingly ineffective in large cities filled with poor immigrants and displaced rural Americans. In this situation, madness was seen as dangerously disruptive of an already tenuous social order. Further, the few private asylums, with their limited resources and high costs, could not hold all those who needed help and custody. As a result, after 1825, the care of the insane increasingly became the province of states. Although there were multiple reasons why states took on this burden, often they expressed their motives in terms of an economics of compassion. A quick response to and treatment of madness in lunatic asylums, both reformers and legislators argued, would help the ill quickly regain both their health and their social productivity.

Somewhat surprisingly, given the urban and industrial forces that fed asylum building in much of the Northeast, the first public mental hospitals were built in the more rural South, in Virginia, Kentucky, South Carolina, and Maryland. Although the early South Carolina Lunatic Asylum (founded in 1820) saw itself as a curative institution founded on the principles of moral treatment, it quickly found itself limited by inadequate funding and an accumulation of chronic and incurable cases. As elsewhere in the antebellum South, many South Carolinians tended to see the new asylum as appropriate only for those whose families were too poor to provide care at home. Discouraged, Francis T. Stribling, while an assistant physician at Virginia's Western Lunatic Asylum, said of his workplace, "The institution deserves no higher appellation, than a *well-kept prison*."

For the most part, the situation for insane slaves was even worse than for poor whites. The 1840s census, conducted by the office of the secretary of

DOROTHEA DIX

Dorothea Dix was an antebellum reformer who achieved international renown for her efforts on behalf of the mentally ill. Growing up in Massachusetts, she early became an admirer of a number of important Boston reformers, including William Ellery Channing and Samuel Gridley Howe. Involved in charitable work from a young age, she found her life mission while teaching a Sunday School class at a local house of correction. There she discovered several insane persons confined in abysmal conditions. With Howe's help, Dix began an investigation of the insane in poorhouses and jails in Massachusetts. In 1843, she presented to the Massachusetts state legislature what was to be the first of many memorials, summarizing her findings and calling for reform.

Subsequently, Dix initiated a national campaign for state-supported hospitals for the mentally ill. A harsh New England childhood and adolescence had made Dix very demanding—of herself and others—but her high expectations served her well once she became involved in asylum work. Despite bouts of ill health (triggered as often by personal disappointments and stress as by physical frailty), Dix traveled ceaselessly across the country, lobbying for the construction of state mental hospitals. Once in Texas, after her stagecoach became mired in mud, she even spent the night in the bottom of a gully. Without a permanent home, Dix spent much of her life moving between boardinghouses, the homes of wealthy friends and relatives, and hotels. While she was often accused of exaggerating the poor condition of local asylums and even, when convenient, inventing the sad stories she presented to newspapers and legislatures, Dix had an extraordinary political career. Particularly remarkable were her activities in Washington, D.C., on behalf of a bill that would have granted federal land-grant monies to mental hospitals. Although eventually Dix's bill was vetoed by President Franklin Pierce in 1857, by then she had become a familiar figure in the U.S. Congress. Her political activism and, in particular, her lobbying stood in notable contrast to her often-proclaimed support for traditional views of female virtues and her hostility to the women's rights movement.

Subsequently, Dix's career took a downturn. Despite her long opposition to the antislavery movement, Dix supported the Union after the outbreak of the Civil War. Named general superintendent of nurses for the Northern army in the 1860s, she found herself unable to maintain, let alone build, administrative power. As the young nurse Louisa May Alcott noted, the women who worked under Dix did not like her; she was seen as good-intentioned but strange, fussy, and ineffective. In old age, having survived most of her family and friends, Dix lived in a suite at the New Jersey State Lunatic Asylum in Trenton until her death in 1887.

Source: Based on Brown, *Dorothea Dix: New England Reformer.*

---

state, John C. Calhoun, allegedly revealed that the rate of insanity among the free blacks of the North was almost five times greater than that among slaves in the South. Calhoun used this data to defend the institution of slavery; within the South, it also helped to justify the exclusionary policies of many asylums. A notable exception was Virginia's Eastern State Hospital at Williamsburg, where John M. Galt, after 1841, placed black males in the wards with whites and set up separate quarters for black females. Although he reported that his white patients often responded by treating the blacks as servants, as the Civil War grew closer, Galt was forced to abandon his experiment.

In Philadelphia in 1844, thirteen heads of lunatic asylums, both public and private, came together to form the Association of Medical Superintendents of American Institutions for the Insane (later the American Psychiatric Association). The first head of the new organization, Thomas Kirkbride of the Pennsylvania Hospital, was an important spokesperson for the emerging medical specialty of psychiatry, arguably the first medical specialty in American medicine outside of surgery. Raised a Quaker and trained at the University of Pennsylvania Medical School, Kirkbride was intensely interested in the architecture and organization of the asylum. He wrote voluminously on a range of practical issues, from the location of ducts and pipes in the well-built institution, the proper size and location of buildings and the best placement of water closets, to classification strategies for patients, attendant training, and therapy programs. Although later criticized for paying more attention to buildings than patients, Kirkbride was convinced that by solving technical matters of construction and maintenance he was solving the problem of insanity. In contrast to eighteenth-century asylums that had resembled houses, nineteenth-century institutions had carefully laid-out central administration buildings, from which often radiated long, straight wings where inmates lived. These large, multistory buildings represented, in visual form, the faith of Kirkbride and his colleagues in the redemptive power of institutions.

Although committed to environmental explanations of madness and therefore to moral treatment, antebellum asylum superintendents did not reject medicine, using drugs and diet to regulate, strengthen, and, when necessary, quiet. Particularly committed to somatic explanations and therapies was John Perdue Gray of the New York State Lunatic Asylum in Utica, who would become notorious for his reliance on sedatives and on restraints like the so-called Utica crib to control the violent. Initially, superintendents claimed, asylum therapeutics were enormously successful. For example, in 1834, Samuel Woodward of the Worcester State (Lunatic) Hospital discharged 82 percent of his recent cases as recovered. However, by the 1850s, as chronic patients had begun to accumulate in the back wards of state institutions, asylum superintendents became markedly less optimistic about their ability to cure the insane.

ASYLUM LIFE AND POLITICS AFTER 1865

Even before the end of the Civil War, state lunatic asylums had come under attack from a variety of sources. This situation worsened as the nineteenth century advanced. Former patients like Elizabeth Packard led campaigns to make involuntary commitment more difficult and to expose the often harsh conditions of asylum life, especially in the back wards. State legislators, unhappy with the high cost of patient care, discussed and in some states implemented cheaper kinds of custodial institutions, often with large farms where inmates worked long hours. For example, patients who had not recovered after several years of treatment at the New York State Lunatic Asylum were transferred to the Willard Asylum for the Chronic Insane, opened in 1869 in Willard, New York, from which few were ever discharged. Many states also set up regulatory boards, called lunacy commissions, to oversee the asylum superintendents. Their intent was to make state-funded institutions more efficient and to prevent abuse and wrongful confinement. Predictably, asylum superintendents disagreed strongly with this and other oversight measures, arguing (unsuccessfully) that they would destroy the doctors' autonomy and politicize asylum management (a prescient claim). At the same time, explanations of insanity became increasingly pessimistic and hereditarian. Crowded, underfunded state institutions increasingly relied upon restraints and medicines, rather than moral treatment, to enforce internal order. Doctors who had once seen themselves as fathers to their patients began to use military and factory metaphors to characterize the organization of their institutions.

While these changes and problems were distressing to families, they continued to send mentally ill members to large, crowded asylums. The decision to do so was rarely made easily or quickly. Although asylum doctors insisted that recent cases of insanity were the most treatable, most families preferred to confine madness within familial rather than asylum walls. They tolerated delusions, eccentricities, and threats of violence for months, even years, sending deranged relatives to state asylums only when they suddenly became dramatically worse, threatening harm to persons or property, or lost their caretakers.

In general, the greater a family's or community's social resources, the longer it postponed institutionalization. On the other hand, once that decision finally was made, it was hard to reverse. State asylums could not turn away patients with legal commitment papers nor could they initiate commitments, but they could and did control who was released. Many of the less fortunate, especially at institutions for the chronic, were simply forgotten by everyone except their ward attendants.

ORIGINS OF THE PUBLIC SCHOOL MOVEMENT

Like asylums and prisons, public schools were promoted in the mid-nineteenth century as a way of instilling order in the increasingly diverse and rapidly changing population of the United States. From the 1830s through the 1850s, under the banner of the common school movement, reformers reshaped almost every aspect of public schooling in the Northeast, including its administration, curriculum, and finances. Among the best known of common school reformers were Horace Mann of Massachusetts and Henry Barnard of Connecticut. Both had begun as Whig legislators, interested in a range of reform causes, before they decided to focus on children. In 1834, Mann supported legislation to establish a permanent school fund from the sale of public land and state taxes and, in 1837, he became secretary of the new Massachusetts Board of Education. Barnard had a similar career, moving from Connecticut to Rhode Island in 1845 to become the state's first commissioner of education. The new common school, as envisioned by these men and their compatriots, was to offer a moral education. The intent was to teach respect for authority, habits of industry, and republican political values, along with reading, writing, and arithmetic.

Winning support for this new experiment in state-funded education was not easy. Even in Massachusetts, a coalition of reformers, merchants, financiers, and industrialists had to fight hard for legislative approval of common school funding and a state board of education. Opponents saw compulsory school taxation as an attack on private property and state school boards as a threat to local autonomy. The resulting battles, bitter in states like Pennsylvania and New York, were even more intense in the Midwest. Once won, they led to a network of district schools, often very different from one another in quality and size. Although American school reformers had borrowed European pedagog-

ical innovations, their common school system, funded by a combination of local taxes, state funds, and tuition, was very different from the national arrangements beginning to emerge in Europe during these years.

Also complicating the expansion of the common school movement was the indifference and, in some cases, outright hostility of workers and immigrants, especially Irish Catholics, toward the project. In New York City, for example, a public school system had been established in 1842, in part to deal with problems of vagrancy and delinquency. Yet, barely half of the city's children attended by midcentury. Many came from families who needed their wages; others saw little of value in a curriculum centered on (Protestant) moral education and character building. Finally, in 1853, the New York State legislature passed the Truancy Act. This authorized local magistrates to compel parents of children between seven and fourteen who lacked "lawful occupation" to send those children to school for at least four months a year. If they refused, the child could be sent to a refuge, orphanage, or juvenile reformatory. A similar law had passed in Massachusetts the preceding year. For the first time, the state and its agents could detain children who had not committed a crime. However, compulsory education laws did not become universal across the United States until 1918, more than fifty years later.

Despite the involvement of many clergy in the common school movement, the United States developed (by nineteenth-century standards) a thoroughly secularized educational system. In large part, this seems to have been the result of the growing fear of Catholics before the Civil War, which led state legislators to banish aid to all nonpublic institutions in order to keep it from Catholic schools. Too poor to support both common and parochial schools, Irish Catholics in particular resented this decision. They saw the common schools as invented for the purpose of turning their children against them, and indeed the curriculum and texts were profoundly hostile toward Ireland and Catholicism.

POPULAR EDUCATION AFTER THE CIVIL WAR

In the second half of the nineteenth century, the public school system spread from the Northeast to the rest of the country. In addition, high schools began to be built, especially in wealthier communities. These provided a link between common schools and colleges and universities. The South,

RELIGION AND SCHOOL REFORM: THE ELIOT SCHOOL INCIDENT

As the movement to fund public common schools in the United States gathered force, it provoked opposition from Roman Catholics, among others. Cities like Boston, with large Irish populations, became the site of heated conflicts. Schools in Irish neighborhoods were overcrowded and of poor quality; the curriculum expressed the values of the dominant Protestants. In March 1859, this situation produced what became known as the Eliot School incident. After an Irish-Catholic student at the Eliot School, Thomas Wall, refused to read aloud from the Protestant King James Bible, he was suspended. Although Wall was reinstated quickly, the situation worsened when a local priest instructed his Sunday catechism class to follow Wall's lead. The boy was blamed for the new problems and a school administrator beat his hands severely with a cane. After about one hundred Catholic boys, including Wall, were suspended from the school, another three hundred refused to return.

Acting to restore order, Boston's Bishop Fitzpatrick asked parents to send their children back to school; he also protested to the Boston School Committee about the Protestant practices of the public schools. Although the committee subsequently decided that no child should be forced to recite anything contrary to his religious principles, often the new rule was disregarded. In 1861, the superintendent of public schools urged that Boston segregate poor children into a separate system of privately funded vocational schools. Eliminating those "too low down in the depths of vice, crime, and poverty, to be reached by the benefits of public education" (a thinly veiled reference to the Irish), he declared, would "purify and elevate the character of the public schools." Not until the Irish gained significant political power in Boston after the Civil War did the situation for Irish children in the public schools substantially change.

Source: Based on Galenson, *Journal of Urban History.*

however, continued to lag behind the rest of the country. In general, southern rural schools provided rather minimal educational experiences to their black and white children, compared to their urban or northern counterparts. Rural education was seen as a part-time complement to the seasonal labor demands of an agricultural area. As in the North, the common or public school system in the South was produced by state legislatures. The general trend was toward segregated schools. The few attempts at mixed schools ended with Reconstruction in 1877.

Before the Civil War, African American slaves had received no education and even free African Americans in the North often were excluded from public schools. After the Civil War, in the South, there were three sources of educational change: the

United States Congress, northern philanthropists, and southern legislatures (the most reluctant). From 1865 through 1872, the congressionally established Freedman's Bureau established schools for newly freed blacks. By 1869, almost 114,000 students attended Bureau schools, which emulated the curriculum of the New England common schools and were staffed largely by northern schoolteachers. In addition to the standard curriculum, these teachers added "industrial training," intended to give freed slaves the skills required to become farmers, mechanics, seamstresses, and laundresses. This tradition of industrial education extended into the first black secondary schools and universities as well. Although badly underfunded, the mere existence of colored agricultural and mechanical (A&M) colleges, established with Morrill Act land-grant money (which provided grants of land to state colleges), angered white southerners, especially plantation owners who feared that black education would threaten their supply of agricultural labor.

Northern philanthropists and missionary societies also played an important role in the establishment of high schools and colleges in the postwar South, setting up the Hampton Institute in Virginia and Fisk University in Tennessee. In terms of black-white relations, the histories of these schools are complicated. From the beginning, some prominent freedmen, including the abolitionist Frederick Douglass, were angered by the paternalism of some of the reformers and their tendency to treat their black students, whatever their age, as children. Despite such limitations these institutions offered much greater opportunities than the segregated public schools reluctantly mandated by post-Reconstruction southern legislatures.

By 1877, public education in the United States had changed dramatically. At the beginning of the nineteenth century, most states had a complex mixture of public and private academies, funded in a variety of ways, without a standardized curriculum or formal state-level supervision. By the end, every state in the Union had some sort of district school system, which included both common or elementary and secondary schools. Many had public institutions of higher learning as well. In the 1830s, most teachers were male; by the 1870s, teachers were largely female, working for substantially lower wages than their male counterparts. Yet, despite these common trends, there continued to be an enormous range of schooling opportunities across America. In nineteenth-century America, as in the twentieth, money was a crucial determinant of educational opportunity and experience. Its lack forced some out of school into full-time jobs and often restricted the number of teachers employed by a school district, the length of the school year, and the diversity of curricular offerings. In the Northeast, where more than 50 percent of school-age children lived, nearly 90 percent attended school. In the South, however, home to more than one-third of American children and to almost all the black children, only about 70 percent attended school. This diversity, in offerings and educational experiences, helps to explain the wide range of ability to read and write among those broadly designated as "literate."

By the end of the nineteenth century, Americans no longer saw themselves as embarked on an exciting quest to build a perfect society. Exhausted by the trauma of the Civil War, discouraged by the ever-increasing populations in prisons and mental hospitals, frightened rather than exhilarated by the size and diversities of urban areas, some reformers gave up in despair and others turned to increasingly elitist agendas for change. At the same time, groups that had played relatively minor roles in earlier efforts moved closer to the center of the political stage, from labor union activists to the small but impassioned anti-lynching groups. Whatever the arena of reform energy, however, the faith in institutions as vehicles of social change, which so energized nineteenth-century Americans, had lost much of its persuasive power.

See also **Patterns of Reform and Revolt** *(in this volume);* **Humanitarianism; Social Reform** *(volume 2); and other articles in this section.*

BIBLIOGRAPHY

Reform: General

Bird, Isabella Lucy. *The Englishwoman in America.* 1856. Reprint, Madison, Wisc., 1966.

Martineau, Harriet. *Society in America.* Vol. 1. New York, 1837.

Mintz, Steven. *Moralists and Modernizers: America's Pre–Civil War Reformers.* Baltimore and London, 1995.

Rothman, David J. *The Discovery of the Asylum; Social Order and Disorder in the New Republic.* Baltimore, 1971.

Prisons and Reformatories

Ayers, Edward. *Vengeance and Justice: Crime and Punishment in the Nineteenth-Century American South.* New York, 1984.

Freedman, Estelle B. *Their Sisters' Keepers: Women's Prison Reform in America, 1830–1930*. Ann Arbor, Mich., 1981.

Pisciotta, Alexander W. *Benevolent Repression: Social Control and the American Reformatory-Prison Movement*. New York, 1996.

Rafter, Nicole Hahn. *Partial Justice: Women in State Prisons, 1800–1935*. Boston, 1981.

Schneider, Eric. *In the Web of Class: Delinquents and Reformers in Boston, 1810–1930*. New York, 1992.

Asylums

Dwyer, Ellen. *Homes for the Mad: Life inside Two Nineteenth-Century Asylums*. New Brunswick, N.J., 1987.

Brown, Thomas J. *Dorothea Dix: New England Reformer*. Cambridge, Mass., 1998.

Gamwell, Lynn, and Nancy Tomes. *Madness in America: Cultural and Medical Perceptions of Mental Illness before 1914*. New York, 1995.

Grob, Gerald N. *The Mad among Us: A History of the Care of America's Mentally Ill*. New York, 1994.

McCandless, Peter. *Moonlight, Magnolias, and Madness: Insanity in South Carolina from the Colonial Period to the Progressive Era*. Chapel Hill, N.C., 1996.

Scull, Andrew. *Social Order/Mental Disorder: Anglo-American Psychiatry in Historical Perspective*. Berkeley, Calif., 1989.

Tomes, Nancy. *A Generous Confidence: Thomas Story Kirkbride and the Art of Asylum-Keeping, 1840–1883*. Cambridge, Mass., 1984.

Common Schools

Galenson, David W. "Ethnicity, Neighborhood, and the School Attendance of Boys in Antebellum Boston." *Journal of Urban History* 24, no. 5 (July 1998): 603–626.

Gutek, Gerald L. *Education in the United States: An Historical Perspective*. Englewood Cliffs, N.J., 1998.

Kaestle, Carl F., and Eric Foner, eds. *Pillars of the Republic: Common Schools and American Society, 1780–1860*. New York, 1990.

Katz, Michael. *The Irony of Early School Reform: Educational Innovation in Mid-Nineteenth-Century Massachusetts*. Cambridge, Mass., 1968.

Nasaw, David. *Schooled to Order: A Social History of Public Schooling in the United States*. New York, 1979.

EVANGELICAL THOUGHT

Mark Y. Hanley

Evangelical thought in the mid-nineteenth century had its own integrity apart from the Calvinist orthodoxy that united most eighteenth-century Protestants and the conservative fundamentalist and social gospel movements that divided a later generation. Although the revival fires of the Second Great Awakening flickered by the 1830s, evangelicals during these middle decades turned to elaborate organizational strategies, new print technology, and sheer numbers in an effort to deepen their spiritual imprint on America and the world.

Broad doctrinal consensus across denominational lines also magnified evangelicals' confidence. Tragically, they divided their moral energy and triumphalist spiritual vision along sectional lines in the 1840s, contributing directly to the outbreak of the American Civil War.

ESSENTIAL DOCTRINES

Like their forebears, evangelicals drew upon the historic doctrines of the Protestant Reformation and its guiding lights, Martin Luther and John Calvin. That heritage gave preeminent place to personal faith in Christ as the means of salvation and to Scripture as the sole authoritative guide to God's redemptive plan.

Keeping with changes brought by the Second Great Awakening that had swept America earlier in the century, mid-nineteenth-century evangelicals explained the Christian experience as a "new birth." Although denominational language and theological emphasis varied, they generally agreed that Christianity required a radical spiritual transformation of the individual. This meant personal spiritual conversion through repentance, faith in Christ and his atonement for sin (justification), and, finally, affirmation of one's regeneration through a life of personal piety and acts of charity and benevolence (sanctification).

John Wesley, Methodism's eighteenth-century founder, was instrumental in defining the new evangelical order. His ministry in Britain and America revived an Arminian theology that endowed all of humanity with the free will to experience a sudden, heart-changing moment of spiritual regeneration and renewal followed by a life of personal holiness. Methodism's aggressive appeal to common people widened the theological opening and prompted both formal and practical revisions of the Calvinist doctrines that had guided most American Protestants since the early colonial era.

Calvinism's historic message of sin, salvation, and judgment remained the doctrinal centerpiece of orthodoxy, of course, but its underlying assumptions of total human depravity and the predestination of souls chafed against a culture bent on democracy and freedom of choice. In place of Calvinism's "limited atonement"—the belief that Christ died only for those whom he elected to save—champions of the new evangelicalism eased the burden of original sin and declared all honest seekers eligible to respond to Christ's call. While Calvinism taught the imputation of Adam's guilt, the new evangelicalism emphasized an inherited *propensity* to sin and held individuals liable for their own acts of defiance.

This seeming renovation of human ability and choice mirrored expanding personal freedom in the nation's emergent democratic culture. It also had limits. Calvinist Old School Presbyterians and Arminian Methodists, for example, agreed that human sinfulness established a fatal divide between God and man and that only personal faith in Christ could seal the breach. Methodists, no less than Calvinists, rejected salvation through good works. The trinitarian theology guiding all evangelicals attributed conversion to the work of the Holy Spirit and spurned any notion that individuals could "save themselves." To be sure, denominational splits, occasional heresy trials, and shrill denunciations by such Calvinist defenders as Charles Hodge and his

Princeton Seminary colleagues roiled evangelical waters. Broad theological agreement, however, controlled these exchanges of friendly fire.

Most importantly, evangelical ministers of all shades adopted a practical style of preaching that cast the salvation net broadly. Many Baptists continued to accept Calvinist constraints, for example, but the exponential growth of the denomination in the nineteenth century reveals the most relevant components of their Confession of Faith: the "blessings of salvation are made free to all" and "it is the immediate duty of all to accept them." Even many Congregationalists and Presbyterians, anchors of the old Calvinist orthodoxy, turned a sympathetic ear to revivalists such as Charles Finney, who preached an Arminianized Calvinism that called all seekers to repent and be saved.

Because this spiritual working consensus allowed for substantial variety and theological change over time, historians often disagree as to evangelicalism's precise definition and denominational boundaries. Generally speaking, Baptists and Methodists accounted for 70 percent of evangelicals in 1860. The formerly dominant Presbyterians and Congregationalists did not keep pace, but their clergy remained the intellectual leaders of the evangelical community. Lutherans, Disciples of Christ, and low-church Episcopalians also housed substantial evangelical contingents.

The organizational strategies of these groups reveal an evangelical establishment committed to universal appeal, not exclusivity. Virtually every major group supported both foreign and domestic missionary outreach. Collective enterprises such as the American Tract Society, the American Sunday School Union, and the American Bible Society demonstrated the capacity of core evangelical beliefs to produce transdenominational cooperation.

Ironically, common theological ground and a shared commitment to global outreach did not prevent fractious internal struggles over the relationship between doctrinal priorities and cultural commitments. On the eve of the Civil War, Methodists and Baptists had splintered into seventeen separate bodies. Many scholars count these divides among the significant causes of the nation's political disunion in 1860. The broad struggle to define the right relationship between Christianity and culture reveals much about how evangelicals reconciled a theology focused on transcendent aims with a collective commitment to achieve global Christian triumph.

A POSTMILLENNIAL WORLDVIEW

Evangelicals assumed that God remained providentially interested in human affairs, and they assigned substantial, though subordinate, significance to the temporal outcomes of collective effort. They ordered their earthly hopes around a "postmillennial" understanding of God's plans. That is, they believed that the gospel message would ultimately spread worldwide and introduce a thousand years of Christ's spiritual reign on earth.

The millennium would be a time of peace, general prosperity, and the triumph of Christian principles prior to Armageddon and Christ's final triumph over Satan. Consequently, postmillennialism inoculated evangelicals against pessimism and despair, while at the same time magnifying their capacity for self-criticism and cultural dissent. It enabled them to find temporal as well as eternal significance in domestic revivals, missionary outreach, and social reform. Older Calvinist notions of revivals as "seasons" of spiritual renewal dispensed at God's pleasure gave way to a pragmatic approach calling for steady advance of the gospel. Noted evangelist Charles Finney's influential *Lectures on Revivals of Religion* (1835) and *Lectures to Professing Christians* (1837) denounced spiritual complacency as a willful spurning of Christ's desire for all to immediately repent and be saved. Under Finney's judgment, the churches had no excuse.

EVANGELICALS AND THE NATION

In the wake of financial panic and depression that struck in 1837, Americans regained lost confidence in the 1840s through the opening of the Oregon Trail, vast territorial gains from the Mexican War, and the glitter of California gold. Evangelicals' optimistic, progressive spiritual vision seemingly paralleled the young nation's bullish vision of national expansion and material gains. Much of that congruence, however, was more apparent than real.

Many scholars argue that evangelicals easily blended sacred and secular progress in a unified stream with Americans enjoying special, "chosen" status in the eyes of God. National progress and the global advance of republicanism more or less marked progress toward the millennium. Liberal dispensations of patriotic eloquence in ministers' Fourth of July and Thanksgiving orations lend support to such interpretations. One zealous minister feted Independence Day by linking the "incarnation of the Son of God and the birth of Representative

AMERICAN TRACT SOCIETY

There is perhaps no better window onto mainstream evangelical thought in mid-nineteenth century America than the avalanche of tracts and books produced by the American Tract Society (ATS).

Established by East Coast Congregationalists in 1825 and headquartered in New York City, the society by 1850 boasted ten thousand members and annual receipts topping $100,000. In the early 1840s the society's commissioners established a "colportage" system. Thirty-one regional agents and colporteurs drawn from at least eight denominations worked to broaden the distribution of books and tracts reinforcing core evangelical beliefs.

Books were ordinarily sold, but profit was not the goal. Indeed, recent scholars have explained ATS literature as essentially hostile to the market forces shaping American culture.

Leaders took particular pride in the populist nature of tracts and publications designed specifically for ordinary people and containing only those "great truths of salvation in which the mass of evangelical Christians can agree." Consistent with that guideline, the Society's 522 General Series tracts delivered a steady diet of evangelistic messages focused on sin, salvation, and final judgment. Some, such as those designed to rescue seamen from profligate lives in American ports, had a distinctly paternalistic tone. Others warred generally against "intemperance and other prevalent vices."

An emphasis on the eternal benefits of individual spiritual transformation, however, overwhelmed all other themes. Titles of some of the most widely distributed pieces—*The Lost Soul, Prepare to Meet Thy God, I've No Thought of Dying Soon,* and *Are You Ready?*—reveal the society's highly personal and spiritual approach. Most pieces delivered the message through dramatic dialogues or sentimental stories of wandering souls finding new direction along the evangelical path to salvation.

Several tracts called new believers to "labor for the conversion of the world," reflecting the common evangelical assumption that the spread of the gospel message would ultimately produce the millennial reign of Christ on Earth. More commonly, they warned that life's uncertainties loomed larger than any millennial hopes. Christ could just as easily come "as a thief in the night," leaving the unrepentant to face "everlasting destruction."

The society also published hundreds of thousands of copies of classic works, reflecting a determination to give a timeless cast to the evangelical message. The society's Evangelical Family Library, for example, featured the works of seventeenth and eighteenth century English dissenters, including Richard Baxter's *Call to the Unconverted* (1657) and John Bunyan's *Pilgrim's Progress* (1678). Baxter's and Bunyan's works were even produced in raised-letter editions for the blind.

Tract Society publications sounded an alarm for unrepentant souls, and in the members' self-prescribed role of providing a religious literature "for the people," they used technology and sophisticated organization to magnify the popular appeal that underwrote evangelical success.

Republicanism" (Scott, p. 75) as the two greatest days in the history of humanity.

Occasional public outpourings, however, are not reliable guides to the core principles that shaped evangelical responses to the culture. More important is the much larger body of regular sermons and instructive discourse directed specifically to the believing community. Collectively, they reveal significant ambivalence toward the culture's definition of progress and a jealous regard for the transcendent, spiritual dimension of faith.

Francis Wayland, the president of Brown University and a leading Baptist theologian of the age, captured the essence of this determination: "In the Old Testament we find nations addressed, and the communications from God are to them. . . . In the New Testament we perceive nothing of the kind. The gospel of Jesus Christ is a communication made from God to *each individual*." The Presbyterian minister and leading antislavery advocate Joseph P. Thompson sharply divided the purposes of Christ's spiritual kingdom and the material interests of nominal Christendom: "The good will that commerce bears to the nations has the ledger for its textbook and prices current for its commentary; and the pages of this gospel are written alternately in letters of gold and in letters of blood." "Christianization," he explained, must "make men disciples of this religion, disciples of Christ himself, by publishing his gospel to all mankind" (Thompson, pp. 835, 825). Such proscriptions did not erase evangelical cultural commitments or material interests, but they did establish clear boundaries between religion and republicanism.

EVANGELICALS AND REFORM

The preeminent place evangelicals accorded to individual spiritual redemption did not preclude interest in broader social and moral reforms, particularly with regard to the temperance and antislavery movements. Scholars who emphasize religion as a vehicle of social control deployed by cultural elites find particular significance in evangelical reform efforts, but again, caution is appropriate here. Certainly the work of some ministers, particularly by the late 1870s, anticipated what one scholar calls the "moralization of belief." Most evangelicals at midcentury, however, still understood reform within the context of historic doctrines and transcendent spiritual aims, not as a positivist commitment to social engineering and material improvements.

Liberal (mainly Unitarian) clergymen and secular reformers who advocated a more worldly Christian agenda met substantial resistance from mainstream evangelical leaders. In the workaday preaching of ordinary ministers, reform themes rarely upstaged the call for individual salvation and personal piety. The Congregationalist divine Austin Phelps described the call for personal redemption as the essential focus of evangelical effort. To reduce Christianity to a "manual of universal progress" useful primarily for its "salutary bearings on organized society" merely affirmed the culture's penchant for reform at the expense of those "critical transitions of destiny . . . on which individual destiny for eternity is suspended" (Phelps, pp. 294–295). In sum, most evangelicals strove to maintain a relationship between religion and reform that gave clear precedence to the former.

Three basic principles guided their approach to reform. First, evangelicals did not seek personal salvation through moral or social reform efforts nor did they believe that political prohibitions against alcohol, sabbath-breaking, or slavery represented a fast track to the millennium. They retained a Puritan impulse to make community law and life conform to Christian principles, to be sure, but they endowed such efforts with limited significance. Evangelicals believed that spiritual rebirth produced a vast chasm in moral understanding and capacity between the believer and those outside the fold. Consequently, they had limited expectations from social and political initiatives dependent on force or appeals to reason and the natural moral sense of the community.

Typical is the Congregationalist John Humphrey's insistence that the earth must remain "to saints as Babylon." Secular leaders, he admitted, might cooperate with believers as "amiable, cheerful, and intelligent men," but they could never "relish their society, or love them in their spiritual character" (Humphrey, pp. 64–65). Evangelicals did not reject legal or institutional remedies, but they shrank from dependence on state power, even in republican form, as an inferior path to the godly society. Community prohibitions against slavery, alcohol, or Sunday mail delivery, in other words, marked progress toward the millennium only as they represented the fruit of deeper, spiritual transformations.

This individualistic approach to reform found its most extreme expression in Christian perfectionism. With roots reaching back to Wesley's emphasis on a Christian life of personal holiness, perfectionism assumed that the Holy Spirit gave believers the

382

CATHARINE BEECHER

The mid-nineteenth century marked the beginning of the modern women's rights movement and the coming of age of such activists as Elizabeth Cady Stanton, Victoria Woodhull, Susan B. Anthony, and Margaret Fuller. Catharine Beecher, however, ranks as the mid–nineteenth century's preeminent female guardian of evangelical views on gender roles.

A member of evangelicalism's "first family" in the nineteenth century, Beecher as a young woman labored under the sometimes smothering influence of her father Lyman, one of the most prominent ministers in America. Her critical engagement with the incipient women's rights movement, however, was decidedly her own. Throughout her long life, she opposed women's suffrage, liberal divorce laws, birth control, and especially the movement of women into the "poisonous atmosphere" of the industrial workplace.

Beecher admitted women's intellectual capacity for political participation, but condemned it as a distraction from their "distinctive and more important duties" in the home. Writing in 1871, she claimed that "a large majority of American women would regard the gift of the ballot, not as a privilege conferred, but as an act of oppression, forcing them to assume responsibilities belonging to man, for which they are not and can not be qualified" (Beecher, *Suffrage*, p. 7).

Beecher worked from a solid evangelical foundation, but she rejected her father's hard-edged Calvinism even as she defended female domesticity. Her quarrel was not, as she explained, with the "fact" of humanity's depraved behavior but with Calvinism's emphasis on human accountability deriving from original sin rather than from the willful disobedience of individuals.

Far from wanting to transform Christianity into a mere moral code, Beecher expected her doctrinal revisions to "remove insurmountable difficulties from just and generous minds in accepting the Bible as Divine authority." Her carefully integrated social and spiritual vision rejected political activism in favor of an alternative expression of female power centered on the moral nurturing of young children in home and school.

Beecher established female seminaries in Hartford, Connecticut, and Cincinnati, Ohio, and worked through the Ladies Society for Promoting Education in the West to call a legion of single women into service as educators in the nation's common schools. Marriage, however, obliged a woman to submit to male authority and become "chief minister" to the moral and spiritual training of children in the home.

Beecher reasoned that this biblically assigned role augmented female social power. Women alone represented the great "preventive" agency that could inoculate the "common people" against the corruptions of the marketplace and the political platform. The politician's struggles against corruption, she explained, simply reflected a society's collective domestic failure to nurture piety and moral rectitude in the young. Consequently, women's unique moral responsibilities actually exceeded the importance of male authority in the public sphere. A woman could "go to her minister for aid," but, at bottom, *"she must decide for herself"* how to lead new generations to the *"life of the soul*, and for ETERNITY!" (Hanley, p. 110).

Beecher's opposition to women's suffrage did not soften with age. In the decade before her death in 1878, she became increasingly troubled by the strident public voice and secular social agendas of suffrage advocates such as Victoria Woodhull. She remained to the end an apostle of biblically prescribed gender roles as the foundation of individual spiritual hope and earthly moral order.

capacity to live in sinless obedience to God's moral law. Evangelist Charles Finney made Oberlin College the epicenter of such beliefs within mainstream evangelicalism. From pulpit and lecture platform, he told believers to "merge their own will entirely in the will of God."

Phoebe Palmer, ignoring gender barriers to her formal ordination, hoisted the same perfectionist banner among Methodists and became a leading lay evangelist of the day. She promoted spiritual renewal throughout the country and eventually joined Finney in a revival tour of Britain. In a culture increasingly devoted to individual freedom and personal choice, they called for absolute submission to the Divine Will. The holiness doctrine remained a controversial topic among evangelicals, but perfectionism really amounted to a difference in degree rather than kind when compared to a general evangelical emphasis on personal piety.

While they expected few Christians to achieve a state of sinless perfection, Finney and Palmer did prescribe lives of personal and social striving. Palmer, for example, established a mission to provide social assistance in the Five Points district of New York. Under Finney's presidency, Oberlin provided higher education for women and served as a beacon in the antislavery cause. Yet neither evangelist placed social transformation above the individual life of holiness. Such efforts testify to a firm yet cautious evangelical embrace of social reform.

The second principle of evangelical reform drew from St. Augustine's dictum that because communities and nations had no eternal existence, God meted out their collective punishments and rewards only in earthly time. More importantly, since believers did not assume protection from God's providential wrath, they recognized a practical interest in their neighbors' behavior. President Abraham Lincoln's second inaugural address in 1865 borrowed liberally from this evangelical script. Setting aside his usually guarded religious views, Lincoln confessed nationwide culpability in the sin of slavery and called for humility and repentance in the wake of God's bloody vengeance.

Finally, evangelicals forcefully advocated "human instrumentality" as God's appointed means of effecting both spiritual revival and material reforms. This emphasis drew both from free-will theology and from New Testament examples of discipleship. Conversion remained the work of the Holy Spirit, but the divine plan called for human assistance in the physical transmission of the gospel message. Evangelicals eagerly employed transportation advances, steam-driven cylinder presses, and sophis-

ticated organization as adjuncts to this crusade. Many argued that the progress of civilization now mandated "systematic benevolence" to replace the random efforts of the past.

Yet clergymen worried that in emphasizing human agency, they also risked undermining the historic role of the church and their own spiritual commitments. God would effect global spiritual transformation only "through the church," Pennsylvania minister David Riddle cautioned. The heralds of civilization and progress beguiled by technology, intellectual achievement, money, or national ambitions deserved only "the astonishment and admiration of worms like themselves" (Riddle, pp. 20–23). Another minister bluntly declared that Christians now struggled against a modern liberal culture demanding that Christianity become a "religion of reform, and the rights of man and human progress, or it shall not be at all" (Harris, pp. 285–286). Such concerns reveal an evangelical community committed to social reform but not to a social gospel.

EVANGELICALS AND THE WORLD

Evangelicals interpreted their commitments to moral reform and individual spiritual growth within a broader theological framework that centered on fulfilling the "Great Commission." Ministers assumed that Christ's final charge to "preach the gospel to every creature" carried concomitant guarantees of victory: the gospel message would ultimately achieve a controlling global influence and provide the foundation for the promised millennium. Indeed, the middle decades of the nineteenth century can be viewed as the high-water mark of evangelical triumphalism in America.

The Great Commission required laborers in foreign fields, and the founding of the American Board of Commissioners for Foreign Missions (ABCFM) in 1810 provided the flagship of that effort. Presbyterians and Congregationalists dominated the officially independent ABCFM, while Methodists and Baptists established their own home and foreign mission programs.

Evangelicals insisted that the believer's peculiar spiritual capacities placed the burden of outreach exclusively upon the church universal. The gospel message, ministers regularly claimed, needed no "auxiliaries." Francis Wayland reduced the cause to the simplest terms: "The kingdom of Christ is extended as the number of true believers is increased, and as new members are added to his spiritual body, and in no other manner."

At the same time, ministers regularly touted America's republican system and political freedoms as providentially established advantages in carrying out their global charge. Consequently, keeping religion from being overwhelmed by their own patriotism became one of the great evangelical struggles of the age.

The keynote sermons delivered at ABCFM annual meetings provide one example of evangelical resolve in keeping doctrinal and millennial principles at the forefront of a transcultural missionary enterprise. Ministers incorporated domestic listeners into a broader human collective and called for a radically altered world order grounded in Christian moral principles. Just as the spiritual regeneration of each believer defied definition as "reform," so too the millennial razing of the existing social and moral status quo would be realized only as individual conversions multiplied and replaced the desires of fallen humanity with anticipations of eternal bliss beyond the millennial paradise.

The Congregationalist minister and long-time ABCFM president Mark Hopkins stated the case plainly: Christians could expect the gospel to "revolutionize and radically transform society," only as they resisted a worldly dependence on "[removing] directly specific forms of evil" and nurtured a "simple desire to preach Christ and him crucified, and to save men" (Hopkins, p. 442). In sum, this approach to the Great Commission blended Protestant triumphalism with a full measure of self-critique and cultural dissent.

EVANGELICALS AND THE SLAVERY QUESTION

The transcendent hopes and global perspective inspired by the Great Commission did not provide immunity from internal strife and the cultural parochialism that led to the Civil War. Indeed, the clergy's appeal for a millennium of brotherhood, equality, and submission to divine will ironically fueled much of the moral intransigence that divided North and South.

In perhaps the most visible foreshadowing of the secession crisis, Baptists and Methodists formally divided along sectional lines in the 1840s. Doctrinal issues had already split Presbyterians into Old and New School wings in 1837, but many southern clergymen cited the New School's northern focus and thinly disguised antislavery cast as equally decisive.

With respect to slavery, evangelicals simply could not reproduce a working social consensus comparable to what they had achieved on spiritual fronts. That failure deprived the nation of institutional resources that could have averted war.

Northern churches supplied the deepest cultural reservoir of antislavery sentiment, but southern religious leaders, particularly in the border states, had also commonly condemned slavery earlier in the century. Many supported the American Colonization Society, a group opposed to slavery but also committed to resettling free blacks outside the United States. Typically, however, southern divines defended their section and indicted their northern counterparts on social, political, and spiritual grounds.

First, they condemned antislavery evangelicals for sullying spiritual waters with political activism. They especially accused radical abolitionists of sanctioning civil disobedience and promoting open hostility toward the government. As one Kentucky Baptist declared, it is "improper for ministers, churches or associations to meddle with emancipation from slavery, or any other political subject, and as such, we advise ministers and churches to have nothing to do therewith, in their religious capacities" (Bailey, p. 128).

Second, on a practical, spiritual level, southern preachers accepted the hard reality that access to black souls depended on acquiescence to the cultural status quo. They preached the hope of heaven to blacks in segregated settings, while prescribing a life of obedience, passivity, and contentment with lives of servitude on this earth. Their pleas for black repentance, conversion, and Christian fellowship, of course, validated the slave's humanity and equality before God. Ministers dodged the bullet, however, by defending established racial hierarchies as part of God's inscrutable providential will.

Finally, since they found no clear biblical proscriptions against human bondage, many southern ministers shed their apologetic tone by the 1850s and followed their section's increasingly strident defense of slavery as a positive social good. Blacks' racial inferiority, they declared, left slaves dependent on the paternalistic guidance and material provisions of benevolent masters. Cases of physical brutality and emotional cruelty represented the sinful transgressions of individual slave owners, not fundamental flaws in the southern system.

Virginia Baptist minister Thornton Stringfellow, recalling the Old Testament examples of Abraham, Isaac, and Jacob, concluded that because God had "singled out the greatest slaveholders of that age, as the objects of his special favor," slavery must still provide "great opportunities to exercise grace and glorify God" (McKitrick, p. 91). The Charleston, South Carolina, minister Thomas Smyth publicly condemned slavery at a London gathering of the Evangelical Alliance in 1847. By 1861 his published defense called it a "providential remedial agency for accomplishing wise and benificent results" (Holifield, p. 152).

Northern evangelicals rejected such strategems as a gross manipulation of Scripture truths. Emboldened by political struggles to gain sectional advantage in the western territories, they increasingly accepted front-line duties in pronouncing slavery a national sin and an embarrassing blight on American republicanism. Ministers dismissed southerners' claims of benevolent intentions as feeble posturing in light of the system's capacity to destroy individual lives, divide families, and violate the slave's natural rights. They pointed as well to its moral toll and soul-threatening impact on slave masters.

A minority of evangelicals joined radicals such as William Lloyd Garrison in declaring the Constitution a proslavery document and demanding immediate abolition. Garrison agreed with southern claims that the Constitution endorsed slavery and ultimately shook his own faith in taking the southern point that Scripture supported it as well. More commonly, evangelicals focused on slavery as a moral evil requiring a spiritual revolution in the hearts and minds of individual Southerners.

Harriet Beecher Stowe's novel *Uncle Tom's Cabin*, first published in serial form and then as a novel in 1852, established the benchmark of northern evangelical attitudes toward slavery. The daughter of the leading northern theologian Lyman Beecher, Stowe drew inspiration more from her evangelical sensibilities than from extensive contact with southern life to produce the most celebrated antislavery treatise of the age. In recounting the life and tragic death of Tom, a Christ-like figure driven by moral fervor and spiritual discipline, Stowe systematically exposed the hollowness of southern defenses.

The stark villainy of Tom's nemesis, the northern-born Louisiana planter Simon Legree, provides the climactic portrait of the slave system's complete moral bankruptcy. Stowe's tack, however, was not Garrisonian. Legree is lured and corrupted by the South's oppressive system, but Stowe puts her faith in individual spiritual enlightenment, not political force or institutional pressure. Christian conscience must produce a deeper moral revolution,

she believed, before legal and structural changes could be effective.

Unfortunately, northern evangelicals did not generate a comparable crusade for black social and political equality. Stowe's character Tom, for example, thrives on moral rectitude and spiritual capacity, not a probing, assertive intellect. Similarly, evangelical institutions often resisted the egalitarian implications of their own message. Methodists, open to integrated worship in the eighteenth century, gradually instituted segregated seating during worship. Prominent evangelicals such as Lyman Beecher supported the American Colonization Society and attacked abolitionism as driven by fanatical, irrational zeal. Black congregants' ad hoc resistance to discrimination finally compelled the minister Richard Allen to establish the African Methodist Episcopal Church in 1816.

Yet in an age when few whites could conceive of anything like a world of full racial equality, evangelicals continued to sustain basic doctrinal principles that exposed their own limiting cultural attitudes. While some southern intellectuals such as Josiah Nott honed a "scientific" racism that identified blacks as a separate and inferior species of humanity, evangelicals remained committed to universalist doctrines that emphasized humanity's common origins and shared guilt before God.

They also accepted slavery's demise as an essential feature of the coming millennium. Focusing on the instrumentality of the church as a worldwide body of believers eroded the legitimacy of cultural pride and nationalistic boasts. To identify the Christian cause with "selfish nationality, or pride, or carnal reasoning," one minister declared, would disrupt "the plans and counsels of Infinite Love" (Skinner, p. 45). A Chicago pastor asked those believers who "caviled at [the doctrine] of human unity and equality" to confront the fact that it was the "centre of our religion." God's commandment to preach the gospel to every creature counseled "no distinction between the Caucasian, the Tartar, the Malay, the Negro, and the Indian. . . . *Every man* is a brother in one great family" (Patterson, pp. 17, 14). Such preaching did not liberate evangelicals from cultural racism, but it did help preserve the intellectual resources for constructing a more just society.

EVANGELICALS AND THE CIVIL WAR

The sectional political conflict over slavery that gave way to bloody struggle in 1861 owed much to the institutional and moral polarization of evangelical groups. The national revival of 1857 and 1858 that reached particular intensity in northeastern cities prompted many to pray for sectional reconciliation but even more for an end to the scourge of slavery. Northern believers on the eve of Lincoln's election had grown comfortable with public declarations against both the South's peculiar sin and northern complacency that together invited divine vengeance. Sin once identified, northern ministers agreed, required repentance and removal, not compromise.

Once fighting began, evangelicals generally closed ranks with their respective sections. Soldiers on both sides carried Bibles into battle and accepted the war as a holy crusade. Southerners generally concluded that their spiritual counterparts in the North had abandoned piety and simplicity for the sordid business of politics and for sponsoring northern economic interests. A few ministers urged restraint. Preaching in dedication of the Presbyterian Church of the Confederacy in 1861, the celebrated southern theologian James Henley Thornwell told his audience to eschew spiritual recriminations and accept the war as a political dispute since the Bible authorized no moral crusade either for or against slavery.

Northern churchmen accepted the conflict as a national catharsis, one that would abolish slavery and chasten their own section for the greed that had preserved an unholy alliance with slavery. Some of them assigned apocalyptic and millennial significance to the war, promising their flocks that from the carnage would rise unprecedented opportunity to spread the gospel. Among the more farsighted, the Congregationalist luminary Horace Bushnell insisted that Christian principles mandated obligation well beyond victory and peace. With regard to slavery, Bushnell told a Yale University audience, "we are not to extirpate the form and leave the fact." Unless the "old habit of domination" is replaced by "gentleness and consideration," the social order would be "turned into a hell of poverty and confusion." A better day could "never be secured, till the dejected and despised race are put upon the footing of men, and allowed to assert themselves" (McLoughlin, p. 155).

Southern evangelical hopes for leniency and conciliation from their northern counterparts eroded in the wake of Lincoln's assassination. Pulpit eulogies across the North lamented the murder as indicative of an unrepentant South and provided a powerful social base for Radical Republicans determined to impose a new order on the defeated Confederacy. "Vengeance upon wickedness is taken through human instrumentality," one northern minister declared. "And woe to the government that fails to do the mission of God" (Chesebrough, p. 61).

Unfortunately, the moral activism that Bushnell and many radicals demanded steadily waned over the course of Reconstruction as the nation looked toward restoring material prosperity rather than securing black rights.

TOWARD THE TWENTIETH CENTURY

With few exceptions, sectional evangelical divides hardened in postwar America and gave regional expression to modernist controversies that threatened to further erode spiritual consensus. Evangelicals confronted higher intellectual criticism of the Bible, as well as internal discord over the relationship between theology and the natural sciences and the appropriate social role of the churches.

As early as the 1840s, they began worrying about what ministers called a "new infidelity" that threatened to replace Christian supernaturalism with what the French intellectual Auguste Comte christened as a "new religion of humanity." Eighteenth-century deists attacked openly, evangelical leaders explained, while the faith's newest enemies, heavily inspired by liberal German theologians and philosophers such as Friedrich Schleiermacher and Ludwig Feuerbach, replaced abrasive assaults on Scripture with a positive celebration of human potential. Redemption from tyranny and human injustice, Feuerbach declared, depended on changing "the friends of God into friends of man, believers into thinkers, worshippers into workers, candidates for the other world into students of this world" (Hanley, p. 115). This new positivism did not reduce orthodox Christianity's role in achieving human progress; it removed it altogether.

Evangelical fears of being ignored rather than engaged further intensified with the publication of *On the Origin of Species by Means of Natural Selection,* by Charles Darwin, in 1859. Liberal and conservative evangelicals alike recoiled from a theory of human evolution that ignored the creative hand of God. Together, philosophical positivism and evolutionary naturalism sent evangelicals scrambling to preserve historic theological moorings and contend for the social relevance of the faith.

The old doctrinal consensus that had supported evangelicals' cultural power, however, did not hold in the half century following Reconstruction. Liberals within the mainline churches declared individual conversion and personal piety to be inadequate responses to the rise of industrial capitalism and rapid urbanization. They sought a more accommodating theology that could achieve both intellectual respectability and social relevance. The Christian hope, the northern Baptist leader Walter Rauschenbusch declared at the turn of the century, must be a "social hope" that "involved the whole social life of man."

Conservatives, on the other hand, opted for doctrinal rigidity and a defense of the faith's "fundamentals," a stand that would place them in a front-line defense against twentieth-century modernism. While they held fast to the old claims for conversion, piety, and scriptural inerrancy, funda-mentalists (a term not widely used until the 1920s) abandoned their forebears' postmillennial confidence in the certainty of missionary triumph. Instead, they continued their aggressive missionary efforts under a "premillennial" banner that discounted human striving and promised millennial restoration only through the cataclysmic, physical return of Christ.

Neither modernism nor internal strife proved fatal to an evangelical community whose numbers and social power overshadowed the influence of liberal Protestantism in the late twentieth century. Yet evangelicals will likely never again claim the triumphalist outlook or cultural dominance that marked their experience in the middle decades of the nineteenth century.

See also **The New England Theology from Edwards to Bushnell; The Transformation of American Religion: 1776–1838** *(in this volume);* **Evangelical Protestants; God, Nature, and Human Nature** *(volume 2).*

BIBLIOGRAPHY

Primary Sources

Anderson, Richard. *Foreign Missions: Their Relations and Claims.* New York, 1869.

Anderson, Rufus. *Memorial Volume of the First Fifty Years of the American Board of Commissioners for Foreign Missions.* Boston, 1862.

Beecher, Catharine. *The True Remedy for the Wrongs of Woman.* Boston, 1851.

———. *Woman Suffrage and Woman's Profession.* Hartford, Conn., 1871.

Bushnell, Horace. *Sermons for the New Life.* New York, 1867.

Finney, Charles G. *Lectures to Professing Christians.* New York, 1837.

Fish, Henry C. *Primitive Piety Revived.* Boston, 1856.

Harris, Samuel. "Demands of Infidelity Satisfied by Christianity." *Bibliotheca Sacra* 13 (April 1856).

Hopkins, Mark. *Miscellaneous Essays and Discourses.* Boston, 1847.

Humphrey, John. "The Carnal Mind." In *Sermons of John Humphrey.* Edited by Herman Humphrey. New York, 1856.

McLoughlin, William, ed. *American Evangelicalism, 1800–1900: An Anthology.* New York, 1968.

Noll, Mark A., ed. *The Princeton Theology, 1812–1821.* Grand Rapids, Mich., 1983.

Patterson, Robert W. "Sermon before the American Board of Commissioners for Foreign Missions." Boston, 1859.

Phelps, Austin. "The Theory of Preaching." *Bibliotheca Sacra* 14 (April 1857).

Riddle, David. "A Sermon Preached before the American Board of Commissioners for Foreign Missions." Boston, 1851.

Rupp, I. Daniel. *An Original History of the Religious Denominations.* Philadelphia, 1844.

Scott, W. A. "Hope of Republics." *National Preacher* 23 (January 1849).

Skinner, Thomas H. "Progress, the Law of Missionary Work." Boston, 1843.

Thompson, Joseph P. "Christian Missions Necessary to a True Civilization." *Bibliotheca Sacra* 14 (October 1857).

Wayland, Francis. *Sermons to the Churches.* New York, 1858.

———. *Letters on the Ministry of the Gospel.* Boston, 1863.

Wheatley, Richard. *The Life and Letters of Mrs. Phoebe Palmer.* 1881. Reprint, New York, 1984.

Secondary Works

Abzug, Robert H. *Cosmos Crumbling: American Reform and the Religious Imagination.* New York, 1994.

Bailey, David T. *Shadow on the Church: Southwestern Evangelical Religion and the Issue of Slavery, 1783–1860.* Ithaca, N.Y., 1985.

Bercovitch, Sacvan. *The American Jeremiad.* Madison, Wis., 1978.

Bozeman, Theodore Dwight. *Protestants in an Age of Science: The Baconian Ideal and Ante-Bellum Religious Thought.* Chapel Hill, N.C., 1977.

Carwardine, Richard J. *Evangelicals and Politics in Antebellum America.* New Haven, Conn., 1993.

Cashdollar, Charles. *The Transformation of Theology, 1830–1890: Positivism and Protestant Thought in Britain and America.* Princeton, N.J., 1989.

Chesebrough, David. *No Sorrow Like Our Sorrow: Northern Protestant Ministers and the Assassination of Lincoln.* Kent, Ohio, 1994.

Conkin, Paul K. *The Uneasy Center: Reformed Christianity in Antebellum America.* Chapel Hill, N.C., 1995.

Dayton, Donald W., and Robert K. Johnston, eds. *The Variety of American Evangelicalism.* Knoxville, Tenn., 1991.

Farmer, James Oscar, Jr. *The Metaphysical Confederacy: James Henley Thornwell and the Synthesis of Southern Values.* Macon, Ga., 1986.

Goen, C. C. *Broken Churches, Broken Nation: Denominational Schisms and the Coming of the Civil War.* Macon, Ga., 1985.

Hanley, Mark Y. *Beyond a Christian Commonwealth: The Protestant Quarrel with the American Republic, 1830–1860.* Chapel Hill, N.C., 1994.

Hardesty, Nancy A. *Women Called to Witness: Evangelical Feminism in the Nineteenth Century.* Nashville, Tenn., 1984.

Hardman, Keith J. *Charles Grandison Finney, 1792–1875: Revivalist and Reformer.* Syracuse, N.Y., 1987.

Hughes, Richard T., and C. Leonard Allen. *Illusions of Innocence: Protestant Primitivism in America, 1630–1875.* Chicago, 1988.

Holifield, E. Brooks. *The Gentlemen Theologians: American Theology in Southern Culture, 1795–1860.* Durham, N.C., 1978.

Hutchison, William R., and Hartmut Lehmann, eds. *Many Are Chosen: Divine Election and Western Nationalism.* Minneapolis, Minn., 1994.

Johnson, Curtis D. *Redeeming America: Evangelicals and the Road to Civil War.* Chicago, 1993.

Loveland, Anne C. *Southern Evangelicals and the Social Order, 1800–1860.* Baton Rouge, La., 1980.

McKitrick, Eric. L., ed. *Slavery Defended: The Views of the Old South.* Englewood Cliffs, N.J., 1963.

McLoughlin, William G. *The American Evangelicals, 1800–1900.* New York, 1968.

Marty, Martin. *Protestantism in the United States: Righteous Empire.* 2d ed. New York, 1986.

Moorhead, James H. *American Apocalypse: Yankee Protestants and the Civil War, 1860–1869.* New Haven, Conn., 1978.

Noll, Mark A. *One Nation Under God? Christian Faith and Political Action in America.* San Francisco, 1988.

Raser, Harold E. *Phoebe Palmer: Her Life and Thought.* Lewiston, N.Y., 1987.

Smith, Timothy L. *Revivalism and Social Reform: American Protestantism on the Eve of the Civil War.* 2d ed. Baltimore, 1980.

Turner, James. *Without God, without Creed: The Origins of Unbelief in America.* Baltimore, 1985.

MORAL PHILOSOPHY

Allen C. Guelzo

American philosophy, between the death of the Congregational clergyman Jonathan Edwards in 1758 and the publication of the psychologist-philosopher William James's *The Principles of Psychology* in 1890, has long been described as dormant and defensive, dominated by a superficial "common sense" realism imported from eighteenth-century Scotland, and yielding pride of place in its collegiate curriculums to a version of applied ethics known as moral philosophy. Since the work of the scholars D. H. Meyer, Theodore Dwight Bozeman, Daniel Walker Howe, and Bruce Kuklick in the 1970s and 1980s, this dismissal of nineteenth-century moral philosophy has undergone serious re-examination, and a more complex recognition of the depth and vigor of realist moral philosophy in American intellectual history has emerged. The term "moral philosophy" has come to have two uses, the first making it a general synonym for Scottish common sense realism in nineteenth-century American thought, and the second referring specifically to moral philosophy as an ethics inquiry which employed a particular epistemology to arrive at a consensus about moral duty and obligation. Taken in the first sense, moral philosophy was a response to the excesses of English empiricism and the fear that the limitations of empiricism (as illustrated by the Scottish philosopher David Hume) would make it impossible to describe human nature or prescribe human behavior. Similarly, it was also a response to the need religious thinkers had to accommodate themselves epistemologically to Newtonian science, and to demonstrate that knowledge and behavior not only displayed regularity, but displayed it in ways that would make belief in God probable, and lead from there to Christianity. In the second sense, moral philosophy was a specifically American response to the need for a usable public philosophy in the atmosphere of the new republic, where religion was barred from offering legal norms and expectations for behavior, and where intellectual, sectarian, and ethnic diversity threatened to make the pursuit of destructive self-interest the only common goal. "The stability of our republican institutions must depend upon the progress of general intelligence and virtue," warned Charles Finney, the Protestant revivalist-turned-academic, in 1846, for if "public and private virtue sink to that point below which self-control becomes impossible, we must fall back into monarchy, limited or absolute; or into civil or military despotism; just according to the national standard of intelligence and virtue." As such, moral philosophy outlined an ambitious intellectual program which would provide a common but rigorous moral platform for civil life and restore through indirect prescriptive "influence" the authority for moral regulation lost by Christian churches after the American Revolution.

ORIGINS OF AMERICAN MORAL PHILOSOPHY

It has been customary to date the beginnings of American moral philosophy to the arrival from Scotland of John Witherspoon as the president of the College of New Jersey (now Princeton University) in 1768. Actually, the shape of American moral philosophy was already apparent in anti-revivalist Old Calvinists in New England in the 1760s, in the unpublished lectures of Francis Alison at the College of Philadelphia, and in more religiously unorthodox forms in the American patriots Thomas Jefferson, Benjamin Franklin, and Benjamin Rush. It also owed a substantial debt to English natural law moralists, beginning with Bishop Joseph Butler and his celebrated *Analogy of Religion* (1736), and Archdeacon William Paley's *Principles of Moral and Political Philosophy* (1785). What is true, however, is that the nascent American moral philosophers took a large share of their cues from Scottish Enlightenment philosophical sources and, in particular, Francis Hutcheson and Thomas Reid.

Scotland, like America, was a province of the British Empire, far from the center of imperial

John Witherspoon (1723–1794). Presbyterian leader, signer of the Declaration of Independence, and president of the College of New Jersey (later Princeton University). LIBRARY OF CONGRESS

culture, but for that very reason freer to develop indigenous strains of philosophical inquiry unhampered by the deadening requirement of conformity to the Church of England. The Enlightenment arrived in Scotland in the 1720s, in tandem with Scottish commercial prosperity, and with it, Scotland's universities—Edinburgh, St. Andrew's, and Glasgow—devoted much of their energy to the challenge of several unresolved philosophical problems spun off by English thinkers. Chief among these problems was the dilemma posed by John Locke's empiricism. According to Locke, all knowledge in the mind was based upon sensations, as physical substances impacted the human senses and the resulting sensations were transmitted to the mind. But that raised the question of where moral knowledge came from. Moral facts, obviously, did not make physical impacts on human senses. Did this mean that moral facts were an illusion of the mind? Bishop George Berkeley, the Anglo-Irish philosopher and clergyman, shrewdly observed that the mind actually knows nothing but its own ideas. It

actually has no evidence for whether those ideas come from physical sensations or spiritual ones, since no one can ever get outside of one's own mind to check. There might, in fact, be no physical substances at all, but merely spiritual causes for the mind's ideas that the mind mistakes for physical ones. This leveled the playing field between physical sensation and moral knowledge, but it was too radical an alternative to attract more than a few eighteenth-century thinkers.

By limiting knowledge to the ideas represented to minds by sensation, Locke also generated criticism from Francis Hutcheson of Glasgow, who objected that minds are not merely passive receptors of representations, and that minds entertain ideas which mere sensations or combinations of sensations have no way of generating. A painting, which is only oil on canvas, gives rise to a perception of beauty, which is irreducible to sensation; a virtuous act arouses the response of approbation, a response incommensurate with information supplied only by sensation. This implied for Hutcheson the existence of a power or capacity in every mind that he called the "moral sense" which ensures that beauty, harmony, and virtue are recognized as real relations (and therefore, moral perceptions are not merely fluctuating personal or cultural prejudices). No matter how varied the situations or experiences, the moral sense enables a mind to sort through the mass of sensations and perceive what is true, right, and beautiful. Although this argument managed to put ethics on some kind of objective footing, it was also tantamount to saying theologically that one might be able to know what is right without any need for God or revelation. But despite the disapproval of the Scottish Presbyterian establishment, Hutcheson's moral sense theory emerged as the Scottish reply to Lockean thought.

The second problem generated by English empiricism grew out of Bishop Berkeley's objection to Locke's shaky distinction between primary and secondary qualities in the objects of sensation, and David Hume's subsequent assertion that, given empiricism, minds have no foundation for understanding even causality. Hume provoked Thomas Reid in Reid's *Inquiry into the Human Mind on the Principles of Common Sense* (1764) to reply that there was a common practical consensus that a reality exists outside the mind and its ideas, and that this common sense (as opposed to representationalism) allows us to experience objects and their relations directly, without mediating ideas. Objects are thereby presented immediately to consciousness, and doubt of their reality is therefore absurd. To interpose ideas as mediators between minds and objects, Reid warned, is to invite skepticism. "To Dr. Reid belongs the credit of showing the utter falsity of the ideal theory," wrote the scholar Joseph Haven in 1871. "He took the ground that the existence of any such representative images . . . is wholly without proof, nay more, is inconceivable; that while we can conceive of an image of form or figure, we cannot conceive of an image of sound, or of taste or smell."

Reid's reasoning allowed him to draw three conclusions, which became the core of American moral philosophy:

1. Not only do minds directly perceive objects, but the process of perception involves an act of judgment as part of the perception which intuitively confirms the outwardness and reality of an object.
2. This intuitive judgment, or common sense, also reveals to minds certain fundamental moral relations between, or moral qualities within, objects of knowledge.
3. Minds understand that there is an objectively real world beyond the mind's ideas, both morally and physically, and afterward construct a picture of this world inductively, working from real specific sensations toward larger, but still real, constructions of reality.

This common sense moral philosophy had a double appeal. For Enlightenment thinkers who hoped to find an objective basis for morality which still resembled Christianity, moral philosophy allowed desire and intuition to blend together and provide a sense of objectivity and universality to personal moral inclinations. At the same time, it would allow traditional theologians to find a secure platform for talking about ethics, free from both the skepticism of David Hume as well as the personalistic demands of counter-Enlightenment pietism that all ethical questions be dissolved into declarations about divine grace and volition. Too often, complained the American educator Noah Porter in 1885, ethics have "followed . . . philosophy and psychology by a natural and necessary consequence" into materialism and atheism, whereas moral philosophy would reconnect ethics to theology and restore "the sensibilities and judgments of duty in respect to the Family, the State, and the Kingdom of God." Porter, with a view to critiquing the German philosopher Immanuel Kant as well as Hume, distinguished ethics as a system of rational arrangement, "exclusive of any reference to fundamental principles or scientific grounds," whereas moral philosophy would provide the connection between epistemology and behavior which not only "rises to more comprehensive, or penetrates to more profound, inquiries" but also explains the root causes and structure of ethics. The assurance that systems of morality could be built inductively from the judgments of the "moral sense" also allowed moral philosophy to advertise itself as a matter of science, a "science of duty" (in the American educator Mark Hopkins's phrase). Moreover, by appealing to natural intuitions of moral truths, a Christian ethicist with an evangelistic agenda could begin on a neutral ground of judged "facts," and proceed inductively to build a case for Christian belief which the nonbeliever could no more honestly deny than beauty in a Rembrandt painting.

EMERGENCE OF AN AMERICAN MORAL PHILOSOPHY

Despite the availability of the Scottish philosophers to other Americans before 1768, the arrival of John Witherspoon at Princeton that year really was a watershed event in the formation of American moral philosophy. Witherspoon was a Scot, and therefore offered a direct connection to the mainstream of Scottish Enlightenment thinking; he was a talented and aggressive administrator and teacher; and he was a moderate Calvinist divine who was quite determined to hold the line for Calvinist religious orthodoxy without falling before the squalling demands of Calvinist revivalists (of which there were several at Princeton, where Jonathan Edwards had briefly been the president before his death).

Witherspoon's first task was to take a clear stand against the emotional, revivalistic piety of Jonathan Edwards. It did not help Edwards's reputation or Witherspoon's mind that Edwards had also imported a Berkeleian-style critique of Locke into his theological writings. Although Witherspoon considered himself fully as much a Calvinist as Edwards in theological terms, he deplored Edwards's philosophical movement toward immaterialism as a response to Locke. In his later treatises, Edwards had moved far enough into immaterialism that it was not clear whether he believed that there existed a stable substance or essence beneath the working consciousness (which brought matters very near to Humean skepticism). Edwardsean ministers, especially Joseph Bellamy, Samuel Hopkins, and Nathanael Emmons, pushed this critique even further as part of their program for focusing attention on the will, and the responsibility of people to respond immediately and without hesitation to the demand to repent. In the case of the most radical Edwardseans, the urge to make the will central to consciousness went to the point of denying the traditional Calvinist doctrine of inherent human depravity, since any notion of an inherent substance, depraved or not, might qualify the accountability one could impute to the will. Witherspoon dealt with the Edwardseans by evicting many of them from strategic positions within Princeton, suppressing popular Edwardsean books, and reshaping the college curriculum around his own orthodox version of Scottish common sense moral philosophy.

Witherspoon's other great task was to deal with the legacy of the American Revolution, which not only freed America from British imperial control, but at the same time freed it from dependence upon (or even gratitude to) any form of Christian denomination or theology. As the first western nation to eliminate all references to God or to Christian churches from its political instrument (the 1787 federal Constitution), the political leaders of the United States were largely men of the Enlightenment. (Witherspoon was the only clergyman included among the delegates to the Continental Congress.) But Witherspoon anticipated the need within republican political philosophy for an authoritative ideology of civic virtue, something which existing secular political republican theory lacked but which he believed that a moralized Christianity could provide, to the benefit of both the state and Christianity. Unlike the Edwardseans, with their demand for a perfectionist private virtue based on the response of the will to the demands of a morally rigorous Christianity, Witherspoon offered as the best basis for civic virtue an apparently neutral moralism secured by appeals to the "moral sense" rather than the will. This allowed him to formulate a public ethic, ostensibly secular and rational, but de facto Christian. On that basis, the federal government could be appealed to, not for direct support of Christianity, but for indirect support through civil laws regulating violations of "common" morality.

If Witherspoon represented the most important voice in the development of American moral philosophy, he was seconded in the first decades of the American republic by a broad variety of moderate Calvinist college presidents and theologians, including Ezra Stiles and Timothy Dwight of Yale (as the grandson of Edwards, Dwight was an especially important convert to common sense moral philosophy), Samuel Stanhope Smith at Princeton (Witherspoon's son-in-law), and David Tappan at Harvard. But the real flowering of American moral philosophy waited until the 1820s, when a variety of talented academic thinkers made Scottish-style common sense realism into something close to an American national philosophy, and made the moral philosophy treatise its most typical genre. These thinkers included Francis Wayland of Brown University, Archibald Alexander and Charles Hodge of Princeton Theological Seminary, Nathaniel William Taylor of Yale Divinity School, John Leadley Dagg of Mercer University, Joseph Haven of Amherst College and the University of Chicago, James Walker, Andrew Preston Peabody, and Francis Bowen of Harvard, Noah Porter of Yale, James McCosh of Princeton, and even the quondam revivalists Charles Grandison Finney and Asa Mahan of Oberlin College and their disciple, James Harris Fairchild.

OUTLINE OF MORAL PHILOSOPHY

Most American students before the Civil War encountered moral philosophy as a freestanding collegiate course by that name, usually taught by the college president in the senior year, or in the form of the treatises written by moral philosophers. Wayland's *Elements of Moral Science* (1835) sold over 200,000 copies in the sixty years it was in print, and Mark Hopkins described it in 1872 as "the most popular work on morals published in this country." Wayland was followed by Alexander's *Outlines of Moral Sciences* (1852) and Porter's *The Elements of Moral Science, Theoretical and Practical* (1885) among the dominant treatises. Many of the moral philosophers used these, and sometimes their own books, as college texts. At Harvard, James Walker assigned Butler and Reid, while Francis Bowen used Reid for teaching junior moral philosophy and Wayland with the seniors.

In its specific shape, moral philosophy differed from ethics in that (1) it refused to confine itself purely to appeals to natural law, and often culminated in demonstrations that ethical enquiry could be shown to have entire compatibility with Christian theology; (2) it discovered norms for public behavior in individually and privately discovered intuitions of morality, and had no sense of morality as a social consensus; (3) it attempted to cast moral discoveries in the same lawlike language and through the same methodology as science; and (4) it created a common moral supernarrative for all humankind, including subnarratives that prescribed social, political, and economic behavior.

Moral philosophy accommodated itself nicely to classical notions of natural law, with the addition that moral feelings now also play a role in the perception of that law. Although some moral philosophers espoused a teleological approach to ethics—that the goal rather than the means were the principal criterion in determining ethical fitness—hardly any dallied with outright utilitarianism, which taught that "the greatest good for the greatest number" was the ethical summum bonum. Francis Wayland attacked both associationist and utilitarian explanations of moral conduct in *The Elements of Moral Science*: "I believe the idea of a moral quality in actions to be ultimate, to arise under such circumstances as have been appointed by our Creator, and that we can assign for it no other reason, than that such is his will concerning us." Some, like Mark Hopkins, prided themselves on dethroning William Paley, which Hopkins acknowledged had been "the text-book here [at Williams College] and generally in our colleges" when he began teaching in 1830. Overall, the moral philosophy enterprise was slanted toward deontological ethics, and toward deontology's tendency to make obligation and duty, rather than the inherent rightness of an action, the measure of right behavior. Alexander and Bowen believed that minds intuit the rightness or wrongness of specific acts, but the principal ethical burden was in obeying their imperatives to action; Wayland and Hopkins believed that what the mind intuits is the relationships and rules of doing, rather than the rightness of the act themselves. Archibald Alexander dismissed as "a common mistake" the notion that "there must be something like a general rule or law, which the mind applies, as the workman does his rule, to ascertain whether the quality of the action be good or bad." Alexander believed that "we are conscious of no such process," and that "when a moral action is viewed . . . the mind perceives its quality, and is conscious of no other mental process."

Mark Hopkins, on the other hand, argued in *Lectures on Moral Science* (1862) that "the Choice of supreme end is generic" and "made . . . in a sense only once," and is thereafter "constantly repeated, since it is only under this that other choices are made." But even then, Hopkins wanted it clearly understood that he was not endorsing Kantian proposals for a categorical imperative, presented to the will by the practical reason; and Finney objected to Kant and "all rightarians" for disconnecting ethics from religion, the opposite of what moral philosophy intended.

The fundamental premise of all the moral philosophers was the existence of some sort of moral "faculty" or "sense" which intuitively and directly apprehended objects and simultaneously offered a moral judgment about them. "As all men, when reason is developed, have a faculty by which they can discern a difference between objects of sight which are beautiful and those who are deformed," wrote Archibald Alexander, "so all men possess the power of discerning a difference between actions, as to their moral quality. The judgment thus formed is immediate, and has no relation to the usefulness or injuriousness to human happiness, of the objects contemplated." Noah Porter acknowledged that there might be some disagreement as to whether the "moral sense" was an independent faculty "superadded to the intellect, sensibility, and will, with the other recognized human powers, like a separate attachment or gearing to a machine," or a feature of the intellect "as an inlet or discerner of moral relations or conceptions," or perhaps even a feature of the emotions, "a special sensibility . . . originating certain feelings." Francis Wayland spoke of "this faculty" (which he identified as "conscience") as "an ever-present faculty," since it "always admonishes us, if we will listen to its voice" and we "may always know our duty, if we will but inquire for it." But James Harris Fairchild, in his *Moral Philosophy; or, The Science of Obligation* (1869), preferred to construe the "moral sense" as a collective intuition of the mind as a whole: "In aid of our rational faculty of conscience and judgment, we seem to have a spontaneous instinctive judgment, a kind of moral taste which acts instantaneously upon the contemplation of many courses of conduct."

What was common to all these definitions was the conviction that the judgments of this moral sense were "*immediate; not a matter of inference, not a roundabout reflective process*," according to Joseph Haven in *Mental Philosophy: Including the Intellect, Sensibilities, and Will* (1871). "The mind is so constituted that it cannot but affirm obligation to will the good or the valuable," asserted Charles Finney, "as soon as the idea of the good or valuable is developed." The need for the moral sense to act immediately on the faculties of the mind meant that the operations of the moral sense had to be both complex and simple: *complex*, in that the moral sense had to work equally on all the other faculties, but *simple* in that the operations were rapid and direct. All the moral philosophers agreed that genuine moral agency and accountability rested on the possession of a functioning reason, properly coordinated emotions, and above all a free will (although Calvinist moral philosophers were quick to reconcile notions of human freedom with the confessional requirement of acknowledging divine predestination). Joseph Haven wrote that, if it was necessary to speak in terms of a process, then the intellect was the first target of the moral sense. "Whatever comes in as a motive to influence the mind in favor of, or against a given course, must in the first instance address itself to the understanding, and be comprehended by that power, before it can influence the mental decisions." Mark Hopkins declared that "it is thought that is the condition of feeling, and governs it." Yet, even Haven was leery of granting the intellect too much preeminence. After all, even "the intellectual perception of the right is followed . . . by a certain class of feelings or emotions, usually called moral sensibilities and it is the *feeling* . . . and not the *knowing* . . . that is directly in contact with the will."

It is one measure of the long shadow of Edwards in nineteenth-century American philosophy that, despite Witherspoon's suspicions of Edwardsean volitionalism, the will fascinated the moral philosophers. Noah Porter sharply disagreed with associational psychologists and "cerebralists of all classes" that "every mental and emotional state is the effect of some action *on,* or *in,* or *from* the brain." Haven, in fact, declared that the will "is, in many respects, at once the most important and the most difficult of the three [faculties]" upon which the "moral sense" operates.

> Whatever control we have over ourselves, whether as regards the bodily or mental powers, whatever use and disposition it is in our power to make of the intellectual faculties with which we are endowed, and of the sensibilities which accompany or give rise to those intellectual activities, and of the physical organization which obeys the behests of the sovereign mind, whatever separates and distinguishes us from the mere inanimate and mechanical forces of nature on the one, or the blind impulses of irrational brute instinct on the other; for all this, be it more or less, we are indebted to that faculty which we call the Will. (*Mental Philosophy,* pp. 517–518)

The moral philosophers were careful to distance themselves from the Edwardseans in their insistent reiterations of the freedom of the will. "Without freedom of some kind, connected with an act at some point," averred Mark Hopkins, "all are agreed that there can be no obligation or responsibility." And yet, even then, the figure of Edwards restrained the latitude they gave to the term "free." "To a free and rational act of willing, the conception of an end is necessary," Hopkins added. Or if not an end, at least some form of attractive motive. "The power to choose is *not a power to choose without a motive,*" Noah Porter warned, or else, in the interests of freedom, moral philosophers might end up disconnecting the will from the operation of the moral sense altogether. Still, whatever freedom was by definition, it certainly existed as fact, since the perception of freedom was itself a self-evident intuition of the moral sense. Alexander, an "Old School" Calvinist Presbyterian but a thoroughgoing opponent of the Edwardseans, had no hesitation in declaring that "man is conscious of liberty, and nothing can add to the certainty which he has that he is a free agent." And his Unitarian counterpart, Andrew Preston Peabody, joined him in affirming that "we have the direct evidence of consciousness . . . not only of doing what we choose, but of exercising our free choice among different objects of desire, between immediate and future enjoyment, between good and evil."

This presented Alexander with the difficulty of appearing to deny a Calvinist understanding of the will as bound by a depraved human nature. But it paid the important dividend of explaining why immediate intuitions of moral law, and the operations of the moral sense, did not automatically result in a common code of human behavior or a consistent pattern of human ethics. The will, being self-evidently free, had the power to resist the operations of the moral sense, since the will could resist or even pervert the intellect and the emotions. Even when the moral sense operated directly on the will, they might behave, according to Mark Hopkins, "like two vessels grappled in conflict. . . . Will the man come into harmony with himself and with God, or will he not? This question no one can decide for another, and the act required is so simple and elementary that no one can tell another how to do it." This did not, however, make the operation of the moral sense less lawlike; it merely indicated that it functioned under a different kind of causal law than physics or chemistry. "The order of sequence which moral law seeks to regulate," explained John Leadley Dagg in his *Manual of Theology* (1857), "is that which subsists between the command and the action, not between the action and its consequences."

Whether the will might refuse to do its duty, however, was one matter; what could not be in doubt was the instantaneous recognition of duty or obligation by the intellect under the operation of the moral sense. "Moral science is the science of duty," Noah Porter said, echoing Hopkins, and its whole work was "to give the results of careful observations, subtle and exhaustive analyses, clear and complete definitions, verified inductions, logical deductions, in the form of a consistent, articulated, and finished system" of personal human obligation. Knowing what was right and doing what was right were "not precisely synonymous," wrote Joseph Haven, "yet [they] are nearly equivalent.... Show me a thing is *right,* and you show me a reason, and the best of all reasons, why I *ought* to do it." Noah Porter agreed that "ethically considered, a right is synonymous with a moral claim."

This was an important assertion for the moral philosophers, because this was the point which allowed them to disclaim any under-the-table theological agendas. Duty and obligation arose in this case not from divine decree or divine revelation but from the authoritative, natural, and universal operation of a moral sense. Noah Porter firmly declared that "moral distinctions are not originated by the arbitrary *fiat* or *will of the Creator.*" Joseph Haven added, "There is a sense in which Deity himself is subject to this eternal and immutable law of right.... An action is right, not *because* God wills it; on the contrary, *he wills it because it is right.*" Yet the very power of the moral sense to impose duty on its own strength could be converted, at the end, into a concluding analogical argument for the existence of God. "The feeling or moral obligation which accompanies every perception of right and wrong, seems to imply, that man is under law," wrote Archibald Alexander, but "if we are under law there must be a lawgiver, a moral governor, who has incorporated the elements of his law into our very constitution." "In the constitution of man moral philosophy would find his end," announced Mark Hopkins. "In the end it would find revealed the will of God." And not only the existence of God, but God's attributes, as well. Reasoning by analogy, Noah Porter asked in *The Elements of Moral Science*:

> If a spiritual force, when intimately connected with matter, can accomplish physical changes [like dutiful behavior] what shall we say of the capacity of the Eternal Spirit to effect many more and vastly greater changes, if indeed he is not more nearly related to the forces of nature than the human spirit is to the body? He would be a rash man who would deny that He who created and upholds these forces by his immanent and upholding power, may so manifest, direct, and combine them as to accomplish any physical effect which he pleases, in answer to prayer, in entire consistency with the laws which he has imposed upon them. (p. 564)

"The analogy of the human soul," concluded Porter, "furnishes a decisive argument in favor of the conclusion, that the creator and thinker is One Being."

THE COLLAPSE OF MORAL PHILOSOPHY

Moral philosophy owed its appeal to an ambidextrous ability to satisfy the expectations of the Enlightenment for a rational and natural ethics, and the requirements of the American Protestant churches for an apologetical ethics which would secure Christian orthodoxy from skepticism. It performed this task surprisingly well, and in a surprising diversity of settings, for over a century. But between 1865 and 1890, much of the impetus of the moral philosophers was lost. The publication of the English naturalist Charles Darwin's *Origin of Species* in 1859 subverted not only the Christian doctrine of creation, but any notion of teleology and purposefulness in the universe and in humankind. At the same time, the increasing sophistication of psychological experimentation in the 1870s transformed psychology from being a subjectively measured subset of philosophy to a laboratory science of its own, thereby challenging the efforts of the moral philosophers to give a "scientific" reading of human nature. Still, it was not so much a move toward scientific objectivity as it was the new intellectual loyalties of the psychologists themselves, in the direction of materialism, Darwinian evolution, and an associationalist psychology with its roots back in Locke, which proved most lethal to the academic moralists.

The moral philosophers also lost ground in more practical ways. Almost from the beginning, moral philosophy had been domesticated within academic rather than religious or political institutions. But American higher education moved after 1860 toward ever-greater levels of professionalization and specialization which cut against the status of moral philosophy as a synthetic and nondisciplinary subject. Given the divided confessional loyalties of the moral philosophers, it proved impossible for them to organize a self-protective academic association of their own. Moreover, the increasing diversity of the American population made it advisable for college administrations to downplay religious overtones in their curriculums and, on the model of the Harvard president Charles Eliot, to reconstruct their faculties with a view to valorizing research and experimentation rather than the upholding of public morality. Above all, the moral philosophers had made promises about the intuitive recognition of moral truth which could not be lived up to in the midst of the greatest ethical challenge in American public life, the controversy over slavery. No consensus emerged among the moral philosophers on a question where their own writings had promised self-evident answers, and the moral morass of the post–Civil War era further discounted their pledge to produce a reliable civic morality.

By the 1890s, moral philosophy was exhausted, in terms of both its writings and its personnel. Francis Bowen was eased into retirement at Harvard by William James in 1889; the last great moral philosophy textbook, *Our Moral Nature*, appeared from James McCosh in 1892, four years after his own retirement from the presidency of Princeton, where he had been Eliot's great critic; Noah Porter had left the helm of Yale in 1886 and died in 1892. Nevertheless, in its day, moral philosophy was an ambitious effort to unite ethics, epistemology, and scientific method in a single system, and it offered a convincing alternative to the individual hedonism and social homogenization and centralization promoted by the moral philosophers' pragmatist successors.

See also **Philosophy from Puritanism to the Enlightenment; The Transformation of Philosophy** *(in this volume);* **Analytic Philosophy** *(volume 2).*

BIBLIOGRAPHY

Primary Sources

Alexander, Archibald. *Outlines of Moral Science.* New York, 1860.

Blare, Joseph L., ed. *American Philosophic Addresses, 1700–1900.* New York, 1946.

Dagg, John Leadley. *Manual of Theology, In Two Parts.* Charleston, S.C., 1859.

Fairchild, James Harris. *Moral Philosophy; or, The Science of Obligation.* New York, 1869.

Finney, Charles Grandison. *Lectures on Systematic Theology.* Vol. 1. Oberlin, Ohio, 1846.

Haven, Joseph. *Mental Philosophy: Including the Intellect, Sensibilities, and the Will.* Boston, 1871.

——. *Moral Philosophy: Including Theoretical and Practical Ethics.* Boston, 1859.

Hedge, Levi. *Elements of Logick; or, A Summary of the General Principles and Different Modes of Reasoning.* Buffalo, N.Y., 1854.

Hickok, Laurens Perseus. *Empirical Psychology; or, The Science of Mind from Experience.* Boston, 1882.

Hopkins, Mark. *The Law of Love and Love as a Law; or, Moral Science, Theoretical and Practical.* New York, 1869.

——. *Lectures on Moral Science Delivered before the Lowell Institute.* Boston, 1872.

——. *An Outline Study of Man; or, The Body and Mind One System.* New York, 1878.

McCosh, James. *The Method of Divine Government, Physical and Moral.* New York, 1851.

——. *Realistic Philosophy Defended in a Philosophic Series.* New York, 1887.

Peabody, Andrew Preston. *A Manual of Moral Philosophy.* New York, 1873.

Porter, Noah. *The Elements of Moral Science, Theoretical and Practical.* New York, 1885.

Walker, James. *Reason, Faith, and Duty: Sermons Preached Chiefly in the College Chapel.* Boston, 1877.

Wayland, Francis. *The Elements of Moral Science.* Boston, 1851.

——. *Sermons Delivered in the Chapel of Brown University.* Boston, 1849.

Secondary Sources

Adams, Todd L. "The Commonsense Tradition in America." *Transactions of the Charles S. Peirce Society* 24 (winter 1988): 1–31.

Bozeman, Theodore Dwight. *Protestants in an Age of Science: The Baconian Ideal and Antebellum American Religious Thought.* Chapel Hill, N.C., 1977.

Flower, Elizabeth, and Murphey, Murray G. *A History of Philosophy in America.* Vol. 1. New York, 1977.

Guelzo, Allen C. "'The Science of Duty': Moral Philosophy and the Epistemology of Science in Nineteenth-Century America." In *Evangelicals and Science in Historical Perspective,* edited by David N. Livingstone et al. New York, 1999.

Hoeveler, J. David. *James McCosh and the Scottish Intellectual Tradition.* Princeton, N.J., 1981.

Hovenkamp, Herbert. *Science and Religion in America, 1800–1860.* Philadelphia, 1978.

Howe, Daniel Walker. *Making the American Self: From Jonathan Edwards to Abraham Lincoln.* Cambridge, Mass., 1997.

———. *The Unitarian Conscience: Harvard Moral Philosophy, 1805–1861.* Cambridge, Mass., 1970.

Kuklick, Bruce. *Churchmen and Philosophers: From Jonathan Edwards to John Dewey.* New Haven, Conn., 1985.

Madden, Edward H. "Francis Wayland and the Scottish Tradition." *Transactions of the Charles S. Peirce Society* 21 (summer 1985): 301–326.

Madden, Edward H., and James E. Hamilton. *Freedom and Grace: The Life of Asa Mahan.* Metuchen, N.J., 1982.

Meyer, D. H. *The Instructed Conscience: The Shaping of the American National Ethic.* Philadelphia, 1972.

O'Donnell, John M. *The Origins of Behaviorism: American Psychology, 1870–1920.* New York, 1985.

Stevenson, Louise L. *Scholarly Means to Evangelical Ends: The New Haven Scholars and the Transformation of Higher Learning in America, 1830–1890.* Baltimore, 1986.

Wilson, Daniel G. *Science, Community, and the Transformation of American Philosophy, 1860–1930.* Chicago, 1990.

AMERICAN ROMANTICISM

David M. Robinson

When Ralph Waldo Emerson called for "an original relation to the universe" in 1836 (*Collected Works*, vol. 1, p. 7), he was attempting to provide an American language for the new conceptions of human nature, human society, and the natural world that had swept through Europe in the previous four decades. Although his version of the "Romantic" consciousness would be contested, extended, and modified by other American thinkers and artists, he signaled his culture's hunger for these new views of experience and suggested how the Romantic insistence on originality coalesced with an American identity founded on new beginnings.

Although Romanticism was given unique forms of expression in America, its origins were European, and the narrative of American Romanticism begins with the transmission of Romantic texts, concepts, and attitudes to America. The relative thinness of any existing literary and artistic culture in the new republic made it particularly receptive to such influences. Romantic art and expression helped fill the demand for a distinctive cultural identity that political independence had encouraged, providing the means for expressing what was felt to be a uniquely national experience and identity. It also afforded, through its utopian proclivity and its emphasis on unrealized human potentiality, the basis for a critique of the shortcomings of the new nation and its culture.

"Romanticism" is a notoriously unsettled term, open to a wide and sometimes divergent assortment of definitions. In an influential analysis of its multiple connotations, the philosopher Arthur O. Lovejoy declared that "the word 'romantic' has come to mean so many things that, by itself, it means nothing. It has ceased to perform the function of a verbal sign" (*Essays in the History of Ideas*, p. 232). Lovejoy's preference for the term "romanticisms" is a reminder of its various and sometimes conflicting emphases. But the ubiquity of the term as a period designator in cultural history also suggests its necessary role as the signifier of an important shift in consciousness in the late eighteenth and early nineteenth centuries. In the broadest sense, this shift can be understood as a series of intellectual and artistic responses to the perceived unraveling of the eighteenth-century view of the stable order of the universe and the rational nature of human experience. The breakdown of the ordered view of the universe that we associate with the Enlightenment generated two related but quite different responses. It infused Romantic thinking with a desire for more comprehensive and inclusive methods of perception and knowledge that included the rational but also pointed beyond it toward a realm of the emotions, the imagination, and the transcendent. But the rejection of the explanatory adequacy of the rational also pushed the Romantics toward an exploration of the darker realms of experience that we associate with pain, suffering, fear, the supernatural, the subconscious, mental instability, and violence. This dark or "gothic" element of the Romantic sensibility inverted the Romantic quest for meaning into a devastating revelation of the terror of experience.

At the center of this quest for meaning was the Romantic self—aspiring and heroic but also often fearful and suffering. Through a concentration on the self, which always threatened to become excessively egotistical, the Romantics confronted what they saw as the fragmentation of the world around them. The struggle to achieve some form of unity—spiritual, emotional, or social—thus became a central focus. Emerson, Henry David Thoreau, and Walt Whitman expressed the optimistic and affirmative side of the self in American literature; the darker and more skeptical side was articulated by Edgar Allan Poe, Nathaniel Hawthorne, and Herman Melville. Because the fragmentation to which the Romantics responded was social as well as psychological, the questing Romantic ego was accompanied in many cases by a similarly Romantic longing for the restoration of a lost human community. The hope for unity and harmony that was central to the

Romantic quest had important social and political implications.

ROMANTIC FICTION AND THE AMERICAN "ROMANCE"

In the preface to *The House of Seven Gables* (1851), Hawthorne argued for a certain freedom of imaginative conception and expression in the writing of fiction, especially with respect to the reader's expectation of a probable or realistic account of ordinary events. Hawthorne noted that an author who writes a "Novel" must "aim at a very minute fidelity, not merely to the possible, but to the probable, and ordinary course of man's experience." But he claimed "a certain latitude" from these expectations for the author of a "Romance," who may present the nature of experience "under circumstances, to a great extent, of the writer's own choosing or creation." Hawthorne's distinction allowed for elements of what he termed "the Marvellous" in fiction, and released him from the obligation to reproduce a detailed and precise rendering of the fabric of the social world. Even though, as Nina Baym has shown, Hawthorne's distinction between the novel and the romance was idiosyncratic for its day (*Novels, Readers, and Reviewers*, pp. 225–235), few critical pronouncements have proved to be as influential and as controversial.

In his important study *The American Novel and Its Tradition* (1957), Richard Chase pointed to the romance, as Hawthorne described it, as the form that gave the novel in America a distinctive identity. The American novel differed from the English novel, Chase argued, "by its perpetual reassessment and reconstitution of romance within the novel form" (p. viii). While Chase's claim has been contested, it seems clear that such authors as Charles Brockden Brown, James Fenimore Cooper, William Gilmore Simms, Poe, and Melville understood the heroic and mythic potential of the kind of fiction that would fall under Hawthorne's definition, and that their perception of these possibilities is an important element in the development of America's cultural self-examination.

ROMANCE AND AMERICAN MYTH

In part because of its lack of emphasis on realistic social detail, the romance became an instrument for the expression of human possibility, in which the aspiring and heroic dimension of experience could become the author's predominant concern.

While Americans embraced the idea of democratic equality as a fundamental cultural value, they also thirsted for the hero who could embody and enact their faith in the possibility of human endeavor. This general predilection toward the heroic was fortified by the widely shared cultural perception of the richness and the corresponding challenge of the natural world in North America. The trials and adventures of settling the frontier, it was believed, called out the worthiest of human traits, and in the contest with nature, Americans might absorb nature's awesome power.

The most important version of this frontier champion was Cooper's Leatherstocking, or Natty Bumppo, the central figure of five romances—*The Pioneers* (1823), *The Last of the Mohicans* (1826), *The Prairie* (1827), *The Pathfinder* (1840), and *The Deerslayer* (1841)—in which Cooper exploited with increasingly conscious intention the mythological qualities of his character, framing the experience of the western frontier as an epic past in which heroic attainment and tragic loss were inextricably intertwined. In his influential reading of the Leatherstocking novels, the English novelist D. H. Lawrence stressed Cooper's importance as an American mythmaker, whose "lovely half-lies . . . form a sort of American Odyssey" (*Studies in Classic American Literature*, p. 50). In formulating his new mythology of the American frontier, Cooper emphasized the heroic but did not overlook the darkness and violence that was part of the western expansion. His Leatherstocking novels achieve their weight and authority because they articulate both America's confident sense of purpose and assured achievement in its western expansion, and its stifled sense of the tragic price of that achievement.

Cooper's mythological depiction of the American frontier depended upon the overpoweringly sublime landscapes of the North American continent, and many interpreters have noted his visual power as the creator of "some of the loveliest, most glamorous pictures in all literature" (*Studies in Classic American Literature*, p. 55). By making his hero a man who helped civilization "overcome" nature by conforming to nature's knowledge, Cooper emphasized an elemental tension in American culture's conception of itself.

While Cooper portrayed this tension in broader social and cultural terms, Melville used the romance to illuminate this tension as a religious or metaphysical one, taking the ocean as the untamed wilderness against which his heroes had to strive. In *Moby-Dick; or, The Whale* (1851) he fused a detailed description of a whaling voyage with a penetrating

"Both Jaws, like Enormous Shears, Bit the Craft Complete in Twain." Illustration for *Moby-Dick*. UNDATED. © BETTMANN/CORBIS

nature's awesome detachment from human definitions and desires.

The vast western frontier and the open sea were the backdrops for the epic romances of Cooper and Melville. For their contemporaries Hawthorne and Poe, the mind, the will, and the conscience were the unmapped and unconquered territories. Hawthorne, a friend and major influence on Melville, recognized that fiction could serve as a means of moral and psychological exploration; his stories and novels are relentless investigations into the dynamics of human moral failings. His masterpiece, *The Scarlet Letter* (1851), narrates the aftermath of an adulterous affair between a New England Puritan minister, Arthur Dimmesdale, and Hester Prynne, who tenaciously refuses to name Dimmesdale to her outraged village authorities as the father of her child and lives among them as a proud outcast. Prynne's bold defiance of the community's attempts to subdue her and Dimmesdale's anguished inability to confess his sin publicly provide Hawthorne with the entry into the hidden origins of human motives that characterize the best of his fiction.

Hawthorne was fundamentally a moralist, and his fiction revolves around the portrayal of sin and its aftermath. But Hawthorne represented sin less as the transgression of a set of moral rules or an existing social code than the violation of the essential integrity of the self that resulted from one individual's reduction of another to mere use value. Hawthorne's tales repeatedly probe the failure of human relationships; in stories such as "The Birthmark" (1843) and "Rappaccinni's Daughter" (1844) he portrays the devastating possessiveness of an egomaniacal male who destroys a woman he presumably loves in pursuit of his own gratification. Such a failure to respect another's separate and individual value injures both the victim and the victimizer and renders impossible the productive union of individuals, especially men and women. But Hawthorne's identity as a moralist is complicated by his intellectual predisposition toward determinism, the lurking suspicion, evident in most of his works, that men and women are compelled to sin by their very nature.

Melville, who read Hawthorne while he was completing *Moby-Dick,* broached the same questions in his analysis of the character of Ahab. Did he freely choose his grim quest for the white whale or was he impelled to it by forces beyond his conscious control? Like Hawthorne, he wrestled with the inevitable dilemma between a moral critique of human actions and a recognition that those actions may not be the product of free moral choice.

study of two men using the voyage as a vehicle for their search for identity and self-understanding. The protagonist is the monomaniacal Captain Ahab, who has identified a particular white whale as the avatar of all human suffering. Ahab is described by the diffident narrator Ishmael, who observes Ahab with an appalled yet fascinated curiosity.

Melville's Ahab, a man of profound intelligence and implacable will, has the same capacity for heroism that Cooper attributed to Leatherstocking. But his remarkable powers are turned to the ends of a wholly egotistical pursuit of vengeance. His angry attempt to strike back at the mysterious force that injured him has a certain majesty, however, when we understand that Ahab conceives it as an attempt to reestablish the lost justice of the universe. Melville uses Ahab's self-consuming pursuit of the whale to illustrate both the caustic egotism of the Romantic self-consciousness and the principle of

---

MOBY-DICK: THE MEANING OF THE WHITE WHALE

Herman Melville's awareness of the importance of symbolic interpretation is indicated not only in his own use of symbols in *Moby-Dick,* but in his depiction of his characters' attempts to read the signs and omens of experience. Captain Ahab explains his pursuit of the white whale as an attempt to strike out at the injustice of the universe:

> All visible objects, man, are but as pasteboard masks. But in each event—in the living act, the undoubted deed—there, some unknown but still reasoning thing puts forth the mouldings of its features from behind the unreasoning mask. If man will strike, strike through the mask! How can the prisoner reach outside except by thrusting through the wall? To me, the white whale is that wall, shoved near to me. Sometimes I think there's naught beyond. But 'tis enough. He tasks me; he heaps me; I see in him outrageous strength, with an inscrutable malice sinewing it. That inscrutable thing is chiefly what I hate; and be the white whale agent, or be the white whale principal, I will wreak that hate upon him.

Source: *Moby-Dick; or, The Whale.* Edited by Harrison Hayford, Hershel Parker, and G. Thomas Tanselle. Evanston, Ill., and Chicago, 1988. Chapter 36, p. 164.

While the book's narrator, Ishmael, shares Ahab's sense that the whale embodies some inexpressibly dark fact about the universe, he finds the whiteness of the whale, in its suggestions of blankness and emptiness, the most significant and terrifying thing about him:

> Is it that by its indefiniteness [whiteness] it shadows forth the heartless voids and immensities of the universe, and thus stabs us from behind with the thought of annihilation, when beholding the white depths of the milky way? Or is it, that as in essence whiteness is not so much a color as the visible absence of color, and at the same time the concrete of all colors; is it for these reasons that there is such a dumb blankness, full of meaning, in a wide landscape of snows—a colorless, all-color of atheism from which we shrink?

Source: Ibid., Chapter 42, p. 194.

While Hawthorne may have feared the worst about human freedom, his stories resist a determinist apathy through their careful delineation of motive and their cautionary tone. But the inner demons that Hawthorne exposes, even through his attempts to censure them, are the central subject of Poe's explorations of the unstable mind pushed to extremes by grief, obsession, and terror. Adapting the conventions of gothic fiction to his particular psychological uses, Poe investigated the power of the dark impulses that compel human actions. Among his most popular works is the poem "The Raven" (1845), which describes in a mesmerizing rhythm the haunting presence of a raven whose repeated "Nevermore" forces the poem's devastated narrator to admit the permanence of his lover's death. His best stories, "Ligeia" (1838) and "The Fall of the House of Usher" (1839), incorporate elements of the darkly supernatural into what are finally explorations of the subconscious minds of their central characters. The narrator of "Ligeia" describes his intense love affair with the beautiful and mysterious Ligeia, who guides him through the world of metaphysical investigation, but whose tragic death traumatizes him. She later seems to return, through a remarkable exercise of will, to murder the woman the narrator married after her death and, in a shocking ending, to resurrect herself in the body of her victim. Poe structures his ghost tale so that it may also be read as the narrative of a daydream, an illusion, or a fantastic alibi, in which the narrator is actually responsible for the death of his wife. In "The Fall of the House of Usher" we are told of the gradual mental disintegration of Roderick Usher, who, mistakenly or willfully, has entombed his twin sister, Madeleine, alive. Haunted by an extreme acuteness of all his senses and expressing himself subconsciously through symbolic art and poetry that seem to be dictated by inner fears and urges, Usher represents the Romantic consciousness at its most intense, fragile, and self-destructive.

Both stories achieve their impact in large part through Poe's employment of gothic settings, the eerily decorated chamber in which the phantom of Ligeia appears to poison the narrator's wife, and the decaying Usher mansion, whose very stones are sentient and seem to imprison Roderick and his sister. Using these settings to reflect the workings of the mind, Poe extended his investigation of terror, chaos, and death as the dark alternatives to the better-known Romantic values of joy, unity, and the possibility of perpetual rebirth. The fiction of Melville, Hawthorne, and Poe thus forms a skeptical, tragically oriented alternative to the affirmative and optimistic pronouncements of the New England Transcendentalists Ralph Waldo Emerson, Margaret Fuller, and Henry David Thoreau, and their chief poetic disciple, Walt Whitman.

SENTIMENTAL FICTION AND SOCIAL REFORM

Scholars of Romantic literature have typically concerned themselves with works that were considered "high" art, even though many of the Romantics were passionate democrats who aspired to a broad and universal readership. Late-twentieth-century reevaluations of the popular literature of the nineteenth century have been spurred by a renewed interest in women's writing and a greater recognition of the importance of the literary marketplace in the shaping of Romantic literature. These studies have yielded a new picture of the literary history of the era, one in which works that were previously dismissed as formulaic and "sentimental" are now recognized as texts that performed a significant cultural function.

While Hawthorne and Melville have had a place at the center of the American literary canon for most of the twentieth century, they struggled for readership in a market that became increasingly dominated by women readers and women authors. Dismissed as aesthetically uninteresting, and largely forgotten by the mid-twentieth century, novelists such as Catharine Maria Sedgwick, Fanny Fern (Sara Payson Willis Parton), E. D. E. N. Southworth, Susan Bogert Warner, Maria Susanna Cummins, and Augusta Jane Evans (later Wilson) nevertheless had a significant role in molding the attitude and self-conception of American women. Some literary historians have found that women's sentimental novels were grounded in what Baym has termed "a moderate, or limited, or pragmatic feminism" (*Woman's Fiction*, p. 18), in which the authors demonstrate that the false assumption of women's complete dependency can and should be replaced with a new belief in women's capability for self-reliance.

Among the more representative and popular of such novels are Warner's *The Wide, Wide World* (1851), Cummins's *The Lamplighter* (1854), Southworth's *The Hidden Hand* (1859), and Evans's *St. Elmo* (1866). Baym described the recurrent plot of such novels as the struggle of a young girl to recognize "the necessity of winning her own way in the world" after she has lost "the supports she had rightly or wrongly depended on to sustain her throughout her life" (*Woman's Fiction*, p. 11). The novels were suffused with a profound religious sentiment and reflected an era that was marked by a rigid separation of male and female spheres of influence. While they taught patience and self-sacrifice, and in many ways reinforced the idea of a proper woman's sphere in the home, they also adapted the Romantic values of self-direction and self-sufficiency to the situation of women. In this sense they also reflect an era in which the ideology of feminism, articulated in such essays as one by Margaret Fuller, published as *Woman in the Nineteenth Century* (1845), was gaining wider acceptance.

It was not until the 1970s that scholars began to explore the incipient feminism in women's novels. Until then the novels had been largely remembered for their sentimental accounts of the acute suffering of their heroines, and their emotion was deemed excessive when seen from the perspective of later realist and modernist aesthetic principles. But such portrayals of suffering, the emotional core of the novels, can be understood, as Jane Tompkins argues, as the sign that the authors were dealing with "the psychological dynamics of living in a condition of servitude" (*Sensational Designs*, p. 172), a state of subjection that, when fully recognized, can become an important basis for the advocacy of change.

SENTIMENTALISM AND ANTISLAVERY LITERATURE

The political potential of the sentimental mode also helped to create a rich antislavery literature, of which Harriet Beecher Stowe's *Uncle Tom's Cabin* (1852) was the most influential example. The social powerlessness of the heroines of sentimental novels was amplified in the abject condition of the slave, and just as the sentimental mode had shaped the attitudes of readers toward feminism, it also added momentum to the growing public intolerance of the legality of slavery. Stowe made slavery "real" to a northern readership, giving familiar shape to people who were victims not only of human callousness and cruelty but of a legal institution that inevitably corrupted or victimized all those under its power. In Uncle Tom she created a compellingly sympathetic martyr-hero, a man whose moral commitment and spiritual constitution could never be destroyed, even though his life and worldly hopes were. Tom's Christ-like virtues of compassion, humility, incorruptibility, forbearance, and strength made slavery seem to be an assault on the essence of religion and a threat to the values that Stowe's readers identified as the foundations of a civilized society.

Stowe was not, of course, the first to recognize that literature was one of the most powerful of antislavery tools, and her novel is built on both the conventions of sentimental fiction and the rich legacy of antislavery advocacy in the sermon, oration, and political treatise that developed in New England in the 1830s and 1840s. Also arising from this context is the *Narrative of the Life of Frederick Douglass* (1845), one of America's most significant autobiographies, a compelling account of Douglass's struggle for self-education and self-emancipation. His story is quintessentially that of the self-made man, "the most thoroughly self-constructed person in the whole nineteenth century," as Daniel Walker Howe has observed (*Making the American Self,* p. 149). Through his embodiment of this primary American cultural myth of the rise from obscurity to prominence, Douglass secured for the slave, the person presumably without a social identity, inclusion in the American social system and demonstrated that slavery was an institution fundamentally alien to America's defining cultural values.

Douglass's *Narrative* succeeds through its detailed explanations of the abuse, both physical and psychological, of the slaves and his contrasting account of his persistent efforts to overcome his condition and claim his full human identity. The same narrative of heroically persistent efforts to overcome slavery's abuses marks Harriet Jacobs's *Incidents in the Life of a Slave Girl* (1861), a text only recently verified by Jean Fagan Yellin as Jacobs's authentic narrative of her experience of slavery and her escape

from it (*Incidents,* pp. xiii–xxxiv). Jacobs's experience, which she tells through the character of Linda Brent, was strikingly unusual. After years of struggling against her master's threats to violate her sexually, she escaped and hid in the cramped garret of her grandmother's house, where her relatives concealed her for nearly seven years before she could arrange for the safety and freedom of her children and finally escape to the North herself.

In her vivid account of her efforts to resist her master's plots to abuse her sexually and in her expressions of her apprehensions about the fate of her children, Jacobs offers a powerful dramatization of the emotional and psychological cruelty of slavery, emphasizing the extreme vulnerability of the slave who was also a woman. Like Douglass's *Narrative,* Jacobs's story is a heroic one; the heroine's strengths are her moral self-possession, her courage, her resourcefulness, and her remarkable patience, virtues that are supplemented by a supportive network of family, friends, and antislavery allies in the North, who finally help her secure her freedom. Nowhere are the Romantic themes of heroic resistance to evil and the achievement of freedom and self-possession better articulated than in antislavery narratives like those of Douglass and Jacobs.

ROMANTICISM IN THE SOUTH

In the South, Romanticism took a somewhat different form, reflecting and reinforcing the sense of a distinctive southern culture and ultimately contributing to the emergence of a southern nationalism that led to secession. Southerners found Romantic literature reprinted, discussed, and imitated in such journals as the *Southern Literary Messenger* and *Southern Quarterly Review* and were also receptive to Romantic authors such as Thomas Carlyle, Thomas Moore, Lord Byron, and Felicia Hemans. They developed a particular affinity for the Waverley Novels of Sir Walter Scott, in whose Romantic depictions of medieval chivalry they found an idealized version of southern plantation culture. Scott's novels infused the archaic feudal culture of Scotland with notions of knightly honor and a spirit of heroic endeavor and resistance, spawning a devotion in the South to what Rollin G. Osterweis terms "the chivalric ideal, with its emphasis on the cult of manners, the cult of woman, the cult of the gallant knight, the loyalty to caste" (*Romanticism and Nationalism in the Old South,* pp. 48–49).

These attitudes, developing at a period of intensifying alienation from the North, contributed to a

THE DEATH OF UNCLE TOM

Harriet Beecher Stowe depicts the slave Uncle Tom as the epitome of all the Christian virtues, making her novel a symbolic narrative of the battle between good and evil, in which the slave is pitted against the persons, laws, and institutions supporting slavery. Uncle Tom dies at the hands of the cruel overseer Simon Legree, but even as Legree beats him, Tom forgives and tries to convert him:

> Tom looked up to his master, and answered, "Mas'r, if you was sick, or in trouble, or dying, and I could save ye, I'd *give* ye my heart's blood: and, if taking every drop of blood in this poor old body would save your precious soul, I'd give 'em freely, as the Lord gave his for me. O Mas'r! don't bring this great sin on your soul! It will hurt you more than 't will me! Do the worst you can, my troubles'll be over soon; but, if ye don't repent, yours won't *never* end!"

Source: Harriet Beecher Stowe, *Uncle Tom's Cabin; or, Life among the Lowly.* Edited by Kathryn Kish Sklar. New York. 1982. Chapter 40, pp. 479–480.

growing sense of a unique cultural identity in a region that was actually quite diverse socially and economically, but which shared an increasing defensiveness about the moral and legal legitimacy of the institution of slavery. The cultural self-consciousness with which the South received Romantic values, attitudes, and images provided what Michael O'Brien terms "the framework" under which "the shared hypothesis of Southern culture" could develop (*Rethinking the South*, p. 55). This process of cultural separation accelerated in 1831–1832, Osterweis argues, because of the founding of William Lloyd Garrison's antislavery periodical *The Liberator*, a slave insurrection led by Nat Turner, and a series of debates on slavery in the Virginia legislature.

The novels of William Gilmore Simms, a novelist characterized by Mary Ann Wimsatt as "the representative antebellum Southern man of letters" ("William Gilmore Simms," p. 108), reflect the influence of Scott and the building mood of defiant regional consciousness in the antebellum South. Central to Simms's role as a spokesman for southern history and southern identity is his series of seven novels on the American Revolutionary War in South Carolina, featuring the exploits of General Francis Marion, the "Swamp Fox": *The Partisan* (1835); *Mellichampe* (1836); *The Kinsmen*, later retitled *The Scout* (1841); *Katharine Walton* (1851); *The Sword and the Distaff*, later retitled *Woodcraft* (1852); *The Forayers* (1855); and *Eutaw* (1856). These romances of the revolution gave the war a decidedly southern hue and suggested a historical precedent for a civil war for independence. Simms consciously adopted the framework for the historical romance established by Scott in these works, modifying it, as C. Hugh Holman shows, only by increasing the amount and specificity of the historical material that establishes the context of the novels. "Where Scott used history for the purposes of romance," Holman explains, "Simms used the romance for the purposes of social history" (*The Roots of Southern Writing*, p. 57). Even though Simms's romances by no means glorified the violence of the war, they intersected with the chivalric emphasis on battle as a necessary enactment of identity and values and offered a more directly accessible point of historical reference for a sense of nationalism in the South.

AMERICAN ROMANTIC POETRY

American poets embraced the sentimentalism that was a manifestation of the Romantic emphasis on the emotions, and a popular body of national poetry flowered through such poets as William Cullen Bryant, John Greenleaf Whittier, and Henry Wadsworth Longfellow, known as the "fireside" poets because of their prominent place in family reading around the hearth. Lydia Huntley Sigourney and Julia Ward Howe, female poets who wrote in the sentimental tradition, have also received significant twentieth-century historical reappraisals. The work of these sentimental poets varied widely from lyric poems to verse on historical and political topics, but they gained their place in the national consciousness for their descriptions of nature (Bryant); of family, home, and village life (Longfellow, Whittier, and Sigourney); and for the depiction of family loss and grief (Sigourney). Longfellow, Whittier, and Howe also made significant antislavery statements in their verse.

While the sentimental poetry of Longfellow, Whittier, Sigourney, and others has long been dismissed because of the shift in aesthetic tastes that are called modernism, it stands as an example of the potential of poetry to articulate widely held social and cultural values. But Romanticism also, and perhaps more familiarly, names the revisionist attitude that challenged conventional norms and was marked by a seemingly unquenchable thirst for newness and innovation.

Walt Whitman, whose *Leaves of Grass* Emerson greeted with extraordinary praise in 1855, was revolutionary in two respects: he articulated a radical version of the Romantic self and completely revised the prevalent conceptions of poetic form, particularly the poetic line. Whitman took to new extremes assumptions about human nature and the natural world that Emerson and other Transcendentalists had broached and insisted on the equality, and the essential identity, of the material and the spiritual. For Whitman, the human body and human sexuality were elements of a divine nature and crucial aspects of a whole and balanced human personality. His frank affirmation of the body made him one of the most controversial literary figures of the nineteenth century. But for Whitman the recognition of the divinity of the human body was part of a larger vision of the monistic unity of the cosmos, a repudiation of the dualistic vision of the opposition of body and mind, material and spiritual, that had characterized much of the tradition of Western thinking. "I hear and behold God in every object," he wrote, "yet understand God not in the least" ("Song of Myself," section 48).

Whitman's striking innovation in poetic form helped to reinforce the challenging freshness of his ideas. Discarding the conventions of rhyme, regularized stanza form, and the measured length of the poetic line, Whitman instead developed long, exclamatory lines whose length was dictated not by artificial convention but the necessity of the expression of an idea or image, and the measure of voiced breath. Writing a poetry that was grounded in human speech, both the dialogue of conversation and the declamatory quality of oratory, Whitman created a style that was unique and difficult to imitate but encouraged later poets to experiment in new poetic forms.

Whitman entitled his first volume of poems *Leaves of Grass,* using the grass as the symbol of his connection to the earth and organic life, and also seeing its individual leaves, alike in identity to all others but nevertheless uniquely separate, as a sign of the unity in diversity of human beings. This volume became his life work; he made significant expansions of it in 1856 and 1860 and made six further revisions and expansions until a final edition was published in 1892, the year of his death.

Whitman's innovations were not, however, the only influential poetic departures in the American Romantic era. The poems of Emily Dickinson, largely unknown until the twentieth century, are now recognized as one of the most important literary achievements in the nineteenth century, and Dickinson, known as a poet in her lifetime only to a circle of her family and friends, is now a central figure in the American literary canon. What Whitman achieved through the expansion of the poetic line and the repetition and multiplication of poetic phrasing, Dickinson achieved through an intense and powerful compression. Her poems are characteristically brief and marked by extreme ellipses, strikingly vivid imagery, original metaphor, and rich thematic ambiguity. Dickinson's poems explore a set of themes that are central to Romanticism, notably in their depiction of the quest of the self for identity and self-understanding and in their exploration of the mind in states of extreme stress. But they also look forward to the modernist sensibility in their fragmentary or disconnected forms and in their evocation of the painful loss of a sense of the order of experience. Only a handful of Dickinson's poems were published in her lifetime, though many were given to friends or family who knew her as a talented poet. The early editions of her work contained editorial alterations, regularized punctuation, and unauthorized titles that now seem to mar the unusual and appealingly unconventional form of her poems as she left them in manuscript. Dickinson's letters, similarly brilliant in their idiosyncratic forms of expression, also constitute an important literary legacy.

ROMANTICISM, LANDSCAPE, AND THE ARTS

The Romantic devotion to nature was also reflected in the wide interest in landscape representation in nineteenth-century American painting. The Hudson River valley, picturesque and only partially tamed by the westward expansion of population, provided the subject matter for the Hudson River school of painting, the first significant artistic movement in America. Thomas Cole, the leading figure in this movement and the most significant early American landscape painter, embraced the unique subject matter that the still untamed wilderness offered to the American artist. His "Essay on American Scenery" (1836) discussed the uniquely beautiful aspects of the North American forests and waterways, but also emphasized the impermanence of these scenes as the western expansion led to the clearing and settling of the land. Cole's paintings depicted the grandeur of the American wilderness, but typically included human figures or signs of human settlement, thus emphasizing the comparative smallness of the human figure in the landscape, but also suggesting the enormous changes to the land that were inherent in the continued growth of the American nation.

Cole's concern about the future of American civilization was expounded in a series of allegorical paintings entitled *The Course of Empire*, which he exhibited in 1836. Cole depicted the cycle of human civilization in five stages, *The Savage State, The Arcadian or Pastoral State, The Consummation of Empire, Destruction,* and *Desolation*. While his series ostensibly portrayed the rise and fall of an ancient empire, it clearly implied the future of America, then emerging from its pastoral state toward its consummation as an empire. This use of an interlinked series of paintings with an explicit narrative and theme was also employed in a later series of paintings, *The Voyage of Life*, first exhibited in 1840. These paintings trace the human life cycle in four stages, *Childhood, Youth, Manhood,* and *Old Age*, portraying a human figure carried down the river of time, with the landscape darkening and becoming ominous before the subject reaches, in *Old Age*, a body of placid water where he sees an angel gesturing toward a stream of sunlight from an opening in the darkened sky. Both somber and expectant in its moods, *The Voyage of Life*, like *The Course of Empire*, captures the complex mixture of energetic hope and brooding apprehension that give Cole's paintings much of their emotional power.

The most culturally significant and artistically accomplished expression of Romantic assumptions in American art was the emergence in the middle nineteenth century of a style of "luminist" painting. Growing out of the Hudson River school of landscape painters, the luminists concentrated on rendering a particular quality of meditative stillness in the landscape, an effect achieved in part through their representation of light. Among the most prominent and accomplished of the luminist painters are Fitz Hugh Lane, John Frederick Kensett, Martin Johnson Heade, Jasper Francis Cropsey, Sanford Robinson Gifford, Frederic Edwin Church, and Albert Bierstadt, whose works were the focal point of "American Light," an important exhibition at the National Gallery of Art in 1980. Finding in the American landscape a unique and compelling subject for representation, the luminists developed a distinctive form of expression, characterized by Barbara Novak as efforts to create "intimate" and "quietistic" visual impressions in which the landscape became the medium for transcendence and spirituality (Novak, *Nature and Culture*, p. 28). Fundamental to the luminists' objective was the achievement of a mood of "sublimity through repose" (p. 39), an aesthetic aspiration that revised in important ways the concept of the "sublime" as described by the eighteenth-century British statesman Edmund Burke. In contrast to Burke's emphasis on the enormous scale and power of nature and its capacity to evoke emotions of wonder and awe, the luminists attempted to achieve the "apprehension of silent energy" (p. 39) in the landscape, an apprehension through which the viewer could find a more contemplative and introspective relationship with the formative power suggested by the scene.

The ability to suggest the transcendent qualities of the natural world, and thus create the mood of meditative quiet to which the luminists aspired, depended largely on their depiction of natural light. Using "minute tonal modulations" of color, luminist painters disguised or concealed brushstrokes, thus achieving the suggestion of "light as pure emanation" on their canvases (Novak, in Wilmerding, ed., *American Light*, p. 25). This depiction of the transcendent quality of light was most often captured through the representation of expanses of still water that reflected the sky and thus served as a mirrorlike medium in the landscape, blending the horizon and the landscape into a unified impression of harmonious repose and natural unity through a suffusion of radiant light. Novak and other scholars have seen an important kinship between the luminists' vision of a meditative spirituality in nature and the connection between nature and the transcendent asserted by American Romantic writers such as Emerson, Thoreau, and Whitman. For both painters and poets, the landscape was a manifestation of transcendent energy and power, and to gain full awareness of a particular natural place was an enlightening and transformative experience. These artists conferred both an intense responsiveness and a reverential awe upon nature, attitudes that gathered popular momentum throughout the nineteenth century and have remained an important and influential element of American public consciousness into the twenty-first century.

Developments in nineteenth-century American architecture and landscape design also reflected the impact of Romantic values, largely through a new emphasis on landscape and garden design that accommodated and made use of natural features, moving away from more formal and highly structured models. Andrew Jackson Downing was a leader in fostering this progression, advancing his theories of landscape design in *A Treatise on the Theory and Practice of Landscape Gardening, Adapted to North America* (1841). Downing advocated careful planning of landscapes, but argued that geometrical designs for gardens and grounds were not always appropriate for North America. He stressed instead a close attention to the natural characteristics of the specific settings, in which existing growth and plantings of species native to the specific area were the foundation of the designs.

Collaborating with architects Alexander Jackson Davis and Calvert Vaux, Downing also became an extremely influential advocate of good taste and appropriate planning in the design of North American homes. He encouraged the adoption of the Gothic Revival style, especially as developed in the English rural cottage, and also promoted Italian and Swiss styling, as alternatives to the Greek Revival mode popular in the early nineteenth century. His *Cottage Residences* (1842), the first widely read house pattern book in America, provided plans and illustrations for houses appropriate for rural and suburban residences in North America. The book was less a builder's guide than a work intended to educate a broader audience in domestic architecture

and pragmatic guidance in the process of planning a home. Downing's publications served the multiple roles of advocacy for alternative styles of architecture, illustrations and plans for home construction, and the creation of a greater awareness of the necessity of design and fostering a more educated architectural taste in the American middle class.

THE END OF THE ROMANTIC ERA

As Morse Peckham has noted, "romanticism" designates both "general and permanent characteristics of mind, art, and personality, found in all periods and in all cultures," and "a specific historical movement in art and ideas which occurred in Europe and America in the late eighteenth and early nineteenth centuries" ("Toward a Theory of Romanticism," p. 5). The Romantic period of American literature began to fade in the 1860s and 1870s with the emergence of realism as a fictional ideal. Mark Twain's well-known satire "Fenimore Cooper's Literary Offenses" (1895) indicates how the realists built their literary agenda in large part around the repudiation of Romantic assumptions and procedures. In the fiction of Twain, William Dean Howells, Henry James, Edith Wharton, and others, the dedication to a precise rendering of the reality of the social world displaced Hawthorne's argument that the writer of fiction could claim "a certain latitude" in the depiction of historical reality. No similarly dramatic shift in American poetry occurred until the early twentieth century, with the emergence of modernist poets such as Robert Frost, T. S. Eliot, and Wallace Stevens. Romanticism continued to operate, however, as an influential force on subsequent authors of both fiction and poetry in the twentieth century, and key authors from the Romantic period continue to attract both readers and critical and biographical attention.

See also **The Classical Vision; Realism in Art and Literature** *(in this volume);* **The Natural World; God, Nature, and Human Nature** *(volume 2);* **Painting; Fiction; Poetry; Biography** *(volume 3); and other articles in this section.*

BIBLIOGRAPHY

The theory of Romanticism, what the term signifies and which works and authors should be termed "Romantic," has been the subject of extensive critical discussion. In Arthur O. Lovejoy's influential "On the Discrimination of Romanticisms," *PMLA* 39 (1924): 229–253, reprinted in his *Essays in the History of Ideas* (Baltimore, 1948), pp. 228–253, he notes the multiple and conflicting uses of the term. Particularly lucid and helpful versions of the theory of Romanticism have been developed by René Wellek, "The Concept of Romanticism in Literary History," in his *Concepts of Criticism,* edited by Stephen G. Nichols (New Haven, Conn., 1963), pp. 128–198; Morse Peckham, "Toward a Theory of Romanticism," *PMLA* 66 (March 1951): 5–23; and M. H. Abrams, *The Mirror and the Lamp: Romantic Theory and Critical Tradition* (New York, 1953).

R. P. Adams, in "Romanticism and the American Renaissance," *American Literature* 23 (January 1952): 419–432, presents a helpful application of Peckham's views to American literature. Among participants in the Romantic movement, Ralph Waldo Emerson gives the most complete account of Romantic values and assumptions. Consult *Collected Works of Ralph Waldo Emerson,* edited by Alfred R. Ferguson et al., 5 vols. (Cambridge, Mass., 1971–1994). Readers should also consult the bibliography included in the chapter on "Transcendentalism" in this work.

The most important single critical work on American Romanticism is F. O. Matthiessen's *American Renaissance* (New York, 1941), centering on the symbolic vision and democratic commitment of five authors who published key works in the years 1850–1855: Emerson, Hawthorne, Melville, Thoreau, and Whitman. Matthiessen's book defined the field of nineteenth-century American literary studies and was extended and augmented by Charles Feidelson's *Symbolism and American Literature* (Chicago, 1953) and R. W. B. Lewis's *The American Adam: Innocence, Tragedy, and Tradition in the Nineteenth Century* (Chicago, 1955). Michael T. Gilmore's *American Romanticism and the Marketplace* (Chicago, 1985) is an important consideration of the effect of market forces on American Romantic literature.

Lawrence Buell's *New England Literary Culture from Revolution through Renaissance* (New York, 1986) offers important considerations of several New England Romantic authors in their immediate historical and geographical context. Robert Weisbuch's *Atlantic Double-Cross: American Literature and British Influence in the Age of Emerson* (Chicago, 1986) considers the literary interchange between America and England during the Romantic period, and Leon Chai's *The Romantic Foundations of the American Renaissance* (Ithaca, N.Y., 1987) is an informative description of the transmission of Romanticism from Europe to America.

Discussions of American Romantic fiction have been heavily influenced by the concept of the "romance," as defined by Hawthorne in his preface to *The House of Seven Gables* (Boston, 1851; reprinted as vol. 2 of *The Centenary Edition of the Works of Nathaniel Hawthorne,* 23 vols., edited by William Charvat et al., Columbus, Ohio, 1965). Richard Chase's influential *The American Novel and Its Tradition* (New York, 1957) argues that the romance gave American fiction a distinctive form and draws from D. H. Lawrence's groundbreaking essay on Cooper in his *Studies in Classic American Literature* (New York, 1923; reprinted New York, 1964). Late-twentieth-century critics of early American fiction have attempted to challenge, refine, or broaden Chase's perspective, emphasizing other forms or definitions of the "romance" and reassessing the overlooked significance of the enormously popular "sentimental" novels written by women.

Important studies of the development of American fiction, from a vast critical literature, include Joel Porte, *The Romance in America: Studies in Cooper, Poe, Hawthorne, Melville, and James* (Middletown, Conn., 1969); Ann Douglas, *The Feminization of American Culture* (New York, 1977); Nina Baym, *Woman's Fiction: A Guide to Novels by and about Women in America, 1820–1870* (Ithaca, N.Y., 1978); Michael Davitt Bell, *The Development of American Romance: The Sacrifice of Relation* (Chicago, 1980); Nina Baym, *Novels, Readers, and Reviewers: Responses to Fiction in Antebellum America* (Ithaca, N.Y., 1984); Mary Kelley, *Private Woman, Public Stage: Literary Domesticity in Nineteenth-Century America* (New York, 1984); Evan Carton, *The Rhetoric of American Romance: Dialectic and*

Identity in Emerson, Dickinson, Poe, and Hawthorne (Baltimore, 1985); Philip Fisher, *Hard Facts: Setting and Form in the American Novel* (New York, 1985); Jane P. Tompkins, *Sensational Designs: The Cultural Work of American Fiction, 1790–1860* (New York, 1985); Cathy N. Davidson, *Revolution and the Word: The Rise of the American Novel* (New York, 1986); Edgar A. Dryden, *The Form of American Romance* (Baltimore, 1988); William A. Ellis, *The Theory of the American Romance: An Ideology in American Intellectual History* (Ann Arbor, Mich., 1989); Susan K. Harris, *Nineteenth-Century American Women's Novels: Interpretive Strategies* (New York, 1990); Joyce W. Warren, ed., *The (Other) American Traditions: Nineteenth-Century Women Writers* (New Brunswick, N.J., 1993); E. Miller Budick, *Engendering Romance: Woman Writers and the Hawthorne Tradition, 1850–1990* (New Haven, Conn., 1994); and Budick, *Nineteenth-Century American Romance: Genre and the Construction of Democratic Culture* (New York, 1996).

For a consideration of Romanticism in the antebellum South, see Rollin G. Osterweis, *Romanticism and Nationalism in the Old South* (New Haven, Conn., 1949). Osterweis's analysis is reconsidered in Michael O'Brien, *Rethinking the South: Essays in Intellectual History* (Baltimore, 1988). The process of nationalism in the antebellum South is analyzed by Drew Gilpin Faust, *The Creation of Confederate Nationalism: Ideology and Identity in the Civil War South* (Baton Rouge, La., 1988). For discussions of William Gilmore Simms as a southern writer, see C. Hugh Holman, *The Roots of Southern Writing: Essays on the Literature of the American South* (Athens, Ga., 1972), and Mary Ann Wimsatt, "William Gilmore Simms," in *The History of Southern Literature*, edited by Louis D. Rubin Jr., et al. (Baton Rouge, La., 1985, pp. 108–117).

For a comprehensive overview of Cole's artistic career, see Ellwood C. Parry III, *The Art of Thomas Cole: Ambition and Imagination* (Newark, Del., 1988). Cole's "Essay on American Scenery" was published in *American Monthly Magazine* 1 (January 1836): 1–12; it is reprinted in John Conron, ed., *The American Landscape: A Critical Anthology of Prose and Poetry* (New York, 1973): 568–578. For interpretations of the cultural significance of his work, see Joy S. Kasson, "The Voyage of Life: Thomas Cole and Romantic Disillusionment," *American Quarterly* 27 (1975): 42–56; Tony Tanner, "Notes for a Comparison between American and European Romanticism," pp. 25–45 in his *Scenes of Nature, Signs of Men* (Cambridge and New York, 1987); Stephen Daniels, *Fields of Vision: Landscape Imagery and National Identity in England and the United States* (Princeton, 1993); and Angela Miller, *The Empire of the Eye: Landscape Representation and American Cultural Politics, 1825–1875* (Ithaca, N.Y., 1993).

The luminist painters are discussed in Barbara Novak, *Nature and Culture: American Landscape and Painting, 1825–1875* (New York, 1980), and in John Wilmerding, ed., *American Light: The Luminist Movement, 1850–1875* (Washington, D.C., 1980). The latter volume records the 1980 exhibition on luminism at the National Gallery of Art, and includes essays on various aspects of luminism by a number of scholars. Andrew Jackson Downing's career and theories in landscape design and architecture are traced in David Schuyler, *Apostle of Taste: Andrew Jackson Downing, 1815–1852* (Baltimore, 1996).

TRANSCENDENTALISM

David M. Robinson

"That which is best in nature, the highest prize of life," the American poet and essayist Ralph Waldo Emerson declared in 1842, "is the perception in the private heart of access to the Universal" (*Early Lectures,* 3:381). Emerson's message of the individual's immediate access to divinity was the central doctrine of Transcendentalism, America's most significant early intellectual and cultural movement. Rooted in the Unitarian dissent to Calvinist theology and the later evangelical revivals of the Great Awakening of the 1740s, Transcendentalism emerged in 1830s New England as a movement of religious awakening and reform within the new Unitarian denomination. Transcendentalism expressed the desire of Emerson and a number of other young ministers for new forms of thought and worship, and correspondingly new forms of social organization and artistic expression.

Affirming the innate spiritual potential of the individual as a cardinal principle, the Transcendentalists believed that the inner harmony glimpsed in their holistic spiritual vision and exemplified in nature could also be translated into the world of human social relations. Brook Farm and Fruitlands, short-lived but significant experiments in cooperative living, signified the desire of many of the Transcendentalists to find an alternative to America's emerging market economy. Their contributions to the discourse on antislavery and women's rights also indicated that this movement of religious protest soon became a vehicle for political dissent.

RELIGIOUS ORIGINS

As the dissent to Calvinism grew in the middle and late eighteenth century, a new theological party emerged to oppose the doctrines of innate depravity and election to grace. Believing that these central tenets of Calvinism falsified the nature of God and compromised human dignity and free will, a group of liberal ministers in the Boston area offered a new theology that depicted God in more benevolent terms, and placed the human will in a more primary role in the process of salvation. The liberals took on the name Unitarian and coalesced into a religious denomination during the first three decades of the nineteenth century, establishing a stronghold at Harvard University and in the established churches in Boston and eastern Massachusetts.

The American clergyman William Ellery Channing articulated the fundamental concepts of Unitarianism in a series of sermons and addresses in the 1820s and 1830s, developing a more positive view of the nature of God, emphasizing the importance of reason in determining religious belief, and stressing self-culture as a key to the religious life, a process of continuing inner growth founded on the innate spiritual potential within every individual. Channing's message helped provide a sense of identity and common purpose for Unitarians, and was enormously appealing to a younger generation of aspiring ministers, the most notable of whom was Emerson.

EMERSON'S EMERGENCE

Emerson was the son of a Unitarian minister, William Emerson, and counted several generations of New England ministers in his ancestry. He struggled, however, with the decision to enter the ministry himself, fearing that his shyness and distaste for theological reasoning would hold him back. But he saw in Channing a quite different model for the ministry, as many of his peers did. Channing was less a dry theologian than an inspiring poet and orator, who emphasized the moral imagination as the key to preaching and to the religious life. Emerson undertook theological studies at Harvard despite a battle with a life-threatening tubercular condition, and assumed the pastorate of the Second Church of Boston in 1829.

In his sermons and the extensive journals that he kept for his reading, observation, and speculation, Emerson developed a religious vision similar to Channing's but which seized on certain of Channing's ideas and pushed their implications much further. Emerson was reading extensively in the Greek philosopher Plato, in the Neoplatonic and Christian mystical traditions, and in new forms of idealism originating in eighteenth- and nineteenth-century German Romantic philosophers and transmitted by the poet Samuel Taylor Coleridge and the essayist-historian Thomas Carlyle. As he advanced his own version of the doctrine of self-culture, he accentuated the divine nature of the conscience or moral sense, seeing this as the means by which the human personality was linked to God, and conceptualizing the recognition and cultivation of this "God within" as the essence of the religious life. This idea of the God within, expanded and reinforced by Emerson's reading in idealist philosophy, his interest in science and natural history, and his increasing skepticism of Jesus as a supernatural figure rather than a prophet and teacher, led Emerson to resign his Boston pulpit in 1832. After traveling to Europe in 1832 and 1833, an expansive and empowering journey for him, he returned to begin a career as a lecturer and essayist, and published *Nature* in 1836, the first full articulation of the Transcendentalist philosophy.

Nature had an enormous impact on younger intellectuals, who saw in it both a new kind of poetry and metaphysics, and a call to action to reformulate the religious life of their denomination and country. Describing both a mystical awareness that "the currents of the Universal Being circulate through me" (*Collected Works,* 1:10) and an intense attentiveness to the details of a physical world that we would see "with new eyes," Emerson urged his readers to know "that the world exists for you" (*Collected Works,* 1:44), challenging them to a reawakened sense of purpose and importance.

THE BEGINNINGS OF A MOVEMENT

Emerson's message of self-culture and a reawakened perception of the world was empowering to a generation dissatisfied with what they felt was an arid and passionless theology that, despite Channing's example, characterized Unitarian preaching. They also took Emerson's message as a hopeful sign of dissent from the narrowing and competitive qualities of America's entrepreneurial economy. Emerson characterized the Transcendentalist as a young person who felt starved intellectually and spiritually in America's overly pragmatic culture, and confined by its constricted and unfulfilling vocational choices. "We are miserable with inaction. We perish of rest and rust. But we do not like your work" (*Collected Works,* 1:212). His message was meant to reopen the world to them and restore a sense of purpose and hope.

As Emerson moved out of the ministry into his career as a public lecturer and essayist in the late 1830s, several other younger Unitarian ministers began to coalesce around him as the champion of the "new views." Frederic Henry Hedge, James Freeman Clarke, Theodore Parker, George Ripley, Orestes Brownson, Convers Francis, Christopher Pearse Cranch, and John Sullivan Dwight, among others, began to see themselves as a dissenting or insurgent party, bound together by both their alienation from the Unitarian status quo and a visionary hopefulness for purposive and progressive change. They were joined by other intellectuals such as Margaret Fuller, Henry David Thoreau, Bronson Alcott, Jones Very, Elizabeth Hoar, and Elizabeth Palmer Peabody, whose work was more literary or educational, and who were also drawn to Emerson's leadership and literary example.

In periodic meetings of what came to be known as the "Transcendental Club," they shared reading, opinions, and plans and, more importantly, found reassurance in the support of their like-minded colleagues. Openness to new concepts and innovative modes of expression, including Romantic literature, German idealist metaphysics, and Asian religions, was an important hallmark of their identity. Their common ethical orientation was toward a somewhat more radical version of the self-culture that Channing had preached, with a greater emphasis on the authority and freedom of the individual conscience. They linked this emphasis on individual dignity and freedom with a democratic and egalitarian political outlook that disposed them to support movements of political reform that were having an important impact on American culture. Their common philosophical assumption was that "intuition" was the source of truth, a wholly internal process of assent that was not dependent on tradition, convention, or external authority. The religious sentiment, Emerson wrote, "is guarded by one stern condition. . . . It is an intuition, It cannot be received at second hand" (*Collected Works,* 1:80). In this sense, the Transcendentalists rejected the empiricism of the English philosopher John Locke and held that truth was an inner revelation, not the

RALPH WALDO EMERSON'S ADDRESSES AND ESSAYS

Historical Christianity has fallen into the error that corrupts all attempts to communicate religion. As it appears to us, and as it has appeared for ages, it is not the doctrine of the soul, but an exaggeration of the personal, the positive, the ritual. It has dwelt, it dwells, with noxious exaggeration about the *person* of Jesus. The soul knows no persons. It invites every man to expand to the full circle of the universe, and will have no preferences but those of spontaneous love. But by this eastern monarchy of a Christianity, which indolence and fear have built, the friend of man is made the injurer of man. The manner in which his name is surrounded with expressions, which were once sallies of admiration and love, but are now petrified into official titles, kills all generous sympathy and liking.

(The Divinity School "Address," *Collected Works,* 1:82)

Nothing is at last sacred but the integrity of your own mind. Absolve you to yourself, and you shall have the suffrage of the world. I remember an answer which when quite young I was prompted to make to a valued adviser who was wont to importune me with the dear old doctrines of the church. On my saying, What have I to do with the sacredness of traditions, if I live wholly from within? my friend suggested—"But these impulses may be from below, not from above" I replied, "They do not seem to me to be such; but if I am the Devil's child, I will live then from the Devil." No law can be sacred to me but that of my nature.

("Self-Reliance," *Collected Works,* 2:30)

To fill the hour,—that is happiness; to fill the hour, and leave no crevice for a repentance or an approval. We live amid surfaces and the true art of life is to skate well on them. Under the oldest mouldiest conventions, a man of native force prospers just as well as in the newest world, and that by skill of handling and treatment. He can take hold anywhere. Life itself is a mixture of power and form, and will not bear the least excess of either. To finish the moment, to find the journey's end in every step of the road, to live the greatest number of good hours, is wisdom.

("Experience," *Collected Works,* 3:35)

product of external perception. For similar reasons, they questioned the authority of historical traditions, called for the reformation and revitalization of the church, and advocated innovative methods of education that were more dialogic and less hierarchical.

Emerson's *Nature* was published along with three other major statements of Transcendentalism in 1836: Brownson's *New Views of Christianity, Society, and the Church,* William Henry Furness's *Remarks on the Four Gospels,* and Ripley's *Discourses on the Philosophy of Religion Addressed to Doubters*

Who Wish to Believe. Emerson furthered this intellectual momentum with two important public addresses, "The American Scholar" (1837) and the Divinity School "Address" (1838), the latter a commencement speech at the Harvard Divinity School that ignited a major theological controversy. Emerson argued there that the biblical miracles were irrelevant to the foundation of true religion, which was instead dependent on the inner qualities of the soul. "To aim to convert a man by miracles, is a profanation of the soul. A true conversion, a true Christ, is now, as always, to be made, by the reception of beautiful sentiments" (*Collected Works*, 1:83). Moreover, he argued that Jesus' claim to supernatural authority had been distorted in the history of the church. Jesus had claimed a divinity that was potentially available to all men and women: "One man was true to what is in you and me" (*Collected Works*, 1:81). But perhaps most important to the Harvard Divinity School graduates about to enter the ministry, he criticized the lifeless and routine preaching responsible for "the famine of our churches." "Where now sounds the persuasion, that by its very melody imparadises my heart and so affirms its own origin in heaven?" (*Collected Works*, 1:85). Reaction to "Address" varied within the Unitarian community, but it was singled out by the influential Harvard professor and denominational leader Andrews Norton as a new form of "infidelity," a dangerous departure from fundamental Christian precepts.

Norton's critique of Emerson indicated a division within the Unitarian denomination over how far liberal theology could go in rejecting the supernatural elements of Christianity, such as the miracles and the divinity of Jesus, a controversy that became even more heated after an 1841 ordination sermon by Theodore Parker, "A Discourse on the Transient and Permanent in Christianity." Parker extended Emerson's emphasis on a religious sentiment that transcended the mythological elements of Christianity by drawing a distinction between the impermanent historical and cultural manifestations of religious belief on the one hand and the lasting principles and sentiments upon which Christianity and all human religions are founded on the other. "In respect of doctrines as well as forms," Parker wrote, "we see all is transitory." However, he assured his audience, "what is of absolute value never changes" (Miller, *The Transcendentalists*, pp. 275, 281). By reaffirming what he termed the "permanent" aspects of Christianity, Parker was also advancing the Transcendentalists' aspirations for a universal religion, one that was composed of the common, underlying elements of the various world religions. Like Emerson, Parker assumed a universally human religious sentiment or orientation, which manifested itself in varying historical and cultural forms. To embrace this universal essence of religion meant to devalue or perhaps discard altogether the identifiable Christian qualities of religion, an unacceptable proposition for many Unitarians, who, like Norton, were unwilling to give up their Christian identities. The controversy over Transcendentalism deepened after Parker's sermon, and the denomination remained divided until the 1890s between radical theological modernists like Parker, and more moderately liberal Unitarians who wanted to retain a connection with their Christian heritage and identity.

LITERARY AND AESTHETIC ACCOMPLISHMENTS

As the theological controversy developed and intensified in the 1840s, the Transcendentalists also undertook innovative artistic work and progressive projects in the political arena that expressed the same assumptions that guided their theological insurgency. Emerson's essays and addresses were striking not only for their radical religious ideas but also for their highly metaphoric and poetic style, a kind of poetry in prose that constituted a major aesthetic achievement. Emerson also championed the art of poetry and took under his wing a number of younger poets and writers. He helped to establish one of the most important early literary magazines in America, the *Dial*. Edited first by Margaret Fuller and then by Emerson from 1842 to 1844, the *Dial* combined religion, politics, poetry, book reviews, and translations of foreign works, an eclectic combination that bespoke the Transcendentalists' wide-ranging intellectual interests. The magazine provided an important outlet for a number of poets and essayists, featuring early works by Thoreau, Fuller, Very, Cranch, Ellery Channing (the nephew of William Ellery Channing), Alcott, and others, establishing itself as an organ for experimental styles and ideas.

The Transcendentalists' advancement of the cause of new European literature and philosophy, and their openness to Asian sacred texts, were also important aspects of their cultural work. Fuller's passionate advocacy of the German poet Goethe's writing, upholding his example of worldly wisdom and balance against a prevailing New England sus-

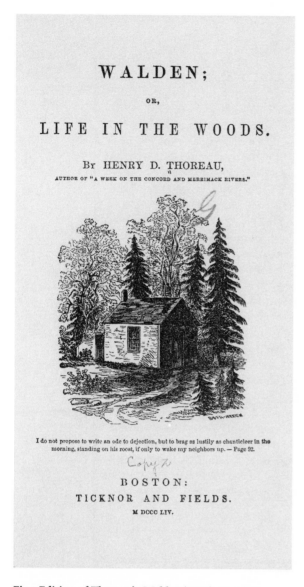

WALDEN;

OR,

LIFE IN THE WOODS.

By HENRY D. THOREAU,

AUTHOR OF "A WEEK ON THE CONCORD AND MERRIMACK RIVERS."

I do not propose to write an ode to dejection, but to brag as lustily as chanticleer in the morning, standing on his roost, if only to wake my neighbors up. — Page 92.

BOSTON:

TICKNOR AND FIELDS.

M DCCC LIV.

First Edition of Thoreau's *Walden* (1854). © CORBIS

into the mould of these new times." He termed Transcendentalism "Idealism as it appears in 1842" (*Collected Works,* 1:201), thus connecting his ideas with the tradition of Plato, whom he regarded as history's most important philosopher. Similarly, Thoreau's *Walden* (1854) is saturated with references to the Greek and Roman classics, the Bible, and the sacred literature of Asia; and Fuller's *Woman in the Nineteenth Century* (1845) is centrally concerned with examples from classical mythology. Both of these intellectual tendencies, toward the new and the experimental, and toward the ancient and the sacred, found expression in the *Dial,* which proved, despite its relatively short life, to be an enormously enabling project for Emerson and his circle.

The opportunities for new expression provided by the *Dial* helped further the development of many of its contributors, especially Thoreau and Fuller. Following Emerson's example of image-rich, highly metaphoric prose, but with a much deeper commitment to the study of nature and a surer sense of extended literary structure, Thoreau published *Walden,* his autobiographical account of a two-year stay in the woods near Walden Pond, widely regarded as a classic of nineteenth-century literature. "I went to the woods because I wished to live deliberately," he wrote, "to front only the essential facts of life, and see if I could not learn what it had to teach, and not, when I came to die, discover that I had not lived" (in Shanley, p. 90). Thoreau's wisdom quest was thus a more secularized version of the Transcendentalists' commitment to revitalize religion by returning to the most fundamental sources of insight and inspiration; he used the natural world, especially the pond in its changing character over the year, as his oracle and measure of authority, dramatizing Emerson's earlier claim that nature mirrored the soul and could serve as a source of self-discovery.

Thoreau's shaping of his narrative over an extended seven-year period (he left the pond in 1847 and published *Walden* in 1854) resulted in a structure dictated by the course of the year and its changing seasons, with a penultimate chapter on spring that equates the awakening of the pond and the woods around it with his own spiritual rejuvenation and renewed sense of moral purpose. Its richly textured and heavily allusive prose, and its exemplification of an organic form, one in which structure is determined not by the imposition of an artificial framework but rather by the internal logic of the developing argument, represent the highest aesthetic aspirations of the Transcendentalist movement. Thoreau continues to be revered both as a

picion of his moral soundness, is a key example of the Transcendentalists' sense of a cultural mission to sensitize the hardened pragmatism of their culture. John Sullivan Dwight became an ardent champion of Beethoven as an exemplar of a new era in music, and in 1852 he founded *Dwight's Journal of Music,* America's most significant early musical periodical. The Transcendentalists also upheld the writings of Wordsworth, Coleridge, and Carlyle, serving as critical advocates for English Romanticism and absorbing those works into their own contributions to American literature.

Despite this identification with change and newness, Emerson argued that Transcendentalist ideas were "not new, but the very oldest of thoughts cast

---

HENRY DAVID THOREAU AT WALDEN

Then to my morning work. First I take an axe and pail and go in search of water, if that be not a dream. After a cold and snowy night it needed a divining rod to find it. Every winter the liquid and trembling surface of the pond, which was so sensitive to every breath, and reflected every light and shadow, becomes solid to the depth of a foot or a foot and a half, so that it will support the heaviest teams, and perchance the snow covers it to an equal depth, and it is not to be distinguished from any level field. Like the marmots in the surrounding hills, it closes its eye-lids and becomes dormant for three months or more. Standing on the snow-covered plain, as if in a pasture amid the hills, I cut my way first through a foot of snow, and then a foot of ice, and open a window under my feet, where, kneeling to drink, I look down into the quiet parlor of the fishes, pervaded by a softened light as through a window of ground glass, with its bright sanded floor the same as in summer; there a perennial waveless serenity reigns as in the amber twilight sky, corresponding to the cool and even temperament of the inhabitants. Heaven is under our feet as well as over our heads. . . .

I learned this, at least, by my experiment; that if one advances confidently in the direction of his dreams, and endeavors to live the life which he has imagined, he will meet with a success unexpected in common hours. He will put some things behind, will pass an invisible boundary; new, universal, and more liberal laws will begin to establish themselves around and within him; or the old laws be expanded, and interpreted in his favor in a more liberal sense, and he will live with the license of a higher order of beings. In proportion as he simplifies his life, the laws of the universe will appear less complex, and solitude will not be solitude, nor poverty poverty, nor weakness weakness. If you have built castles in the air, your work need not be lost; that is where they should be. Now put the foundations under them.

(*Walden*, pp. 282–283, 323–324)

---

prophet of the simple life within an entrepreneurial and consumerist culture and an early voice of an environmental ethic in which respect for the natural world must take prominence in all human decisions and activities.

TRANSCENDENTALISM AND POLITICAL DISSENT

Although it has been widely admired and extensively studied as a work of art, *Walden* lives in American culture as more than an aesthetic accomplishment, given its articulation of an important dissent to mainstream social, economic, and ethical assumptions. In his criticism of excessive materialism and consumption, and of the deadening work necessary to sustain them, Thoreau attacked what he felt was a warped system of values at the heart of American culture. Thoreau dramatized his dissent to American political culture in his refusal to pay his poll tax in 1846, an act that led to his arrest and an overnight stay in the Concord, Massachusetts, jail, the subject of his 1849 essay "Resistance to Civil Government" (better known as "Civil Disobedience"). Thoreau emphasized the immorality of the war with Mexico and the continuance of legal slavery in America, and urged acts of resistance as both an ethical duty and a means of advancing political reform.

Thoreau's social critique was one aspect of a larger attempt among the Transcendentalists to question existing social and political norms, and to advocate a democratic, egalitarian, and cooperative

Margaret Fuller (1810–1850). © BETTMANN/CORBIS

social structure. Margaret Fuller adapted the Emersonian stress on self-reliance and the inherent dignity and divinity of the individual to feminist purposes, expanding an earlier *Dial* essay into *Woman in the Nineteenth Century,* one of the most important American treatises on women's rights. Fuller argued that women faced restrictive and debilitating barriers to their development, and stressed the need for women to find new modes of self-expression, both in work and in private and family life. Such harmonious development, in which all aspects of the personality, intellectual, emotional, aesthetic, and social, were cultivated to their full potential, was crucial for both women and men. Exemplifying these principles as a leader of "conversations" for women in the late 1830s, Fuller eventually became an essayist and commentator for the *New York Tribune* and traveled to Italy in 1847, where she reported on, and became committed to, the independence movement led by the Italian revolutionary Giuseppe Mazzini. Returning to America in 1850, Fuller and her husband and child were killed in a shipwreck, leaving her projected history of the Italian Revolution uncompleted. The loss of her voice was a profound setback to the development of American culture.

Fuller's work on women's rights had stressed the intellectual and intuitive capabilities of women, and condemned the social barriers to self-culture that faced women of Fuller's era. In *Woman* she noted the close links between the women's movement and the antislavery movement, seeing the restrictions on women as akin to the enslavement of the African Americans. Fuller's sense of the political urgency and moral gravity of the slavery crisis accorded with the antislavery commitment of many of the Transcendentalists. Though reluctant to give up his literary and philosophical work for direct political involvement, Emerson nevertheless gave important antislavery addresses in the mid-1840s, noting Britain's success in ending slavery in the West Indies. But he was enraged with the passage of the Fugitive Slave Law in 1850, and responded with a series of withering attacks on slavery in the next decade, works that had been largely overlooked until the scholar Len Gougeon's 1990 study of Emerson and antislavery. Emerson and Thoreau developed a great respect for the radical abolitionist John Brown, whom Thoreau defended in a public address before his execution, and eulogized afterward as a modern-day saint. Brown was "a transcendentalist above all, a man of ideas and principles," Thoreau declared. "No man in America has ever stood up so persistently and effectively for the dignity of human nature" (Glick, *Reform Papers,* pp. 115, 125). Theodore Parker gained a wide following as one of the nation's best-known antislavery preachers from his pulpit at the Twenty-eighth Congregational Society in Boston, using his oratorical skills to portray slavery as the nation's great moral challenge. For the Transcendentalists the existence of slavery was a violation of the deepest principle of the dignity of the individual, and they sensed that the political struggle over slavery and the Civil War were crucial tests of the moral fate of the nation.

UTOPIAN COMMUNAL EXPERIMENTS

While the slavery issue rose in intensity during the 1840s and 1850s, becoming the dominant political and moral issue of the time, it was to many of the Transcendentalists only one aspect of a more profoundly flawed social arrangement that perpetuated wide disparities in income and unequal distribution of property, a competitive and narrowing arena of work, and the overconsumption of unnecessary and debilitating products. Thoreau sounded this note most clearly in *Walden,* arguing forcefully that "most of the luxuries, and many of the so-called

MARGARET FULLER'S WRITINGS

Male and female represent the two sides of the great radical dualism. But, in fact, they are perpetually passing into one another. Fluid hardens to solid, solid rushes to fluid. There is no wholly masculine man, no purely feminine woman.

I believe that, at present, women are the best helpers of one another.

Let them think; let them act; till they know what they need.

We only ask of men to remove arbitrary barriers. Some would like to do more. But I believe that it needs for a woman to show herself in her native dignity, to teach them how to aid her; their minds are so encumbered with tradition.

(*Woman in the Nineteenth Century,* pp. 68–69, 101)

I am not what I should be on this earth. I could not be.

My nature has need of profound and steadfast sentiment, without this it could have no steadfast greatness, no creative power.

I have been since we parted the object of great love from the noble and the humble. I have felt it towards both; Yet a kind of chastened libertine I rove, pensively, always, in deep sadness, often O God help me; is all my cry. Yet I have very little faith in the paternal love, I need; the government of the earth does seem so ruthless or so negligent.

I am tired of seeing men err and bleed. I am tired of thinking, tired of hoping. I take an interest in some plans, *our* socialism, for instance, for it has become mine, too, but the interest is shallow as the plans. They are needed, they are even good, but man will still blunder and weep, as he has done for so many thousand years.

(From a letter from Rome to William Henry Channing, 10 March 1849, *The Letters of Margaret Fuller,* vol. 5, pp. 205–206)

comforts of life, are not only not indispensable, but positive hindrances to the elevation of mankind" (p. 14). He believed that "the mass of men lead lives of quiet desperation" (p. 8) in a fruitless pursuit of satisfaction through ownership and consumption, and urged an extreme simplification of economic activities as the first step toward a restoration of dignity and meaningfulness in life.

Thoreau's alienation from the economic mainstream of American life led to his quite individual experiment in solitary living at Walden Pond, but other Transcendentalists saw more promise in collective acts to implement alternative modes of economic organization. The most famous of these was the Brook Farm commune, organized by George Ripley in 1841. Ripley envisioned a collective that would include a farm and school, and in which the members would share in both duties and rewards in an environment that would be egalitarian, emotionally supportive, and intellectually stimulating. While Emerson expressed support, but refused to join, Ripley gathered an interesting group at Brook

BROOK FARM

In 1841 George Ripley led a group of men and women to establish Brook Farm, one of the most important utopian experiments of the era. Ripley had been a colleague and admirer of Ralph Waldo Emerson, and a persuasive advocate of the "new views" in theology that were characterized as Transcendentalism. Ripley had resigned the pastorate of his Purchase Street Church in that year, explaining his departure in terms that illuminate the entire Transcendentalist movement. "There is a class of persons who desire a reform in the prevailing philosophy of the day," he wrote. "These are called Transcendentalists, because they believe in an order of truths which transcends the sphere of the external sense. Their leading idea is the supremacy of mind over matter. Hence they maintain that the truth of religion does not depend on tradition, nor historical facts, but has an unerring witness in the soul." Ripley went on to connect his belief in a transcendent order of truth to the necessity of social and political reform. "The purpose of Christianity, as I firmly believe, is to redeem society as well as the individual from all sin" (Miller, pp. 255, 256).

Ripley enacted this belief in establishing the community at Brook Farm, intending to demonstrate on a small scale his hope for a reformed society. Elizabeth Palmer Peabody described the purpose of the experiment in an 1844 issue of the *Dial:*

> In order to live a religious and moral life worthy of the name, they feel it is necessary to come out in some degree from the world, and to form themselves into a community of property, so far as to exclude competition and the ordinary rules of trade;—while they reserve sufficient private property, or the means of obtaining it, for all purposes of independence, and isolation at will. They have bought a farm, in order to make agriculture the basis of their life, it being the most direct and simple in relation to nature. (Miller, *The Transcendentalists,* p. 466)

Brook Farm underwent a significant intellectual reorientation when the commune officially embraced the doctrines of Charles Fourier and undertook to become a Fourierist phalanx, a step that signified a deeper commitment to socialist experimentation and a more radical dissent to conventional society. Though Brook Farm had a certain success, providing an atmosphere of friendly cooperation, shared ideals, and aesthetic endeavor, it disbanded in 1847, largely because of the financial devastation caused when their nearly completed central building was destroyed by fire in 1846. Brook Farm is in part remembered, however, through a novel by one of its more disgruntled and skeptical members, Nathaniel Hawthorne. *The Blithedale Romance* (1852) is based on his own experience as an early member of Brook Farm, and it paints a rather dark picture of the motives and accomplishments of the utopian reformers of the period. Brook Farm remains one of the most interesting socialist experiments in nineteenth-century America, however, recalling a time in which the assumptions of the industrial and market economy of the United States was under serious critique.

Farm, including the novelist Nathaniel Hawthorne, who, though far from a Transcendentalist in his philosophy, saw Brook Farm as a possible way to allow him to balance physical labor with his desire to write fiction. The experiment failed for Hawthorne, and he later criticized it in his novel *The Blithedale Romance* (1852). Even though Brook Farm was disbanded in 1847, it achieved some success as an experiment in communal living. Ripley had founded the commune on broadly socialist, or "associationist" principles, but after its establishment led the commune into a more explicit avowal of Fourierist socialism, a theory of social organization based on the writings of the French utopian Charles Fourier. Interpreted and expounded by his American disciple Albert Brisbane, Fourier's work had great impact in America in the 1840s and 1850s. His criticism of family life with its inflexible roles and rules appealed to many nineteenth-century reformers, and his vision of a social organization in which each person worked cooperatively according to his or her inclinations and desires seemed to bridge the theoretical gap between individual freedom and collective unity that troubled many utopian and dissenting political thinkers. Eventually a number of communes or "phalanxes" were founded in America with some allegiance to his principles, and Fourier's name became attached to a general critique of the nature of middle-class life as it had developed in the early industrial period.

Bronson Alcott and the British reform theorist Charles Lane launched Fruitlands, a different utopian experiment, in 1844, a short-lived disaster for Alcott and his family. Fruitlands was smaller and much less well organized than Brook Farm, and it seemed to embody Alcott's lilies-of-the-field faith that good intentions and noble hopes would produce successful results. In some conflict about aims and procedures, Alcott and Lane were forced to recognize that their experiment could not succeed under the existing conditions, and Fruitlands was disbanded after only seven months. Alcott, a controversial teacher who had earlier been forced to close his Temple School as his enrollment dwindled, had placed much hope in Fruitlands; its collapse was a crushing blow to his dream of establishing a fulfilling alternative to conventional life. Both Fruitlands and Brook Farm were efforts to reconcile the Transcendentalists' religious aspirations with the state of modern society, and were undertaken with the belief that a new social organization could help individuals to develop and express their innate spiritual potential. They were attempts to enact Emerson's encouragement to see the world as open to transformation.

THE LEGACY OF TRANSCENDENTALISM

Transcendentalism left an important but complex legacy for American culture, one which historians and literary critics continue to analyze. In particular, Emerson's political legacy has been controversial because his advocacy of individualism can be given both a progressive and conservative interpretation. Some historians find that his advocacy of self-reliance ultimately lends support to the entrepreneurial individualism and mistrust of collective action that have been damaging aspects of America's competitive economy and consumption-driven value system. Others find him a fountainhead of American progressive thinking, seeing his emphasis on individual conscience as a necessary condition of effective political dissent and a guard against the uncritical acceptance of political and cultural authority. Important to this view of Emerson's progressive political legacy are his antislavery addresses and his later role as an ethical philosopher in conflict with the materialism and superficiality of American culture.

Though Emerson has been subject to criticism by philosophers for his lack of systematic method and an optimistic naïveté, his philosophical link to the pragmatist school of psychologist-philosophers William James and John Dewey, his influence on the German philosopher Friedrich Nietzsche, and his contributions to ethics and democratic theory have been persuasively brought forward in the 1980s and 1990s. His influence on American literature, especially American poetry, has been universally recognized, and he has been seen as an enabling voice and example for a diverse array of later poets, including Walt Whitman, Emily Dickinson, Robert Frost, Wallace Stevens, A. R. Ammons, and Gary Snyder.

Thoreau shares Emerson's divided political legacy as an advocate of individualism, but his "Resistance to Civil Government," with its account of his act of nonviolent civil disobedience, has had a powerful appeal to twentieth-century readers and to progressive political leaders such as Mahatma Gandhi and Martin Luther King Jr. Moreover, Thoreau has come to be seen as a founder of the American environmental movement, an early ecologist whose poetic appreciation of nature and engagement in empirical field research have contributed significantly to a modern ecological worldview. Thoreau exemplified a value system that replaced purely

The Fruitlands Farmhouse at the Fruitlands Museum, Harvard, Massachusetts. "They look well in July. We shall see them in December," wrote Emerson after visiting the utopian community in 1843. The group had disbanded by the end of January 1844. © LEE SNIDER/CORBIS

human material interests with a larger concern for the health of the entire planet and its various ecosystems.

Thoreau's influence as a founding voice in environmentalism is paralleled by the increasing recognition of Margaret Fuller's role as a crucial early theorist of feminism whose legacy was obscured by the attempts of her friends and family to smooth over and conventionalize her radicalism after her tragic early death. Fuller is coming to be seen not only as an important early feminist, but also as a central figure in the development of the Transcen-

dentalist movement, who was less Emerson's student than his friend and sometime critic. Her later journalistic work in New York, in which she became more outspoken as a social critic, and her support of and involvement in the Italian Revolution are also increasingly regarded as essential clues to her character as well as indications of the political dimension of Transcendentalism. Indeed, it seems as if readers in the late twentieth century often looked to the Transcendentalists as a reflection of their own cultural aspirations, making the "new views" of the 1830s once again new.

See also **Pastoralism and the Rural Ideal; New England** *(volume 2);* **Individualism and the Self** *(volume 3); and other articles in this section.*

BIBLIOGRAPHY

An excellent bibliographical guide on Transcendentalism, covering primary sources, manuscript material, biography, and criticism through 1981, is *The Transcendentalists: A Review of Research and Criticism,* edited by Joel Myerson (New York, 1984). Later developments in scholarly editions and criticism can be followed in the chapter "Emerson, Thoreau, Fuller, and Transcendentalism" in the annual volume *American Literary Scholarship* (Durham, N.C.).

Ralph Waldo Emerson

Authoritative modern editions of Emerson's work include:

Emerson, Ralph Waldo. *Collected Works.* Edited by Alfred R. Ferguson et al. 5 vols. to date. Cambridge, Mass., 1971–.

——. *Complete Sermons.* Edited by Albert J. von Frank et al. 4 vols. Columbia, Mo., 1989–1992.

——. *Early Lectures.* Edited by Robert E. Spiller, Stephen E. Whicher, and Wallace E. Williams. 3 vols. Cambridge, Mass., 1959–1972.

——. *Emerson's Antislavery Writings.* Edited by Len Gougeon and Joel Myerson. New Haven, Conn., 1995.

——. *Journals and Miscellaneous Notebooks.* Edited by William H. Gilman et al. 16 vols. Cambridge, Mass., 1960–1982.

——. *Selected Letters.* Edited by Joel Myerson. New York, 1997.

For works not yet included in the ongoing *Collected Works* edition, consult Ralph Waldo Emerson, *The Complete Works of Ralph Waldo Emerson* (Centenary Edition), edited by Edward Waldo Emerson, 12 vols. (Boston, 1903–1904).

The ongoing Princeton University Press edition of *The Writings of Henry D. Thoreau,* 12 volumes to date (1971–) includes both Thoreau's published works and his important multivolume *Journal.* Also included in this edition are *Walden,* edited by J. Lyndon Shanley (1971) and *Reform Papers,* edited by Wendell Glick (1973).

The Works of Transcendentalists

Important editions of the works of other Transcendentalists include:

Channing, William Ellery. *William Ellery Channing: Selected Writings.* Edited by David Robinson. Mahwah, N.J., 1985.

Fuller, Margaret. *The Letters of Margaret Fuller.* Edited by Robert Hudspeth. 6 vols. Ithaca, N.Y., 1983–1994.

——. *"These Sad but Glorious Days": Dispatches from Europe, 1846–1850.* Edited by Larry J. Reynolds and Susan Belasco Smith. New Haven, Conn., 1991.

——. *Woman in the Nineteenth Century.* Edited by Larry J. Reynolds. New York, 1997.

Very, Jones. *Jones Very: The Complete Poems.* Edited by Helen R. Deese. Athens, Ga., 1993.

The Transcendentalist Movement

One of the most important resources for the study of the Transcendentalist movement is Perry Miller's anthology and historical interpretation, *The Transcendentalists: An Anthology* (Cambridge, Mass., 1950). For an excellent brief history of the movement, see Barbara L. Packer, "The Transcendentalists" in *The Cambridge History of American Literature,* vol. 2, edited by Sacvan Bercovitch (New York, 1995).

An important pair of reference tools are the *Biographical Dictionary of Transcendentalism* and the *Encyclopedia of Transcendentalism,* edited by Wesley T. Mott (Westport, Conn., 1996).

The religious backgrounds to the movement are discussed by Conrad Wright in *The Beginnings of Unitarianism in America* (Boston, 1955) and in Daniel

Walker Howe, *The Unitarian Conscience: Harvard Moral Philosophy, 1805–1861* (Middletown, Conn., 1988).

F. O. Matthiessen, *American Renaissance: Art and Expression in the Age of Emerson and Whitman* (New York, 1941) contains widely respected chapters on Emerson and Thoreau.

For the definitive history of the *Dial*, with a valuable collection of biographies of its contributors, see Joel Myerson, *The New England Transcendentalists and the* Dial: *A History of the Magazine and Its Contributors* (Rutherford, N.J., 1980).

For a discussion of the connections between the Transcendentalists' religious vision and their literary work, see Lawrence Buell, *Literary Transcendentalism: Style and Vision in the American Renaissance* (Ithaca, N.Y., 1973). Buell's *New England Literary Culture* (New York, 1986) is a comprehensive study of the literary history of the region, including the work of the Transcendentalists. Daniel Walker Howe, *Making the American Self: Jonathan Edwards to Abraham Lincoln* (Cambridge, Mass., 1997) offers important discussions of Channing, Fuller, and Thoreau in the context of the American discourse on self-culture.

Political and Social Aspects of Transcendentalism

For perspectives on the political and social aspects of the movement, especially their utopian experiments, see Taylor Stoehr, *Nay-Saying in Concord* (Hamden, Conn., 1979); Richard Francis, *Transcendental Utopias: Individual and Community at Brook Farm, Fruitlands, and Walden* (Ithaca, N.Y., 1997); and Carl J. Guarneri, "Brook Farm and the Fourierist Phalanxes: Immediatism, Gradualism, and American Utopian Socialism," in *America's Communal Utopias,* edited by Donald E. Pitzer (Chapel Hill, N.C., 1997).

Biographies

There are a number of excellent biographies of various members of the Transcendentalist movement. Among the most significant on Emerson are Ralph L. Rusk, *The Life of Ralph Waldo Emerson* (New York, 1949) and Robert D. Richardson Jr., *Emerson: The Mind on Fire* (Berkeley, Calif., 1995). For important biographical work on Thoreau, see Walter Harding, *The Days of Henry Thoreau* (Princeton, N.J., 1992) and Robert D. Richardson Jr., *Henry David Thoreau: A Life of the Mind* (Berkeley, Calif., 1987).

Other important biographies of Transcendentalists include:

Belbanco, Andrew. *William Ellery Channing: An Essay on the Liberal Spirit in America.* Cambridge, Mass., 1981.

Capper, Charles. *Margaret Fuller: An American Romantic Life, The Private Years.* New York, 1992. The book is the first of a projected two volumes.

Cole, Phyllis. *Mary Moody Emerson and the Origins of Transcendentalism: A Family History.* New York, 1998.

Crowe, Charles. *George Ripley: Transcendentalist and Utopian Socialist.* Athens, Ga., 1967.

Gittleman, Edwin. *Jones Very: The Effective Years, 1833–1840.* New York, 1967.

Von Mehren, Joan. *Minerva and the Muse: A Life of Margaret Fuller.* Amherst, Mass., 1994.

Critical Literature

There is a voluminous critical literature on Transcendentalism; the following volumes offer an initial guide to various aspects of the movement and its key figures:

RALPH WALDO EMERSON

Barish, Evelyn. *Emerson: The Roots of Prophecy*. Princeton, N.J., 1989.

Cavell, Stanley. *Conditions Handsome and Unhandsome: The Constitution of Emersonian Perfectionism*. Chicago, 1990.

Cayton, Mary Kupiec. *Emerson's Emergence: Self and Society in the Transformation of New England, 1800–1845*. Chapel Hill, N.C., 1989.

Gougeon, Len. *Virtue's Hero: Emerson, Antislavery and Reform*. Athens, Ga., 1990.

Lopez, Michael. *Emerson and Power: Creative Antagonism in the Nineteenth Century*. DeKalb, Ill., 1996.

Mott, Wesley T. *"The Strains of Eloquence": Emerson and His Sermons*. University Park, Pa., 1989.

Packer, Barbara. *Emerson's Fall: A New Interpretation of the Major Essays*. New York, 1982.

Poirier, Richard. *The Renewal of Literature: Emersonian Reflections*. New York, 1987.

Robinson, David M. *Apostle of Culture: Emerson as Preacher and Lecturer*. Philadelphia, 1982.

——. *Emerson and the Conduct of Life*. Cambridge, Mass., 1993.

Sealts, Merton M., Jr., *Emerson on the Scholar*. Columbia, Mo., 1992.

Whicher, Stephen E. *Freedom and Fate: An Inner Life of Ralph Waldo Emerson*. Philadelphia, 1953.

HENRY DAVID THOREAU

Buell, Lawrence. *The Environmental Imagination: Thoreau, Nature Writing, and the Formation of American Culture*. Cambridge, Mass., 1995.

Cavell, Stanley. *The Senses of* Walden: *An Expanded Edition*. San Francisco, 1981.

Milder, Robert. *Reimagining Thoreau*. Cambridge, Mass., 1995.

Paul, Sherman. *The Shores of America: Thoreau's Inward Explorations*. Urbana, Ill., 1958.

Peck, H. Daniel. *Thoreau's Morning Work: Memory and Perception in* A Week on the Concord and Merrimack Rivers, *the Journal, and* Walden. New Haven, Conn., 1990.

Sattelmeyer, Robert. *Thoreau's Reading: A Study in Intellectual History with Bibliographical Catalogue*. Princeton, N.J., 1988.

Shanley, J. Lyndon. *The Making of Walden*. Chicago, 1957.

Walls, Laura Dassow. *Seeing New Worlds: Henry David Thoreau and Nineteenth-Century Natural Science*. Madison, Wisc., 1995.

MARGARET FULLER

Chevigny, Bell Gale. *The Woman and the Myth: Margaret Fuller's Life and Writings*. Boston, 1994.

Ellison, Julie. *Delicate Subjects: Romanticism, Gender, and the Ethics of Understanding*. Ithaca, N.Y., 1990.

Zwarg, Christina. *Feminist Conversations: Fuller, Emerson, and the Play of Reading*. Ithaca, N.Y., 1995.

COMMUNITARIANISM

Carl J. Guarneri

EUROPEAN AND AMERICAN ORIGINS

The communitarian worldview encompasses two beliefs: first, that models of a rational or godly social order can be constructed in small settlements; and, second, that society as a whole can be perfected through their example. This worldview has its origins in premodern European sources such as Greek theories of ideal republics, sectarian Christian visions of the Second Coming of Jesus Christ, and utopian fantasies of faraway perfect worlds. Yet communitarianism crystallized into a coherent program only in the nineteenth century, when hopes for a millennial kingdom on earth became commonplace in the Anglo-American world and when popular reform movements provided a viable alternative to piecemeal political change on the one hand, or violent revolution on the other.

Although many Protestant millennial sects originated in Europe, and theories of utopian socialism came from Great Britain and France, it was in the United States that communitarianism became a prominent branch of reform and the largest number of communal experiments were attempted. The young American nation's open doors beckoned to political exiles, and its freedom attracted religious dissenters. Especially in newly settled regions, cheap land was available for immigrant colonies and sectarian communal settlements. From colonial times, America had been promoted as paradise on earth, a land of economic opportunity, or a "virgin land" on which the social compact could begin anew. This mythology, encoded on the national seal which proclaimed "A New Order of the Ages," inspired immigrant and native-born groups who hoped to turn their utopian theories or dreams into reality.

The communitarian program of social reform through model experiments accorded with early-nineteenth-century Americans' sense that their society was young, pliant, and perfectible. Like other popular crusades such as home missions, antislavery, and land reform, the communitarian move-ment was premised upon the assumption that the newly settled townships of the West would decisively shape the American future. Utopian socialists argued that society in the United States had to take advantage of its youth to plant a way of life that would prove impervious to the ills of urban industrialism, problems that were already apparent on the European horizon and were threatening to cross the Atlantic. Thus communitarians voiced a revisionist version of American "exceptionalism," the popular notion that the New World was exempt from the conflicts and ills of the old one. They promised to extend America's distinctive difference into the modern age and in the process to realize a communal rather than individualistic version of the American dream.

During the antebellum period, communitarian groups emerged from more specific social and cultural forces as well. The evangelical Second Great Awakening, which swept through inland towns in the 1820s and 1830s, produced converts anxious to practice Christianity in their daily lives. A severe economic depression in the half decade after 1837 left bankrupted farmers and unemployed craftsmen available for cooperative enterprises. The same wave of reform enthusiasm that created the temperance and abolitionist movements predisposed middle-class northerners to new ideas about improving society. Radical abolitionists, peace advocates, feminists, and health reformers were drawn to community experiments at the same time that communal dwellers became vegetarians or attended antislavery and woman's rights meetings. Communitarian experiments culminated the quest to perfect society by promising a total transformation of lifestyles. No wonder the Transcendentalist philosopher Ralph Waldo Emerson, characterizing his times as an age of reform, reported to the essayist-historian Thomas Carlyle in 1840, "We are all a little wild here with numberless projects of social reform. Not a reading man but has a draft of a new community in his waistcoat pocket" (Guarneri, *The Utopian Alternative*, p. 13).

Between 1825 and the Civil War at least a hundred such utopian communities were established. Compared to abolitionist or temperance societies, their membership was small. The population of the Shaker communities peaked at about six thousand in 1840, while the Fourierist phalanxes of the following decade enrolled perhaps seven thousand members. Some communities were as small as a dozen true believers and most lasted no more than a few years. Yet the influence of these groups spread far beyond their numbers. They attracted thousands of sympathetic visitors and their arrangements were analyzed in the reform press. Their repudiation of individualism struck a responsive chord among social critics and their projects created a communitarian tradition that endured into the twentieth century.

COMMUNAL SECTS

Among the largest and most durable utopian societies in antebellum America were German-speaking sects that traced their origins to various Anabaptist offshoots of the Protestant Reformation. George Rapp, a German farmer and lay preacher who quarreled with the Lutheran Church, left for America in 1803. Two years later he and 750 followers incorporated as the Harmony Society and settled in western Pennsylvania.

Quiet and industrious, the Harmonists (also known as Rappites) built prosperous agricultural settlements at three successive sites: Harmony, Pennsylvania (from 1805 to 1814), a second village with the same name in Indiana (from 1815 to 1824), and their final community called Economy (1825), located north of Pittsburgh. Until he died in 1847, Rapp ruled the group as a genial autocrat. Members signed over all their property to the community; they pledged to live in celibacy; and they prayed for the Second Coming as depicted in Father Rapp's weekly sermons. Eventually, celibacy and the unwillingness to proselytize non-Germans took their toll: by 1900 only a handful of elderly Harmonists were left, and the Economy community died with them.

Besides Harmony, several other pietistic communities flourished in the antebellum period, including German groups at Zoar, Ohio (from 1817 to 1898), and Amana, Iowa (from 1843 to 1932), as well as the Swedish settlement of Bishop Hill, Illinois (from 1846 to 1862). None of these, however, were as large or successful as the most influential communal sect of the era, the Shakers.

Officially named the United Society of Believers in Christ's Second Appearing, the Shakers earned their nickname by the convulsions and dances that accompanied their early rituals. Ann Lee (Mother Ann), an unschooled blacksmith's daughter from Manchester, England, joined the small sect and took several followers to America after a series of visions in which she was told that sexual intercourse was the original sin and that the millennial church would take root in the New World. Her followers settled in the Albany, New York, area, but not until 1787, three years after her death, did the group form its first true communal settlement.

Mother Ann's successors, male and female Shakers who were skillful organizers, codified her theology and set down the rules that governed their religious rituals and communal routines. The Shakers' religious views were distinctive and led to an austere but compelling way of life. They believed that God was both male and female in nature; Jesus represented the masculine "Christ spirit," and Mother Ann the feminine. Since her birth signaled the Second Coming, true believers now lived in the millennial kingdom and had to follow its laws. "The Resurrection Order" required communal sharing of goods and strict celibacy; it also mandated the spiritual equality of men and women. Shaker settlements were organized with a careful gender parallelism; there were separate quarters for the sexes, and eldresses as well as elders governed "families" of about sixty members. Since women assumed influential roles it was no surprise that they often formed a majority in Shaker communities.

The hard work, isolation, and self-denial of Shaker life was balanced by emotional release through the ritual dances that were part of Shaker services. There were also periodic spirit visitations that resembled the religious revivals of the world outside. Taught that work was akin to prayer, Shaker artisans created simple and sturdy furniture that found a ready national market, and they perfected a host of labor-saving inventions.

Since the Shakers spoke English they could recruit American-born members more easily than the German sects, and the group's celibacy made it necessary for survival. Their preachers converted many men and women who were touched by local evangelical revivals and were ready to bridge moments of spiritual ecstasy with weeks of practical Christian living. Shaker communities also took in orphans and children left by widowers, giving them the choice at age eighteen whether to stay. Their way of life proved so attractive that by the 1830s there were twenty-three Shaker villages from Maine to Kentucky and the sect enjoyed an economic prosperity that spurred the curiosity of European visitors as well as American reformers. These proved to be the Shakers' peak years; beginning in the 1850s the United Society entered a long, slow demographic decline that was nearly complete by the late twentieth century.

Strictly speaking, religious communalists like the Rappites and Shakers were only halfway communitarians; they believed in godly communities but they were convinced that human redemption would come through spiritual renewal rather than social engineering. They focused on preparing for the afterlife rather than the here and now. The longer they lasted, however, the more they adopted the language of social reform instead of theology to describe their way of life. And the religious sects' example of successful communal living became the ballast that steadied other communitarians' hopes even as many secular experiments capsized around them.

UTOPIAN SOCIALISTS

Pietistic communities like the Rappites and Shakers tended to last much longer than the secular utopian socialist groups. Their members were held together by religious ideals, isolated themselves from the rest of society, and were willing to defer to charismatic leaders or other authority figures. By contrast, utopian-socialist movements were joined by contentious, independent-minded local artisans and entrepreneurs. In the few cases these communities managed to persist, such as the French Icarians, it was due more to their shared foreign language and ethnicity than to their social doctrines. Most utopian-socialist experiments were torn by doctrinal disputes and struggled to find a secular faith that could be as compelling as religious bonding.

A case in point was the Owenites, who began communal life with great fanfare and a ready-made settlement but squandered their assets in just a few years. Robert Owen was a successful industrialist who managed the vast cotton mills at New Lanark, Scotland. From innovations in working and educational arrangements he introduced there, Owen deduced his theory that "the character of man is . . . always formed for him" by his surroundings. This was a first step to full-fledged communitarianism. Soon Owen was advocating the establishment of model agricultural and manufacturing villages as prototypes of a rational and just society. Owen rejected the Bible and formal religion in favor of "reason"; he criticized private property and endorsed divorce and birth control. Thus Owenism was among the first secular and professedly scientific critiques of capitalist individualism, but it allowed utopian socialism to be tainted from the outset with allegations of promoting "communism" (the abolition of private property) and "free love."

Toward the end of 1824 Owen sailed for the United States, where he charmed literary and business elites and even addressed Congress twice. Spending more than half of his fortune, he purchased the tidy village that the Rappites had constructed in Indiana and rechristened it New Harmony. Despite Owen's prestige and the community's fine property, New Harmony proved to be an organizational fiasco. The buildings became overcrowded after Owen issued a blanket invitation to all comers; Owen's frequent absences and changes of mind created a leadership vacuum; and ideological factions developed that subsequently split the community into three separate settlements. After several reorganizations failed to create unity, New Harmony dissolved in 1827 when its debts became due. Owen's ideas were still powerful enough to inspire almost a dozen other short-lived ventures, including the reformer Frances "Fanny" Wright's Nashoba community in Tennessee, an unusual interracial experiment that proposed to educate and emancipate African Americans.

By the 1840s Owenism was eclipsed by a second outburst of utopian socialist organizing based on the theories of Charles Fourier. An obscure and eccentric French bachelor, Fourier, like Owen, decided that the ills of competitive society could be cured by small cooperative communities organized under the principles of "social science." In Fourier's case, however, communal circumstances would be arranged to fit human nature rather than vice versa. By intricately analyzing the "passions" of the human personality, Fourier deduced that each model settlement, or "phalanx," should house 1,620 persons and provide enough gardens, workshops, and cultural amenities to assure a fulfilling existence as members rotated among them. Fourier believed that labor should be pleasurable and human relations governed by unfettered "attraction," and his writings obsessively spelled out the elaborate work groups and multiform sexual arrangements that the "Harmonic" society of the future would create.

Fourier died in 1837 without setting foot in the New World, but his doctrines were brought to America by an idealistic and wealthy young convert from western New York, Albert Brisbane. Brisbane shrewdly extracted Fourier's practical communal plans from his more controversial theories so that the phalanx was made to fit the perfectionist aims and moral rhetoric of antebellum reform. His persistent propaganda, boosted by a daily column in the popular *New York Tribune,* created a burst of Fourierist organizing in the northern states almost overnight. In the decade after 1842 nearly thirty miniature American phalanxes were established from Massachusetts to Iowa, and in 1853 Brisbane convinced Fourier's most important French disciple, Victor Considerant, to plant a colony of Fourierist exiles in Texas.

Life at the more successful Fourierist communities, such as the Wisconsin and North American Phalanxes, was quite pleasant and far more attuned to middle-class tastes than Shaker villages. But many of the phalanxes struggled with unproductive farms, heavy mortgages, and internal disputes over religion and living arrangements. Most disbanded after a few years. The North American Phalanx succumbed to a fire in 1856 and Wisconsin Phalanx members sold their farm for a profit in order to establish family farms nearby.

Fourier's "social science" decreed that coopera-

tive mechanisms would abolish greed and religious disputes, but Fourierist communities, like Owen's New Harmony, did not demand the discipline and self-sacrifice that could achieve group harmony. By changing converts' hearts and prescribing their behavior, the religious sects were more realistic than utopian socialists about how to achieve communal success with human materials. Then, too, despite their founders' radical theories, the actual Owenite and Fourierist communities did not depart far enough from conventional social practices to compel members' allegiances when outside pressures were felt. When comparing them with the pietistic societies, it becomes clear that the more a community deviated from American norms, the better its chance of survival, albeit as a small sect rather than a plausible model for society as a whole.

AMERICAN ORIGINALS

Somewhere between the two types of communitarianism originating in Europe, the Rappite-Shaker brand of religious pietism and the Owenite-Fourierist secular utopian socialism, stood native-born communities that blended features of both. These in-

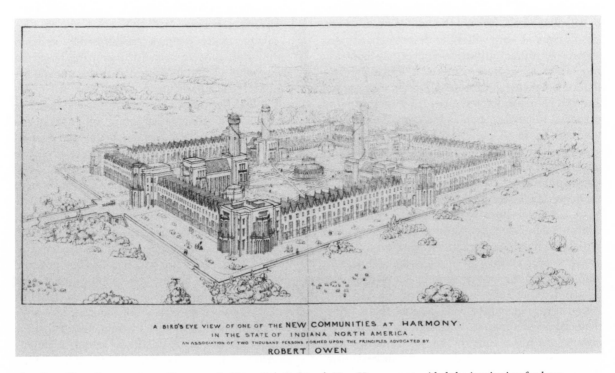

A BIRD'S EYE VIEW OF ONE OF THE NEW COMMUNITIES AT HARMONY. IN THE STATE OF INDIANA NORTH AMERICA. AN ASSOCIATION OF TWO THOUSAND PERSONS FORMED UPON THE PRINCIPLES ADVOCATED BY ROBERT OWEN

Plan for a New Community at Harmony, Indiana. Robert Owen's New Harmony provided the inspiration for later experimental communities. © CORBIS

***Brook Farm* (1844) by Josiah Wolcott.** The scene shows the entrance to the community and several buildings, including the Hive, Shop, Eyrie, Cottage, and Pilgrim House. It also shows the foundations for the new Phalanstery, which burned to the ground in March 1846, prior to its completion. COURTESY OF THE MASSACHUSETTS HISTORICAL SOCIETY

cluded experiments at Hopedale (from 1842 to 1856), Fruitlands (1843), and Northampton (from 1842 to 1846) in Massachusetts as well as the anarchist commune at Modern Times (from 1851 to 1864) on New York's Long Island. The most famous were those at Brook Farm and Oneida.

Brook Farm, founded in West Roxbury, Massachusetts, in 1841 by the Unitarian minister George Ripley, originated in discussions of the Boston-area Transcendental Club. Transcendentalism was an idealistic sensibility and a set of attitudes about humanity and nature rather than a coherent doctrine. Yet its influence was obvious in the plan Ripley announced to Ralph Waldo Emerson to "insure a more natural union between intellectual and manual labor," to spread educational and material benefits to all, and "to prepare a society of liberal, intelligent, and cultivated persons, whose relations with each other would permit a more simple and wholesome life, than can be led amidst the pressure of our competitive institutions" (Swift, *Brook Farm,* pp. 15–16). Emerson and the Transcendentalist author Margaret Fuller were too resolutely individu-

alistic to join Brook Farm, but the novelist Nathaniel Hawthorne lived at the community for several months in 1841 before deciding that farmwork did not improve his writing.

Brook Farm was in fact a serious experiment in social reform. The community ran a successful school with a liberal arts curriculum that combined learning with doing. After the community converted to the Fourierist plan in 1844, it published an influential weekly journal that spread communitarian ideas and it broadened its membership to include more artisans than ministers and teachers. Still, the greater structure of Fourierism did not rescue Brook Farm's struggling farm and craft industries, and the community was forced to sell its property after a fire destroyed its new communal dwelling in 1846.

Despite its brief life, Brook Farm became more celebrated than other antebellum communities, partly because of the famous writers associated with it but also due to its infusion of communal living with culture and charm. Brook Farm offered its unmarried majority the harmless flirting and intellectual stimulation of a coeducational campus years before that experience was available in the outside world.

Oneida went much further than Brook Farm in its mingling of the sexes, and as a consequence attracted more notoriety than praise. Like Brook Farm, it sprang from New England theology, but it was the product of evangelical Protestantism rather than Transcendentalism. Its founder, John Humphrey Noyes, was a restless lawyer and clergyman who endorsed perfectionism, one of the most extreme evangelical doctrines. Noyes decided that once a person was saved he or she became perfect—incapable of sinning. Applied to groups, Noyes's perfectionism asserted that duplicating the kingdom of heaven on earth entailed sharing goods and "spiritual wives" communally. In the 1830s Noyes gathered a handful of disciples near his family homestead in Putney, Vermont. By 1846 they had organized communally and enraged townspeople so thoroughly that Noyes had to flee to avoid charges of adultery. In 1848 the Putney group joined other Perfectionists at Oneida in upstate New York.

"Bible communism" as practiced at Oneida involved "complex marriage," a system of carefully controlled free love which assured that community members would practice sexual intercourse as "a joyful act of fellowship" with many partners and without forming monogamous relationships. To avoid unwanted pregnancies and to free Oneida's women for other tasks, Noyes promoted a form of birth control called "male continence," or intercourse without ejaculation. In 1869 Noyes also began experimenting with planned reproduction, or "stirpiculture," as he called it. The most spiritually advanced community members were chosen by committee and "scientifically combined" to produce even more perfect young communitarians. The rules and regulations governing sexuality at Oneida thus demanded self-control and obedience to hierarchy as much as sensuality. These and other community norms were enforced by sessions of "mutual criticism" where members were reproved publicly by the group. Complex marriage worked so efficiently that remarkably few children were conceived accidentally at Oneida. But Noyes's insistence upon acting as "first husband" to virgin females in the community led to dissension and his prohibition of conventional marriage forced some Oneida couples to elope.

In spite of sexual tensions among its members and opposition from the outside world, Oneida flourished, thanks to its production of handicrafts and especially its manufacturing of animal traps.

Over a period of three decades Oneida's comfortable Mansion House was expanded to include wings and finally became a fully enclosed quadrangle. The community grew less isolated as younger members were educated in outside colleges and Noyes himself developed interests in social science and secular socialism. This decline in religious fervor fed dissent over Noyes's rule and merged with confusion over who would become the aging leader's successor. Conflict grew so heated that Noyes escaped into Canadian exile in 1879 and the community voted to turn itself into a joint-stock company two years later. The fact that several Oneidans quickly paired off and exchanged vows suggests that complex marriage had not completely replaced Victorian norms among the Perfectionists.

Noyes's Oneida was among the most original American communal experiments. It blended the Protestant theology and strict discipline of the pietistic communities with the utopian socialists' interest in science and social reform. This combination helped Oneida to survive into a more secular age; it also made the community reflect the entire spectrum of antebellum communitarianism.

THE ANTEBELLUM MOVEMENT

Communities set up by the Shakers, Owenites, Fourierists, and Oneidans spanned a spectrum from "free love" to celibacy in their sexual practices and from communal property to relative individualism in their economic arrangements. Yet virtually all groups expressed a deep yearning to evolve a more equitable and communal society around them; in Noyes's words, to realize "the enlargement of home—the extension of family union beyond the little man-and-wife circle to large corporations" (*History of American Socialisms*, p. 23). Celibacy and free love shared the notion that private and exclusive intimate relationships diverted loyalties from the common good. Even communitarians who allowed conventional marriage, such as the Amana Inspirationists and the Fourierists, socialized domestic work and educated children communally. In an age of "separate spheres" for men and women, communitarians practiced a limited feminism. They did not reject conventional sex roles so much as blur the distinction between public and private lives and attempt to infuse daily life with "masculine" and "feminine" traits in perfect harmony with each other. Women voted and they took leadership positions more often than in conventional society, but they often found plenty of discrimination to protest. Especially in struggling settlements, communitarian women were so overburdened with child-rearing and domestic work that the New Moral World offered nothing better than the old immoral one.

It is convenient to divide communitarian experiments into religious and secular groups, but this distinction can be misleading. Most communal groups relied upon a revival-like conversion experience, voiced millennial hopes, and asserted the harmony of science and revelation. Whether at Shaker villages, New Harmony, Modern Times, or the North American Phalanx, antebellum communitarians located near one another, shared common doctrinal origins, saw members migrate between settlements interchangeably, borrowed communal techniques, and traded goods. Their goal of restructuring American society into a just and godly commonwealth made them allies in a loosely structured communitarian movement. Noyes recognized the connectedness of what he called the "great American socialistic revival" of the antebellum years when he heard "echoes" of Shakerism in the Owenite communities and called his own Oneida the reincarnation of Brook Farm (p. 24).

By the Civil War most communities founded during the great wave of experimentation in the 1830s and 1840s had failed. Events in the outside world, such as the booming prosperity of the gold rush and the growing dominance of the antislavery struggle, combined with internal disputes and inefficiencies to doom them. Yet the communitarian movement's influence was felt in other ways. The Owenites and Fourierists helped to place trade unions, free public schools, and worker cooperatives on the labor movement's agenda. New Harmony's educational system included the first American kindergarten and became a model for the nation. Fourierist arguments found their way into the sectional debate between the South's chattel slavery and the "wage slavery" of the modernizing North. Brook Farm inspired Hawthorne's novel *The Blithedale Romance* (1852), prompted Emerson's landmark essay "Self-Reliance" as a riposte, and jump-started several important journalistic careers. Nearly all communal experiments served as educational environments whose "alumni" actuated the group's ideals in such arenas as politics, education, the professions, and reform.

THE COMMUNITARIAN LEGACY

Communitarianism did not simply end after the Civil War. Dozens of small colonies continued to sprout between 1870 and the First World War, especially in California and the West. Gradually, however, the communitarian idea lost its larger frame of reference as the institutions of individualism became too entrenched to supplant and the scale of urban settlements grew too large to make communes a viable alternative. Late-nineteenth-century colonies were refuges of true believers or demonstrations of particular principles to be introduced into the larger society; they were rarely seen as the actual germs of a full-scale, renovated social pattern.

Still, echoes of communitarian ideals could be heard in other calls for social reform: feminist plans for cooperative households, the labor movement's push for cooperative workshops, designs for urban parks, various back-to-the-land movements, and futuristic visions such as Edward Bellamy's enormously popular utopian novel, *Looking Backward, 2000–1887* (1888). In the 1960s the communitarian tradition was revived as one wing of a young people's countercultural offensive against conventional society. Members of more than three thousand short-lived rural communes, for the most part unaware of their nineteenth-century predecessors, experimented with alternative lifestyles before breaking off to rejoin the American mainstream. Although the full-fledged communitarian program has been rendered obsolete, as long as America's dominant individualistic culture fails to satisfy the urge for beloved community, enclaves of religious and secular dissenters will coalesce in response.

See also **Moral Philosophy; Transcendentalism; Popular Intellectual Movements: 1833–1877** *(in this volume);* **Utah and Mormonism; Anti-Statism** *(volume 2);* **Technological Enclaves** *(volume 3); and other articles in this section.*

BIBLIOGRAPHY

Bestor, Arthur. *Backwoods Utopias: The Sectarian Origins and the Owenite Phase of Communitarian Socialism in America, 1663–1829.* Philadelphia, 1970. Includes a "checklist of communitarian experiments" to 1860.

Chmielewski, Wendy, Louis J. Kern, and Marlyn Klee-Hartzell, eds. *Women in Spiritual and Communitarian Societies in the United States.* Syracuse, N.Y., 1993.

Clark, Christopher. *The Communitarian Moment: The Radical Challenge of the Northampton Association.* Ithaca, N.Y., 1995.

Foster, Lawrence. *Religion and Sexuality: The Shakers, the Mormons, and the Oneida Community.* Urbana, Ill., 1984.

Guarneri, Carl J. *The Utopian Alternative: Fourierism in Nineteenth-Century America.* Ithaca, N.Y., 1991.

Harrison, John F. C. *Quest for the New Moral World: Robert Owen and the Owenites in Britain and America.* New York, 1969.

Hayden, Dolores. *Seven American Utopias: The Architecture of Utopian Socialism, 1790–1975.* Cambridge, Mass., 1975.

Kanter, Rosabeth Moss. *Commitment and Community: Communes and Utopias in Sociological Perspective.* Cambridge, Mass., 1972.

Klaw, Spencer. *Without Sin: The Life and Death of the Oneida Community.* New York, 1993.

Nordhoff, Charles. *The Communistic Societies of the United States.* New York, 1965. First published in 1875, this survey includes accounts of the author's visits to several communities.

Noyes, John Humphrey. *History of American Socialisms.* New York, 1966. Originally published in 1870, this compilation includes many documents on Fourierism and outlines Noyes's theories on communitarian history.

Pitzer, Donald E., ed. *America's Communal Utopias.* Chapel Hill, N.C., 1997. Includes chapters on the major antebellum groups and a comprehensive bibliographical essay.

Spann, Edward K. *Hopedale: From Commune to Company Town.* Columbus, Ohio, 1992.

Stein, Stephen J. *The Shaker Experience in America.* New Haven, Conn., 1992.

Sutton, Robert P. *Les Icariens: The Utopian Dream in Europe and America.* Urbana, Ill., 1994.

Swift, Lindsay. *Brook Farm: Its Members, Scholars, and Visitors.* New York, 1900.

Wunderlich, Roger. *"Low Living and High Thinking" at Modern Times, New York, 1851–1864.* Syracuse, N.Y., 1986.

WOMEN IN THE PUBLIC SPHERE, 1838–1877

Glenna Matthews

In the years just before and just after the Civil War, the public sphere in the United States was expanding dramatically, and women's relationship to it was changing equally dramatically. The change with respect to women can be summarized briefly: in 1838 women played almost no public role, and in 1877—still lacking the vote, still unable to serve on juries—women had begun to forge a powerful suffrage movement, certain women were participating in the public political discourse, and the nation had ratified the Fourteenth Amendment to the Constitution, which would eventually be used to fight sex discrimination. What's more, organized American womanhood had done much to humanize society. As for the public sphere itself, it was growing because of democratic ferment and because of new forms of organization and communication in the nineteenth century.

In the context of the present article, the "public sphere" includes, but is not confined to, the state. Beyond electoral politics and the institutions of governance, beyond the judicial system, lies the realm of civil society or the public sphere independent of the state. Civil society includes various means for influencing public opinion such as lecturing, writing (either for periodicals or in the form of political fiction), labor activism, collective action in voluntary associations, public demonstrations, and, to a certain extent, the realm of religion. All of these forms of civil society were growing between 1838 and 1877, and women were expanding their participation therein, and hence their role in the public sphere. Women were also expanding their economic role in these years of vibrant national economic growth. While it is true that the economy is its own discrete realm apart from politics and civil society, it is also true that as women have been integrated into the economy as individuals participating on their own, their involvement has had the spillover effect of enhancing their public participation more generally.

But even as there was progress for women between 1838 and 1877, this progress was not distributed equally either by class, by race, by region, or by religion. Those women who were white Anglo-Saxon Protestants living in the Northeast in cities or small towns were far likelier to play a visible role than their rural or southern or Catholic or non-white/ethnic sisters. This said, there was a courageous network of African American women abolitionists in the period before the Civil War and a burgeoning black women's club movement after it.

WOMEN AND THE STATE

In charting the relationship between American women and the state over the course of American history, it would be difficult to overstate the importance of the doctrine of coverture, which influenced the legal systems of all of the original colonies. English common law mandated that a married woman be civilly dead, "covered" by her husband's status. (The long-standing custom of referring to a married woman as "Mrs. John Smith" is only one of many surviving relics of coverture.) The historian Linda Kerber has argued that the underlying assumption behind coverture was that the husband was entitled to unrestricted physical access to his wife's body. Should she be allowed to play a responsible political or economic role, then some action of hers might cause her husband to forfeit that access. For example, should she enter into a contract and default, she would be vulnerable to debtor's prison, thus removing her from her husband's bed and board. Should she be subject to such obligations of citizenship as military service, she would necessarily be absent from her marital duties. As Kerber has put it, a woman's domestic/marital obligations have trumped the civic ones for much of history. In consequence, a woman's relationship to the state has been through her husband, mediated by his status as a citizen. Until the early 1900s, he cast the vote for the household (depending on his own access to the franchise, as determined by racial and property-ownership restrictions at various times in American history). In short, her route to full citizenship has been circuitous at best.

Ideas that flourished at the time of the American Revolution began to create a breach in the barrier that stood between women and a direct relationship with the state. A generation of scholarship has explored the impact of Revolution-era republicanism on American society. This political ideology was born in Rome and reinvented during the Renaissance as civic humanism. Because it so influenced the founders, its linkage of private virtue and public life made possible a new, if not necessarily co-equal, political role for women. Women, as wives and mothers, would foster virtue in their children and promote patriotic values in their homes and in this way participate in the civic culture. Moreover, during the years before the outbreak of hostilities with Great Britain, a consumer boycott had been the patriots' most effective weapon to deploy against their British rulers, thus giving substance to the idea of a linkage between the political and the domestic. Finally, the transatlantic shift in political and social ideas that is known as the Enlightenment had begun to undermine traditional views of gender. For all of these reasons, white American women began to receive an improved education in the years following the founding of the new nation, and this would prove essential to the progress they made in the nineteenth century.

In the antebellum period a few American women, beneficiaries of these changes, began to challenge their second-class status as citizens. The suffrage movement began with a small number of women, whose entry into the public sphere was catalyzed by their strong antislavery views, asserting that they were citizens in their own right and able to speak out publicly. The first-ever public meeting devoted to women's rights—including suffrage—took place in Seneca Falls, New York, in 1848, followed by a series of women's rights conventions in the years leading up to the Civil War. After the war ended, there was a schism in the nascent movement, because some white and black men and women thought that enfranchising African American men was the highest priority at that juncture, and that women of both races could take a backseat to the needs of the terribly vulnerable freedmen. Others disagreed, arguing that, for example, the Fourteenth Amendment—which placed the word "male" next to the word "voters" for the first time—would be a terrible setback for women. As a result, as of the late

Elizabeth Cady Stanton (1815–1902) Speaks at the First Woman's Rights Convention. Defining the convention's purpose, Stanton stated, "We have met to uplift woman's fallen divinity upon an even pedestal with man's. And, strange as it may seem to many, we now demand our right to vote according to the declaration of the government under which we live." © BETTMANN/CORBIS

1870s there were two discrete suffrage organizations, the American Woman Suffrage Association, which accepted the Reconstruction amendments, and the National Woman Suffrage Association, which did not. The latter was the one led by the two best-known suffragists, Susan B. Anthony and Elizabeth Cady Stanton.

The suffrage movement was absolutely essential to improving women's status as citizens, but it was not the only means by which women were connecting themselves to the institutions of governance in the mid-nineteenth century. Recent scholarship shows that women were beginning to demonstrate loyalty to political parties in various ways, primarily by attending political rallies. In 1840, for example, twelve hundred women in Richmond, Virginia, listened to a speech by the orator and politician Daniel Webster in which he exhorted them to uphold public virtue. As another instance of this phenomenon, women attended the Lincoln-Douglas political debates in Illinois in 1858. In short, their inability to vote did not mean that women were uninterested in electoral politics.

A few women were highly visible partisan politicians in the mid-nineteenth century. Perhaps the best known was Pennsylvania's Anna Elizabeth Dickinson, a fiery Republican orator who came to public attention in the 1860s. Dickinson's career is all the more remarkable when it is remembered that women gave no public speeches at all until the antebellum period.

A Quaker from Philadelphia, Dickinson was an ardent believer in the antislavery cause. She gave her first public address in 1860 at the age of seventeen. After the Civil War broke out, she became so effective an advocate for the Radical Republican cause—defining the war's focus to be the abolition of slavery—that she was highly sought after for her oratorical skills. On one occasion she addressed an audience of five thousand people at Cooper Union in New York. On another, she spoke to the House of Representatives on the subject of the Freedmen's Bureau—with President Abraham Lincoln in the audience. On these occasions she was not speaking in the vein of general moral uplift, but rather making specific public policy recommendations.

With a small but growing suffrage movement and a larger group of women who might not have been willing to endorse the then-radical cause of suffrage but who were taking a demonstrable interest in important issues of the day, American women were growing in their capacity to be full citizens owing to changes in the legal system. The first significant reform—the first truly consequential erosion of coverture—came with the passage of married women's property laws, beginning in the late 1830s and continuing on with a variety of reforms of marriage laws throughout the nineteenth century. These reforms were essential before women could play an independent role in politics or public life—as well as for women's protection within the marriage itself. For example, Mary Livermore, one of the outstanding female leaders in the North during the Civil War, described in her memoirs her successful attempt to raise money for humanitarian purposes during the conflict. This was, however, an effort tinged with the humiliation of learning that she could not enter into a contract toward that end without her husband's cooperation.

In addition, what would eventually become the fundamental tool for attacking both discriminatory laws and practices prejudicial to women's interests, the Fourteenth Amendment to the Constitution, was ratified in 1868 as one of the keystones of legal protection for African Americans. Clearly defining citizenship for the first time, it would obviously affect all women, not just those who were black. On the one hand, the amendment seemed a setback to many suffragists because it employed the term "male voters." On the other hand, its language encouraged pioneering activists to file suit on behalf of women's rights. They seized on the amendment's guarantees of "equal protection" and "due process" to citizens in the maintenance of their "privileges and immunities" to argue that, for example, a woman should be admitted to the bar to practice law in the state of Illinois. The U.S. Supreme Court found against Myra Bradwell in *Bradwell v. Illinois* in 1873 and would not, in fact, apply the Fourteenth Amendment to women's rights until *Reed v. Reed* in 1971. The ratification of the Fourteenth Amendment was important for women not because of any immediate payoff, but because the Constitution did not remotely offer any remedy for gender-

Anna Elizabeth Dickinson. A fiery orator, Dickinson (1842–1932) published an article in William Lloyd Garrison's *Liberator* at age fourteen. ARCHIVE PHOTOS

437

based discrimination until this amendment became a part of it.

WOMEN AND CIVIL SOCIETY

The changes in the relationship between American women and the state in the mid-nineteenth century were fundamental and epochal. But relative to the magnitude and breadth of the change in the realm of civil society—they were the first halting baby steps—women were taking giant strides in activism in the public sphere independent of the state. Public activism was emerging because women were challenging the underlying cultural assumptions that had made "public woman" an invidious term; a term that equated a would-be powerful woman with the biblical Jezebel. To be a public woman connoted the kind of sexual uncleanness associated with prostitution.

Public activity had been proscribed in many ways and for many reasons. In the first place, an ironclad convention had dictated that a respectable woman should never speak in public. Further, in most Christian denominations she was forbidden from preaching. She was supposed never to publish anything she wrote, especially using her own name. (Indeed, there used to be a saying that a respectable woman's name appeared in the newspaper only three times: when she was born, when she married, and when she died.)

The first significant challenge to these assumptions came from the Quakers, a radical sect born during the turmoil of seventeenth-century England and transplanted to the New World colony of Pennsylvania shortly thereafter. Questioning many societal as well as religious norms, members of the Society of Friends—as the Quakers were officially known—believed in the authority of the Inner Light as echoing the voice of God. With this type of validation of their unconventional insights available to them, they came to the conclusion that women could preach as well as men. By the antebellum period a few other denominations had joined the Quakers in opening the pulpit to women, most significantly the African Methodist Episcopal Church in a few instances.

These religious challenges to the cultural prohibition against women speaking in public were especially important because the New Testament words of St. Paul had been so powerful a means for silencing women. In fact, "Let your women keep silence in your churches," St. Paul counseled in a letter to the Corinthians (1 Cor. 14:34, King James),

and this admonition was then applied liberally to many circumstances both within and outside the walls of a church in subsequent centuries. Worth noting is the fact that in the predominantly Protestant United States of the time, one nineteenth-century women's rights activist after another felt impelled either to challenge or reinterpret St. Paul as a preparation for challenging the gender status quo.

A few women were preaching in the early nineteenth century, but far more were joining voluntary associations connected with their churches. This occurred during the burst of evangelistic fervor in the Early Republic that is known as the Second Great Awakening, a period which saw changes set in motion that would affect the lives of American women for many years to come. For the first time in American history significant numbers of women were organizing, forming religiously based female networks of benevolence. At first, they confined themselves to such "safe" subjects as, for example, promoting missionary efforts, but over time some of these women's groups provided a foundation for dealing with far more controversial issues such as the abolition of slavery. These networks were critical to the emergence of women into public efficacy within the generation that came to maturity during the 1830s. In effect, many a Protestant church served as a training ground for female activism, following the path blazed by the Quakers.

The generation of women that came to maturity in the 1830s also benefited from many of the other changes in the society and in the economy that were unfolding around them. First, the growth of the market and the dawning of factory-based production meant that more women had access to such commercially available goods as soap and textiles. Without having to produce such products themselves, they had more time to devote to the world outside the home. Second, economic development was creating new employment opportunities for women, most significantly as teachers and as factory workers. Third, women were beginning to show the effects of the increased investment in education, including the education of women (except for higher education). Moreover, the culture had begun to sentimentalize motherhood in unprecedented ways and this valorization of their gender gave women a shield with which to deflect criticism as they created their networks of involvement in the world outside the home. Finally, the sheer physical growth of the new nation and the rapidly changing means of transportation necessarily undermined conventional ideas about "woman's sphere." A wife traveling by railroad to meet her husband who had gone ahead to a new settlement, for example, was breaking new ground for her sex, whether she intended to be a pioneer or not.

These, then, were the building blocks of women's new role in civil society that began to take off in the 1830s: better-educated women with more time and more freedom of movement, many of whom were organized into female networks. That mainstream American society so venerated mothers was limiting in some ways—consider the woman who did not want to conform to conventional gender norms—but also a source of immense cultural authority for the vast majority of women. How and why would they use their newfound authority?

WOMEN ACTIVISTS, 1838–1877

It would be impossible to list more than a small fraction of the many, many remarkable women who came to public attention in the mid-nineteenth century. Indeed, there was scarcely a corner of America that did not benefit from the extraordinary release of female energy during these years. From the treatment of the insane, to the education of children in the West, to advocacy for enslaved African Americans, to addressing the needs of prostitutes, women began to tackle the job of improving the lives of their fellow Americans. Still not fully citizens on the same basis as men, women organized, they circulated petitions, they raised money, they lectured, and they publicized the need for reform. On some occasions—such as in the case of the suffrage movement or the labor activism of mill workers—they also advocated for themselves.

Among the most significant breakthrough figures were the pioneers of public speaking, courageous women who paid a high price for their willingness to be innovators. The first woman to give a public political speech to both men and women in the United States—as far as historians have been able to determine—was the Scottish-born freethinker Frances "Fanny" Wright. A thoroughgoing radical committed to a broad range of reforms including "free love," Wright first spoke on 4 July 1828 in New Harmony, Indiana. For a brief period the statuesque and flamboyant Wright enthralled audiences in several parts of the country, but she soon flamed out, becoming a pariah. The next woman to give a public political address was Maria Miller Stewart, an African American. Her story is a truly remarkable one.

Born in Hartford, Connecticut, in 1803 and orphaned at the age of five, the young Maria Miller became an indentured servant, a contract that would last until she was fifteen. While in bonded service and with no access to school, she managed to acquire an education by means of after-hours ventures into her employer's library. She married James Stewart in 1826, was widowed in 1829, and shortly thereafter was defrauded of her inheritance by his executors.

She fought back publicly. Inspired by the dawning abolitionist movement in the Northeast, she gave four speeches in Boston in 1832 and 1833, speeches that were devoted to the situation of free blacks. In so doing, she became the first American-born woman to give a public address. But the experience was evidently too painful to maintain for an extended period of time. In addition to the stage fright that anyone might suffer in such a situation, there was the additional burden of anxiety attending the act of flouting so deep-seated a societal convention, hence running the risk of forfeiting one's reputation for respectability.

Sarah and Angelina Grimké, southern-born abolitionists who moved north, were the next American women to defy tradition and give public political speeches, beginning in the mid-1830s. In fact, having witnessed the cruelties of slavery firsthand, they became the first women to be paid abolitionist agents. When they undertook to give their lectures in New England, they were officially denounced by the Congregationalist clergy as having overstepped the bounds of propriety. They were also the butt of many cruel jokes. Not surprisingly, they, too, retired to the sidelines after a few years, but not before they had set a powerful example that other courageous pioneers would soon follow.

By the 1850s a number of women regularly appeared on the lecture platform, usually to address either the antislavery cause or women's rights or both. It still took rare courage, but this second wave of female speakers did not burn out as quickly as the first wave had. Those who lectured during the 1850s included both white women, such as Lucy Stone and Antoinette Brown Blackwell, and black women, such as Sojourner Truth and Frances Watkins Harper. Blackwell deserves special mention, because in 1853 she became the first American woman to be ordained as a minister by a mainstream Protestant denomination, the Congregationalists.

The spoken words of women pioneers reached a small but significant number of their fellow Americans. On the other hand, the written words of female authors reached many millions and pro-

439

foundly changed the political discourse of the whole nation. Indeed, President Abraham Lincoln is said to have remarked when he met Harriet Beecher Stowe, the author of *Uncle Tom's Cabin,* during the Civil War: "So you are the little woman who wrote the book that made this great war?"

But before discussing the most important woman writer—Stowe—one must examine the context for her literary work. A new genre of fiction written by women for a primarily but not exclusively female audience had come into prominence beginning in the 1830s and continuing into the 1870s. Twentieth-century scholars have labeled it "domestic fiction," because the novels belonging to the genre explored in a largely realistic way the daily lives of ordinary women and young girls. Often celebrating the competence of housewives, these novels found a vast readership. Most important of the cultural "work" they performed was their unprecedented valorization of female subjectivity. The heroines of domestic fiction were not figures of romance daydreaming about Mr. Right, but rather women striving to learn how to be self-supporting, morally responsible adults, adept at domestic tasks.

Like the church-based women's networks, some of which evolved into networks dealing with controversial issues, domestic novels evolved from being didactic and relatively conventional into vehicles for disseminating radical ideas about gender and many other issues. A few novelists wrote with thinly disguised anger about the inequities of the marriage laws, for example. Others painted memorable portraits of the difficulties of being suddenly required to earn a living. Thus when Stowe transformed the domestic novel into the means for arousing the conscience of the country—and the world—about slavery, she was working within the context of an already politicized genre.

Stowe, the daughter of one of the nation's best-known clergymen, was herself a housewife when she wrote *Uncle Tom's Cabin.* Married to another clergyman who had a hard time adequately supporting the family, Stowe began to write occasional light prose for the popular *Godey's Lady's Book.* Then Congress passed the Fugitive Slave Act as part of the Compromise of 1850. This law was the price exacted by southern states for going along with the admission of California to the union as a free state. Detested in much of the North, the new law inspired Stowe to attempt her first novel as a record of what she saw as the sinful way that slavery permitted human beings to treat one another. At first serialized, the novel she wrote eventually sold some 3 million copies—in a country with a population of 25 mil-

lion. The first installment of *Uncle Tom's Cabin* appeared in the 5 June 1851 issue of the *National Era.* Within a short time, the country was galvanized into discussing it, even in the South, where it was loathed just as heartily as it was admired elsewhere. Stowe succeeded in imbuing the crusade against slavery with all the sacredness attached to purity of family life in the American society of the mid-nineteenth century, because she dramatized the ways in which "the peculiar institution" undermined the slave family: children sold down the river away from their mothers and husbands and wives separated against their will—with the latter being vulnerable to sexual predation by their masters. Some of Stowe's most admirable characters are highly competent housewives, such as the Quaker Rachel Halliday, whose home is a station on the Underground Railroad for escaping slaves.

In effect, Stowe was enjoining her fellow housewives to use the means at their disposal to put pressure on politicians to end slavery. Though women could not vote, there were many other things they *could* do, she pointed out in "An Appeal to the Women of the Free States," published in 1854. First of all, they must master the intricacies of the debate. She then suggested:

> In the second place, women can make exertions to get up petitions, in their particular districts, to our national legislature. They can take measures to communicate information in their vicinity. They can employ lecturers to spread the subject before the people of their town or village. They can circulate the speeches of our members in Congress, and in many other ways secure a full understanding of the present position of our country.

Stowe was one of the key figures who helped call into being a female public in the North in the years leading up to the Civil War. That is, in addition to the structural changes at the societal level already happening, there were outstanding women writers who were fostering female activism by writing a "script" for it. Another was Lydia Maria Child, the author of a best-selling book of domestic advice, who evolved into an eloquent and passionate spokeswoman for human freedom. By the 1850s Child was publishing regularly in one of the nation's outstanding newspapers, the *New York Tribune,* including a piece featuring a heroic Kansas housewife fighting for her antislavery beliefs. The net result of the combination of social change and the injunctions to female involvement by respected women authors was that during the war itself northern women established some ten thousand soldiers' aid societies and broke new ground for their sex in a plethora of ways from battlefront visitation to fund-raising to organizing humanitarian supplies to circulating petitions for emancipation on a massive scale.

Besides the activism called into being by abolitionism and suffrage, another important manifestation of female political energy lay in the labor organizing of New England mill workers. By 1860 some sixty thousand women were employed in the region's textile factories. When they were first recruited from surrounding farm families in the 1820s and 1830s, factory owners had built supervised dormitories for them, so that the young women would not be unchaperoned. Living and working so closely together had nurtured a sisterhood that manifested itself in a willingness to strike on more than one occasion in the 1830s. For example, eight hundred women "turned out" or struck in February 1834. Though no lasting labor organization resulted from these pioneering strikes, the mill workers set an example of courage and determination that would echo down the decades.

From the above account it is clear that the capacity to play a public role was shaped by factors that were unavailable to many women: time, for example, was hard to come by for a woman in a rural area who might still have been fabricating daily necessities. Time would also have been much less available to a poor woman. Another liability for thousands of women was the fact that gender norms in the South were far more tradition-bound than in the North—at least in part because abolition and women's rights were so intertwined and the former was anathema as a subject of discussion in the South. (In fairness, it should be pointed out that there *were* a number of southern women writers of domestic fiction who articulated a regional defense, including those who wrote in response to *Uncle Tom's Cabin*.) Therefore the female public remained inchoate in the South until after the Civil War. There was a strong relationship between public activism by women and investment in female education, and therefore those areas that were slower to invest—once again, principally the South—were also slower to see public women.

Women of color faced the biggest obstacles, because both racism and sexism impeded their entry into public roles. (The wonder is that so many African American women played so active a role early on.) In the first place, they were *not* beneficiaries of public education on the same basis as white women and would not be for generations to come. Another major obstacle lay in the fact that many a white woman "reformer" let it be known that she did not

choose to affiliate with an organization to which women of color also belonged. Further, some women of color had immigrated from countries with restrictive gender norms of their own, and as a result it might take decades for women from the group to participate in civil society as freely as their white counterparts. The historian Judy Yung has demonstrated that for one group, Chinese American women in San Francisco, for example, each generation built on the pathbreaking innovations of its mothers until a true breakthrough into public efficacy came during the mid-twentieth century.

A STRONG VOICE

Women achieved much during the middle years of the nineteenth century. In so doing, they demonstrated courage, tenacity, vision, generosity of spirit, adherence to democratic values—and, on occasion, the usual human fallibility. The generation that came to maturity toward the end of the Reconstruction era would break new ground both in terms of public activism and professional achievement, in large part because higher education was beginning to be a realistic option with a significant number of colleges and universities having become coeducational and with the great burgeoning of women's colleges in the years after the Civil War. Moreover, in 1874 was born a powerful and militant temperance organization, the Woman's Christian Temperance Union, which would become the first national, grassroots network of women—one ultimately dedicated to suffrage and reform as well as to prohibition. The following decade the social worker Jane Addams founded Hull-House in Chicago, setting in motion the settlement house movement whereby middle-class women moved into urban slums to put their skills to work serving the poor. Scholars still debate how much good the settlements did for their clients, but no one can deny that they precipitated enormously effective advocacy by the care providers and ever-greater visibility for women in the public sphere.

An event that took place in 1872 both symbolized the gains women had already made and pointed the way to the voting, running-for-office future: that year Susan B. Anthony cast votes at the state and congressional elections in her hometown of Rochester, New York, to test whether the Fourteenth and Fifteenth Amendments enfranchised women. (A handful of less famous women attempted to vote also, but their acts of rebellion have been little recognized in the history books.) A jury indicted her for illegal voting and a court levied a fine, but the authorities never collected it, thus denying her the chance of fighting her case through the court system. She lost—and she did not live to see the ratification of the Nineteenth Amendment granting woman suffrage in 1920. But she had announced that "failure is impossible," and about that she was right, both in the narrow sense of winning the right to vote and in the larger sense of closing the gap between male and female citizenship. Nearly one hundred years after her brave attempt to seize the rights of full citizenship, the U.S. Supreme Court would begin to apply to cases of gender discrimination the very Fourteenth Amendment she had first opposed and then tried to employ.

See also **Gender and Political Activism** *(in this volume);* **Women** *(volume 2);* **Family; Sexuality; Gender** *(volume 3).*

BIBLIOGRAPHY

Overviews

Ginzberg, Lori D. *Women and the Work of Benevolence: Morality, Politics, and Class in the Nineteenth-Century United States.* New Haven, Conn., 1990.

Kerber, Linda K. *No Constitutional Right to Be Ladies: Women and the Obligations of Citizenship.* New York, 1998.

Matthews, Glenna. *The Rise of Public Woman: Woman's Power and Woman's Place in the United States, 1630–1970.* New York, 1992.

Ryan, Mary P. *Women in Public: Between Banners and Ballots, 1825–1880.* Baltimore, 1990.

Scott, Anne Firor. *Natural Allies: Women's Associations in American History.* Urbana, Ill., 1991.

Case Studies of Activist Women

Hewitt, Nancy. *Women's Activism and Social Change, Rochester, N.Y., 1822–1872.* Ithaca, N.Y., 1984.

Lebsock, Suzanne. *The Free Women of Petersburg: Status and Culture in a Southern Town, 1784–1860.* New York, 1984.

Ryan, Mary P. *Cradle of the Middle Class: The Family in Oneida County, New York, 1790–1865.* Cambridge, Mass., 1981.

Varon, Elizabeth R. *We Mean to Be Counted: White Women and Politics in Antebellum Virginia.* Chapel Hill, N.C., 1998.

Abolition and Suffrage

Dubois, Ellen Carol. *Feminism and Suffrage: The Emergence of an Independent Women's Movement in America, 1848–1869.* Ithaca, N.Y., 1978.

Jeffrey, Julie Roy. *The Great Silent Army of Abolitionism: Ordinary Women in the Antislavery Movement.* Chapel Hill, N.C., 1998.

Venet, Wendy Hamand. *Neither Ballots nor Bullets: Women Abolitionists and the Civil War.* Charlottesville, Va., 1991.

Yee, Shirley J. *Black Women Abolitionists: A Study in Activism, 1828–1860.* Knoxville, Tenn., 1992.

Biography

Cazden, Elizabeth. *Antoinette Brown Blackwell: A Biography.* Old Westbury, N.Y., 1983

Karcher, Carolyn. *The First Woman in the Republic: A Cultural Biography of Lydia Maria Child.* Durham, N.C., 1995.

Lerner, Gerda. *The Grimké Sisters from South Carolina: Pioneers for Woman's Rights and Abolition.* New York, 1971.

Morris, Celia. *Fanny Wright: Rebel in America.* Urbana, Ill., 1992.

Painter, Nell. *Sojourner Truth: A Life, A Symbol.* New York, 1996.

Sterling, Dorothy. *Ahead of Her Time: Abbey Kelley and the Politics of Antislavery.* New York, 1991.

Literary Culture

Carby, Hazel V. *Reconstructing Womanhood: The Emergence of the Afro-American Woman Novelist.* New York, 1987.

Kelley, Mary. *Private Woman, Public Stage: Literary Domesticity in Nineteenth-Century America.* New York, 1984.

Moss, Elizabeth. *Domestic Novelists in the Old South: Defenders of Southern Culture.* Baton Rouge, La., 1992.

DOMESTICITY AND SENTIMENTALISM

Carolyn Haynes

After several publishers rejected the manuscript, in December 1850 George Putnam's firm decided to release *The Wide, Wide World*, a lengthy first novel by a relatively unknown American writer, Susan Warner. Little did Putnam know that by 1853, the novel would have undergone sixteen editions in the United States, one of which sold 80,000 copies. Fifty years later, the book was still in demand with cumulative sales estimated at a half-million dollars. Despite its unprecedented success, Warner's novel was not the only mid-nineteenth-century fictional work to boast such popularity. The novelist Harriet Beecher Stowe's *Uncle Tom's Cabin* (1852) eclipsed Warner's novel, topping out at over 2 million copies in English and in translation all over the world. At least one other American novel released in the 1850s sold over 100,000 copies, and many more exceeded 10,000 copies. Moreover, these novels were advertised, reviewed, anthologized, dramatized, parodied, and even enshrined in marbled duodecimo collected editions to be consigned to posterity. As G. M. Goshgarian put it, "The age of the best-seller had arrived" (*To Kiss the Chastening Rod*, p. 2).

The sudden popularity of the American novel, however, did not occur without controversy and criticism. The most popular novels of the mid- to late nineteenth century were not only written by women such as Stowe, Warner, E. D. E. N. Southworth, and Maria Cummins, but they were sentimental—centering on home truths as well as cherished cultural icons and landmarks. The sentimental narrative highlighted spirited emotion and sympathetic identification—the act of imagining oneself in another's position—usually with the downtrodden (the poor, lame, elderly, or widowed). Moreover, sentimentalism was not limited to fiction; it permeated a wide range of cultural forms, including advice books, statues, portraits and photographs, sermons, pamphlets, begging letters, lyric poems, fashion advertisements, temperance testimonials, and conversion narratives. Several male novelists, such as Nathaniel Hawthorne, did not take kindly to this transformation in the United States cultural industry. According to him, a "d—d mob of scribbling women" with their lackluster "trash" had outshined their more brilliant, male competitors.

A century and a half later, Hawthorne's view still presided in some literary circles. As Goshgarian noted in 1992, "The quality of the writing America bought [in the 1850s] plummeted in proportion as the quantity soared" (p. 2). What was this cultural phenomenon known as sentimentalism? How did it relate to domesticity and gender? Why did it arise, and how should its upsurge and longevity be interpreted? These are the questions explored in this article.

Sentimentality is not simply a rhetorical mode or literary genre; rather it is a practical consciousness or set of actions: "The sentimental complex . . . situates the reader or viewer: that is, the act of emotional response the work evokes also produces the sentimental subject who consumes the work. This production crucially involves a movement of sympathy, in all its anxious appeals, across race, class, and gender lines" (Samuels, *The Culture of Sentiment*, p. 6). Moreover, because it was so often set in the domestic realm, sentimentalism, according to the writer Rosemarie Garland Thomson, should be seen as "the affective and relational component of domesticity" (in *Nineteenth-Century American Women Writers*, p. 128). Thus, sentimentalism must be studied within the context of domesticity, that larger ideology and set of practices that structured women's and men's places and roles in the nineteenth century. Although the concept of domesticity shifted throughout the nineteenth century, it fundamentally held a division of labor that assigned women to the privatized realm of the home, which became the site and source of feeling, religion, morality, child rearing, purity, and order. By contrast, domesticity relegated men to the public world of politics, economic production, money, and other

Harriet Beecher Stowe (1811–1896) from a Rare Photo.
Much of Stowe's inspiration to write *Uncle Tom's Cabin*
came from the death of her young son in 1849.
© BETTMANN/CORBIS

activities outside the home. While men were imagined as worldly, competitive, ruthless, and in need of moral guidance, women were cast in just opposite terms, as sheltered, submissive, pious, and pure. The strength of the domestic ideology was that it redefined women, not as inferior to men (as had been done before), but as different from them. Women were given a separate and, in some ways, morally superior role to that of men.

The editor and author Sarah Josepha Hale celebrated the differences between women and men in her 1845 poem "Empire of Woman," designating the outward world for men and reserving the holier empire of wife and motherhood for women. The proliferation of this type of sentimental popular culture fostered what the scholar Barbara Welter termed the "cult of true womanhood" in her 1966 article of the same name, a belief in the home as woman's natural place and the family as her paramount interest. Sentimental renditions of domesticity idealized maternity, family life, and a pious, pure, and submissive notion of womanhood. When *Mother's Magazine* first appeared in 1833, it inaugurated a long tradition of female editors offering advice on household and child care. Instead of viewing children as original sinners (as the Calvinists had done), the new sentimental view advocated a notion of children as blank slates on which mothers could inscribe the correct message. Numerous advice writers implored mothers to inculcate virtue in their children since fathers were occupied with business affairs. Similarly, the educator-author Catharine Beecher and Harriet Beecher Stowe advised women how to take best advantage of cooking, heating, and lighting innovations to manage efficient, happy homes. In the 1850s a plethora of recipe books emerged with detailed instructions for cakes, cookies, and desserts, encouraging elaborate domesticity and investing meals with emotional significance.

Sentimental culture helped both to maintain domesticity and to transform it. It focused on and valorized women's virtuousness and piety and used them as rationales to enter into and reform the public realm through moral suasion. Sympathy—the quintessential sentimental emotion—entails attachment to others. As moral exemplars of sympathy, women were able to engage with the downtrodden, sinful, and sensational individuals and aspects of society in a "safe" way. Barred traditionally from access to the public realm, women were nevertheless imagined by sentimental culture as being responsible for and best suited to purging society of corruption. Under the banner of sentiment, women marched into the public world to enact humanitarian reform.

Women, such as the educator-reformer Frances Willard and Harriet Beecher Stowe, lectured, wrote, protested, and organized campaigns for such varied causes as abolition, temperance, suffrage, education, dress reform, and sanitation, as well as against such vices as prostitution, lynching, prisons, poverty, and obscenity. They utilized sentimental tropes and rhetoric to advance their causes. Proclaimed the novelist-essayist Lillie Devereux Blake, "The national housekeeping is all out of order for want of that virtue, love of order, and, above all, conscientiousness which woman especially represents" (*Woman's Place Today*, p. 147). Similarly, Frances Willard, founder of the Women's Christian Temperance Union, underlined the power of woman's maternal instinct: "Mother-love works magic for humanity. . . . Mother-hearted women are called to be the saviors of the race" (Hardesty, "Minister," p. 97). Implicit in Willard's statement is the conviction that women are aligned with virtue and piety and are destined to improve those around them. In the mid- to late 1800s, Dr. Elizabeth Blackwell attempted to enhance her own professional viability through a similar appeal to domesticity and sentimentalism. Considered the first woman doctor of modern medicine, Blackwell implied that women doctors, by virtue of their femininity, had a particular aptitude for the medical field which stressed healthy "habits . . . formed by . . . the silent working of influences, hour by hour and day by day, that are invisible and cannot be measured, that seem valueless, taking item by item . . . and yet in the aggregate . . . mould body and soul" (*Essays,* vol. 2, pp. 243–244).

Not all women, however, wanted to or could conform to sentimental domestic norms. Writers and reformers like Lydia Maria Child, Margaret Fuller, Frances "Fanny" Wright, Amelia Bloomer, Lucretia Mott, and Elizabeth Cady Stanton, for example, protested the double standard embodied in domestic sentimentalism. Written in the early 1840s, Child's *Letters from New York* refutes the ideals of submissive purity and piety applied to women alone and argues that the world would be improved if men adopted feminine virtues. Invoking the Declaration of Independence, Elizabeth Cady Stanton and Lucretia Mott, along with three hundred other men and women, drafted in 1848 a Declaration of Sentiments that rejected domesticity and gendered standards of behavior as the basis for women's rights. Not only did these delegates enumerate the ways that men behaved tyrannically toward women, but they demanded property rights, child custody in the event of death or divorce, equal job opportunities, and voting rights.

While some women rejected sentimental notions of domesticity, race and poverty kept others outside of its bounds. Not only did poverty ensure lower standards of living and consumption, but it meant that women in the household were forced to earn money and lacked the resources and time to create the sentimental household. According to the historian Christine Stansell, their lives were a "catch-as-catch-can struggle to make ends meet . . . [and] a ceaseless round of scraping, scrimping, borrowing, and scavenging" (*City of Women,* p. 46). Instead of the intricate furnishings of middle-class households, rag rugs and stick furniture sufficed in overcrowded dwellings. High population densities led to lower standards of living, poorer sanitation, and more health problems for poor city women and their families.

The sacred home and the sentimental virtues of piety, purity, and submissiveness were also unavailable to the approximately 6 percent of free blacks

and to the enslaved women who remained trapped in an abusive pattern of agricultural labor. Slavery, economic hardship, and racial prejudice denied African American women the liberties white women most prized, including the right to marry, to bear and raise children, and to practice religion, as well as the right to personal safety from sexual terrorism. The historian Robert Fogel estimated that one in every eleven unions between slaves ended through the sale of one or both partners. Once joined, enslaved women attempted to create as comfortable a domestic environment for themselves and their families as possible, sacrificing sleep and using ingenuity and creativity for domestic chores. They held quilting parties, grew additional food in makeshift gardens, and made clothes for their families. The historian Deborah Gray White argued that because both partners had complementary roles with neither holding economic power over the other, enslaved families were more egalitarian than white, middle-class ones. Yet, according to the writer bell hooks, once emancipation happened and African American women assimilated white American values, they came to believe that field work degraded women and aspired to sentimental, domestic ideals. In fact, narratives written by formerly enslaved women either bemoan their inability to live up to the ideals of true womanhood or self-consciously appropriate the conventions of sentimental domesticity in order to critique the racism and sexism of slavery and of the northern, white middle classes.

Finally, domestic sentimentalism had little relevance for Native American women who valued interdependence in social and economic relations. For example, among the Pueblo people, prospective marriage partners exchanged equal amounts of wealth, indicating each partner's parity of importance. The historian Ramón Gutiérrez reported that Pueblo households were preeminently a female domain of love and ritual in which men moved in with their wives' families, laboring for the good of the household. The Great Plains Indians prized stamina in both sexes since both sexes were required to follow the buffalo. Mid- and late-nineteenth-century westward expansion, however, disrupted many Native American customs and displaced Native Americans under brutal, harsh conditions.

Most American families, then, due to their economic, racial, or ethnic situation, were not able to live up to the ideals of domestic sentimentalism. Yet, despite the fact that these sociocultural norms applied only to a narrow sector of the United States population, the cult of sentimental domesticity was ever-present in the fabric of American culture and set the terms of women's roles that prevailed throughout most of the nineteenth century and that are arguably still in existence today.

ORIGIN AND CAUSES OF SENTIMENTALISM AND DOMESTICITY

While white, middle-class women were peculiarly linked to sentimentalism during the nineteenth century, the concept of sentimentalism in America dates back at least to 1630 when the American colonist and first governor of Massachusetts John Winthrop argued in *A Modell of Christian Charity* that the American community must be "knit together" as a single body. According to him, one's loyalty to the community must not be fundamentally contractual or political in nature; rather, it should be familial. Moreover, he believed that women and domesticity were essential elements in maintaining sacred, familial community. This emphasis on domesticity as the linchpin of American society continued, according to Douglas Anderson, through the revolutionary and Civil War periods: "Winthrop's example suggests that American spiritual and intellectual life was 'feminized'—or at least domesticated—long before the nineteenth century. Moreover, it was a conscious process of domestication, every bit as deliberate as the domestication of Washington . . . or the maternal shawl that Abraham Lincoln appropriated at least partly as a dimension of his wartime image as the mourning national parent" (*A House Divided*, p. 5). Anderson's claim is not surprising when historians consider that many Enlightenment theorists who strongly influenced the Founding Fathers posited sympathy as the affective tie that holds a society together. As the Scottish economist Adam Smith argued in his *Theory of Moral Sentiments* (1759), "It is by the imagination only that we can form any conception of what we are [the] sensations [of our brother on the rack]. . . . By the imagination we place ourselves in his situation, we conceive ourselves enduring all the same torrents, we enter as it were into his body and become in some measure the same person with him" (p. 9).

Smith's ideas were revived by American revolutionaries. Thomas Paine's *Common Sense* (1776), for example, argued the need for colonists to redirect their affection and affiliation from the parent country of England to their own flesh and blood on the American continent. In his military resignation in 1784, George Washington's "voice faultered and sunk, and the whole house felt his agitations" (Bur-

nett, *Letters of Members of the Continental Congress*, p. 394). The poet Walt Whitman captured the sentimentalism of the moment in "The Sleepers." He described how Washington "cannot repress the weeping drops" while he "encircles [his officers'] necks with his arm and kisses them on the cheek, / He kisses lightly the wet cheeks one after another." Washington's and Paine's effective use of sentiment to create national community and connection were not unique. According to the historian Andrew Burstein, many of the nation's early political and intellectual leaders, such as Thomas Jefferson, deliberately utilized sentimental rhetoric, gestures, and narrative to bolster the foundation of the republic: "Emphasizing human compassion, they established a pattern of philanthropic mission, spiritual renewal, and global conversion still discernable at the end of the twentieth century" (*Sentimental Democracy*, p. xiv).

By the middle of the nineteenth century, however, American sentimentality had gained much greater prominence and had become singularly associated with the feminine, domestic world. According to the editors Mary Chapman and Glenn Hendler, it became "less directly identified with public virtue and benevolence and more associated with women's moral, nurturing role in the private sphere of the bourgeois family" (*Sentimental Men*, p. 3). The writer Lora Romero noted, "By 1830 the nature of woman's contribution to society had become a regional obsession among Anglo-American intellectuals of the northeastern United States, and by virtue of the dominance of this region's population over cultural production, it necessarily became a national obsession as well" (*Home Fronts*, p. 14). The question, then, emerges as to why sentimentalism and domesticity became in the mid-nineteenth century so deeply inscribed in American culture and affiliated with the feminine. As in the case of any complex cultural shift, this change appears to be caused by multiple interrelated forces.

The historian Betty DeBerg argued that the emergence of domesticity and sentimentality can be explained by a shift away from the early industrial era of the previous century when men defined themselves through several key roles: patriarch; landowner or skilled laborer; and warrior (*Ungodly Women*, p. 14). The mass exodus from the farms and into the city (and a wage economy) disrupted this traditional understanding and function of manhood. Fewer men could own large tracts of land, pass down their wealth or skills to their sons, or demonstrate physical prowess. Thus, a new notion of manhood, which maintained men's superior position over women yet was more congruent with the changing economy, emerged. No longer able to be the heroes on the battlefield defending their family honor, men instead became economic warriors in a business world increasingly depicted "as unsavory and strenuous in which ruthlessness and aggression were prized" (p. 18). A fixed income, a middle-class home, and a virtuous wife and family replaced bravery, physical strength, and property as the markers of successful manhood. Moreover, assigning women to the private sphere worked to assuage the moral and ethical conflicts in capitalism. "Uneasy about the profit motive, about exploiting those less fortunate, about using deceptive means to sell their goods, about ruthless and often unfair competition against other businessmen" (p. 19), the home was constructed as the refuge from the vicious world of business. By remaining in the private sphere, women did not threaten masculine power or identity.

Another reason that women could devote so much attention to the home and the emotional realm was the onslaught of immigrants in the nineteenth century. Between 1815 and 1865, some 5 million immigrants arrived in the United States, primarily from Ireland, Germany, and Scandinavia. Single women were especially well represented among the Irish immigrants. Desperate for jobs, they became the cheap labor upon which the cult of domesticity depended, taking low-paid jobs in textile and shoe factories and working in middle-class kitchens, and thereby giving housewives free time to devote to child care and leisure activities. Rising population densities, advancing birth control techniques (such as abstinence, coitus interruptus, douching, and then condoms which were available at midcentury), and increasing education levels of white, middle-class women served to decrease the average family size and to shorten the child-bearing period. Higher standards of cleanliness, warmer dwellings, and better nutrition contributed to lower infant mortality rates and child health. Thus, at midcentury, a new model of the middle-class family emerged, with greater emphasis on the welfare of individual members. With more time on their hands, fewer children to raise, and more sentimental literature reinforcing the importance of childhood, mothers began to lavish much more of their emotional and economic resources on their children.

With the rise of a capitalist economy and living standards and a decline in birth rates came an increase in consumerism and what the historian Lori Merish called a sense of "pious materialism" (*American Literary History*, 1:1, p. 3). No longer expected

to work on the family farm, middle-class women had the time and ability to purchase material goods to prove their domestic refinement and demonstrate their husbands' status. As Merish noted, "In sentimental texts 'outside' signifies the absence of domestic warmth, both emotional and physical: it signifies exclusion from care and interest; it signifies 'neglect.' . . . Individuals want to cross the threshold from outside to inside, from street to household; everybody wants a 'good home'" (p. 7). And a good home included all of the material comforts and proper amenities. Not only was a home supposed to display all of the necessary utilitarian goods such as furniture and food, but it also had to be replete with nonfunctional items such as plants, pets, trinkets, and fancywork that signified that the lady of the house had the money, leisure time, and the sentimental proclivity to care for or produce such things. Consumerism, then, played a key role in fueling sentimentalism and domesticity.

Domesticity and sentimentalism were not only sparked and maintained by economics and demographics. Religion—and in particular, the gradual disestablishment of it which was begun in 1777 and completed in 1833—also contributed to their ascent. Disestablishment meant that states no longer required its citizens to attend and maintain certain churches. Instead, a new, voluntary system emerged in which no denomination had automatic precedence over any other and no person had any obligation to attend worship or to support religion beyond his or her desire to do so" (Douglas, *The Feminization of American Culture*, p. 24). No longer assured of congregation, salary, or status, suddenly United States Protestant ministers had to begin recruiting congregants. Thus, they began to soften some of their harsher and unpopular themes such as original sin, predestination, and infant damnation and began to place greater emphasis on a merciful and loving God, a feminine and suffering image of Christ, and the importance of feelings over reason. In addition, they began to make specific appeals to women and to domestic ideology. Noted the Reverend Daniel C. Eddy, "Home is woman's throne, where she maintains her royal court, and sways her queenly authority. It is there that man learns to appreciate her worth, and to realize the sweet and tender influences which she casts around her . . . and there she fills the sphere to which divine providence has called her" (*The Young Woman's Friend*, p. 23). Similarly, another minister, William Thayer, commented, "Indeed such is woman's influence, we may add, that she decides social morality. If her standard of excellence is high, the society in which she moves will be elevated. If otherwise, the morals of the community will be loose. Let her treat religion lightly, and the men will rail about it as infidels of the lowest school" (*The Poor Girl and True Woman*, p. 55).

As a result of these transformations, attendance in mainline Protestant churches rose remarkably. Although women had formed the congregational majority in Protestant churches since the Great Awakening, their presence continued to rise perhaps in response to this new, gentler form of Protestantism. By the second half of the nineteenth century, close to 75 percent of churchgoers were women; by century's end, women comprised the overwhelming majority of the United States domestic and foreign missionary force. Throughout the century, women were pivotal in founding and organizing numerous benevolence organizations and served as the principal educators in Sunday schools. By 1870, 165 women listed themselves as ministers, and many more served as prayer leaders, deaconesses, and evangelists. As leaders and the main members of congregation, women thus helped to maintain the sentimental and domestic thrust of Protestant religion throughout the 1800s.

Finally, the cult of sentimentalism and domesticity fueled and was fueled by America's growing nationalism and the impending domestic and foreign threats to it. Just as sentimentalism may have emerged in response to the unsavory ruthlessness of capitalism, it also may have developed as a means of coping with the harsh, racist, and imperialist realities of Manifest Destiny and slavery. The sentimentalization of the American home and of the downtrodden individuals in society helped both to erase and to call attention to the inequities in American society. This function became most apparent in Stowe's blockbuster novel, *Uncle Tom's Cabin*. By imploring her readers to sympathize with disenfranchised slaves, Stowe foregrounded filial devotion toward a liberal, democratic state where everyone is considered equal and deserving of happiness. Yet, at the same time that she called for the abolition of slavery and the reinstitution of a more united nation by appealing to her readers' sympathy, she also so overly sentimentalized her African American characters that they lacked any real individuality or agency and thus reinforced pernicious racial stereotypes.

Besides being the most popular sentimental novel of the nineteenth century, *Uncle Tom's Cabin* has also been the most widely reviewed text by twentieth-century scholars of domesticity and sentimentalism. Predictably, the interpretations of sen-

timental, domestic texts and objects have varied widely. The final section of this article reviews the dominant critical interpretations of sentimentalism and domesticity. While American sentimentalism has traditionally been viewed in direct opposition to the dominant male tradition of rugged individualism and as a cause of a cultural decline, it also was a complex, conflicted, and powerful force, helping both to advance national and international social reform and to maintain status quo ideals.

INTERPRETATIONS OF SENTIMENTALISM AND DOMESTICITY

One of the arguments in twentieth-century American criticism has been that the dominant nineteenth-century male tradition set itself in direct opposition to the domestic concerns that dominated women's sphere. This viewpoint extends back at least to 1940, when Herbert Ross Brown issued *The Sentimental Novel in America*. Brown argued that sentimental writers failed to enlighten their readers to the "great national drama" and the pressing social questions of the time, such as Manifest Destiny and the rising middle class. As a prominent example, he noted that the "most conspicuous failure of the sentimentalists was their inability to solve the irrepressible problem of slavery" (Samuels, p. xxvi). Two decades later, Leslie Fiedler sounded a similar critique in his *Love and Death in the American Novel* (1960); yet he added an explicit gendered component to his derision of sentimentalism. In his eyes, what made "the American novel ... different from its European prototypes" (p. 11) was its focus on the white male's flight from the woman-centered home into the wilderness inhabited by dark men. For Fiedler, American literature was distinct for its valorization of masculine frontier heroes such as Natty Bumppo and Daniel Boone and its distance from the "sentimental travesties" of domestic fiction. While Fiedler recognized the English novelist Samuel Richardson's role in popularizing the sentimental tradition, he argued that "when women became the chief authors as well as the chief characters of the novel," the result was "a blight, a universal influence which was also a universal calamity" (pp. 82, 75).

The critical derision of sentimental culture culminated in *The Feminization of American Culture* (1977) in which the historian Ann Douglas chastised sentimentality for its "debased religiosity [and] sentimental peddling of Christian belief for its nostalgic value," its "dishonesty," and its conservative anti-intellectualism (pp. 6, 12). She also blamed the rise of domesticity and sentimentalism for the banishment of masculinity and the rise of modern mass culture. According to her, sentimentalism guaranteed the loss of the finest values in Calvinist Protestantism without any replacement of a legitimate form of feminism. Brown, Fiedler, and Douglas to varying degrees all contributed to a rigid demarcation between a laudable, political progressive and masculine high cultural tradition and an inferior, conservative, feminine, popular cultural tradition. Such a viewpoint still presides among some late-twentieth-century critics. In 1986 Richard H. Brodhead wrote that Herman Melville "worked in the same . . . literary and social milieu" as the domestic novelists "but . . . stands not just in a different but in virtually the opposite relation to [domestic fiction] and its cultural accommodations" (*The School of Hawthorne,* p. 20).

Some scholars have offered criticism on slightly different grounds. Unlike Brown who castigated sentimentalism for ignoring important social issues such as slavery, some late-twentieth-century critics noted that sentimentalism often did offer representations of race and slavery. But they lamented "the impotence of sentiment to effect significant change. Sentimental feeling . . . cannot in any way protect individuals against enslavement. Even more troubling, it does little to move individuals to change the system" (Budick, in *Homes and Homelessness,* pp. 309–310). While sentimental objects and texts may have attempted to motivate readers to change their feelings, they never took the extra step of advocating a new law, such as the legal abolition of slavery, or of arguing for specific human rights. Moreover, the exhibition and commercialization of sentimentalism further displaced a genuinely political sense. Even more strident than the claim for the political inefficacy of sentimentalism are the arguments of Saidiya V. Hartman and Laura Wexler, who contended that sentimental texts and images often served to subjugate and dominate marginalized groups. Hartman noted, "Rather than bespeaking the mutuality of social relations or the expressive and affective capacity of the subject, sentiment . . . facilitated subjection, domination, and terror precisely by preying upon the flesh, the heart, and the soul" (*Scenes of Subjection,* p. 5). Analyzing stories of young Native American girls at the Hampton Institute, Wexler revealed how sentimental educational texts used "tender violence" to induce accommodation to white, middle-class culture.

In response to mounting criticisms, in 1985 the academician Jane Tompkins launched an influential defense of sentimentalism. Tompkins argued that rather than "turning away from the world into self-absorption and idle reverie," sentimentalists like Harriet Beecher Stowe were striving for nothing less than a revolution of the world "in the name of the 'family state' under the leadership of Christian women" (*Sensational Designs,* pp. 143–144). Sentimentalists aimed to overturn a thoroughly unjust society, to create a society based on motherly love, and to offer victims of slavery the hope of an afterlife. Instead of lulling their audiences into complacency, these writers—according to Tompkins—helped shaped their readers into sympathetic respondents to the plight of the disadvantaged. Indeed, Stowe's work had such resonating effects that when she was greeted at the White House, President Abraham Lincoln supposedly exclaimed, "So this is the little lady who made this big war" (Wilson, *Patriotic Gore,* p. 3).

Philip Fisher and others have also pointed out the radical potentiality of sentimentalism that "trains and explicates new forms of feeling" by extending subjectivity to marginalized groups and individuals (*Hard Facts,* p. 18). Through sentimental texts, white Americans came to see formerly "subhuman" groups such as blacks, Native Americans, handicapped, and the poor as recognizably human. By "endowing black slaves with feelings, reconstructing them as objects of love rather than objects of use," sentimentalists were able to animate the formerly "dead" with "the preservative impulses of moral and aesthetic sensibility, situating them within the bonds of domestic intimacy" (Merish, *American Literary History,* p. 19).

Other critics emphasized the way sentimentalism and domesticity provided a relatively safe and acceptable way for white, middle-class women to gain public and political power. According to these critics, sentimentality can be interpreted as part of a protofeminist politics. Under the banner of sentimentalism, women assumed leadership roles in religious, reform, and benevolent movements and, by doing so, forged connections, through sympathy and emotion, with women of differing classes, cultures, and religions. In 1877 Frances Willard led prayers and recruited members for her temperance reform organization at some of the prominent American evangelist Dwight Moody's revivals before groups numbering as many as 9,000 persons. By 1897 the Women's Christian Temperance Union had a membership of over 2 million members. By the same year, women comprised 1,000 of the Salvation Army's 1,854 American officers. By 1882 at least 16 women's missionary societies had dispatched 694 single female missionaries and raised almost 6 million dollars. According to Barbara Welter in a 1980 article she wrote for *Women in American Religion*, by 1880 women constituted over 57 percent of the active missionary force.

Domesticity charged by its affectional component, sentiment, helped to forge distinct gender roles for the nineteenth-century white middle class. But the boundaries between the public masculine realm and the feminine private one were permeable. The private, feminized space of the home both permeated and buttressed the public, male arena of politics and the marketplace, and sentimental values were used to support women's entry into the wider civic realm. In the 1990s, critics began to accentuate the permeability of another gendered boundary—that between male, rugged individualism and female sentimentalism. As Douglas Anderson wrote, "It is much too simple to continue to assume, for example, that Hawthorne, Thoreau, Melville, and Whitman constitute a canonical aesthetic tradition that is opposed in subject and style to the sentimental domestic spirit of their day" (*A House Divided*, p. 5). According to Anderson and an array of other critics, numerous canonical male writers such as Herman Melville, Nathaniel Hawthorne, Henry David Thoreau, Ralph Waldo Emerson, Mark Twain, Walt Whitman, Oliver Wendell Holmes, Frank Norris, and Theodore Dreiser "all deploy the discourse of sentiment in their works" (Chapman and Hendler, *Sentimental Men*, p. 7). Lora Romero went even further to break down dualistic gendered assumptions by questioning whether women actually were the primary producers and consumers of sentimental texts. She noted that not only has no scholar "attempted to verify his or her claims about the gender composition of the antebellum novel-reading audience through primary data," but "even if . . . the best-selling novels of the period written by women outsold the best-sellers written by men, the book-publishing industry was almost entirely in the hands of men" (*Home Fronts*, p. 13). The latter point, of course, greatly complicates the issue of who actually controlled or was controlled by the culture of sentimental domesticity.

Regardless of who produced or consumed it or whether it was used for radical or reactionary ends, nineteenth-century sentimental domesticity was a vibrant discourse because it offered men and women meaningful and rich symbols and an expansive logic through which to perceive and take action in their world. It was powerful precisely for its permeability. Those who were allowed inside the domestic realm depended on the political, economic, religious, racial, or gendered agenda at hand. Moreover, although it enjoyed its heyday in the period between 1830 and 1870, the ideology of sentimentalism and domesticity did not cease as the nineteenth century's end approached. Women's postwar campaign for the vote and their increasing influx into the professions of education, medicine, religion, and social services helped to propel a new, more institutionalized form of domesticity and to build the seeds for the system of social welfare that became one of the hallmarks of the twentieth century.

See also **Conflicting Ideals of Colonial Womanhood; Gender, Social Class, Race, and Material Life** *(in this volume);* **Women** *(volume 2);* **Family; Gentility and Manners** *(volume 3); and other articles in this section.*

BIBLIOGRAPHY

Albers, Patricia, and Beatrice Medicine. *The Hidden Half: Studies of Plains Indian Women.* Washington, D.C., 1983.

Anderson, Douglas. *A House Divided: Domesticity and Community in American Literature.* Cambridge, Mass., 1990.

Barnes, Elizabeth. *States of Sympathy: Seduction and Democracy in the American Novel.* New York, 1997.

Blackwell, Elizabeth. *Essays in Medical Sociology.* Vol. 2. New York, 1972.

Blake, Lillie Devereux. *Woman's Place Today.* New York, 1883.

Bordin, Ruth. *Frances Willard: A Biography.* Chapel Hill, N.C., 1986.

Brereton, Virginia Lieson, and Christa Ressmeyer Klein. "American Women in Ministry: A History of Protestant Beginning Points." In *Women in American Religion,* edited by Janet James. Philadelphia, 1980.

Brodhead, Richard H. *The School of Hawthorne.* New York, 1986.

Brown, Herbert Ross. *The Sentimental Novel in America, 1789–1860.* Durham, N.C., 1940.

Budick, Emily Miller. "When a Home Is Not a House: Nineteenth-Century American Fiction and the Domestication of the Nation." In *Homes and Homelessness in the Victorian Imagination,* edited by Murray Baumgarten and H. M. Daleski, pp. 307–321. New York, 1998.

Burnett, Edmund C., ed. *Letters of Members of the Continental Congress.* Vol. 7. Washington, D.C., 1934.

Burnham, Michelle. *Captivity and Sentiment: Cultural Exchange in American Literature, 1682–1861.* Hanover, N.H., 1997.

Burstein, Andrew. *Sentimental Democracy: The Evolution of America's Romantic Self-Image.* New York, 1999.

Camfield, Gregg. *Sentimental Twain: Samuel Clemens in the Maze of Moral Philosophy.* Philadelphia, 1994.

Carby, Hazel V. *Reconstructing Womanhood: The Emergence of the Afro-American Woman Novelist.* New York, 1987.

Chapman, Mary, and Glenn Hendler, eds. *Sentimental Men: Masculinity and the Politics of Affect in American Culture.* Berkeley, Calif., 1999.

Child, Lydia Maria. *Letters from New York.* 1843. Reprint, edited by Bruce Mills, Athens, Ga., 1998.

Cott, Nancy F. *The Bonds of Womanhood: "Woman's Sphere" in New England, 1780–1835.* New Haven, Conn., 1977.

DeBerg, Betty A. *Ungodly Women: Gender and the First Wave of American Fundamentalism.* Minneapolis, Minn., 1990.

Douglas, Ann. *The Feminization of American Culture.* New York, 1988.

Eddy, Daniel Clark. *The Young Woman's Friend; or, The Duties, Trials, Loves, and Hopes of Woman.* 1859.

Elmer, Jonathan. "Terminate or Liquidate? Poe, Sensationalism and the Sentimental Tradition." In *The American Face of Edgar Allan Poe,* edited by Shawn Rosenheim and Stephen Rachman, pp. 91–120. Baltimore, 1995.

Fiedler, Leslie A. *Love and Death in the American Novel.* New York, 1992.

Fisher, Philip. *Hard Facts: Setting and Form in the American Novel.* New York, 1985.

Fogel, Robert William. *Without Consent or Contract: The Rise and Fall of American Slavery.* New York, 1989.

Ginzberg, Lori D. *Women and the Work of Benevolence: Morality, Politics, and Class in the Nineteenth-Century United States.* New Haven, Conn., 1990.

Goshgarian, G. M. *To Kiss the Chastening Rod: Domestic Fiction and Sexual Ideology in the American Renaissance.* Ithaca, N.Y., 1992.

Gutiérrez, Ramón A. *When Jesus Came, the Corn Mothers Went Away: Marriage, Sexuality and Power in New Mexico, 1500–1846.* Stamford, Conn., 1991.

Hardesty, Nancy A. "Minister or Prophet? Or As Mother?" In *Women in New Worlds: Historical Perspectives on the Wesleyan Tradition,* vol. 1, edited by Hilah F. Thomas and Rosemary Skinner Keller. Nashville, Tenn., 1981.

———. *Women Called to Witness: Evangelical Feminism in the Nineteenth Century.* Nashville, Tenn., 1984.

453

Hartman, Saidiya V. *Scenes of Subjection: Terror, Slavery, and Self-Making in Nine-teenth-Century America.* New York, 1997.

hooks, bell. *Ain't I a Woman: Black Women and Feminism.* Boston, 1981.

Merish, Lori. "Sentimental Consumption: Harriet Beecher Stowe and the Aesthetics of Middle-Class Ownership." *American Literary History* 1, no. 1 (spring 1996): 1–33.

Noble, Marianne. "An Ecstasy of Apprehension: The Gothic Pleasures of Sentimental Fiction." In *American Gothic: New Interventions in a National Narrative,* edited by Robert K. Martin and Eric Savoy, pp. 163–182. Iowa City, Iowa, 1998.

Romero, Lora. *Home Fronts: Domesticity and Its Critics in the Antebellum United States.* Durham, N.C., 1997.

Ryan, Mary P. *Women in Public: Between Banners and Ballots, 1825–1880.* Baltimore, 1990.

Samuels, Shirley. "Introduction." In *The Culture of Sentiment: Race, Gender and Sentimentality in Nineteenth-Century America,* edited by Shirley Samuels. New York, 1992.

Schultz, Elizabeth. "The Sentimental Subtext of *Moby-Dick:* Melville's Response to the 'World of Woe.'" *ESQ* 42, no. 1 (1996): 29–49.

Smith, Adam. *The Theory of Moral Sentiments.* Edited by D. D. Raphael and E. L. Macfie. Oxford, 1976.

Stansell, Christine. *City of Women: Sex and Class in New York, 1789–1860.* Urbana, Ill., 1987.

Stowe, Harriet Beecher. *Uncle Tom's Cabin.* 1852. Reprint, New York, 1981.

Thayer, William. *The Poor Girl and True Woman; or, Elements of Woman's Success.* Boston, 1859.

Thomson, Rosemarie Garland. "Crippled Girls and Lame Old Women: Sentimental Spectacles of Sympathy in Nineteenth-Century American Women's Writing." In *Nineteenth-Century American Women Writers: A Critical Reader,* edited by Karen Kilcup, pp. 128–145. Oxford, 1998.

Tompkins, Jane. *Sensational Designs: The Cultural Work of American Fiction, 1790–1860.* New York, 1985.

Warner, Susan. *The Wide, Wide World.* 1850. Reprint, New York, 1987.

Welter, Barbara. "The Cult of True Womanhood." *American Quarterly* 18 (summer 1966): 151–174.

———. "She Hath Done What She Could: Protestant Women's Missionary Careers in Nineteenth-Century America." In *Women in American Religion,* edited by Janet James. Philadelphia, 1980.

Wexler, Laura. "Tender Violence: Literary Eavesdropping, Domestic Fiction, and Educational Reform." In *The Culture of Sentiment,* edited by Shirley Samuels, pp. 9–38. New York, 1992.

White, Deborah Gray. *Ar'n't I a Woman? Female Slaves in the Plantation South.* New York, 1985.

Whitman, Walt. "The Sleepers." In *Complete Poetry and Selected Prose,* pp. 546–547, New York, 1982.

Wilson, Edmund. *Patriotic Gore: Studies in the Literature of the American Civil War.* 1962. Reprint, Boston, 1984.

Yellin, Jean Fagan. *Women and Sisters: The Antislavery Feminists in American Culture.* New Haven, Conn., 1989.

SECESSION, WAR, AND UNION

Allen C. Guelzo

Unlike civil wars based on competing ethnicities or religions, the American Civil War (1861–1865) arose from a complex conflict of ideology and geography. The ideological conflict clustered around both political and moral poles. The political aspect concerned the different jurisdictions of the American federal and state governments, and whether the states had the right of secession from the federal Union; the moral aspect concerned the morality of black slavery as a labor system and its incompatibility with the universal freedoms articulated at the founding of the American republic. But actual conflict over these ideas only arose when they intersected with the dynamics of American geography. Those who defended slaveholding, and who believed that the federal government had no power to curtail it, were concentrated in the fifteen contiguous states of the American South where black slavery had been legalized. This created a potential political mass, fully capable of organizing itself and taking coordinated action, up to the point of joint secession and reorganization as a separate nation-state.

Geography also played another role in triggering civil war. The opening of the American West through the Louisiana Purchase (1803) and the Mexican Cession (1848) set off an escalating cycle of tension between the Southern slave states and the Northern free states. Southerners believed that since slaves were legal property, carrying slaves with them into the new territories was as fully justified as the common right of carrying any other property. Few Northerners were committed to abolishing black slavery, but they had no wish to see it spread as a labor system outside the Southern states, and many hoped that confining it to the South would guarantee its slow and painless extinction. The prospect of expansion angered Northerners and led to the organization of a Northern-based political party, the Republicans, in 1856. Four years later, the Republicans were able to elect their candidate, Abraham Lincoln, as president, on a no-extension platform.

The Southern states viewed the Republican victory as a political hijacking of the federal government, and between December 1860 and May 1861 eleven of the fifteen slave states announced that they had seceded from the federal Union and created a separate nation, the Confederate States of America. Their seizures of federal property in those states, especially the attack on Fort Sumter in Charleston Harbor in April 1861, forced the Lincoln administration to act. Lincoln denied that a right of secession existed in law and insisted that the Confederacy was merely a domestic insurrection which he intended to suppress. The suppression turned out to be long and costly. But the costs ran against the Confederates, who could not withstand the long-term strain imposed by the North's superior resources.

The Civil War ended in April 1865, along with the permanent abolition of slavery and the occupation of the Southern states by federal armies. As an ideological war, the principal victory was won for free labor over slavery and for the supremacy and survival of the federal Union. But the carnage of the war placed a discouraging hand on the confidence of significant sectors of American culture, especially American Protestant Christianity and American moral philosophy, laying the foundations for the rise of secularism and pragmatism.

THE IDEA OF THE UNION

The Civil War posed in a dramatic way two political questions which had remained ambiguous since the founding: whether the Constitution had created a perpetual Union of states, and what sovereignty that Union possessed. Those who argued for the permanence and sovereignty of the Union cited four practical considerations to promote their claims. The Union must be perpetual and sovereign so that (*a*) it could devise policies to protect the common interests of the states against foreign political encroachment and economic competition, (*b*) it could monitor and arbitrate commercial and legal disputes among the states, (*c*) it could reduce cultural differences that might weaken or threaten American stability, and (*d*) it could supervise expansion and ensure that new additions of territory to the United States would be organized along the same republican principles as the first states.

By the 1830s the idea of the Union had acquired almost mystical overtones. It was invoked as the guarantee of American prosperity, as the location of disinterested republican patriotism, and as a symbol of cultural harmony. In 1847, Alexander Stephens of Georgia could declare, "The Union is not only the life, but the soul of these States." The most famous voice for this almost-sacred notion of national Union was Daniel Webster, whose peroration to his second Senate debate in 1830 with Robert Hayne linked the very survival of American freedom to the Union:

> While the Union lasts, we have high, exciting, gratifying prospects spread out before us. . . . When my eyes shall be turned to behold for the last time the sun in heaven, may I not see him shining on the broken and dishonored fragments of a once glorious Union; on States dissevered, discordant, belligerent; on a land rent with civil feuds, or drenched, it may be, in fraternal blood! Let their last feeble and lingering glance rather behold the gorgeous ensign of the republic . . . not a stripe erased or polluted, nor a single star obscured, bearing for its motto, no such miserable . . . words of delusion and folly, "Liberty first and Union afterwards"; but everywhere, spread all over in characters of living light . . . that other sentiment, dear to every true American heart,—Liberty *and* Union, now and for ever, one and inseparable! (C. M. Wiltse, ed., *The Papers of Daniel Webster*, vol. 2, pp. 287–348)

The idea of the Union retained and strengthened its practical appeal as well. The successful recruitment and development of the various Protestant denominations (whose memberships and organizations were national rather than sectional), the new American professional and scholarly organizations, and American higher education and law all assumed the priority of the Union. The great series of U.S. Supreme Court decisions handed down through the long tenure of Chief Justice John Marshall (1801–1835) all underscored the superiority of the federal government and the immunity of contract, both in commerce and land, from interference by local and state authorities. Above all, the supremacy of the Union was key to Henry Clay's "American System" of government-sponsored economic development, protective tariffs for American manufacturing, and federally-funded "internal improvements."

The Union had the greatest appeal to those whose worlds were still being made in the nineteenth century. But this meant that it was likely to generate less enthusiasm in the overwhelmingly agrarian world of the South than in Webster's Northern states. Southern politics was dominated by a landed gentry whose interests were better served by local or state protections of their institutions—including slavery—than by identification with the national Union. The charismatic John Randolph of Roanoke spoke for many Southerners when he announced that the founders had never intended to create more than a league of sovereign states: "The Constitution is not the work of the amalgamated population of the then existing confederacy, but the offspring of the States." The states made the Union, and they could unmake it if they desired. "They have only to refuse to send members to the other branch of the Legislature [the Senate], or to appoint Electors of President and Vice-President, and the thing is done."

Southern skepticism about national sovereignty was articulated as early as 1798, in the Virginia and Kentucky resolutions, which declared that the Union was only a compact of already-sovereign states and that federal legislation which overrode that sovereignty (in this case, the Alien and Sedition acts) could be nullified by the states. More southern resistance to the sovereignty of the Union surfaced in the 1820s and 1830s over Indian removal. When the Creek and Cherokee tribes appealed to federal treaties and courts to resist eviction by southern state governments, irritated southerners threatened resistance to federal intervention on the grounds of state sovereignty. In 1832, fury over the tariffs proposed by Henry Clay's "American System" drove South Carolinians to nullify federal tariff legislation.

Although a confrontation between South Carolina and President Andrew Jackson was averted, the tariff crisis gave a platform to John C. Calhoun (who emerged as the great champion of South Carolina) to articulate a view of the Union as limited and temporary. The Union, Calhoun argued, is only "the government of a community of States, and not the government of a single State or nation." The sheer diversity of American ethnic and sectional politics and culture made the idea of a paramount national Union impossible. "So numerous and diversified are the interests of our country, that they could not be fairly represented in a single government." Calhoun demanded that this "diversity of interests" be fairly recognized for what it was, and that future federal legislation be subjected to a subsequent round of concurrent approval by the states. Without that as a shield against creeping Unionism, Calhoun saw no alternative for South Carolina but withdrawal from the Union. In contrast to the Unionists, curtailment of the Union was most attractive to those who believed that the best world had already been made and did not need improving, except perhaps in terms of geographical expansion.

It was not only regions which divided over the idea of the Union. The Democratic Party, founded by Jefferson (one of the authors of the Virginia and Kentucky resolutions) and dominated by southern agricultural interests, tended to define the Union mostly in terms southerners found comfortable. James Fenimore Cooper, in *The American Democrat* (1838), repeated the basic contention that "the government of the United States was formed by the several states of the Union" and "all power which is not granted to the federal authority, remain in the states themselves." But many Democrats, especially Andrew Jackson, actively deplored the efforts of Calhounite extremists "to sow the seeds of discord between different parts of the United States and to place party divisions directly upon geographical distinctions." Meanwhile, the Whig Party (which rose in the 1830s under Henry Clay to become the opposition party to Jackson) revered the Union as a metaphor for the overall Whig strategy of promoting national economic development and cultural homogeneity. For Clay, the Union was both end and means. "If anyone desire to know the leading and paramount object of my public life," Clay wrote in 1844, "the preservation of the Union will furnish the key." And as proof of that devotion, the national compromise legislation the Whigs crafted for avoiding conflict and saving the Union in 1820, in 1832, and again in 1850 became their greatest public policy legacy.

The issue which proved the most resistant to compromise was slavery. Until the 1850s, northerners had maintained a reluctant silence over slavery on the assumption that the great Missouri Compromise of 1820 (which barred slavery from most of the Louisiana Purchase) was a gentlemen's agreement which forbade them from meddling with slavery so long as slavery sought no expansion. After the Mexican Cession and the Kansas-Nebraska Act, that agreement seemed to have been thrown to the winds by an aggressive and expansionist "slave power" in the South. Angry northerners called for the restoration of the Missouri Compromise, or for the repeal or defiance of national legislation (like the

Fugitive Slave Act of 1850) that protected slavery. Through the 1850s, three attitudes toward the Union emerged or hardened: (a) southern Calhounites now openly attacked the Union as a threat to southern states' rights, cultural autonomy, and economic health, (b) northern antislavery Whigs and Democrats united, not so much in opposition to slavery as in opposition to southern threats of disunion, and experimented with "fusion" politics, and (c) northern abolitionists, such as William Lloyd Garrison, applauded disunion as a way of disencumbering the North morally from contamination by slavery. The Whigs gradually expired as a viable national party after 1852, allowing a successful "fusion" of northern Whigs and numerous antislavery Democrats to take shape as the new Republican Party. Many onetime Whigs of the Northwest and upper South struggled to create still another Union-saving strategy. But the Republican electoral triumph in November 1860 was the South's handwriting on the wall.

The Republican president, Abraham Lincoln, was an "old Henry Clay Whig" whose basic instinct was to find a path of compromise without making concessions to the South. For the first year of the war Lincoln strove to downplay the slavery issue and confine his war aims purely to the restoration of the Union. He had three reasons for this minimalism. First, the strategic slave states of the upper South—Missouri, Kentucky, Maryland, Delaware—had not joined the Confederates, and Lincoln feared that any effort to strike directly at slavery would drive those states into secession and make the restoration of the Union hopeless. Second, what remained of the Northern Democrats was still politically substantial, and might rally to a presidential call to restore the Union but not to a crusade to liberate black slaves. Third, he was convinced that the Confederacy represented only a coup by the plantation aristocrats, and that loyal Southern Unionists would soon retake control if the North aimed only at restoring the "Constitution as it is, the Union as it was."

Far from responding to Lincoln's genteel Unionism, however, the outnumbered Confederates fought the Union armies to a surprising standstill, relying on slave labor behind the lines to release its white citizens for military service. This led Lincoln to conclude that there was no way to restore the Union *except* by striking at slavery, as the chief prop of secession. Lincoln not only freed the Confederacy's slaves by military decree in his Emancipation Proclamation of 1 January 1863 but also proceeded to arm and recruit former slaves and free blacks and turn them against their onetime Southern masters. Lincoln never ceased hoping that Southern Unionism would eventually rise and overthrow the secessionist regime of the Confederacy. His re-election campaign in 1864 ran a Southern Unionist, Andrew Johnson, as vice president and temporarily reinvented the Republican Party as the "National Union" Party. But it was the war, not Unionism, which ground down the Confederates and brought them to surrender in the spring of 1865.

THE WAR AS REVOLUTION

The Southern Confederacy adopted two ways of talking about itself in political terms. The first insisted that secession was legal and justifiable, and only represented the resumption of powers temporarily surrendered to the old federal government at the time of the ratification of the federal Constitution. "The right of the people to self-government in its fullest and broadest extent has been a cardinal principle of American liberty," declared Judah Benjamin. "By the same power under which one Legislature can repeal the act of a former Legislature, so can one convention of the people duly assembled . . . it is in strict and logical deduction from this fundamental principle of American liberty, that South Carolina has adopted the form in which she has declared her independence." Arguments for legal continuity were embodied in the new Confederate Constitution, which was adopted in February 1861 and which reproduced most of the provisions of the old federal Constitution: a bicameral legislature, an executive president, and an independent judiciary. And although the Confederate preamble specified that each of the eleven Southern states was acting in "its sovereign and independent character," even the Confederates acknowledged that this would form a "permanent federal government." If anything, it would be an improved version of the old government, suppressing the spirit of party politics and holding up a model of republican unity, simplicity, and self-denial.

Other Confederate voices were impatient with such conservatism, and preferred to speak of the Confederacy as a revolution. The onetime Unionist Alexander Stephens declared that the Confederacy was an entirely new kind of nation, and secession "one of the greatest revolutions in the annals of the world," because the Confederacy was "the first in the history of the world" to be deliberately founded on "the great truth that the negro is not equal to the white man." This would make the creation of the Confederacy not only a revolution against the federal government but against liberal political economy and the Enlightenment as well. "The Southern Revolution of 1861," wrote George Fitzhugh in 1863, "was . . . a solemn protest against the doctrines of natural liberty, human equality and the social contract, as taught by Locke and the American sages of 1776, and an equally solemn protest against the doctrines of Adam Smith, Franklin, Say, Tom Paine and the rest of the infidel political economists."

Some Confederates hoped that this antiliberal turn might parallel the monarchical restorations in post-1848 Europe and reorder social and political relationships which had become too coarse and democratized under the old Constitution. The principal Richmond newspaper noticed "Confederate citizens expressing distrust of the permanency of Democratic institutions in this country; sighing for gradations of rank, hinting that 'the mob' ought not to rule." Others, like the pious Confederate general Thomas Jonathan ("Stonewall") Jackson, hoped that such a counter-Enlightenment revolution might allow for a reestablishment of Christianity in an explicitly Christian republic and compel "the Confederate States . . . to adjust the working of their institutions" to "recognize the rights of God more distinctly" so "that the Christian Church should put forth more saving power in society."

Such antiliberal postures played directly into the hands of Abraham Lincoln, who claimed that secession was neither a legal action nor a revolutionary one, but rather an antidemocratic insurrection staged by the slave-holding elite and enforced by its military. Although Lincoln fully agreed with Benjamin's first premise, that "the people" always have a "*revolutionary* right to dismember, or overthrow . . . the existing government . . . whenever they shall grow weary of it," he did not see in Southern secession anything which resembled a practical movement of the people. The Confederacy was "a Power existing in pronunciamento only," and Lincoln believed in 1861 that "it may well be questioned whether there is . . . a majority of the legally qualified voters of any State . . . in favor of disunion." Two years later, Lincoln reiterated that "the strength of the rebellion, is its military—its army."

That absence of genuine popular uprising deprived the Confederacy of any revolutionary justification and threw it back onto the legal argument about the possibility of secession, an argument which Lincoln rejected with contempt. "Our States have neither more, nor less power, than that reserved to them, in the Union, by the Constitution—

no one of them ever having been a State *out* of the Union," Lincoln explained in 1861. What secession really represented was not the employment of a legitimate legal option but another form of attack on liberal democracy, this time philosophical rather than revolutionary:

> This is essentially a People's contest. On the side of the Union, it is a struggle for maintaining in the world, that form, and substance of government, whose leading object is, to elevate the condition of men—to lift artificial weights from all shoulders— to clear the paths of laudable pursuit for all—to afford all, an unfettered start, and a fair chance, in the race of life. (Basler and Basler, eds., *The Collected Works of Abraham Lincoln,* vol. 4, p. 438)

Curiously, it is Lincoln who is most often cast as the "revolutionary" of the Civil War era. This charge was leveled during the war by disgruntled Southerners who believed that Lincoln's administration would became the model for "consolidated" national government (marked by tariffs, government-funded public projects, and a new national banking system) and by Northern civil libertarians who charged that Lincoln was responsible for unlawful suspensions of the writ of habeas corpus, as well as for military arrests and trials of civilians in the North. This ascription was renewed in a much more complimentary sense by twentieth-century progressives who hailed Lincoln for creating a modern centralized state, and for successfully replacing liberty and the Constitution as the preeminent national ideological values with equality and the Declaration of Independence.

Odd as it is to be praised and condemned for the same actions, Lincoln was actually much more cautious and restrained than either view assumes. Lincoln's domestic agenda of tariffs and banking was really only an extension of Henry Clay's "American System." Much as he termed the war a rebellion, Confederate captives were treated as prisoners of war rather than as insurrectionists. Lincoln made no provision for postwar treason trials of Confederate officials, proposed no drastic postwar retribution, and discouraged making the war an excuse for a "remorseless revolutionary struggle." What might be construed as Lincoln's one genuinely revolutionary act—the Emancipation Proclamation—warned against slave uprisings and treated emancipation as a wartime confiscation measure (similar to the confiscation of enemy military property). It was not Lincoln but the radicals of the Republican Party who most nearly resembled revolutionary figures by calling for the destruction of Confederate state identities upon reconquest, the extension of broad civil equality to the freedpeople, and the reconstruction of the Southern economy along liberal free-labor lines. But few of the radical plans came to fruition, and even those that did were hedged by doubts within the radical wing itself.

THE WAR AS INTELLECTUAL SOLVENT

Lincoln's caution in directing the war was matched by the response of most Northern and Southern intellectuals. A significant number of the families of prominent Northern intellectuals were involved in the war—Oliver Wendell Holmes's son and namesake was severely wounded at Antietam in 1862; William James's brother, Garth Wilkinson James, was commissioned as an officer with the black troops of the Fifty-fourth Massachusetts and was wounded in 1863 in their famous attack on Battery Wagner; Horace Binney, the grandson and namesake of the famed Philadelphia jurist, served as a lieutenant in the 118th Pennsylvania; Charles Grandison Finney's son-in-law Jacob Dolson Cox rose to become a major general. But few of them were prepared for the war as an intellectual event, and in case after case, the war produced not vindication but severe cultural confusion and dislocation.

Although abolitionist radicalism was supposed to have its epicenter in Massachusetts, a surprising number of New England intellectuals struggled to ignore the war altogether, either by avoiding military service (like Charles Sanders Peirce), going abroad (like Charles William Eliot), or by simply averting their eyes (like Ralph Waldo Emerson, who discouraged his son Edward from enlisting and who had little to say about the war until after emancipation). The blue-blood elite of the mid-Atlantic, represented by Horace Binney, George Templeton Strong, Henry Bellows, and George Boker, were generally more supportive of the war. "The people of whom my family and friends are to be a part will never again be fooled with the notion of a confederation of sovereigns," Binney wrote defiantly in 1861, "but belong confessedly and openly to *one nation . . .* as much as to one God." But many (like Strong) were dismissive of Lincoln as an inexperienced bumbler, and many others hoped that the demands of the war might provide an opportunity, as much for restoring their own class to social and political leadership as for restoring the Union.

The war was greeted with far greater enthusiasm by Protestant evangelicals. The antislavery agitation of the prewar decades had split the major denominations into separate northern and southern halves—Southern and Northern Baptists, Southern and Northern Presbyterians, and so forth—presaging the division of the Union itself, and feeding Southern confidence that disunion could be achieved painlessly and peacefully. Northern evangelicals, who were predominantly antislavery, hoped the war would help them achieve denominational reunion and larger spheres of influence in public life. Some had so blended Unionism and revivalism that the war brought them to the point of promising the millennium as a reward for Union victory.

The actual experience of the war and Reconstruction held very different lessons, and much greater disappointments, than any of these Northerners had expected. This was largely because few Americans anticipated the scale of violence and dislocation the war would bring. The United States in 1860 lacked a deep military tradition. The wars fought by Americans within the living memory of the Civil War generation had been limited in scope, and the Civil War armies were overwhelmingly composed of temporary volunteers. Nothing had prepared Americans for the savagery, carnage, and terror they met with on Civil War battlefields. For figures like Ambrose Bierce, Robert Ingersoll, and Mark Twain, the shattering encounter of combat undercut all confidence in the serene, reasonable verities of Christianity. Even the devout James A. Garfield admitted to William Dean Howells that at the sight of "dead men whom other men had killed, something went out of him, the habit of his lifetime, that never came back again: the sense of the sacredness of life and the impossibility of destroying it." Civilians, too, had to endure disruption, flight, and the decimating losses of neighbors and relatives. The character in Elizabeth Phelps's *Gates Ajar* (1871) who receives word of her brother's death in the army felt "as if the world were spinning around in the light and wind and laughter, and God just stretched down His hand one morning and put it out."

The war also struck a blow at the respectability of American philosophy. The prevailing tradition of collegiate moral philosophy, rooted in the popular textbooks of Francis Wayland, Francis Bowen, and Mark Hopkins, had promised reliable answers to questions of public ethics based on the certainty of natural law and the intuitions of a "moral sense." But the moral philosophers had divided disastrously and embarrassingly over the most obvious question in public ethics, slavery, and that division undercut the authority with which they could speak to any other issue. Hardly any part of Northern society was more conspicuous by its silence during the war than its public philosophers; the burden of defending the Union cause fell instead to lawyers like Binney, Francis Lieber, and Charles Janeway Stille, or literati like Edward Everett Hale and James Russell Lowell. Its most important poetry came from a noncombatant, Walt Whitman, and its most important art forms were the popular song and the parlor print. Little wonder that by the mid-1870s, Charles Sanders Peirce and William James in Cambridge had already begun to lay the foundations of a pragmatism which would decisively sweep away moral philosophy's preoccupation with epistemological foundationalism and substitute for it a philosophy of practice and satisfaction.

Northern evangelicals, likewise, found little resembling the millennium in the goatish greed of the postwar years. In a gesture of reconciliation, Lincoln had warned at the close of the war that no confident pronouncements about God's purposes were really possible. North and South "read the same Bible, and pray to the same God, and each invokes His aid against the other," Lincoln observed in his Second Inaugural. Both could not be right. If anything, both had been wrong about God's intentions, and both had been punished equally for slavery by this war. Bereft of certainty that they alone had enjoyed God's approval, Northern evangelicals also faced renewed attacks on the veracity of the Bible from Darwinian science and a steady disengagement of the Protestant churches from public life, as if too much had been staked and lost on the Civil War to justify any further such risks. "I am somewhat startled at the decay of faith . . . and of scepticism among men of the world," complained Princeton Seminary's Charles Hodge. "Among the masses speculative faith a few years ago seemed to be the rule. I fear the reverse is true now."

For no one, however, did the war pose greater intellectual tragedies than for Southerners. Southern intellectuals like Edmund Ruffin, George Fitzhugh, and James Henry Hammond had struggled for a place as thinkers in the agrarian world of slave-holding society, and they hoped they had found it before the war by organizing themselves as the first phalanx of Southern apologists for slavery. Ruffin believed that slavery was "an institution of divine origin, and manifestly designed and used by the all-wise and all-good Creator to forward his beneficent purposes." The coming of the war offered them the additional opportunity to make themselves into the arbiters of the South's values. "The political revolution in which we are now engaged makes necessary an intellectual one," claimed a North Carolinian, and the *Southern Literary Mes-*

senger urged Southern writers to discern "the great social and philosophic truths" which lay behind the war.

Yet many of the Southern intellectuals were harassed with doubts about the legitimacy of slavery. James Henley Thornwell, the most talented of the South's theologians, could only defend slavery as a social necessity, not as a divine institution. "Upon an earth radiant with the smile of heaven, or in the Paradise of God, we can no more picture the figure of a slave than we can picture the figures of the halt, the maimed, the lame, and the blind," Thornwell warned. On the eve of the war, he privately confessed that "he had made up his mind to move . . . for the gradual emancipation of the negro, as the only measure that would give peace to the country." Once the war began those doubts were temporarily silenced, and Southern intellectuals bent to the task of intellectual nation-building by delineating a uniquely Southern version of American culture, even down to the formulation of "Confederate" mathematics and grammar textbooks. But the slow collapse of Confederate military strength and infrastructure, and the unwillingness of foreign nations to interfere on the South's behalf, forced Southerners to confront the demoralizing possibility that God had abandoned them and that they had blindly dedicated themselves to an error. "The idolized expectation of a separate nationality, of a social life and literature and civilization of our own . . . all this has perished," mourned the Richmond Presbyterian pastor Moses Hoge, "and I feel like a shipwrecked mariner thrown up like a seaweed on a desert shore."

For both North and South, the Civil War proved to be an unhinging event, undermining philosophies of certainty and theologies of providence, and opening a path toward secularism, experimentation, and the crassest forms of commercial indulgence. A great suffering had been endured, slavery abolished, and the Union saved. But the suffering had become detached from meaning, and the freed slaves given little more than mere freedom. Only the Union survived without ambivalence.

See also **The Idea of the South; Antebellum Charleston; Anti-Statism** *(volume 2); and other articles in this section.*

BIBLIOGRAPHY

The Idea of the Union

Blau, Joseph, ed. *Social Theories of Jacksonian Democracy.* New York, 1954.

Calhoun, John C. *Union and Liberty: The Political Philosophy of John C. Calhoun.* Edited by Ross M. Lence. Indianapolis, Ind., 1992.

Cheseborough, David B., ed. *God Ordained This War: Sermons on the Sectional Crisis, 1830–1865.* Columbia, S.C., 1991.

Cooper, James Fenimore. *The American Democrat.* Cooperstown, N.Y., 1838.

Foner, Eric. *Free Soil, Free Labor, Free Men: The Ideology of the Republican Party before the Civil War.* New York, 1970.

Guelzo, Allen C. *The Crisis of the American Republic: A History of the Civil War and Reconstruction Era.* New York, 1995.

Holt, Michael F. *The Rise and Fall of the American Whig Party: Jacksonian Politics and the Onset of the Civil War.* New York, 1999.

Watson, Harry L. *Liberty and Power: The Politics of Jacksonian America.* New York, 1990.

Welter, Rush. *The Mind of America, 1820–1860.* New York, 1975.

White, G. Edward. *The Marshall Court and Cultural Change, 1815–1835.* New York, 1991.

The War as Revolution

Aaron, Daniel. *The Unwritten War: American Writers and the Civil War.* New York, 1973.

461

Belz, Herman. *Abraham Lincoln, Constitutionalism, and Equal Rights in the Civil War Era*. New York, 1998.

Beringer, Richard E., et al. *Why the South Lost the Civil War*. Athens, Ga., 1986.

Binney, Charles C. *The Life of Horace Binney*. Philadelphia, 1903.

Faust, Drew Gilpin. *The Creation of Confederate Nationalism: Ideology and Identity in the Civil War South*. Baton Rouge, La., 1988.

Frederickson, George M. *The Inner Civil War: Northern Intellectuals and the Crisis of the Union*. New York, 1965.

Freidel, Frank, ed. *Union Pamphlets of the Civil War*. 2 vols. Cambridge, Mass., 1967.

Lincoln, Abraham. *The Collected Works of Abraham Lincoln*. Edited by Roy P. Basler and Christian B. Basler. 9 vols. New Brunswick, N.J., 1953.

Moorhead, James H. *American Apocalypse: Yankee Protestants and the Civil War, 1860–1869*. New Haven, Conn., 1978.

Paludan, Phillip Shaw. *A People's Contest: The Union and the Civil War, 1861–1865*. New York, 1988.

Rable, George C. *The Confederate Republic: A Revolution against Politics*. Chapel Hill, N.C., 1994.

Strong, George Templeton. *Diary of the Civil War, 1860–1865*. Edited by Allan Nevins. New York, 1962.

Thomas, Emory M. *The Confederate Nation, 1861–1865*. New York, 1979.

Wakelyn, Jon L., ed. *Southern Pamphlets on Secession, November 1860–April 1861*. Chapel Hill, N.C., 1996.

The War as Intellectual Solvent

Carter, Paul A. *The Spiritual Crisis of the Gilded Age*. DeKalb, Ill., 1971.

Faust, Drew Gilpin. *A Sacred Circle: The Dilemma of the Intellectual in the Old South, 1840–1860*. Baltimore, 1977.

James, Henry. *Charles W. Eliot: President of Harvard University, 1869–1909*. 2 vols. New York, 1930.

Kazin, Alfred. *God and the American Writer*. New York, 1997.

Rose, Anne C. *Victorian America and the Civil War*. New York, 1992.

Stevenson, Louise L. *The Victorian Homefront: American Thought and Culture, 1860–1880*. New York, 1991.

Stowell, Daniel W. *Rebuilding Zion: The Religious Reconstruction of the South, 1863–1877*. New York, 1998.

Wilson, Edmund. *Patriotic Gore: Studies in the Literature of the American Civil War*. New York, 1962.

POPULAR INTELLECTUAL MOVEMENTS,
1833–1877

Robert C. Fuller

The main distinction between popular intellectual movements and formal academic philosophy has little to do with the sophistication of their ideas. Instead, what most distinguishes an intellectual movement as "popular" is how its ideas are intended to be applied or consumed. Scholars are typically interested in analyzing ideas in terms of their historical or logical connections. Popular audiences, on the other hand, are concerned with the more practical issue of finding ideas that can help them symbolize or resolve problems arising in the context of everyday life. For this reason popular intellectual movements frequently reveal less about the intrinsic nature of ideas than about the needs, desires, and expectations of the persons who become interested in them. And, thus, although we cannot expect popular intellectual movements to reveal much about formal philosophy, we can expect them to provide a unique window into the lives and concerns of the Americans who turn to them for help in making sense of their lives.

Much of popular intellectual life in antebellum America stemmed from two distinct sources. The first of these was the subtle change in Protestant doctrine brought about by the rapid proliferation of revival meetings known as the Second Great Awakening. As the American nation grew more confident and expanded rapidly into its western frontiers during the first three decades of the nineteenth century, there was a surge of interest in revival meetings. These revival meetings intended to win converts to one of the era's evangelical Protestant denominations. But unlike previous outbursts of revival activity, this religious awakening all but ignored traditional views of predestination and instead emphasized the individual's free will to decide for salvation. Bible-based revivalists traveled on lecture circuits throughout the country seeking to win converts to a gospel that placed increasing importance upon humans' own abilities to avail themselves of God's miraculous powers. Revivalists of this era downplayed Protestantism's historical emphasis upon humanity's innate depravity and instead focused upon particular sins (e.g., intemperance, Sabbath breaking, unchastity). The Second Great Awakening thus implied that if Americans could overcome these sins they might—by their own will and effort—restore humanity's right relationship to God and to the providential forces that God has implanted for humans in nature. In this way revivalist activity stimulated a faith in human perfectibility that meshed well with the country's geographic and economic expansion.

Those who attended these revival meetings leapt to the further conclusion that society, too, was capable of immediate renovation if it could first be brought into alignment with God's will. Antebellum Americans assumed that social evils were simply a collection of individual acts of selfishness and could therefore be eliminated once and for all through the deliberate efforts of persons who had already received God's grace. Converted Americans joined together in voluntary societies designed to rescue persons from the kinds of ignorance or vice that would prevent their salvation. The earliest of these voluntary societies were devoted to the establishment of churches, the creation of Sunday schools, and the distribution of Bibles or religious literature. As the nineteenth century progressed, the spirit of voluntaryism launched by the Second Great Awakening gave rise to societies dedicated to such causes as temperance, the abolition of slavery, and female suffrage. Thus, all in all, the revival meetings of the Second Great Awakening unleashed a "romantic perfectionism" in American thought. By promulgating the belief that human nature is open to divinely inspired renovation in the twinkling of an eye, the Second Great Awakening gave popular American thought a distinctive bent toward perfectionism and utopian optimism.

A second principal source of antebellum intellectual life was the Transcendentalist movement that emerged out of 1830s New England. George Ripley, William Ellery Channing, Bronson Alcott, Margaret

Fuller, and Henry David Thoreau were among those who tried to create a new religious outlook centered upon the mystical or transcendental dimension of human experience itself. It was, however, the poet and clergyman Ralph Waldo Emerson who became the movement's preeminent spokesperson. His publication of *Nature* in 1836 signaled Americans' astonishing level of interest in spiritual ideas that were completely independent of the Bible or traditional religious understandings of sin and salvation. Emerson celebrated the potential of every person to have an immediate, personal experience of God without any of the trappings of institutional religion. He claimed that nature itself can trigger such experiences in us. When alone in nature, Emerson wrote, we are all capable of momentarily putting aside our normal rational outlook and entering into states of mystical reverie in which we can feel "the currents of Universal Being" flowing into, and energizing, our lives. Emerson's Transcendentalist philosophy thus had no place for notions such as sin, guilt, or contrition. Instead, it communicated the more optimistic message that—at least potentially—we are all inwardly connected to a higher, spiritual energy that is the ultimate source of all health, vitality, and creativity throughout the universe.

What Americans found exciting about Emerson's Transcendentalist philosophy was that it implied that every person is capable of being the recipient of what he called "an influx of Divine Mind into our mind." The Transcendentalist gospel was one of optimistic individualism. It suggested that each and every person has inner access to a higher source of energy that is capable of effecting instantaneous change or growth in one's life. And, thus, even though Transcendentalism and Protestant revivalism were rooted in wholly different sets of intellectual assumptions, they communicated strikingly similar messages to American audiences. Both exuded an optimism and belief in progress. Both stressed the necessity of individuals undergoing an inner experience whereby an unseen, spiritual power would descend into and wholly transform lives. And, finally, both believed that individuals who had undergone such an interior transformation would become God's instruments for the progressive renovation of American culture. Together, these two influential sources of nineteenth-century American thought created a certain optimistic and progressive-minded outlook that contemporaries called ultraism. Ultraism, as described by the historian Whitney R. Cross, was a "combination of activities, personalities, and attitudes creating a condition of society which could foster experimen-

tal doctrines." Mormonism, Shakerism, Adventism, and communitarianism were all among the experimental doctrines that emerged out of ultraism's quest for new ways of bringing people into harmony with a higher order of life. So, too, were a host of new medical philosophies and radical psychologies that promised reliable techniques for aligning individuals with the deepest currents of nature.

SECTARIAN MEDICAL PHILOSOPHIES

It should not be surprising that a high percentage of the nineteenth century's popular intellectual movements were in some way concerned with either physical or psychological healing. There is no greater test of an idea's practical value than its ability to deliver health, wholeness, and personal vitality. Most of these popular medical systems were rooted in philosophical assumptions that were broadly spiritual in nature. That is, sectarian medical philosophies were typically expressions of the progressivism and belief in the power of spiritual agencies that the Protestant revivalists and Transcendentalists had put into popular circulation.

One of the earliest of these sectarian medical philosophies was propounded by the New Hampshire farmer Samuel Thomson. Thomson's distrust of the era's "regular physicians" prompted him to develop a novel healing philosophy based upon his study of simple herbal and botanical remedies. The premise of the Thomsonian healing system was that there is only one cause of diseases, cold, and one cure, heat. By combining steam baths with botanics such as cayenne pepper, Thomson was able to assure patients that he had restored "heat" to their systems and thus set them back on the road to recovery. Thomson's methods spared patients the harsh bleedings and mercurial drugs that the era's regular physicians utilized. Nor did the Thomsonian system entail much cost to the patient, who could study and apply Thomson's methods cheaply without dependence upon haughty physicians. Indeed, a professed goal of the Thomsonian movement was "to make every man his own physician." Thomsonianism was, in essence, supplying the medical counterpart to the Second Great Awakening's "romantic perfectionism." Paralleling the message of revivalist preachers, Thomsonians told their audiences that worldly happiness is intended by both divine and natural law. Thomsonian principles implied that disease is by no means a deserved reprimand from a wrathful God, but instead a natural phenomenon and thus subject to laws that human reason can discover and systematically apply. Thomsonian advocates assured people that all they had to do to avail themselves of God's progressive plan was to assume willful responsibility for their own physiological salvation. Thus, it is not surprising that Thomsonianism spread along precisely the same geographical lines that revivalist preachers had traveled spreading the new theological mood of optimism and perfectionism.

A second sectarian medical philosophy, homeopathy, emerged more or less concurrently with the public's gradual loss of enthusiasm for the Thomsonian system. Homeopathy was the creation of the German physician Samuel Hahnemann, who postulated that a drug that causes a particular illness in a healthy person will cure that same illness in a sick person. This principle, which Hahnemann termed *similia similibus curantur* (like is cured by like) was soon supplemented by a second homeopathic concept: that very diluted doses of a drug are actually more potent than large doses. Homeopathy was introduced to the United States by the physician Hans Gram, who, after studying the system in Europe, opened an office in New York. By 1833 a homeopathic college had been formed and a national association of homeopathic physicians soon followed. Throughout the 1800s approximately 10 percent of the country's medical schools and medical school graduates were adherents of homeopathic principles. One reason for the popularity of homeopathy was that it, like Thomsonianism, was far less likely to assault patients' own recuperative powers than the conventional physicians' use of bleeding and poisonous drugs.

There were, however, other intellectual and cultural factors responsible for the positive reception that homeopathy received in the United States. Homeopathic spokespersons placed greater importance upon nature and the individual's own recuperative powers than did conventional physicians. In addition, they made vague references to the "spiritlike" activity of the tiny doses of medicine that they employed. These references caught the imagination of many intellectuals seeking innovative answers to the perennial question of the relationship of the world of matter to the world of spirit. Homeopaths seemed to insinuate that matter, while not exactly an expression of spirit, was at least receptive to spiritual infusions. For this reason their healing system was avidly investigated by many followers of Transcendentalism and others who had become disillusioned with the materialism seemingly implied by the Enlightenment worldview that permeated the era's science. Most of the directions

in which they pushed were soon to be reinforced by the metaphysical movements Swedenborgianism and mesmerism.

Other sectarian medical systems also acted as catalysts of popular intellectual thought. Hydropathy, for example, attracted thousands of Americans who had grown leery of the regular physicians and instead sought curative measures that seemed more wholesome and natural. Hydropathy, or water-cure, was first introduced to Americans by Joel Shew. Shew, along with his associate Russell Trall, opened a water-cure institute in Lebanon Springs, New York, in 1845. Their institute became the first of many such health retreats set up throughout the United States where people could go to relax, take fresh water baths, drink plenty of water, exercise, and be instructed about proper diet, sleep, or clothing. Hydropathy drew eclectically from Thomsonianism, homeopathy, and the emerging dietary therapies taught by individuals such as the reformer Sylvester Graham, the Adventist preacher Ellen White, and the physician John Harvey Kellogg (of Kellogg's breakfast cereal fame). Hydropathy, like the dietary therapies, taught that in their natural state humans are the perfect work of God; humanity's present degenerated physical state is the result of thousands of years of willful disregard of the divinely ordained principles of healthy living. The water-cure movement thus suggested that all impediments to health and human progress could be removed by a better understanding of physical law. Its teachings were not only physiological but also moral insofar as they sought to restore people to their proper relationship with God's providential powers. There were, then, several interconnected factors responsible for hydropathy's ideological appeal: it offered noninvasive hygienic principles in place of drug-based therapeutics; it provided distinct opportunities for a "conversion" to a new worldview in a revival-like setting; and it fostered self-determination through changes in personal habits while promoting a reformist social outlook toward the class- and gender-based status quo.

Hydropathy eventually became entangled with so many of the era's progressive causes that it gradually lost its distinctive character and became loosely incorporated into a number of diet and exercise philosophies. Shew and Trall were among the first to associate hydropathy's reform principles with those being championed by the day's forward thinkers, William Alcott, Lucy Stone, Amelia Bloomer, Susan B. Anthony, and Horace Greeley. Trall also formed a partnership with the New York publishers and metaphysical dilettantes Orson Fowler, Lorenzo

Fowler, and Samuel R. Wells, who make for an interesting story about popular intellectual life in their own right.

Not only did the Fowlers and Wells personally dabble in water-cure, phrenology, vegetarianism, mesmerism, Grahamism (after the American reformer Sylvester Graham), and spiritualism, but they published the most significant books on these topics. Additionally, they brought all these diverse beliefs to the attention of the American reading public on the same advertisement pages. In doing this, the Fowlers and Wells were undoubtedly justified. For whether logically compatible or not, metaphysical theories of all kinds were linked by the popular intellectual climate. A good many Americans were dissatisfied with orthodox theology and were seeking progressive-minded insights into the higher laws of nature. Eclecticism and broad-minded synthesis appealed to those seeking a philosophy fit for a new age in which religion and science might be combined in some kind of transcendent intellectual synthesis. The Fowlers and Wells were among the first commercial publishers to ensure that popular intellectual movements would be targeted to those whose religious and philosophical interests ventured beyond either conventional science or religion.

METAPHYSICAL MOVEMENTS

One of the most widespread and influential intellectual movements from the 1830s onward was that of Swedenborgianism. Emanuel Swedenborg was an eminent Swedish scientist who had made significant contributions in such varied fields as physics, astronomy, and anatomy before undergoing a series of mystical experiences in which he claimed to have been granted "perfect inspiration." Swedenborg, whose more than thirty volumes of spiritual writings were brought to the attention of Americans by Emerson and other Transcendentalists, appealed to those wishing to find a spirituality that went beyond routine church affairs. His own mystical experiences were seen as proof that the truths of religion could be known through inward illumination, thus freeing the essence of religion from the literal reading of Scriptures. Swedenborg's visions revealed that the universe is more fascinating and expansive than humans had ever dared to imagine. He explained that humans inhabit a multidimensional universe comprised of several interpenetrating and successively "higher" dimensions of existence—the physical, mental, spiritual, and angelic, among others.

Key to Swedenborg's system was his doctrine of "correspondence," which allowed American audiences to view Swedenborg's philosophy as simultaneously scientific and metaphysical. The concept of correspondence stated that every dimension of existence is imperceptibly connected with all other dimensions. The most important implication of this metaphysical doctrine was that harmony in any one dimension of life depends upon establishing rapport with other levels on the cosmic scale. All true progress proceeds according to influences received from above. When inner harmony or resonance between realms is established, energy and guiding wisdom from the higher level can flow into and exert causal power within the lower level. Swedenborg thus proclaimed that men and women are all inwardly constructed so as to be able to receive "psychic influx" from higher dimensions of reality. A further implication was that through diligent study and prolonged introspection anyone is able to obtain the requisite spiritual capacity to make such contact with higher spiritual planes. According to Swedenborg, the benefits were numerous: the instantaneous healing of both physical and emotional disorders; spontaneous insight into cosmological secrets; conversations with angelic beings; and intuitive understanding of the hidden spiritual meaning of Scripture.

Swedenborg's confidence in the soul's capacity for limitless development contrasted sharply with traditional Protestantism's insistence upon human depravity. His doctrines thus appealed to many of the other experimental doctrines and sectarian groups that populated the nineteenth-century religious landscape. Communitarians, Transcendentalists, homeopathic physicians, spiritualists, and wealthy dilettantes such as the American philosopher and author Henry James Sr. were encouraged by his exciting descriptions of invisible spiritual worlds. It was, however, mesmerism that most thoroughly connected with Swedenborgianism's belief in humanity's intimate connection with "higher" spiritual dimensions and in humanity's capacity to avail itself of invisible spiritual energies for the total renovation of its personal life.

Between 1836 and the early 1850s, a number of itinerant lecturers introduced Americans to the European-born metaphysical philosophy known as mesmerism. The Austrian physician Franz Anton Mesmer's "science of animal magnetism" had already attracted the attention of European intellectuals and popular audiences alike. Mesmer believed that he had detected the existence of a superfine substance or fluid that had previously eluded sci-

PHRENOLOGY: BOTH FAD AND SCIENCE

One of the most fascinating popular intellectual movements of the late 1830s and 1840s was phrenology. Phrenology was the creation of two German physicians, Franz J. Gall and Johann K. Spurzheim, who attempted to chart the physiology of the brain in the late 1790s. Their theory posited that each personality trait (e.g., honesty, frugality, sloth, intemperance) is controlled by its own distinct organ within the brain. They surmised that the size of each brain organ would thus roughly indicate how powerful that particular psychological function would be in a given person's life. Further assuming that the shape of the skull corresponds to the organs beneath it, they deemed it possible to discern a person's character by examining the size and shape of each section of the skull.

The first to promote phrenology was the physician Charles Caldwell of Transylvania University in Lexington, Kentucky, who first lectured on the topic as early as 1821. Lecture tours by Spurzheim in 1832, the British phrenologist-mesmerist Robert Collyer in 1839, and the Scottish phrenologist George Combe between 1828 and 1840 all brought considerable new attention to this forward-looking attempt to establish a scientific method for studying human personality. Particularly important for the spread of phrenology was the backing it received from the publishing trio of Orson Fowler, Lorenzo Fowler, and Samuel R. Wells. Their publishing company, located in New York, sold books, pamphlets, and plaster casts of the skull with appropriate phrenological markings.

Throughout the 1840s phrenology continued to attract the attention of intellectuals and social reformers. Henry Ward Beecher, Horace Greeley, Horace Mann, and Sarah Grimké were among those who believed that phrenology could be of invaluable help in reform movements of every kind. Intellectuals and reformers suggested the value of phrenology for such fields as education, religion, medical treatment of the mentally ill, and even the rehabilitation of criminals. It was claimed, for example, that a trained phrenologist could examine the shape of someone's head and make precise diagnoses as to which intellectual or moral faculties were structurally deficient. Compensatory programs could then be designed and specifically adapted to the individual's mental and moral development. For instance, a person diagnosed with a deficient organ of honesty could be asked to read and memorize appropriate moral lessons, thereby helping to strengthen otherwise underdeveloped sections of the brain. Some phrenologists proposed placing leeches on criminals' heads in order to siphon off the strength from their organs of deceit and larceny.

Phrenology's fairly swift exit from the American intellectual scene after the 1840s was not dictated by any full-scale refutation of its theories. It would be a few more decades before advances in physiological psychology would undermine its scientific credibility among popular audiences. Instead, phrenology's major shortcoming was that its master image of human personality was too static to be compatible with the pragmatic temper of the American people. Revivalism and Transcendentalism alike had reinforced Americans' belief that human nature is susceptible to an influx of a higher spiritual energy capable of effecting an immediate and total renovation of personality. Phrenology never made allowance for the wider cultural ethos—and suffered the consequences. Many of those initially attracted to phrenology's scientific promise soon found a more congenial psychological theory in mesmerism.

entific notice. He maintained that this invisible fluid, which he named animal magnetism, is evenly distributed throughout the healthy human body. His theory postulated that if an individual's supply of animal magnetism is thrown out of equilibrium, one or more bodily functions will consequently be deprived of sufficient amounts of this vital force and will thus begin to falter. Mesmer proclaimed that "there is only one illness and one healing." Since any and all illnesses can ultimately be traced back to a disturbance in the body's supply of animal magnetism, Mesmer claimed, medical science could be reduced to a simple set of procedures aimed at supercharging a patient's nervous system with this mysterious, life-giving energy.

Over time Mesmer and his pupils developed techniques for putting their patients into a peaceful trance that was thought to make them especially receptive to the inflow of animal magnetism. "Mesmerized" patients felt inwardly transformed. They reported feeling prickly sensations running up and down their bodies that they interpreted to be the inflow of animal magnetism. Upon awaking from their sleeplike trance, they invariably reported relief from such disorders as rheumatism, digestive problems, nervousness, liver ailments, and heart pain. Still more unusual was the fact that many appeared to enter even deeper states of trance and allegedly performed extraordinary mental feats such as acute intelligence, telepathy, clairvoyance, and precognition. What began as a novel healing theory was, by the time it reached American audiences, quickly developing into a psychological theory of humanity's ability to tap into metaphysical dimensions of experience.

Hundreds of individuals throughout New England became practitioners of the science of animal magnetism. Some opened offices in their hometowns, while others became itinerant lecturers who specialized in giving stage demonstrations of mesmerism's power to heal and to activate formerly undetected psychological abilities. Most of mesmerism's adherents were drawn from those middle- and upper-class Americans who styled themselves progressive thinkers (including a good many who belonged to either the Unitarian or Universalist religious denominations) and who dabbled in other metaphysical philosophies such as Transcendentalism or Swedenborgianism. Mesmerism's healing feats were taken as empirical proof of the Transcendentalist and Swedenborgian belief in the existence of higher spiritual worlds and of the capacity of humans to avail themselves of an "influx" of life-renovating spiritual energies. American audiences

thus believed that mesmerism was heralding a revolution not only in science, but in religion as well. Many mesmerist authors such as George Bush merged mesmerism and Swedenborgianism with the hope of deriving a single intellectual system that could unite their scientific and spiritual interests. Whitney R. Cross described popular culture's synthesis of diverse metaphysical theories by noting, "Before they ever heard of Mesmer or Swedenborg, they expected new scientific discoveries to confirm the broad patterns of revelation as they understood them: to give humankind ever-more-revealing glimpses of the preordained divine plan for humanity and the universe. They expected all such knowledge would demonstrate the superiority of ideal over physical or material force, and that it would prove the relationship of a person's soul to the infinite spiritual power."

Yet another metaphysical movement emerged in 1848 when mysterious knocking sounds were heard by Kate and Maggie Fox in their home in Hydesville, New York. Once the two young girls overcame their initial fright, they bravely asked if there was any invisible presence responsible for this knocking and, if so, for it to make appropriate rapping responses. A series of raps came in apparent response. Soon the Fox sisters were engaging in protracted dialogues with a spirit of a murdered peddler whose remains were thought to be buried in their cellar. The Fox sisters' ostensible ability to communicate with the dead set loose a wave of religious and philosophical enthusiasm that came to be known as spiritualism.

The spiritualist movement appealed to Americans on two distinct levels. The first was related to spiritualism's bold claim to have proven the existence of life after death and to make communication possible with departed loved ones. Spiritualist mediums claimed to be adept at entering into special trance states in which they could channel messages from the spiritual world. These mediums, many of whom were women in an era in which positions of religious leadership were otherwise closed, were often able to use "spirit guides" to make predictions about their clientele's lives or to offer spiritual advice. Some said they were able to read people's auras and others conducted séances in which spirits might speak by using their vocal chords or by a technique called "automatic writing." In such ways spiritualist mediums were strikingly successful at meeting people's enduring need to confirm the existence of an afterlife and know about their departed loved ones' continued well-being. While popular in the late 1840s and imme-

---

GEORGE BUSH'S *MESMER AND SWEDENBORG*

George Bush, a professor at New York University and one of the nation's foremost proponents of Swedenborgianism, wrote a book in 1847 entitled *Mesmer and Swedenborg*. Bush's text captures the era's enthusiasm for philosophical and psychological ideas that might open up a new metaphysical understanding of humanity's relationship to a higher spiritual order of things. Bush's hope was to alert his readers to the fact that "when taken together, the investigations of the mesmeric state point to an entirely new class of facts in psychology." The class of facts that Bush had in mind pertained to the phenomena surrounding the deepest levels of the mesmeric trance state. Bush claimed to have experimented with mesmerism and found clear evidence that entranced subjects make connection with a higher plane of consciousness and spontaneously display instances of extrasensory perception, telepathy, and clairvoyance. He took this as empirical confirmation of what the Swedish scientist Emanuel Swedenborg had taught all along. In Bush's estimation, Swedenborg and Mesmer both advocated the doctrine "that man is a spirit as to his interiors and that his spiritual nature in the body often manifests itself according to the laws which govern it out of the body."

Mesmerist psychology offered Bush and others attracted to Swedenborgian metaphysics what appeared to be a scientific analysis of the mind "just at that point where anthropology welds itself to Theology." Bush noted that mesmerized subjects "speak as if, to their own consciousness, they had undergone an inward translation by which they had passed out of a material into a spiritual body. . . . The state into which a subject is brought by the mesmerizing process is a state in which the spirit predominates for the time being over the body." It struck Bush that the "facts" of mesmerism gave scientific backing to Swedenborg's eloquent metaphysical writings and for this reason heralded the dawn of a new era in American spiritual thought. As he put it, "On the whole it must, we think, be admitted that the phenomena of mesmerism taken in conjunction with the developments of Swedenborg, open a new chapter in the philosophy of mind and in man's relations to a higher sphere."

---

diately after the Civil War, spiritualism never gave rise to any successful organizations and much of the intellectual curiosity it generated became absorbed by the Theosophical Society that emerged in the late 1870s.

Spiritualism also influenced popular intellectual life at a second, more philosophical level. In 1843 an apprentice cobbler by the name of Andrew Jackson Davis attended a lecture-demonstration on mesmerism in his hometown of Poughkeepsie, New York. Davis volunteered to come up to the stage to serve as a subject and, as it turned out, he proved to be adept at entering into the deepest levels of the mesmeric trance. After several months of experimenting with self-induced mesmeric trances, Davis suddenly found himself communicating with a host of departed spirits—including the spirit of Emanuel Swedenborg. Swedenborg and other celestial sages dictated lengthy messages concerning spiritual matters. Friends feverishly recorded every word so that Davis might later publish them. Although the various books written "by and through" Andrew Jackson Davis are somewhat ponderous and vague, they nonetheless espouse a respectable spirituality. Davis and other spiritualist authors such as Thomas Lake Harris managed to combine Transcendentalism, mesmerism, and Swedenborgianism into a mystical spirituality that many middle-class Americans found to be a viable alternative to the scriptural religion of the churches. Spiritualism presented Americans with quasi-empirical "proof" that they were connected with a wider spiritual universe from which they might expect guidance, healing, and increased vitality. The metaphysical vision that spiritualists popularized was picked up by theosophy in the late 1800s and early 1900s and remained a powerful component of the many "New Age" philosophies that have historically engaged Americans' spiritual curiosities.

MIND CURE AND THE POWER OF POSITIVE THINKING

In 1838 a clockmaker by the name of Phineas Parkhurst Quimby attended a lecture-demonstration on mesmerism being given in his hometown, Belfast, Maine. Quimby was so astonished at this display of the mind's remarkable powers that he began his own study of the science of animal magnetism. With the passage of time, however, Quimby became increasingly skeptical that animal magnetism alone could account for all of his therapeutic successes. Like many other mesmerists, he realized that his patients' beliefs and expectations of cure had a lot to do with their rapid recoveries. But Quimby ventured further and arrived at the more radical conclusion that his patients' beliefs and attitudes had caused their illnesses in the first place. He suggested that if a person "is deceived into a belief that he has, or is liable to have a disease, the belief is catching and the effects follow from it." Put differently, "All sickness is in the mind or belief . . . to cure the disease is to correct the error, destroy the cause, and the effect will cease."

Quimby's "discovery" of the mental origins of disease prompted him to become the first psychotherapist in American history. People throughout New England flocked to his office to be helped with their various physical and emotional disorders. Quimby first listened to them and then helped them redirect their thinking in more life-affirming ways. His therapeutic activities were guided by his conviction that "disease is something made by belief or forced upon us by our parents or public opinion. . . . Now if you can face the error and argue it down you can cure the sick." And cure he did. By 1865 he had treated more than twelve thousand people, most of whom left his office with glowing enthusiasm for Quimby's philosophy of mind over matter.

Although it was very popular, Quimby's theory was not wholly psychological or mentalistic. There was still a metaphysical dimension to this theory, inspired by Swedenborgianism and mesmerist philosophy. Quimby continued to affirm that the ultimate cause of either health or healing is the invisible spiritual energy that Mesmer termed animal magnetism. Quimby's argument was that a person's beliefs and mental attitudes function like control valves—they determine whether the conscious mind is connected to, or severed from, this health-bestowing metaphysical energy. His "Mind Cure" philosophy was based upon the principle that one's beliefs can either open one up to, or close one off from, the spiritual power that promotes health and vitality. Thus when Quimby counseled his patients to maintain healthy, optimistic thoughts he was trying to do more than just adjust their belief system. He was also trying to help bring about the inner transformation necessary to restore a productive relationship with a higher, metaphysical power.

Quimby's teachings had enormous influence over popular intellectual life in the second half of the nineteenth century. One of Quimby's patients, Mary Baker Eddy, developed his teachings into one of the five largest religious denominations to have emerged in American religious history. Mary Baker Eddy arrived at Quimby's doorstep in 1862 a helpless physical and mental wreck. The mesmeric healer cured her afflicted body and, in the process, filled her receptive mind with new ideas. Once healed, Mrs. Eddy resolved that she too would take up a career in mental healing. Soon after Quimby's death, Mary Baker Eddy transformed the lessons she had learned from her mesmeric mentor into the doctrinal foundations of the Church of Christ, Scientist (Christian Science). Her principal text, *Science and Health with a Key to the Scriptures* (1875), sold over 400,000 copies by the time of her death in 1910.

Three of Quimby's other patients also played an important role in developing his ideas in ways that would attract the attention of thousands of Americans from the 1860s to the early 1900s. Annetta Dresser, Julius Dresser, and Warren Felt Evans parlayed their tutelage under Quimby into successful careers as authors and lecturers of what was initially referred to as the philosophy of Mind Cure and what eventually became known as the New Thought movement. Evans was clearly the most influential of these writers, with his *Mental Cure* (1869) and *Mental Medicine* (1872) going through seven and fifteen editions, respectively, by 1885. Evans's principal message was that individuals can enhance their inner receptivity to the inflow of a divine energy that will automatically usher in physical health, emotional serenity, and economic vitality. Evans and the dozens of other New Thought authors developed a "power of positive thinking" philosophy that met the spiritual and psychological needs of Americans who were otherwise at a loss for how to find their bearings in a world rapidly being transformed by immigration, urbanization, and industrialization. Most middle-class Americans in the 1870s were no longer able to make sense of the world around them, let alone impose order upon it. The New Thought movement gave them a vocabulary and set of self-help exercises to take systematic control of their inner lives, inspiring hope that they could find the secret of both spiritual composure and worldly success.

See also **Individualism and the Self** *(volume 3) and other articles in this section.*

BIBLIOGRAPHY

Albanese, Catherine. *Corresponding Motion: Transcendental Religion and the New America.* Philadelphia, 1977.

Boston Thomsonian Manual 3 (15 November 1837): 21.

Braden, Charles S. *Spirits in Rebellion: The Rise and Development of New Thought.* Dallas, Tex., 1963.

Braude, Ann. *Radical Spirits: Spiritualism and Women's Rights in Nineteenth-Century America.* Boston, 1989.

Carroll, Bret. *Spiritualism in Antebellum America.* Bloomington, Ind., 1998.

Cayleff, Susan. *"Wash and Be Healed": The Water-Cure Movement and Women's Health.* Philadelphia, 1987.

Cross, Whitney R. *The Burned-Over District: The Social and Intellectual History of Enthusiastic Religion in Western New York, 1800–1850.* Ithaca, N.Y., 1950.

Davies, John. *Phrenology: Fad and Science.* New Haven, Conn., 1955.

Davis, Andrew. *The Magic Staff: An Autobiography of Andrew Jackson Davis.* 1857. Reprint, Pomeroy, Wash., 1998.

Ellenborger, Henri. *The Discovery of the Unconscious.* New York, 1970.

Emerson, Ralph Waldo. *The Early Lectures of Ralph Waldo Emerson.* Cambridge, Mass., 1959.

Fuller, Robert C. *Mesmerism and the American Cure of Souls.* Philadelphia, 1982.

Kaufman, Martin. *Homoeopathy in America: The Rise and Fall of a Medical Heresy.* Baltimore, 1971.

Nissenbaum, Stephen. *Sex, Diet, and Debility in Jacksonian America.* Westport, Conn., 1980.

Quimby, Phineas P. *The Quimby Manuscripts.* New York, 1924.

Shew, Joel. *Handbook of Hydropathy: The Treatment and Prevention of Diseases by Means of Water.* Brooklyn, N.Y., 1991.

Thomson, Samuel. *Narrative of the Life and Medical Discoveries of Samuel Thomson.* New York, 1972.

Wrobel, Arthur, ed. *Pseudo-Science and Society in Nineteenth-Century America.* Lexington, Ky., 1987.

SOUTHERN INTELLECTUAL LIFE

Douglas Ambrose

The Old South, Henry Adams claimed in *The Education of Henry Adams* (1907), expressed "no need or desire for intellectual culture in its own right." Although many scholars and commentators since Adams have shared his overall assessment of antebellum southern intellectual pursuits, most now recognize that the Old South had a vibrant and extensive intellectual life. The unfortunate tendency to judge southern intellectual life according to a New England–based norm has prevented many observers of that intellectual life from considering it on its own terms. But the antebellum and Civil War South and its intellectual life differed in fundamental ways from the North and from the rest of the nineteenth-century Western world. Those differences arose primarily if not exclusively from slavery. For the Old South was not simply a society with slaves, it was a slave society. Slavery permeated nearly every facet of life for blacks and whites, men and women, slaveholders and nonslaveholders. Recognizing the Old South as a slave society does not, however, mean that southern intellectual life consisted only of the defense of slavery. Southern intellectuals wrote novels, short stories, and poems and produced significant works in political economy, law, history, the sciences, theology, and political and social thought. Only by examining these products can one appreciate the achievements and limitations of southern intellectual life and understand the ways slavery did and did not influence the development and expression of southern thought.

INSTITUTIONS

Publishing Although the South was home to a good number of printers, publishing houses were rare. For some observers, both in the nineteenth and twentieth centuries, the paucity of southern publishers reflected the pervasive anti-intellectual, or at least unintellectual, climate of the South. This climate, some argue, arose in the post-Jeffersonian South as the need to defend slavery and the triumph of evangelicalism led southerners into an ever-increasing intellectual isolation, out of touch with the main currents of Western thought. But such views of southern intellectual and cultural life are increasingly hard to sustain, as historians argue persuasively that neither a broad proslavery consensus nor evangelicalism necessarily hindered southern interest in and appreciation of the intellectual debates of the age.

Southern elites read widely, and their personal libraries and the periodicals that circulated among them testify to their interest in the entire range of contemporary intellectual endeavors. Access to books did, however, prove somewhat difficult for people in the countryside, which in the South meant the vast majority of the population. As a slave society, the South lacked an extensive internal market network. Its big cities—New Orleans, Charleston, Mobile—tied the South to the wider Atlantic trading complex, but the South lacked an integrated network of small cities and towns that, in the North for example, facilitated the circulation of commodities, including books. But to recognize that southerners published few books and faced difficulties acquiring those published elsewhere does not mean that their intellectuals could neither write nor read or that they could not, in short, engage in intellectual activity. Indeed, southern intellectuals did not write many books. The much more popular means of intellectual expression was the periodical or literary magazine. These publications, popular throughout antebellum America, proliferated in the South in the generation before the Civil War. In the periodical literature of the Old South one finds the clearest and fullest expressions of southern intellectual and cultural life.

Most periodicals had a short life. Only a few survived for more than a few years, the most important being the *Southern Literary Messenger* (1834–1864), *Southern Quarterly Review* (1842–

1857), and *Commercial Review of the South and West*, better known as *DeBow's Review* (1847–1861). There were also important agricultural journals that promoted, among other things, the application of science to agriculture. Like the literary journals, most of these efforts died quickly, but some, including the *Southern Agriculturist, Farmers' Register, Southern Planter, Southern Cultivator,* and *American Cotton Planter,* had longer lives. Religious periodicals also appeared in the decades before the war. The most influential of these were the *Southern Presbyterian Review* and the *Methodist Southern Christian Advocate.* The editors of these journals, and of the countless other short-lived ones, regularly complained that the South lacked the critical masses of both writers to contribute to their journals and readers to subscribe to them. Southern authors were mainly urban lawyers, teachers, ministers, merchants, and politicians, along with some planters, but few were professional writers who earned their living through writing.

No one articulated the complaints of southern editors more eloquently and forcefully than William Gilmore Simms, novelist, poet, essayist, editor, and the foremost man of letters in the antebellum South. An editor of several literary magazines, Simms lamented that his "contributors—men, generally, in our country, devoted to other professions, . . . can only write . . . at moments of leisure." The editor, he continued, "is necessarily compelled to wait upon them for their articles, which, good, bad or indifferent, he is compelled to publish" (from Simms's *Letters,* vol. 1, pp. 196–197). Simms also described "other evils," including difficulties in collecting payments from subscribers. As with the book trade, southern periodical publishing suffered from both demographic diffusion and an inadequate distribution network.

Some scholars have suggested that a low literacy rate also contributed to the difficulties faced by southern periodicals. Slave illiteracy was the norm, but literacy was practically universal among southern elites. And the literacy rates of nonelite whites were quite high: more than 75 percent in most states and even higher in some. But most whites lacked the means and the desire to become consumers of periodical literature. It is hardly surprising that most periodicals with a limited base of support failed, since most elite southerners, like most elite northerners, did not subscribe to periodicals. That rate of failure did limit the extent of critical discourse in the South, but it did not prevent such discourse. Southern intellectuals continued to establish periodicals even into the Civil War years, and

although many ceased publication during the war, many resumed publication during Reconstruction.

The frequent appearance of the word "Southern" in titles of antebellum periodicals speaks to many southerners' desire to create vehicles for the expression of a distinct sectional and, by the 1850s, national cultural voice. For some, especially in the 1830s and 1840s, a southern literature's purpose was to contribute to the development of a broader American literature. But by the 1850s more and more southern writers called for a literature—in the broadest sense—that celebrated and reinforced the South's differences from and superiority to the North. This change reflected the sincere adherence of southern intellectuals to their social order and the values it espoused: hierarchy, interdependence, and inequality. As the South came under increasing attack, southern intellectuals, from novelists to theologians, utilized the periodical press to defend and promote their slave society, although they continued to devote most of their writings to topics—such as the influence of German Romanticism on the fine arts, the intricacies of Hegelian philosophy, and the merits of Tennyson's poetry—that had little if anything to do with slavery or the political crisis. Nevertheless, by the time of the Civil War, "Southern" in a title usually denoted a set of values and beliefs that stood in sharp contrast to that in the North and in the wider Atlantic world.

Education Southerners only began to create public school systems in the 1840s, and only Kentucky and North Carolina had statewide systems in place before the Civil War. But southern elites, both in cities and on plantations, received adequate educations. Many southern students attended schools and colleges in the North, but the southern states contained an impressive number of colleges. In the decade before the Civil War, a higher percentage of southern white youths attended college than did northern youths, and the South was home to far more female colleges than the North. Colleges grew slowly until the 1820s, but exploded thereafter. Following the eighteenth-century lead of North Carolina, both states and religious denominations established colleges and universities. Although a good number of these schools hardly merited the name "college," some, including South Carolina College, William and Mary, the University of Virginia, and the University of Georgia, were respectable institutions. And southern theological seminaries, particularly the Presbyterian Columbia Theological Seminary in Columbia, South Carolina, and the Protestant Episcopal Theological Seminary in Alexandria, Virginia, provided quality educations for southern ministers and educators. James Henley Thornwell, the Old South's most formidable theologian and a prominent professor and editor, attended and later taught at Columbia Theological. Leonidas Polk, the first Episcopal bishop of Louisiana, founder of the University of the South, and a general in the Confederate Army, attended the Episcopal seminary in Alexandria. That the South was not home to a Harvard or Princeton hardly means that southerners remained in intellectual darkness.

The curricula at most colleges remained focused on the classics, with a smattering of moral philosophy and natural philosophy, throughout the antebellum era. The preponderance of classical curricula has led some scholars to conclude that southern colleges stagnated and failed to keep pace with the intellectual developments of the mid-nineteenth century, especially in the natural sciences. But several schools, including Transylvania University in Kentucky and the University of Georgia, dramatically expanded their commitment to the study of the sciences and differed little from most northern colleges in integrating the sciences into their curricula. Nor did southern evangelicalism squelch academic inquiry, although the famous case of the religious skeptic Thomas Cooper, who was forced out of the presidency of South Carolina College in 1834, does suggest that there were limits to how far one could challenge the religious consensus on southern campuses. But at least through the Civil War years, most colleges saw no fundamental conflict between science and religion. Many schools included courses on "evidences of christianity" in their curricula, convinced not only that no conflict existed between biblical revelation and the empirical study of the natural world, but that such empirical research would verify revelation. The familiar image of southern religion as a "mindless" ecstatic religion of the heart reflects only a part of reality, and certainly not the most important part of religious institutions of higher education. In those institutions, the head mattered far more than the heart.

In their emphasis on the classics, their increasing commitment to the sciences, and their belief in a rational Christian theology, southern colleges did not differ dramatically from northern ones. But important differences existed, especially in the decade or two leading up to the Civil War. Many southerners demanded that their colleges become more aggressively and explicitly "southern," purge themselves of "yankeeisms," and train their students to be ardent defenders of the southern social order. For some, the call for more "southern" schools was part of a larger plea for more institutions that would collectively promote southern intellectual and cultural development even as they allowed southerners to participate in the intellectual discourse of the transatlantic world. The culmination of these efforts to create a southern education was the founding of the University of the South at Sewanee, Tennessee, in 1857. Led by the efforts of several Episcopal bishops, including James Hervey Otey of Tennessee, Stephen Elliott of Georgia, and especially Leonidas Polk of Louisiana, the founders of the university appealed to southerners' desire for a centrally located, well-funded, and thoroughly southern university. The bishops raised nearly $500,000 by 1859 when construction began. Their ambitious plans called for the creation of thirty-two departments or schools, each headed by a professor with a staff of tutors and assistant professors. The Civil War destroyed the university's buildings, its endowment, and the grand vision of its founders.

Learned Societies Southerners, like their northern counterparts, created a number of literary and scientific societies in the decades before the Civil War. As these societies tended to be located in cities and large towns, it is not surprising that the North saw more of them than did the South. Charleston, South Carolina, was home to a number of the most important societies, including the Apprentices Library Society, the South Carolina Literary and Philosophical Society, the Charleston Horticultural Society, and, most notably, the Elliott Society of Natural History, which was founded in 1853. Other significant societies were the New Orleans Academy of Sciences and the Maryland Academy of Science and Literature. These societies, like the periodicals, sought to provide intellectually interested individuals with a means of disseminating knowledge and, in so doing, help their society's mental, cultural, and material progress. Many of the societies sponsored public lectures, some published proceedings, and some established museums and libraries. Like the periodicals, many learned societies had short lives, since even Charleston and New Orleans lacked populations large enough to ensure the membership needed to sustain the societies and their functions.

Intellectual Life of Common White Folks Although southern common white folk did not, in general, write for or subscribe to periodicals, attend college, or join learned societies, they did have cultural and intellectual lives that found expression in a number of ways, primarily through folklore and storytelling. But the most important institutional base of those intellectual and cultural lives was evangelical Christianity.

Evangelical Christianity provided both a language and a set of beliefs that enabled nonelite southerners to make sense of the world and to act within it. Outsiders, including elite and urban southerners, often denounced the religion of the plain folk as emotional twaddle, but late-twentieth-century studies display a greater appreciation of that religion's coherence and depth. Although evangelicalism could promote a degree of egalitarianism, because it emphasized that God was no respecter of persons, for most white southerners its more powerful message served to support hierarchy in general and the hierarchy within southern households in particular. Southern evangelicalism recognized that people occupied different stations in life, and it insisted that individuals recognize their stations and the duties that flowed from them. Wives, children, and slaves were to obey those God had placed over them, while husbands, parents, and masters were to protect and guide their dependents. There thus existed a certain tension within southern society between the values of the household and those of the polity, where a rhetoric of equality found expression. But the equality of white men in the public realm depended on their position of superordination within the hierarchically structured household. Sermons and church courts reinforced this view of the households and thus helped shape southern notions of what constituted a proper social order.

SUBJECTS OF STUDY

Southern intellectuals were aware of and actively contributed to the developments in Western thought. The problem for many students of southern intellectual life is that they tend to devote far too much attention to the one field—high literature—in which southern contributions were least noteworthy. Only by looking at other fields can one appreciate the extent of southern participation in the intellectual and cultural life of the nineteenth-century Western world and the ways in which that participation marked them as southerners.

Political Economy Throughout the antebellum era, southern political economists contributed to discussions of political economy on two levels. George Tucker and Jacob Cardozo were two of the most distinguished economic thinkers in antebel-

lum America, and Thomas Cooper and Thomas Roderick Dew were respectable political economists. The South also produced several less sophisticated but competent writers who popularized economic issues in a variety of publications. The most noteworthy of these included Louisa S. McCord, who translated and promoted the works of the French political economist Claude-Frédéric Bastiat, and James D. B. DeBow, publisher of the influential *DeBow's Review*. All of these economic commentators worked within the broad parameters of classical political economy, which grew out of the writings of Adam Smith, David Ricardo, and Thomas Malthus, among others. Since classical political economy proved hostile to slavery, many southerners—including some of the above-named authors—struggled to reconcile their commitment to slavery with the claims of the emerging "science" of economics. By the Civil War many ardent defenders of slavery had rejected the premises of classical political economy and chose instead to emphasize the moral and "sociological" benefits of their social system.

Like many other southern intellectuals, Tucker pursued a number of interests. He wrote biographies and novels, including *The Valley of the Shenandoah* (1824), practiced law, and served in the U.S. Congress (1819–1825) before settling down as professor of moral philosophy at the University of Virginia in 1825 at the age of fifty. From his appointment until his death in 1861, he devoted himself almost entirely to political economy. Tucker's most notable contributions arose from his work on population trends and statistics, best exemplified in his famous analysis of the 1850 census, *Progress of the United States in Population and Wealth in Fifty Years* (1855). Like Cardozo, with whom he shared much, Tucker believed that population growth and industrialization would eventually undermine slavery by rendering slave labor unprofitable. Neither Tucker nor Cardozo thought that such developments would improve the working class' material conditions; insecurity and starvation would be the necessary elements of economic progress.

Dew followed Tucker and Cardozo in his analysis of the economics of slavery. Claiming that "no people had the generosity to liberate their slaves, until it became their interest to do so," Dew believed that slavery declined when population density rendered it unprofitable. He even speculated in his famous "Review of the Debate [on the Abolition of Slavery] in the Virginia Legislature of 1831 and 1832" that the rise of cities and manufacturing would encourage free laborers to migrate to Virginia and that, "in due time, the abolitionists will find the most lucrative system working to their hearts' content, increasing the prosperity of Virginia, and diminishing the evils of slavery" (from *The Pro-Slavery Argument: As Maintained by the Most Distinguished Writers of the Southern States,* p. 478). But Dew the political economist collided with Dew the social analyst when he contemplated this scenario. Arguing that "the history of the world has too conclusively shown, that two races, differing in manners, customs, language and civilization can never harmonize upon a footing of equality. One must rule the other or exterminating wars must be waged" (from *The Pro-Slavery Argument: As Maintained by the Most Distinguished Writers of the Southern States,* p. 410). Dew concluded that social peace necessitated slavery. The political economy of Dew (and Tucker and Cardozo) could not defend slavery as the proper relation between labor and capital at all times and places. Only by appealing to noneconomic arguments, in this case racist ones, could Dew defend the southern social order as anything other than a stage in economic development. Because of the classical political economy's intrinsic hostility to the idea of permanent slavery, its practitioners and advocates became increasingly subordinated either to those, like Dew, who elevated social necessity over economic theory, or to those, like George Fitzhugh or Henry Hughes, who rejected classical political economy as incompatible with the slavery that they promoted as morally and socially superior to all other labor systems.

Law Southern legal thought, like southern economic thought, followed Great Britain's lead, but slavery posed dilemmas that southern legal theorists and jurists had to resolve themselves. Although the South did not develop a distinct legal system, the need to confront issues related to slavery produced some of the most interesting and innovative aspects of southern legal thought. Thomas R. R. Cobb's *An Inquiry into the Law of Negro Slavery in the United States of America* (1858) is the only major work on slave law that emerged from the antebellum South, but case law reveals in dramatic fashion the contradictions and difficulties southerners encountered when trying to reconcile the dominant legal traditions with their social system.

Perhaps the best-known example of the way in which slavery led southern law away from northern and British law is the ruling by the North Carolina Supreme Court justice Thomas Ruffin in *State v. Mann* (1829). In deciding the question of whether John Mann, who had hired a slave and then shot and wounded her when she attempted to run off, was guilty of assault and battery, Ruffin noted that "the Court is compelled to express an opinion upon the extent of the dominion of the master over the slave in North Carolina." Rejecting any analogous cases in criminal or civil law, Ruffin concluded that Mann could not be guilty. "The power of the master must be absolute," he wrote, "to render the submission of the slave perfect. . . . We cannot allow the right of the master to be brought into discussion in the courts of justice. The slave, to remain a slave, must be made sensible that there is no appeal from his master; that his power is in no instance usurped; but is conferred by the laws of man at least, if not by the laws of God" (quoted in Rose, *A Documentary History of Slavery in North America*, pp. 221–223). Actually, most states and courts in the antebellum South did attempt to limit the cruelty masters could inflict on their slaves. Jurists, clergy, and laymen, led by the distinguished judge John Belton O'Neall of South Carolina, insisted on reforming slave codes to better protect slaves and their families, and statutes required masters to treat slaves with humanity and not inflict cruel punishment on them. Every southern state made the murder of a slave by his master a capital crime. But since slaves could not testify against their masters, most of these laws proved unenforceable. Ruffin articulated the logic of slavery with brutal clarity, and he reminded his fellow southerners that slavery did indeed make southern law—and southern society—different from that of the North and Britain.

History One sign of the way in which southern intellectual work has been relegated to the margins of American intellectual history is the neglect of the South Carolinian William Henry Trescot, who has justly been called "the father of the writing of diplomatic history in the United States." While other southerners produced popular historical and biographical works, Trescot wrote sophisticated histories of American foreign policy in the revolutionary and early national eras, including *The Diplomacy of the Revolution* (1852) and *The Diplomatic History of the Administrations of Washington and Adams, 1789–1801* (1857). Trescot, like so many other southern intellectuals, wore many hats. He was a lawyer by training, the assistant secretary of state in 1860, a southern nationalist, a member of the South Carolina legislature during the Civil War, and, after 1877, a special negotiator for the State Department. Overshadowed by the works of his northern contemporaries George Bancroft and Henry Adams, Trescot nonetheless advanced a view of history that ascribed to nations the same basic life cycle as individuals and asserted that "the conflict of opposing national interests" produced "progress by antagonism." He also maintained that within a nation, "the governing interest will have been matured through the contrast of opposing parties" (quoted in David Moltke-Hansen, *Dictionary of Literary Biography,* vol. 30, pp. 310–319). Trescot conveyed this understanding of the historical process, which demonstrates his debt to contemporary romantic thought, in an elegant prose style and, more important, made American diplomacy a subject of serious historical study.

Literature The idea that the South lacked a vibrant intellectual life has relied most heavily on its lack of great literature. W. J. Cash, in his famous book *The Mind of the South* (1941), stated this notion succinctly: "the whole South produced . . . no novelist but poor Simms to measure against the Northern galaxy headed by Hawthorne and Melville and Cooper . . . no poet deserving the name save Poe—only half a Southerner" (p. 96). Although Cash inaccurately characterized the intellectual life of the Old South, there is no arguing that its literary output did not equal that of the North. On one level, this disparity resulted less from cultural influences than from demographic ones. Given the slave states' proportionately smaller literate population, to produce one Edgar Allan Poe was, in quantitative terms, roughly equivalent to the larger free states producing a Herman Melville and a Nathaniel Hawthorne.

But novelists and poets other than Simms and Poe did inhabit the Old South, and the scholars who have studied them and their writings have sought to understand why their works have not become canonical. Some believe that the need to defend slavery and racism so dominated the southern mind that true literature could not emerge; southern writers were primarily propagandists and polemicists, not artists. But most scholars now recognize that slavery did not prevent southern writers from engaging in the major literary movements, especially Romanticism, that were sweeping the Western world. Southern novelists and poets borrowed and adopted contemporary literary conventions to express their values and their distinct ethos. In this way, slavery did indeed shape southern literature and, according to some historians, does explain why most of that literature has fallen into obscurity. Most southern authors of merit, including Simms, Henry Timrod (the poet laureate of the Confederacy), Augusta Jane Evans, John Pendleton Kennedy,

Augustus Baldwin Longstreet, and Nathaniel Beverley Tucker, supported slavery. Their commitment to their social order distinguished them from most other "modern" writers, whose sense of alienation from their surroundings constituted the core of their art. The individualism—the notion that truth resides within the self and that art reflects the struggle of the self against society and its constraints—that characterized much of northern and Western literature failed to capture the imaginations of southern writers. Instead, they displayed in their art an alternative model of "modernity." Not the isolated, alienated intellectual, but the stable, harmonious, and hierarchical community lay at the center of their vision. For many the plantation served as the model social order. Even though they shared much with nonsouthern writers, including a hostility to the vulgarities and corruptions of the marketplace, they attempted to use forms and conventions derived from a world increasingly dominated by the values of freedom and individualism to defend a social order and a worldview antithetical to those values. Their work, not surprisingly, reveals contradictions and tensions that reflect the larger dilemma of a southern slave society in a capitalistic, bourgeois world. Southern authors failed to develop the literary forms that could express in an artistically distinct way the worldview of their unique modern slave society.

Science Although some historians argue that slavery inhibited scientific development, particularly technological innovations within industries such as iron manufacturing, most scholars have found that slavery did not stifle interest in science. Although the South could not match the northeastern region of the country in terms of the number of scientific publications, participation in national scientific associations, and the founding of scientific journals and societies, the level of scientific activity in the South matched that found in other nonurban parts of the United States. The South actually increased its interest in and commitment to science in the years leading up to the Civil War. That it continued to lag behind the Northeast testifies again to the lack of urban centers, not to some tendency of slave societies to suppress thought. Nor did religion significantly inhibit the growth of science. Although some geologists did encounter hostility and suspicion from religious leaders and laity, most scientists pursued their work with little if any interference. The one exception to this rule were the advocates of polygenesis, the notion that blacks constituted a different species than whites and thus must have been created separately from them. Religious leaders, especially the South Carolina Lutheran John Bachman, defended the scriptural idea of a single creation. Bachman's *The Doctrine of the Unity of the Human Race* (1850) sought to reconcile science and the Bible by demonstrating that humans were one species with infinite varieties. The limited appeal of polygenesis in the South resulted from both religious hostility to an idea that contradicted Scripture and scientific arguments that challenged its contentions.

Most southern scientists focused on the biological and geological sciences and tended to neglect the physical sciences and mathematics. Although science became more professional in the decades preceding the Civil War, many planters adopted scientific approaches on their farms. Articles on soil composition, plant nutrition, and other aspects of "scientific agriculture" filled the more than one hundred agricultural journals that appeared in the South before 1860. While not all planters embraced scientific solutions to agricultural problems, many large planters eagerly adopted and contributed to the development of scientific agriculture. Perhaps the most famous scientific planter was Edmund Ruffin of Virginia. He experimented with marl and wrote the extensive *An Essay on Calcareous Manures* (1852), which he hoped would enable farmers on exhausted soils to reclaim the land's productivity. Although he was never happy with the popular response to his proposals, his work encouraged others to pursue scientific solutions to the practical problems of agriculture.

The most famous scientists to emerge from the South were the Virginians Matthew Fontaine Maury and William Barton Rogers and the Georgian Joseph LeConte. Maury was the foremost oceanographer in America and author of the popular *The Physical Geography of the Sea* (1855). Maury's use of deep-sea soundings helped locate the Atlantic plateau, which made possible the laying of the transatlantic cable in 1858. Rogers was professor of natural philosophy at William and Mary from 1828 to 1835, when he moved to the University of Virginia and became the state geologist as well. His primary scientific contribution derived from his work on the state geological survey, which he conducted in the late 1830s and early 1840s. He became the first president of the Massachusetts Institute of Technology in 1862. LeConte studied zoology and geology with the eminent Louis Agassiz at Harvard University in the early 1850s and then returned to Georgia to teach at Ogelthorpe University and the University of Georgia. In 1857 he relocated to South

Carolina College. A supporter of the Confederacy, he served as a chemist for the Confederate government. After the war he again taught at South Carolina College, until 1869, when he accepted a position at the new University of California, where he remained until his death in 1901.

Theology One cannot appreciate southern intellectual and cultural life in the nineteenth century without recognizing the vital role religion played in the lives of most southerners. Although most people think of southern religion as simple, enthusiastic evangelicalism, the South did produce both sophisticated theologians and passionate backwoods preachers. And the gulf separating these two groups was not as great as some might think. Certainly, most southerners lacked the ability to discuss the nuances of antebellum theology, but they shared with southern divines a commitment to "rational orthodoxy"—a religious worldview that assumed a compatibility between reason and revelation.

The South remained hostile to religious liberalism throughout the antebellum and Reconstruction eras, in part because of the association of religious liberalism with abolition and other dangerous social causes. But the southern commitment to orthodoxy was not simply the result of anxiety over slavery. As the debate between proslavery southern religious leaders and their antislavery northern counterparts demonstrates, much more was at stake in the eyes of southerners than the religious sanction of slaveholding. Again and again, southern ministers and theologians turned to the Bible and produced persuasive evidence that Scripture supported slavery. Although they readily acknowledged that individual masters often abused their authority, they argued that such abuse demonstrated the sinfulness of the master, not the institution itself. They challenged northern opponents to prove through Scripture that slavery was inherently sinful. To southerners, the northerners' appeal to the "spirit of the Bible" over its actual words bespoke a dangerous trend in liberal theology. Once the letter of Scripture was forsaken in favor of a subjectively defined "spirit," nothing would stop individuals from deciding for themselves what was and what was not divinely sanctioned on the basis of their consciences. As the great Presbyterian minister and theologian James Henley Thornwell warned, "Let the authority of the Bible be destroyed, and Christianity must soon perish from the earth. Put its doctrines upon any other ground than a 'thus saith the Lord,' and every one of them will soon be denied" ("The Standard and Nature of Religion," p. 25). Southerners watched as more and more northerners slid from orthodoxy to Unitarianism to spiritualism to atheism, and in the process denied the doctrines of Original Sin, the Incarnation, the Trinity, the Virgin Birth, and the divinity of Jesus, among others. For these southerners, the defense of orthodoxy became much more than a means to defend slavery; in a very real sense it was the defense of Christianity itself.

The defeat of the Confederacy did not destroy the rational orthodoxy of southern theologians, although religious liberalism did spread in the decades after the war. The most interesting aspect of the religious response to defeat was the belief that God had punished the South for its sins, especially the sins associated with slavery. But as they had before the war, southern ministers distinguished between the behavior of masters, which deserved divine chastisement, and slavery itself, which they continued to defend as divinely sanctioned. As the Presbyterian Robert L. Dabney, one of the South's leading theologians after the death of Thornwell in 1862, remarked in his 1867 *A Defence of Virginia: (And through Her, of the South)*, "A righteous God, for our sins towards Him, has permitted us to be overthrown by our enemies and His" (p. 356). Military defeat ended slavery and the Confederacy, but it would take more than that to change southerners' conviction that their social order was ordained by God.

Social and Political Thought Most discussions of southern contributions to antebellum political thought begin and end with John C. Calhoun. Although Calhoun deserves such attention, he was not the only significant political or social thinker of the Old South. Southern intellectuals, especially in the two decades preceding the Civil War, developed a political and social vision that increasingly challenged free-labor society and the egalitarian and individualistic direction of much of Western thought. Although most southerners continued to espouse the political egalitarianism that grew out of Jacksonian democracy, they drew a sharp line between the political equality of white heads of households and the social hierarchies of those households and the society itself.

Calhoun's posthumously published *A Disquisition on Government* (1851) is the most important work of political philosophy to emerge from the antebellum South. Although Calhoun was deeply interested in advancing the cause of the South, he was also seriously concerned with the larger problems of politics—the nature of man and government, the relation of liberty and power in a democracy, and

the problems of an extended republic. By vesting significant interests with a veto power over the enactment and implementation of federal law, Calhoun sought a constitutional means to protect the minority South from northern tyranny. But by making the *Disquisition* a work of political theory rather than a pragmatic policy guide, Calhoun meant to and did contribute to the still lively debate within American constitutional thought over the vexing question of the rights of minorities in a democracy.

In some ways, Albert Taylor Bledsoe, although not as well known as Calhoun, reveals more clearly than Calhoun the dramatic departure of southern social thought from that of mainstream Western culture, including the North. Bledsoe taught mathematics at several colleges and universities, wrote provocative and learned theological texts, and produced *An Essay on Liberty and Slavery* (1856), which both defended southern slavery and attacked free labor and its attendant ideology of individualism. Although Bledsoe defended the concept of natural rights, which other southerners, including Calhoun, attacked, he ridiculed the notion that individual rights trumped the claims of the community over its members. "Civil society," he wrote, "arises, not from a surrender of individual rights, but from the right originally imposed upon all by God himself—a duty which must be performed, whether the individual gives his consent or not." It therefore followed that "the rights of the individual are subordinate to those of the community," since individual rights could only be realized within society, not in freedom from it (pp. 110–111).

Bledsoe's insistence on the primacy of the community over the individual found even more forceful expression in the writings of the Virginian George Fitzhugh and the Mississippian Henry Hughes, two of the South's most passionate proslavery ideologues. Fitzhugh, in *Sociology for the South: or, The Failure of the South* (1854), *Cannibals All! or, Slaves Without Masters* (1857), and numerous journal articles, and Hughes, in *Treatise on Sociology, Theoretical and Practical* (1854), pushed the southern social vision to its extreme. Not only did they repudiate social compact theory and insist that individuals were born into society from which they derived duties and obligations, they embraced slavery as the most humane and natural form of social organization for all societies, regardless of their racial composition or level of economic development. Both attacked free labor and the social conflict, atomization, and the selfishness it promoted. In the "competitive society" of free labor, Fitzhugh insisted, "capital exercises a more perfect compulsion over free laborers than human masters over slaves; for free laborers must at all times work or starve." In the South, however, "slaves are supported whether they work or not" (*Cannibals All!*, p. 32). Only by instituting unfree labor could society provide for all its members and thereby ensure domestic peace. As Hughes stated, "Men must not be free-laborers. For if they are some must starve" (*Treatise on Sociology*, p. 197). In the writings of Fitzhugh and Hughes, one best grasps the South's intellectual revolution against a social vision grounded in freedom, equality, and individual rights. These and countless other southerners offered an alternative vision in which the principles of interdependence, hierarchy, and the subordination of the individual to the community would provide the stability and order necessary for civilization. Only by recognizing that vision can one both appreciate the gulf that separated antebellum southerners not only from northerners but from most of the people of the Western world and understand just how revolutionary the Civil War was for southern intellectual and cultural development. Stripped of the material basis of slavery, southerners proved incapable of maintaining that vision in the decades after the war. Although regional variations would continue, never again would the southern intellectual and cultural life diverge so thoroughly from that of the rest of the nation.

See also **The Classic Vision** *(in this volume);* **White and the Construction of Whiteness; The Idea of the South; Antebellum Charleston; New Orleans** *(volume 2); and other articles in this section.*

BIBLIOGRAPHY

Bledsoe, Albert Taylor. *An Essay on Liberty and Slavery.* Philadelphia, 1856.

Calhoun, John C. *A Disquisition on Government.* In *Union and Liberty: The Political Philosophy of John C. Calhoun.* Edited by Richard K. Cralle. Columbia, S.C., 1851. Reprint, edited by Ross M. Lence. Indianapolis, Ind., 1992.

Cash, W. J. *The Mind of the South.* New York, 1941.

Dabney, Robert L. *A Defence of Virginia: (and through Her, of the South) in Recent and Pending Contests against the Sectional Party.* New York, 1867.

Dew, Thomas Roderick. "Review of the Debate in the Virginia Legislature, 1831–1832." In *The Pro-Slavery Argument: As Maintained by the Most Distinguished Writers of the Southern States.* Charleston, S.C., 1852.

Fitzhugh, George. *Cannibals All! or, Slaves without Masters.* Edited by C. Vann Woodward. Cambridge, Mass., 1960. Originally published in 1857.

Genovese, Eugene D. *The Slaveholders' Dilemma: Freedom and Progress in Southern Conservative Thought, 1820–1860.* Columbia, S.C., 1992.

Holifield, E. Brooks. *The Gentlemen Theologians: American Theology in Southern Culture, 1795–1860.* Durham, S.C., 1978.

Hughes, Henry. *Treatise on Sociology, Theoretical and Practical.* Philadelphia, 1854.

Kaufman, Allen. *Capitalism, Slavery, and Republican Values: American Political Economists, 1819–1848.* Austin, Tex., 1982.

Lounsbury, Richard C., ed. *Louisa S. McCord: Political and Social Essays.* Charlottesville, Va., 1995.

Morris, Thomas D. *Southern Slavery and the Law, 1619–1860.* Chapel Hill, N.C., 1996.

Numbers, Ronald L., and Todd L. Savitt, eds. *Science and Medicine in the Old South.* Baton Rouge, La., 1989.

O'Brien, Michael. *Rethinking the South: Essays in Intellectual History*. Baltimore, 1988.

O'Brien, Michael, and David Moltke-Hansen, eds. *Intellectual Life in Antebellum Charleston*. Knoxville, Tenn., 1986.

Rose, Willie Lee, ed. *A Documentary History of Slavery in North America*. New York, 1976.

Rubin, Louis D., Jr., Blyden Jackson, Rayburn S. Moore, Lewis Simpson, and Thomas Daniel Young, eds. *The History of Southern Literature*. Baton Rouge, La., 1985.

Simms, William Gilmore. *The Letters of William Gilmore Simms*. 5 vols. Collected and edited by Mary C. Simms Oliphant, Alfred Taylor Odell, and T. C. Duncan Eaves. Columbia, S.C., 1952–1956.

Thornwell, James Henley. "The Standard and Nature of Religion." In *The Collected Writings of James Henley Thornwell*. 4 vols. Edited by John B. Adger and John L. Giradeau. Edinburgh, Pa., 1974.

SCIENCE AND RELIGION

Paul Jerome Croce

The strained relationship between science and religion in the middle of the nineteenth century presented Americans with one of their first challenges in diversity. During the first half of the century, all human knowledge was widely regarded as comfortably integrated. The social overlap of scientists and religious thinkers well represented this outlook. In addition, the harmony of reflections about nature and the divine were powerful glues at the core of this synthesis. However, by the end of the century, scientific inquiry developed theoretical justifications and institutional structures separate from religious realms. The bloom of intellectual and cultural diversity that emerged in the wake of these independent inquiries (often in support of science, but sometimes in reaction to all that it stood for), and that have exploded in the twentieth century, began with the breakup of harmony between science and religion from the 1830s to the 1870s. This fissure was the modern precursor of the contemporary split between the "two cultures," as C. P. Snow famously called the humanities and the sciences in the twentieth century, and the mother-lode of our modern pluralism.

The introduction of Darwinism and the widespread influence of evolutionary theories after the 1859 publication of *The Origin of Species* set the terms of debate about science and religion in the ensuing decades. Despite a widespread perception of the warfare of science and religion generated by the theory of species development based on natural selection, the conflict motif was actually only one major view among many in the 1860s and 1870s. At least as important as the irreligious scientific naturalism of Darwinism was the probabilistic nature of his hypothesis and his method of inquiry. And on both fronts—the content and the methods of Darwinism—its revolutionary impact developed force because of gradual changes in science as practiced over the preceding decades.

There have been two major interpretations of the relation of science and religion in the nineteenth century. The traditional view, emerging even at the time, was that the two fields were at war with each other, with enlightened, rational science vanquishing obscurantist religion. The dramatic clarity of the conflict view, as expressed in John William Draper's *History of the Conflict between Religion and Science* (1874) and Andrew Dickinson White's *A History of the Warfare of Science with Theology in Christendom* (1896), was so forceful that it still shapes popular opinions as the folk wisdom of our culture concerning science and religion. A recent revisionist trend, however, emphasizes that many scientists retained their religious beliefs and that many religious believers welcomed new scientific theories; this more recent view expands the separation between science and religion into a spectrum. Although there were a fair number of scientific boosters and religious traditionalists on either end who hoped—or we might even say, hoped and prayed—for the warfare motif to justify their own polarized position, the conventional wisdom now maintains that a general harmony prevailed between science and religion at least until the early twentieth century. And yet that harmony was often hard won, and it went through two major phases.

HARMONY AND TENSION

Until about 1860, science and religion were widely perceived to be in harmony, although the increasingly separate practices of science and religion made reconciliation if their insights more and more difficult. After 1860, tensions between science and religion increased, with a few intellectuals trumpeting the change and most striving mightily to retain the harmony. Meanwhile, change in the methods of science suggested new paths to reconciliation of science and religion through their mutual uncertainty. These remained as hints, unrecognized by most, but gathering force for further development in the twentieth century.

The nineteenth-century emphasis on harmony between science and religion was in some ways a response to the Enlightenment. The most radical, anticlerical phases of the intellectual movement to expand the influence of human reason never gained much of a foothold in America. More Americans sympathized with the Scottish "common sense" phase of the Enlightenment, which emphasized trust in the untutored natural ability of the human mind and heart to discover the true and the good, and which encouraged the moderate belief that science and urbanity could support the more humble drives for religion and morality. What Henry May has called the Didactic Enlightenment encouraged inquiry into the natural world on the model of Francis Bacon's empiricism, which emphasized fact-gathering and caution in proposing theories. Proponents of the didactic perspective treated the facts of nature as evidence for the designing hand of the divine following the natural theology of William Paley. By the early nineteenth century, religious leaders, although aware of the radically antireligious potential in the Enlightenment, found they could reverse its secular thrust by actually enlisting science to support religion. Boasting about the "altered tone of science," Lewis Green, minister and president of Hampden-Sidney College, said in 1842, "The whole spirit of physical investigation has been revolutionized in the present century; and . . . the stupid Atheistic Materialism of the last century, has almost totally disappeared."

The religious enthusiasm for science coincided with more secular attitudes because science was also welcomed as a source of patriotic pride and a tool for economic growth. New knowledge of the natural world flooded in with the reports of travel and settlement in the west, and technological innovations helped to spark America's great economic growth. Throughout this period, however, science had only a minimum of institutional infrastructure with the founding of the *American Journal of Science and Arts* in 1819 and a few scientific schools (notably Rensselaer Institute, Troy, New York, founded in 1824; Yale University's Sheffield Scientific School, 1846; and Harvard University's Lawrence Scientific School, 1847). By contrast schools and departments for the training of young scientists flourished after 1860, spurred by the demands of the Civil War and of industrial growth in the ensuing years. More common in the earlier period were the local scientific and natural history societies and lyceums, which were havens for serious but amateur scientific inquiries by professional men with scientific curiosity. With the gender specializations of the time, women gravitated toward the writing of children's primers, scientific illustrations, and popularizations, and these often served as scientists' first enthusiastic steps in their fields. Religion's place in this form of science was wary and watchful, curious but not overtly critical.

With the growth of scientific knowledge and the first pressures toward specialization, the local societies proved inadequate by the 1840s. National organizations, including the Smithsonian Institution and the American Association for the Advancement of Science, established professional standards, encouraged research presentations and publications, and in general promoted the "increase and diffusion" of scientific knowledge, as the Smithsonian charter put it. The government, most notably the Coast Survey (whose name changed to the Coast and Geodetic Survey in 1878) employed one-third of antebellum scientists. In addition, colleges added prominent scientists to their faculty. For example, Harvard hired the prolific and influential botanist Asa Gray in 1842 and in 1848, persuaded the Swiss geologist and zoologist Louis Agassiz to join the faculty and take up permanent residence in the United States, where he had already been visiting for two years. Although very different personally, and with contrasting approaches to science that would take them to opposite sides of the debate over Darwinism, they were both deeply religious and shared the view that scientific research offered no threat to religious belief.

Meanwhile, evangelical religion of the time did not resist science, but instead was either indifferent or quietly supportive of the design argument. The revivalist and educator Charles Grandison Finney, for example, said flatly that "studying science is studying the works of God." Nature understood by science provided evidence for Christianity, which contributed to the public authority of Christian churches. And nonscientific intellectuals, such as the Transcendentalists, the diverse followers of Emanuel Swedenborg's spiritual philosophy, and other romantic thinkers, following Ralph Waldo Emerson's maxim that "every natural fact is a symbol of some spiritual fact," assumed that investigation of the natural world would support religious insight. These romantic thinkers were in the vanguard of a revolution against Baconian science, and its complement in religion, natural theology, which looked to the orderly empirical facts of nature for proof of the divine. But while their German-inspired idealism was philosophically opposite to empiricism, it reinforced the same theme of harmony between science and religion, albeit on dif-

LOUIS AGASSIZ

Louis Agassiz was a professor of natural history at Neuchâtel in Switzerland when the Lowell Institute invited him to Boston. His spotting of glacial action on first arriving in America set the tone for his quarter century of enthusiastic leadership of American science: "I sprang on shore and . . . was met by the familiar signs, the polished surfaces, the furrows and scratches, the line engravings of the glacier . . . and I became convinced . . . that here also this great agent had been at work."

In 1846, Agassiz was already world famous for his vast knowledge and encyclopedic classification of fish (his special expertise) and the whole animal kingdom, and for his theory of glacial action during an ancient ice age. His special appeal in America, where his lectures were even hawked on street corners, was his idealistic, religious approach to science. Glaciers were "God's great plough" clearing landscapes to make room for special creations, and as Ralph Waldo Emerson said, "he made anatomy popular *by the aid of an idea*"—the conviction that the whole natural world was organized by divine plan.

Agassiz's theory of special creation made him an odd bedfellow with southern pro-slavery advocates when he theorized that blacks were created separately from whites. He maintained his loyalties to his adopted city, however, and was a vigorous Unionist during the Civil War. Darwin's theory of natural selection clashed directly with his theories of glacial action and the fixity of species in their current terrain. However, his enthusiasm inspired nonscientific amateurs and a whole generation of late-nineteenth-century scientists—many of whom, such as Joseph LeConte, blended his idealism with evolutionism in the development of American neo-Lamarckianism. Agassiz himself, however, resisted the tide of scientific opinion and firmly rejected Darwinism and evolutionism for the rest of his life.

Jean Louis Rodolphe Agassiz (1807–1873). Founder of the Museum of Comparative Zoology at Harvard University. ARCHIVE PHOTOS

the awesome workings of the divine. Henry David Thoreau represented another stream of Romanticism in his blending of empiricism and idealism, which linked science and religion through his spiritual but factual natural history investigations, conducted in the spirit of the German polymath scientist Alexander von Humboldt's empirical naturalism.

For all their disagreements, practitioners of science and religious adherents, empiricists and idealists, shared the conviction that scientific work would not conflict with the essential truths of religion. Aware that some still "kept distrustful eyes on science," the mineralogist and geologist James Dwight Dana was confident that it would bring "new revelations of profound truths direct from God's works." The theologian James Henley Thornwell said, "Geology and the Bible must kiss and embrace each other, and . . . [t]he earth can never turn traitor to its God."

Religious leaders were generally even more enthusiastic than scientists about science's support of religion. For scientists, religious connections were becoming more like rhetorical ornaments placed at the introduction and conclusion of scientific addresses. Their religious beliefs, while personally wel-

ferent terms. In place of emphasizing factual evidence, romantic thinking effectively domesticated the harsh proofs of science by proposing that the complicated results of scientific pursuit were actually part of the wonders of the natural world and

Asa Gray (1810–1888), World-renowned Botanist.
During their correspondence for several years before
On the Origin of Species was published, Gray educated
Darwin about North American plants from his personal
herbarium. Following the publication of Darwin's work in
1859, Gray publicly defended Darwin's theory in the
United States. © BETTMANN/CORBIS

come, were becoming increasingly irrelevant to the
actual work of scientific research. For example, Gray
heard Agassiz lecture on his triumphal visit to the
United States the year before he was hired at Harvard, and noted that the pious zoologist's "references to the Creator were so natural and unconstrained as to show that they were never brought in
for effect." Although Gray was a strong religious
believer, he could not accept religious references applied just for pious show.

THE EMERGING DIVIDE

The ebbing away from religion came gradually, and
when antireligious conclusions were made explicit
in the 1840s, most scientists readily defended religion's harmony with their fields of inquiry. In 1844,
the Englishman Robert Chambers argued for the

evolutionary change of species in *The Vestiges of
Creation.* He published it anonymously in rightful
expectation of hostility for its purely material explanations. The book's reception gave Darwin himself caution about publishing his more thorough
and persuasive account of species development.

Just as scientific investigations were conducted
without reference to science, so too did religious
believers become more distant from science. The
increasingly privatized religion of the heart in the
early to middle nineteenth century was the culmination of the Reformation assault on the institutional church, other eighteenth-century evangelical
impulses, and the special challenges of churches in
the New World where religious believers generally
worked through voluntary organizations but resisted the more formal hierarchies of European culture. Sentimentalized religion, with close ties to
women's culture and popular religion, was not
overtly antagonistic to science, but left little reason
for a religious interest in science; on the contrary,
it suggested a strict separation of science and sentiment, echoing the separate spheres of men and
women. Although religious believers tacitly assumed scientific support of religious belief, most
simply ignored the insights of science and paid little
attention to its gradual steps away from religion.

Although average believers were moved by private feelings and religious sentiments, religious intellectuals and church leaders worried more about
their connection to science. They noticed the
growth of scientific knowledge, recalled the more
radical phases of the Enlightenment, and felt moved
to reconcile science with traditional doctrine. Intellectuals at Princeton or New Haven, for example,
had more motivation than the typical churchgoer
to connect their religion to the hopes for harmony
that science might be able to offer. Their apologetics
offered a twist on an old intellectual tradition in the
Western world. In place of arguing for the compatibility of science and religion based on unquestioning faith in divine existence and providential governance of the world, mid-nineteenth-century
intellectuals were so aware of fundamental doubts
that they felt they could no longer rely on assumptions of faith, but instead searched anxiously for
scientific proofs of religion. Their quest for a faith
with scientific certainty dovetailed with the passionate assurances then appearing in other parts
of American religion and culture, including the
millennial zeal of revivalists, the earnest creation of
new religions, and the fierce call for Manifest
Destiny.

꙰

CHOLERA EPIDEMICS: DIVINE PUNISHMENT OR NATURAL DISASTER?

After 1817, cholera became a global disease, spreading from local pockets in the Far East, first to Persia and Russia, and then across Europe to the Americas and the rest of the world. It was an unwelcome stowaway with the vast migrations of people in the nineteenth century and improvements in the transportation and marketing of goods. Urban centers, with their large concentrations of people, but not yet with public health standards or even much order in public works, were fallow fields for the cholera epidemics that swept in periodically through the century. And it was a reaper not only grim, but also swift and lurid, turning its victims cold and darkened, with painful cramps and thorough dehydration—all in the span of as little as one day. Before the German physiologist Robert Koch isolated the organism causing cholera, *Vibrio comma,* in 1883, the disease was wholly mysterious and terrifying, and it inspired a broad range of religious and scientific explanations.

In 1832, 1849, and 1866, the United States suffered major outbreaks of cholera, and as the historian Charles Rosenberg points out, the cultural responses to the disease serve as a microcosm of secularizing trends over these decades. One minister, in "A Sermon Preached August 3, 1832, A Day Set Apart in the City of New-York for Public Fasting, Humiliation and Prayer. . ." regarded cholera as a "scourge, a rod in the hand of God." Although liberals objected to this stern talk, they retained a place for the divine in their explanations, even if they assumed that God operated exclusively through secondary laws.

The argument about natural laws controlling even God's will gained still more adherents by 1849. Spiritual and physical concerns about the spread of disease mingled, for example, in a New Bedford newspaper editorial: "Prayer, without at the same time forsaking sin and doing right, is an utter mockery, and deserves a curse. We must now cleanse and purify ourselves." There was growing concern, as the president of the Wisconsin State Medical Society lamented, about human "ignorance of the nature and the character of the pestilence." Distinct impressions were forming that concentrations of filth and unwashed food contributed to the spread of cholera, but efforts to combat the disease, whether from religious or scientific circles, were utterly powerless. This contributed not only to secularization, but also to skepticism about the medical profession and to the growth of nonmainstream medical systems, especially hydropathy and homeopathy, which were generally more successful than "regular practitioners" in combating the disease.

When the scourge returned in 1866, there was still no cure, but there was some hope for prevention of its spread. The medical profession, bolstered by the organization of the Sanitary Commission during the Civil War and reinforced by scientific studies of contamination in food and water supplies, set up Boards of Health, first in New York, for the reform of public health in the degraded urban centers. There was now almost no public mention of religion in relation to cholera, except those who, like one Methodist preacher, proposed that he could not minister to "the souls of man . . . while their bodies are thus crowded and packed in such filthy abodes." This shows the eagerness during this era to enlist mankind in God's work, and yet there is no assumption of divine Providence guiding the course of the world.

In thirty-four years, cholera had shifted in the public imagination from a spiritual crisis to a social problem.

Darwin's theory of species development through natural selection and the enthusiasm for professional and nonreligious science that came in its wake brought the religious leaders' worst fears to life. Building the argument for species change on the analogy with selective breeding of domesticated species and supporting it with an abundant array of facts from the burgeoning sciences of botany, embryology, geography, geology, morphology, physiology, and zoology, Darwin's theory presented a fundamental challenge to the conventional wisdom about harmony between science and religion. First, the presentation was wholly naturalistic, without a place for the divine or even any religious flourishes; second, with the struggle for existence as the engine of change, Darwinism implied a world without mercy and morality; and third, the central hypothesis was presented as a plausible explanation but not as a proof. The theory of natural selection operated in a different conceptual universe from the urge to find proof for religion in the benign facts of nature.

In the context of the earlier generation's commitment to certainty, Darwin's theory of natural selection was both religious and scientific heresy. With its attention to constant change and minute variations within species pools, the scientific "heresy" produced new paths for research spurring investigation into vast eons of time, exploration of broad expanses of geography, and close attention to details in individual creatures. In suggesting and justifying large amounts of new inquiry into nature, Darwinism reinforced trends toward professionalization and specialization in the sciences.

Although Darwinism was greeted with some spirited scientific resistance, most notably from Louis Agassiz, and was honored more in general as evolutionism than for its particular arguments, its success coincided with a great upsurge of institution building in higher education. By the 1870s, some of the leading colleges took the first steps along these lines: the chemist Charles Eliot became president of Harvard in 1869 and emphasized scientific training as part of the buildup of a strong masculine character in preparation for cultural leadership; and after training at Yale's Scientific School and serving as president of the University of California, Daniel Coit Gilman in 1876 became president of the Johns Hopkins University, which pioneered by prioritizing research, especially in science, instead of undergraduate education. Even outside universities, science became a point of widespread public curiosity and respect by the 1870s, as evidenced by the publication of *Appleton's Journal* "for scientific news" (from 1867) and *Popular Science Monthly* (from 1872), the creation of scientific columns in *Harper's* (from 1869) and *Galaxy* (from 1871), and the addition of the word "science" to the subtitle of the *Atlantic*.

Religious figures were slower to respond to Darwinism. Taking heart from the scientific opponents to Darwinism during the 1860s, many religious leaders treated it as a tempest in a scientific teapot. Applying the logic of the previous generation in reverse, they assumed that any theory that did not reinforce religious belief must not be good science. In addition, although the Civil War promoted institution building in science, it inhibited serious reflection on science and its implications.

By 1870, with evolutionism entrenched in scientific circles, religious thinkers finally turned their attention to the theological implications of the "transmutation hypothesis," as the theory was called by theologians and clerics. Only at this point did religions even begin to separate in response to Darwinism, on paths that became the polarized mainstays of twentieth-century American religion. Comparing Darwin's hypotheses with the ideal of Baconian empiricism and also horrified by the purely naturalistic amorality of the theory, conservatives rejected Darwinism on scientific and religious grounds. For example, the Episcopal clergyman and University of Pennsylvania Provost Daniel Goodwin wrote scathingly that Darwinism "expressly refuses to recognize any necessary or determinate law of development or variation; and throws itself upon the illimitable ocean of accident."

Asa Gray took the lead for a blending of Darwinism and religion. Not concerned with the naturalistic displacement of God from providential action and primary causes, he retained a picture of the divine as a mysterious reclusive force, like a hidden, forceful wind behind all worldly action; "natural selection is not the wind," Gray argued, "but the rudder which . . . shapes the course." These religious words from a scientist supported liberal theologians such as Henry Ward Beecher and James Woodrow who presented evolution as God's approach to the creation and governance of the world. Religious thinkers endorsing evolutionism without the technical specifics of Darwinism found support among late-nineteenth-century professional scientists: geology and physics provided no clear evidence for the fabulous time spans required for the operation of natural selection, and the science of genetics had not yet developed to provide biological reasoning to endorse the processes of natural selection. For scientists and liberal theologians, evolution was a way of comprehending progress, by compromising on Darwin's harsh picture of nature in favor of incorporating the Enlightenment biologist Jean Baptiste de Lamarck's theory that acquired traits could shape future species change. American neo-Lamarckians depicted evolution on a shorter time span and with more optimistic opportunities for voluntary improvement than were allowed with the chance mutation and inheritance mechanisms of Darwinism.

SCIENTIFIC THEORY AND HYPOTHESIS

Most supporters of evolution treated innovations in science, including Darwinism, as fully authoritative or even certain. After all, science had the prestige of professional status, and it was associated with the marvelous technological innovations that thrilled the average citizen. But scientists themselves increasingly treated their theories as Darwin did: as hypotheses. Darwin himself wrote, in a letter to fellow scientist Gray, that he sought throughout his theory "to establish a point as a probability by induction and to apply it as hypotheses to other parts and see whether it will solve them."

Two young students of science at Harvard in the 1860s, Charles Sanders Peirce and William James, noticed this core of uncertainty beneath the social confidence of science. As early as 1868, James wrote that Darwin's theory "at best helps to accumulate a probability," but he recognized that "the great value of the hypothesis [is] in setting naturalists to work. . . . It is doubtless provisional, but none the less serviceable for that." And in 1877, Peirce wrote with more logical precision that Darwinism is a result of the "statistical method applied to biology" because "Darwin, while unable to say what the operation of variation and natural selection in any individual case will be, demonstrates that in the long run they will, or would adapt animals to their circumstances." Out of their youthful discussions about the nature and methods of science, especially Darwinism, in the 1860s and 1870s, Peirce and James de-

veloped the theory of pragmatism, although it did not take on that name publicly until 1898. Before it was a name, pragmatism grew in the shadow of Darwinism, from a recognition of the uncertain and therefore hypothetical and constructed but also useful nature of science; and in the context of mid-nineteenth-century debates about the relation of science and religion, pragmatism emerged as a new way to reconcile science and religion. While it avoided the early-nineteenth-century expectation of harmony between the two fields based on their mutual certainty, pragmatism inaugurated a tradition that embraced modern science and drew parallels between its methods and the character of religious belief—based on their mutual uncertainty.

In the early nineteenth century, scientific and religious truths were usually presented in terms of proof and certainty. However, by the end of the century, propositions in these fields had fewer universal assurances: hypotheses qualified the expression of scientific theories; liberal religious commentators used the language of metaphor and ambiguity; and conservatives held on to the methods of the earlier generation. During the middle of the century, not only did the practice of science and religion reach a fundamental separation, but also the seeds were planted for the liberal-conservative split in religious views of science over the question of how much certainty was required to sustain belief. And so, the warfare of science and religion was not wholly inaccurate, but rather it was a polemical, popularized exaggeration of a very real trend. Meanwhile, professional students of science and religion embraced the uncertainty of steady inquiry and ambivalence in each field, while most of the public was still eager for scientific proof and religious assurance. This fraying of the culture over fundamental truths broke the edifice of consensus in nineteenth-century American culture and cracked the expectation of uniformities in thought and culture. And into the breach created by the changing relations of science and religion, countless other intellectual and cultural diversities followed.

See also **The Rise of Biblical Criticism and Challenges to Religious Authority; The Struggle over Evolution; Pragmatism and Its Critics** *(in this volume);* **The Scientific Ideal** *(volume 3).*

BIBLIOGRAPHY

Books

Bozeman, Theodore Dwight. *Protestants in an Age of Science: The Baconian Ideal and Ante-bellum American Religious Thought.* Chapel Hill, N.C., 1977.

Bruce, Robert V. *The Launching of Modern American Science, 1846–1876*. New York, 1987.

Burnham, John C. *How Superstition Won and Science Lost: Popularizing Science and Health in the United States*. New Brunswick, N.J., 1987.

Cashdollar, Charles D. *The Transformation of Theology, 1830–1890: Positivism and Protestant Thought in Britain and America*. Princeton, N.J., 1989.

Conser, Walter H., Jr. *God in the Natural World: Religion and Science in Antebellum America*. Columbia, S.C., 1993.

Croce, Paul Jerome. *Science and Religion in the Era of William James*. Vol. 1, *Eclipse of Certainty, 1820–1880*. Chapel Hill, N.C., 1995.

Cummings, Sherwood. *Mark Twain and Science: Adventures of a Mind*. Baton Rouge, La., 1988.

Daniels, George H. *American Science in the Age of Jackson*. New York, 1968.

Dupree, A. Hunter. *Asa Gray: American Botanist, Friend of Darwin*. Baltimore, 1988.

Fleming, Donald. *John William Draper and the Religion of Science*. Philadelphia, 1950.

Hawkins, Hugh. *Between Harvard and America: The Educational Leadership of Charles W. Eliot*. New York, 1972.

Hovenkamp, Herbert. *Science and Religion in America, 1800–1860*. Philadelphia, 1978.

Hull, David L. *Darwin and His Critics: The Reception of Darwin's Theory of Evolution by the Scientific Community*. Chicago, 1973.

Kohlstedt, Sally Gregory. *The Formation of the American Scientific Community: The American Association for the Advancement of Science, 1848–1860*. Urbana, Ill., 1976.

——. "Parlors, Primers, and Public Schooling: Education for Science in Nineteenth-Century America." *Isis* 81, no. 308 (1990): 425–445.

Kuklick, Bruce. *Churchmen and Philosophers: From Jonathan Edwards to John Dewey*. New Haven, Conn., 1985.

Lindberg, David C., and Ronald L. Numbers. *God and Nature: Historical Essays on the Encounter between Christianity and Science*. Berkeley, Calif., 1986.

May, Henry. *The Enlightenment in America*. New York, 1976.

Moore, James R. *The Post-Darwin Controversies: A Study of the Protestant Struggle to Come to Terms with Darwin in Great Britain and America, 1870–1900*. New York, 1979.

Oleson, Alexandra, and Sanborn Conner Brown, eds. *The Pursuit of Knowledge in the Early Republic: American Scientific and Learned Societies from Colonial Times to the Civil War*. Baltimore, 1976.

Rabinowitz, Richard. *The Spiritual Self in Everyday Life: The Transformation of Personal Religious Experience in Nineteenth-Century New England*. Boston, 1989.

Rosenberg, Charles. *The Cholera Years: The United States in 1832, 1849, and 1866*. Chicago, 1987.

Snow, C. P. *The Two Cultures and the Scientific Revolution*. New York, 1961. The Rede lecture, 1959.

Stevenson, Louise L. *Scholarly Means to Evangelical Ends: The New Haven Scholars and the Transformation of Higher Learning in America, 1830–1890.* Baltimore, 1986.

Turner, James. *Without God, without Creed: The Origins of Unbelief in America.* Baltimore, 1985.

Part 4

COMMERCIAL AND NATIONAL CONSOLIDATION: 1878–1912

OVERVIEW:
1878–1912

Susan Curtis

Between 1878 and 1912, Americans experienced two contradictory impulses—social consolidation and cultural rebellion. Social consolidation, emphasizing economic and social interdependence and collective thought and action, undergirded the transformation of economic life from the 1860s to the 1890s, by which time the United States emerged as the industrial leader of the world. Industrialization spread from its traditional stronghold in the Northeast across the Midwest into the mining and ranching regions of the West and through the "New South." Rail lines crisscrossed the nation, drawing even remote areas into national and international markets. Captains of industry solidified their position of dominance in the U.S. economy and society as more and more Americans depended on them for goods, services, and employment.

At the same time, this rapidly consolidating economy and society created the conditions for widespread cultural rebellion. Dissonance between prevailing cultural ideas and lived experience lay at the heart of the rebellion. The corporate order fundamentally altered the experience of work and the organization of family and communal life in the United States, but time-worn Victorian platitudes about hard work, self-control, "separate spheres," and social advancement could not make sense of these changes. Moreover, industrial expansion drew into the matrix of production a population marked increasingly by race, ethnic, and class differences, but the constitutional promises of equality before the law did not prevent lynching of African Americans, outbursts of nativist hysteria against immigrants, or violent eruptions of class warfare.

Economic confidence co-existed with social anxiety. Corporate interdependence spawned bitter class struggles. An incorporating economy eventually required the incorporation of diverse people into the body politic and into the public culture. The triumph of consolidation and the transformation of American culture left the nation reeling, as the cherished individualism of the new nation gave way to a social ethos and as reveries in the parlor gave way to ragtime music, cakewalk dances, amusement parks, and vaudeville theater. As the Harvard English professor Barrett Wendell put it, "We are submerged beneath a conquest so complete that the very name of us means something not ourselves." Between 1878 and 1912, the United States remade itself and struggled simultaneously for self-recognition.

INCORPORATING ECONOMY

The incorporation of the American economy, in the broadest sense, set in motion the process of social and cultural change that defined the gilded age. The growth of large-scale enterprises implied in this meaning of incorporation did not begin in 1878. But in the fifty years following the end of the Civil War, the economy had come to be dominated by them. Businessmen, officially wedded to the ideal of individual entrepreneurship, experimented with a variety of corporate forms to assure their success. As the nation's economy came to rely on heavy industries like steel production, the mining and refining of valuable ores and minerals, the movement of goods and people in an extensive network of rails, roads, and shipping lanes, it was bound together in a series of interlocking regional, national, and international markets. Interdependence rapidly overtook the American ideal of self-reliance.

In order to accomplish large-scale productivity, corporate magnates reorganized the workplace, making it more impersonal, efficient, dominated by machines, and driven by time. The efficient manufacture of standardized products changed the nature and meaning of manual labor. Division of labor diminished the importance of artisanal creativity and depended instead on the maximal use of time. A managerial revolution contributed to this process and created a new class of professionals who were neither entrepreneurs nor wage workers. The growth of corporations rested on ideas and assumptions that cut against the grain of liberal individualism, laissez-faire government, and the Victorian promise of success as the reward for hard work and self-control.

As they reorganized their companies and the nature of production, industrialists redefined the free enterprise system. While many captains of industry had amassed the capital necessary to finance machine-powered mass production and national marketing as individual entrepreneurs, the promise of industrialism and economic incorporation lay in attracting investors and limiting individual liability. Railroad moguls soon learned that profits generated by the construction of rail lines quickly gave way to a daily struggle to keep lines running without losing money. They tried to attract large corporate users by offering economic incentives like lower rates and rebates at the expense of customers, like farmers, with small, more irregular shipments. As these measures failed to bring the desired financial result, railroad owners entered into pooling agreements to fix prices at a profitable level. Other industrialists experimented with new corporate forms. Beginning in the 1880s, many companies created trusts that would achieve legally what pools could not. Trusts preserved the appearance of individual competing firms, but they demanded that each company exchange common stock for trust certificates and abide by policies made by a board of trustees. When declared illegal by the Sherman Antitrust Act of 1890, trusts largely gave way to holding companies, which turned independent competitors into subsidiaries of a single entity. Although not explicitly illegal, these new companies clearly endorsed monopoly. Defenders of free enterprise in practice worked to bind the invisible hand of capitalism.

This early phase of large-scale industrialization prompted a nationwide debate about the appropriate relationship between business activity and government provision for the common good. Discriminatory rates, struck down initially by state laws enacted by legislatures sympathetic to farmers' pleas for fair play, called into being the intervention of the state. The Interstate Commerce Commission, established in 1887 as the first regulatory agency in the United States, oversaw commercial traffic across state boundaries and introduced the potential for more aggressive measures by the government to protect the interests of individual citizens against the consolidated power of the corporation. Budding regulation did not mean that the government assumed a hostile relationship to incorporated business. Not only had land grants promoted the construction of a transcontinental railroad, but the ratification of the Fourteenth Amendment in 1868 had legitimized new forms of economic organization. Such initiatives as the Open Door policy also opened new markets to American entrepreneurs. Moreover, businesses, once hostile to the idea of government regulation, eventually saw in a regulatory state a chance to impose order on their industries and weed out smaller competitors. Nevertheless, in justifying the regulation of railroad practice, advocates spelled out new responsibilities for the state that would be taken up by the Populist, or People's, Party in the 1890s and the progressives of both Republican and Democratic Parties in the first decades of the twentieth century.

Corporate organization of work, refashioning of the marketplace, and tussling with governmental restraint, taken together, reshaped American society, economic life, and cultural expression. Sheer output put to rest Malthusian predictions of widespread social disaster in the face of growing populations and modern conditions, as cited in the hastily written pamphlet distributed in the late 1790s. Indeed, industrial production far outstripped the basic subsistence needs of the rapidly expanding U.S. population. The vast network of railroads ended the isolation of "island communities" across the country, connecting small-town Americans to national trends. By 1900 the United States had become the undisputed leader of the world, producing more than 30 percent of the goods manufactured worldwide. The principles of mass production extended from heavy industries to a plethora of consumer-oriented industries—clothing, household furnishings, processed food, and small household gadgets—bringing a different standard of living within reach of the middle class. Economic incorporation made ready use of new technologies, which were patented in unprecedented numbers. In these ways the consolidation of economic resources and efforts to stay the invisible hand of the market profoundly affected the daily lives of most Americans—in the city and in the countryside. Enthusiasm for the widespread benefits of modernization, however, clashed with anxiety about work and self-worth, class conflict in a democracy, and the relationship between "wealth" and "commonwealth."

WORKING-CLASS IDEOLOGY IN THE AGE OF CONSOLIDATION

Not everyone enjoyed the benefits of an incorporating economy. Those whose lives were most directly affected by the new organization of work—laboring men and women—responded angrily to the changed conditions. The ideological devaluation of workers to the process of production, which was compounded by the growing impersonality of workplaces employing hundreds of hands, shook the foundations of the American work ethic as well as personal bases for individual identity. Organizations of labor had existed since the early nineteenth century. Those groups imbibed the language of republicanism, sought self-improvement through literacy, and took seriously the call to democratic participation in the Age of Jackson. Laborers preserved craft traditions and standards of workmanship in the antebellum years when factories and mills first began to gather wage workers into industrial production. Post–Civil War laborers, however, faced greater challenges to their autonomy and skill and responded by creating and working for organizations that articulated principles in opposition to those of the business community.

Opposition from workers to the new conditions wrought by big business philosophy and industrial modes of production exploded at the dawn of the era of consolidation. The Great Strike of 1877, precipitated by a sudden and drastic reduction in wages of railroad workers, exposed the ideological chasm that separated employers from their employees. Anger erupted in Baltimore, Pittsburgh, Chicago, St. Louis, and San Francisco and escalated into mob violence as workers fought what they perceived as attacks on their ability to fulfill the cultural roles of breadwinner and workingman and on the work ethic they had believed was inviolable. Local, state, and federal troops quelled the uprising at the request of railroad owners. Aware that social chaos could emerge from class conflict, owners justified their drastic actions as essential to the maintenance of social order and free enterprise in the United States.

The Great Strike of 1877, eventually put down with force, set the tone for class struggle in the ensuing two decades. Through existing and newly formed unions, workers articulated ever more clearly their particular class interests and their opposition to the industrial capitalist system. In so doing, they tried to preserve the value of labor by refashioning the work ethic in collective terms. The Knights of Labor reflected a desire by workers to share with investors and employers the fruits of their labor. Recognizing the indispensability of both labor and capital, the Knights of Labor argued in favor of cooperative economic forms. This cooperative impulse ran counter to the emerging view of businessmen that labor represented a cost of production. Concomitant with the cooperative ideal, the Knights of Labor also refused to cling to an older view of laborers as individual agents. "An injury to one," they declared, "is an injury to all." They thus called for class solidarity.

Under the leadership of Terence V. Powderly, the Knights of Labor pushed for—and sometimes established—cooperatives that linked ownership and work. Few such cooperatives competed successfully with highly capitalized enterprises. Authorizing strike actions only as a last resort, Powderly's Knights of Labor hoped that organized workers negotiating with reasonable businessmen could produce harmony in the nation's workplaces. The successful strikes against the robber baron Jay Gould's railroads in 1885 attracted thousands of laborers to the organization. But their lack of commitment to striking as a last resort and their desire for a more aggressive, militant union ultimately undermined the viability of the union and the cooperative ideal.

At the same time that the membership of the Knights of Labor grew most dramatically, other labor philosophies began to emerge as well. Advocates of the eight-hour day, for example, hoped to use the collective power of organized workers to wrest concessions from capitalists. Socialists, hoping to bring the entire order of competition and class division to an end, made appeals to workers on the basis of a communal ideal, sometimes rooted in the Christian tradition and other times in materialist philosophy. The American Railway Union president Eugene V. Debs's socialism, which defined work as a source of personal identity and required the commitment of strong communities to the common good and the mutual respect between rich and poor, employer and employee, arose from a desire to defend both republican virtue and traditional manliness.

When a rally at the Haymarket Square in Chicago in 1886 ended in the explosion of a bomb and the deaths of Chicago policemen on hand to maintain order, and the news media depicted participants—including the Knights of Labor—as irresponsible and dangerous radicals, support for Powderly's organization began to evaporate. The American Federation of Labor began making a different kind of class-based appeal to workers. Arguing that industrial production was not likely to disappear, the American Federation of Labor's most powerful spokesman, Samuel Gompers, advocated that labor use its collective power to insist upon greater benefits, better wages and hours, and improved working conditions. The American Federation of Labor's philosophy grew out of the realization that workers could not afford the goods they created, and it relied on the desire of workers to share in the abundance by demanding a better wage.

By 1900 a small minority of workers belonged to unions, but the labor organizations, their leaders, and the celebrated strikes of 1877, 1885–1886, 1892 (the Amalgamated Steelworkers' strike against the steel industrialist Andrew Carnegie's plant at Homestead, Pennsylvania), and 1894 (Debs's American Railway Union's strike against the Pullman Palace Car Company) had established terms in which much of the social debate would be argued. Indeed, class divisions in a democratic society posed a cultural problem difficult to resolve.

THE YEOMAN FARMER AND COMMERCIAL REALITIES

Class warfare raised profound concerns about the viability of the American democratic experiment. The economist Thorstein Veblen's identification of a "leisure class" devoted to "conspicuous consumption" and Henry Demarest Lloyd's *Wealth against Commonwealth* (1894) both exposed the frayed strands of republican ideology in an age of industrialism. Utopian novels like William Dean Howells's *A Traveler from Altruria* (1894) and Edward Bellamy's *Looking Backward, 2000–1887* (1888) pointed to the chasm that yawned between Americans' egalitarian hopes and their lived experience. One of the most pointed attacks on the consolidating national economy came from America's farmers. The agrarian revolt of the 1890s contributed to the mounting disaffection from dominant cultural ideals and imagined a new role for the government that would flower after 1900.

The growth of commercial agriculture after the Civil War depended on new technology and expanded networks of transportation, unmistakable emblems of industrial consolidation. While steel plows, reapers, and threshers had appeared before the Civil War, demand for them did not increase appreciably until steamships, railroads, and the transatlantic cable facilitated the sale of large-scale surpluses. Eager to take part in the expanding network of exchange, farmers, whose numbers rose almost fourfold between 1850 and 1900, opened more than 300 million acres of land to cultivation in that same span of time. The attraction of new markets at home and overseas, however, masked the number of competitors in the field. Thanks to rapidly expanding markets, U.S. farmers competed with Argentines, Canadians, Russians, and Australians for a livelihood. From 1870 to 1900, farmers faced the commercial reality of steadily declining commodity prices. Although the economic crisis was not felt with the same intensity by farmers in all regions and agricultural sectors, it deepened in the 1880s and 1890s. As many farmers saw it, unfair shipping rates and an inadequate money supply were responsible for their economic misery. They did persuade state legislatures (and the federal government) to pass laws to regulate the railroads, but efforts to expand the currency with paper money languished.

Like the Knights of Labor, some farmers pushed for cooperation. In the South and the West, local political groups, known as Farmers' Alliances, bypassed local merchants and purchased supplies in bulk at wholesale prices. They railed against the "money power" and the various trusts, appealing to the most hard-pressed farmers. By the late 1880s, more than 6 million members took part in Farmers' Alliances. Southern leaders like Tom Watson of Georgia tried to downplay divisive race issues in the hope of achieving broader economic and political goals. Other leaders advanced a plan that called for the construction of government-run warehouses, where producers could store grain until prices rose to favorable levels. This vision of government-sponsored cooperation reflected their desire to restore a commonwealth ideal even as it pointed toward a more active, interventionist state.

By the early 1890s, farmers voiced their critique of corporate America and their vision in the platform for the People's Party. Authored by Ignatius Donnelly, the platform outlined a sweeping political program of public ownership of essential modes of transportation and communication, direct democracy, and the expansion of the money supply through the free coinage of silver and a bimetal currency. Perhaps as important as any specific plank in the platform were the terms used by Donnelly to explain the social conflict. Donnelly saw the nation riven into two warring camps, identified variously as "tramps" and "millionaires" and the "people" and the "interests."

The People's Party won some seats in 1892, but performed poorly in the presidential race. Four years later, the Populist Party redoubled its efforts. Lacking a single unifying leader and hearing the echo of some of their most cherished ideals in the oratory of William Jennings Bryan, a young free-silverite from Nebraska, the Populists nominated Bryan as their presidential candidate even though he already had accepted the nomination of the Democratic Party. Bryan could not overcome the advantages held by his opponent, William McKinley. Republicans amassed a campaign fund that exceeded that of the Democrats and Populists combined by more than ten times. The Republican strategist Mark Hanna deployed media images and messages that presented Bryan and his supporters as crackpots. White supremacists in the South engaged in fraudulent practices using race to divide black and white voters. The lopsided election led to the demise of the third-party movement.

The ideals of the movement lived on in Progressives' extension of government involvement in the economy and in social welfare in the early twentieth century. And despite the easing of the farm crisis with an upturn in commodity prices, due in part to overseas expansion, the haunting images of the pinched isolation of America's rural population rendered by Hamlin Garland in *Main-Travelled Roads* (1893) and the novelist Frank Norris in *The Octopus* (1901) left many Americans to question the truths they had inherited.

CULTURAL REBELLION AND THE QUEST FOR AUTHENTICITY

Economic consolidation and the varied responses to it produced a clash of ideas and values that in turn generated cultural transformation. Those who defended the industrial order rested their position on social Darwinism. Applying Charles Darwin's insights into the evolutionary process to the distribution of wealth and power in a free human society, they offered a fatalistic view of America's social order. Darwin had posited that natural selection favored species and individuals within a species with the traits necessary for survival in a natural war of all against all. Taking their cues from the popular phrase "survival of the fittest," social Darwinists argued that those who enjoyed the strongest position in human society had simply proven their mettle in the social struggle for survival. Those in subordinate positions lacked intelligence, strength, adaptability, and prowess and had achieved the highest station they could or should hope to reach. The logic of social Darwinist thought dictated against intervention in the social arena with ameliorative measures, social welfare, or assistance to the poor.

By the 1890s, however, too many Americans had discovered the flaws in this cultural and ideological imperative. Coal miners in the state of Missouri, for instance, reported to investigators from the state's

Bureau of Labor that in spite of steady work and financial vigilance, 90 percent could not make ends meet. Other laboring and farming groups protested that those who labored most diligently starved while the spoils of industry went to those who labored least. Moreover, many had found the twin pillars of the Victorian ideal—domesticity and self-control—had crumbled before the demands of industry as women and children had to supplement the income of men in dangerous, exploitative jobs in factories, mills, fields, and sweatshops. Americans in the 1890s witnessed a widespread cultural rebellion against an ideology that no longer made sense in an urban, industrial nation.

In the realm of literature, writers rebelled against the convention of culture as uplift by experimenting with new forms and subject matter. They explored the underside of modern life in novels that exposed the social forces that overrode individual will. Prostitution, bankruptcy, and "tramping," once viewed as personal failures, they demonstrated, could be the product of a society out of kilter. Unhappy marriages and racial "passing" raised problems once considered unfit subjects for polite readers. Writers who experimented with dialect writing not only resisted the standard of literature as a form of self-improvement, but also gave voice to the polyglot reality of the United States. Some attempted to replicate black speech patterns in works that contributed to the incorporation of black idiom into American speech. Local colorists added the broad pronunciation of New England, and others presented the mangled English of such immigrant groups as Germans and Irish. Beginning in the 1890s comedians like "Ned" Harrigan earned national fame by bringing the broken brogue of various immigrant types to the stage.

The literary impulses of realists, naturalists, local colorists, and dialect writers found a ready counterpart in the world of art. The American painter Robert Henri and a group of young painters began "making pictures from life." Turning away from the stuffy sentimentalism of Victorian artists and the breathtaking landscape painters of the preceding generation, "The Eight" tried to capture the vitality of urban street life, to expose the gritty reality of industrial America and tenement districts, and to replace natural landscapes with technology-dominated cityscapes. Some experimented with impressionism, using perspective to destabilize the constancy of reality. Others let the subjects of their canvases speak for a new aesthetic. They all rebelled against the standards set and maintained by the National Academy and the Society of American Artists, and when they staged an independent exhibition in 1908 they became known as the "Ashcan School."

The Ashcan School did not use art to advance an agenda of social reform, but their work did create a visual record of real industrial and urban conditions that dovetailed with the more overt critiques of writers, muckraking journalists, and social activists. By contrast, many photographic artists promoted serious consideration of prevailing social conditions and recorded images of social groups often ignored by the comfortable middle class. In their own way, Jacob A. Riis, Lewis Hine, and Edward Curtis rebelled against photography's appeal to middle-class vanity and its utility in recording the dimensions of the western lands. They brought to light hidden, unflattering realities in an era of consolidation. Riis's exposé of the "other half" drew attention to urban squalor, poverty, and foreign ways, which inspired a debate about the terms of the social contract in the 1890s. Hine's haunting photographs of child laborers documented the sordid truth that the burden of industrial production too often fell on frail shoulders. Curtis's portraits of Native American warriors, which toured the nation in the early 1900s, introduced the "vanishing race" to many who thought it had long since disappeared. Curtis's show pricked the conscience of a modern society whose voracious demands for land and resources had brought about the demise of the "noble savages" they now viewed through misty eyes. Edward Steichen demonstrated the subversive possibilities of photographic portraiture when his famous photograph of the American financier and industrialist J. P. Morgan, with its stark contrasts and glinting, daggerlike armrest, offered a vivid commentary on the ruthlessness of the capitalist class. Photography thus served as an important tool of social criticism.

Upheavals in literature, art, and photography drew strength from the contradictions between the dominant ideology and lived experience. These contradictions troubled religious leaders as well. In the 1880s and 1890s, the clergyman Walter Rauschenbusch and Washington Gladden decried the individualistic Protestantism they had imbibed in their youth and proclaimed a new, social, gospel. They called for a new view of salvation based on the commitment to social betterment, an embrace of Jesus' example of selfless devotion to the downtrodden, and a revitalization of church life through service. The social gospel sought to replace individual regeneration with social reform and set in motion programs that self-consciously ran counter to social Darwinist belief.

The social gospelers' rebellion against the beliefs of their elders rested as well on the quest for authenticity expressed in the world of art and letters. Drawing on higher criticism, which subjected the Bible to historical analysis, social gospelers' teaching emphasized the historical Jesus. They recast the fair-haired, soft, androgynous Jesus of the Victorian imagination as a burly, muscular man of principle and action. The carpenter's son and friend of fishermen was a physically powerful man who could have ousted the money changers from the temple. This Jesus spoke to the working people and fired the imagination of activists determined to right the wrongs of industrial America. While the social gospel did not absolve sinners of individual wrongdoing, it did shift the emphasis in liberal Protestant thought away from eventual, heavenly rewards and toward the work of building the Kingdom of God on earth and feeling the rewards of salvation in the here and now. By 1908 most Protestant denominations endorsed the social creed articulated by the Methodist minister Frank Mason North, and by the end of the era of consolidation—1911–1912—many took part in a nationwide campaign to attract boys and men to revitalized church life in the Men and Religion Forward movement. Social gospel thought, reflected in the settlement house movement, undergirded much of the social legislation initiated by Progressives in the early 1900s.

Cultural upheaval extended to the intellectual realm as well. The philosopher and psychologist William James's "pragmatic method" as a quest for truth through experience proposed a view of the universe as contingent and open to revision. Historians like James Harvey Robinson called for a "new history" that would take account of the whole of human experience rather than just the political and martial elements. The new history and pragmatic philosophy called for the collapsing of boundaries between academic disciplines and between the imagined divide between idealism and materialism. They reflected the impact of industrialism on received wisdom and the modernist impulse to integrate opposing elements into a coherent whole. Sociology and psychology likewise flourished in the era of consolidation. Pioneering social investigators like W. E. B. Du Bois sought root causes of social division, and theorists like Lester Frank Ward undermined the supposed naturalness of existing social structures. Interest in adolescence as a special transitional phase of human development reflected psychologists' interest in the impact of modern life on identity formation. All these intellectual endeavors shook faith in immutable truth.

REDEFINING AMERICAN CULTURE

Americans in all walks of life struggled to find meaning in the society emerging from economic consolidation. They struggled as well to know what it was to be "American." These interrelated quests were called into being by the palpable changes in the way most Americans lived and by the visible heterogeneity of the nation at the turn of the century. The reality of women and children in the workplace as well as the allure of consumer items forced many men and women to reevaluate their expectations for marriage and family life. Millions of immigrants from around the globe arrived at U.S. ports of entry, and thousands of African Americans migrated from the South to the West, Northeast, and Midwest as factory and domestic jobs opened up to them. As they expressed their dreams, desires, and beliefs in leisure activities, in songs and dances, in foodways, and in politics, Americans produced a vibrant popular culture that upended Victorian propriety and created new opportunities for business activity.

The "true woman" of the Victorian imagination had always been an ideal type, but as industrialization advanced after 1877, Americans found it ever more difficult to believe. The much-debated "new woman"—active, intelligent, public-minded, and daring—arose as more women sought higher education, work outside the home, and leisure pursuits. The new ideal, however, clashed with traditional conceptions of family life. Rising divorce rates, growing numbers of female professionals, the companionate family, and the selling power of the artist Charles Dana Gibson's "girls" as the American ideal of femininity attested to the changing attitudes. Both men and women, frustrated by modern work, sought relief from the tedium in a variety of new activities. Amusement parks, spectator sports, vaudeville theater, and dance halls created leisure activities meant to rejuvenate tired working bodies and increasingly were seen as the reward for work. Most importantly, these new popular cultural forms downplayed propriety in favor of exuberance and expressiveness, and they drew heavily on influences from ethnic and racial minorities.

Ragtime music, for example, blended African American rhythms and European harmonies into the first quintessentially American music. It skyrocketed in popularity from the 1890s on, and by 1912 it was featured in a performance of the all-black Clef Club Orchestra at Carnegie Hall. Similarly, all-black musical theater troupes organized by such duos as Bert Williams and George Walker and J. Rosamond Johnson and Bob Cole appeared on stages across the nation—even on Broadway's "Great White Way"—turning black music, dance, idiom, and humor into the stuff of American entertainment. While nativists deplored degenerate influences of the new immigrants on American life, Americans eagerly shared in their foodways, self-deprecating humor, and exotic dances as dining out and going to cabarets gained legitimacy. Theater circuits, sheet music publishers and recording companies, and restaurateurs all traded on the attraction of these expressions from the "other half" of American life. Furthermore, the networks of communication and transportation that extended the reach of corporations into the farthest corners of the nation also delivered the cultural offering of socially marginalized citizens to their white, native-born, and middle-class countrymen and -women.

Cultural incorporation far outstripped social equality, however. By the early 1900s, various forms of diversion had bifurcated along class lines into highbrow and lowbrow forms of entertainment. The Chinese Exclusion Act of 1882, the 1907 Gentlemen's Agreement that limited Japanese immigration, and white supremacist ideas betrayed deep-seated racism. Anti-immigration forces, eugenicists, and lynch mobs erected both social and ideological barriers to full citizenship for African Americans and immigrants. While immigrants found champions among the muckrakers, settlement house workers, and progressive social reformers and eventually gained the privileges accorded to whites, African Americans and other people of color struggled to claim their birthright as Americans. By the end of this period, the National Association for the Advancement of Colored People and the Negro Business League had begun to perform the function of like associations in the organizational society, articulating group consciousness and acting collectively to spur change.

By 1912, many agreed with the Midwestern writer Floyd Dell that a "new spirit suddenly [had] come to birth in America." Social consolidation and cultural rebellion had transformed the nation in the previous three decades. Corporations dominated economic life. Regulation and social reform formed the agenda of the state, bidding farewell to laissez-faire principles. Collective thought and action pervaded work, religion, and popular entertainment. The once-isolated nation had become involved overseas and had begun to bear a striking resemblance to Europe with its class divisions, corruption, and decadence. In thirty-five years, the United

States had become an industrial giant, a diverse nation bound together by markets and mass communication. And as Americans grappled with the implications of what kind of a people they had become, they created a cultural life that reflected social diversity, contingency and relativity, and social responsibility—the foundation for budding modernism in the years to come.

BIBLIOGRAPHY

Primary Sources

Addams, Jane. *Twenty Years at Hull-House*. New York, 1910.

Bellamy, Edward. *Looking Backward, 2000–1887*. Boston, 1888.

Chopin, Kate. *The Awakening*. Chicago, 1888.

Dreiser, Theodore. *Sister Carrie*. New York, 1900.

George, Henry. *Progress and Poverty*. New York, 1880.

James, William. *Pragmatism*. New York, 1907.

Lloyd, Henry D. *Wealth against Commonwealth*. New York, 1894.

Riis, Jacob A. *How the Other Half Lives: Studies Among the Tenements of New York*. New York, 1890.

Ross, Edward Alsworth. *Sin and Society: An Analysis of Latter-Day Iniquity*. Boston, 1907.

Sinclair, Upton. *The Jungle*. New York, 1906.

Steffens, Lincoln. *The Shame of the Cities*. New York, 1904.

Twain, Mark. *The Adventures of Huckleberry Finn*. New York, 1885.

Secondary Sources

Crunden, Robert. *Ministers of Reform: The Progressives' Achievement in American Civilization, 1889–1920*. New York, 1982.

Curtis, Susan. *A Consuming Faith: The Social Gospel and Modern American Culture*. Baltimore, 1991.

Erenberg, Lewis. *Steppin' Out: New York Nightlife and the Transformation of American Culture, 1890–1930*. Chicago, 1981.

Goodwyn, Lawrence. *Democratic Promise: The Populist Movement in America*. New York, 1976.

Heilbroner, Robert L. *The Economic Transformation of America*. New York, 1977.

Kasson, John F. *Amusing the Million: Coney Island at the Turn of the Century*. New York, 1978.

Lears, T. J. Jackson. *No Place of Grace: Antimodernism and the Transformation of American Culture, 1880–1920*. New York, 1981.

Levine, Lawrence W. *Highbrow/Lowbrow: The Emergence of Cultural Hierarchy in America*. Cambridge, Mass., 1988.

May, Elaine Tyler. *Great Expectations: Marriage and Divorce in Post-Victorian America*. Chicago, 1980.

Painter, Nell Irvin. *Standing at Armageddon: The United States, 1877–1919*. New York, 1987.

Palmer, Bruce. *"Man Over Money": The Southern Populist Critique of American Capitalism*. Chapel Hill, N.C., 1980.

Rodgers, Daniel. *The Work Ethic in Industrial America, 1850–1920*. Chicago, 1974.

Rydell, Robert. *All the World's a Fair: Visions of Empire at American International Expositions, 1876–1916*. Chicago, 1984.

Trachtenberg, Alan. *The Incorporation of American Culture and Society in the Gilded Age*. New York, 1982.

Wald, Priscilla. *Constituting Americans: Cultural Anxiety and Narrative Form*. Durham, N.C., 1995.

Wiebe, Robert. *The Search for Order, 1877–1920*. New York, 1967.

URBAN CULTURAL INSTITUTIONS

Steven Conn

When Andrew Carnegie died in 1919, he already had memorials in Xenia, Ohio, Gainesville, Texas, and Ferndale, California. The memorials in these far-flung towns, of course, were libraries funded through Carnegie's extraordinary philanthropy, and such libraries could, by 1919, be found in cities and small towns from Massachusetts to California.

Carnegie's libraries stand now as among the most widespread and beloved examples of a remarkable period of institution building that began in the years after the Civil War and drew to a close roughly during the 1920s. In addition to opening libraries, Americans during these years founded symphony orchestras and opera companies, filled new museums with priceless treasures, expanded and redefined higher education, and created permanent foundations to perpetuate their philanthropies. The result, it is not an exaggeration to say, was a cultural landscape transformed into one whose defining contours are largely recognizable to us today.

The typical Carnegie library was built in stone, lined with oak, and done in a reserved, neoclassical style. These imposing buildings, often the grandest in town, were meant to suggest solidity and timelessness. And the grandeur of the buildings reflected the grandeur of the ideas they embodied.

Such grand institutions as Carnegie's libraries, therefore, stood in contrast to those Americans built in the first half of the nineteenth century. Charles Willson Peale founded the nation's first significant museum in Philadelphia in the late eighteenth century, but it never had a permanent home or a secure financial footing, and thus did not long survive the founder's death. While parts of the museum eventually landed in Baltimore, the large enterprise Peale created dissolved. In the absence of aristocratic or government patronage—an absence often lamented by artists and cultural commentators—the new republic's institutions tended to be small, private, and locally focused. Leading citizens in several cities founded atheneums that served as lending libraries, picture galleries, and social clubs. These varied in their exclusivity from place to place, though it is probably safe to say that none were open to the public in the way Carnegie's libraries would be.

America's antebellum cultural landscape was sprinkled with colleges, especially in New England. Many had been founded during the colonial era, including most of those that would later constitute the Ivy League. Others, especially throughout the Midwest as far as Wisconsin, were founded by New Englanders as they migrated westward and tried to replicate the town greens and college quads they had left behind. Though numerous, American colleges of this period had a limited cultural impact. They enrolled tiny numbers of young, white men—with a few experimental exceptions like Oberlin in Ohio and Berea in Kentucky, no women were permitted to enter these enclaves. And colleges functioned often to provide students with only a rudimentary gloss of classical learning, combined with denominationally specific theology.

The theater thrived in America's small but booming cities and provided residents with a wide range of entertainment: circus acts, Shakespearian scenes, German art songs, and black minstrelsy. And for those Americans, a majority still, who lived in small towns or in isolated farm settlements, entertainment came when troops of itinerant performers touring the country came and set up their tents. Yet while the culture of theater and traveling show might well have been more vibrant in the antebellum period than it would be later on, most of the cultural institutions founded in these years proved as fleeting as circus tents. Many of these institutions, like Peale's museum or Nathan Dunn's Chinese Museum, did not cross the great divide of the Civil War. Those institutions that did, like colleges, underwent profound transformations in the postbellum world.

CULTURAL INSTITUTIONS AFTER THE CIVIL WAR

In 1855, shortly before the outbreak of the Civil War, Henry Ward Beecher, the influential occupant of the pulpit at Brooklyn's Plymouth Congregational Church, wrote: "There can never be too many libraries, too many cabinets, too many galleries of art, too many literary men, too much culture" ("Christian Liberty in the Use of the Beautiful," in *Star Papers*, p. 296). Beecher wrote these words as an expression of certain ideals; after the dust of war settled, however, some Americans took them almost as a kind of challenge. The period of institution building that followed the war sat at the intersection of several related transformations in American life. First, the Civil War both marked and helped inaugurate the rise and maturation of the country's industrial economy. By the 1890s, after a generation of explosive and erratic growth, the value of the industrial economy eclipsed the value of the agricultural economy, and big business had become genuinely "big."

The new generation of cultural institutions grew from the money generated by this new economy. One obvious distinction between pre- and postwar cultural institutions was the sheer size of the latter, and the liberality with which they were funded. The museums, libraries, and universities of this generation in particular stand as monuments to the robber barons who gilded the age. Retail giant Marshall Field put his name on Chicago's museum of natural history with a donation of one million dollars, to cite one example. In addition to hundreds of libraries around the country, Carnegie also put his name on both a museum and a university in his adopted hometown of Pittsburgh. Some of the wealthy industrialists who built these institutions did so as a way of legitimating their money and redeeming themselves. Through institutional philanthropy, Leland Stanford could prove to a suspicious and dubious public that he was more than an imperious railroad baron, and American Tobacco's James Duke could demonstrate that cigarettes had a higher purpose.

Social Uplift and Social Control Just as big business became properly big in the years after the Civil War, so too did American cities expand dramatically, as they filled with millions of new immigrants looking for jobs in the growing industrial economy. The transformation of the American city, both in size and ethnic composition, created a second rationale for building cultural institutions. For many older-stock Americans who saw their fortunes shrinking and their influence fading, the city became a major cause for hand-wringing. The city came to embody all the dark forces—labor unions, political radicals, Jews and Catholics from southern and eastern Europe—that threatened to corrode the virtue of the republic. Congregationalist minister Josiah Strong fretted in his 1885 book, *Our Country: Its Possible Future and Its Present Crisis*, about a variety of evils facing the nation: immigration, Romanism, intemperance, and socialism. These all came together in chapter 11, titled "The City." "The city," Strong warned, "has become a serious menace to our civilization because in it each of the dangers we have discussed is enhanced and all are focalized."

Cultural institutions might provide the antidote for the increasing societal fractures and growing urban disorder that these old-stock Americans perceived. Among the first urban institutions created to respond to the new American city were large parks like Philadelphia's Fairmount Park, Boston's Public Garden, and most especially New York City's Central Park. These green spaces were built upon the premise, nostalgic perhaps, that the loss of contact with nature led city dwellers down a series of "unhealthful" paths, including crime and other antisocial behavior. By providing city residents with access to trees, fresh air, and restrained strolling, the proponents of parks hoped to mitigate the ills of city living.

Just as fresh air and green trees might save urban souls, many cultural institutions were shaped, either theoretically or literally, by a group of aesthetes, social philosophers, reformers, and academics who believed increasingly in the restorative power of culture. Drawing on the writings of John Ruskin, Matthew Arnold, and Charles Eliot Norton, among others, institution builders hoped to improve the culturally impoverished lives of Americans by giving them access to the timeless and the ideal.

In this sense, of course, cultural institutions subscribed to a highly specific, elite notion of what constituted "culture" and how it should be appreciated, and they did not bother to question these assumptions about the relationship between high culture and social uplift. As Beecher put it, in his essay "Christian Liberty in the Use of the Beautiful": "The power of mind at the top of society will determine the ease and rapidity of the ascent of the bottom." If old stock Americans of the post–Civil War generation could no longer shape national politics the way their families had in the past, and if their position in the economic hierarchy was slipping, then some turned to "culture" and the institutions that enshrined it as a way of exerting influence on the nation's taste, morals, and intellectual development. The line separating social uplift from social control in these institutions blurred for some commentators, then as now.

To walk through the doors of a museum or library meant adhering to a set of forms and rules set by those who ran the institution. Sometimes this led to highly publicized controversies. Many institutions found their policy of Sunday closure under attack. For those in charge, the policy reflected a Protestant sensibility to observe the Sabbath; for working people who wanted to patronize these institutions, Sunday was their only day off. Public pressure in the 1880s forced the Metropolitan Museum of Art to open its doors on Sundays; the conflict was portrayed in the press as a "masses" versus the "classes" struggle. Perhaps still miffed over this battle, the Met's board voted in 1897 to ban the wearing of overalls in the museum. When a plumber came to the museum still dressed in the offending garments, he was unceremoniously tossed out. The resulting storm of bad press forced yet another retreat by a shamefaced Met.

If social control, in the harshest sense of that term, exaggerates what went on in these institutions, it is fair to say that those who did control new cultural institutions changed some of the terms on which people could enjoy them. While big, public museums were new for Americans, the theater and opera had long histories in the United States, but by the end of the nineteenth century the way audiences enjoyed these entertainments changed. Whereas an antebellum audience might enjoy a few Shakespearean scenes, an aria or two, and an animal act as a night's bill, by the end of the century things like Shakespeare, the opera and symphonic music had become, in the words of one historian, "sacralized."

This "sacralization" changed not only what was performed and how, but who came to those performances and how they behaved. Under the influence of conductor Theodore Thomas, who was the founding conductor of the Chicago Symphony in 1890, symphonic music was now performed in its entirety rather than in selected snippets. Audiences were now expect to listen attentively and quietly; they were not to applaud until the entire piece was finished. Clapping or singing along and demands for repeat playings or encores were no longer acceptable audience practice. Going to the symphony became the cultural equivalent of attending church. After all, as conductor Thomas put it in 1898:

"Bach, Handel, Mozart, and Beethoven were sons of God!"

What happened in the symphony hall happened in the "legitimate" theater and the opera house as well. Gone now was the audience participation of the antebellum period, and with it, a certain sense of inclusiveness. High culture, as represented by the likes of Shakespeare and Mozart, became increasingly the province of a cultural elite with enough taste, training, and cultural refinement to appreciate these geniuses properly. Gone, too, was an earlier sense that all Americans shared and had access to these figures. Live entertainment, through institutions like opera companies and symphony orchestras, reflected a sense of class stratification by the late nineteenth century. Ironically, while art objects and library books became available to an unprecedentedly large public at this time, the audience for theater and classical music probably shrank concurrently.

The Scientific Organization of Institutions

America's postbellum institutions attempted to give solid form to the ways in which knowledge and intellectual life were changing in the mid-nineteenth century. Charles Darwin arrived in America at almost exactly the moment that the Civil War broke out. But Darwin's theories about the natural world were only one set of shocks to the world view of the mid-Victorians. Developments across a host of fields—physics, chemistry, archaeology, and literary analysis to name only a few—fundamentally challenged or changed the ways in which Americans (and others) understood the world. As Henry James famously, if inscrutably, wrote: "The Civil War marks an era in the history of the American mind." Though that observation might refer to any number of postwar developments, it is surely true that the changes in America's intellectual life were connected in important ways to changes in the country's cultural institutions.

While institutions of various kinds proliferated, they all shared some sense of being "scientifically" organized. The influence of a scientific sensibility— a commitment to rationality, order, and the demonstration that the human mind could command and control the world—pervaded libraries, museums, and universities. As a result, those who shaped institutions in the last third of the nineteenth century drew sharp distinctions between themselves and their antebellum predecessors. For this new generation of cultural elites, the institutions of the earlier era had been randomly organized, arranged without any attention to scientific systematics, and thus did not promote the useful knowledge required to uplift those whom these institutions had targeted. Writing about American museums in 1904, David Murray could proudly claim that the museum of 1897 "is far in advance of the museum of 1847" (*Museums, Their History and Their Use*, pp. 187–188).

There had indeed been museums, libraries, and colleges in antebellum America. However, under the influence of postwar intellectual shifts, dedicated to a new sense of audience, and enriched by America's industrial fortunes, the very ideas that defined what cultural institutions should be stood transformed almost beyond recognition. Museums were among the most dynamic of this new generation of institutions. Even a cursory list of the museums founded in the postwar years demonstrates the remarkable energy with which Americans built new museums. Among the best-known were the Metropolitan Museum of Art and the American Museum of Natural History in New York City, the Philadelphia Museum of Art, the Art Institute and the Field Museum of Natural History in Chicago, and the Detroit Institute of Arts.

These museums, and dozens of others besides, were not built merely to serve as great warehouses. Rather, they were designed to institutionalize different bodies of knowledge and the way the boundaries around those fields were changing. In an 1895 essay, the Smithsonian Institution's assistant secretary, George Brown Goode, outlined six categories of museums: art, history, natural history, technology, anthropology, and commerce. For Goode these categories represented the most efficient way in which the sum of the knowledge about the world could be divided, and how, therefore, it could best be put on display for the public in grand, new museums. As it happened, only Philadelphia among American cities actually endeavored to create this encyclopedia set of museums. By the 1930s Philadelphia had, in addition to the oldest natural history museum in the country, the first major museums devoted to anthropology, an enormous new art museum, and the only American commercial museum.

If no other city completed the set, many cities built natural history museums, and the form of the nineteenth-century natural history museum essentially became the model for all the others. At a very general level, natural history museums collected specimens, classified them, and arranged them in displays that illustrated the orderly development of life from its oldest, simplest forms to its most recent, most complex. In this way they made sense for visitors of the evolutionary ideas that were swirling in the public consciousness. While Darwin might suggest an arbitrary world without design, the highly designed galleries of the natural history museum demonstrated that the natural world still had a recognizable logic and an essential order.

Many cities also built art museums. The drive to build these institutions reflected the belief that art ennobled and that Americans, perhaps more than any other people, needed ennobling. They were also erected to correct what some saw as a national embarrassment; namely, that the United States, unlike European nations, had no proper, permanent art museum. Art museums, like their natural history counterparts, were not supposed to be simply haphazard collections of whatever objects an institution could accumulate. Art museums, too, aspired to synoptic completeness. As with all kinds of museums, the educative value of the art museum would be lost, it was believed, if the objects were not collected, classified, and displayed in a thorough, "scientific" way. In 1864 James Jackson Jarves, an art collector and art theorist, argued in his book, *The Art Idea*, that museums needed to assemble collections that would enable visitors to come away with an understanding of the entire historical development of Western art. Though Jackson had no luck selling his own collection to the patricians of Boston to serve as the basis of such a museum, art museum builders did largely take his ideas as a model. Whether the museum displayed art, archaeology, or natural history, however, the design and purpose of these museums was largely the same: to display the whole of a particular body of knowledge in miniature, and to present it to the public in an orderly and educational way.

Reforming Higher Education In 1866 philosopher John Fiske could still write with some accuracy that the "whole duty" of a college consisted of training the "mental faculties" of students who were pursuing "varied and harmonious activity," and of providing those students with "the means of acquiring a thorough elementary knowledge of any given branch of science, art, or literature" ("University Reform," in *Darwinism and Other Essays*, 1969 reprint, p. 292). That description might well cover the activities of the very best of America's antebellum colleges. Ten years later it would no longer suffice.

The year 1876 marks the founding of The Johns Hopkins University, signalling, as conveniently as any marker, the beginning of the modern era in American higher education. In fact, a number of factors contributed to the transformation of American higher education in the years after the Civil

War. Politically, the Morrill Act of 1862 paved the way for the growth of large public universities, especially west of the Appalachians. In addition, and as in so many other areas of American life, a new generation of leaders emerged to replace the more staid, conservative administrators who had dominated the colleges through the middle years of the nineteenth century. Men like Theodore Dwight Woolsey and Mark Hopkins, who presided over Yale and Williams, respectively, in the mid-nineteenth century, resisted educational innovation and kept those institutions anchored to religious concerns. With the passing of this older generation, American colleges and universities were freer to experiment with new educational ideas.

More important than these, though, was a growing sense that knowledge, especially in the sciences but in other fields as well, was changing and expanding much faster than the old, hidebound college curricula could accommodate. Seizing their moment, the new generation of educational leaders redefined the mission of higher education to include a commitment to abstract, "original" research and (like their brethren in other institutions) practical public service and the cultivation of public taste. In the pursuit of original research, American universities modeled themselves to some extent on their German counterparts. Many in the new generation had had a taste of German seminars and, they returned impressed enough to recreate those seminars in American classrooms. This emphasis on creating new knowledge, rather than preserving traditions, served to distinguish the college from the university, the old institutions from the new. As Edwin Slosson wrote in 1909: "The essential difference between a university and a college is the way they look. The university looks forward and the college looks backward. The aim of one is discovery; the aim of the other is conservation." In this way, the new university drew a distinction between general training and specialized training, between undergraduate and graduate students. As Daniel Coit Gilman, president of Hopkins, put it in an 1876 speech: "The University is a place for the advanced and special education of youth who have been prepared for its freedom by the discipline of a lower school" (*University Problems in the United States*, p. 13).

One hallmark of the new universities was their commitment to graduate training, and the goal of graduate training was the doctor of philosophy (Ph.D.) degree, which became the coin of the academic realm. Graduate programs measured the prestige of universities in the new arithmetic of higher education, even though graduate students constituted a small part of the national student body: in 1900 there were 237,500 undergraduates in the nation, and less than 5,700 graduate students. Universities also reorganized themselves to reflect the ways in which knowledge was shifting and fragmenting by institutionalizing bodies of knowledge in a broadening array of semiautonomous departments. When Gilman pondered taking the presidency of the newly created Johns Hopkins, he fantasized about a new kind of institution where "the usual college machinery . . . may be dispensed with [where] each head of a great department, with his associates in that department . . . shall be as far as possible free from the interference of other heads of departments." By creating these institutional homes, universities and their constituent departments became part and parcel of the growing specialization of professionalized knowledge. Members of university departments often played an active role in new and specialized professional associations that grew up at the same time as the departments.

This first phase of university development came to a climax in the 1890s. By then, many older institutions had transformed themselves under the leadership of dynamic institution builders. Among the first were Charles W. Eliot at Harvard, William Pepper at Pennsylvania, and James B. Angell at Michigan to name just three. These established universities were joined by the 1890s by three new ones—Chicago, Clark in Massachusetts, and Stanford in California—each founded to carry out its particular vision in higher education. Their establishment capped a thirty-year period of theorizing about and experimenting with different versions of what a university might be. As Pennsylvania provost Pepper put it to a dinner crowd in 1891: "Until fifteen years ago the gradual decline and decay of our college system was feared. . . . But this has not only checked, but reversed. . . . Our universities and colleges have emancipated themselves from hampering traditions, and are expanding into a great university system admirably adapted to the needs of the American people."

The dramatic changes in American higher education in the late nineteenth and early twentieth centuries should be kept in perspective. Between 1900 and 1910, student enrollments at colleges and universities grew almost 25 percent, from 4.01 percent of the student-aged population to 4.84 percent. Which is to say that America's colleges and universities remained bastions of exclusivity and did not directly reach the public in the way that libraries or even museums did. But the changes that took place on American campuses in these years set the stage for their later growth, not merely in size, but in prestige and intellectual authority as well. Wherever the center of American intellectual life might have been at the beginning of the nineteenth century, by the dawn of the twenty-first century that center has surely been occupied by American colleges and universities.

Enlarging and Rationalizing Libraries

William Rainey Harper, the University of Chicago's founding president, noted in a 1894 speech at the dedication of Colorado College's new library that "a quarter of a century ago the library in most of our institutions, even the oldest, was scarcely large enough . . . to deserve the name library." The situation had much improved, Harper told his audience. Though he was talking only about college libraries, his retrospective remarks might well have been made about American libraries in general. Thus, twelve years later Melvil Dewey, perhaps America's foremost library scientist, could confidently proclaim: "The name 'library' has lost its etymological meaning and means not a collection of books, but the central agency for disseminating information, innocent recreation, or best of all, inspiration among people."

Libraries were probably the most common institution in antebellum American life, but they were largely homespun affairs. In countless American small towns, these libraries were often founded by the wealthiest businessman or most prominent town father. As often as not, a local librarian shoe horned an eclectic collection of books into an old house now serving as the town library. Just as other institutions, however, libraries found themselves the focus of concerted efforts to expand after the Civil War, and to do so according to new systems of organization and design. In the most general sense, a new generation of library builders reorganized the arrangement of books on the shelves and reconfigured the interior spaces of the library itself. In these endeavors, no figure looms larger than Dewey.

Dewey's luster as a librarian has faded somewhat since his invention—the decimal classification system that bears his name—has largely been supplanted. Still, he deserves credit for creating a rational, decimal system for organizing books within a library collection, and for disseminating that system so that libraries around the country adopted a uniform practice. Randomness and local custom were replaced with a system of numbers, which meant that library patrons could find the books they wanted quickly and efficiently, regardless of the library they happened to be using. Just as natural scientists created taxonomies of the natural world and put specimens on display in museums to illustrate those taxonomies, so too Dewey created a scientific system for the organization of books, and he thus stands as America's Linneaus of the library.

Dewey's concern with rationalizing library practice, however, extended beyond the tags on the spines of books. He was central as well to creating the field of library science and professionalizing it. Under his direction, the first school of library science was established in 1887 at Columbia University (though it was closed almost immediately because Dewey admitted women to the program without telling Columbia's administration). Professionally trained and credentialed librarians played an important role in shaping the design of the new library buildings springing up around the country in the late nineteenth and early twentieth centuries, thanks in no small part to the efforts of Carnegie's philanthropy. Working with architects, librarians insisted on creating library spaces that incorporated new technologies and new ideas so that they could control their domains in the most efficient way possible. And while libraries did not conform to a single plan, it is fair to say that many shared certain characteristics: card catalogues, separate spaces for younger readers, and a commanding position for the circulation desk. By 1910 librarian Arthur Bostwick could trumpet the creation of the "modern library idea," which included work with children, broad public support, cooperation with the schools, and branch libraries to reach urban residents who did not patronize the central library.

CULTURAL PHILANTHROPY, THE WORKING CLASS, AND URBAN AMERICA

Through the building of libraries, Andrew Carnegie expressed his particular philanthropic ideas. Carnegie, especially in his writings, fancied himself philanthropy's philosopher, and his essays can be read both as self-serving justifications and as instructions to his fellow robber barons to attend to the nation's public good. Carnegie's library project thus embodied many of the contradictions of the cultural institution building that began during the Gilded Age. On the one hand, Carnegie genuinely believed that libraries could serve as a source of inspiration and uplift for America's ordinary people. On the other hand, he, like many who funded these new institutions, viewed those people—especially the urban working classes—with some combination of suspicion, contempt, and fear. For Carnegie and the others, cultural institutions reflected both a democratic impulse to make books and art and learning widely available, and a desire to use culture as a way of controlling or at least restraining a public that often confused and confounded them.

When Carnegie's project stopped in 1917, after almost thirty years, money provided by him had built nearly 1,700 libraries. They stand as perhaps the most ubiquitous features on the cultural landscape created in the last quarter of the nineteenth century and the first quarter of the twentieth. But because of that ubiquity, perhaps, it has been forgotten just how remarkable the building of those libraries—and museums and universities and parks—really was. The United States officially became an urban nation when the census of 1920 announced it. In fact, for a generation before that America's cultural life was increasingly connected to its urban life. The institutions built in the years after the Civil War shaped the culture of those cities, and of the nation besides, and created a sense of a shared public sphere. Cities used their public cultural institutions as a yardstick by which to measure their own greatness.

It is not surprising, therefore, that as many of the cities which grew to prominence during these years face troubled futures at the turn of the twenty-first century, they turn back to these now venerable institutions as a source of economic support and civic salvation. As America's older industrial cities in particular try to figure out new uses for themselves in the postindustrial world, cultural institutions have assumed a new prominence both as tourist destinations and thus as generators of revenue, and as sources of a city's distinctiveness and pride. Those places that built an extensive cultural infrastructure at the turn of the twentieth century will find it much easier to make this transition than those cities that did not. From this distance, the legacy of those industrialists and other elites who built this extraordinary constellation of cultural institutions looks important indeed.

See also **The Harlem Renaissance** *(in this volume);* **The City; New York City; Chicago; Philadelphia; The San Francisco Bay Area; Detroit; Cincinnati; New Orleans** *(volume 2);* **Culture for Mass Audiences; Salons, Coffeehouses, Conventicles, and Taverns; Libraries; Museums** *(volume 3).*

BIBLIOGRAPHY

Bremner, Robert H. *The Public Good: Philanthropy and Welfare in the Civil War Era.* New York, 1980.

Conn, Steven. *Museums and American Intellectual Life, 1876–1926.* Chicago, 1998.

Horowitz, Helen Lefkowitz. *Culture and the City: Cultural Philanthropy in Chicago from the 1880s to 1917.* Lexington, Ky., 1976.

Levine, Lawrence. *Highbrow/Lowbrow: The Emergence of Cultural Hierarchy in America.* Cambridge, Mass., 1988.

Oleson, Alexandra, and John Voss, eds. *The Organization of Knowledge in Modern America, 1860–1920.* Baltimore, 1979.

Van Slyck, Abigail A. *Free to All: Carnegie Libraries and American Culture, 1890–1920.* Chicago, 1995.

Veysey, Laurence R. *The Emergence of the American University.* Chicago, 1965.

PATTERNS OF REFORM AND REVOLT

Eugene E. Leach

In the years 1878–1912 Americans' experience parted company with their aspirations, and a dynamic political economy grew at odds with a fragmenting culture. Ideas about reform and revolt reflected efforts to reduce these dissonances, on the one hand by tempering aspirations, on the other by learning to understand the forces that were remaking the society. Americans struggled to adjust their ways of thought to the realm of objective structures and events, to make their ideas more accurate guides to social experience and more supple tools for governing it.

Prior to the Civil War, when memories of the American Revolution were green, immigration was scant, and industrialization had barely begun, Americans' visions of social felicity were markedly utopian and uniform. The good society would be a Christian republic built on the precepts of the Bible and the Declaration of Independence. It would guarantee both the liberty and the security of its members. It would be a roughly egalitarian society of small producers residing in small towns, selling goods on local markets characterized more by cooperation than by competition. The political economy of this good society would be indistinguishable from its moral economy; virtue would be rewarded in the marketplace as well as in politics; wealth and power would gravitate to the righteous. The common religion would be a fervent but undogmatic Protestant Christianity; the common political creed would be a sturdy republicanism that prized civic virtue and cast a suspicious eye on government. Government would indeed be limited, the state small, its power decentralized.

This vision of a Christian republic entranced oppressed groups almost as much as it attracted the white Protestant males of the governing class. Subtract from it the assumption of white supremacy and free blacks would share in it; control for native-born Americans' xenophobic prejudices and immigrants would embrace it; remove the unexamined patriarchalism of the day and most women would

embrace it too. It shaped the rhetoric of politicians and the voting behavior of ordinary citizens. It shaped, as well, the means and ends of reformers and rebels.

Three aspects of this vision deserve emphasis. First, it was a vision of a classless utopia, free of inherited privilege, rich in opportunities for advancement, with sufficient material to provide for the needs of all. Second, it was an ahistorical vision of a society arrested at the pastoral stage of development. Extracted from a past presumed to be a record of sin, war, and oppression, the young republic would be delivered into a prelapsarian state of timeless harmony and rectitude. This yearning to escape from history derived mainly from Protestant millennialism, but the ahistoricity of American thought revealed itself almost everywhere: in the assumptions of classical economics, in the writings of the Transcendentalists, even in the writings of historians like George Bancroft.

Third and finally, confident that America was exceptional and the past escapable, a great many Americans believed it possible to build their timeless Christian republic. To be sure, it often seemed that America was getting dragged back into old-world historical patterns. The vision of an Edenic communal republic was subverted by the social realities of slavery, sin, political corruption, infidelity, drinking, the division of labor, the squalor of cities, and the arrival of aliens. But the mission of antebellum reformers lay precisely in eliminating these impurities. This species of utopian reform was common to Garrisonian abolitionism, to prohibitionism, and to a host of other movements.

In the 1860s and 1870s history caught up with the millennialist reformers. Union victory in the Civil War put in power a Republican leadership and a class of industrial entrepreneurs who aggressively set about transforming the political economy. As industrialization accelerated, the antebellum vision of a pastoral Christian republic grew increasingly implausible. Perhaps most sobering of all was the specter of class warfare, once thought an old-world deformity. The depression of the 1870s suggested to many farmers and workers the existence of a conspiratorial capitalist elite (later dubbed the Money Power). On the other hand, the railroad strikes of 1877 revealed to the middle and upper classes the existence of a Social Problem posed by the "dangerous classes" below them. Blame was attributed to revolutionary ideologies from Europe, especially Marxism and anarchism. A culture that sanctified antebellum visions of justice, harmony, and self-sufficiency was increasingly at odds with a postbellum political economy that was generating ever-greater social inequities, diversities, and dependencies, along with an ever-faster tempo of change.

Literally millions of Americans sought reform or threatened revolt in the Gilded Age. It is useful to distinguish five orientations among them. Two groups sought sweeping social change. One consisted of Protestant, middle-class, visionary reformers who could trace their lineage back to the antebellum adepts of the Christian republic. The other, much less numerous, was made up of anarchists, socialists, and communitarians who championed radical revisions of the class and gender orders in America. Except for the first group, these orientations differed from their millennialist forerunner by striving to restructure American society rather than to save it.

Three other groups differed from these utopians and radicals by virtue of the relative modesty and concreteness of their goals. They were realists whose purpose was not to reinvent America but to become part of it or to expand their influence within it. The first of these groups structured their reform endeavors closely to mirror their class interests. Suffragists, civil rights activists, and many labor reformers fell into this category. To the second realist grouping belonged middle-class Protestant men, liberal Republicans, and civil service reformers. These gentlemen reformers were fighting to recover influence and respect they felt they were losing to the parvenu industrialists and political bosses. This group, too, was defending its class interests. But it was seeking real or imagined lost authority, while those in the first group were fighting for what they had never had.

Third, there was a loose grouping of reform organizations that straddled the boundaries between national redemption and class interests. Christian millennialist themes and dreams of dramatic change were prominent in the ideologies of the Knights of Labor, Farmers' Alliances, Greenbackers, and Populists. Also prominent, however, were specific objectives that reflected concrete class interests.

UTOPIANS AND RADICALS

One response to the corruptions and injustices of the Gilded Age was to hold fast to the moralist, millennialist, utopian traditions of antebellum reform. This was the course preferred by many native-born Protestants of the middle class. Their fidelity to this tradition reflected their piety, their alienation from industrializing America, and their anxious conviction that only fundamental reform could restore the nation to righteousness and themselves to leadership. They regarded themselves as "solid citizens," productive, disinterested, and patriotic. But in fact this group feared downward mobility. Their anxiety about their condition was reflected in their attraction to grand visions of sweeping social change. Repelled by the venal politicians and decadent capitalists who were gaining ascendancy over them, appalled by the turbulent proletarians who seemed to menace them from below, men of the Protestant middle class gravitated toward panaceas that would restore them to their rightful positions of leadership in a classless republic. They remained faithful to the ideal of a Christian republic of small producers that had animated reformers earlier in the century.

The historian John L. Thomas finds "a whole company of Gilded Age humanitarians and reformers who were convinced that they saw on the far horizon the millennial community toward which Americans were resolutely marching" (*Alternative America*, pp. 116–117). The company included ministers and lay leaders of the Protestant social gospel, a movement whose stress on Christian works and Christian ethics harked back to the perfectionist faith of antebellum revivalists like Charles Grandison Finney. The social group sponsored critiques of unregulated capitalism and its materialist rationales. The movement's sources included liberal theology and British Christian socialism; its adversaries included Herbert Spencer, laissez-faire economics, and scholastic theological systems. A few social gospelers embraced socialism, but all espoused a vigorous Christian moralism. The movement's first national leader was Washington Gladden, a Congregation minister of Columbus, Ohio, who tirelessly called on the churches to act against poverty and social injustice. The preeminent expositor of the social gospel was Walter Rauschenbusch, the Baptist son of a German missionary, who found his vocation in the Hell's Kitchen slum district of New

York City, where he held a pulpit from 1886 to 1897. Turning away from traditional theology and superficial piety, Rauschenbusch put ethics at the center of Christianity. In *Christianity and the Social Crisis* (1907), the foremost manifesto of the social gospel, Rauschenbusch expressed the vivid and naive hope that the Kingdom of God was within Americans' reach: "The swiftness of evolution in our own country proves the immense latent perfectibility in human nature" (p. 422).

Akin to the social gospelers were a group of reformers who recast into secular terms essentially religious modes of social thought. Henry George was a representative figure and probably the most significant member of this group. Though unchurched, he had a pious upbringing and remained a man of strong religious conviction throughout his life. From his youth he dreamed of bliss in a pastoral America. Writing to a sister in 1861, the twenty-one-year-old George expressed his yearning to escape "the fierce struggle of our high civilized life, and . . . get away from cities and business . . . and live content with what Nature and our own resources would furnish." "How I long for the Golden Age," he continued, "for the promised Millennium, when each will be free to follow his best and noblest impulses, unfettered by the restrictions and necessities which our present state of·society impose upon him" (*Alternative America,* p. 14).

George proceeded to elaborate this yearning into an original (if lopsided) critique of classical economics, developed from the viewpoint of a fervent egalitarian. In 1879, having established himself as a journalist in San Francisco, George published a book, *Progress and Poverty,* or as the subtitle puts it, "an inquiry into the cause of industrial depressions and of increase of want with increase of wealth." Attacking Thomas Malthus, John Stuart Mill, and social Darwinians, George contended that the cruel paradox of poverty amid plenty arose from "social maladjustments" rather than any implacable natural law. "With man the limit of subsistence is, within the final limits of earth, air, water, and sunshine, dependent upon man himself" (pp. 138–139). The source of poverty, George explained, lay in the malignant effects of monopolization of land. The key to resolving the problem lay in imposing a confiscatory tax on the profits of rent on land. This "single tax" would cure all the economic and moral ills of industrial capitalism, preventing depressions and reopening avenues of opportunity. Moreover the revenues generated by a tax on rent would fund a host of public amenities. The single tax was, in short, a panacea that would painlessly transport

America to "a transpolitical and transhistorical realm of social harmony" (*Alternative America,* p. 119). Eloquent and reassuring, *Progress and Poverty* struck a chord with the middle-class public. The book sold hundreds of thousands of copies and launched George into a brief third-party political career.

Widespread longing for "the Golden Age" soon made a best-seller of a second utopian tract, this one a romantic novel published in 1888. Like Henry George, Edward Bellamy was an idealistic journalist with a religious cast of mind, his father having been a Baptist minister. Bellamy's *Looking Backward* propelled a genteel time traveler through an improbable plot whose purpose was to depict a perfected America in the year 2000. In this utopia all productive property belonged to the state. Adult males spent their working years in an industrial army; women belonged to a ladies' auxiliary. Property was distributed on roughly egalitarian principles, but power was not; only retired male workers voted, and artists and professionals enjoyed special privileges. When the time traveler asks how the placid and efficient America of 2000 emerged from the class-divided and unstable America of 1888, he is told that the transition occurred by a sort of spontaneous mass conversion. The trusts had already concentrated property in private hands, Bellamy explained. That simplified the next logical step conveying it all to the commonwealth. As with *Progress and Poverty,* Bellamy's book quickly became the basis of a movement, Nationalism, dedicated to making the utopia real. With reluctance the retiring Bellamy became a public reformer, and hundreds of Nationalist Clubs were started, mostly among educated middle-class Protestants, in all regions except the South.

Conservative detractors saw socialism in the single tax and the industrial army. Serious socialists knew better. Karl Marx dismissed George as a crackpot, and though many American-born socialists found much to admire in *Looking Backward,* to most radicals the book was at best a sugar-coated primer in collectivist principles. Their skepticism was well justified. George, Bellamy, and social gospel writers indeed dissented from the economic orthodoxies of their day. But where socialists looked forward to a secular workers' state, George and Bellamy looked backward to an imagined landscape of blissful Christian community. The class they sought to convert was their own, the respectable middle class that continued to believe in the millennial mission of the United States. Like social gospelers and other reformers of their kind, they had little confidence in the working class, they vigorously rejected doctrines of class conflict and revolution, and they were profoundly uncomfortable with industrialism. The single tax was a magical device that, by breaking the stranglehold of monopolists on land, would invite workers back to family farms. Though Bellamy gingerly embraced a sanitized collectivism, his utopia was a undemocratic society purged of blue-collar workers as well as blacks and immigrants. Both *Progress and Poverty* and *Looking Backward* were not so much blueprints for practical reform as they were nostalgic reveries of restoration and escape.

There was a radical Left, too, on the American scene, but its reputation much exceeded its real influence. Thus the wildcat railroad strikes of 1877 were widely blamed on immigrant revolutionaries who existed only in propaganda and myth. Many workers rejected the dominant creed of competitive individualism in favor of ethnic solidarity and mutualist values, but few converted to the cause of overthrowing capitalism. The recurrent labor protests of the late nineteenth century were inspired by homegrown standards of economic justice and the heritage of 1776, not by the revolutions of 1848 or the Paris Commune of 1871. Moreover there were deep ideological and cultural divisions on the Left. Native-born radicals were often put off by the materialism, determinism, and penchant for violence they saw in the writings of European ideologues like Karl Marx, Ferdinand Lasalle, and Michael Bakunin. Instead of striving to master the universal laws of history, undoctrinaire American radicals were drawn to reformist schemes that reflected the peculiar history of the United States. The historian Paul Buhle notes that German-American socialists were admired for their discipline and learning but criticized for "hair-splitting on theoretical matters and organization-splitting on practical ones" (*Marxism in the USA*, p. 37). Marx rebuked his own disciples in the United States for failing to bridge the gap between European ideals and American conditions. Many native-born as well as immigrant radicals eventually lost their faith and went over to the enemy.

Nonetheless radicals played a part in promoting the incessant class tensions and occasional revolts of the period. In 1877 socialists of the small Workingmen's Party, successor to Marx's First International Workingmen's Association, helped lead a brief general strike that united black and white workers in St. Louis. Later calling itself the Socialist Labor Party, this group drew most of its support from German immigrant communities. Through its native-born leaders it succeeded in influencing some branches of the Knights of Labor and some unions of skilled workers. After 1890 the SLP took on greater militance under the leadership of the Lassellean Daniel DeLeon. Socialists in the labor movement came close to gaining a formal endorsement of their goals by the American Federation of Labor in 1894. Immigrant anarchists who opposed any "domination or authority of one man over another" built vibrant subcultures among German and Bohemian immigrants in cities like Chicago and Cincinnati, complete with their own recreation programs and armed militia companies, until they were repressed following the Haymarket bombing incident of 1886.

The career of Samuel Gompers illustrated a pattern of pragmatic adjustment that characterized many labor radicals. As a young immigrant Gompers learned Marxist doctrines of proletarian revolt in New York cigar-making shops. But once launched into a career of labor organizing, Gompers soon dropped radical visions to pursue narrow "bread and butter" unionist goals. By the 1890s Gompers had become a vocal anti-socialist, championing unions as the "business organizations" of the working class. A few working-class leaders moved in the opposite direction. Eugene V. Debs, a conservative officer of the Brotherhood of Locomotive Firemen in the 1870s and 1880s, emerged in the early 1890s as a proponent of industrywide organizing, as a leader of the Pullman Strike, and finally, after a brief jail term, as a socialist.

EARLY REALISTS

Other Gilded Age reformers had little interest in the sweeping social transformations contemplated by socialists, anarchists, social gospelers, single-taxers, and Nationalists. Many of them revered the ideal of the Christian republic, with the utopians; many had strong reservations about capitalism, with the socialists. But these reformers were neither utopians nor socialists. They were realists about history, power, class, and their own prospects. Their purposes as reformers were more narrow and concrete, their means more practical and gradualist, than those of the radicals and utopians. What decisively set these realists apart from the radicals and utopians was, in the first instance, their prudential relationship to power. Most of them represented interest groups that had been excluded from full citizenship. Their first priority was to gain the means to govern their own destinies. They were set apart, too, by their acceptance (however grudging) of the world that industrial capitalism had made, and their candid pursuit of class-specific interests within that world. Their purpose was not transformative but adaptive; rather than save humankind or reconstitute lost community, they worked to improve the lot of selected groups in a society whose complexity and pluralism they did not question.

Whether or not they were Darwinians, realists had an evolutionist sensibility. Unlike the utopians, the realists viewed history as a process that could be altered by prudent intervention, but not stopped. Many were, in fact, indebted to the revisionist Darwinism of Lester Frank Ward, a sociologist who held that the intelligence of humans removed them from the natural struggle for survival and made them capable of directing their own evolution.

The bounded horizons of the realist mentality were captured by Frederick Jackson Turner in his celebrated 1893 paper, "The Significance of the Frontier in American History." Long exempted from history's laws by geographic bounties, it argued, America was now running out of space, as much for social invention as for western settlement. Another expression of the realists' outlook was the pioneering work of the sociologist Edward A. Ross, who analyzed the mechanisms by which society bends individuals to its norms in *Social Control* (1901). Ross held that in the new century it would be as futile to flee from industrial capitalism as it would be impossible to overthrow it. It would be futile, too, to continue to imagine that America could be exempted from history's strictures. Americans would have to imagine reform within the confinements of their time and place.

Good Government and Moral Reformers

One group of realists was, in terms of their class position and values, not very different from the middle-class followers of George and Bellamy. These were the "good government" reformers, or as snide detractors sometimes called them, the "goo-goos." Throughout the Gilded Age they battled against corruption and vice at every level of government. Most were men of property who felt displaced and diminished by the new industrial order. Staunch Protestants and sincere republicans, they saw themselves as gentlemen whose education, rectitude, and disinterestedness uniquely qualified them to lead their communities. They struggled to reassert their influence on many fronts. In the realm of high culture they were among the prime movers behind the genteel magazines, symphonies, art museums, art societies, and historical societies that stood for

Anglo-Saxon civilization against the barbarism of robber barons and immigrant workers. They were particularly outraged by corrupt politicians who either took bribes from businessmen or manipulated workers.

The good government orientation first crystallized in the Liberal Republicans or mugwumps who, unable to stomach the scandals of the Grant administration or the alleged chicanery of the radical governments in the Reconstruction South, bolted from the Republican Party in 1872. Through the 1880s the mugwumps denounced the venality of their party's establishment, with little effect. More successful were good government types who crusaded at the municipal level, beginning with the overthrow of the flamboyantly crooked Tweed Ring in New York City in 1873. From the late 1880s through the 1890s, Republican reformers challenged the sway of political machines in New York, Cleveland, Toledo, and other cities.

The Liberal Republicans and most other good government reformers were liberals in the sense that prevailed in the nineteenth century: They adhered to the liberal political philosophy of John Locke and John Stuart Mill and the "classical" school of economics founded by Adam Smith, Thomas Malthus, and David Ricardo. Suspicious of state power, dead set against any sort of economic regulation, outraged by corruption, insensitive to the plight of the poor, liberals held that unfettered markets were the surest engines of material and moral progress. In these regards their opinions followed the orthodoxy of their time; they would have felt perfectly comfortable at the party to celebrate the centennial of Smith's *The Wealth of Nations* held at Delmonico's restaurant in New York in 1876. Theirs was the conservative point of view of men of education and property who were repelled equally by parvenu industrialists, resentful workers, and urban political bosses. Their favorite causes were electoral and civil service reform. By these means the good government reformers would take authority away from politicians, vulnerable to public opinion and private temptation, and give it to trained civil servants, chosen for their positions by merit and examination. The idea was to get as much government power as possible into the light and into the hands of gentlemen like themselves. Perhaps the pinnacle of their achievement in the Gilded Age was the passage in 1883 of the Pendleton Act, which appreciably expanded the federal civil service.

First cousins to the goos-goos were moral reformers, men and women alike, who battled prostitution, gambling, drunkenness, contraceptive devices,

and other vices they associated with the lower orders of the soulless modern city. They ranged from
Puritanical obsessives like Anthony Comstock, tireless anti-smut crusader, to shrewd politicians like
Theodore Roosevelt, who became police commissioner in an administration pledged to clean up
New York City.

Reforms for Excluded Groups   If the mugwumps
and moral reformers sought to defend privileges
they feared they were losing, other realists fought to
gain rights or protections they had always been denied. Among excluded groups striving for inclusion,
the most numerous was women. During the Gilded
Age thousands of middle-class women organized
tirelessly to win fundamental legal rights, protection
from the violence and neglect caused by male drinking, laws to guard the health of working women and
children, and above all the suffrage.

Since 1869 suffragists had been divided into two
ideological camps. The militant National Woman
Suffrage Association (NWSA), led by Elizabeth
Cady Stanton and Susan B. Anthony, marched under the banner of full equality and natural rights,
holding to the republican principles they had first
invoked at the seminal meeting in Seneca Falls, New
York, in 1848. The militants rejected appeals based
on roles or qualities that distinguished women from
men. Instead they insisted that as human beings and
as citizens, women deserved every right enjoyed by
men, emphatically including the vote. Some militants attacked the myth of a woman's sphere, and
at the movement's fringes some challenged the
sanctity of marriage. Members of the moderate
American Woman Suffrage Association (AWSA)
were more prone to compromise with Victorian stereotypes of female domesticity and delicacy. Their
thinking descended in part from earlier concepts of
"republican motherhood" and from the "domestic
feminism" of women like the Beecher sisters; they
petitioned for rights based on women's gender-
specific talents and social contributions. By this way
of thinking, not only women's natural rights but
their special gifts entitled them to the vote.

The NWSA and AWSA came together in 1890
as the National American Woman Suffrage Association (NAWSA) on terms that reflected the growing
realism of American reform in general and the
growing conservatism of suffrage reformers in particular. The historian Aileen Kraditor has documented the gradual migration in suffragist thought
from idealistic principles of justice and natural
rights to expedient arguments designed to win the
support of male power brokers. In 1894 the aging

Anthony published an eloquent pamphlet titled
Suffrage a Natural Right. In 1918 Carrie Chapman
Catt, the master strategist of the final push for a
constitutional amendment, professed not to care
whether suffrage was a right, a duty, or a privilege;
it was enough to know that "whatever it is, the
women want it" (Kraditor, *The Ideas of the Woman
Suffrage Movement,* p. 45).

This shift toward prudential and strategic thinking in suffragism mirrored developments in the
temperance movement, the longest-running reform
endeavor of the nineteenth century. Temperance,
suffragism, and political shrewdness converged in
the career of Frances Willard, who built the
Women's Christian Temperance Union (WCTU)
into the largest women's organization and one of
the most potent reform organizations of the Gilded
Age. Under Willard's leadership, temperance
women moved from prayer and petition for a narrow prohibitionist program to lobbying and leaflet-
ing for a comprehensive agenda of women's causes,
including a carefully reasoned argument for the
vote. The Anti-Saloon League (1895), an organization led by male ministers, focused narrowly on
prohibition, but it took even further the trend toward tight organization and political expedience begun by the WCTU and the NAWSA.

Suffrage and temperance agitation were old
movements by the 1890s. Alongside them, often in
cooperation with them, new movements of reform
captured the ambitions and the sympathies of
middle-class women eager to break free of the
"women's sphere." Jane Addams described both the
objective necessity for settlement houses in the misery of immigrant slums, and the subjective necessity
posed by the hunger of idealistic, educated women
to engage the world. By 1910 there were more than
four hundred settlement houses providing social
services and lobbying for government services in
cities across the country. The movement was sponsored intellectually by roughly equal parts of democratic idealism, Christian faith, confidence in
social science, the doctrine of women's nurturing
gifts, and feminism. The National Consumers
League (NCL), led by Florence Kelley (devoted to
pressuring retail stores to treat their employees de-
cently), the Women's Trade Union League (offering
assistance to female unionists), and many other
women's organizations and clubs proclaimed their
determination to enter the public world, with or
without the vote.

Civil rights reformers, too, turned increasingly
to formal organizations and concrete agendas, as
they struggled against deepening currents of scien-

tific racism and segregation. Ida B. Wells risked her life to crusade publicly against lynching in the 1890s, then took part in the formation of the National Association for the Advancement of Colored People (NAACP) in 1909. The model of racial reform most favored by both white and black establishments until World War I remained the careful accommodationist and self-help program of Booker T. Washington. But beginning around the turn of the century, the scholarly W. E. B. Du Bois began urging a revival of the spirit of Frederick Douglass and William Lloyd Garrison, calling for immediate civil equality and militant resistance to disfranchisement, discrimination, and lynching. This was the direction taken by the new NAACP, which soon cut its teeth protesting the racist film epic *Birth of a Nation,* released in 1915, and the rebirth of the Ku Klux Klan during the same year.

Farmers' and Workers' Movements The Knights of Labor, Farmers' Alliances, Greenbackers, and Populists constituted the most ambiguous grouping of Gilded Age reformers. In their sense of righteousness and their enthusiasm for comprehensive reform, these movements of workers and farmers resembled the utopians. Greenbackers and Alliance people indulged in fanciful imaginings about the magic of currency inflation, and the Knights sometimes expressed nostalgia for the artisanal regime that had preceded industrialization. In their sharp criticism of the wage system, the unregulated power of railroads, trusts, and banks, and the inequities generated by the capitalist economy, these groups often skirted close to the socialists. (Socialists played prominent roles in many branches of the Knights.) But in their sense of oppression and their clear-eyed determination to defend their class interests, they stood in the ranks of the realists.

The growing convergence of reform thought during the 1890s was reflected in an attempt to put together a grand coalition behind the Populists in 1896. But the project of joining social gospelers, single-taxers, and Nationalists with Knights and Populists failed, because the interests of farmers, workers, and the middle class remained too far apart. Despite certain sharings of vision and value, farmers and workers had made the leap into history and politics, whereas single-taxers, Nationalists, and others of their ilk had not.

In a significant sense the co-optation of the Populists and other reformers by William Jennings Bryan's Free Silver campaign in 1896 proved the last hurrah for the utopian currents in American reform thought. Free Silver, almost as dreamy a panacea as the single tax, went down to defeat along with Bryan. Looking back to the agrarian past more resolutely than they gazed into the urban-industrial future, advocates of the silver nostrum represented a shrinking body of American opinion. In 1896 the majority voted for a presidential candidate, William McKinley, whom they trusted to stabilize the regime of industrial capitalism, not to dismantle it. By the turn of the twentieth century, as Lawrence Goodwyn has argued, radical dissent and revolt had been purged from the spectrum of realistic political possibilities. The die had been cast not just for reform, but for an increasingly institutionalized and moderate style of reform.

Radicalism did not vanish in the new century. In 1901 Eugene V. Debs, Victor Berger, and others started a new Socialist Party of America that proved less sectarian and more adaptable than the Socialist Labor Party. In 1905 "Big Bill" Haywood of the obstreperous Western Federation of Miners declared that "the working class and the employing class have nothing in common" at the founding of a defiant alternative to the AFL, the Industrial Workers of the World. This new labor federation adopted doctrines of class struggle and syndicalist tactics of direct action in the workplace. A lively socialist press ran the gamut from J. A. Wayland's homespun weekly *The Appeal to Reason,* sent to hundreds of thousands of readers from its offices in Kansas, to foreign language newspapers all over urban America. When Debs ran for the presidency on the SPA ticket in 1912 he won the votes of nearly 1 million men, from ex-Populist farmers in Oklahoma to Jewish garment workers in New York. In the same year the Wobblies led immigrant textile workers in Lawrence, Massachusetts, to victory in a dramatic strike.

Yet radical ideas remained on the margins of American culture and politics. The Wobblies never advanced beyond romantic guerilla raids against industrial capitalism, and though Debsian socialism renounced all revolutionary aims, it never overcame the ethnic divisions, the loyalty to the old parties, or the bourgeois values of most workers. In 1912 more workers and farmers voted for the Democrat Woodrow Wilson and the renegade Republican Theodore Roosevelt, two progressive reformers, than for the Socialist Debs.

PROGRESSIVES

The patterns of Gilded Age reform thought that pointed the way to the future belonged less to the protesters of 1896 than to liberal Republicans, civil service advocates, and female crusaders for social justice who had emerged in the 1880s. These were the ancestors of the many movements between 1897 and 1917 that historians loosely group under the rubric "progressivism," as Richard Hofstadter contended in his seminal *The Age of Reform* (1955). Progressives came in a hectic array of ideological shapes and social sizes, but at the center of this many-sided movement were urban middle-class Americans who were determined to bring order and morality to a wayward society. They were determined, too, to recover for themselves the cultural authority they felt people of their class had lost.

In these purposes the progressives resembled—indeed many of them had previously been—genteel realists of the Gilded Age: the mugwumps, anti-vice crusaders, the ladies of the WCTU and the NCL, and the men and women of the settlement house movement. Like earlier genteel realists, the progressives were well-off and well-educated white Protestants dismayed by the squalor, the immorality, the waste, and the potential for working-class revolution they saw in the cities. Most of the progressives, too, were elitists animated by a spirit of noblesse oblige and civic piety. In 1896 the voters among them were more likely to have picked McKinley than Bryan. Theodore Roosevelt liked to call himself a "progressive conservative," commenting that "the only true conservative is the man who resolutely sets his face toward the future" (Blum, *The Republican Roosevelt*, p. 5). All of these characteristics made progressives more acceptable to the society's key power brokers than were other groups of reformers.

Progressivism was the mode of reform that emerged following the failure of the utopians and radicals, when middle-class reformers fully engaged with the political and economic realities of an industrialized America. Progressivism reflected a set of historical circumstances that made reformers less desperate to transform their society, less disposed to escape it, and more confident they could manage it. Chief among these was the defeat of Bryan and the Populists in 1896. With the forces of revolt in retreat, with the menace of class war beaten back (but with class antagonisms still seething), with a triumphant corporate elite ready to make strategic concessions to workers and consumers and critics, the way was opened for a new movement of *managerial* reform.

Often college- or university-educated, progressives had more respect for formal ideas and intellectual expertise than previous groups of reformers. Many were academics. Their path to progressive reform was paved by growing discontent with a priori, formalist, determinist, and atomistic modes of thought. Inherited systems of ideas seemed increasingly incapable of interpreting experience in a dynamic and plural industrial society. In modern science, progressives found the tools for the understanding and purposive change that they desired. Without ceasing to be pious moralists, the progressives confidently embraced the scientific method. In 1914, at the apex of progressive optimism, Walter Lippmann rhapsodized on the power science gave modern people to "master" their social world. "The scientific spirit is the discipline of democracy, the escape from drift, the outlook of a free man" (*Drift and Mastery*, p. 151).

If there was a universal intellectual authority among progressives, it was no statesman, philosopher, or economist but rather a scientist, Charles Darwin. By demonstrating the dynamism and plasticity of nature, Darwin's *On the Origin of Species* (1859) opened up new vistas of thought about human nature and human society. Evolutionary science legitimized change and bred a passion for empirical inquiry. Along with muckraking exposés, the progressive movement produced hundreds of painstaking investigations of social problems, underwritten by settlements like Hull-House, universities like Chicago and Wisconsin, charitable foundations like Russell Sage, and finally by federal and state government.

Expertise, Democracy, and Individualism Respecting the scientific method, progressives also respected experts trained in its use. Scientific expertise signified objectivity, fairness, disinterestedness, efficiency, and continuity, all qualities much valued by progressive reformers. It also promised an ideal melding of knowledge with power: knowledge making power responsible, power making knowledge effective. Progressive campaigns often began with an investigation and often ended with the creation of a panel of experts or a new government bureau staffed by experts on labor arbitration panels, boards of health, boards of charities, park commissions, the Federal Trade Commission, the Children's Bureau of the U.S. Labor Department, and so on.

The progressives' fondness for bureaucratic remedies reflected not only their conviction that social problems needed to be approached objectively, but also their belief that problems needed to be continuously managed. They preferred policy—rational, predictable—to the unpredictable and sometimes corrupt play of democratic politics. By the same token they distrusted panaceas and dramatic interventions of all sorts. Social disorder, dysfunction, and injustice were too imbedded in complex social processes, they typically believed, to be resolved simply by enacting a law or passing down a judicial decision. Such simplistic "solutions" were likely to bring about new disorders or injustices. The purpose of responsible intervention in social processes was not to remake society but to reestablish order and achieve equilibrium, to keep the social machine running. Social problems demanded constant monitoring and the application of regulatory power finely calibrated to the precise problem at hand.

Enamored of expertise, bureaucracy, and active government, progressives were less than passionate about democracy. They were sincere republicans (whether Republicans or Democrats) in the meaning of that term early in the nation's history; they believed in political institutions that respected and reflected public opinion but that placed power in the hands of men of education, property, and civic virtue. They were sincere foes of anything that smacked of plutocracy, of men buying power. Direct, unmediated democracy, however, carried for most progressives troubling connotations of demagogy, disorder, and power yielded into unqualified hands. Jane Addams traced her democratic faith straight to Abraham Lincoln, an associate of her father, and she was deeply devoted to the welfare of the immigrant workers of Chicago. She was a representative progressive, however, in her disgust with machine politics and her enthusiasm for boards of arbitration and study commissions staffed by individuals like herself. Better Alexander Hamilton's distrust of democratic excess, Herbert Croly asserted, than Thomas Jefferson's confusion of democracy with "extreme individualism" and pandering egalitarianism. Americans needed not more freedom, but more disciplined use of the freedom they already possessed. Croly said: "A more highly socialized democracy [one directed by a powerful state] is the only practical substitute on the part of convinced democrats for an excessively individualized democracy" (*Promise of American Life*, p. 25).

Another intellectual pillar of progressivism was its commitment to the concept of human sociality. Progressives discarded the several forms of individualism—analytic, economic, and ethical—that permeated classical economics, evangelical theology, liberal political theory, and almost every other body of orthodox Victorian thought. Bringing together Darwin, research in psychology, and threads of socialism and the social gospel, they took the position that human beings are intrinsically social animals and societies are dense and fragile webs of reciprocal relationships. There is a public interest, they believed, which cannot be reduced to a sum of private interests. It is the legitimate business of the state not just to protect property and keep the peace, but actively to defend the public interest and sustain the general welfare. Quite apart from the dictates of morality, the simple facts of human interdependency, growing ever greater in modern societies, demanded social planning and an activist state.

Progressives found a congenial philosophy in the radical empiricism of William James and John Dewey, who taught that the world is plural, plastic, always changing, and knowable only by experience. Ideas are not copies of reality, these "pragmatists" held, but rather tools for manipulating the environment. Utility is the test of truth, and endless inquiry will yield more truth than any fixed or closed intellectual system. James influenced a number of reform intellectuals. Dewey urged the application of experimental methods to social problems and himself participated in reform movements, especially in the field of education.

Progressives also found inspiration and validation in revisionist historical scholarship. Rejecting the filiopietism of writers like George Bancroft, the Columbia historian Charles Beard proposed that the Constitution was designed to secure the property of men of wealth. "Progressive historians" like Beard pictured the American past as a record of struggle between democracy and capitalism, "the people" and "the interests," which established a context for contemporary campaigns to curb the power of trusts and banks.

The Social Science The intellectual currents that proved most fertile for progressives flowed through the infant social sciences. Scientific study of society was new in this period, and so was the reliance of politicians and civil servants on scientific expertise. Political science virtually grew up with progressive reform. A young scholar named Woodrow Wilson anticipated several progressive reform themes in *The State* and in *Congressional Government*, both published in the 1880s; in 1915, a Columbia political scientist named Benjamin De Witt wrote *The Progressive Movement*, the best early book on the movement. The "new psychology" of Sigmund Freud was beginning to influence reform intellectuals like Walter Lippmann after 1910. Most important to reformers, however, were developments in economics and sociology.

Graduate students began to bring the "new economics" back from German universities in the 1870s. Stimulated by scholars like Karl Knies and Adolf Wagner, young American economists attacked their elders' veneration of market laws, laissez-faire policies, and utilitarian ethics. They were especially intent on desanctifying and demystifying the market, which, they insisted, is a highly imperfect and an often cruel mechanism. When the interplay of supply and demand fails to yield efficiency and justice, the state has a positive duty to intervene in economic affairs. In 1885 these renegades formed a reform-oriented American Economic Association to espouse, as its leader Richard T. Ely declared, "the ethical school of economics."

Ely's ideas were heterodox in part because his experience and connections were so diverse. His intellectual career involved him in the overthrowing of old icons and old barriers alike. According to the historian James Kloppenberg, Ely "stood at the crossroads of the social gospel, the labor movement, the professionalization of social science, and the politics of progressivism" (*Uncertain Victory,* p. 207). After teaching at Johns Hopkins University, Ely joined another reform economist, John R. Commons, at the University of Wisconsin, where a vigorous partnership was formed between university researchers and the reform administration of Governor Robert LaFollette. Henry Carter Adams of the University of Michigan, John Bates Clark of Columbia University, and Simon Patten of the University of Pennsylvania were other prophets of the "new economics." In time they, their brand of economics, and the whole progressive movement, grew more established. Their careers exemplified, as the historian Leon Fink says of Commons, "the general turn taken by social scientists from the moral and agitational stance of the critical outsider to a position of technical expertise and influence among policy-making elites" (*Progressive Intellectuals,* p. 66).

While Ely and his colleagues were questioning received wisdom in economics, the new discipline of sociology was challenging the laissez-faire principles imbedded in the monolithic intellectual system invented by the English polymath Herbert Spencer. A truer social Darwinist than Darwin, Spencer taught that harsh laws of natural selection governed evolution in both animal species and human societies. Any tampering with these laws by governments or philanthropies would subvert the harmonies of nature. Hugely popular in the United States, Spencer's first book, published in 1851, was titled, tellingly, *Social Statics.* In 1883 the pioneering

sociologist Lester Frank Ward answered Spencer's fatalism with *Dynamic Sociology,* in which he rejected the theory of continuity between biological and social evolution. Possessing intelligence, Ward argued, humans can shape their environments, and thus can determine the course of their own development. In the 1890s Ward was joined by other proponents of an activist sociology such as Edward A. Ross of Stanford, Charles Horton Cooley of Michigan, and Albion Small of Chicago, who made the *American Journal of Sociology,* founded in 1895, a forum for social welfare research. Far the best of early sociological studies was W. E. B. Du Bois's 1899 investigation of black Philadelphia, but in this time of deepening racism Du Bois's color and his subject marginalized his work.

Progressivism fused the old Protestant moralism with a new faith in empiricism, education, and science. It represented, as Charley Forcey has argued, a "new liberalism," retaining the old liberal veneration for liberty and property but renouncing faith in the market and recognizing the necessity for an activist state. Progressivism can also be understood as the marriage of American reform with industrial capitalism. Many of the most significant progressive reforms clustered in a field that the French economist Charles Gide called "social economy": ameliorative efforts "within the constraints of political economy itself—to temper, socialize, and mutualize the pains of the capitalist transformation" (Rodgers, *Atlantic Crossings,* p. 12). Progressives held that the industrial economy had grown up too chaotically and brutally as an engine for producing goods; now it had to be civilized and made into the foundation for a decent society.

Perhaps most importantly, progressivism was imbued with a sense of history as an ongoing, unending process which, though dauntingly complex, could be explained, directed, and controlled. It followed that reform demanded constant adaptation, a perpetual dialogue between facts and ideals. The better future that was "the promise of American life," the publicist Herbert Croly wrote in 1909, would have to be "planned and constructed rather than fulfilled of its own momentum" (*Promise of American Life,* p. 6). The *New Republic,* a progressive journal, sounded a keynote of the new reform ethos when it declared in 1915, "We can put our ideals behind us and worship them, or we can put them ahead of us and struggle toward them." It exhorted Americans to put "a new experimental idealism" in place of their "old immutable idealism" (Forcey, *The Crossroads of Liberalism,* p. 21).

See also **Reform Institutions; Gender and Political Activism; Radical Alternatives; Racialism and Racial Uplift** *(in this volume);* **Social Reform; Socialism and Radical Thought; Anti-Statism** *(volume 2);* **Rhetoric; Marxist Approaches** *(volume 3).*

BIBLIOGRAPHY

Addams, Jane. *Twenty Years at Hull-House.* New York, 1960.

Bellamy, Edward. *Looking Backward, 2000–1887.* Edited by Cecelia Tichi. New York, 1982.

Blum, John Morton. *The Republican Roosevelt.* Cambridge, Mass., 1965.

Boyer, Paul. *Urban Masses and Moral Order in America, 1820–1920.* Cambridge, Mass., 1978.

Buhle, Paul. *Marxism in the USA.* London, 1987.

Cott, Nancy F. *The Grounding of Modern Feminism.* New Haven, Conn., 1987.

Croly, Herbert. *The Promise of American Life.* New York, 1964.

Feffer, Andrew. *The Chicago Pragmatists and American Progressivism.* Ithaca, N.Y., 1993.

Fine, Sidney. *Laissez-Faire and the General-Welfare State: A Study of Conflict in American Thought, 1865–1901.* Ann Arbor, Mich., 1956.

Fink, Leon. *Progressive Intellectuals and the Dilemmas of Democratic Commitment.* Cambridge, Mass., 1997.

Forcey, Charles. *The Crossroads of Liberalism: Croly, Weyl, Lippmann and the Progressive Era, 1900–1925.* New York, 1961.

George, Henry. *Progress and Poverty: An Inquiry into the Cause of Industrial Depressions and of Increase of Want with Increase of Wealth.* 1879. Reprint, New York, 1940.

Goodwyn, Lawrence. *The Populist Moment: A Short History of the Agrarian Revolt in America.* New York, 1978.

Hofstadter, Richard. *The Age of Reform: From Bryan to F.D.R.* New York, 1955.

Howe, Frederic C. *The City: The Hope of Democracy.* Seattle, 1967.

Howe, Irving. *Socialism and America.* New York, n.d.

Kloppenberg, James T. *Uncertain Victory: Social Democracy and Progressivism in European and American Thought, 1870–1920.* New York, 1986.

Kraditor, Aileen S. *The Ideas of the Woman Suffrage Movement, 1890–1920.* New York, 1981.

Lippmann, Walter. *Drift and Mastery: An Attempt to Diagnose the Current Unrest.* Madison, Wis., 1985.

Quandt, Jean B. *From the Small Town to the Great Community: The Social Thought of Progressive Intellectuals.* New Brunswick, N.J., 1970.

Rodgers, Daniel T. *Atlantic Crossings: Social Politics in a Progressive Age.* Cambridge, Mass., 1998.

Thomas, John L. *Alternative America: Henry George, Edward Bellamy, Henry Demarest Lloyd, and the Adversary Tradition.* Cambridge, Mass., 1983.

Weinstein, James. *The Corporate Ideal in the Liberal State, 1900–1918.* Boston, 1968.

Westbrook, Robert B. *John Dewey and American Democracy.* Ithaca, N.Y., 1991.

White, Morton. *Social Thought in America: The Revolt Against Formalism.* Boston, 1957.

NATIONALISM AND IMPERIALISM

Cecilia Elizabeth O'Leary

From the Republic's founding, militarism and conflict played pivotal roles in the construction of American identity as settlers fought Indian wars for land. In the 1800s the ideology of manifest destiny justified the U.S.-Mexican War and the acquisition of half of Mexico's territory. By the dawn of the twentieth century, the Spanish-American War coupled with capitalist expansion and the successful conclusion of the bloodiest civil war of the nineteenth century had not only assured the existence of a continental United States but had also launched the nation as an emerging world power. The words "nationalism" and "imperialism" became part of public culture as the United States reinvented itself as a modern nation-state after the Civil War, and jockeyed for colonial possessions and economic influence in eastern Asia, the Caribbean, Latin America, and the Pacific. The United States entered a stage of high imperialism with the 1898 war against Spain for control of Cuba and colonies halfway across the world in the Philippines. The belief that national culture needed to be revitalized by war and military preparedness soared in popularity as discourses of male warrior heroism, white supremacy, and manifest destiny framed economic visions of dominance in the capitalist world economy.

NATIONALISM

Nationalism, a modern ideological and cultural innovation, requires conscious political intervention and sustained popular mobilization. Unlike other countries whose governments took an active role in constructing the content and rituals of national culture, citizen-volunteers took the lead in the United States. At the end of the nineteenth century, the United States entered into an age of patriotism. Fears about whether such a polyglot, racially and ethnically heterogeneous nation was truly tied together motivated nationalists to pursue cultural unification. A spectrum of groups invented, popu-

larized, and disseminated many of the nationalist symbols and rituals—the Pledge of Allegiance, flags over the public schools, Memorial Day, veterans' parades—that we now take for granted. Veterans' organizations and educators, politicians and journalists, men and women, capital and labor, reactionaries and reformers, white supremacists and anti-racists, immigrants and the native born all competed for sufficient cultural authority to impose their interpretation of what it meant to be an American.

Nationalism, never just a neutral point of identity and allegiance, continuously reproduces and reflects structures of economic, social, and cultural power. Although nations might claim to be timeless, consensual, and monolithic, they are crisscrossed with divisions and conflicting interests. Nationalism sutures these differences into a unified, albeit unstable, sense of national identity and purpose. Narratives of the nation—rituals, histories, heroes, holidays, monuments—make it easier for disparate social groups to imagine themselves part of a national family, even in the face of inequality and injustice. The United States, however, is also one of the few countries in which a citizen can be cast out of the body politic and denounced as un-American because of political beliefs or failure to meet racial, ethnic, gender, class, or religious criteria imposed by the dominant society. When belonging is seen as a choice rather than a birthright, discourses about national identity and mission have very real consequences.

Between the Civil War and World War I, there was considerable conflict over whose memories, icons, and rituals would represent what it meant to be an American. Anti-liberalism confronted emancipatory traditions forged during the Civil War and Reconstruction, when a national citizenship guaranteed citizenship rights regardless of race for the first time. Democratic rights for all Americans met with fierce opposition from white supremacists, who upheld a race-based concept of national identity. Those who advocated civic-oriented concepts of an educated citizenry vied with martial brands of unquestioning nationalism. Organized labor wielded nationalism in its advocacy of the right of workers to share in capitalism's bounty, while capitalists denounced strikers as un-American. Women's groups used their participation in patriotic movements to move from the margins into the center of civic culture. Americanizers embraced an optimistic belief in the country's power to transform immigrants, while nativists organized for immigration restriction. During the Spanish-American War anti-imperialists condemned expansionists for turning a republic into a colonial empire. In the years leading up to World War I, preparedness advocates competed with peace groups and isolationists for the hearts and minds of the American public.

IMPERIALISM

At the turn of the century, the United States joined the great power rivalry that was redividing the world. Great Britain, France, Germany, Italy, the Netherlands, Belgium, Japan, and the United States seized most of Africa and the Pacific for political and economic reasons. Where traditional empires survived in Asia, their independence was drastically compromised by spheres of influence set up by competing Western powers. These conflicts largely took place outside of Europe and the Americas. The United States had already asserted its hegemony over Latin America during the first half of the nineteenth century. In 1823, President James Monroe issued the Monroe Doctrine and warned that any direct European intervention into the Western Hemisphere would be considered a challenge to the peace and safety of the United States. Not limited to interventions in the Western Hemisphere, the United States mobilized its armed forces to promote commercial interests in countries as distant as Japan, China, Angola, and Hawaii between 1853 and 1893.

Unlike the British Empire, which controlled its system of colonies through direct political rule administered out of its imperial center in England, the United States typically asserted its power through investments, ownership of natural resources, and political manipulation. Armed interventions only took place when it appeared that U.S. interests might be threatened. Of course, the great exceptions to isolationism and strategies of indirect domina-

tion were the wars of continental conquest in North America.

MANIFEST DESTINY

The United States is a nation founded by white settlers who relied on enslaved Africans to fuel early economic growth and relied on the forced removal of Indians to ensure continental expansion. The ideology of manifest destiny justified the drive to become a continental power as a God-given right. Manifest destiny became one of the most important defining concepts for the United States, institutionally embedded and working in harness with other historical forces to transform expansionism into a "normal" practice. A popular painting in the 1870s, titled *American Progress,* reads as a visual text on expansion. A white woman, reminiscent of early representations of Liberty but now crowned with the Star of Empire, floats above the westward advance of manly settlers, wagons, carriages, trains, and telegraph wires. Indians, who are only barely visible, flee into the painting's margins. An imperialist logic justified military conquests, broken treaties, and forced removal of the land's original inhabitants as the nation moved West. Indian Wars raged through 1890, when the massacre of two hundred Sioux men, women, and children took place at Wounded Knee on a South Dakota reservation. The same year, the Bureau of the Census declared the end of the frontier.

The imperatives of the southern slave economy impelled geographic expansion into the West. Pro-slavery forces demanded expansion for a variety of social, political, and economic reasons. The United States first moved into the Southwest by annexing Texas in 1845; it then seized half of Mexico in 1848 after instigating a war over a disputed border. At the war's end, the United States had not only secured the Rio Grande River as Texas's southern border, but had also conquered the territory that makes up all of present-day Arizona, California, New Mexico, Nevada, and Utah and part of Colorado. Militarism and nationalism became dramatically bound to each other in the symbol of the Stars and Stripes, which the press associated with images of bloodshed in victorious battles against Mexico. For the first time, the U.S. Army carried the national colors into combat on foreign soil.

Although the nation fought the U.S.-Mexican War as a divided country, the conflict significantly deepened nationalist consciousness. While anti-slavery forces in the Northeast opposed the Mexican

War and pacifists denounced the war as an aggressive attack on a weak neighbor, the mood of the country as a whole favored the victorious troops who relentlessly marched south under the banner of manifest destiny. Henry David Thoreau criticized the nation-state for making men into machines who marched "against their common sense and consciences." But while Thoreau saw the "file of soldiers" as "agents of injustice," many more Americans saw them as embodiments of Jefferson's Empire for Liberty (*Walden*, p. 637).

Newspapers fired their readers' imaginations with images of the "children of the Revolution" raising the Stars and Stripes over the "Halls of Montezuma and spreading THE EMPIRE OF FREEDOM" as far as Mexico City. Heroic newspaper serials about George Washington circulated among U.S. Army regiments in Mexico. "Shall we not follow the Banner of the Stars from the bloody height of Bunker Hill," read the men, to "the golden city of Tenochtitlan?" (Lippard, pp. 524–525). At the war's end in 1848, Mexican settlers who had lived in the Southwest for two hundred years found themselves foreigners in their own land.

The United States was not, however, ready to become a major power outside the Western Hemisphere. Following the Civil War, priority was given to internal development and the U.S. merchant marine dwindled to a few outdated wooden sailing ships. Rapid industrialization and the completion of transcontinental railroads sharpened business appetites for foreign markets and the possibility of establishing outposts in Samoa and the Hawaiian Islands gained in significance. In 1894 American businessmen in Hawaii, who owned most of the sugar plantations there, led a rebellion and set up a provisional government. They proclaimed the Republic of Hawaii and made Sanford B. Dole its first president. The public did not yet support such direct imperialist interventions in distant lands, and requests for annexation failed until a popular imperialism inspired by the Spanish-American War led to passage of a joint resolution in 1898 to make Hawaii part of the territory of the United States.

THE SPANISH-AMERICAN WAR

The United States became a serious rival within the world capitalist system when it went to war with Spain in 1898 over the last vestiges of the latter's empire in the Caribbean and the Pacific. The ideological relationship between nationalism and imperialism intensified as militarists like Theodore Roosevelt championed the need for white male warriors to safeguard the "home of the brave" and spearhead the "civilizing" of Cuba, Puerto Rico, and the Philippines. Initially, public opinion had been divided over whether to go to war with Spain over the "liberation" of Cuba. The United States had previously not intervened on behalf of Cuban struggles for independence that took place throughout the 1800s. But in 1895, when an independence movement erupted once again and José Martí y Pérez met his untimely death on an expedition to liberate Cuba, the press finally began to carry stories of Spanish atrocities. When the U.S. warship *Maine* mysteriously exploded in waters of Havana's harbor on 15 February 1898, newspaper editors held Spain responsible and agitated for retribution. White and black Americans, inspired by the idea of establishing an independent Cuban republic, supported going to war. Jingoists, on the other hand, seized upon the opportunity to expand national influence through the creation of a colonial empire.

When President William McKinley asked Congress to use the army and navy to win Cuban freedom from Spain, Hearst's *New York Journal* printed full-page images of the Stars and Stripes with headlines announcing: "WE'RE FIGHTING FOR HUMANITY, FREEDOM" (*New York Journal*, 1 May 1898, p. 1). In Memorial Day services around the country, veterans fired cannons, children executed flag drills, and speakers linked the battle for liberty during the Civil War with the liberation of Cuba. Women, who had created Memorial Day out of personal rituals of remembrance of the horrors of the Civil War, immediately endorsed the Spanish-American War. While individual chapters of the Woman's Relief Corps, the largest organization of patriotic women, joined the movement for "peace and arbitration" at the turn of the century, the nationalist path of a rising world power led the group to side with an imperialism couched in the language of idealism.

The ideological core of Memorial Day, the celebration of loyalty to the nation, ultimately required the Woman's Relief Corps to join military mobilizations rather than oppose them. The potentially subversive quality of Memorial Day rituals, with their pathos and inchoate critique of war, never materialized. Instead, Memorial Day played an important part in the imaginative web of national identity described by Benedict Anderson, in which strangers joined in a fraternity, and despite structures of inequality, come to feel they can march off to war as comrades. The Woman's Relief Corps succeeded in creating a cultural bridge between the nation's past and its future through Memorial Day by bolstering an unquestioning patriotism focused on the nation's triumphs rather than its unrealized promise.

Before the government even made the official call for National Guard units, states mobilized thousands of volunteers for the war effort. Symbolic of the increasing reconciliation between the white North and white South, former Confederates served as high-ranking officers in the U.S. military for the first time since before the Civil War. President William McKinley courted votes by awarding major generals' commissions to "Fightin' Joe" Wheeler of Alabama and Fitzhugh Lee of Virginia. Theodore Roosevelt also welcomed southern recruits, including former Harvard classmates and hardened frontier fighters from the Texas Rangers into his Rough Riders. Immigrants, proletarians, and black Americans, however, were excluded from the regiment's ranks.

In a little less than three months, Spain agreed to sign a peace treaty. "VICTORY!!" declared the *New York Journal* above the wings of an enormous eagle. "COMPLETE! GLORIOUS! THE MAINE IS AVENGED!" (2 May 1898, p. 1). Drawing upon the language of manifest destiny, the Spanish-American War was reshaped into a religious mission. "Old Glory is God's chosen banner," proclaimed a Civil War veteran. "When our flag was raised on these islands and proclaimed freedom and independence to the inhabitants, it was like a voice from heaven." National hubris, missionary zeal, and a racist paternalism toward the "poor, ignorant people" of Cuba, Puerto Rico, and the Philippines proved a powerful combination. A popular imperialism ignited the country with visions of Anglo-Saxon Americans civilizing the "inferior" peoples of the world (Women's Relief Corps, p. 289).

U.S.-PHILIPPINES WAR

War did not stop with defeat of Spain. After months of debate, the Senate ratified a treaty that promised independence to Cuba but turned over the Philippines, Puerto Rico, and Guam to the United States for $20 million. Cuban independence never materialized while the Filipinos, who also had fought for independence from Spain, now faced occupation by the United States. The war to liberate Cuba turned into a war of conquest in the Philippines.

The United States significantly reshaped its foreign relations when it made the fateful decision to acquire colonies whose people would be denied the rights of citizenship and statehood. Imperialism thwarted the independence struggle of the Filipino peoples and dramatically impacted the ways that Americans saw themselves. The majority of the nation was firm in its belief that the military intervention to liberate Cuba was noble, but there was less agreement over what to do with the spoils of what had been transformed into an imperialist war.

Although President McKinley declared that imperialism was "alien to American sentiment, thought and purpose," intervention in the Philippines looked very much like the power politics engaged in by European colonialists. Faced with the contradiction between ideals and reality, war enthusiasts drew upon scientific racism to justify the need to expand an enlightened colonialism to "inferior" peoples. The nation's presses described the acquisition of extra-continental territories in the more acceptable language of advancing an empire of democracy, or an empire of liberty. Christianity wedded ideas of mission and destiny together. John Ireland, a Civil War veteran and Catholic archbishop, maintained that "America is too great to be isolated from the world around her." A major Protestant magazine implored its readers not "to abandon some part of the world" when it is the responsibility of the Christian church "to take the world." Some businessmen couched calls for intervention in terms of commercial uplift, but others did not shy away from describing the Philippines as a stepping stone toward making the Pacific into a "highway" for commercial expansion in Asia. Men like Henry Cabot Lodge embraced the geopolitics of European rivalry outright, arguing that "the great nations of the earth are competing in a desperate struggle for the world's trade, and in that competition . . . we must not be left behind" (Stephanson, pp. 90, 92–93, 95–96).

Despite the popularity of appeals for the righteousness of American expansionism, opposition to the war in the Philippines took on a much broader scope than what opponents of the U.S.-Mexican War had been able to mount in the 1840s. A broad spectrum of constituencies opposed the acquisition of the Philippines. Some argued that it violated the basic right of government by consent. Radicals denounced the war as capitalist robbery, and mainstream figures such as Andrew Carnegie and former President Grover Cleveland raised their voices in opposition. Samuel Gompers, leader of the American Federation of Labor, feared that the Philippines would become a source of cheap labor. Still other anti-imperialists viewed Filipinos as an inferior race who, like former Africans enslaved in the United States, could not be assimilated into American citizenship. Mark Twain, famous author, newspaper contributor, and lecturer, became a fervent anti-imperialist during the Spanish-American War. In 1900 he wrote, "I left these shores ... a red-hot imperialist. I wanted the American eagle to go screaming into the Pacific. It seemed tiresome and tame for it to content itself with the Rockies. Why not spread its wings over the Philippines, I asked myself?" But Twain quickly came to believe that "we have gone there to conquer, not to redeem" (*New York Herald,* 15 October 1900).

The Anti-Imperialist League, founded in November 1898, included capitalists and workers, politicians and educators, progressives and reactionaries, and white supremacists and pluralists who were unified only by their opposition to colonial expansion. Members represented a mixture of Republicans, Mugwumps, and Democrats, many of whom had stood on opposite sides of political battles in the past. The League distributed pamphlets, sponsored speeches, and published letters in newspapers from soldiers figuring in the Philippines to demonstrate the cruelty of the war. Letters described the use of torture and the burning of villages. One soldier wrote, "Last night one of our boys was found shot and his stomach cut open. Immediately orders were received from [the] General ... to burn the town and kill every native in sight" (Morison, Merk, and Freidel, p. 88). Yet despite the participation of such well-known figures as Jane Addams, Mark Twain, Andrew Carnegie, William Jennings Bryan, and former president Cleveland, the Anti-Imperialist League never developed into a significant opposition.

The black press initially welcomed the liberation of Cuba. Some blacks, however, balked at the prospect of American troops fighting against Filipinos who, as some African Americans saw it, were in a battle for civil rights. Other African Americans countered that black men needed to prove their patriotism in order to gain citizenship rights. Lynchings at home, however, coupled with disillusionment over the racist treatment of returning troops, left black communities deeply ambivalent. Emilio Aguinaldo, leader of the independence movement, asked black soldiers why they fought on the side of a nation that so clearly despised them. Many black soldiers agreed and desertion rates were unusually high. A black church leader warned that the ascendance of "race supremacy" was undermining the "finest impulses of American citizenship" (Durham, p. 3).

Justified as a military campaign to spread democratic principles in the Philippines and uplift "our little brown brothers," the strategy of total war there echoed the wars of annihilation fought against American Indians. Many high-ranking officers who had honed their military skills while fighting Apaches, Comanches, Kiowas, and Sioux transferred the tactics used in conquering the West to the new imperial frontier. The invention of racial hierarchies, in which people of color were dehumanized as "savage," eased acceptance of the need for military violence.

Filipino resistance held strong and it took three years of grueling guerrilla warfare before the United States finally consolidated its control. U.S. soldiers burned down villages, shot fleeing Filipinos, raped Filipino women, and engaged in torture, all in the name of extending American freedom. News of atrocities generated anti-imperialist criticism as many questioned how the United States could remain a republic while subjugating people halfway around the world. Despite these sentiments, however, a mass peace movement never materialized.

IMPERIALISM, RACE, AND GENDER

The war provided a structural basis for the ideological alliance of white supremacists in the South and advocates of imperialism in the North. In a speech urging the annexation of the Philippines, Senator Albert Beveridge reveled in the opportunity the war provided for the "most virile, ambitious, impatient, militant manhood the world has ever seen" (*Major Problems,* pp. 389–391). Beveridge tied his view of reinvigorated masculine power to a white male body seeped in potent sexuality and martial violence.

Though the nation briefly extolled black soldiers as American heroes during the summer of 1898, the Spanish-American War did not result in any new enthusiasm for expanding civil rights. Instead, the war served to reinforce racism at home. In Kansas City, Missouri, the townspeople invited the white First Cavalry into their homes and furnished them with free meals in the local restaurants. The Ninth Cavalry, whose black members had also fought valiantly, were not even allowed to stand up and get a bite to eat at the restaurant counters.

Entrepreneurial capitalists, eager to take advantage of the new nationalism, appropriated patriotic sentiments so that their products would appeal to whites both North and South. Popular music sheets began to include the Confederate general Robert E. Lee in their lists of American heroes. Western adventure stories transformed former Indian fighters into soldiers battling against the new villains of civilization: men with Spanish-sounding names and brown complexions.

Widely read magazines depicted as heroes the men who had answered Rudyard Kipling's call to "take up the white man's burden" (*McClure's Magazine,* 12 February 1899). A widely used photograph pictured a white U.S. soldier carrying within the folds of the Stars and Stripes three children symbolizing Cuba, Puerto Rico, and the Philippines who needed civilizing. In popular culture the Spanish-American War was represented as a civilizing duty rather than a violent war of imperialist conquest.

Out of the Spanish-American War, Theodore Roosevelt emerged as the most powerful embodiment of the new American hero. A master craftsman of cultural symbolism, he promulgated a new interpretation of twentieth-century manhood that celebrated a virile masculinity forged in imperial conquest. Roosevelt's nationalism contained a gendered and racialized structure of authority in which white women bore the responsibility for producing the nation's children and white men the responsibility for national regeneration through expansion.

The spirit of the frontier lived on in Roosevelt's call to take up the challenge of empire. Just as a righteous war had been fought against Indian "savages," American men needed to "civilize" the Filipinos. Roosevelt's Rough Riders physically and symbolically embodied the link between manifest destiny and the new imperialism. William F. "Buffalo Bill" Cody's Wild West show popularized this view in its production of "San Juan Hill." Across the United States and on stages in Europe, actors linked the struggle between white men and Indians in the West to all contemporary struggles between "progressive" and "savage" races in the modern world.

CONCLUSION

At the turn of the century, an aggressive foreign policy and economic intervention became central components of U.S. relations within the capitalist world economy. As the nation's industrial strength grew, the United States increasingly turned its attention from domestic development to global affairs. Whether insisting on an Open Door policy in the Far East, imposing the Monroe Doctrine in the Western Hemisphere, or collaborating with American corporations that made Latin America into their private domains for investments, the United States increasingly found itself in rivalry with Europe for power and economic influence and, in the case of the Philippines, China, and Mexico, against revolutions that challenged American political authority and economic domination.

Few Progressives opposed the new imperialism, seeing social reform at home as compatible with the extension of American ideals around the world. In 1904 the Roosevelt Corollary to the Monroe Doctrine established the United States as the policeman of the hemisphere. Both Progressives and imperialists upheld the right to intervene to correct social disorder, whether in the slums of New York's East Side or in a Latin American country whose people needed to be "civilized."

As a militant nationalism merged with the rhetoric of an idealistic imperialism, veterans' organizations, educators, and politicians revised U.S. history to better meet the exigencies of expansion. At the cost of national amnesia and what W. E. B. Du Bois would later condemn as "lies agreed upon," the commemoration of the fiftieth anniversary of Gettysburg rewrote Civil War history (*Black Reconstruction,* p. 714). One year before Europe launched World War I, the 1913 anniversary embodied a memory of the Civil War suitable for a twentieth-century nation aspiring to become a hegemonic imperialist power. More than fifty thousand Civil War veterans, tens of thousands of guests, and numerous political dignitaries attended the four-day national performance. In the name of national solidarity, the memory of Emancipation, which shared the anniversary year of 1863 with Gettysburg, was forgotten. The association of liberty and nationhood forged during the Civil War was replaced by a romanticized militarism in which a shared national racism allowed former Confederates to be transformed into blood brothers of white northerners, the two reunited to realize a global destiny. A nationalism defined by "whiteness" asserted itself against double-edged fears of the New Negro and new immigration.

"It matters little to you or to me now," the reunion's chairman told the crowds, "what the causes were that provoked the War of the States in the Sixties." What mattered, he asserted, was that veterans from the Union and the Confederacy survived to see their sons stand shoulder to shoulder to "sweep San Juan Hill, sink Spanish fleets in Santiago and Manila Bays, and thundering at the gates of Peking, establish our country as a power second to none on earth" (Schoonmaker, pp. 95–96).

See also **Expansion and Empire** *(in this volume);* **Artistic, Intellectual, and Political Refugees; Nationalism; International Relations and Connections; Anti-Statism** *(volume 2).*

BIBLIOGRAPHY

Primary Works

Beveridge, Albert J. "Senator Albert J. Beveridge's Salute to Imperialism, 1900." In *Major Problems in American Foreign Policy: Documents and Essays,* edited by Thomas G. Patterson. Vol. 1. 3d ed. Lexington, Mass., 1989.

Du Bois, W. E. B. *Black Reconstruction in America: An Essay toward a History of the Part Which Black Folk Played in the Attempt to Reconstruct Democracy in America, 1860–1880.* 1935. New York, 1970.

Durham, J. S. "Emancipation Address." *Christian Recorder,* 10 January 1901.

Gatewood, Willard B., Jr. *"Smoked Yankees" and the Struggle for Empire: Letters from Negro Soldiers, 1898–1902.* Urbana, Ill., 1971.

Kipling, Rudyard. "The White Man's Burden." In *Anti-Imperialism in the United States, 1898–1935,* edited by Jim Zwick. Philadelphia, 1970. ⟨http://www.boondocksnet.com/ail98–35.html⟩ (30 May 2000).

Library of Congress, Hispanic Division. *The World of 1898: The Spanish American War.* ⟨http://lcweb.loc.gov/rr/hispanic/1898/index.html⟩ (September 2000).

Lippard, George. *Washington and His Generals; or, Legends of the Revolution.* Philadelphia, 1847.

Morison, Samuel Eliot, Frederick Merk, and Frank Friedel. *Dissent in Three American Wars.* Cambridge, Mass., 1970.

Roosevelt, Theodore. *The Rough Riders.* New York, 1902.

Schoonmaker, J. M. *Fiftieth Anniversary of the Battle of Gettysburg.* Harrisburg, Pa., 1913.

Stephanson, Anders. *Manifest Destiny: American Expansion and the Empire of Right.* New York, 1995.

Thoreau, Henry David. "Civil Disobedience." In *Walden and Other Writings of Henry David Thoreau.* 1849. Edited by Brooks Atkinson, New York, 1950.

Woman's Relief Corps. *Journal of the Sixteenth Convention, 1898.* 1898. Reprint, Boston, 1911.

Secondary Works

Anderson, Benedict. *Imagined Communities: Reflections on the Origin and Spread of Nationalism.* Rev. ed. London, 1991.

Bederman, Gail. *Manliness and Civilization: A Cultural History of Gender and Race in the United States, 1880–1917.* Chicago, 1995.

Beisner, Robert L. *From the Old Diplomacy to the New, 1865–1900.* 2d ed. Arlington Heights, Ill., 1986.

———. *Twelve against Empire: The Anti-Imperialists, 1898–1900.* New York, 1968.

Chaudhuri, Nupur, and Margaret Strobel, eds. *Western Women and Imperialism.* Bloomington, Ind., 1990.

Cosmas, Graham A. *An Army for Empire: The United States Army in the Spanish-American War.* Columbia, Mo., 1971.

Eley, Geoff, and Ronald Grigor Suny. *Becoming National: A Reader.* New York, 1996.

Gatewood, Willard B., Jr. *Black Americans and the White Man's Burden, 1898–1903.* Urbana, Ill., 1975.

Gould, Lewis L. *The Spanish-American War and President McKinley.* Lawrence, Kans., 1982.

Hall, Stuart, David Held, and Tony McGrew, eds. *Modernity and Its Futures.* Cambridge, Mass., 1992.

Hobsbawm, Eric. *The Age of Empire, 1875–1914.* London, 1987.

Hoganson, Kristin L. *Fighting for American Manhood: How Gender Politics Provoked the Spanish-American and Philippine-American Wars.* New Haven, Conn., 1998.

Kaplan, Amy, and Donald E. Pease, eds. *Cultures of United States Imperialism.* Chapel Hill, N.C., 1994.

LaFeber, Walter. *The New Empire: An Interpretation of American Expansion, 1860–1898.* 35th anniv. ed., Ithaca, N.Y., 1998.

McClintock, Anne. *Imperial Leather: Race, Gender, and Sexuality in the Colonial Contest.* New York, 1995.

McCullough, David G. *The Path between the Seas: The Creation of the Panama Canal, 1870–1914.* New York, 1977.

Miller, Stuart Creighton. *"Benevolent Assimilation": The American Conquest of the Philippines, 1899–1903.* New Haven, Conn., 1982.

O'Leary, Cecilia Elizabeth. *To Die For: The Paradox of American Patriotism.* Princeton, N.J., 1999.

Rosenberg, Emily S. *Spreading the American Dream: American Economic and Cultural Expansion, 1890–1945.* New York, 1982.

Rydell, Robert W. *All the World's a Fair: Vision of Empire at the American International Expositions, 1876–1916.* Chicago, 1984.

Slotkin, Richard. *Gunfighter Nation: The Myth of the Frontier in Twentieth-Century America.* New York, 1992.

Wallerstein, Immanuel. *The Essential Wallerstein.* New York, 2000.

Williams, William Appleman. *Empire as a Way of Life: An Essay on the Causes and Character of America's Present Predicament.* New York, 1980.

Zinn, Howard. *A People's History of the United States, 1492–Present.* Rev. ed. New York, 1995.

GENDER, SOCIAL CLASS, RACE, AND MATERIAL LIFE

Jeanne Halgren Kilde

Sometime in the late 1890s, the evangelist Rachel Wild Peterson of Denver, Colorado, was invited to address the women of that city's Woman's Christian Temperance Union at the Trinity Methodist Episcopal Church on the subject of a home planned for "fallen women." Peterson described her experience in her 1905 autobiography:

> Trinity Church is one of the leading churches of our city and the leading society ladies of the city attend it. I felt more like being led out, after I have taken my seat among the speakers, there was so much style and fashion in evidence. I began to imagine I looked as much out of place as a pig would be in the parlor. One might wonder why I felt so. One reason was I did not think to put on my kid gloves, as I was not in the habit of wearing them, and not stopping to think of the stylish place I was to speak in. I felt as strange as if I had come in bare-headed. Not one of the platform nor in the audience, as far as I could see, but whom had on kid gloves except me. Try to imagine how I felt! You could hear the rustle of the silk dresses and the air was laden with rich perfumes from their delicate handkerchiefs. But there I was, wondering what to do with my big, coarse, red hands. One could not help seeing I was embarrassed; and you surely would have pitied me. However I was compelled to make the best of it. (p. 213)

Kid gloves, in this anecdote, symbolize a constellation of meanings that cause Peterson great anxiety. Social class and refinement are easily read into this single material product, and exclusion and isolation are the result. It is not her lack of a silk dress that annoys her, for such was simply out of her financial reach. The lack of gloves, though, is a breach of etiquette similar to the lack of head covering. Left exposed are her red hands, the hands of a working woman. Peterson's poverty is on display, and she likens herself to the barnyard animal completely out of place within a home. Gloves would have modestly covered her reality.

Significantly, Peterson does own gloves. Her isolation was not an absolute; had she brought them, she might have indicated her alignment with the

women of the church, her internalizing of a belief in aspiration. They would mask the reality of her social situation. Yet her red hands, the reader knows, would always separate from that audience. Even supporting the apparel of the wealthy women, Peterson would not be of their class. Still, the distance could be reduced. Kid gloves would have produced a kind of leveling, even though it would be nothing more than a shared fiction of equality.

Peterson's story illustrates a number of ways in which material objects function within complex signification systems, particularly those of class and gender. First, the anecdote highlights the fact that in the final decades of the nineteenth century the mass production of material items like kid gloves held out the tantalizing promise of a shrinkage of the chasm between social classes. While material possessions may have been a relatively reliable indicator of wealth and status in the generations prior to the Industrial Revolution, mass production increasingly rendered them ineffective in this regard. But much of this "leveling" was of a specific type. Had Peterson worn her gloves she would have signaled her acquiescence to a shared value. The gloves would have indicated that she located herself within the social category of "respectability," if not precisely the middle class itself. In this case, although the gloves would have leveled some of the perceived moral distance deemed to exist between the poor and the rich, the social distance would have remained.

Furthermore, the story illustrates the profound way in which women in particular had learned to define themselves through their possessions, internalizing a consumer ethic that would drive industrial production right up to the present. Women, or more specifically white, middle-class women, did not have red hands; they did have kid gloves, which were to be worn at all times in public. Further, they owned silk dresses and attended churches like the one Peterson visited. Part of Peterson's anxiety is due to the fact that her lack of kid gloves indicates that she is not acquiescing to the dominant ideal for white womanhood, the dominant gender ideal.

This analysis illustrates the ways in which cultural historians think about the relationships among the four categories of this essay—gender, social class, race, and material life. Moreover, it points up some of the unique challenges posed by the enormous social and cultural transformations that occurred during the period in question, from 1878 to 1912. Although that period was one of distinctive national and commercial consolidation and incorporation, it was also one of enormous expansion. During the period, the population of the United States more than doubled. Much of the increase came through immigration. The gross national product increased almost fivefold between 1880 and 1920, and much of this new wealth was created through the development of new products. More than sixty thousand patents were issued in the United States between 1876 and 1915.

People's lives changed dramatically. The population grew more diverse. More than 5 million people entered the United States from northern and western Europe between 1880 and 1900, and another 8 million came from eastern and southern Europe between 1890 and 1910. Immigrants from Asia numbered over 400,000 between 1900 and 1920. These immigrants joined native-born Americans of many social groups—native-born Anglo-Americans, including German, French, Irish, Scots, and Scandinavian Americans, whose families had arrived in earlier waves of immigrants; African Americans, released from slavery; Latino Americans in the Southwest; and Native Americans, embattled in a fight with the U.S. government for their very existence. These people increasingly moved into urban areas, though small town and rural life remained predominant. They worked at new jobs producing goods on a scale unimagined by their grandparents. They lived in new types of houses with a vast variety of new products, and they did new things in their spare time and with their spare cash. The sheer number of lifestyle choices took on an unprecedented vastness.

Such rapid transformation significantly altered the ways in which Americans understood themselves, their society, and their places within that society. Just as Peterson used kid gloves to discuss her position within the group at Trinity Church, Americans created a plethora of systems to impose meaning upon the potential chaos of change. The most critical of those systems to cultural historians have been gender, social class, and race. Although these categories have long been considered socially created, cultural historians examine them as culturally constructed ideological systems whose function is to create and maintain social hierarchies that privilege certain groups above others. During this period of enormous growth, these ideological systems served as consolidating and incorporating factors, labeling, categorizing, and judging individuals and groups in ways that privileged the values and lifestyles of the new middle class and that encouraged the growth of an economic system based upon industrial and consumer capitalism.

Although social history has yielded much information on gender, class, and racial ideologies, the connections between gender, class, and race constructions and the economies of capitalism have been revolutionized by the cultural historian's growing interest in material culture. While scholars have long investigated how societies negotiate ideas and create themselves through written and spoken language, relying heavily upon documents to understand cultural ratiocination, late-twentieth-century studies have asserted that these processes advance through material means as well. The historian Barbara Fields reminds us that while doctrines, which lend themselves to verbal expression, can easily be imposed and handed down to later generations, ideologies, which are highly complex meaning systems, "must be constantly created and verified." Material artifacts—whether objects, buildings, or landscapes—do precisely this, creating and verifying as well as maintaining gender, class, and racial ideologies through two processes: signification and reification. Signification refers to the ways in which artifacts, buildings, and landscapes embody and articulate sociocultural meanings. Functioning as a kind of language, material culture carries complex messages within a variety of meaning systems. Peterson's kid gloves, for instance, carried messages about gender and class. Material culture, however, not only offers eloquent testimony to society's values, priorities, aspirations, and limitations, but it also constitutes one of the very processes that create cultural meaning and ideologies. Operating well beyond simple signification, a society's material production is constitutive of cultural meaning. Kid gloves helped create, verify, and maintain those very ideas about social class and gender. Given the astounding transformations that took place in the late nineteenth and early twentieth centuries, this period has proven fertile territory for cultural historians interested in these specific categories of cultural productions.

CONSTRUCTION OF SOCIAL CLASS THROUGH MATERIAL LIFE

As the population expanded and the variety of choices made available through new kinds of consumer goods and employment burgeoned, concerns grew over locating individuals within the precise social categories. On the one hand, this process ensued through the development of class awareness or class consciousness, as certain groups such as factory workers or suburban homeowners recognized shared interests. For example, factory workers, recognizing their shared position of powerlessness against employers, attempted to come together through union activity in order to improve their working situations. In addition, social class definitions evolved as groups developed distinctive lifestyles based on their relative economic power and political power. In both of these processes material life created, verified, and maintained distinctions between social classes.

Buildings, Space, and Landscapes Transformations in the material aspects of American life produced remarkable alterations in the working lives of all Americans regardless of class or sex during the late nineteenth century. During a period that saw enormous industrial and commercial expansion, the sheer variety of new work locales transformed the very experience of working in the United States. Warehouses, department stores, office buildings, retail centers, libraries, restaurants, schools, theaters, amusement parks, train and streetcar stations, and tenement flats and sweatshops constituted the plethora of locations in which new types of work were performed. Many of these buildings effectively separated laborers into distinct groups, identified quite readily through the location of their labor.

The factory and office building alike located workers in hierarchical layers that carried clear meanings to those familiar with the context. Whether pouring molten iron on the foundry floor or stoking the furnace in a basement, the lowest class of laborers performed the most onerous and worst-paid labor in the "bowels" of such workplaces. With the development of elevators, vertical differentiation grew explicit; as a building rose, so did the status of workers, with clerks on the lower public floors, managers and accountants on mid-level floors, and owners and partners on the top. Similarly, service and public entrances, stairways, and rooms ranked those located within them. In

this way, buildings did not simply reflect hierarchical rank but actually constituted or reified that system in a very profound manner.

On a larger scale, vast landscapes also indicated social class position. As cities became increasingly industrialized, those who could afford to move away from the soot, smoke, and congestion of the city center did so. With new streetcar systems making possible the opening of suburban land several miles from cities, wealthy and middle-class families moved out of the city, usually building single-family homes on spacious plots. Residence in a new suburb itself signaled middle- (or sometimes upper-) class status, while residence in the city center indicated a lower rank in the social hierarchy.

Homes themselves reified ideas about social class. Residence in the city remained marked by multiple-family dwellings and congestion. Buildings never meant for residence were subdivided into small flats, often accommodating more than one family. Tenement buildings, consisting of numerous small apartments of two or three rooms, offered few amenities. A single toilet and water faucet per building was common. Intense housing shortages in cities, exacerbated by the growing population, meant that even tenement flats came dearly. While families might live together, single men and women boarded wherever they could.

Middle-class status was increasingly defined through home ownership. In fact, during this period the middle-class home became a totemic standard of a fully legitimate and therefore "American" lifestyle. Middle-class homes stood as islands on suburban plots several times larger than the house, and the resulting lawns and gardens became buffer zones between the public street with its diverse social makeup and the homogeneous private home. Inside the home, rooms became specialized to a great degree, with boys' and girls' bedrooms, parlor, dining room, kitchen, pantry, parents' room, and, in the homes of the wealthy, a library, study, music room, and conservatory. The novelist William Dean Howells commented extensively in *A Hazard of New Fortunes* (1889) and *The Rise of Silas Lapham* (1885) on the foibles of middle-class and nouveaux riches families as they struggled to define their social class through the location of their residences and the rooms within.

Rural homes were also influenced by these middle-class trends, and farmhouses grew larger during the period, with the addition of sex-segregated bedrooms. Indicative of the potential for resisting the dominant standard of the period, however, was

---

DOMESTIC WORK AND APPLIANCES

New appliances altered the shape of middle-class women's days. Ranges, iceboxes, and porcelain kitchen sinks with running water and drains transformed the ways that women prepared, preserved, and stored food. Such food products as baking powder, cold cereal, and canned soups significantly altered American diets as well. The central coal furnaces located in the basements of middle-class homes relocated the daily collecting of fuel and dumping of ashes while redefining those chores as men's labor. The ongoing battle with greasy soot continued, however. As sanitary fixtures with sand drawers below gave way to water closets, women's labor shifted from dumping to cleaning. All the new porcelain fixtures—bathtubs, toilets, sinks—needed regular cleaning. In fact, cleaning standards increased markedly during the period, even though the popularity of carpets, draperies, table and mantle cloths, as well as decorative bric-a-brac and abundant furniture, made cleaning an increasingly specialized and time-consuming chore. In the kitchen, specialized cooking pans and utensils, china dishes, silver flatware, and table linens all required regular cleaning and though the presence of running water and sinks along with commercially produced soaps made the task less onerous, it needed to be done more often than before. What was gained in terms of effort was lost in terms of time. The laundering of clothing and linens remained one of the most burdensome household tasks, even with the invention of the wringer washer, precisely because families owned more clothing, which needed to be washed more often as standards for cleanliness rose. Middle-class women, for whom the gender ideal discouraged productive labor, hired working-class women to perform these tasks. Many African American women found domestic service the only means available to them to make money. Unmarried immigrant women found jobs as cooks and general domestic servants. Thus, the middle-class lifestyle rested on a foundation of the labor of working-class women.

---

the adoption by immigrants of the building patterns and techniques of their nation of origin. For example, German farmers in the upper Midwest often resisted the American middle-class model of parlor, dining room, and kitchen, adopting instead the traditional German two-room plan for the main floor of their farmhouses.

Material Objects   While the location and spaces of work and residence were clear indicators of social class, material objects, particularly mass-produced goods whose production and consumption fueled the industrial capitalist economy, were equally important components in the creation, verification, and maintenance of social class ideology. Their precise messages and roles, however, proved more ambiguous.

Consumption, or more precisely consumerism—the purchase, display, and use of products—

became a hallmark of middle-class status. As the sociologist Thorstein Veblen argued in 1899, "the consumption of luxuries . . . is a consumption directed to the comfort of the consumer himself, and is, therefore, a mark of the master" (*The Theory of the Leisure Class*, p. 45). With the growth of white-collar positions with salaries well above those of laborers, this "mark of the master" came within the reach of many more families, although less than 20 percent of all Americans could count themselves in this class in 1900. Significantly, Veblen continued, consumerism carried distinctive gender meanings in that it created new roles for men and women of middle-class families. Men were viewed as producers of wealth; they went away to their jobs and returned home to enjoy the material benefits of the income. Women, or more precisely wives, took on the new role of consumer, spending that wealth in ways that "comforted" their families. The very fact that the gender ideal for middle-class wives was that they did not perform productive labor indicated the conspicuous leisure that wealth allowed.

The single-family home became the focus of much consumer behavior, and it was incumbent upon the middle-class housewife to properly fill her family's house with goods. Each room required its own furnishings, and mass production made available an abundance of furniture, textiles, wallpapers, paints, carpets, lamps, ornaments, and appliances. Clutter was the dominant aesthetic. Elsie de Wolfe, pursuing the new feminine occupation of interior decorator, urged that rooms be filled so that only paths through furnishings remained. Thus, shopping became a critical part of a middle-class woman's life. New retail establishments, particularly department stores, not only supplied the opportunity to purchase these goods, but also catered to the needs of female shoppers, offering such amenities as home delivery, lounges, playrooms for the children of shoppers, and restaurants and tea-rooms to attract them.

If the middle-class lifestyle was characterized by the conspicuous incorporation of material goods within the home, rural and urban laboring families were far from immune to the growing consumerism and materialistic ethic. Working-class families in cities and on farms filled their homes with ornaments and furnishings as well, acknowledging the value of consumption despite their limited capacity to participate. Photographs, novels, and personal narratives demonstrate that upholstered furniture, accent tables, lamps with decorative shades, pictures and calendars, ornamental fringes of paper and textiles, carpeting, and wallpaper all appeared in working-class homes. More than simply emulating the behavior of those higher in social class, however, these consuming workers reified the notions of respectability, class, and gender that such consumption implied. Although some argue that the availability of goods facilitated the possibility of social mobility, in fact, it actually defined what mobility entailed. Mobility was found in consumption, in owning things. Numerous novelists of the period illustrated consumption as a means of escaping from a particular social class identity. In Anzia Yezierska's 1925 novel *Bread Givers*, for example, one of the several sisters defies the role of the good daughter who hands her meager earnings over to her mother by spending her income on herself, on such items as a toothbrush, a bar of soap, a hand towel, and a tablecloth. For her, these goods embody the values of middle-class respectability and signify her desire to move beyond her current station.

However, in significant ways material culture, or its consumption, also worked against the hegemonic imposition of social class categories and middle-class values. The historian Kathy Peiss has examined the meanings attached to material objects, particularly clothing, by working-class women. She argues that access to mass-produced clothing created the attractive potential for mimicking wealthy lifestyles, if not actually living them. Yet the highly ornamented hats, hairpieces, coats, and shoes bought and worn by shopgirls of the period signaled more than just a desire to appear to be of a higher social ranking. Women infused these material objects with a strong sense of American identity, with their desire for pleasure and romance, and with strong messages about individual expressiveness and autonomy. Through their clothing, working women could construct an identity unlimited by the actual wages they earned or conditions under which they lived. Thus, though dominant meaning systems were strong, the potential for resistance and for infusing into objects new, personal, and unintended meanings was possible. Such resistance to dominant meanings and the infusion of personal meaning into material life is seen in the character of another sister in Yezierska's novel. Sara, searching for her own identity, flees her parents' house, ultimately trading the heavy furnishings of her mother's home for a sparsely furnished but scrupulously clean flat.

Leisure Another area in which material consumption and social class were closely linked was that of leisure. The expansion of the clerical and white-collar workforce created a significant population with larger numbers of nonwork hours available for recreation. At the same time, electric lighting, which spread rapidly in the late 1890s, significantly expanded the hours available for recreation far into the night, even for workers who labored long hours in the factory or sweatshop. Transportation systems, particularly streetcar lines, were expanded to bring people to new entertainment locales such as amusement parks and resorts. Although recreation had always been highly dependent on income and closely associated with specific social classes, during the late nineteenth and early twentieth centuries these characteristics slowly began to break down.

Leisure, as the historian Richard Butsch points out, was transformed into consumption during this period. Access to new entertainment venues was ticket-dependent, and material objects themselves became increasingly central to recreation. Bicycling, perhaps the most popular recreational activity of the period, in that it attracted the most participants, required simply a bicycle. Sporting equipment of all types, however, underwent great changes as equipment companies like A. G. Spalding and Brothers learned that they could bring in large profits through sales of baseball equipment to nonprofessionals. Baseballs, bats, and gloves (different ones for different positions) were hawked by companies that increasingly defined the very game of baseball itself, publishing official rule books along with official equipment. Golf, football, and basketball all became increasingly dependent on the manufacture and sale of equipment.

Social class and gender distinctions blurred. For example, even though bicycling was deemed highly inappropriate for women, they quickly adopted the practice, attracted by the physical exercise and the increased mobility. While bicycles were widely available, their cost and the limited leisure hours of the working class determined that bicycling remained predominantly a middle-class activity. Golf and football, which originated among elites, generally remained the pastimes of the economically advantaged, although football drew spectators from a wide cross-section of the populace. Rowing, a sport that also garnered a vast array of spectators, attracted college men as well as craftsmen and artisans. Gymnasia, bowling alleys, and billiards and pool halls attracted both middle- and working-class men.

The period also offered growing opportunities and sites for mixed-sex recreation. Theaters of all types were built throughout the nation, and while vaudeville attracted families of all social strata, burlesque was dominated by a male audience. Amusement parks like Coney Island in Brooklyn, New York; Cedar Point in Toledo, Ohio; and Riverside in Chicago offered carnival-like buildings, games, rides, dance floors, and restaurants and were attended by the working and middle classes as well as rural families. Dance halls were particularly popular among working-class women and their presence attracted numerous men. In fact, earlier patterns of gender-specific recreation were strongly compromised during this period as new commercial recreational sites catered to couples and families.

CONSTRUCTION OF RACIAL IDEOLOGIES THROUGH MATERIAL LIFE

In addition to creating, verifying, and maintaining social hierarchies, the material life of this period was also a part of the construction of racial ideologies, by embodying increasingly polarized views of

blackness and whiteness. Jim Crow segregation was made real through defining space within buildings. Whites-only hotels and restaurants, "colored" and white restrooms and drinking fountains were easily labeled. But labels were not always necessary. Custom, not signs, placed African Americans at the back of streetcars and in third-class railroad cars; nevertheless, the racial meanings attached to these spaces were easily read by those familiar with racial ideology.

Mass-produced material objects also played a distinctive role in racial ideologies during the Jim Crow period. Items like cookie jars depicting "Aunt Jemima," pepper shakers in the shape of "Uncle Mose," and a host of other memorabilia (now valued as black collectibles) were popular among both northern and southern whites. These items embodied and broadcast racist stereotypes that served to separate whiteness from blackness. As Kenneth W. Goings argues, such objects gave expression to the conception of black people as childlike, happy, and devoted to white employers. Uncle Mose, whether depicted in a pepper shaker or on a cereal box, was an ever-kind, ever-simple, never-threatening black man. Images and objects that depicted sexually available black women, watermelon-obsessed children, and intellectually challenged black men defined not only a racist view of black people but also implied their opposite as characteristic of whites. Further, whiteness was also defined in the appreciation of the so-called humor embodied in these objects. Although not all whites acquiesced to this perspective, such graphically derogatory images of the racial "other" appealed to whites who believed the ideology of racial polarization. Goings points out that these objects also participated in the creation of a new ideology, an "invented tradition," in Eric Hobsbawm's terminology, that substituted a new ideological image to mask the reality of the slavery period it ostensibly depicted. Aunt Jemima, whether embodied in a smiling cookie jar, in a pancake mix advertisement, or in a movie, was always pleased to cook for "her" white family. Her very presence attested to the idea that plantation life and slavery itself was perfectly suited to black people. In this way, material culture gave shape and tangibility to social, racial, and gender ideologies.

Native Americans were also presented to white society in a way that closely connected them with their material life or, more precisely, the primitive nature of their material life, and here again, the processes of inventing traditions and racial othering through material culture are evident. Producing romanticized pictures of Native Americans for a

C. Allan Gilbert Magazine Poster, 1898. Young women at this private, single-sex college challenged traditional notions of middle-class femininity by participating in athletics such as bicycling and field hockey. SOLTON AND JULIA ENGEL COLLECTION. RARE BOOK AND MANUSCRIPT LIBRARY, COLUMBIA UNIVERSITY

growing middle-class white market, white frontier photographers assumed they were documenting a dying race, so rather than depict their subjects' current lifestyles, they had them hold or wear material objects that conveyed how different and anomalous Native American life was in relation to that of their customers. Animal skins, buckskin clothing, porcupine quill necklaces and beaded decorations, woven blankets, headdresses, baskets, pottery, tipis, hogans, and canoes all reinforced the idea of the "otherness" of Native American life. In fact, some photographers carried trunkloads of such artifacts with them in order to randomly "dress" their subjects to depict difference. Even the well-known Edward S. Curtis, who was more scrupulous than most in attempting to maintain authenticity, posed subjects with objects unfamiliar to them. A certain beaded shirt, the art historian Barbara Davis re-

ports, appears in photographs of at least sixteen different men from three different tribes, and the historian Margaret Blackwell learned that friends of many of Curtis's Haida subjects in the Pacific Northwest assert that the men were given long-haired wigs to disguise their short haircuts. Such indiscriminate treatment of cultural artifacts not only misrepresented each tribe and individual depicted but also helped to invent the notion of a generic "Indian" experience. The important cultural differences constructed in these photographs lay between the Native American subjects and the white consumers, not among tribal cultures, which were seen as interchangeable. The significance of the difference was read in the ideology of racial devolution. All of these Native American subjects belonged to a race that would soon disappear.

Photography, in fact, became a very popular means of inventing traditions and constructing racial identities during this period. A series of photographs by Frances Johnston, intended to extol the benefits of education for black and Indian people, was commissioned and published by the Hampton Institute, a black vocational school in Virginia, in 1899. Johnston used her camera to illustrate "before" and "after" effects of a Hampton education. For example, in one "before" depiction, an elderly couple dressed in ragged clothing prays over their meager supper in a dark and ramshackle cabin. In the "after" picture, a well-dressed black couple sits with their two children at a dining room table covered in a linen cloth and laden with china dishes and silver flatware. A piano, framed paintings, and a stairway leading to a second story are further indications of the middle-class status of this black family. Here, the family has adopted the lifestyle along with the values of the white middle class: consumption, cleanliness, and controlled physical behavior are the mark of the educated family.

CONSTRUCTION OF GENDER THROUGH MATERIAL LIFE

Particularly among the middle class, gender construction through material life proved to be a battleground, as many women struggled against the ways in which material life was used to restrict their participation in society. One clear example of this is bicycling. Young women adopted this activity, although they were warned against it by their elders, who feared it would irrevocably harm a woman's reproductive capacity. Similarly, women's clothing became a contested topic, as reformers urged women to give up "tight-lacing" and even abandon body-restricting corsets. The hourglass shape imposed on the female body by the corset was a symbol of ideal womanhood, even though it was achieved through severe discomfort and even damage to the body. Moreover, tight-lacing discouraged women from engaging in any type of exertion, thus reifying the ideal of a middle-class (or elite) woman as a nonproducer. While many women attempted to live up to this ideal, others struggled against it. Only in the post–World War I era would the ideal of womanhood change substantially enough to eliminate tight-lacing altogether.

The buildings and landscapes of the late nineteenth and early twentieth centuries also imposed gender ideologies. Although most public buildings were considered almost exclusively male species, a few mixed-sex spaces appeared during this period. Libraries incorporated men's and women's reading rooms as well as sex-segregated lavatories. Churches also incorporated such sex-segregated rooms, as well as kitchens, dining rooms, and nurseries for women's use. Tearooms and soda fountains appeared in retail areas to serve a predominantly female clientele. Similarly, department stores catered to women's needs. Generally speaking, however, women's activities within public spaces were severely restricted precisely because the spaces were recognized as excluding of women. Working women were deemed to be something less than ideal women because of their location within the "promiscuous" public arena. To carry a typewriter into an office building and seek employment was to violate that gender ideal. Thousands of women did it, however, and thereby challenged the very conception of what constituted proper female behavior. As these women, having adopted many of the values of the middle class, particularly the consumerist ethic, pursued their business within public places, gender constructions gradually shifted. The meanings attached to office buildings slowly faded and new meanings took their place.

Thus it is with all the ideological systems under consideration here. Ideas about gender, social class, and race are in constant flux. And the function of material life in creating, verifying, and maintaining those ideologies also changes. The late nineteenth and early twentieth centuries saw enormous activity in these areas precisely because of the rapid transformations that occurred within each.

See also **Conflicting Ideals of Colonial Womanhood; American Romanticism; Domesticity and Sentimentalism; Gender, Social Class, Race, and Material Life; Manhood; The Bahavioral and Social Sciences** *(volume 1);* **Women and Family in the Suburban Age; Women** *(in this volume); and other articles in this section.*

BIBLIOGRAPHY

Blackman, Margaret B. "Posing the American Indian." *Natural History* 89 (October 1980): 69–74.

Butsch, Richard. *For Fun and Profit: The Transformation of Leisure into Consumption.* Philadelphia, 1990.

Calvert, Karin. *Children in the House: The Material Cultural of Early Childhood, 1600–1900.* Boston, 1992.

Clark, Clifford E., Jr. *The American Family Home, 1800–1960.* Chapel Hill, N.C., 1986.

Cohen, Lizabeth A. "Embellishing a Life of Labor: An Interpretation of the Material Culture of American Working-Class Homes, 1885–1915." In *Material Cultural Studies in America,* edited by Thomas J. Schlereth. Nashville, Tenn., 1982.

Cross, Gary. *Time and Money: The Making of Consumer Culture.* New York, 1993.

Davis, Barbara A. *Edward S. Curtis: The Life and Times of a Shadow Catcher.* San Francisco, 1985.

Fields, Barbara Jeanne. "Slavery, Race, and Ideology in the United States of America." *New Left Review* 181 (May/June 1990): 95–118.

Goings, Kenneth W. *Mammy and Uncle Mose: Black Collectibles and American Stereotyping.* Bloomington, Ind., 1994.

Hardy, Stephen. "'Adopted by All the Leading Clubs': Sporting Goods and the Shaping of Leisure, 1800–1900." In *For Fun and Profit: The Transformation of Leisure into Consumption,* edited by Richard Butsch. Philadelphia, 1990.

Hayden, Dolores. *The Grand Domestic Revolution: A History of Feminist Designs for American Homes, Neighborhoods, and Cities.* Cambridge, Mass., 1981.

Heinze, Andrew. *Adapting to Abundance: Jewish Immigrants, Mass Consumption, and the Search for American Identity.* New York, 1990.

Jones, Jacqueline. *Labor of Love, Labor of Sorrow: Black Women, Work, and the Family, from Slavery to the Present.* New York, 1985.

Katzman, David. *Seven Days a Week: Women and Domestic Service in Industrializing America.* New York, 1978.

McDannell, Colleen. *The Christian Home in Victorian America, 1840–1900.* Bloomington, Ind., 1986.

McMurry, Sally Ann. *Families and Farmhouses in Nineteenth-Century America: Vernacular Design and Social Change.* New York, 1988.

Nasaw, David. *Going Out: The Rise and Fall of Public Amusements.* New York, 1993.

Peiss, Kathy. *Cheap Amusements: Working Women and Leisure in Turn-of-the-Century New York.* Philadelphia, 1986.

Peterson, Fred W. *Building Community, Keeping the Faith: German Catholic Vernacular Architecture in a Rural Minnesota Parish.* St. Paul, Minn., 1998.

Peterson, Rachel Wild. *The Long-Lost Rachel Wild; or, Seeking Diamonds in the Rough.* Denver, Colo., 1905.

Schlereth, Thomas J. *Cultural History and Material Culture: Everyday Life, Landscapes, and Museums.* Ann Arbor, Mich., 1990.

——. *Victorian America: Transformations in Everyday Life, 1876–1915.* New York, 1991.

Veblen, Thorstein. *The Theory of the Leisure Class: An Economic Study in the Evolution of Institutions.* New York, 1899.

Wright, Gwendolyn. *Moralism and the Modern Home: Domestic Architecture and Cultural Conflict in Chicago, 1873–1919.* Chicago, 1980.

Yezierska, Anzia. *Bread Givers, A Novel.* 1925. Reprint, New York, 1975.

GENDER AND POLITICAL ACTIVISM

Vivien Sandlund

In 1886, an Irish immigrant woman named Leonora Barry began her new job as an organizer and lecturer for the Knights of Labor, then the fastest-growing labor union in the United States. Barry traveled around the country, observing working conditions, lobbying for protective labor legislation, and seeking to organize new union locals. After a trip to Auburn, New York, in 1887, she wrote, "I found the working-women of this city in a deplorable state. . . . There were long hours, poor wages, and the usual results consequent upon such a condition." Barry described similar conditions in Rhode Island among workers of both sexes, with "its industries being for the most part in the control of soulless corporations, who know not what humanity means—low pay, long hours, . . . the employment of children, in some cases, who are mere infants." But Barry found reason for hope as well. She reported after a visit to Danbury, Connecticut, in 1888 that among women hatmakers, "wages are fairly good, conditions very good, as this industry is thoroughly organized" (Baxandall and Gordon, *America's Working Women*, pp. 99–101). She expressed enthusiasm that so many women were then organizing to win better wages and working conditions.

Barry's story is remarkable for several reasons. First, this young immigrant woman had risen from a position as a hosiery worker to become the nation's first female professional union organizer. For a woman, and a poor woman, to attain such a visible public position was extraordinary in nineteenth-century America. Second, Barry focused her efforts on organizing women as well as men, despite the prevailing view that women belonged in the home, not in factories or other public workplaces. Barry herself believed that women ideally belonged at home. In 1889, she wrote, "I wish it were not necessary for women to learn any trade but that of domestic duties. . . . But . . . that is impossible under present conditions" (Baxandall and Gordon, p. 102). Barry and the male leadership of the Knights

of Labor thus accepted the presence of women in the workplace and committed their union to organizing women. Though most Americans at the time still insisted that women were naturally suited for domesticity and economic dependence on men, women already had become a large and permanent part of the industrial labor force.

The emergence of women as industrial workers was not entirely new in the 1880s. Since the early nineteenth century, some industrial employers had sought out women as a labor force. The best-known example was the Lowell, Massachusetts, textile industry. But the factory system was still new in America before the Civil War, and the numbers of women employed were relatively small.

After the Civil War, the expansion of the industrial system in the northern United States drew thousands of women, men, and even children into factories and sweatshops. This rapid industrialization helped to attract millions of immigrants from central, southern, and eastern Europe as well as from Asia. The new arrivals took whatever jobs they could find, and entire families often entered the wage labor force. Most immigrants crowded into the eastern cities of New York or Philadelphia, or into the newer midwestern industrial cities like Chicago and Cleveland. There they formed ethnic communities, called Little Italies or Chinatowns.

Industrialization in the northern United States in the latter decades of the nineteenth century fueled massive immigration and the rapid growth of cities. Industrialization, immigration, and urbanization in turn created new social problems that drew both women and men into social reform causes, like Leonora Barry's work in labor reform. These major economic and social changes served to break down the traditional roles of women and men and also the ideas about gender and sex roles that Americans had embraced through most of the nineteenth century. Because of industrialization, immigration, urbanization, and resulting social reform movements, women were drawn increasingly out of the home and into the public arena, and women and men both came to see appropriate gender roles in new ways. Americans gradually relinquished the idea that women belonged only in the home, or that men and women were designed by God to occupy rigidly separate spheres. The early twentieth century would produce a "new woman," one who marched with determination into the previously male worlds of work and politics.

GENDER IDEALS BEFORE THE CIVIL WAR

Americans had always viewed women as different from men, but in the decades before the Civil War, physicians, ministers, teachers, and popular writers put increased emphasis on the differences between the sexes and the distinct roles they believed men and women were suited to play. Books and popular magazines aimed at the new middle class promoted the view that women were naturally suited for the domestic sphere, where they were to be gentle and loving nurturers to husbands and children. Nineteenth-century popular literature urged women to develop the attributes of what the historian Barbara Welter has called "True Womanhood," qualities that Welter has identified as "piety, purity, submissiveness, and domesticity" (Norton and Alexander, *Major Problems in American Women's History*, p. 115). Woman's domain was the home, and her highest calling was to be a dutiful wife and mother. She was not to work outside the home, especially after marriage. Legally and socially, married women had no independent existence; they were "covered" by their husbands under a legal doctrine known as coverture. In most states, any property that a woman brought to a marriage became the property of her husband.

If the ideal woman in antebellum America was pious, pure, submissive, and domestic, the ideal man was her opposite and complement. He was independent, courageous, and responsible for his family, willing to take risks, and always willing to serve his country and to prove his heroism in war. His domain was the public sphere, the world of business, politics, and military service.

Of course, the true woman and her opposite, the true man, were cultural ideals and not the reality for many Americans. Even as middle-class Americans were seeking to emulate these ideals, poor families usually had little hope of meeting such genteel standards. Poor men sometimes failed to support their families, and growing numbers of destitute women wandered city streets in search of work,

sometimes falling into prostitution. Free black men rarely earned enough money for their wives to stay home, and African American women frequently worked as laundresses, cooks, or domestic servants, occupations in which they competed with Irish immigrant women. For the millions who were enslaved, masters denied their human property the right to marry at all. They forced men and women to work side by side in the fields, denying slaves the opportunity to divide their labor by sex. Slave masters also raped their female slaves with impunity. By exercising nearly complete control over slave families, masters denied black men any role as husbands and providers, and they hampered efforts by black women to create a maternal, domestic sphere.

EARLY CHALLENGES TO PREVAILING GENDER IDEALS

Some Americans in the antebellum years actively challenged mainstream views of proper behavior for women and men. Abolitionist women, committed to ending slavery, spoke out in public and often found themselves jeered and even physically attacked for daring to make speeches in front of mixed-sex audiences. These activist women and their male supporters went on to forge an independent movement for women's rights. The most controversial of their demands was that women be given the right to vote nationwide. Following their historic Seneca Falls women's rights convention in 1848, women's rights activists worked for both women's equality and abolition. They also held regular women's rights conventions until the Civil War, when most supported the Union cause.

In the Reconstruction era following the Civil War, women's-rights activists split over the issue of support for the Fifteenth Amendment, which prohibited states from denying the right to vote on the basis of race, color, or previous condition of servitude. Some activists, notably Elizabeth Cady Stanton and Susan B. Anthony, were outraged that the amendment did not prohibit states from denying the right to vote on the basis of sex. The amendment as written would guarantee the vote to black men but not to women. Stanton and Anthony and their followers took a stance against the Fifteenth Amendment, and they organized into the National Woman Suffrage Association. Other activists disagreed with Stanton and Anthony and supported the Fifteenth Amendment as a step toward universal suffrage. Leaders Lucy Stone and Henry Blackwell formed a second organization, the American

Woman Suffrage Association, committed to supporting both the Fifteenth Amendment and women's suffrage. The Fifteenth Amendment was finally ratified in 1870, without guaranteeing votes for women. Ironically, despite the language of the amendment, most black men subsequently lost the vote in the South, first through violent intimidation by the Ku Klux Klan and later through legal devices such as poll taxes and literacy tests. Neither women nor southern black men would be guaranteed the unfettered right to vote in the nineteenth century.

SOCIAL CHANGE AND REFORM ACTIVISM IN THE GILDED AGE

The decades after Reconstruction, dubbed the Gilded Age by Mark Twain and William Dean Howells, were years when industrialization, immigration, and urbanization produced both enormous wealth and grinding poverty. The final collapse of Reconstruction in 1877 left southern blacks largely at the mercy of the white majority, as Republicans removed federal troops from the South. Republicans in the White House and Congress turned their attention away from protecting the rights of African Americans toward expanding the industrial economy. Despite the long-term efforts of women's rights activists on behalf of both abolition and women's equality, Victorian gender ideals and standards of behavior remained largely intact in 1878. The women's suffrage movement was still weak and divided, and most Americans, including women, insisted that women had no business in politics.

Though they were excluded from voting, women did organize for reform in the 1870s and 1880s. Women of various backgrounds had been active since the antebellum era in opposing alcohol consumption. A number of women's-rights activists, including Susan B. Anthony, had started their reform careers in the temperance crusade. Temperance drew both conservative and radical women to its ranks. These women saw drunkenness as a woman's concern, because they believed that alcohol destroyed families. They pointed to men who spent their earnings on drink, leaving wives and children destitute.

In the post–Civil War depression of 1873, women in small towns in the Midwest suddenly embraced temperance with renewed fervor. Women feared that, in the climate of depression, men would turn more to drink and state legislatures would loosen the liquor laws. In Hillsboro, Ohio, seventy women marched into local saloons and prayed that they be shut down. The Hillsboro action inspired a wave of similar protests by women across the northern United States, who succeeded in driving alcohol out of 250 towns. The energized women went on to create a national organization, the Woman's Christian Temperance Union (WCTU). Its president from 1879 to 1899 was Frances Willard, a labor reformer and women's suffrage activist.

The WCTU grew into the largest women's reform organization of the nineteenth century. The organization embodied the assumptions about gender that prevailed in the nineteenth century, and it attracted women of all class backgrounds, regions, and political leanings. Women thereby moved into the public sphere to a limited degree, became socially involved, and still worked on behalf of Victorian motherhood, domesticity, and support for traditional family arrangements. Their all-women's reform organization reflected the traditional view that women belonged in a separate sphere from men. Yet, through their organization, women temperance activists had a powerful impact on the political system. Ultimately, in the twentieth century, the WCTU and the Anti-Saloon League would succeed in winning passage of a prohibition amendment. Temperance was thus an example of women's nineteenth-century activism that had far-reaching results and that drew ordinary, conservative women into the arena of politics.

For Americans the 1880s were a time of glowing hopes and tragic disappointments, of growing wealth and expansion of the middle class but also of wrenching depressions, bitter strikes, and labor violence. The new industrial economy was subject to sudden downturns, called panics, which prompted employers to cut wages and eliminate jobs. In 1877, railroad workers angry over a wage cut went on strike in Martinsburg, West Virginia, and then across the country. Federal troops finally put down the Great Strike of 1877 after workers destroyed railroad property and tore up tracks. The workers lost this battle, but the struggle for labor reform had just begun. In the 1880s and 1890s, American workers engaged in more than twenty thousand strikes, demanding shorter hours, higher wages, safer working conditions, and recognition of their unions. Though most striking industrial workers were men, women workers also engaged in strikes in the latter decades of the nineteenth century. Many of these strikes were spontaneous walkouts by workers who were unorganized, and in most instances employers succeeded in breaking the strikes by women without making any improvement in working conditions.

Most male trade union leaders shared the prevailing Victorian view that women belonged at home, and they were not generally enthusiastic about the growing numbers of women entering the paid labor force. Labor unions fought for male wages high enough to support an entire family, and union leaders generally viewed women workers as threats to higher wages. Employers nearly always paid women less than men and often hired women to keep wages down. In 1900, the average weekly wage for women factory workers was seven dollars, three dollars less than the average weekly wage for unskilled male workers. Union leaders were inclined, therefore, to resist the influx of women into the paid labor force.

However, by the 1890s, women were entering the labor force in such great numbers that union leaders began to take a different stance: they began trying to organize women in an effort to keep wages up for all workers. The Knights of Labor had been first to try to organize women, but the Knights collapsed in the late 1880s. The American Federation of Labor, headed by Samuel Gompers, emerged in 1886. After some initial resistance, Gompers reluctantly hired women to organize other women. Slowly, labor unions came to accept the presence of women in the workplace and to include women in the union movement.

Despite the labor conditions and widespread unrest in the United States, poor people in Europe and Asia saw America as the golden land, where anyone could get rich and live in freedom. Between 14 and 20 million immigrants arrived on American shores between 1880 and World War I, in search of jobs, freedom, and better lives. Steamships made immigration both possible and affordable for poor people, and millions came through Ellis Island in New York City and other ports of entry. Industrial employers saw immigrants as a source of cheap labor that they could use to fill the growing numbers of unskilled jobs.

The massive influx of immigrants quickly swelled the population of cities. The new immigrants crowded into tenements in the industrial North, on New York's Lower East Side or in Chicago's Packingtown. To afford the rents in tenement houses, families often rented floor space to boarders. Six to eight adults and half a dozen children might be crammed into a tiny three-room flat on the Lower East Side. On hot summer nights, the rooftops and fire escapes were filled with people sleeping outdoors to escape the stifling heat of the tenements. Despite the efforts of immigrant families to create pleasant living spaces, poor sanitation and

crowding led to the outbreak of contagious diseases. Tuberculosis, cholera, and typhus took the lives of children as well as adults. Most tenement houses lacked toilets in the early years, and people often threw their waste out the windows rather than walk five stories down to the outhouse.

Working conditions for immigrants were often horrid in the late nineteenth and early twentieth centuries. At Andrew Carnegie's steel mills, workers labored twelve hours a day, six days a week. Their only holiday was the Fourth of July. A Hungarian nobleman was distressed by what he saw when he visited the communities of Hungarian immigrants who worked in the steel mills near Pittsburgh. He wrote, "Wherever the heat is most scorching, the smoke and soot most choking, there we are certain to find compatriots bent and wasted with toil" (Handlin, *This Was America*, p. 408).

At the turn of the century, 20 percent of children under the age of sixteen worked for wages, many of them in factories and mines. In the Pennsylvania coal mines, young boys went to work at the age of twelve. One miner wrote in 1902, "There were five of us boys. One lies in the cemetery—fifty tons of rock dropped on him" ("A Miner's Story" in *The Independent*, 12 June 1902). Young women also suffered from dangerous working conditions and starvation wages in factories. In his 1890 book *How the Other Half Lives*, the reformer Jacob Riis examined the plight of working girls such as this typical young worker in a New York factory: "She averages three dollars a week. Pays $1.50 for her room; for breakfast she has a cup of coffee; lunch she cannot afford. One meal a day is her allowance" ("The Working Girls of New York"). Many more women and children sewed garments or made artificial flowers in tenement sweatshops or at home. They were typically paid by the piece and often worked long into the night. Young Sadie Frowne worked in a sweatshop in Manhattan. She wrote, "The machines go like mad all day, because the faster you work the more money you get. Sometimes in my haste I get my finger caught and the needle goes right through it. . . . I bind the finger up with a piece of cotton and go on working" (Stein, *Out of the Sweatshop*, pp. 60–61).

WOMEN IN PROGRESSIVE REFORM

Industrial conditions, crowded, unhealthy slums in cities, and the perceived power of giant monopolies spawned the strong and effective Progressive movement in the 1890s. It attracted large numbers of women into social reform and ultimately helped to transform nineteenth-century gender roles and ideals.

In 1889, Jane Addams and Ellen Gates Starr founded Hull-House in Chicago, a "settlement house" whose purpose was to bring elite social reformers into a poor immigrant neighborhood to provide the immigrants with education and services. Jane Addams was the quintessential elite reformer. She was born in 1860 to a well-off family in northern Illinois. She met Starr when the two women were students at Rockford Female Seminary. The two friends each sought to build independent lives and careers, without husbands. But to do so in the nineteenth century was both difficult and controversial; few careers were then open to women beyond teaching, nursing, and missionary work.

Addams briefly attended medical school, but she soon lost interest. She began to feel that her true calling might be working with the poor. Her thoughts were confirmed in 1888, when she and Starr visited Toynbee Hall Settlement House in London. There they saw wealthy young people living and working with the poor of London's East End. The experience prompted Starr and Addams to devise a plan for a settlement house of their own. Addams used her substantial inheritance to fund the undertaking, and in the summer of 1889 the two women rented a house from the Hull family and moved to Halsted Street in Chicago. The neighborhood consisted mostly of immigrants.

Having found a way to be independent and socially useful, Addams and Starr spent their entire lives at the settlement house, living and working in a community of mostly women reformers. Neither woman married, and Jane Addams had a life partner named Mary Rozet Smith. In a period when women still lived in a largely separate sphere from men and routinely formed passionate friendships, the relationship did not draw public scrutiny or criticism.

Hull-House became a multipurpose community center, offering classes in literature, art, history, and science, as well as practical classes in the English language, sewing, cooking, and crafts. Immigrants came to Hull-House for social activities, lectures, and day care for their children. Writers and political leaders from around the country visited Hull-House, and social reformers used the house as a base for trade-union organizing and political action in the wider community.

By 1910 reformers had created four hundred settlement houses in cities around the United States.

Like Addams and Starr, they hoped to improve life for poor immigrants through education and charitable assistance. Over time they sought to do more. Progressive reformers aimed to clean up the cities and improve sanitation and public health. They aimed to improve factory conditions and to eliminate tenement sweatshops through the passage of protective labor legislation. They sought to abolish child labor. The tried to organize unions, particularly among women workers. In the early twentieth century, reformers and labor union activists in New York City created the Women's Trade Union League, a cross-class alliance of working-class women and elite social reformers whose purpose was to promote union organizing among women.

The Progressive movement included both men and women, but they often worked in separate organizations. In part this was a legacy of the nineteenth-century belief that women and men are fundamentally different in temperament and interests and ought to inhabit separate spheres. Men and women were unaccustomed to working together in mixed-sex organizations. Women's closest bonds and friendships were usually with other women. Progressive women activists tended to focus their organizing primarily among women, on behalf of women and children. They sought to unite women in a universal sisterhood that crossed class boundaries.

The Progressive movement, and the settlement house movement in particular, drew women into the public arena in new ways. In Chicago, Florence Kelley, a resident of Hull-House, conducted investigations that revealed that children as young as three were working for wages. Her research led to passage of the first Illinois law banning child labor. Progressive Governor John Peter Altgeld then appointed Kelley as chief factory inspector for the state. For a woman to hold such a position was unprecedented, and the zealous reformer worked diligently to uncover violations of the law. Kelley lost her job when the governor was not reelected, and she was forced to leave Hull-House in search of other work. She moved to New York and began to direct the National Consumers League, which collected evidence of working conditions faced by women in factories and informed consumers how their products were made. Reformers then used the evidence to support state legislation aimed at protecting women workers. Kelley also pushed for the creation of a federal bureau to protect children, and the United States Children's Bureau was established in 1912.

The goals of progressive reformers varied widely. Some, like Florence Kelley, challenged the industrial system directly and sought new legislation to limit the power of employers. Others sought instead to reform the habits of immigrants, to Americanize them, and to imbue them with middle-class beliefs. Settlement house leaders sought both to change the immigrants and to change the system that surrounded them.

As women of all classes became more involved in social reform activities at the turn of the century, they moved from charity work and providing individual assistance to pushing for social change. Direct experiences with immigrants and the working poor in the cities led many progressives to make a stronger critique of the social order. Over time, progressive reformers of both sexes embraced government action to challenge the power of monopolies, to regulate industries for the protection of workers and consumers, to clean up the cities, and to stop lynching and attacks on African Americans and immigrants. Progressive journalists, dubbed muckrakers by Theodore Roosevelt, sought to expose the abuses of the industrial system and to mobilize public action for change.

PROGRESSIVE VICTORIES IN PROTECTING WORKERS

Progressives were successful in many of their efforts to protect women and children from the industrial system. They succeeded in either enacting or strengthening laws in thirty-nine states to limit the working hours of women. They also won passage of various state laws banning or limiting child labor, although the federal government did not successfully enact a nationwide ban until the New Deal of the 1930s.

Protective legislation for women raised a new debate about the extent to which women should be treated as the equals of men or given special legal protections. In 1908, an Oregon employer, Curt Muller, challenged the constitutionality of a state law limiting the working hours of women in factories and laundries. Muller's attorney argued before the Supreme Court that the Oregon law discriminated against women by limiting only their hours and not the hours of men. The attorney who argued in support of the law was the progressive Louis Brandeis. He presented a brief that contained extensive evidence gathered by Florence Kelley's National Consumers League of the detrimental effects of long working hours on the health of women. The Supreme Court upheld the Oregon law, citing the need for legislation that would protect women, whose

roles as mothers were endangered by long and arduous working conditions. Conflict over the Oregon law initiated a debate among women's rights activists that would last until the 1960s. Did protective labor legislation aimed specifically at women constitute sex discrimination, or did such legislation advance the cause of women in industry? Progressives like Florence Kelley supported protective legislation, while proponents of legal equality, like the women's suffrage leader Alice Paul, opposed such legislation.

Laws regulating industry and protecting all workers got a boost from a tragedy in 1911. For more than a decade, organizers had sought to unionize women garment workers to win higher wages and safer working conditions. In 1909 some thirty thousand garment workers, 80 percent of them women, struck in New York City and Philadelphia demanding union recognition. The strike failed, however, and the garment workers remained unorganized. Then in March 1911, fire broke out in the Triangle Shirt Waist factory in New York City. Women were trapped on the upper floors because the company had locked the doors to the stairs to prevent employee theft. There were no fire extinguishers and only one fire escape that led nowhere. Fire department ladders and hoses could not reach the upper floors of the building. Dozens of desperate young women jumped to their deaths to escape the flames. One hundred and forty-six workers, mostly women, died in the fire. The Triangle Shirt Waist fire prompted New York legislators to pass some of the strongest workplace safety legislation in American history. It was a victory for progressive reformers and labor activists, a victory won only with the loss of many lives.

PROGRESSIVE REFORMERS AND AFRICAN AMERICANS

While many Progressives focused on the plight of immigrants, few paid comparable attention to the problems facing African Americans. Prior to World War I, most African Americans still lived in the South, where many struggled under desperate poverty as sharecroppers and tenant farmers. In this period, a small but steady stream of migrants began moving to the industrial North in search of jobs, better education, and better opportunities. Industrial cities had black communities at the turn of the century, as well as a black middle class. But race discrimination was a northern as well as a southern problem, and most African Americans were denied jobs in industry except during strikes, with black workers often excluded from white unions. When blacks were hired for permanent jobs, they were given only the lowest-paid and most dangerous positions. The Great Migration of African Americans to the North would not begin until World War I, when the war economy created a demand for new factory laborers.

Black and white progressive reformers did come together at the turn of the century to try to stop lynching. In the South especially, mobs of whites frequently took the law into their own hands, pulling accused black criminals from jails and murdering them in gruesome fashion, sometimes torturing their victims before hanging them from trees. Victims of lynching were sometimes found with their ears or genitals cut off; some were burned alive before they were hanged. White mobs turned lynching into a spectator sport, and whites even sent postcards with photographs of lynchings to friends and relatives. The perpetrators of lynching often sought to justify their brutality by claiming to defend white southern womanhood from black rapists. Most lynch victims were never convicted of rape, and a man could be lynched simply for being politically active and for threatening the whites in power. As many as 3,500 black people, mostly men, may have been lynched in the period between the end of Reconstruction and the 1950s.

In the early 1890s, a black woman newspaper editor in Memphis, Ida B. Wells, wrote a series of editorials decrying the barbarity of lynching. An angry white mob retaliated by destroying her press and threatening her life. She was forced to move to the North to avoid being lynched herself. There she continued to speak and write about the horror of mob violence aimed at African Americans.

In 1910, the now-married Wells-Barnett worked with other black and white activists in the North to organize the National Association for the Advancement of Colored People. Its goals included challenging southern segregation and stopping lynching. The NAACP worked diligently for passage of a federal anti-lynching bill, but the measure never passed. The struggle did focus public attention on the problem, however, and the number of lynchings declined in the twentieth century. Wells-Barnett continued her anti-lynching crusade, and she also worked for women's suffrage.

THE PROGRESSIVE MOVEMENT AND WOMEN'S SUFFRAGE

Of all the progressive goals, women's suffrage most directly challenged traditional gender roles at the

Ida B. Wells, Journalist (1862–1931). Wells's parents died of malaria when she was fourteen. Several years later she began working as a teacher to support her siblings. While teaching, she started publishing articles in black newspapers under the pen name "Iola." © BETTMANN/ CORBIS

turn of the century. Both male and female Progressives generally supported votes for women. Most saw the women's vote as a means of ensuring that progressive legislation would pass, because they believed that women were more likely than men to be concerned about the welfare of other women and especially children. They believed that women were naturally more moral and would clean up the corrupt political system once they entered the world of politics. Progressives thus brought some older nineteenth-century ideas about gender to their new, twentieth-century reform efforts.

The women's suffrage movement had stagnated in the late nineteenth century, as only four states, all in the West, granted women full suffrage. In 1890, the two separate women's suffrage organizations created during Reconstruction merged into the National American Woman Suffrage Association, or NAWSA. Elizabeth Cady Stanton was chosen as the organization's president, and her friend Susan B. Anthony succeeded her two years later. The organization pursued a dual strategy of seeking to win the vote state by state and also of pushing for a constitutional amendment to grant women the vote nationwide.

In the early twentieth century, the movement received an infusion of new energy from young progressive reformers who stepped into the leadership of the struggle and pioneered new strategies. More women were graduating from college. They found themselves still restricted in career options, and many were impatient with their inability to vote and eager to take more dramatic action. American suffragists also received a jolt of inspiration from England, where some British women's suffragists, led by the Pankhurst family, staged mass marches, heckled members of Parliament, and engaged in radical civil disobedience and even riots. Young American suffragists, while generally less militant than the Pankhursts, were fascinated and moved by the radical strategies employed by a portion of the British movement.

Elizabeth Cady Stanton died in 1902, but her daughter, Harriot Stanton Blatch, carried on the struggle. Blatch had lived much of her adult life in England, where she worked in the British women's suffrage movement. After her mother's death, she returned to live in the United States. In New York she began to organize among working-class women on the Lower East Side, employing tactics she had learned in Britain. She hoped to make the American movement more militant and visible.

Blatch sought to build a cross-class women's alliance for suffrage. She found working women, especially Jewish women, eager to participate, and they organized the first mass suffrage parades through the city. Working women also handed out leaflets at factories, staged rallies and demonstrations, and campaigned at baseball games, beaches, and amusement parks. These actions initially provoked criticism from older women's suffrage activists. Many Americans viewed women demonstrating in public as shocking and unfeminine. But the suffrage parades and other actions gave the issue of votes for women new visibility among workingmen. As more women marched, their husbands and sons began to think differently about the issue.

Black women also engaged in the suffrage struggle, despite resistance from white women's suffrage groups. White leaders feared that the presence of black women in the movement would turn white southerners against women's suffrage. However, black women insisted on being involved, and they formed their own women's suffrage organizations and black women's clubs.

Opposition to women's suffrage came from various quarters, including conservative women's groups, who believed that voting would take women out of their traditional domestic roles, and from the liquor industry, which foresaw women voting for prohibition of alcohol. The liquor interests paid for political advertisements that painted a grim picture of men's future if women should win the vote. The ads portrayed women in pants, ruling over men and households, with men in aprons reduced to housekeepers and drudges.

Despite the opposition, by the time of Woodrow Wilson's election to the presidency in 1912, the women's suffrage movement had begun to generate new momentum. Suffrage activists won the vote in five new states in 1912, including California. In 1915, Carrie Chapman Catt of Iowa, an experienced and savvy organizer, stepped in to lead NAWSA to the final suffrage victory. Catt devised a strategy to win both voting rights in individual states and passage of a women's suffrage amendment to the Constitution. It was called the Anthony Amendment, named for Susan B. Anthony, who died in 1906.

When the United States entered the Great War in 1917, Catt called on her followers to throw their support behind the war effort while continuing to push for women's suffrage. Radicals led by the Quaker Alice Paul defied Catt and began picketing the White House, an action that infuriated her. In the end, despite this conflict, Catt's strategy worked to build support in Congress and to convince President Wilson to support the Anthony Amendment. By the end of World War I, public support for women's suffrage was strong enough for the amendment to pass the Congress and the required three-quarters of the states, though just barely. The Anthony Amendment became part of the Constitution in 1920.

IMPACT OF THE PROGRESSIVE MOVEMENT ON GENDER ROLES

The women's suffrage victory was the culmination of the broader movement for progressive reform that emerged in the late nineteenth century and reached its height with the election of Wilson as president in 1912. The Progressive movement aimed to address and correct the social and economic problems caused by industrialization, immigration, and urbanization. At first, Progressives did not necessarily intend to change gender relations in fundamental ways, and many clung to nineteenth-century ideas. Progressive women tended to organize with and for women and children, in a sphere separate from men. Yet their successful reform activism drew progressive women into the public, political arena, and the women's suffrage movement directly challenged the assumption that politics belonged exclusively to men. Over time, progressive activists pushed to expand the opportunities available to women, and in doing so, they laid the groundwork for a more heterosocial and more nearly equal society.

Progressive reform, coupled with the increasing entry of women into the paid labor force and the greater mixing of men and women in large cities, helped to transform assumptions about women's proper roles as well as the actual roles that women could and did play. In the twentieth century, Americans would come to see men and women as more similar than different. This fundamental change in assumptions would gradually open new opportunities for both sexes, but especially for women.

See also **Women in the Public Sphere: 1838–1877** *(in this volume);* **Women** *(volume 2); and other articles in this section.*

BIBLIOGRAPHY

Addams, Jane. *Twenty Years at Hull-House.* Edited with an introduction by Victoria Bissell Brown. Boston, 1999. This is the classic description of Hull-House by its famous founder and leader Jane Addams. Editor Brown provides an analysis and overview of Addams's life and work.

Baxandall, Rosalyn, and Linda Gordon, eds. *America's Working Women: A Documentary History, 1600 to the Present.* New York, 1995. This is a collection of primary documents by and about the history of working women in America.

Bordin, Ruth. *Frances Willard: A Biography.* Chapel Hill, N.C., 1986. This is a study of the complex life of the president of the Woman's Christian Temperance Union in the late nineteenth century. Besides supporting temperance and Christianity, Willard was an avowed socialist, labor reformer, and women's suffrage activist. Her story reveals the mixture of conservatism and radicalism among some progressive reformers.

Buhle, Mari Jo, and Paul Buhle, eds. *The Concise History of Woman Suffrage: Selections from the Classic Work of Stanton, Anthony, Gage, and Harper.* Urbana, Ill., 1978. This is an edited version of the six-volume *History of Woman Suffrage* by the women who led the movement: Elizabeth Cady Stanton, Susan B. Anthony, Matilda Joslyn Gage, and Ida Husted Harper. The study spans the entire seventy-two-year history of the movement.

Diliberto, Gioia. *A Useful Woman: The Early Life of Jane Addams.* New York, 1999. This is a new biography of Jane Addams that ends in 1899, when Addams was thirty-nine years old. The author explores the roots of Addams's commitment to the poor.

Dubois, Ellen Carol. *Feminism and Suffrage: The Emergence of an Independent Women's Movement in America, 1848–1869.* Ithaca, N.Y., 1999. This is an illuminating analysis of the rise of the nineteenth-century women's movement from its origins within the abolition movement.

———. *Harriot Stanton Blatch and the Winning of Woman Suffrage.* New Haven, Conn., 1997. This is an excellent analysis of the thinking and significance of the twentieth-century women's suffrage leader and the daughter of Elizabeth Cady Stanton, who sought to build an alliance of working-class and elite women.

Evans, Sara M. *Born for Liberty: A History of Women in America.* New York, 1989. This textbook on the history of American women is widely used in undergraduate classrooms and gives a fine overview of the subject.

Fink, Leon. *Workingmen's Democracy: The Knights of Labor and American Politics.* Urbana, Ill., 1985. This study of the Knights analyzes the ideology and political strategies of this unique nineteenth-century labor union.

Fink, Leon, ed. *Major Problems in the Gilded Age and Progressive Era: Documents and Essays.* Lexington, Mass., 1993. This is a collection of primary documents and scholarly essays spanning the period from the 1880s until World War I.

Flexner, Eleanor. *Century of Struggle: The Woman's Rights Movement in the United States.* Cambridge, Mass., 1996. This is a revised edition of an older history of the nineteenth-century struggle for women's rights, originally published in 1959. It remains one of the best treatments of the suffrage movement and other women's efforts to win equal rights.

Giddings, Paula. *When and Where I Enter: The Impact of Black Women on Race and Sex in America.* New York, 1996. This study examines black women reformers and their impact on U.S. history.

Gilmore, Glenda. *Gender and Jim Crow: Women and the Politics of White Supremacy in North Carolina, 1896–1920.* Chapel Hill, N.C., 1996. This is a study of middle-class black women's political activism in the Jim Crow South.

Handlin, Oscar, ed. *This Was America: True Accounts of People and Places, Manners and Customs, as Recorded by European Travelers to the Western Shore in the Eighteenth, Nineteenth, and Twentieth Centuries.* Cambridge, Mass., 1949. This is a primary source collection of travel accounts by visitors to the United States.

Hunter, Tera. *To 'Joy My Freedom: Southern Black Women's Lives and Labors after the Civil War.* Cambridge, Mass., 1997. This is an important study of the political and social activism of black women domestic workers in Atlanta. The author illuminates the lives and struggles of urban working-class black women, a group previously ignored by scholars.

Jones, Jacqueline. *Labor of Love, Labor of Sorrow: Black Women, Work, and the Family from Slavery to the Present.* New York, 1986. This is a fine overview of black women's work in U.S. history.

Kessler-Harris, Alice. *Out to Work: A History of Wage-Earning Women in the United States.* New York, 1983. This is still the best comprehensive overview of working women in U.S. history.

Norton, Mary Beth, and Ruth M. Alexander, eds. *Major Problems in American Women's History: Documents and Essays.* Lexington, Mass., 1996. This is a collection of primary sources in women's history and secondary essays by scholars.

Riis, Jacob A. *How the Other Half Lives: Studies among the Tenements of New York.* Introduction and notes by Luc Sante. New York, 1997. This is a new edition of the classic Progressive Era study of tenement life by the Danish immigrant and reformer Jacob Riis. Originally published in 1890, the book includes Riis's famous photographs of tenement life in New York and his commentary on the various immigrant groups, their lives, and their work.

Sinclair, Upton. *The Jungle.* New York, 1990. This is possibly the most famous and influential novel of the Progressive Era. The book exposed conditions in the meatpacking plants of Chicago and highlighted the suffering of poor immigrant workers. It was first published in 1906.

Sklar, Kathryn Kish. *Florence Kelley and the Nation's Work: The Rise of Women's Political Culture, 1830–1900.* Vol. 1. New Haven, Conn., 1997. This first volume of a planned two-part biography of Florence Kelley is a masterful study of women's progressive reform activism and its impact in the nineteenth century.

Spruill Wheeler, Marjorie. *One Woman, One Vote: Rediscovering the Woman Suffrage Movement.* Troutdale, Ore., 1995. This is a collection of primary writings and secondary essays by scholars on the women's suffrage movement.

Stein, Leon, ed. *Out of the Sweatshop: The Struggle for Industrial Democracy.* New York, 1977. This is a collection of primary documents by workers and reformers.

Wells-Barnett, Ida B. *Crusade for Justice: The Autobiography of Ida B. Wells.* Edited by Alfreda M. Duster. Chicago, 1972. Wells-Barnett's autobiography details her work as an anti-lynching and racial justice crusader as well as her work in progressive reform, in organizing black women's clubs, and in women's suffrage. She describes the founding of the NAACP and the anti-black riots after World War I.

————. *Southern Horrors and Other Writings: The Anti-Lynching Campaign of Ida B. Wells, 1892–1920.* Edited and with an introduction by Jacqueline Jones Royster. Boston, 1997. This slender volume contains Wells-Barnett's most significant writings on the subject of lynching, including "Southern Horrors," "A Red Record," and "Mob Rule in New Orleans." Editor Jacqueline Jones Royster discusses the nature and extent of lynching in turn-of-the-century America.

Woloch, Nancy. *Muller v. Oregon: A Brief History with Documents.* Boston, 1996. This short book analyzes the debate over protective legislation for women workers and the history of U.S. Supreme Court rulings on the issue. The book includes the text of various Supreme Court decisions, including the ruling in *Muller* v. *Oregon,* which upheld a state law limiting the working hours of women.

For further research on gender and political activism, go to the website entitled "Women and Social Movements in the United States, 1830–1930" at http://womhist.binghamton.edu/projectmap.htm. The website has been prepared by graduate students at the State University of New York at Binghamton. It provides primary documents that address significant issues in the history of women and social reform.

MANHOOD

Amy S. Greenberg

In Henry James's 1886 novel *The Bostonians,* Basil Ransom spoke for a generation of American men when he bemoaned the loss of manliness as a personal and cultural value in America. "The whole generation is womanized; the masculine tone is passing out of the world," Ransom complained. "It's a feminine, nervous, hysterical, chattering, canting age, an age of hallow phrases and false delicacy and exaggerated solicitudes and coddled sensibilities. . . . The masculine character, the ability to dare and endure, to know and yet not fear reality, to look the world in the face and take it for what it is . . . that is what I want to preserve, or rather . . . recover" (p. 343). White men in the era of commercial and national consolidation were obsessed with manhood, both their own and that of others. As a response to perceived threats to male prerogative from women, from the working class, and from African Americans, the ideal of white American manhood in this period was contested and remade in a manner that allowed men to assert their dominance over others.

Shifts in the ways men and women understood masculinity were the result of changes in the nature and organization of work, in gender roles, in family structure, and in capitalism. Men uncomfortable with transformations in the capitalist economic structure idealized the norms of manhood held by previous generations, the "ability to dare and endure, to know and yet not fear reality, to look the world in the face," as James put it, and in the process significantly distorted those ideals. An emergent standard of manhood, characterized by vigorous athleticism, fears of feminization, and a discourse that idealized "primitive" masculinity, with its unrestrained passion and savagery, was widely adopted in the last decades of the nineteenth century. As a result, many men, especially in the middle class, began to celebrate behavior that a previous generation had fought to restrain. While manhood is best understood as a process (linking male anatomy and male identity to the exercise of power), rather than a historical constant, by the late nineteenth century a new ideal of manhood was clearly evident in American business activities, in male patterns of recreation, in American cultural life, and in American foreign policy. Variations in the meaning of manhood continued to exist in this era, as they always had, but a new virile or martial ideal of manhood left its imprint on virtually every aspect of American life and culture at the dawn of the twentieth century.

MANHOOD BEFORE THE CIVIL WAR

During the antebellum period a wide variety of styles of manhood co-existed in America. An emergent urban working-class male culture was organized around drinking, gambling, theatergoing, frequenting prostitutes, and, above all, physical violence. Urban workers repaired from their workplaces to saloons, where they found the camaraderie and respect missing from their jobs. They also found fistfights, dogfights, and rat-baiting contests organized by saloon keepers as entertainment. One primary way working-class men earned the respect of their peers was through their physical strength and ability to dominate others. Indeed, physical violence was central to urban working-class masculine culture, which celebrated both bare-knuckle boxing, as well as less orchestrated exhibitions of virility. Personal acts of physical violence were common within saloon culture, and common also among working-class street-gang members.

In the southern backcountry, rivermen and others involved in dangerous occupations also engaged in violence, specifically when honor was at stake. Southern planters also believed that upholding honor was essential to the protection of their manhood and family name; but for these men, protection of honor was less likely to involve fistfights, and more likely to involve stylized displays such as nose-pulling and dueling. Many yeoman farmers who generally eschewed violence nevertheless conceived of their family, community, and political world in starkly patriarchal terms.

In contrast, many northern men, especially those holding white-collar jobs, placed less value on upholding personal honor than on conforming to the values of evangelical Christianity. They remained sober, practiced personal control, and focused their energies on success in the workplace. Many of these men joined literary clubs or temperance and other reform organizations. For these men, manhood was demonstrated through self-restraint and moral vigilance.

Some social organizations took a middle path, foremost among them the urban volunteer fire department. They drew men of different occupations and ethnic backgrounds together in celebration of a manhood that was expressly physical in nature, but did not condone violence. Fire companies offered some of the trappings of the middle class—fine houses, libraries, even an occasional piano—along with the physicality and excitement of working-class culture. Volunteer fire companies offered men an opportunity to race, parade, wear a uniform, and match strength with other like-minded men, regardless of occupation, and to dedicate leisure hours to a chivalrous voluntary ideal.

THE CIVIL WAR TO THE EARLY TWENTIETH CENTURY

A heightened concern with the health and vigor of American manhood emerged in the decades after the Civil War, and culminated in violence. When Jack Johnson, the first African American heavyweight boxing champion, defeated white former champion Jim Jeffries in 1910, race riots convulsed every southern state, and a number of northern states as well. To white American men, Johnson's victory was not the victory of one black man, but a final sign of the failure of white American manhood to prove itself. The extent of disorder following Johnson's victory can only be explained in the context of America's growing obsession with manhood, and the perception by white American men that their racial and social dominance was under attack.

Economic factors were partially responsible for the rising levels of concern. The continued rapid expansion of low-level clerical work and a series of crippling depressions between 1873 and 1897 closed off avenues of success that middle-class men of an earlier generation had taken for granted. The authority of middle-class men faced a variety of external threats. Starting in the 1830s American political culture adopted a distinctively masculine character, a character opposed to the self-restraint of evangelical manhood. Partisan rallies featured both alcohol and processions of manly fire and military companies, and election day voting often occurred in saloons. Working-class men gained increasing control over party machinery in many places, and middle-class men who ran for office, especially if they ran on reform platforms, were frequently labeled effeminate by opponents. Labor unrest, beginning with the Great Strike of 1877, posed the possibility of class warfare, as did continued heavy immigration.

Women appeared to pose their own threat to American manhood. Nineteenth-century biology proclaimed that conception was the result of the meeting of two very different and complementary forces: that of the passive female, whose eggs remained stationary in wait of the active spermatozoa, and the active male, whose sperm would aggressively search out the egg and complete the work of union. The moment of each individual's origin, therefore, contained within it the essence of the proper and naturally sanctioned roles of the sexes. To be masculine was to be in movement, active and aggressive, while to be feminine was to remain passive and receptive to the overtures of the male. Men and women, in this schema, were not only different, but complementary, and fundamentally opposed.

But many men felt that the natural order of things was being challenged. Middle-class men grew up in an increasingly "feminized" culture, taught the values of self-restraint and moral virtue by mothers who by the 1830s occupied the primary parenting role in the home. Female novelists penned novels that celebrated passionlessness and the domestic authority of heroines while ministers preached a feminized version of the gospel to overwhelmingly female congregations. The idealization of the feminine extended to the world of medicine as well. Men institutionalized in asylums in the nineteenth century were frequently diagnosed as "insane by reason of excessive masculinity." Asylum staff members devised therapeutic settings that were deliberately feminized in an effort to cure their hyper-masculine patients. In a cultural milieu increasingly focused on the virtues of Victorian domesticity, the role of men was not easily negotiated.

When the woman's movement began to agitate for female suffrage and increased rights for women, men of all classes felt their position threatened. As women gained increasing influence outside the home, men responded by loudly asserting their own manhood. As the *American University Magazine* commented in a January 1896 article, the "intense desire to win" exhibited by both participants and fans of college football "is the outcome of what is best in these young men, their manliness, their courage, their pluck. . . . May the day never come when contests of this kind are considered degrading and handed over to professional brutes, for then manliness will be at a discount, and effeminacy at a premium. We may have to have a 'new' and masculine woman, but let us not have a 'new' and feminine man." The ubiquitous concern with the meaning of manhood that is evident in the cultural products of late-nineteenth-century America was in large part the anxious offspring of the increasing influence and assertiveness of women in society.

The Civil War also enforced the value of physical and moral toughness in society, not only by rewarding soldiers with exactly these qualities, but also by destroying some of the idealistic power of the competing norms of evangelical Christianity. The resulting postbellum culture was suffused with a martial imagery. The American men who emerged from the Civil War alive were a toughened and more cynical group than those who entered it, with a starker view of life and manhood. While many of them embraced the increasingly bureaucratized work world, they also began to engage in compensatory ideals of virile manhood. The new man balanced his Christian morality with the hardened understanding that life was a struggle, and that success required constant competition and vigilance. The new man was forceful, athletic, physically and mentally tough, and aggressively pursued challenge. The new man disavowed feminine culture, and erred on the side of passion rather than its opposite, restraint. Men of all classes now celebrated aggressive behavior that had once been associated with working-class culture. By the 1870s, this virile or martial ideal of manhood had assumed a cultural dominance in America.

MANHOOD ON THE OFFENSIVE

Neurasthenia, the archetypal Victorian ailment, was widely diagnosed by neurologists beginning in the 1880s. A disorder of excessive nervousness, when diagnosed in men it was assumed to be the result of engagement in purely mental endeavors. Doctors located the cause of this derangement in the stresses of the modern industrial order; mental exertion without the healthful balance of physicality. The sudden emergence of this disease convinced many

that middle-class manhood had grown weak, and that working-class men, virtually never diagnosed with neurasthenia, possessed a virility lost to middle-class men.

At the same moment that neurasthenia identified one failure of middle-class American manhood, homosexual activity was reinterpreted from criminal behavior to disease. Medical investigation into the "problem" of the homosexual male was another way in which perceived threats to American manhood emerged as a subject of social concern. Muckraking newspapers reported on both male homosexuality and urban vice districts and furthered the impression that American manhood was swiftly degenerating.

American men responded to the perceived threats to their manhood with a variety of strategies, all of which reveal the ascendancy of the new martial ideal of manhood. Some high schools worked to recruit male teachers in order to provide "appropriate" behavioral models for male students. Mainline Protestant denominations attempted to restrain the feminine influence in religion. The Men and Religion Forward movement of 1911–1912 took as its goal to locate the "1,000,000 missing men" from church congregations. The educator and psychologist G. Stanley Hall claimed in the 1890s that the key to promoting virility in men was to allow boys to practice their primitive savagery. "Primitive" activities by boys could thus combat neurasthenia in men. While previous generations of parents had punished fighting, Hall suggested that salvation lay in encouraging that same violent behavior in their sons.

Interest in primitive cultures was not limited to educators, but was widespread among men looking to the virile model of manhood. The greatest cultural expression in the primitive ideal emerged in a pulp novel with enormous cultural resonance. In 1912 Edgar Rice Burroughs created *Tarzan of the Apes,* introducing America to a twentieth-century symbol of primitive masculinity tempered by Victorian morality. Like many men of his generation, Burroughs found his business efforts thwarted by the limited opportunity offered in the large-scale corporate world. He was also rejected by Theodore Roosevelt's Rough Riders. He found success at last with Tarzan, the invincible man who wins the respect of other men and the love of an ideal woman, not only through his fearlessness, animal instinct, and muscle-clad physique, but through the exercise of physical violence against African men as well. As the child of English aristocrats, Tarzan managed to uphold an ideal of white middle-class manhood while at the same time prevailing through the practice of violent primitive behavior. Published in book form in 1914 after being serialized in eight major newspapers, *Tarzan of the Apes* became one of the best-selling novels of the early twentieth century.

The hope that white manhood could be redeemed through violence against blacks was unfortunately not limited to fiction. Prior to 1889, lynching was a frontier practice of vigilante justice, and white men were the usual victims. Starting in the 1890s, southern whites began lynching black men in large numbers. They constituted the lynch mob as the central element in a reign of racial terror that continued well into the new century. In 1892 alone, 161 African Americans were murdered by lynch mobs. Victims of lynch mobs were often tortured and then mutilated after death.

Southern whites justified lynching as the only response to the uncontrolled sexuality of the black male. Lynchings almost always originated in accusations of the rape of white females, accusations that nearly always lacked any factual basis and camouflaged the racist motivations of the lynch mob. The myth of the black rapist, accepted at face value by most of the northern public as well, reveals the need of southern white men in this period to bolster their own male power and authority. Repeated lynchings of black men helped to bolster the newly aggressive ideal of manhood by allowing white southerners to portray themselves as paragons of manhood. By claiming to be the fearless and aggressive protectors of white womanhood they fulfilled the requirements of the new martial manhood in a particularly horrific manner.

Physical fitness and athletics offered another less violent means of strengthening and reasserting the virility of American manhood. By the 1850s, leading New England thinkers like Edward Everett Hale and Ralph Waldo Emerson called on American men to adopt a "muscular Christianity" in reaction to the perceived increasing feminization of polite society. An increasing interest in sports among all segments of male society was evident in the 1840s and 1850s. By the 1870s, most American men had embraced sport as the means to physical and mental development. College students began to flock to football and basketball games. As the Pennsylvania State University 1887 yearbook proclaimed, "What helps to make the perfect man/A pattern from Dame Nature's plan?/Athletics." By the turn of the century, team sports and physical fitness were seen as crucial to the development of manhood. President Theodore Roosevelt argued that the occasional death of a college football player was justified by the virility-building qualities of the sport. The Young Men's Christian Association, or YMCA, proved central to institutionalizing physical exercise and athletic competition in the gilded age. By 1900 there were 261 YMCA gymnasiums across America that offered extensive sports programs, including courses in amateur sparring, calisthenics, weight lifting, football, and swimming. The underlying ideology of the YMCA was that athletics promoted moral health, especially when practiced in a clean, moral atmosphere. Clean sports could teach the values of competition, discipline, and leadership to young men, values that would help them prevail in the strife-ridden world of capitalist America.

Men also asserted their manhood through fraternal rituals. Fraternal organizations began to arise in the 1870s and 1880s, with close to eight hundred different organizations in existence by the early 1920s. During the last third of the nineteenth century, almost half of the total adult male population belonged to a fraternal order. The essence of fraternalism was the articulation of masculine identity. The lodge room was a masculine space, and lodge members considered themselves brothers. Outstanding characteristics of these orders were the mixed-class characters of most lodges, and the performance of elaborate initiation rituals associated in some way with the rites of primitive men, virtually all of which were created after the 1830s and declined in popularity in the early twentieth century.

Fraternal rituals seem to have helped men distance themselves from the values and emotional ties of women. Rituals for the Improved Order of Red Men, the first fraternal order in the United States, subjected inductees to such trials as shooting down imaginary eagles in order to win a "hunting" trophy, as well as ritualistic attempted executions. The Knights of Pythias required that initiates into the highest order brave skeletons and snakes, and voluntarily jump onto a bed of nails. Elders subjected new members to ordeals designed to test the initiate's bravery before admitting him to the tribal family. The hyper-masculine playacting of fraternal brotherhoods offered men another means to express their martial ideal of manhood.

The extent to which older standards of manly behavior were discredited in the gilded age is evident in the language of the period. New phrases reflected a newly aggressive vision of manhood. "Stuffed shirt," "Sissy," and "Pussy-foot" were newly coined terms that served to denigrate behavior considered manly and restrained only a generation before. At the same time the term "masculine," once a fluid adjective, took on definite meaning. To be "masculine" by the 1890s was to be aggressive, sexual, and physically forceful, by then highly esteemed characteristics. The ideal of the male body was also transformed in this period. During the era of the Civil War, the ideal male body was wiry and trim, but by the 1890s, the "perfect" body more closely resembled that of a prize fighter, with well-defined muscles and obvious strength. The newly muscled body, and the rise of both athletics and fraternal rituals, allowed men to externalize their masculine virtues. This marked a shift away from manhood as a primarily moral condition to an externally visible fact that was easily accessible to strangers and acquaintances alike.

MANHOOD AT WORK AND AT WAR

Transformations in the world of work reflected the rise of the new ideal of manhood. While some professions, including law and medicine, began to elevate expertise above the more manly virtues of bravery and independence in the nineteenth century, the values of the new manhood were clearly evident elsewhere in the work world. White-collar men began to describe their sedentary labors with a martial language, investing their daily routine with the emotional intensity of hand-to-hand combat. Business became a "battle" where everyday events were described in the language of war. In a warlike business environment, only the fiercest competitor could hope to prevail. As William James Tilley wrote in his 1889 success manual, *Masters of the Situation, or Some Secrets of Success and Power,* "[Life is] a struggle in which we go forth armed and equipped to contend with our fellows. . . . The great fact confronts one at the outset of his career. From the cradle to the grave, indeed, the strife continues" (p. 582). Gilded-age success manuals, a newly popular genre, assured men that success was a matter of throwing oneself into the fray without fear. At the same time, these manuals described true success as the achievement of manhood. To develop a virile, self-disciplined, and powerful character was in the end a greater achievement than money, fame, or riches.

Working men adopted the new manhood to their own purposes. Both technological change and the rise of the factory system decimated the old apprentice system that had previously marked a boy's passage into manhood. Apprenticeships not only socialized boys into the working world of men, but the passage from apprentice to master promised the ability to earn a living wage and start a family of one's own. While skilled labor suffered in the transition to factory work, many unskilled but physically fit men found that their physical attributes were rewarded in the working conditions of the factory. On the factory floor, strength, endurance, and youth were valued over the painstaking training at a premechanized craft. Trade unions, which had long excluded women, began in the age of mechanization to set tougher standards for admission, standards that reflected the new martial ideal of manhood. An increasing valorization of physical health and ruggedness, as well as psychological toughness, replaced the earlier and increasingly anachronistic value placed in unions on certification and training. By claiming the right to decide who was manly enough to practice a trade, union members regained some of the control over admission to the trade lost in the move away from certification. Ironically enough, middle-class men adopted some of the trappings of working-class manhood just as the latter group faced a real crisis in establishing their economic independence.

The new ideal of manhood not only imbued the business world with the language of war, but helped propel the nation into battle. The renegotiation of manhood in the late nineteenth century created a desire among men for martial challenges, and thus justified entry into both the Spanish-American and Philippine-American Wars. Americans looked to war as a means to address anxieties about manhood. As the Civil War generation faded away, war could create a new generation of martial heroes. War would develop courage and physical strength, challenge men grown soft from the sedentary life, foster fraternalism, and highlight the differences between men and women. Supporters of war with Cuba argued that war would allow American men to bolster their chivalry and honor. That the Spanish-American War was a success was proven to many observers in its effect on manhood. According to the historian Henry Watterson in *History of the Spanish-American War* (1898), the war was "above all" a success in that it "elevated, broadened, and vitalized the manhood of the rising generation of Americans" (p. viii). Colonialism was advocated for similar reasons. The experience of protecting the "childlike" and "womanlike" Filipinos could work to strengthen white male character. War and man-

Theodore Roosevelt and the Rough Riders. Though second in command, Roosevelt made an indelible image for himself in the Spanish-American War. © BETTMANN/CORBIS

hood were thus intimately linked at the turn of the century.

COMPETING IDEALS OF MANHOOD

The new manhood was never hegemonic, and competing ideals of male behavior co-existed, not always peacefully, with the dominant ideal. African American men in the North and South sought to emulate the gender norms of white America throughout the nineteenth century, but were not always successful. Since for white Americans manhood involved personal independence and the ability to support a family, African American women also withdrew from the labor force whenever possible, and husbands assumed the role of breadwinner. The difficulty of supporting a family in the segregated and discriminatory labor market of gilded-age America meant, however, that African American women, and frequently children, were generally forced to work outside the home. This was especially true for black sharecroppers. As a result, black men sometimes felt that their manhood was challenged, although they also grounded their own gender identity in their ability to protect female relations from physical and sexual attack by whites. Whatever their feelings, black men were less likely than whites to

embrace the new manhood, perhaps because they were not rewarded by white society for doing so. Black veterans of both the Civil War and Spanish-American War found that their accomplishments failed to result in concrete social or economic progress. First generation immigrants also hesitated to embrace the new martial manhood, and generally clung to gender norms learned in the home countries, although second and third generation immigrants from many traditions were quick to adapt to the norms of the larger society.

Historians have documented close male relationships and expressions of affection between middle-class men throughout this period; homosocial relationships were closer in style to the friendships of middle-class women than to the dominant ideal of physical competition and barely contained violence. In this pre-Freudian era, intimate male relationships posed few problems for men as long as love did not involve sexual behavior. For these men emotional openness did not signify effeminacy, as it did within the newly dominant martial ideal.

Those men who did engage in sexual behavior with one another offered another alternative to the new ideal of manhood. A wide variety of gender roles existed within the culture of gay sexuality before this sexual behavior was stigmatized as "inverted" and opposed to normal heterosexual activ-

THEODORE ROOSEVELT

Theodore Roosevelt became the ultimate symbol of turn-of-the-century manhood despite inauspicious beginnings. Roosevelt was the adored scion of a wealthy family. A small, asthmatic child, he took seriously his father's advice to engage in regular strenuous exercise. The young Roosevelt adored adventure stories, especially tales of cowboys and other western men of action, and idealized these visions of manhood rather than that of the restrained men of his family. As a young New York State assemblyman in the 1880s, he was ridiculed for his fancy clothes and high voice, and branded effeminate by the press. In a culture where political power and manhood were intertwined, a political leader who failed to project a virile image faced difficulty maintaining his political legitimacy. Aware that his future depended on a change, Roosevelt cultivated an image of a frontiersman and rancher, publishing stories of his adventures on his cattle ranch in North Dakota. His new image proved wildly popular. In his race for mayor of New York, Roosevelt was praised more for his physical stamina and love of fighting than his political platform. He gained national fame in 1898 at the age of thirty-nine when he resigned as assistant secretary of the navy and led the first U.S. volunteer cavalry regiment into the Spanish-American War. Known as the Rough Riders, the regiment was made up of western cowboys and frontiersmen, along with a sprinkling of Ivy League–educated athletes. The combination of men was designed to display the superior manhood of America, and to highlight the way that a shared masculine ethos could unify men of different backgrounds. An effective self-promoter, Roosevelt encouraged several journalists to follow the Rough Riders and keep the public informed of their manly exploits. When Roosevelt returned from the war he was probably the most famous man in America. After serving as governor of New York, in 1900 he was elected vice president of the United States, in large part because of his advocacy of virile imperialism. As one Massachusetts delegate said, "His life to us is an embodiment of those qualities which appeal everywhere to American manhood." After President McKinley's assassination in 1901, Roosevelt assumed the presidency. His campaign for election in 1904 also highlighted his role in the war.

Throughout his career, Roosevelt advocated an active and aggressive approach to both life and politics that greatly appealed to a wide spectrum of American men. In his view, the key to success in both international relations and personal fulfillment was for American men to develop and utilize their superior manhood. Like many other Americans, Roosevelt feared the decay of American manhood through the sedentary pursuits of a commercial economy. He advocated vigorous outdoor activity as a means to revitalize the "virile virtues," and advocated a return to an idealized "strenuous life" so that America's men could maximize their virile potential at home and abroad. In his view, no activity was more revitalizing than war. In his public speeches and writings he urged the nation to take control of Puerto Rico, Cuba, and the Philippines, and repeatedly invoked the specter of race war if white Americans should fail to rise to the challenge. It was the mission of America, according to Roosevelt, to assert imperialistic control over inferior men everywhere. Imperialism was thus a means of avoiding effeminacy as well as the "white man's burden." In Roosevelt's cosmology, American manhood was not simply an issue of personal relations, but the key to advancing civilization.

CONTINUED NEXT PAGE

Men who declined to follow America's path to empire were ridiculed by Roosevelt as "lazy," "timid," and "over-civilized weaklings." Anti-imperialists were nothing more than cowards who "made a pretense of humanitarianism to hide and cover their timidity" and to "excuse themselves for their unwillingness to play the part of men." Roosevelt criticized his own president and boss in the same terms in 1898, when the president refused to clamor for war. His opinion that "McKinley has no more backbone than a chocolate éclair," was one widely shared by the press.

At the close of his presidential career, Roosevelt continued to publicly advocate and practice the strenuous life, most notably on an eleven-month safari to Africa where he and his team killed 296 big-game animals, including nine lions. So great was the public's interest in Roosevelt's safari that journalists, unable to satiate the voracious public with fact, began to fabricate exploits for him that stressed his hyper-masculine persona. Roosevelt was a potent cultural symbol both because he personified the American masculine ethos of the late nineteenth century, and because his psychological concerns were ones he shared with a wide spectrum of American men.

ity in the early twentieth century. Some men took on the persona of woman as "fairies" and engaged in sexual activities with men who in all matters except the sexual act defined virile manhood, from policemen and sailors to successful businessmen.

Others historians have documented a turn-of-the-century "masculine domesticity" shared by suburban fathers. These men seem to have been uninterested in proving their manhood among other men. They gladly exchanged the camaraderie of the tavern and gym for the pleasures of the hearth, and made their wives, not other men, their primary companions. These men also voluntarily took on an increasing role in child rearing, and expressed pleasure in the ability to spend time with their children.

These alternatives existed on the fringes of mainstream culture, for the most part, and did not threaten the widely held gender norms that coalesced into the martial manhood of the gilded age. Regardless of how realistic their fears were, men responded to changes in their society by enshrining manly virtues and physical prowess. The new ideal of manhood offered white American men a means to assuage their fears, but reassurance was often purchased at the expense of those who by race, gender, or nationality, were deemed inferior to themselves.

See also **The Athlete as Cultural Icon** *(in this volume);* **Success; Individualism and the Self; Sexuality; Gentility and Manners** *(volume 3) and other articles in this section.*

BIBLIOGRAPHY

Primary Sources

Burroughs, Edgar Rice. *Tarzan of the Apes.* New York, 1914.

James, Henry. *The Bostonians.* 1886. Reprint, New York, 1965.

Roosevelt, Theodore. *American Ideals, the Strenuous Life, Realizable Ideals: The Works of Theodore Roosevelt.* Vol. 14. Edited by Herman Hagedorn. New York, 1926.

Tilley, William James. *Masters of the Situation, or Some Secrets of Success and Power.* New York and St. Louis, Mo., 1889.

Watterson, Henry. *History of the Spanish-American War.* St. Louis, Mo., 1898.

Secondary Sources

Bederman, Gail. *Manliness and Civilization: A Cultural History of Gender and Race in the United States, 1880–1917.* Chicago, 1995.

Carnes, Mark C., and Clyde Griffen, eds. *Meanings for Manhood: Constructions of Masculinity in Victorian America.* Chicago, 1990.

Chauncey, George. *Gay New York: Gender, Urban Culture, and the Making of the Gay Male World, 1890–1940.* New York, 1994.

Clawson, Mary Ann. *Constructing Brotherhood: Class, Gender, and Fraternalism.* Princeton, N.J., 1989.

Gatewood, Willard B., Jr. *Black Americans and the White Man's Burden, 1898–1903.* Urbana, Ill., 1975.

Gorn, Elliott J. *The Manly Art: Bare-Knuckle Prize Fighting in America.* Ithaca, N.Y., 1986.

Greenberg, Amy S. *Cause for Alarm: The Volunteer Fire Department in the Nineteenth-Century City.* Princeton, N.J., 1998.

Greenberg, Kenneth S. *Honor and Slavery: Lies, Duels, Noses, Masks, Dressing as a Woman, Gifts, Strangers, Humanitarianism, Death, Slave Rebellions, the Proslavery Argument, Baseball, Hunting, and Gambling in the Old South.* Princeton, N.J., 1996.

Hilkey, Judy. *Character is Capital: Success Manuals and Manhood in Gilded Age America.* Chapel Hill, N.C., 1997.

Hoganson, Kristen. *Fighting for American Manhood: How Gender Politics Provoked the Spanish-American and Philippine-American Wars.* New Haven, Conn., 1998.

Leverentz, David. *Manhood and the American Renaissance.* Ithaca, N.Y., 1989.

Macleod, David I. *Building Character in the American Boy: The Boy Scouts, YMCA, and their Forerunners, 1870–1898.* Madison, Wisc., 1983.

Morris, Edmund. *The Rise of Theodore Roosevelt.* New York, 1979.

Rotundo, E. Anthony. *American Manhood: Transformations in Masculinity from the Revolution to the Modern Era.* New York, 1993.

REALISM IN ART AND LITERATURE

Winfried Fluck

The term "realism" carries associations of special accuracy and objectivity in the representation of reality. However, an "objective" representation of reality is impossible, because each representation of reality is at the same time also its interpretation. The realism of one generation will therefore become another generation's convention. Therefore, the use of the term must be understood as a rhetorical strategy to claim special authority for a particular interpretation of reality. In literature this truth-claim is based on the aesthetic illusion of a direct, unmediated reflection of reality, the so-called "reality effect," which is created by such formal devices as the elimination of authorial interference, a richly detailed description, and a deliberately "unliterary" use of everyday language.

In this essay, the term "realism" is not restricted to the description of a particular artistic movement. It is used to outline a general tendency among American writers and painters in the period after the Civil War. At its most basic level, this movement toward more realistic forms of representation was based on the assumption that human beings become better or more authentic people when they get in touch with reality; consequently, realists challenged art to defy received academic standards and worn-out romantic conventions. After nineteenth-century realism was dismissed by the avant-garde of the twentieth century, critics lost sight of the fact that realism, too, was once an avant-garde movement that provoked considerable hostility because of its unadorned, "degrading" images of humanity.

EARLY BEGINNINGS OF REALISM IN AMERICA

Like Romanticism, realism was a belated arrival in American culture. Although it had emerged in Europe in the 1840s and Americans were well aware of this development, there was no concerted attempt to imitate European developments (which, as

a rule, were regarded as unnecessarily immoral). Although American realism shared some goals with European realism such as the focus on the commonplace or the striving for objectivity in representation, it developed distinct forms of its own. In literature, only the Russian authors Ivan Turgenev (on William Dean Howells and Henry James) and later Leo Tolstoy (on Howells) had any significant influence; in their paintings, Thomas Eakins and Winslow Homer rejected European models even more radically. Thus, in contrast to Europe, American realism did not start out as a movement with clearly defined goals. The term is used throughout the period after the Civil War, but not consistently before the 1880s and even then hardly ever in reference to a well-defined aesthetic theory.

In literature, realism emerged in the gradual, piecemeal revision of existing forms and genres. Rebecca Harding Davis's tale "Life in the Iron Mills" (1861), for example, is based on a strictly religious view of reality. However, within that frame, it provides one of the first and most distressing descriptions of the effects of industrialization. Elizabeth Stoddard's novel *The Morgesons* (1862) draws attention to another important influence in its transformation of the domestic novel of female development into a remarkably original bildungsroman whose realistic tendencies are unequaled in the literature of the decade. John William De Forest's Civil War novel *Miss Ravenel's Conversion from Secession to Loyalty* (1867) uses the genre of the historical novel to present uncompromising descriptions of battle scenes. Regional art that tried to give a faithful, albeit picturesque and often idealized, portrayal of a particular section of the country provided another important source for the development of American realism. And, as literary historians have acknowledged only recently, the novelist Nathaniel Hawthorne, although decidedly antirealistic in his symbolic modes of writing, had a remarkable influence on the development of American realism through his unrelenting studies of the psychology of inner conflict.

REALISM IN LITERATURE

The growing support of realism as a new, decidedly "modern," literary form was, above all, the work of a group of intellectuals and writers centered around the literary magazine *Atlantic Monthly*. Their goal was to increase the influence of literature on American life in order to provide a counterforce to the dangers of increasing materialism, dramatized in political satires such as Mark Twain and Charles Dudley Warner's *The Gilded Age* (1873) or Henry Adams's *Democracy* (1880). In literature, American realism emerged out of the attempts of a "modern" faction of the American gentry to gain influence on American society through the development of a form of literature that addressed issues of contemporary importance and provided a candid, nonidealized portrait of the current state of American civilization. For this purpose, the novel seemed far better suited than poetry. The age of realism is therefore the period in which the genre of the novel became the leading literary form. In order to be taken seriously, however, the novel had to go beyond traditional models, such as the domestic romance (with its strong sentimentalism) or the metaphysical romance (with its penchant for remote lands of the imagination). Even the historical novel was no longer considered adequate, because it dealt with the extraordinary events of the past and not the commonplace reality of the present. In Twain's devastating essay "Fenimore Cooper's Literary Offenses" (1895) and his young adult books *The Adventures of Tom Sawyer* (1876) and *Adventures of Huckleberry Finn* (1884), the historical novel is ridiculed as adolescent fantasy.

Scholars of realism consider the two major realists of the period to be William Dean Howells, who started out as editor of the *Atlantic Monthly* and gradually gained a reputation as the dean of American letters in the Gilded Age, and Henry James, who began his literary career as a reviewer of contemporary novels and then gained first recognition with a study of Nathaniel Hawthorne. Both were on friendly terms and shared similar views about the need of the novel to discard an outworn romanticism. Their early novels, in many respects still conventional, focus on nonheroic characters (usually a young woman who is regarded as representative of national conditions), favor everyday events and contemporary settings, give priority to character analysis over plot, proudly emphasize the "eventlessness" of the narrative, and toy with the elimination of the traditional happy ending. These shifts in emphasis, which led critics of the new analytical school of writing to criticize the realistic novel as a dreary literature of dissection, have their common goal in a redefinition of the function of literature: if the novel is to have an impact on American life, it has to address the reader not as an immature adolescent who likes to indulge in pleasant daydreams, but as an adult. While the historical novel incited the imagination with grandiose scenarios of self-empowerment, the realist novel began to address the reader as a democratic equal with whom an ongoing dialogue about the promise and remaining shortcomings of American life could be established on the basis of common sense and common experience.

This redefinition of the reader as democratic equal explains realism's characteristic formal strategies. In place of the omniscient narrator of the historical novel, the dramatic method of the realistic novel reduced the role of its narrator, sometimes to invisibility. Readers were no longer told by the narrator what to think, but were encouraged to see with their own eyes. Similarly, the wealth of descriptive detail typical of the realist novel not only created a reality effect, but also challenged the reader's observational and interpretive abilities. These formal strategies became linked to a view of American society which, in the opinion of the realists, had not yet realized its full potential because it was still in the grip of religious "superstition," aristocratic "Old World" notions of culture, and obsolete literary genres like the romance (Twain, in fact, attributed the Civil War to the damaging influence that the historical romances of Sir Walter Scott had had on the American South).

Realists believed that the spell of these cultural traditions could only be broken by experience. Experience is crucial because it validates or falsifies claims, corrects fantasies, and reconnects the individual with reality. In the realist novel, it is experience that eventually tells characters like Huck Finn, Silas Lapham, or Isabel Archer what is true and false, right and wrong. If there is a common denominator that links the diverse forms of American realism—ranging from the historical and the political novel to travel literature and local color writing to the novel of manners and the utopian novel, and including novels so vastly different in style and structure as Twain's *Huckleberry Finn*, Howells's *The Rise of Silas Lapham* (1885), and James's *The Portrait of a Lady* (1881)—it is not an elusive norm of objectivity, nor a concern with the social question, but the attempt to describe exemplary learning processes in which the main characters finally come to trust their own observations and experiences as the only reliable source of knowledge.

Thus, the generic starting point of American realism is the Victorian story of social apprenticeship in which individual victories or failures stand for national possibilities. This story appears in three major thematic settings:

1. Tales of courtship and marriage that are redefined as test cases of the individual's ability to perceive reality adequately. Howells's early novels *Their Wedding Journey* (1872) and *A Chance Acquaintance* (1873), as well as his much more daring novel of divorce, *A Modern Instance* (1882), provide typical examples, as do James's early novels *The American* (1877), *Washington Square* (1880), and *The Portrait of a Lady*.

2. The encounter between an innocent, socially and sexually still inexperienced American and a morally corrupt Europe that has not yet liberated itself from its aristocratic past. This "international tale" can be found in Howells's travel book *Venetian Life* (1866) and his novels *A Foregone Conclusion* (1875) and *Indian Summer* (1886). In his novels *The American, Roderick Hudson* (1876), *Daisy Miller* (1879), *The Portrait of a Lady, The Ambassadors* (1903), *The Wings of the Dove* (1902), and *The Golden Bowl* (1904), James brought the form to perfection.

3. Tales of an unrestrained, not yet sufficiently "civilized" social ambition in which the American businessman has to learn the lesson that money is not everything in life. Howells's *The Rise of Silas Lapham*, Twain's *The Gilded Age* and *A Connecticut Yankee at King Arthur's Court* (1889), and Henry B. Fuller's *The Cliff-Dwellers* (1893) and *With the Procession* (1895) are impressive novels about the failure to transform economic success into cultural values.

William Dean Howells, however, became disillusioned in the 1880s in response to the growing inequalities in American society and, under the influence of Leo Tolstoy, transformed the realist novel into the social novel, in which individual growth is no longer considered sufficient to deal with the remaining problems of American society (see his *The Minister's Charge*, 1887; *Annie Kilburn*, 1889; and *A Hazard of New Fortunes*, 1890). In the social novel,

the realist novel opens itself toward the harsher realities of American life. It leaves the drawing room and, with a mixture of fear and fascination, begins to move out into the street, as for example in the "slumming party" of Hjalmar Boyeson's novel *Social Strugglers* (1893). As a rule, however, there remains a safe distance between the urban underside and the middle-class onlooker in this genre. For Howells, in continuing a tradition of female reform novels such as Rebecca Harding Davis's *Margaret Howth* (1862) and Elizabeth Stuart Phelps's *The Silent Partner* (1871), a form of Christian socialism remained the only hope for American society achieving equality with nonviolent means. This promise of a radical, yet peaceful, economic and social transformation also explains the immense popularity of Edward Bellamy's utopian novel *Looking Backward 2000–1887* (1888), in which the self-elimination of a wasteful and unjust capitalist system is achieved by advanced technology and the efficient management of resources. For a brief period, the appeal of the genre of the utopian novel was enormous. Between 1888 and 1900, roughly 160 to 190 utopian novels were published in the U.S. Even Howells participated in the trend with his utopian novel *A Traveler from Altruria* (1894).

At about the same time, James, too, extended the novel of social apprenticeship into critical portrayals of social movements (consider his *The Bostonians*, 1886; *The Princess Casamassima*, 1886), before he began to redefine the problem of individual growth as the problem of heightened consciousness. His intriguingly enigmatic tales of the 1890s (*The Aspern Papers*, 1888; "The Figure in the Carpet," 1896; *What Maisie Knew*, 1897; and *The Turn of The Screw*, 1898) emphasize the close, inextricable connection between perceiving and imagining reality. In his late, great novels *The Wings of the Dove, The Ambassadors,* and *The Golden Bowl,* heightened consciousness becomes not only a defense of the individual against manipulation by others but a possibility for counteraction. For this heightened sense of awareness, his complex novels provide a model as well as a training ground; consequently, James, who was always careful to distinguish the representation of reality from mere photographic fidelity, wrote extensively on *The Art of Fiction* (1884), laid the foundations for the theory of the novel in the twentieth century, and developed innovative forms of narration such as the narrative perspective of a center of consciousness in *The Ambassadors,* which already points toward experimental modernism.

In contrast to Howells and James, Mark Twain never even toyed with the idea of being a "realist." However, he shared the realist's aim of liberating American culture from reality-distorting cultural conventions. Twain's literary humor draws its appeal and explosive force from the collision between cultural "training" and the corrective powers of common sense and lived experience. At first, Twain regarded the idealization of a feudal European past as the main culprit of what was still wrong with American culture. In Twain's *The Innocents Abroad* (1869), a self-styled "American vandal" burlesques Old World pretensions. *Tom Sawyer, The Prince and the Pauper* (1882), and *Huckleberry Finn* expose the perverse consequences of a cultural training that distorts common sense. Eventually, however, Twain began to lose faith in the saving powers of common sense. *A Connecticut Yankee at King Arthur's Court* reveals unexpected dimensions of ambition and aggression in the American common man who is to transform medieval England into a modern-day democracy. *The Tragedy of Pudd'nhead Wilson* (1894), a tale of murder in which two babies are exchanged shortly after their birth, dramatizes the arbitrariness of the idea of race; the posthumously published *The Mysterious Stranger* (1916), an unauthorized assembly of several fragments, is the culminating point of Twain's growing disillusion with the "dam'ned human race."

While Howells and James modernized the novel of manners and the domestic novel, Twain's work points to another important branch of American realism, that of regional writing. Literary regionalism had first gained national attention through the vernacular humor of the American Southwest. It reemerged as local color writing in the 1870s and 1880s, promoted by literary magazines in response to a growing demand by East Coast readers who looked back nostalgically to a preindustrial America that seemed to vanish rapidly. Local color stories are tales of cultural contact and cultural confrontation in which the peculiar customs of certain regions of the United States are exhibited in either humorous, or melodramatic, encounters between local characters and a representative of the civilizatory centers of the East. Bret Harte's sentimental stories of California miners whose rough exteriors hide hearts of gold, and Twain's tongue-in-cheek tall tales such as "The Celebrated Jumping Frog of Calaveras County" (1865) and the stories collected in his travel book *Roughing It* (1872) made the genre popular in the East.

In the wake of the popular local color stories about the West, each region with a sufficiently "colorful" image developed its own specialists. The works of George Washington Cable (*Old Creole Days,* 1879; *The Grandissimes,* 1880), Grace King (*Balcony Stories,* 1893) and Kate Chopin (*Bayou Folk,* 1894; *A Night in Acadie,* 1897) evoke a South of noble aristocratic codes, strong passions, and a lingering fear of miscegenation. The writings of Edward Eggleston (*The Hoosier School-Master,* 1871) and Mary Noailles Murfree (*In the Tennessee Mountains,* 1884) depict a Midwest of rugged, eccentric individuals. Harriet Beecher Stowe, in books like *Oldtown Folks* (1869) and *Poganuc People* (1878), Rose Terry Cooke in numerous stories, Sarah Orne Jewett in *The Country of Pointed Firs* (1896), and Mary Wilkins Freeman in *A New England Nun and Other Stories* (1891) and her social reform novel *The Portion of Labor* (1901) present a quaint, barren New England in which women struggle for independence at the cost of loneliness and poverty. Altogether, literary historians consider local color writing a distinct and influential form of American realism whose sometimes quaint regionalism should not distract readers from the fact that it was exactly this innocent surface that permitted the articulation of wishes and symbolic acts of self-assertion—acts that could only be expressed in the displaced form of this genre.

In its unsparing, disillusioned tone, the local color literature especially of Jewett and Freeman became one of the first forms of women's writing that found recognition among members of the literary establishment. This recognition came at a price, however, because it also trapped these writers in the local color convention. The same is true of the development of black writing. After the Civil War, white southern writers like Thomas Nelson Page had established a highly romanticized plantation literature centered around the figure of a sagacious ex-slave who looked back nostalgically at the time before the war. In Joel Chandler Harris's stories (*Uncle Remus: His Songs and His Sayings,* 1880), this formula is enriched by the figure of the cunning trickster-figure Brer Rabbit; in Charles W. Chesnutt's story collection *The Conjure Woman* (1899) it is transformed into a clever play through which the plans of the white plantation owner are constantly undermined. But when Chesnutt, the first black writer of the South to gain national recognition, tried to go beyond the formula in his novels *The House behind the Cedars* (1900) and *The Marrow of Tradition* (1901) in order to address the problem of race relations more openly, he lost his (white) public. Other ethnic writers, such as the Jewish American author Abraham Cahan, suffered a similar fate. He, too, remained most popular where he was ethnically most "colorful," as in his story "Yekl: A Tale of the New York Ghetto" (1896).

In the work of writers like Jewett, Freeman, and Chesnutt, the promise of regionalism—to provide a source of identity and possible regeneration—is already subtly undermined. Instead, the region turns into a hostile environment that paralyzes those who cannot muster the courage to leave. This grim regionalism achieves full expression in books like Edgar Howe's novel *The Story of a Country Town* (1883), and especially Hamlin Garland's tales in *Main-Travelled Roads* (1891) and *Prairie Folks* (1893), sometimes also dubbed "prairie realism." Garland's tales signal the arrival of a new generation of writers who will soon criticize the realism of William Dean Howells's generation as too timid and "genteel"—a generational conflict that finds its most spectacular expression in Sinclair Lewis's Nobel Prize acceptance speech of 1930. In this speech, he voiced the view of a younger generation of realists by calling Howells "a pious old maid whose greatest delight was to have tea at the vicarage." This critique was anticipated in 1911 by George Santayana's sweeping dismissal of the nineteenth-century American culture as "genteel tradition" ("Genteel Tradition," in *Winds of Doctrine*, vol. 7 of *The Works of George Santayana*, pp. 127–150).

The crisis of classical American realism that occurred around the turn of the century is reflected in the crisis of the story of individual growth. Examples can be found in the stories of religious crises such as Margaret Deland's novel *John Ward, Preacher* (1888) or Harold Frederic's remarkable novel *The Damnation of Theron Ware* (1896), where individual development appears as an effect of impression management and self-deception. In Henry Adams's posthumously published *The Education of Henry Adams* (1907), a compendium of major intellectual currents of the nineteenth century, the idea of self-development is still evoked by the title, but only in order to be rejected categorically in Adams's unsparing self-examination. Edith Wharton's portrayals of "empty" upper-class heroines like Lily Bart in *The House of Mirth* (1905) or Undine Spragg in *The Custom of the Country* (1913), both entrapped in a system of conspicuous consumption, subvert traditional Victorian ideals of female development. The most radical rejection, however, is provided by Kate Chopin's novel *The Awakening* (1899), which replaces the story of development with a story of sensual and sexual awakening in which Victorian self-control is no longer a source of strength but of imprisonment. Chopin's "scandalous" novel of female self-assertion, combining realism with impressionism, was so far ahead of its time that it was rejected by the public, forgotten, and only rediscovered in the late 1960s by the women's movement.

Radical rejection of the Victorian idea of individual growth also lay at the center of the American naturalism that emerged in the 1890s, again without ever becoming a clearly identifiable school of thought. There are critics who consider naturalism merely an extension of realism's attempt to provide faithful representations of reality; however, it is more accurate to speak of a new literary movement, because naturalist writing was generated by a radically different view of reality. While realism's depiction of reality is based on a Victorian trust in the possibility of moral progress and civilizatory development, naturalism focuses on instinctual drives and environmental forces that threaten to overpower civilizatory self-control at any given moment. Beneath the thin veneer of civilization, elemental forces are lurking that the individual cannot hope to control or contain. The novelist Frank Norris therefore dismissed the novels of Howells as "teacup tragedies" and provided an effective contrast between the new naturalist writing and classical realism: "Terrible things must happen to the characters of the naturalistic tale. They must be twisted from the ordinary, wrenched out from the quiet, uneventful round of every-day life, and flung into the throes of a vast and terrible drama that works itself out in unleashed passions, in blood, and in sudden death" ("Zola as a Romantic Writer," 1896, quoted in *The Literary Criticism of Frank Norris*, edited by Donald Pizer, pp. 71–72). The statement not only aptly summarizes the naturalist project; it also foregrounds naturalism's experimental thrust. Since "terrible things" and unleashed passions are not part of everyday life, a faithful depiction of common experience cannot be sufficient. In order for the novel to be successful, the literary text must go beyond the everyday in order to uncover the hidden forces that shape reality. Naturalism's unrepentant melodramatic sensationalism must thus be seen as an experimental device to explode the deceptive surface reality of "common experience."

In Stephen Crane's most important works, influenced strongly by his journalistic background, the ghetto (*Maggie: A Girl of the Streets*, 1893) and the Civil War (*The Red Badge of Courage*, 1895) present such forces, while in his superb short story "The Open Boat" (1898), man is at the mercy of overpowering nature. The characters of Norris's novel *McTeague* (1899) are driven by stark primitive passions; in the ambitious project of a "wheat trilogy" (*The Octopus,* 1901; *The Pit,* 1903), which his early death prevented him from completing, Norris wanted to demonstrate the anonymous power of a natural phenomenon like wheat in the three stages of production, distribution, and consumption. For Jack London, the most popular of the American naturalists, basic instincts for power and survival dominated all aspects and areas of life (*The Call of the Wild,* 1903; *The Sea Wolf,* 1904). Theodore Dreiser's daring novel *Sister Carrie* (1900) sees humans as victims of an anthropological lack. Because of the continuing impact of archaic instincts, they are not fully capable of rational self-control; on the other hand, they also lack the instinctual guidance of animals and are thus doomed to fight a losing battle between desire and reason. Two major types of story emerged from this naturalist redefinition of what "really" constitutes reality: melodramas of destruction (as seen in *Maggie, McTeague,* and *The Octopus*) and adventure tales of regeneration through the loss of civilizatory inhibitions (*The Sea Wolf, The Red Badge of Courage, Sister Carrie*). In Upton Sinclair's muckraking novel about the meat-packing industry, *The Jungle* (1906), socialism finally provides a rescue from the play of Norris's "terrible things," as it does in the later work of Jack London (*The Iron Heel,* 1907; *Martin Eden,* 1909).

REALISM IN PAINTING AND PHOTOGRAPHY

The development of an American form of pictorial realism was slower and less consistent than that of literary realism, mainly because there was even less of an institutional base for it. There had been an immensely popular school of genre painting in the Jacksonian period that anticipated the local color school of the gilded age, but nature painting, considered by many as the supreme embodiment of the idealizing potential of the fine arts, still remained the dominant mode in the period after the Civil War. Realism first entered pictorial representation through photography, in the Civil War photographs of Matthew Brady and Alexander Gardner (*Photographic Sketch Book of the Civil War,* 1866) which, despite the difficulties of handling the still cumbersome equipment, produced some striking pictures of the squalor of war. Carleton E. Watkins's and Timothy H. O'Sullivan's photos of the spectacular landscapes of the American West gave impetus to the nature preservation movement that led to the

establishment of national parks. Photography also played an important role in social reform, as seen in Jacob Riis's documentary pictures of tenement life in New York, published as the influential report *How the Other Half Lives* (1890), and Lewis Hine's documentation of the abuses of child labor for the National Child Labor Committee. At the same time, photography as a medium also began to attract artists like Edward Steichen and Alfred Stieglitz, whose photograph *The Steerage* (1907) illustrates a new confidence in the expressive power of a carefully composed realistic representation.

In painting, Winslow Homer's work provides the best illustration for the gradual emergence of a specifically American form of realism. Homer started out with sketches of the Civil War for *Harper's Weekly.* His postwar paintings of outdoor life and youths at play (*Snap the Whip,* 1872) present a fundamental break with the genre painting of the Jacksonian period in that they avoid the idyllic and the sentimental. Sports, physical exercise, sailing, and hunting are preferred topics and depict a youthful and vigorous America. In Homer's paintings individual and society remain in precarious but successful balance (*Breezing Up,* 1876). However, in the 1880s Homer's art underwent a dramatic change of mood. In somber pictures of rough seas, pounding storms, and heroic individuals who struggle against primeval forces of nature, the drama of survival and death becomes his work's major theme. Pictures like *The Fox Hunt* (1893), *The Gulf Stream* (1899), and *Right and Left* (1909) exhibit the heroism of the struggle for survival in paintings of cold beauty.

Thomas Eakins, considered by many the greatest American painter of the nineteenth century, transferred Homer's existential heroism to American social life and redefined it as the quiet heroism of sportsmen and professionals who claim the public sphere as space for the practice and exhibition of their skills. In its focus on a thoroughly "profane" activity, Eakins's best-known early picture, *Max Schmitt in a Single Scull* (1871), illustrates not only his preference for topics considered highly unorthodox by the academic establishment of the time but also his interest in the concrete physical aspects of daily life. This eminently "physical" realism also dominates such studies of the human body as the painting *The Swimming Hole* (c. 1884). For Eakins, the scientist and the artist are kindred spirits, as his most famous picture, the controversial *The Gross Clinic* (1875), demonstrates forcefully. The painting depicts a famous surgeon at work, shown in the heroic pose of an individual who is drawing his

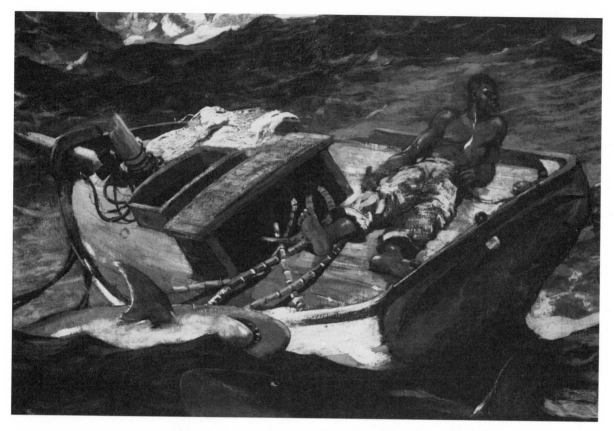

Winslow Homer, *The Gulf Stream* (detail). Oil on canvas, 1899. The study for this painting was done during Homer's winter trips to the Bahamas in 1884–1885 and 1898–1899. © FRANCIS G. MAYER/CORBIS

sense of self-worth from his professional mastery. Surgery here becomes a metaphor for the realist artist. In its uncompromising realism, the painting violated the still-dominant genteel sensibilities of the age. Painted for the art exhibition at the Centennial Exposition of 1876 in Philadelphia, the picture was not shown in the art building but in the U.S. Army Post Hospital exhibit. Eakins never fully recovered from this relegation. His paintings of the 1880s and 1890s show individuals with inner power but also in retreat, absorbed in their own world (*Miss Amelia C. van Buren*, c. 1890). This retreat of the human can also be observed in the trompe l'oeil still-life painting of William Harnett and Frederick Peto, which expresses a fascination with the sheer physicality of common everyday objects.

The fate of Eakins shows that even the "age of realism" was still dominated by a view of art as a realm of "higher" values. This belief in art as a medium of aesthetic transcendence found a modernized expression in an epigonal form of American impressionism, an internationally oriented aestheticism, and various forms of symbolism. The painter Mary Cassatt, an expatriate and active participant

in the French impressionist movement, played an important part in the transition from realism to modernism. But, at the same time, a realist tradition continued in the paintings of the so-called ashcan school, through which the reality of urban life finally entered American painting. These pictures by Robert Henri, George Bellows, John Sloan, and Everett Shinn are deliberately daring in their choice of a "common" subject matter; at the same time, their somber, yet highly expressive, depictions of street life, urban amusements, and colorful urban characters reveal a fascination with the vitality of the new metropolis. This depiction is best seen in Bellows's painting of the ghetto (*The Cliff Dwellers,* 1913) or his rendition of a "primitive" boxing match (*Both Members of this Club,* 1909); as well as Sloan's picture of the elevated (*Six O'Clock,* 1912). In contrast to Eakins, by whom they were influenced, these pictures lack psychological depth, which the artists replaced with aesthetic expressiveness, advancing in their own way the gradual transformation of realism that began after 1900.

The international style called modernism that was the result of these changes in expression defined itself against realism and soon put abstraction in the place of faithful representation. But in the process, modernism forgot that its own development would have been impossible without the realist disenchantment of art. Not modernism, but realism, was the first modern movement in literature and the arts, although, in view of the diversity of realistic tendencies in the period covered in this essay, it seems more fitting to speak of a variety of American realisms instead of one single movement.

See also **Fine Arts in Colonial America; The Arts in the Republican Era; American Romanticism; The Harlem Renaissance; The Artist and the Intellectual in the New Deal** *(in this volume);* **Postmodernism and the Arts** *(volume 2);* **Painting; Sculpture; Public Murals; Fiction** *(volume 3).*

BIBLIOGRAPHY

Borus, Daniel. *Writing Realism: Howells, James, and Norris in the Mass Market.* Chapel Hill, N.C., 1989.

Brodhead, Richard. *Cultures of Letters: Scenes of Reading and Writing in Nineteenth-Century America.* Chicago, 1993.

Conn, Peter. *The Divided Mind: Ideology and Imagination in America, 1898–1917.* Cambridge, Mass., 1983.

Doezema, Marianne. *American Realism and the Industrial Age.* Cleveland, Ohio, 1980.

Fetterly, Judith, and Marjorie Pryse, eds. *American Women Regionalists 1850–1910.* New York, 1992.

Goodrich, Lloyd. *Thomas Eakins.* 2 vols. Cambridge, Mass., 1982.

———. *Winslow Homer.* New York, 1959.

Hakutani, Yoshinobu, and Lewis Fried, eds. *American Literary Naturalism: A Reassessment.* Heidelberg, Germany, 1975.

Johns, Elizabeth. *Thomas Eakins: The Heroism of Modern Life.* Princeton, N.J., 1983.

Kaplan, Amy. *The Social Construction of American Realism.* Chicago, 1988.

Martin, Jay. *Harvest of Change: American Literature, 1865–1914.* Englewood Cliffs, N.J., 1967.

Orvell, Miles. *The Real Thing: Imitation and Authenticity in American Culture, 1880–1940.* Chapel Hill, N.C., 1989.

Pizer, Donald. *The Theory and Practice of American Literary Naturalism: Selected Essays and Reviews.* Carbondale, Ill., 1993.

———, ed. *The Cambridge Companion to American Realism and Naturalism: Howells to London.* New York, 1995.

———, ed. *The Literary Criticism of Frank Norris.* New York, 1976.

Santayana, George. "The Genteel Tradition in American Philosophy." In *Winds of Doctrine,* vol. 7 of *The Works of George Santayana.* New York, 1937, pp. 127–150.

Shi, David E. *Facing Facts: Realism in American Thought and Culture 1850–1920.* New York, 1995.

Trachtenberg, Alan. *The Incorporation of America: Culture and Society in the Gilded Age.* New York, 1982.

Zurier, Rebecca, Robert W. Snyder, and Virginia M. Mecklenburg. *Metropolitan Lives: The Ashcan Artists and Their New York.* New York, 1995.

THE TRANSFORMATION OF PHILOSOPHY

Bruce Kuklick

THE RISE OF AMERICAN PHILOSOPHY

In the eighteenth and most of the nineteenth century, philosophers in America were part of a wider and more fundamental dialogue of speculative thought that had several strands. Perhaps most important were parish ministers, primarily scattered through New England, whose main concern was to explore the truths of Presbyterian and Congregational Calvinism as they had been distinctively formulated in America from the seventeenth century on. This circle of thinkers includes Jonathan Edwards, Horace Bushnell, and Ralph Waldo Emerson.

Another branch of American speculative thought was located in the divinity schools that grew up in the Northeast, the South, and the old Midwest. The divinity school theologians had the preeminent institutional power base in the nineteenth century: they trained the ministers and controlled much learned publication. Their outlook tended to be more narrow and sectarian than those speculators who were not professors of divinity, but it is difficult to argue that they were not the intellectual equals of the men outside the divinity schools. Henry Ware of the Harvard Divinity School, Nathaniel William Taylor of the Yale Divinity School, Henry Boynton Smith of the Union Theological Seminary, and Edwards Amasa Park of the Andover Theological Seminary belong to this cadre.

A final group of speculators were formally known as philosophers. Some men unconnected to institutions were so called, such as the banker-thinker Alexander Bryan Johnson. But more influential were the holders of chairs in mental, moral, or intellectual philosophy in the American colleges of the nineteenth century. Their function, effectively, was to lend theoretical support to the more clearly theological concerns of the divinity school theologians and the most serious active ministers. The philosophers were inevitably ministers and committed Protestants themselves, but in addition to showing that reason was congruent with faith they also elaborated on the grounds of the social order and politics, and commented on the affairs of the world. Notables here include Francis Bowen of Harvard, James McCosh of the College of New Jersey (now Princeton University), and Noah Porter of Yale.

The American speculative tradition was formed from three intersecting dialogues of ministerial amateurs, divinity school theologians, and college philosophers. From the time of Jonathan Edwards to the end of the nineteenth century, the intellectual space that religion and theology occupied in American intellectual life shrank in a revolutionary way. Divinity schools lost their primacy and, indeed, many closed their doors; at the same time, small colleges such as Yale and Princeton were, in the space of thirty years, transformed into larger, internationally recognized centers of learning. New public and private universities commanded national attention—for example, Johns Hopkins University, Cornell University, the University of Chicago, the University of Michigan, and the University of California (Berkeley).

In this new institutional and social setting, an intellectual revolution that had its locus in England—the writing of the naturalist Charles Darwin in *The Origin of Species* (1859)—prompted the emergence in the United States of innovative and characteristic schemes of thought, oriented around the doctrines of what came to be known as pragmatism. The new setting and innovative thought resulted in the emergence of American philosophy. As opposed to the speculative tradition, not one of whose members figures as a significant philosopher, the three leading pragmatists—Charles Sanders Peirce, William James, and John Dewey—are recognized as compelling twentieth-century thinkers.

The American philosophy, created between 1880 and 1920, was rooted in the ideas of the earlier nineteenth-century college philosophers. But separating an earlier speculative era and a later philosophical one is meant to make a substantive point: the latter is distinctive and includes the names of the pragmatists and their philosophical cousins with whom contemporaries conjure. This tradition provided the framework for the ideas of twentieth-century political theorists and reflective social scientists. More important, the post–Civil War philosophers were relatively unconnected to the standard tropes of American thought around them; the young pragmatists and their peers rejected many of the ideas of their elders, generated new ones, and made their way in secular universities and not church-related colleges.

SCOTTISH REALISM

The intellectual view of the men in the older, speculative tradition was a version of what was called Scottish realism. The position emerged in Scotland at the end of the eighteenth century as the first competent attempt to answer the Scottish philosopher David Hume's antireligious skepticism. In America the Scots Thomas Reid and Dugald Stewart were regarded as defenders of common sense and true religion. Against Hume's skepticism, the two argued that the mind directly apprehends the natural world—hence the approbative label "Scottish realism"—and the truths of Christianity.

In the United States, Scottish ideas were taken up in different ways by different thinkers to serve different communal purposes in a variety of local and doctrinal cultures; the ideas themselves changed over one hundred years. Yet the Scottish position standardly joined three components: an epistemology, or theory of how the mind comes to know what it does; a psychology, or assertions about the nature of the mind and how it works; and a theory of science, or an argument about how people accumulate systematic knowledge about the world.

Epistemology According to David Hume, at the basis of people's knowledge of the world are sensations, the momentary contents of consciousness that individuals have before them at a given time. Observing the ordered changes in these sensations, people construct a world and predict the alterations in it. But this knowledge is based on custom and habit, not reason; and people do not have what Hume termed "rational" grounds for their beliefs, grounds that had any indubitable basis. The basis for a belief system is not logic and deduction, but the uncertainty that accompanies the experiential

evidence of the senses. From a theoretical point of view, Hume was a skeptic. He believed no argumentative foundation exists for beliefs, which are only the practical extrapolations from what is given to a single individual. Moreover, even this practical basis for activity was limited to empirical data; there is no room at all for commitment to knowledge beyond the senses.

In America, the Scottish epistemology denied the premise of Hume's skepticism, that people are directly aware only of the contents of consciousness; rather, people grasp things as they are in themselves and, therefore, as they really interact. According to this way of thinking, physical objects, and also the mind itself are "presented" to people. In consciousness people know each basic substance; common sense teaches that the five external senses and consciousness—the internal sense—give people a direct apprehension of the external world and of the mind itself. To deny such common sense is not just a philosopher's trick but self-destructive; belief about the world and the self is necessary to any sort of reasoning.

In assuming he could show the impossibility of knowledge, Hume presupposed the reasoning he ruled out. What did it mean for him to say people only know the phenomena that pass before their minds? He adopted a standpoint from which he could look at what was in his consciousness and claim it told him truly of the relation of objects to mind; but this presupposed what he wished to deny—that consciousness could adequately depict itself and the external world.

This reductio ad absurdum clinched the epistemological case against Hume. The reasoning involved in demonstrating that skepticism presupposes a framework that cannot be doubted was called "the principles of common sense." Individual truths of this importance were known as "intuitions," which were described as being given, and could not be yielded without surrendering thought itself. In the United States, intuition guaranteed the mind's grasp of all sorts of truths about the world.

Psychology American speculators from the late eighteenth century developed what present-day scholars would call psychological theories of the mind. They were all responding to Jonathan Edwards, who had been required reading since the middle of the eighteenth century. For Edwards, the mind is not so much an entity but a function, and there are two reciprocally related functions—cognition and volition. Edwards advanced his views mainly as a way of elaborating a deterministic position on the troubling question of human freedom for Calvinism. In the nineteenth century his solution provoked much opposition that found comfort in a different conception of mind and that divided the mental realm into a series of separate powers.

For the opposition to Edwards and for many Scottish realists, the mind has three functions, not two, and they are more clearly separated into ontological faculties. The understanding is not so much an activity as a substance that does the cognizing. The affections are capable of emotion, and the will, another substance, has the capacity for choice. Thus, in human behavior, the reason (or understanding or cognition) sets goals; the affections provide the motives; and the will makes action possible.

Psychology in the nineteenth century was elaborated by college philosophers, but most clearly served a theological purpose. It was an ancestor of present-day psychology, but lodged in a religious conversation and without an experimental component. The faculty psychology gave theologians a way to respond to Edwards on the will; they believed the will is a separate and freely acting entity. Disciples of the Scots in the United States shifted discussion away from the Edwardsean functionalist view of mind to a three-substance view.

Theory of Science The Scottish realists defended a theory of science that was known as taxonomic or naturalist, following the position of the early naturalist-philosopher Sir Francis Bacon. "Natural philosophers" observed the world around them systematically and from their observations induced generalizations (theories) about the world that gained the status of laws of nature, if these theories were sustained and acceptable.

It was premised that the American scientist is a methodical observer, even a collector. The observations are presumed to be "objective," that is, they depend on the impartial character of the scientists' findings and their ability to see what actually exists. The naturalist did not engage in philosophy, that is, metaphysics; empirical theories were considered different from hypotheses or speculations. The difference was just that theories had been "induced" from the facts collected. The precise nature of this kind of Baconian induction was mysterious. Ostensibly the scientist teased out of the information universal statements that were more than merely the sum of all the individual data; yet the statements or theories did not go beyond what was given in any unwarranted way. *That* would be metaphysics, speculative hypothesizing. Finally, although the practice

of science in America did not in all ways conform to this ideal, the biological sciences *were* heavily naturalistic. The more strictly empirical Baconian philosophy of science *was* compatible with much of the science.

Overall, the Scottish epistemology was static. It held that the mind knows an externally existing universe, and itself is substantive. Scottish psychology studied an entity that has certain features or characteristics. The philosophy of science was based on recipe: to obtain scientific knowledge, the natural philosopher followed certain rules, more or less mechanistically.

THE TRANSFORMATION OF SCOTTISH REALISM

The progenitor of pragmatism was in some ways an extreme development in Scottish realism. In the course of the nineteenth century, realism underwent alterations that pushed it, in various times and in various ways, to meet local intellectual crises. The pragmatists of the end of the century expounded ideas that emerged from a matrix of Scottish problems but denied what the Scots asserted.

Throughout the nineteenth century, Scottish realism in America, as a living intellectual tradition, developed in response to intellectual movements in Europe. Of most significance in the Old World was a turning away from the Scots as an answer to Hume and a turning toward German thought. The German philosopher Immanuel Kant, too, had answered Hume, and in the nineteenth century his answer had become preeminent. Kant believed the mind is active and shapes the physical world to make it, indeed, the physical world. European thinkers began to give up realism as a solution to skepticism in favor of Kant's constructionalism. Kant's answer to Hume eschewed skepticism because people's knowledge of the world is guaranteed by the fact that knowledge is defined by the rules the mind itself imposes. Hume's phenomena were already impregnated by the categories of the mental. After Kant, the German philosopher Georg Wilhelm Friedrich Hegel carried forward this analysis by urging that phenomena themselves are only a manifestation of a greater mind that is to be understood in historical time. This background meant that pragmatism was closely connected to philosophical idealism, the commitment to the primacy of mind (as against the material world). In the United States, Scottish realism progressively became less certain of the independent existence of the external world, as it gave ground to these German efforts to rebut skepticism.

The crucial challenge to the Scottish position in America came with the intellectual community's response to Charles Darwin. American scientists and speculators argued, but an evolutionary comprehension of life rapidly became conventional. This comprehension quickly put a robust commitment to Reformed Protestantism on the defensive and contributed greatly to the decline of the centrality of theology in American higher education. Many thinkers found it impossible to accept the traditional story of creation and the doctrine of Original Sin and redemption. Darwin called into question the substance of older beliefs. Darwin's emphasis on long-term change and adaptation in the evolution of organisms also called into question fixed and unalterable intuitions. The new biological science relied heavily on the hypothetical powers of the human mind in framing explanations of the fossil record and reasoned to conclusions beyond the available evidence. In addition to questioning the substance of older beliefs, Darwin also questioned the method by which scholars arrived at these beliefs.

Within the burgeoning university system, pragmatism arose to reconstruct the philosophic worldview eroded by the Germans and fatally undermined by Darwin. The pragmatists transformed realism to meet the demands of their own time: the loss of some Protestant certainties, a new approach to the life sciences, and changes in the understanding of the history of living creatures.

Epistemology Whereas Scottish epistemology was static, that of the pragmatists was dynamic and interactive. Legitimate knowledge of the world was ascertainable, but the pragmatists defined knowledge not in terms of the intuitional grasp of a preexisting external object. Rather, according to pragmatists, knowledge functions as the human ability to act in an only semihospitable environment. What people know to be true are modes of action that secure their satisfactory adjustment to this environment. Beliefs are true if they survive; they are competitively tested by experience.

The pragmatists used Darwinian concepts in the service of philosophy. Nonetheless, at another level pragmatism's use of Darwin permitted the reinstatement, in a chastened fashion, of beliefs that could be called religious if not Protestant. Pragmatists emphasized the way that ideas actually establish themselves in communities of investigators and what their acceptance means. If beliefs about the spiritual prosper in the world, they can be considered true. The world is, in part, what human beings collectively make of it. Thus, scholars often refer to pragmatism as a form of communitarian idealism.

Psychology For pragmatists, consciousness is not a *thing*, it is a *function*. Pragmatic psychology stressed not what the psyche is, but what behavior defines the mental. According to this doctrine, the mind does not have being, but is a form of doing. As psychology emerged as a separate empirical discipline in the new university system, the Edwardsean functional view again gained credibility, although now its activity was found to be self-generated and not a product of God's power. That is, by the end of the nineteenth century, a different voluntaristic psychology arose.

Theory of Science New scientific practices in the late nineteenth century were not limited to psychology. Innovation was key to biologists whose taxonomic undertaking became more theoretical. Indeed, in the period after the Civil War the entire structure of knowledge was changing, and the practices of men of mind (and later women) were altering. In a new set of disciplines—the social sciences—a dialogue arose that examined the factors that, over time, gave rise to differences in the world's cultures. In the pragmatist theory of science, rules were not emphasized, but the practice of scientists was; what was important was what the varied communities of scientists did.

PRAGMATISM IN THE UNIVERSITY

Harvard Two main academic variants of pragmatism emerged at the end of the nineteenth century. One was centered in Cambridge, Massachusetts, around Harvard University, the nation's premier institution of higher learning, and the many schools along the East Coast, the Midwest, and the West that came under its sway—Cornell, Yale, Princeton, Pennsylvania, Johns Hopkins, Michigan, and California, among others. Cambridge pragmatism took its cues from the mathematical and natural sciences, as well as psychology. In overthrowing Scottish realism, it relied on Kant, not Hegel, and thus tended to shy away from social commitment.

In the 1870s a number of Cambridge intellectuals loosely connected to Harvard met regularly in a Metaphysical Club, where an early statement of pragmatism was enunciated by the intellectual Charles Peirce. Peirce lectured at Harvard and taught for a few years at Johns Hopkins, but was one of the last thinkers of significance in the United States without a professorial position. His friend William James did become a professor at Harvard and distinctively elaborated the pragmatism associated with that university. Jamesean pragmatism was itself molded not just by Peirce but by James's colleague from California and Hopkins, Josiah Royce. Royce and James together defined the "Golden Age of American Philosophy" at Harvard, and pragmatic themes may be found in the work of their younger colleagues, the philosopher-humanist George Santayana, the philosopher Ralph Barton Perry, and the psychologist Edwin B. (E. B.) Holt.

Peirce developed his abstruse philosophy, which he at one point renamed "pragmaticism" to distinguish it from James's "pragmatism," from the 1860s until his death. Peirce's most influential contribution was made in a series of essays published in *Popular Science Monthly* in 1878, the most important one being "How to Make Our Ideas Clear."

Peirce put forward two connected ideas in these essays. The first was that truth is defined by the ongoing investigations of a community of scientists, extended indefinitely in time. According to Peirce, the explorations of this community are self-correcting and subject to continuous scrutiny. The aim of its work is to reach an agreed opinion and its results define what is real. The beliefs of this community might at any time be wrong, but over time, the beliefs asymptotically approach a true opinion.

Peirce's other idea concerned his definition of scientific concepts: they are meaningful to the extent that they can be expressed by linking behavior in an experimental situation to the expected effects of acting on the concept in question. This is a strict version of pragmatism, defined as "operationalism." For a substance to be hard is for it, in carefully defined settings, not to be able to be scratched. Hardness means only this, and nothing more. Peirce emphasized empirical consequences, and the lack of clarity in any nonscientific methods of thinking.

William James's *Principles of Psychology* (1890) introduced this experimental method to what in the United States had often been an introspective science of the soul. Although James resisted concluding that the mind could be reduced to behavior, he did allow that it has a complicated relation to human action in the world. According to James, mind and world are mutually defined in their interaction;

WILLIAM JAMES ON PRAGMATISM AND AMERICAN PHILOSOPHY

PRAGMATISM

Pragmatism is considered by scholars to be James's cornerstone work; here James explained his ideas as a certain style of philosophizing:

> Pragmatism represents a perfectly familiar attitude in philosophy, the empirical attitude, but it represents it in a less objectionable form than it has ever yet assumed. A pragmatist turns his back resolutely and once for all upon a lot of inveterate habits dear to professional philosophers. He turns away from abstraction and insufficiency, from verbal solutions, and from bad *a priori* reasons, from fixed principles, closed systems, and pretended absolutes and origins. He turns toward concreteness and adequacy, toward facts, toward actions, and toward power. That means the empiricist temper regnant, and the rationalist temper sincerely given up. It means the open air and the possibilities of nature, as against dogma, artificiality and the pretence of finality in truth. At the same time it does not stand for any special results. It is a method only. (*Pragmatism*, reprint, 1975, p. 31)

JAMES TO SANTAYANA

In 1905 James wrote his student George Santayana about the younger generation of professional philosophers:

> [I have] a queer sense of the gray-plaster temperament of our bald-headed young Ph.D.'s, boring each other at seminaries, writing those direful reports of literature in the "Philosophical Review" . . . fed on "books of reference," and never confounding "Aesthetik" with "Erkentnisstheorie." Faugh! I shall never deal them again. . . ! (*The Letters of William James*, edited by Henry James. Boston, 1926. Vol. 2, pp. 228–229)

---

mind certainly does not passively look out at the real, but partially constructs it in human action.

In 1898, in a famous address entitled "Philosophical Conceptions and Practical Results" given at the University of California, James made clear his indebtedness to Peirce and expanded on his own ideas. In this talk and his later *Pragmatism* (1907), he defined truth as the "cash value" that ideas have. True ideas fit in with other beliefs and are verified in experience. Most crucially, however, they are satisfactory and work in the world. Because James considered the emotional effects that ideas have and not, like Peirce, only their consequences in the laboratory, James formulated a view in which religious beliefs are true if they can be shown to guide humankind prosperously through experience.

James's pragmatism was an extreme individualistic version of the doctrine, and at Harvard contrasted with the position of his colleague Royce. Royce was explicitly known as an idealist and emphasized not just the role of the mind but of an absolute mind, an overarching conscious experience at the heart of the cosmos. Overlooked by many historians, idealism was a lively part of professional dispute in post–Civil War American philosophy, and gave birth to the most arcane studies in mathematical logic. Royce's *The Religious Aspect of Philosophy* (1885) and two-volume *The World and the Individual* (1899, 1901) deeply influenced Peirce, James, and John Dewey. All of these thinkers adhered to the idealistic principle—that existence does not transcend consciousness, that nothing exists outside the mind—highlighted in Royce. At the same time, many Jamesean themes occurred in Royce, so much so that he called his position "absolute pragmatism."

Chicago-Columbia   The second variant of pragmatism became prominent some fifteen years later in the 1890s at the University of Chicago and, after the turn of the century, at Columbia University. This variant, indebted more to Hegel than to Kant, found its inspiration in the new social sciences and psychology, as opposed to mathematics and the natural sciences. It had a cultural dimension lacking in the pragmatism of Harvard. Dewey, arguably the most important intellectual that America produced in the twentieth century, delineated this brand of pragmatism. His academic power was felt in the Midwest, at universities including Michigan, Minnesota, Illinois, and Chicago. After he moved from Chicago to Columbia in 1904, his commanding presence was felt even more potently in the scholarly world of New York City—City College, New York University (NYU), and the New School for Social Research, in addition to Columbia; and preeminently in the high cultural life of the city. Dewey was most successful in establishing a school of likeminded thinkers: Edward S. Ames, James R. Angell, George Herbert Mead, Addison W. Moore, and James H. Tufts of Chicago; Herbert Schneider, John Herman Randall, and Irwin Edman of Columbia;

Morris Raphael Cohen of City College; and Sidney Hook of NYU.

Dewey spoke with the heavy ponderousness of an academic philosopher, armed with a learned jargon acquired though expert training. He later recalled that he was inspired by his reading of James's *Principles of Psychology,* but in working his way out of a religious crisis in the 1880s, Dewey himself had transformed German and English neo-Hegelian thought, of which he was an early proponent, into his version of pragmatism, called "instrumentalism." He codified his ideas in two books: *Studies in Logical Theory* (1903), an edition of essays by the Chicago school of thinkers, of whom Dewey was the leader; and his own collected essays, *The Influence of Darwin on Philosophy* (1910).

Instrumentalism was grounded in a Darwinian vision of the evolution of life. According to this philosophy, experience is *cognitive*; that is, one element in it actually signals the occurrence of a following element. The experience becomes *cognized* when an organism recognizes the signaling aspect of experience and is able to shape behavior based on expectations of what would occur under certain conditions. Indeed, cognized experience is the criterion of the emergence of mind in nature; the intelligence that distinguishes the progressive development of culture is just a pattern of activity that reveals the use of one experience to predict or control subsequent experiences.

The great leap forward in human life, for Dewey, occurred in early modern Europe with the scientific revolution. Western man learned to manipulate his experience of the physical world and, through technology, to increase his material wealth and to advance immeasurably his physical well-being.

According to Dewey, knowledge is never a static relation in which a disembodied mind knows the external world. Mind is only the name given to a peculiar active connection the organism has to its environment. When an organism behaves in an appropriate way (controlling its responses in terms of expected responses), mind can be said to exist. We are, in fact, better off talking of the mental—an adjective describing a way of behaving—than of mind—a noun. Similarly, truth is a characteristic of acting and thus adverbial and not substantive. According to this argument, human beings act truly when they are able satisfactorily to predict or control future experience on the basis of understanding the connection of a present experience to a future experience. Dewey's theory of truth thus had a limited notion of traditional versions of objectivity, and instead urged that knowledge successfully integrates

578

present experience with guided activity that will deliver desired future experiences.

Dewey ushered in American intellectual life in the twentieth century by calling for the extension of the thinking of the scientific revolution to the realm of the social and moral. In his early career he was known for his work on children's education, *The School and Society* (1900). According to this work, the same sort of method that had allowed people to control the natural world would allow them to control society for the betterment of humankind. Intelligent examination of the problems of men would, most significantly, revolutionize the irrational and unhelpful aspects of politics; social problems would be solved; and moral dilemmas could be resolved in the same manner as technical or scientific questions—by patient exploration of the causes or consequences of phenomena.

Dewey's ideas about the instrumental investigation of culture served as the scholarly justification for the academic social sciences—economics, political science, and sociology—that came to maturity in the early years of the twentieth century.

AMERICAN PHILOSOPHY

By the early decades of the twentieth century, American philosophy was appreciated in the international learned world, and pragmatism had become the standard position of the philosopher in the American university system. Its centrality to learned disputation was felt in many ways. In the discipline itself in the United States, pragmatists controverted various forms of idealism, centered in Royce's work.

Among young scholars, pragmatism easily lent support to scientifically oriented philosophies, to various forms of realism, and to more sharply etched variants of pragmatism itself. Most notable are three responses to pragmatism: the critical realism of Roy Wood Sellars of Michigan and Arthur O. Lovejoy of Hopkins accepted an independently existing physical universe known by science but complexly mediated by mind; the conceptual pragmatism of C. I. Lewis of Harvard developed themes from Royce and James but took them well beyond original pragmatist thought and based its views in a study of the foundations of logic; and the logical empiricism of Ernest Nagel at Columbia combined this same interest in logic with an instrumentalism indebted to Dewey.

In Europe, the acceptance of American thought as mature was indicated by the invitation of Royce, in 1899–1900, and James, in 1901–1902, to deliver the Gifford Lectures in Scotland. Pragmatism was recognized as the distinctive American philosophy, and an option among twentieth-century worldviews. Pragmatism generated followers in England and Italy, and sympathizers in France such as the philosopher Henri Bergson. The philosophy was important enough to be denounced by German thinkers and received close criticism from the English logician and philosopher Bertrand Russell. American idealisms and sophisticated realisms also had counterparts in foreign lands and were respected within a Western philosophical community.

In the American university, outside the discipline of philosophy, pragmatism was widely understood, especially in the writings of John Dewey, to provide the conceptual foundation for work in the social sciences; and philosophy itself had a high prestige as that scholarly enterprise that provided the theoretical guide to modern university study.

For the educated upper middle class outside the system of higher learning the pragmatists gave a justification for work in the world that had a religious tinge, but was recognizably modern, forward looking, and scientific. American philosophers had replaced theologians as the arbiters of ultimate questions. The system of higher education in which they functioned had put a premium on expertise and the credential of higher degrees; a doctorate in philosophy rather than a popular lecture forum became the criterion for possessing wisdom. John Dewey became the paragon of a thinker. He was securely in the professorial ranks, but just as surely he contributed to public life.

This particular transformation in the role of philosophy in American culture proved fleeting. Academic philosophers had stepped onto center stage from 1880 to 1920, during the same period that the university system matured. Their prominence was caused not just by the decline of religious understanding but by the flowering of the doctrines of a few gifted individuals. When pragmatism and its adjacent philosophies became a standard part of the professionalized university curriculum, not only was there a falling off of intellectual achievement, but philosophy eventually lost its wider role in the nonacademic intellectual world. By the time of Dewey's retirement from Columbia in 1930, philosophy had become merely another academic discipline.

See also **Philosophy from Puritanism to the Enlightenment; Moral Philosophy; Pragmatism and Its Critics** *(in this volume);* **Analytic Philosophy; New Philosophical Directions** *(volume 2);* **The History of Ideas** *(volume 3).*

BIBLIOGRAPHY

Primary Works

Dewey, John. *The Influence of Darwin on Philosophy, and Other Essays in Contemporary Thought.* New York, 1910.

——. *The School and Society.* Chicago, 1899.

——, et al. *Studies in Logical Theory.* Chicago, 1903.

James, William. *Pragmatism, A New Name for Some Old Ways of Thinking; Popular Lectures on Philosophy.* New York, 1907. Reprint, Cambridge, Mass., 1975.

——. *The Principles of Psychology.* 2 vols. New York, 1890.

McCosh, James. *The Intuitions of the Mind.* 3d ed. rev. New York, 1872.

Peirce, Charles S. *Peirce on Signs: Writings on Semiotic by Charles Sanders Peirce.* Edited by James Hoopes. Chapel Hill, N.C., 1991.

Porter, Noah. *The Human Intellect.* New York, 1868.

Royce, Josiah. *The Religious Aspect of Philosophy: A Critique of the Bases of Conduct and of Faith.* 1885. Reprint, New York, 1965.

——. *The World and the Individual.* 2 vols. 1899, 1901. Reprint, New York, 1959.

Secondary Works

Brent, Joseph. *Charles Sanders Peirce: A Life.* Rev. and enl. ed. Bloomington, Ind., 1998.

Kloppenberg, James T. *Uncertain Victory: Social Democracy and Progressivism in European and American Thought, 1870–1920.* New York, 1986.

Kuklick, Bruce. *Churchmen and Philosophers: From Jonathan Edwards to John Dewey.* New Haven, Conn., 1985.

——. *The Rise of American Philosophy: Cambridge, Massachusetts, 1860–1930.* New Haven, Conn., 1977.

Marsden, George. *The Soul of the American University.* New York, 1994.

Reuben, Julie A. *The Making of the Modern University: Intellectual Transformation and the Marginalization of Morality.* Chicago, 1996.

Schneider, Herbert W. *A History of American Philosophy.* 2d ed. New York, 1963.

Simon, Linda. *Genuine Reality: A Life of William James.* New York, 1998.

Veysey, Laurence R. *The Emergence of the American University.* Chicago, 1965.

Westbrook, Robert B. *John Dewey and American Democracy.* Ithaca, N.Y., 1991.

THE RISE OF BIBLICAL CRITICISM AND CHALLENGES TO RELIGIOUS AUTHORITY

Charles H. Lippy

BIBLICAL CRITICISM AND COMMON SENSE REALISM

American Christians, especially Protestants, have long been a people who took the Bible seriously—or at least they claimed to do so. The Puritans, whose influence dominated American Christian life throughout the colonial period, were convinced that their visions for both religious and common life reflected the teachings of the Bible, albeit filtered through a Calvinist lens. For much of the nineteenth century, a widespread acceptance of biblical truth continued to undergird the many strands of Protestantism that flourished in the United States. Divisions of opinion had not yet widened into seemingly unbridgeable rifts between those who based their understanding of that truth on a presumably literal rendering of the biblical text and those who did not. From the era of American independence, a tacit assumption that biblical truth was self-evident pervaded much of Protestant life. By the end of the nineteenth century, however, that assumption no longer prevailed as scholars and then preachers began to apply new methods and interpretive constructs to the biblical text in order to discern its meaning.

The conviction that the meaning of Scripture was self-evident derived from Scottish common sense realism, a philosophy that became embedded in American intellectual life through the labors of the clergyman John Witherspoon, who became president of the College of New Jersey (now Princeton University) in 1768. Associated primarily with the philosophers Thomas Reid and Dugald Stewart, common sense realism had roots in both Enlightenment currents and a moderate Calvinism that sustained one wing of Scottish Presbyterianism. Reid and Stewart insisted that a real freedom, grounded in reason, enabled humans to have the power to act in the world (not just react). Sense experience, taken responsibly, could thus yield truth about the natural world; hence there was a natural

affinity with a Baconian understanding of science. At the same time, an inner sense, intuition, could likewise make reliable judgments about moral truth based on what was self-evident. Reacting against the empirical skepticism of the Scottish philosopher David Hume, common sense proponents may have held too high an evaluation of the natural powers of reason and sense experience. However, their thinking resonated well with the democratic impulses that pervaded much of American religion and culture in the nineteenth century. After all, if common sense were in some way equally accessible to all, then religious truth could readily be discerned by ordinary folk. One did not necessarily need religious professionals to offer a single interpretation of religious teaching; what was true should be self-evident to all.

Corollaries of common sense realism for biblical authority and interpretation were significant. The biblical text became the property of ordinary folk since common sense would expose the self-evident meaning of the text. It went against common sense reasoning to think that God would communicate with humanity in ways that were convoluted and subject to ready misunderstanding. Extending a principle rooted in the Protestant Reformation of the sixteenth century, this approach in theory meant that no external authority such as a priest or pastor had to interpret the text so ordinary folk could grasp its meaning; they could intuit it for themselves. Hence religious authority resided, in theory, in the Bible as the self-evident word of God, but in fact it also resided in individuals who read the Bible for themselves and used that common sense basic to all to understand its meaning as the word of God.

In operation, the common sense method differs from what later generations called a literal interpretation. The mind could intuit that some Scripture was to be understood allegorically. Other passages might have a symbolic meaning along with a surface meaning. Common sense would automatically sort that out. Nor was there any conflict between common sense perceptions and viewing the Bible as inspired, the very word of God. Intuition easily fathomed what inspiration meant. Hence Scripture remained different from other literature, for it pointed to truth about God, about human nature, about salvation, about good and evil. That truth alone set the Bible apart from other texts. But common sense strategies did not mean that there would be uniformity when it came to applying the self-evident truths of Scripture to daily life, to explication of Christian doctrine, or to ways of organizing the church, whether one thought of polity or of worship. As intense as disputes over the application of Scripture might be, there remained an underlying conviction that in the final analysis essential truth was obvious. Thus American Protestants could clash over whether immersion was the only sanctioned mode of baptism or whether having bishops was the only leadership structure reflected in the New Testament. But none doubted that the Bible spoke of both. Common sense realism thereby endowed Protestants with an abiding confidence as they used the Bible, and it buttressed claims that various teachings and practices were grounded in the truths of Scripture.

By the end of the nineteenth century, that confidence had eroded in intellectual religious circles and was beginning to unravel among the Christian rank and file. What spurred the gradual collapse of common sense approaches to the Bible was the emergence of biblical criticism and its gradual acceptance by many of the nation's leading theological school professors, many of whom had pursued graduate study in Germany. In Europe, especially in the German universities, theories that seemed to undermine biblical authority were gaining a hearing and attracting a growing number of advocates in the opening decades of the nineteenth century—just when common sense was assuring American Protestants of the sanctity and authority of Scripture. Although there are clear antecedents in the writings of the French theologians Louis Cappel and Richard Simon in the seventeenth and early eighteenth centuries, by the 1830s German scholars were beginning to publish works in which they explored the Bible and Christian origins, using the same tools that they would employ to explore other texts and movements. Their aim was not to undermine Christian truth, but to broaden understanding of the meaning of Scripture and the development of Christian doctrine and institutions.

Ferdinand Christian Baur, the longtime theology professor at the University of Tübingen, shattered traditional understanding of Christian origins in his study of the pastoral epistles of the New Testament that appeared in 1835. In that study, Baur drew on Hegelian principles (after the German idealist philosopher Georg Wilhelm Friedrich Hegel) to argue that conflict among early Christians over church organization was resolved or synthesized in what became the Catholic Church. His later work on Paul (1845) questioned whether the apostle was indeed the author of all the epistles attributed to him, and a study of the gospels that appeared in 1847 argued that the Gospel of John echoed themes of second-century gnostic teaching and was therefore devoid of value in trying to understand the historical Jesus. The philosopher David Friedrich Strauss, who also lectured at Tübingen and operated from a Hegelian perspective, jolted the European religious world in 1835 when he claimed in his *Life of Jesus Critically Examined* that all four gospels reflected a process of mythologizing the figure of Jesus, layering supernatural elements onto early legend between the time of Jesus' death and their composition. Several decades earlier, the orientalist Johann Gottfried Eichhorn, on the faculty at the University of Göttingen, began advocating and refining theories suggested by the French physician Jean Astruc in the eighteenth century that the Old Testament book of Genesis reflected several strands of writing and was unlikely to be the work of a historical Moses.

At first, such historical criticism attracted little attention in the United States. Nor did the appearance of the English naturalist Charles Darwin's *Origin of Species* generate much response among the American Christian public when it was published in 1859. American Protestants were perhaps too absorbed in fashioning what the historian Robert T. Handy dubbed "a Christian America" and coping with the debates over slavery and secession to become absorbed in European intellectual endeavors. But after the Civil War, when American universities began to develop graduate programs modeled after those of the German universities, it became fashionable for American academics, including theologians and biblical scholars, to study abroad. Very often what they imbibed was a critical method that had moved well beyond what Baur, Eichhorn, and Strauss had used, although later nineteenth-century German theologians such as Albrecht Ritschl, Wilhelm Herrmann, and Adolf von Harnack clearly recognized the shortcomings in their predecessors' work.

What exactly went into the critical methods that were so influential in the late nineteenth century and how did they come to be seen as threats to the integrity of Christianity by some? The critical methods of biblical interpretation began with a concern for the accuracy of the biblical text. Since no original manuscripts of any sections of the Bible are known to have survived, scholars always work from later manuscripts in crafting what they believe to be the most accurate rendering in Hebrew or Greek. Particularly where there are multiple readings in surviving ancient manuscripts, comparison with other early translations such as the Septuagint or the Vulgate may also come into play. Careful examination of the Hebrew texts of the Pentateuch, for example, led scholars to question whether the so-called Books of Moses actually came from a single hand or represented layers of tradition put into written form at different times and then combined through an editorial process that might have spanned centuries.

Questions of textual accuracy logically lead to queries about authorship, audience, and dating. Here biblical criticism works much like literary criticism in general; indeed, the principles are pretty much the same. The assumption is that knowing as much as possible about the circumstances and overall context prevailing when a particular book of the Bible was written facilitates understanding of how its message was received when it was first known, why a writer might have chosen to develop specific themes, and what relationship one document might have with another. Some scholars put primary emphasis on literary form, convinced the particular genre used has significance for understanding the meaning of the writing. For example, when scholars examined the parables recorded in the gospels, they pondered why the literary form of the parable was chosen to communicate a particular teaching or idea. Others recognized the affinities between the creation stories in the Hebrew Bible and cognate tales in other religions and were as willing to label the biblical accounts as myth as they were the others. For them, myth simply meant that a story lacked historical or scientific basis, not that it was without value. Indeed, biblical critics insisted that myth communicated vital truths about human nature and the character of life.

Not all these approaches to biblical criticism were as fully developed in the last third of the nineteenth century, when American theological students began to study in German universities in increasing numbers, as they are today. But the basic theories and methods were in place and gradually made their way into the curricula of some of the leading Protestant seminaries in the United States as those who had imbibed biblical criticism as students in Germany became professors themselves. For a time, few outside the academy paid much attention to biblical criticism, but as seminary graduates became pastors and drew on biblical criticism as they prepared sermons to preach to their flocks, the ideas began to filter down to the common people. When critical method appeared well on its way to becoming entrenched in many theological schools, its detractors began to make their opposition known.

Those who spurned critical method did not necessarily reject all its tenets or results. In particular, those who labored to construct the Hebrew and Greek texts of the Bible as accurately as they could were embraced by the opponents of critical method overall. The key issue was whether biblical criticism undermined the idea of inspiration. Christianity had long claimed that Scripture was inspired by God; the common sense realism that had come to the fore in providing philosophical support for much American Protestant thinking in no way challenged tacit acceptance of inspiration. But now the dilemma became determining precisely what inspiration meant and exactly what about the actual text of the Bible was inspired. To opponents, biblical criticism held the potential to demolish the authority of Scripture by undermining inspiration. Critical method, with its emphasis on context and the like, seemed to elevate the human element over the divine in the composition of Scripture. Comparing Bible stories with parallels in other traditions could readily lead to denying the common presumption that Christianity represented God's absolute and final revelation to humanity in a form superior to all others. Those who feared the impact of biblical criticism understood that it was a small step from labeling some passages as myth or, in the case of the Book of Jonah, as religious fiction to denying that Scripture had any historical accuracy. Common sense realism had seen science as an ally, assuming that the postulates of science could never contradict the self-evident meaning of Scripture. Now it seemed that unless scientific method and hypotheses could verify the assertions of Scripture, biblical critics would be prepared to dismiss Scripture altogether. Such, of course, overstated the case, but the fears were real that critical method, unless it were checked, would utterly demolish the faith of ordinary folk.

All these concerns come into sharper relief in a controversy that emerged primarily within northern Presbyterian circles in the United States and centered on a dispute that arose initially between the two seminary professors who served as co-editors of the new

Presbyterian Review, Archibald Alexander Hodge of Princeton Theological Seminary and Charles Augustus Briggs of Union Theological Seminary. The two seminaries were the primary sponsors of the journal. While both Hodge and Briggs came from Presbyterian backgrounds steeped in the evangelical Calvinism that dominated much American Protestantism, Briggs had pursued graduate education at the University of Berlin after completing an initial theological degree at Union. Hodge, the son of the well known Princeton Presbyterian theologian Charles Hodge, did not study abroad, although he served briefly as a missionary in India. Disagreements between the two about the nature of Scripture and the value of critical method emerged almost as soon as they undertook joint editorship of the fledgling *Presbyterian Review* in 1880.

Hodge co-authored an article for the *Review,* later published separately, with his Princeton colleague Benjamin Breckinridge Warfield, who had studied for a year in Europe. The first of a *Review* series of eight pieces on biblical interpretation and entitled simply "Inspiration," the essay defended what Princeton theologians regarded as the verbal inspiration of the Bible or "inerrancy," a word that would come to plague later generations caught up in controversies over fundamentalism and the resurgence of evangelicalism in the closing decades of the twentieth century. What Hodge and Warfield meant was that the very words of the original autographs, the first written forms of any biblical document, were directly inspired by God and therefore were without error, or inerrant. Inspiration thus came close to being a mechanical process; the humans responsible for actually recording the words of the biblical text did so as amanuenses who simply put down what God dictated. Discrepancies or errors might have crept in as the texts were copied by scribes and transmitted to later generations, but in the original they contained the very words of God. Consequently what Scripture taught was also infallible. Here Hodge and Warfield continued to draw on common sense realism to some extent, for they assumed that the meaning of the text, even in translation, would be apparent; they did not sufficiently recognize that both translation and exposition are modes of interpretation and therefore not necessarily self-evident.

Briggs, however, championed the tools of biblical criticism. In the second article in the series, Briggs outlined the scholarly objections to verbal inspiration, suggesting as well that the approach taken in "Inspiration" was moot since no original autographs survived. The response to these two articles revealed that a deep division prevailed in Presbyterian circles over approaches to biblical interpretation. Briggs went on to amplify his views in *Biblical Study: Its Principles, Methods, and History* (1883). This collection prompted little reaction, perhaps because Briggs had previously published all the articles separately. But the rancor prevailing between Briggs and Hodge led first to the dissolution of the *Presbyterian Review* in 1889. It may also have influenced both the topic and tone of Briggs's 1891 address at Union when he assumed the newly endowed Robinson professorship in biblical theology. Echoing themes that resonated in the evangelical liberalism then gaining ground in American theology, Briggs insisted on the authority of the Bible for Christian belief and practice, but in the manner of the polemic he denounced inerrancy, verbal inspiration, and claims that Scripture was historically and scientifically accurate in every detail.

Briggs and others who promoted critical method also found an outlet for their views in a journal, the *Biblical World,* founded in 1880 by William Rainey Harper, the first president of the University of Chicago. Harper was committed to broad dissemination of the results of biblical criticism. One venue for that was the university's fledgling divinity school. The journal was another, perhaps more significant, means, for its readership would include not only scholars but pastors and preachers.

Hodge, other theologians of the Princeton school, and many Presbyterian pastors recoiled at what Briggs promulgated. Within the denomination, moves were taken to shore up what proponents insisted was Christianity's historic understanding of biblical authority and to prevent the "heresy" espoused by Briggs and other biblical critics from further infecting the churches. The northern Presbyterian General Assembly meeting in Portland, Oregon, in 1892 adopted what became known as the "Portland Deliverance." Building on the views articulated by Hodge and Warfield, the statement required candidates for the professional ministry to sign a document affirming their belief in verbal inspiration of the Bible and in the authority of Scripture because it was the inerrant word of God. A similar view undergirded the "Five Points Deliverance" adopted in 1910 that became a bedrock of nascent Fundamentalism.

The most well-known use of the Portland Deliverance came when charges of heresy were lodged against Briggs. Earlier the General Assembly had sought to intervene by approving a report calling for Briggs's removal from the Robinson professorship. Union balked. A trial conducted by the Presbytery of New York had already resulted in the dismissal of the case against Briggs, although its verdict expressed disapproval of the positions he defended. Those determined to ferret out all dangerous teaching appealed the dismissal of the charges to the 1892 General Assembly. While the proceedings there became a tangle of parliamentary red tape, the mood was evident. The assembly sustained the appeal, necessitating a subsequent trial conducted by the Synod of New York, and on its final day of deliberation adopted the archconservative Portland Deliverance. The ensuing trial, with Briggs's attackers now having the Portland Deliverance for support, led to Briggs's suspension from the Presbyterian ministry in 1893—he later became an Episcopal priest—and Union Theological Seminary's severing its formal ties with the northern "New School" Presbyterianism that had given it birth. But the episode by no means ended the widening rift in much American Protestantism between advocates of biblical criticism and those who thought it dangerous to vital faith. In time, the ongoing debates would fuse with those surrounding the validity of theories of evolution rooted in Darwinian thought. Together they would feed into the Fundamentalist-modernist controversy that came to a head in the 1920s.

CHANGES IN THE INDUSTRIAL, SOCIAL, AND RELIGIOUS LANDSCAPE

Debates over verbal inspiration, the historical and scientific accuracy of the Bible, and methods of interpretation were only one cluster of challenges to traditional authority within American Protestantism, especially in its evangelical expression. At the same time that critical method was making its way into American theological circles, the very character of the nation was changing. The forces that propelled that change also posed new risks for Protestant bodies, especially those of an evangelical bent, that had for decades dominated American religious life. Between the end of the Civil War and the outbreak of World War I, the United States effectively moved from being a rural nation to an urban one. The 1890 census showed that the western frontier had been closed as the population distribution spanned the continent, while the 1920 census revealed that for the first time the majority of Americans lived in urban areas. Urbanization in turn gained momentum from the tremendous increase in immigration that came in those decades, an immigration that changed the religious complexion of the nation as well. The rapid industrialization that

came in the late nineteenth century joined with urbanization and immigration to bring dramatic shifts in the economic base of the United States. What implications did these have for the authoritative sway the evangelical Protestant denominations had exercised?

Industrialization unwittingly gave impetus to a cultural trend long under way, namely relegating religion more and more to a domestic sphere that was throughout the Victorian era increasingly regarded as the domain of women. The family had been a functioning economic unit when the nation was primarily agrarian. It was different in industrial America. Income-producing work was done outside the home, continuing the gradual transformation of the home—a process that had begun even before the Civil War—into a domestic space distinct from all else. With the home primarily the realm of women, religious nurture and the cultivation of vital faith—once a shared family responsibility in much American Protestantism—became part of women's sphere. As the home became the locus for religious experience and expression, the churches lost authority indirectly. For both Catholics and Protestants, the move to see religious nurture and development as private, domestic matters that were the responsibility of women received testimony in the surge in religious periodicals and popular literature intended for domestic use. Locating vital religion in the domestic arena did not mean that the churches suddenly ceased to be important. It did suggest, however, that religious institutions exercised less direct control over how the public perceived religious truth and found direction for their lives.

While religious authorities, whether in an abstract form like a denomination or a more personal one like a pastor or priest, could not regulate what people did in their own homes, they could have some say in the resources that people drew on to cultivate this more privatized religiosity, such as religious periodicals. Here the tie to concerns over biblical interpretation becomes apparent. If ordinary folk were reading materials that presumed the validity of critical methods and the conclusions reached through their use, then they might entertain all the doubts that those opposed to biblical criticism feared. They would come to question the authority of the Bible, many of the basic doctrines of the Christian tradition, and ultimately the absoluteness and finality of Christian revelation. The emerging domestic patterns that came with urbanization and industrialization increased what was at stake in the debates over critical method.

Even the clergy saw its status shifting. Industrial magnates displaced preachers in terms of prestige and power, and men who once looked upon professional ministry as a vocation for the most gifted and talented increasingly turned to other careers. In the cities, "princes of the pulpit" such as Phillips Brooks and Henry Ward Beecher for a time commanded the attention and respect of the urban elite, but their practical influence was dwindling and would pretty well evaporate in the opening decades of the twentieth century. After all, if critical method undermined the authority of the Bible and if relegation of vital piety to the home whittled away at the authority of the churches, proclamation of the word of God in erudite sermons also lost its power as a matter of course.

Consigning religious cultivation to the home and thus to the sphere of women eroded traditional religious authority in other ways. Men increasingly carved out a separate sphere for themselves, distinct from home, church, and workplace. The age of rapid industrialization also brought significant growth in the number of fraternal orders and lodges targeted toward a male constituency and a tremendous increase in the number of men who affiliated with them, continuing an upward spiral until the time of the Great Depression. Fraternal orders, such as the Masons and the Odd Fellows, to some extent superseded both home and church, though not necessarily as direct competitors. Ritual ceremonies within the lodges took on the character of religious services. Analysts have demonstrated that many of the rituals themselves drew not only on biblical language, but on imagery that was distinctly feminine and domestic. In this context, the canons of biblical criticism mattered little, for the fraternal movement appropriated Scripture for its own purposes, providing a link to what was familiar from the past in the new urban, industrial context.

By 1910 some Protestant leaders wondered whether the churches were in danger of completely losing men as committed adherents. The Men and Religion Forward movement of 1911–1912, a carefully orchestrated series of rallies conducted simultaneously in urban centers across the country (with smaller-scale events planned for towns and villages), had as its goal bringing a million more men onto the rolls of Protestant churches. While the movement was a failure in that regard, it did help the churches for a time refocus their ministry to add programs that would attract men. Churches built gymnasiums to house sports programs, for example, that were thought to appeal to men. Many of those same programs also served a broader constit-

uency in the larger cities, where immigrants sought to carve a place for themselves.

Massive immigration fueled rapid industrialization by bringing thousands into the laboring ranks who were willing to work in poor conditions for low wages. Yet this immigration also contributed to the disintegration of traditional religious authority. Between 1870 and 1910, immigrants entering the United States totaled nearly 26 million—nearly four times the number that had arrived during the previous fifty years. Most came from central, southern, and eastern Europe. Like other immigrants, they brought their own religious styles with them, but only a minority were identified with the kinds of evangelical Protestantism that enjoyed dominant influence in American religious life. Most were Roman Catholic, Eastern Orthodox, or Jewish. Cities that were ports of entry, especially New York, took on a different religious complexion. Josiah Strong, the prominent general secretary of the Evangelical Alliance, called attention to the ways in which this religious diversity, as well as the difference in cultural styles of the immigrants, could demolish the Protestant way of life so integral to American identity, especially among those in positions of political and economic power. His *Our Country* (1885) is a call to action, summoning evangelical Protestants to convert the immigrants to evangelical Protestantism as the best means to Americanize them. A sense of urgency pervades Strong's work; the erosion of traditional religious authority was too apparent.

Most immigrants came first to eastern cities; so, too, did thousands of in-migrants. Industry beckoned young men and women to leave rural America for the cities, raising hopes of a better life with a presumably more secure financial base. In the opening decades of the twentieth century, the "Great Migration" of African Americans from the rural South to the urban North added to the challenges presented by urban, industrial life. This in-migration, both black and white, also altered the religious character of the cities, even if its base was largely Protestant. Simply put, a religious dissonance became obvious when a rural African American style was juxtaposed with that prevailing among the black churches of the urban North. Perhaps to a lesser extent, but nonetheless a real force, the same held in the predominantly white churches as young men and women brought a rural evangelical piety with them as they sought to fulfill their dreams in the emerging urban, industrial economy. While churches and denominations made moves to accommodate the thousands flocking to the cities, they had to compete with the other urban institutions for the allegiance of the people. Traditional authority was once again in transition.

The scope of industrialization that transformed the nation would not have been possible without significant gains in practical science and technology. Here, too, there are connections to the decline of the religious authority that had prevailed in an earlier era. Apart from its links to understanding the biblical accounts of creation, Darwinian theory posed an intellectual threat all its own, for it seemed to make the authority of science superior to that of revealed religion. The rapid expansion of industry in the late nineteenth century, made possible in part by technological advances, also boosted the authority extended to practical science. Applied science seemed poised to offer such vast improvements in the quality of life that most human problems would vanish. In other words, what the Protestant faithful expected in the heavenly realm was in the process of becoming an empirical reality.

As well, the philosophical underpinnings provided by Scottish common sense realism collapsed, pushed aside in part because the practical realities of science seemed to relegate revealed knowledge to the periphery. Biblical criticism was itself something of a science, at least in its commitment to sustained, logical analysis, and a willingness to accept conclusions based on that analysis that might put traditional doctrinal formulations at risk. Behind much of the critical method and the theological constructions that followed from it lay a philosophical idealism most often associated with the German thinker Georg Wilhelm Friedrich Hegel. The dialectical approach of Hegel and his passion for bringing thesis and antithesis together in a logical synthesis challenged the assumptions of common sense reasoning. If the meaning of the biblical text were not self-evident, then its authority could not be absolute.

A scientific approach to Scriptures was not the only shift that spurred religious change. With immigrants and in-migrants all bringing new religious ways to the burgeoning cities, and the domestic sphere replacing the churches as cradles of vital spirituality, the authority of evangelical Protestantism and its hold on American religious life were confronting unprecedented challenges. Little wonder then that the rise of biblical criticism and its rethinking of the authority of Scripture, of the very word of God, provoked such controversy. When all the threads were woven together, they created a tapestry in which the face of traditional religious authority was obscure. A century later, a fresh chapter in the story would open as evangelical Protestants rekindled an interest in biblical authority, moving in rather different directions from those that rocked American Protantism when biblical criticism began its ascendancy.

See also **Pragmatism and Its Critics; Religious Liberalism, Fundamentalism, and Neo-Orthodoxy** *(in this volume);* **God, Nature, and Human Nature** *(volume 2);* **Hermeneutics and American Historiography** *(volume 3); and other articles in this section.*

BIBLIOGRAPHY

Barr, James. *The Bible in the Modern World.* Philadelphia, 1990.

Briggs, Charles A. *The Authority of Holy Scripture: An Inaugural Address.* New York, 1891.

———. *Biblical Study: Its Principles, Methods, and History.* New York, 1883.

Brown, Ira V. "The Higher Criticism Comes to America, 1880–1900." *Journal of Presbyterian History* 38 (1960): 192–212.

Brown, Jerry Wayne. *The Rise of Biblical Criticism in America, 1800–1870: The New England Scholars.* Middletown, Conn., 1969.

Carnes, Mark. *Secret Ritual and Manhood in Victorian America.* New Haven, Conn., 1989.

Carpenter, Joseph E. *The Bible in the Nineteenth Century.* New York, 1903.

Carter, Paul A. *The Spiritual Crisis of the Gilded Age.* DeKalb, Ill., 1971.

Grave, S. A. *The Scottish Philosophy of Common Sense.* Westport, Conn., 1973.

Handy, Robert T. *A History of Union Theological Seminary in New York.* New York, 1987. Chapters 3 and 4 are especially relevant.

Hatch, Nathan O., and Mark A. Noll, eds. *The Bible in America: Essays in Cultural History.* New York, 1982.

Hodge, Archibald Alexander, and Benjamin Breckinridge Warfield. "Inspiration." *Presbyterian Review* 2 (April 1881): 225–260. Reprinted in book form as *Inspiration.* Grand Rapids, Mich., 1979.

Hoffecker, W. Andrew. *Piety and the Princeton Theologians.* Nutley, N.J., 1981.

McDannell, Colleen. *The Christian Home in Victorian America, 1840–1900.* Bloomington, Ind., 1986.

Marsden, George M. *Fundamentalism and American Culture: The Shaping of Twentieth Century Evangelicalism, 1870–1925.* New York, 1980.

Niebuhr, H. Richard, and Daniel D. Williams, eds. *The Ministry in Historical Perspective.* San Francisco, 1983.

Noll, Mark A. *Between Faith and Criticism: Evangelicals, Scholarship, and the Bible in America.* Grand Rapids, Mich., 1991.

———, ed. *The Princeton Theology, 1812–1921: Scripture, Science, and Theological Method from Archibald Alexander to Benjamin Breckinridge Warfield.* Grand Rapids, Mich., 1983.

Pals, Daniel L. *The Victorian "Lives" of Jesus.* San Antonio, Tex., 1982.

Presbyterian Review 1–10 (1880–1889).

Rogers, Max Gray. "Charles Augustus Briggs: Conservative Heretic." Ph.D. dissertation, Columbia University, 1964.

Sawyer, M. James. *Charles Augustus Briggs and Tensions in Late Nineteenth-Century American Theology.* Lewiston, N.Y., 1994.

Schlesinger, Arthur M. *A Critical Period in American Religion, 1875–1900.* 1932. Reprint ed., Philadelphia, 1967.

Strong, Josiah. *Our Country.* 1885. Reprint edited by Jurgen Herbst. Cambridge, Mass., 1963.

Stuart, Moses. "Are the Same Principles to Be Applied to the Bible as to Other Books?" *Biblical Repository* 2 (January 1832): 125–137.

Warfield, Benjamin Breckinridge. *Inspiration and the Authority of the Bible.* Philadelphia, 1948.

Wills, David F., ed. *The Princeton Theology/Reformed Theology in America.* Grand Rapids, Mich., 1989.

THE STRUGGLE OVER EVOLUTION

Jon H. Roberts

CHARLES DARWIN'S THEORY AND ITS PRECURSORS

In 1859 the English natural historian Charles Darwin published *On the Origin of Species by Means of Natural Selection; or The Preservation of Favoured Races in the Struggle for Life*. In this work, which represented the culmination of more than twenty years of thought, fieldwork, and wide-ranging investigation, Darwin rejected what he later called the "dogma of special creations" in favor of the idea that species are the product of descent from preexisting species (*Descent of Man*, vol. 1, p. 153). Underlying this project was a desire to describe the history of life in terms of the operation of the same kind of agencies—*natural* agencies—that scientists were using to account for other phenomena.

Darwin predicated his theory on three propositions. First, he observed that individuals within a species frequently existed in larger numbers than could be sustained by the environment and that this superfecundity led to a struggle for existence among those individuals. Second, Darwin noted that differences, or variations, seemed to occur "at random" among individuals within a species. Some of those variations conferred advantages in the struggle for existence, thereby making it more likely that individuals possessing those variations would survive to leave offspring. Finally, Darwin observed that there was typically a resemblance between parents and offspring. Accordingly, he reasoned that when individuals who had been "naturally selected" in the struggle for existence bred, they would pass on the variations that had given them an advantage to their progeny.

Darwin was aware that as long as the environment remained constant, the process that he described would do little more than maintain the stability of existing species. He emphasized, however, that during the course of the history of the planet, the environment had undergone almost constant, albeit usually gradual, change. In this state of affairs, organisms possessing variations best adapted to new conditions would be most likely to survive and reproduce. After many generations, populations of organisms that had triumphed in the ongoing struggle for limited resources would have diverged sufficiently greatly from original ancestral populations to be considered new species.

Although the logic of Darwin's argument made the relevance of his work to the origin of the human species obvious, his desire to render his theory as noncontroversial as possible prompted him to avoid addressing the question head-on in the *Origin of Species*. However, after several works by others during the 1860s applied Darwin's theory to human origins, Darwin made his own views concerning the issue explicit. In his *The Descent of Man, and Selection in Relation to Sex* (1871) Darwin not only traced humanity's physical characteristics to earlier species, but he blurred the distinction between the intellect of human beings and the mental capacities of other animals. He even described humanity's "moral sense" in evolutionary terms, as a product of a highly developed "social instinct" and a superior intellect.

Darwin was certainly not the first to attribute the history of life to a process of "transmutation," or "development," or as it would later be termed, "evolution" (by the last quarter of the nineteenth century the terms were used interchangeably). For more than a century prior to the publication of the *Origin of Species* a number of thinkers had invoked evolutionary ideas in accounting for the history of the organic world. Within the English-speaking world the most widely read work of this kind was written by the Scottish publisher Robert Chambers and published anonymously: *Vestiges of the Natural History of Creation* (1844). In this work Chambers made the transmutation of species only one element in a more comprehensive process of gradual, lawful, predetermined change that took place throughout the natural world.

THE SCIENTIFIC RESPONSE

Neither *Vestiges* nor other works espousing the development hypothesis prior to the *Origin of Species* received favorable treatment from the scientific community. The vast majority of natural historians were convinced that species were "fixed" within immutable boundaries. Not only did most regard the fixity of species as a precondition of biological inquiry, but they were convinced that empirical evidence confirmed their belief in the immutability of species. For one thing, observation of living organisms suggested that the need to adapt to the environment imposed strict limits on the degree to which an individual within a species might vary. No less importantly, the fossil record appeared to lack evidence for the kind of gradual change that Darwin had postulated; rather, paleontological data seemed to indicate that species in different strata were discontinuous.

Most Anglo-American scientists were committed Christians who believed that each species had been specially created by God. They were forced, however, to adopt a posture of what Darwin scornfully referred to as "reverent silence" in confronting the question of precisely how God had introduced those species into the world (*Origin of Species,* p. 483). Some natural historians believed that species had been created by miraculous divine fiat. Others assumed that they had appeared on earth as the product of an as-yet-undiscovered natural law. Still others were content to regard speciation as an unfathomable mystery.

Notwithstanding their inability to describe the process of "special creations" in detail, most American natural historians initially confronted Darwin's theory with a skeptical eye. In 1860 Harvard University's Louis Agassiz, the most distinguished natural historian in the United States and an indefatigable opponent of the transmutation hypothesis, informed readers of the *American Journal of Science* that Darwin's arguments had not altered his views one whit. Agassiz, whose thought represented a merger of philosophical idealism with a scrupulous examination of natural history, invoked a variety of stock arguments to support his conclusion that species were individual ideas in the mind of God. Darwin's theory, Agassiz wrote, was "a scientific mistake, untrue in its facts, unscientific in its method, and mischievous in its tendency" (Lurie, *Louis Agassiz,* p. 298).

Although the majority of scientists who initially responded to Darwin's theory agreed with Agassiz, a few, most notably the botanist Asa Gray, were committed to ensuring that the Darwinian hypothesis received fair play in the United States. In 1860 Gray, who was Agassiz's colleague at Harvard and for some years one of Darwin's confidants, wrote a series of articles directed at both the scientific community and the general public. Gray acknowledged that Darwin's theory had not yet been established on unassailable grounds. He insisted, however, that it would be unreasonable to reject it out of hand, for it represented a legitimate attempt to extend scientific investigation into the history of life.

During the decade after publication of the *Origin of Species,* Darwin's views received the respectful hearing that Gray had demanded. In part this is because Darwin was a respected natural historian who had presented the most persuasive case yet for the mutability of species. But just as importantly, most scientists wanted to widen the realm in which scientific discourse could be applied, and they were therefore sympathetically inclined toward a theory that ascribed the origin of species to a natural process. In contrast to the doctrine of special creations, which implied that the relationship of organisms through time was simply a plan in the mind of God, the transmutation hypothesis made that relationship an appropriate subject for scientific investigation.

During the 1860s and early 1870s the investigations of natural historians, viewed through the prism of the Darwinian hypothesis, yielded suggestive evidence in support of an evolutionary interpretation of the history of life. Between 1865 and 1875 most natural historians in the United States embraced the theory of organic evolution as their working hypothesis. Indeed, by 1877 the eminent paleontologist O. C. Marsh was asserting that "to doubt evolution is to doubt science" (Roberts, *Darwinism and the Divine,* p. 85).

If, however, Darwin succeeded in convincing natural historians to abandon their commitment to special creations, he enjoyed decidedly less success in persuading them of the primacy of natural selection. Although most credited natural selection with weeding out the unfit and preserving the fit, they subordinated its importance to other mechanisms, such as the use and disuse of structures, the influence of the environment, and large mutational variation, in bringing about the evolution of species. Even Darwin himself, as subsequent editions of the *Origin of Species* revealed, placed less and less emphasis on natural selection. Nevertheless, in common parlance, both within the scientific community and outside it, "Darwinism" came to refer to the broader theory of the evolution of species by modification as well as the narrower theory of evolution by means of natural selection.

At the same time that scientists were considering the theory of organic evolution, some thinkers were seeking to broaden the realm within which evolution operated to the entire universe. The most notable of these efforts was the work of the English philosopher Herbert Spencer, whose exposition of "cosmic evolution" received a good deal of attention in the United States. However, although Spencer managed to gain the support of a few committed disciples, such as the philosopher-historian John Fiske and Edward L. Youmans, editor of *Popular Science Monthly,* his views were much more widely read than accepted. Accordingly, in an effort to keep discussion of the evolutionary controversy within manageable limits, the remainder of this essay confines itself to the response of Americans to the theory of organic evolution.

ORGANIC EVOLUTION AND AMERICAN RELIGIOUS THOUGHT

Unfortunately, historians are unable to ascertain the views of most Americans concerning the transmutation hypothesis or even the number who were familiar with that hypothesis. It is clear, however, that within the American intellectual community, the scientific community's conversion to the theory of organic evolution had a profound impact on thought and discourse.

No realm of American thought was more significantly affected than religion. In order to appreciate the stakes at issue for American religious thinkers in discussions of the origin of species, it is necessary to understand that prior to the scientific community's endorsement of the transmutation hypothesis, American clergymen and theologians, especially within the Christian tradition, had placed enormous emphasis on the doctrine of special creations in explicating and defending many of the most cherished tenets of their worldview. Theists had long regarded the adaptation of organisms to the conditions of their existence as the most compelling evidence they could muster for their claim that the world was the product of a divine designer. In addition, defenders of Christianity had pointed to the periodic appearance of new species as proof of their view that God exercised ongoing providential control over the affairs of the world. Indeed, in a universe that scientists were rendering ever more intelligible in terms of natural law, many religionists had invoked special creations to defend the very

principle of miraculous supernatural interposition within natural history. Finally, many religious thinkers had maintained that the fossil record, which seemed to disclose a "progressive" pattern culminating in the appearance of the human species, attested to the special status of human beings in the eyes of God.

As long as natural historians withheld their allegiance from the transmutation hypothesis, most clergymen and theologians in the United States viewed that hypothesis as simply one of a number of efforts that were being made in the nineteenth century to masquerade unbelief in the guise of science. Accordingly, in dealing with the Darwinian hypothesis, prior to about 1875 they devoted most of their attention to emphasizing its scientific deficiencies. During the late nineteenth and early twentieth centuries, however, after it had become clear that the overwhelming majority of natural historians had endorsed the theory of organic evolution, religious thinkers focused on the theory's theological implications. The most avid participants in this endeavor were mainline Protestants, for proponents of that set of traditions had long been most enthusiastic in calling upon science to defend their worldview. Although opinion leaders within the smaller Protestant sects, Roman Catholicism, and Judaism did not entirely ignore the issues raised by evolutionary thought, their primary emphasis lay elsewhere, in evangelization efforts, "bricks and mortar" issues, or determined efforts to detach themselves from the larger currents of American society.

Even the most cursory assessment of the theological implications of evolution made it apparent that Darwinism was difficult, if not impossible, to square with traditional formulations of Judeo-Christian thought in three important realms. The first concerned the existence of God and the nature of God's relationship to the world. The problem was not that Darwin's theory was impossible to reconcile with theism. It was rather that by ascribing the existence of species well adapted to their environments to an evolutionary process that could be described in terms of naturalistic agencies, Darwin's work undermined the force of the most commonly formulated argument from design and drastically reduced the number of instances of alleged divine supernatural intervention within nature. Second, Darwinism proved difficult to harmonize with prevailing expositions of Judeo-Christian anthropology. By placing the human species within a more general evolutionary process, Darwin's theory seemed to jeopardize belief in humanity's special kinship with God and even the unique redemptive nature of the divine-human encounter. Third, the Darwinian hypothesis seemed to call into question the divine inspiration of the Bible by positing a view of natural history that is irreconcilable with the scriptural account of the origin of human beings, the fall of humanity, and a number of other fundamental doctrines.

In responding to these challenges, religious intellectuals in the United States found themselves sharply divided. The majority, convinced that failure to embrace a theory that had gained the support of the scientific community would lead to a mass exodus of educated believers from the ranks of the faithful, joined the scientific community in endorsing the transmutation hypothesis. Those thinkers worked to reformulate the central tenets of the Judeo-Christian worldview to bring them into accord with the implications of that hypothesis. Among these "accommodationists," it is possible to discern a spectrum of opinion ranging from those who believed that they could reconcile their faith with the theory of evolution by making relatively minor adjustments in biblical and theological interpretation to those who used the theory of evolution as a springboard for fundamentally reconstructing theology.

Clerics, theologians, and philosophers who sought to show that evolutionary theory left theism intact employed a variety of strategies. Some urged that while natural agencies could account for the *survival* of the fittest, only a divine Designer could adequately explain the *arrival* of the fit—the appearance of the favorable variations on which the evolution of organisms depended. Others, espousing a more broadly focused argument from design, argued that the very intelligibility of evolution and other natural processes attested to the existence of a rational Creator; in confronting nature, minds were meeting Mind. Still others defended theism by appealing to the testimony of the "religious consciousness" as to humanity's dependence on a divine Absolute.

Most accommodationists recognized, however, that their task went well beyond reconstructing arguments for the existence of a divine Creator and Designer. The theory of organic evolution had also significantly narrowed the realm in which supernatural intervention seemed operative in the world, thereby challenging traditional understandings of God's relationship to nature. In addressing this issue, most evolutionists within the American religious community placed greater emphasis on the doctrine of God's immanence. Divine activity, they urged, should not be equated with supernatural fiat. Rather *all* activity within nature should be seen as the manifestation of the divine energy of an immanent deity. This prompted many thinkers, such as the Methodist clergyman and philosopher B. F. Cocker, to assert that God's "will and his power are the only real forces in nature" (Roberts, *Darwinism and the Divine*, p. 139). For proponents of that position, natural laws and processes were simply descriptions of the ways in which God typically achieves his providential ends.

Religious evolutionists also asserted that the central tenets of Judeo-Christian anthropology could be reconciled with the development hypothesis. Discussing human creation with both Genesis and the transmutation hypothesis in mind, the Protestant clergyman Lyman Abbott quipped that he would just "as soon have a monkey as a mud man for an ancestor" (*Darwinism and the Divine*, p. 177). Many other religionists pointed out that the central theological affirmation in the biblical story of human creation is that human beings had been created in God's image. The particular mode by which God had chosen to create the human species, they argued, did nothing to alter the legitimacy of that affirmation; human nature and the means by which humanity originated were separate issues.

Still, although they were prepared to ascribe the origin of the human species to the process of evolution, accommodationists within the religious community were typically much more intent than Darwin and many other evolutionists on emphasizing the differences between the mental and moral attributes of human beings and those of other animals. They also stressed that those differences were theologically crucial. In particular, they maintained that human beings are capable of acting in accordance with divinely decreed values and ideals that are different in kind from the utilitarian motives animating other organisms. Admittedly, human beings do not always act in ways that are consistent with those values and ideals. Nevertheless, responsibility to subordinate one's "brute-inheritance" to higher impulses is an important characteristic of the human condition, and failure to do so constitutes sinful behavior.

Accommodationists also made concerted efforts to show that the transmutation hypothesis posed little danger to the credibility of divine revelation. Toward that end, some suggested that in order to reconcile the Bible with evolutionary thought, little more was needed than to interpret the biblical phrase "let the earth bring forth" in evolutionary terms. By the last quarter of the nineteenth century, however, the strategy of altering interpretations of the meaning of biblical phrases to bring them into closer harmony with the latest views of scientists was wearing thin. Most accommodationists chose instead to emphasize that the Scriptures were intended to reveal the structure and dynamics of the divine-human encounter, not to provide a scientific description of natural phenomena. Here, as in discussing God's relationship to the natural world, many religious thinkers found the doctrine of divine immanence helpful. By emphasizing that God was immanent in history as well as in nature, many clergy and theologians broadened the very meaning of divine revelation. No less importantly, they framed revelation itself within an evolutionary context. The books of the Bible, they suggested, should be seen as a series of important stages in God's gradual revelation to humanity or—just as accurately—of humanity's gradually clearer apprehension of the divine. For thinkers who adopted this position, the Bible remained important as a source of the life, teachings, and resurrection of Jesus and many other historical events. Nevertheless, the notion that the Bible was the word of God increasingly gave way to the idea that it simply *contained* God's word. This freed religious thinkers from having to try to reconcile each biblical passage with the latest findings of modern scholarship. It also allowed them to maintain that the fruits of scientific and historical investigation, as well as the promptings of the "religious consciousness," were vehicles of God's revelation to humanity.

The efforts of religious thinkers to reformulate the Judeo-Christian worldview to bring it into accord with the theory of organic evolution may well have succeeded in convincing many educated Americans to remain within their religious traditions. Those efforts did little, however, to counter the widening of the realm within which "methodological naturalism" seemed appropriate in describing the external world. To an extent that has not yet been adequately measured, many Americans during the late nineteenth and early twentieth centuries continued to embrace religion but tended to confine expression of their faith to the private sphere of their lives; religious perspectives were increasingly excluded from thought and discourse concerning nature and society.

Not all American intellectuals within the religious community were prepared to make their peace with Darwinism. In fact, even after the scientific community had rendered its verdict in favor of the theory of organic evolution, a sizable minority of religious thinkers continued to view that theory with a jaundiced eye. There were two major reasons for this. First, this minority expressed concern that one of the casualties inflicted by the scientific worldview in general and evolution in particular was a lively sense of God's supernatural intervention in the cosmos. Supernaturalism, they believed, not only provided evidentiary support for the doctrine of divine providence, but it also helped justify the notion that the biblical authors had been divinely inspired. Opponents of the transmutation hypothesis therefore denounced efforts to place all divine activity within the framework of natural law and expressed hostility toward tendencies to stress God's immanence at the expense of God's transcendence. An overweening emphasis on divine immanence, they warned, moved dangerously in the direction of pantheism.

Second, most opponents of the evolutionary hypothesis were concerned about its impact on belief in the veracity of biblical testimony and, ultimately, the doctrine of divine inspiration itself. This was especially true of American Protestants of a conservative bent. Those thinkers held that the transmutation hypothesis was irreconcilable with the scriptural account of not only the creation of each species "after its kind" but the creation of human beings and virtually every other biblical doctrine relating to the scheme of redemption. This concern prompted M. E. Dwight, an Iowa clergyman, to warn readers in 1884 that if the human species had descended from lower forms of life,

> then the Scriptures are in fatal error, not simply with regard to man's advent on the globe, but in all their doctrines concerning his original and present spiritual condition, the method of his recovery and his future destiny—that is, their entire system of spiritual teaching, for which they were confessedly given, is at fault. (*Darwinism and the Divine*, p. 212)

Religious thinkers who dissented from the scientific community's verdict concerning organic evolution frequently emphasized the fallibility, hubris, and speculative quality of that community's conclusions concerning the natural world. By contrast, they asserted, the Bible provides error-prone humanity with a complete, inerrant, and clear view of the essential elements of the divine-human encounter. For many of the thinkers who endorsed this contrast, rejecting the conclusions of scientists regarding the transmutation hypothesis had a liberating effect; it encouraged them to adopt the kind of muscular view of biblical authority that culminated in the rise of fundamentalism.

EVOLUTION, PSYCHOLOGY, AND SOCIAL THEORY

In contrast to clergy and theologians, who engaged in fierce controversy over evolution, most other American thinkers who addressed themselves to questions relating to human nature and society during the late nineteenth and early twentieth centuries chose to situate their ideas within a Darwinian framework. The triumph of the evolutionary paradigm in biology also shaped psychology and social theory in other, less direct, but important ways: it seemed to confirm the value of the historicist approach to human affairs and lent credence to the idea that the human mind and behavior, like other phenomena, could be described in terms of intelligible natural processes.

Of all the human sciences, psychology was most immediately and fundamentally affected by the Darwinian revolution. In 1859, even before he made his views on human evolution explicit, Darwin had predicted that his theory would place psychology "on a new foundation" by showing that mental processes, like physical structures, had developed incrementally through transmutation (*Origin of Species*, p. 488). Subsequent developments in psychology confirmed that prediction. By bringing the mind within the purview of evolutionary analysis, Darwin's work privileged the "scientific method" as the means of yielding knowledge of human nature and gave strong support to the long-standing hope that a comprehensive science of human nature could be developed. It thus served to promote the agenda of many American academic psychologists in the late nineteenth century who were seeking to create a new, scientific psychology detached from its traditional moorings in philosophy departments.

The evolutionary perspective also shaped the substance of American psychological research. Prompted at least in part by their awareness of the gradualism implicit in evolutionary thought, many psychologists in the United States embraced comparative and developmental approaches to mind and behavior; children and other animals became important subjects of psychological investigation. No less importantly, the evolutionary categories of heredity, adaptation, and variation became central in the thinking of the "new psychology."

One of the areas of psychological research most obviously invigorated by evolutionary thought was the study of the origin, existence, and varieties of instinct. One effect of Darwin's efforts to emphasize the continuity of important human mental characteristics with those of other animals was to highlight the salience of instinct. Predictably, many psychologists, especially those intent on emphasizing the link between biology and psychology, made instinct central in accounting for the actions of human beings and other organisms alike.

American psychologists also recognized, however, that within environments undergoing change, habits and instincts did not always promote successful adaptation. This insight, coupled with the Darwinian conviction that the mind possesses survival value, played an important role in shaping the research program of the functional psychologists. The central tenet of functional psychology, which remained the dominant "school" of American psychology throughout the late nineteenth and early twentieth centuries, was that mental processes contribute to the ability of organisms to alter their habits and adapt to new conditions. As early as the 1870s, and most compellingly in his groundbreaking *Essays in Psychology* (1890), William James held that consciousness had evolved at least in part because it was useful in enabling organisms to make choices "out of the manifold experiences present to it at a given time," to establish goals, and to vigorously pursue them (p. 46). Consciousness, James declared, was "a *fighter for ends*" (*Principles of Psychology*, vol. 1, p. 144). A similar view prompted many psychologists, such as John Dewey and James Rowland Angell, to investigate the ways in which mind and body interact to foster adaptation and survival. During the early twentieth century, efforts to determine the survival value of consciousness increasingly gave way to concern with behavior. By 1913, the emphasis on behavior within psychology led John B. Watson, the father of behaviorism, to insist that consciousness should be avoided altogether in psychological discourse and that the province of psychology should be limited to the study of behavior. Nothing in the behaviorist message, however, did anything to make the adaptation of organisms to their environment less central as a focus of psychological research.

Finally, evolution helped to foster interest in the differing abilities of human beings to respond effectively to their surroundings. Recognition of this variability gave rise to great interest among psychologists in individual psychological differences. It also prompted inquiries as to the relative role of heredity and environment in accounting for those differences.

The role of the theory of organic evolution in shaping social theory has been a much discussed but highly controversial topic since the mid-1900s. One reason historians have had difficulty in reaching consensus is that evolutionary conceptions of social change preceded Darwin's work, and it is difficult to determine the relative importance that history, anthropology, philology, and biology played in formulating theoretical descriptions of society in the late nineteenth and early twentieth centuries. All that can be said with confidence is that the transmutation hypothesis helped diffuse the idea that change is a crucial category of scientific analysis.

Also, historians have had difficulty reaching agreement about the role of biological evolution in social theory because of the way that the issue has characteristically been framed. Ever since 1945, when Richard Hofstadter published his influential *Social Darwinism in American Thought,* the nature and influence of "social Darwinism" have dominated discussion of the relationship between evolution and American social theory. This is unfortunate, for while virtually all social thinkers after 1875 embraced the transmutation hypothesis and while many employed Darwinian vocabulary—"struggle," "selection," "survival," and the like—in describing interactions among individuals, classes, nations, and races, the uses to which they put that rhetoric were so diverse that we are not well served by employing "social Darwinism" as a descriptive term for a determinate set of ideas.

Certain generalizations about the role of the theory of organic evolution in shaping social thought do seem warranted. First, the theory was used as a terminological and conceptual resource for a multitude of different social theories. Second, acceptance of the transmutation hypothesis fostered naturalistic and positivistic approaches to social phenomena. The success of the theory of organic evolution in accounting for the history of life without the need to invoke supernatural intervention helped encourage virtually every major American social thinker in the late nineteenth and early twentieth centuries to take the position that one of the most important tasks of social science was to describe and explain social phenomena naturalistically. Similarly, Darwin's success in bringing human beings within the orbit of scientific analysis generated confidence that the scientific method could be applied to the analysis of human interaction. Third, Darwinism's emphasis on the importance of adaptation prompted American social theorists, especially in the period prior to 1900, to think of social interaction as one of the means by which individuals adapted to the larger environment. The fascination of theorists with the issue of adaptation can be seen with particular clarity in their persistent interest in the *function* of social practices and institutions.

Within American social theory, the fault line most clearly related to the theory of organic evolution concerned the importance of the human intellect in determining the structure and operation of society. Some social thinkers, most notably Yale's William Graham Sumner, minimized the role of conscious intelligence and purpose and emphasized instead the centrality of humanity's struggle with nature and the importance of practices and institutions—"folkways"—gradually built up through trial and error. Others, such as Lester Frank Ward, whose influential works in sociology eventually led to his obtaining a professorship in that subject at Brown University in 1906, emphasized that with the advent of the human species, a fundamentally new power came into the world: the "thinking, knowing, foreseeing, calculating, designing, inventing, and constructing faculty" (Boller, *American Thought,* p. 66). Thanks to this "psychic factor," Ward argued, human beings could make choices, develop practices and institutions, and arrive at strategies that enable them to alter the social environment rather than simply adapt to it.

During the course of the late nineteenth and early twentieth centuries, an ever-increasing number of social thinkers in the United States made a point of distinguishing the products of human intelligence and learning, which they grouped within the rubric of culture, from biological factors in determining societies' structure and operation. One of the factors that gave impetus to this effort was the work of the German biologist August Weismann in the late 1880s. Weismann destroyed the basis for belief in the Lamarckian concept of the inheritance of acquired characteristics by showing that the responses of organisms to the environment during their lifetimes are not passed on through heredity to their offspring. This forced social thinkers to treat the cultural environment and heredity as independent variables. It took some time for Weismann's views to be fully accepted. As of 1912, most theorists accorded both culture and biology important roles in shaping human behavior. Nevertheless, they were giving much more attention to cultural factors than had Charles Darwin, who was more intent on emphasizing the continuity between human beings and other animals and the salience of biological factors in accounting for human social behavior. In so doing, they began the process of detaching social theory from biology that became so conspicuous in the period after 1920.

See also **Science and Religion** *(in this volume);* **God, Nature, and Human Nature; Anthropology and Cultural Relativism** *(volume 2); and other articles in this section.*

BIBLIOGRAPHY

Primary Sources

Darwin, Charles. *The Descent of Man, and Selection in Relation to Sex.* 2 vols. 1871. Reprint, Princeton, N.J., 1981.

———. *On the Origin of Species by Means of Natural Selection; or, The Preservation of Favoured Races in the Struggle for Life.* 1859. Reprint, Cambridge, Mass., 1964.

James, William. *Essays in Psychology.* Cambridge, Mass., 1983.

———. *The Principles of Psychology.* 3 vols. 1890. Reprint, Cambridge, Mass., 1981.

Secondary Sources

GENERAL BACKGROUND

Boller, Paul F., Jr. *American Thought in Transition: The Impact of Evolutionary Naturalism, 1865–1900.* Chicago, 1969.

Bowler, Peter J. *Evolution: The History of an Idea.* Berkeley, Calif., and Los Angeles, 1984.

Gruber, Howard E., and Paul H. Barrett. *Darwin on Man: A Psychological Study of Scientific Creativity.* New York, 1974.

Numbers, Ronald L. *Darwinism Comes to America.* Cambridge, Mass., 1998.

Persons, Stow, ed. *Evolutionary Thought in America.* New Haven, Conn., 1950.

Ruse, Michael. *The Darwinian Revolution: Science Red in Tooth and Claw.* Chicago, 1979.

Russett, Cynthia Eagle. *Darwin in America: The Intellectual Response, 1865–1912.* San Francisco, 1976.

DARWINISM AND AMERICAN SCIENCE

Dupree, A. Hunter. *Asa Gray 1810–1888.* Cambridge, Mass., 1959.

Lurie, Edward. *Louis Agassiz: A Life in Science.* Chicago, 1960.

DARWINISM AND AMERICAN RELIGIOUS THOUGHT

Appleby, R. Scott. "Exposing Darwin's 'Hidden Agenda': Roman Catholic Responses to Evolution, 1875–1925." In *Disseminating Darwinism: The Role of Place, Race, Religion, and Gender,* edited by Ronald L. Numbers and John Stenhouse, pp. 173–208. New York, 1999.

Livingstone, David N. *Darwin's Forgotten Defenders: The Encounter between Evangelical Theology and Evolutionary Thought.* Grand Rapids, Mich., 1987.

Moore, James R. *The Post-Darwinian Controversies: A Study of the Protestant Struggle to Come to Terms with Darwin in Great Britain and America, 1870–1900.* New York, 1979.

Numbers, Ronald L. *The Creationists.* New York, 1992.

Roberts, Jon H. *Darwinism and the Divine in America: Protestant Intellectuals and Organic Evolution, 1859–1900.* Madison, Wis., 1988.

———. "Darwinism, American Protestant Thinkers, and the Puzzle of Motivation." In *Disseminating Darwinism: The Role of Place, Race, Religion, and Gender,* edited by Ronald L. Numbers and John Stenhouse, pp. 145–172. New York, 1999.

Swetlitz, Marc. "American Jewish Responses to Darwin and Evolutionary Theory, 1860–1890." In *Disseminating Darwinism: The Role of Place, Race, Religion, and Gender,* edited by Ronald L. Numbers and John Stenhouse, pp. 209–246. New York, 1999.

EVOLUTION, PSYCHOLOGY, AND SOCIAL THEORY

Bannister, Robert C. *Social Darwinism: Science and Myth in Anglo-American Social Thought.* Philadelphia, 1979.

Bellomy, Donald C. "'Social Darwinism' Revisited." *Perspectives in American History,* n.s., 1 (1984): 1–129.

Degler, Carl N. *In Search of Human Nature: The Decline and Revival of Darwinism in American Social Thought.* New York, 1991.

Hawkins, Mike. *Social Darwinism in European and American Thought, 1860–1945: Nature as Model and Nature as Threat.* New York, 1997.

Hofstadter, Richard. *Social Darwinism in American Thought.* 2d ed. Boston, 1955.

O'Donnell, John M. *The Origins of Behaviorism: American Psychology, 1870–1920.* New York, 1985.

Richards, Robert J. *Darwin and the Emergence of Evolutionary Theories of Mind and Behavior.* Chicago, 1987.

Stocking, George W., Jr. *Race, Culture, and Evolution: Essays in the History of Anthropology.* New York, 1968.

RACIALISM AND RACIAL UPLIFT

Carolyn Williams

In the period following Reconstruction up to the eve of World War I, a number of American intellectuals, political leaders, and social activists became increasingly concerned about the issue of race. Actually, the primary emphasis was on Anglo-Saxonism and Protestantism. Many feared that the dominant Anglo-Saxon cultural and racial base of American society was being eroded and even co-opted. Threats were perceived in a number of areas, particularly in the rising tide of immigration from southern and eastern Europe, China and Japan, and Latin America and the demands by newly emancipated African Americans for inclusion in the American mainstream. Some sought reactionary measures, including immigration restriction and segregation. Others advocated "racial uplift," that the various groups raise themselves to the level of Protestant Anglo-Saxonism or "Anglo-conformity."

INCLUSION VERSUS COLONIZATION

This concept of racial uplift did not suddenly emerge in the late nineteenth century. It actually was born with the new American nation in the late eighteenth century. As the new government took shape, opposing views appeared about who was an American and who was eligible for incorporation. Benjamin Franklin feared the "Europeanization" of Anglo-America. Others adhered to the view of Thomas Jefferson, that newcomers from Europe could be absorbed into this new Anglo-Saxon nation. Jefferson even believed that non-Europeans, at least Native Americans, were capable of adopting the dominant Anglo-American culture and ultimately could be absorbed. However, Jefferson and the majority of European Americans felt that African Americans were not capable of such elevation. Hence, the solution he proposed was emancipation and colonization, that is, relocation of black people outside the United States.

Jefferson's views on race were not based solely on his personal observations and experiences; they were also informed by the opinions of experts of the day. In the eighteenth century scientists began to take a serious look at the concept of race. Concurrently, Europeans began to encounter apes in Africa. This unfortunate concurrence of events caused Europeans to attribute a special kinship between the animals with a strong resemblance to human beings and the people who inhabited sub-Saharan Africa, the same populations that were being enslaved and exported to the New World settlements being established by Europeans. The ultimate result was a decided racist perspective of Africans and non-Europeans generally. (Another species of ape was also found in Latin America, where the labor of the people and the land was exploited and seized by Europeans.) The pronouncements of European scientists about a hierarchy of the human genre relegating non-Europeans to the lower rungs of the ladder, and the subjugation of the peoples and the political and economic conquest of Africa, America, and Asia, reinforced views of a superior European civilization. In addition, by the eighteenth century Great Britain was the most dominant power of the European world, heightening notions of a superior Anglo-Saxon civilization.

The belief in an inherent black inferiority that could not be eradicated, leading to the conclusion that deportation was the sensible answer, represented the dominant perspective of Anglo-America until the Civil War. President Abraham Lincoln demonstrated the persistence of this outlook by his efforts until a few months before he announced the Emancipation Proclamation in 1863 to solicit support for colonization, rather than emancipation and inclusion. New threats also marked the antebellum period, especially the rising number of Catholic and European immigrants. The response was nativist groups, particularly the American or Know-Nothing Party, which was founded in 1849 as the Secret Order of the Star-Spangled Banner but became an official political organ of the American nativist movement.

Westernized Africans such as the former slaves Olaudah Equiano and Phillis Wheatley and an emerging African American educated elite in the late eighteenth and early nineteenth centuries were distressed and alarmed by the negative views of Africans and Africa, which was regarded as devoid of civilization and dubbed the "dark continent." In addition, those who opposed this negative depiction of Africans and Africa lacked evidence, that is, a body of scholarship to dispute the European view of Africa. They did, however, possess proof that Africans, at least their descendants in America, Europe, and the European diaspora, were not inherently inferior or genetically incapable of reaching the heights of the accomplishments of Europeans and their descendants in America, as Jefferson implied in his *Notes on the State of Virginia* (1785). The proof was themselves. They stressed the fact that, given the opportunity to acquire an education and Christianity (Protestant Christianity), black people or "African Anglos," as they sometimes styled themselves, could also be lifted to the level of Anglo Americans.

Consequently, as the new nation emerged from the revolution, African Americans responded by preaching a gospel of racial uplift. Whether they were assimilationists pursuing integration or black nationalists advocating separatism, westernized African American leaders and prominent blacks of the African diaspora consistently stressed the need for "elevation of the race" (a more common antebellum term for racial uplift) from the debased condition that resulted from slavery and racial oppression.

New dimensions were added to this discussion when colonization became a special threat following the second war of independence of the United States—the War of 1812. In 1817 the American Colonization Society was founded. This organization would eventually encompass individuals of varying political orientations and views about slavery and people of African descent. It included slaveholders like Henry Clay and James Madison and genuine abolitionists like Benjamin Lundy. Although they were barred from formal membership in the American Colonization Society, some African Americans, such as the black shipowner Paul Cuffe, were strong supporters of colonization.

Other blacks opposed colonization and urged emancipation and elevation of the race as the solution to America's "race" problem. During the decades preceding the Civil War, a growing number of black leaders spoke out and even organized to oppose colonization. Instead of deportation, the black elite proposed that they themselves serve as role models for the masses of blacks and encourage them to pursue education and cultivate the Protestant ethic of industry, hard work, frugality, and self-restraint. This was the same formula for success that the educator and former slave Booker T. Washington and others would proclaim in the postbellum period as a means of improving their condition and diminishing white racial prejudice. They believed that if it could be demonstrated that African Americans could lift themselves from the degraded condition of slavery and racial oppression to a level of cultural refinement and civilization, whites would be more willing to accept them as full citizens.

Others, like the physician and reformer Martin Delany, who was a strong advocate of emigration back to Africa (as long as this relocation was voluntary and controlled by black people), believed that not only would a return of civilized (westernized) black Protestants to Africa benefit the emigrants, but it would also help to lift Africa from a state of backwardness. Delany and other African Americans generally felt that Africans and their descendants who had mastered European or European American culture and the Protestant religion would elevate the continent of Africa. The most concrete expression of this was the African Civilization Society, founded in the 1850s, which stated among its chief goals "the civilization and Christianization of Africa, and of the descendants of African ancestors in any portion of the earth, wherever dispersed, and generally the elevation of the colored population of our country, and of other lands." This statement was issued in 1858, the year after the U.S. Supreme Court declared in the Dred Scott decision that black people, by virtue of their African ancestry, were not American citizens. The implication of the African Civilization Society objective, and a recurring theme in both assimilationist and black nationalist thought, was that by "uplifting" the continent of Africa, black people in "England and America would experience a corresponding elevation of status." The problem of racism, however, persisted. Notions about the inferior nature of non-Anglos and those who were not Protestant Christians and the unwillingness of white Protestant Americans to include others as full and equal members of the American nation and society were issues of heated debate as the conflict about slavery escalated.

THE RISE OF NATIVISM

Whites sympathetic to the plight of African Americans endorsed the racial uplift solution for blacks but were largely indifferent to the struggle of the foreign born, who were regarded with hostility. In the 1840s and early 1850s, a massive immigration of Irish Catholics and Germans, many of whom were Catholic, led to increasing ethnic tensions. The question was whether they could and should be elevated. The answer was usually negative. The fact that most of these new arrivals clustered in their own separate communities or neighborhoods helped arouse the suspicion and distrust of Americans of older stock. Native-born and even immigrant Protestants viewed the Catholic newcomers as bearers of an alien culture. Extremists regarded the new immigrants as a particular threat to the American republic.

The response was the formation of local nativist parties, especially the Know-Nothing Party, which pledged "to resist the insidious policy of the Church of Rome" and to elect "none but native born Protestant citizens." In addition to the nativist elite, the Know-Nothings also appealed to native-born workers who feared competition from low-paid immigrants. In the elections of 1854–1855 the Know-Nothings were successful in four New England states; they swept Maryland, Kentucky, and Texas; and seemed to replace the Whigs as an alternative to the Democrats. By 1856, due to the decrease in the rate of immigration and conflict over the extension of slavery, the Know-Nothings experienced a serious decline in that year's presidential election, which led to the party's ultimate demise.

NATIVE AMERICANS AND RACIAL UPLIFT

Prior to the massive immigration that led to the nativist movement, another group became the center of attention—Native Americans. In fact, until the Jacksonian period, racial uplift was the official policy of the U.S. government toward Native Americans. From the administration of George Washington (1789–1796) to the presidency of John Quincy Adams (1825–1829), the Jeffersonian perspective that the indigenous people were genetically on the same level as Europeans but culturally backward informed U.S. policy toward Native Americans. The solution was to encourage them to adopt the culture of whites. As individuals lifted themselves to Euro-American standards, they would be incorporated into the Anglo-American mainstream. A chief motivation for this was the eventual peaceful acquisition of Native American land. The men were en-

couraged to give up hunting and replace it with plow agriculture. The women were urged to relinquish their political power in the tribes to an exclusive male leadership in order to conform to European and European American gender relations. In the antebellum period this policy was pursued most aggressively in the southeastern United States, where a large number of native people lived on land coveted by Anglo-Americans. Christian missionaries, Scottish merchants, and government agents assigned to instructing Native American women in appropriate female responsibilities and employments, such as spinning and weaving, were dispatched or given permission by the U.S. government to deal with the Creek, Cherokee, Choctaw, Chickasaw, and Seminole Indians.

Racial uplift, however, did not prove to be the solution for those Indians regarded as the Five Civilized Tribes. Instead of peaceful inclusion, there was forced expulsion and confinement to Indian Territory in the West. By the Civil War the concentration of the eastern Indians into impoverished ethnic enclaves was completed. The period after the war was marked by the military subjugation of the Plains Indians, who were the last of the free and autonomous indigenous people, with a great deal of their culture intact. Following their conquest, the policy shifted to one of aggressive acculturation. A growing number of "friends" of the Indians believed that after the death of the cultural being called an "Indian," a new acculturated American would rise.

Protestant churches had lobbied for a program of salvation of Native Americans through assimilation from the time of conquest and annexation of the West. The culmination of this process was the Dawes General Allotment Act of 1887, in which the communal basis of Native Americans experienced a mortal wound. They were forced to divide up their communal territory into individual lots, and Native American children were taken from their families and placed in Christian boarding schools to complete their "elevation." The Dawes Act provided for the banning of Indian religious and sacred ceremonies, the telling of legends and myths, and resulted in the imprisonment or exile of shamans and medicine men. Indian schools forbade native languages, clothes, hairstyles, and other fashions. The following quote, made by a Native American boy in 1887 at a conference on the Dawes Act at Lake Mohonk in New York, proved to be a poignant prophecy of the impact of the education program mandated by this law: "I believe it will kill the Indian that is in me and leave the man and citizen."

601

THE NEW IMMIGRANT WAVE

As efforts to stamp out Native American cultures proceeded in the late nineteenth century, new groups arrived who were regarded as threats to the dominant white Anglo-Saxon Protestant (WASP) culture. Waves of immigrants began to arrive from Europe, Asia, and Latin America, many of whom were Catholics, Jews, or members of other non-Christian religions. Concurrently, intellectuals were provided with new theories that reinforced Anglo-Saxonism and could be used to stress Anglo conformity. The adaptation of Charles Darwin's theory of evolution by the English philosopher Herbert Spencer was widely circulated, debated, and incorporated in the American intellectual community. In fact, Spencer's views had even greater acceptance and impact in the United States than in England.

Spencer drew on Darwin's explanation of the role of natural selection in the survival of species. Darwin argued that organisms change through variations that facilitate survival and thus perpetuate themselves. Spencer believed that different groups of people represent different levels of evolution. Also, the quality of the civilization produced by a people reflected the stage of their biological evolution. According to Spencer, the dominant or superior races or groups possessed greater mental complexity as well as greater mental mass. These traits would be evident in their conquest of primitive and inferior races or groups. Some people were equipped by nature to survive and conquer. The natural capacities of others meant they were meant to be conquered and to serve.

The rapidly growing nation with an increasingly diverse population was in many respects an ideal laboratory to test and observe how this theory based on the natural world articulated the human social world. The fact that of the many groups, from the first settlers to new arrivals, the Anglo-Saxon Protestant was the most successful in the struggle for survival in America confirmed for many the "fitness" of this group and provided definitive evidence of the superiority of WASPs. Also, observations of developments in the nation at that time, particularly in the urban areas, increased the negative views of the new arrivals from eastern and southern Europe, Asia, and Latin America. Most new immigrants lived in poverty and conditions that barely seemed decent or civilized, which reinforced notions of racial superiority and inferiority. The need to find solutions to these threats posed by the new immigrants to the superior Anglo-Protestant culture thus became more immediate.

One major solution explored was exclusion and repression. Asian groups on the West Coast were the first targets of laws limiting or banning immigration outright. In 1882 Congress passed the Chinese Exclusion Act in response to the growing number of immigrants from China. The Japanese, many of whom were recruited by American employers, were confronted with a similar response when the Japanese government affirmed in 1907–1908 in a "Gentleman's Agreement" that it would stop the emigration of laborers to the United States. Regional laws such as the Alien Land Act (1913) passed in California and a mounting tide of racial violence against Asians in various parts of the West accompanied the repressive national laws. Apart from the efforts of some missionaries, particularly to rescue young Chinese women from prostitution, few measures were taken by private citizens or government agents to "uplift" Asians to WASP heights. Many of the older residents viewed them as too alien and incapable of being absorbed into the so-called American melting pot.

Other missionaries, a number of them women, migrated to the American West to engage in a campaign to anglicize the Mexican people who had become residents of the United States as a result of the war with Mexico (1846–1848). In addition to a natural and traditional northern movement of the people of Mexico, Americans who were establishing the mining and railroad industries, as well as the large farms and ranches that would evolve into the agribusiness sector of the late-nineteenth-century and early-twentieth-century American economy in the West, stepped up efforts to recruit labor from south of the border. The growing Hispanic population heightened the apprehensions of many Americans and recent European immigrants that the Latino and Catholic people would also dominate the labor force, interfering with the progress of white workers.

POST–CIVIL WAR AFRICAN AMERICANS

African Americans in the South experienced difficulties similar to those of nonwhites in the West. Although American blacks had been technically elevated to a political status of free and equal citizens by the passage of the Thirteenth (1865), Fourteenth (1868), and Fifteenth (1870) Amendments, violence coupled with oppressive legislation prevented their economic, political, and social ascension. In 1865 and 1866 southern states passed black codes, which restricted the movements of newly freed slaves and relegated the majority of them to the plantation system in which they had formerly labored. The Ku Klux Klan and other terrorist groups used violence to keep the southern black population "in its place." As they rapidly regained control of various states, southern white politicians passed laws providing for literacy tests, poll taxes, and "grandfather" clauses, thus disenfranchising blacks and separating the races in all areas from birth to death. The government measure that sealed the fate of black Americans, especially those in the South, for nearly a century was the *Plessy v. Ferguson* Supreme Court decision in 1896, which provided for constitutional protection of separate-but-equal statutes. *Plessy* affected all measures that mandated the separation of races, therefore affecting all people of color in the United States. The media, popular culture, especially minstrel shows, and such scholarship as the William Archibald Dunning school of Reconstruction history perpetuated images of black people as genetically inferior and dangerous, helping support the new racial order of the United States.

The majority of black people in the South, shackled by poverty and intimidation, were prevented from challenging the unjust system directly. Instead, they found ways to resist the negative depiction of themselves and fight racial prejudice by embracing a new gospel of racial uplift. Their chief spokesman, but certainly not the only African American leader to espouse these views, was the educator and former slave Booker T. Washington. The title of his widely read autobiography, *Up from Slavery* (1901), put forth the message of racial uplift that was the foundation of Washington's views. Similar to his antebellum antecedents, Washington did not accept the allegation that black people were by nature inferior. He pointed to slavery and the lack of opportunity generally as the reasons for the low position of the masses of African Americans. Blacks, and he used himself as a prime example, were capable of lifting themselves from the degraded status that was the result of generations of bondage.

The surest way of accomplishing this, Washington argued, was to embrace the Anglo-Protestant ethic. In an address to the Harvard University Board of Overseers, Washington indicated his assessment of the necessity of Anglo conformity. "This country demands that every race shall measure itself by the American standard. By it a race must rise or fall, succeed or fail." In his autobiography Washington explained that in the early years of Tuskegee Institute, the school he founded in 1881, Native American students (designated "colored" by the racial policies of the day) were placed in the school to

Booker T. Washington (1856–1915). Photograph taken in 1903. Washington was the principal developer of Tuskegee Normal and Industrial Institute, now Tuskegee University, as well as the school's president from its opening in 1881 until his death. © BETTMANN/CORBIS

educate them in American culture. In the autobiography Washington stated, "no white American ever thinks that any other race is wholly civilized until he wears the white man's clothes, eats the white man's food, speaks the white man's language, and professes the white man's religion." Washington demonstrated in his words and actions that he was willing to do this and urged African Americans to follow his example in their struggle to lift themselves.

W. E. B. Du Bois, who became a major critic of Washington's program for black advancement, particularly Washington's advocacy of technical rather than academic education and the emphasis on economic measures rather than political agitation and organization, pointed out in an 1897 *Atlantic Monthly* article entitled "Strivings of the Negro People," the psychological dilemma of African Americans with regard to Anglo conformity:

After the Egyptian and Indian, the Greek and Roman, the Teuton and Mongolian, the Negro is a sort of seventh son, born with a veil, and gifted with second sight in this American world,—a world

603

which yields him no self-consciousness, but only lets him see himself through the revelation of the other world. It is a peculiar sensation, this double-consciousness, this sense of always looking at one's self through the eyes of others, of measuring one's soul by the tape of a world that looks on in amused contempt and pity. One ever feels his two-ness,—an American, a Negro; two souls, two unreconciled strivings; two warring ideals in one dark body, whose dogged strength alone keeps it from being torn asunder.

In his review of Washington's autobiography, Du Bois also indicated why Washington was promoted by the white power structure. First, Washington addressed the fears of white southerners (and white Americans generally) by asserting that he would not challenge the racial hierarchy and status quo. In the 1895 address that first brought Washington to national prominence, an address to a white audience at the Cotton States and International Exposition in Atlanta, Georgia, he proclaimed, "In all things that are purely social we can be as separate as the fingers, yet one as the hand in all things essential to mutual progress." In a letter to Theodore Roosevelt in 1904, Washington repeated his acquiescence and that of black people generally with segregation. "So far as I can discern," he wrote, "the Negro in no part of the country feels it necessary to have purely social intercourse with the white man, nor does he hanker after it."

In addition to allaying white (Anglo-Saxon) fears about mixing with "lower races," Washington, as Du Bois pointed out, "learned thoroughly the speech and thought of triumphant commercialism and the ideals of material prosperity." Washington's central message of racial uplift was cloaked in the language of commerce. In the momentous Atlanta address, Washington stated, "If anywhere there are efforts tending to curtail the fullest growth of the Negro, let these efforts be turned into making him the most useful and intelligent citizen. Effort or means so invested will pay a thousand per cent interest." In 1897 in Boston on the occasion of the dedication of a memorial to Robert Gould Shaw, the young white New Englander who died leading a regiment of black soldiers, the Fifty-fourth Massachusetts, during the Civil War, Washington stated, "Tell them that the sacrifice was not made in vain, that up from the depth of ignorance and poverty, we are coming . . . we are gaining. . . . Tell them that we are learning that standing ground for the race must be laid in intelligence, industry, thrift, and property."

THE GOSPEL OF WEALTH

Washington's clever merger of the ideology of racial uplift with economics echoed the sentiments of the Scottish immigrant Andrew Carnegie, a successful industrialist and one of the chief creators of the "gospel of wealth" of the Gilded Age. Carnegie, who donated money for the creation of a library at Tuskegee, embraced much of Spencer's social Darwinism. While accepting the underlying assumption of the superiority of the Anglo-Protestant, Carnegie applied Spencer's theory to explain competition between individuals, rather than between groups or races. In his Gospel of Wealth article, published in the *North America Review* in 1889, he stated, "We must accept and welcome the concentration of business, industrial and commercial, in the hands of a few and the law of competition between these as being not only beneficial, but essential to the future progress of the race." Once men with special abilities acquired their fortunes, one major way in which the "race" would benefit, is that these wealthy men would use portions of their fortunes for public purposes. In the *North America Review* article Carnegie stated his belief in the duty of "men of wealth to administer his estate best calculated to produce the most beneficial results to the community."

Carnegie believed it was essential that men with great wealth apply their resources to projects that would work good for the community. According to Carnegie, "There remains only one mode of using great fortunes. . . . [that is, help usher in] a reign of harmony founded upon the most intense Individualism. . . . Under its sway we shall have an ideal State, in which the surplus of wealth of the few will become, in the best sense, the property of the many and can be made a much more potent force for the elevation of race than if distributed in small sums to the people themselves." He felt that "the possibilities for the improvement of the race lie embedded in the present law of the accumulations of wealth." One of the most worthwhile endeavors was to donate money for the establishment of public libraries, "where the treasures of the world contained in books [would] be open to all forever without money and without price." He thought "rich men should be thankful to busy themselves in organizing benefactions from which the masses of their fellows will derive lasting advantages, and thus dignify their lives."

But, he cautions, "In bestowing charity, the main consideration should be to help those who will help themselves; to provide part of the means by which those who desire to rise: to assist but rarely or never to do all. Neither the individual nor the race is improved in almsgiving. Those worthy of assistance, except in rare cases, seldom require assistance. The really valuable men of the race never do, except in case of accident or sudden change." Carnegie's emphasis on the survival of the "fittest" in the contest between individuals saved him from the extreme laissez-faire position of Spencer and many of his followers and the racism that was supported by social Darwinism.

SOCIAL DARWINISM

Herbert Spencer was opposed to free libraries, public education, and other scholastic institutions supported by the state. He felt this would result in the degeneration of society rather than improvement. For example, he believed that free libraries facilitated the dissemination of inferior literature or "trashy" fiction and that people should pay for the education of their children and not rely on the state. In the ideal Spencerian society, there would be no social legislation, poor relief, or regulation of industry, or any legislation that would interfere with the natural laws of society. Conflicts between groups would result in the natural outcome of the inferior groups being destroyed by superior groups. As Spencer's views were being digested by Americans and others, many social scientists, particularly those involved with the new disciplines of sociology and psychology, began to apply this outlook to help articulate their observations and conclusions regarding society.

In the 1860s one of the major consequences of Darwin's views, which were being discussed by American intellectuals and scientists like Asa Gray, one of the first major promoters of Darwin's views in the United States, was the application of these theories to race. That is, some believed that the different races were either members of one species or the result of different species. Both views were used to support theories of racial inferiority and superiority. Many monogenists regarded different races as representing different levels of evolution, from the primitive to the civilized. Polygenists noted the order of advancement of different species. Therefore, the acceptance of Darwin's theory on monogenism did little to dispel the growing racist thought of the nineteenth century.

Spencer's adaptation of Darwin's biological argument to the social structure helped reinforce no-

tions of ranking different races from the inherent primitive to the natural superior categories. In fact, it was Spencer who contributed the phrases "struggle for existence" and "survival of the fittest," which were used to explain and rationalize developments within national borders, individual societies, and global politics during this age of imperialism in the late Victorian era. Social Darwinism constituted the cornerstone of the concept of Anglo-Protestant superiority. Both conservatives and liberals in all areas, from the academic community of the social sciences, business education, and political science to the wider application of these theories, reinforced this view.

JANE ADDAMS AND HULL-HOUSE

One important departure from this view was represented by Jane Addams and the reformers at Hull-House in Chicago. Addams created a new theory of racial uplift that was rooted in democracy. Hull-House, founded in 1889, evolved out of a desire of young middle- and upper-class American men and women to share the advantages of their heritage and experiences with the poor and foreign-born in Chicago. From the beginning, however, rather than the paternalistic approach articulated by Carnegie and others, in which the "better people" would lead the masses, Addams explained—in an 1892 address, "The Subjective Necessity for Social Settlements," given at the School of Applied Ethics in Plymouth, Massachusetts—that the chief goal of Hull-House reformers "was to make the entire social organism democratic. . . . To move beyond merely the extension of the franchise to immigrants, blacks, and others while ostracizing these groups socially, feeling no duty to invite him to our houses." In the same address Addams stated that the goal was to recapture "the true democracy of the early Church," and that the first Christians "did not denounce, nor tear down the temples . . . [and] identified with slaves. They longed to share the common lot that they might receive the constant revelation."

In a 1908 address to the National Education Association, Addams explained that one central revelation the Hull-House reformers had was the wealth of culture that existed in the various immigrant communities that were often overlooked:

> If the body of teachers in our great cities could take hold of the immigrant colonies, could bring out of them their handicrafts and occupation, their traditions, their folk songs and folk lore, the beautiful

stories which every immigrant colony is ready to tell and translate; could get the children to bring these things into school as the material from which culture is made and the material upon which culture is based, they would discover that by comparison that which they give them now is a poor, meretricious and vulgar thing. Give these children a chance to utilize the historic and industrial material which they see about them, and they will begin to have a first consciousness of ease in America, a first consciousness of being at home.

Addams's remarks echo the sentiments Du Bois had expressed in the *Atlantic Monthly* article:

The history of the American Negro is the history of the strife,—this longing to attain self-conscious manhood, to merge his double self into a better and truer self. In this merging he wishes neither of the older selves to be lost. He does not wish to Africanize America, for America has too much to teach the world and Africa; he does not wish to bleach his Negro blood in a flood of white America.... He wishes to make it possible for a man to be both a Negro and an American without being cursed and spit upon by his fellows, without losing the opportunity of self development.

Addams and Du Bois were working toward a new concept of racial uplift as the twentieth century dawned. They strove to shape the United States into a society where the human dignity of each individual was acknowledged and the contributions of the many peoples and cultures who shaped America was celebrated.

See also **Race as a Cultural Category; Slavery and Race** *(in this volume);* **Race, Rights, and Reform; African Americans** *(volume 2);* **Race; Class; Marxist Approaches** *(volume 3); and other articles in this section.*

BIBLIOGRAPHY

Addams, Jane. "The Necessity for Social Settlements." In *Jane Addams on Education,* edited by Ellen Condliffe Lagemann. New York and London, 1985.

———. "The Public School and the Immigrant Child." In *Jane Addams on Education,* edited by Ellen Condliffe Lagemann. New York and London, 1985.

Du Bois, W. E. B. "Strivings of the Negro People." In *African American Political Thought, 1890–1930: Washington, Du Bois, Garvey, and Randolph,* edited by Cary Wintz. Armonk, N.Y., 1996.

Gordon, Milton M. "Assimilation in America." In *Forging the American Character,* 2d ed., vol. 2, *Readings in United States History Since 1865,* edited by John R. M. Wilson. Upper Saddle River, N.J., 1997.

Gossett, Thomas F. *Race: The History of an Idea in America.* Dallas, Tex., 1963.

Hofstadter, Richard. *Social Darwinism in American Thought.* Rev. ed. New York, 1959.

Horrocks, Thomas. "The Know Nothings." In *Forging the American Character,* 2d ed., vol. 1, *Readings in United States History to 1877,* edited by John R. M. Wilson. Upper Saddle River, N.J., 1991.

Jordan, Winthrop. *White over Black: American Attitudes toward the Negro, 1550–1812.* Chapel Hill, N.C., 1968.

Moses, Wilson Jeremiah. *The Golden Age of Black Nationalism, 1850–1925.* Hamden, Conn., 1978.

Summers, Mark Wahlgren. *The Gilded Age; or, The Hazard of New Functions.* Upper Saddle River, N.J., 1997.

Utley, Robert M. *The Indian Frontier of the American West, 1846–1890.* Albuquerque, N. Mex., 1984.

Wall, Joseph Frazier, ed. *The Andrew Carnegie Reader.* Pittsburgh, Pa., 1992.

Washington, Booker T. *Up from Slavery.* New York, 1901.

Wintz, Cary D., ed. *African American Political Thought, 1890–1930: Washington, Du Bois, Garvey, and Randolph.* Armonk, N.Y., 1996.

Part 5

WORLD WAR I, THE 1920s, AND THE GREAT DEPRESSION

OVERVIEW: FROM THE GREAT WAR THROUGH THE GREAT DEPRESSION

Casey Nelson Blake

The cultural history of the United States during the years between the end of World War I and that of World War II is marked by movements of extraordinary integration and disintegration. On the one hand, this period witnessed the consolidation of a consumer culture that stamped a vision of the good life on the imaginations of millions of people in the United States and abroad, and the creation of the most coherent variant of American patriotism in the country's history. On the other hand, these were years of nightmarish death and suffering on a heretofore unimaginable scale, of mass dislocation and migration of people during a period of economic crisis and total war, and of intellectual, religious, cultural, and political movements that attracted many Americans with their promise of a definitive break from the dominant traditions in their country's history. If these years bequeathed to subsequent generations a confident vision of the promise of American life, they also left memories of turmoil and doubt that haunted American culture until the end of the twentieth century.

THE STRUGGLE OVER "AMERICANISM"

The Wilson administration's prosecution of World War I, with its relentless campaign against the "domestic enemy" at home, unleashed a wave of vindictive nationalism that targeted ethnic and racial minorities, the radical Left, and urban intellectuals as threats to an "America" identified with rural and small-town citizens of northern European, Protestant stock. The passage of Prohibition during the war, the 1919 race riots in East St. Louis and Chicago, the election of Warren G. Harding to the White House in 1920, the revival of the Ku Klux Klan (and its rapid expansion into the Midwestern heartland), and the passage of the National Origins Act of 1924 all stand as familiar signposts for a period that sought "normalcy" and an end to the cultural and political experimentation of the prewar

era. Likewise, the Americanization courses and rituals demanded of immigrant workers and their children in factories and schools testify to a deep desire by elite groups—and by many first- and second-generation immigrants themselves—to create a more homogeneous American ideal.

That said, the Americanization efforts of the immediate postwar period were neither unchallenged nor monolithic. Intellectuals, writers, and artists raised on the prewar discussions among advocates of ethnic pluralism and cosmopolitanism continued to maintain allegiances that contradicted efforts to uphold "one-hundred-percent Americanism." Cultural anthropologists like Ruth Benedict and Margaret Mead turned the new discipline's lens on the cultural practices of Americans, juxtaposing assumptions their fellow citizens had taken for granted with the "patterns of culture" evidenced elsewhere on the globe, all in the service of a reformist agenda that was simultaneously cosmopolitan, progressivist, and feminist. The postwar expatriation and repatriation of modernist writers and critics that Malcolm Cowley famously chronicled in *Exile's Return* (1934) had as its inspiration the hope for a more cosmopolitan reconfiguring of American arts and letters. The Harlem Renaissance of the 1920s simultaneously spoke to a desire to explore the particularity of African American expressive culture and the belief that the rewriting of U.S. cultural history as a story of racial and ethnic mixing might enable the democratization of the nation's segregated institutions and public life. Meanwhile, the postwar period witnessed the flourishing of a powerful regionalist movement in culture and intellectual life, particularly in the South and Midwest, that challenged the ascendancy of a univocal national culture in the name of local traditions and genres.

Nor was the Americanization process itself monolithic. In the end, it was *The Jazz Singer*—the 1927 film starring Al Jolson—and not D. W. Griffith's *Birth of a Nation* (1915) that best captured the possibilities and limitations of the "American"

609

identity available to immigrants in the years after World War I. Griffith's paean to the Reconstruction-era Klan as a band of white, Protestant-producerist brothers proved too narrow a vision for an industrial, ethnically polyglot society. By contrast, *The Jazz Singer* opened the doors of national identity to second-generation immigrants willing—as was the Jolson character "Jack Robin" (formerly "Jakie Rabinowitz")—to shed old-world traditions for an ethnically mixed urban popular culture. In the first decades of the twentieth century, ethnic mixing in dance halls, movie theaters, baseball parks, and other urban venues allowed for the creation of an "ethnic" working-class identity distinct from both the moralizing uplift of the WASP educated classes and the traditionalist values of the first generation of migrants. This was an alternative road to "Americanization" that beckoned with the promise of openness and freedom from traditional constraints. That openness existed on the "white" side of the color line, however, as workers of southern and eastern European descent often gained access to American status by defining themselves in opposition to African American culture. It was only in unusual venues—some jazz circles in the 1920s, or, later, among the most militant cadres of labor's CIO and the Communist-led popular front in the 1930s, that this alternative Americanism reached out to include African Americans, let alone Mexican Americans or Asian Americans.

Fordism   A similar pattern emerged in the history of consumer culture in this period. Historians disagree as to when exactly the United States became a consumption-oriented society; market forces certainly shaped the values and behavior of North American peoples from the time of the arrival of the first European settlers and West African slaves to the continent. The discrete elements of a consumer culture—the mass-production economy of the second industrial revolution (with its revolutionary electrochemical discoveries), the assembly line and Taylorized work, the new film and advertising industries, and a therapeutic attitude that identified success with a vision of self-realization without the traditional referents of God, nation, and family—were all in place by the start of the conflict in Europe. But it was during the 1920s that urban, middle-class Americans began to participate extensively in an economy organized around industrial and white-collar work, relatively higher wages, installment buying, and the stimulation of consumer desire for novelty purchases. As noted at the time by commentators from Sinclair Lewis (in his novel, *Babbitt*, 1922) to Robert S. and Helen M. Lynd (in their sociological study *Middletown*, 1929), this economy brought with it a revolution in values, dissolving older communal ties of neighborhood, religion, and family with the promise of individual fulfillment while also promoting what critics considered a new conformism. The ascendancy of Henry Ford as a culture hero of the 1920s—the prophet of "Fordismus," as Germans called the quasi-socialist form of capitalism hailed by Marxists, fascists, and technocrats around the globe—epitomized these developments. Pioneer of the assembly line, the five-dollar day, and installment buying, Ford made the automobile the central product of the postwar economic boom and the dominant symbol of middle-class success.

But as with the new Americanism of the postwar period, the ascendant consumer culture of these years met with significant resistance, whether from religious traditionalists on the right or from feminist or progressive advocates of consumer education on the left. Evangelical and fundamentalist Protestants struggled to keep the culture of the market at bay, and with it the secular challenge to orthodox belief most often associated with Darwinism. Conservative intellectuals such as Irving Babbitt, Joseph Wood Krutch, and—by the late 1920s—Walter Lippmann bemoaned the corrosion of traditional loyalties and beliefs by the "acids of modernity." Their critique was seconded by the Agrarian group of southern intellectuals, whose manifesto, *I'll Take My Stand*, praised the organic, "natural" hierarchy of the Old South against the rootless individualism and moral relativism of a consumer society. More liberal and leftist critics of consumer culture, such as the Lynds, often sounded like the Agrarians in their lament for a lost communal order, though their response was to call for educational and safety measures to empower citizens as knowledgeable consumers. Even those Americans who eagerly participated in the consumer market did so for their own purposes, in many cases choosing certain goods (such as "race records" aimed at an African American market, for example) to solidify preexisting identities, or selectively drawing on both the mass-produced wares on sale at chain stores and the custom items still available at mom-and-pop stores that balanced the bottom line with personal attention to customers' needs and circumstances. The consumption of a particular item was not in itself evidence of a cultural revolution among members of the new middle class. The Lynds acknowledged that the family automobile facilitated traveling to family reunions and church gatherings even as it

610

allowed teenagers to socialize without adult chaperones. Consumer culture could dissolve and reinforce traditional bonds and commitments

On closer inspection, the therapeutic values of self-realization and personal growth that attended the consumer culture of the postwar years also appear to have had diverse, even contradictory meanings. Advertising copywriters associated the good self with limitlessness, abundance, and freedom from all constraints—and, of course, the purchase of new consumer goods. But during this same period, Protestant social gospelers, Catholic personalists, and many secular intellectuals on the progressive Left continued to define personal growth in collective terms, insisting that true self-realization required commitments beyond the self. The moral language of selfhood was at the very least bifurcated, with many Americans firmly convinced that their "best" selves were most in evidence in the contexts of spiritual fellowship and political solidarity with others. The 1920s also witnessed the emergence of a genre of cultural and social criticism—best represented by Lewis's *Babbitt* and the Lynds' *Middletown,* along with H. L. Mencken's tirades against the "booboisie"—that has ever since attracted a middle-class readership uneasy about its own embrace of consumer values.

The capitals of the new consumer culture—New York and Hollywood—themselves generated contradictory artistic and intellectual impulses in this period. New York's supremacy as the literary, cultural, and financial capital of the United States was cemented during the years around the war, and the city's unique position as a site of intense, innovative cultural exchange across ethno-racial and class lines made it a haven for refugees from the remnants of Victorian sensibility in the heartland. It is not surprising that the city was the home for intellectuals who coalesced in the first significant intelligentsia in the country's history. Committed to cultural and political radicalism, modernist experimentation in the arts, feminism, and sexual experimentation, the New York intelligentsia found sustenance in new publishing houses and new journals—from *Seven Arts* and the *Masses* in the 1910s to *Partisan Review* in the 1930s—that fostered essays joining cultural and social criticism to autobiographical reflection. Whether in Greenwich Village or in Harlem, the city's intellectual class found itself in a deeply ambivalent relationship to the ascendant consumer culture of the era. Its members embraced jazz, film, and other new genres of cultural production that spoke to the vitality of urban-industrial life, yet they were also appalled by the power and

reach of the culture industries of the metropolis, which in many cases rewarded them richly for their talents.

As capital of the film industry, Hollywood attracted second-generation Jewish immigrants in search of a new livelihood and a new identity as Americans; such people went on to produce western after western along with other films glorifying a mythic ideal of a homogeneous frontier or rural culture. But there were also many others in the industry who sought—especially during the Great Depression—to put cinema in the service of political radicalism. On both coasts, then, the centers of the most intense cultural mixing fueled the invention of a monolithic, national popular culture as well as intellectual resistance to that culture.

Not surprisingly, foreign observers often understood better than Americans the volatile mix of cultural currents at work in the 1920s. European artists and intellectuals—particularly Weimar-era Germans—were especially acute in depicting those tensions. Bauhaus architects and other modernists noted the clash between neo-Victorian adornment and raw technological power in American cityscapes. The brilliant Weimar-era German film *Metropolis* (1927) linked the supposedly "primitive" rhythms of jazz to futuristic vistas of a city that resembled nothing more than New York. No wonder that the dada artist Man Ray noted that "Dada is impossible in New York. New York is Dada" (in Scott and Rutkoff, *New York Modern,* p. vii).

THE NEW DEAL AND THE POPULAR FRONT

The contradictory impulses of the 1920s—promoting cultural-social integration and dissent—were kept in check by the prosperity of the period. But the Great Depression brought those tensions to the surface, as unprecedented economic suffering, mass dislocation, labor strife, and a dramatic leftward shift in American political culture seemed, however briefly, to call into question the country's historic commitments to individualism, capitalist enterprise, and limited government. The apparent paralysis of the two established parties during the worst years of hardship, in the early 1930s, radicalized many liberal-progressive intellectuals who, like their mentor John Dewey, began to explore socialist political and economic alternatives. Intellectuals such as Lewis Mumford and other left-leaning communitarians promoted programs for regional and urban planning that combined elements of European socialism and more local forms of decentralist utopianism. Such people often assumed that the new, militant Congress of Industrial Organization—a labor federation of mostly ethnic, blue-collar workers in the mass-production industries—would usher in a laborite political party that would push for dramatic state controls of the market.

To a large extent, hopes for a native variant of socialist thought and practice foundered by mid-decade, for two reasons: the success of Franklin Roosevelt's New Deal in preempting challenges from a laborite Left; and the emergence of the popular front movement, led by the Soviet-inspired Communist Party, as the driving force in radical and reformist activities among intellectuals, artists, and activists who sought a more thoroughgoing reconstruction of American society. Communist Party leader Earl Browder's famous declaration that "Communism is twentieth-century Americanism" fit perfectly with the organicist-populist understandings of national identity that fueled the New Deal's remarkable cultural projects. Together, the New Deal and the Popular Front channeled the radical hopes of the depression era into a political program of welfarist liberalism and a cultural enterprise that reinforced central elements of the American creed, even as it made them available to outsiders on the margins of the society.

Contemporary observers and subsequent historians have fiercely debated the political consequences of the "second" American renaissance of the 1930s, which generated an outpouring of documentaries, literature, music, film, and painting chronicling the experiences and the moral wisdom of ordinary Americans during the depression. Did such work reify a folkish, unanimous vision of a singular national culture—a less poisonous version of what Nazi and fascist regimes were producing in Europe—or did it result in a significant democratization of arts and letters, as African Americans and immigrants from Europe and Mexico articulated a fuller conception of the country's history and identity? Cultural documents from the period suggest the futility of a simple answer. Were folkloric murals depicting a static, rural past more representative of the era than the great Marxist historical work of W. E. B. Du Bois, *Black Reconstruction in America* (1935)? Was the technocratic corporatism celebrated in the World's Fair of 1939–1940 a better summing-up of the decade's aspirations than the 1940 John Ford film rendition of John Steinbeck's novel *The Grapes of Wrath* (1939)? The Ford film itself confounds reductionist readings of the culture of the 1930s. Unlike Steinbeck's dark conclusion,

the Ford film closed with two reflections on the meaning of the response of the oppressed Okies to the economic and ecological catastrophe of the Dust Bowl: Tom Joad's promise to continue the struggle as a radical organizer and Ma Joad's determined, but politically ambiguous, affirmation of the capacity of "The People" to survive. Tom's oath inspired Woody Guthrie to write "Tom Joad" immediately after watching the film; a half-century later, Bruce Springsteen summoned up "The Ghost of Tom Joad" as a specter of refusal in Newt Gingrich's America. Yet Ma's ode to the tenacity of common people fed nicely into the sentimental nationalism of official propaganda during World War II. Resistance and reaffirmation coexisted within the same film, poem, mural, and photograph throughout the decade.

THE MODERNIST CHALLENGE

The 1930s also witnessed the coalescence of a modernist sensibility in the arts and intellectual life that often took the form of a self-conscious critique of left-liberal orthodoxy. The figures associated with *Partisan Review* and, later, *Politics* magazine sought to defend the idea of an intellectual avant-garde and the autonomy of aesthetic experience against left ideas of "commitment," championing the modernist achievements of conservative or apolitical writers such as T. S. Eliot, James Joyce, Marcel Proust, Ezra Pound, and William Faulkner and their counterparts in the visual arts. The defense of complexity and psychological interiority in the arts also resulted in increasingly fierce denunciations of "mass culture" that went well beyond the earlier critiques of middle-class conformity by Lewis, the Lynds, and others in the 1920s. Likening "kitsch" and "masscult" to the official art of fascist and Stalinist regimes, modernist critics such as Clement Greenberg and Dwight Macdonald—and the refugee German Marxists of the Frankfurt school who were writing in the United States at the same time—raised the specter of a "soft" cultural totalitarianism that celebrated the wisdom of the folk even as it subjected them to ever greater control and manipulation.

The growing modernist mood in artistic and intellectual circles found an echo in American Protestantism, which under the leadership of Reinhold Niebuhr moved from the confident progressivism of the social gospel period to a liberalism that insisted on the divided nature of the self, the inescapability of evil, and the limits of all reformist aspirations even as it demanded that believers enter the rough-and-tumble world of political reform. Tragedy, limits, responsibility, and realism were the bywords of a chastened liberalism that bore obvious traces of the renascent modernist sensibility. Richard Wright ended his memoir of his days in the Communist Party, *American Hunger*—not published in full until 1977—with the hope that art and ethico-religious reflection might better serve human aspirations than did the politics that had attracted him for much of the 1930s.

Two great reflections on the events of the 1930s, published in the following decade, reflected the new mood in left-liberal circles. Both the extraordinary "anti-documentary" by James Agee and Walker Evans, *Let Us Now Praise Famous Men* (1941), and Robert Penn Warren's novel about the Huey Long era in Louisiana, *All the King's Men* (1946), charted the moral limits of liberalism and asserted the priority of existential human dilemmas over any promise of automatic political and social reform. Similarly, the classic wartime film *Casablanca* (1942) depicted its lead character, Rick Blaine (played by Humphrey Bogart), as a far darker, more internally conflicted figure than Tom Joad or any other 1930s Hollywood icon. Blaine is a Niebuhrian hero whose agonized decision to commit to the Allied cause is made with the full knowledge that the means and ends of such a cause are likely to be imperfect at best.

Casablanca stands as an excellent example of the complex relationship that the culture of the wartime era had to the memory of the depression years. While on one level the film is a work of wartime propaganda that offers a "conversion narrative" for viewers on the eve of the Allied assault on North Africa, it is also a work of great moral seriousness that acknowledges the memory of 1930s radicalism and the deep wounds that the war would inflict on private life and the individual soul. The Bogart character is a former leftist living in the shadow of dashed hopes who chooses ultimately to sign up for a new cause, even at the expense of love and personal happiness. The film's gritty realism about the personal and political toll of the shift from 1930s radicalism to wartime mobilization resurfaced, after the war, in the far more triumphalist *It's a Wonderful Life* and *The Best Years of Our Lives* of 1946. However sentimental, even these films acknowledged that the victorious good life they celebrated was haunted by years of economic hardship, social tension, and personal suffering. At its most effective, wartime popular culture negotiated the political and cultural shift from "The Red Decade" to "The Good Fight" by paying homage to aspirations and fears that were within easy reach of most Americans' memories.

The war prompted a dramatic dislocation of people across the globe that had long-lasting consequences for American culture. Jewish and leftist intellectuals in flight from Nazism arrived in the United States during the 1940s from central and eastern Europe, in many cases taking positions in universities. They brought with them a commitment to modernist art and architecture and a familiarity with the great historicist tradition in the social sciences rooted in Karl Marx, Sigmund Freud, and Max Weber. The emergence of abstract expressionism in painting, the triumph of the International Style in architecture, and the ascendancy of the social sciences in the postwar American university are all inconceivable without their arrival.

Migration within the North American continent had cultural consequences as well. The almost overnight emergence in the South and West of industrial cities devoted to military production, the swelling of long-established manufacturing cities such as Detroit with new migrants from the South, and the conscription of some 16 million in the armed forces resulted in a mixing of cultural traditions and styles—especially among working-class Americans—that would yield innovations in many genres immediately after the war. Popular music especially reflected these cultural translations across ethno-racial and regional lines, as musical traditions from the black and white South, and from Latin America, collided to produce rock and roll and other new musical and cultural styles that galvanized a new youth culture after the war. The Zoot Suit riots in Los Angeles, the "double-V" struggle of African Americans to make the victory against fascism a victory against racism at home, and the riots in Harlem and Detroit during the war signaled the emergence of a new militancy among younger Mexican and African Americans and the rise to national attention of a politics organized around issues of racial justice. Likewise, the entrance of women into the paid marketplace in large numbers laid the groundwork for the "second-wave" feminism of the postwar period. The social upheaval of the war years thus left an egalitarian legacy in cultural styles and heightened Americans' awareness of the ways in which international influences and ethno-racial conflict at home shaped their values and modes of expression.

The consequences of the war for the country's moral imagination are more difficult to determine. The internment of thousands of Japanese-American citizens, the mass killing of millions in the Holocaust, and the use of aerial bombardment and then atomic weapons to bring the war against the Axis to an end are all issues of grave concern to anyone looking back on World War II from the perspective of the early twenty-first century. It is striking how little such horrific events figured in the culture of the war and its immediate aftermath. Norman Rockwell's upbeat series of "Four Freedoms" posters, Henry Luce's pronouncements about the "American century," and Henry Wallace's contrasting prediction of an emerging "people's century" all display an innocent optimism about human nature and postwar possibilities at odds with later views of the war, which saw the Holocaust and Hiroshima as turning points in human history. Throughout the war years, it was the rare intellectual who drew attention to "our" atrocities or noted the parallels between Nazi tactics and those of their opponents. Although the Holocaust would have to wait until the 1950s and 1960s to receive sustained reflection and analysis from American intellectuals, the obliteration of Hiroshima and Nagasaki did provoke the outrage of isolated critics, such as Lewis Mumford and Dwight Macdonald, who claimed—in Mumford's words—that "Hitler had . . . won the war" by infecting all nations with a toxic moral callousness and indifference to human suffering (*Sketches*, p. 436). But Mumford and Macdonald were a distinct minority in a country eager to put years of war and social upheaval behind it.

That said, there is no doubt that the horrors of the early 1940s, and the hardships of the decade before them, left a mark on popular memory that would militate against the triumphalist culture of the cold war era. Antiwar activists during the 1960s called their adversaries in the Pentagon "Eichmanns" and, following the lead of the young Bob Dylan, revived the folk-culture stance of the 1930s. Years later, Art Spiegelman's two-volume cartoon memoir, *Maus* (1986, 1991), brilliantly demonstrated how the Holocaust shaped the psyches of the children of survivors and unnerved the complacent optimism of others living in more peaceful, prosperous times. Even those postwar Americans who took a more positive view of their country's recent history had to acknowledge the unsettling lessons of the years between the end of World War I and the dropping of atomic bombs on Japan. During the 1950s and 1960s, television viewers became accustomed to the annual ritual of watching Frank Capra's *It's a Wonderful Life* around the Christmas holiday, warming to the film's sentimental affirmation that this life—the wonderful life of an imaginary Bedford Falls that had proven its decency by defeating Nazism—was the best of all possible lives. And yet Capra's film also spoke to a profound dread that the beloved little community of Bedford Falls might yet succumb to social chaos and violent rule by the rich and powerful, a threat envisioned in the imaginary Pottersville sequence that gave the film some of its most visually compelling moments. The moral and civic achievements of the New Deal era, the democratic values that had seemingly triumphed in the great antifascist struggle, were all precarious and in constant jeopardy. A ruthless, unchecked market, the brutal imposition of order by the wealthy, and the disintegration of communal values into a desperate individualism—as Capra's film made abundantly clear, these possibilities lurked just beneath the surface of the wonderful American life that stood victorious at war's end.

BIBLIOGRAPHY

Ashton, Dore. *The New York School: A Cultural Reckoning.* New York, 1973.

Baker, Houston, Jr. *Modernism and the Harlem Renaissance.* Chicago, 1987.

Bender, Thomas. *New York Intellect: A History of Intellectual Life in New York City.* New York, 1987.

Blake, Casey Nelson. *Beloved Community: The Cultural Criticism of Randolph Bourne, Van Wyck Brooks, Waldo Frank, and Lewis Mumford.* Chapel Hill, N.C., 1990.

Blum, John Morton. *V was for Victory: Politics and American Culture During World War II.* New York, 1976.

Bodnar, John. *Remaking America: Public Memory, Commemoration, and Patriotism in the Twentieth Century.* Princeton, N.J., 1992.

Boyer, Paul S. *By the Bomb's Early Light: American Thought and Culture at the Dawn of the Atomic Age.* New York, 1985.

Cohen, Lizabeth. *Making A New Deal: Industrial Workers in Chicago, 1919–1939.* New York, 1990.

Cooney, Terry A. *Balancing Acts: American Thought and Culture in the 1930s.* New York, 1995.

Corn, Wanda M. *The Great American Thing: Modern Art and National Identity, 1915–1935.* Berkeley, Calif., 1999.

Cowley, Malcolm. *Exile's Return.* New York, 1934, 1951.

Denning, Michael. *The Cultural Front: The Laboring of American Culture in the Twentieth Century.* London and New York, 1996.

Doss, Erika. *Benton, Pollock, and the Politics of Modernism: From Regionalism to Abstract Expressionism.* Chicago, 1991.

Douglas, Ann. *Terrible Honesty: Mongrel Manhattan in the 1920s.* New York, 1995.

Erenberg, Lewis A. *Steppin' Out: New York Nightlife and the Transformation of American Culture, 1890–1930.* Chicago, 1981.

———. *Swingin' the Dream: Big Band Jazz and the Rebirth of American Culture.* Chicago, 1998.

Fox, Richard Wightman. *Reinhold Niebuhr: A Life.* New York, 1985.

Graebner, William. *The Age of Doubt: American Thought and Culture in the 1940s.* Boston, 1991.

Haskell, Barbara. *The American Century: Art and Culture, 1900–1950.* New York, 1999.

Hoeveler, J. David. *The New Humanism: A Critique of Modern America, 1900–1940.* Charlottesville, Va., 1977.

Hollinger, David A. *In the American Province: Studies in the History and Historiography of Ideas.* Bloomington, Ind., 1985.

Huggins, Nathan Irvin. *Harlem Renaissance.* New York, 1971.

Hughes, Thomas P. *American Genesis: A Century of Invention and Technological Enthusiasm.* New York, 1989.

Hutchinson, George. *The Harlem Renaissance in Black and White.* Cambridge, Mass., 1995.

Kammen, Michael. *American Culture, American Tastes: Social Change and the Twentieth Century.* New York, 1999.

Koolhaas, Rem. *Delirious New York: A Retroactive Manifesto for Manhattan.* New York, 1994.

Lasch, Christopher. *The New Radicalism in America: The Intellectual as a Social Type, 1889–1963.* New York, 1965.

Lears, Jackson. *Fables of Abundance: A Cultural History of Advertising in America.* New York, 1994.

Lipsitz, George. *Rainbow at Midnight: Labor and Culture in the 1940s.* Urbana, Ill., 1994.

Marchand, Roland. *Advertising the American Dream: Making Way for Modernity, 1920–1940.* Berkeley, Calif., 1985.

Marsden, George M. *Fundamentalism and American Culture: The Shaping of Twentieth-Century Evangelicalism, 1870–1925.* New York, 1980.

McCarraher, Eugene. *Christian Critics: Religion and the Impasse in Modern American Social Thought.* Ithaca, N.Y., 2000.

Mumford, Lewis. *Sketches from Life: The Early Years.* New York, 1982.

Ogren, Kathy J. *The Jazz Revolution: Twenties America and the Meaning of Jazz.* New York, 1989.

O'Meally, Robert G., ed. *The Jazz Cadence of American Culture.* New York, 1998.

Pells, Richard W. *Radical Visions and American Dreams: Culture and Social Thought in the Depression Years.* New York, 1973.

Ray, Robert B. *A Certain Tendency of the Hollywood Cinema, 1930–1980.* Princeton, N.J., 1985.

Rogin, Michael. *Blackface, White Noise: Jewish Immigrants in the Hollywood Melting Pot.* Berkeley, Calif., 1996.

Rosenberg, Rosalind. *Beyond Separate Spheres: The Intellectual Roots of Modern Feminism.* New Haven, Conn., 1982.

Scott, William B., and Peter M. Rutkoff. *New York Modern: The Arts and the City.* Baltimore, 1999.

Stott, William. *Documentary Expression and Thirties America.* Chicago, 1986.

Susman, Warren I. *Culture as History: The Transformation of American Society in the Twentieth Century.* New York, 1984.

Sumner, Gregory D. *Dwight Macdonald and the Politics Circle: The Challenge of Cosmopolitan Democracy.* Ithaca, N.Y., 1996.

Westbrook, Robert. *John Dewey and American Democracy.* Ithaca, N.Y., 1991.

INDUSTRIALISM AND ITS CRITICS

Andrew Feffer

In the early days of the Republic, when most people worked on farms, in local commerce, or in small-scale manufacturing, "industry" commonly meant hard work. Its moral implications were governed largely by a Protestant ethic that took industriousness and its worldly accomplishments for evidence of divine blessing. Thus, a pillar of the community built his reputation on the regularity and profits of his labor in the field, countinghouse, or workshop. But as soon as one asked the question, "For whom and for what purpose is this work being done?" the notion of industry lost its apparent simplicity: Did one pursue economic gain, wealth, and luxury at the expense of others? Or, did obligations to the commonwealth set limits on individual enterprise? Did one work for oneself in an intrinsically rewarding occupation, the products of which embodied the skill and creativity of one's vocation? Or, did one work for a master and lose the independence of judgment and will that came with economic self-sufficiency?

After the Civil War, corporations and mechanized factory production displaced small manufactories and workshops, while the working day increasingly came under a regime of wage labor. On this new social and economic ground, Americans erected a modern outlook, simultaneously giving new meaning to the old term "industry" and new complexity to their existing concerns about civic responsibility, dependency, and community obligation.

Viewed simply as the capacity to produce goods, modern American industrialism promised an end to economic scarcity and a future of apparently limitless social progress. Yet, as the pursuit of profit brought unprecedented combinations of wealth and political power, the conviction grew that industrial development could injure as well as benefit the Republic. Existing notions of good citizenship did not rest comfortably with the spirit of enterprise that reigned over the Gilded Age (1865–1900). The new industrial elite, richer and less tied to community

and place than earlier elites, seemed to many to be acting contrary to the public interest, accumulating enormous fortunes to indulge their personal taste for luxuries and exercising vastly disproportionate clout in the increasingly corrupt worlds of local and national politics. On the other side of the emerging class divide, it seemed that independence, creativity, and craftsmanship steadily evaporated from workshops and occupations. It was no longer a simple task to measure character and moral standing by the fruits of one's labor, increasingly debased to drudgery in New England mills and New York City sweatshops (already familiar institutions by the 1840s). And as corporations dominated markets, one's tenure as a wage laborer looked less and less like a temporary stop on the road to becoming a freeholding farmer, a self-employed businessman, or an independent artisan, social stations believed by many to be prerequisites for responsible citizenship.

THE ETHIC OF INDUSTRIALISM

There were of course numerous defenders of the new industrialism. Acknowledging the evolution of industry into an overwhelmingly powerful social and economic interest, social Darwinists such as Andrew Carnegie and William Graham Sumner nevertheless argued that neither Protestant nor republican values were compromised by the rule of free-market competition and capital accumulation. One's riches, according to Sumner, reflected not only an individual capacity to produce marketable goods, but also the achievement of the "race," its advancement from a primitive to a civilized state in which the labor and sacrifices of earlier generations allowed greater industrial productivity and the accumulation of social wealth. It was nothing new to say that personal enrichment benefited the rest of humanity, or that the wealthy were entitled to their surplus of political power: Sumner merely translated an old argument into the nascent language of Darwinian biology. Nor was it surprising that a self-made millionaire like Carnegie agreed, even though, unlike Sumner, he believed the wealthy bore an obligation to redistribute their profits through cultural and educational institutions. For both, as for many other affluent Americans at the time, any disparities of wealth and status reflected the actual distributions of talent and industriousness that are natural to a modern, technologically advanced, and prosperous society. To legislate a change in that balance of economic power would compromise industrial prosperity: "Much better this great irregularity than universal squalor," Carnegie declared.

Sumner and Carnegie were not entirely wrong, even if their arguments were self-serving. The new industrial order was in large part achieved through the investment of personal wealth in burgeoning corporations, where mechanized production and enormous industrial sites allowed unparalleled efficiencies and economies of scale. Yet the accumulation of capital was only part of the picture. Equally important was a restructuring of industrial relations that transformed simple manufacturing into modern mass production.

Frederick Winslow Taylor's notorious innovations in factory management were emblematic of this revolution in the nature of work. Refining conventional industrial practices, Taylor methodically broke down craft traditions, intensifying the division of labor by shifting the conception and control of production from employees to a new and expanding level of engineers and middle management. Routinizing tasks to an unprecedented degree, Taylor also pitted employees against each other by introducing differential piece rates and bonus payment systems. The advocates of Taylor's and similar methods of scientific management were as eager to justify modern industrialism as Sumner and Carnegie. They claimed that, by increasing efficiencies and reducing costs, the new managerial techniques would bring greater prosperity and industrial peace. Taylor went even further. Scientific management, he insisted, "democratizes industry" under a "rule of law," moving labor-management relations from an arbitrary system of authority to one based on scientific truth.

DEMOCRACY AND INDUSTRY

Many Americans, however, perceived the relationship between industrialism and democracy differently than Taylor. They condemned the orgy of Gilded Age profit making and the modernization of manufacturing for disrupting stable communities and undermining representative government and, by the turn of the century, increasingly blamed the persistence of class strife on irresponsible industrial leadership. Yet, as critics tried to discipline industrialism, to make it serve the public good, they uncovered the weaknesses and confusions of time-honored political traditions, especially their incapacity for reconciling democratic expectations with industrial growth and the modern mass society that came with it. By the end of World War II, industrial democracy, the goal of a generation of intellectuals and social reformers, would remain an elusive ideal even as it became a commonplace in our political speech.

If managers like Taylor confused democracy with efficiency and economic growth, their employees generally did not. The historian David Montgomery and others have argued that until the 1920s much working-class opposition to industrialism invoked a republican tradition antithetical to Taylorism, emphasizing the virtue of productive labor as a basis for true citizenship, while defending the economic and occupational independence of small proprietors, artisans, and skilled workers. Striving to maintain workers' control over the conditions of employment, such "producerism" branched in several radically democratic directions, including the organization of unskilled workers in the Knights of Labor (founded 1869) and the immensely successful electoral campaigns of the Socialist Party under Eugene V. Debs (founded 1901). Debs argued that modern industrial capitalism corrupted the republic by degrading the worth of its citizens in the name of efficiency and the pursuit of profit. In the modern factory, Debs declared, "the human must be reduced to a hand. No head, no heart, no soul—simply a hand. A thousand hands to one brain—the hands of workingmen, the brain of a capitalist" (*Writings and Speeches*, p. 124). While American workers never embraced socialism with the fervor of their European counterparts, Debs's popularity crested in the 1912, 1916, and 1920 presidential elections, supported not only by craft workers and machine operators but also by agricultural laborers and farmers from formerly populist strongholds in Texas, Oklahoma, and Louisiana.

Searching for the means to restore public control to the nation's industrial life, middle-class intellectuals employed rhetoric that shared much in common with Debs's brand of working-class republicanism. In cities such as Boston and Chicago professionals joined forces with artisans to form an Arts and Crafts movement that flourished during the first decades of the twentieth century. Influenced by John Ruskin, William Morris, and the British Pre-Raphaelites most Arts and Crafts enthusiasts simply cultivated an aesthetic sensibility that would shelter their private lives from the ravages of industrialism and the artlessness of mass production. Pitting art against the machine, they endorsed the sale of handicrafts as an alternative to consumption of mass-produced goods, eventually turning their movement to the promotion of good taste in household decor, in publications such as *House Beautiful* and the *Ladies Home Journal.* Yet, other Arts and Crafts adherents, such as Oscar Lovell Triggs, founder of Chicago's Industrial Arts League, offered the spirit of craftsmanship as a basis for "restoring a soul" to mass production. Ruskin and Morris's communal antimodernism also permeated the reform agenda of major settlement houses, where Arts and Crafts activism mixed with moderate socialism and liberal Christianity. At Chicago's Hull-House (founded 1889), Ellen Gates Starr's classes typified that settlement's critical view of industrial life, as did the Hull-House labor museum, where Jane Addams and her colleagues reacquainted immigrant children with the fading artisan traditions of their home countries. Knowledge of the arts, Addams and Starr argued, did not merely add a fringe on the end of the working day but grounded the labor of an individual in the vital work of a community, a connection lost as displaced rural families collected in city neighborhoods.

Few intellectuals of this generation, however, would have returned the nation to a preindustrial age, even if they romanticized traditional communities. Like most Americans, intellectuals and reformers of the Progressive Era (1900–1917) considered industrial progress inevitable. Criticizing Arts and Crafts nostalgia for the age of handicraft, the architect Frank Lloyd Wright insisted art and machine were compatible and that the instinct of craftsmanship could coexist with the new mass production technology. Instead, it was the concentration of power, the fact that "society is still a sound aristocrat," as the philosopher John Dewey put it, which posed the central problem of industrial life as they saw it. Like Dewey, they hoped to make industrial relations "subordinate to human relations," believing only that preindustrial communities and artisanal occupations offered democratic principles and practices by which modern industrial society could be reconstructed.

PROGRESSIVE INTELLECTUALS AND THE LABOR MOVEMENT

Taming and humanizing industry would be no easy task, especially if that meant importing the solidarities of idealized community life into the world of modern market relations. By the turn of the century, intellectuals, moved by the great labor disputes of the previous three decades, conceded that trade-union representation through collective bargaining was a necessary means, appropriate as a counterbalance to the overwhelming power of corporate employers. Led by radical democrats such as the economist Richard Ely and socialists such as Debs and Florence Kelley, some progressive intellectuals even found themselves avid sponsors of the labor movement, especially its efforts during the 1910s to organize rapidly expanding mass-production industries such as garments, textiles, and meatpacking. The celebrated outpouring of sympathy for Paterson, New Jersey, silk workers in their 1913 strike (feted by the Greenwich Village Left at New York's Madison Square Garden) was only the most visible edge of the emerging coalition of progressive and left-wing intellectuals with labor. Massive garment strikes in Chicago and New York between 1909 and 1915 enlisted substantial support from academics, clerics, and middle-class reformers, mobilized in large part by leading settlements, by Margaret Dreier Robins's Women's Trade Union League (founded 1903) and by liberal churchmen like Walter Rauschenbusch.

Within that coalition competing versions of industrial democracy were staked out. Radically democratic forms of worker control (for example, management by shop committees) enjoyed strong support among democratic socialists such as Debs and syndicalists such as William Z. Foster. Even some conventionally progressive reformers like the social psychologist George Herbert Mead and the *New Republic* editor Herbert Croly endorsed a participatory organization of labor-management relations, if only because, as Mead argued, it would increase the efficiency and responsiveness of industry. The lawyer and future Supreme Court justice Louis Brandeis came to a similar position in the 1910s, arguing that only profit-sharing and worker management could guarantee the survival of democracy in an industrial setting. Such moderate versions of workplace democracy, however, were offered in a

"The Spirit of May Day." From the 28 April 1917 issue of the IWW newspaper *Solidarity*. The Industrial Workers of the World were formed to unite all workers, regardless of race, color, creed, or sex. The IWW organized workers by industry, differing from the American Federation of Labor, which organized workers according to a specific skill. © UNDERWOOD & UNDERWOOD/CORBIS

spirit of conciliation and compromise usually missing from more radical proposals. Resisting the notion that the growing antagonism between workers and industrialists represented an irreconcilable conflict of class interests, intellectual advocates of industrial democracy often looked askance at the more militant and uncompromising strategies of Debsian socialists or the anarcho-syndicalists who filled the ranks of insurrectionary organizations such as the Industrial Workers of the World (IWW), founded 1905. For progressive intellectuals, even those verbally committed to the democratic reform of industry, workers and their employers still shared a common ground in the moral economy of productive labor and a common interest in the health of their companies. In the words of Addams, this moderate position pursued "the larger solidarity which includes labor and capital," taking "a larger steadier view" than the worker "smarting under a sense of wrong" or the capitalist "ignoring human passion" (*Hull-House Maps and Papers,* pp. 196, 200, 202). And if progressive critics of industrialism sometimes followed contemporaries such as Kelley, William English Walling, and Upton Sinclair into the socialist movement (as did Starr, for example), they tended to end up as advocates of the gradual

collectivization of wealth and social resources under the banners of Fabianism or guild socialism.

The imperative to reconcile labor and capital to some extent explains the attraction of progressive intellectuals to cultural and educational means of ameliorating industrial conflict and restoring community and craft to modern life. Warning that schools were increasingly resembling factories, Dewey, Mead, and their colleagues at the University of Chicago joined local labor leaders in efforts to pass child-labor and compulsory education laws and to redistribute the intellectual fruits of technological and scientific progress by means of a universal common school system run on a democratic basis. The goal of such an educational democracy, as Dewey termed it, was similar to that of Addams, drawing like hers on romantic, antimodernist, and producerist critiques of industrial life. Progressive educators hoped to reestablish a closer, organic connection between book learning and the daily practices of a productive community, to be achieved in part by adding craft and art courses and by organizing the curriculum around a critical history of industry and agriculture. Dewey predicted such schools would compensate for the industrial division of labor culturally, by bringing together opposing class perspectives in their diverse graduates, who would be trained equally for "intellectual" and "manual" occupations.

THE PROMISE OF REGULATION

Meanwhile, critics of industry pursued the establishment of local and national legislation that would invest responsibility for the regulation of industrialism in the state. The promise of American life, its future as a democratic republic and as a prosperous nation, Croly concluded in his influential 1909 treatise, could only be achieved by loosing ideological attachments to the myth of an open and unregulated market. While progressives made enormous gains in the regulation of manufacturing, resistance prevailed through the 1920s, especially to more social democratic restrictions on investments, to the protection of labor rights, and to rules governing working conditions and the terms of employment. From the landmark case *Lochner v. New York* (1905) until the passage (and judicial survival) of the Wagner and Fair Labor Standards Acts (1935 and 1938, respectively), conservative Supreme Court rulings protecting freedom of contract threw up almost insurmountable obstacles to the efforts to regulate factory conditions and the length of the workday.

Conservative opposition, however, was not the only brake on legislating a more humane industrialism. An emphasis on social obligation and dependency competed in the progressive political culture with liberal traditions stressing individual rights over social responsibilities. To open a wedge for more extensive government controls, Florence Kelley, leading campaigns to end child and sweatshop labor, pioneered successful efforts to ground regulation of hours and working conditions in common-law protection of women and children. Kelley built a case on an ethical and legal framework that elevated the good of the commonwealth (seen in the particular case of women in terms of the value of motherhood to the community) over individual rights to freedom of contract. Tying criticism of industry and the regulation of working conditions to the protection of women, however, reinforced conventional notions of female inequality, pitting the pursuit of protective labor legislation against the movement for the passage of the Equal Rights Amendment in the 1920s, which Kelley (despite her commitment to the empowerment of women) opposed. Similar ambiguities characterized the positions of Croly and Brandeis, for whom regulation

skirted the boundaries of statist socialism in order to protect rights and enhance citizenship.

Despite the apparently widespread agreement among progressive intellectuals on the need for industrial regulation and trade-union representation, on the eve of the Great War industrial democracy remained a controversial notion. Differences hung in part on the vague, illusory, and often mutually inconsistent concepts of community and democracy drawn from the republican tradition, on middle-class fears of industrial strife, and on the persistent liberal conflation of democracy with economic opportunity and the protection of property rights. An important turning point in the attitudes of American intellectuals in general, the war deeply split socialists and progressives, with some long-term critics of industry such as Dewey, Croly, and Walling supporting the war effort, and others, such as Addams and Debs, opposing it. The successes of the War Industries Board and the National War Labor Board at temporarily regulating industrial production, mediating industrial disputes, and prodding the captains of industry to recognize collective bargaining rights convinced many progressives that industrial democracy was in the making. Many of them mobilized for the war effort, as propagandists and as planners in newly formed federal agencies. Yet, for the sake of building a tenuous regulatory framework and achieving a temporary acknowledgment of labor's perspective, intellectuals readily abandoned other democratic principles. Few of the war's supporters protested the banning of antiwar literature from the mails or the jailing and deportation of large numbers of socialist and anarchist opponents to the war, including some of America's most prominent critics of managerial authority, such as Debs, the Socialist Party's Kate Richards O'Hare, and the IWW's Bill Haywood. The spirit of "cooperation" that rationalized support for war mobilization and justified the repression of dissent could only be understood, argued the cultural critic Randolph Bourne, as a concession to the power of corporations to determine national priorities and manipulate a hysterical public.

INDUSTRIAL DEMOCRACY OR
BENEVOLENT DESPOTISM?

As would become evident in its aftermath, industrial planning during the war focused on efficiency at the expense of workplace democracy. That experience would set the pattern for future industrial reform. By the early 1920s, after a disastrous wave of strikes in 1919 and an extensive repression of political dissent, the climate of debate had changed. During the 1910s the coalition of labor and reform intellectuals had achieved in parts of selected industries (notably garment manufacturing) union recognition, third-party arbitration, and other contractual and institutionalized means of regulating the terms of employment. While industry abandoned much of the regulatory framework set up during war mobilization, on the basis of such accomplishments labor leaders like Sidney Hillman of the garment workers union and reformers such as Brandeis, whose settlement of the 1909 New York garment strike became a model for peaceful industrial relations, believed that a new age of industrial relations waited around the corner. Such beliefs reflected in part a declining interest of reformers and labor leaders alike in the participatory side of industrial reform and a growing commitment instead to a more moderate redistributive justice (in the form of wage increases and welfare benefits) that would renew opportunities for workers to move into the middle class. This position was strongly endorsed by the Wisconsin economist John Rogers Commons, who contended in *Industrial Government* (1921) that workers wanted "wages, hours, and security without financial responsibility." The failures of past attempts at cooperative ownership demonstrated to Commons that labor cannot by nature manage industry or participate directly in ownership. Industrial democracy, he maintained, is best achieved through the cooperation of labor with enlightened management to increase the national standard of living through industrial efficiency.

If Commons sounded like Taylor, it was in part because faith in enlightened management pervaded the intellectual life of the 1920s, encouraged by the consideration some industrialists gave to the criticisms leveled against industry over the previous forty years. It had become increasingly evident, even to some of the most zealous promoters of scientific management, that modern industry's systematic erosion of initiative and will from daily labor irrevocably undermined the credibility of a moral economy based on the work ethic and threatened the stability of urban communities that supplied labor for industry. By the time World War I began, such issues had become matters of public record and discussion. In his 1916 investigation of Taylorism, the sociologist Robert Franklin Hoxie echoed many of the objections of organized labor when he pointed out that scientific management limited the power of employees to negotiate the terms of employment, in principle granting management complete control of production. Whatever their theoretical claims, Hoxie concluded, in practice Taylorism and competing schools of scientific management instituted a "benevolent despotism" that intentionally subverted workplace solidarity and the quasi-democratic control employees had once exercised over their work lives. But, like others (including many labor leaders and socialists), Hoxie treated scientific management as a necessary evil: The industrial revolution inevitably broke down craft traditions anyway, he conceded, while Taylorism increased productivity, potentially enabling a rise in base wage-rates.

Hoxie's stance in many respects typified criticism of industry after the war, as the managerial revolution took on a more human face. There were indeed enlightened industrial leaders, such as General Electric's chairman Gerard Swope, who, taking advice from reformers like the industrial psychologist Elton Mayo and settlement activists like Addams and Alice Hamilton (founder of American industrial hygiene), introduced welfare programs and new personnel management techniques at such firms as GE and National Cash Register. Expressing contempt for Taylorist schemes to increase output through the use of piece rates, bonuses, and speedup, Mayo, who ran a long-term study of alternative production methods at Western Electric's Hawthorne plant in Chicago, called on managers to view the worker as "part of a whole," and address the employee's need for interest, solidarity, initiative, and recreation in the workplace environment. Labor management relations would be subsumed thereby into the larger field of "human relations," guided by the rational science of social and behavioral psychology.

Far from revolutionizing industry, however, the human relations approach reinforced managerial power, encouraging the belief that managers, guided by an enlightened interest in the good of the company and the efficiency of production, could defy the profit motive and other imperatives of the marketplace. Such views were shared across the political spectrum, by radical economists like Thorstein Veblen, who believed that a new managerial stratum, embodying the traditional ethic of craftsmanship, would value the technologies of production above private property, and by progressives such as Croly, who, despite his support for worker participation, concluded that reorganizing industrial production along such technocratic lines was the only means of establishing a true industrial democracy. A technocratic belief in the neutrality and good faith of the new managerial elite was also popular among socialists, like the GE engineer Charles Steinmetz, who considered the concentration of capital a precondition for social and political revolution and believed that the efficient functional organization of production and decision-making in corporations offered a model for good government based on meritocracy.

This was not the sort of industrial democracy envisioned twenty years earlier, either by Debs or Dewey. Intentionally or not, such reforms as Mayo's often increased, rather than reduced, the inequalities of the corporate workplace, widening the gap between factory labor and managerial expertise, ultimately doing little to turn a lifetime of drudgery into a rewarding occupation. While the subjects of Mayo's Hawthorne experiments reported higher job satisfaction as a result of the more humane organization of the work environment, they still enjoyed little control over managerial decisions. In their critical evaluation of corporate economic and legal relations, Adolf A. Berle and Gardiner C. Means warned of the authoritarian tendencies of the managerial bureaucracies taking over corporate enterprise. Nevertheless, like Veblen and Croly, they also endorsed managerial prerogatives and the new technocratic order that came with them, as a manner of collectivizing production, as well as elevating social and community needs over the profit seeking of stockholders. The appearance in 1932 of the Berle and Means study was timely: Their argument anticipated the establishment the following year of firmer government control, especially in financial markets, at the time held substantially responsible for the economic collapse of 1929.

THE PROBLEM OF THE PUBLIC

Critics of industrialism long recognized that it wrought its effects on American civic culture not simply through the transformation of work, but also by reshaping the nation's social geography. Industrial development and managerial restructuring created economic incentives for recruiting large numbers of unskilled workers from Asia, southern and eastern Europe, Latin America, Canada, and the rural United States, most of whom amassed in rapidly growing northern and Midwestern cities. The social and moral degradation of life in those cities became the subject of numerous nativist jeremiads, such as Josiah Strong's *Our Country* (1885), decrying the rising tide of immigration and predicting the moral and civic decay of the Protestant republic at the hands of "romanism," socialism, and intemperance.

Antiurban sentiments also nourished radical populist and progressive movements, for example, the People's Party in the 1890s and the Farmer-Labor Party of the 1930s. Pastoral strains ran through the progressive and socialist movements, evident in Pre-Raphaelite aesthetic sensibilities and an inclination to believe in the morally regenerative virtues of the countryside (such as that which guided the socialist Scott Nearing's retreat to Vermont during the Great Depression). Even conservative writers could yield radical, if not radically democratic, critiques of modern industry. In their uncompromising 1930 manifesto *I'll Take My Stand* (replete with explicit racism and nostalgia for an imaginary Old South), the Southern Agrarians exhorted southerners to embrace an agrarian and presumably more humane way of life instead of the materialism and "brutal and hurried" labors of modernity. While John Crowe Ransom's invocation in the manifesto of southern gentility rang false in the context of Jim Crow, the Southern Agrarians nonetheless marked off a critical vantage point from which to challenge industrial capitalism's unbridled conquest of nature.

While sharing conservative and antimodernist mistrust of industrial life, urban liberal and socialist critics of industrialism tended to accept the modern industrial city as a given, even while they struggled to change it into a more humane environment. The abhorrence of urban misery became a commonplace in the Progressive Era, graphically publicized in the literary exposés of novelists such as Theodore Dreiser and Anzia Yezierska and the reports and photos of muckraking journalists such as Jacob Riis, Lincoln Steffens, Lewis Hine, and Upton Sinclair. Like Strong, although without his moral fervor or bigotry, some progressives initially perceived social order to be threatened by the influx of non-Protestant factory labor. Yet, "Americanizing" these immigrant populations became only one of the many strategies for reconstructing the communitarian foundations that Victorians believed undergirded the stability of the body politic. As social science drifted toward primarily secular concerns, the specific cultural backgrounds of the urban population became less important than the fact of deracination and dislocation. The erosion of community and family by the uprooting of peasants from supposedly traditional societies in Europe preoccupied reformers such as Addams and her settlement colleagues Sophonisba Breckinridge and Grace Abbott. Low family wages, factory employment of young women, and the temptations of the saloon and the city streets, they argued, all contributed to juvenile crime, prostitution, alcoholism, and civic disorder. Thus, in Hull-House's pioneering study of urban social geography, *Hull-House Maps and Papers* (1895), the map of community life and the network of associations among immigrants was almost as important as documenting deplorable sanitary and housing conditions.

Related questions appeared in the work of the Chicago sociologist Robert Ezra Park about the capacity of urban populations to act as part of a rational citizenry. Under the influence of economic necessity, unhinged from traditional frameworks of belief, manipulated by advertising and poorly informed by the news media, immigrant working class populations drifted somewhere between behaving like an impulsive crowd and acting as a responsible public. Elton Mayo conceptually framed his Hawthorne experiments in a like manner, by a concern about "extensive social disintegration" and the erosion of the work ethic. Such apprehension recurred throughout the 1920s, motivating pathbreaking anthropological and sociological studies of life and attitudes in industrial communities, such as William I. Thomas and Florian Znaniecki's *The Polish Peasant in Europe and America* (1927) and Robert and Helen Lynd's *Middletown* (1929). It also appears in unexpected places, such as Margaret Mead's *Coming of Age in Samoa* (1928), offered as an effort to understand through comparative ethnography the effects of a chaotic and morally unanchored "American civilization" on the "difficulties and maladjustments of youth." Led by a new generation of cultural critics such as Waldo Frank and Lewis Mumford, American intellectuals became increasingly wary of the "mass culture" that governed urban life, even as the American population embraced that culture with rising enthusiasm.

Yet, troubled though they may have been by the corrosive effects of the "acids of modernity," social scientists nonetheless believed it possible to reconstitute the public democratically, even amidst the squalor of industrial cities, by expanding political participation, democratizing education, and investigating and publicizing the problems of modern society. Such faith in the democratic spirit, espoused most prominently in the interwar period by Dewey, did not convince the journalist Walter Lippmann, who in the 1920s persistently questioned the capacity of common citizens to constitute a self-governing public in an overwhelmingly complex world: none were educated or intelligent enough, nor sufficiently resistant to the manipulations of the press and ad-

vertising, to comprehend the intricacies of social and political governance. The individual must relinquish some part of his or her authority, Lippmann concluded, to those with specialized knowledge or expertise. Despite his experience in socialist and progressive movements, Lippmann did not trust the forms of ethnic, social, and political solidarity (within which informed citizenship could be constituted) offered as alternatives to market individualism. Nor did cultural critics like Frank and Mumford, who, though influenced by Deweyan pragmatism, lacked the philosopher's trust in political institutions and grew more and more reliant on elite forms of cultural regeneration to resurrect organic communitarian ideals.

FROM CULTURAL FRONT TO POSTWAR CONSENSUS

This new mistrust of public life in mass industrial society conformed to declining expectations for democratizing industry, as labor relations became predicated on negotiating industrial peace, increasing efficiency, and raising productivity and wages. Meanwhile, the few intellectuals and labor activists who entered the communist movement took a somewhat different approach, translating the popular democratic traditions of earlier socialism and radicalism into an embrace of mass society and mass politics, with few or none of Lippmann's reservations about the public's capacity for self-governance. Founded in the wake of the 1917 Bolshevik Revolution, the Communist Party's initial critique of industrialism emerged from conventional Marxism as well as the pragmatic syndicalism of William Z. Foster, who rose to national prominence as the leader of efforts to organize the meatpacking and steel industries in the late 1910s and who directed the party's labor activism through the 1920s. Culturally, intellectually, and politically, communism floundered through the 1920s, riven by internal factionalism and undermined by inconsistent directives from Moscow.

The stock market crash of 1929 and ensuing depression, however, brought a dramatic leftward shift in the political climate, rekindling anticapitalist movements and with them intellectual and cultural critiques of corporate industrialism. Writers, artists, critics, and academics collected around socialist, communist, and anarchosyndicalist organizations that proliferated in cities across the country, largely in conjunction with the rise of industrial unionism under the Congress of Industrial Organizations (founded 1935), giving birth to a cultural movement that would transform American arts and letters in the years before World War II. While diverse in political affiliation, many of these groups circulated within what the historian Michael Denning has called the "cultural front," the amorphous cloud of cultural and political activism at the center of which stood the Communist Party. While it was similar to working-class republicanism in believing in the nobility of toil, this new cultural Left offered a critique of industrialism and a vision of industrial democracy with relatively little stake in preserving premodern forms of democratic solidarity. Meanwhile, the noncommunist Left organized its own cultural critiques of capitalism and industrial life that disavowed the authoritarian designs of the Soviet Union. Much of the critical vocabulary for discussing the emergence of mass culture in industrial and postindustrial society we owe to progressives and anti-Stalinists like Mumford, Dwight Macdonald, and the writers and critics associated with publications like the *Partisan Review*.

As the mood of the nation shifted, reformers found in the Great Depression the opportunity to change the organization of the American political economy. The coalition that brought Franklin Delano Roosevelt to power in the election of 1932, however, had neither a unified vision nor a single guiding philosophy. In the first years of the New Deal, President Roosevelt's amalgam of regulatory reform and fiscal intervention began extending state power to control markets, labor relations, and in-vestment capital. The achievement of a labor bill of rights in the Wagner Act and the Fair Labor Standards Act seemed to signal the advent of the kind of industrial reform that had animated earlier movements for industrial democracy. Yet, the more aggressive regulatory state proposed by New Dealers such as Thurman Arnold and W. Jett Lauck, which would have changed some of the institutional relations of industrial capitalism, lost out in the late 1930s to advocates of government fiscal intervention to stimulate economic growth. This more conservative Keynesianism was aimed primarily at raising and sustaining the level of mass consumption without significantly changing or regulating capitalism. Much as earlier defenders of industrialism had conflated industrial efficiency and high wages with democracy, the new outlook of the 1940s offered Americans economic growth and higher living standards in place of democratic control over their work lives or even a moderately social democratic regulatory state.

It was by such growth, prosperity, and industrial peace, managed within the favorable labor contracts of the late 1940s and government's fiscal management of the economy, that Americans came to define industrial democracy in the postwar period. It occupied what the historian Arthur Schlesinger Jr., called the "vital center" of American political life. From that center most dissenting views were soon excluded and with them the more trenchant critiques of industrialism that had flourished earlier in the century.

See also **The Culture and Critics of the Suburb and the Corporation; The Design of the Familiar** *(volume 2);* **Technology; Technological Enclaves** *(volume 3); and other articles in this section.*

BIBLIOGRAPHY

Berle, Adolf A., and Gardiner C. Means. *The Modern Corporation and Private Property.* New York, 1968.

Blake, Casey Nelson. *Beloved Community: The Cultural Criticism of Randolph Bourne, Van Wyck Brooks, Waldo Frank, and Lewis Mumford.* Chapel Hill, N.C., 1990.

Boris, Eileen. *Art and Labor: Ruskin, Morris, and the Craftsman Ideal in America.* Philadelphia, 1986.

Carnegie, Andrew. "The Gospel of Wealth." In *Words That Made American History.* Edited by Richard Current, John A. Garraty, and Jules Weinberg. Boston, 1978.

Commons, John R., et al. *Industrial Government.* New York, 1921.

Croly, Herbert. *Progressive Democracy.* New York, 1914.

———. *The Promise of American Life.* New York, 1909.

Debs, Eugene V. "Unionism and Socialism." *Appeal to Reason* report (1904) reprinted in *Writings and Speeches of Eugene V. Debs,* pp. 95–125. New York, 1948.

Denning, Michael. *The Cultural Front: The Laboring of American Culture in the Twentieth Century.* London, 1997.

Dewey, John. "The Ethics of Democracy." In *The Early Works of John Dewey.* Edited by Jo Ann Boydston. Carbondale, Ill., 1969. Vol. 1, pp. 227–249.

———. *The Public and Its Problems.* Chicago, 1954.

Feffer, Andrew. *The Chicago Pragmatists and American Progressivism.* Ithaca, N.Y., 1993.

Fink, Leon. *Progressive Intellectuals and the Dilemmas of Democratic Commitment.* Cambridge, Mass., 1997.

Fraser, Steve, and Gary Gerstle, eds. *The Rise and Fall of the New Deal Order, 1930–1980.* Princeton, N.J., 1989.

Gilbert, James Burkhart. *Designing the Industrial State: The Intellectual Pursuit of Collectivism in America, 1880–1940.* Chicago, 1972.

Haber, Samuel. *Efficiency and Uplift: Scientific Management in the Progressive Era, 1890–1920.* Chicago, 1964.

Hoxie, Robert Franklin. *Scientific Management and Labor.* New York, 1915.

Johanningsmeier, Edward P. *Forging American Communism: The Life of William Z. Foster.* Princeton, N.J., 1994.

Lasch, Christopher. *The True and Only Heaven: Progress and Its Critics.* New York, 1991.

Lippmann, Walter. *The Phantom Public.* 1925. Reprint, New Brunswick, N.J., 1993.

Mayo, Elton. *The Human Problems of an Industrial Civilization.* New York, 1977.

Montgomery, David. *The Fall of the House of Labor: The Workplace, the State, and American Labor Activism, 1865–1925.* New York, 1987.

Noble, David. *America by Design: Science, Technology, and the Rise of Corporate Capitalism.* New York, 1977.

Park, Robert Ezra. *On Social Control and Collective Behavior: Selected Papers.* Edited by Ralph H. Turner. Chicago, 1967.

Residents of Hull-House. *Hull-House Maps and Papers.* 1895. Reprint, New York, 1970.

Rock, Virginia, ed. *I'll Take My Stand: The South and the Agrarian Tradition, by Twelve Southerners.* Baton Rouge, La., 1977.

Rodgers, Daniel T. *The Work Ethic in Industrial America, 1850–1920.* Chicago, 1978.

Salvatore, Nick. *Eugene V. Debs: Citizen and Socialist.* Urbana, Ill., 1982.

Sklar, Katherine Kish. *Florence Kelley and the Nation's Work: The Rise of Women's Political Culture, 1830–1900.* New Haven, Conn., 1995.

Strum, Philipa. *Brandeis: Beyond Progressivism.* Lawrence, Kans., 1993.

Taylor, Frederick Winslow. *Principles of Scientific Management.* 1911. Reprint, Chicago, 1967.

Wald, Alan. *The New York Intellectuals: The Rise and Decline of the Anti-Stalinist Left from the 1930s to the 1980s.* Chapel Hill, N.C., 1987.

Zimmerman, Joan. "The Jurisprudence of Equality: The Women's Minimum Wage, the First Equal Rights Amendment, and *Adkins v. Children's Hospital,* 1905–1923." *Journal of American History* 78 (June 1991): 188–225.

CULTURAL MODERNISM

Dickran Tashjian

THE AMERICANIZATION OF MODERNIZATION

In *The Autobiography of Alice B. Toklas,* published in 1933, Gertrude [Stein] has Alice say:

> Gertrude Stein always speaks of America as being now the oldest country in the world because by the methods of the civil war and the commercial conceptions that followed it America created the twentieth century, and since all the other countries are now either living or commencing to be living a twentieth century of life, America having begun the creation of the twentieth century in the sixties of the nineteenth century is now the oldest country in the world. (p. 96)

By the reversals of Stein's logic, the New World of America became the Old and the European Old World became the New. Or rather, through the accelerations of advanced machine technology, a transformed United States came to spread the gospel of modernity throughout Europe, which, exhausted after World War I, found itself being made over in the image of a mechanized America.

As Stein noted, these developments did not occur overnight, and the years of World War I followed by the 1920s and 1930s were decisive in the Americanization of modernization. New energy sources (oil and electricity) harnessed to mechanized systems of production resulted in the moving assembly line, developed most notably at Henry Ford's automobile plant in 1913. In the aftermath of World War I, the United States shifted its industrial might from the war to the home front, thereby standing at the forefront of what was widely recognized as the machine age. In addition to a broad range of durable goods, American factories began to manufacture other machines for domestic use. Thus, mass production mechanized the home as well as the workplace. In this unprecedented opportunity for mass consumption, the kitchen became the domestic site of electrical appliances, rivaled only by the garage for the automobile, superseding the stable or barn for the horse. It would

not be far-fetched for Americans to think of their homes as "a machine for living," as the Swiss architect Le Corbusier put it in the 1920s.

By 1930, less than a half century after the frontier had closed, the United States was no longer a rural nation, its landscape transformed by growing urban areas as well as new roads and bridges to accommodate the automobile. A majority of Americans were moving to the city, whose modernity was symbolized by high-rise Manhattan in New York. Paris reluctantly ceded its claim as the world's modern city to New York, whose tall buildings were made possible by elevators and their steel skeletal frames. New York is "a complete work of art," marveled the young artist Marcel Duchamp, interviewed upon his arrival from Paris in 1915. Five years later, he gave up the title of artist and declared himself to be an engineer—tacit recognition that the engineer had become the heroic figure of the machine age.

GROWTH OF A MODERN CULTURE

To see Manhattan as a work of art is to lend a cultural form to the process of modernization. If modernization profoundly changed the social landscape, modernism referred to the cultural possibilities of this new world dominated by machines. Almost inevitably, then, machines were invested with symbolic values. As early as 1913, the American painter John Marin celebrated a Manhattan that was "alive," with "great forces at work" in his watercolors of exploding, fragmented skyscrapers. "If these buildings move me they too must have life. Thus the whole city is alive . . . and the more they move me the more I feel them to be alive," Marin claimed (*Camera Work,* nos. 42–43, April–July, 1913, p. 18). Some ten years later, in *Broom,* an American little magazine published in Paris, French critic Jean Epstein expanded upon Marin's enthusiastic observation: "All these instruments: the telephone, microscope, magnifying glass, cinematograph, lens, microphone, gramophone, automobile, kodak, aeroplane, are not merely dead objects" (Epstein, "New Conditions," *Broom* 2, April 1922, p. 10).

Adding the burgeoning mass media and the new forms to his list of technological wonders, Epstein argued that "these machines become part of ourselves, interposing themselves between the world and us, filtering reality as the screen filters radium emanations. Thanks to them, we have no longer a stable, clear, continuous, constant notion of an object." Anticipating media guru Marshall McLuhan, Epstein recognized the way that technology becomes an extension of ourselves while emphasizing the disorientation that results from these innovations. Epstein was also offering an explanation for the visual dislocations and fragmentations of cubism, an avant-garde movement begun by Pablo Picasso and Georges Braque before World War I. Their visual experiments challenged the pictorial conventions of Renaissance perspective and its fixed point of view.

Ultimately, Epstein was acknowledging the subtle changes in human perception and consciousness caught up in this new world of advanced technology. Thus, the purchase of a radio meant more than finding space for it in the living room. Mere entertainment perhaps, but it was also a new way of perceiving, hence knowing, the world. In short, advanced technology brought about profound changes in American culture—changes in the values, attitudes, and ideas that inform patterns of behavior. Entering the machine age, Americans became engaged in the culture of modernism, partly a home-grown response to modernization and partly a European importation.

THE 1913 ARMORY SHOW

If Europe lagged behind the United States in modernization, the Old World, with its entrenched academies, emerged as the site of avant-garde formations that produced a disturbing new art that would be construed as "modern" in the United States. Having settled in Paris in 1903, Gertrude Stein was soon attracted to the avant-garde paintings of Henri Matisse and Pablo Picasso, acknowledged leaders of fauvism and cubism, respectively. Their work was featured at a landmark exhibition in New York City held at the Sixty-ninth Regiment Armory in 1913.

It was there that Epstein's ideas were dramatically brought home to Americans, though not with a clarity that the distance of a decade would bring to his essay of 1929 in *Broom*. The Armory Show had been organized by an association of American artists who were dissatisfied with the meager exhibition opportunities that were available in an art world dominated by conservative academies in New York, Boston, and Philadelphia. What was conceived as an American showcase was soon expanded to include contemporary European artists, as an energetic deputation to Europe managed to round up some of the most advanced work available. Needless to say, avant-garde European art eclipsed most of the American art on view at the Armory.

In presenting a vast farrago of European avant-garde artists, the Armory Show was an iconoclastic event that took on scandalous proportions through the mass media. The Europeans were variously branded as revolutionaries, crazies, degenerates, or charlatans. Such epithets, however, should not be dismissed simply as exaggerations, any more than they were mere metaphors for the unfamiliar. Conservative American art critics and the public alike engaged in denigration of a literal sort, because they sensed that avant-garde art represented a new way of seeing and hence a new way of knowing the world. Old habits and modes of perception were threatened all the more intensively, because aesthetic developments and visual styles appeared compressed in the Armory display. Whereas "modern" poetry in the guise of imagism had been introduced in 1912 to a limited readership in *Poetry*, Harriet Monroe's Chicago-based magazine, Americans became widely aware of modern art through the Armory Show, which was highly publicized. It subsequently traveled to Chicago and closed in Boston.

American artists who considered themselves progressive were dismayed to discover that they had been outflanked by European work. Some, however, were converted to the new art. Stuart Davis, for example, was moved upon viewing the exhibition to avow that he "would quite definitely have to become a 'modern' artist" (Sims, *Stuart Davis*, p. 20). Only nineteen years old in 1913, Davis would take the better part of the next decade to assimilate the formal lessons of the Armory Show and achieve a "colonial cubism," as he would later title a painting.

The Armory Show was a two-pronged affair. While the exhibition had all the earmarks of a revolution to an unprepared American public (and artists as well), the show was also conservatively pitched by its proponents as an educational event in an effort to win over the uninitiated. Adverse criticism indicated the difficulties of importing European avant-garde art into American networks of galleries, museums, and private collections. Since it was all too easy to conflate an avant-garde movement or "ism" with anarchism, viewed as a live, bomb-throwing movement threatening corporate America, it was far better to speak euphemistically of "modern art," as a way to domesticate and sanitize avant-garde art, its formal qualities stripped of threatening cultural and political implications. Modernism as a generic label filled the bill, allowing the new art to be seen as international and timeless, above the political fray.

Even so, modern art was but slowly assimilated into American society and culture. Only by late 1929 did the Museum of Modern Art (MOMA), backed by the Rockefellers and other wealthy patrons of the arts, open its doors in Manhattan. MOMA was viewed as heir to the Armory Show. None other than Lloyd Goodrich, who became director of the Whitney Museum of American Art, made the connection in witnessing "the final apotheosis of modernism and its acceptance by respectable society" (Lynes, *Good Old Modern,* p. 65). With its first loan exhibition of the late-nineteenth-century paintings of Gauguin, Cézanne, Seurat, and van Gogh, MOMA embarked upon establishing a high modernist canon in American culture.

The long-term trade-offs were costly for the avant-garde, as evidenced by MOMA's 1936 exhibition of Dada, Surrealism, and Fantastic Art, the latter an element running through two major movements that extended back to World War I. Just as the Italian Futurists, who glorified the machine and war prior to the World War, were excluded from the Armory Show because they wanted to exhibit as a group, Alfred H. Barr denied the request of the French poet André Breton to mount a separate exhibition for the Surrealists, whose experimental art and poetry in the 1920s explored the unconscious and sexual themes. The subsequent exhibition turned into a sprawling spectacle, one in which Breton, as the Surrealist leader, was lost in the shuffle, and more crucially, one in which the radical political interests of the Surrealists was muted. Dadaism, an internatioinal movement from which Surrealism developed, attacked the horrors of World War I by espousing nonsense, anarchism, and nihilism. The movement was similarly subdued when the militant German communist John Heartfield, still protesting the obscenities of Nazi rule, was omitted from the exhibition.

ALFRED STIEGLITZ AND HIS CIRCLE

Watching the Armory Show from the sidelines was the preeminent photographer Alfred Stieglitz, who ran the Little Galleries of the Photo-Secession, otherwise known as 291 because of its address on lower Fifth Avenue in Manhattan. Stieglitz began exhibiting paintings at 291 in 1908, thanks to his friendship with Edward Steichen, a photographer who was also a painter at the time. Through Steichen's Parisian contacts, Stieglitz exhibited Picasso, Rodin, and Matisse prior to the Armory Show. At America's entry into World War I in 1917, Stieglitz shut down 291 and then opened the Intimate Gallery in 1925, which was superseded by An American Place in 1929 on Madison Avenue until his death in 1946. Despite their tenuous existence, his galleries served as intermittent social centers for an aspiring American avant-garde.

By the 1920s Stieglitz shifted his interest from the European avant-garde to a small group of American painters forging an American modernism: Arthur G. Dove, John Marin, Marsden Hartley, and Charles Demuth. Stieglitz met Georgia O'Keeffe, then an unknown painter, during World War I (they married in 1924). While all of these artists painted in a nonrepresentational manner, Dove having perhaps anticipated Wassily Kandinsky in painting the first modern abstraction, they all nonetheless remained to varying degrees rooted in a recognizable image, often tied to the natural landscape. (O'Keeffe's early watercolor landscapes deployed lush abstract washes.) With the exception of O'Keeffe, these artists had all established their visual signatures in their modernist quest during World War I. Indeed, Hartley and Marin had been well represented at the Armory Show.

Of the group, Demuth was the most urbane, his sensibility bound to the city, whether painting watercolors of the gay scene, Duchamp on the town in Greenwich Village, or witty and ironic images of industrial architecture. After an early period of painting Manhattan's structures (the Woolworth Building, Brooklyn Bridge), Marin devoted his efforts primarily to the Maine coast. Only O'Keeffe in the 1920s took up the challenge of New York (and the difficulties of being part of Stieglitz's male coterie) to paint skyscrapers, most notably, *City Night* (1926).

Stieglitz became increasingly isolated from his circle during the 1920s and 1930s, as the artists scattered from New York. Because of diabetes, Demuth was restricted to his hometown of Lancaster, Pennsylvania. By the end of the 1920s, O'Keeffe spent more and more of her time in the Southwest, joined for a while by the photographer Paul Strand, who had become Stieglitz's protégé during World War I. After a largely unsettled existence, Hartley finally returned to Maine; Dove lived on a sailboat off Long Island Sound; and Marin lived in Maine and New Jersey. Their lives, then, had a double tether, one end in New York, where Stieglitz held court at An American Place, and the other at various locations throughout the country. While they found it impossible to ignore their machine age environment, they were finally attracted to the natural landscape in their art.

ART FROM A MACHINE

Part of Stieglitz's strategy in championing nonrepresentational painting at 291 was to establish the integrity of photography as an art form in its own right. Since the invention of photography in the nineteenth century, academic painters had argued that the new medium could not possibly rank among the fine arts because the image was made by a machine. In response, photographers tried to emulate painting by taking soft-focus images of genteel subjects deemed worthy of fine art. They also manipulated the negative and the subsequent print in ways that would lend it the semblance of, say, an impressionist painting.

Early in his career, Stieglitz successfully adopted "pictorial" photography, as it was called, winning several awards in Europe in the process. Around 1910, however, as he began to take photographs of Manhattan, he came to change his mind. Railroad yards, steamers, skyscrapers, construction sites— these seemed beyond the realm of the genteel; the dynamic growth of Manhattan called for a different approach. He turned to "straight" photography, which required sharply focused images without manipulation of negative or print. Photographs that seemed artless and direct were thought to be somehow commensurate with the bold presence of this raw and powerful urban scene.

Stieglitz took the offensive on the occasion of the Armory Show by giving himself an exhibition at 291. His journal *Camera Work* (1903–1917), which presented the debates over the artistic and aesthetic possibilities of the camera, increasingly advocated straight photography. Stieglitz ironically called his photographs "snapshots" as a way to test their antiartistic qualities against the latest European art, which in its abstract tendencies also had

been derided by conservative critics as beyond the pale of art. Stieglitz's stratagem turned the tables on the academicians. His photographs, which exploited the capacity of the camera for mimetic representation, pointed out the inadequacies of academic painting and in the process validated modernist nonrepresentation as a way of seeing and painting.

Paul Strand became the heir to straight photography. His prints were published in the last two issues of *Camera Work* (1917). Not only did he survey New York, its buildings and its people, but he also took close-ups of bowls, which transformed a still life into an abstraction, thereby suggesting that the boundaries between painting and photography were permeable. In 1921 Strand joined forces with Charles Sheeler, a straight photographer (and painter), to make *Manhatta*, a short film that celebrated modern New York with subtitles taken from Walt Whitman.

MARCEL DUCHAMP AND THE READY-MADE

In 1915 Duchamp arrived a celebrity in New York. His *Nude Descending a Staircase, No. 2* (1912) in the Armory Show had captured the public imagination as emblematic of all that was wrong with modern art: "an explosion in a shingle factory" or "the rude descending a staircase during rush hour," it was called. Duchamp was serenely prepared to send some more shock waves through the New York art world. In 1913 he had set aside painting when he mounted a bicycle wheel with its front fork on a stool. The implicit motion of his descending nude was here gained by a mere flick of the wheel, laconically titled *Bicycle Wheel*. The following year he selected a rack for drying wine bottles, which he called *Bottlerack*. Generically, he called these enigmatic objects "ready-mades" because they were mass-produced artifacts that he but minimally manipulated.

In 1917 Duchamp went public with his ready-mades, which had been known only to a few who visited his studio. American artists finally organized a follow-up to the Armory Show, no less massive in size, but with a twist. The organizers (including Stieglitz) of this exhibition of "Independents" decided to eliminate juries as a way to stand in contrast to their academic colleagues. To highlight their egalitarian outlook, the committee declared that anyone could enter work in the exhibition upon payment of a modest entry fee.

Duchamp decided to test these principles by submitting a urinal, titled *Fountain* and signed

Marcel Duchamp, *Nude Descending a Staircase, No. 2.*
Oil on canvas, 58 × 35 in., 1912. The stir created by
Duchamp's work at the Armory Show offers a sense of the
cultural environment of the era, a time when many of
America's most important artists emigrated to Europe.
© BURSTEIN COLLECTION/CORBIS

Duchamp's submission of a mass-produced urinal to an art exhibition dramatically integrated the
industrial network with the art network—two systems of production that had hitherto been thought
incommensurate and hence incompatible. Duchamp brilliantly exposed the way that modernism
and modernization were related. In the process he
ambiguously expanded the cultural category of art
to include machines and machine-made artifacts.
The controversy surrounding the ready-made *Fountain* indicates, however, the extent to which modernism and modernization stood in uneasy relation.
That an established institution such as MOMA
could mount a popular exhibition titled *Machine
Art* in 1934 reveals how, in fewer than twenty years,
the machine had infiltrated American culture.

DEBATE OVER THE MACHINE

The 1920s opened with the controversy over the
machine still raging. In 1919 the novelist and cultural critic Waldo Frank published an indictment of
industrial society in *Our America.* Fearing alienation and spiritual starvation bred by the machine,
Frank sought a "mystical" America predicated on
the nationalism of the poet Walt Whitman. Set
against Frank was the young expatriate writer Matthew Josephson, who in a series of articles for *Broom*
celebrated an America taken over by the machine
and intoxicated by the mass media: "the Billposters
enunciate their wisdom, the Cinema transports us,
the newspapers intone their gaudy jargon; where . . .
skyscrapers rise lyrically to the exotic rhythms of
jazz bands which upon waking up we find to be
nothing but the drilling of pneumatic hammers on
steel girders" ("The Great American Billposter,"
Broom 3, 1922, p. 305).

Josephson derived his position from Robert
Coady, a New York art dealer, who in 1916–1917
published *The Soil,* a journal that called for the creation of American art out of things American, found
primarily in the popular arts, ranging from vaudeville and the movies to advertising. "Our art is, as
yet, outside of our art world," he declared. It was
to be found in the spirit of the machine age. The
enthusiasm for things American among Josephson's
Parisian friends was also contagious, summed up in
1930 by the poet Philippe Soupault in *The American
Influence in France.* Yet sheer enthusiasm, no more
than condemnation, simply begged the questions
posed by the social and cultural impact of advanced
technology. Did machines threaten to turn human
beings into automatons? Short of such dehumani-

pseudonymously "R. Mutt." *Fountain* was found offensive by many of the organizers, and, after intense
debate, the urinal was rejected and hidden behind
a screen; it was later removed by Duchamp and
taken to 291, where Stieglitz photographed it. In
protest, the "Richard Mutt Case" was bruited in *The
Blind Man* (No. 2, 1917, p. 5; unsigned), a journal
initially intended to celebrate the independents.
Fountain was incisively defended. It was hardly "immoral," because urinals were often on public display in plumbing shops. Most crucially, the issue of
mass production was irrelevant, because Duchamp
had "chosen" the object and given it a new context
in an art exhibition. The essay concluded by claiming
that "the only works of art America has given are her
plumbing and her bridges."

zation, what was the impact of advanced technology on traditional culture? How might artists respond to this overwhelming presence? Then as now, answers were difficult to come by, compelling the critic Oliver Sayler to survey the issues facing art and culture in the machine age in a 1930 collection of essays titled *Revolt in the Arts.*

SPIRITUALIZING THE MACHINE

One of the first salvos in this controversy was fired at the start of the 1920s by T. S. Eliot with his multi-voiced poem, *The Waste Land* (1922). The title suggests a sweeping indictment of contemporary civilization, characterized by spiritual drought: indifferent and unfeeling lovers ("the young man carbuncular," the "typist home at teatime"), gray London crowds of living dead, office workers regimented by the clock ("when the human engine waits / like a taxi throbbing"), and robotic women ("she smoothes her hair with automatic hand"). As for the arts, the poem offers only a parodic "Shakespeherian Rag." Modern life clearly held little prospect for spiritual regeneration recorded in ancient vegetation myths and promised by Christian resurrection.

An indignant William Carlos Williams registered his protests in poetry and prose. Although he admired the formal innovations of *The Waste Land,* he believed that the expatriate Eliot had set back the development of American poetry by living abroad. Williams, a physician in Rutherford, New Jersey, sought a distinctly American poetry by making "contact," as he put it, with the local, with the particulars of American life. Like Josephson, Williams carried on Coady's call for the creation of an American art out of things American.

Williams was a committed modernist with an urban sensibility. In seeking friendships with visual artists, he centered on the avant-garde group of painters surrounding Stieglitz, especially Hartley and Demuth. For Williams, contact meant opening up one's self to the immediacy of fresh experience. "The new, the everlasting new!" became his credo. Hence, his celebration of "Spring and All" (1923) is up against the spiritual despair expressed in the opening lines of *The Waste Land:* "April is the cruellest month, breeding / Lilacs out of the dead land."

Spending much of his time in the industrial decay of Paterson, New Jersey, treating immigrant patients, Williams observed "the stiff curl of wildcarrot leaf" "by the road to the contagious hospital" (Litz and MacGowan, eds., "Spring and All," *Com-*

William Carlos Williams (1883–1963). Photograph, c. 1958. In addition to his poetry Williams wrote early essays on the work of literary modernists such as Gertrude Stein and James Joyce. © BETTMANN/CORBIS

plete Collected Poems, vol. 1, 1986, p. 183). Beyond these marginal signs of natural growth crowded out by the roadway, he could appreciate in another poem "the broken / pieces of a green / bottle," lying among "cinders," "between walls" of the hospital's back wings, "where / nothing / will grow" (Litz and MacGowan, eds., "Between Walls," *Complete Collected Poems,* vol. 1, 1986, p. 453.)—unlike Eliot, who despaired over the litter in the Thames.

Snatching some spare time from his busy practice, Williams would sneak into Manhattan to visit his fellow artists. On his way to Marsden Hartley's apartment one evening he "saw the figure 5 / in gold / on a red / firetruck / moving / tense / unheeded / to gong clangs / siren howls" ("The Great Figure," *Sour Grapes,* 1921, p. 78). Charles Demuth later painted a colorful poster portrait of his friend, utilizing multiples of the figure five in gold to dramatize visually a fleeting urban experience.

In contrast to Williams, whose poems were often deceptively short and simple in appearance, Hart Crane embarked upon an ambitious project, partly inspired by Eliot's "epic" poem. The young poet from Ohio lived in a Brooklyn apartment looking out on the Brooklyn Bridge, a major engineering feat of the late nineteenth century. He decided to a write a long poem that would celebrate the bridge and in the process create a modern myth, a structure of belief that would refute *The Waste Land.* Crane's poem, titled simply *The Bridge* (1930), perhaps as a way to universalize the Brooklyn span, became a series of poems bound together by the narrator's quest for spiritual salvation.

From a "Harbor Dawn" (brilliant for its clarity of images and the sun on the cables of the bridge), the narrator speaks from the shadows of the bridge's piers and makes his plea: "Unto us lowliest sometime sweep, descend / And of the curveship lend a myth to God." The narrator then crosses America by rail (on the "Twentieth-Century Limited," accompanied by hoboes) into the nation's pioneer past and back through the purgatory of New York's subway ("The Tunnel") to emerge finally seeking redemption on Brooklyn Bridge at night: "Oh Thou whose radiance doth inherit me," he cries, "hold thy floating singer late!" he pleads, but ends with a plaintive question, "Is it Cathay . . . ?"

In a limited edition, published in Paris in 1930 by the Black Sun Press of Harry and Caresse Crosby, Crane included three exquisite photographs of the Brooklyn Bridge taken by the young photographer Walker Evans from the perspective of the piers beneath. Another artist, Joseph Stella, perhaps closer in spirit to Crane's project, anticipated the poet by painting a large canvas of Brooklyn Bridge in 1919, and then continued with a monumental five-panel *New York Interpreted* in 1922, with the bridge as its centerpiece. Stella was an immigrant associated with the Italian Futurists, who were fascinated by the power of the machine during World War I.

Stella's bridge paintings achieve a shimmering surface movement that echo Crane's bridge, "silver-paced . . . some motion ever unspent in thy stride." More than formal affinities, however, was the way that the painter shared the poet's spiritual concerns. In an essay published the same year as *The Bridge,* Stella recounted his own experiences while standing on the bridge at night: "in the middle alone—lost . . . crushed by the mountainous black impenetrability of the skyscrapers—here and there lights resembling suspended falls of astral bodies or fantastic splendors of remote rites . . . I felt deeply moved, as if on the threshold of a new religion or in the presence of a new DIVINITY" ("The Brooklyn Bridge," *Transition* 16–17, 1929, pp. 86–88). No wonder that Stella's hieratic multipanels evoke stained-glass cathedral windows, in turn alluding to the gothic vaults of Brooklyn Bridge.

THE MACHINE AGE IN FULL SWING

With industrial production for mass consumption in full gear, the 1920s enjoyed unprecedented prosperity, evidenced by the ubiquitous automobile. The car became a symbol of affluence, celebrated by F. Scott Fitzgerald in *The Great Gatsby* (1925). The millionaire Gatsby's "gorgeous car" is "a rich cream color, bright with nickel . . . terraced with a labyrinth of wind-shields that mirrored a dozen suns" (p. 49). Fitzgerald's sense of New York glamour, "the racy, adventurous feel of it at night," its "constant flicker of men and women and machines," would carry over into the Depression-ridden 1930s in the films of Fred Astaire and Ginger Rogers, dancing across Manhattan.

While in 1925 Gatsby's car was "swollen here and there in its monstrous length with triumphant hat-boxes and supper-boxes and tool-boxes," the automobile became svelte and streamlined in the 1930s. Intended for reducing wind and air resistance to enhance speed and fuel efficiency, streamlining went beyond trains, planes, and automobiles to become a visual style of the Great Depression era. Teardrop shapes accompanied by three parallel lines, run horizontally to connote motion and speed, informed commercial architecture such as gas stations. Streamlining was the signature building style of the 1933–1934 Century of Progress International Exposition in Chicago. The sinuous lines and curves of streamlined "moderne" coexisted with the popular linear elegance and geometry of art deco, introduced at the 1925 Exposition Internationale des Arts Decoratifs et Industriels Modernes in Paris.

The moderne style obviously symbolized speed and everything up to date. It also exuded an erotic aura: Fred Astaire and Ginger Rogers were just plain sexy in their moderne penthouse apartments. No wonder that manufacturers appropriated the style for appliances such as irons, toasters, blenders, and lamps. While these machines alleviated heavy labor in the home, they also lifted the spirits of women caught in the depression to dream of their matinee idols during housework. The successful designer Walter Loewy even went so far as to compile charts showing the evolution of streamlined machines paralleled by the streamlined female body.

Moderne and art deco styling suggests that machines possessed an aesthetic dimension, even if only a small elite thought to consider them as works of art. The desire to enhance the visual appeal of new products flooding the American market precipitated the rise of the industrial designer, who superseded the engineer in the 1930s. Lesser known than Paul Frankel, Walter Dorwin Teague, and Norman Bel Geddes was Warren MacArthur, who patented his designs for aluminum furniture in 1930. Displaying a virtuoso use of this new metal, which is lightweight and sturdy, MacArthur manufactured a wide variety of chairs, couches, and tables whose spare geometric elegance alluded to the functionalism of classic Shaker furniture.

THE END OF AN ERA

The economic depredations of the depression belied the optimism of machine age designers. During the summer of 1936, Walker Evans joined *Fortune* magazine on leave from the Farm Security Administration, where he had been a photographer for Roy Stryker's Resettlement Administration. *Fortune* asked him to collaborate with their staff writer James Agee on a photo essay about tenant farmers in the South. Living in intimate contact with three families in Alabama, Evans and Agee produced an extraordinary documentary in photographs and narrative that *Fortune* rejected. Their book was eventually published in 1941 as *Let Us Now Praise Famous Men*. Evans's portraits of these men, women, and children and his photographs of their dilapidated homes, with walls covered with the detritus of advertisements serving as insulation, reiterated his *American Photographs* of 1938, which captured automobile graveyards, abandoned houses, and mill towns. Here was a rural America that had been left behind.

While Fitzgerald's extravagant prose took lush though ambivalent measure of an affluent and privileged class, Agee's was no less extragavant, even strained, in an attempt to convey the tangible experiences of those families caught in a desperate economic vise. His incantations echoed the stripped language pioneered by Stein and turned to novelistic use by Ernest Hemingway to dramatize a brutal world war and its devastating effects on American expatriates in Paris during the 1920s. Agee stole this modernist cleansing of language for praise of lives damaged beyond repair, left only for remembrance and spiritual redemption through worlds made fresh and raw for a reader's unmediated reception. Different though they were, these writers all stood on common ground in a fast need to invent a language that might be adequate for a world changing rapidly for better and worse.

Thus in Manhattan a building boom brought in rapid succession the Chrysler Building (1930), the world's tallest skyscraper for eleven months, and then the Empire State Building, which rose to 1,250 feet in less than two years (1930–1931). Lewis Hine, who began photographing industrial working conditions at the start of the century, documented construction of the Empire State Building in a series of breathtaking photographs of men at work. At about the same time, Diego Rivera, the Mexican muralist who had inspired the mural movement under the Works Progress Administration, painted his monumental murals of the Ford Motor Company plant at River Rouge for the inner courtyard of the Detroit Art Institute. These were indeed efforts to praise American workers.

The decade closed with the 1939 New York World's Fair, a utopian venture in design that promised the "world of tomorrow" for Americans. Dominated by industrial designers, the sleek white buildings with their moderne decor enticed visitors to see and try all the gadgets of the future. Alexander Calder, a third-generation sculptor (who was trained as an engineer), was commissioned to fabricate a motorized outdoor complex for the fairgrounds. For the Ford Motor Company Pavilion, Isamu Noguchi built the large *Chassis Fountain* out of enlarged automobile parts, echoing the "hubcaps" that adorn the Chrysler Building.

Although war had been declared in Europe, there were no signs of the conflict at the fair. Of course, Germany was not invited to the fair; Czechoslovakia, which had been overrun by Nazi Germany maintained a nominal but defiant presence with its pavilion; and the Soviet Union withdrew after the first year of the fair. Soon, the parachute jump, a popular amusement ride, would be commandeered by the U.S. Army for training troops. In an ironic turn that would be overwhelmingly tragic, the machine age that came out of World War I moved toward global conflict once again.

See also **The Culture and Critics of the Suburb and the Corporation; The Culture of Self-Improvement; Popular Culture in the Public Arena; Poststructuralism and Postmodernism; Anthropology and Cultural Relativism** *(volume 2);* **Ethnicity and Race; Cultural Studies** *(volume 3); and other articles in this section.*

BIBLIOGRAPHY

Primary Sources

Agee, James, and Walker Evans. *Let Us Now Praise Famous Men.* Boston, 1941.

Crane, Hart. *The Bridge.* New York, 1930.

Duchamp, Marcel. "A Complete Reversal of Art Opinions by Marcel Duchamp, Iconoclast." *Arts and Decoration* 5 (September 1915): 427–428.

Eliot, T. S. *Collected Poems, 1909–1962.* New York, 1963.

Epstein, Jean. "The New Conditions of Literary Phenomena." *Broom* 2, no. 1 (April 1922): 10.

Fitzgerald, F. Scott. *The Great Gatsby.* New York, 1925.

Frank, Waldo. *Our America.* New York, 1919.

Josephson, Matthew. "The Great American Billposter." *Broom* 3, no. 4 (November 1922): 304–312.

Litz, A. Walton, and Christopher MacGowan, eds. *The Complete Collected Poems of William Carlos Williams.* Vol. 1 (1909–1939). New York, 1986.

Marin, John. "Water-Colors by John Marin." *Camera Work* 42–43 (April–July 1913): 18.

Museum of Modern Art. *Machine Art.* New York, 1934.

"The Richard Mutt Case." *The Blind Man* 2 (May 1917): 5.

Sayler, Oliver. *Revolt in the Arts: A Survey of the Creation, Distribution, and Appreciation of Art in America.* New York, 1930.

Soupault, Philippe. *The American Influence in France.* Seattle, Wash., 1930.

Stein, Gertrude. *The Autobiography of Alice B. Toklas.* New York, 1933.

Stella, Joseph. "The Brooklyn Bridge." *Transition* 16–17 (1929): 86–88.

Williams, William Carlos. "The Great Figure." In *Sour Grapes.* Boston, 1921.

Secondary Sources

Banham, Reyner. *Theory and Design in the First Machine Age.* New York, 1967.

Brown, Milton W. *The Story of the Armory Show.* Greenwich, Conn., 1963.

Detroit Institute of Arts. *The Rouge: The Image of Industry in the Art of Charles Sheeler and Diego Rivera.* Detroit, Mich., 1978.

D'Harnoncourt, Anne, and Kynaston McShine, eds. *Marcel Duchamp.* New York, 1973.

Flink, James J. *The Automobile Age.* Cambridge, Mass., 1988.

Giedion, Siegfried. *Mechanization Takes Command: A Contribution to Anonymous History.* New York, 1969.

Homer, William J. *Alfred Stieglitz and the American Avant-Garde.* Boston, 1979.

Hultén, K. G. Pontus. *The Machine: As Seen at the End of the Machine Age.* New York, 1968.

Kaplan, Wendy, ed. *Designing Modernity: The Arts of Reform and Persuasion, 1885–1945.* New York, 1995.

Lichenstein, Claude, and Franz Engler, eds. *Streamlined: A Metaphor for Progress.* Zurich, Switzerland, n.d.

Lynes, Russell. *Good Old Modern: An Intimate Portrait of the Museum of Modern Art.* New York, 1973.

Meikle, Jeffrey. *Twentieth-Century Limited: Industrial Design in America, 1925–1939.* Philadelphia, 1979.

National Gallery of Art. *Alexander Calder, 1898–1976.* Washington, D.C., 1998.

Nye, David. *Electrifying America: Social Meanings of a New Technology, 1880–1940.* Cambridge, Mass., 1990.

Rydell, Robert W. *The World of Fairs: The Century-of-Progress Expositions.* Chicago, 1993.

Silk, Gerald. *Automobile and Culture.* New York, 1984.

Sims, Lowrey Stokes. *Stuart Davis: American Painter.* New York, 1991.

Smith, Terry. *Making the Modern: Industry, Art, and Design in America.* Chicago, 1993.

Steinman, Lisa M. *Made in America: Science, Technology, and American Modernist Poets.* New Haven, Conn., 1987.

Stott, William. *Documentary Expression and Thirties America.* New York, 1973.

Tashjian, Dickran. *Skyscraper Primitives: Dada and the American Avant-Garde, 1910–1925.* Middletown, Conn., 1975.

Tichi, Cecelia. *Shifting Gears: Technology, Literature, and Culture in Modernist America.* Chapel Hill, N.C., 1987.

Wilson, Richard Guy, Dianne H. Pilgrim, and Dickran Tashjian. *The Machine Age in America, 1918–1941.* New York, 1986.

ANTI-MODERN DISCONTENT BETWEEN THE WARS

Karen Lucic

MODERNISM AND MODERNITY

This essay examines the anti-modern and retrospective impulses in early-twentieth-century American culture. As T. J. Jackson Lears has demonstrated, the late nineteenth century gave rise to various retreats from modernity in such manifestations as the fascination with medieval handcrafts, Eastern religions, and Christian mysticism. Skepticism about modernity persisted into the twentieth century and involved a wide spectrum of responses—critique, evasion, regression, ambivalence, and confusion—often exacerbated by insecurity about national identity. These diverse reactions derived from differing class backgrounds, professional affiliations, and individual sensibilities, but even the most vehement negations still generally accommodated modernity in some form.

In order to understand the complexity of this aspect of American culture, it is necessary to distinguish between "modernism" and "modernity," because scholars and students often confuse the two terms. In the discussion that follows, *modernity* refers to the characteristic social, economic, and material forms of modern life, such as a consumerist ethos, bureaucratic organization, global economies of scale, and technologically sophisticated methods of production, distribution, and entertainment. *Modernism* denotes the various modes of cultural expression that have, since the mid-nineteenth century, challenged Western conventions of visual or literary representation. Modernism encompasses a multitude of individual artists' "signature styles," but broadly, it involves reformulating expressive language, often using new materials and addressing both traditional and novel subjects in innovative ways.

One of the most intriguing paradoxes of the era is the fact that many modernist artists secretly or openly reviled modernity. Admittedly, they often lived unconventional lives, flouting the social and cultural norms of their Victorian predecessors. Ex-hilarated by the intoxicating pace of the city, the power of industrial forms, and unprecedented developments in transportation, communication, advertising, and consumerism, this generation relentlessly examined contemporary themes. Beginning in the 1910s, images of factories, machines, and skyscrapers proliferated in painting and photography. In the next decade, novelists mimicked the language of ad copy and tabloid journalism. The era gave rise to a highly self-aware, nativist strain of modernism, but an undercurrent of confusion and dissent almost always accompanied the celebratory clamor.

From the beginning, the task of forging an American modernism meant confronting the daunting preeminence of the European—and especially the French—vanguard. Eagerly studying developments from abroad, modernists in the United States simultaneously sought to establish a distance from them. As the poet William Carlos Williams put it, "We looked upon the French with a certain amount of awe because we thought they had secrets about art and literature which we might gain. We were anxious to learn, and yet we were repelled too" (in Rourke, *Charles Sheeler,* p. 49). After World War I, critics such as Van Wyck Brooks, Randolph Bourne, and Robert Coady intensified the call for cultural self-sufficiency. A conflict developed between the desire to make an art congruent with the largely abstract, nonlocalized idiom of the international avant-garde and the need to identify American modernism as a uniquely national manifestation. Such contradictory agendas endowed the art of this country with a peculiar self-consciousness about its status.

In fact, cultural insecurity was not unique to the pioneering modernists. Since the colonial period, American writers and artists had been criticized for being derivative and unsophisticated; over the centuries, each generation developed strategies for coping with derision and neglect. In the interwar years, modernists shrewdly annexed themes and images that evoked the nation's prestige as the capital of the

Machine Age, responding to assessments, such as that of the French expatriate Marcel Duchamp, that "the only art America has given are her plumbing and her bridges." The world recognized the nation's preeminence in industrial production, technological expertise, and urban development. By associating with these prestigious features of commerce and industry, artists and writers tried to raise the status of America's cultural production. The focus on modernity in American modernism was therefore in part an expedient in the task of identity formation and in part an engaged, visceral fascination with the new. This emphasis on contemporaneity did not preclude, however, a concurrent interest in reconstructing a viable American heritage, nor thoroughgoing critiques of the very phenomena modernists were using to establish cultural prestige.

AVERSION AND AMBIVALENCE

Aversion to modernist art emerged with America's first exposure to the European vanguard and persisted throughout the interwar years. In 1913 the academic artist Kenyon Cox shrilly denounced the works exhibited at the Armory Show in New York: "To have looked at it is to have passed through a pathological museum where the layman has no right to go" (*Harper's Weekly*, 15 March 1913, p. 10). Early responses to Gertrude Stein's literary modernism were similarly strident. One critic exclaimed, "After a hundred lines of this I wish to scream, I wish to burn the book, I am in agony.... Someone has applied an egg-beater to my brain" (*Atlantic Monthly*, September 1914, p. 432). Such sentiments characterize mainstream attitudes toward vanguard styles throughout most of the twentieth century, representing one of the most tortured responses to modern developments during the era.

Not surprisingly, World War I also stimulated a deep hostility toward modernity. The war seemed to concretize the twentieth century's worst horrors, exploiting as it did advanced technology, industrial processes, and bureaucratic control for maximum human and material devastation. Its psychological effects lingered through the next two decades, as was evident in the fiction of Ernest Hemingway and John Dos Passos.

Other social developments—the advent of the assembly line, the accelerated pace of life, unprecedented scientific and artistic developments, and an explosion of skyscraper construction—at times inflicted anguish, yet they also energized contemporary observers. New York City generated particularly ambivalent responses. Alfred Stieglitz's photograph *The Hand of Man* (1902) depicts a gritty, ominous, but awesomely powerful locomotive whose smoke obliterates the sky. This work illustrated the eclipse of nature in the outlying industrial zones of the metropolis. Images of Manhattan repeatedly focused on the monumental grandeur of the skyline but banished the human element. The modernist painter George Ault dubbed Manhattan skyscrapers "tombstones of capitalism," and the critic Lewis Mumford wrote a scathing assessment of contemporary urban life:

> We have shirked the problem of trying to live well in a régime that is devoted to the production of T-beams and toothbrushes and TNT.... The urban worker escapes the mechanical routine of his daily job only to find an equally mechanical substitute for life and growth and experience in his amusements.... The movies, the White Ways, and the Coney Islands, which almost every American city boasts in some form or other, are means of giving jaded and throttled people the sensations of living without the direct experience of life—a sort of spiritual masturbation. ("The City," p. 13)

Clearly, commentators were troubled not only by the environmental changes brought on by the Machine Age but also by the psychological costs. Modern selfhood began to be characterized as fragmented and mechanized, mirroring the urban and industrial environment of the era. As Thorstein Veblen noted, "men have learned to think in the terms in which technological processes act" (p. 17).

The scion of an illustrious Boston family, Henry Adams was a prescient if unlikely student of technology's impact on the self. He wrote *The Education of Henry Adams* in 1905, although it was not published until 1918, when it immediately became a best-seller. The text characterized twentieth-century life as one of unfathomable multiplicity, in contrast to the unity of past times. Modern science and technology had created the dynamo, a new quasi-religious symbol of infinity. But they were also responsible for unleashing anarchic energies that could not be controlled or even understood, as Adams noted in Paris at "the Gallery of Machines at the Great Exposition of 1900, with his [Adams's] historical neck broken by the sudden irruption of forces totally new" (p. 382). Rejecting nineteenth-century notions of progress, Adams realized that the advent of the Machine Age represented a watershed in human history—one that overturned all moral, psychological, and spiritual foundations and offered nothing certain to replace them.

Adams's ambivalence toward modernity is not surprising, given his advanced age and his idealization of the past. More unexpected is the multi-valent view held by young members of the vanguard, such as T. S. Eliot, whose early poetry uncannily parallels Adams's perception of modern fragmentation. An expatriate living in London, Eliot created devastating portraits of modern enervation and impotence, combining learned allusions to classic texts, fragmented voices, and shockingly unexpected turns of phrases, such as the first lines of "The Love Song of J. Alfred Prufrock" (1917): "Let us go then, you and I,/When the evening is spread out against the sky/Like a patient etherised upon a table." Eliot's most famous work, *The Waste Land* (1922), is "a heap of broken images" in which the multiple narrators "can connect nothing with nothing." Moving from Kew to Carthage, from Shakespeare to ragtime, the poem is a modernist dirge, a death knell for a civilization. It is also a celebration of the power of language, which modern consciousness has liberated in unprecedented ways.

The 1920s spawned many other literary innovators, who also responded ambivalently to modernity's transformations. The Great War had actually catapulted America into industrial dominance and prosperity; the country's productive capacities multiplied thirteenfold in the war's aftermath. In addition, new products, innovations in advertising, packaging and distribution, installment financing, and greater, more widely (if still unevenly) distributed wealth created a nation of avid consumers. As Lears and Roland Marchand have shown, advertisers exploited Americans' need to establish autonomy and control in an increasingly impersonal and bureaucratized society. Through slogans, images, and shrewdly crafted campaigns, advertising employed a therapeutic model of consolation for Americans' modern anxieties. At the same time, it enforced greater homogenization of values through an ethos of mass consumption. Sinclair Lewis's *Babbitt* (1923) and F. Scott Fitzgerald's *The Great Gatsby* (1925) perceptively satirize this new consumerist mentality and underscore the hollowness of American materialism.

Some chose to remove themselves physically from the hypermodernity of the American scene. Many of the country's most influential writers—Eliot, Stein, Hemingway, Ezra Pound—preferred living in foreign capitals. Artists who incorporated skyscrapers and factories in their work, such as Stieglitz, Georgia O'Keeffe, and Charles Sheeler, maintained rural retreats far from the frenzy of the metropolis. Modernist art colonies sprang up in remote, rustic regions like Woodstock, New York, and Ogunquit, Maine. In the general populace, the flight from the cities to the suburbs intensified during the interwar era. Such gestures represent concrete if complex attempts to escape urban chaos, overcrowding, and heterogeneity.

The Great Depression renewed attacks on metropolitan life and the capitalist industrial system. After the stock market crash of 1929, Fitzgerald came to "the awful realization that New York was a city after all and not a universe, [and] the whole shining edifice that he had reared in his imagination came crashing to the ground" ("My Lost City," p. 37). In response to the Ford Motor Company's violent suppression of worker protest, Dos Passos wrote in 1936: "when the country on cracked shoes, in frayed trousers, belts tightened over hollow bellies . . . started marching from Detroit to Dearborn, asking for work . . . all they could think of at Ford's was machineguns" (*The Big Money*, p. 56). The social realist painters Raphael Soyer and Ben Shahn challenged class divisions and inequities through depictions of unemployed workers, bread lines, and displaced immigrants. Walker Evans's photographs of automobile junkyards and consumer detritus represented yet another jaundiced investigation of American materialism, exemplifying the critique of modernity characteristic of the decade.

USES OF THE AMERICAN PAST

Interestingly, both modernists and traditionalists used the American past to ameliorate a sense of rootlessness in modern life. A nationalistic form of antiquarianism represented one of the most straightforward forms of anti-modern reaction in the early twentieth century. Stimulated by the 1876 centennial celebrations around the country and the rapid destruction of old buildings due to industrial and urban development, antiquarians preserved relics of a heroic colonial past in shrines such as Memorial Hall at Deerfield, Massachusetts. In the twentieth century, photographer, preservationist, and furniture manufacturer Wallace Nutting sold over ten million photographic souvenirs of colonial buildings, often including figures dressed in period costumes. In addition, he restored four historic houses and began making reproductions of seventeenth-century New England furniture in 1917. These revivalist settings were designed to infuse domestic life with a sense of homey simplicity in order to counteract the chaotic proliferation of mass-produced goods.

Such emulation of the past coincided with the Arts and Crafts movement's goal to reestablish

Walker Evans, *Coal Miner's House, Scotts Run, West Virginia.* Photograph, 1936. Evans worked for the Farm Security Administration during the Great Depression, documenting rural poverty in the South. But some of his photographs are also indictments of the false promises of American advertising and commercial culture. LIBRARY OF CONGRESS

handcraft as morally superior to the dehumanizing aspects of industrial labor. At the turn of the century, Henry Chapman Mercer founded the Moravian Pottery and Tile Works in Doylestown, inspired by the all-but-extinct Pennsylvania German pottery traditions of the region. Mercer revived local preindustrial handicrafts because he felt the lives of ordinary, anonymous settlers embodied the real significance of the American past. Yet as his business acquired national renown, it attracted unlikely patrons—tycoons of industry and the mass media, such as William Randolph Hearst, who decorated his palatial "castle" at San Simeon, California, with Mercer tiles. Gustav Stickley, whose sturdy Arts and Crafts furniture gained great popularity in the early twentieth century, extolled the virtues of hand production in his influential journal, *The Craftsman* (published 1901–1916). Yet his furniture was largely mass produced in his Syracuse, New York, factory.

Wooden dowels, suggesting medieval techniques of furniture construction, covered the modern metal screws that actually held Stickley's pieces together. Theory and practice often diverged in the American Arts and Crafts movement, as with many other retrospective manifestations during the period.

For some lovers of the past, reviving antiquated designs meant resurrecting patriotic fervor as well, because they saw the stark simplicity of the earliest American forms as embodying the strength of colonial character. In fact, distrust of the urban working class and anti-immigrant prejudice also fueled the antiquarian retreat from the present. By the early 1920s, about half the nation's population consisted of first- or second-generation immigrants, and of the 28 million new arrivals since 1880, most were eastern or southern European. This massive influx of unfamiliar foreigners threatened those who conceived of an ideal America as composed of pure New England or aristocratic southern stock, and in response, the government imposed strict immigration restrictions. Re-creations of the American past usually excluded ethnic diversity as well as signs of the harsher realities of the colonial period: slavery, disease, poverty, rudimentary hygiene, and intolerance. The restoration of colonial Williamsburg, begun in 1927 and funded by the industrialist John D. Rockefeller Jr. was an especially sanitized and excessively opulent re-creation of Virginia's colonial capital.

Antiquarians of the late nineteenth century prized historic artifacts less for their aesthetic features than for their associations with legendary individuals or colonial values. They embraced the American past as an explicit critique of industrial modernity, and therefore, the "colonial" epoch for them extended into the antebellum period. Their selective interest in the past ceased with the Victorian era when the evidence of mass production appeared in material culture. In the twentieth century, the colonial revival continued to develop in tandem with antiquarian and preservationist concerns, but issues of connoisseurship prevailed, as did a preference for the lavish high-style designs of the eighteenth century over the stark utilitarianism of early English colonization. This was evident in the landmark opening of the American Wing at New York's Metropolitan Museum of Art in 1924. Although the period rooms included seventeenth-century examples, elaborate suites of Queen Anne and Chippendale furniture predominated.

As the colonial revival became the most popular style of the era, dual tendencies developed: expensive reproductions of colonial furniture, silver, and architecture grew more archaeologically "correct," while middlebrow manifestations of the style were freer and increasingly accommodated modernity. Especially in suburbia, colonial revival houses embraced modern spatial ideals: open, informal plans, extensive glass windows and doors, and terraces and porches connecting interior and exterior spaces. Kitchens and bathrooms were identical to those in modernist dwellings—highly efficient "machines for living." Nevertheless, the comforting traditional exteriors of such houses conferred a sense of stability and continuity in the face of disorienting change.

The most idiosyncratic amalgamation of past and present occurred in Henry Ford's outdoor history museum, Greenfield Village, surrounding the automobile manufacturer's birthplace in Dearborn, Michigan. Founded in the late 1920s, the museum encompassed an eclectic display of replicated his-

toric buildings—such as Philadelphia's Independence Hall—with actual structures, like Thomas Edison's laboratory, transported from their original locations. Ford once declared that "history is bunk," but like earlier antiquarians, he amassed huge numbers of old tools and other useful artifacts, which caused one commentator to muse: "The creator of the assembly-belt civilization is in love with the old handcraft civilization. Henry Ford adores the horse-and-buggy. It is as if Stalin went in for collecting old ledgers and stocktickers" (in Hosmer, *Preservation Comes of Age*, p. 94). What made Greenfield Village unique was that Ford presented the American preindustrial craft tradition as prefiguring the twentieth-century assembly line. Regarding a reconstructed display at the Village, an official publication entitled *Looking Forward through the Past* declared: "Look at the black smith shop of seventy-five years ago. The smithy with its bellows, forge, and anvil, is one of the lineal ancestors of the great automobile plants of today" (Ford Motor Co., c. 1930s, unpaged). Therefore, Ford conceived of simple rural technology as groundwork for his own entrepreneurial achievements in large-scale industry.

The modernist quest for the "usable past" also aligned history with the present, providing a foundation for art, rather than—as in Ford's case—for industry. Initially formulated by the literary scholar Van Wyck Brooks in the years following World War I, the usable past project involved a searing critique of American society and values. In his 1918 essay "On Creating a Usable Past," Brooks wrote:

> The present is a void, and the American writer floats in that void because the past that survives in the common mind of the present is a past without living value. But is this the only possible past? If we need another past so badly, is it inconceivable that we might discover one, that we might even invent one? (p. 339)

Brooks initiated a fundamental reevaluation of America's literary past, challenging the established canon of nineteenth-century genteel literati. In the wake of Brooks's efforts, William Carlos Williams, Lewis Mumford, and others championed largely forgotten writers like Herman Melville, Walt Whitman, and Mark Twain. To this literary group, Mumford added architects like H. H. Richardson and artists such as Albert Pinkham Ryder. In her important study *American Humor* (1931), Constance Rourke expanded the quest for a usable past to include vernacular expressions, like folktales and popular theater. Artists, collectors, and museum curators further amplified the quest by assembling and

Edward Hopper, *Early Sunday Morning.* Oil on canvas, 1930. Hopper's mysterious paintings of the city almost completely avoided the skyscraper, the new icon of urban vitality that so entranced his modernist contemporaries. Instead, he found inspiration in the often criticized remnants of Victorian architecture in New York. COLLECTION OF WHITNEY MUSEUM OF AMERICAN ART, NEW YORK

exhibiting Appalachian crafts, folk sculpture and painting, and Shaker furniture.

Members of the Ogunquit artists' colony—Hamilton Easter Field, Yasuo Kuniyoshi, Robert Laurent, and others—were among the first to collect American folk art. Following Henri Matisse and Pablo Picasso's interest in tribal art, they assembled such nonacademic material as a way to inspire and legitimize their own modernist work. Patrons of the avant-garde, like Abby Aldrich Rockefeller, soon followed their lead, finding folk art complementary to modernism. Folk art became institutionalized when Holger Cahill organized the first major exhibition at the Newark Museum in 1930, later reassembled at the Museum of Modern Art. Dubbed the art of the "American Primitives" or the "Common Man," folk objects served the interwar generation's need to construct an anonymous, collective, and native foundation for their creative efforts. This counteracted the modernist sense of isolation and belatedness as a provincial offshoot of the European vanguard.

This modernist agenda fundamentally distinguishes the usable-past quest from the antiquarianism and colonial revivalism of the era, and by the 1930s, it revolutionized the notion of an American cultural heritage. As Ann Douglas has argued, the modernists expunged the refinement and moral uplift of nineteenth-century "feminine" traditions. Modernists excoriated the false fronts and gingerbread bargeboards of Victorian architecture as signs of America's shallow and derivative culture. (Working against the grain, the painters Charles Burchfield and Edward Hopper, along with Walker Evans, often incorporated these forms into their work and appreciated, in Hopper's words, their "hideous beauty.") Proponents of the usable past advocated an unornamented, nonacademic heritage that not surprisingly accorded with current modernist aesthetic preferences and values. However, both the antiquarian and the modernist embrace of the American past involved an attempt to compensate for a perceived void in the present.

FOREIGN REVIVALS

The interwar years also gave rise to revivals of foreign styles, which were especially attractive to institutions and the mercantile elites. The Gothic Revival, persisting well into the twentieth century, prevailed in the construction of churches and edu-

642

cational facilities, notably at the universities of Yale, Princeton, and Duke. One of its major proponents, Ralph Adams Cram, designed important buildings such as the Graduate School (1913) and University Chapel (1928) at Princeton and the Cathedral of St. John the Divine in New York (begun 1892; Cram took over in 1911). For Cram, a devout Anglican, the Gothic was not merely a style but a force that symbolized an idealized medieval society unified by shared religious enthusiasm. Cram railed against modern capitalism, imperialism, and materialism and criticized the post-Renaissance "riot of individualism." He felt that since Gothic forms embodied organic wholeness and spiritual inspiration, his buildings could restore communal unity and remedy modern secularization and fragmentation.

More eclectic in his revivalism was Cram's longtime partner, Bertram Grosvenor Goodhue. One of his most famous buildings, St. Bartholomew's Church, New York City (1914–1919), is ostensibly Romanesque revival in style. But of its design, Goodhue confessed that "it will look more like Arabian Nights or the last act of *Parsifal* than any Christian church" (Goodhue to George Horsfield, 16 February 1919, Avery Library Archive, Columbia University). Addison Mizner employed an even more fanciful approach to revivalism in his opulent houses for the nouveaux riches in Palm Beach, Florida. After the war, Mizner developed a fanciful "Spanish-style" for palatial dwellings, with red tile roofs, white stuccoed walls, and palm-lined patios. Such theatricality and conspicuous display chart the distance traveled between Cram and Mizner's uses of past. Mizner's was not a critical, moralizing architecture but one that offered status and a pleasurable retreat from industrial modernity into an exotic fantasy of the past. Similar escapist longings are evident in contemporaneous high-budget Hollywood movies, such as *Male and Female* (1919), *The Sheik* (1921), and *The Thief of Bagdad* (1924).

In the decorative arts, period revival furnishings dominated the American market. English Tudor, Spanish baroque, and eighteenth-century French revival designs vied for popularity with colonial American styles. Typically, Park Avenue apartments were decorated as country manors or aristocratic chateaux. Although some commentators noted an incongruity between the modernity of the American cityscape and the conservative nature of domestic interiors, most newly prosperous patrons sought out traditional symbols of elevated status. Influential tastemakers like Emily Post assured buyers that such forms were a guarantee of refined taste and a venerable heritage. The elitist promotion of revival furnishings seemed to offer a way to distinguish oneself in the increasingly homogeneous commercial culture of the 1920s and 1930s, but the mass marketing of revivalist designs actually undercut the effort to be unique. In addition, the conspicuous veneers, applied ornaments, and elaborate carvings were machine-made, creating a discontinuity between the furnishings' symbolic associations of traditional handcrafted luxury and the methods of industrial manufacture. Some wealthy homeowners decorated with authentic European antiques, but most consumers happily purchased affordable reproductions.

The synthesis of past and present was even more complex in the modern decorative arts and architecture of the period. Buildings as innovative and diverse as Frank Lloyd Wright's Los Angeles houses of the 1920s and the New York skyscrapers designed by Eli Jacques Kahn incorporated forms and motifs borrowed from Pre-Columbian precedents. The art moderne style, popularized in this country following the 1925 *Exposition Internationale des Arts Décoratifs et Industriels Modernes* in Paris, drew its inspiration from the exquisite forms and techniques of eighteenth-century French cabinetmaking. A concurrent resurgence in neoclassicism was accompanied by more exotic borrowings from Egyptian, Mesopotamian, archaic Greek, and Middle Eastern designs. Yet unlike the makers of period reproductions, designers such as Frederick Carder, Paul Frankl, Erik Magnussen, and Walter Dorwin Teague modernized their sources. Forms were stripped down and geometricized; Bakelite and chrome replaced ebony and silver. Such designs emanated a stylish sophistication more daring than that of period reproductions. But those who purchased these items also desired to separate themselves from the anonymity of mass culture through distinctive acts of consumption and display.

Classicism acquired new meaning in the sculpture at Rockefeller Center, New York (1931–1939). Consisting of fourteen art deco buildings, the Center displayed a decorative program that celebrated the progress of humanity—an ironic choice given current economic and social conditions. Sculptors created classically inspired heroic figures, updated with modernistic stylizations. Paul Manship designed an imposing gilded bronze statue of Prometheus for Rockefeller Plaza, and Lee Lawrie crafted a muscular Atlas shouldering a mammoth celestial sphere facing Fifth Avenue. Amid the towering modern skyscrapers, these works relied on the strength and authority of classical culture to mask the weakness of industrial capitalism during the

Marsden Hartley, *Indian Composition.* Oil on canvas, c. 1914–1915. Ironically, Hartley was in Berlin when, motivated by primitivist impulses, he initiated his study of American Indian sources. Decrying the state of modernism in America, he claimed that the Native Americans possessed the only authentic and original art and advised others to study the American Indian in order to discover the land's unexplored sources of creativity. THE FRANCES LEHMAN LOEB ART CENTER, VASSAR COLLEGE, POUGHKEEPSIE, NEW YORK. GIFT OF PAUL ROSENFELD. 1950.1.5

1930s. As with the other examples in this section, a well-established foreign heritage—adapted to modern conditions—advanced the ideological or class-conscious motives of the patron.

PRIMITIVISM

Yet another avenue of escape from the present was imaginary regression into the "primitive." Primitivism involves the belief in the superiority of primal human existence, especially in contrast to the perceived ills of modern society. This phenomenon again had earlier roots, but it gained momentum in the twentieth century as many individuals sought to evade overcivilization by contact with primeval selfhood. Many sought contact with tribal peoples as a remedy for modern ennui, less through face-to-face interactions than through various forms of symbolic mediations.

The Harlem Renaissance of the 1920s—a movement of literary figures, visual artists, and other members of the black intelligentsia—explored African heritage as a possible foundation for contemporary creative achievements. White America also tried to gain symbolic access to "primitive" energies through African American music, such as spirituals, minstrelsy, ragtime, jazz, and the blues. In nightclubs, Broadway shows, and speakeasies, patrons thrilled to the syncopated rhythms of "jungle music" and the overtly sexual performances of Josephine Baker and Bessie Smith. Popular white musicians and songwriters such as Paul Whiteman and Irving Berlin often appropriated black musical forms (without crediting their sources). Such music inspired fantasies of transcending modern civiliza-

644

tion's inhibiting grip on behavior and the imagination. Jazz was also characterized as the country's most unique art, free from European derivation yet lauded throughout the world.

Primitivism also sparked interest in Native American culture, and this led to enthusiastic study of indigenous peoples, especially in the Southwest and on the Northwest coast, where inhabitation had been continuous since prehistoric times. Ethnographers such as Franz Boas and Ruth Bunzel conducted extensive fieldwork, documenting oral culture and religious practices. Museum professionals and private individuals, such as R. Stewart Culin and George Heye, collected Native American artifacts on a massive scale for the Brooklyn Museum and the Museum of the American Indian. The "salvage paradigm" that motivated these efforts turned on the conviction that indigenous peoples, who represent the "childhood" of modern civilization, were destined to vanish. In a society increasingly perceived as dangerously adrift, social scientists avidly studied the American Indian in part to recover a world of primal emotional intensity and instinctive religious awe. Therefore, they tried to "salvage" not only endangered artifacts but also a stable sense of self-origin amid the uncertainties of their own era.

Visual artists and poets appropriated Native American culture for similar reasons, seeking to endow their work with emotive authenticity and exotic, non-Western stylizations. In 1914 the modernist Marsden Hartley executed a series of largely abstract paintings that incorporated Native American designs and symbols. On 12 November 1914, he wrote to his patron Stieglitz that he found himself "wanting to be an Indian—to paint my face with the symbols of that race I adore . . . & face the sun forever—that would seem the true expression of human dignity" (Beinecke Rare Book and Manuscript Library, Yale University). By the end of the 1920s, many other artists, weary of urban life, made pilgrimages to remote areas of the West, especially New Mexico. Georgia O'Keeffe, Paul Strand, Ansel Adams, John Marin, and numerous others looked to the indigenous people and the arid, monumental landscape as a means of revitalization. The British expatriate D. H. Lawrence, who established a ranch north of Taos, counseled, "America must turn again to catch the spirit of her own dark, aboriginal continent. . . . Americans must take up life where the Red Indian . . . left it off" ("America, Listen to Your Own," p. 69). Mary Austin, a longtime resident of Santa Fe, made just such an effort, taking Native American chants as a model for her poetry.

Modernists felt that Native American material perfectly complemented their avant-garde aspirations. Realizing the power and richness of previously undervalued indigenous traditions, they also assuaged their own feelings of dislocation and alienation from mainstream culture by an imaginary retreat into a timeless world of social integration and oneness with nature.

Primitivism therefore shares a common motivation with the concurrent revivals of the era. Modern individuals in a mobile and technologically sophisticated world were seeking a sense of rootedness in the past. Paradoxically, such therapeutic forms of regression almost invariably accommodated present realities, and throughout the era, American culture remained fundamentally modern: committed to unfettered individualism, to the enhanced control over nature afforded by the machine, and to innovation as the favored form of cultural capital. But Americans filtered their experience of modernity through various lenses, often blurring it through displacement and denial instead of bringing it into sharp focus.

See also **The Ideal of Spontaneity; Poststructuralism and Postmodernism; Postmodernism and the Arts** (*volume 2*); **Technological Enclaves** (*volume 3*); *and other articles in this section.*

BIBLIOGRAPHY

Primary Sources

Adams, Henry. *The Education of Henry Adams.* 1918. Reprint, Boston, 1973.

Austin, Mary. *The American Rhythm.* New York, 1923.

Brooks, Van Wyck. "On Creating a Usable Past." *Dial,* 11 April 1918, p. 339.

Dos Passos, John. *1919.* New York, 1932.

———. *The Big Money.* New York, 1936.

Eliot, T. S. *The Waste Land, and Other Poems.* New York, 1962.

Fitzgerald, F. Scott. *The Great Gatsby.* New York, 1925.

———. "My Lost City." 1932. In *The Crack Up,* edited by Edmund Wilson. New York, 1956.

Hartley, Marsden. "Red Man Ceremonials: An American Plea for American Esthetics." *Art and Archaeology,* January 1920, pp. 7–14.

Hemingway, Ernest. *A Farewell to Arms.* New York, 1929.

Lawrence, D. H. "America, Listen to Your Own." *New Republic,* 15 December 1920, pp. 68–70.

Lewis, Sinclair. *Babbitt.* New York, 1922.

Mumford, Lewis. *The Brown Decades: A Study of the Arts in America, 1865–1895.* New York, 1931.

———. "The City." In *Civilization in the United States,* edited by Harold E. Stearns. 1922. Reprint, Westport, Conn., 1971.

Rourke, Constance. *American Humor: A Study of the National Character.* New York, 1931.

———. *Charles Sheeler: Artist in the American Tradition.* New York, 1938.

Veblen, Thorstein. *The Place of Science in Modern Civilisation, and Other Essays.* New York, 1919.

Williams, William Carlos. *In the American Grain.* New York, 1925.

Secondary Sources

Bradbury, Malcolm, and James McFarlane, eds. *Modernism, 1890–1930.* New York, 1976.

Corn, Wanda M. *The Great American Thing: Modern Art and National Identity, 1915–1935.* Berkeley, Calif., 1999.

Davies, Karen [Lucic]. *At Home in Manhattan: Modern Decorative Arts, 1925 to the Depression.* New Haven, Conn., 1983.

Douglas, Ann. *Terrible Honesty: Mongrel Manhattan in the 1920s.* New York, 1995.

Fox, Richard W., and T. J. Jackson Lears, eds. *The Culture of Consumption: Critical Essays in American History, 1880–1980.* New York, 1983.

Hosmer, Charles B., Jr. *Preservation Comes of Age: From Williamsburg to the National Trust, 1926–1949.* Charlottesville, Va., 1981.

Lears, T. J. Jackson. *No Place of Grace: Antimodernism and the Transformation of American Culture 1880–1920.* New York, 1981.

Lucic, Karen. *Charles Sheeler and the Cult of the Machine.* Cambridge, Mass., 1991.

Marchand, Roland. *Advertising and the American Dream: Making Way for Modernity, 1920–1940.* Berkeley, Calif., 1985.

Orvell, Miles. *The Real Thing: Imitation and Authenticity in American Culture, 1880–1940.* Chapel Hill, N.C., 1989.

THE POPULAR ARTS

James P. Cullen

One can perhaps best begin to appreciate the significance of the popular arts in America, not simply in one generation but in the entire twentieth century, by looking at the work of the magazine writer and cultural critic Gilbert Seldes. At the beginning of his 1924 book *The Seven Lively Arts,* Seldes makes a wry allusion to one event no one was likely to forget—the Great War—as a means of talking about another event no one was likely to remember. "Lest the year 1914 should not otherwise be distinguished in history," he wrote, "it may be recorded that it was then, or a year earlier, or possibly a year later, that the turning point came in the history of the American moving picture" (p. 14).

According to Seldes, that turning point was the merger of three now largely forgotten movie studios—Fine Arts, Kay-Bee, and Keystone—into the aptly named Triangle Film Corporation. Why was this merger important? Certainly not as a business proposition (Triangle collapsed a few years later); this was only one of a number of such deals, and Seldes could think of "nothing more doleful as a subject of conversation than the social-economics of the moving picture" (p. 15). And, notwithstanding the opinions of observers at the time and film historians since, its importance did not lie in the fact that a critically acclaimed director—D. W. Griffith, who has often been cited as the father of modern cinema because of such films as *The Birth of a Nation* (1915) and *Intolerance* (1916)—was involved in the deal.

Instead, the real significance of Triangle for Seldes was that it ratified the emergence of another producer-director, Mack Sennett, as the premier moviemaker of his time. Sennett was known for wildly popular slapstick comedies, the most famous of which were his Keystone Kops pictures. Fast-paced, anarchic, and often cheerfully violent, Sennett's movies fully exploited the potential of the new medium of film in ways his typically working-class audience could immediately grasp and appreciate.

For Seldes, Sennett's centrality was not simply a matter of his popularity (though he noted that as far as the financial backers of Triangle were concerned, it was Sennett, not Griffith, that mattered). Rather, he was asserting that Sennett was a great artist—greater than Griffith and many other leaders of film and other media who strived for self-conscious sophistication. "For us to appreciate slapstick may require a revolution in our way of looking at the arts. Having taken thought on how we now look at the arts," he concluded in his typically understated manner, "I suggest that the revolution is not entirely undesirable" (p. 33).

Whatever the broader historical relevance of Seldes's views on Sennett and the genre of slapstick comedy, his comments about them are particularly suggestive about popular culture as a whole between 1914 and 1939—the crucible in which it became recognizably modern. From his remarks one can extrapolate a number of useful generalizations about the period.

THE DIVIDE BETWEEN "HIGH" AND "LOW" CULTURE

To greater or lesser degrees, there has always been a widely held distinction between elite arts (for example, portrait painting, symphonic music, ballet) and more vernacular ones (folk songs, theater, handicrafts). But rarely has this divide been more pronounced than it was in the early twentieth century, particularly on the part of modernist intellectuals who focused intensively—some might say obsessively—on distinguishing between them. At the core of modernism, which as an aesthetic movement crystallized at the turn of the century, was an impatience with, even rejection of, traditions like narrative in fiction, melody in music, and mimetic representation in the visual arts, all of which were viewed as dulling clichés. In part, this concern reflected the crudity and soullessness of cultural life in an age of mechanical reproduction. And yet at the very moment Gertrude Stein and the Lost Generation of American expatriates were wandering around Parisian salons and cafés lamenting their anomie, some of the most durable and meaningful work of the twentieth century was being produced and experienced elsewhere: on the Mississippi riverboats where Louis Armstrong played jazz; on the pages of newsprint where George Herriman published his much beloved comic strip "Krazy Kat"; in the vaudeville theaters where Fred Astaire perfected the moves that would characterize his work in the movie musical. Highbrow critics and artists would occasionally note, and even draw inspiration from, such work. But any admiration of this kind was typically offered as a confession bracketed by a tone of irony or an insistence that it could not be taken altogether seriously. (One exception that proved the rule were the films of Sennett's protégé, Charlie Chaplin.) The caution with which Seldes approached popular culture was typical. His willingness and ability to engage with it on its own terms was not.

THE IMPACT OF INDUSTRIAL CAPITALISM

Technological innovation and the rapid growth of large corporations transformed many aspects of American life in the decades following World War I, but the impact of such developments was most dramatic in popular culture. It is one thing to perform a song or stage a drama before a live audience. It is another when that song or drama is recorded to be played later, and still another when that song or drama can be distributed to millions of people who can experience it virtually on demand.

But the technical and commercial capabilities of new media such as film, radio, musical recording, and television not only magnified artistic expression but also gave rise to new genres of expression (like the radio serial, a kind of oral theater that became a forerunner of the situation comedy). Seldes's admiration for Sennett was less a matter of Sennett's ability to use old techniques in new situations than his acuity in exploiting the unique characteristics of film. In no other medium, for example, could throwing a pie in an actor's face be quite so vivid or emotionally powerful.

Moreover, industrial capitalism transformed the context in which art was produced. To put it simply, making a movie and getting it into theaters requires more talent—and more money—than any one person can typically provide. And the people who had access to both (like Sennett and later Chaplin) were in a position to acquire an unprecedented amount of power and notoriety. The years immediately preceding and following World War I were notable for their rapid elaboration of organizations like film studios, radio networks, and record companies that could efficiently produce a steady stream of entertainment for profit. At the turn of the century, such organizations were either nonexistent or barely recognizable as such. In 1924 their growth and consolidation had become an unremarkable fact of life. And by World War II they were so fully elaborated that they became the template for new media. The development and uses of television, for example, proceeded down tracks put down in the interwar decades (by many of the same people, among them Seldes, who became a programming executive at CBS).

FORM VS. CONTENT

One of the most striking patterns about the history of American popular culture generally is the nature of the struggle to control it. Beginning with the advent of the penny press in the early nineteenth century, new cultural forms were typically created by elites with access to capital and technology. Printing presses, movie projectors, recording equipment, and other forms of popular culture were usually introduced at the high end of the nation's social structure and diffused downward. But as these forms evolved, it became increasingly apparent that the economic—and, especially, the artistic—viability of these forms depended on their *content* of popular culture: the particular books, movies, shows, or other texts that commanded large audiences. Ordinary working people were the key to those large audiences; they made popular culture truly popular. Perhaps even more important is that, unlike the labor market, residential patterns, or even democratic government, popular culture afforded a unique degree of economic, social, and even political opportunity for otherwise marginalized constituencies in American society. Historically, African Americans, immigrants, homosexuals, and women have been far better represented here than just about anywhere else. (Mack Sennett, for example, came from a working-class Irish Catholic background.)

This openness was quite apparent in the early decades of the twentieth century, which was pivotal less because of a notably open social climate than because the new media created an unusually large cultural vacuum for outsiders to fill. The classic case in point is for Jews in the film industry. At the turn of the century, the inventor Thomas Edison sought a monopoly over the medium by acquiring control of key patents for film, cameras, and projectors. By 1909 he succeeded but largely ignored the movies themselves. By contrast, a remarkable group of eastern European immigrants on the exhibition end of the industry—Adolph Zukor, Marcus Loew, Carl Laemmle, the Warner brothers, and others—were acutely attuned to the kinds of movies that audiences wanted to see and, through a complex series of legal and financial maneuvers, were able to set up a cartel of so-called "movie moguls" that lasted until well after World War II. This period was also notable for the impressive array of Jewish performers, among them Fanny Brice, Al Jolson, and Eddie Cantor, who assimilated and adapted American culture to their purposes.

But blacks were the supreme example of the form-content distinction. Systematically denied the most fundamental kinds of economic, social, or political power, they were nevertheless able to make incalculable contributions to the nation's cultural life—indeed, one might go so far as to say that it was the presence of a heterogeneous African American presence more than any other factor that made American culture truly American. This presence took many forms. The most obvious, of course, were figures with mainstream interracial appeal, like Bert Williams, a multitalented entertainer who laid the foundations for a black comic tradition that runs through Flip Wilson, Richard Pryor, and beyond. Less popular but more enduringly influential figures—jazz singer Billie Holiday is a good example—began their careers within relatively insular black communities such as Harlem in New York City or the South Side of Chicago but went on to attain lasting influence and renown for the rest of the century. That immense influence went far beyond imitators in the popular arts; it also spilled into avowedly elite culture. In the world of classical music, for instance, composers as diverse as Antonín Dvořák, George Gershwin, and Leonard Bernstein at various times have incorporated African American strains into their work.

For all these common patterns, however, it is difficult to convey the significance of the interwar years without some effort to recount at least a few notable developments within particular media.

THE FILM INDUSTRY

The Great War was good for the movie moguls. Besides allowing them to gain control of 98 percent of the domestic market and 85 percent of the international market (Sklar, *Movie-Made America*, p. 47), the industry's close collaboration with the U.S. government's Committee on Public Information to produce Allied propaganda offered an opportunity for industry leaders to demonstrate their patriotism (movie stars Charlie Chaplin, Mary Pickford, and Douglas Fairbanks burnished their images by making a tour to promote Liberty Bonds). Such ties may have played a role in the Justice Department's relative lack of zeal in investigating the industry's anticompetitive practices and its willingness to allow internal censorship tools like production codes rather than rely on formal government regulation. The ensuing decades are widely viewed as the golden age of the medium: data from 1946, the eve of its decline at the advent of television, showed that 90 million people went to movie theaters every week, accounting for ninety cents of every amusement dollar (Ray, *A Certain Tendency*, p. 129).

Three major developments, all interrelated, were central to the American cinema's evolution between the world wars. The first was the rise of Hollywood as the film capital of the world. Actually, this process was well under way even before World War I; film production can be dated as early as 1907, when a Chicago studio set up shop there. A steady stream of New Yorkers followed, attracted by good weather, varied landscapes, and a cheap, pliable labor force. But by the early 1920s, Hollywood was more than a practical production site: it had become the repository of collective hopes and fears.

Perhaps the purest embodiment of Hollywood as a living symbol for dream life were Fairbanks and Pickford, who divorced their spouses, married each other in 1920, and moved into in a baronial home they dubbed "Pickfair" in the hamlet of Beverly Hills (which, like nearby Hollywood, had recently become part of Los Angeles). In the words of the film historian Richard Schickel, "No one has quite recaptured the freshness, the sense of perpetually innocent, perpetually adolescent narcissism that Douglas Fairbanks brought to the screen" (*His Picture in the Papers*, p. 1). Pickford, commonly known as "America's Sweetheart," was cherished as an eternal child; well into her thirties she was playing characters in golden curls and frilly dresses in what were popularly known as "Mary" pictures. Pickford and Fairbanks would eventually divorce (1935), and their preeminence as movie stars would be displaced in favor of dream couples like Clark Gable and Carole Lombard, but they established archetypes and lifestyles that remain part of American movie culture to this day.

The second major innovation of the interwar years was technical: the advent of sound, which revolutionized the industry in the late 1920s. Actually, this technology had been available since the beginning of the decade, but producers were reluctant to use it because they had invested a great deal in silent film production and were loath to make the expensive adaptations sound required. Its introduction by Warner Brothers in a series of short films in the mid-1920s was something of a gimmick to boost the financially struggling studio. A 1926 feature film, *Don Juan*, featured a recorded soundtrack by the New York Philharmonic. But at one point during the filming of the 1927 film *The Jazz Singer*, which had no sound, the irrepressible vaudevillian actor Al Jolson blurted out, "You ain't heard nuthin' yet, folks! Listen to this!" Struck by the remark, producer Sam Warner added another 250 words of dialogue to the film, which became a huge hit. From that point on, sound movies became the new standard.

The third major development of this period was the creation of the so-called studio system, which reached its height between the late 1920s and mid-1940s. Early film producers like Edison had tried to make actors anonymously interchangeable parts, but it became apparent to others very quickly that the public would take to particular figures. In fact, one goal of the Triangle Film Corporation was to attract established Broadway stars into one company stable. The plan failed—in large measure because theatrical talent and glamour did not always translate to the silver screen—but it did significantly drive up the salaries commanded by bona fide movie stars.

To deal with the high cost of filmmaking, the movie moguls created a densely interlocking infrastructure of talent (dramatic and technical), production facilities, managers, and capital. Actors signed with a studio, which paid them a flat fee and had the right to employ them in any of its productions. A studio could also loan an actor's services to another studio, pocketing the difference between the fee and the actor's salary. In addition, studios rented space to each other and bought, financed, or distributed pictures through their vertically controlled chains of movie theaters. Such techniques allowed the studios to produce a large number of pictures with factorylike efficiency.

Hollywood operated with a similar mass-production mentality on the aesthetic plane as well, producing a line of different genres to appeal to different segments of the market. A series of discrete storytelling traditions—the Western, the horror film, the screwball comedy, the musical—elaborated their own cinematic traditions. By highbrow conventions of uniqueness and elite appeal, such movies were routinely dismissed as junk, but in drawing upon, adapting, and subverting widely shared cultural conventions, these movies had tremendous audience appeal. Thus, while the 1942 film *Casablanca* might leave a lot to be desired from a standpoint of modernist experimentation, its combination of brisk direction by Michael Curtiz, nuanced acting by Humphrey Bogart and Ingrid Bergman, and imaginative reconfigurations of genre conventions (a romantic love story where the guy does not get the girl; a fable of political commitment set in an atmosphere of cynicism and corruption) make this cheap, fast Warner Brothers production one of the most beloved films of all time.

RADIO

Originally developed at the turn of the century for nautical uses, radio technology was used for land and air as well as sea operations during World War I. In the years that followed, however, its creators and boosters struggled to find a way for it to become the fixture of everyday life they believed it could be. After the war, General Electric (GE), the Radio Corporation of America (RCA), and American Telephone and Telegraph (AT&T) pooled their various patents into a cartel. They believed most of their revenues would come from selling equipment ("ham" radio transmission and reception over long distances was something of a fad at the time). But in 1920 an executive at Westinghouse, a company that lagged behind its rivals, noticed that an engineer with the company had begun playing records from a transmitter in his home in Pittsburgh and that a local department store was advertising receivers as the means to hear them. In other words, the goal was not two-way radio communication but broadcasting from one point to many recipients. By 1930, radio was reaching 40 percent of American families (Czitrom, *Media and the American Mind*, p. 79) and was well on its way to becoming the staple form of popular culture in American life.

The question—and this is something that took more than a decade to become clear—was how it was to become a staple of American life. At first, broadcasting was a freewheeling affair, as churches, unions, schools, and private companies received licenses from the federal government for particular

DIFFERENT WAVELENGTHS

Before there was *Seinfeld,* before there was *All in the Family,* even before *The Honeymooners,* there was *Amos 'n' Andy.* The radio show began as a fifteen-minute serial out of a Chicago station in 1928 and rapidly became a national half-hour fixture five or six nights a week. Never has popular culture been more popular. At its peak, *Amos 'n' Andy* was listened to by one in three Americans: movie theaters played it in their lobbies; Atlantic City merchants broadcast it on the Boardwalk; and when the show was over, utility companies reported drops in water pressure. It was eventually broadcast on television.

The title characters of *Amos 'n' Andy* were played by Charles Correll and Freeman Gosden, white actors who extended the minstrel tradition of the nineteenth century by portraying black ones. Gosden played Amos, a sly "Zip Coon" figure. Correll played Andy, a stereotypical Sambo. The following is an excerpt from the radio broadcast of 30 October 1929, the day after the stock market crash. It suggests the complex mixture of racism and identification with which the white Americans regarded African Americans:

> *Andy:* Well Lightnin',' 'course I'd like to give you a job but de business repression is on right now.
> *Lightnin':* Whut is dat you say, Mr. Andy?
> *Andy:* Is you been keepin' yo' eye on de stock market?
> *Lightnin':* Nosah, I ain't ever seed it.
> *Andy:* Well, de stock market crashed.
> *Lightnin':* Anybody get hurt?
> *Andy:* Well, 'course, Lightnin', when de stock market crashes it hurts us bizness men. Dat's what puts de repression on things.

This is a complicated exchange. In part, its humor stems from Lightnin's uncannily appropriate concern over people being hurt and Andy's evocative malapropism for the depression (*Amos 'n' Andy*'s term "repression" is a better one than is generally used, an Illinois paper later editorialized). Moreover, the term "repression" may have had even more resonance for African Americans in particular than most whites imagined, an irony that some blacks surely noted. Finally, any admiration for the acuity and even wisdom expressed here must be balanced against the childlike simplicity and condescension with which it is rendered. Such complexities and cross-currents are typical of even the most seemingly simple popular culture.

Source: Arthur Frank Wertheim. *Radio Comedy.* New York, 1979, p. 37.

wavelengths. Gradually, and amid much resistance, a system of wired networks controlled by the National Broadcasting Company (NBC) and the Columbia Broadcasting System (CBS) became dominant. (ABC was carved out of NBC as the result of an antitrust action in 1941.) The networks broadcast live entertainment that was paid for by sponsors, who typically bought a block of time to advertise their products repeatedly over the course of a program.

Radio programming took a variety of forms. News was important; Edward R. Murrow, for example, became a giant of journalism as a result of his broadcasts from Germany on the eve of World War II. The legendary intimacy President Franklin Delano Roosevelt achieved with the American people was derived in large measure from his "fireside chats" that were broadcast into American homes during the Great Depression. But the most beloved types of programs were radio serials. Some, like the

THE (SWING) JAZZ AGE

Years after his conversion to Islam and on the eve of his assassination, a weary Malcolm X recalled the popular culture of his youth with a clarity and affection that stood in stark contrast to his feelings about much else in American life. He was particularly enchanted by the jazz of legendary figures like Count Basie, Fletcher Henderson, and Duke Ellington, pioneers of the so-called swing music that first emerged in the mid-1930s. The following excerpt from his autobiography describes his experiences as a shoeshine boy at nightclubs in Boston and New York before World War II.

"Showtime!" People would start hollering about the last hour of the dance. Then a couple dozen really wild couples would stay on the floor, the girls changing to low white sneakers. The band now would really be blasting, and all the other dancers would form a clapping, shouting circle to watch that wild competition as it began, covering only a quarter or so of the ballroom floor. The band, the spectators and the dancers would be making the Roseland Ballroom feel like a big rocking ship. The spotlight would be turning, pink, yellow, green, and blue, picking up the couples lindy-hopping as if they had gone mad. "Wail, man, wail!" people would be shouting at the band; and it *would* be wailing, until first one and then another couple just ran out of strength and stumbled off toward the crowd, exhausted and soaked with sweat. Sometimes I would be down there inside the door jumping up and down in my gray jacket with the whiskbroom in my pocket, and the manager would have to come and shout at me that I had customers upstairs.

Source: Malcolm X, with the assistance of Alex Haley. *The Autobiography of Malcolm X.* Rev. ed. New York, 1992, p. 51.

dramas sponsored by soap companies—hence the name "soap operas"—were daytime shows whose principal appeal was to women. Others, like the wildly popular black comedy *Amos 'n' Andy,* appealed to all audiences.

Radio was also a source of live music. Most musical performances were limited by radio's technological capabilities, but the situation improved in the mid-1920s with the introduction of the electric microphone, which could transmit a greater range of voices. "Sweet music," or "crooning," followed. The big, brassy voice of Al Jolson did not translate to radio well; the more mellow style of Bing Crosby made him the biggest pop singer of the era. Whatever the artistic merits of such performers—one critic compared crooning to the sound of mashed potatoes dropping—they vividly illustrated the way technology could shape popular taste.

Radio also helped lay the foundations for later musical revolutions. Large stations—like WSM in Nashville, Tennessee, home of the legendary *Grand Ole Opry* hour—could be heard hundreds of miles away, which allowed isolated rural people to make cultural contact with other musical communities around the country and made national stars out of figures like Jimmie Rodgers and the Carter Family. Such broadcasts were absolutely pivotal in the evolution of blues, jazz, and country music. Without them it would be hard to explain Elvis Presley, for example, who was born in 1935 and grew up listening to such shows.

THE RECORDING INDUSTRY

A kind of radio programming that was not common in the 1920s and 1930s was one taken for granted today: recorded music. In part, this was because of the poor sound quality of records when broadcast. But it was also because the American Society of Composers, Authors, and Publishers (ASCAP) set such high fees for rights that radio stations avoided records. It was not until the 1950s, when the proliferation of television led to a transformation of radio, that broadcasting and records began to seem like a synergetic fit.

The record industry came into its own during the dance crazes of the 1910s. Sales of phonographs, which were based on developments in the 1870s of "talking machines" by Thomas Edison and Alexander Graham Bell, reached 500,000 in 1914 (Schlereth, *Victorian America*, p. 193). In particular, the "Victrola," manufactured by the Victor Talking Machine Company, turned what had been a generally unwieldy contraption into a standard piece of furniture in the typical middle-class home. The spread of phonographs stoked a growing market for prerecorded music. Record production peaked at 100 million in 1921 (Maltby, *The Passing Parade*, p. 42).

Both in form and content, the pop music world, like radio broadcasting, was centered in New York. The dominant style was the Tin Pan Alley tradition forged in vaudeville and other forms of theater—and which drew on and diffused across other musical traditions around the country. By the 1930s, the spread of big band jazz into the mainstream of popular culture helped spark the creation of the first true pop idol, Frank Sinatra, who began his career in the late 1930s as a singer with the Harry James band.

Yet the record industry was perhaps the least secure of the new electronic media of the interwar years. In 1925 sales were only half of what they had been four years earlier. And the Great Depression was devastating to the industry; a mere 6 million records were sold in 1932, less than one-tenth of the 1921 figure (Maltby, p. 102).

PRINT CULTURE

The advent of new media did not simply destroy old ones, which in many cases adapted—or simply persisted with smaller, but, perhaps as a result, more devoted, audiences. For most of the nineteenth century, popular culture had been a culture of print, whether in newspapers, magazines, books, or other formats (e.g., sheet music). In the twentieth century, by contrast, the written word was often a building block for newer media, whether as a source of inspiration (countless novels were adapted into movies) or as an important structural element (like radio scripts, which were written ahead of time to be delivered over the airwaves).

Print culture also underwent internal shifts that reflected technological as well as demographic changes. The sensationalistic dime novel, which had largely petered out by 1900, got a new lease on life in the 1920s and 1930s in the so-called pulp magazines that catered to working-class audiences. Journalism also underwent changes. Newspapers like the *New York Daily News* (founded in 1919) gave photography greater play than ever, and the creation of the first "newsweeklies"—*Time* was founded in 1923, *Newsweek* a decade later—emphasized a more staccato reporting style that reflected the faster pace of the times.

Still other facets of print culture sought to affirm continuity with the past and bridge a widely perceived cultural divide. The much-beloved illustrations of Norman Rockwell, which graced the covers of magazines like the *Saturday Evening Post* for almost fifty years beginning in 1916, paid homage to a timeless small-town America at the very moment the nation's population was concentrated in cities. *Readers Digest*, first published in 1922, and the Book-of-the-Month Club, founded in 1926, sought to aid self-help-minded Americans in navigating an often dizzying array of cultural choices and developments and reassure them that Victorian values of cultivation had not altogether vanished. Critics of this so-called middlebrow culture noted that such approach all too often reduced complex ideas to inane cocktail party chatter. But a sense that American society was dauntingly, even frighteningly, beyond comprehension was by no means limited to what writer H. L. Mencken dismissively referred to as the "booboisie."

THE IMPACT OF THE GREAT DEPRESSION

The Great Depression severely damaged popular culture industries. Hollywood weathered the initial shock relatively well; theater attendance actually rose in 1930, and while it declined in 1931, studios and exhibitors generally remained in the black. By 1932, however, some major players—among them Paramount, Universal, and Fox—were either in bankruptcy or undergoing reorganization.

Such setbacks here and elsewhere proved temporary. Part of the reason was structural. The implementation of the Roosevelt administration's National Recovery Administration (NRA) in 1933, for example, granted movie studios important concessions that allowed them to regain and even strengthen their positions. By the time the NRA was declared unconstitutional and the passage of the Wagner Act in 1935 gave new power to unions, the industry had largely stabilized.

But in a real yet unquantifiable way, the survival, even prosperity, of the popular arts was a function of their essential character. Relative to other forms of art, they remained highly accessible: once a family invested in a radio (something that was likely to have occurred before the stock market crash), entertainment was cheap and plentiful. Popular culture was also highly sensitive to the interests and feelings of ordinary people; a spate of gangster films in the early 1930s, typified by *Little Caesar* (1930), *The Public Enemy* (1931), and *Smart Money* (1931), dramatized the appeal of characters who took matters into their own hands in a time of widely perceived powerlessness. Pressure from interest groups softened such appraisals—the star of *The Public Enemy*, James Cagney, played a government agent in *"G" Men* (1935)—but producers of popular culture literally could not afford to ignore the desires of their audiences, even if they could respond only in a veiled or coded way.

THE CULTURAL DIVIDE NARROWS

The 1930s was also a decade when, literally and figuratively, émigré intellectuals came home. This partial rapprochement between intellectuals and the masses, which became especially pronounced in mid-decade, was a product of the larger global situation. The rise of fascism in Germany and Italy, combined with the show trials in the Soviet Union and Joseph Stalin's directive for the creation of a popular front with capitalist countries, led former skeptics to reconsider the possibilities of the United States. T. S. Eliot and Ezra Pound stayed abroad, but F. Scott Fitzgerald came home; his unfinished final novel, *The Last Tycoon* (1941), portrayed a

movie mogul modeled on MGM executive Irving Thalberg. Hollywood, for its part, evinced a notable sense of political consciousness and social realism in the 1930s. A film like John Ford's *The Grapes of Wrath* (1940), while softening some of the edges of John Steinbeck's 1939 best-selling novel, remains an unusually vivid document of what life was like for millions of Americans. Even the ultimately uplifting films of Frank Capra—among them *Mr. Deeds Goes to Town* (1936), *You Can't Take It With You* (1938), and especially *Mr. Smith Goes to Washington* (1939)—often evinced a gritty realism that gave such "Capracorn" its credibility with large audiences.

This is not to say, of course, that the core assumptions of modernism were repudiated or that attacks on the "booboisie" or the "Sahara of the Bozart" disappeared. H. L. Mencken was—and is—far better known than Gilbert Seldes. But by the time Adolf Hitler invaded Poland in September 1939, the popular arts in the United States had not simply assumed forms that would prove durable in the postwar era. They had also become a source of tradition and inspiration to succeeding generations around the world. Popular artists also showed some ability to appreciate and adapt elite culture elements into their work. Walt Disney distinguished himself as a gifted animator in his early cartoons of the mid-1920s and early 1930s, and made a huge conceptual as well as logistical leap in creating the first animated feature film, *Snow White and the Seven Dwarfs*, in 1937. He went still further in blending striking visual images and classical music in *Fantasia* (1940), which cemented his reputation as one of the defining artists of the twentieth century.

See also **The Design of the Familiar; Popular Culture in the Public Arena** *(volume 2);* **Elite vs. Popular Cultures; Culture for Mass Audiences; Film; Radio; Drama; Fiction; Music; Dance; Marxist Approaches** *(volume 3); and other articles in this section.*

BIBLIOGRAPHY

General Histories and Studies

Butch, Richard. *The Making of American Audiences: From Stage to Television, 1750–1990.* New York, 2000.

Cullen, Jim. *The Art of Democracy: A Concise History of Popular Culture in the United States.* New York, 1996. Survey history from the rise of the novel to the advent of the Internet.

Czitrom, Daniel J. *Media and the American Mind: From Morse to McLuhan.* Chapel Hill, N.C., 1982. Explores connections between technology and culture.

Levine, Lawrence W. *The Unpredictable Past: Explorations in American Cultural History.* New York, 1993. Collection of essays from a major historian with a special focus on popular culture and African American culture generally and the 1920s and 1930s in particular.

Maltby, Richard, ed. *The Passing Parade: A History of Popular Culture in the Twentieth Century.* New York, 1989. Lavishly illustrated, statistically rich survey.

Nasaw, David. *Going Out: The Rise and Fall of Public Amusements.* New York, 1993. Useful blend of older arts like vaudeville alongside newer ones such as film.

Schlereth, Thomas. *Victorian America: Transformations in Everyday Life, 1876–1915.* New York, 1991.

Seldes, Gilbert. *The Seven Lively Arts.* New York, 1924. Enlarged ed. New York, 1957. A founding text in the study of popular culture. The 1957 edition is annotated to include Seldes's observations from the perspective of a generation later.

Susman, Warren. *Culture as History: The Transformation of American Society in the Twentieth Century.* New York, 1984. Collected articles from a giant in the field with particular focus on the interwar period.

Film

Carey, Gary. *Doug and Mary: A Biography of Douglas Fairbanks and Mary Pickford.* New York, 1977.

Gabler, Neal. *An Empire of Their Own: How the Jews Invented Hollywood.* New York, 1988. Social history of the movie moguls.

Haskell, Molly. *From Reverence to Rape: The Treatment of Women in the Movies.* Rev. ed. Chicago, 1987. Good material on the 1920s, 1930s, and the genre known as "women's film."

O'Connor, John E., and Martin A. Jackson, eds. *American History/American Film: Interpreting the Hollywood Image.* 2d ed. New York, 1988. Includes a series of richly contextualized essays on major films from the interwar years.

Ray, Robert B. *A Certain Tendency of the Hollywood Cinema, 1930–1980.* Princeton, N.J. 1985.

Schatz, Thomas. *The Genius of the System: Hollywood Filmmaking in the Studio Era.* New York, 1988. Superb history and analysis of American cinema's golden age.

Schickel, Richard. *His Picture in the Papers: A Speculation on Celebrity in America Based on the Life of Douglas Fairbanks, Sr.* New York, 1973.

Sklar, Robert. *Movie-Made America: A Cultural History of American Movies.* Rev. ed. New York, 1995. The standard account.

Radio

Barnouw, Erik. *A Tower in Babel.* Vol. 1 of *A History of Broadcasting in the United States.* New York, 1966. Survey from the dean of broadcasting studies. Parts of this account are included in Barnouw's *Tube of Plenty: The Evolution of American Broadcasting,* rev. ed. (New York, 1990).

McChesney, Robert W. *Telecommunications, Mass Media, and Democracy: The Battle for Control of U.S. Broadcasting, 1928–1935.* New York, 1993. Detailed account of the lost opportunities for public broadcasting and the rise of commercial radio.

Smulyan, Susan. *Selling Radio: The Commercialization of American Broadcasting, 1920–1934.* Washington, D.C., 1994. Cultural history of early radio programming and audience resistance to advertising.

Wertheim, Arthur Frank. *Radio Comedy.* New York, 1979.

Popular Music

Collier, James Lincoln. *The Making of Jazz: A Comprehensive History.* Boston, 1978.

Ehrenberg, Lewis A. *Steppin' Out: New York Nightlife and the Transformation of American Culture, 1890–1930.* Rev. ed. Chicago, 1984. Covers theater, dance, nightclubs, and other venues where popular music flourished.

Hobsbawm, Eric. *The Jazz Scene.* Rev. ed. New York, 1993. Superb primer by a noted British historian.

Holiday, Billie, with William Dufty. *Lady Sings the Blues.* New York, 1956; rev. ed., New York, 1992. Classic memoir that serves as an evocative social history.

Malone, Bill C. *Country Music U.S.A.* Rev. ed. Austin, Tx., 1985. The definitive history.

Print Culture

Radway, Janice A. *A Feeling for Books: The Book-of-the-Month-Club, Literary Taste, and Middle-Class Desire.* Chapel Hill, N.C., 1997. A simultaneously personal and comprehensive treatment of the subject from its origins to the present.

Rubin, Joan Shelley. *The Making of Middlebrow Culture.* Chapel Hill, N.C., 1992. Highly regarded study focuses on the interwar decades.

THE HARLEM RENAISSANCE

George Hutchinson

> I was there. I had a swell time while it lasted. But I thought it wouldn't last long. . . .
> For how could a large and enthusiastic number of people be crazy about Negroes
> forever? But some Harlemites thought the millennium had come. They thought the
> race problem had at last been solved through art plus Gladys Bentley. They were sure
> the New Negro would lead a new life from then on in green pastures of tolerance
> created by Countee Cullen, Ethel Waters, Claude McKay, Duke Ellington, Bojangles,
> and Alain Locke. (Hughes, *The Big Sea*, p. 228)

Langston Hughes's satirical 1940 characterization of the movement in which he was a central figure, the movement now known as the Harlem Renaissance, helped set a pattern of thinking about it that has remained strong ever since. It frames in retrospect a brief vogue of the 1920s in which Hughes had participated while maintaining an ironic distance that absolves him of complicity in the movement's alleged naïveté. Thus, two antithetical yet vitally linked notions emerge that run through all later commentary: a "Negro vogue" that flamed up and died quickly, a failed attempt to solve the "race problem" through the arts, involving a lot of superficial interracial glad-handing at parties and promotions; and a less glamorous, unnamed process of artistic self-development on the part of individuals who were wise to the game all along, realistic about the position of the black artist in American society, and determined to be true to their crafts.

Despite claims that what is now referred to as the Harlem Renaissance was a failure, a sense that it was also peculiarly important remains. Black schoolchildren for decades after the 1920s were instilled with pride in the accomplishments of some of its luminaries, chiefly Countee Cullen, Langston Hughes, James Weldon Johnson, and W. E. B. Du Bois. Aimé Césaire and Léopold Sédar Senghor attested to the inspiration it gave them for the negritude movement among chiefly Francophone African and black Caribbean intellectuals. And despite a rather low scholarly rating given the movement by many from the 1960s on, there seems to have been a grudging recognition that the Harlem Renaissance set the foundations for all later African American art and writing, indeed that it left an inescapable legacy to people of African descent not only in the United States but throughout the world. If the movement failed to overcome racial prejudice and transform American society, as an intellectual and cultural movement it was indeed a turning point. Moreover, it established positions in American cultural institutions upon which later generations would build.

WHY HARLEM?

Commonly referred to as a "Negro renaissance" by contemporaries, the phenomenon had roots outside New York City, and indeed outside the United States; Harlem, however, provided the movement with its symbolic capital and its institutional center of gravity. There one found a complex and culturally productive concentration of peoples of African descent: recent migrants from the rural South, immigrants from the Caribbean and Latin America, native New Yorkers, and a burgeoning black professional class hailing from all sections of the United States. Moreover, black Harlem was a new community that seethed with energy and hope, indeed with a kind of optimism that came to characterize much of the artwork and publicity of the "New Negro."

At the beginning of the 1920s, Harlem was regarded by many as a healthful and attractive residential area, with broad, tree-lined avenues and sidewalks, handsome brownstones, and plenty of fresh air. Blacks of the middle and professional classes had begun moving into the area from about 1900; by 1910 whites were fleeing as the "Negro" section expanded, displacing Italians and Jews, who had themselves only recently displaced the earlier

Langston Hughes, c. 1922. Following poems in *Opportunity* and *The Crisis*, Hughes's first book, *The Weary Blues*, was published in 1926. NICKOLAS MURRAY/ GEORGE EASTMAN HOUSE/ARCHIVE PHOTOS

German settlers. In 1928 black Harlem still occupied less than two square miles between 114th and 156th streets, between the East River and St. Nicholas Avenue, but it was famous throughout the world.

Harlem featured an extraordinary cross-section of black social groups and cultural institutions, including an active branch of the New York Public Library that served as a community cultural center and by the mid-1920s had the greatest collection of texts and materials concerning black history ever assembled. Its theaters, nightclubs, and dance halls attracted an international clientele, many of whom came for a taste of the exotic. Its churches ranged from storefront Pentecostal operations to the African Methodist Episcopal "Mother Zion" Church to staid Protestant Episcopal churches, including some of the wealthiest black congregations in the country. "Negro" branches of the YMCA and YWCA participated in the cultural ferment and encouraged it; in the late 1920s, the Dunbar Apartments (America's first black cooperative apartment complex)

housed a veritable "who's who" of black movers and shakers in every field—medicine, law, social work, business, journalism, the arts, and education. The "Mecca of the New Negro," as Alain Locke dubbed it for a special 1924 issue of the magazine *Survey Graphic,* drew top talent from throughout the black world. However, daily life was anything but glamourous for most Harlemites; many women, for example, could make a living only in some form of domestic service. Moreover, much of the money that came into the section went right back out to white owners of stores, apartment buildings, and entertainment houses, while the neighborhoods grew increasingly congested and crime rates rose.

An important force in the overall phenomenon of the "Black Metropolis" in the early 1920s, the Jamaican exile Marcus Garvey attracted a mass following to his United Negro Improvement Association, which merged calls for racial autonomy with admiration for European-style empire and capitalist economics; he later boasted that he had been one of the first fascists. His goal: to reclaim Africa for Africans and build a great black empire, in part by repatriating blacks of the Western Hemisphere to their ancestral homeland. Garvey's grand parades and rallies accounted for part of the excitement of Harlem in the early 1920s. Unlike the great civil rights leaders of the era such as W. E. B. Du Bois, James Weldon Johnson, and Ida B. Wells-Barnett, Garvey wanted nothing to do with integration or "Americanism"; he even met with leaders of the Ku Klux Klan in 1922, agreeing on the importance of racial nationalism and the dangers of amalgamation. By 1923 many mainstream black leaders were calling for the U.S. attorney general to crush his movement. Former supporters began abandoning and even attacking him, and by 1925 he was imprisoned for mail fraud, his Black Star Line (a steamship company for émigrés to Africa) a catastrophic failure. But to the extent that Garvey helped inspire widespread pride in blackness and a desire for social and economic autonomy, his movement contributed greatly to the cultural ferment of the age.

The Harlem Renaissance is unusual among literary and artistic movements for its close relationship to organizations fighting for civil rights and social reform, almost all of them based in New York. Crucial to its support were the black magazines *The Crisis,* edited by Du Bois for the National Association for the Advancement of Colored People (NAACP); *Opportunity,* edited by Charles S. Johnson for the National Urban League; and *The Messenger,* initially a black socialist journal edited chiefly by A. Philip Randolph with Chandler Owen and George S. Schuyler, among others. *Negro World,* the newspaper of Marcus Garvey's United Negro Improvement Association, also played a role, but few of the major authors of the Harlem Renaissance identified with Garvey's Back to Africa movement. *The Crisis, Opportunity,* and *The Messenger* stressed the Americanism of African Americans together with Pan-Africanism. A tension as well as complementarity between American cultural nationalism and black cultural nationalism informed their support of new black efforts in art, literature, and music. In *The Crisis,* for example, Du Bois and the literary editor Jessie Fauset assailed the hypocrisy of white America while claiming, in the words of one of Fauset's fictional heroes, "There is nothing more supremely American than the colored American, nothing more made-in-America, so to speak." As the abolitionist Frederick Douglass stressed decades earlier, African Americans not only believed in and understood the value of the ideals expressed in the Declaration of Independence more deeply than any other citizens, they had also, allegedly, given the United States its only distinctive cultural forms. This combination of convictions formed one of the most consistent ideological positions of an otherwise extremely diverse and at times contradictory movement. Another major concern was resurrecting the image of Africa and fostering solidarity of the "darker races" against white domination.

Both of these ideological touchstones help explain the optimism of the movement. Black intellectuals worldwide regarded World War I as a tremendous blow to the prestige of European civilization, revealing its supposed exhaustion—a point often attested to by European and white American modernists themselves. A cycle of history appeared to be closing, and the "darker races" were coming back into their own, reclaiming their cultural and political authority. Within the United States, left-wing American cultural nationalists sought to detach American culture from English culture and to call a native culture into being from previously denigrated sources. African American writers and artists viewed their own work within the context of such efforts, which seemed to offer them a strategic position for pressing their claims on the nation, while at the same time serving as an avant-garde movement for worldwide black cultural resurgence.

The diversity of ideologies and cultural orientations and of periodicals and activist organizations brought together in uptown Manhattan made it the nerve center of black modernism. But connections with "white" institutions in New York City were also crucial; New York was the publishing capital of the nation and rapidly becoming a literary and artistic capital of global proportions. It was the home of a wide variety of "little" magazines, educational institutions, libraries, and intellectual circles that proved particularly important to aspiring black writers. Marxist periodicals competed with liberal and conservative ones, old-line publishers with new ones that were founded, in many cases, by Jews. Institutions such as the Rand School and the New School for Social Research spread new and often radical ideas that affected many black writers; Columbia University and New York University housed departments of anthropology, philosophy, and literature, at which a number of black intellectuals studied and, perhaps as important, contributed to significant transformations in American intellectual history, of which the Harlem Renaissance was a part.

CULTURAL AND AESTHETIC THEORY

Important to the intellectual context of the movement were new theories of race and culture that developed, particularly in New York, in the first two decades of the twentieth century. For example, the work of the Columbia University anthropologist Franz Boas in cultural and physical anthropology as well as linguistics and folklore was appropriated by a diverse array of black intellectuals—including Zora Neale Hurston, his student—to further their own programs. His views also help account for the new quality of interest among some white intellectuals in African American arts in the 1920s. Boasian anthropology undermined some of the most powerful assumptions of racist social science, including the popular conception that some "races" were inherently more advanced or more suited to American democracy than others and the view that cultural attributes derived from inherent racial traits. Boasian views thus buttressed the arguments of those African Americans who insisted on not only their equality with whites but also their cultural Americanness. But the new anthropology also could be recruited to support the concept of cultural pluralism, in that Boas insisted that the art or language of any group could be understood only according to its own formal characteristics and canons of interpretation.

The theory of cultural pluralism, which gained currency in the late 1910s and the 1920s, opposed the melting-pot concept as undemocratic and un-American. According to cultural pluralists, Ameri-

Zora Neale Hurston. In the early 1920s Hurston began publishing stories in various magazines. When her story "Spunk" appeared in *Opportunity* in 1925, it drew the attention of her literary peers. YALE COLLECTION OF AMERICAN LITERATURE, BEINECKE RARE BOOK AND MANUSCRIPT LIBRARY. REPRODUCED BY PERMISSION OF CARL VAN VECHTEN PAPERS

sciousness depends. Art thus supplies the values and meanings in terms of which actions and experiences are evaluated in any culture. Aesthetic experience and judgment become a form of social participation, essential to the building of community and the interactive orientation of diverse individuals and groups to a common world. Implicit in this theory is the notion that social groups will develop different aesthetic traditions, not as a function of inborn ethno-racial characteristics but in response to distinct historical conditions and experiences. Such thinking, broadly circulating on the American cultural left and explicitly adopted by such black editors and promoters as Charles S. Johnson, encouraged artists to develop forms and techniques out of the black heritage and particularly out of those art forms that had been produced in most intimate relation to the daily life of the masses.

Such aesthetic views, however, could also easily shade into primitivist tendencies that merely modified and sustained racial stereotypes, often encouraged by the popularization of Freudian psychology in the United States at this time. The African American modernists were always potentially subject to white fantasies about the sensuality, spirituality, and instinctive artistry of a supposedly exotic race unspoiled by a mechanistic and soul-deadening civilization. Indeed, some of the work and publicity of the period clearly exploits the contemporary appeal of the primitive and exotic. As important as this tendency was, however, it was never all-pervasive, and critiques and satires of exotic primitivism were a significant aspect of the Harlem Renaissance itself.

can civilization should develop as a sort of federation of ethnoracial groups harmonizing with each other but cultivating their own group customs and ideals. These ideals derived from historical experience and spiritual values specific to each group.

Strains of philosophical pragmatism, sometimes crossed with Marxian theory, also played a role in new aesthetic orientations associated with the Harlem Renaissance. Art, in this view, was not above or apart from daily activity but something that gives the final touch of meaning to all experience and reveals the fundamental qualities of every people. But for art to recover its proper role, it must regain the continuity with normal processes of living that it had lost in Western high culture. Artistic labor, in this view, brings the aesthetic aspect inherent in all human experience to a level of consummation that helps train the sensibilities upon which ethical con-

MUSIC

Black music provided the pulse of the Harlem Renaissance and of the so-called Jazz Age generally. The migration of African Americans to the North after about 1915 brought with it the musical forms first developed in the South, such as blues and jazz. The founding of the "race records" industry, beginning with Okeh's Original Race Records label in 1921, helped popularize the blues, and female blues singers quickly came into high demand. Well-known performers included Mamie Smith, Alberta Hunter, Ma Rainey, and Bessie Smith, some of whom had been performing for years but found themselves famous after their recordings were released. Male blues singers started recording in the mid-1920s. The lyrics of the blues have a wide range, but undoubtedly the best-known in the 1920s and 1930s, such as "Saint Louis Blues,"

tended to be lamentations of personal disaster (often loss of love) through which the performer transmuted painful experience into an empathetic process of aesthetic satisfaction. The music was often composed in performance, playing off a conventional melody or harmony, and it used instruments in startling new ways that seemed to imitate the human voice or, in the urban blues, the sounds of the city. The lyrics, moreover, had their own sort of poetic form in uses of meter and rhyme as well as rich imagery and metaphor, synecdoche and understatement. Frequently ironic, often bawdy, the music seemed to express in secular form the very longings and philosophical perspectives of the black working class. Literary intellectuals, especially of the bohemian sort, increasingly valued the blues as an indigenous cultural form of the nation's most oppressed people, a secular equivalent of the spirituals, and an antidote to Anglo-American Puritanism as well as black bourgeois assimilationism.

Out of the blues came jazz, and as New Orleans jazz performers migrated to Chicago and other points north during World War I, they brought their music with them, giving the decade of the 1920s the character of a "jazz age." So-called classic jazz was performed by small bands that included a trio of trumpet, clarinet, and trombone and a rhythm section of piano, bass, and drum. Collective improvisation and polyphony characterized the music, and, like blues musicians, jazz performers made previously unheard sounds come out of their instruments through new, improvised techniques. For such reasons, along with the fast pace of much of the music and the dances that developed with it, jazz came to be regarded by many as the quintessential modern, and American, art form.

In the 1920s orchestras grew in size and incorporated new instruments, making collective improvisation impossible. Moreover, younger musicians with college or conservatory training emerged. The transformation became clear when the first big band was organized in New York City by Fletcher Henderson and Don Redman. Henderson and Redman arranged the music in advance, allowing for solo improvisations. Louis Armstrong became the first great jazz soloist when he moved from King Oliver's Creole Jazz Band in Chicago to Fletcher Henderson's band in New York in 1924. Between that year and 1936, the size of the band grew to sixteen players, and similar big bands came to prominence, such as those led by Cab Calloway, Duke Ellington, Chick Webb, and Jimmie Lunceford. Not surprisingly, artists in other areas, including literature and fine arts, began attempting to create equivalents to jazz in their own media. Such attempts were not, by any means, restricted to black or even American artists; indeed, white producers and musicians notoriously appropriated "black" forms and techniques, often without acknowledging the source, while black performers were pushed into the background. The dance forms associated with jazz, most famously the Charleston (also a product of mid-1920s Harlem), became international fads and began to transform not only the field of dance but drama and musical theater as well.

The international appeal of jazz, along with the sheer self-confidence and virtuosity of the musicians and their vital connection with African Americans as a people, clearly encouraged black intellectuals in other fields to turn increasingly to specifically Negro aesthetic forms as a basis for innovation and cultural self-expression. This tendency appeared in the realm of concert music as well as literature.

Black concert musicians in the 1920s turned to folk music as a source of ideas for composition and performance, adopting the rhythms, harmonies, and melodies of blues, spirituals, and jazz. Roland Hayes, one of the stars of the New Negro movement who gained international acclaim as a concert singer beginning in the 1920s in New York, expressed the ethos of many artists of the Harlem Renaissance:

> My people have been very shy about singing their crude little songs before white folks. They thought they would be laughed at—and they were! And so they came to despise their own heritage. . . . If, as I truly believe, there is purpose and plan in my life, it is this: that I shall have my share in rediscovering the qualities we have almost let slip away from us; and that we shall make our special contribution—only a humble one, perhaps, but our very own—to human experience. (In Southern, *The Music of Black America*, p. 402)

The 1920s was a period of expanding opportunity for black concert musicians. Although discrimination often barred the way, for the first time in history major orchestras performed works by black composers, opera companies used black performers in leading roles, and symphony and radio orchestras were conducted by black musicians.

The 1920s also saw the beginning of regular appearances of professional black choruses in concert, theater, and film—most notably the Hall Johnson choir, which gave particularly distinctive performances of spirituals. But undoubtedly the most popularly noted phenomenon of black musical advance was the invasion of Broadway. Not since 1909 had a show written and produced by blacks been seen on Broadway, and even that one (*Mr. Lode of*

The Fletcher Henderson Orchestra, 1924. Featuring Louis Armstrong on trumpet, Fletcher Henderson on piano, Coleman Hawkins on tenor saxophone, and Don Redman on alto saxophone, the Henderson Orchestra was, in 1924, the best jazz band in the world. FRANK DRIGGS/ARCHIVE PHOTOS

Koal, starring Bert Williams) was constrained by minstrel show conventions to an extent far greater than the works of the 1920s. In 1921 *Shuffle Along,* by Eubie Blake and Noble Sissle, opened on Broadway and, according to Eileen Southern, established a model that would shape the format of black musicals for the next sixty years. Sissle and Blake turned to Harlem folk sources and made few concessions to white audience expectations. From this time on, black artists had increasing freedom to develop their own ideas for black musical theater—although this remained only a relative freedom, always constrained by the dominance of white producers and audience demands. In the 1920s black-produced shows came to Broadway again and again, and many white-produced shows featured black casts. The success of such shows fueled the optimism of the Harlem Renaissance, despite worsening socioeconomic conditions in Harlem itself.

LITERATURE

The literary Harlem Renaissance was so complex and diverse that scholars sometimes question whether it should even be called a "movement," but its diversity was crucial to its vitality and importance. If one quality can be said to lie at the center of the literary movement, it would be race pride. But beyond that one finds little agreement, for the actors involved disagreed (often vehemently) about what race pride entailed. George Schuyler lampooned the very idea of Negro art in America as "hokum" artificially stimulated by white decadents. Countee Cullen resisted any suggestion that traditional forms of English poetry were inappropriate for black poets and suspected that the new, more experimental styles often played into the interests of whites to ghettoize black authors and lead them away from the finely chiseled expression of eternal verities with universal appeal. On the other hand, for such writers as Langston Hughes, Zora Neale Hurston, and Sterling A. Brown, black writing must resist the "urge within the race to whiteness" by finding in the aesthetic forms developed by the black masses—whether urban working class or rural peasantry—the bases of black literary modernism, for these often unnamed artists of the people had created an art of, by, and for black people themselves.

Such notions on the part of emerging black writers did not, of course, develop in isolation. Indeed, they responded in part to the call of American cultural nationalists such as Van Wyck Brooks, Waldo Frank, and Randolph Bourne for an American culture independent of English tradition, developed from native experience and forms of expression, in vernacular forms. Hughes's early models were Carl Sandburg and Walt Whitman. Edgar Lee Masters's *Spoon River Anthology* (1916), with its distinct voicing of a diverse assortment of Midwesterners, "high" and "low," inspired a broad range of black authors, including Hughes, Hurston, Schuyler, and Melvin B. Tolson. Moreover, this native modernism was part of a global phenomenon that included the Irish Renaissance and left-wing anticolonial and cultural nationalist movements in India and Latin America. The Irish Renaissance was repeatedly held up by white and black intellectuals as an example for African American authors.

Central to the movement was the effort of black artists to reconceptualize "the Negro" in modern terms, independent of white myths and stereotypes that had distorted African Americans' views of themselves and their heritage—independent, too, of Victorian moral values and bourgeois embarrassment about those features of African American life that whites might take to confirm racist beliefs. An anthology edited by Alain Locke, *The New Negro: An Interpretation* (1925), helped announce this new movement to the world and attempted to massage the diverse and often conflicting positions of the artists into a coherent cultural manifesto. Critical to this project was the distinction Locke made between an older generation that had devoted its art chiefly to racial self-defense and propaganda and a new one that no longer allowed a "counterattitude" to limit its artistic experimentation. In particular, the younger authors Locke favored—such as Jean Toomer and Hughes—turned to the black folk heritage for inspiration in both subject matter and form, attempting to define new, characteristic racial idioms.

Toomer's *Cane* (1923), a dense and multigeneric experiment, seemed to many a radical new departure in writing about the South, centered in African American folk life yet dealing with that life in ways never seen or heard before. It refrained from moralizing, while the tones, phrases, symbols, and rhythms of black folk music and jazz provided its underlying structural motifs, weaving together its diverse sketches, poems, short stories, and dramatic narratives. The book broke free of the self-defensiveness that had seemed to limit earlier efforts and revealed a new, relatively frank treatment of black female sexuality. And while it unambiguously exposed the brutal force of white supremacy, it did so without seeming melodramatic or preachy. For many young black writers, *Cane* marked the path of the literary future. Ironically, however, even as he wrote *Cane*, Toomer thought of himself not as a "new Negro" but as the first conscious member of a new race—the "American race." He denied identification with the Negro renaissance and regarded the "Negro" label as limiting and inappropriate for his work.

In marked contrast, Hughes put Negro identity at the heart of his artistic project and became a crucial protagonist of the Harlem Renaissance, above all because of his explorations of black vernacular speech and lyrical forms. He began with free verse attempts to capture the experiences, longings, and frustrations of the masses. Gradually, perhaps influenced by the work of Sandburg and Vachel Lindsay with American folk song and the rising impact of black popular music, he experimented with verse forms, language, and subject matter drawn directly from the blues and then from jazz. A crucial development in black literary history, Hughes's direction was anticipated by James Weldon Johnson, who used the rhythms, idioms, and stylistic embellishments of popular black preaching style as the formal integuments of his poem "The Creation" (1920), a sermon in free verse. Such experiments broke black poetry free of the conventions of the genteel, often nostalgic and condescending dialect tradition that had constrained Paul Laurence Dunbar as well as Johnson himself. Later, Brown in poetry and Hurston in prose advanced the vernacular tradition of African American literature, which has grown increasingly powerful ever since.

In contrast to the vernacular poets, many black poets continued to write in traditional English literary forms, although in some cases turning these forms to new uses. Claude McKay, a radical socialist born and raised in Jamaica (where he had published two volumes of verse chiefly in Jamaican dialect) was a master of the sonnet, which he used as the vehicle for a wide range of lyrics concerning love, exile, nostalgia, political invective, and—most famously—racial defiance. McKay also published interesting and controversial novels—notably *Home to Harlem* (1928), which many accused of exploiting exotic primitivism, and *Banjo* (1929), which dealt with the black proletariat in an international context, set in the port of Marseilles.

Countee Cullen also preferred traditional English poetics to the vernacular forms favored by Hughes, but in other respects his poetry differs from McKay's, being more traditional in its emotional timbre and moral appeal and less radical in its political implications. Cullen was the favorite poet of the black middle class of the 1920s (one of the Harlem branches of the New York Public Library was later named for him), and he gained considerable attention in the white-dominated poetic world as well, mainly among critics still enamored of late Romantic and Edwardian verse. Cullen flirted with, but ultimately rejected, the notion of a distinct Negro aesthetic as propounded by his friend Locke. Although proud of his race and not averse to using racial subject matter, he felt that great poetry must transcend racial identity. Indeed, a great deal of poetry published by African Americans during the 1920s and early 1930s, particularly by women, was not concerned with racial subject matter; love poetry and nature poetry, often indistinguishable from similar poetry by whites, abounded in the pages of black newspapers and magazines.

In prose, highly moralistic and melodramatic fiction certainly continued to appear, but the range of new approaches to black fiction from the 1920s through the 1930s was unprecedented and laid the foundations on which later generations would build. Women's fiction is especially noteworthy in this regard. Jessie Fauset, for example, wrote novels of manners focusing chiefly on black middle-class characters, revealing the confusions in their lives caused by racism and class anxieties. On the whole, however, her fiction ended up affirming black bourgeois values and the program of racial uplift, while counterposing the idealistic Americanism of the Negro against the hypocrisy and spiritual bankruptcy of white Americans. Nella Larsen's fiction, also diverging from folk experiments, offers a complex, original, and genuinely tragic exploration of black and mulatto women's psychology along with brilliantly perceptive treatments of sexuality, social class, and interracial relationships. Raised by a Danish working-class mother (her father was West In-

dian) in a white Chicago family that rejected her, Larsen challenged as radically as any author of the time the myths of race and the role of the patriarchal family (with its anxious control of female sexuality) in maintaining racial and class hierarchies.

In contrast to Larsen's work, Hurston's chief importance is in her transformation of novelistic form through the adaptation of narrative patterns, language, imagery, and point-of-view that had developed in oral tradition, independent of the heritage of the European novel. Like Larsen, however, Hurston challenged male authority over black female sexuality and inspired later generations of black women writers by the confidence she showed in a female-centered, "womanist" (to borrow Alice Walker's term) voice and point-of-view, most effectively exemplified in *Their Eyes Were Watching God* (1937), which speaks to the agency of ordinary people making life meaningful within circumstances only partly of their own choosing.

VISUAL ARTS

Visual artists were less plentiful—and remain far less well-known—than writers in the Harlem Renaissance, but they also broke new ground and established foundations for later generations of African American artists. Central to much of their work was the effort to wrest control over images of their people from the white culture industry. The photographer James VanDerZee moved to Harlem from Lenox, Massachusetts, in 1905, initially with musical ambitions. Like the Photo-Secession group surrounding Alfred Stieglitz at the time, VanDerZee saw the potential for developing photography as a deliberate art form. He experimented from early on with atmospheric effects, diffused light, and soft focus, though it is also true that much of his work is of primarily documentary interest, providing a rich visual record of Harlem in the 1920s. Making his living as a highly successful portrait photographer out of a studio on 135th Street, he showed Harlem at its best in handsome images of individuals or groups, carefully composed and often hand-tinted or retouched. In this respect, his work offers a significant response to the concern for how the Negro would be portrayed, how one might present African Americans in images closer to those they had of themselves than to those most whites seemed to expect.

Prior to World War I, black painters and sculptors rarely concerned themselves with African American subject matter, let alone with inventing new artistic styles based on black aesthetic traditions. By the end of the 1920s this had changed immensely.

Meta Warrick Fuller anticipated the change with her 1914 sculpture *Ethiopia Awakening,* which not only dealt explicitly with racial subject matter but also seemed to prophesy a Pan-African Negro renaissance. Appearing from a distance like a piece of Egyptian funerary sculpture, on closer inspection it reveals a black woman wrapped like a mummy from the waist down but with her upper torso living and aspiring upward, her head crowned with an Egyptian queen's headdress—suggesting rebirth from a long sleep, a sense of nationhood, and hope. Egyptianism and Ethiopianism had been important aspects of late-nineteenth-century black nationalism and would remain significant touchstones for nationalist feeling and ideology, but as African cultures became better known in the West, West African cultural models gained in importance, revealing a greater sense of the historical backgrounds of African American culture itself and thus helping bridge the gap between Africanist tendencies and interest in reinterpreting and re-evaluating African American culture and experience.

The discovery and use of West African sculpture by European modernists, along with unprecedented exhibits held by Alfred Stieglitz and Albert C. Barnes of sub-Saharan art as art rather than as ethnographic specimens, inspired black artists and aesthetic theorists. Alain Locke called for black artists to look to African art for new aesthetic techniques and release from the influence of Western representations of black people. The interest in black folklore and modern urban experience also inspired new treatments of everyday life in African American communities. This trend did not go unchallenged by middle-class African Americans who felt it played to white expectations; indeed, some of the first and most influential, as well as controversial, work along these lines was actually painted by the German immigrant Winold Reiss, who faced a storm of criticism for his essentially realistic portraits of ordinary Harlemites, only to be defended and even lauded by black writers and artists who admired his work. Aaron Douglas, encouraged by black acquaintances in New York, left Kansas City for Harlem after seeing the 1925 "Harlem: Mecca of the New Negro" issue of *Survey Graphic,* with Reiss's portrait of Roland Hayes on its cover.

Douglas, who studied for two years under Reiss after arriving in New York, became the most recognized artist of the Harlem Renaissance after he turned from traditional landscape painting to rec-

ognizably Negro subject matter and a modern style influenced by art deco, the flat profile designs of ancient Egyptian art and Greek vase painting, and what he called the abstract qualities of the spirituals. Perhaps his most influential work of the 1920s was a series of illustrations for James Weldon Johnson's *God's Trombones* (1927), in which Douglas transformed traditional white Christian iconography by putting black subjects in central roles and evoking (like Johnson's poems) the identification of black Americans with the suffering of Jesus and other central motifs of the Bible. His stylized, silhouette-like renderings of Negro physical features, imbued with qualities of both spiritual yearning and implicit dignity, became a signature of the movement. Douglas also borrowed from African art in new ways; overall, the affirmation of Negro consciousness and experience was perhaps nowhere more evident than in his artwork, which in the 1930s showed an even more overt interest in interpreting the collective historical experience of African Americans, subtly inflected with a new Marxist orientation, as in his series *Aspects of Negro Life* (1934).

This interest in new, uncompromising presentations of modern American history from a black perspective would be taken further by Jacob Lawrence, usually considered a post-Renaissance artist but who was trained in Harlem in the 1920s and 1930s and whose work clearly built upon foundations laid in the 1920s by Douglas, among others. Despite Douglas's importance, most black painters of the 1920s spent little time in Harlem. Paris was the mecca of black painters and sculptors in that decade. However, traveling exhibits and awards presented by the Harmon Foundation from 1927 to 1933 encouraged African American work in the fine arts. Notable artists included Palmer C. Hayden, who interpreted black folklore and the customs of black southerners in his paintings; Archibald J. Motley, a Chicago artist best known for his paintings of black social life; the sculptors Richmond Barthé and Augusta Savage (who became an influential art teacher in Harlem in the 1930s); and the painters Sargent Johnson, William H. Johnson, Hale Woodruff, and Lois Mailou Jones. Many of these people produced their best work in the 1930s and helped cultivate the next generation. Indeed, the Harlem Renaissance in painting, especially, might be regarded as a phenomenon more of the 1930s than of the 1920s, as the depression forced many artists to return from Europe and brought them together in a critical mass they had never previously known. Not only did New York become a center of art education, with important new schools, galleries, and museums, but the federal arts project under the New Deal's Works Progress Administration, picking up where the Harmon Foundation left off in 1933, provided an unprecedented level of patronage. Harlem thus became the incubator of an entire generation of artists that would extend the legacy of the New Negro movement, though often in ostensible rejection of its example. Whether they knew it or not, the Harlem Renaissance had demonstrated that black artists could achieve authority over the images of their own people; and, in the words of Mary Schmidt Campbell, the New Negro artists had "define[d] a visual vocabulary for Black Americans" (*Harlem Renaissance*, p. 13). Later black artists would have a set of positions on Negro art against which they could extend, modify, or define themselves.

In hindsight, the most significant aspects of the Harlem Renaissance for the historian cluster around the emergence of a semiautonomous field of cultural expression embracing elite as well as popular forms, self-consciously working to develop distinctly Negro aesthetics and to win black artists new institutional footholds in the broad terrain of Western modernism. While the movement—like most artistic movements—could not achieve its most ambitious social aims, it was nonetheless a turning point in American cultural history.

See also **African Americans** *(volume 2);* **Painting; Fiction; Poetry** *(volume 3); and other articles in this section.*

BIBLIOGRAPHY

Anderson, Jervis. *This Was Harlem: A Cultural Portrait, 1900–1950.* New York, 1982.

Baker, Houston A. *Modernism and the Harlem Renaissance.* Chicago, 1987.

Bontemps, Arna, ed. *The Harlem Renaissance Remembered.* New York, 1972.

Campbell, Mary Schmidt, David Driscoll, David Levering Lewis, and Deborah Willis Ryan. *Harlem Renaissance: Art of Black America.* New York, 1987.

Clarke, John Henrik, ed. *Harlem: A Community in Transition.* New York, 1964.

Cruse, Harold. *The Crisis of the Negro Intellectual.* New York, 1967.

Douglas, Ann. *Terrible Honesty: Mongrel Manhattan in the 1920s.* New York, 1995.

Floyd, Samuel A., Jr., ed. *Black Music in the Harlem Renaissance.* New York, 1990.

Hemenway, Robert E. *Zora Neale Hurston: A Literary Biography.* Urbana, Ill., 1977.

Huggins, Nathan Irvin. *Harlem Renaissance.* New York, 1971.

Huggins, Nathan Irvin, ed. *Voices from the Harlem Renaissance.* New York, 1976.

Hughes, Langston. *The Big Sea: An Autobiography.* New York, 1940.

——. "The Negro Artist and the Racial Mountain." *Nation* 122 (1926): 692–694.

Hull, Gloria T. *Color, Sex, and Poetry: Three Women Writers of the Harlem Renaissance.* Bloomington, Ind., 1987.

Hutchinson, George. *The Harlem Renaissance in Black and White.* Cambridge, Mass., 1995.

Lewis, David Levering. *When Harlem Was in Vogue.* New York, 1981.

Locke, Alain, ed. *The New Negro: An Interpretation.* New York, 1925.

Martin, Tony. *Literary Garveyism: Garvey, Black Arts, and the Harlem Renaissance.* Dover, Mass., 1983.

Ogren, Kathy J. *The Jazz Revolution: Twenties America and the Meaning of Jazz.* New York, 1989.

Rampersad, Arnold. *The Life of Langston Hughes.* 2 vols. New York, 1986–1988.

Singh, Amritjit. *The Novels of the Harlem Renaissance: Twelve Black Writers, 1923–1933.* University Park, Pa., 1976.

Southern, Eileen. *The Music of Black Americans: A History.* 3d ed. New York, 1997.

Wall, Cheryl A. *Women of the Harlem Renaissance.* Bloomington, Ind., 1995.

Watson, Steven. *The Harlem Renaissance: Hub of African-American Culture, 1920–1930.* New York, 1995.

Williamson, Joel. "Harlem and After." In *New People: Miscegenation and Mulattoes in the United States.* Baton Rouge, La., 1980.

Wintz, Cary, ed. *The Harlem Renaissance, 1920–1940.* 7 vols. New York, 1996.

THE BEHAVIORAL AND SOCIAL SCIENCES

Hamilton Cravens

THE HAWTHORNE STUDIES

In 1924 the National Research Council selected Western Electric's Hawthorne Works, with some 30,000 workers and located on Chicago's West Side, as the locus for a routine study of worker productivity based on the shopworn ideology of scientific management. A group of electrical engineers from the Massachusetts Institute of Technology (MIT) constituted the research team. They assumed that workers were rational individuals who responded to incentives and their absence, all the while calculating their individual good. The researchers took their notions from Frederick Winslow Taylor, the most famous of the time-and-motion experts of the early twentieth century, who in turn had fashioned his system of ideas from classical laissez-faire liberalism and individualistic psychology. The engineers selected two small groups of workers. They kept the conditions of the control group constant and varied the factory's physical environment for the experimental group. They began with illumination, trying to see how increasing or decreasing the lighting in the work environment would influence the experimental group's productivity. They were astonished. Worker productivity increased independently of variation in illumination. They eventually realized that lighting was but one factor, and perhaps a minor one at that, in worker productivity. Obviously, many other factors could be involved; what they might be was the question.

Management authorized more research. The second round of tests began in the spring of 1927. The researchers returned with new assumptions and goals. They wanted now to understand the total environment and all its dynamics, including why the workers behaved in certain ways, which certainly did not square with the assumptions of both Tayloresque scientific management and rationalist, laissez-faire economics, according to which each individual sought to maximize advantage and wealth and minimize trouble and dimin-

ished income. The research continued for some years. It cost more than a million dollars—a spectacular sum for civilian scientific research then—and consumed many thousands of hours of time from the workers. MIT professors from a variety of specializations, not just electrical engineering, had joined the research team. They probed the relationships among working conditions, monotony, and fatigue. The researchers isolated six women who assembled relays in a room adjacent to the main relay assembly room. After observing the women under normal conditions for a while, they moved them into an experimental room to help them adjust to their new circumstances. Next, the women experienced a variety of working situations. The experimenters recorded their conversations and behavior, as well as any changes in productivity. As before, the workers responded by being more productive in the new environment. No matter what improvements the researchers introduced—higher wages, rest pauses, flexible working hours, even free nutritious lunches—the women worked more efficiently than before. When the researchers withdrew these improvements (save for higher wages), the women responded by working less efficiently. As each perquisite was reintroduced, they worked harder and better. The researchers learned that each factor in the environment was so dependent on every other one that no factor could be considered apart from any other—a result that researchers had not anticipated or accounted for in their theoretical prognostications and simulations. They realized, however, that the women were now a social unit and mutually participated in making the group's important decisions, a rather unnerving discovery from management's standpoint, to be sure.

The managers of Western Electric wanted to know more about these social networks among the workers. George Elton Mayo of the Harvard University Graduate School of Business Administration now led the research team. Mayo and his colleagues began their work in November 1931, and finished

669

six and a half months later. They observed fourteen male bank-wiring operators without altering any of the work conditions. The workers had created very complicated and involved social organizations, complete with their own social rules to regulate production and means of identifying and punishing deviant behavior, the latter being actions not sanctioned by the workers' group norms. Thus, the workers constituted a team whose members sought to protect and preserve the group's own survival and prosperity. Their ultimate purpose was job security. Their weapon was their control of production. Not surprisingly, the workers took a rather uppity attitude toward management and disagreed with most of its notions about pay, working conditions, and the like.

Mayo concluded that the group determined individual performance. That hoary old shibboleth of classical liberal political economy and of Tayloresque scientific management, that workers responded as individuals positively or negatively to working conditions based on rationalist and individualist notions of advantage or disadvantage, simply did not hold water. It was pure supposition—and little else. Western Electric managers were fascinated. Mayo and his colleagues had shown that the workers controlled output and often in so natural and subtle a way that few, if any, could tell what was going on. But if all was not rationalist calculation, then perhaps there were ways of manipulating the workers' behavior. Mayo argued that the crucial element was psychological, not material or economic. How much management made laborers think they "belonged" to the organization in active and positive ways and specific perquisites on the job, such as wages or working conditions, had little consequence, save as proof positive of the factory's psychological climate. Thus, the women increased their output because they were active participants in the study and thus wished it well. They flattered themselves as having been consulted by the company and taken into the confidence of their supervisors—in short, they believed themselves partners in the enterprise. The men, on the other hand, felt threatened by the researchers' presence and observations; they openly banded together to control production, thus protecting themselves as a group. It was group dynamics that mattered—behavioral science, that is. And that was the crucial insight that Mayo and his team hit upon in their work.

Managers implemented these ideas about group dynamics, and chance played a major role. Coincidentally, the company had been interviewing employees about its various programs for its workers.

Company interviewers, however, found that the workers would not stick to the topics management selected. Instead, they aired their views about what concerned them. Managers soon changed tactics; Mayo's lessons now made sense. The interviewers allowed the interviewees to prattle on about whatever pleased them. They applauded the company for making all manner of improvements at work, which in fact had never been contemplated, let alone achieved. They were gratified and complimented by being interviewed. That management appeared to value their opinions made them feel as though they belonged to the organization and were recognized as valuable members of it. Thus, management realized that the workers could be manipulated, if not downright duped, into becoming more productive and loyal by simply being listened to; no expensive wage and fringe benefit programs or elaborate worker-oriented schemes were necessary. It was only important to have company representatives listen to employees. Western Electric appointed long-term, well-liked company employees as counselors, telling them to focus on the employees' attitudes toward problems, never the problems themselves. In 1936 there were but five such counselors and twenty-nine in 1941; employee productivity appeared to improve as workers felt they were a part of the company and its operations.

A new generation of human relations professionals, specialists in the behavior of small groups and employee-management situations, appeared to help out America's larger corporations and institutions with their problems with their managers and workers. Questions of the physical context of the workplace or of material interests receded into the background, as issues of attitudes, and what could be done about them, came to the fore. Worker productivity was a state of mind. But happily, from management's perspective, it could still be understood and resolved as a problem in group dynamics or, more simply, behavioral science. It was the *behavior* of people in groups that Mayo and his corporate clients wished to understand and use.

The Hawthorne experiments were thus symptomatic of a new development in the social disciplines: the emergence of the behavioral sciences. Up to this point in time the social sciences were static, not dynamic, and were concerned with traits and characteristics rather than behavior and conduct. Thus, Taylorism and its parallels in late nineteenth and early twentieth century scientific management were concerned with the average abilities of workers in particular settings. The Hawthorne experiments, and the interesting interpretations that Mayo and his associates made of them, were strikingly different from the underlying conceptions of social science before the 1920s. Notions of social science between the 1870s and the 1920s might be characterized as representing natural and social reality, as if they were a hierarchical system of discrete and unique parts that nevertheless added up to a larger whole. Each part was separate from every other. Only in combination, all in their right or assigned places in the hierarchy, could the parts become the larger whole at its most efficient. Centralization, segregation, and differentiation were the watchwords of the notion of reality as a system. For the social sciences in particular this had specific implications. The national population was a system of social groups of differing weight and thus value; each type was distinct, and all individuals within that type approximated a particular mean for all group traits to be measured. Some groups were simply more valuable, because they were more talented, than others. Each type or group bred true—its history and behavior were entirely predictable.

THE EMERGENCE OF THE BEHAVIORAL SCIENCES

If the prewar view depicted reality as a hierarchical system, that of the interwar years could be dubbed a network, or an interdependent system of systems. In the prewar view, parts were distinct, segregated, different; in the interwar years they were so integrated that a change could not occur in one without widespread changes throughout all the others. Parts within the new systems had little identity or intrinsic nature by themselves. All won some of their character from their relationships to the other parts, and because each part interacted with others, all relationships were indefinite and relative. When new stimuli came into the network, the balance among the existing parts was undermined. The consequence was unpredictable adjustment and compensation throughout the entire whole. Put simply, in the pre-1920s system, the parts added up to the whole, no more and no less, whereas in the post-1920s network, the whole was greater than or different from the product of the parts.

Thus, the important new development in these years was the emergence of the behavioral sciences, the study of human behavior in the "real world." This new perspective came to influence all the social sciences. It was evident early among the psychologists, whose interest in psychological consciousness in the early 1900s led to more serious questioning of what consciousness might be. Increasing discontent over a new generation of experimentally oriented psychologists, who were coming to the fore in the 1910s in their profession, led within a few years to renunciation of the concept itself and proclamation that what should be the proper study of psychologists was the behavior of their subjects, whether animal or human. It was John Broadus Watson, an up-and-coming psychologist at Johns Hopkins University, who first introduced the concept into his discipline's formal discourse in a famous paper in 1913, "Psychology as the Behaviorist Views It."

By the 1920s the behavioral point of view dominated the study of the human mind; it was the discipline's paramount and overriding ideology. Above all, psychologists considered behaviorism a call for objective experimentation; it was not a liberal reformist environmentalist philosophy. Watson, the alleged founder of behaviorism in psychology, did not believe in such environmentalist ideas, as some historians have carelessly assumed. In his scientific writings on behavioral psychology, he posited the interaction of the organism and the environment, the organism being an aggregate of innate, mute anatomical structures waiting to be awakened by environmental stimuli at the right point of the developmental cycle. Thus, the basis of behavior was programmed into the species' genetic and constitutional structures. It was this deterministic message of Watson's that psychologists carried over into the interwar era. And it was a group determinism, with Watson, because in all of his studies of animals and children, he was interested in the behavior of the average cat, or rat, or infant in categories or groups, not in studying the life histories of individual cats, rats, or babies. He did seem to stress the total environment as formative, but only after he was forced to leave Johns Hopkins because of his sexual misadventures and when he was working for the J. Walter Thompson Advertising Agency and trying to keep his scientific fame—or notoriousness—alive by writing sensational potboilers on raising children.

Indeed, it was the new science of child development where the behavioral science point of view crystallized first in psychological social science. At Yale University, Arnold Lucius Gesell studied the maturation of infants and children, that is, at what stages of life a typical infant could do any number of physical tasks, such as standing up or walking; here it was the maturation of the innate physical and physiological anatomical structures that determined "typical" behavior in infants and young children. The maturation hypothesis, with its stark biological determinism, became one of the key theses of child development. The field's other major theory, that the intelligence quotient was fixed at birth, received considerable support from the work of Stanford University psychologist Lewis M. Terman's genius project, in which almost a thousand California schoolchildren of genius IQ range provided the data for the nation's first longitudinal study of human traits and conduct. Terman's ultimate goal was to show that geniuses were all-around superior people, which sat well with his elitist social views; he and his associates studied and restudied their subjects five times by the 1950s and came to include all manner of behavioral patterns as well as mental capacities. They took what constituted "group snapshots," studying all persons in the sample as if they were a group at various times, rather than tracking individuals over time, and in that sense there were no individuals apart from the group. Individual persons were buried in the study as examples of variations from the group norm on particular characteristics, but individual persons qua individuals were not a part of the project. This group determinism might seem bizarre today, but it was pervasive in the behavioral sciences in the years between the two world wars.

The new theories of human conduct assumed that individuals could be categorized in particular groups, or, more precisely, that no individual could exist apart from his or her "group" identity. And this group orientation existed for behavioral scientists in a variety of disciplines. They thought of a social and economic scale of occupations and class, with the highest white-collar occupations being equated with the best educated and wealthiest classes and so on down to the poorest of the working classes. In fact, the Harvard economist Frank Taussig was one of the first behavioral scientists to work out such a scale in the early 1920s. F. Stuart Chapin, a sociologist, and Florence Goodenough, a psychologist, at the University of Minnesota devised an occupational scale in the early 1930s, in which they combined Taussig's occupational scale with a standardized inventory of household possessions—books, furniture, appliances—as a way of pinpointing a family's exact position on the larger social and economic taxonomy of social classes.

GROUP BEHAVIOR

In the 1930s social and behavioral scientists invented a discourse of group behavior, theories, ideologies, and specific studies whose authors and champions could be found at but one place: the State University of Iowa's Child Welfare Research Station. But before notions of group behavior could be worked out, it was essential to cut behavioral theory loose from the rationalistic and positivistic intellectual baggage that social science had carried forth from the eighteenth and nineteenth centuries. At the Institute of Human Relations at Yale University, several behavioral scientists used the nonrationalist work of Sigmund Freud to reorient individual psychology—the precondition to inventing group behavior as anything other than the study of rationalistic individuals in the aggregate—a sterile approach indeed, especially for the study of behavior.

Freudian psychodynamics seemed to promise much more. Thus, the social anthropologist John Dollard published *Caste and Class in a Southern Town* (1937), in which he deployed Freudian notions of frustration and aggression to explain race relations in the then heavily segregated American South. At the same time, however, Dollard displaced the American reliance on learning theory for the German action theory, the difference being that learning theorists used experiments to determine how long it took any organism to learn certain tasks, whereas action theorists devised experiments to account for action of any kind in the present with whatever investigation of past circumstances seemed relevant to the case at hand.

A younger researcher at Yale, Robert R. Sears, had been attempting for several years to test experimentally whether Freudian psychodynamics could be verified. Sears was interested in large molar units of behavior, such as fear, rage, love, and the like, not the narrow syllogisms of conventional American behavior learning theory. He was working out an experimental basis for Freudian psychodynamics. After a year or so of elaborate and involved discussions and experiments with other colleagues, Sears and his associates published a landmark study in action theory, *Frustration and Aggression* (1939), in which individual action with regard to frustration and aggression was worked out with great intricacy. Their basic hypothesis was that aggression always resulted from frustration. As conscientious, even self-conscious, theorists, Sears and his associates first addressed the matter of definitions and principles. Then they applied their hypothesis to such phenomena as socialization, crime, and adolescence. Freely admitting the role of contingency in human affairs, they were no rigid determinists or simplistic biological reductionists. Their stimulus-response formulations were always statements of if-then propositions. They took an expansive view of the complexities of culture and society as they impinged on individual behavior and the behavior of individuals toward one another. Now there was the possibility of theories of group behavior, because elements of rationality and irrationality could be mixed into theories of individual and of group conduct.

At the Iowa Child Welfare Research Station at the State University of Iowa, Kurt Lewin, a brilliant Gestalt psychologist and refugee from Nazi Germany, had been conducting experiments in action psychology for years, as applied to children. The work of Lewin and his students on small group dynamics in several experimental situations was notable as seminal to the nascent field of group psychology. Here the central assumption was that there was a psychological field that defined the action—the behavior—of all individuals in the group in any situation, including how the group atmosphere motivated its members to act in certain ways. Examples were the "democratic," "authoritarian," or "laissez-faire" mask-making clubs for ten-year-olds; or (during World War II itself), programs to improve civilian morale by creating small groups that would encourage people to get along better or consume organ meats; and programs designed to train group leaders in the proper behavior for democratic group leadership. In 1942 Sears was appointed director of the Iowa Station. In a few short years he and Lewin created two traditions of group behavior studies, or group dynamics. Sears added a marriage of cultural anthropology and group psychology, laced with Freudian psychodynamics, in order to work out both an experimental basis for Freudian theory, if any, as a way to revivify child development as a field and to construct new, dynamic notions of group behavior. Lewin and Sears differed in that Lewin, the Jewish refugee scientist, tried to work out a group psychology of democratic principles, whereas Sears, a man of liberal beliefs with relatively little interest in current affairs, fashioned theories of group Freudian psychodynamics almost totally devoid of any political content or significance, but of great scientific interest to behavioral scientists nationally and even internationally. Lewin and Sears soon departed from the Iowa Station for greener academic pastures; thereafter, group psychology developed in many centers of behavioral science.

CHILD DEVELOPMENT AND EDUCATION

Public education expanded to incorporate new groups at both ends of the age distribution, that is, preschool children and high school pupils who were not college-bound or on a definite vocational track, which meant mainly working-class adolescents, white and nonwhite. Child development research centers sponsored preschool education as a way of gaining access to a research population. At such institutions, which rapidly spread to embrace children of upper- and middle-class white families, children were taught manifold interrelated patterns of social and intellectual behavior, so that they would act as well-adjusted, academically capable pupils in kindergarten. The so-called life adjustment movement was even more interesting and involved millions, not several thousands, as did preschool education. In the decades from the 1920s to the 1950s the share of high-school-age Americans who won their diplomas rose from about one-third to one-half of their cohort. And the expansion of secondary education that caused the life adjustment movement followed. The movement's guru was Charles Prosser, a leader in vocational education, who by the late 1930s had realized that with universal high school education, perhaps 60 percent of the pupils were not sufficiently talented to be either on a college or a specific vocational track; these youths, therefore, needed a general "adjustment to life" curriculum. They were the children of unskilled and semiskilled working-class families with poor incomes and cultural environments; they tended to begin school later than others, made bad grades, did poorly on standardized intelligence and achievement tests, had little commitment to school, and seemed less emotionally mature and stable. Thus, their behavior, actual and potential, was the issue.

Prosser launched the life adjustment movement through the U.S. Office of Education. The program was to emphasize a curriculum that fit the "needs" of these children for such things as practical arts, home and family life, health and physical fitness—to adjust to life in society's bottom half, in other words. The other 40 percent, the college-bound and those to be trained in highly skilled vocations, had curricula that prepared them for better niches in the socioeconomic order. No curricula changes resulted from the life adjustment movement after its formal launching in 1945–1946; the necessary "reforms" had already taken place in most school districts around the country. It was the life adjustment movement's function to publicize the new ideology already implanted in the nation's secondary institutions as the consequence of the universalization of high school attendance and the dissemination of the notion of automatic promotion in the nation's public schools. By the early 1950s the life adjustment movement was under heavy attack from critics who wanted intellectual or, at least, academic substance in the nation's high schools.

COMMUNITY STUDIES

Urban and rural social science sprang from urban and rural sociology, or the study of society in city and countryside. Until the 1920s sociology was as much a reform movement as an academic field—thus its strong emphasis on charities and corrections and on social work, which was sociology's customary academic curriculum before the 1920s. In that decade the University of Chicago and Columbia University emerged as national centers of graduate training in the field; the work they sponsored among faculty and graduate students could be dubbed behavioral social science. Faculty and students at the University of Chicago focused on two themes. One was the so-called interactionist social psychology, the how and why of human interaction with others in primary and secondary groups. The primary groups are those in which there is face-to-face contact. The secondary are the more impersonal ones—what such great German sociologists as Friedrich Toennes had characterized as the distinction between Gemeinschaft (community) and Gesellschaft (society), the one more identified with the traditional community, the other with the modern industrial social order, sometimes known as the "Gemeinschaft grouse," that is, the complaint that the old-time traditional society had been undone by modern industrialism. Thus, it was the kind of behavior that could and did occur that mattered to the social interactionist school of social psychologists, behavior that was activated by symbolic behavior, such as gestures, language, rituals, playing various social roles, and the like. It was possible to belong to primary and secondary groups at the same time—it was the possibilities of behavior that tipped the scale. This kind of social psychology was thus attitudinal or mentalistic. The whole or integrated personality was possible when the individual was able to balance the various social roles (and thus patterns of behavior) that he or she was obliged to play.

Community studies—the study of the city—also pioneered at Chicago, under the leadership of such figures as Robert E. Park, Ernest W. Burgess, Roderick McKenzie, and Louis Wirth. According to the Chicago school, the city was the arena of conflict of various ethnic groups competing for survival and dominance in the urban-industrial revolution. As the natural area of ethnic and racial conflict of industrialism, the city was seen as a series of concentric circles, each a natural area for a group, with all groups competing as best they could in their particular ecological niches. Thus, the city as a whole was an organism that was greater than or different from the sum of its parts, each part or natural area interdependent with all others, so that, as McKenzie put it, to interfere with one aspect of the larger system of systems, no matter how seemingly marginal, threatened to have incalculable consequences throughout the entire system. Again, it was behavior that mattered, not mere traits or taxonomic categorization. Whether or not individual members of the Chicago school were liberal reformers, their professional and disciplinary ideology was profoundly conservative.

Sociologists at Chicago and Columbia, together with some firebrands here and there, also insisted that sociology go beyond the charities and corrections emphases of the Progressive Era and Gilded Age and become a positivistic or objectively true social and behavioral science. In these interwar decades, they sought to compile lists of scientific terms and concepts for social phenomena, to apply statistical techniques to social phenomena, especially regression analysis and coefficients of correlation. But they also used simple arithmetic, meaning percentages of raw data. Probably the nation's most celebrated advocate of positivistic sociology was George A. Lundberg of the University of Washington, who taught in the 1940s and 1950s that sociology as an objective behavioral science can rescue society by discovering the underlying principles or laws of social integration and cohesion.

RURAL SOCIOLOGY

Rural sociology had its roots in the country life movement of the early twentieth century, whose leaders sought to improve the quality of rural life in America, believing that it was the agricultural community that was the fundamental element of stability in the rapidly industrializing nation. The perception that rural communities were deteriorating galvanized rural reformers into action. As an academic enterprise rural sociology had its base in the several dozen land-grant colleges and their extension services scattered across the nation. When Congress enacted the Smith-Lever Act of 1914, it made possible federal matching funds from the U.S. Department of Agriculture for cooperative work with the land-grant colleges and permitted work in the social as well as the natural sciences. Rural sociology focused on the study of the countryside as a center of ameliorative campaigns. Of course, the land-grant colleges never commanded as much prestige as such liberal arts research universities as Chicago and Columbia; biases against rural people and institutions were strong in the interwar years. But rural sociologists and their fellow travelers, the county extension agents for home economics, rural community life, preschool education, and the like, became an important part of rural America. Since rural sociologists even more than urban sociologists wished to save and to modernize the people and natural areas (that is, communities) they studied, it was those patterns of behavior that rural folks exhibited that warranted attention, scrutiny, investigation, interpretation, and—quite possibly—behavioral reformation. In *Farm Children: An Investigation of Rural Child Life in Selected Areas of Iowa* (1930), the University of Iowa professor Bird T. Baldwin and his associates provided a point-by-point comparison of rural children in two "typical" small towns in Iowa. One was modern and progressive, the other not, and the study argued that stagnant rural communities could be modernized and brought up to snuff through the standard remedies of modernity, such as preschool and regular public education, the development of up-to-date community institutions to provide social cohesion, and the distribution of modern means of public health.

THE GOVERNMENT AND THE ECONOMY

And what of the marketplace, of the classical laissez-faire economics that had dominated American political economy in one form or another since the days of Thomas Jefferson? In the interwar decades politicians and professors of both major political parties changed the public-private nexus of capitalism and the marketplace in important and sometimes unpredictable ways, thus making both economic policy and academic or scientific economics a new social and behavioral science. And as the shift to a consumer society became manifest in the interwar years, politicians and professors of political economy alike worked out ways to estimate the behavior of all groups and persons within the larger public-private economy. In the 1920s it was entrepreneurs of enterprise and Republicans, whether academics or not, who led the way.

In 1921, doubtless on the advice of men of enterprise and following the example of at least a dozen of the states, the administration of President Warren G. Harding created the Bureau of the Budget, an office within the executive branch, which for the first time created the federal government's budget, thus usurping the power of Congress to appropriate funds by having its committees prepare the federal budget. By the late 1920s the bureau had retrieved the initiative for federal action from Congress and moved it to the White House, thus greatly augmenting the power of the president in setting the parameters of federal policy initiation and enforcement. From the scientific side, the bureau's technicians used various statistical techniques to estimate the total amount of money in the marketplace. At the same time, Secretary of Commerce Herbert Hoover was encouraging this kind of statistical work among his scientists and also attempting to gather such information from other executive departments (such as the Departments of Agriculture and the Interior) in order to make public to all entrepreneurs, large and small, the size of the nation's market or economy so that, armed with such information, entrepreneurs could compete, regardless of size, on an equal footing.

From efforts such as these, and of the Columbia University economist Wesley Clair Mitchell, who made studies of the business cycle his specialty, economists in the interwar years began to gather information on the size of the national economy, in order to estimate such phenomena as aggregate demand for particular items. As Mitchell argued, the economy was an organic whole that was greater than or different from the sum of its parts, and yet it was an equilibrium of many distinct yet interrelated structures and processes. From such a perspective, what mattered was the behavior of the various groups in the larger economy. Hoover's interest as secretary of commerce and as president was to use the federal government's moral suasion and information to encourage the private sector to regulate itself voluntarily through fair trade laws (which eliminated discounting), high tariffs, and other such interventions in the economy.

When the Democrats became the majority party in 1932, the New Dealers looked at the economy not much differently than the so-called "New Era" Republicans, that is, as a large system of systems, of many distinct yet interrelated groups in the economy. The major disagreement between Democrats and Republicans was what to do about downturns in the business cycle—with Mitchell's equilibrium, that is. The Republicans were content to tinker with preventive measures, while the New Dealers were committed to doctoring after the fact of depression: experimentation with various methods of restoration of total aggregate demand, such as increased government spending on public works (an old idea save on the federal level); cutting back on supply (as with farm commodities, an idea parallel to the tariff); expansion of the money supply, as with taking the national currency off the gold standard (another old idea); and even investments in various kinds of social insurance (again, an old idea save for the federal government). But federalism was maintained even under the twin emergencies of the Great Depression and total war, with only a limited role for the federal government, and full cooperation of the states until the middle 1940s, when the balance began to shift toward the federal government in terms of initiative and funding.

By that time economists and political office-holders had come to be concerned chiefly with the economic behavior, not so much the economic abilities, of their fellow citizens in the aggregate, and the door was thus open to the full and conscious importation of John Maynard Keynes's ideas on total aggregate demand and how to prevent depressions—by spending enough public funds when the economy cooled down to prevent a downturn and tightening the public purse's strings in good times to prevent inflation. Franklin D. Roosevelt's cutting of the budget in 1936 caused a serious recession by 1939, and only the entry of the United States into World War II in 1941 got the nation's economy out of the recession, which demonstrates the incompleteness of the adoption of Keynesian economics in the 1930s. The enactment by Congress of the Full Employment Act of 1946, which committed the national government to maintaining full employment regardless of what it took, a promise honored more in the breach than in the execution, demonstrated how far the Keynesian intellectual revolution had gone, presumably facilitated by the emergency of total war and how the new behavioral point of view had transformed political economy and, for that matter, the whole of the social sciences.

See also **Intelligence and Human Difference; Psychology, the Mind, and Personality; Anthropology and Cultural Relativism** (volume 2); **Individualism and the Self; Ethnicity: Early Theories; Ethnicity and Race; Race; Class; The Social Sciences; Cultural Studies; Social Construction of Reality** (volume 3).

BIBLIOGRAPHY

Baldwin, Bird T., et al. *Farm Children: An Investigation of Rural Child Life in Selected Areas of Iowa.* New York, 1930.

Barber, William J. *Designs within Disorder: Franklin D. Roosevelt, the Economists, and the Shaping of American Economic Policy, 1933–1945.* New York, 1996.

———. *From New Era to New Deal: Herbert Hoover, the Economists, and American Economic Policy, 1921–1933.* New York, 1985.

Baritz, Loren. *The Servants of Power: A History of the Use of Social Science in American Industry.* Middletown, Conn., 1960.

Cravens, Hamilton. *Before Head Start: The Iowa Station and America's Children.* Chapel Hill, N.C., 1993.

———. *The Triumph of Evolution: The Heredity-Environment Controversy, 1900–1941.* Baltimore, 1988. Originally published in 1978.

Cremin, Lawrence A. *The Transformation of the School: Progressivism in American Education, 1876–1957.* New York, 1961.

Dollard, John. *Caste and Class in a Southern Town.* New Haven, Conn., 1937.

Graebner, William. *The Engineering of Consent: Democracy and Authority in Twentieth-Century America.* Madison, Wis., 1987.

Hinkle, Roscoe C., Jr., and Gisela J. Hinkle. *The Development of Modern Sociology: Its Nature and Growth in the United States.* New York, 1954.

Hunt, Joseph McVicker. *Intelligence and Experience.* New York, 1960.

Lewin, Kurt. "Field Theory and Experiment in Social Psychology: Concepts and Methods." *American Journal of Sociology* 44 (1939): 868–896.

Marcus, Alan I., and Howard P. Segal. *Technology in America: A Brief History.* 2d ed. New York, 1999.

McKenzie, Roderick. *The Metropolitan Community.* New York, 1933.

Mitchell, Wesley Clair. *Business Cycles: The Problems and Its Setting.* New York, 1927.

Prosser, Charles. *Secondary Education and Life.* Cambridge, Mass., 1939.

Sears, Robert R. *Survey of Objective Studies of Psychoanalytic Concepts: A Report.* New York, 1943.

——, et al. *Frustration and Aggression.* New Haven, Conn., 1939.

Terman, Lewis M., et al. *Genetic Studies of Genius.* 5 vols. Stanford, Calif., 1926–1957.

United States Office of Education. *Life Adjustment Education for Every Youth.* Washington, D.C., 1948.

United States President's Research Committee on Social Trends. *Recent Social Trends in the United States.* 2 vols. New York, 1933.

Watson, John Broadus. *Behavior: An Introduction to Comparative Psychology.* New York, 1914.

——. *Psychology from the Standpoint of a Behaviorist.* Philadelphia, 1919.

PRAGMATISM AND ITS CRITICS

Christopher Phelps

Pragmatism, the most important philosophical tradition to originate in the thought of American intellectuals, is often interpreted as a quintessential expression of American culture. Celebrants have seen in pragmatism America's democratic, practical mind-set, disparagers the anti-intellectualism of the most thoroughly commercial society in the world. Despite the important American philosophers whose names are associated with pragmatism, however, at no time has a majority of American professional philosophers embraced pragmatism. The claim that pragmatism and American character are identical also obscures the philosophy's European precursors and slights the multiple countries, from China to Mexico, whose intellectuals, despite divergent cultural histories, have contributed to pragmatism.

To be sure, pragmatism, like every philosophy, carries traces of the country, period, and social purposes for which it was originally employed. The key pragmatist philosophers sometimes gestured in the direction of can-do practicality, commonsense know-how, and impatience with theory, all putatively American characteristics. Yet those who would equate pragmatism with the American character, narrow practicality, or capitalist culture risk distortion, despite the mythic resonance of these suggestions. Pragmatists have generally sought to refashion the nation they found, conceiving of their project as reconstructive, experimental, meliorative, and future-oriented rather than a mirror of existing America.

Pragmatism has had two peaks of influence. In the first and most influential, lasting from the late nineteenth century through World War II, pragmatism was created and elaborated by its founders. This high point of creativity and cultural recognition was followed by a long period of relative obscurity. Pragmatism did not figure in intellectual, cultural, or philosophical discourse in the cold war epoch as it had between 1900 and 1940. In an unanticipated revival of the 1980s and 1990s, however, pragmatism took on new forms, achieved new vitality, and won new prestige in a variety of disciplines, if only a toehold in philosophy proper.

Pragmatism defies convenient definition if only because the major pragmatist thinkers differed substantially in interest, temperament, and emphasis. Many writers, for instance, have observed great discrepancies between the philosophy's two major phases. If a single concern dominated pragmatism's first generation—chief among them Charles Sanders Peirce, William James, and John Dewey—it was the attempt to create a salutary relationship between science and culture. But Richard Rorty, the dominant figure in neo-pragmatism, is so little attached to scientific method and so strongly influenced by the "linguistic turn" that some commentators have doubted that what now goes by the name of pragmatism has any meaningful connection to its ancestral ideas, despite Rorty's evident affection for Dewey.

On the other hand, a shared philosophical *culture,* if not doctrinal uniformity, does connect the two pragmatist moments, making it possible to speak coherently of a pragmatist tradition. Across time, pragmatists have understood their approach as a means of overcoming the ceaseless quarrels engendered by conventional schools of philosophy. To classical pragmatists and neo-pragmatists alike, most of the issues that have engaged philosophy through the ages are contrivances that act as impediments to simpler and preferable modes of thinking. Rather than prolong such a waste of time masquerading as profundity, pragmatists maintain, philosophy would better realize its ambition of enhancing intelligence and improving human life by giving up the quest for certitude, which leads mainly to dogmatism and infinite disputation about how to establish proper metaphysical foundations for truth. Philosophers, pragmatists say, should instead recognize the provisional, fallible status of all knowledge. In place of the many conceptions of philosophy that have claimed to apprehend a single,

William James, Psychologist and Philosopher (1842–1910). © BETTMANN/CORBIS

final, ultimate truth, pragmatists posit a world of plural, changing, partial truths. To pragmatists, philosophy is not a source of insight into supreme reality or even a source of knowledge as much as it is an invitation to moral wisdom and exploration. All of this can make pragmatism seem not a philosophy as much as a way of doing without one, as the Italian pragmatist Giovanni Papini famously put it.

CHARLES SANDERS PEIRCE: THE PRAGMATIC MAXIM

Few philosophies have so precise a date of birth as pragmatism, which as an account of human thinking came into existence in 1898, when William James introduced the term in a lecture he delivered in Berkeley, California, on "Philosophical Conceptions and Practical Results." Then approaching the height of his stature as the leading intellectual of his day, James was a Harvard professor and author of the immensely successful *Principles of Psychology* (1890) who belonged to one of the most intellectually distinguished families of late-nineteenth-century America. "To attain perfect clearness in our

thoughts of an object," James stated at Berkeley, ". . . we need only consider what effects of a conceivably practical kind the object may involve—what sensations we are to expect from it, and what reactions we must prepare. Our conception of these effects, then, is for us the whole of our conception of the object, so far as that conception has positive significance at all."

In so announcing pragmatism, James drew heavily upon the work of Charles Sanders Peirce, even calling pragmatism "the principle of Peirce," and thus attracting new attention to a series of articles that Peirce had published twenty years before in the *Popular Science Monthly,* which languished, half forgotten. Although neither "The Fixation of Belief" (1877) nor "How to Make Our Ideas Clear" (1878) contain the word "pragmatism," Peirce apparently had coined the term as early as the early 1870s, when both he and James belonged to a metaphysical discussion club in Cambridge, Massachusetts. Peirce's essays, governed by a logical rigor and technical exactness altogether absent from James's evocative prose, were of paramount importance for subsequent pragmatists.

Although sympathetic to the modern rejection of medieval scholasticism and its premise that authority is the basis for truth, Peirce was just as firmly opposed to the Cartesian supposition that skepticism and intuition, or introspection, should be the starting point for philosophy. Doubt, he maintained, was not willed but erupts spontaneously when beliefs that otherwise exist unquestioned encounter strong external counterarguments or counterevidence: "The irritation of doubt causes a struggle to attain a state of belief." If doubt prompts thought rather than the other way around, what is the optimal method for restoring intellectual satisfaction? In "The Fixation of Belief," Peirce maintained that three traditional methods—tenacity, authority, and the Kantian a priori—were incapable, despite their respective power, of really putting doubt to rest. Only science, he argued, because accountable to reality and community, may settle belief in such a way that it will become the basis for new rules for action, new habits. "How to Make Our Ideas Clear" supplemented these theses with a theory of meaning, namely that clarity in a concept is achieved when the whole of its practical effects are considered. What makes us designate a diamond as "hard," for example, according to Peirce, is not its inherent metaphysical "properties" but rather its ability to scratch rather than be scratched. Peirce expressed this method in what famously came to be known as the "pragmatic maxim": "Consider what effects, that might conceivably have practical bearings, we conceive the object of our conception to have. Then, our conception of these effects is the whole conception of the object."

Despite a formulation of scientific method positivistic in its assumption that accrual of incontrovertible facts would provide definite knowledge of reality, Peirce's *Popular Science Monthly* articles expressed in germinal form all the core elements of the first-generation conception of pragmatism: a theory of mind that views concepts or ideas as plans for action, a theory of meaning in which ideas are best understood and clarified by assessment of the whole of their consequences, a theory of truth that judges ideas according to the scientific method of observation and verification, and a concept of inquiry crediting the search for knowledge to the stimulus of doubt when expectations are shattered after ideas are confounded by experience.

The word "pragmatism" itself has antecedents in ancient Greek thought and German idealism, where, in both instances, it pertained to action and conduct. This is what the first generation of pragmatists had in mind when they embraced the term as an apt designation for their method. The pragmatists hoped to evoke a close relationship between ideas and action, consequences and practice—not narrow utility, disregard for principle, or acquiescence in the existing social order, meanings that attach to "pragmatic" in the American vernacular. Philosophical pragmatists sought rather to illuminate the vibrant interchange of thought and experience, theory and practice. Knowledge, pragmatists believe, means little if isolated from its surroundings and effects. "To connect thought with existence," stated the French sociologist Émile Durkheim in a lecture delivered at the Sorbonne in 1913, "to connect thought with life—this is the fundamental idea of pragmatism" (p. 407).

WILLIAM JAMES: THE WILL TO BELIEVE

No one did more in the first decade of the twentieth century to proselytize for pragmatism than William James. After training in medicine, James's early work was in psychology, where he helped give rise to the school of functionalism, which, borrowing from advances in evolutionary biology, held that the mind arranged experience for a human organism adapting constantly to a changing environment. To James, pragmatism was not a system but a method, and not a new method but one variously employed by earlier philosophers, such as Aristotle, John Locke, George Berkeley, and David Hume, if only in fragments—making pragmatism, as he famously put it, "a new name for some old ways of doing things." James proved an eloquent explicator of the implications of the pragmatic maxim. "It is astonishing," he wrote, "to see how many philosophical disputes collapse into insignificance the moment you subject them to this simple test of tracing a concrete consequence. . . . The whole function of philosophy ought to be to find out what definite difference it will make to you and me, at definite instants of our life, if this world-formula or that world-formula be the true one." James saw in pragmatism "a method of settling metaphysical disputes that otherwise might be interminable."

In this manner, James extended the pragmatic maxim to cover truth as well as meaning. The veracity of ideas, he thought, as well as their signification, is determined by their practical consequences. James also went beyond Peirce in his articulations of a sense of the world as fluid, plastic, changing, and dynamic. Pragmatism, held James, requires setting aside thoughts of eternal verity: "It means the open air and possibilities of nature, as against dogma, artificiality, and the pretence of finality in truth." In an ever-shifting environment, "concrete truths" could be established, he held, but those truths are subject to reassessment. Knowledge is the sum of plural and temporal approximations, all subject to revision and refinement. Pragmatism, therefore, eschews fixed theories: "She has in fact no prejudices whatever, no obstructive dogmas, no rigid canons of what shall count as proof. She is completely genial. She will entertain any hypothesis, she will consider any evidence."

A further distinction between James and Peirce resided in their respective views about science and culture. Prominent in Peirce's philosophy of science was a community of inquirers that would weed out error through mutual examination, verification, and correction. Ultimately, Peirce believed, scientific communities would come to accept those truths that best depict reality. This was not the dispensation of James. Immersed in psychology and Protestantism, James cast pragmatism in a far more individualistic—and therefore inconsistently realist—manner. To James, theories were instruments for organizing experience rather than transcripts of reality. He was open to considering the effects of *holding* a given proposition as well as the effects of the proposition itself, and was even attracted by cases in which belief was a precondition for making a given idea *become* true.

The philosophical effects of these modifications loom largest in James's writings on religion. Pragmatism's value for James was intertwined with a subject that had been very important to him personally in a psychological crisis that had shaken his early adulthood: how religious belief and hope in meaningful activity can be sustained in an age of science. In his essay "The Will to Believe" (1896), James suspended the scientific injunction to verify when there is no evidence to contradict or affirm a momentous hypothesis, such as the existence of God. Given the impossibility of certitude in all spheres of knowledge, James maintained, demands for absolute proof of God are absurd. James upheld "the right to believe" despite lack of evidence as long as the hypothesis "is live enough to tempt our will." In *Pragmatism* (1907), James described pragmatism as "a happy harmonizer of empiricist ways of thinking with the more religious demands of human beings," and in *The Varieties of Religious Experience* (1902) he defended belief in God on the basis of beneficial psychological effects that the idea of God might have.

Critics accused James of fostering a subjective theory of truth—what is true is what is useful, and what is useful is what works for *me*. His philosophy of religion, they charged, called into doubt the transcendence of metaphysics that pragmatism was supposed to provide, inviting mysticism in what was tantamount to a will to "*make* believe." The critics' ranks included a disgruntled Peirce, who characterized James's literary presentation of the pragmatic maxim as "not very deep," and finally renamed his own point of view "pragmaticism," a word "ugly enough to keep it safe from kidnappers." Defenders, on the other hand, have noted the heavy qualifications James placed upon cases where a leap of faith is permissible—momentous, unavoidable dilemmas without immediate prospect of evidence upon which to base a judgment—and have pointed out that since believing in whatever one pleases will be inexpedient, or fail to work, James's criteria are not as subjective as they might appear. That claim did not persuade many who thought James's themes of expedience and satisfactoriness willfully left the door ajar to flights of fancy.

JOHN DEWEY: INQUIRY AND DEMOCRACY

The thought of John Dewey, who lived from the Civil War to the cold war, marks the culmination of classical pragmatism. After an early period as a He-gelian idealist, Dewey, who studied philosophy at the Johns Hopkins University, was won to pragmatism in the 1890s along with a group of his University of Chicago colleagues. From the outset James considered Dewey, along with Oxford University's F. C. S. Schiller, exemplary of the new sensibility. There were, however, important differences of emphasis. What in Peirce was a theory of meaning, what in James became as well a theory of truth with particular significance for psychology and religion, became in Dewey yet more expansive—indeed, all encompassing. A prolific, diligent philosopher, Dewey explored education, political theory, the social sciences, psychology, logic, ethics, and aesthetics. Dewey's "experimental naturalism" or "instrumentalism" located knowledge within an ongoing temporal process of creative intelligence, or inquiry, rendering pragmatism thoroughly social and informed by democratic values. By the interwar years, Dewey enjoyed a public stature and recognition as great as, if not greater than, James achieved in the first decade of the twentieth century, giving him ample opportunities to address the very "public" at the heart of his ethical and political philosophy.

In a trait residual from his idealism, Dewey's thought is holistic, such that one may isolate almost any of his writings and find allusions that open windows onto the whole of his worldview. His famous educational theories, for example, as elaborated in *The School and Society* (1899) and *Democracy and Education* (1916), involve insights drawn from evolutionary biology, pragmatist theories of knowledge, and social reform impulses. Dewey opposed education premised on punitive discipline and unidirectional transmission of information for the same reason that he opposed any concept of thinking that separated mind from nature. Dewey thought it a mistake to build an educational philosophy on the assumption of a detached spectator rather than an "agent-patient, doer, sufferer, and enjoyer" who continually evolves within significant environments. Because knowledge is inseparable from practice, he emphasized "learning by doing," meaning an educational atmosphere that recognizes children's social, creative, investigative, and artistic instincts. To Dewey, who tested his ideas in a Laboratory School that he and his first wife, Alice Chipman Dewey, established at Chicago University in 1896, educational reform would require more than classroom technique. The artificial separation of thought from action was tied to historical class divisions separating intellectuals from production, culture from living experience, and intelligence from work.

The reform of education would require a reconstruction of philosophy combined with societywide democratic transformation.

From the neo-Thomists of the 1930s to neoconservatives in the 1970s, conservative thinkers have blamed Dewey's educational philosophy for moral relativism, identifying it with romanticism, the view that children should be free to do whatever they please. Abandonment of moral and ethical absolutes, conservatives argue, results in declining standards. Pragmatism did represent a challenge to authoritarian traditionalism in religion, state, and ideology. But Dewey's educational philosophy was not amoral. It was infused with values and ideals: cooperation, personality, democracy. Dewey advocated a student-focused process of *guided* activity that would, through varied problem-solving experiments and exercises, encourage children to formulate hypotheses and test them experimentally to arrive at general understandings. The point of doing things was that children get the *idea.*

The connection Dewey drew between thought and action held great appeal for educated middle-class readers who found in pragmatism a justification for their social reform activity. The notion of reforms as "working hypotheses" (in the salient phrase of pragmatist psychologist George Herbert Mead) influenced settlement house organizer Jane Addams, Supreme Court justice Oliver Wendell Holmes, historian Charles Beard, and the principled critic of racism W. E. B. Du Bois, among others. Dewey, in works like *The Public and Its Problems* (1927), *Individualism Old and New* (1930), and *Freedom and Culture* (1939), rejected atomistic individualism and laissez-faire liberalism as anachronistic, and called for a deep, thoroughgoing, cooperative democracy in social, civil, industrial—and not just political—life. His involvement in movements like the League for Independent Political Action of the 1930s reflected his declaration in his essay "The Need for a Recovery of Philosophy" (1917) that "philosophy recovers itself when it ceases to be a device for dealing with the problems of philosophers and becomes a method, cultivated by philosophers, for dealing with the problems of men."

Stylistically, Dewey rarely matched James's effervescence. Holmes remarked that Dewey wrote as "God would have spoken had He been inarticulate but keenly desirous to tell you how it was." The cultural critic Lewis Mumford did not even offer that backhanded compliment when he called Dewey's writing as "fuzzy and formless as lint." Yet Dewey was hardly the worst of prose stylists. Anyone who tries to puzzle out the precise meaning of the "me" and the

"I" in Mead's pragmatist psychology, for example, may run right back to Dewey as a paragon of clarity. Dewey's intentions, furthermore, are sufficiently transparent that many views attributed to him by others are obviously inconsistent with his philosophy, making many criticisms of his positions tendentious, although the dreamy quality of his prose may account in part for misreadings by friends and opponents alike.

A failure to respect Dewey's own conception of "scientific intelligence," for instance, has led to charges of elitism against a philosopher who believed in the capacity of everyone to use scientific method, given improved social organization and education. A philosopher who rejected "expertise" along with all forms of unquestioned authority becomes a technocrat when interpreted by some critics. His references to "social control"—an amorphous phrase that to Dewey implied a steady extension of rational, democratic deliberation over the whole of social affairs, or "cooperative experimental intelligence" as against "drift and casual improvisation"—have been taken to imply an ominous program of social engineering. Interpretations of Dewey as an elitist have a difficult time explaining his conviction that "the cure for the ailments of democracy is more democracy."

Confusion is all the more understandable given the influence of journalist Walter Lippmann, who in *Drift and Mastery* (1914), *Public Opinion* (1922), and *The Phantom Public* (1925) promoted a "realistic" modern liberalism that encouraged professional and scientific experts to govern in the benevolent interest of a befuddled, gullible public. Lippmann was first in a line of chastened liberals, among them historian Arthur Schlesinger Jr., to make pragmatism synonymous with antiradical liberalism. By midcentury, however, the realists, Schlesinger included, would take special pleasure in repudiating Dewey. Protestant theologian Reinhold Niebuhr led the way in *Moral Man and Immoral Society* (1932), which attacked Dewey for an excessively optimistic, sentimental liberalism lacking any comprehension of raw self-interest and the coerciveness of groups.

Yet Lippmann and the rest of the right-tacking liberals at the early *New Republic* had some reason to believe that they were on a Deweyan path, given Dewey's support for American entry into World War I on the grounds that it would deepen world democracy. That stance and its illusions produced the most famous criticism of Dewey, "The Twilight of Idols" (1917) by Greenwich Village rebel Randolph Bourne. Bourne faulted Dewey for his assumptions about a store of public rationality at a time of patriotic bellicosity, for failing to recognize that not all events are plastic, among them wars of empire, and for fostering an instrumentalism more attentive to means than ends—objections that would inform many later broadsides against pragmatism, including Mumford's condemnation of the "pragmatic acquiescence" in *The Golden Day* (1926). Yet even in expressing grave disappointment in Dewey, Bourne's thought remained pragmatist: "A philosophy upon which I had relied to carry us through no longer *works*," he wrote, while summoning the memory of James, who opposed American imperialism in 1898, as contrasting hero. The Bourne-Dewey debate thus was internal to pragmatism, especially given Dewey's implicit postwar concessions to Bourne's criticism.

The controversy over pragmatism and the American social system did not stop with Bourne. One prominent line of thought has viewed pragmatism as the shallow mindset of a business civilization. The British philosopher Bertrand Russell, for example, equated Deweyan instrumentalism with cultural barbarism, just as James's metaphor of the "cash value" of ideas invited similar criticism. Another view has interpreted Dewey as the philosopher par excellence of the new political-managerial capitalism of the twentieth century, dominated by large-scale bureaucratic organization. The Frankfurt school founder Max Horkheimer's *Eclipse of Reason* (1947) and some New Left critics of "corporate liberalism" considered Deweyan pragmatism the embodiment of a technocratic-administrative outlook. Charges of accommodation inform radical accounts as varied as Christopher Lasch's *The New Radicalism in America* (1965) and vulgar Marxist interpretations of Dewey as a petty bourgeois ideologist or imperialist warmonger.

At odds with these varieties of left-wing opposition to pragmatism stands a sympathetic body of radical thought, beginning with William English Walling's *The Larger Aspects of Socialism* (1913), which has held the logical end-point of the Deweyan moral project to be the abolition of class rule. The most advanced expression of this case came from Dewey's student Sidney Hook, a revolutionary democratic socialist during the 1920s and 1930s. Drawing upon pragmatism to propose a Marxism free of dogma, Hook observed striking similarities between Dewey's history of philosophy and historical materialism, as well as between Deweyan method and Marx's talk of practice in his theses on Feuerbach. As for Dewey himself, while he traveled to Mexico in 1937 to investigate the charges made against the exiled Russian revolutionist Leon Trot-

sky in the Moscow trials, it appears he never studied Marx or twentieth-century Marxism seriously. He was suspicious of class struggle and given to mischaracterize it as the exclusive means recommended by Marx. Dewey's environment of the professional and reformist middle class undoubtedly shaped his conviction that exploitation and inequality could be overturned by purely deliberative, educational means. But pragmatism, democracy, and socialism were compatible in Dewey's view, and interpretations that brand Dewey an apologist for capital, a technocrat, or a corporate liberal—not to mention accolades laying claim to him for conventional liberalism—are misguided. They cannot account for Dewey's criticism of the New Deal because it left the system in the hands of a plutocracy, his votes for socialist candidates, or his explicit rejection in *Liberalism and Social Action* (1935) of "piecemeal policies undertaken *ad hoc*," in favor of "radical" measures and a "socialized economy."

The radical Dewey, however, was lost to amnesia among cold war liberals, whose more conservative interpretation of pragmatism was ratified by the postwar rightward direction of Hook and Max Eastman, another former leftist Deweyan, whose positions conceded much to the resigned tragic realism of Lippmann and Niebuhr. Tom Hayden read Dewey when drafting *The Port Huron Statement* (1962) for the Students for a Democratic Society, but most young radicals of the 1960s saw Dewey as father to the failed modern liberal statist project that had eventuated in the Vietnam War.

THE PRAGMATIST RENEWAL

In the several decades following the death of Dewey, Cornel West notes, pragmatism lay "dormant in the American unconscious, venerated by parochial epigoni, depreciated by myopic specialists, yet seriously interrogated by few." In Europe, phenomenology, existentialism, structuralism, and other theoretical trends reinforced imperviousness to pragmatism. In the Anglo-American philosophical discipline, analytic approaches were predominant. A few scholars, such as H. S. Thayer and Charles Morris, wrote about pragmatism, but the past tense seemed necessary when describing its glory days. The ice slowly began to melt in philosophy when, though the discipline as a whole remained solidly analytic, individual philosophers like W. V. O. Quine, Nelson Goodman, and Wilfred Sellars took on pragmatist colorations. In Europe, philosopher Jürgen Habermas, heir to the Frankfurt school, drew respectfully upon Dewey for his theory of "communicative rationality." The most significant reconsideration of pragmatism, however, came after publication of *Philosophy and the Mirror of Nature* (1979) by Richard Rorty.

Educated at the University of Chicago and Yale University, Rorty taught at Princeton University from 1961 to 1982 on what seemed an accomplished but typically analytical path. *Philosophy and the Mirror of Nature* was the treasonous defection of an insider. Challenging the entire tradition in which he was steeped, Rorty called Ludwig Wittgenstein, Martin Heidegger, and Dewey the three greatest philosophers of the twentieth century and argued against the idea that mind represents nature, or external reality. Rorty has reached an extensive academic audience with this version of pragmatism as anti-realism. In the *Consequences of Pragmatism* (1982), Rorty denied the possibility of grounding beliefs on anything other than one's own conversations, and in *Contingency, Irony, and Solidarity* (1989) he proposed a "liberal ironist" aware of the limitations of "her" own "vocabulary," aware of the contingency of commitments but nevertheless holding out the possibility of a solidarity premised upon mutual recognition of human suffering. Whereas Dewey sought a recovery of philosophy, Rorty devalued if not jettisoned it in favor of conversational cultural criticism. Rorty himself took up teaching literature students at the University of Virginia and Stanford, and he has been given to saying that journalism and novels provide better moral inspiration than philosophy.

A full-scale pragmatist renaissance ensued in the 1980s, with multiple manifestations. In philosophy, the realist Hilary Putnam came to a Deweyan pragmatism very different in sensibility from Rorty's, while Richard Shusterman's *Pragmatist Aesthetics* (1992) applied Deweyan insights to hip-hop music. New interpretations of pragmatism's past by historians like Bruce Kuklick, David Hollinger, and James T. Kloppenberg illuminated its sources in liberal Protestant culture, its relationship to American thought and character, and the transatlantic context of its ascendance. Pragmatism enjoyed new favor in legal studies, political theory, and even women's studies, where in *Pragmatism and Feminism* (1996) Charlene Haddock Seigfried held pragmatism philosophically optimal for feminists given its rejection of such gendered dualisms as subjectivity and objectivity, emotion and reason, and caring and judgment.

One way to speak to the post-1968 intellectual context in which pragmatism has flourished is to say that not all contemporary pragmatists are neo-pragmatists. The thought of Peirce, James, and Dewey attracts many scholars and intellectuals because of the hope that pragmatism offers of an approach not blinded by absolutism, cognizant of the fluidity and diversity of experience, yet respectful of rationality and scientific method, unlike so much contemporary cultural theory. Pragmatism appeals to them precisely because of its refusal to throw overboard a commitment to truth and intelligence, its recognition of the provisional status of all truths, and its eschewal of nihilism, irrationalism, and skepticism. But to those who may best be described as neo-pragmatist—most prominently Rorty—pragmatism holds attraction for a different reason. To neo-pragmatists, pragmatism is an American idiom for what might be called the postmodernist (though Rorty resists the label) sensibility, namely antifoundationalism and contingency.

Literary critic Richard Poirier's *Poetry and Pragmatism* (1992), for example, informed by "linguistic skepticism," has come in for strong challenge by other pragmatists, who argue that although language was significant for James and Dewey they thought of experience as occurring at varying levels of consciousness and in multiple tones and hues, not restricted to its linguistic elements. Among the leading thinkers to so engage neo-pragmatism has been the philosopher Richard J. Bernstein. Bernstein views pragmatism as offering a vital possibility for overcoming the damaging, bitter antagonism between continental and Anglo-American philosophy, and he sees in pragmatism a striking anticipation of problems now designated "postmodern." In contradistinction to neo-pragmatists, however, he emphasizes the original pragmatist commitments to communities of inquirers, social engagement, and, especially, "fallibilism" as opposed to skepticism or relativism. Revisable truths operating as working hypotheses, suggests Bernstein, ought not be thrown out along with the quest for metaphysical certitude.

One animating debate in contemporary pragmatism concerns pragmatism's political ramifications. Robert Westbrook's *John Dewey and American Democracy* (1991) argues that participatory democracy, not conventional liberalism, is at the center of Dewey's vision. In a similar vein, Cornel West's *The American Evasion of Philosophy* (1989) touches upon many unusual figures, from Ralph Waldo Emerson to W. E. B. Du Bois, in a genealogy culminating in West's own "prophetic pragmatism," a democratic socialism informed by African American religious traditions. Other left-leaning or liberal writers, however, have cautioned to varying degrees against upholding Dewey as an intellectual model for the American Left. Few on either side have been drawn toward Rorty's "postmodern bourgeois liberalism" or his flag-waving in *Achieving Our Country* (1998), but Rorty's increasingly sharp differentiation of his political perspective from that of the very cultural Left that formed so much of his readership in the 1980s makes it plain that pragmatism remains unfolding and unfinished, much like the world it imagines.

See also **Science and Religion; The Rise of Biblical Criticism and Challenges to Religious Authority; The Struggle over Evolution** *(in this volume);* **Anthropology and Cultural Relativism** *(volume 2).*

BIBLIOGRAPHY

Bernstein, Richard J. *The New Constellation: The Ethical-Political Horizons of Modernity/Postmodernity.* Cambridge, Mass., 1992.

Blake, Casey Nelson. *Beloved Community: The Cultural Criticism of Randolph Bourne, Van Wyck Brooks, Waldo Frank, and Lewis Mumford.* Chapel Hill, N.C., 1990.

Bourne, Randolph Silliman. *The Radical Will: Randolph Bourne Selected Writings, 1911–1918.* Edited by Olaf Hansen. Berkeley, Calif., 1977.

Brint, Michael, and William Weaver, eds. *Pragmatism in Law and Society.* Boulder, Colo., 1991.

Cotkin, George. *William James, Public Philosopher.* Urbana, Ill., 1994.

Critchley, Simon, Jacques Derrida, Ernesto Laclau, and Richard Rorty. *Deconstruction and Pragmatism.* London, 1996.

Dewey, John. *The Early Works 1882–1898, The Middle Works 1899–1924,* and *The Later Works 1925–1953.* Edited by Jo Ann Boydston. 37 vols. Carbondale, Ill., 1967–1991.

Dickstein, Morris, ed. *The Revival of Pragmatism: New Essays on Social Thought, Law, and Culture.* Durham, N.C., 1998.

Diggins, John P. *The Promise of Pragmatism: Modernism and the Crisis of Knowledge and Authority.* Chicago, 1994.

Durkheim, Emile. "Pragmatism and Sociology." In *Lectures on Sociology and Philosophy,* edited by Kurt H. Wolff, 386–436. New York, 1964.

Feffer, Andrew. *The Chicago Pragmatists and American Progressivism.* Ithaca, N.Y., 1993.

Geras, Norman. *Solidarity in the Conversation of Humankind: The Ungroundable Liberalism of Richard Rorty.* New York, 1995.

Gunn, Giles B. *Thinking Across the American Grain: Ideology, Intellect, and the New Pragmatism.* Chicago, 1992.

Habermas, Jürgen. *Knowledge and Human Interests.* Boston, 1971.

——. *Toward a Rational Society.* Boston, 1970.

Hollinger, David A. *In the American Province: Studies in the History and Historiography of Ideas.* Bloomington, Ind., 1985.

Hollinger, Robert, and David Depew, eds. *Pragmatism: From Progressivism to Postmodernism.* Westport, Conn., 1995.

Horkheimer, Max. *Eclipse of Reason.* New York, 1947.

Hook, Sidney. *From Hegel to Marx: Studies in the Intellectual Development of Karl Marx.* 1936. Reprint, New York, 1994.

Hoopes, James. *Community Denied: The Wrong Turn of Pragmatic Liberalism* Ithaca, N.Y., 1998.

James, William. *The Works of William James.* Edited by Frederick H. Burkhardt. 19 vols. Cambridge, Mass., 1975–1988.

Kloppenberg, James. "Pragmatism: An Old Name for Some New Ways of Thinking?" *Journal of American History* 83 (1996): 100–138.

———. *Uncertain Victory: Social Democracy and Progressivism in European and American Thought, 1870–1920.* New York, 1986.

Kuklick, Bruce. *The Rise of American Philosophy: Cambridge, Massachusetts, 1860–1930.* New Haven, Conn., 1977.

Lamont, Corliss, ed. *Dialogue on John Dewey.* New York, 1959.

Lippmann, Walter. *Drift and Mastery.* New York, 1914.

Livingston, James. *Pragmatism and the Political Economy of Cultural Revolution, 1850–1940.* Chapel Hill, N.C., 1994.

Lovejoy, Arthur O. *The Thirteen Pragmatisms, and Other Essays.* Baltimore, 1963.

Mead, George Herbert. *Selected Writings.* Edited by Andrew J. Reck. Chicago, 1981.

Mills, C. Wright. *Sociology and Pragmatism.* New York, 1966.

Mitchell, W. J. T., ed. *Against Theory: Literary Studies and the New Pragmatism.* Chicago, 1985.

Morris, Charles. *The Pragmatic Movement in American Philosophy.* New York, 1970.

Mouffe, Chantal, ed. *Deconstruction and Pragmatism.* London, 1996.

Mumford, Lewis. *The Golden Day: A Study in American Experience and Culture.* New York, 1926.

Niebuhr, Reinhold. *Moral Man and Immoral Society: A Study in Ethics and Politics.* New York, 1932.

Perry, Ralph Barton. *The Thought and Character of William James.* 2 vols. Boston, 1935.

Phelps, Christopher. *Young Sidney Hook: Marxist and Pragmatist.* Ithaca, N.Y., 1997.

Pierce, Charles Sanders. *The Writings of Charles S. Peirce: A Chronological Edition.* Edited by the editors of the Peirce Edition Project. 30 vols. Bloomington, Ind., 1982– .

Poirier, Richard. *Poetry and Pragmatism.* Cambridge, Mass., 1992.

Putnam, Hilary. *Pragmatism: An Open Question.* Cambridge, Mass., 1995.

———. *Renewing Philosophy,* Cambridge, Mass., 1992.

Rorty, Richard. *Achieving Our Country: Leftist Thought in Twentieth-Century America.* Cambridge, Mass., 1998.

———. *Consequences of Pragmatism: Essays, 1792–1980.* Minneapolis, Minn., 1982.

———. *Contingency, Irony, and Solidarity.* Cambridge, Mass., 1989.

———. *Essays on Heidegger and Others: Philosophical Papers.* Vol. 2. Cambridge, Mass., 1991.

————. *Objectivity, Relativism, and Truth: Philosophical Papers.* Vol. 1. Cambridge, Mass., 1991.

————. *Philosophy and the Mirror of Nature.* Princeton, N.J., 1979.

————. *Truth and Progress: Philosophical Papers.* Vol. 3. Cambridge, Mass., 1998.

Schlipp, Paul Arthur, ed. *The Philosophy of John Dewey.* Evanston, Ill., 1939.

Shusterman, Richard. *Practicing Philosophy: Pragmatism and the Philosophical Life.* New York, 1997.

————. *Pragmatist Aesthetics: Living Beauty, Rethinking Art.* Oxford, 1992.

Seigfried, Charlene Haddock. *Pragmatism and Feminism: Reweaving the Social Fabric.* Chicago, 1996.

Thayer, H. S. *Meaning and Action: A Critical History of Pragmatism.* Indianapolis, Ind., 1968.

West, Cornel. *The American Evasion of Philosophy: A Genealogy of Pragmatism.* Madison, Wisc., 1989.

Westbrook, Robert B. *John Dewey and American Democracy.* Ithaca, N.Y., 1991.

White, Morton G. *Social Thought in America: The Revolt against Formalism.* New York, 1949.

Wiener, Philip P. *Evolution and the Founders of Pragmatism.* Cambridge, Mass., 1949.

RADICAL ALTERNATIVES

David C. Engerman

In 1906, the German sociologist Werner Sombart asked the most famous question about American radicalism: "Why is there no socialism in the United States?" Only thirty-five years later, the former radical Eugene Lyons decried the "Stalinist penetration of America." Such divergent assessments are hardly unusual in the controversial history of American radicalism. This essay traces three themes in American radicalism in the period between Sombart's and Lyons's writings: First, the inverse relationship between prosperity and the strength of radical movements; Sombart himself blamed "roast beef and apple pie" for limiting American radicalism. Second, American radical organizations and individuals were profoundly affected by foreign events. Even before Karl Marx's International Working Men's Association (the First International) collapsed in the 1870s, radical and reform movements proclaimed their internationalism. The Bolsheviks' ascent to power in Russia in 1917 more dramatically recast American radicalism through the Russian-dominated Communist International and also indirectly, as Americans closely followed Soviet events. Finally, American radicals grappled with the relationship of radical politics to radical artistic expression through the first half of the twentieth century: How should art serve the revolution? Should a work of art be considered radical by dint of its themes, its author, or its mode of expression? In painting, drawing, and especially writing, American radicals sought to answer these questions.

American radicalism reached peak influence in national politics, local politics, unionism, and intellectual circles between 1906 and 1941. Tellingly, each of these peak moments happened at different times, revealing the complexity and even cross-purposes of different spheres of radical activity. Given the extraordinary range of "radical alternatives," this essay considers only those alternative movements—whether artistic, labor-related, or political—that located capitalism as a central cause of social problems.

THE SOCIALIST PARTY OF AMERICA

The strongest American radical organization of Sombart's time was the Socialist Party of America (SPA), founded in 1901. Like the huge corporations it challenged, the party itself came into being as the result of a merger: the labor organizer Eugene V. Debs brought his American Railway Union together with dissidents from the small and sectarian Socialist Labor Party, whose defectors included most of the key figures in turn-of-the-century radicalism. The party quickly attracted a diverse and loyal following. First were rural radicals in the Midwest, who read newspapers like the Missouri-based *National Rip-Saw* and the Kansas-based *Appeal to Reason;* their numbers included many disappointed by the demise of populism in the 1890s. The rural radicals were joined on the left wing of the SPA by the syndicalists, especially those associated with the Wobblies (Industrial Workers of the World, or IWW). Founded in 1905, the IWW and its leader, "Big Bill" Haywood, quickly earned fame and notoriety for their confrontational battles in western and midwestern mines. Third, a polyglot group of immigrant organizations comprised the largest single element in the SPA. Yiddish-speaking Jews from New York's Lower East Side were the largest of these foreign-language federations, but Finns, western Slavs, Germans, and Irish also had sizable contingents. The fourth group, municipal socialists, included the most conservative members of the party. Led by mayors such as Victor Berger (Milwaukee, Wisconsin) and George Lunn (Schenectady, New York), municipal socialists shared much with major-party politicians: they ran ethnic-based party machines, doled out patronage, and worked (as one business executive put it) "hand in glove" with major corporations. Critics termed such mayors not socialists but "slow-cialists," though Berger himself preferred to emphasize Socialists' practical achievements by using the term "constructivists." Finally, numerous intellectuals were attracted to the SPA:

∽⧜∼

MAX AND CRYSTAL EASTMAN

Brother and sister Max and Crystal Eastman stood at the crossroads of American radicalism in the 1910s and 1920s, and their lives reveal much about the fate of radical movements. Born to two ministers, both siblings abandoned their parents' religious beliefs but maintained and expanded their unconventional views. Arriving in Greenwich Village to work in the settlement houses, Crystal earned a law degree from New York University in 1907, living with a remarkable group of activists and attorneys. Max, engaged to the sculptor-activist Ida Rauh from that group, frequented their apartment. Crystal soon used her training to promote industrial safety and workers' rights; her study of the Triangle Shirtwaist Factory fire in 1911 concluded that only a revolution would improve factory conditions. She also helped found key organizations of the era, from the Women's International League for Peace and Freedom to the American Civil Liberties Union. While not a regular member, Crystal worked closely with a group of women calling themselves Heterodoxy. The group brought bohemians together with social scientists, socialists, lawyers, and writers. Breaking away from the central tenets of domesticity, purity, and motherhood that united earlier women's movements, Heterodoxy set the stage for twentieth-century feminism.

Max, meanwhile, had studied philosophy with John Dewey and in 1913 began editing the *Masses* (which ran from 1911 to 1917), the flagship radical magazine of the era. As its masthead indicated, it was to be "a revolutionary and not a reform magazine . . . directed against rigidity and dogma wherever it is found . . . a magazine whose final policy is to do as it pleases and conciliate nobody, not even its readers." (This last task was made possible by the quiet benefaction of a vice president of New York Life Insurance Company.) The twenty thousand or so subscribers to the *Masses* read political reportage from luminaries like Mary Heaton Vorse, Walter Lippmann, and William English Walling—but also distinguished fiction and poetry by the likes of Carl Sandburg, Amy Lowell, and Sherwood Anderson and drawings by Ashcan school artists.

After the *Masses* was shut down by the postmaster general in 1917, Max and Crystal helped create the *Liberator;* the immediate impetus was to publish the revolutionary writer John Reed's dispatches from Russia—the basis for Reed's *Ten Days That Shook the World* (1919). More political than its predecessor, the *Liberator* proved to be a crucial conduit for information about the Bolsheviks as well as domestic labor actions. Standing with "one foot in Bohemia" and "the other in the revolutionary movement" (as the co-editor Joseph Freeman put it), the magazine attracted a readership of about eighty thousand. But Eastman himself was unable to reconcile this split; he left for Russia in 1922, eventually smuggling out the Bolshevik leader Vladimir Ilich Lenin's last testament, a document highly critical of the Communist leader Joseph Stalin. With Max's departure, Crystal quit her *Liberator* post and worked as a freelance journalist and activist—primarily because she was unable to land a suitable job. She shuttled back and forth between New York and London, working on feminist and radical causes, until her death in 1928. Upon quitting the *Liberator,* Max and Crystal turned it over to the Communist Party, which established two editorial boards to oversee it, one for politics and another for art. This organizational dualism, however, faltered, and the magazine became a more typical Communist Party organ, renamed *Workers' Monthly.*

CONTINUED NEXT PAGE

690

Max's long career after the *Liberator* incurred the wrath of American radicals. He angered them with increasingly vociferous criticisms of Stalinism—especially for the lack of cultural freedom—in the 1930s. By the 1950s, Eastman exemplified another trend of interwar American radicals, becoming an outspoken conservative who defended Senator Joseph McCarthy (as a "clear-headed patriot") and fought both philosophical and political battles against leftists.

some, like the self-described "gentleman socialist" William English Walling, played a major role in party leadership. Others, like the black activist W. E. B. Du Bois, maintained close ties with SPA members but had more fleeting terms of actual party membership. A small number of Christian socialists, led by the Reverend Edward E. Carr, joined the intellectuals. The broad base of the SPA, with five or more distinct elements in the party, boosted membership and influence but also created internal dissension.

By any quantitative measure, the Socialist Party was gathering steam when Sombart asked his famous question. SPA electoral support expanded quickly: Debs polled roughly 100,000 votes in the 1900 presidential election, the first of his five campaigns. By 1904, over 400,000 voters opted for Debs's SPA ticket. The SPA vote peaked in 1912, when Debs polled almost 900,000—6 percent of the electorate. Debs insisted that his campaigns sought "a majority of Socialists, not of votes"; by that measure, the party grew even more quickly. Membership jumped dramatically, from 10,000 at the founding (1901) to 42,000 by 1908 and 118,000 by 1912. Socialists also achieved significant success in local elections, winning major offices in seventy-four cities and towns—as far east as Rockaway, New Jersey, and as far west as Berkeley, California. Socialist periodicals received similarly wide attention—as many as three hundred newspapers in fifteen languages; the largest of these were *Appeal to Reason* (over 750,000 circulated weekly) and the *Jewish Daily Forward* (140,000 daily).

As the SPA expanded, tensions between its various constituencies grew accordingly. Haywood and his IWW colleagues favored matching employers' anti-union violence by initiating acts of sabotage, while intellectuals and municipal socialists shunned such tactics. The question of violence eventually led to a major falling-out of party leadership right at its prewar apex. In 1913, conservative members of the SPA executive board pushed through a resolution banning sabotage and violence. Many syndicalists left the party soon thereafter, devoting their energies to the major textile strikes of 1911 and 1912.

GREENWICH VILLAGE'S BOHEMIAN RADICALS

At the very time the organized American Left reached its prewar peak, a very different, and distinctly unorganized, radicalism flourished in New York's Greenwich Village. Rebelling against what they saw as small-town Victorian strictures on personal behavior, these Village radicals rejected the inherited patterns of artistic expression and social life. Whether gathered in salons and cafés or clustered around small literary magazines, these intellectuals tried to work out a distinctly modern way of relating to the world, free of repression from capitalist organization and societal expectations. Only a handful of these Villagers belonged to the SPA. Measured by the number of influential periodicals emanating from lower Manhattan, the literary and artistic output of the Village's years of prewar ferment was impressive; the *New Republic, Seven Arts,* and the *Dial* all were born in the Village of the 1910s.

If any single year marked the climax of what the historian Henry May called "the end of American innocence," it was 1913. Two quite different enterprises emerged from Mabel Dodge's salon that year: first, the International Exhibition of Modern Art (widely known as the Armory Show) brought European modernism, most famously the Paris-based artists Marcel Duchamp and Pablo Picasso, to American shores in what one critic called "the Great Event in the history of American art." With help from the avante-garde American writer Gertrude Stein in Paris and Dodge in New York, organizers assembled thirteen hundred paintings, drawings, and sculptures to demonstrate the newest trends in both American and European art. The most controversial work, Duchamp's *Nude Descending a Staircase, No. 2* (1912) provoked both satire and

The Masses, c. 1912. Piet Vlag founded the journal in New York in 1911, and the following year appointed Max Eastman editor. Its contributors, including Randolph Bourne, Helen Keller, and Upton Sinclair, also shared management duties in this cooperatively run publication. LIBRARY OF CONGRESS

criticism; one New York newspaper, by sponsoring a "find the nude" contest, called attention to the work's nonrepresentational forms. American contributions by the American realist Robert Henri and the rest of Henri's group "The Eight" painted in a rather conventional style (by European standards), but sought to express their radical politics instead by depicting America's urban poor. Critics, citing their scenes of the underside of urban life, soon gave the group a new name: the Ashcan School.

Amid the preparations for the Armory Show, Dodge's salon—most notably the revolutionary writer-activist John Reed, who was especially close to Dodge—engaged in more explicitly political activities. After visiting the ongoing silk workers' strike in Paterson, New Jersey, Reed and friends sought to attract both attention and funds to the strikers' cause. They organized the Paterson Pageant, a reenactment of the strike, in Manhattan's Madison Square Garden. Mounted for only one night, the program featured reprises of speeches that Reed, the labor organizer Elizabeth Gurley

Flynn, and Bill Haywood had made in Paterson. The stars of the show were twelve hundred strikers who had marched down Fifth Avenue before the pageant and overwhelmed even the ample facilities of the Garden. The final result of this event, which offered its own vision of proletarian art, revealed the tensions between workers and intellectuals: while raising some five thousand to ten thousand dollars for the strike fund (far less than expected), the pageant contributed to the ultimate failure of the strike: taking advantage of picket lines depleted for the evening, employers brought scab workers into the Paterson factories that very night. New forms of expressive art, then, could be not only distant from but even detrimental to radical politics.

WORLD WAR AND REVOLUTION

The onset of the European war in 1914 presented another fundamental challenge to radicals. The collapse of the Socialist International (also known as the Second International, a federation of socialist parties and trade unions) as European socialist parties opted for national defense over international solidarity, led to disputes within the SPA. Across Europe, pledges not to enter a "capitalist war" were quickly forgotten in a frenzy of patriotism. The American party's staunch antiwar stance attracted some new followers, helping to rebuild after the post-1912 hemorrhage in membership. At the same time, though, an influential segment of the membership—including intellectuals like William English Walling—supported the American war effort and made damaging public breaks from the party.

Far more devastating for radical movements in general was the suppression of dissent that accompanied the war. The Espionage and Sedition Acts of 1917 and 1918 sharply limited the range of permissible criticism of the United States government, banning actions that encouraged disloyalty or brought the government into disrepute. Citizens faced lengthy jail sentences while noncitizens were threatened with deportation. The postmaster general was especially vigorous in enforcement, endangering many if not most Village magazines. Over one thousand activists were convicted under these laws; Debs received a ten-year sentence for describing the war in class terms.

The declaration of Soviet power in Russia in November 1917 wholly transformed American leftism. The Bolsheviks, led by the revolutionary Vladimir Ilich Lenin, declared power in the name of the Soviets, workers councils dominated by socialist parties. A destructive civil war ensued, as British, French, and American troops joined monarchists and would-be dictators in fighting the Bolsheviks. The Bolshevik Revolution changed the nature of American leftism. Gone were the days when socialism could be theorized in the abstract; all leftists had to come to terms with Russia's professed socialism. The revolution itself repelled many American socialists, especially moderate intellectuals and municipal socialists who quickly joined anti-Soviet organizations and supported American intervention in Russia. For others, events in Russia fired their enthusiasm for socialism. The radical John Reed, already in Russia, sent dispatches that idolized and idealized Lenin and the Bolsheviks. Though short-lived, communist revolts in central Europe further inspired American radicals.

Even those American socialists inspired by Russian events soon split into warring factions, with not one but two groups leaving the SPA to form rival communist parties. In August 1919, Reed and many American-born radicals formed the Communist Labor Party after being barred—by Chicago police officers—from an SPA meeting. At the same time, other left-wing members of the SPA formed the Communist Party of America, led by Nicholas Hourwich and Louis C. Fraina; this party was dominated by those from the foreign-language federations of the SPA, especially the Russians.

Most socialists' dealings with the police, however, were far less innocuous than separating feuding factions. The end of the war saw a sharp rise in the official repression of increasingly militant leftist and pro-union activism in the United States. From the Seattle general strike in winter 1919 to the Boston police strike that summer, workers fought for higher wages and the right to unionize. In both of these major strikes—and in dozens of smaller ones—officials accused the strikers of trying to establish a Bolshevik America. Radical militancy took violent forms: postal officials uncovered an anarchist plot to send letter-bombs to politicians leading the charge against the "Reds," including Attorney General A. Mitchell Palmer. Race riots in Chicago, Washington, and East St. Louis and major strikes accelerated throughout the year, all of which were blamed (however misleadingly) on radicals. Palmer stepped up surveillance of leftist organizations, establishing the Bureau of Investigation (later the Federal Bureau of Investigation or FBI) headed by the young and eager J. Edgar Hoover. Noncitizen suspects had few legal rights; about two hundred fifty, including the anarchists Emma Goldman and Alexander Berkman, were deported to Soviet Russia

on the USS *Buford*, dubbed the "Soviet Ark," in December 1919. At the same time, law enforcement officers stepped up the campaign with the so-called "Palmer raids," rounding up as many as four thousand supposed radicals in thirty-three cities. The accused ranged from socialists to union leaders to a bakery cooperative in Lynn, Massachusetts. While the foreign born made up a significant portion of the membership in American socialist parties, the *Buford* example reveals how opponents painted leftism as, literally, an alien ideology.

The red scare and the divisiveness among left-wing parties decimated the movement. Membership dropped precipitously in all of the major parties. The SPA lost well over half its members to splinter parties. The only bright spot for American leftists in this period was Debs's final presidential bid in 1920. He organized a major campaign from his jail cell, polling 920,000 votes in an electorate newly expanded to include women.

FACTIONALISM AND DECLINE IN THE 1920s

The thrill of revolution had worn off by the early 1920s. In Russia, Bolsheviks shifted from the glory of revolution and the heroism of civil war battles to the more mundane tasks of economic reconstruction and the extension of political power. Wartime and postwar repression took a heavy toll on American radical movements, while interparty disputes further alienated many activists.

The Moscow-dominated Communist International (also known as the Third International and Comintern), established in 1919, pressured American parties to end their factional infighting. Both parties sought to join Comintern, but it insisted that the parties unite. Even after this uneasy unification was accomplished, new tensions emerged, this time over the creation of an aboveground party organ. Fraught with factionalism for the remainder of the decade, American Communists continually relied on Comintern to resolve conflicts—so much so that it eventually established an American Commission to handle such issues. After significant struggle, the Comintern eventually brought most of the parties together, under the name Communist Party of the United States of America (CPUSA), in 1929. Other American Communists turned away from Comintern completely, shifting their allegiance to the exiled (later deported and eventually assassinated) Russian theorist and agitator Leon Trotsky. James P. Cannon led the initial splinter group away from the

Communist Party in 1928 to form the Communist League of America. Never a mass movement, the various Trotskyist organizations attracted numerous intellectuals and writers despite a series of doctrinal disputes in the 1930s.

Greenwich Village radicalism also flagged after the war: many of those disappointed by the rising conformism and consumption fled America entirely, joining the expanding group of expatriates in Paris. Disillusioned by wartime America or harassed by authorities, others wandered away from radicalism—so much so that one dispirited reformer wondered, "Where Are the Pre-War Radicals?" in a 1925 article in *Survey* magazine. While some writers of the "lost generation" focused on a literary modernism devoid of explicit political content, the novelist John Dos Passos and others experimented with a disjointed and multivocal style that combined fictional and nonfictional narratives.

Dos Passos's political and artistic career exemplified the twists and turns of literary radicalism in the interwar years. Radicalized by his Harvard experience, Dos Passos served as an ambulance driver in World War I, proclaiming that his "only hope" was in revolution. His first major novel, *Manhattan Transfer* (1925), depicted the disjointed and frenetic life in New York through the telling of hundreds of seemingly scattered episodes. His magnum opus was the *USA* trilogy, published in the early 1930s, in which he perfected the voice of the "artist-reporter." The books interweave a fictional plot and characters with reportage both real and invented. As one of the major achievements of literary radicalism, the trilogy told the story of the United States from 1900 until the Great Depression. Dos Passos's political career balanced radicalism with anarchist tendencies ("Organization is death," he concluded during his wartime service). Throughout the early 1930s, Dos Passos was a reliable fellow-traveler, insulting non-Communists for their lack of commitment; in one famous episode, he opined that voting for the socialists in the 1932 election was like drinking "near-beer," which could deliver the taste but not the punch. By the late 1930s, though, Dos Passos drifted from Communism, in large part because of Soviet anti-Trotsky activities during the Spanish Civil War. Extreme individualism eventually won out over radicalism, and Dos Passos by the 1960s was firmly in the right wing of the Republican Party.

The Socialist Party found its national role greatly reduced in the 1920s. Unprecedented prosperity reduced the appeal of radical politics in urban areas. The agricultural recession, meanwhile, led to the rise of farmer-labor parties in the Midwest. Mid-western radicals—once the Socialist Party's largest constituency—abandoned the SPA, leaving the party's strength primarily among foreign-born workers living in eastern cities. While the downward trend had started in the war years—New York accounted for only 7.5 percent of the SPA vote in 1916, but 22 percent in 1920—it accelerated in the early 1920s. Growing hostility to foreigners—most visible with the passage of the draconian Immigration Act of 1924—isolated immigrants who remained an important constituency for socialists and communists. Perennial presidential candidate Debs, furthermore, left no natural successor; leaders like Berger (by then a U.S. representative) were ineligible by virtue of their foreign birth.

African American politics and culture provided one notable exception to the broad pattern of decline in worker militancy and intellectual energy. The Harlem Renaissance brought together an impressive array of writers, artists, and theorists, all exploring themes of racial identity and radical social transformation. But once again, the relationship between radical art and politics led to conflict; as the poet Langston Hughes infused his poems with direct commentary on racism and capitalism, for instance, leading lights of the Renaissance distanced themselves from his work. Only one periodical, the trade unionist A. Philip Randolph's *The Messenger,* successfully bridged the political and cultural radicalism of the 1920s. Randolph, an SPA member for five years following World War I, combined activism within the SPA with racially oriented political organizations such as the International League of Darker Peoples. Randolph became most famous for leading the Brotherhood of Sleeping Car Porters against the formidable Pullman Company—as well as against racism in white unions.

Through the rosy haze of the consumerist complacency and the age of political normalcy, one controversy did bring together radicals in the 1920s: a drawn out murder case against two Italian anarchists, Nicola Sacco and Bartolomeo Vanzetti. Accused in 1920 of killing two factory employees during a robbery, Sacco and Vanzetti confused their case by offering misleading testimony in order to conceal their anarchist activities. Not only radicals but also "responsible liberals" like the future Supreme Court justice Felix Frankfurter fought for Sacco and Vanzetti's acquittal. The fight was long and ultimately unsuccessful; the two Italians were executed in August 1927, amid a blizzard of last-minute legal and public appeals. The execution quickly became the focus of radicals' anger—*The New Masses,* for instance, railed against "Lynchers in Frockcoats," while the muckraking socialist author Upton Sinclair deplored the case in *Boston*.

AMERICAN COMMUNISM IN THE EARLY DEPRESSION

American radical movements of all sorts—political parties, unions, pro-Soviet organizations, and literary magazines—took advantage of both domestic and international circumstances to expand in the early 1930s. Soviet plans for rapid industrialization began in 1926, quickly attracting the attention of American radicals and liberals enthralled by the concept of central planning and rapid modernization. Economic policies also carried political implications, as the Bolshevik leader Joseph Stalin eliminated his rivals and proclaimed the goal of "socialism in one country." The Soviets' compromises with capitalism, which Americans associated with Soviet economic policy in the 1920s, were replaced by visions of mechanized collective farms and huge factories. The Soviet economy appeared even stronger in relative terms after the stock market crash of 1929 and the arrival of the Great Depression across the United States and Europe.

More militant Soviet policy had a direct effect on American radicalism with the promulgation of Comintern's Third Period policies in 1928: aggressive electoral politics, dual unionism (establishing Communist Party–run unions to compete with non-Communist ones); and self-determination for southern blacks. While Communist-led unions grew only slowly, CPUSA's new militancy brought increases in party membership and especially in the ranks of fellow travelers (those working within Communist-led organizations though not formal CPUSA members). Unemployment Councils found large constituencies in depression-wracked cities, while the party's defense of nine African Americans accused of rape in Scottsboro, Alabama, widely known as the "Scottsboro Boys," significantly raised the profile of the Communists among northern and southern blacks.

Intellectuals were even more likely than workers to explore the expanded range of radical alternatives in the early 1930s. Magazines like V. F. Calverton's *Modern Quarterly* (from 1933 to 1937, *Modern Monthly*) and a much revivified *New Masses* published first-rate literature and social analysis from distinctly leftist perspectives. Reportage from the likes of the journalists Whittaker Chambers and Meridel Le Sueur kept intellectuals informed about strikes and workers movements across the country. Marxist literary criticism also reached new heights.

Granville Hicks's *Great Tradition* (1933) sought to trace a strain of radical critique through American literary history. A magazine initially aligned with Communist Party literary policy, the *Partisan Review,* offered a more activist view, calling on critics to engage in "direct participation."

The decade also marked the high point of the proletarian literature movement, which strove to narrate workers' lives from their own point of view. From the journalist Mike Gold's literary experimentation in the 1920s, the movement spread rapidly through the Communist Party's John Reed Clubs. By 1932 over one thousand club members promised to defend the Soviet Union, to further the revolutionary labor movement, and to fight against fascism, racism, and bourgeois ideas. These clubs resolved the tension between radical art and radical politics in favor of the latter, preferring didactic rehearsals of injustice to experimentation with forms and styles. Similar moves took place in other genres, as leftists explored newly politicized forms of theater and film. In what would become a standard trajectory for many intellectuals, the author Richard Wright joined the John Reed Club because of its interest in nurturing proletarian writers, but eventually grew disgusted with their politics of ideological purity and broke away.

NON-COMMUNIST RADICALISM IN THE EARLY DEPRESSION

The Socialist Party of America enjoyed a renaissance in the early 1930s, primarily because of the indefatigable work and personal charisma of the party's new head, Norman Thomas. A direct descendent of the social gospel movement, Thomas served as an editor with the *Nation* and the short-lived *New York Leader.* His 1928 presidential bid, like Eugene Debs's campaigns, attracted both party members and voters. His 1929 campaign for New York mayor brought Thomas further support, especially in churches and universities. Thomas co-founded the League for Independent Political Action, which brought together the leading lights of America's Left intellectuals (including the philosopher John Dewey, Du Bois, the *Nation* editor Oswald Garrison Villard, and the theologian Reinhold Niebuhr) to promote socialist causes. With League support, Thomas garnered 880,000 votes in the presidential campaign. By comparison, about 100,000 voted for the labor agitator William Z. Foster and the CPUSA ticket, with its Third Period platform, "Towards a Soviet America."

Union activity reversed after the decline of the 1920s, spurred especially by President Franklin D. Roosevelt's pro-labor legislation. From Kentucky coalfields to California strawberry fields, a new generation of organizers led new industrial unions. In 1934 alone, a violent general strike shut down San Francisco; a strike incapacitated the Toledo, Ohio, auto industry; and a Trotskyist-supported Teamsters strike divided Minneapolis, Minnesota.

Interparty hostility prevented any unification of radical efforts. Communists lashed out at any organization that they saw as compromising with capitalism, hardly limiting themselves to vitriolic attacks on Trotsky and his followers. Following the Comintern logic that workers might be misled by faux radicals now that the collapse of capitalism was near at hand, American Communist Party members condemned socialists and other non-Communists as "social fascists." In one infamous episode, Communist Party members violently disrupted a New York rally in support of Austrian socialists suppressed by the German chancellor Adolf Hitler. The Communist Party also mocked the radical author Upton Sinclair's gubernatorial bid in California in 1934. Under the social reform movement he organized, End Poverty in California, Sinclair won the Democratic nomination (though not President Roosevelt's support) but was called "Hitler-like" in Communist Party newspapers.

As the depression deepened, many Americans were attracted to radical organizations well outside the Communist fold. One of the most interesting and enduring of these was the Catholic Worker movement, organized by Dorothy Day and lasting beyond her death in 1980. Inspired by the writings of Jack London and Upton Sinclair in her teenage years, Day joined the Socialist Party of America in 1916 (while a student in Illinois) and soon thereafter moved to New York. Working as a writer for the socialist *Call*, Day interviewed left-wing luminaries such as Russian exile Leon Trotsky. With the start of World War I, Day joined Max Eastman's *Masses* and was the principal editor for the issue on the war that began the battles with the United States government. A fixture on the Greenwich Village bohemian scene, Day worked with IWW, argued with Mike Gold and John Dos Passos, and frequented the famous speakeasy "Hell Hole," where she was frequently regaled by playwright Eugene O'Neill's recitations.

After giving birth to a daughter out of wedlock in 1926, Day rethought her life and emerged as a devout Catholic. Asked by her bewildered bohemian companions why she joined such a famously conservative institution, Day replied that the Catholic Church was home to the poor masses of America. Undertaking an assignment for the Catholic magazine *Commonweal*, Day met Peter Maurin, a French Catholic intellectual of peasant origins. Day found Maurin's plan for a spiritually infused radicalism compelling and soon thereafter took up many of his goals. She created a newspaper, the *Catholic Worker* (which debuted on May Day 1933), serving for decades as its editor, chief writer, and moving force. She also sought to establish alternatives to industrial capitalism in urban areas and rural farming communes. The first such alternative, House of Hospitality, opened in 1933 in New York's Lower East Side; by 1940 at least forty houses were in operation.

Within a few years, the Catholic Worker movement had many adherents; over 150,000 subscribed to its monthly newspaper in 1936. But the outbreak of the Spanish Civil War, pitting radical forces against the fascist- and Catholic-supported royalists, presented a challenge. Rather than pick one side or the other, Day and the *Catholic Worker* took a staunch pacifist position against the war: "Both Sides Fight Like Savages," blared one headline. Day's pacifism, visible in her earlier work with the magazine the *Masses* during World War I, cost the movement many supporters as World War II neared. As American radicals and conservatives alike came to accept the inevitability of fighting the Nazis, the *Catholic Worker*'s antiwar position left it isolated from its traditional sources of support; circulation dropped to one-third of its 1936 level. While Day's own radicalism was born of the socialist and bohemian tendencies of the pre–World War I era, in other ways her movement was a successor to religiously inspired radical movements that have shaped important aspects of American history, from the abolitionist movement to the social gospel of the late nineteenth century. Day fashioned a powerful and influential vision of social justice shaped not by Marx (whose writings, by her own admission, she "didn't understand") but by Catholic teachings.

Not all radical movements of the interwar era were left of center. A number of popular and powerful but ephemeral right-wing movements attracted significant attention throughout the 1930s. These movements peaked in the early 1930s and were already rife with internal dispute by the 1936 presidential election, after which surviving groups and their leaders resorted increasingly to a combination of anti-Semitism and Communist-bashing. Like Day, these right-wing leaders typically emerged from religious backgrounds and claimed an interest in social justice, but otherwise they shared little with the *Catholic Worker* and other such left-wing movements.

Father Charles Coughlin, for instance, was ordained in the Catholic Church in 1916 and in the mid-1920s began experimenting with radio broadcasts as a means of reaching a larger audience with his sermons and religious parables. With the onset of the depression, though, Coughlin's message veered toward the secular and the political. He excoriated bolshevism and socialism as anti-Christian while also condemning President Herbert Hoover's ineffective responses to the deepening economic crisis. Aside from Hoover, Coughlin blamed international bankers, whom he saw as part of a conspiracy to take over the world. He supported Franklin D. Roosevelt's candidacy in 1932 and even claimed partial credit for Roosevelt's victory. After President Roosevelt failed to enact some of Coughlin's pet proposals, though, the priest turned his invective against the president, both through radio speeches and through the newly created National Union for Social Justice. In the 1936 election, Father Coughlin joined forces with other right-wing populists under the banner of the Union Party. This new third party included refugees from the "Share the Wealth" movement led by Louisiana governor Huey Long (until his assassination in 1935), the Old Age Revolving Pension Plan led by Frances Townsend, and supporters of Gerald L. K. Smith.

Smith, a protestant preacher, was another key figure in right-wing populism in the 1930s. He began his career as a Protestant preacher and by the mid-1930s had joined Governor Long's machine. Smith was a vociferous opponent of the political Left, painting the New Deal as a form of Communism—in fact, an especially pernicious form in that it left economic power in the hands of old-line magnates like the Roosevelts and the Rockefellers. Smith and his magazine, the *American Progress*, repeatedly insisted that the 1936 election pitted the New Deal's "red flag" against the "Stars and Stripes."

For both Coughlin and Smith, anti-Communism merged into anti-Semitism. Both figures had reputations for hate-mongering before and during the Union Party presidential campaign in 1936; Smith's public standing, for instance, was wounded by a newsreel on "The Lunatic Fringe" that played up his narrow definition of who counted as "Americans." After the collapse of the 1936 campaign, both Coughlin and Smith became more vocal in their anti-Semitism. Coughlin in 1938 republished the notorious *Protocols of the Elders of Zion*, a World War I–era forgery purporting to reveal the Jewish conspiracy to take over the world. His magazine, *Social Justice*, also reprinted some speeches of Nazi propaganda minister Joseph Goebbels and defended the Nazi Party for its anti-Communism. Smith's strongest anti-Semitic statements came a few years later. After being pushed out of the "Share the Wealth" movement in 1936, Smith founded the Committee of One Million (with a membership of nine) as a platform for his anti-union and anti-Communist politics. He campaigned for a seat in the United States Senate in 1939 (as a Republican) but lost handily. Through these activities, Smith became acquainted with auto magnate Henry Ford, and it is likely that Smith's growing anti-Semitism was encouraged by these contacts. His new magazine, the *Cross and the Flag*, published Smith's ever-more-vehement anti-Semitic and anti-Communist commentaries throughout the 1940s and 1950s; he blamed the Jews for everything from the crucifixion of Jesus to the Great Depression and World War II. Both Father Coughlin and Smith were among the most charismatic and effective orators of their day, and their messages of intolerance and hatred—all in the name of the worker—serve as reminders that the radical alternatives of the depression decade came not only from the Left.

THE POPULAR FRONT

The rise of fascism in Germany, combined with the worsening United States economy, brought increased attention for radicalism, especially Communism. Reflecting changes in Moscow's priorities as well as western party initiatives, Comintern reversed its stance in 1935, calling for a popular front of all progressive forces against fascism. Soviet diplomacy took an activist stance, trying in vain to organize a broad alliance against Germany. Amid growing concern with German expansionism, such endeavors found more western support among intellectuals than diplomats. Communist officials in the United States and elsewhere now sought alliances with the same groups they had vilified a few years earlier. Even President Roosevelt, compared to the Italian dictator Benito Mussolini in 1932, was now seen as sufficiently progressive that the 1936 Communist Party presidential candidate Earl Browder called for Roosevelt's victory—but did so quietly, for fear that explicit Communist support would cost Roosevelt votes.

By 1935, Communists had replaced the call for a "Soviet America" with the claim that "Communism is the Americanism of the twentieth century."

Like the critic Granville Hicks earlier, Browder portrayed the Communists as successors to an indigenous radical tradition. Dual unionism was abandoned, and party organizers—considered the best and most energetic—helped organize numerous locals for the new Congress of Industrial Organizations (CIO), a breakaway organization originally part of the more conservative American Federation of Labor. Large organizing efforts in high-profile industries like steel and automobiles brought early successes to both the CIO and the Communist Party.

The popular front was especially influential among artists and intellectuals. The dissolution of the doctrinaire John Reed clubs in 1934 and the creation of the League of American Writers in 1935 suggested new directions for left-wing literary work. The League made fewer political demands on its members, but limited entry to published authors— a sharp contrast to the John Reed clubs' preference for inexperienced writers from the working class. Many famous writers, including John Steinbeck and Lillian Hellman, most without party affiliation, loaned their names to the League, and even the popular lecturer Dale Carnegie and the once-ridiculed Upton Sinclair participated in League events. The CPUSA supported a proliferation of other affiliated organizations: the American Artists Congress, National Lawyers Guild, National Committee for the Defense of Political Prisoners, Hollywood Anti-Nazi League, and countless others.

The League soon entered into a major conflict with the renegade New York John Reed club and its ever-more-influential *Partisan Review*. By 1937, the *Review* editors Philip Rahv and William Phillips, joined by the writers Mary McCarthy and Dwight Macdonald, had led the magazine out of the CPUSA fold and allied it instead with the party's number-one enemy: Leon Trotsky. The growing tensions between Communist Party members (who ignored or dismissed ever-more-obvious indications of Joseph Stalin's deadly policies) and anti-Stalinists were centered around the *Partisan Review* and came to define intellectual life in New York from the late 1930s well into the 1950s. The two sides engaged in all-out intellectual combat in print, at rallies, and in the City College of New York lunchrooms that soon produced the next generation of New York intellectuals: Daniel Bell, Nathan Glazer, Irving Kristol, and Irving Howe. Among the most important radical causes in the late 1930s was the Spanish Civil War. While British, French, and American diplomats declared neutrality, the Italian and German governments supplied General Francisco Franco with

military hardware. The American contingent in Comintern's International Brigades—named, in true popular front fashion, the Abraham Lincoln Brigade—attracted about three thousand Americans determined to fight on the front line against fascism. Franco's military machine quickly overran these untrained troops, killing as many as half of the Americans and leading one participant to wonder whether they had been named after Lincoln because "he, too, was assassinated." In spite of the fatal results, the Spanish conflict attracted widespread attention among leftists throughout the United States and Europe; the novelists Ernest Hemingway and George Orwell both wrote major works about the war.

The popular front prospered because of a confluence of internal and external factors. The CPUSA's turn toward "Americanism," soon ratified by Comintern policy, encouraged a far wider scope of membership and activities. Remarkable successes in unionization reflected not only the organizers' ability to recruit workers but also a political environment far more favorable to labor; the 1935 National Labor Relations Act, for instance, sharply curtailed union-busting violence. International events also played a crucial role. German militarism was on the increase, with the annexations of Austria and Czechoslovakia as well as intensifying anti-Jewish activities. In Spain, as well as in their efforts for a collective security arrangement in Europe, the Soviets successfully portrayed themselves as the only bulwark against fascism.

THE COLLAPSE OF THE POPULAR FRONT

If international events were partially responsible for the rise of the popular front, they also contributed mightily to its demise. The Soviet show trials from 1936 to 1938, during which senior Bolshevik leaders were executed for outrageous accusations of espionage, heated up conflicts between American Stalinists and anti-Stalinists. Many leftists maintained their support for the Soviet Union, either backing the prosecutors' accusations, or placing Soviet opposition to fascism above domestic policies, or explaining the trials as an example of Russia's brutal traditions. But increasing doubts were sown among less credulous leftists. John Dewey and Waldo Frank (the president of the League of American Writers until 1937) articulated their doubts about the trials and soon incurred blistering attacks from the Communist Party.

Even more damaging for the American radical movements was the announcement of a Nazi-Soviet Pact in August 1939. After 1935, thousands of radicals had flocked to the Communist Party in support of the Soviets' antifascist diplomacy. But overnight the party line shifted from collective security against fascism to neutrality in a war between capitalists. Fallout in autumn 1939 was immediate and dramatic. Over one hundred of the eight hundred members of the League of American Writers quit, leaving it all but bereft of officers. The CIO soon passed anti-Communist resolutions—and Communists in the union offered no opposition. Trotskyists and others who had compared Stalinist Russia with Nazi Germany claimed vindication.

There were also domestic reasons for radicals' ills. The American Federation of Labor stepped up its long-standing efforts against radical unionists. In 1938, the Republican politician Martin Dies Jr. established the House Committee on Un-American Activities, which soon held hearings on alleged Communist conspiracies in union organizing and numerous Democratic Party projects. The "yellow journalist" extraordinaire William Randolph Hearst, meanwhile, joined Dies and others in condemning both the New Deal and Communism in the popular media.

The high hopes and eventual betrayal of those attracted to radical alternatives in the 1930s had a significant but delayed impact. After the German attack on the Union of Soviet Socialist Republics in 1941, the Americans and Soviets were military allies. The official mood turned friendly, in spite of continuing spying activities. Earl Browder even disbanded the CPUSA in 1944, creating the Communist Political Association. Yet after the war, official knowledge of Soviet espionage, coupled with the willingness of many ex-Communists to testify about the activities of themselves and their colleagues, provided much of the energy for the United States senator Joseph McCarthy's anti-Communist crusade. Long after McCarthy's censure in 1954, former participants and historians still battle over the meanings of American radicalism in the interwar period.

See also **Patterns of Reform and Revolt** *(in this volume);* **The Ideal of Spontaneity; American Expatriate Artists Abroad; Working Class; Liberalism; Social Reform; Socialism and Radical Thought** *(volume 2);* **Twentieth-Century Economic Thought; Journals of Opinion; Periodicals; Painting; Marxist Approaches** *(volume 3); and other articles in this section.*

BIBLIOGRAPHY

The spirited and even self-destructive debates that have defined American radicalism have created a tremendously useful source base for historians. Many of the key analyses of Communist Party history, for instance, were written by one-time members of the party, or by longtime critics. Theodore Draper, the author of two influential books critical of the party for its fealty to the Comintern, for instance, participated in heated radical debates while at City College of New York in the 1930s; his *Roots of American Communism* (New York, 1957) and *American Communism and Soviet Russia, the Formative Period* (New York, 1960) set the terms for later debate about the relationship between the Comintern and the American Party. Historians more sympathetic to radicalism have tried to defend the movement on different grounds: Irving Howe and Lewis Coser, *The American Communist Party, A Critical History, 1919–1957* (Boston, 1957), accused the party of betraying radicalism. More recent historians have emphasized the rank-and-file members and their political and literary activities; see, for instance, Fraser M. Ottanelli, *The Communist Party of the United States: From the Depression to World War II* (New Brunswick, N.J., 1991), and, for a provocative reinterpretation of left-wing culture, Michael Denning, *The Cultural Front: The Laboring of American Culture in the Twentieth-Century* (London, 1996). Critics on the Right have struck back with newly available documents from Soviet archives suggesting the extent of financial support and political interference from Moscow; see, most recently, Harvey Klehr, John Earl Haynes, and Kyrill M. Anderson, *The Soviet World of American Communism* (New Haven, Conn., 1998) and Harvey Klehr, John Earl Haynes, and Fridrikh Igorevich Firsov, *The Secret World of American Communism* (New Haven, Conn., 1995).

The connection between historical interpretation and an author's own politics is further evident in important works on party history. James Weinstein, *The Decline of Socialism in America, 1912–1925* (New York, 1967), for instance, wrote from the perspective of a 1960s socialist student. Harvey Klehr, *The Heyday of American Communism: The Depression Decade* (New York, 1984), provided a critical but broad and admirably thorough overview. David A. Shannon, *The Socialist Party of America: A History* (New York, 1955), written at the height of McCarthyism, offered a surprisingly even-handed perspective. Robin D. G. Kelley, *Hammer and Hoe: Alabama Communists during the Great Depression* (Chapel Hill, N.C., 1990) gave an impassioned and well-documented argument about the appeal of the Communist Party for African Americans in the South.

The contributions of Left-inclined writers in the early twentieth century has led to a spate of excellent works of literary history. Henry F. May, *The End of American Innocence: A Study of the First Years of Our Own Time, 1912–1917* (New York, 1959) and Daniel Aaron, *Writers on the Left: Episodes in American Literary Communism* (New York, 1961) produced both exceptionally important and sensitive books that defined the field for decades and still merit reading. John Patrick Diggins, *The Rise and Fall of the American Left* (New York, 1992) wrote a sweeping overview of the intellectual history of the Left, stressing a generational approach. Greenwich Village's busiest year is well described in Martin Green, *New York 1913: The Armory Show and the Paterson Strike Pageant* (New York, 1988). On the fate of prewar radicals in the 1920s, see the autobiographical essays in Frederic Howe, "Where Are the Pre-War Radicals?" *Survey* 55 (1 February 1926): 556–566. Radical intellectuals of the 1930s have been the subject of numerous recent works; see especially Alan M. Wald, *The New York Intellectuals: The Rise and Decline of the Anti-Stalinist Left from the 1930s to the 1980s* (Chapel Hill, N.C., 1987); Terry A. Cooney, *The Rise of the New York Intellectuals: "Partisan Review" and Its Circle* (Madison, Wisc., 1986); Caren Irr, *The Suburb of Dissent: Cultural Politics in the United States and Canada during the 1930s* (Durham, N.C., 1998); and Judy Kutulas, *The Long War: The Intellectual People's Front and Anti-Stalinism, 1930–1940* (Durham, N.C., 1995).

Some more specialized works describe key episodes and individuals in American radicalism. Antiradicalism, an American tradition as old as radicalism itself, has been the subject of far fewer works. For a useful review, see M. J. Heale, *American Anticommunism: Battling the Enemy Within, 1830–1970* (Baltimore, 1990). The only full-scale work on post–World War I antiradical campaigns remains Robert K. Murray, *Red Scare: A Study in National Hysteria, 1919–1920* (Minneapolis, Minn., 1955). America's Spanish experience is chronicled in Peter N. Carroll, *The Odyssey of the Abraham Lincoln Brigade: Americans in the Spanish Civil War* (Stanford, Calif., 1994). Labor struggles are sympathetically described in Jeremy Brecher's revised and expanded edition of *Strike!* (Boston, 1997). Nancy F. Cott's incisive and important *Grounding of Modern Feminism* (New Haven, Conn., 1987) sketches the intellectual frameworks for post-suffrage feminism and presents some key feminists in radical circles (and vice versa). Bohemian radical life in New York is elegantly described in Christine Stansell, *American Moderns: Bohemian New York and the Creation of a New Century* (New York, 2000). The life of one of America's most important radicals is described in William L. O'Neill, *The Last Romantic: A Life of Max Eastman* (Oxford, 1978). There are many superb biographies of leading figures, including new works on Communist Party leaders (and rivals) Earl Browder and William Z. Foster. The most compelling and important biography for this period is Nick Salvatore's *Eugene V. Debs: Citizen and Socialist* (Urbana, Ill., 1982). On Dorothy Day, see

Mel Piehl, *Breaking Bread: The Catholic Worker and the Origin of Catholic Radicalism in America* (Philadelphia, 1982) and Nancy L. Roberts, *Dorothy Day and the* Catholic Worker (Albany, N.Y., 1984). On right-wing populists, see Alan Brinkley, *Voices of Protest: Huey Long, Father Coughlin and the Great Depression* (New York, 1982) and Leo P. Ribuffo, *The Old Christian Right: The Protestant Far Right from the Great Depression to the Cold War* (Philadelphia, 1983).

Scholarly reference works are indispensable for in-depth research. See Mari Jo Buhle, Paul Buhle, and Dan Georgakas, eds., *Encyclopedia of the American Left* (Oxford, 1998), which combines short articles with a brief list of key works. For a thorough list of scholarly works and memoirs on a variety of topics, consult John Earl Haynes, *Communism and Anti-Communism in the United States: An Annotated Guide to Historical Writings* (New York, 1987).

THE ARTIST AND THE INTELLECTUAL
IN THE NEW DEAL

Terry A. Cooney

On a spring night in 1935, a handful of people gathered at the home of Henry Alsberg to discuss the ambitions and ideas they were bringing to the organization of the Federal Arts Projects, or Federal Project One, an offspring of the recently created Works Progress Administration (WPA). Hallie Flanagan arrived with Harry Hopkins, a friend of President Franklin Roosevelt and the newly appointed head of the WPA, who was urging Flanagan to accept the directorship of the Federal Theatre Project. Among the others present, Holger Cahill had signed on to lead the Federal Art Project, Nikolai Sokoloff had agreed to run the Federal Music Project, and the host, Henry Alsberg, had undertaken to manage the Federal Writers Project. It was "one of those evenings," Flanagan reported later, "when everything seemed possible."

Cahill led the discussion, preaching his conviction that "government subsidy was the next logical step in the development of American art, not an art that would be an occasional unrelated accompaniment to everyday existence, but a functioning part of our national life." All agreed that the most important challenge to such a nationwide movement in the arts was "the people," for "they must be made to believe that they had important work to do." The job of the national directors of the Federal Arts Projects was to define what that work would be. Alsberg began to describe his plan for a series of guides that would describe every state in the Union and help the nation know itself better. Cahill spoke of an Index of American Design prepared by artists and photographers that would record the history of American furniture, painting, architecture, needlework, glassware, and other practical arts. Sokoloff outlined an ambitious project to establish symphony orchestras across the entire country. Drawn in by the occasion, Flanagan suggested a plan for "dramatizing contemporary events in a series of living newspapers that would have a rapid, cinematic form and an emphasis on many people doing small bits rather than roles demanding a few stars." As

they departed, Hopkins urged Flanagan to take the theater directorship. It could not go to someone with a narrow commercial consciousness from the established New York theater: "This is an American job" (Flanagan, pp. 18–20).

CONTEXTS PAST AND PRESENT

Explicitly, or by implication, the discussions of this evening marked a number of major themes moving forward from the early decades of the twentieth century to shape the relationship of artists and writers to the New Deal. Many in the arts saw the United States of the 1920s as a commercially driven society preoccupied with getting and spending, a society that would necessarily keep the arts at arms length and limit their power. One path available to the arts, patronage by the wealthy, pointed toward too cloying a social embrace, and aesthetic creation for social elites aroused persistent anxieties over restricted audiences and class divisions. Another path, the pursuit of a purer and more independent art, led toward that modernist isolation Edmund Wilson had explored in *Axel's Castle* (1931) at the beginning of the decade, holding little hope of social relevance for the arts. The Federal Arts Projects eschewed both these paths and dreamed of new possibilities. As Cahill's remarks suggest, the directors wanted to make the arts a "functioning" part of social and cultural life across the nation, to claim a place that would clearly be near the center and not on the periphery, and to establish in the public consciousness a new level of legitimacy and recognition for the arts. The artist would be integrated with society and contribute to its collective awareness, overcoming older concerns about irrelevance and isolation while blunting newer diagnoses of alienation in either their Marxist or Freudian forms. Wholeness seemed possible, with federal support.

The directors aspired as well to erase long-established feelings of American cultural inferiority

W. H. AUDEN ON THE WPA

The Arts Project of WPA was, perhaps, one of the noblest and most absurd undertakings ever attempted by any state. Noblest because no other state has ever cared whether its artists as a group lived or died. . . . Yet absurd, because a state can only function bureaucratically and impersonally—it has to assume that every member of a class is equivalent or comparable to every other member—but every artist, good or bad, is a member of a class of one.

Source: Anzia Yezierska, *Red Ribbon on a White Horse*, New York, 1950.

and to cultivate commitment and distinctiveness. References to "an American art," as contemporaries often understood, involved ideas that were not just national but nationalistic. Many American intellectuals—particularly after Van Wyck Brooks's proclamations in *America's Coming-of-Age* (1915) about the development of a unique American culture—had anxiously sought signs of maturation in literature and the arts and of the emergence of a rich American culture that no longer needed to defer to Europe. This tradition looked eagerly for great artists and great works. By the early 1930s some intellectuals, including the author Constance Rourke, offered a variant answer to concerns about American cultural limitations by reframing notions of what counted as culture and placing a high value on native traditions of humor, story, craft, and creativity. (Rourke would be named editor of the Index of American Design as WPA workers set out to record the breadth and depth of the American practical arts.) Radicals at the same moment longed for a new level of culture in the United States based on proletarian artists and writers (some of whom might show greatness) while others sought affirmation of American distinctiveness within traditions of frontier settlement and rural democracy. In all of its forms, the urge to affirm American distinctiveness found reinforcement in a nationalist impulse that was widespread during the decade. Americans of the 1930s, Warren Susman has pointed out, pursued with newly self-conscious attentiveness notions of American identity and an American dream. After 1935 this quest to define national character and tra-

ditions gained urgency as the growing power of fascism in Europe prompted Americans to reexamine the nature and sources of their democratic practice. Thus, the Federal Arts Projects' attentiveness to "the development of American art" expressed over time both sincere cultural ambition and necessary political awareness.

Any federal program in the 1930s confronted issues about the structure of the American polity. From the earliest New Deal efforts toward recovery and reform, questions about the relationship between national, state, and local authority were endemic. Relief programs, like much of the New Deal, mixed federal direction with structures of state and local implementation. The question of how centralized the authority over the arts projects should be provoked continuing controversy, and state or local directors sometimes put their own stamp on programs just as they did when construction projects were at stake rather than paintings or plays. If efforts to maintain federal rules and standards chafed against local and state authority, they also created friction between the projects and individual artists. The national directors generally believed that publicly funded arts projects must serve a useful national purpose. A competing outlook celebrated the individual artist's freedom and championed public subsidies for artists to create whatever products they pleased. Even WPA expectations of regular work hours that could be tracked for appropriate payments provoked tensions with some artists' need or desire to work at odd times or for irregular periods. (The WPA could not, for example, control the speed at which paint dried.) The federal arts projects combined benevolence and obtrusiveness, both from the point of view of local authorities and from that of individual artists, which made the directors' position difficult.

Perhaps the greatest challenge derived from the limitations inherent in the framework that supported the projects. The WPA was a relief program, and the primary responsibility of the arts projects was to put people to work, not to design a renovation of American culture. Whatever their plans for advancing the arts, the directors would be expected to make use predominantly of people registered as unemployed and needy. In a handful of larger cities there might be ample artistic or literary talent among those on relief, but in many parts of the country finding qualified workers was not easy. The WPA also reflected tensions within the New Deal's attitude toward relief: employment projects sought to bolster a sense of self-worth by providing meaningful work yet hoped to avoid lasting commitments or direct competition with private employment. The practical dilemmas of implementing arts projects consistent with such assumptions were daunting in themselves and were made more so by the behavior of private groups. The American Federation of Musicians (AFM), for example, pressured the Federal Music Project to meet the standards embodied in its union rules (implying equivalence between relief and private employment) yet complained if project productions threatened to compete with private ventures. Project directors might have aspired toward lasting contributions but they worked within a programmatic framework that assumed a temporary existence and that remained anxious about what too much success might mean.

The tentative plans put forward by the directors masked incompletely a series of unresolved questions and potential impediments that derived not only from the fresh challenges of defining public programs in the arts but also from wider tensions in American politics and culture. Projects that attempted to reach across the country and across constituencies within each branch of the arts threatened to disturb those multiple communities of opinion and commitment that could normally live in relative peace, in part through relative separation from one another. If high hopes were characteristic of the federal arts projects, so too were struggles with practicality, opposition, and difference.

EARLY PROGRAMS

The WPA arts projects had shorter-lived predecessors earlier in the New Deal. Several of these emerged under the Civil Works Administration (CWA), which functioned on an emergency basis from December 1933 through June 1934 to provide relief during the first winter of the Roosevelt presidency. The CWA Public Works of Art Project (PWAP) directed by Edward Bruce managed during its brief history to encounter a number of the issues that would resonate through later arts programs. Bruce sought to employ talented artists of superior ability who would justify their federal sponsorship by creating art of evident high quality. For Harry Hopkins, who was running the CWA, artists were primarily unemployed workers who needed help from a relief program regardless of ability. When Bruce identified the appropriate subject matter for PWAP art as the American scene, and when an assistant opined that "one solitary masterpiece would be worth the whole project," the administration of the PWAP aligned itself with those who sought to

build a distinctively American art that could claim a place equivalent to European traditions (Contreras, *Tradition and Innovation*, p. 42). Yet abstract artists who felt that they represented the most advanced art complained that the preference for representational art reflecting the American scene cut them off from appropriate opportunities. Pleas for PWAP employment on behalf of recognized artists including William Gropper and the brothers Soyer (Moses, Isaac, and Raphael) underlined the economic need that was present yet also suggested the trickiness of bringing politically active artists into a federal program. On a PWAP project at the Coit Memorial Tower in San Francisco, a few radical artists departed from the approved design to paint emblems and slogans associated with the Communist Party. Artists and writers unions on the left rallied against any restrictions as censorship and proclaimed that artists must be free to chose what they painted, while others declared that artists had no right to be paid from public funds to indulge their politics. There was no broad agreement on purposes and principles that should guide federally supported arts projects under the umbrella of relief.

PROJECTS OUTSIDE THE WPA

A more sustained program, the Section of Fine Arts (the Section), appeared under the Treasury Department. The Section drew funds primarily from federal construction budgets and provided works of art mainly for new public buildings. Operating from 1934 to 1943, slightly longer than the WPA Federal Art Project (FAP), the Section did not owe its existence to relief funding within a larger program and was thus freer to define its own procedures and goals. Clearly, the content of works commissioned as part of public building projects could not be left solely to the artists' discretion. With Edward Bruce as director once more, the Section committed itself to seeking art of the highest quality and providing impetus to the broader development of American art. The Section at times hired recognized artists directly, and it awarded most commissions through blind competitions based on aesthetic judgments not economic need. Bruce continued to encourage a distinctive style as Section artists sought to express a national cultural identity and to define further an art of the "American Scene," a movement often associated with painters Thomas Hart Benton, John Steuart Curry, Grant Wood, and Reginald Marsh. Positioning itself between more conservative traditions of historical painting and the advancing forces of abstraction, Section art, one scholar has argued, "aimed squarely for the artistic center, endorsing a representational style updated with modernist gestures" (Melosh, *Engendering Culture*, p. 7). That style differed not only from abstraction but also from the classicist preferences of the Commission of Fine Arts in Washington, D.C., producing lingering squabbles over the place of realist art. A realist style also meant that despite Bruce's best efforts to avoid controversy, the meaning of symbols, images, and words within Section paintings would on occasion provoke political and religious opposition.

Of the thousands of paintings and sculptures produced for post offices and public buildings by Section artists, a large share depicted pioneer or agricultural life. Although the subject matter was hardly new, this fresh stream of art contributed to an intensifying contrast during the depression between different images of rural America. One set of images told a story of extreme agricultural depression, insect infestations, drought, dust storms, and tenants losing their homes, a picture that would be memorably engraved in John Steinbeck's *The Grapes of Wrath* (1939) and in the New Deal documentaries of Pare Lorentz, *The Plow That Broke the Plains* (1936) and *The River* (1937). Another set of images pointed to rural and agricultural life as the cure for industrial woes (as in the case of the southern Agrarians) or as the source of true American values. Section art, Barbara Melosh has argued, domesticated representations of the frontier and celebrated agricultural life as the source of American democracy. Depictions of frontier violence, especially between Indians and whites, was "actively censored" by Section administrators, and frontier hardship faded before an emphasis on "the neighborly cooperation of settlers, the bounty of the land, and the fruits of family labor." Section paintings and sculpture masked gender differences as well to depict men and women as partners in farm labor, and the family farm became "an icon of an idealized social and moral landscape." The affirmation of nationhood and national character implicit in these works of art gave them a patriotic tenor that provided a degree of political cover, whatever disputes over style or content the Section faced.

An extensive New Deal program of photography might well have been part of an arts program as well but was in fact housed in the Farm Security Administration (FSA). Along with photojournalists working entirely or in part outside of federal agencies (especially Margaret Bourke-White and Walker Evans), FSA photographers including Dorothea Lange, Arthur Rothstein, and Marion Post provided important interpretive statements on rural life in the 1930s, often framed as documentary. The photographs showed powerful images of farms under pressure, of drought-stricken fields, of the forced migration of Okies and Arkies toward California, yet left out images of agricultural rebellion or conflict. They emphasized the character of individual people, striking human endurance, and the meaningfulness of objects and events in day-to-day lives, avoiding the depraved or derelict. In pointing toward endurance, dignity, and strength as elements of American character and culture, the FSA photographs invited broad identification and national affirmation. In this, these selective documentary photographs shared much with the idealized images of Section painting.

FEDERAL ART PROJECT

In the arts project under the WPA, the Index of American Design affirmed by another path the worth of common people and the strength of American traditions, upholding their creativity and consequence by the very act of recording with attentiveness and care the patterns through which ordinary Americans had enhanced the functional objects in their lives. For the FAP, the Index provided one kind of project that could indeed employ large numbers of relief workers with limited skills in work deemed useful to the public, serving a patriotic end. Edward Bruce had been offered leadership of the FAP but had turned it down, believing professional standards and aesthetic quality would be sacrificed in an effort to relieve unemployment. Holger Cahill hesitated for different reasons but finally took the job. Cahill had accumulated experience with folk and popular as well as modern art. His convictions combined with the function of the FAP as a relief program opened the project to artists with varying styles. Whereas the Section was largely under centralized control, the FAP had many units and a structure of state-by-state administration for a program that at its peak employed 5,300 artists. To Cahill, art was a proper concern of government and an essential part of a healthy everyday life. Art belonged not just to the upper classes but to everyone. Dismissing the singular importance of quality, he insisted that "Art is not a matter of rare, occasional masterpieces." Cahill promoted the formation of WPA Community Art Centers (controversial and wasteful for conservatives), sought to stimulate community participation, and hoped to change American culture for the longer term.

For Cahill anything done by an American qualified as American art; no particular style or content claimed national pride of place. He sought to reach the public and to convey that inclusive notion through FAP public exhibitions, which brought both enthusiastic praise and dismissive criticism of the quality of many of the works. In general, Cahill tried to win within the framework of the WPA freedom for artists to paint what they wished, and he continued to hope for some form of integration between the fine and practical arts and between the artist and society. FAP artists for the most part did avoid sharp controversies over the themes of their work. And through the Index of American Design, Community Art Centers, and public murals celebrating community life, the FAP presented a positive record of contributions to social unity and national enrichment. Just how the FAP should be judged as an intellectual and artistic venture, however, remains open to debate. If one scholar holds that the Section was traditional in hiring first-rate artists on commission and the FAP innovative for putting artists on salary with freedom to work as they chose, another reverses these judgments to find the FAP traditional in treating the artist as a romantic individual and the Section comparatively innovative in its efforts "to create a truly public art." The FAP at the very least provided opportunities for a number of strong young artists and employment for thousands more, meeting its primary purpose of relieving unemployment and preserving skills, if not its more capacious ideals.

FEDERAL MUSIC PROJECT

The Federal Music Project (FMP) proved an even more substantial success as a relief program. Musicians had been especially hard hit by unemployment, as the depression accelerated an ongoing decline in the use of live musicians attributable to sound tracks on films, recording devices, radio, canned music, and the impact of prohibition on clubs and nightlife. In 1933 the American Federation of Musicians (AFM) estimated that two-thirds of all musicians were unemployed, including twelve thousand out of fifteen thousand musicians around New York City. Six months after its founding, the FMP was employing fifteen thousand workers on a national basis, more than any of the other arts projects, and it was reaching more people through its performances than any other program. Yet the FMP proved the least controversial of the projects and has attracted the least attention. There are perhaps sev-

eral reasons for this. First, FMP director Nikolai Sokoloff was committed to promoting what he somewhat narrowly regarded as the best music, yet he understood the purposes of the FMP and responded flexibly when necessary to maintain public support. Second, Sokoloff recognized that all WPA projects were subject to criticism and attack, and he worked especially to avoid claims of radical or antipatriotic activities within the FMP. His task was no doubt eased because it was generally harder to identify explicit social commentary in musical performances than in painted symbols or the written word. Moreover, the AFM, the dominant union among professional musicians, was affiliated with the American Federation of Labor, which tended to be unsympathetic to radicals. Third, the FMP under Sokoloff encouraged the development and recognition of American composers and American music, providing a stage for past and present works and for American conductors. Project leaders worked consciously to construct programs around patriotic themes, acutely aware of the larger political context for the FMP's existence.

Sokoloff believed that the FMP should promote the cultivated music of the concert hall, which he regarded as distinctly superior to popular or vernacular music. The project formed orchestras across the country, provided free or minimal-cost concerts, and took performances into schools, hospitals, and other public venues to reach wide audiences, all with the conviction that providing the experience of art music was part of a democratic vision that would create better citizens. Although inclined toward paternalism, this conviction reflected a confidence in public judgment and a faith in the power of education well expressed in staff member Frances McFarland's assertion that "the masses of people will absorb what is best, given the opportunity." Sokoloff favored classically trained musicians and wanted to pay them at a higher scale than popular performers, but he gave in to AFM insistence on standard pay. About 12 percent of FMP employees were black musicians, an exceptional record compared to the .001 percent in the Federal Writers Project in 1937. Yet African Americans were largely confined to segregated units, limiting opportunities for the few formally trained black musicians despite the popularity of all-black choruses, opera groups, dance bands, and folk singers. Even so, African American music and performers provided one source of changes that would begin to blur the lines between cultivated and popular music and encourage the development of distinctive American voices in complex relationship with Sokoloff's preferences. Led by Aaron Copland and Roger Sessions, a number of American composers had already been moving toward seeking broader contact with American audiences, bringing recognizable American themes to art music. Left-leaning composers who in the early 1930s had rejected popular or folk music out of sympathy with efforts to create a new proletarian culture changed course with the Popular Front after 1935 and championed the value of vernacular expression, notably in Charles Seeger's work with folk music. These directions marked an accelerated development of American musical identity in the 1930s that was reinforced through the opportunities created by the FMP.

FEDERAL THEATRE PROJECT

If the FMP mounted public arts programs with limited political controversy, the Federal Theatre Project (FTP) encouraged social consciousness, stimulated vigorous opposition, and consequently, led a short life. Hallie Flanagan had indicated that she wanted to dramatize contemporary events in "rapid, cinematic form," reflecting open anxieties about the impact of the film industry on theater, and she told project leaders that theater must "grow up" and address the "changing social order." The FTP found early opportunity to claim social engagement and score points on Hollywood by mounting productions of Sinclair Lewis's *It Can't Happen Here* (1935) in twenty-one cities simultaneously. MGM had purchased the film rights to Lewis's novel then dropped the project, fearing the book's satire of dictatorship and extreme politics would hurt film markets in Germany and Italy. The FTP productions, opening before a total of about twenty thousand people on 27 October 1936, won wide publicity and positioned the FTP as a champion of principle. Because the productions had different casts and took on different slants in different localities, quality and interpretation varied: Des Moines might present the play as anti-Communist even as the Communists regarded it as antifascist, while varying critics declared it favored either Republicans or Democrats. Not only the influence of local directors and casts but also the varying regional and ideological sensitivities of viewers affected the perceived politics of what was presumably the same play. The FTP would support new writers and many of the best-known playwrights of the day, and scripts emerged across a spectrum including religious pageants, activist labor plays, and public

Flyer from the WPA Production *Power*. A Living Newspaper production that explored public issues.

health education. Among the productions that attracted the greatest attention were those of T. S. Eliot's *Murder in the Cathedral* and the Harlem unit's production of *Macbeth* with an all-black cast organized and directed by John Houseman and Orson Welles. Yet in both theater and politics, the FTP would perhaps best be known for its Living Newspapers.

Exploring current public issues through a series of short dramatic scenes, the Living Newspapers embodied Flanagan's desire to bring cinematic form to the stage and introduced the FTP's most significant innovation. Appropriately for a relief program, the Living Newspapers could employ relatively large numbers of actors of limited skill; less appropriately, they combined energetic theatre with open partisanship. In productions including *Injunction Granted, Power, One-Third of a Nation,* and *Triple-A Plowed Under,* the Living Newspapers turned fragments of public controversy into arguments for fair labor standards, public ownership, public housing, and agricultural price supports, taking positions clearly in support or to the left of the New Deal. Contemporary responses, even from those sympathetic to the messages, quickly identified the productions as propaganda, a term Flanagan was willing to accept with only limited qualification (Mathews, pp. 114–15, 220). Although the form was at times highly effective, the narrow social outlook of Living Newspaper productions was apparent in *Triple-A Plowed Under*. There, New York writers depicted "an embattled and militant rural America through plots and characters borrowed from the genre of the labor play," a radical template applied in striking contrast to the images of united agrarian purposefulness in New Deal art (Melosh, p. 53). The FTP in fact had a strong urban bias, and struggling with WPA rules, union pressures, and commercial theater interests, it proved unable to build a strong national program, gravitating toward a few metropolitan centers. This lack of national effectiveness and the presence of politically controversial productions made the FTP a vulnerable target for opponents of the New Deal and purveyors of indignant anticommunism. Hearings before the House Committee on Un-American Activities, headed by Martin Dies, in 1938 led to the death of the FTP in 1939, well before the end of the other arts projects. The hearings were at times unfair and the issues distorted. Yet it was also true that every director of an arts project had faced the need to balance personal convictions and the preferences of project employees against requirements for federal support and the realities of political context. In this balancing, Flanagan proved the least sensitive and the least successful. And the opposition roused by the politics of the FTP contributed to a legacy of suspicion toward federal support for the arts more generally.

FEDERAL WRITERS' PROJECT

The Federal Writers' Project (FWP) under Henry Alsberg had at least as many radicals on its relief rolls as the FTP: Stalinist and Trotskyist writers sniped (or swiped) at each other regularly in New York and other major cities. The FWP juggled issues of freedom similar to those in the FAP, allowing some workers to do creative writing on their own, publishing the best of the results, and in the process assisting young authors including Richard Wright and Saul Bellow. Like other projects, the FWP inherited smaller programs from earlier relief efforts, doing good service by collecting oral histories from

former slaves, compiling American folklore, and gathering information on particular groups or locales. And like other projects, the FWP aspired to assist large numbers of people, to establish itself across the nation, and to complete respectable work with employees of widely varying ability. The overarching enterprise for the FWP, and the best demonstration of its usefulness, came in the American Guide Series, a collection of volumes covering every state accompanied by some 330 books and pamphlets on special topics. In addition to general essays and a section on cities, each state guidebook contained a section that provided a mile-by-mile tour down every major highway, slowing to describe the smallest points of interest along the way. National editors pushed local directors to find the distinctive and colorful, the unique and the various. And they did, with the Chicago director calling on a staff of established and rising writers while a 20-year-old director in North Dakota wrote most of the guide herself.

The guides represented a changing use of "facts" during the 1930s as the largely negative documentation of social suffering during the depression turned toward a largely positive recording of stories, memories, and persistence. They also worked as a ready justification and defense for the WPA and the FWP. Lewis Mumford was quick to seize the possibilities when he called the series "the finest contribution to American patriotism that has been made in our day," a comment seemingly crafted with conservatives in mind. Left-wing novelist Robert Cantwell took a different tack, noting the oddities, false starts, and failures recorded in the guides, yet he ultimately admired the demonstrated ability of Americans to take "extraordinary happenings in their stride" and posited a people defining their character through disparateness and variety. In their emphasis on diversity and detail, the FWP guides reinforced a wider pattern in American intellectual life at the end of the 1930s that increasingly associated American identity and democratic values with a multiplicity of interests and with cultural heterogeneity. Pressured to define national values in contrast to Nazi Germany and Soviet Russia (sometimes linked by the end of the thirties as "totalitarian" societies), Americans found unity in their differences and virtue in their plurality.

THE END OF THE ARTS PROJECTS

The stronger conservative opposition to the New Deal and federal expenditures after 1938, of which the Dies Committee represented an extreme form, placed Federal Arts Projects on the defensive. World War II ended them. The economic recovery associated with the war removed the justification for federal relief programs and with it the job of providing employment for artists. President Roosevelt, who had never assumed projects supporting art would be permanent, brought all of them to an end by mid-1943, indicating that the WPA had "earned its honorable discharge." Before the question had been settled, Archibald MacLeish at the request of the WPA Commissioner brought a group of project administrators and writers, musicians, and artists together in 1941 to discuss whether government support for the arts should continue. Even within this interested group, the discussions "immediately and permanently bogged down," Richard McKinzie remarked, as to whether, apart from their relief functions, the projects were worth the cost and "who and what the government should subsidize" if relief was not a consideration. Questions about whether art judged qualitatively was an elite activity inconsistent with democracy remained unresolved. Deep divisions persisted over who deserved recognition as an artist. Some artists (as have some scholars since) assumed any governmental sponsorship threatened censorship (or hegemonic control), while administrators, politicians, and the public

tired of the special treatment and procedural exceptions artists seemed to demand. Conflicts within and between clusters of artists, organizations, and programs obstructed any prospect of building public or political support for continuing governmental funding as war took center stage.

In closing down the projects, the government created no process for evaluating or preserving the works produced. Orchestras and theater groups disbanded. The American Guide Series found a home on library shelves. Murals in post offices and public buildings disappeared in many cases when the next freshening of the walls took place, and individual paintings were often disposed of ungraciously. Jackson Pollock's paintings for the WPA were sold for five dollars in 1945 and have largely disappeared. For all their limits of execution and legacy, however, the Federal Arts Projects did demonstrate that public spending could improve the level of contact with painting, music, and their own cultural traditions for millions of Americans across the land. They also contributed to an examination of American aesthetic possibilities, past and present, that nourished a coalescing sense of national identity and confidence in the arts and in literature. In doing so, the projects helped strengthen the foundation for strong American development in the arts after World War II.

See also **Intellectuals and Ideology in Government** *(volume 2);* **The Visual Arts; The Role of the Intellectual; Government; Public Murals** *(volume 3).*

BIBLIOGRAPHY

Primary Sources

Cantwell, Robert. "America and the Writers' Project." *New Republic* 98 (April 26, 1939), 323–325.

Flanagan, Hallie. *Arena.* New York, 1940.

Mumford, Lewis. "Writers' Project." *New Republic* 92 (October 20, 1937), 306–307.

O'Connor, Francis V. *Art for the Millions: Essays from the 1930s by Artists and Administrators of the WPA Federal Art Project.* Greenwich, Conn., 1973.

Secondary Sources

Baigell, Matthew. *The American Scene: American Painting of the 1930's.* New York, 1974.

Bindas, Kenneth J. *All of This Music Belongs to the Nation: The WPA's Federal Music Project and American Society.* Knoxville, Tenn., 1995.

Contreras, Belisario R. *Tradition and Innovation in New Deal Art.* Lewisburg, Penn., 1983.

Cooney, Terry A. *Balancing Acts: American Thought and Culture in the 1930s.* New York, 1995.

De Hart, Jane Sherron. *The Federal Theatre, 1935–1939: Plays, Relief, and Politics.* Princeton, N.J., 1967.

Harris, Jonathan. *Federal Art and National Culture: The Politics of Identity in New Deal America.* New York, 1995.

Hurley, Forrest Jack. *Portrait of a Decade: Roy Stryker and the Development of Documentary Photographs in the Thirties.* Baton Rouge, La., 1972.

Marling, Karal Ann. *Wall-to-Wall America: A Cultural History of Post Office Murals in the Great Depression.* Minneapolis, Minn., 1982.

McKinzie, Richard D. *The New Deal for Artists.* Princeton, N.J., 1973.

Melosh, Barbara. *Engendering Culture: Manhood and Womanhood in New Deal Public Art and Theater.* Washington, D.C., 1991. At the end of this volume, Melosh offers an extensive "Inventory of Section Murals and Sculptures," listing them by location.

Park, Marlene, and Gerald E. Markowitz. *Democratic Vistas: Post Offices and Public Art in the New Deal.* Philadelphia, 1984.

Penkower, Monte Noam. *The Federal Writers' Project: A Study in Government Patronage of the Arts.* Urbana, Ill., 1977.

Purcell, Edward A., Jr. *The Crisis of Democratic Theory: Scientific Naturalism and the Problem of Value.* Lexington, Ky., 1973. Purcell explores the need to define democratic values in opposition to fascism during the later 1930s.

Rubin, Joan Shelley. *Constance Rourke and American Culture.* Chapel Hill, N.C., 1980.

Stott, William. *Documentary Expression and Thirties America.* New York, 1973.

Susman, Warren I. *Culture as History: The Transformation of American Society in the Twentieth Century.* New York, 1984.

RELIGIOUS LIBERALISM, FUNDAMENTALISM, AND NEO-ORTHODOXY

Charles H. Lippy

The era between the world wars brought tremendous ferment in U.S. Protestant theological circles. One major strand of thought, the fundamentalism that still exerted considerable influence at the end of the twentieth century, assumed the basic contours that remained with it for decades. Liberalism, often seen as fundamentalism's opposite but actually a complex of theologies ranging from personalism to scientific modernism, reached its apogee and began to move out of favor. What became known as neo-orthodoxy emerged in part out of dissatisfaction with both fundamentalism and liberalism but also in response to changing intellectual currents. All three currents echoed other currents cascading through the larger society. All had roots that stretched back earlier, including ties to theological movements in Europe. None was thus uniquely American, but all had distinctive Protestant American expressions that deserve scrutiny.

Behind all three currents lie intellectual advances of the latter half of the nineteenth century that also in many cases had an impact on Reform Judaism, although the results were different. Many of those advances became quickly entrenched in German universities, although some emerged first in Great Britain. German schools, for example, established themselves as places for application of critical methods in the study of sacred texts, the comparative analysis of religious traditions, and the initial formulations of liberal theology identified early in the nineteenth century with Friedrich Schleiermacher and later with thinkers such as Adolf von Harnack and Albrecht Ritschl. Britain was home to Charles Darwin, whose *On the Origin of Species* (1859) helped make nascent evolutionary theory a force with which theology had to grapple. From Britain, too, came the early statement of dispensationalism, a set of theological presuppositions that had great influence in some fundamentalist circles.

Higher criticism of sacred texts for Christianity meant probing questions about authorship, audience, dating, and context for the documents that make up the Bible. It meant looking at a sacred text just as one looked at other documents composed in the past. Proponents believed that rational inquiry opened up more of the original intent and meaning behind Scripture; opponents felt critical method placed Scripture on a plane with secular literature, since the analytical tools were identical and therefore undermined belief in divine inspiration of Scripture. By the 1920s fundamentalism rejected much of the results of higher criticism, while liberalism affirmed them.

The comparative study of religion worked much the same way. In the nineteenth century, thanks largely to the labors of missionaries in Asia, western Christians gained their first sustained exposure to religious traditions like Hinduism and Buddhism. Initially, many saw these as polytheistic perversions of true religion, but some (including many missionaries) recognized that religious traditions the world over wrestled with the same issues in providing a framework for meaning in life. Spurring comparative study of religion was the conviction that by examining how each tradition struggled with the same issue—the meaning of death, for example—one would understand better what each had to say and how cultural context shaped particular forms of religious expression. In the 1920s fundamentalists remained skeptical about comparative study of religion, convinced that it would destroy the superiority of Christianity to other religions and deny that Christianity alone captured ultimate truth. Those in the liberal camp had a more positive valuation, believing that such comparative study uncovered a religious consciousness common to all humanity.

While later generations immediately identified evolutionary theory with Charles Darwin, geologists had earlier developed theories regarding the age of the earth based on examination and tentative dating of various geological strata. The geological approach seemed benign from a theological perspective; it did not necessarily challenge a traditional doctrine of creation to account for the origins of the earth, but merely pushed the date of creation back, given the speculation about the age of various strata. Even Darwin's approach was not regarded as dangerous in all theological circles. What made it a threat to some was the principle of natural selection, Darwin's explanation of the process by which evolution occurred. For many, especially those in the fundamentalist orbit, natural selection seemed an outright denial of a miraculous creation ex nihilo, marking the beginning of chronological time. It was a small step from questioning the traditional doctrine of creation to challenging the veracity of the scriptural texts behind it. Coupled with critical approaches to Scripture, Darwin's theories appeared to deny the authenticity of Scripture. Without Scripture, the foundations of Christian theology would crumble. Evolutionary theory and critical method also influenced Roman Catholic modernism, which presented a stronger challenge to the traditional Thomistic underpinnings of Catholic theology in Europe than in the United States.

One particular episode symbolized the rift between fundamentalism and liberalism, bringing into public view the strengths and weaknesses of both positions. In 1925 in Dayton, Tennessee, the high school biology teacher John Scopes was found guilty of violating the state law that prohibited the teaching of evolutionary theory in the public schools. The sensationalism of the trial discredited fundamentalism in intellectual circles, and, despite the verdict, liberalism seemed triumphant. Although fundamentalism enjoyed an intellectual resurgence in the later decades of the twentieth century, neither fundamentalism nor liberalism expanded its intellectual character significantly after the 1920s.

LIBERALISM

Facile interpretation traditionally has claimed that because liberalism embraced modernism, it was a positive movement within theology. By contrast, fundamentalism was anti-modern and, therefore, a negative reaction against everything liberalism affirmed. The reality goes much deeper. Both were products of their age. Both were modern in that they reflected the intellectual and cultural context of their times. Because fundamentalist theologians saw themselves as defending Christian belief attacked by liberals, it is instructive to look first at what actually characterized the liberal position.

In American Protestant theology, liberalism first began to take shape in the social gospel, whose primary theologian was Walter Rauschenbusch, and then in personalism, a philosophical-theological approach developed initially by Borden Parker Bowne. The social gospel emerged largely because Rauschenbusch and others articulated a theology that spoke to the conditions of industrializing America. As a student and then a seminary professor, Rauschenbusch spent time in Germany, where he imbibed liberal thought that emphasized the unity of humanity as the creation of a loving God and the necessity of ethical behavior to reflect the image of God in all persons. In the context of urban, industrializing America, Rauschenbusch believed such ethical conduct demanded church support for labor's cause in conflicts between workers and industrialists. The ethical teachings of the ancient Hebrew Prophets and of Jesus, when applied to the modern situation, required owners to pay workers a living wage so they could carry out their divinely mandated responsibilities for their families without undue hardship. Concerns for labor conditions prompted a parallel development in American Catholic theology, especially in the thought of John A. Ryan.

The social gospel thus looked positively on the possibility of creating an ethical and just social order. But when the atrocities of World War I forced theologians to consider anew the penchant for humans to engage in morally evil conduct, despite the example of the Prophets and Jesus, it seemed naive. Nevertheless, a sensitivity to the importance of ethics became embedded in much of American Protestant thought as a result of the social gospel, particularly in what in the 1920s was called liberalism or modernism.

Implicit in the social gospel's emphasis on ethical behavior and a just society was another hallmark of liberal thought, a stress on the immanence of God. For many, the God of traditional Protestant theology was aloof and removed from the daily affairs of humanity and so transcendent as to be unapproachable by mere mortals. To social gospel thinkers and later liberals, highlighting the immanence of God was a way to bring the divine into active engagement with the contemporary world. For later fundamentalists, transcendence was essential to the character of God but did not make God aloof and unapproachable. Rather, to fundamentalists and others of a more traditional ilk, in Jesus Christ, one fully human and fully divine, God took the initiative to close the gap.

Developing liberalism, like fundamentalism, recognized that the fascination with science and scientific method fueled by Darwin's evolutionary theory held potential danger for theology. If fundamentalists rejected scientific claims challenging their understanding of the Bible, liberals tried to integrate science and religion. Bowne's personalism was one of the first efforts in that regard, coming to fruition in the thought of two of his students, Albert C. Knudson and Edgar Sheffield Brightman. Bowne recognized that those taken with science could advance a mechanistic theory of the world, leaving little room for religious faith. He also understood that mechanistic views often led to determinism. In contrast, Bowne developed a concept of God as infinite energy, a ground of being undergirding objective reality but, given the nature of humanity, personal in its character. This personal dimension linked humanity to God, and the constant expression of divine energy sustaining creation seemed compatible with scientific understanding. It accounted for both constancy and change without recourse to determinism.

Bowne was primarily a philosopher; Knudson, also at Boston University, was the first to build a theological system based on personalism. For him, the human personality, including rational faculties and self-consciousness, reflected the divine personality, that which is ultimately real. Human self-consciousness included freedom. Although Knudson rejected a traditional understanding of original sin, he insisted that humans could misuse their freedom and therefore stood in need of redemption. That redemption was effected through the God-consciousness of Christ, manifested particularly in Christ's love. Experiencing that love, humans could choose to place trust in God and thereby use their freedom to work with God and thus better reflect the divine personality. There was also a practical payoff; this cooperative relationship with God increased happiness in this life and gave life greater meaning.

Brightman, Knudson's colleague, moved even further from traditional formulations of basic doctrine. While Brightman made sharper distinctions than Knudson between human personality and the personality of God, he boldly claimed that although God as creator was both ultimate and eternal, God was also limited by creation itself and therefore finite. Brightman was grappling to reconcile the existence of sin and evil with the personality of God, who was always loving and good. By positing a finitude in the being of God, Brightman could affirm

that God, like humans, was actively struggling to overcome sin and evil.

Other theologians identified with liberal currents moved in different directions. For example, William Adams Brown was among the more carefully systematic of liberal theologians. Brown understood the theological task to be the interpretation of the basics of Christianity in terms relevant to the contemporary situation. He willingly labeled his efforts a "new theology," in that he tried to show that Christian faith was in harmony with a scientific outlook. For him, theological reflection emerged not from unchanging truths but from the lived experience of human beings as products of their own time. Even the Bible was not a fixed and final account of divine revelation, but a living record of a range of religious experiences from a variety of contexts. Brown unabashedly saw his approach as liberal; he assumed that different human experiences would bring differences in the fine points in theological nuance. In line with German liberal theologians like Harnack, Brown sought to define the essence of Christianity, and, like the Germans and others, he found that essence in a Christ who revealed the moral character of God and thus also in ethical conduct on the part of Christian believers. The centrality of the Christ figure to Brown's thought led some to label his position "christocentric liberalism." Others called it "evangelical liberalism."

Like Knudson, Brown found a practical dimension to ethical living. Greater human happiness would result, and human society would continue evolving into the Kingdom of God. In this regard, Brown echoed the belief in progress implicit in the social gospel and its equating the divine kingdom with an ideal society. For Brown, as for social gospel advocates, the Christian faithful were called to practical service, and in addition to teaching at New York's Union Theological Seminary, Brown was involved with settlement houses in New York slums, efforts to reform municipal government, labor unions, and a variety of other social causes.

In another city, the longtime professor and dean of the University of Chicago Divinity School Shailer Mathews pushed liberal thinking even further. Mathews and his historian colleague Shirley Jackson Case pioneered the sociohistorical method in analyzing Christian belief. Presuming that particular doctrinal formulations and even religion itself evolved over time, the sociohistorical method meant that any particular statement of belief was both dependent on and reacting to the social-historical context, the way of viewing the world or what Mathews called the "social mind" of its time. Because this method drew on the scientific perspective of the day, the label "scientific modernism" was attached to Mathews's position; one of his best-known works was *The Faith of Modernism* (1924), in which he argued that the theological task was never finished, because the context in which it occurred was always evolving and changing.

Mathews, like Brown, was taken with the idea of the Kingdom of God, although he regarded it as a future, eschatological phenomenon, not anything linked to empirical society. To this extent, he moved beyond German liberalism as well. Also like Brown, he highlighted the moral dimension of Jesus' teaching. For him, religious commitment was a "loyalty to Jesus" that demanded application of ethical values to specific situations. Convinced that some liberal theology had sold out to culture in this particular area, he claimed that loyalty to Jesus always involved a tension between believers and the culture around them. This basic tension between faith and culture would invigorate the development of neo-orthodox theology before the end of the 1920s.

Perhaps the extreme of liberalism came in the naturalism and more radical empiricism of thinkers such as John Dewey and Henry Nelson Wieman, but their primary and most creative work came in the 1930s, after more classical liberalism had already begun to wane. Some would question whether either approach was a Christian theology proper. While a generation of pastors imbibed liberal thought as seminary students became conduits for its reaching the masses, perhaps the most vibrant popular voice of liberalism was Harry Emerson Fosdick, longtime pastor of New York's Riverside Church and radio preacher whose voice was familiar to millions. Fosdick marked out the battle lines between liberalism and fundamentalism in his 1922 sermon "Shall the Fundamentalists Win?" Through anthologies of his sermons, Fosdick helped a lay audience understand that a moderate liberalism could bring genuine personal happiness and inner peace.

FUNDAMENTALISM

Even before Fosdick preached his sermon attacking fundamentalism, fundamentalist theology had received sustained exposition in a series of pamphlets, *The Fundamentals*, published first in 1910. At bottom, fundamentalist thinking sought to be faithful to a particular understanding of the Bible text, namely that the Bible was not only divinely inspired but without error in any details. The idea of biblical inerrancy that assumed greater importance later in the century has roots here. This view of Scripture led to the conviction that core Christian beliefs or doctrines, particularly those concerned with Jesus Christ, were likewise unchanging. If the more liberal questioned the historicity of the miracles of Jesus recorded in the Gospels, fundamentalists found in them proof of the divinity of Christ. If liberals concluded that because Asian stories about the miraculous birth of the Buddha shared features with New Testament accounts of the birth of Jesus, neither should be taken as historically accurate, fundamentalists insisted that the virgin birth of Jesus, his bodily resurrection, and a physical Second Coming were basic to genuine Christian affirmation.

These ideas gained currency in many Protestant circles before any systematic statement of them, largely through summer Bible conferences and widespread use of the *Reference Bible,* prepared by Cyrus I. Scofield and first published in 1909. These conferences and the Scofield *Reference Bible* presumed not only the basic points of fundamentalism, but a hermeneutic known as premillennial dispensationalism, first advanced in Britain by John Nelson Darby, founder of the Plymouth Brethren. Premillennial dispensationalism claimed that history, from divine creation to the Second Coming of Christ, was divided into large time blocks or dispensations. In each dispensation, God revealed truth to humanity and offered humanity appropriate means of salvation, but always with a disastrous ending as humans rejected what God offered. What gave excitement to premillennial dispensationalism was its assertion that the church age, the present, was quickly winding down. Such developments as evolutionary theory, higher criticism, and comparative religion were signs of present-day corruption, making the Second Coming of Christ imminent. Always, however, theologians offered a more nuanced understanding than this popular fascination with the supernatural and with premillennial dispensationalism. Through the 1920s the major theologians who gave fundamentalism an intellectual base had association with the Princeton Theological Seminary. Among the more influential were Benjamin Breckinridge Warfield and J. Gresham Machen.

Warfield's most notable contributions concerned biblical inspiration. By inspiration, Warfield meant that God was the author or responsible power for every idea, fact, or principle—whether spiritual or physical—contained in the Bible. He thus moved from inspiration per se to advocating a form of inerrancy. Unlike many later voices for inerrancy, Warfield as a biblical scholar recognized that higher criticism was correct in understanding how the biblical text had been transmitted over the centuries. He knew that no original biblical manuscripts remained or had been found and that discrepancies, usually minor ones, existed among the oldest surviving manuscript fragments. In addition, he was an astute enough historian to allow for possible copying errors made by scribes. Hence, Warfield argued that inerrancy in a strict sense applied only to the original autographs, not to later copies that could contain human errors. Similarly, he rejected the claim, advocated by some liberals, that core doctrines of the Christian faith were based on rational absurdities, as in proving the divinity of Christ by means of miracles that contradicted reason. Warfield countered that there simply was no longer any way to verify miracles or disprove them.

From a Calvinist, Presbyterian background, Warfield also attacked ideas foundational to liberal thought. For example, while many liberals accepted Schleiermacher's locating religious experience in a feeling of absolute dependence on the divine, Warfield rejected such speculation and reasserted the primacy of divine providence as the beginning point of religious experience. Curiously, Warfield did not reject every formulation of evolutionary theory generally accepted by liberals. Rather, he struggled to reconcile Darwinian theory with Scripture by emphasizing the all-encompassing providence of God. Both providence and sovereignty were at the core of John Calvin's thought, and, in Warfield's hands, divine providence became the divine force that nudged evolution along. Warfield, however, could never sanction the rejection of scriptural authority that others thought a necessary accompaniment of evolutionary theory, nor could he jettison the biblical account of creation in favor of a nontheistic process of natural selection.

Although Machen, like Warfield, wrote significant works in biblical studies, his primary contribution to the struggle between fundamentalism and liberalism was his *Christianity and Liberalism* (1923). An astute scholar, Machen appreciated the social and cultural context in which the theological battle took place, but he believed that the same intellectual and technological advances that had enriched the quality of life in the West had also created a theological monster in liberalism. Machen regarded liberalism as a religion distinct from authentic Christianity, not a theological movement within

Christianity, because of its assumptions. One such assumption, emerging from the fascination with comparative religion and the use of critical method in biblical study, was historicism, or the conviction that all theological assertions were contingent on the circumstances in which they were formulated. There were no absolute truths in liberalism, according to Machen, but only relative, tentative expressions of ethical principles changed with the times.

In *Christianity and Liberalism*, Machen attacked liberal thinkers for insisting that the historical Jesus was only a moral example, not a supernatural Savior born of a virgin. Machen, like Warfield, thus regarded biblical statement as historical fact, not symbol. In Machen's view, liberalism was simply a naturalistic religion that proffered salvation by imitating the moral behavior of Jesus but without an atonement. Liberalism's downplaying doctrine troubled Machen perhaps more than anything else, because he believed that doctrine based on scriptural testimony was essential to Christianity. Hence, liberalism did not simply modify or alter traditional Christianity, but substituted for Christianity a shallow, near paganism that, contrary to Scripture, denied all that was supernatural. If liberal thinkers like Brown saw personal experience as providing the context for articulating theological postulates, for a fundamentalist like Machen, doctrinal propositions provided the basis for appraising personal experience.

Machen lived through the bitter denominational battles among northern Presbyterians and Baptists that accompanied the fundamentalist-modernist controversy of the 1920s, reluctantly leaving the Presbyterian Church and his post at Princeton Theological Seminary because he believed them to be infected by liberalism and therefore not expressions of true Christianity. Machen helped start a new denomination, the Orthodox Presbyterian Church, and a new seminary, where unfettered biblical truth could reign. In reality, however, both Warfield and Machen, along with their fundamentalist allies, were engaged in much more than trying to preserve embattled biblical truths. Historians have demonstrated that there were cultural dimensions undergirding fundamentalist thought more obvious perhaps in materials in the popular religious press than in the tomes of the theologians. One issue more evident there, for example, is a concern for gender roles and shifts in the structure of family life that accompanied the nation's move from being a rural, agrarian nation to an urban, industrial nation, a move effectively completed by 1920, when the census showed that a majority of the nation's people lived in urban areas.

NEO-ORTHODOXY

Fundamentalist thought and liberal theology in its many guises had taken their essential form by the early 1920s. Neo-orthodoxy, a name that signals a desire to restate in fresh ways classical themes of the theological tradition, was in its embryonic stages at the end of the decade. Some refer to the movement as "neo-Reformation" or "new Reformation" theology, both because its early voices had roots in the Reformed denominations once heavily influenced by Calvin's thought and because the classical themes it emphasized were prominent in the sixteenth century Reformation and thus had roots in Martin Luther's thought as well as Calvin's. Others labeled the movement "neoliberalism," a less common term, since its earliest formulators began to rethink their own theological positions because of growing dissatisfaction with liberal theology.

It is too facile, though not entirely untrue, to see neo-orthodoxy as a reaction to extreme fundamentalism and liberalism or as a middle ground between the two. Neo-orthodoxy affirmed liberalism's insistence that literary and historical methods be applied to Scripture, but it still maintained that Scripture was a vehicle for divine revelation. But neo-orthodoxy saw liberalism's conviction that human society was moving steadily toward becoming the Kingdom of God as naive, resting on an uncritical endorsement of progress. Instead of steady progress, human limitation or sin stood out in neo-orthodox assessment of the human situation. The ravages of World War I and then the Great Depression served as reminders that flaws still marked humanity's common life. Like fundamentalism, neo-orthodoxy thus found value in traditional doctrinal categories.

Not only did the prevalence of sin mute an easy idealism for neo-orthodox thinkers, but a keen sense of the transcendence of God—what the nineteenth-century Danish theologian and philosopher Søren Kierkegaard called the "infinite qualitative difference" between humanity and God—overwhelmed them. Consequently, like fundamentalism, neo-orthodoxy maintained that divine revelation, not human experience, was the starting point for theological reflection. But like liberalism, neo-orthodoxy owed much of its impetus to continental developments, particularly the early thought of the theological giant Karl Barth and that of Emil Brunner, both from Switzerland. While Barth had the greater influence overall, in nascent neo-orthodoxy Brunner's thinking had more impact simply because his works were available in English translation before most of Barth's works. The forays into New Testament theology by the German theologian Rudolf Bultmann were also vital, particularly his efforts to "demythologize" while still using a dialectical method akin to that of Barth.

Among American Protestant thinkers, three of the most prominent in shaping neo-orthodoxy were the brothers H. Richard Niebuhr and Reinhold Niebuhr and Edwin Lewis. H. Richard Niebuhr, longtime professor at Yale Divinity School, drew on strains of liberalism in *The Social Sources of Denominationalism* (1929), in which he made social-historical context and economic class dominant criteria in determining the nature and beliefs of religious groups. Liberalism's fascination with the Kingdom of God informed Niebuhr's *The Kingdom of God in America* (1937), but by then neo-orthodoxy's abandonment of liberalism's easy identification of the kingdom with a particular manifestation of human culture is evident; here Niebuhr understood that different notions of the kingdom were theological critiques of culture, not merely acceptance of cultural norms.

Of Niebuhr's early writing, *The Meaning of Revelation* (1941) most clearly manifested theological themes of neo-orthodoxy. Niebuhr argued that all revelation was historically conditioned, coming to humans in the context of particular times and places; hence, one formulation of theological truth might not speak to the human situation in a different time and place. Although here he sounds like a liberal, he also insisted that what was revealed was, nevertheless, objective truth, the God who stands above as well as within history. Thus, he refused to fall into the relativism that critics condemned in liberalism. Instead, he maintained a constant tension between God and the setting or means by which God was revealed. No manifestation of the sovereign God was itself absolute, because it was contingent on historical context; yet all manifestations pointed to and communicated that which was absolute. In his more mature work, Niebuhr proposed that same tension carried over into the relationship between authentic Christian faith and culture. He cast aside both the liberal embrace of culture and the fundamentalist rejection of culture for a stance that was both part of culture yet critical of culture.

Reinhold Niebuhr, H. Richard Niebuhr's older brother, advanced what he saw as a more realistic posture than liberalism (or fundamentalism) with regard to how theology and society interacted. His years as a pastor in Detroit, where he tried to apply liberal theological views to social conditions in one of the nation's major urban, industrial centers, convinced him of the bankruptcy of traditional liberal thought as he began a distinguished teaching career at Union Theological Seminary. Like European thinkers such as Barth and Brunner, Reinhold Niebuhr saw how sin and the conditions of human finitude dashed idealistic hopes that human society could ever become the empirical Kingdom of God on earth. As the United States moved from the stock market crash of 1929 into the Great Depression, Niebuhr wrote *Moral Man and Immoral Society* (1932), in which he argued that while individual human life, with all its sin and shortcomings, had the possibility for redemption—the heart of the Christian gospel—corporate life was infinitely more complex because collective egotism could never be eliminated. Proximate justice, not the fullness of the kingdom, was all that could be hoped for.

As humanity stood on the brink of World War II, in 1939 Niebuhr delivered his famous Gifford lectures, later published as *The Nature and Destiny of Man* (1941–1943). There he restated the classic Christian doctrine of human nature and original sin, stressing human selfishness and limitation. But that was not the final word. Human destiny, revealed in Christ, contained the possibility of overcoming sin. Human destiny also pushed beyond time, for human destiny informed by faith reached its culmination only at the eschaton. Until then, every triumph over sin was only partial, for every manifestation of justice exposed new injustice to which humanity had been blind. The tension foundational to neo-orthodox theology is thus present in Reinhold Niebuhr's thought as it was in his brother's, but here it is the tension between reality and the ideal, between what can be achieved in the context of time and space and what awaits fulfillment beyond the limits of historical circumstance.

Like the Niebuhr brothers, Edwin Lewis reflected the basic tenets of a liberal theology in his early writing. What pushed him beyond liberalism to embrace emerging neo-orthodoxy was not only his familiarity with Barth's thinking, but also his work as coeditor of the *Abingdon Bible Commentary* (1939), a leading one-volume reference tool of its day. Work on the commentary drew Lewis into deep exploration of the biblical text and thus to a theology based on biblical revelation, with its profound understanding of sin and evil and the consequent need for atonement and redemption offered to humanity by God in Christ. Lewis's move to neo-orthodoxy resounded in *A Christian Manifesto* (1934), in which he completely repudiated the naturalistic basis of much liberal thought and called for a return to supernaturalism. But Lewis never embraced the same sort of supernaturalism that was at the heart of fundamentalism. Rather, as a neo-orthodox theologian, he recognized a tension between the supernatural and the historical conditions in which the supernatural was revealed.

By the mid-1930s, in much of mainstream American Protestantism, liberal theology was increasingly on the margins, although it never disappeared, or in the hands of those so smitten by reason and science that they often seemed prepared to jettison all matters of faith. Fundamentalism as an intellectual current was also on the periphery, thanks more to power struggles within denominations that kept those of fundamentalist inclination outside the ranks of power. But although on the periphery, fundamentalism as both a theology and a movement within American Protestantism quietly grew until it returned to the forefront in the closing decades of the twentieth century. Neo-orthodoxy was the theology of the moment. Perhaps, on a popular level, that can best be seen through the pulpiteer Harry Emerson Fosdick. In 1922 his sermon "Shall the Fundamentalists Win?" rallied liberals to defend their theology, drew the battle line between fundamentalists and liberals, and forced fundamentalists to close ranks. In 1935 Fosdick preached another well-known sermon, "Beyond Modernism," which was published in the *Christian Century*. The popular epitome of liberalism now called on persons of faith to confront and critique society, not simply to accommodate theology to prevailing cultural fancies. Neo-orthodoxy in time faced its own challenges, and it became clear that it, too, reflected the historical conditions of its day. But as the 1920s gave way to the decade of the Great Depression, neo-orthodoxy was still on the rise.

See also **The Rise of Biblical Criticism and Challenges to Religious Authority** *(in this volume);* **Evangelical Protestants** *(volume 2);* **Organized Religion** *(volume 3).*

BIBLIOGRAPHY

Ahlstrom, Sydney E. "Continental Influences on American Christian Thought since World War I." *Church History* 21 (1958): 256–272.

Averill, Lloyd J. *American Theology in the Liberal Tradition*. Philadelphia, 1967.

Brightman, Edgar Sheffield. *The Future of Christianity*. New York, 1937.

———. *Personality and Religion*. New York, 1934.

Brown, William Adams. *Modern Theology and the Preaching of the Gospel*. New York, 1914.

———. "The Old Theology and the New." *Harvard Theological Review* 4 (1911): 1–24.

Cauthen, Kenneth. *The Impact of American Religious Liberalism*. 2d ed. Washington, D.C., 1983.

Deats, Paul, and Carol Robb, eds. *The Boston Personalist Tradition in Philosophy, Social Ethics, and Theology*. Macon, Ga., 1986.

Fowler, James W. *To See the Kingdom: The Theological Vision of H. Richard Niebuhr*. 1974. Reprint, Lanham, Md., 1985.

Hart, Darryl G. *Defending the Faith: J. Gresham Machen and the Crisis of Conservative Protestantism in Modern America*. Baltimore, 1994.

Hoffecker, W. Andrew. *The Princeton Piety*. Nutley, N.J., 1981.

Hordern, William. *The Case for a New Reformation Theology*. Philadelphia, 1959.

Hutchison, William R. *The Modernist Impulse in American Protestantism*. 1976. Reprint, Durham, N.C., 1992.

———, ed. *American Protestant Thought in the Liberal Era*. 1968. Reprint, Lanham, Md., 1984.

Knudson, Albert C. *The Doctrine of God*. New York, 1930.

———. *The Doctrine of Redemption*. New York, 1933.

———. *The Philosophy of Personalism: A Study in the Metaphysics of Religion*. New York, 1927.

Lewis, Edwin. *A Christian Manifesto*. New York, 1934.

———. *The Creator and the Adversary*. New York, 1948.

Lovin, Robin. *Reinhold Niebuhr and Christian Realism*. Cambridge, U.K., 1995.

Machen, J. Gresham. *The Christian Faith in the Modern World*. New York, 1936.

———. *Christianity and Liberalism*. New York, 1923.

McLarney, James J. *The Theism of Edgar Sheffield Brightman*. Washington, D.C., 1936.

Marsden, George M. *Fundamentalism and American Culture: The Shaping of Twentieth Century Evangelism, 1870–1925*. New York, 1980.

———. *Understanding Fundamentalism and Evangelicalism*. Grand Rapids, Mich., 1991.

Mathews, Shailer. *The Faith of Modernism*. 1924. Reprint, New York, 1970.

———. *The Social Teaching of Jesus*. New York, 1897.

Niebuhr, H. Richard. *Christ and Culture*. New York, 1951.

———. *The Kingdom of God in America*. New York, 1937.

———. *The Meaning of Revelation*. New York, 1941.

———. *The Social Sources of Denominationalism*. New York, 1929.

Niebuhr, Reinhold. *Moral Man and Immoral Society: A Study in Ethics and Politics.* New York, 1932.

——. *The Nature and Destiny of Man: A Christian Interpretation.* 2 vols. New York, 1941–1943.

Noll, Mark A., ed. *The Princeton Theology, 1812–1921: Scripture, Science, Theological Method from Archibald Alexander to Benjamin Breckinridge Warfield.* Grand Rapids, Mich., 1983.

Peden, W. Creighton, and Jerome A. Stone, eds. *The Chicago School of Theology: Pioneers in Religious Inquiry.* Vol. 1, *The Early Chicago School, 1906–1959.* Lewiston, N.Y., 1997.

Seamands, S. A. *Christology and Transition in the Theology of Edwin Lewis.* Lanham, Md., 1987.

Toulouse, Mark G., and James O. Duke, eds. *Makers of Christian Theology in America.* Nashville, Tenn., 1999.

Voskuil, Dennis N. "American Protestant Neo-Orthodoxy and the Search for Realism, 1925–1939." *Ultimate Reality and Meaning* 8 (1985): 277–287.

Warfield, Benjamin B. *The Works of Benjamin B. Warfield.* 10 vols. Grand Rapids, Mich., 1991.

THE ATHLETE AS CULTURAL ICON

Daniel A. Nathan

From the Great War through the Great Depression, sports were a prominent part of twentieth-century American social and cultural life. They reflected and reinforced various, sometimes contradictory, attitudes and ideologies, and they provided many Americans with an important means to express themselves. Successful athletes often personified specific values and represented particular ethnic, racial, and religious constituencies. In terms of their popularity and cultural meaning, some athletes were more significant than others. A select few managed to transcend their sports. Athletes such as Jack Dempsey, Babe Ruth, Red Grange, Babe Didrikson Zaharias, and Joe Louis were widely perceived to be vibrant cultural icons. For myriad reasons besides their athletic accomplishments, these and other sports personalities earned tremendous adulation—and, in most instances, a great deal of money—and served as powerful symbols of success, daring, and rugged individualism. In some ways they confirm the idea that different historical moments and communities demand and produce different types of heroes. This essay examines the cultural significance and symbolism associated with some of the most prominent American athletes during the late 1910s through the 1930s. Historians often describe the 1920s and the early 1930s as the "Golden Age of American Sport," primarily because numerous superstar athletes competed at about the same time. In addition, a complex nexus of historical, social, and cultural forces and contexts contributed to the heightened national enthusiasm for sports during the period.

CONTEXTS FOR THE GOLDEN AGE

Physical recreation had long been part of American society by the early twentieth century. In addition to the games played by the indigenous peoples of North America, immigrants transported folk games from Europe to colonial America. The settlers of New England and the mid-Atlantic region engaged in physical recreation in moderation; blood sports, gambling, and amusements on the Sabbath were commonly outlawed. In seventeenth- and early-eighteenth-century Virginia, horse racing and cockfighting were popular among the gentry; poor and middle-class whites often emulated their social betters and had their own vernacular recreations; and, in their limited free time, slaves held their own athletic competitions. By the mid-eighteenth century, cities such as Baltimore, Boston, New York, and Philadelphia were becoming centers of leisure and recreation. As the eighteenth century drew to a close, sport as we know it had not yet taken shape, but its outlines could be seen.

During the early and mid-nineteenth century, despite the criticism of some upper-middle-class Victorian reformers, sport became more popular. "Between 1820 and 1870," writes the historian Melvin L. Adelman, "American athletics became increasingly organized and commercialized, marked by the emergence of national standards and competition, specialized player roles, a burgeoning sports information system, and ideological sanctions promoting the moral and social benefits of sport" (*A Sporting Time*, p. xi). Even before the Civil War, baseball was emerging as the "national pastime." After the war, returning soldiers, many of whom played baseball during lulls in the fighting, helped inspire interest in the game. In 1869 the first professional team was formed (the Cincinnati Red Stockings), and in 1876 the National League was founded. By the end of the century, baseball was regularly extolled as a democratic and, in spite of its occasional rowdyism, respectable social institution. Although the latter was not true of prizefighting, it too was popular. In fact, historian Elliott J. Gorn argues that John L. Sullivan, the world heavyweight prizefighting champion from 1882 to 1892 and the last of the bare-knuckle champions, was "the greatest American hero of the late nineteenth century" (*The Manly Art,* p. 247). Still, sport did not achieve anything like its present position in American culture until the turn of the century.

Many factors contributed to sport's increased national popularity and social significance—and the heightened iconic status of prominent American athletes—during the 1910s and beyond. One of the earliest and most persistent explanations for the rise of sport was that it functioned as a kind of social safety valve or surrogate frontier or battlefield, one where traditional (that is, masculine) values—aggressiveness, courage, individualism, strength, and toughness—could be exhibited and subsequently celebrated. Historian Roderick Nash suggests that, against a backdrop of anxiety-producing cultural and social change, "it was comforting to find in sports a ritualistic celebration of the major components of the national faith" (*The Nervous Generation*, p. 127). After World War I many Americans (especially young males) seemed to yearn for heroes "with whom to identify in order to clarify (or at least fabricate) their own identity," writes the historian Peter G. Filene. "Not having found him on the battlefield, they looked to the gridiron and the diamond" (*Him/Her/Self,* p. 157). Thus, for many people, sport (and by extension interest in athletic heroes) was not simply an escapist activity; rather, it was a site of personal and cultural meaning.

Another important reason for the ascendancy of sport after World War I was its intensified relationship with the news media. By the end of the nineteenth century, sport had become a daily staple in most metropolitan newspapers. Popular conceptions of sport, much like the nation itself, underwent significant transformations. For many urban, middle-class Americans, some sports emerged as legitimate leisure time pursuits. They had become activities, whether engaged in as a spectator or a participant, that served social and ideological purposes. At the same time, notes historian Frank Luther Mott, sporting news "came to be segregated on special pages, with special make-up, pictures, and news gathering style" (*American Journalism*, p. 579). Several powerful publishers, such as Charles A. Dana of the *New York Sun* and Joseph Pulitzer of the *New York World*, stepped up the pace that James Gordon Bennett Sr. had established earlier in the century in his *New York Herald* of providing more space to sporting news. In 1883 Pulitzer's *World* was the first newspaper to establish "a separate sports section, with its own editor and writers" (Stevens, "The Rise of the Sports Page," p. 6). Pulitzer's competitors followed his lead.

During this period numerous talented reporters and columnists devoted their attention to sports.

"What is sometimes overlooked about that glorious era of competition," argues the sportswriter John Kieran, "is that there were writers worthy of the great competitors of those dazzling days" (Danzig and Brandwein, p. ix). Those men included Heywood Broun, Paul Gallico, Frank Graham, Ring Lardner, W. O. McGeehan, Westbrook Pegler, Grantland Rice, Damon Runyon, and Arch Ward, among others. In general, two types of sportswriting dominated the era: the "Gee Whiz" and "Aw Nuts" schools. The former style (which Broun, Gallico, and Rice practiced) portrayed athletes uncritically and romantically; the latter (plied by Lardner, McGeehan, and Pegler) portrayed athletes critically and cynically. During most of the 1920s and 1930s, there were more "Gee Whiz" writers, and their stories were more popular and influential. Reflecting on the era, the sportswriter Robert Lipsyte contends that the "so-called Golden Age of Sports, the 1920s and early 1930s, was really the 'golden age of sportswriting.' The glories of the Babe, the Manassa Mauler [Jack Dempsey], the Four Horsemen [of Notre Dame football fame], were tunes composed on portable typewriters by gifted, ambitious, often cynical men who set customs and standards of sports journalism that are being dealt with to this day" (*Sportsworld*, p. 170).

Technological advances also contributed to sport's importance and vibrancy. Bigger, faster printing presses and improved distribution methods enabled newspapers to reach more readers than ever before. The new medium of radio—the nation's first commercial radio station, KDKA in Pittsburgh, began operating in 1920—developed quickly and had far-reaching effects on American social life. In terms of athletics, writes historian Benjamin G. Rader, radio "brought a totally new experience of sports to the fan. Now the fan did not have to await his morning newspaper; he instantly shared the drama transpiring on the playing field" (*In Its Own Image,* p. 23). By 1929, when approximately 40 percent of American families owned a radio, millions of fans were listening to championship prizefights and World Series broadcasts. With transportation developments, such as more efficient and less expensive automobiles and buses (and improved roadways), travel time and costs were reduced, and such advances created many new opportunities for athletes, teams, and fans. Collectively, these and such developments as improved sports equipment and training methods, and their constant refinements, contributed to the prominence athletes and organized sports achieved during these years.

It is important to note that, in addition to John L. Sullivan, there were iconic American athletes before the 1920s. James "Gentleman Jim" Corbett earned national acclaim in 1892 by defeating Sullivan to become the heavyweight champion. Jack Johnson achieved a different kind of iconic status in 1908 when he became the first African American heavyweight champion. Reviled and caricatured by white Americans and the media, the extroverted and ostentatious Johnson was a notorious public figure who flouted many of society's most rigidly enforced racial conventions. Johnson's public persona and symbolism were so powerful that his resounding victory over former champion and "Great White Hope" Jim Jeffries in 1910 sparked a wave of race riots. Two years later, at the Olympic Games in Stockholm, Sweden, Jim Thorpe, a two-time All-American in college football who was of Native American descent, won the decathlon, the pentathlon, and unprecedented respect, including that of the Swedish king, Gustav V, who proclaimed, "Sir, you are the greatest athlete in the world." Since it was the self-acclaimed national pastime, baseball had more than its fair share of iconic figures before the late 1910s. In the late nineteenth century, ballplayers like Mike "King" Kelly, Adrian "Cap" Anson, and Denton "Cy" Young earned widespread admiration. During the first two decades of the twentieth century, Christy Mathewson, Ty Cobb, Walter Johnson, Honus Wagner, and Grover Cleveland Alexander were frequently heralded as the game's brightest stars.

JACK DEMPSEY AND THE "SWEET SCIENCE"

The heavyweight champion Jack Dempsey was the first iconic American athlete after World War I. Compared to modern heavyweights, Dempsey was not a big man (six feet, one inch and 190 pounds), but his humble origins, boxing style, and public persona contributed to his tremendous popularity and iconic status. Born in 1895 to poor Irish immigrants in Manassa, Colorado, William Harrison Dempsey took the name "Jack" after the famous "Nonpareil" Jack Dempsey, a mid-nineteenth-century middleweight. For much of his youth, Dempsey was a hobo, riding the western rails, looking for work, and fighting hundreds of barroom brawls. In 1917 he came under the tutelage of Jack "Doc" Kearns, who became his manager and publicist. Following a series of carefully chosen fights, Dempsey faced Jess Willard for the heavyweight championship on 4 July 1919. Although smaller than Willard (who was past his prime), Dempsey knocked him down seven times on the way to a third-round victory. Thus began Dempsey's seven-year, two-month reign as heavyweight champion. Dempsey successfully defended his title five times, including memorable bouts with the popular French war hero Georges Carpentier and the Argentine Luis Firpo, and lived an extravagant and highly publicized life. For many Americans, the seemingly invincible, aggressive, yet friendly and fun-loving Dempsey embodied the nation's rugged frontier past. "No intellectual, he exuded animal ferocity in the ring. He displayed little scientific finesse," writes historian William J. Baker. "He was a fighter of perpetual motion whose dramatic flamboyance was peculiarly suited to the new age of the automobile, jazz, and brash American confidence" (*Sports in the Western World*, p. 222).

Historians have pointed out that Dempsey's fights with Gene Tunney highlight the cultural symbolism ascribed to each man. They first fought on 23 September 1926 in Philadelphia, with the clever, clean-cut ex-marine Tunney outpointing the rusty champion in ten rounds in front of 130,000 spectators. Their rematch a year later in Chicago featured a record-setting $2.6 million gate. For six rounds Tunney outboxed Dempsey, but in the seventh Dempsey knocked Tunney down with a barrage of punches. However, the referee's count was delayed because Dempsey did not immediately go to a neutral corner. This gave Tunney precious time to recover. After the controversial "long count," Tunney regained command of the fight and retained his title, winning the ten-round bout on points. Besides the inherent drama of these fights, there were also occasions for commentators and fans to interpret their cultural significance. As Gorn puts it, "Each boxer came to represent key values in American life, and the two men together in the ring symbolized central tensions and contradictions of the 1920s" ("The Manassa Mauler and the Fighting Marine," p. 32). Tunney was portrayed as the embodiment of traditional middle-class values, like the Protestant work ethic, clean living, and patriotism. The version of masculinity he represented was characterized by his self-control, self-improvement, and "scientific" approach to boxing. By contrast, Dempsey was understood to be a spontaneous, hyperaggressive, fast-living brawler, an outlaw, and noble savage. Even if the media exaggerated and exploited the differences between Dempsey and Tunney, their fights exemplified the ways in which athletic icons sometimes personified cultural values and conflicts.

Dempsey and Tunney were not the only iconic prizefighters during these years. For some Jewish immigrants and many of their children, boxers such as lightweight champion Benny Leonard (1917–1925), who is considered the outstanding Jewish American athlete of the first third of the century, and Barney Ross, who once held three titles simultaneously (lightweight, junior welterweight, and welterweight in 1934–1935), countered popular anti-Semitic stereotypes about Jewish masculinity and physicality. They also provided American Jews in the 1920s and 1930s with "a special source of ethnic pride and acceptance," argues historian Peter Levine (*Ellis Island to Ebbets Field*, p. 153). Although their iconic status was less pervasive and mainstream than that of Dempsey or Tunney, Leonard, Ross, and other Jewish boxers were local and ethnic heroes and vibrant symbols of Jewish American success and toughness, in much the same way that John L. Sullivan was for many Irish Americans in the late nineteenth century, and the way Rocky Graziano and Rocky Marciano were for many Italian Americans in the 1940s and 1950s. When Joe Louis won the heavyweight championship in 1937, he similarly provided millions of African Americans with a powerful symbol of racial pride and strength during a time of pervasive racism.

BABE RUTH AND THE NATIONAL PASTIME

"The Ruth is mighty and shall prevail." So wrote Heywood Broun after George Herman "Babe" Ruth of the New York Yankees hit two home runs in the second game of the 1923 World Series (quoted in Einstein, p. 58). Babe Ruth was the most compelling and dominant athlete of his era. His near mythic exploits (on and off the field) and exuberant personality endeared him to millions of Americans, and his iconicity endures. "Ruth is better remembered than contemporary Presidents Harding, Coolidge, and Hoover," writes the biographer Marshall Smelser, "better than the contemporary ethical hero Lindbergh, better than the foxy hero Cobb" (*The Life That Ruth Built*, p. 555).

Born and raised in Baltimore's slums, Ruth was a neglected, mischievous child. In 1902 Ruth's parents sent their seven-year-old son to St. Mary's Industrial School for Boys, a reformatory and orphanage where he excelled at baseball. In 1914 Ruth, a lithe and unrefined left-handed pitcher, signed with the minor league Baltimore Orioles of the International League. That July, Ruth's contract was sold to the Boston Red Sox. The following year

Babe Ruth (1895–1948). The resonance of this popular photo bespeaks Ruth's heroic status as the "Sultan of Swat." © BETTMANN/CORBIS

was Ruth's first full season in the major leagues, and his pitching and hitting helped Boston win the American League (AL) pennant and the World Series. For the next four years, Ruth flourished as a pitcher and helped the Red Sox win two more World Series, but his hitting ability was obvious, and in 1919 he was shifted to the outfield so he could play every day. That year was his breakthrough season, as he hit a record twenty-nine home runs and led the AL in runs scored and runs batted in. The following January the financially strapped Red Sox sold Ruth to the New York Yankees.

Unperturbed by the intense media attention he received for his playing and profligate lifestyle—he indulged himself with fast cars and women, stylish clothes, rich food and drink—Ruth smashed his own home run record by hitting fifty-four in 1920. Amid the hoopla surrounding Ruth's heroics, the Black Sox scandal, in which eight members of the Chicago White Sox allegedly conspired with gamblers to intentionally lose the 1919 World Series, came to the public's attention. For many, it was a devastating revelation. It has long been maintained that Ruth, with his raffish lifestyle and power hitting, rejuvenated—indeed, transformed—baseball after the Black Sox scandal. It is commonly held that, having shattered his own home run record in 1920, the year that the World Series imbroglio was revealed, Ruth galvanized popular interest in the game in 1921, when he hit fifty-nine home runs. To the delight of the baseball establishment, it seemed that most fans "were more interested in speculating about what the Babe would do for an encore in 1921 than they were in rehashing the delinquencies of the White Sox," maintains Ken Sobol (*Babe Ruth and the American Dream*, p. 135). More so than Judge Kenesaw Mountain Landis, who was hired in 1920 as baseball's first commissioner to give the game the appearance of propriety, Ruth revitalized professional baseball. Thus, in terms of baseball history and mythology, he was (and remains) the game's great savior. Over the rest of his career, which lasted until 1935, Ruth assaulted the record book. He led the AL in home runs twelve times. He hit 714 home runs, batted in a record 2,213 runs, and had a lifetime batting average of .342. In 1927 he hit a single-season record sixty home runs, a feat unsurpassed until 1961.

Yet Ruth's meaning cannot be reduced to statistics or records. Like all of the athletes examined in this essay, Ruth meant many things. Clearly, Ruth was a vibrant cultural symbol for his age. Moreover, to understate the matter, much of the public loved Ruth. They did so partly because he represented the realization of the American dream and partly because of his rambunctiousness. "No modern athletic hero exceeded Babe Ruth's capacity to project multiple images of the brute power, the natural, uninhibited man and the fulfillment of the American success dream," writes Benjamin G. Rader. "Ruth was living proof that the lone individual could still rise from mean, vulgar beginnings to fame and fortune, to a position of public recognition equaled by few men in American history" ("Compensatory Sport Heroes," p. 12). Whereas Ty Cobb and John McGraw were calculating, temperamental, self-made men, and Christy Mathewson, Walter Johnson, and Lou Gehrig were humble, gracious role models, Ruth was the ultimate prowess hero, crudely powerful and widely beloved. As Smelser puts it, Ruth "is our Hercules, our Samson, Beowulf, Siegfried. No other person outside of public life so stirred our imaginations or so captured our affections" (p. 560). Of course, the power of a cul-

tural icon always owes something to timing. And historian Warren I. Susman correctly notes that Ruth "was the perfect creation for an increasingly mechanized world that still hungered for the extraordinary personality, that tired of the Model T automobiles and yet was also appreciative of their virtues—wanting only something more, something bigger than life" (*Culture as History*, p. 148).

Although Ruth may have been America's preeminent athletic hero during his career, many contemporaneous baseball players were icons as well. His Yankees teammate and first baseman Lou Gehrig, who batted .340 with 493 home runs and played in a record 2,130 consecutive games during his career, was greatly respected as a paragon of virtue. Gehrig's heroic status was enhanced by the fact that his career and life were cut tragically short by an incurable neurological disease, amyotrophic lateral sclerosis, better known today as Lou Gehrig's disease. Baseball had many other stars during these years, such as the sluggers Rogers Hornsby, Jimmie Foxx, and Mel Ott and the pitchers Robert "Lefty" Grove, Carl Hubbell, and Jerome "Dizzy" Dean. Since baseball had been long linked to such American ideals as democracy, individualism, and meritocracy and was deeply ingrained in the American psyche as the national pastime, it is not surprising that these men were extremely popular. But organized baseball was racially segregated until 1947, and the major and minor leagues were not truly national, democratic, or meritocratic during the years examined here.

Beginning in 1920, African American ballplayers played in their own leagues. The Negro Leagues provided pride, pleasure, and opportunity for black people. Many African Americans were obviously good enough to play in the white major leagues. At least two such players achieved iconic status—pitcher Leroy "Satchel" Paige and catcher Josh Gibson, both of whom are in the National Baseball Hall of Fame. Paige was a charismatic showman who pitched in the Negro Leagues for more than twenty years before joining the Cleveland Indians in 1948, when he was past forty. "Like Ruth, who had so dominated major league baseball earlier, the long and lean Paige uncontestedly occupied center stage of black baseball in the 1930s and 1940s," notes Rader. "Like Ruth, he possessed awesome skills. An aura of excitement always hung about him, an anticipation that he might perform the unexpected or do the impossible" (*Baseball*, p. 146). Gibson, sometimes described as the "Babe Ruth of the Negro Leagues," walloped approximately 800 career home runs over the course of his seventeen-year career.

"Gibson was the ultimate hitter. He hit with power, for a high average, and seldom struck out. He was a blue-collar slugger without the glitz and glamour of his major league counterparts," observes Negro League researcher Larry Lester. "Gibson will be the eternal monarch of home run kings. He dominated the game with majestic power like none before him" (Clark and Lester, *The Negro Leagues*, p. 42). Unfortunately, until the late twentieth century, these two players and many other African American athletes were invisible to most Americans.

RED GRANGE AND THE GRIDIRON

Harold "Red" Grange was an All-American halfback as a sophomore at the University of Illinois in 1923. It was his singular performance on 18 October 1924 that thrust him onto the national scene. In Champaign, Illinois, in front of 67,000 fans, Grange scored four touchdowns in the first twelve minutes of a victory over the previously undefeated University of Michigan. He took the opening kickoff ninety-five yards for a touchdown, ran from scrimmage for two more, returned a punt fifty-six yards for another, ran for a fifth touchdown, and passed for a sixth. The Chicago sports editor Warren Brown dubbed the elusive Grange the "Galloping Ghost."

Although he was a star high school athlete in Wheaton, Illinois, Grange was not heavily recruited to play college football and had to be pressured by his friends to try out for the Illinois team. Strong, fast, and nimble, Grange had a great college career, at a time when college football was remarkably popular. In three seasons he scored thirty-one touchdowns and was a three-time All-American. After his final game for Illinois in 1925, Grange again made national headlines when he announced that he was leaving school and had signed a contract to play professional football for the Chicago Bears of the fledgling and not yet reputable National Football League (NFL). It was a controversial decision that generated extensive debate, for it "openly flaunted the myth of the college athlete as a gentleman-amateur who played merely for the fun of the game and the glory of his school," writes Rader ("Compensatory Sport Heroes," p. 16). Grange brought credibility and attention to the professional game as he drew huge crowds during a nationwide seventeen-game barnstorming tour. The following year Grange and his agent, C. C. "Cash and Carry" Pyle, formed the American Football League to rival the NFL. After one season, the league folded. Grange sat out the 1928 season with a knee injury, and in 1929 he returned to the Bears, for whom he excelled as a defensive back.

Grange had a noteworthy pro career and was a charter member of the Professional Football Hall of Fame, but his iconicity derived only partly from his gridiron success. Just as important were his humble origins and rapid rise to fame and fortune, his fortuitous timing, and his humble, Midwestern image. Like Dempsey and Ruth, Grange personified the American dream of success and exhibited awe-inspiring power. Grange also came of age at the right time, precisely when the sport and media coverage of it were burgeoning, and when many Americans yearned for daring, larger-than-life heroes. However, Grange differed from Dempsey and Ruth in that he was widely perceived to be a modest, hardworking, and clean-living athlete. The historian John M. Carroll argues, "Grange's stature was enhanced by the popular perception created by the media that he was a product of the West and represented frontier values that were being threatened in an increasingly industrial and urban nation" (*Red Grange*, p. 213). Grange seemed to reaffirm traditional virtues during a time of cultural and social transformation. While an American original who represented his age, Grange was simultaneously seen as a kind of throwback who embodied older values and evoked an earlier era.

BABE DIDRIKSON, HELEN WILLS, AND THE "WEAKER SEX"

Organized sport in the United States was a male-dominated institution during this period. It thus reflected American gender relations and society. But just as this era witnessed dramatic changes in the status and behavior of women, it also saw women's sports grow significantly. Several women athletes achieved iconic status. Europeans like Suzanne Lenglen, a flamboyant French tennis player who won the Wimbledon and French singles titles six times each from 1919 to 1926, and Sonja Henie, a graceful Norwegian who won the world's figure-skating championship for ten consecutive years (1927–1936) and three Olympic gold medals (1928, 1932, 1936) before becoming a movie star, revolutionized their respective sports. There were also numerous extraordinary American women athletes. In 1926 Olympic medalist Gertrude Ederle earned worldwide acclaim after she became the first woman (and only the sixth person) to swim the English Channel, breaking the previous record by approximately two

Babe Didrikson at the Women's National Track Championships, 1931. In addition to her extraordinary feats in track and golf, Didrikson won championships in billiards, speed skating, cycling, swimming, shooting, squash, and tennis; she pitched in several major league exhibition games, and was a three-time All-American in basketball. © BETTMANN/CORBIS

hours. In golf, Glenna Collett Vare won the U.S. Amateur a record six times during the 1920s and 1930s and was a charter member of the International Women's Golf Hall of Fame. If one thinks of aviation as an athletic endeavor, and many people did at the time, Amelia Earhart deserves attention because she made national headlines in 1928 as the first woman to fly across the Atlantic, with Wilmer Stutz and Louis Gordon, and then made a solo flight in 1932. She subsequently set several aviation records. Like Charles Lindbergh, Earhart was lavishly celebrated for her independence, daring, and courage.

Mildred "Babe" Didrikson Zaharias exhibited the same qualities, although her appearance (slender and muscular) and attitude (often blunt and brash) were frequently criticized as "mannish," especially early in her career. The greatest all-around athlete of the period, Didrikson was born in Texas to working-class, Norwegian American immigrants. As a girl and young woman the tomboyish Didrikson excelled in many sports—some of which were reserved for boys and men. She played baseball, basketball, football, tennis, and volleyball; she boxed, bowled, cycled, skied, and swam. In 1932 Didrikson single-handedly won the Women's National Amateur Athletic Union track championship, competing in all eight events. That same year, she won two gold

medals and one silver at the Los Angeles Summer Olympics; she might have won more, but the rules at the time mandated that women could only participate in three events. Years later, Didrikson became the greatest woman golfer in the world, winning fifty-three amateur and professional tournaments, seventeen consecutively. The Associated Press voted Didrikson the Female Athlete of the Year a record six times and in 1950 named her Female Athlete of the Half Century. But because she challenged and rejected conventional notions of femininity, at least early in her career, Didrikson often received negative media coverage and was sometimes derisively described as a "muscle moll," an appellation she detested. Still, she captured the imagination of much of the public and did a great deal to dispel stereotypes of female physical inferiority.

Of all the women athletes of the era, the tennis player Helen Wills Moody, who won a total of nineteen Wimbledon, French, and U.S. singles titles between 1923 and 1938, "was probably the best known and most typical," writes historian Allen Guttmann (*Women's Sports*, p. 151). Wills was born in Centerville, California, in 1905 to an affluent, privileged family. The impassive, coolly efficient Wills learned to play tennis at the Berkeley Tennis Club and was state champion in 1921. Two years later, she won

729

the first of her seven U.S. singles titles. "Her fresh face, girlish beauty, and trademark plain white visor enhanced her reputation as a simple yet poised and graceful young champion," writes historian Susan K. Cahn. "Within a few short years she achieved the status of national hero, revered by the public as 'the American girl' or simply 'our Helen'" (*Coming On Strong*, p. 31). Unlike the theatrical Bill Tilden, the most popular and successful male tennis player of the period (he won ten U.S. and Wimbledon singles titles in the 1920s), Wills was remarkably self-controlled and methodical, on and off the court. Thus, in addition to dominating women's tennis—from 1927 to 1932 she did not lose a set in singles—Wills, who was modest, well-behaved, and attractive, also embodied the era's prevailing notion of traditional femininity. For these reasons, Guttmann contends that "more than Earhart and much more than Didrikson and Ederle, Helen Wills Moody seemed to embody the athletic ideals of the era. Physically gifted, properly educated, dedicated to her sport but not obviously, crassly, materialistically aggressive, she was a superior athlete who remained conventionally feminine" (*Women's Sports*, p. 153). Considering the contexts in which she played, it is understandable why Wills was America's most widely admired woman athlete.

JESSE OWENS AND JOE LOUIS: "CREDITS TO THEIR RACE"

Although the United States was rigidly segregated and plagued by racial inequality during these years, the track star Jesse Owens and the boxer Joe Louis nonetheless became the first African American athletes to be embraced by white America. They did so because they were excellent athletes, and—while they were inspiring to many African Americans—they did not disrupt the racial status quo. Owens was born in Alabama, the son of a sharecropper and the grandson of a former slave, and moved to Cleveland, Ohio, when he was a boy. Owens burst on the national scene on 25 May 1935 as a sophomore track star at Ohio State University when he broke three world records and equaled another at the Big Ten championships. Owens eventually won a record eight National Collegiate Athletic Association individual outdoor titles. His crowning moment came in 1936, when he set three world records, tied another, and won four gold medals (in the 100-meter dash, 200-meter dash, the 400-meter relay, and the long jump) at the Summer Olympics in Berlin, which were presided over by Adolf Hitler and were held against the backdrop of Aryan propaganda. It was one of the most remarkable performances in the history of the modern Olympics and received a great deal of media attention. Shortly after the games, Owens turned professional and later the Associated Press named him the Athlete of the Year. A national celebrity, Owens was humble, patriotic, and (some critics have noted) deferential to whites. Many sportswriters, both black and white, wrote that he was a gentleman and "a credit to his race." "Heroes inspire others to pursue visions of greatness," writes William J. Baker, "and Owens certainly did that. For blacks of his generation, especially, he was an inspirational model of success" (*Jesse Owens*, p. 235). Paradoxically, despite his athletic accomplishments, for many years Owens struggled financially, as opportunities were severely limited for African Americans and other racial and ethnic minorities.

Like Owens and many other African Americans at the time, Joe Louis was born into a poverty-stricken family of southern sharecroppers and moved to a northern city, Detroit. He dropped out of school when he was seventeen, worked at the Ford Motor Company, and excelled as an amateur boxer, turning professional in 1934. Over the next three years, Louis went 28–1 (his lone loss was in 1936 to former champion Max Schmeling of Germany) and beat three former champs before capturing the heavyweight title on 22 June 1937, knocking out James J. Braddock in eight rounds. The first African American heavyweight titleholder since the controversial Jack Johnson, Louis and his managers worked hard to craft a public image that was antithetical to that of Johnson and thus acceptable to white America. The result of their handiwork was a quiet, unassuming, Bible-reading, patriotic champion. To his supporters, Louis "challenged stereotypes, instilled hope and provided models for racial advancement," contend historians Dominic J. Capecci Jr. and Martha Wilkerson. "Galahad-like, fighting clean and complimenting opponents, he enhanced black respectability" ("Multifarious Hero," p. 7). A year after Louis won the title, he avenged his 1936 loss to Schmeling with a thrilling, brutal first-round knockout. Because Schmeling was associated with Nazi aggression, Louis's victory was seen as a triumph for America and democracy, and the "Brown Bomber" was transformed into a national icon. At the time, however, he was already a transcendent hero to millions of African Americans. "Figures like Joe Louis were so important because they were never perceived as isolated men but rather as an integral part of the entire network of black culture," argues historian Lawrence W. Levine. "Because he was enshrined as a culture hero, everything Joe Louis did was seen in symbolic terms" (*Black Culture and Black Consciousness,* p. 436). In short, Louis was a mythic hero for many Americans.

How one assesses Owens and Louis as cultural icons depends upon one's perspective. For some, they represent the classic American success story of talent and hard work overcoming such daunting obstacles as poverty and racism. For others, they symbolize racial pride, strength, and accomplishment. For still others, they seem (in retrospect) to be obsequious accommodationists—although historian David K. Wiggins points out that both men "often couched their complaints of racial discrimination in words acceptable to whites" (*Glory Bound,* p. 210). At the height of their fame and long afterward, "Louis and Owens were credited with opening doors for others in and apart from sport," writes the sociologist Othello Harris. "If those who followed behaved like them, African Americans were told, sport and other institutions would be more accepting of black presence" ("The Role of Sport in the Black Community," p. 314). As Harris suggests, that claim is debatable.

CONCLUSION

The athletic icons examined here suited, reflected, and contributed to the character of their historical moment. They all captivated much of the public and most achieved something like mythic status in their lifetimes. But as talented as they were, in many instances these athletes became icons largely because they reaffirmed or symbolized dominant cultural values or because they reinforced exhausted ideologies and national myths. With few exceptions, they rarely challenged social norms or boundaries or took controversial political positions—as later athletic icons, such as Jackie Robinson, Muhammad Ali, and Billie Jean King would. Babe Ruth flaunted some social conventions with his unrepentant hedonism, but he was also America's preeminent spendthrift as the nation shifted from a producer to a consumer culture. Joe Louis struck blows for racial advancement, but he also deliberately cultivated a docile public image that would not threaten white America. This is not to take anything away from their athletic accomplishments, which were remarkable. Rather, it is to note the ways that these athletic icons were representative symbols of their era.

See also **Popular Culture in the Public Arena** *(volume 2);* **Elite vs. Popular Cultures; Culture for Mass Audiences** *(volume 3).*

BIBLIOGRAPHY

General Works

Adelman, Melvin L. *A Sporting Time: New York City and the Rise of Modern Athletics, 1820–1870.* Urbana, Ill., 1986.

Baker, William J. *Sports in the Western World.* Totowa, N.J., 1982.

Betts, John R. *America's Sporting Heritage, 1850–1950.* Reading, Mass., 1974.

———. "Sporting Journalism in Nineteenth-Century America." *American Quarterly* 5 (spring 1953): 39–56.

Cahn, Susan K. *Coming on Strong: Gender and Sexuality in Twentieth-Century Women's Sport.* New York, 1994.

Danzig, Allison, and Peter Brandwein, eds. *Sport's Golden Age: A Close-Up of the Fabulous Twenties.* New York, 1948.

Dyreson, Mark. "The Emergence of Consumer Culture and the Transformation of Physical Culture: American Sport in the 1920s." *Journal of Sport History* 16 (winter 1989): 261–281.

Edmonds, Anthony O. "The Second Louis-Schmeling Fight: Sport, Symbol, and Culture." *Journal of Popular Culture* 7 (summer 1973): 42–50.

Evensen, Bruce J. *When Dempsey Fought Tunney: Heroes, Hokum, and Storytelling in the Jazz Age.* Knoxville, Tenn., 1996.

Filene, Peter G. *Him/Her/Self: Sex Roles in Modern America.* New York, 1975.

Fox, Stephen R. *Big Leagues: Professional Baseball, Football, and Basketball in National Memory.* New York, 1994.

Gallico, Paul. *Farewell to Sport.* New York, 1950. Originally published in 1938.

Gorn, Elliott J. "The Manassa Mauler and the Fighting Marine: An Interpretation of the Dempsey-Tunney Fights." *Journal of American Studies* 19 (April 1985): 27–47.

Gorn, Elliott J., and Warren Goldstein. *A Brief History of American Sports.* New York, 1993.

Guttmann, Allen. *A Whole New Ball Game: An Interpretation of American Sports.* Chapel Hill, N.C., 1988.

———. *Women's Sports: A History.* New York, 1991.

Harris, Othello. "The Role of Sport in the Black Community." *Sociological Focus* 30 (October 1997): 311–319.

Levine, Lawrence W. *Black Culture and Black Consciousness: Afro-American Folk Thought from Slavery to Freedom.* Oxford, U.K., 1977.

Levine, Peter. *Ellis Island to Ebbets Field: Sport and the American Jewish Experience.* New York, 1992.

Lipsky, Richard. *How We Play the Game: Why Sports Dominate American Life.* Boston, 1981.

Lipsyte, Robert. *Sportsworld: An American Dreamland.* New York, 1975.

Lipsyte, Robert, and Peter Levine. *Idols of the Game: A Sporting History of the American Century.* Atlanta, Ga., 1995.

Mott, Frank Luther. *American Journalism: A History.* 3d ed. New York, 1962. Originally published in 1941.

Nash, Roderick. *The Nervous Generation: American Thought, 1917–1930.* Chicago, 1970.

Paxson, Frederic L. "The Rise of Sport." *Mississippi Valley Historical Review* 4 (September 1917): 143–168.

Pope, S. W. *Patriotic Games: Sporting Traditions in the American Imagination, 1876–1926.* New York, 1997.

Rader, Benjamin G. *American Sports: From the Age of Folk Games to the Age of Televised Sport.* 3d ed. Englewoods Cliffs, N.J., 1996.

———. "Compensatory Sport Heroes: Ruth, Grange, and Dempsey." *Journal of Popular Culture* 16 (spring 1983): 11–22.

———. *In Its Own Image: How Television Has Transformed Sports.* New York, 1984.

Smith, Leverett T. *The American Dream and the National Game.* Bowling Green, Ohio, 1975.

Stevens, John. "The Rise of the Sports Page." *Gannett Center Journal* (fall 1987): 1–11.

Susman, Warren I. *Culture as History: The Transformation of American Society in the Twentieth Century.* New York, 1984.

Wiggins, David K. *Glory Bound: Black Athletes in a White America.* Syracuse, N.Y., 1997.

Williams, Peter. *The Sports Immortals: Deifying the American Athlete.* Bowling Green, Ohio, 1994.

Individual Sports and Biographies

Alexander, Charles C. *John McGraw.* New York, 1988.

———. *Ty Cobb.* New York, 1984.

Baker, William J. *Jesse Owens: An American Life.* New York, 1986.

Capecci, Dominic J., Jr., and Martha Wilkerson. "Multifarious Hero: Joe Louis, American Society and Race Relations during World Crisis." *Journal of Sport History* 10 (winter 1983): 5–25.

Carroll, John M. *Red Grange and the Rise of Modern Football.* Urbana, Ill., 1999.

Cayleff, Susan E. *Babe: The Life and Legend of Babe Didrikson Zaharias.* Urbana, Ill., 1996.

Clark, Dick, and Larry Lester, eds. *The Negro Leagues Book.* Cleveland, Ohio, 1994.

Creamer, Robert W. *Babe: The Legend Comes to Life.* New York, 1974.

Crepeau, Richard C. *Baseball: America's Diamond Mind, 1919–1941.* Orlando, Fla., 1980.

Einstein, Charles, ed. *The Baseball Reader: Favorites from the Fireside Books of Baseball.* New York, 1983.

Gorn, Elliott J. *The Manly Art: Bare-Knuckle Prize Fighting in America.* Ithaca, N.Y., 1986.

Heller, Peter. *"In This Corner . . . !": Forty World Champions Tell Their Stories.* New York, 1973.

Jones, Robert T., Jr., and O. B. Keeler. *Down the Fairway: The Golf Life and Play of Robert T. Jones, Jr.* New York, 1927.

Mead, Chris. *Champion: Joe Louis; Black Hero in White America.* New York, 1985.

Peterson, Robert. *Only the Ball Was White: A History of Legendary Black Players and All-Black Professional Teams.* New York, 1992. Originally published in 1970.

Rader, Benjamin G. *Baseball: A History of America's Game.* Urbana, Ill., 1992.

Rice, Grantland. *The Tumult and the Shouting: My Life in Sport.* New York, 1954.

Roberts, Randy. *Jack Dempsey: The Manassa Mauler.* Baton Rouge, La., 1984. Originally published in 1979.

Robinson, Ray. *Iron Horse: Lou Gehrig in His Time.* New York, 1990.

———. *Matty, An American Hero: Christy Mathewson of the New York Giants.* New York, 1993.

Ruth, Babe, as told to Bob Considine. *The Babe Ruth Story.* New York, 1948.

Seymour, Harold. *The Golden Years.* Vol. 2 of *Baseball.* New York, 1989.

Smelser, Marshall. *The Life That Ruth Built: A Biography.* New York, 1975.

Sobol, Ken. *Babe Ruth and the American Dream.* New York, 1974.

Sperber, Murray. *Shake Down the Thunder: The Creation of Notre Dame Football.* New York, 1993.

Voigt, David Q. *American Baseball: From the Commissioners to Continental Expansion.* Vol. 2 of *American Baseball.* University Park, Pa., 1970.